Lecture Notes in Computer Science 12371

More information about this series at http://www.springer.com/series/7412

Andrea Vedaldi · Horst Bischof ·
Thomas Brox · Jan-Michael Frahm (Eds.)

Computer Vision – ECCV 2020

16th European Conference
Glasgow, UK, August 23–28, 2020
Proceedings, Part XXVI

 Springer

Editors
Andrea Vedaldi (iD)
University of Oxford
Oxford, UK

Horst Bischof (iD)
Graz University of Technology
Graz, Austria

Thomas Brox (iD)
University of Freiburg
Freiburg im Breisgau, Germany

Jan-Michael Frahm
University of North Carolina at Chapel Hill
Chapel Hill, NC, USA

ISSN 0302-9743   ISSN 1611-3349 (electronic)
Lecture Notes in Computer Science
ISBN 978-3-030-58573-0   ISBN 978-3-030-58574-7 (eBook)
https://doi.org/10.1007/978-3-030-58574-7

LNCS Sublibrary: SL6 – Image Processing, Computer Vision, Pattern Recognition, and Graphics

This Springer imprint is published by the registered company Springer Nature Switzerland AG
The registered company address is: Gewerbestrasse 11, 6330 Cham, Switzerland

Foreword

Hosting the European Conference on Computer Vision (ECCV 2020) was certainly an exciting journey. From the 2016 plan to hold it at the Edinburgh International Conference Centre (hosting 1,800 delegates) to the 2018 plan to hold it at Glasgow's Scottish Exhibition Centre (up to 6,000 delegates), we finally ended with moving online because of the COVID-19 outbreak. While possibly having fewer delegates than expected because of the online format, ECCV 2020 still had over 3,100 registered participants.

Although online, the conference delivered most of the activities expected at a face-to-face conference: peer-reviewed papers, industrial exhibitors, demonstrations, and messaging between delegates. In addition to the main technical sessions, the conference included a strong program of satellite events with 16 tutorials and 44 workshops.

Furthermore, the online conference format enabled new conference features. Every paper had an associated teaser video and a longer full presentation video. Along with the papers and slides from the videos, all these materials were available the week before the conference. This allowed delegates to become familiar with the paper content and be ready for the live interaction with the authors during the conference week. The live event consisted of brief presentations by the oral and spotlight authors and industrial sponsors. Question and answer sessions for all papers were timed to occur twice so delegates from around the world had convenient access to the authors.

As with ECCV 2018, authors' draft versions of the papers appeared online with open access, now on both the Computer Vision Foundation (CVF) and the European Computer Vision Association (ECVA) websites. An archival publication arrangement was put in place with the cooperation of Springer. SpringerLink hosts the final version of the papers with further improvements, such as activating reference links and supplementary materials. These two approaches benefit all potential readers: a version available freely for all researchers, and an authoritative and citable version with additional benefits for SpringerLink subscribers. We thank Alfred Hofmann and Aliaksandr Birukou from Springer for helping to negotiate this agreement, which we expect will continue for future versions of ECCV.

August 2020

Vittorio Ferrari
Bob Fisher
Cordelia Schmid
Emanuele Trucco

Preface

Welcome to the proceedings of the European Conference on Computer Vision (ECCV 2020). This is a unique edition of ECCV in many ways. Due to the COVID-19 pandemic, this is the first time the conference was held online, in a virtual format. This was also the first time the conference relied exclusively on the Open Review platform to manage the review process. Despite these challenges ECCV is thriving. The conference received 5,150 valid paper submissions, of which 1,360 were accepted for publication (27%) and, of those, 160 were presented as spotlights (3%) and 104 as orals (2%). This amounts to more than twice the number of submissions to ECCV 2018 (2,439). Furthermore, CVPR, the largest conference on computer vision, received 5,850 submissions this year, meaning that ECCV is now 87% the size of CVPR in terms of submissions. By comparison, in 2018 the size of ECCV was only 73% of CVPR.

The review model was similar to previous editions of ECCV; in particular, it was double blind in the sense that the authors did not know the name of the reviewers and vice versa. Furthermore, each conference submission was held confidentially, and was only publicly revealed if and once accepted for publication. Each paper received at least three reviews, totalling more than 15,000 reviews. Handling the review process at this scale was a significant challenge. In order to ensure that each submission received as fair and high-quality reviews as possible, we recruited 2,830 reviewers (a 130% increase with reference to 2018) and 207 area chairs (a 60% increase). The area chairs were selected based on their technical expertise and reputation, largely among people that served as area chair in previous top computer vision and machine learning conferences (ECCV, ICCV, CVPR, NeurIPS, etc.). Reviewers were similarly invited from previous conferences. We also encouraged experienced area chairs to suggest additional chairs and reviewers in the initial phase of recruiting.

Despite doubling the number of submissions, the reviewer load was slightly reduced from 2018, from a maximum of 8 papers down to 7 (with some reviewers offering to handle 6 papers plus an emergency review). The area chair load increased slightly, from 18 papers on average to 22 papers on average.

Conflicts of interest between authors, area chairs, and reviewers were handled largely automatically by the Open Review platform via their curated list of user profiles. Many authors submitting to ECCV already had a profile in Open Review. We set a paper registration deadline one week before the paper submission deadline in order to encourage all missing authors to register and create their Open Review profiles well on time (in practice, we allowed authors to create/change papers arbitrarily until the submission deadline). Except for minor issues with users creating duplicate profiles, this allowed us to easily and quickly identify institutional conflicts, and avoid them, while matching papers to area chairs and reviewers.

Papers were matched to area chairs based on: an affinity score computed by the Open Review platform, which is based on paper titles and abstracts, and an affinity score computed by the Toronto Paper Matching System (TPMS), which is based on the paper's full text, the area chair bids for individual papers, load balancing, and conflict avoidance. Open Review provides the program chairs a convenient web interface to experiment with different configurations of the matching algorithm. The chosen configuration resulted in about 50% of the assigned papers to be highly ranked by the area chair bids, and 50% to be ranked in the middle, with very few low bids assigned.

Assignments to reviewers were similar, with two differences. First, there was a maximum of 7 papers assigned to each reviewer. Second, area chairs recommended up to seven reviewers per paper, providing another highly-weighed term to the affinity scores used for matching.

The assignment of papers to area chairs was smooth. However, it was more difficult to find suitable reviewers for all papers. Having a ratio of 5.6 papers per reviewer with a maximum load of 7 (due to emergency reviewer commitment), which did not allow for much wiggle room in order to also satisfy conflict and expertise constraints. We received some complaints from reviewers who did not feel qualified to review specific papers and we reassigned them wherever possible. However, the large scale of the conference, the many constraints, and the fact that a large fraction of such complaints arrived very late in the review process made this process very difficult and not all complaints could be addressed.

Reviewers had six weeks to complete their assignments. Possibly due to COVID-19 or the fact that the NeurIPS deadline was moved closer to the review deadline, a record 30% of the reviews were still missing after the deadline. By comparison, ECCV 2018 experienced only 10% missing reviews at this stage of the process. In the subsequent week, area chairs chased the missing reviews intensely, found replacement reviewers in their own team, and managed to reach 10% missing reviews. Eventually, we could provide almost all reviews (more than 99.9%) with a delay of only a couple of days on the initial schedule by a significant use of emergency reviews. If this trend is confirmed, it might be a major challenge to run a smooth review process in future editions of ECCV. The community must reconsider prioritization of the time spent on paper writing (the number of submissions increased a lot despite COVID-19) and time spent on paper reviewing (the number of reviews delivered in time decreased a lot presumably due to COVID-19 or NeurIPS deadline). With this imbalance the peer-review system that ensures the quality of our top conferences may break soon.

Reviewers submitted their reviews independently. In the reviews, they had the opportunity to ask questions to the authors to be addressed in the rebuttal. However, reviewers were told not to request any significant new experiment. Using the Open Review interface, authors could provide an answer to each individual review, but were also allowed to cross-reference reviews and responses in their answers. Rather than PDF files, we allowed the use of formatted text for the rebuttal. The rebuttal and initial reviews were then made visible to all reviewers and the primary area chair for a given paper. The area chair encouraged and moderated the reviewer discussion. During the discussions, reviewers were invited to reach a consensus and possibly adjust their ratings as a result of the discussion and of the evidence in the rebuttal.

After the discussion period ended, most reviewers entered a final rating and recommendation, although in many cases this did not differ from their initial recommendation. Based on the updated reviews and discussion, the primary area chair then made a preliminary decision to accept or reject the paper and wrote a justification for it (meta-review). Except for cases where the outcome of this process was absolutely clear (as indicated by the three reviewers and primary area chairs all recommending clear rejection), the decision was then examined and potentially challenged by a secondary area chair. This led to further discussion and overturning a small number of preliminary decisions. Needless to say, there was no in-person area chair meeting, which would have been impossible due to COVID-19.

Area chairs were invited to observe the consensus of the reviewers whenever possible and use extreme caution in overturning a clear consensus to accept or reject a paper. If an area chair still decided to do so, she/he was asked to clearly justify it in the meta-review and to explicitly obtain the agreement of the secondary area chair. In practice, very few papers were rejected after being confidently accepted by the reviewers.

This was the first time Open Review was used as the main platform to run ECCV. In 2018, the program chairs used CMT3 for the user-facing interface and Open Review internally, for matching and conflict resolution. Since it is clearly preferable to only use a single platform, this year we switched to using Open Review in full. The experience was largely positive. The platform is highly-configurable, scalable, and open source. Being written in Python, it is easy to write scripts to extract data programmatically. The paper matching and conflict resolution algorithms and interfaces are top-notch, also due to the excellent author profiles in the platform. Naturally, there were a few kinks along the way due to the fact that the ECCV Open Review configuration was created from scratch for this event and it differs in substantial ways from many other Open Review conferences. However, the Open Review development and support team did a fantastic job in helping us to get the configuration right and to address issues in a timely manner as they unavoidably occurred. We cannot thank them enough for the tremendous effort they put into this project.

Finally, we would like to thank everyone involved in making ECCV 2020 possible in these very strange and difficult times. This starts with our authors, followed by the area chairs and reviewers, who ran the review process at an unprecedented scale. The whole Open Review team (and in particular Melisa Bok, Mohit Unyal, Carlos Mondragon Chapa, and Celeste Martinez Gomez) worked incredibly hard for the entire duration of the process. We would also like to thank René Vidal for contributing to the adoption of Open Review. Our thanks also go to Laurent Charling for TPMS and to the program chairs of ICML, ICLR, and NeurIPS for cross checking double submissions. We thank the website chair, Giovanni Farinella, and the CPI team (in particular Ashley Cook, Miriam Verdon, Nicola McGrane, and Sharon Kerr) for promptly adding material to the website as needed in the various phases of the process. Finally, we thank the publication chairs, Albert Ali Salah, Hamdi Dibeklioglu, Metehan Doyran, Henry Howard-Jenkins, Victor Prisacariu, Siyu Tang, and Gul Varol, who managed to compile these substantial proceedings in an exceedingly compressed schedule. We express our thanks to the ECVA team, in particular Kristina Scherbaum for allowing open access of the proceedings. We thank Alfred Hofmann from Springer who again serve as the publisher. Finally, we thank the other chairs of ECCV 2020, including in particular the general chairs for very useful feedback with the handling of the program.

August 2020   Andrea Vedaldi
                                                                        Horst Bischof
                                                                        Thomas Brox
                                                                    Jan-Michael Frahm

Organization

General Chairs

Vittorio Ferrari   Google Research, Switzerland
Bob Fisher   University of Edinburgh, UK
Cordelia Schmid   Google and Inria, France
Emanuele Trucco   University of Dundee, UK

Program Chairs

Andrea Vedaldi   University of Oxford, UK
Horst Bischof   Graz University of Technology, Austria
Thomas Brox   University of Freiburg, Germany
Jan-Michael Frahm   University of North Carolina, USA

Industrial Liaison Chairs

Jim Ashe   University of Edinburgh, UK
Helmut Grabner   Zurich University of Applied Sciences, Switzerland
Diane Larlus   NAVER LABS Europe, France
Cristian Novotny   University of Edinburgh, UK

Local Arrangement Chairs

Yvan Petillot   Heriot-Watt University, UK
Paul Siebert   University of Glasgow, UK

Academic Demonstration Chair

Thomas Mensink   Google Research and University of Amsterdam,
The Netherlands

Poster Chair

Stephen Mckenna   University of Dundee, UK

Technology Chair

Gerardo Aragon Camarasa   University of Glasgow, UK

Tutorial Chairs

Carlo Colombo   University of Florence, Italy
Sotirios Tsaftaris   University of Edinburgh, UK

Publication Chairs

Albert Ali Salah   Utrecht University, The Netherlands
Hamdi Dibeklioglu   Bilkent University, Turkey
Metehan Doyran   Utrecht University, The Netherlands
Henry Howard-Jenkins   University of Oxford, UK
Victor Adrian Prisacariu   University of Oxford, UK
Siyu Tang   ETH Zurich, Switzerland
Gul Varol   University of Oxford, UK

Website Chair

Giovanni Maria Farinella   University of Catania, Italy

Workshops Chairs

Adrien Bartoli   University of Clermont Auvergne, France
Andrea Fusiello   University of Udine, Italy

Area Chairs

Lourdes Agapito   University College London, UK
Zeynep Akata   University of Tübingen, Germany
Karteek Alahari   Inria, France
Antonis Argyros   University of Crete, Greece
Hossein Azizpour   KTH Royal Institute of Technology, Sweden
Joao P. Barreto   Universidade de Coimbra, Portugal
Alexander C. Berg   University of North Carolina at Chapel Hill, USA
Matthew B. Blaschko   KU Leuven, Belgium
Lubomir D. Bourdev   WaveOne, Inc., USA
Edmond Boyer   Inria, France
Yuri Boykov   University of Waterloo, Canada
Gabriel Brostow   University College London, UK
Michael S. Brown   National University of Singapore, Singapore
Jianfei Cai   Monash University, Australia
Barbara Caputo   Politecnico di Torino, Italy
Ayan Chakrabarti   Washington University, St. Louis, USA
Tat-Jen Cham   Nanyang Technological University, Singapore
Manmohan Chandraker   University of California, San Diego, USA
Rama Chellappa   Johns Hopkins University, USA
Liang-Chieh Chen   Google, USA

Yung-Yu Chuang	National Taiwan University, Taiwan
Ondrej Chum	Czech Technical University in Prague, Czech Republic
Brian Clipp	Kitware, USA
John Collomosse	University of Surrey and Adobe Research, UK
Jason J. Corso	University of Michigan, USA
David J. Crandall	Indiana University, USA
Daniel Cremers	University of California, Los Angeles, USA
Fabio Cuzzolin	Oxford Brookes University, UK
Jifeng Dai	SenseTime, SAR China
Kostas Daniilidis	University of Pennsylvania, USA
Andrew Davison	Imperial College London, UK
Alessio Del Bue	Fondazione Istituto Italiano di Tecnologia, Italy
Jia Deng	Princeton University, USA
Alexey Dosovitskiy	Google, Germany
Matthijs Douze	Facebook, France
Enrique Dunn	Stevens Institute of Technology, USA
Irfan Essa	Georgia Institute of Technology and Google, USA
Giovanni Maria Farinella	University of Catania, Italy
Ryan Farrell	Brigham Young University, USA
Paolo Favaro	University of Bern, Switzerland
Rogerio Feris	International Business Machines, USA
Cornelia Fermuller	University of Maryland, College Park, USA
David J. Fleet	Vector Institute, Canada
Friedrich Fraundorfer	DLR, Austria
Mario Fritz	CISPA Helmholtz Center for Information Security, Germany
Pascal Fua	EPFL (Swiss Federal Institute of Technology Lausanne), Switzerland
Yasutaka Furukawa	Simon Fraser University, Canada
Li Fuxin	Oregon State University, USA
Efstratios Gavves	University of Amsterdam, The Netherlands
Peter Vincent Gehler	Amazon, USA
Theo Gevers	University of Amsterdam, The Netherlands
Ross Girshick	Facebook AI Research, USA
Boqing Gong	Google, USA
Stephen Gould	Australian National University, Australia
Jinwei Gu	SenseTime Research, USA
Abhinav Gupta	Facebook, USA
Bohyung Han	Seoul National University, South Korea
Bharath Hariharan	Cornell University, USA
Tal Hassner	Facebook AI Research, USA
Xuming He	Australian National University, Australia
Joao F. Henriques	University of Oxford, UK
Adrian Hilton	University of Surrey, UK
Minh Hoai	Stony Brooks, State University of New York, USA
Derek Hoiem	University of Illinois Urbana-Champaign, USA

Timothy Hospedales	University of Edinburgh and Samsung, UK
Gang Hua	Wormpex AI Research, USA
Slobodan Ilic	Siemens AG, Germany
Hiroshi Ishikawa	Waseda University, Japan
Jiaya Jia	The Chinese University of Hong Kong, SAR China
Hailin Jin	Adobe Research, USA
Justin Johnson	University of Michigan, USA
Frederic Jurie	University of Caen Normandie, France
Fredrik Kahl	Chalmers University, Sweden
Sing Bing Kang	Zillow, USA
Gunhee Kim	Seoul National University, South Korea
Junmo Kim	Korea Advanced Institute of Science and Technology, South Korea
Tae-Kyun Kim	Imperial College London, UK
Ron Kimmel	Technion-Israel Institute of Technology, Israel
Alexander Kirillov	Facebook AI Research, USA
Kris Kitani	Carnegie Mellon University, USA
Iasonas Kokkinos	Ariel AI, UK
Vladlen Koltun	Intel Labs, USA
Nikos Komodakis	Ecole des Ponts ParisTech, France
Piotr Koniusz	Australian National University, Australia
M. Pawan Kumar	University of Oxford, UK
Kyros Kutulakos	University of Toronto, Canada
Christoph Lampert	IST Austria, Austria
Ivan Laptev	Inria, France
Diane Larlus	NAVER LABS Europe, France
Laura Leal-Taixe	Technical University Munich, Germany
Honglak Lee	Google and University of Michigan, USA
Joon-Young Lee	Adobe Research, USA
Kyoung Mu Lee	Seoul National University, South Korea
Seungyong Lee	POSTECH, South Korea
Yong Jae Lee	University of California, Davis, USA
Bastian Leibe	RWTH Aachen University, Germany
Victor Lempitsky	Samsung, Russia
Ales Leonardis	University of Birmingham, UK
Marius Leordeanu	Institute of Mathematics of the Romanian Academy, Romania
Vincent Lepetit	ENPC ParisTech, France
Hongdong Li	The Australian National University, Australia
Xi Li	Zhejiang University, China
Yin Li	University of Wisconsin-Madison, USA
Zicheng Liao	Zhejiang University, China
Jongwoo Lim	Hanyang University, South Korea
Stephen Lin	Microsoft Research Asia, China
Yen-Yu Lin	National Chiao Tung University, Taiwan, China
Zhe Lin	Adobe Research, USA

Haibin Ling	Stony Brooks, State University of New York, USA
Jiaying Liu	Peking University, China
Ming-Yu Liu	NVIDIA, USA
Si Liu	Beihang University, China
Xiaoming Liu	Michigan State University, USA
Huchuan Lu	Dalian University of Technology, China
Simon Lucey	Carnegie Mellon University, USA
Jiebo Luo	University of Rochester, USA
Julien Mairal	Inria, France
Michael Maire	University of Chicago, USA
Subhransu Maji	University of Massachusetts, Amherst, USA
Yasushi Makihara	Osaka University, Japan
Jiri Matas	Czech Technical University in Prague, Czech Republic
Yasuyuki Matsushita	Osaka University, Japan
Philippos Mordohai	Stevens Institute of Technology, USA
Vittorio Murino	University of Verona, Italy
Naila Murray	NAVER LABS Europe, France
Hajime Nagahara	Osaka University, Japan
P. J. Narayanan	International Institute of Information Technology (IIIT), Hyderabad, India
Nassir Navab	Technical University of Munich, Germany
Natalia Neverova	Facebook AI Research, France
Matthias Niessner	Technical University of Munich, Germany
Jean-Marc Odobez	Idiap Research Institute and Swiss Federal Institute of Technology Lausanne, Switzerland
Francesca Odone	Università di Genova, Italy
Takeshi Oishi	The University of Tokyo, Tokyo Institute of Technology, Japan
Vicente Ordonez	University of Virginia, USA
Manohar Paluri	Facebook AI Research, USA
Maja Pantic	Imperial College London, UK
In Kyu Park	Inha University, South Korea
Ioannis Patras	Queen Mary University of London, UK
Patrick Perez	Valeo, France
Bryan A. Plummer	Boston University, USA
Thomas Pock	Graz University of Technology, Austria
Marc Pollefeys	ETH Zurich and Microsoft MR & AI Zurich Lab, Switzerland
Jean Ponce	Inria, France
Gerard Pons-Moll	MPII, Saarland Informatics Campus, Germany
Jordi Pont-Tuset	Google, Switzerland
James Matthew Rehg	Georgia Institute of Technology, USA
Ian Reid	University of Adelaide, Australia
Olaf Ronneberger	DeepMind London, UK
Stefan Roth	TU Darmstadt, Germany
Bryan Russell	Adobe Research, USA

Mathieu Salzmann	EPFL, Switzerland
Dimitris Samaras	Stony Brook University, USA
Imari Sato	National Institute of Informatics (NII), Japan
Yoichi Sato	The University of Tokyo, Japan
Torsten Sattler	Czech Technical University in Prague, Czech Republic
Daniel Scharstein	Middlebury College, USA
Bernt Schiele	MPII, Saarland Informatics Campus, Germany
Julia A. Schnabel	King's College London, UK
Nicu Sebe	University of Trento, Italy
Greg Shakhnarovich	Toyota Technological Institute at Chicago, USA
Humphrey Shi	University of Oregon, USA
Jianbo Shi	University of Pennsylvania, USA
Jianping Shi	SenseTime, China
Leonid Sigal	University of British Columbia, Canada
Cees Snoek	University of Amsterdam, The Netherlands
Richard Souvenir	Temple University, USA
Hao Su	University of California, San Diego, USA
Akihiro Sugimoto	National Institute of Informatics (NII), Japan
Jian Sun	Megvii Technology, China
Jian Sun	Xi'an Jiaotong University, China
Chris Sweeney	Facebook Reality Labs, USA
Yu-wing Tai	Kuaishou Technology, China
Chi-Keung Tang	The Hong Kong University of Science and Technology, SAR China
Radu Timofte	ETH Zurich, Switzerland
Sinisa Todorovic	Oregon State University, USA
Giorgos Tolias	Czech Technical University in Prague, Czech Republic
Carlo Tomasi	Duke University, USA
Tatiana Tommasi	Politecnico di Torino, Italy
Lorenzo Torresani	Facebook AI Research and Dartmouth College, USA
Alexander Toshev	Google, USA
Zhuowen Tu	University of California, San Diego, USA
Tinne Tuytelaars	KU Leuven, Belgium
Jasper Uijlings	Google, Switzerland
Nuno Vasconcelos	University of California, San Diego, USA
Olga Veksler	University of Waterloo, Canada
Rene Vidal	Johns Hopkins University, USA
Gang Wang	Alibaba Group, China
Jingdong Wang	Microsoft Research Asia, China
Yizhou Wang	Peking University, China
Lior Wolf	Facebook AI Research and Tel Aviv University, Israel
Jianxin Wu	Nanjing University, China
Tao Xiang	University of Surrey, UK
Saining Xie	Facebook AI Research, USA
Ming-Hsuan Yang	University of California at Merced and Google, USA
Ruigang Yang	University of Kentucky, USA

Kwang Moo Yi	University of Victoria, Canada
Zhaozheng Yin	Stony Brook, State University of New York, USA
Chang D. Yoo	Korea Advanced Institute of Science and Technology, South Korea
Shaodi You	University of Amsterdam, The Netherlands
Jingyi Yu	ShanghaiTech University, China
Stella Yu	University of California, Berkeley, and ICSI, USA
Stefanos Zafeiriou	Imperial College London, UK
Hongbin Zha	Peking University, China
Tianzhu Zhang	University of Science and Technology of China, China
Liang Zheng	Australian National University, Australia
Todd E. Zickler	Harvard University, USA
Andrew Zisserman	University of Oxford, UK

Technical Program Committee

Sathyanarayanan
   N. Aakur
Wael Abd Almgaeed
Abdelrahman
   Abdelhamed
Abdullah Abuolaim
Supreeth Achar
Hanno Ackermann
Ehsan Adeli
Triantafyllos Afouras
Sameer Agarwal
Aishwarya Agrawal
Harsh Agrawal
Pulkit Agrawal
Antonio Agudo
Eirikur Agustsson
Karim Ahmed
Byeongjoo Ahn
Unaiza Ahsan
Thalaiyasingam Ajanthan
Kenan E. Ak
Emre Akbas
Naveed Akhtar
Derya Akkaynak
Yagiz Aksoy
Ziad Al-Halah
Xavier Alameda-Pineda
Jean-Baptiste Alayrac

Samuel Albanie
Shadi Albarqouni
Cenek Albl
Hassan Abu Alhaija
Daniel Aliaga
Mohammad
   S. Aliakbarian
Rahaf Aljundi
Thiemo Alldieck
Jon Almazan
Jose M. Alvarez
Senjian An
Saket Anand
Codruta Ancuti
Cosmin Ancuti
Peter Anderson
Juan Andrade-Cetto
Alexander Andreopoulos
Misha Andriluka
Dragomir Anguelov
Rushil Anirudh
Michel Antunes
Oisin Mac Aodha
Srikar Appalaraju
Relja Arandjelovic
Nikita Araslanov
Andre Araujo
Helder Araujo

Pablo Arbelaez
Shervin Ardeshir
Sercan O. Arik
Anil Armagan
Anurag Arnab
Chetan Arora
Federica Arrigoni
Mathieu Aubry
Shai Avidan
Angelica I. Aviles-Rivero
Yannis Avrithis
Ismail Ben Ayed
Shekoofeh Azizi
Ioan Andrei Bârsan
Artem Babenko
Deepak Babu Sam
Seung-Hwan Baek
Seungryul Baek
Andrew D. Bagdanov
Shai Bagon
Yuval Bahat
Junjie Bai
Song Bai
Xiang Bai
Yalong Bai
Yancheng Bai
Peter Bajcsy
Slawomir Bak

Mahsa Baktashmotlagh
Kavita Bala
Yogesh Balaji
Guha Balakrishnan
V. N. Balasubramanian
Federico Baldassarre
Vassileios Balntas
Shurjo Banerjee
Aayush Bansal
Ankan Bansal
Jianmin Bao
Linchao Bao
Wenbo Bao
Yingze Bao
Akash Bapat
Md Jawadul Hasan Bappy
Fabien Baradel
Lorenzo Baraldi
Daniel Barath
Adrian Barbu
Kobus Barnard
Nick Barnes
Francisco Barranco
Jonathan T. Barron
Arslan Basharat
Chaim Baskin
Anil S. Baslamisli
Jorge Batista
Kayhan Batmanghelich
Konstantinos Batsos
David Bau
Luis Baumela
Christoph Baur
Eduardo
  Bayro-Corrochano
Paul Beardsley
Jan Bednavr'ik
Oscar Beijbom
Philippe Bekaert
Esube Bekele
Vasileios Belagiannis
Ohad Ben-Shahar
Abhijit Bendale
Róger Bermúdez-Chacón
Maxim Berman
Jesus Bermudez-cameo

Florian Bernard
Stefano Berretti
Marcelo Bertalmio
Gedas Bertasius
Cigdem Beyan
Lucas Beyer
Vijayakumar Bhagavatula
Arjun Nitin Bhagoji
Apratim Bhattacharyya
Binod Bhattarai
Sai Bi
Jia-Wang Bian
Simone Bianco
Adel Bibi
Tolga Birdal
Tom Bishop
Soma Biswas
Mårten Björkman
Volker Blanz
Vishnu Boddeti
Navaneeth Bodla
Simion-Vlad Bogolin
Xavier Boix
Piotr Bojanowski
Timo Bolkart
Guido Borghi
Larbi Boubchir
Guillaume Bourmaud
Adrien Bousseau
Thierry Bouwmans
Richard Bowden
Hakan Boyraz
Mathieu Brédif
Samarth Brahmbhatt
Steve Branson
Nikolas Brasch
Biagio Brattoli
Ernesto Brau
Toby P. Breckon
Francois Bremond
Jesus Briales
Sofia Broomé
Marcus A. Brubaker
Luc Brun
Silvia Bucci
Shyamal Buch

Pradeep Buddharaju
Uta Buechler
Mai Bui
Tu Bui
Adrian Bulat
Giedrius T. Burachas
Elena Burceanu
Xavier P. Burgos-Artizzu
Kaylee Burns
Andrei Bursuc
Benjamin Busam
Wonmin Byeon
Zoya Bylinskii
Sergi Caelles
Jianrui Cai
Minjie Cai
Yujun Cai
Zhaowei Cai
Zhipeng Cai
Juan C. Caicedo
Simone Calderara
Necati Cihan Camgoz
Dylan Campbell
Octavia Camps
Jiale Cao
Kaidi Cao
Liangliang Cao
Xiangyong Cao
Xiaochun Cao
Yang Cao
Yu Cao
Yue Cao
Zhangjie Cao
Luca Carlone
Mathilde Caron
Dan Casas
Thomas J. Cashman
Umberto Castellani
Lluis Castrejon
Jacopo Cavazza
Fabio Cermelli
Hakan Cevikalp
Menglei Chai
Ishani Chakraborty
Rudrasis Chakraborty
Antoni B. Chan

Kwok-Ping Chan
Siddhartha Chandra
Sharat Chandran
Arjun Chandrasekaran
Angel X. Chang
Che-Han Chang
Hong Chang
Hyun Sung Chang
Hyung Jin Chang
Jianlong Chang
Ju Yong Chang
Ming-Ching Chang
Simyung Chang
Xiaojun Chang
Yu-Wei Chao
Devendra S. Chaplot
Arslan Chaudhry
Rizwan A. Chaudhry
Can Chen
Chang Chen
Chao Chen
Chen Chen
Chu-Song Chen
Dapeng Chen
Dong Chen
Dongdong Chen
Guanying Chen
Hongge Chen
Hsin-yi Chen
Huaijin Chen
Hwann-Tzong Chen
Jianbo Chen
Jianhui Chen
Jiansheng Chen
Jiaxin Chen
Jie Chen
Jun-Cheng Chen
Kan Chen
Kevin Chen
Lin Chen
Long Chen
Min-Hung Chen
Qifeng Chen
Shi Chen
Shixing Chen
Tianshui Chen

Weifeng Chen
Weikai Chen
Xi Chen
Xiaohan Chen
Xiaozhi Chen
Xilin Chen
Xingyu Chen
Xinlei Chen
Xinyun Chen
Yi-Ting Chen
Yilun Chen
Ying-Cong Chen
Yinpeng Chen
Yiran Chen
Yu Chen
Yu-Sheng Chen
Yuhua Chen
Yun-Chun Chen
Yunpeng Chen
Yuntao Chen
Zhuoyuan Chen
Zitian Chen
Anchieh Cheng
Bowen Cheng
Erkang Cheng
Gong Cheng
Guangliang Cheng
Jingchun Cheng
Jun Cheng
Li Cheng
Ming-Ming Cheng
Yu Cheng
Ziang Cheng
Anoop Cherian
Dmitry Chetverikov
Ngai-man Cheung
William Cheung
Ajad Chhatkuli
Naoki Chiba
Benjamin Chidester
Han-pang Chiu
Mang Tik Chiu
Wei-Chen Chiu
Donghyeon Cho
Hojin Cho
Minsu Cho

Nam Ik Cho
Tim Cho
Tae Eun Choe
Chiho Choi
Edward Choi
Inchang Choi
Jinsoo Choi
Jonghyun Choi
Jongwon Choi
Yukyung Choi
Hisham Cholakkal
Eunji Chong
Jaegul Choo
Christopher Choy
Hang Chu
Peng Chu
Wen-Sheng Chu
Albert Chung
Joon Son Chung
Hai Ci
Safa Cicek
Ramazan G. Cinbis
Arridhana Ciptadi
Javier Civera
James J. Clark
Ronald Clark
Felipe Codevilla
Michael Cogswell
Andrea Cohen
Maxwell D. Collins
Carlo Colombo
Yang Cong
Adria R. Continente
Marcella Cornia
John Richard Corring
Darren Cosker
Dragos Costea
Garrison W. Cottrell
Florent Couzinie-Devy
Marco Cristani
Ioana Croitoru
James L. Crowley
Jiequan Cui
Zhaopeng Cui
Ross Cutler
Antonio D'Innocente

Rozenn Dahyot
Bo Dai
Dengxin Dai
Hang Dai
Longquan Dai
Shuyang Dai
Xiyang Dai
Yuchao Dai
Adrian V. Dalca
Dima Damen
Bharath B. Damodaran
Kristin Dana
Martin Danelljan
Zheng Dang
Zachary Alan Daniels
Donald G. Dansereau
Abhishek Das
Samyak Datta
Achal Dave
Titas De
Rodrigo de Bem
Teo de Campos
Raoul de Charette
Shalini De Mello
Joseph DeGol
Herve Delingette
Haowen Deng
Jiankang Deng
Weijian Deng
Zhiwei Deng
Joachim Denzler
Konstantinos G. Derpanis
Aditya Deshpande
Frederic Devernay
Somdip Dey
Arturo Deza
Abhinav Dhall
Helisa Dhamo
Vikas Dhiman
Fillipe Dias Moreira
  de Souza
Ali Diba
Ferran Diego
Guiguang Ding
Henghui Ding
Jian Ding

Mingyu Ding
Xinghao Ding
Zhengming Ding
Robert DiPietro
Cosimo Distante
Ajay Divakaran
Mandar Dixit
Abdelaziz Djelouah
Thanh-Toan Do
Jose Dolz
Bo Dong
Chao Dong
Jiangxin Dong
Weiming Dong
Weisheng Dong
Xingping Dong
Xuanyi Dong
Yinpeng Dong
Gianfranco Doretto
Hazel Doughty
Hassen Drira
Bertram Drost
Dawei Du
Ye Duan
Yueqi Duan
Abhimanyu Dubey
Anastasia Dubrovina
Stefan Duffner
Chi Nhan Duong
Thibaut Durand
Zoran Duric
Iulia Duta
Debidatta Dwibedi
Benjamin Eckart
Marc Eder
Marzieh Edraki
Alexei A. Efros
Kiana Ehsani
Hazm Kemal Ekenel
James H. Elder
Mohamed Elgharib
Shireen Elhabian
Ehsan Elhamifar
Mohamed Elhoseiny
Ian Endres
N. Benjamin Erichson

Jan Ernst
Sergio Escalera
Francisco Escolano
Victor Escorcia
Carlos Esteves
Francisco J. Estrada
Bin Fan
Chenyou Fan
Deng-Ping Fan
Haoqi Fan
Hehe Fan
Heng Fan
Kai Fan
Lijie Fan
Linxi Fan
Quanfu Fan
Shaojing Fan
Xiaochuan Fan
Xin Fan
Yuchen Fan
Sean Fanello
Hao-Shu Fang
Haoyang Fang
Kuan Fang
Yi Fang
Yuming Fang
Azade Farshad
Alireza Fathi
Raanan Fattal
Joao Fayad
Xiaohan Fei
Christoph Feichtenhofer
Michael Felsberg
Chen Feng
Jiashi Feng
Junyi Feng
Mengyang Feng
Qianli Feng
Zhenhua Feng
Michele Fenzi
Andras Ferencz
Martin Fergie
Basura Fernando
Ethan Fetaya
Michael Firman
John W. Fisher

Matthew Fisher
Boris Flach
Corneliu Florea
Wolfgang Foerstner
David Fofi
Gian Luca Foresti
Per-Erik Forssen
David Fouhey
Katerina Fragkiadaki
Victor Fragoso
Jean-Sébastien Franco
Ohad Fried
Iuri Frosio
Cheng-Yang Fu
Huazhu Fu
Jianlong Fu
Jingjing Fu
Xueyang Fu
Yanwei Fu
Ying Fu
Yun Fu
Olac Fuentes
Kent Fujiwara
Takuya Funatomi
Christopher Funk
Thomas Funkhouser
Antonino Furnari
Ryo Furukawa
Erik Gärtner
Raghudeep Gadde
Matheus Gadelha
Vandit Gajjar
Trevor Gale
Juergen Gall
Mathias Gallardo
Guillermo Gallego
Orazio Gallo
Chuang Gan
Zhe Gan
Madan Ravi Ganesh
Aditya Ganeshan
Siddha Ganju
Bin-Bin Gao
Changxin Gao
Feng Gao
Hongchang Gao

Jin Gao
Jiyang Gao
Junbin Gao
Katelyn Gao
Lin Gao
Mingfei Gao
Ruiqi Gao
Ruohan Gao
Shenghua Gao
Yuan Gao
Yue Gao
Noa Garcia
Alberto Garcia-Garcia
Guillermo
    Garcia-Hernando
Jacob R. Gardner
Animesh Garg
Kshitiz Garg
Rahul Garg
Ravi Garg
Philip N. Garner
Kirill Gavrilyuk
Paul Gay
Shiming Ge
Weifeng Ge
Baris Gecer
Xin Geng
Kyle Genova
Stamatios Georgoulis
Bernard Ghanem
Michael Gharbi
Kamran Ghasedi
Golnaz Ghiasi
Arnab Ghosh
Partha Ghosh
Silvio Giancola
Andrew Gilbert
Rohit Girdhar
Xavier Giro-i-Nieto
Thomas Gittings
Ioannis Gkioulekas
Clement Godard
Vaibhava Goel
Bastian Goldluecke
Lluis Gomez
Nuno Gonçalves

Dong Gong
Ke Gong
Mingming Gong
Abel Gonzalez-Garcia
Ariel Gordon
Daniel Gordon
Paulo Gotardo
Venu Madhav Govindu
Ankit Goyal
Priya Goyal
Raghav Goyal
Benjamin Graham
Douglas Gray
Brent A. Griffin
Etienne Grossmann
David Gu
Jiayuan Gu
Jiuxiang Gu
Lin Gu
Qiao Gu
Shuhang Gu
Jose J. Guerrero
Paul Guerrero
Jie Gui
Jean-Yves Guillemaut
Riza Alp Guler
Erhan Gundogdu
Fatma Guney
Guodong Guo
Kaiwen Guo
Qi Guo
Sheng Guo
Shi Guo
Tiantong Guo
Xiaojie Guo
Yijie Guo
Yiluan Guo
Yuanfang Guo
Yulan Guo
Agrim Gupta
Ankush Gupta
Mohit Gupta
Saurabh Gupta
Tanmay Gupta
Danna Gurari
Abner Guzman-Rivera

JunYoung Gwak
Michael Gygli
Jung-Woo Ha
Simon Hadfield
Isma Hadji
Bjoern Haefner
Taeyoung Hahn
Levente Hajder
Peter Hall
Emanuela Haller
Stefan Haller
Bumsub Ham
Abdullah Hamdi
Dongyoon Han
Hu Han
Jungong Han
Junwei Han
Kai Han
Tian Han
Xiaoguang Han
Xintong Han
Yahong Han
Ankur Handa
Zekun Hao
Albert Haque
Tatsuya Harada
Mehrtash Harandi
Adam W. Harley
Mahmudul Hasan
Atsushi Hashimoto
Ali Hatamizadeh
Munawar Hayat
Dongliang He
Jingrui He
Junfeng He
Kaiming He
Kun He
Lei He
Pan He
Ran He
Shengfeng He
Tong He
Weipeng He
Xuming He
Yang He
Yihui He

Zhihai He
Chinmay Hegde
Janne Heikkila
Mattias P. Heinrich
Stéphane Herbin
Alexander Hermans
Luis Herranz
John R. Hershey
Aaron Hertzmann
Roei Herzig
Anders Heyden
Steven Hickson
Otmar Hilliges
Tomas Hodan
Judy Hoffman
Michael Hofmann
Yannick Hold-Geoffroy
Namdar Homayounfar
Sina Honari
Richang Hong
Seunghoon Hong
Xiaopeng Hong
Yi Hong
Hidekata Hontani
Anthony Hoogs
Yedid Hoshen
Mir Rayat Imtiaz Hossain
Junhui Hou
Le Hou
Lu Hou
Tingbo Hou
Wei-Lin Hsiao
Cheng-Chun Hsu
Gee-Sern Jison Hsu
Kuang-jui Hsu
Changbo Hu
Di Hu
Guosheng Hu
Han Hu
Hao Hu
Hexiang Hu
Hou-Ning Hu
Jie Hu
Junlin Hu
Nan Hu
Ping Hu

Ronghang Hu
Xiaowei Hu
Yinlin Hu
Yuan-Ting Hu
Zhe Hu
Binh-Son Hua
Yang Hua
Bingyao Huang
Di Huang
Dong Huang
Fay Huang
Haibin Huang
Haozhi Huang
Heng Huang
Huaibo Huang
Jia-Bin Huang
Jing Huang
Jingwei Huang
Kaizhu Huang
Lei Huang
Qiangui Huang
Qiaoying Huang
Qingqiu Huang
Qixing Huang
Shaoli Huang
Sheng Huang
Siyuan Huang
Weilin Huang
Wenbing Huang
Xiangru Huang
Xun Huang
Yan Huang
Yifei Huang
Yue Huang
Zhiwu Huang
Zilong Huang
Minyoung Huh
Zhuo Hui
Matthias B. Hullin
Martin Humenberger
Wei-Chih Hung
Zhouyuan Huo
Junhwa Hur
Noureldien Hussein
Jyh-Jing Hwang
Seong Jae Hwang

Sung Ju Hwang
Ichiro Ide
Ivo Ihrke
Daiki Ikami
Satoshi Ikehata
Nazli Ikizler-Cinbis
Sunghoon Im
Yani Ioannou
Radu Tudor Ionescu
Umar Iqbal
Go Irie
Ahmet Iscen
Md Amirul Islam
Vamsi Ithapu
Nathan Jacobs
Arpit Jain
Himalaya Jain
Suyog Jain
Stuart James
Won-Dong Jang
Yunseok Jang
Ronnachai Jaroensri
Dinesh Jayaraman
Sadeep Jayasumana
Suren Jayasuriya
Herve Jegou
Simon Jenni
Hae-Gon Jeon
Yunho Jeon
Koteswar R. Jerripothula
Hueihan Jhuang
I-hong Jhuo
Dinghuang Ji
Hui Ji
Jingwei Ji
Pan Ji
Yanli Ji
Baoxiong Jia
Kui Jia
Xu Jia
Chiyu Max Jiang
Haiyong Jiang
Hao Jiang
Huaizu Jiang
Huajie Jiang
Ke Jiang

Lai Jiang
Li Jiang
Lu Jiang
Ming Jiang
Peng Jiang
Shuqiang Jiang
Wei Jiang
Xudong Jiang
Zhuolin Jiang
Jianbo Jiao
Zequn Jie
Dakai Jin
Kyong Hwan Jin
Lianwen Jin
SouYoung Jin
Xiaojie Jin
Xin Jin
Nebojsa Jojic
Alexis Joly
Michael Jeffrey Jones
Hanbyul Joo
Jungseock Joo
Kyungdon Joo
Ajjen Joshi
Shantanu H. Joshi
Da-Cheng Juan
Marco Körner
Kevin Köser
Asim Kadav
Christine Kaeser-Chen
Kushal Kafle
Dagmar Kainmueller
Ioannis A. Kakadiaris
Zdenek Kalal
Nima Kalantari
Yannis Kalantidis
Mahdi M. Kalayeh
Anmol Kalia
Sinan Kalkan
Vicky Kalogeiton
Ashwin Kalyan
Joni-kristian Kamarainen
Gerda Kamberova
Chandra Kambhamettu
Martin Kampel
Meina Kan

Christopher Kanan
Kenichi Kanatani
Angjoo Kanazawa
Atsushi Kanehira
Takuhiro Kaneko
Asako Kanezaki
Bingyi Kang
Di Kang
Sunghun Kang
Zhao Kang
Vadim Kantorov
Abhishek Kar
Amlan Kar
Theofanis Karaletsos
Leonid Karlinsky
Kevin Karsch
Angelos Katharopoulos
Isinsu Katircioglu
Hiroharu Kato
Zoltan Kato
Dotan Kaufman
Jan Kautz
Rei Kawakami
Qiuhong Ke
Wadim Kehl
Petr Kellnhofer
Aniruddha Kembhavi
Cem Keskin
Margret Keuper
Daniel Keysers
Ashkan Khakzar
Fahad Khan
Naeemullah Khan
Salman Khan
Siddhesh Khandelwal
Rawal Khirodkar
Anna Khoreva
Tejas Khot
Parmeshwar Khurd
Hadi Kiapour
Joe Kileel
Chanho Kim
Dahun Kim
Edward Kim
Eunwoo Kim
Han-ul Kim

Hansung Kim
Heewon Kim
Hyo Jin Kim
Hyunwoo J. Kim
Jinkyu Kim
Jiwon Kim
Jongmin Kim
Junsik Kim
Junyeong Kim
Min H. Kim
Namil Kim
Pyojin Kim
Seon Joo Kim
Seong Tae Kim
Seungryong Kim
Sungwoong Kim
Tae Hyun Kim
Vladimir Kim
Won Hwa Kim
Yonghyun Kim
Benjamin Kimia
Akisato Kimura
Pieter-Jan Kindermans
Zsolt Kira
Itaru Kitahara
Hedvig Kjellstrom
Jan Knopp
Takumi Kobayashi
Erich Kobler
Parker Koch
Reinhard Koch
Elyor Kodirov
Amir Kolaman
Nicholas Kolkin
Dimitrios Kollias
Stefanos Kollias
Soheil Kolouri
Adams Wai-Kin Kong
Naejin Kong
Shu Kong
Tao Kong
Yu Kong
Yoshinori Konishi
Daniil Kononenko
Theodora Kontogianni
Simon Korman

Adam Kortylewski
Jana Kosecka
Jean Kossaifi
Satwik Kottur
Rigas Kouskouridas
Adriana Kovashka
Rama Kovvuri
Adarsh Kowdle
Jedrzej Kozerawski
Mateusz Kozinski
Philipp Kraehenbuehl
Gregory Kramida
Josip Krapac
Dmitry Kravchenko
Ranjay Krishna
Pavel Krsek
Alexander Krull
Jakob Kruse
Hiroyuki Kubo
Hilde Kuehne
Jason Kuen
Andreas Kuhn
Arjan Kuijper
Zuzana Kukelova
Ajay Kumar
Amit Kumar
Avinash Kumar
Suryansh Kumar
Vijay Kumar
Kaustav Kundu
Weicheng Kuo
Nojun Kwak
Suha Kwak
Junseok Kwon
Nikolaos Kyriazis
Zorah Lähner
Ankit Laddha
Florent Lafarge
Jean Lahoud
Kevin Lai
Shang-Hong Lai
Wei-Sheng Lai
Yu-Kun Lai
Iro Laina
Antony Lam
John Wheatley Lambert

Xiangyuan lan
Xu Lan
Charis Lanaras
Georg Langs
Oswald Lanz
Dong Lao
Yizhen Lao
Agata Lapedriza
Gustav Larsson
Viktor Larsson
Katrin Lasinger
Christoph Lassner
Longin Jan Latecki
Stéphane Lathuilière
Rynson Lau
Hei Law
Justin Lazarow
Svetlana Lazebnik
Hieu Le
Huu Le
Ngan Hoang Le
Trung-Nghia Le
Vuong Le
Colin Lea
Erik Learned-Miller
Chen-Yu Lee
Gim Hee Lee
Hsin-Ying Lee
Hyungtae Lee
Jae-Han Lee
Jimmy Addison Lee
Joonseok Lee
Kibok Lee
Kuang-Huei Lee
Kwonjoon Lee
Minsik Lee
Sang-chul Lee
Seungkyu Lee
Soochan Lee
Stefan Lee
Taehee Lee
Andreas Lehrmann
Jie Lei
Peng Lei
Matthew Joseph Leotta
Wee Kheng Leow

Gil Levi
Evgeny Levinkov
Aviad Levis
Jose Lezama
Ang Li
Bin Li
Bing Li
Boyi Li
Changsheng Li
Chao Li
Chen Li
Cheng Li
Chenglong Li
Chi Li
Chun-Guang Li
Chun-Liang Li
Chunyuan Li
Dong Li
Guanbin Li
Hao Li
Haoxiang Li
Hongsheng Li
Hongyang Li
Houqiang Li
Huibin Li
Jia Li
Jianan Li
Jianguo Li
Junnan Li
Junxuan Li
Kai Li
Ke Li
Kejie Li
Kunpeng Li
Lerenhan Li
Li Erran Li
Mengtian Li
Mu Li
Peihua Li
Peiyi Li
Ping Li
Qi Li
Qing Li
Ruiyu Li
Ruoteng Li
Shaozi Li

Sheng Li
Shiwei Li
Shuang Li
Siyang Li
Stan Z. Li
Tianye Li
Wei Li
Weixin Li
Wen Li
Wenbo Li
Xiaomeng Li
Xin Li
Xiu Li
Xuelong Li
Xueting Li
Yan Li
Yandong Li
Yanghao Li
Yehao Li
Yi Li
Yijun Li
Yikang LI
Yining Li
Yongjie Li
Yu Li
Yu-Jhe Li
Yunpeng Li
Yunsheng Li
Yunzhu Li
Zhe Li
Zhen Li
Zhengqi Li
Zhenyang Li
Zhuwen Li
Dongze Lian
Xiaochen Lian
Zhouhui Lian
Chen Liang
Jie Liang
Ming Liang
Paul Pu Liang
Pengpeng Liang
Shu Liang
Wei Liang
Jing Liao
Minghui Liao

Renjie Liao
Shengcai Liao
Shuai Liao
Yiyi Liao
Ser-Nam Lim
Chen-Hsuan Lin
Chung-Ching Lin
Dahua Lin
Ji Lin
Kevin Lin
Tianwei Lin
Tsung-Yi Lin
Tsung-Yu Lin
Wei-An Lin
Weiyao Lin
Yen-Chen Lin
Yuewei Lin
David B. Lindell
Drew Linsley
Krzysztof Lis
Roee Litman
Jim Little
An-An Liu
Bo Liu
Buyu Liu
Chao Liu
Chen Liu
Cheng-lin Liu
Chenxi Liu
Dong Liu
Feng Liu
Guilin Liu
Haomiao Liu
Heshan Liu
Hong Liu
Ji Liu
Jingen Liu
Jun Liu
Lanlan Liu
Li Liu
Liu Liu
Mengyuan Liu
Miaomiao Liu
Nian Liu
Ping Liu
Risheng Liu

Sheng Liu
Shu Liu
Shuaicheng Liu
Sifei Liu
Siqi Liu
Siying Liu
Songtao Liu
Ting Liu
Tongliang Liu
Tyng-Luh Liu
Wanquan Liu
Wei Liu
Weiyang Liu
Weizhe Liu
Wenyu Liu
Wu Liu
Xialei Liu
Xianglong Liu
Xiaodong Liu
Xiaofeng Liu
Xihui Liu
Xingyu Liu
Xinwang Liu
Xuanqing Liu
Xuebo Liu
Yang Liu
Yaojie Liu
Yebin Liu
Yen-Cheng Liu
Yiming Liu
Yu Liu
Yu-Shen Liu
Yufan Liu
Yun Liu
Zheng Liu
Zhijian Liu
Zhuang Liu
Zichuan Liu
Ziwei Liu
Zongyi Liu
Stephan Liwicki
Liliana Lo Presti
Chengjiang Long
Fuchen Long
Mingsheng Long
Xiang Long

Yang Long
Charles T. Loop
Antonio Lopez
Roberto J. Lopez-Sastre
Javier Lorenzo-Navarro
Manolis Lourakis
Boyu Lu
Canyi Lu
Feng Lu
Guoyu Lu
Hongtao Lu
Jiajun Lu
Jiasen Lu
Jiwen Lu
Kaiyue Lu
Le Lu
Shao-Ping Lu
Shijian Lu
Xiankai Lu
Xin Lu
Yao Lu
Yiping Lu
Yongxi Lu
Yongyi Lu
Zhiwu Lu
Fujun Luan
Benjamin E. Lundell
Hao Luo
Jian-Hao Luo
Ruotian Luo
Weixin Luo
Wenhan Luo
Wenjie Luo
Yan Luo
Zelun Luo
Zixin Luo
Khoa Luu
Zhaoyang Lv
Pengyuan Lyu
Thomas Möllenhoff
Matthias Müller
Bingpeng Ma
Chih-Yao Ma
Chongyang Ma
Huimin Ma
Jiayi Ma

K. T. Ma
Ke Ma
Lin Ma
Liqian Ma
Shugao Ma
Wei-Chiu Ma
Xiaojian Ma
Xingjun Ma
Zhanyu Ma
Zheng Ma
Radek Jakob Mackowiak
Ludovic Magerand
Shweta Mahajan
Siddharth Mahendran
Long Mai
Ameesh Makadia
Oscar Mendez Maldonado
Mateusz Malinowski
Yury Malkov
Arun Mallya
Dipu Manandhar
Massimiliano Mancini
Fabian Manhardt
Kevis-kokitsi Maninis
Varun Manjunatha
Junhua Mao
Xudong Mao
Alina Marcu
Edgar Margffoy-Tuay
Dmitrii Marin
Manuel J. Marin-Jimenez
Kenneth Marino
Niki Martinel
Julieta Martinez
Jonathan Masci
Tomohiro Mashita
Iacopo Masi
David Masip
Daniela Massiceti
Stefan Mathe
Yusuke Matsui
Tetsu Matsukawa
Iain A. Matthews
Kevin James Matzen
Bruce Allen Maxwell
Stephen Maybank

Helmut Mayer
Amir Mazaheri
David McAllester
Steven McDonagh
Stephen J. Mckenna
Roey Mechrez
Prakhar Mehrotra
Christopher Mei
Xue Mei
Paulo R. S. Mendonca
Lili Meng
Zibo Meng
Thomas Mensink
Bjoern Menze
Michele Merler
Kourosh Meshgi
Pascal Mettes
Christopher Metzler
Liang Mi
Qiguang Miao
Xin Miao
Tomer Michaeli
Frank Michel
Antoine Miech
Krystian Mikolajczyk
Peyman Milanfar
Ben Mildenhall
Gregor Miller
Fausto Milletari
Dongbo Min
Kyle Min
Pedro Miraldo
Dmytro Mishkin
Anand Mishra
Ashish Mishra
Ishan Misra
Niluthpol C. Mithun
Kaushik Mitra
Niloy Mitra
Anton Mitrokhin
Ikuhisa Mitsugami
Anurag Mittal
Kaichun Mo
Zhipeng Mo
Davide Modolo
Michael Moeller

Pritish Mohapatra
Pavlo Molchanov
Davide Moltisanti
Pascal Monasse
Mathew Monfort
Aron Monszpart
Sean Moran
Vlad I. Morariu
Francesc Moreno-Noguer
Pietro Morerio
Stylianos Moschoglou
Yael Moses
Roozbeh Mottaghi
Pierre Moulon
Arsalan Mousavian
Yadong Mu
Yasuhiro Mukaigawa
Lopamudra Mukherjee
Yusuke Mukuta
Ravi Teja Mullapudi
Mario Enrique Munich
Zachary Murez
Ana C. Murillo
J. Krishna Murthy
Damien Muselet
Armin Mustafa
Siva Karthik Mustikovela
Carlo Dal Mutto
Moin Nabi
Varun K. Nagaraja
Tushar Nagarajan
Arsha Nagrani
Seungjun Nah
Nikhil Naik
Yoshikatsu Nakajima
Yuta Nakashima
Atsushi Nakazawa
Seonghyeon Nam
Vinay P. Namboodiri
Medhini Narasimhan
Srinivasa Narasimhan
Sanath Narayan
Erickson Rangel
   Nascimento
Jacinto Nascimento
Tayyab Naseer

Lakshmanan Nataraj
Neda Nategh
Nelson Isao Nauata
Fernando Navarro
Shah Nawaz
Lukas Neumann
Ram Nevatia
Alejandro Newell
Shawn Newsam
Joe Yue-Hei Ng
Trung Thanh Ngo
Duc Thanh Nguyen
Lam M. Nguyen
Phuc Xuan Nguyen
Thuong Nguyen Canh
Mihalis Nicolaou
Andrei Liviu Nicolicioiu
Xuecheng Nie
Michael Niemeyer
Simon Niklaus
Christophoros Nikou
David Nilsson
Jifeng Ning
Yuval Nirkin
Li Niu
Yuzhen Niu
Zhenxing Niu
Shohei Nobuhara
Nicoletta Noceti
Hyeonwoo Noh
Junhyug Noh
Mehdi Noroozi
Sotiris Nousias
Valsamis Ntouskos
Matthew O'Toole
Peter Ochs
Ferda Ofli
Seong Joon Oh
Seoung Wug Oh
Iason Oikonomidis
Utkarsh Ojha
Takahiro Okabe
Takayuki Okatani
Fumio Okura
Aude Oliva
Kyle Olszewski

Björn Ommer
Mohamed Omran
Elisabeta Oneata
Michael Opitz
Jose Oramas
Tribhuvanesh Orekondy
Shaul Oron
Sergio Orts-Escolano
Ivan Oseledets
Aljosa Osep
Magnus Oskarsson
Anton Osokin
Martin R. Oswald
Wanli Ouyang
Andrew Owens
Mete Ozay
Mustafa Ozuysal
Eduardo Pérez-Pellitero
Gautam Pai
Dipan Kumar Pal
P. H. Pamplona Savarese
Jinshan Pan
Junting Pan
Xingang Pan
Yingwei Pan
Yannis Panagakis
Rameswar Panda
Guan Pang
Jiahao Pang
Jiangmiao Pang
Tianyu Pang
Sharath Pankanti
Nicolas Papadakis
Dim Papadopoulos
George Papandreou
Toufiq Parag
Shaifali Parashar
Sarah Parisot
Eunhyeok Park
Hyun Soo Park
Jaesik Park
Min-Gyu Park
Taesung Park
Alvaro Parra
C. Alejandro Parraga
Despoina Paschalidou

Nikolaos Passalis
Vishal Patel
Viorica Patraucean
Badri Narayana Patro
Danda Pani Paudel
Sujoy Paul
Georgios Pavlakos
Ioannis Pavlidis
Vladimir Pavlovic
Nick Pears
Kim Steenstrup Pedersen
Selen Pehlivan
Shmuel Peleg
Chao Peng
Houwen Peng
Wen-Hsiao Peng
Xi Peng
Xiaojiang Peng
Xingchao Peng
Yuxin Peng
Federico Perazzi
Juan Camilo Perez
Vishwanath Peri
Federico Pernici
Luca Del Pero
Florent Perronnin
Stavros Petridis
Henning Petzka
Patrick Peursum
Michael Pfeiffer
Hanspeter Pfister
Roman Pflugfelder
Minh Tri Pham
Yongri Piao
David Picard
Tomasz Pieciak
A. J. Piergiovanni
Andrea Pilzer
Pedro O. Pinheiro
Silvia Laura Pintea
Lerrel Pinto
Axel Pinz
Robinson Piramuthu
Fiora Pirri
Leonid Pishchulin
Francesco Pittaluga

Daniel Pizarro
Tobias Plötz
Mirco Planamente
Matteo Poggi
Moacir A. Ponti
Parita Pooj
Fatih Porikli
Horst Possegger
Omid Poursaeed
Ameya Prabhu
Viraj Uday Prabhu
Dilip Prasad
Brian L. Price
True Price
Maria Priisalu
Veronique Prinet
Victor Adrian Prisacariu
Jan Prokaj
Sergey Prokudin
Nicolas Pugeault
Xavier Puig
Albert Pumarola
Pulak Purkait
Senthil Purushwalkam
Charles R. Qi
Hang Qi
Haozhi Qi
Lu Qi
Mengshi Qi
Siyuan Qi
Xiaojuan Qi
Yuankai Qi
Shengju Qian
Xuelin Qian
Siyuan Qiao
Yu Qiao
Jie Qin
Qiang Qiu
Weichao Qiu
Zhaofan Qiu
Kha Gia Quach
Yuhui Quan
Yvain Queau
Julian Quiroga
Faisal Qureshi
Mahdi Rad

Filip Radenovic
Petia Radeva
Venkatesh
  B. Radhakrishnan
Ilija Radosavovic
Noha Radwan
Rahul Raguram
Tanzila Rahman
Amit Raj
Ajit Rajwade
Kandan Ramakrishnan
Santhosh
  K. Ramakrishnan
Srikumar Ramalingam
Ravi Ramamoorthi
Vasili Ramanishka
Ramprasaath R. Selvaraju
Francois Rameau
Visvanathan Ramesh
Santu Rana
Rene Ranftl
Anand Rangarajan
Anurag Ranjan
Viresh Ranjan
Yongming Rao
Carolina Raposo
Vivek Rathod
Sathya N. Ravi
Avinash Ravichandran
Tammy Riklin Raviv
Daniel Rebain
Sylvestre-Alvise Rebuffi
N. Dinesh Reddy
Timo Rehfeld
Paolo Remagnino
Konstantinos Rematas
Edoardo Remelli
Dongwei Ren
Haibing Ren
Jian Ren
Jimmy Ren
Mengye Ren
Weihong Ren
Wenqi Ren
Zhile Ren
Zhongzheng Ren

Zhou Ren
Vijay Rengarajan
Md A. Reza
Farzaneh Rezaeianaran
Hamed R. Tavakoli
Nicholas Rhinehart
Helge Rhodin
Elisa Ricci
Alexander Richard
Eitan Richardson
Elad Richardson
Christian Richardt
Stephan Richter
Gernot Riegler
Daniel Ritchie
Tobias Ritschel
Samuel Rivera
Yong Man Ro
Richard Roberts
Joseph Robinson
Ignacio Rocco
Mrigank Rochan
Emanuele Rodolà
Mikel D. Rodriguez
Giorgio Roffo
Grégory Rogez
Gemma Roig
Javier Romero
Xuejian Rong
Yu Rong
Amir Rosenfeld
Bodo Rosenhahn
Guy Rosman
Arun Ross
Paolo Rota
Peter M. Roth
Anastasios Roussos
Anirban Roy
Sebastien Roy
Aruni RoyChowdhury
Artem Rozantsev
Ognjen Rudovic
Daniel Rueckert
Adria Ruiz
Javier Ruiz-del-solar
Christian Rupprecht

Chris Russell
Dan Ruta
Jongbin Ryu
Ömer Sümer
Alexandre Sablayrolles
Faraz Saeedan
Ryusuke Sagawa
Christos Sagonas
Tonmoy Saikia
Hideo Saito
Kuniaki Saito
Shunsuke Saito
Shunta Saito
Ken Sakurada
Joaquin Salas
Fatemeh Sadat Saleh
Mahdi Saleh
Pouya Samangouei
Leo Sampaio
  Ferraz Ribeiro
Artsiom Olegovich
  Sanakoyeu
Enrique Sanchez
Patsorn Sangkloy
Anush Sankaran
Aswin Sankaranarayanan
Swami Sankaranarayanan
Rodrigo Santa Cruz
Amartya Sanyal
Archana Sapkota
Nikolaos Sarafianos
Jun Sato
Shin'ichi Satoh
Hosnieh Sattar
Arman Savran
Manolis Savva
Alexander Sax
Hanno Scharr
Simone Schaub-Meyer
Konrad Schindler
Dmitrij Schlesinger
Uwe Schmidt
Dirk Schnieders
Björn Schuller
Samuel Schulter
Idan Schwartz

William Robson Schwartz
Alex Schwing
Sinisa Segvic
Lorenzo Seidenari
Pradeep Sen
Ozan Sener
Soumyadip Sengupta
Arda Senocak
Mojtaba Seyedhosseini
Shishir Shah
Shital Shah
Sohil Atul Shah
Tamar Rott Shaham
Huasong Shan
Qi Shan
Shiguang Shan
Jing Shao
Roman Shapovalov
Gaurav Sharma
Vivek Sharma
Viktoriia Sharmanska
Dongyu She
Sumit Shekhar
Evan Shelhamer
Chengyao Shen
Chunhua Shen
Falong Shen
Jie Shen
Li Shen
Liyue Shen
Shuhan Shen
Tianwei Shen
Wei Shen
William B. Shen
Yantao Shen
Ying Shen
Yiru Shen
Yujun Shen
Yuming Shen
Zhiqiang Shen
Ziyi Shen
Lu Sheng
Yu Sheng
Rakshith Shetty
Baoguang Shi
Guangming Shi

Hailin Shi
Miaojing Shi
Yemin Shi
Zhenmei Shi
Zhiyuan Shi
Kevin Jonathan Shih
Shiliang Shiliang
Hyunjung Shim
Atsushi Shimada
Nobutaka Shimada
Daeyun Shin
Young Min Shin
Koichi Shinoda
Konstantin Shmelkov
Michael Zheng Shou
Abhinav Shrivastava
Tianmin Shu
Zhixin Shu
Hong-Han Shuai
Pushkar Shukla
Christian Siagian
Mennatullah M. Siam
Kaleem Siddiqi
Karan Sikka
Jae-Young Sim
Christian Simon
Martin Simonovsky
Dheeraj Singaraju
Bharat Singh
Gurkirt Singh
Krishna Kumar Singh
Maneesh Kumar Singh
Richa Singh
Saurabh Singh
Suriya Singh
Vikas Singh
Sudipta N. Sinha
Vincent Sitzmann
Josef Sivic
Gregory Slabaugh
Miroslava Slavcheva
Ron Slossberg
Brandon Smith
Kevin Smith
Vladimir Smutny
Noah Snavely

Roger
   D. Soberanis-Mukul
Kihyuk Sohn
Francesco Solera
Eric Sommerlade
Sanghyun Son
Byung Cheol Song
Chunfeng Song
Dongjin Song
Jiaming Song
Jie Song
Jifei Song
Jingkuan Song
Mingli Song
Shiyu Song
Shuran Song
Xiao Song
Yafei Song
Yale Song
Yang Song
Yi-Zhe Song
Yibing Song
Humberto Sossa
Cesar de Souza
Adrian Spurr
Srinath Sridhar
Suraj Srinivas
Pratul P. Srinivasan
Anuj Srivastava
Tania Stathaki
Christopher Stauffer
Simon Stent
Rainer Stiefelhagen
Pierre Stock
Julian Straub
Jonathan C. Stroud
Joerg Stueckler
Jan Stuehmer
David Stutz
Chi Su
Hang Su
Jong-Chyi Su
Shuochen Su
Yu-Chuan Su
Ramanathan Subramanian
Yusuke Sugano

Masanori Suganuma
Yumin Suh
Mohammed Suhail
Yao Sui
Heung-Il Suk
Josephine Sullivan
Baochen Sun
Chen Sun
Chong Sun
Deqing Sun
Jin Sun
Liang Sun
Lin Sun
Qianru Sun
Shao-Hua Sun
Shuyang Sun
Weiwei Sun
Wenxiu Sun
Xiaoshuai Sun
Xiaoxiao Sun
Xingyuan Sun
Yifan Sun
Zhun Sun
Sabine Susstrunk
David Suter
Supasorn Suwajanakorn
Tomas Svoboda
Eran Swears
Paul Swoboda
Attila Szabo
Richard Szeliski
Duy-Nguyen Ta
Andrea Tagliasacchi
Yuichi Taguchi
Ying Tai
Keita Takahashi
Kouske Takahashi
Jun Takamatsu
Hugues Talbot
Toru Tamaki
Chaowei Tan
Fuwen Tan
Mingkui Tan
Mingxing Tan
Qingyang Tan
Robby T. Tan

Xiaoyang Tan
Kenichiro Tanaka
Masayuki Tanaka
Chang Tang
Chengzhou Tang
Danhang Tang
Ming Tang
Peng Tang
Qingming Tang
Wei Tang
Xu Tang
Yansong Tang
Youbao Tang
Yuxing Tang
Zhiqiang Tang
Tatsunori Taniai
Junli Tao
Xin Tao
Makarand Tapaswi
Jean-Philippe Tarel
Lyne Tchapmi
Zachary Teed
Bugra Tekin
Damien Teney
Ayush Tewari
Christian Theobalt
Christopher Thomas
Diego Thomas
Jim Thomas
Rajat Mani Thomas
Xinmei Tian
Yapeng Tian
Yingli Tian
Yonglong Tian
Zhi Tian
Zhuotao Tian
Kinh Tieu
Joseph Tighe
Massimo Tistarelli
Matthew Toews
Carl Toft
Pavel Tokmakov
Federico Tombari
Chetan Tonde
Yan Tong
Alessio Tonioni

Andrea Torsello
Fabio Tosi
Du Tran
Luan Tran
Ngoc-Trung Tran
Quan Hung Tran
Truyen Tran
Rudolph Triebel
Martin Trimmel
Shashank Tripathi
Subarna Tripathi
Leonardo Trujillo
Eduard Trulls
Tomasz Trzcinski
Sam Tsai
Yi-Hsuan Tsai
Hung-Yu Tseng
Stavros Tsogkas
Aggeliki Tsoli
Devis Tuia
Shubham Tulsiani
Sergey Tulyakov
Frederick Tung
Tony Tung
Daniyar Turmukhambetov
Ambrish Tyagi
Radim Tylecek
Christos Tzelepis
Georgios Tzimiropoulos
Dimitrios Tzionas
Seiichi Uchida
Norimichi Ukita
Dmitry Ulyanov
Martin Urschler
Yoshitaka Ushiku
Ben Usman
Alexander Vakhitov
Julien P. C. Valentin
Jack Valmadre
Ernest Valveny
Joost van de Weijer
Jan van Gemert
Koen Van Leemput
Gul Varol
Sebastiano Vascon
M. Alex O. Vasilescu

Subeesh Vasu
Mayank Vatsa
David Vazquez
Javier Vazquez-Corral
Ashok Veeraraghavan
Erik Velasco-Salido
Raviteja Vemulapalli
Jonathan Ventura
Manisha Verma
Roberto Vezzani
Ruben Villegas
Minh Vo
MinhDuc Vo
Nam Vo
Michele Volpi
Riccardo Volpi
Carl Vondrick
Konstantinos Vougioukas
Tuan-Hung Vu
Sven Wachsmuth
Neal Wadhwa
Catherine Wah
Jacob C. Walker
Thomas S. A. Wallis
Chengde Wan
Jun Wan
Liang Wan
Renjie Wan
Baoyuan Wang
Boyu Wang
Cheng Wang
Chu Wang
Chuan Wang
Chunyu Wang
Dequan Wang
Di Wang
Dilin Wang
Dong Wang
Fang Wang
Guanzhi Wang
Guoyin Wang
Hanzi Wang
Hao Wang
He Wang
Heng Wang
Hongcheng Wang

Hongxing Wang
Hua Wang
Jian Wang
Jingbo Wang
Jinglu Wang
Jingya Wang
Jinjun Wang
Jinqiao Wang
Jue Wang
Ke Wang
Keze Wang
Le Wang
Lei Wang
Lezi Wang
Li Wang
Liang Wang
Lijun Wang
Limin Wang
Linwei Wang
Lizhi Wang
Mengjiao Wang
Mingzhe Wang
Minsi Wang
Naiyan Wang
Nannan Wang
Ning Wang
Oliver Wang
Pei Wang
Peng Wang
Pichao Wang
Qi Wang
Qian Wang
Qiaosong Wang
Qifei Wang
Qilong Wang
Qing Wang
Qingzhong Wang
Quan Wang
Rui Wang
Ruiping Wang
Ruixing Wang
Shangfei Wang
Shenlong Wang
Shiyao Wang
Shuhui Wang
Song Wang

Tao Wang
Tianlu Wang
Tiantian Wang
Ting-chun Wang
Tingwu Wang
Wei Wang
Weiyue Wang
Wenguan Wang
Wenlin Wang
Wenqi Wang
Xiang Wang
Xiaobo Wang
Xiaofang Wang
Xiaoling Wang
Xiaolong Wang
Xiaosong Wang
Xiaoyu Wang
Xin Eric Wang
Xinchao Wang
Xinggang Wang
Xintao Wang
Yali Wang
Yan Wang
Yang Wang
Yangang Wang
Yaxing Wang
Yi Wang
Yida Wang
Yilin Wang
Yiming Wang
Yisen Wang
Yongtao Wang
Yu-Xiong Wang
Yue Wang
Yujiang Wang
Yunbo Wang
Yunhe Wang
Zengmao Wang
Zhangyang Wang
Zhaowen Wang
Zhe Wang
Zhecan Wang
Zheng Wang
Zhixiang Wang
Zilei Wang
Jianqiao Wangni

Anne S. Wannenwetsch
Jan Dirk Wegner
Scott Wehrwein
Donglai Wei
Kaixuan Wei
Longhui Wei
Pengxu Wei
Ping Wei
Qi Wei
Shih-En Wei
Xing Wei
Yunchao Wei
Zijun Wei
Jerod Weinman
Michael Weinmann
Philippe Weinzaepfel
Yair Weiss
Bihan Wen
Longyin Wen
Wei Wen
Junwu Weng
Tsui-Wei Weng
Xinshuo Weng
Eric Wengrowski
Tomas Werner
Gordon Wetzstein
Tobias Weyand
Patrick Wieschollek
Maggie Wigness
Erik Wijmans
Richard Wildes
Olivia Wiles
Chris Williams
Williem Williem
Kyle Wilson
Calden Wloka
Nicolai Wojke
Christian Wolf
Yongkang Wong
Sanghyun Woo
Scott Workman
Baoyuan Wu
Bichen Wu
Chao-Yuan Wu
Huikai Wu
Jiajun Wu

Jialin Wu
Jiaxiang Wu
Jiqing Wu
Jonathan Wu
Lifang Wu
Qi Wu
Qiang Wu
Ruizheng Wu
Shangzhe Wu
Shun-Cheng Wu
Tianfu Wu
Wayne Wu
Wenxuan Wu
Xiao Wu
Xiaohe Wu
Xinxiao Wu
Yang Wu
Yi Wu
Yiming Wu
Ying Nian Wu
Yue Wu
Zheng Wu
Zhenyu Wu
Zhirong Wu
Zuxuan Wu
Stefanie Wuhrer
Jonas Wulff
Changqun Xia
Fangting Xia
Fei Xia
Gui-Song Xia
Lu Xia
Xide Xia
Yin Xia
Yingce Xia
Yongqin Xian
Lei Xiang
Shiming Xiang
Bin Xiao
Fanyi Xiao
Guobao Xiao
Huaxin Xiao
Taihong Xiao
Tete Xiao
Tong Xiao
Wang Xiao

Yang Xiao
Cihang Xie
Guosen Xie
Jianwen Xie
Lingxi Xie
Sirui Xie
Weidi Xie
Wenxuan Xie
Xiaohua Xie
Fuyong Xing
Jun Xing
Junliang Xing
Bo Xiong
Peixi Xiong
Yu Xiong
Yuanjun Xiong
Zhiwei Xiong
Chang Xu
Chenliang Xu
Dan Xu
Danfei Xu
Hang Xu
Hongteng Xu
Huijuan Xu
Jingwei Xu
Jun Xu
Kai Xu
Mengmeng Xu
Mingze Xu
Qianqian Xu
Ran Xu
Weijian Xu
Xiangyu Xu
Xiaogang Xu
Xing Xu
Xun Xu
Yanyu Xu
Yichao Xu
Yong Xu
Yongchao Xu
Yuanlu Xu
Zenglin Xu
Zheng Xu
Chuhui Xue
Jia Xue
Nan Xue

Tianfan Xue
Xiangyang Xue
Abhay Yadav
Yasushi Yagi
I. Zeki Yalniz
Kota Yamaguchi
Toshihiko Yamasaki
Takayoshi Yamashita
Junchi Yan
Ke Yan
Qingan Yan
Sijie Yan
Xinchen Yan
Yan Yan
Yichao Yan
Zhicheng Yan
Keiji Yanai
Bin Yang
Ceyuan Yang
Dawei Yang
Dong Yang
Fan Yang
Guandao Yang
Guorun Yang
Haichuan Yang
Hao Yang
Jianwei Yang
Jiaolong Yang
Jie Yang
Jing Yang
Kaiyu Yang
Linjie Yang
Meng Yang
Michael Ying Yang
Nan Yang
Shuai Yang
Shuo Yang
Tianyu Yang
Tien-Ju Yang
Tsun-Yi Yang
Wei Yang
Wenhan Yang
Xiao Yang
Xiaodong Yang
Xin Yang
Yan Yang

Yanchao Yang
Yee Hong Yang
Yezhou Yang
Zhenheng Yang
Anbang Yao
Angela Yao
Cong Yao
Jian Yao
Li Yao
Ting Yao
Yao Yao
Zhewei Yao
Chengxi Ye
Jianbo Ye
Keren Ye
Linwei Ye
Mang Ye
Mao Ye
Qi Ye
Qixiang Ye
Mei-Chen Yeh
Raymond Yeh
Yu-Ying Yeh
Sai-Kit Yeung
Serena Yeung
Kwang Moo Yi
Li Yi
Renjiao Yi
Alper Yilmaz
Junho Yim
Lijun Yin
Weidong Yin
Xi Yin
Zhichao Yin
Tatsuya Yokota
Ryo Yonetani
Donggeun Yoo
Jae Shin Yoon
Ju Hong Yoon
Sung-eui Yoon
Laurent Younes
Changqian Yu
Fisher Yu
Gang Yu
Jiahui Yu
Kaicheng Yu

Ke Yu
Lequan Yu
Ning Yu
Qian Yu
Ronald Yu
Ruichi Yu
Shoou-I Yu
Tao Yu
Tianshu Yu
Xiang Yu
Xin Yu
Xiyu Yu
Youngjae Yu
Yu Yu
Zhiding Yu
Chunfeng Yuan
Ganzhao Yuan
Jinwei Yuan
Lu Yuan
Quan Yuan
Shanxin Yuan
Tongtong Yuan
Wenjia Yuan
Ye Yuan
Yuan Yuan
Yuhui Yuan
Huanjing Yue
Xiangyu Yue
Ersin Yumer
Sergey Zagoruyko
Egor Zakharov
Amir Zamir
Andrei Zanfir
Mihai Zanfir
Pablo Zegers
Bernhard Zeisl
John S. Zelek
Niclas Zeller
Huayi Zeng
Jiabei Zeng
Wenjun Zeng
Yu Zeng
Xiaohua Zhai
Fangneng Zhan
Huangying Zhan
Kun Zhan

Xiaohang Zhan
Baochang Zhang
Bowen Zhang
Cecilia Zhang
Changqing Zhang
Chao Zhang
Chengquan Zhang
Chi Zhang
Chongyang Zhang
Dingwen Zhang
Dong Zhang
Feihu Zhang
Hang Zhang
Hanwang Zhang
Hao Zhang
He Zhang
Hongguang Zhang
Hua Zhang
Ji Zhang
Jianguo Zhang
Jianming Zhang
Jiawei Zhang
Jie Zhang
Jing Zhang
Juyong Zhang
Kai Zhang
Kaipeng Zhang
Ke Zhang
Le Zhang
Lei Zhang
Li Zhang
Lihe Zhang
Linguang Zhang
Lu Zhang
Mi Zhang
Mingda Zhang
Peng Zhang
Pingping Zhang
Qian Zhang
Qilin Zhang
Quanshi Zhang
Richard Zhang
Rui Zhang
Runze Zhang
Shengping Zhang
Shifeng Zhang

Shuai Zhang
Songyang Zhang
Tao Zhang
Ting Zhang
Tong Zhang
Wayne Zhang
Wei Zhang
Weizhong Zhang
Wenwei Zhang
Xiangyu Zhang
Xiaolin Zhang
Xiaopeng Zhang
Xiaoqin Zhang
Xiuming Zhang
Ya Zhang
Yang Zhang
Yimin Zhang
Yinda Zhang
Ying Zhang
Yongfei Zhang
Yu Zhang
Yulun Zhang
Yunhua Zhang
Yuting Zhang
Zhanpeng Zhang
Zhao Zhang
Zhaoxiang Zhang
Zhen Zhang
Zheng Zhang
Zhifei Zhang
Zhijin Zhang
Zhishuai Zhang
Ziming Zhang
Bo Zhao
Chen Zhao
Fang Zhao
Haiyu Zhao
Han Zhao
Hang Zhao
Hengshuang Zhao
Jian Zhao
Kai Zhao
Liang Zhao
Long Zhao
Qian Zhao
Qibin Zhao

Qijun Zhao
Rui Zhao
Shenglin Zhao
Sicheng Zhao
Tianyi Zhao
Wenda Zhao
Xiangyun Zhao
Xin Zhao
Yang Zhao
Yue Zhao
Zhichen Zhao
Zijing Zhao
Xiantong Zhen
Chuanxia Zheng
Feng Zheng
Haiyong Zheng
Jia Zheng
Kang Zheng
Shuai Kyle Zheng
Wei-Shi Zheng
Yinqiang Zheng
Zerong Zheng
Zhedong Zheng
Zilong Zheng
Bineng Zhong
Fangwei Zhong
Guangyu Zhong
Yiran Zhong
Yujie Zhong
Zhun Zhong
Chunluan Zhou
Huiyu Zhou
Jiahuan Zhou
Jun Zhou
Lei Zhou
Luowei Zhou
Luping Zhou
Mo Zhou
Ning Zhou
Pan Zhou
Peng Zhou
Qianyi Zhou
S. Kevin Zhou
Sanping Zhou
Wengang Zhou
Xingyi Zhou

Yanzhao Zhou
Yi Zhou
Yin Zhou
Yipin Zhou
Yuyin Zhou
Zihan Zhou
Alex Zihao Zhu
Chenchen Zhu
Feng Zhu
Guangming Zhu
Ji Zhu
Jun-Yan Zhu
Lei Zhu
Linchao Zhu
Rui Zhu
Shizhan Zhu
Tyler Lixuan Zhu

Wei Zhu
Xiangyu Zhu
Xinge Zhu
Xizhou Zhu
Yanjun Zhu
Yi Zhu
Yixin Zhu
Yizhe Zhu
Yousong Zhu
Zhe Zhu
Zhen Zhu
Zheng Zhu
Zhenyao Zhu
Zhihui Zhu
Zhuotun Zhu
Bingbing Zhuang
Wei Zhuo

Christian Zimmermann
Karel Zimmermann
Larry Zitnick
Mohammadreza
   Zolfaghari
Maria Zontak
Daniel Zoran
Changqing Zou
Chuhang Zou
Danping Zou
Qi Zou
Yang Zou
Yuliang Zou
Georgios Zoumpourlis
Wangmeng Zuo
Xinxin Zuo

Additional Reviewers

Victoria Fernandez
   Abrevaya
Maya Aghaei
Allam Allam
Christine
   Allen-Blanchette
Nicolas Aziere
Assia Benbihi
Neha Bhargava
Bharat Lal Bhatnagar
Joanna Bitton
Judy Borowski
Amine Bourki
Romain Brégier
Tali Brayer
Sebastian Bujwid
Andrea Burns
Yun-Hao Cao
Yuning Chai
Xiaojun Chang
Bo Chen
Shuo Chen
Zhixiang Chen
Junsuk Choe
Hung-Kuo Chu

Jonathan P. Crall
Kenan Dai
Lucas Deecke
Karan Desai
Prithviraj Dhar
Jing Dong
Wei Dong
Turan Kaan Elgin
Francis Engelmann
Erik Englesson
Fartash Faghri
Zicong Fan
Yang Fu
Risheek Garrepalli
Yifan Ge
Marco Godi
Helmut Grabner
Shuxuan Guo
Jianfeng He
Zhezhi He
Samitha Herath
Chih-Hui Ho
Yicong Hong
Vincent Tao Hu
Julio Hurtado

Jaedong Hwang
Andrey Ignatov
Muhammad
   Abdullah Jamal
Saumya Jetley
Meiguang Jin
Jeff Johnson
Minsoo Kang
Saeed Khorram
Mohammad Rami Koujan
Nilesh Kulkarni
Sudhakar Kumawat
Abdelhak Lemkhenter
Alexander Levine
Jiachen Li
Jing Li
Jun Li
Yi Li
Liang Liao
Ruochen Liao
Tzu-Heng Lin
Phillip Lippe
Bao-di Liu
Bo Liu
Fangchen Liu

Hanxiao Liu
Hongyu Liu
Huidong Liu
Miao Liu
Xinxin Liu
Yongfei Liu
Yu-Lun Liu
Amir Livne
Tiange Luo
Wei Ma
Xiaoxuan Ma
Ioannis Marras
Georg Martius
Effrosyni Mavroudi
Tim Meinhardt
Givi Meishvili
Meng Meng
Zihang Meng
Zhongqi Miao
Gyeongsik Moon
Khoi Nguyen
Yung-Kyun Noh
Antonio Norelli
Jaeyoo Park
Alexander Pashevich
Mandela Patrick
Mary Phuong
Bingqiao Qian
Yu Qiao
Zhen Qiao
Sai Saketh Rambhatla
Aniket Roy
Amelie Royer
Parikshit Vishwas
  Sakurikar
Mark Sandler
Mert Bülent Sarıyıldız
Tanner Schmidt
Anshul B. Shah

Ketul Shah
Rajvi Shah
Hengcan Shi
Xiangxi Shi
Yujiao Shi
William A. P. Smith
Guoxian Song
Robin Strudel
Abby Stylianou
Xinwei Sun
Reuben Tan
Qingyi Tao
Kedar S. Tatwawadi
Anh Tuan Tran
Son Dinh Tran
Eleni Triantafillou
Aristeidis Tsitiridis
Md Zasim Uddin
Andrea Vedaldi
Evangelos Ververas
Vidit Vidit
Paul Voigtlaender
Bo Wan
Huanyu Wang
Huiyu Wang
Junqiu Wang
Pengxiao Wang
Tai Wang
Xinyao Wang
Tomoki Watanabe
Mark Weber
Xi Wei
Botong Wu
James Wu
Jiamin Wu
Rujie Wu
Yu Wu
Rongchang Xie
Wei Xiong

Yunyang Xiong
An Xu
Chi Xu
Yinghao Xu
Fei Xue
Tingyun Yan
Zike Yan
Chao Yang
Heran Yang
Ren Yang
Wenfei Yang
Xu Yang
Rajeev Yasarla
Shaokai Ye
Yufei Ye
Kun Yi
Haichao Yu
Hanchao Yu
Ruixuan Yu
Liangzhe Yuan
Chen-Lin Zhang
Fandong Zhang
Tianyi Zhang
Yang Zhang
Yiyi Zhang
Yongshun Zhang
Yu Zhang
Zhiwei Zhang
Jiaojiao Zhao
Yipu Zhao
Xingjian Zhen
Haizhong Zheng
Tiancheng Zhi
Chengju Zhou
Hao Zhou
Hao Zhu
Alexander Zimin

Contents – Part XXVI

EfficientFCN: Holistically-Guided Decoding for Semantic Segmentation

Jianbo Liu[1], Junjun He[2], Jiawei Zhang[3], Jimmy S. Ren[3],
and Hongsheng Li[1(✉)]

[1] CUHK-SenseTime Joint Laboratory, The Chinese University of Hong Kong,
Shatin, Hong Kong
liujianbo@link.cuhk.edu.hk, hsli@ee.cuhk.edu.hk
[2] Shenzhen Key Lab of Computer Vision and Pattern Recognition,
Shenzhen Institutes of Advanced Technology, Chinese Academy of Sciences,
Beijing, China
[3] SenseTime Research, Beijing, China

Abstract. Both performance and efficiency are important to semantic segmentation. State-of-the-art semantic segmentation algorithms are
mostly based on dilated Fully Convolutional Networks (dilatedFCN),
which adopt dilated convolutions in the backbone networks to extract
high-resolution feature maps for achieving high-performance segmentation performance. However, due to many convolution operations are
conducted on the high-resolution feature maps, such dilatedFCN-based
methods result in large computational complexity and memory consumption. To balance the performance and efficiency, there also exist encoder-
decoder structures that gradually recover the spatial information by combining multi-level feature maps from the encoder. However, the performances of existing encoder-decoder methods are far from comparable
with the dilatedFCN-based methods. In this paper, we propose the EfficientFCN, whose backbone is a common ImageNet pretrained network
without any dilated convolution. A holistically-guided decoder is introduced to obtain the high-resolution semantic-rich feature maps via the
multi-scale features from the encoder. The decoding task is converted
to novel codebook generation and codeword assembly task, which takes
advantages of the high-level and low-level features from the encoder. Such
a framework achieves comparable or even better performance than state-
of-the-art methods with only 1/3 of the computational cost. Extensive
experiments on PASCAL Context, PASCAL VOC, ADE20K validate the
effectiveness of the proposed EfficientFCN.

Keywords: Semantic segmentation · Encoder-decoder · Dilated
convolution · Holistic features

1 Introduction

Semantic segmentation or scene parsing is the task of assigning one of the predefined class labels to each pixel of an input image. It is a fundamental yet challenging task in computer vision. The Fully Convolutional Network (FCN) [15],

© Springer Nature Switzerland AG 2020
A. Vedaldi et al. (Eds.): ECCV 2020, LNCS 12371, pp. 1–17, 2020.
https://doi.org/10.1007/978-3-030-58574-7_1

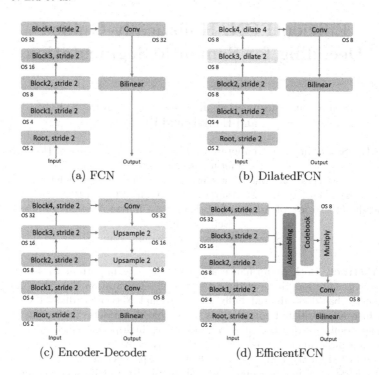

Fig. 1. Different architectures for semantic segmentation. (a) the original FCN with output stride (OS) = 32. (b). DilatedFCN based methods sacrifice efficiency and exploit the dilated convolution with stride 2 and 4 in the last two stages to generate high-resolution feature maps. (c)Encoder-Decoder methods employ the U-Net structure to recover the high-resolution feature maps. (d) Our proposed EfficientFCN with codebook generation and codeword assembly for high-resolution feature upsampling in semantic segmentation.

as shown in Fig. 1(a), for the first time demonstrates the success of exploiting a fully convolutional network in semantic segmentation, which adopts a DCNN as the feature encoder (*i.e.*, ResNet [9]) to extract high-level semantic feature maps and then applies a convolution layer to generate the dense prediction. For the semantic segmentation, high-resolution feature maps are critical for achieving accurate segmentation performance since they contain fine-grained structural information to delineate detailed boundaries of various foreground regions. In addition, due to the lack of large-scale training data on semantic segmentation, transferring the weights pretrained on ImageNet can greatly improve the segmentation performance. Therefore, most state-of-the-art semantic segmentation methods adopt classification networks as the backbone to take full advantages of ImageNet pre-training. The resolution of feature maps in the original classification model is reduced with consecutive pooling and strided convolution operations to learn high-level feature representations. The output stride of the final feature map is 32 (OS = 32), where the fine-grained structural information is discarded. Such low-resolution feature maps cannot fully meet the requirements of semantic segmentation where detailed spatial information is needed. To tackle this problem, many works exploit dilated convolution (or atrous convolution) to enlarge the receptive field (RF) while maintaining the resolution of high-level feature maps. State-of-the-art dilatedFCN based methods [2, 8, 24–26] (shown in Fig. 1(b)) have demonstrated that removing the downsampling operation and replacing convolution with the dilated convolution in the later blocks can achieve superior performance, resulting in final feature maps of output stride 8 (OS = 8). Despite the superior performance and no extra parameters introduced by dilated convolution, the high-resolution feature representations require high computational complexity and memory consumption. For instance, for an input image with 512×512 and the ResNet101 as the backbone encoder, the computational complexity of the encoder increases from 44.6 GFlops to 223.6 GFlops when adopting the dilated convolution with the strides 2 and 4 into the last two blocks.

Alternatively, as shown in Fig. 1(c), the encoder-decoder based methods (e.g. [18]) exploit using a decoder to gradually upsample and generate the high-resolution feature maps by aggregating multi-level feature representations from the backbone (or the encoder). These encoder-decoder based methods can obtain high-resolution feature representations efficiently. However, on one hand, the fine-grained structural details are already lost in the topmost high-level feature maps of OS = 32. Even with the skip connections, lower-level high-resolution feature maps cannot provide abstractive enough features for achieving high-performance segmentation. On the other hand, existing decoders mainly utilize the bilinear upsampling or deconvolution operations to increase the resolution of the high-level feature maps. These operations are conducted in a local manner. The feature vector at each location of the upsampled feature maps is recovered from a limited receptive filed. Thus, although the encoder-decoder models are generally faster and more memory friendly than dilatedFCN based methods, their performances generally cannot compete with those of the dilatedFCN models.

To tackle the challenges in both types of models, we propose the EfficienFCN (as shown in Fig. 1(d)) with the Holistically-guided Decoder (HGD) to bridge the gap between the dilatedFCN based methods and the encoder-decoder based methods. Our network can adopt any widely used classification model without dilated convolution as the encoder (such as ResNet models) to generate low-resolution high-level feature maps (OS = 8). Such an encoder is both computationally and memory efficient than those in DilatedFCN model. Given the multi-level feature maps from the last three blocks of the encoder, the proposed holistically-guided decoder takes the advantages of both high-level but low-resolution (OS = 32) and also mid-level high-resolution feature maps (OS = 8, OS = 16) for achieving high-level feature upsampling with semantic-rich features. Intuitively, the higher-resolution feature maps contain more fine-grained structural information, which is beneficial for spatially guiding the feature upsampling process; the lower-resolution feature maps contain more high-level semantic information, which are more suitable to encode the global context effectively. Our HGD therefore generates a series of holistic codewords in a codebook to summarize different global and high-level aspects of the input image from the low-resolution feature maps (OS = 32). Those codewords can be properly assembled in a high-resolution grid to form the upsampled feature maps with rich semantic information. Following this principle, the HGD generates assembly coefficients from the mid-level high-resolution feature maps (OS = 8, OS = 16) to guide the linear assembly of the holistic codewords at each high-resolution spatial location to achieve feature upsampling. Our proposed EfficientFCN with holistically-guided decoder achieves high segmentation accuracy on three popular public benchmarks, which demonstrate the efficiency and effectiveness of our proposed decoder.

In summary, our contributions are as follows.

– We propose a novel holistically-guided decoder, which can efficiently generate the high-resolution feature maps considering holistic contexts of the input image.
– Because of the light weight and high performance of the proposed holistically-guided decoder, our EfficientFCN can adopt the encoder without any dilated convolution but still achieve superior performance.
– Our EfficientFCN achieves competitive (or better) results compared with the state-of-the-art dilatedFCN based methods on the PASCAL Context, PASCAL VOC, ADE20K datasets, with 1/3 fewer FLOPS.

2   Related Work

In this section, we review recent FCN-based methods for semantic segmentation. Since the successful demonstration of FCN [15] on semantic segmentation, many methods were proposed to improve the performance the FCN-based methods, which mainly include two categories of methods: the dilatedFCN-based methods and the encoder-decoder architectures.

DilatedFCN. The Deeplab V2 [2,3] proposed to exploit dilated convolution in the backbone to learn a high-resolution feature map, which increases the output stride from 32 to 8. However, the dilated convolution in the last two layers of the backbone adds huge extra computation and leaves large memory footprint. Based on the dilated convolution backbone, many works [5–7,26] continued to apply different strategies as the segmentation heads to acquire the context-enhanced feature maps. PSPNet [28] utilized the Spatial Pyramid Pooling (SPP) module to increase the receptive field. EncNet [25] proposed an encoding layer to predict a feature re-weighting vector from the global context and selectively high-lights class-dependent feature maps. CFNet [26] exploited an aggregated co-occurrent feature (ACF) module to aggregate the co-occurrent context by the pair-wise similarities in the feature space. Gated-SCNN [20] proposed to use a new gating mechanism to connect the intermediate layers and a new loss function that exploits the duality between the tasks of semantic segmentation and semantic boundary prediction. DANet [5] proposed to use two attention modules with the self-attention mechanism to aggregate features from spatial and channel dimensions respectively. ACNet [6] applied a dilated ResNet as the backbone and combined the encoder-decoder strategy for the observation that the global context from high-level features helps the categorization of some large semantic confused regions, while the local context from lower-level visual features helps to generate sharp boundaries or clear details. DMNet [7] generated a set of dynamic filters of different sizes from the multi-scale neighborhoods for handling the scale variations of objects for semantic segmentation. Although these works further improve the performances on different benchmarks, these proposed heads still adds extra computational costs to the already burdensome encoder.

Encoder-Decoder. Another type of methods focus on efficiently acquire the high-resolution semantic feature maps via the encoder-decoder architectures. Through the upsampling operations and the skip connections, the encoder-decoder architecture [18] can gradually recover the high-resolution feature maps for segmentation. DUsampling [21] designed a data-dependent upsampling module based on fully connected layers for constructing the high-resolution feature maps from the low-resolution feature maps. FastFCN [22] proposed a Joint Pyramid Upsampling (JPU) method via multiple dilated convolution to generate the high-resolution feature maps. One common drawback of these methods is that the feature at each location of the upsampled high-resolution feature maps is constructed via only local feature fusion. Such a property limited limits their performance in semantic segmentation, where global context is important for the final performance.

3   Proposed Method

In this section, We firstly give a thorough analysis of the classical encoder-decoder based methods. Then, to tackle the challenges in the classical encoder-decoder methods, we propose the EfficientFCN, which is based on the traditional ResNet as the encoder backbone network for semantic segmentation. In our EfficientFCN, the Holistically-guided Decoder (HGD) is designed to recover the high-resolution (OS $=8$) feature maps from three feature maps in the last three blocks from the ResNet encoder backbone.

3.1   Overview

In state-of-the-art DCNN backbones, the high-resolution mid-level feature maps at earlier stages can better encode fine-grained structures, while the low-resolution high-level features at the later stages are generally more discriminative for category prediction. They are essential and complementary information sources for achieving accurate semantic segmentation. To combine the strengths of both features, encoder-decoder structures were developed to reconstruct high-resolution feature maps that have semantic-rich information from the multi-scale feature maps. To generate the final feature map $\tilde{f}_8$ of OS $=8$ for mask prediction, a conventional three-stage encoder-decoder first upsamples the deepest encoder feature map f_{32} of OS $=32$ to generate OS $=16$ feature maps f_{16}. The OS $=16$ feature maps e_{16} of the same size from the encoder is either directly concatenated as $[f_{16}; e_{16}]$ (U–Net [18]) or summed as $f_{16}+e_{16}$ followed by some 1×1 convolution to generate the upsampled OS $=16$ feature maps, $\tilde{f}_{16}$. The same upsampling +

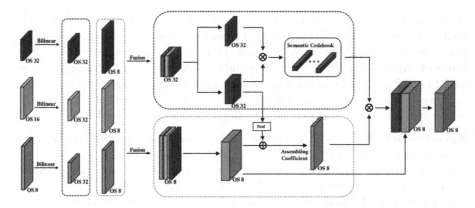

Fig. 2. Illustration of the proposed EfficientFCN model. It consists of three main components. Multi-scale feature fusion fuses multi-scale features to obtain OS = 8 and OS = 32 multi-scale feature maps. Holistic codebook generation results in a series of holistic codewords summarizing different aspects of the global context. High-resolution feature upsampling can be achieved by codeword assembly.

skip connection procedure repeats again for $\tilde{f}_{16}$ to generate $\tilde{f}_8$. The upsampled features $\tilde{f}_8$ contain both mid-level and high-level information to some extent and can be used to generate the segmentation masks. However, since bilinear upsampling and deconvolution layer in the classical decoder are local operations with limited receptive field. We argue that they are incapable of exploring important global context of the input image, which are crucial for achieving accurate segmentation. Although there were some existing attempts [10, 25] on using global context to re-weight the contributions of different channels of the feature maps either in the backbone [25] or in the upsampled feature maps [10]. This strategy only scales each feature channel but maintains the original spatial size and structures. Therefore, it is incapable of generating high-resolution semantic-rich feature maps to improve the recovery of fine-grained structures. To solve this drawback, we propose a novel Holistically-guided Decoder (HGD), which decomposes the feature upsampling task into the generation of a series of holistic codewords from high-level feature maps to capture global contexts, and linearly assembling codewords at each spatial location for semantic-rich feature upsampling. Such a decoder can exploit the global contextual information to effectively guide the feature upsampling process and is able to recover fine-grained details. Based on the proposed HGD, we present the EfficientFCN (as shown in Fig. 1(d)) with an efficient encoder free of dilated convolution for efficient semantic segmentation (Fig. 2).

3.2 Holistically-Guided Decoder for Semantic-Rich Feature Upsampling

To take advantages of both low-resolution high-level feature maps of size OS = 32 and the high-resolution mid-level feature maps of sizes OS = 8 and OS = 16, since the high-level feature maps have already lost most structural details but are semantic-rich to encode categorical information, we argue that recovering detailed structures from them is quite challenging and also non-necessary. Instead, we propose to generate a series of holistic codewords without any spatial order from the high-level feature maps to capture different aspects of the global context. On the other hand, the mid-level high-resolution feature maps have maintained abundant image structural information. But they are from relatively shallower layers and cannot encode accurate enough categorical features for final mask prediction. However, they would still be representative enough for guiding the linear assembly of the semantic-rich codewords for high-resolution feature upsampling. Our proposed Holistically-guided Decoder therefore contains three main components: multi-scale feature fusion, holistic codebook generation, and codeword assembly for high-resolution feature upsampling.

Multi-scale Features Fusion. Given the multi-scale feature maps from the encoder, although we can directly encode the holistic codewords from the high-level $OS = 32$ feature maps and also directly generate the codeword combination coefficients from the mid-level $OS = 16$ and $OS = 8$ feature maps, we observe the fusion of multi-scale feature maps generally result in better performance. For the $OS = 8$, $OS = 16$, $OS = 32$ feature maps from the encoder, we first adopt separate 1×1 convolutions to compress each of their channels to 512 for reducing the follow-up computational complexity, obtaining e_8, e_{16}, e_{32}, respectively. The multi-scale fused $OS = 32$ feature maps m_{32} are then obtained by downsampling e_8, e_{16} to the size of $OS = 32$ and concatenating them along the channel dimension with e_{32} as $m_{32} = [e_8^{\downarrow}; e_{16}^{\downarrow}; e_{32}] \in \mathbb{R}^{1536 \times (H/32) \times (W/32)}$, where $\downarrow$ represents bilinear downsampling, $[\cdot; \cdot]$ denotes concatenation along the channel dimension, and H and W are the input image's height and width, respectively. We can also obtain the multi-scale fused $OS = 8$ feature maps, $m_8 = [e_8; e_{16}^{\uparrow}; e_{32}^{\uparrow}] \in \mathbb{R}^{1536 \times (H/8) \times (W/8)}$, in a similar manner.

Holistic Codebook Generation. Although the mutli-scale fused feature maps m_{32} are created to integrate both high-level and mid-level features, their small resolutions make them lose many structural details of the scene. On the other hand, because e_{32} is encoded from the deepest layer, m_{32} is able to encode rich categorical representations of the image. We therefore propose to generate a series of unordered holistic codewords from m_{32} to implicitly model different aspects of the global context. To generate n holistic codewords, a codeword base map $B \in \mathbb{R}^{1024 \times (H/32) \times (W/32)}$ and n spatial weighting maps $A \in \mathbb{R}^{n \times (H/32) \times (W/32)}$ are first computed from the fused multi-scale feature maps m_{32} by two separate 1×1 convolutions. For the bases map B, we denote $B(x, y) \in \mathbb{R}^{1024}$ as the 1024-d feature vector at location (x, y); for the spatial weighting maps A, we use $A_i \in \mathbb{R}^{(H/32) \times (W/32)}$ to denote the ith weighting map. To ensure the weighting maps A are properly normalized, the softmax function is adopted to normalize all spatial locations of each channel i (the i-th spatial feature map) as

$$\tilde{A}_i(x, y) = \frac{\exp(A_i(x, y))}{\sum_{p,q} \exp(A_i(p, q))}. \tag{1}$$

The i-th codeword $c_i \in \mathbb{R}^{1024}$ can be obtained as the weighted average of all codeword bases $B(x, y)$, *i.e.*,

$$c_i = \sum_{p,q} \tilde{A}_i(p, q) B(p, q). \qquad (2)$$

In other words, each spatial weighting map $\tilde{A}_i$ learns to linearly combine all codeword bases $B(x, y)$ from all spatial locations to form a single codeword, which captures certain aspect of the global context. The n weighting maps eventually result in n holistic codewords $C = [c_1, \cdots, c_n] \in \mathbb{R}^{1024 \times n}$ to encode high-level global features.

Codeword Assembly for High-Resolution Feature Upsampling. The holistic codewords can capture various global contexts of the input image. They are perfect ingredients for reconstructing the high-resolution semantic-rich feature maps as they are encoded from the high-level features m_{32}. However, since their structural information have been mostly removed during codeword encoding, we turn to use the $OS = 8$ multi-scale fused features m_8 to predict the linear assembly coefficients of the n codewords at each spatial location for creating a high-resolution feature map. More specifically, we first create a raw codeword assembly guidance feature map $G \in \mathbb{R}^{1024 \times (H/8) \times (W/8)}$ to predict the assembly coefficients at each spatial location, which are obtained by applying a 1×1 convolution on the multi-scale fused features m_8. However, the $OS = 8$ fused features m_8 have no information on the holistic codewords as they are all generated from m_{32}. We therefore consider the general codeword information as the global average vector of the codeword based map $\bar{B} \in \mathbb{R}^{1024}$ and location-wisely add it to the raw assembly guidance feature map to obtain the novel guidance feature map $\bar{G} = G \oplus \bar{B}$, where $\oplus$ represents location-wise addition. Another 1×1 convolution applied on the guidance feature map $\bar{G}$ generates the linear assembly weights of the n codewords $W \in \mathbb{R}^{n \times (H/8) \times (W/8)}$ for all $(H/8) \times (W/8)$ spatial locations. By reshaping the weighting map W as an $n \times (HW/8^2)$ matrix, the holistically-guided upsampled feature $\tilde{f}_8$ can be easily obtained as

$$\tilde{f}_8 = W^{\top} C. \qquad (3)$$

Given the holistically-guided upsampled feature map $\tilde{f}_8$, we reconstruct the final upsampled feature map $\hat{f}_8$ by concatenating the feature map $\tilde{f}_8$ with the guidance feature map G. Such an upsampled feature map $\hat{f}_8$ takes advantages of both m_8 and m_{32}, and contains semantic-rich and also structure-preserved features for achieving accurate segmentation.

Final Segmentation Mask. Given the upsampled feature map $\hat{f}_8$, a 1×1 convolution can output a segmentation map of $OS = 8$, which is further upsampled back to the original resolution $H \times W$ as the final segmentation mask.

4   Experiments

In this section, we introduce the implementation details, training strategies and evaluation metrics of our experiments. To evaluate our proposed EfficientFCN

Table 1. Comparisons with classical encoder-decoder methods.

Method	Backbone	OS	mIoU%	Parameters (MB)	GFlops (G)
FCN-32s	ResNet101	32	43.3	54.0	44.6
dilatedFCN-8s	dilated-ResNet101	8	47.2	54.0	223.6
UNet-Bilinear	ResNet101	8	49.3	60.7	87.9
UNet-Deconv	ResNet101	8	49.1	62.8	93.2
EfficientFCN	ResNet101	8	55.3	55.8	69.6

model, we conduct comprehensive experiments on three public datasets PASCAL Context [16], PASCAL VOC 2012 [4] and ADE20K [30]. To further evaluate the contributions of individual components in our model, we conduct detailed ablation studies on the PASCAL Context dataset.

4.1 Implementation Details

Network Structure. Different with the dilatedFCN based methods, which remove the stride of the last two blocks of the backbone networks and adopt the dilated convolution with the dilation rates 2 and 4, we use the original ResNet [9] as our encoder backbone network. Thus the size of the output feature maps from the last ResBlock is 32× smaller than that of the input image. After feeding the encoder feature maps into our proposed holistic-guided decoder, the classification is performed on the output upsampled feature map $\hat{f}_8$. The ImageNet [19] pre-trained weights are utilized to initialize the encoder network.

Training Setting. A poly learning rate policy [2] is used in our experiments. We set the initial learning rates as 0.001 for PASCAL Context [16], 0.002 for PASCAL VOC 2012 [4] and ADE20K [30]. The power of poly learning rate policy is set as 0.9. The optimizer is stochastic gradient descent (SGD) [1] with momentum 0.9 and weight decay 0.0001. We train our EfficientFCN for 120 epochs on PASCAL Context, 80 epochs on PASCAL 2012 and 120 epochs on ADE20K, respectively. We set the crop size to 512 × 512 on PASCAL Context and PASCAL 2012. Since the average image size is larger than other two datasets, we use 576 × 576 as the crop size on ADE20K. For data augmentation, we only randomly flip the input image and scale it randomly in the range [0.5, 2.0].

Evaluation Metrics. We choose the standard evaluation metrics of pixel accuracy (pixAcc) and mean Intersection of Union (mIoU) as the evaluation metrics in our experiments. Following the best practice [5,8,25], we apply the strategy of averaging the network predictions in multiple scales for evaluation. For each input image, we first randomly resize the input image with a scaling factor sampled uniformly from [0.5, 2.0] and also randomly horizontally flip the image. These predictions are then averaged to generate the final prediction.

4.2 Results on PASCAL Context

The PASCAL Context dataset consists of 4,998 training images and 5,105 testing images for scene parsing. It is a complex and challenging dataset based

Table 2. Results of using different numbers of scales for multi-scale fused feature m_{32} to generate the holistic codewords.

	{32}	{16, 32}	{8, 16, 32}
pixAcc	80.0	80.1	80.3
mIoU	54.8	55.1	55.3

Table 3. Results of using different numbers of scales for multi-scale fused feature m_8 to estimate codeword assembly coefficients.

	{8}	{8, 16}	{8, 16, 32}
pixAcc	78.9	80.0	80.3
mIoU	47.9	52.1	55.3

on PASCAL VOC 2010 with more annotations and fine-grained scene classes, which includes 59 foreground classes and one background class. We take the same experimental settings and evaluation strategies following previous works [5–7,25,26]. We first conduct ablation studies on this dataset to demonstrate the effectiveness of each individual module design of our proposed EfficientFCN and then compare our model with state-of-the-art methods. The ablation studies are conducted with a ResNet101 encoder backbone.

Comparison with the Classical Encoder-Decoders. For the classical encoder-decoder based methods, the feature upsampling is achieved via either bilinear interpolation or deconvolution. We implement two classical encoder-decoder based methods, which include the feature upsampling operation (bilinear upsampling or deconvolution) and the skip-connections. To verify the effectiveness of our proposed HGD, these two methods are trained and tested on the PASCAL Context dataset with the same training setting as our model. The results are shown in Table 1. Although the classical encoder-decoder methods have similar computational complexities, their performances are generally far inferior than our EfficientFCN. The key reason is that their upsampled feature maps are recovered in a local manner. The simple bilinear interpolation or deconvolution cannot effectively upsample the $OS = 32$ feature maps even with the skip-connected $OS = 8$ and $OS = 16$ feature maps. In contrast, our proposed HGD can effectively upsample the high-resolution semantic-rich feature maps not only based on the fine-grained structural information in the $OS = 8$ and $OS = 16$ feature maps but also from the holistic semantic information from the $OS = 32$ feature maps.

Multi-scale Features Fusion. We conduct two experiments on multi-scale features fusion to verify their effects on semantic codebook generation and codeword assembly for feature upsampling. In our holistically-guided decoder, the semantic codewords are generated based on the $OS = 32$ multi-scale fused feature maps m_{32} and the codewords assembly coefficients are predicted from the $OS = 8$ multi-scale fused feature maps m_8. For the codeword generation, we conduct three experiments to generate the semantic codebook from multi-scale fused features with different numbers of scales. As shown in Table 2, when reducing the number of fusion scales from 3 to 2 and from 2 to 1, the performances of our EfficientFCN slightly decrease. The phenomenon is reasonable as the

Table 4. Ablation study of the number of the semantic codewords.

	32	64	128	256	512	1024
pixAcc	79.9	80.1	80.1	80.3	80.3	80.1
mIoU	54.5	54.9	55.0	55.3	55.5	55.1
GFLOPS	67.9	68.1	68.6	69.6	72.1	78.9

Table 5. Segmentation results of state-of-the-art methods on PASCAL Context and ADE20K validation dataset.

Method	Backbone	mIoU% (PASCAL Context)	mIoU% (ADE20K)	GFlops
DeepLab-v2 [2]	Dilated-ResNet101-COCO	45.7	–	>223
RefineNet [12]	Dilated-ResNet152	47.3	–	>223
MSCI [11]	Dilated-ResNet152	50.3	–	>223
PSPNet [28]	Dilated-ResNet101	–	43.29	>223
SAC [27]	Dilated-ResNet101	–	44.30	>223
EncNet [25]	Dilated-ResNet101	51.7	44.65	234
DANet [5]	Dilated-ResNet101	52.6	–	>223
APCNet [8]	Dilated-ResNet101	54.7	45.38	245
CFNet [26]	Dilated-ResNet101	54.0	44.89	>223
ACNet [6]	Dilated-ResNet101	54.1	**45.90**	>223
APNB [31]	Dilated-ResNet101	52.8	45.24	>223
DMNet [7]	Dilated-ResNet101	54.4	45.50	242
Ours	ResNet101	**55.3**	45.28	**70**

deepest feature maps contain more categorical information than the $OS = 8$ and $OS = 16$ feature maps. For the codeword assembly coefficient estimation, the similar experiments are conducted, where results are shown in Table 3. However, different from the above results, when fewer scales of feature maps are used to form the multi-scale fused $OS = 8$ feature map m_8, the performances of our EfficientFCN show significant drops. These results demonstrate that although the $OS = 8$ feature maps contain more fine-grained structural information, the semantic features from higher-level feature maps are essential for guiding the recovery of the semantic-rich high-resolution feature maps.

Number of Holistic Codewords. We also conduct experiments to survey the effectiveness of the number of codewords in our predicted semantic codebook for feature upsampling. As shown in Table 4, as the number of the semantic codewords increases from 32 to 512, the performance improves 1% in terms of mIoU on PASCAL Context. However, when the number of the semantic codewords further increases from 512 to 1024, the performance has a slight drop, which might be caused by the additional parameters. The larger model capacity might cause model to overfit the training data. In addition, since the assembly coefficients of the semantic codewords are predicted from the $OS = 8$ multi-scale fused feature

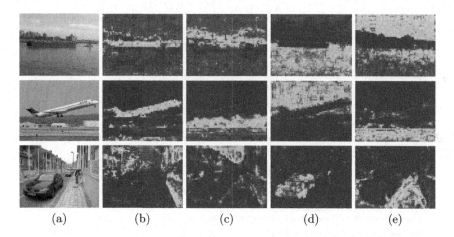

Fig. 3. (a) Input images from the PASCAL Context and ADE20K dataset. (b–e) Different weighting maps $\tilde{A}_i$ for creating the holistic codewords.

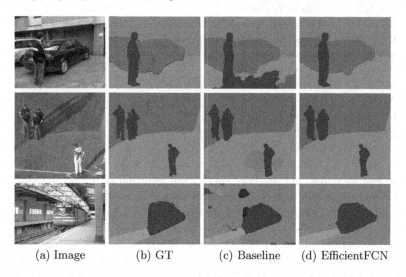

(a) Image   (b) GT   (c) Baseline   (d) EfficientFCN

Fig. 4. Visualization results from the PASCAL context dataset.

m_8, the increased number of the semantic codewords also leads to significantly more extra computational cost. Thus, to balance the performance and also the efficiency, we set the number of the holistic codewords as 256 for the PASCAL Context and PASCAL VOC 2012 datasets. Since PASCAL Context only has 60 classes and we observe the number of codewords needed is approximately 4 times than the number of classes. We therefore set the number of codewords as 600 for ADE20K, which has 150 classes.

Table 6. Results of each category on PASCAL VOC 2012 test set. Our EfficientFCN obtains 85.4 % without MS COCO dataset pre-training and 87.6% with MS COCO dataset pre-training. (For each columns, the best two entries are filled in gray color.)

Method	aero	bike	bird	boat	bottle	bus	car	cat	chair	cow	table	dog	horse	mbike	person	plant	sheep	sofa	train	tv	mIoU%
FCN [15]	76.8	34.2	68.9	49.4	60.3	75.3	74.7	77.6	21.4	62.5	46.8	71.8	63.9	76.5	73.9	45.2	72.4	37.4	70.9	55.1	62.2
DeepLabv2 [2]	84.4	54.5	81.5	63.6	65.9	85.1	79.1	83.4	30.7	74.1	59.8	79.0	76.1	83.2	80.8	59.7	82.2	50.4	73.1	63.7	71.6
CRF-RNN [29]	87.5	39.0	79.7	64.2	68.3	87.6	80.8	84.4	30.4	78.2	60.4	80.5	77.8	83.1	80.6	59.5	82.8	47.8	78.3	67.1	72.0
DeconvNet [17]	89.9	39.3	79.7	63.9	68.2	87.4	81.2	86.1	28.5	77.0	62.0	79.0	80.3	83.6	80.2	58.8	83.4	54.3	80.7	65.0	72.5
DPN [14]	87.7	59.4	78.4	64.9	70.3	89.3	83.5	86.1	31.7	79.9	62.6	81.9	80.0	83.5	82.3	60.5	83.2	53.4	77.9	65.0	74.1
Piecewise [13]	90.6	37.6	80.0	67.8	74.4	92	85.2	86.2	39.1	81.2	58.9	83.8	83.9	84.3	84.8	62.1	83.2	58.2	80.8	72.3	75.3
ResNet38 [23]	94.4	72.9	94.9	68.8	78.4	90.6	90.0	92.1	40.1	90.4	71.7	89.9	93.7	91.0	89.1	71.3	90.7	61.3	87.7	78.1	82.5
PSPNet [28]	91.8	71.9	94.7	71.2	75.8	95.2	89.9	95.9	39.3	90.7	71.7	90.5	94.5	88.8	89.6	72.8	89.6	64.0	85.1	76.3	82.6
EncNet [25]	94.1	69.2	96.3	76.7	86.2	96.3	90.7	94.2	38.8	90.7	73.3	90.0	92.5	88.8	87.9	68.7	92.6	59.0	86.4	73.4	82.9
APCNet [8]	95.8	75.8	84.5	76.0	80.6	96.9	90.0	96.0	42.0	93.7	75.5	91.6	95.0	90.5	89.3	75.8	92.8	61.9	88.9	79.6	84.2
CFNet [26]	95.7	71.9	95.0	76.3	82.8	94.8	90.0	95.9	37.1	92.6	73.0	93.4	94.6	89.6	88.4	74.9	95.2	63.2	89.7	78.2	84.2
DMNet [7]	96.1	77.3	94.1	72.8	78.1	97.1	92.7	96.4	39.8	91.4	75.5	92.7	95.8	91.0	90.3	76.6	94.1	62.1	85.5	77.6	84.4
Ours	96.4	74.1	92.8	75.6	81.9	96.9	92.6	97.1	41.6	95.4	72.9	93.9	95.9	90.6	90.6	77.2	94.0	67.5	89.3	79.8	85.4
With COCO Pre-training																					
CRF-RNN [29]	90.4	55.3	88.7	68.4	69.8	88.3	82.4	85.1	32.6	78.5	64.4	79.6	81.9	86.4	81.8	58.6	82.4	53.5	77.4	70.1	74.7
Piecewise [13]	94.1	40.7	84.1	67.8	75.9	93.4	84.3	88.4	42.5	86.4	64.7	85.4	89.0	85.8	86.0	67.5	90.2	63.8	80.9	73.0	78.0
DeepLabv2 [2]	92.6	60.4	91.6	63.4	76.3	95.0	88.4	92.6	32.7	88.5	67.6	89.6	92.1	87.0	87.4	63.3	88.3	60.0	86.8	74.5	79.7
RefineNet[12]	95.0	73.2	93.5	78.1	84.8	95.6	89.8	94.1	43.7	92.0	77.2	90.8	93.4	88.6	88.1	70.1	92.9	64.3	87.7	78.8	84.2
ResNet38[23]	96.2	75.2	95.4	74.4	81.7	93.7	89.9	92.5	48.2	92.0	79.9	90.1	95.5	91.8	91.2	73.0	90.5	65.4	88.7	80.6	84.9
PSPNet [28]	95.8	72.7	95.0	78.9	84.4	94.7	92.0	95.7	43.1	91.0	80.3	91.3	96.3	92.3	90.1	71.5	94.4	66.9	88.8	82.0	85.4
DeepLabv3[3]	96.4	76.6	92.7	77.8	87.6	96.7	90.2	95.4	47.5	93.4	76.3	91.4	97.2	91.0	92.1	71.3	90.9	68.9	90.8	79.3	85.7
EncNet[25]	95.3	76.9	94.2	80.2	85.2	96.5	90.8	96.3	47.9	93.9	80.0	92.4	96.6	90.5	91.5	70.8	93.6	66.5	87.7	80.8	85.9
CFNet [26]	96.7	79.7	94.3	78.4	83.0	97.7	91.6	96.7	50.1	95.3	79.6	93.6	97.2	94.2	91.7	78.4	95.4	69.6	90.0	81.4	87.2
Ours	96.6	80.6	96.1	82.3	87.8	97.7	94.4	97.3	47.1	96.3	77.9	94.8	97.2	94.3	91.1	81.0	94.3	61.5	91.6	83.5	87.6

Importance of the Codeword Information Transfer for Accurate Assembly Coefficient Estimation. The key of our proposed HGD is how to linearly assemble holistic codewords at each spatial location to form high-resolution upsampled feature maps based on the feature maps m_8. In our HGD, although the OS $= 8$ features have well maintained structural image information, we argue that directly using OS $= 8$ features to predict codeword assembly coefficients are less effective since they have no information about the codewords. We propose to transfer the codeword information as the average codeword basis, which is location-wisely added to the OS $= 8$ feature maps. To verify this argument, we design an experiment that removes the additive information transfer, and only utilizes two 1×1 convolutions with the same output channels on the OS $= 8$ feature maps m_8 for directly predicting assembly coefficients. The mIoU of this implementation is 54.2%, which has a clear performance drop if there is no codeword information transfer from the codeword generation branch to the codeword coefficient prediction branch.

Visualization of the Weighting Maps and Example Results. To better interpret the obtained holistic codewords, we visualize the weighting maps $\tilde{A}$ for creating the holistic codewords in Fig. 3, where each column shows one weighting map $\tilde{A}_i$ for generating one holistic codeword. Some weighting maps focus on summarizing foreground objects or regions to create holistic codewords, while some other weighting maps pay attention to summarizing background contextual regions or objects as the holistic codewords. The visualization shows that the learned codewords implicitly capture different global contexts from the scenes. In Fig. 4, we also visualize some predictions by the baseline DilatedFCN-8s and by our EfficientFCN, where our model significantly improves the visualized results with the proposed HGD.

Comparison with State-of-the-Art Methods. To further demonstrate the effectiveness of our proposed EffectiveFCN with the holistically-guided decoder, the comparisons with state-of-the-art methods are shown in Table 5. The dilatedFCN based methods dominate semantic segmentation. However, our work is still able to achieve the best results compared to the dilatedFCN based methods on the PASCAL Context validation set without using any dilated convolution and has significantly less computational cost. Because of the efficient design of our HGD, our EfficientFCN only has 1/3 of the computational cost of state-of-the-arts methods but can still achieve the best performance.

4.3   Results on PASCAL VOC

The original PASCAL VOC 2012 dataset consists of 1,464 images for training, 1,449 for validation, and 1,456 for testing, which is a major benchmark dataset for semantic object segmentation. It includes 20 foreground objects classed and one background class. The augmented training set of 10,582 images, namely train-aug, is adopted as the training set following the previous experimental set in [26]. To further demonstrate the effectiveness of our proposed HGD. We adopt all the best strategies of HGD design and compare it with state-of-the-art methods on the test set of PASCAL-VOC 2012, which is evaluated on the official online server. As shown in Table 6, the dilatedFCN based methods dominate the top performances on the PSCAL VOC benchmark. However, our EfficientFCN with a backbone having no dilated convolution can still achieve the best results among all the ResNet101-based methods.

4.4 Results on ADE20K

The ADE20K dataset consists of 20 K images for training, 2K images for validation, and 3 K images for testing, which were used for ImageNet Scene Parsing Challenge 2016. This dataset is more complex and challenging with 150 labeled classes and more diverse scenes. As shown in Table 5, our EfficientFCN achieves the competitive performance than the dilatedFCN based methods but has only 1/3 of their computational cost.

5   Conclusions

In this paper, we propose the EfficientFCN model with the holistically-guied decoder for achieving efficient and accurate semantic segmentation. The novel decoder is able to reconstruct the high-resolution semantic-rich feature maps from multi-scale feature maps of the encoder. Because of the superior feature upsampling performance of the HGD, our EfficientFCN, with much fewer parameters and less computational cost, achieves competitive or even better performance compared with state-of-the-art dilatedFCN based methods.

Acknowledgements. This work is supported in part by SenseTime Group Limited, in part by the General Research Fund through the Research Grants Council of Hong Kong under Grants CUHK 14202217/14203118/14205615/14207814/14213616/14208417/-14239816, in part by CUHK Direct Grant.

References

1. Bottou, L.: Large-scale machine learning with stochastic gradient descent. In: Lechevallier, Y., Saporta, G. (eds.) COMPSTAT 2010, pp. 177–186. Springer, Heidelberg (2010). https://doi.org/10.1007/978-3-7908-2604-3_16
2. Chen, L.C., Papandreou, G., Kokkinos, I., Murphy, K., Yuille, A.L.: DeepLab: semantic image segmentation with deep convolutional nets, atrous convolution, and fully connected CRFs. IEEE Trans. Pattern Anal. Mach. Intell. **40**(4), 834–848 (2017)
3. Chen, L.C., Papandreou, G., Schroff, F., Adam, H.: Rethinking atrous convolution for semantic image segmentation. arXiv preprint arXiv:1706.05587 (2017)
4. Everingham, M., Van Gool, L., Williams, C.K., Winn, J., Zisserman, A.: The pascal visual object classes (VOC) challenge. Int. J. Comput. Vis. **88**(2), 303–338 (2010)
5. Fu, J., et al.: Dual attention network for scene segmentation. In: Proceedings of the IEEE Conference on Computer Vision and Pattern Recognition, pp. 3146–3154 (2019)

6. Fu, J., Liu, J., Wang, Y., Li, Y., Bao, Y., Tang, J., Lu, H.: Adaptive context network for scene parsing. In: The IEEE International Conference on Computer Vision (ICCV), October 2019

7. He, J., Deng, Z., Qiao, Y.: Dynamic multi-scale filters for semantic segmentation. In: Proceedings of the IEEE International Conference on Computer Vision, pp. 3562–3572 (2019)

8. He, J., Deng, Z., Zhou, L., Wang, Y., Qiao, Y.: Adaptive pyramid context network for semantic segmentation. In: Proceedings of the IEEE Conference on Computer Vision and Pattern Recognition, pp. 7519–7528 (2019)

9. He, K., Zhang, X., Ren, S., Sun, J.: Deep residual learning for image recognition. In: Proceedings of the IEEE Conference on Computer Vision and Pattern Recognition, pp. 770–778 (2016)

10. Hu, J., Shen, L., Sun, G.: Squeeze-and-excitation networks. In: Proceedings of the IEEE Conference on Computer Vision and Pattern Recognition, pp. 7132–7141 (2018)

11. Lin, D., Ji, Y., Lischinski, D., Cohen-Or, D., Huang, H.: Multi-scale context intertwining for semantic segmentation. In: Proceedings of the European Conference on Computer Vision (ECCV), pp. 603–619 (2018)

12. Lin, G., Milan, A., Shen, C., Reid, I.: RefineNet: multi-path refinement networks for high-resolution semantic segmentation. In: Proceedings of the IEEE Conference on Computer Vision and Pattern Recognition, pp. 1925–1934 (2017)

13. Lin, G., Shen, C., Van Den Hengel, A., Reid, I.: Efficient piecewise training of deep structured models for semantic segmentation. In: Proceedings of the IEEE Conference on Computer Vision and Pattern Recognition, pp. 3194–3203 (2016)

14. Liu, Z., Li, X., Luo, P., Loy, C.C., Tang, X.: Semantic image segmentation via deep parsing network. In: Proceedings of the IEEE International Conference on Computer Vision, pp. 1377–1385 (2015)

15. Long, J., Shelhamer, E., Darrell, T.: Fully convolutional networks for semantic segmentation. In: Proceedings of the IEEE Conference on Computer Vision and Pattern Recognition, pp. 3431–3440 (2015)

16. Mottaghi, R., et al.: The role of context for object detection and semantic segmentation in the wild. In: Proceedings of the IEEE Conference on Computer Vision and Pattern Recognition, pp. 891–898 (2014)

17. Noh, H., Hong, S., Han, B.: Learning deconvolution network for semantic segmentation. In: Proceedings of the IEEE International Conference on Computer Vision, pp. 1520–1528 (2015)

18. Ronneberger, O., Fischer, P., Brox, T.: U-net: convolutional networks for biomedical image segmentation. In: Navab, N., Hornegger, J., Wells, W.M., Frangi, A.F. (eds.) MICCAI 2015. LNCS, vol. 9351, pp. 234–241. Springer, Cham (2015). https://doi.org/10.1007/978-3-319-24574-4_28

19. Russakovsky, O., et al.: Imagenet large scale visual recognition challenge. Int. J. Comput. Vis. **115**(3), 211–252 (2015)

20. Takikawa, T., Acuna, D., Jampani, V., Fidler, S.: Gated-SCNN: gated shape CNNs for semantic segmentation. In: Proceedings of the IEEE International Conference on Computer Vision, pp. 5229–5238 (2019)

21. Tian, Z., He, T., Shen, C., Yan, Y.: Decoders matter for semantic segmentation: data-dependent decoding enables flexible feature aggregation. In: Proceedings of the IEEE Conference on Computer Vision and Pattern Recognition, pp. 3126–3135 (2019)

22. Wu, H., Zhang, J., Huang, K., Liang, K., Yu, Y.: FastFCN: rethinking dilated convolution in the backbone for semantic segmentation. arXiv preprint arXiv:1903.11816 (2019)
23. Wu, Z., Shen, C., Hengel, A.v.d.: Wider or deeper: revisiting the ResNet model for visual recognition. arXiv preprint arXiv:1611.10080 (2016)
24. Yu, F., Koltun, V., Funkhouser, T.: Dilated residual networks. In: Proceedings of the IEEE conference on Computer Vision and Pattern Recognition, pp. 472–480 (2017)
25. Zhang, H., et al.: Context encoding for semantic segmentation. In: The IEEE Conference on Computer Vision and Pattern Recognition (CVPR), June 2018
26. Zhang, H., Zhang, H., Wang, C., Xie, J.: Co-occurrent features in semantic segmentation. In: The IEEE Conference on Computer Vision and Pattern Recognition (CVPR) (2019)
27. Zhang, R., Tang, S., Zhang, Y., Li, J., Yan, S.: Scale-adaptive convolutions for scene parsing. In: Proceedings of the IEEE International Conference on Computer Vision, pp. 2031–2039 (2017)
28. Zhao, H., Shi, J., Qi, X., Wang, X., Jia, J.: Pyramid scene parsing network. In: Proceedings of the IEEE Conference on Computer Vision and Pattern Recognition, pp. 2881–2890 (2017)
29. Zheng, S., et al.: Conditional random fields as recurrent neural networks. In: Proceedings of the IEEE International Conference on Computer Vision, pp. 1529–1537 (2015)
30. Zhou, B., Zhao, H., Puig, X., Fidler, S., Barriuso, A., Torralba, A.: Scene parsing through ADE20K dataset. In: Proceedings of the IEEE Conference on Computer Vision and Pattern Recognition, pp. 633–641 (2017)
31. Zhu, Z., Xu, M., Bai, S., Huang, T., Bai, X.: Asymmetric non-local neural networks for semantic segmentation. In: Proceedings of the IEEE International Conference on Computer Vision, pp. 593–602 (2019)

GroSS: Group-Size Series Decomposition for Grouped Architecture Search

Henry Howard-Jenkins$^{(\boxtimes)}$ (D), Yiwen Li (D), and Victor Adrian Prisacariu (D)

Active Vision Laboratory, University of Oxford, Oxford, UK
{henryhj,kate,victor}@robots.ox.ac.uk

Abstract. We present a novel approach which is able to explore the configuration of grouped convolutions within neural networks. Group-size Series (GroSS) decomposition is a mathematical formulation of tensor factorisation into a series of approximations of increasing rank terms. GroSS allows for dynamic and differentiable selection of factorisation rank, which is analogous to a grouped convolution. Therefore, to the best of our knowledge, GroSS is the first method to enable simultaneous training of differing numbers of groups within a single layer, as well as all possible combinations between layers. In doing so, GroSS is able to train an entire grouped convolution architecture search-space concurrently. We demonstrate this through architecture searches with performance objectives on multiple datasets and networks. GroSS enables more effective and efficient search for grouped convolutional architectures.

Keywords: Group convolution · Network acceleration · Architecture search

1 Introduction

In recent years, there has been a flurry of deep neural networks (DNNs) producing remarkable results on a broad variety of tasks. In particular, grouped convolution has become a widely used tool in some prevalent networks. ResNeXt [28] used grouped convolution for improved accuracy over the analogous ResNets [7]. On the other hand, Xception [3], MobileNet [8], and various others [19,29] have used depthwise convolutions, which are the special case of grouped convolutions where the number of groups is equal to the number of in channels, in a for extremely low-cost inference. With these architectures, grouped convolution has proven to be a valuable design tool for high-performance and low-cost design alike. But, its application to these contrasting performance profiles has so far, to the best of our knowledge, remained relatively unexplored.

Finding a heuristic or intuition for how combinations of grouped convolutions with varying numbers of groups interact within a network is challenging. Grouped convolution, therefore, is presents itself as an ideal candidate for Neural Architecture Search (NAS), which has provided an alternative to hand designed

Electronic supplementary material The online version of this chapter (https://doi.org/10.1007/978-3-030-58574-7_2) contains supplementary material, which is available to authorized users.

A. Vedaldi et al. (Eds.): ECCV 2020, LNCS 12371, pp. 18–33, 2020.
https://doi.org/10.1007/978-3-030-58574-7_2

networks. NAS allows for the search and even direct optimisation of the network's structure. But, the search space for architectures is often vast, with potentially limitless design choices. Furthermore, each configuration must undergo some training or fine-tuning for its efficacy to be determined. This has led to the development of methods which lump multiple design parameters together, which reduce the search space in a principled manner [23], as well as creating the need for sophisticated search algorithms [17,27], which can more quickly converge to an improved design. Both techniques reduce the number of search iterations and ultimately reduce the number of required training/fine-tuning stages.

In this work, however, we do not wish to make assumptions about the grouped convolution manifold. We achieve this with the introduction of a Group-size Series (GroSS) decomposition. GroSS allows us to train the entire search space of architectures *simultaneously*. In doing so, we shift the expense of architecture search with respect to groups away from decomposition and training, and towards cheaper test-time sampling. This allows for the exploration of possible configurations, while significantly reducing the need for imparting bias on the group design hyperparameter selection.

The contributions of this paper can be summarised as follows:

1. We present GroSS decomposition – a novel formulation of tensor decomposition as a series of rank approximations. This provides a mathematical basis for grouped convolution as a series of increasing rank terms.
2. GroSS provides the apparatus for differentiably switching between grouped convolution ranks. Therefore, to the best of our knowledge, it is the first simultaneous training of differing numbers of groups within a single layer, as well as the all possible configurations between layers. This makes feasible, for the first time, a search for rank selection for network compression.
3. We explore this concurrently-trained architecture space in the context of network acceleration. We factorise a small network, as well VGG-16 and ResNet-18, and propose exhaustive and breadth-first searches on CIFAR-10 and ImageNet. We demonstrate the efficacy of the GroSS for rank selection search over a more conventional approach of partial training schedules.

2   Related Work

Grouped convolution has had a wide impact on neural network architectures, particularly due to its efficiency. It was first introduced in AlexNet [14] as an aid for the single network to be trained over multiple GPUs. Since then, it has had a wide impact on DNN architecture design. Deep Roots [9] was the first to introduce group convolution for efficiency, while ResNeXt [28] used grouped convolutions synonymously with concept of *cardinality*, ultimately exploiting the efficiency of grouped convolutions for high-accuracy network design. The reduced complexity of grouped convolution allowed for ResNeXt to incorporate deeper layers within the ResNet-analogous residual blocks [7]. In all, this allowed higher accuracy with a similar inference cost as an equivalent ResNet. The efficiency of grouped convolution has also led to several low-cost network designs. Sifre [20] first introduced depthwise separable convolutions, which were later utilised by

Xception [3]. MobileNet [8] utilised a ResNet-like bottleneck design with depth-wise convolutions for an extremely efficient network with mobile applications in mind. ShuffleNet [29] was also based on a depthwise bottleneck, however, pointwise layers were also made grouped convolutions.

Previous works [5,10,15,25] have applied low-rank approximation of convolution for network compression and acceleration. Block Term Decomposition (BTD) [4] has recently been applied to the task of network factorisation [2], where it was shown that the BTD factorisation of a convolutional weight was equivalent to a grouped convolution within a bottleneck architecture. Wang *et al.* [26] applied this equivalency for network acceleration. Since decomposition is costly, these methods have relied on heuristics and intuition to set hyperparameters such as the rank of successive layers within the decomposition. In this paper, we present a method for decomposition which allows for exploration of the decomposition hyperparameters and all the combinations.

Existing architecture search methods have overwhelmingly favoured reinforcement learning. Examples of this include, but are not limited to, NAS-Net [30], MNasNet [22], ReLeq-Net [6]. In broad terms, these methods all set a baseline structure, which is manipulated by a separate controller. The controller optimises the structure through and objective based on network performance. There has also been work in differentiable architecture search [17,27] which makes the network architecture manipulations themselves differentiable. In addition, work such as [23] aims to limit the network scaling within a performance envelope to a single parameter.

These methods all have a commonality: the cost of re-training or fine-tuning at each stage motivates the recovery of the optimal architecture in as few training steps as possible, whether this is achieved through a trained controller, direct optimisation or significantly reducing the search space. In this work, however, GroSS allows efficient weight-sharing between varying grouped architectures, thus enabling them to be trained at once. This is similar to the task of one-shot architecture search. SMASH [1] use a hypernetwork to predict weights for each architecture. The work of Li *et al.* [16] bares most resemblance to this paper, where randomly sampled architectures are used to train shared-weights.

3 Method

In this section, we will first introduce Block Term Decomposition (BTD) and detail how its factorisation can be applied to a convolutional layer. After that, we will introduce GroSS decomposition, where we formulate a unification of a series of ranked decompositions so that they can dynamically and differentially be combined. We detail the training strategy for training the whole series at once. Finally, we detail the methodology of our exhaustive and breadth-first search.

3.1 General Block Term Decomposition

Block Term Decomposition (BTD) [4] aims to factorise a tensor into the sum of multiple low rank-Tuckers [24]. That is, given an Nth order tensor

$\mathbf{X} \in \mathbb{R}^{d_1 \times d_2 \times \ldots \times d_N}$, BTD factorises $\mathbf{X}$ into the sum of R terms with rank $(d'_1, d'_2, \ldots, d'_N)$:

$$\mathbf{X} = \sum_{r=1}^{R} \mathbf{G}_r \times_1 \mathbf{A}_r^{(1)} \times_2 \mathbf{A}_r^{(2)} \times_3 \ldots \times_N \mathbf{A}_r^{(N)}$$

$$\text{where} \begin{cases} \mathbf{G} \in \mathbb{R}^{d'_1 \times d'_2 \times \ldots \times d'_N} \\ \mathbf{A}_r^{(n)} \in \mathbb{R}^{d_n \times d'_n}, n \in \{1, \ldots, N\} \end{cases} \tag{1}$$

In the above, $\mathbf{G}$ is known as the *core* tensor and we will refer to $\mathbf{A}$ as *factors* matrices. We use the usual notation $\times_n$ to represent the *mode-n* product [4].

3.2 Converting a Single Convolution to a Bottleneck Using BTD

Here, we can restrict discussion from a general, N-mode, tensor to the 4-mode weights of a 2D convolution as follows: $\mathbf{X} \in \mathbb{R}^{t \times u \times v \times w}$, where t and u represent the number of input and output channels, and v and w the spatial size of the filter kernel. Typically the spatial extent of each filter is small and thus we only factorise t and u. To eliminate superscripts, we define $\mathbf{B} = \mathbf{A}^{(1)}$ and $\mathbf{C} = \mathbf{A}^{(2)}$. Therefore, the BTD for convolutional weights is expressed as follows:

$$\mathbf{X} = \sum_{r=1}^{R} \mathbf{G}_r \times_1 \mathbf{B}_r \times_2 \mathbf{C}_r$$

$$\text{where} \begin{cases} \mathbf{G} \in \mathbb{R}^{t' \times u' \times v \times w} \\ \mathbf{B} \in \mathbb{R}^{t \times t'} \\ \mathbf{C} \in \mathbb{R}^{u \times u'} \end{cases} \tag{2}$$

This factorisation of the convolutional weights into R groups forms a three-layer bottleneck-style structure [2]: a pointwise (1×1) convolution $\mathbf{P} \in \mathbb{R}^{t \times (Rt') \times 1 \times 1}$, formed from factor $\mathbf{B}$; followed by a grouped convolution $\mathbf{R} \in \mathbb{R}^{t' \times (Ru') \times v \times w}$, formed from core $\mathbf{G}$ and with R groups; and finally another pointwise convolution $\mathbf{Q} \in \mathbb{R}^{(Ru') \times u \times 1 \times 1}$, formed from factor $\mathbf{C}$. With careful selection of the BTD parameters, the bottleneck approximation can be applied to any standard convolutional layer. This is visualised in Fig. 1.

In Table 1, we detail how the dimensions of the bottleneck architecture are determined from its corresponding convolutional layer, and indicate how properties such as stride, padding and bias are applied within the bottleneck for

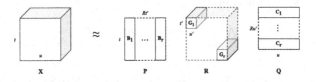

Fig. 1. Formation of bottleneck layers $\mathbf{P}$, $\mathbf{R}$ and $\mathbf{Q}$ from BTD cores and factors.

Table 1. Convolution to grouped bottleneck. The table states how the convolutional parameters are used in the equivalent bottleneck

	Filter Size	C_{in}	C_{out}	Groups	Bias	Stride	Padding
Convolution	$v \times w$	t	u	1	B	S	P
	1×1	t	Rt'	1	–	1	0
Bottleneck	$v \times w$	Rt'	Ru'	R	–	S	P
	1×1	Ru'	u	1	B	1	0

equivalency with the original layer. It is worth noting that we often refer to the quantities t' or u' as the group-size; this quantity determines the number of channels in each group and is equivalent to the rank of the decomposition.

3.3 Group-Size Series Decomposition

Group-size Series (GroSS) decomposition unifies multiple ranks of BTD factorisations. This is achieved by defining each successive factorisation relative to the lower order ranks. Thus we ensure that higher rank decompositions only contain information that was missed by the lower order approximations. Therefore the ith approximation of $\mathbf{X}$ is given as follows:

$$\mathbf{X} = \sum_{r=1}^{R_i} [(\mathbf{g}_r)_i + (\mathbf{G}'_r)_{i-1}] \times_1 [(\mathbf{b}_r)_i + (\mathbf{B}'_r)_{i-1}] \times_2 [(\mathbf{c}_r)_i + (\mathbf{C}'_r)_{i-1}]$$

$$\text{where} \begin{cases} (\mathbf{g}_r)_i, \ (\mathbf{G}'_r)_{i-1} \in \mathbb{R}^{t'_i \times u'_i \times v \times w} \\ (\mathbf{b}_r)_i, \ (\mathbf{B}'_r)_{i-1} \in \mathbb{R}^{t \times t'_i} \\ (\mathbf{c}_r)_i, \ (\mathbf{C}'_r)_{i-1} \in \mathbb{R}^{u \times u'_i} \end{cases} \quad (3)$$

Omitting r from the notation, $\mathbf{g}_i$, $\mathbf{b}_i$ and $\mathbf{c}_i$ represent the additional information captured between the $(i-1)^{\text{th}}$ and i^{th} rank of approximation, and $\mathbf{G}'_{(i-1)}$, $\mathbf{B}'_{(i-1)}$ and $\mathbf{C}'_{(i-1)}$ to represent total approximation from lower rank approximations in the form of cores and factors. However, both the core and factors must be recomputed so that the dimensions match the ranks required R_i, which is not a trivial manipulation.

Instead, we introduce a function, $\Psi_{g \to h}()$, which allows the weights of a grouped convolution to be "expanded". The expanded weight from a convolution with group-size g can be used in a convolution with group-size h, where $h > g$, giving identical outputs:

$$\mathbf{W}_g *_g \boldsymbol{F} \equiv \Psi_{g \to h}(\mathbf{W}_g) *_h \boldsymbol{F} \quad (4)$$

where $\mathbf{W}_g$ is the weight for a grouped convolution, $*_g$ refers to convolution with group-size g, and $\boldsymbol{F}$ is the feature map to which the convolution is applied. We provide an example visualisation of $\Psi()$ in Fig. 2. This allows us to conveniently

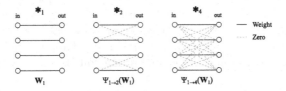

Fig. 2. Visualisation of a depthwise weight, $\mathbf{W}_1$, expanded for convolutions with groups of size 2 and 4.

reformulate the GroSS decomposition in terms of the successive convolutional weights obtained from BTD, rather than within the cores and factors directly. More specifically, we define the bottleneck weights for the Nth order GroSS decomposition with group-sizes, $S = \{s_1, ..., s_N\}$, as follows:

$$\mathbf{R}_N = \Psi_{s_1 \to s_N}(\mathbf{R}_1) + \sum_{i=2}^{N} \Psi_{s_i \to s_N}(\mathbf{r}_i)$$

$$\mathbf{P}_N = \mathbf{P}_1 + \sum_{i=2}^{N} \mathbf{p}_i, \quad \mathbf{Q}_N = \mathbf{Q}_1 + \sum_{i=2}^{N} \mathbf{q}_i \tag{5}$$

$\mathbf{R}_1$, $\mathbf{P}_1$ and $\mathbf{Q}_1$ represent the weights obtained from the lowest rank decomposition present in the series. $\mathbf{r}_i$, $\mathbf{p}_i$ and $\mathbf{q}_i$ represent the additional information that the ith rank decomposition contribute to the bottleneck approximation:

$$\mathbf{p}_i = \mathbf{P}_i - \mathbf{P}_{(i-1)}, \quad \mathbf{r}_i = \mathbf{R}_i - \Psi_{s_{(i-1)} \to s_i}(\mathbf{R}_{(i-1)}), \quad \mathbf{q}_i = \mathbf{Q}_i - \mathbf{Q}_{(i-1)}. \tag{6}$$

This formulation involving only manipulation of the convolutional weights is exactly equivalent to forming the bottleneck components $\mathbf{r}_i$, $\mathbf{p}_i$ and $\mathbf{q}_i$ from $\mathbf{g}_i$, $\mathbf{b}_i$ and $\mathbf{c}_i$, as in the general BTD to bottleneck case.

Further, the grouped convolution weight expansion, $\Psi()$, enables us to dynamically, and differentiably, change the group-size of a convolution. In itself, this is not particularly useful: a convolution with a larger group-size is requires more operations and more memory, while yielding identical outputs. However, it allows for direct interaction between differently ranked network decomposition and, therefore, the representation of one rank by the combination of lower ranks. Thus, GroSS treats the decomposition of the original convolution as the sum of successive order approximations, with each order contributing additional representational power.

Training GroSS Simultaneously. The expression of a group-size s_i decomposition as the combination of lower rank decompositions is useful because it enables the group-size to be dynamically changed during training. The expansion and summation of convolutional weights is differentiable and so training at a high rank, also optimises the lower rank approximations simultaneously. To the best of our knowledge GroSS is the first method that allows weight-sharing between, and training of, convolutions with varying numbers of groups.

We leverage the series form of the factorisation during training, by randomly sampling a group-size for each decomposed layer at each iteration. We sample a group-size s_i for each decomposed layer uniformly. Through uniform sampling, we are able to train each network configuration equally.

3.4 Search

The objective for all the searches performed within in this paper is: given a base configuration, we aim to find an alternative configuration which is more accurate, but offers the same or cheaper inference. We implement two forms of search to achieve this leveraging GroSS decomposition: exhaustive and breadth-first.

Exhaustive. Within the exhaustive search, all possible configurations are evaluated. In this search, we simply filter any configuration with multiply accumulates (MACs) above the respective base configuration. After filtering, we can select the highest accuracy remaining.

Breadth-First Search. Where an exhaustive search is not feasible due to the sheer number of possible configurations, we use a greedy breadth-first search. We first randomly select a configuration which requires fewer operations for inference than the base configuration. We evaluate all neighbouring configurations—those which only require one layer to have it's group-size changed—of the currently selected configuration. We select the neighbour with the highest accuracy that does not exceed the number of MACs as the base configuration for the next step. We repeat this step for a maximum of 25 times, or until there are no more accurate neighbours not exceeding the cost of the base configuration.

This is repeated 20 times. The most accurate configuration from all of the 20 runs is considered the result of the search. Since the search for a base configuration with fewer MACs is contained within the search-space with a higher limit, we perform them incrementally. This results in the same search process, but the first 10 runs are initialised using the top-10 highest accuracy results from the smaller search. We found that this generally led to faster stopping.

4 Application of GroSS

In this section, we explain how we apply GroSS to a several models across datasets. We first detail the dataset on which evaluation is conducted. Next, we describe the network architecture on which perform GroSS decomposition. Finally, we list the procedure for the decomposition and fine-tuning.

4.1 Datasets

We perform our experimental evaluation on CIFAR-10 [13] and ImageNet [14]. CIFAR-10 is a dataset consisting of 10 classes. The size of each image is 32×32.

In total there are 60,000 images, which are split into 50,000 train images and 10,000 testing images. We further divide the training set into a training and validation splits with 40,000 and 10,000 images, respectively. ImageNet consists of 1000 classes, with 1.2 million training images and 50,000 validation images. Since the test annotations are not available, we report our accuracy on the validation set.

4.2 Models

In this paper, we perform on three general network architectures: a custom 4-layer network, VGG-16 [21], and ResNet-18 [7]. Here, we provide an overview of the network definitions, with more details in the supplementary material.

Our 4-layer network has four convolutional layers, with output channel dimensions of 32, 32, 64 and 64, followed by two fully-connected layers of size 256 and 10. In our ImageNet experiments, we use a standard VGG-16 and ResNet-18, identical to those in [21] and [7], respectively. However, we make some changes to the fully connected structure in VGG-16 for training and inference on CIFAR-10. The convolutional layers instead followed by a 2×2 max-pooling and two fully-connected layers of size 512 and 10, respectively. A ReLU layer and dropout with probability of 0.5 is applied between the fully-connected layers.

4.3 Decomposition

We perform GroSS decomposition on our small 4-layer network, as well as VGG-16 [21]. In each case we decompose all convolutional layers in the network aside from the first. Unless otherwise stated, we set the bottleneck width equal to the number of input channels. For the 4-layer network, group-sizes are set to all powers of 2 which do not exceed the bottleneck width for that respective layer. This leads to a total of 252 configurations represented by our decomposition. We decompose each layer in VGG-16 and ResNet-18 into 4 group-sizes: (1, 4, 16, 32). This leads to a total of 4^{12} and 4^{16} configurations represented by the decomposed VGG-16 and ResNet-18, respectively.

Our formulation of GroSS decomposition as a series of convolutional weight differences (expanded weights in the case of the grouped convolution), as detailed by Eq. 5 means that we are able to use an off-the-shelf BTD framework [12]. For each group-size, we set the stopping criteria for BTD identically: when the decrease in approximation error between steps is below 1×10^{-6} for the 4-layer network and 1×10^{-5} for VGG-16, or 5×10^{5} steps have elapsed. We define approximation error as the Frobenius norm between the original tensor and the product of the BTD cores and factors divided by the Frobenius norm of the original tensor. For the 4-layer network, we perform this decomposition 5 times.

4.4 Fine-Tuning

CIFAR-10. After we have performed GroSS decomposition on the network, we then fine-tune on the classification task. For the 4-layer network, we tune for 150 epochs with a batch-size of 256, an initial learning rate of 0.0001 and momentum 0.9. We decay the learning rate by a factor of 0.1 after both 80 and 120 epochs. For VGG-16, we fine-tune with the same SGD parameters and batch-size, however we train for 200 epochs, and decay the learning rate after 100 and 150 epochs. All network parameters are frozen aside from the GroSS decomposition weights. During training, there is a 0.5 probability of horizontal flipping, zero-padding of size 2 is applied around all borders and a random 32×32 crop is taken from the resulting image.

ImageNet. We decompose VGG-16 and ResNet-18 before funetuning on ImageNet. For VGG-16, we train using SGD for a total of 4 epochs with a batch-size of 128, leading to approximately 10^4 iterations. The initial learning rate is set to 10^{-5}, which is decayed by a factor of 0.1 after 2 epochs. Momentum is set to 0.9. Again, all the network parameters are frozen, aside from the decomposition weights. For ResNet-18, we train for 8 epochs in total with a batch size of 512. The initial learning rate is set to 5×10^{-5}, with decay every 2 epochs The images are resized so that the smallest side is of size 256. During training, the resized images are flipped horizontally with a probability of 0.5 and a random 224×224 crop is taken. During testing, we simply take a centre crop from the resized image, hence evaluating 1-crop accuracy.

Individual Configurations. For the decomposition in the conventional manner, *i.e.* a singular group-size configuration, we decompose using exactly the same routine as with GroSS. However, the fine-tuning schedules are slightly modified. On CIFAR-10, we reduce the schedule for our 4-layer network and our CIFAR VGG-16 to 100 epochs. The initial learning rate is increased to 0.001, and decayed at 80 epochs. On Imagenet, we do not freeze the non-decomposed layers. The VGG-16 configurations have a schedule of 6 epochs, with learning rate decay occurring after every 2 epochs. The initial learning rate is kept at 10^{-4}. For ResNet-18 configurations, we increase batch size to 512 and again unfreeze all layers. We run for a total of 12 epochs, with initial learning rate 10^{-3} and decay after 8 and 10 epochs. Due to this being the conventional BTD factoristation strategy, we often refer to this as the *true* accuracy of a configuration.

5   Results

In this section, we demonstrate the effectiveness of GroSS. First, we explore group-size selection for network acceleration through search on our GroSS decomposition. Secondly, we justify the design of GroSS over a more simply using partial training schedules for group configurations.

5.1   Group-Size Search

Here, we evaluate the performance of our search. We split our results by dataset, with our CIFAR-10 results being followed by our results on ImageNet.

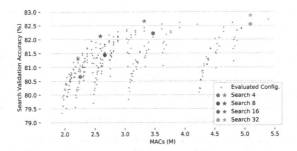

Fig. 3. Exhaustive search for the 4-layer network on CIFAR-10. Each search is colour coded. The circles and stars mark the performance of the baseline and found configuration, respectively.

For each search, we report the change in accuracy of the found configuration over the baseline, as well as the percentage reduction in MACs compared to the baseline. We are primarily concerned with exploring the impact of the number of groups on the performance of the network, rather than other design parameters such as the bottleneck dimensions. In our experimental setup, the inference cost between configurations varies only in the number of groups in each bottleneck. However, there is significant overhead from other layers in the network that remains constant between configurations. Therefore, we report the reduction in total MACs, as well as the contribution from the group layers alone. This provides greater insight into grouped architecture design and the performance of the searches using GroSS.

Table 2. Exhaustive search for our 4-layer network on CIFAR-10

4-Layer Network Configuration	MACs	Accuracy			ΔMACs	
		GroSS	True	ΔAcc.	Total	G.Conv
Full	5.13M	-	83.99 (0.53)	-	-	-
Baseline: 32 32 32	**5.09M**	*82.55 (0.07)*	*83.70 (0.05)*	-	-	-
32 16 64	**5.09M 82.87 (0.14)**		**84.05 (0.07)**	↑ **0.35**	0.00%	0.00%
Baseline: 16 16 16	*3.47M*	*82.22 (0.10)*	*82.94 (0.06)*	-	-	-
VBMF [18]: 16 8 16	**3.33M**	81.76 (0.10)	82.83 (0.10)	↓ 0.11	↓ **4.25%**	↓ **9.09%**
8 16 64	**3.33M 82.66 (0.11)**		**83.88 (0.10)**	↑ **0.94**	↓ **4.25%**	↓ **9.09%**
Baseline: 8 8 8	*2.66M*	*81.44 (0.16)*	*82.86 (0.10)*	-	-	-
2 16 32	**2.59M 82.12 (0.16)**		**83.50 (0.07)**	↑ **0.64**	↓ **2.77%**	↓ **9.09%**
Baseline: 4 4 4	*2.26M*	*80.66 (0.13)*	*82.37 (0.11)*	-	-	-
1 8 16	**2.22M 81.32 (0.16)**		**82.45 (0.15)**	↑ **0.08**	↓ **1.63%**	↓ **9.09%**
Depthwise: 1 1 1	*1.95M*	*79.34 (0.14)*	*81.70 (0.32)*	-	-	-

Table 3. Breadth-first search on our VGG-16 network on CIFAR-10

VGG-16 (CIFAR) Configuration	MACs	Accuracy			ΔMACs	
		GroSS	True	ΔAcc.	Total	G.Conv
Full	314M	-	91.52	-	-	-
32 32 32 32 32 32 32 32 32 32 32 32	121M	90.97	**91.57**	-	-	-
VBMF [18]	118M	90.97	91.31	↓ 0.26	↓ 2.68%	↓ 6.18%
32 4 16 32 16 16 32 16 4 16 32 1	**103M**	**91.31**	91.41	↓ 0.16	↓ 14.6%	↓ 33.7%
16 16 16 16 16 16 16 16 16 16 16 16	94.6M	91.13	91.19	-	-	-
4 4 16 32 16 16 1 32 4 32 16 1	**86.7M**	**91.28**	**91.31**	↑ 0.12	↓ 8.36%	↓ 30.2%
4 4 4 4 4 4 4 4 4 4 4 4	74.9M	90.43	90.90	-	-	-
1 1 1 16 16 4 1 1 4 4 1 4	**74.1M**	**90.97**	**91.14**	↑ 0.24	↓ 1.11%	↓ 12.6%
1 1 1 1 1 1 1 1 1 1 1 1	70.0M	90.24	90.66	-	-	-

CIFAR-10. The results of the exhaustive search on the 4-layer network are shown in Table 2, where the decomposition and tune is performed 5 times for each configuration and the mean and standard deviation are reported decompositions with uniform rank values across layers (4, 8, 16, and 32) are chosen as the baseline configurations for the search, such that we perform search across the range of possible configurations. For each baseline configuration we are able to find an alternative that is more accurate whilst requiring fewer operations. The results of the search are also visualised in Fig. 3.

In the case of our CIFAR-10 VGG-16 network, the 4^{12} configurations produced by our GroSS decomposition are too many to feasibly enable exhaustive evaluation. We, therefore, perform a breadth-first search. The full details of how this search is performed are described in Sect. 3.4. Results for this search on VGG-16 are shown in Table 3.

For the searches on the 4, 8 and 16 baselines, we are able to find configurations which meet the objective. However, in the case of the search below the 32 baseline, the found configuration's true accuracy is less than that of the baseline. We speculate that this is because 32 is the maximum rank in the decomposition. Therefore, the rank of each layer can never be increased above that of the baseline. This means that configurations have less room to manoeuvre in targeting more heavy-duty layers at key stages of the network.

We also include a configuration found through Variational Bayesian Matrix Factorisation (VBMF) [18], which is used for one-shot rank selection in [11]. For both networks, we were able to find more accurate configurations which require fewer or the same number of operations than the VBMF rank selection. In fact, Kim *et al.* [11] note that, although they achieve good network compression results with the result of VBMF, they had not investigated whether this method of rank selection was optimal. The results in Table 2 demonstrate that VBMF is not optimal in this case, and GroSS is an effective tool to determine this.

Table 4. Breadth-first search for VGG-16 and ResNet-18 on ImageNet. * denotes the configuration is using the decomposition structure from [26]

ImageNet Configuration	MACs	GroSS	True	ΔAcc	Total	G.Conv
VGG-16 (Full)	15.49B	-	71.59	-	-	-
16 16 16 16 16 16 16 16 16 16 16 16	*4.75B*	*70.25*	*70.77*	-	-	-
1 32 32 32 16 1 32 16 32 4 32 16	**4.70B**	**70.40**	**70.82**	↑ **0.04**	↓ **0.99%**	↓ **3.65%**
4 4 4 4 4 4 4 4 4 4 4 4	*3.78B*	*69.73*	*70.51*	-	-	-
1 1 4 4 4 4 32 16 1 1 32 1	**3.78B**	**69.97**	**70.63**	↑ **0.12**	↓ **0.14%**	↓ **1.69%**
1 1 1 1 1 1 1 1 1 1 1 1	*3.54B*	*68.98*	*70.28*	-	-	-
[26]: *11 10 14 9 15 16 16 29 33 56 56 56**	*1.16B*	*62.64*	*66.85*	-	-	-
11 10 14 9 15 32 64 58 3 56 7 7*	**1.16B**	**63.11**	**67.22**	↑ **0.37**	↓ **0.39%**	↓ **4.89%**
ResNet-18 (Full)	1.82B	-	69.76	-	-	-
Baseline 16s	*738M*	*60.77*	*65.80*	-	-	-
16 16 4 32 32 32 32 32 16 32 32 32 16 4 32 16	**715M**	**61.25**	**65.84**	↑ **0.04**	↓ **3.18%**	↓ **11.5%**
Baseline 4s	*586M*	*60.02*	*65.46*	-	-	-
1 4 4 1 16 4 1 4 32 4 4 4 16 4 4 4	**585M**	**60.31**	**65.44**	↑ **0.18**	↓ **0.08%**	↓ **0.88%**
1 1 1 1 1 1 1 1 1 1 1 1	*547M*	*58.61*	*65.16*	-	-	-

ImageNet. We now move to a larger, more complex dataset in ImageNet. We perform the same GroSS decomposition and breadth-first search on conventional VGG-16 and ResNet-18 structures. We search against baseline configurations of uniform 4s and 16s. The results are listed in Table 4 and we provide visualisation of the search on VGG-16 in Fig. 4.

We also include results for an alternative decomposition structure and group configuration identical to that used in [26], which we detail in the supplementary material. This decomposition structure aggressively reduces widths in bottleneck layers to achieve a large compression ratio. In our search, we are able to show that the original configuration of groups within this structure is not optimal, with our found configuration leading to a significant improvement in accuracy as well as a slight speed up.

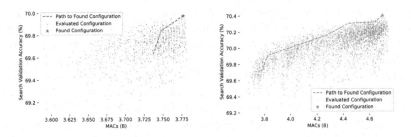

Fig. 4. Visualisation of the VGG-16 breadth-first search on ImageNet. (**Left**) and (**Right**) are the searches against the 4s and 16s baselines, respectively.

The results show that exploration of group selection with GroSS generalises well across datasets and architectures. In every search performed, we found configurations that met the objective of increased accuracy with lower inference cost.

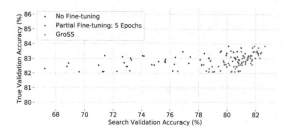

Fig. 5. Search-space vs true validation accuracy for our 4-layer network on CIFAR-10. Here we plot the accuracy of 45 random configurations of our 4-layer network for 3 different methods of obtaining a search-space. The accuracy of each configuration is plotted against its true validation accuracy.

5.2   GroSS vs. Conventional Fine-Tuning

In this section, we justify the need for GroSS by evaluating it against using a partial fine-tuning strategy for each individual configuration. For this, we select 45 random group-size configurations of our 4-layer network and fine-tine according to our individual schedule, which is outlined in Sect. 4.4, giving us a true validation accuracy for each configuration. We can then evaluate the validation accuracy of these same configurations in our GroSS search-space. This procedure allows us to visualise how representative GroSS is of the true accuracy.

For comparison, we also include the validation accuracy of the same configurations with no fine-tuning, as well as with a shortened schedule of 5 epochs. The partial fine-tune could be considered a reasonable solution to reducing the burden of training while performing a configuration search.

We visualise the search-space against the true validation accuracies in Fig. 5. Qualitatively, it can be seen that the validation accuracies produced by GroSS produce a significantly more consistent search space. The points appear to be more tightly distributed and closer to the ideal distribution ($y = x$). To measure this quantitatively, we compute the top-5 average precision of the search spaces. We simulate searches across the entire range of configurations by evaluating the average precision at multiple slices through the search-space. This allows for comparison across the space, not just the most accurate group configurations.

Table 5 lists the results of this average precision computation. GroSS is consistently as good or better than no fine-tuning and the partial schedule at each slice. This leads to a significant improvement in search performance across the range of configurations which is highlighted by the mean average precision.

Table 5. Average precision across the range of the search space. We compute the average precision using the top 5 true validation accuracies as positive recalls. "$X \downarrow$" refers to the average precision computed after the top-X configurations have been removed from the search

Fine-tune strategy	Average precision (top 5)				
	All	10 $\downarrow$	20 $\downarrow$	30 $\downarrow$	Mean
No fine-tuning	43.0	43.8	86.3	69.8	60.7
Partial fine-tuning	35.2	**64.0**	42.5	66.4	52.0
GroSS	**44.1**	63.8	**94.3**	**82.5**	**71.2**

When making the comparison between GroSS and a partial training strategy, it is worth considering the computational requirements of each. Running inference for a new configuration in either of the conventional decompositions requires a new network to be initialised, and weights to be loaded. However, since group-sizes are handled dynamically within a GroSS decomposition, switching between them is essentially free, with no structure change or weight loading. This leads to GroSS having a significant speed improvement for running inference (7 s vs 287 s) over the 45 configurations. This only increases with more configurations tested. For example, the inference for the exhaustive search on the GroSS decomposition of the 4-layer network took only 9 s for 252 configurations. Similarly, the total number of training epochs for the partial training strategy increase linearly with the number of configurations, but remain constant for GroSS. With larger search-spaces, such as those visualised in Fig. 4, the accuracy and performance benefits of GroSS combine to make grouped architecture search feasible where it might not have been before.

6   Conclusions

In this paper, we have presented GroSS, a series BTD factorisation which allows for the dynamic assignment and simultaneous training of differing numbers of groups within a layer. We have shown how GroSS-decomposed layers can be combined to train an entire grouped convolution search space at once. We confirmed the value of these configurations through an exhaustive search and a breadth-first search. We further demonstrate that, without GroSS, these searches would be less effective and dramatically less efficient.

Acknowledgements. We gratefully acknowledge the European Commission Project Multiple-actOrs Virtual Empathic CARegiver for the Elder (MoveCare) for financially supporting the authors for this work.

References

1. Brock, A., Lim, T., Ritchie, J.M., Weston, N.: SMASH: one-shot model architecture search through hypernetworks. arXiv Preprint arXiv:1708.05344 (2017)

2. Chen, Y., Jin, X., Kang, B., Feng, J., Yan, S.: Sharing residual units through collective tensor factorization to improve deep neural networks. In: IJCAI, pp. 635–641 (2018)
3. Chollet, F.: Xception: deep learning with depthwise separable convolutions. In: Proceedings of the IEEE Conference on Computer Vision and Pattern Recognition, pp. 1251–1258 (2017)
4. De Lathauwer, L.: Decompositions of a higher-order tensor in block terms–part II: definitions and uniqueness. SIAM J. Matrix Anal. Appl. **30**(3), 1033–1066 (2008)
5. Denton, E.L., Zaremba, W., Bruna, J., LeCun, Y., Fergus, R.: Exploiting linear structure within convolutional networks for efficient evaluation. In: Advances in Neural Information Processing Systems, pp. 1269–1277 (2014)
6. Elthakeb, A.T., Pilligundla, P., Yazdanbakhsh, A., Kinzer, S., Esmaeilzadeh, H.: ReLeQ: a reinforcement learning approach for deep quantization of neural networks. arXiv Preprint arXiv:1811.01704 (2018)
7. He, K., Zhang, X., Ren, S., Sun, J.: Deep residual learning for image recognition. In: Proceedings of the IEEE Conference on Computer Vision and Pattern Recognition, pp. 770–778 (2016)
8. Howard, A.G., et al.: MobileNets: efficient convolutional neural networks for mobile vision applications. arXiv Preprint arXiv:1704.04861 (2017)
9. Ioannou, Y., Robertson, D., Cipolla, R., Criminisi, A.: Deep roots: Improving CNN efficiency with hierarchical filter groups. In: Proceedings of the IEEE Conference on Computer Vision and Pattern Recognition, pp. 1231–1240 (2017)
10. Jaderberg, M., Vedaldi, A., Zisserman, A.: Speeding up convolutional neural networks with low rank expansions. arXiv Preprint arXiv:1405.3866 (2014)
11. Kim, Y.D., Park, E., Yoo, S., Choi, T., Yang, L., Shin, D.: Compression of deep convolutional neural networks for fast and low power mobile applications. arXiv Preprint arXiv:1511.06530 (2015)
12. Kossaifi, J., Panagakis, Y., Anandkumar, A., Pantic, M.: TensorLy: tensor learning in Python. J. Mach. Learn. Res. **20**(1), 925–930 (2019)
13. Krizhevsky, A., Nair, V., Hinton, G.: The CIFAR-10 dataset (2014). http://www.cs.toronto.edu/kriz/cifar. HTML 55
14. Krizhevsky, A., Sutskever, I., Hinton, G.E.: ImageNet classification with deep convolutional neural networks. In: Advances in Neural Information Processing Systems, pp. 1097–1105 (2012)
15. Lebedev, V., Ganin, Y., Rakhuba, M., Oseledets, I., Lempitsky, V.: Speeding-up convolutional neural networks using fine-tuned CP-decomposition. arXiv Preprint arXiv:1412.6553 (2014)
16. Li, L., Talwalkar, A.: Random search and reproducibility for neural architecture search. arXiv Preprint arXiv:1902.07638 (2019)
17. Liu, H., Simonyan, K., Yang, Y.: DARTS: differentiable architecture search. arXiv Preprint arXiv:1806.09055 (2018)
18. Nakajima, S., Sugiyama, M., Babacan, S.D., Tomioka, R.: Global analytic solution of fully-observed variational Bayesian matrix factorization. J. Mach. Learn. Res. **14**(Jan), 1–37 (2013)
19. Sandler, M., Howard, A., Zhu, M., Zhmoginov, A., Chen, L.C.: MobileNetV2: inverted residuals and linear bottlenecks. In: Proceedings of the IEEE Conference on Computer Vision and Pattern Recognition, pp. 4510–4520 (2018)
20. Sifre, L., Mallat, S.: Rigid-motion scattering for image classification (2014)
21. Simonyan, K., Zisserman, A.: Very deep convolutional networks for large-scale image recognition. arXiv Preprint arXiv:1409.1556 (2014)

22. Tan, M., et al.: MnasNet: platform-aware neural architecture search for mobile. In: Proceedings of the IEEE Conference on Computer Vision and Pattern Recognition, pp. 2820–2828 (2019)
23. Tan, M., Le, Q.V.: EfficientNet: rethinking model scaling for convolutional neural networks. arXiv Preprint arXiv:1905.11946 (2019)
24. Tucker, L.R.: Some mathematical notes on three-mode factor analysis. Psychometrika **31**(3), 279–311 (1966)
25. Vanhoucke, V., Senior, A., Mao, M.Z.: Improving the speed of neural networks on CPUs (2011)
26. Wang, P., Hu, Q., Fang, Z., Zhao, C., Cheng, J.: DeepSearch: a fast image search framework for mobile devices. ACM Trans. Multimed. Comput. Commun. Appl. (TOMM) **14**(1), 6 (2018)
27. Wu, B., et al.: FBNet: hardware-aware efficient ConvNet design via differentiable neural architecture search. In: Proceedings of the IEEE Conference on Computer Vision and Pattern Recognition, pp. 10734–10742 (2019)
28. Xie, S., Girshick, R., Dollár, P., Tu, Z., He, K.: Aggregated residual transformations for deep neural networks. In: Proceedings of the IEEE Conference on Computer Vision and Pattern Recognition, pp. 1492–1500 (2017)
29. Zhang, X., Zhou, X., Lin, M., Sun, J.: ShuffleNet: an extremely efficient convolutional neural network for mobile devices. In: Proceedings of the IEEE Conference on Computer Vision and Pattern Recognition, pp. 6848–6856 (2018)
30. Zoph, B., Vasudevan, V., Shlens, J., Le, Q.V.: Learning transferable architectures for scalable image recognition. In: Proceedings of the IEEE Conference on Computer Vision and Pattern Recognition, pp. 8697–8710 (2018)

Efficient Adversarial Attacks for Visual Object Tracking

Siyuan Liang[1,2], Xingxing Wei[4(✉)], Siyuan Yao[1,2], and Xiaochun Cao[1,2,3(✉)]

[1] Institute of Information Engineering, Chinese Academy of Sciences, Beijing, China
{liangsiyuan,yaosiyuan,caoxiaochun}@iie.ac.cn
[2] School of Cyber Security, University of Chinese Academy of Sciences,
Beijing, China
[3] Cyberspace Security Research Center, Peng Cheng Laboratory,
Shenzhen 518055, China
[4] Beijing Key Laboratory of Digital Media,
School of Computer Science and Engineering, Beihang University,
Beijing 100191, China
xxwei@buaa.edu.cn

Abstract. Visual object tracking is an important task that requires the tracker to find the objects quickly and accurately. The existing state-of-the-art object trackers, i.e., Siamese based trackers, use DNNs to attain high accuracy. However, the robustness of visual tracking models is seldom explored. In this paper, we analyze the weakness of object trackers based on the Siamese network and then extend adversarial examples to visual object tracking. We present an end-to-end network FAN (Fast Attack Network) that uses a novel drift loss combined with the embedded feature loss to attack the Siamese network based trackers. Under a single GPU, FAN is efficient in the training speed and has a strong attack performance. The FAN can generate an adversarial example at 10ms, achieve effective targeted attack (at least 40% drop rate on OTB) and untargeted attack (at least 70% drop rate on OTB).

Keywords: Adversarial attack · Visual object tracking · Deep learning

1 Introduction

Some studies have shown that DNN-based models are very sensitive to adversarial examples [11]. In general, most recent methods for generating adversarial examples rely on the network structure and their parameters, and they utilize the gradient to generate adversarial examples by iterative optimization [3,28]. Adversarial examples have successfully attacked deep learning tasks such as image classification [23], object detection [29], and semantic segmentation [10]. Researching adversarial examples can not only help people understand the principles of DNNs [30] but also improve the robustness of networks in visual tasks [14].

Electronic supplementary material The online version of this chapter (https://doi.org/10.1007/978-3-030-58574-7_3) contains supplementary material, which is available to authorized users.

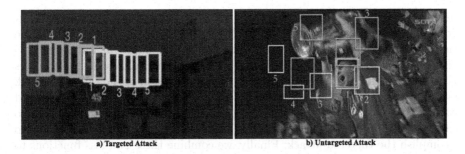

a) Targeted Attack   b) Untargeted Attack

Fig. 1. Two examples of adversarial attacks for VOT. To better show the attacking results, we plot the bounding boxes in the initial frame. The numbers represent the results in the corresponding video frames. The blue box represents the predicted bounding box, and the yellow box represents the ground truth. (Color figure online)

Visual Object Tracking (VOT) [18] aims to predict the object's locations in the subsequent frames in a video when given an object's location in the initial frame. In recent years, deep learning [4] based trackers have achieved excellent performance in many benchmarks. Among them, the SiamFC tracker [1] explores the similarity between video frames by using powerful deep features and has achieved great results in accuracy and robustness for the tracking task. Similar to the Faster R-CNN architecture [25] in object detection, the latest visual object tracking methods are based on the Siamese network, and many variants have been derived, such as SiamVGG [34], SiamRPN [20], SiamRPN++ [19] and so on. Therefore, the significance of investigating the robustness of trackers based on deep learning becomes quite crucial.

In different visual tasks, the attacking targets are different. In image classification task, the target is the classification problem. In the object detection task, the target is the regression (for SSD and YOLO) or classification problem (for Faster-RCNN). In object tracking, VOT searches the most similar regions in each frame with the reference patch. Therefore the target is essentially the similarity metric problem. Thus, attacking the tracking task is totally different from the other image recognition tasks, and the existing attacking methods cannot work well (the results in Sect. 4.4 verify this point).

Regarding the above motivation, in this paper, we study the adversarial attacks on Visual Object Tracking (VOT). **Firstly**, because the adversarial attack on VOT is seldom explored, we give a definition of the targeted attack and untargeted attack in the visual object tracking task. **Then**, we propose an end-to-end fast attack network (FAN) that combines the drift loss and embedded feature loss to jointly perform the targeted and untargeted attacks on VOT. Under the hardware condition of a single GPU, we only need 3 hours off-line training on the ILSVRC15 dataset. In the inference phase, the generator can generate adversarial perturbations in milliseconds speed for the OTB dataset [32] and the VOT dataset [16]. Figure 1 gives two examples. Targeted attack causes the tracker to track object along any specified trajectory. Untargeted attack makes the tracker unable to keep track of the object. Overall, **our contributions** can be summarized as follows: (1) To the best of our knowledge, we are the first one to perform the targeted attack and untargeted attack against the Visual Object Tracking (VOT) task. We analyze the weakness of the trackers based on the Siamese network, and then give a definition of the targeted attack and untargeted attack in this task. (2) We propose a unified and end-to-end attacking method: FAN (fast attack network). We design a novel drift loss to achieve the untargeted attack effectively and apply the embedded feature loss to accomplish the targeted attack. Finally, we combine these two loss functions to jointly attack the VOT task. (3) After three hours of training, FAN can successfully attack VOT and OTB datasets without fine-tuning network parameters. In inference, FAN can quickly produce adversarial examples within 10 ms, which is much faster than iterative optimization algorithms.

2 Related Work

2.1 Deep Learning in Object Tracking

Modern tracking systems based on the deep network can be divided into two categories. The first branch is based on a tracking-by-detection framework [27]. The second branch is mainly based on SiamFC [1] and SiamRPN [20]. For SiamFC, these methods focus on discriminative feature learning [12,34,35], exemplar-candidate pairs modeling [6], and dynamical hyperparameter optimization [7,8]. For SiamRPN, some researchers introduce a more powerful network cascaded model [9] or deeper architecture [19] for region proposal searching. DaSiam [37] proposes a distractor-aware training strategy to generate semantic pairs and suppress semantic distractor. In summary, the Siamese trackers show their superior performance due to the high localization accuracy and efficiency, but most of these trackers are sensitive to the adversarial pertubations of the input data. Therefore, investigating the robustness of these trackers under adversarial attracks becomes crucial.

2.2 Iterative and Generative Adversary

The existing adversarial attacks are based primarily on the optimization algorithm and generation algorithm. The optimization-based adversarial attack discovers the noise's direction by calculating the DNNs' gradient within a certain limit [3]. I-FGSM [17] decomposes one-step optimization into multiple small steps, and iteratively generates adversarial examples for image classification. DAG [33] regards the candidate proposal for RPN [25] as a sample, and iteratively change the proposal's label to attack object detection and segmentation. Another type of adversarial attack is based on the generator, which can quickly generate adversarial perturbations [2]. GAP [24] uses the ResNet generator architecture to misclassify images of ImageNet [5]. UEA [29] generates transferable adversarial examples by combining multi-layer feature loss and classification loss, aiming to achieve an untargeted attack in image and video detection. Due to speed limitations, adversarial attacks based on iterative optimization cannot achieve real-time attacks in the visual object tracking task.

3 Generating Adversarial Examples

3.1 Problem Definition

Let $V = \{I_1, ..., I_i, ..., I_n\}$ be a video that contains n video frames. For simplicity, we take one tracking object as the example, thus $\mathcal{B}^{gt} = \{b_1, ..., b_i, ..., b_n\}$ is used to represent the object's ground-truth position in each frame. The visual object tracking will predict the position $\mathcal{B}^{pred}$ of this object in the subsequent frames when given its initial state. For different datasets, the predicted output is different. In general, four points $b_i \in \mathcal{R}^4$ are used to represent the box.

In SiamFC [1], the tracker $f_\theta(\cdot)$ with parameters θ first transforms the reference frame I_R and annotation b^{init} to get an exemplar region $z = \tau(I_R, b^{init})$, and searches a large area b^{search} in the candidate frame I_C to get a candidate region $x = \tau(I_C, b^{search})$. After feature extraction $\varphi(\cdot)$, a fully-convolutional network is used to calculate the similarity between z and x to get the response score map $\mathcal{S} = f_\theta(z, x) = \varphi(z) * \varphi(x)$. A Cosine Window Penalty (CWP) [1] is then added to generate the final bounding box $b_i = CWP(\mathcal{S})$. CWP can penalize the large offset, making the predicted box not far from the previous box.

$\hat{V} = \{\hat{I}_1, ..., \hat{I}_i, ..., \hat{I}_n\}$ represents the adversarial video. The generator mainly attacks the candidate area $\hat{x}_i = \tau(\hat{I}_i, b_i^{search})$ in the adversarial frame $\hat{I}_i$. The definitions of targeted and untargeted attacks in VOT are given below:

(1) Targeted Attack. The adversarial video $\hat{V}$ guides the tracker to track the object along the specified trajectory $\mathcal{C}^{spec}$, i.e., $\forall i, ||\hat{c}_i - c_i^{spec}||_2 \le \varepsilon$, s.t. $\hat{c}_i = center(CWP(f(z, \hat{x}_i)))$. $center(\cdot)$ gets the prediction center through the prediction box. The Euclidean distance between the prediction center $\hat{c}_i$ and the target center c_i^{spec} should be small. Here we set ε to 20 pixels.

(2) Untargeted Attack. The adversarial video $\hat{V}$ causes the adversarial trajectory $\mathcal{B}^{attack} = \{CWP(f(z, \hat{x}_i))\}_{i=1}^n$ to deviate from the original trajectory $\mathcal{B}^{gt}$ of an object. When the IOU of the prediction box and the ground-truth box is zero, i.e., $IOU(\mathcal{B}^{attack}, \mathcal{B}^{gt}) = 0$, we think that the untargeted attack is successful.

3.2 Drift Loss Attack

Trackers based on the Siamese network are highly dependent on the response map generated by the fully-convolutional network to predict the object's location. Because the SiamFC uses a search area x when predicting the object's location, we can attack this search area to achieve untargeted attack. Over time, the tracker will accumulate the predicted slight offset until the tracker completely loses the object.

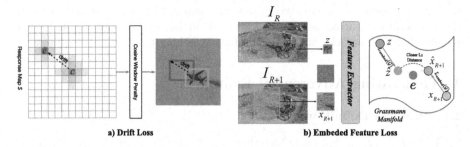

Fig. 2. Overview of the proposed drift loss and embedded feature loss. They are designed for untargeted attack and targeted attack. For details, see Sects. 3.2 and 3.3. (Color figure online)

In Fig. 2a), the darker the color in response map $\mathcal{S}$, the greater the response score. The red area and green area represent the response regions of the adversarial image and clean image. c represents the maximum score in the response map. For a well-trained tracker, the response map of clean examples are generally concentrated on the central area (green area). Thus, we propose a drift loss, which generates adversarial perturbations that drift the activation center of $\mathcal{S}$:

$$l(y, s) = \log(1 + exp(-ys)), \tag{1}$$

where s represents the response score and $y \in (-1, 1)$ represents the label of grid in response map $\mathcal{S}$. The central part of the response map $\mathcal{S}$ (green area) is labeled 1, and the rest is -1. In order to generate adversarial examples, the maximum response value of the non-intermediate response map is greater than the maximum response value of the ground-truth, so the score loss of the response map can be written as:

$$\mathcal{L}_{score}(\mathcal{G}) = \min_{p \in \mathcal{S}^{+1}} (l(y[p], s[p])) - \max_{p \in \mathcal{S}^{-1}} (l(y[p], s[p])), \tag{2}$$

where $p \in \mathcal{S}$ represents each position in the response map. The offset of the prediction box depends on the offset of the activation center in the response map. We want the activation center to be as far away from the center as possible, so the distance loss can be expressed as:

$$\mathcal{L}_{dist}(\mathcal{G}) = \frac{\beta_1}{\delta + \|p_{max}^{+1} - p_{max}^{-1}\|_2} - \xi, \tag{3}$$

where $p_{max}^i = \arg \max_{p \in \mathcal{S}^i}(s[p]), i = +1, -1$ represents position of max activation scores in positive areas or negative areas of response map. δ is a small real number, and β_1 controls weight in distance loss. ξ controls the offset degree of the activation center. Usually, the activation center leaves the central area. The drift loss consisting of score loss and distance loss can be written as:

$$\mathcal{L}_{drift} = \mathcal{L}_{dist} + \beta_2 \mathcal{L}_{score}. \tag{4}$$

3.3 Embedded Feature Loss Attack

Since the targeted attack requires the tracker to track along the specified trajectory, it is different from the untargeted attack. The drift loss in Sect. 3.2 is easy to achieve the untargeted attack, but its attack direction is random, and it cannot achieve targeted attack. The input to the targeted attack are a video V and the specified trajectory's centers C^{spec}. Due to the great difference between the object and background, the response value of the candidate image x_{R+1} and the exemplar image z along the specified trajectory will gradually drop to be lower in the background area. Thus, the targeted attack will soon fail.

For effective targeted attack, we need increase the response value. As shown in Fig. 2b), we want to minimize the L_2 distance between the features of the adversarial exemplar and the specific trajectory area. Thus, we propose embedded feature loss that generates adversarial images $\hat{z}$ and $\hat{x}_{R+1}$. The features of the generated adversarial examples are close to the features of the embedded image e.

$$\mathcal{L}_{embed}(\mathcal{G}) = \|\varphi(q + \mathcal{G}(q)) - \varphi(e)\|_2, \tag{5}$$

In Eq. 5, e represents the specified trajectory area, $q \in \{z, x_{R+1}\}$ represents input video area. z and x_{R+1} represent the exemplar frame and the $R+1$ frame to track. φ represents the feature function, and $\mathcal{G}(q)$ represents adversarial perturbation. After feature extraction, the features of the adversarial image and the embedded image should be as close as possible to achieve targeted attack.

In the training phase, the choice of embedded images is very important. For example, the feature distance between a shepherd dog and a sled dog is smaller than that of a shepherd dog and an Egyptian cat. In the actual attack, we find that attacking a video frame to an object will produce significant perturbations. We use Gaussian noise to replace the object feature in e to optimize Eq. 5, but the specified trajectory remains unchanged.

3.4 Unified and Real-Time Adversary

As shown in Fig. 3, we train a GAN to generate adversarial examples. Necessarily, generating adversarial perturbations can be seen as an image translation task [24]. We generate adversarial perturbations for candidate images in the candidate frames, which are more difficult to perceive in space. We refer to cycle GAN [36] as a generator to learn the mapping from natural images to adversarial perturbations. We adopt the generator proposed in paper [15] and use nine blocks to generate adversarial perturbations. For the discriminator, we use PatchGAN [13], which uses the overlapping image patch to determine whether the image is true or false.

The loss of the discriminator can be expressed as:

$$\mathcal{L}_{\mathcal{D}}(\mathcal{G}, \mathcal{D}, \mathcal{X}) = \mathbb{E}_{x \sim p_{data}(x)}[(\mathcal{D}(\mathcal{G}(x) + x))^2]$$
$$+ \mathbb{E}_{x \sim p_{data}(x)}[(\mathcal{D}(x) - 1)^2]. \tag{6}$$

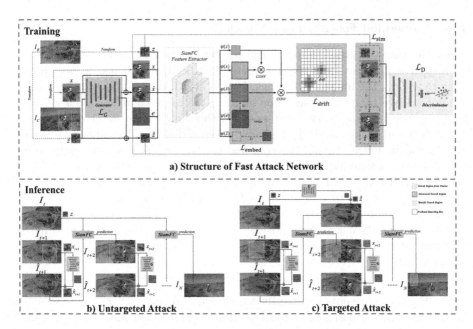

a) Structure of Fast Attack Network

b) Untargeted Attack   **c) Targeted Attack**

Fig. 3. The training and inference framework of FAN. In a), we train the generator and discriminator using the well-trained SiamFC architecture (yellow area + convolution parameters). The losses of the generator and the discriminator are highlighted by the purple parts and blue parts, respectively. We can achieve both a targeted attack and an untargeted attack by adjusting the loss weight of the generator. For untargeted attack b), we only generate adversarial perturbations for search area x in the candidate image I_C. For targeted attack c), we attack both the exemplar image z and the specific search area (the blue part in c), which is determined by the specific trajectory. (Color figure online)

In the training phase, we train the discriminator by minimizing Eq. 6. In order to make the image generated by the generator more realistic, the loss of the generator can be expressed as:

$$\mathcal{L}_{\mathcal{G}}(\mathcal{G}, \mathcal{D}, \mathcal{X}) = \mathbb{E}_{x \sim p_{data}(x)}[(\mathcal{D}(\mathcal{G}(x) + x) - 1)^2]. \tag{7}$$

In addition, we use the L_2 distance as a measure to minimize the loss of similarity so that the adversarial image is closer to the clean image in visual space. The loss of similarity can be expressed as:

$$\mathcal{L}_{sim}(\mathcal{G}) = \mathbb{E}[\|\mathcal{X} - \hat{\mathcal{X}}\|_2]. \tag{8}$$

Finally, the full objective for the generator can be expressed as:

$$\mathcal{L} = \mathcal{L}_{\mathcal{G}} + \alpha_1 \mathcal{L}_{sim} + \alpha_2 \mathcal{L}_{embed} + \alpha_3 \mathcal{L}_{drift}, \tag{9}$$

We propose a **unified network** architecture, which can achieve a targeted attack and untargeted attack by adjusting the hyperparameters. β_1, β_2 make L_{dist} and L_{score} roughly equal. Thus, there is no need for special adjustment. ξ controls the offset degree of the activation center. α_1 and α_3 control the untargeted attack. We fix α_3 and adjust α_1 from the visual quality. α_2 controls embedding image features. We test value from 0.05-0.1 and the precision score improves ten percentage. For the targeted attack, we do not need drift loss, so set α_3 to 0, $\alpha_1 = 0.0024$ and $\alpha_2 = 0.1$. For the untargeted attack, we set α_2 to 0, $\alpha_1 = 0.0016$, and $\alpha_3 = 10$. In Eq. 3, we set $\beta_1 = 1$, $\delta = 1 * 10^{-10}$, $\xi = 0.7$. In Eq. 4, β_2 is set to 10. We use Adam algorithm [22] to optimize generator $\mathcal{G}$ and discriminator $\mathcal{D}$ alternatively. Using a GPU Titan XP, we can get the best weight by iterating about 10 epochs(about 3 hours) on the ILSVRC 2015 dataset.

Since the prediction box of the tracker in the current frame is strongly dependent on the results of the previous frame, we can make the prediction box produce a small error offset and eventually stay away from the ground-truth trajectory. We only add perturbations to the candidate image x for the untargeted attack. For targeted attack, we embed features of embedding images in exemplar states z and candidate images x by adding adversarial perturbations. Although the adversarial attack deals with a large number of videos, the generator can generate adversarial examples in milliseconds. This enables us to complete the **real-time adversarial attack** for visual object tracking.

4 Experiments

4.1 Datasets and Threat Models

We train the generator and discriminator on the training set of the ILSVRC 2015 dataset [26]. We refer to the training strategy in SiamFC [1]. After training is completed, the generator is tested on four challenging visual object tracking datasets without parameter adjustment: OTB2013 [31], OTB2015, VOT2014, and VOT2018 [16]. Specifically, the VOT datasets will be re-initialized after the tracker fails to track. Therefore, it is more difficult to attack VOT datasets than OTB datasets. We use SiamFC based on Alexnet as a white-box attack model. SiamRPN [20], SiamRPN+CIR [35] and SiamRPN++ [19] as black-box attack models.

4.2 Evaluation Metrics

Since the targeted attack and untargeted attack are different, we define their own evaluation criteria, respectively.

Untargeted Attack Evaluation: In the OTB dataset, we use success score, precision score, and success rate as the evaluation criteria. The **success score** calculates the average IOU of the prediction box and the ground-truth. The **precision score** indicates the percentages of the video frames whose euclidean distance between the estimated centers and ground-truth centers is less than the given threshold. The percentage of successful attacked frames to all the frames is the **success rate**.

In the VOT dataset, we measure the accuracy in the videos using the **success score**. Considering the restart mechanism in the VOT dataset, robustness is a more important evaluation metric. **Mean-Failures** refer to calculating the average number of failures for the object tracking algorithm in all datasets.

Targeted Attack Evaluation: The target attack requires the tracker to move according to a specific trajectory, so we use the **precision score** as the evaluation criteria. The higher the precision score, the more effective the targeted attack.

Image Quality Assessment: We use **Mean-SSIM** to evaluate the quality of adversarial videos. Mean-SSIM calculates the average SSIM of frames in videos. The generated adversarial perturbations are difficult to be found when Mean-SSIM is close to 1.

4.3   Untargeted Attack Results

In Table 1, we report the results of the untargeted attack on four tracking datasets. The second and the third columns represent the object tracking results of SiamFC on the clean video and the adversarial video. The drop rate of tracking evaluation metrics for OTB datasets has fallen by at least 72%, indicating that our attack method is effective. For the quality assessment, the highest drop rate is only 7%, which is sufficient to show that adversarial perturbations generated by our attack method are visually imperceptible.

Table 1. Untargeted attacks on VOT and OTB datasets. We use drop rate to measure the attack performance. Large Mean-Failures means the tracker frequently lost objects.

Datasets		Clean videos	Adversarial videos	Drop rate
OTB2013	Success score	0.53	0.14	74%
	Precision score	0.71	0.17	76%
	Success rate	0.66	0.12	**81%**
	Mean-SSIM	1	0.93	7%
OTB2015	Success score	0.53	0.15	72%
	Precision score	0.72	0.18	75%
	Success rate	0.66	0.12	**81%**
	Mean-SSIM	1	0.93	7%
VOT2014	Success score	0.54	0.42	22%
	Mean-failures	28	112	300%
	Mean-SSIM	1	0.94	6%
VOT2018	Success score	0.49	0.42	14%
	Mean-failures	48	246	**413%**
	Mean-SSIM	1	0.97	**3%**

Fig. 4. We visualize the tracking results under the untargeted attack. Yellow represents a ground-truth bounding box and, red represents predicted bounding box by trackers. (Color figure online)

We find that the success rate is the most vulnerable evaluation metrics on the OTB dataset, with a drop rate of 81%. This indicates that our attack method can effectively reduce the IOU between the prediction box and the ground-truth box. Our attack method increases the number of tracking failures as high as 413% on the VOT2018 dataset. Therefore, our attack method can still effectively fool the tracker and cause it to lose objects under the reinitialization mechanism. However, compared with the OTB datasets, there is no significant decrease in the success score on VOT datasets. The reason may be that the success score is still high because the tracker keeps reinitializing the object. According to the definition of untargeted attack, Mean-Failures is more reasonable for evaluating adversarial attacks. Finally, the VOT2018's Mean-SSIM dropped only 3%. Our generator sparsely attacks video frames over time, resulting in that perturbations less difficult to be perceived.

We show an adversarial video in Fig. 4, which is sampled equidistantly in time from left to right. We added slight perturbations in search images to successfully fool the SiamFC tracker. This kind of attack method does not produce too much deviation in a short-time and is difficult to be detected by trackers. The third line represents adversarial perturbations, and FAN can adaptively attack the critical feature areas without prior shapes.

The left-to-right in Fig. 5 are the results of the uniform sampling of a video over time. By comparing the second row and the fourth row, we can see that the responding area of the clean image is concentrated, and the scores are not much different (the green part). However, the adversarial examples generated by FAN start to cause a large range of high scores in the response map and are relatively scattered. These scattered high-scoring areas will fool the SiamFC tracker to make it impossible to distinguish the object. Due to incorrect activation of the response map, the search areas in adversarial examples will gradually shrink over time. The subsequent adversarial perturbations will also increase the degree of

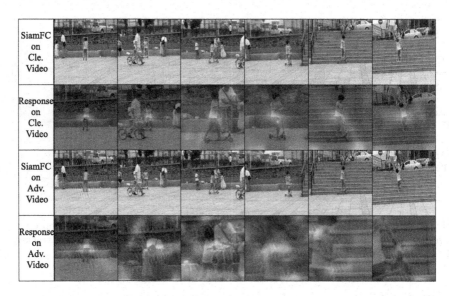

Fig. 5. The visualization of response maps between adversarial examples and clean videos, respectively. Blue indicates low response, and red indicates high response. (Color figure online)

narrowing of the search areas (the extent of the fourth line is reduced differently in equal time). The perturbations gradually decrease in space over time due to the FAN attack on the search areas.

4.4 Comparisons with the Baselines

To better show the performance, we compare our FAN method with the widely used FGSM [11] and PGD [21]. The results are shown in Table 2.

Table 2. The untargeted attacks on OTB2013. Compared with the FAN method, the modified FGSM and PGD methods cannot achieve effective attacks. The percentage represents the drop rate compared to clean video.

Methods	Success score	Precision score	Success rate	Mean-SSIM	Time(s)
FGSM	3%	2%	3%	0.95	0.03
PGD	3%	2%	3%	0.97	3.53
FAN	**74%**	**76%**	**81%**	**0.94**	**0.01**

Because FGSM and PGD are used to attack the image classification task, and cannot directly attack the visual object tracking task. Therefore we make some modifications. In object tracking, tracker searches the most similar regions in each frame with the reference patch. The most similar regions in the response map are labeled 1; the others in the response map are -1. Therefore, for FGSM and PGD, the attack target is to change the correct label in the response map (invert label 1 to -1). We perform experiments on the modified FGSM and PGD methods at OTB2013 and compared them with the FAN method.

The percentages in Table 2 represent the drop rate versus different metrics. We can see that these two methods are not effective for attacking VOT tasks. Besides, the average time for PGD to process a sample is 3.5 s, which is not suitable for attacking a large number of frames. Under the same hardware conditions, our method process a sample only need 0.01 s, and it can effectively attack clean videos.

4.5 Targeted Attack Results

We need to set specific trajectories for the video frames in the dataset to achieve targeted attack. Since the VOT datasets will be reinitialized when the tracker is far away from the ground-truth, there is no point in implementing a targeted attack on the VOT datasets. Our targeted attack method still works because it can cause the tracker to restart multiple times on the VOT dataset. For clean videos in the VOT2014, SiamFC will restart tracking per 108.8 frames. After attacked by our method, SiamFC will restart tracking per 14 frames, which shows our method significantly increases numbers of restart for tracker in the VOT dataset in the targeted attacks.

Table 3. An overview of the targeted attack results. We use precision scores to evaluate targeted attacks. A high precision score means that the tracker's prediction is close to the specified trajectory.

Datasets		Clean videos	Adversarial videos	Drop rate
OTB2013	Precision score	0.69	0.41	40.6%
	Mean-SSIM	1	0.92	8%
OTB2015	Precision score	0.71	0.42	40.8%
	Mean-SSIM	1	0.92	8%

We conduct experiments on OTB2013 and OTB2015 datasets. Manually labeling specific trajectories on these datasets will be time-consuming. Therefore, we generate specific trajectories based on the original annotations. Here we consider the most difficult case of a targeted attack. That is, the generated specific trajectory is completely opposite to the original trajectory. We use the following rules to calculate the bounding box for specific trajectory:

$$b_t^{spec} = \begin{cases} b_0^{gt} & t = 1 \\ 2 * b_{t-1}^{gt} - b_t^{gt} & t \geq 2, \end{cases} \tag{10}$$

where b^{spec} represents the bounding box of specified trajectory, and b^{gt} represents ground-truth in datasets.

In Table 3, the first and second columns represent precision scores of tracker's predicted trajectory on clean videos and adversarial videos. Experiment results show that the tracking system after the targeted attack cannot reach the same precision scores on the clean video. The reason for this result may be that the automatically generated specific trajectory is not the best path that the targeted attack can choose. Even if the targeted attack of visual tracking is more difficult than an untargeted attack, FAN can still successfully attack most videos under the most difficult specific trajectories.

We visualize the results of the targeted attack in Fig. 6. The first and third lines represent bounding boxes on the clean video and the adversarial video. The second line represents the specific trajectories we automatically generated according to Eq. 10. It can be seen that the predicted bounding box by tracker is basically the same as the specific bounding box. The fourth line shows adversarial perturbations from the search region, which is significantly stronger than adversarial perturbations in the untargeted attack. Therefore, the targeted attack is more difficult than the untargeted attack under limited disturbance.

4.6   Transferability to SiamRPN

We use SiamRPN [20], SiamRPN+CIR [35], SiamRPN++ [19] as black-box attack models to verify the transferability of adversarial examples generated by FAN. SiamRPN uses an RPN network to perform location regression and classification on the response map. SiamRPN+CIR uses the ResNeXt22 network

Fig. 6. The results under targeted attacks. Green represents a ground-truth bounding box, cyan represents the specific bounding box, and red represents the predicted bounding box by trackers. The cyan and red boxes are basically the same in time series, which indicates that targeted attack is successful. (Color figure online)

to replace SiamRPN's Alexnet. SiamRPN++ performs layer-wise and depth-wise aggregations to improve accuracy.

Table 4. Transferability of adversarial examples on two datasets.

Methods		SiamFC	SiamRPN	SiamRPN+CIR	SiamRPN++
OTB2013	Success score	74%	55%	46%	33%
	Precision score	76%	47%	58%	35%
	Success Rate	81%	56%	47%	35%
OTB2015	Success score	72%	44%	45%	32%
	Precision score	75%	51%	58%	37%
	Success rate	81%	55%	43%	39%

The experimental results are shown in Table 4. The first column refers to the drop rate of a white-box attack method. The other columns refer to the drop rate of black-box attack methods. We find that black-box attack methods have a lower drop rate than the white-box attack method. It is obvious that black-box attack methods are more difficult than a white-box attack method. Except for the precision score, the performance of the black-box attack in SiamRPN is better than SiamRPN+CIR. This may be due to SiamRPN and SiamFC using the same feature extraction network AlexNet. The black-box attack in SiamRPN++ performs the worst. This is because the architecture of SiamRPN++ can correct some spatial offsets. Even in this case, the drop rate of the black-box attacks can still reach 32%. The results show that our method can still show good transferability for different tracking methods.

5   Conclusion

In this paper, we accomplished the adversarial attacks for the Visual Object Tracking (VOT) task. We analyzed the weaknesses of DNNs based VOT models: the feature networks and the loss function, and then designed different attacking strategies. We firstly presented a drift loss to make the high-score area obtained by adversarial examples be offset with the original area. Then a pre-defined trajectory was embedded into the feature space of the original images to perform the targeted attack. Finally, we proposed an end-to-end framework to integrate these two modules. Experiments conducted on two public datasets verified the effectiveness of the proposed method. In addition, our method not only achieved excellent performance on the white-box attack, but also on the black-box attack, which expanded its application area. Furthermore, the image quality assessment showed that the generated adversarial examples had good imperceptibility, which guaranteed the security of the adversarial examples.

Acknowledgement. Supported by the National Key R&D Program of China (Grant No. 2018AAA010 0600), National Natural Science Foundation of China (No. U1636214, 61861166002, No. 61806109), Beijing Natural Science Foundation (No. L182057), Zhejiang Lab (NO. 2019NB0AB01), Peng Cheng Laboratory Project of Guangdong Province PCL2018KP004.

References

1. Bertinetto, L., Valmadre, J., Henriques, J.F., Vedaldi, A., Torr, P.H.S.: Fully-convolutional siamese networks for object tracking. In: Hua, G., Jégou, H. (eds.) ECCV 2016. LNCS, vol. 9914, pp. 850–865. Springer, Cham (2016). https://doi.org/10.1007/978-3-319-48881-3_56
2. Bose, A.J., Aarabi, P.: Adversarial attacks on face detectors using neural net based constrained optimization. In: 2018 IEEE 20th International Workshop on Multimedia Signal Processing (MMSP), pp. 1–6. IEEE (2018)
3. Carlini, N., Wagner, D.: Towards evaluating the robustness of neural networks. In: 2017 IEEE Symposium on Security and Privacy (SP), pp. 39–57. IEEE (2017)
4. Danelljan, M., Robinson, A., Shahbaz Khan, F., Felsberg, M.: Beyond correlation filters: learning continuous convolution operators for visual tracking. In: Leibe, B., Matas, J., Sebe, N., Welling, M. (eds.) ECCV 2016. LNCS, vol. 9909, pp. 472–488. Springer, Cham (2016). https://doi.org/10.1007/978-3-319-46454-1_29
5. Deng, J., Dong, W., Socher, R., Li, L.J., Li, K., Fei-Fei, L.: ImageNet: a large-scale hierarchical image database. In: 2009 IEEE Conference on Computer Vision and Pattern Recognition (CVPR), pp. 248–255. IEEE (2009)
6. Dong, X., Shen, J.: Triplet loss in siamese network for object tracking. In: Proceedings of the European Conference on Computer Vision (ECCV), pp. 459–474 (2018)
7. Dong, X., Shen, J., Wang, W., Liu, Y., Shao, L., Porikli, F.: Hyperparameter optimization for tracking with continuous deep q-learning. In: Proceedings of the IEEE Conference on Computer Vision and Pattern Recognition (CVPR), pp. 518–527 (2018)
8. Dong, X., Shen, J., Wang, W., Shao, L., Ling, H., Porikli, F.: Dynamical hyperparameter optimization via deep reinforcement learning in tracking. IEEE Trans. Pattern Anal. Mach. Intell. (2019)
9. Fan, H., Ling, H.: Siamese cascaded region proposal networks for real-time visual tracking. In: Proceedings of the IEEE Conference on Computer Vision and Pattern Recognition (CVPR), pp. 7952–7961 (2019)
10. Fischer, V., Kumar, M.C., Metzen, J.H., Brox, T.: Adversarial examples for semantic image segmentation. arXiv preprint arXiv:1703.01101 (2017)
11. Goodfellow, I.J., Shlens, J., Szegedy, C.: Explaining and harnessing adversarial examples. arXiv preprint arXiv:1412.6572 (2014)
12. He, A., Luo, C., Tian, X., Zeng, W.: A twofold siamese network for real-time object tracking. In: Proceedings of the IEEE Conference on Computer Vision and Pattern Recognition (CVPR), pp. 4834–4843 (2018)
13. Isola, P., Zhu, J.Y., Zhou, T., Efros, A.A.: Image-to-image translation with conditional adversarial networks. In: Proceedings of the IEEE Conference on Computer Vision and Pattern Recognition (CVPR), pp. 1125–1134 (2017)
14. Jia, X., Wei, X., Cao, X., Foroosh, H.: ComDefend: an efficient image compression model to defend adversarial examples. In: Proceedings of the IEEE Conference on Computer Vision and Pattern Recognition (CVPR), pp. 6084–6092 (2019)

15. Johnson, J., Alahi, A., Fei-Fei, L.: Perceptual losses for real-time style transfer and super-resolution. In: Leibe, B., Matas, J., Sebe, N., Welling, M. (eds.) ECCV 2016. LNCS, vol. 9906, pp. 694–711. Springer, Cham (2016). https://doi.org/10.1007/978-3-319-46475-6_43

16. Kristan, M., et al.: The visual object tracking VOT2017 challenge results. In: Proceedings of the IEEE International Conference on Computer Vision Workshops, pp. 1949–1972 (2017)

17. Kurakin, A., Goodfellow, I., Bengio, S.: Adversarial examples in the physical world. arXiv preprint arXiv:1607.02533 (2016)

18. Lee, K.H., Hwang, J.N.: On-road pedestrian tracking across multiple driving recorders. IEEE Trans. Multimed. **17**(9), 1429–1438 (2015)

19. Li, B., Wu, W., Wang, Q., Zhang, F., Xing, J., Yan, J.: SiamRPN++: evolution of siamese visual tracking with very deep networks. In: Proceedings of the IEEE Conference on Computer Vision and Pattern Recognition (CVPR), pp. 4282–4291 (2019)

20. Li, B., Yan, J., Wu, W., Zhu, Z., Hu, X.: High performance visual tracking with siamese region proposal network. In: Proceedings of the IEEE Conference on Computer Vision and Pattern Recognition (CVPR), pp. 8971–8980 (2018)

21. Madry, A., Makelov, A., Schmidt, L., Tsipras, D., Vladu, A.: Towards deep learning models resistant to adversarial attacks. arXiv preprint arXiv:1706.06083 (2017)

22. Mathieu, M., Couprie, C., LeCun, Y.: Deep multi-scale video prediction beyond mean square error. arXiv preprint arXiv:1511.05440 (2015)

23. Moosavi-Dezfooli, S.M., Fawzi, A., Fawzi, O., Frossard, P.: Universal adversarial perturbations. In: Proceedings of the IEEE Conference on Computer Vision and Pattern Recognition (CVPR), pp. 1765–1773 (2017)

24. Poursaeed, O., Katsman, I., Gao, B., Belongie, S.: Generative adversarial perturbations. In: Proceedings of the IEEE Conference on Computer Vision and Pattern Recognition (CVPR), pp. 4422–4431 (2018)

25. Ren, S., He, K., Girshick, R., Sun, J.: Faster R-CNN: towards real-time object detection with region proposal networks. In: Advances in Neural Information Processing Systems, pp. 91–99 (2015)

26. Russakovsky, O., et al.: Imagenet large scale visual recognition challenge. Int. J. Comput. Vis. **115**(3), 211–252 (2015)

27. Song, Y., et al.: VITAL: visual tracking via adversarial learning. In: Proceedings of the IEEE Conference on Computer Vision and Pattern Recognition (CVPR), pp. 8990–8999 (2018)

28. Szegedy, C., et al.: Intriguing properties of neural networks. arXiv preprint arXiv:1312.6199 (2013)

29. Wei, X., Liang, S., Chen, N., Cao, X.: Transferable adversarial attacks for image and video object detection. arXiv preprint arXiv:1811.12641 (2018)

30. Wong, E., Kolter, J.Z.: Provable defenses against adversarial examples via the convex outer adversarial polytope. arXiv preprint arXiv:1711.00851 (2017)

31. Wu, Y., Lim, J., Yang, M.H.: Online object tracking: a benchmark. In: Proceedings of the IEEE Conference on Computer Vision and Pattern Recognition (CVPR), pp. 2411–2418 (2013)

32. Wu, Y., Lim, J., Yang, M.H.: Object tracking benchmark. IEEE Trans. Pattern Anal. Mach. Intell. **37**(9), 1834–1848 (2015)

33. Xie, C., Wang, J., Zhang, Z., Zhou, Y., Xie, L., Yuille, A.: Adversarial examples for semantic segmentation and object detection. In: Proceedings of the IEEE International Conference on Computer Vision (ICCV), pp. 1369–1378 (2017)

34. Yin, Z., Wen, C., Huang, Z., Yang, F., Yang, Z.: SiamVGG-LLC: visual tracking using LLC and deeper siamese networks. In: 2019 IEEE 19th International Conference on Communication Technology (ICCT), pp. 1683–1687. IEEE (2019)
35. Zhang, Z., Peng, H.: Deeper and wider siamese networks for real-time visual tracking. In: Proceedings of the IEEE Conference on Computer Vision and Pattern Recognition (CVPR), pp. 4591–4600 (2019)
36. Zhu, J.Y., Park, T., Isola, P., Efros, A.A.: Unpaired image-to-image translation using cycle-consistent adversarial networks. In: Proceedings of the IEEE International Conference on Computer Vision (ICCV), pp. 2223–2232 (2017)
37. Zhu, Z., Wang, Q., Li, B., Wu, W., Yan, J., Hu, W.: Distractor-aware siamese networks for visual object tracking. In: Proceedings of the European Conference on Computer Vision (ECCV), pp. 101–117 (2018)

Globally-Optimal Event Camera Motion Estimation

Xin Peng[1,2], Yifu Wang[3], Ling Gao[1], and Laurent Kneip[1,4(✉)]

[1] Mobile Perception Lab, SIST, ShanghaiTech University, Shanghai, China
kneip.laurent@gmail.com
[2] Shanghai Institute of Microsystems and Information Technology,
Chinese Academy of Sciences, Beijing, China
[3] Australian National University, Canberra, Australia
[4] Shanghai Engineering Research Center of Intelligent Vision and Imaging,
Shanghai, China

Abstract. Event cameras are bio-inspired sensors that perform well in HDR conditions and have high temporal resolution. However, different from traditional frame-based cameras, event cameras measure asynchronous pixel-level brightness changes and return them in a highly discretised format, hence new algorithms are needed. The present paper looks at fronto-parallel motion estimation of an event camera. The flow of the events is modeled by a general homographic warping in a space-time volume, and the objective is formulated as a maximisation of contrast within the image of unwarped events. However, in stark contrast to prior art, we derive a globally optimal solution to this generally non-convex problem, and thus remove the dependency on a good initial guess. Our algorithm relies on branch-and-bound optimisation for which we derive novel, recursive upper and lower bounds for six different contrast estimation functions. The practical validity of our approach is supported by a highly successful application to AGV motion estimation with a downward facing event camera, a challenging scenario in which the sensor experiences fronto-parallel motion in front of noisy, fast moving textures.

Keywords: Event cameras · Motion estimation · Contrast maximisation · Global optimality · Branch and bound

1 Introduction

Camera motion estimation is an important technology with many applications in automation, smart transportation, and assistive technologies. However, despite the fact that a certain level of maturity has already been reached, we keep facing

---

X. Peng, Y. Wang and L. Gao—indicates equal contribution.

Electronic supplementary material The online version of this chapter (https://doi.org/10.1007/978-3-030-58574-7_4) contains supplementary material, which is available to authorized users.

© Springer Nature Switzerland AG 2020
A. Vedaldi et al. (Eds.): ECCV 2020, LNCS 12371, pp. 51–67, 2020.
https://doi.org/10.1007/978-3-030-58574-7_4

challenges in scenarios with high dynamics, low texture distinctiveness, or challenging illumination conditions [5,9]. Event cameras—also called dynamic vision sensors—present an interesting alternative in this regard, as they pair HDR with high temporal resolution. The potential advantages and challenges behind event-based vision are well explained by the original work of Brandli et al. [3] as well as the recent survey by Gallego et al. [10].

Our work considers fronto-parallel motion estimation of an event camera. The flow of the events is hereby modelled by a general homographic warping in a space-time volume, and motion may be estimated by maximisation of contrast in the image of unwarped events [12]. Various reward functions that maximise contrast have been presented and analysed in the recent works of Gallego et al. [11] and Stoffregen and Kleeman [29], and successfully used for solving a variety of problems with event cameras such as optical flow [12,28,32,34,36,37], segmentation [21,27,28], 3D reconstruction [26,32,35,37], and motion estimation [12,13]. Our work focuses on the latter problem of camera motion estimation. However—different from many of the aforementioned works—we propose the first globally optimal solution to the underlying contrast maximisation problem, an important point given its generally non-convex nature.

Our detailed contributions are as follows:

- We solve the global maximisation of contrast functions via Branch and Bound.
- We derive bounds for six different contrast estimation functions. The bounds are furthermore calculated recursively, which enables efficient processing.
- We successfully apply this strategy to Autonomous Ground Vehicle (AGV) planar motion estimation with a downward facing event camera (cf. Fig. 1), a problem that is complicated by motion blur, challenging illumination conditions, and indistinctive, noisy textures. We prove that using an event camera can solve these challenges, hence outperforming alternatives given by regular cameras.

(a) AGV   (b) wood grain foam   (c) $\theta = 0$ (d) $\theta = \hat{\theta}$

Fig. 1. (a): AGV equipped with a downward facing event camera for vehicle motion estimation. (b)–(d): collected image with detectable corners, image of warped events with $\theta = 0$, and image of warped events with optimal parameters $\hat{\theta}$.

2   Contrast Maximisation

Gallego et al. [12] recently introduced contrast maximisation as a unifying framework allowing the solution of several important problems for dynamic vision sensors, in particular motion estimation problems in which the effect of camera motion may be described by a homography (e.g. motion in front of a plane, pure rotation). Our work relies on contrast maximisation, which we therefore briefly review in the following.

An event camera outputs a sequence of *events* denoting temporal logarithmic brightness changes above a certain threshold. An event $e = \{\mathbf{x}, t, s\}$ is described by its pixel position $\mathbf{x} = [x \; y]^T$, timestamp t, and polarity s (the latter indicates whether the brightness is increasing or decreasing, and is ignored in the present work). The core idea of contrast maximisation is relatively straightforward: The flow of the events is modelled by a time-parametrised homography. Given its position and time-stamp, every event may therefore be warped back along a point-trajectory into a reference view with timestamp t_{ref}. Since events are more likely to be generated by high-gradient edges, correct homographic warping parameters will likely lead to a sharp Image of Warped Events (IWE) in which events align along a crisp edge-map. Gallego et al. [12] simply propose to consider the contrast of the IWE as a reward function to identify the correct homographic warping parameters. Note that homographic warping functions include 2D affine and Euclidean transformations, and thus can be used in a variety of vision problems such as optical flow, feature tracking, or fronto-parallel motion estimation.

Suppose we are given a set of N events $\mathcal{E} = \{e_k\}_{k=1}^N$. We define a general warping function $\mathbf{x}_k' = W(\mathbf{x}_k, t_k; \boldsymbol{\theta})$ that returns the position $\mathbf{x}_k'$ of an event e_k in the reference view at time t_{ref}. $\boldsymbol{\theta}$ is a vector of warping parameters. The IWE is generated by accumulating warped events at each discrete pixel location:

$$I(\mathbf{p}_{ij}; \boldsymbol{\theta}) = \sum_{k=1}^N \mathbf{1}(\mathbf{p}_{ij} - \mathbf{x}_k') = \sum_{k=1}^N \mathbf{1}(\mathbf{p}_{ij} - W(\mathbf{x}_k, t_k; \boldsymbol{\theta})), \tag{1}$$

where $\mathbf{1}(\cdot)$ is an indicator function that counts 1 if the absolute value of $(\mathbf{p}_{ij} - \mathbf{x}_k')$ is less than a threshold ϵ in each coordinate, and otherwise 0. $\mathbf{p}_{ij}$ is a pixel in the IWE with coordinates $[i \; j]^T$, and we refer to it as an *accumulator* location. We set $\epsilon = 0.5$ such that each warped event will increment one accumulator only.

Existing approaches replace the indicator function with a Gaussian kernel to make the IWE a smooth function of the warped events, and thus solve contrast maximisation problems via local optimisation methods (cf. [11–13]). In contrast, we show how our proposed method is able to find the global optimum of the above, discrete objective function.

As introduced in [11,29], reward functions for event un-warping all rely on the idea of maximising the contrast or sharpness of the IWE (they have also been denoted as *focus loss functions*). They proceed by integration over the entire set of accumulators, which we denote $\mathcal{P}$. The most relevant ones for us are summarized in Table 1. Note that for L_{Var}, μ_I is the mean value of $I(\mathbf{p}_{ij}; \boldsymbol{\theta})$ over all pixels (a function of $\boldsymbol{\theta}$ itself), and N_p is the total number of accumulators in I. For L_{SoSA}, δ is a design parameter called the *shift factor*. Different from other objectives functions, locations with few accumulations will contribute more to L_{SoSA}. The intuition here is that more empty locations again mean more events that are concentrated at fewer accumulators. L_{SoEaS} is a combination of L_{SoS} and L_{SoE}. Similarly, L_{SoSAaS} is a combination of L_{SoS} and L_{SoSA}.

Let us now proceed to the main contribution of our work, which is a derivation of bounds on the above objectives as required by Branch and Bound.

Table 1. Contrast functions evaluated in this work

Sum of Squares (SoS)	$L_{\text{SoS}}(\boldsymbol{\theta}) = \sum_{\mathbf{p}_{ij} \in \mathcal{P}} I(\mathbf{p}_{ij}; \boldsymbol{\theta})^2$
Variance (Var)	$L_{\text{Var}}(\boldsymbol{\theta}) = \frac{1}{N_p} \sum_{\mathbf{p}_{ij} \in \mathcal{P}} (I(\mathbf{p}_{ij}; \boldsymbol{\theta}) - \mu_I)^2$
Sum of Exponentials (SoE)	$L_{\text{SoE}}(\boldsymbol{\theta}) = \sum_{\mathbf{p}_{ij} \in \mathcal{P}} e^{I(\mathbf{p}_{ij}; \boldsymbol{\theta})}$
Sum of Suppressed Accumulations (SoSA)	$L_{\text{SoSA}}(\boldsymbol{\theta}) = \sum_{\mathbf{p}_{ij} \in \mathcal{P}} e^{-I(\mathbf{p}_{ij}; \boldsymbol{\theta}) \cdot \delta}$
SoE and Squares (SoEaS)	$L_{\text{SoEaS}}(\boldsymbol{\theta}) = \sum_{\mathbf{p}_{ij} \in \mathcal{P}} I(\mathbf{p}_{ij}; \boldsymbol{\theta})^2 + e^{I(\mathbf{p}_{ij}; \boldsymbol{\theta})}$
SoSA and Squares (SoSAaS)	$L_{\text{SoSAaS}}(\boldsymbol{\theta}) = \sum_{\mathbf{p}_{ij} \in \mathcal{P}} I(\mathbf{p}_{ij}; \boldsymbol{\theta})^2 + e^{-I(\mathbf{p}_{ij}; \boldsymbol{\theta}) \cdot \delta}$

3   Globally Maximised Contrast Using Branch and Bound

Figure 2 illustrates how contrast maximisation for motion estimation is in general a non-convex problem, meaning that local optimisation may be sensitive to the initial parameters and not find the global optimum. We tackle this problem by introducing a globally optimal solution to contrast maximisation using Branch and Bound (BnB) optimisation. BnB is an algorithmic paradigm in which the solution space is subdivided into branches in which we then find upper and lower bounds for the maximal objective value. The globally optimal solution is isolated by an iterative search in which entire branches are discarded if their upper bound for the maximum objective value remains lower than the corresponding lower bound in another branch. The most important factor deciding the effectiveness of this approach is given by the tightness of the bounds.

Our core contribution is given by a recursive method to efficiently calculate upper and lower bounds for the maximum value of a contrast maximisation function over a given branch. In short, the main idea is given by expressing a bound over $(N + 1)$ events as a function of the bound over N events plus the contribution of one additional event. The strategy can be similarly applied to all six aforementioned contrast functions, which is why we limit the exposition to the derivation of bounds for L_{SoS}. Detailed derivations for all loss functions are provided in the supplementary material.

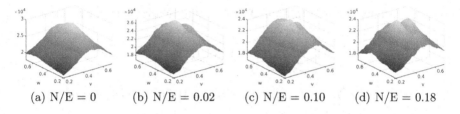

(a) N/E = 0   (b) N/E = 0.02   (c) N/E = 0.10   (d) N/E = 0.18

Fig. 2. Visualization of the Sum of Squares contrast function. The camera is moving in front of a plane, and the motion parameters are given by translational and rotational velocity (cf. Sect. 4). The sub-figures from left to right are functions with increasing Noise-to-Events (N/E) ratios. Note that contrast functions are non-convex.

3.1   Objective Function

In the following, we assume that $L = L_{\text{SoS}}$. The maximum objective function value over all N events in a given time interval $[t_{\text{ref}}, t_{\text{ref}} + \Delta T]$ is given by

$$L_N = \max_{\theta \in \Theta} \sum_{\mathbf{p}_{ij} \in \mathcal{P}} \left[\sum_{k=1}^{N} \mathbf{1}\left(\mathbf{p}_{ij} - W(\mathbf{x}_k, t_k; \theta)\right) \right]^2, \tag{2}$$

where Θ is the search space (i.e. branch or sub-branch) over which we want to maximise the objective. Most globally optimal methods for geometric computer vision problems find bounds by a spatial division of the problem into individual, simpler maximisation sub-problems (cf. [6]). However, the contrast maximisation objective is related to the distribution over the entire IWE and not just individual accumulators, which complicates this strategy.

3.2   Upper and Lower Bound

The bounds are calculated recursively by processing the events and one-by-one, each time updating the IWE. The event are notably processed in temporal order with increasing timestamps.

For the lower bound, it is readily given by evaluating the contrast function at an arbitrary point on the interval Θ, which is commonly picked as the interval center θ_0. We present a recursive rule to efficiently evaluate the lower bound.

Theorem 1. *For search space Θ centered at θ_0, the lower bound of SoS-based contrast maximisation may be given by*

$$\underline{L_{N+1}} = \underline{L_N} + 1 + 2I^N(\eta_{N+1}^{\theta_0}; \theta_0), \tag{3}$$

where $I^N(\mathbf{p}_{ij}; \theta_0)$ is the incrementally constructed IWE, its exponent N denotes the number of events that have already been taken into account, and

$$\eta_{N+1}^{\theta_0} = \text{round}(W(\mathbf{x}_{N+1}, t_{N+1}; \theta_0)) \tag{4}$$

returns the accumulator closest to the warped position of the $(N + 1)$-th event.

Proof. According to the definition of sum of the square focus loss function,

$$L_{N+1} = \sum_{\mathbf{p}_{ij} \in \mathcal{P}} \left[\sum_{k=1}^{N+1} \mathbf{1} \left(\mathbf{p}_{ij} - W(\mathbf{x}_k, t_k; \boldsymbol{\theta}_0) \right) \right]^2$$

$$= \sum_{\mathbf{p}_{ij} \in \mathcal{P}} \left[I^N(\mathbf{p}_{ij}; \boldsymbol{\theta}_0) + \mathbf{1} \left(\mathbf{p}_{ij} - W(\mathbf{x}_{N+1}, t_{N+1}; \boldsymbol{\theta}_0) \right) \right]^2 \qquad (5)$$

$$= a + b + c, \text{ where}$$

$$a = \sum_{\mathbf{p}_{ij} \in \mathcal{P}} I^N(\mathbf{p}_{ij}; \boldsymbol{\theta}_0)^2 ,$$

$$b = 2 \sum_{\mathbf{p}_{ij} \in \mathcal{P}} \left[\mathbf{1}(\mathbf{p}_{ij} - W(\mathbf{x}_{N+1}, t_{N+1}; \boldsymbol{\theta}_0)) I^N(\mathbf{p}_{ij}; \boldsymbol{\theta}_0) \right] ,$$

$$c = \sum_{\mathbf{p}_{ij} \in \mathcal{P}} \left[\mathbf{1}(\mathbf{p}_{ij} - W(\mathbf{x}_{N+1}, t_{N+1}; \boldsymbol{\theta}_0)) \right]^2 .$$

It is clear that $a = L_N$. In c, owing to the definition of our indicator function, only the $\mathbf{p}_{ij}$ which is closest to $W(\mathbf{x}_{N+1}, t_{N+1}; \boldsymbol{\theta}_0)$ makes a contribution, thus we have $c = 1$. For b, the term $\mathbf{1}(\mathbf{p}_{ij} - W(\mathbf{x}_{N+1}, t_{N+1}; \boldsymbol{\theta}_0))$ is simply zero unless we are considering an accumulator $\mathbf{p}_{ij} = \boldsymbol{\eta}_{N+1}^{\theta_0}$, which gives $b = 2I^N(\boldsymbol{\eta}_{N+1}^{\theta_0}; \boldsymbol{\theta}_0)$. Thus we obtain (3). Note that the IWE is iteratively updated by incrementing the accumulator which locates closest to $\boldsymbol{\eta}_{N+1}^{\theta_0}$.

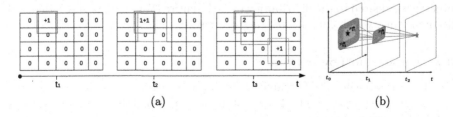

Fig. 3. (a) Incremental update of the IWE. For each new event e, we choose and increment the currently maximal accumulator in the bounding box $\mathcal{P}^\Theta$ around all possible locations $W(\mathbf{x}, t; \boldsymbol{\theta} \in \Theta)$. We simply increment the center of the bounding box if no other accumulator exists. (b) Bounding boxes of two temporally distinct events generated by the same point in 3D.

We now proceed to our main contribution, a recursive upper bound for the contrast maximisation problem. Let us define $\mathcal{P}_i^\Theta$ as the bounding box around all possible locations $W(\mathbf{x}_i, t_i; \boldsymbol{\theta} \in \Theta)$ of the un-warped event. Lemma 1 is introduced as follows.

Lemma 1. *Given a search space $\boldsymbol{\theta} \in \Theta$, for a small enough time interval, if $W(\mathbf{x}_i, t_i; \boldsymbol{\theta}) = W(\mathbf{x}_j, t_j; \boldsymbol{\theta})$ and $0 < i < j \leq N$, we have $\mathcal{P}_i^\Theta \subseteq \mathcal{P}_j^\Theta$. An intuitive explanation is given in Fig. 3(b).*

Lemma 1 now enables us to derive our recursive upper bound.

Theorem 2. *The upper bound of the objective function L_N for SoS-based contrast maximisation satisfies*

$$L_{N+1} = L_N + 1 + 2I^N(\eta_{N+1}^{\hat{\theta}}; \hat{\theta}) \tag{6}$$

$$\leq \overline{L_N} + 1 + 2Q^N = \overline{L_{N+1}}, \tag{7}$$

$$where \; Q^N = \max_{\mathbf{p}_{ij} \in \mathcal{P}_{N+1}^{\Theta}} \overline{I}^N(\mathbf{p}_{ij}) \geq I^N(\eta_{N+1}^{\hat{\theta}}; \hat{\theta})$$

$\mathcal{P}_{N+1}^{\Theta}$ *is a bounding box for the $(N+1)$-th event. $\hat{\theta}$ is the optimal parameter set that maximises L_{N+1} over the interval Θ. $\overline{I}^N(\mathbf{p}_{ij})$ is the value of pixel $\mathbf{p}_{ij}$ in the upper bound IWE, a recursively constructed image in which we always increment the maximum accumulator within the bounding box $\mathcal{P}_{N+1}^{\Theta}$ (i.e. the one that we used to define the value of Q^N. The incremental construction of $\overline{I}^N(\mathbf{p}_{ij})$ is illustrated in Fig. 3(a).*

Proof. (6) is straightforwardly derived from (3). The proof of inequation (7) then proceeds by mathematical induction.

For $N = 0$, it is obvious that $L_0 = \overline{L_0} = 0$. Similarly, for $N = 1$, $L_1 = 1 \leq \overline{L_0} + 1 + 0$, and $Q^0 = I^0(\eta_1^{\hat{\theta}}; \hat{\theta}) = 0$ (which satisfies Theorem 2). We now assume that $\overline{L_n}$ as well as the corresponding upper bound IWE $\overline{I}^n$ are given for all $0 < n \leq N$. We furthermore assume that they satisfy Theorem 2. Our aim is to prove that (7) holds for the $(N+1)$-th event. It is clear that $\overline{L_N} \geq L_N$, and we only need to prove that $Q^N \geq I^N(\eta_{N+1}^{\hat{\theta}}; \hat{\theta})$, for which we will make use of Lemma 1. There are two cases to be distinguished:

– The first case is if there exists an event ϵ_k with $0 < k < N+1$ and for which $\eta_k^{\hat{\theta}} = \eta_{N+1}^{\hat{\theta}}$. In other words, the k-th and the $(N+1)$-th event are warped to a same accumulator if choosing the locally optimal parameters. Note that if there are multiple previous events for which this condition holds, the k-th event is chosen to be the most recent one. Given our assumptions, $\overline{L_{k-1}}$ as well as the $(k-1)$-th constructed upper bound IWE satisfy Theorem 2, which means that $Q^{k-1} \geq I^{k-1}(\eta_k^{\hat{\theta}}; \hat{\theta})$. Let $\mathbf{p}_k \in \mathcal{P}_k^{\Theta}$ now be the pixel location with maximum intensity in $\overline{I}^{k-1}(\mathbf{p}_k)$. Then, the k-th updated IWE satisfies $\overline{I}^k(\mathbf{p}_k) = Q^{k-1} + 1 \geq I^{k-1}(\eta_k^{\hat{\theta}}; \hat{\theta}) + 1$. According to Lemma 1, we have $\mathcal{P}_k^{\Theta} \subseteq \mathcal{P}_{N+1}^{\Theta}$, therefore $\mathbf{p}_k \subseteq \mathcal{P}_{N+1}^{\Theta}$, and $Q^N \geq \overline{I}^k(\mathbf{p}_k) \geq I^{k-1}(\eta_k^{\hat{\theta}}; \hat{\theta}) + 1$. With optimal warp parameters $\hat{\theta}$, events with indices from $k+1$ to N will not locate at $\eta_{N+1}^{\hat{\theta}}$, and therefore $I^{k-1}(\eta_k^{\hat{\theta}}; \hat{\theta}) + 1 = I^N(\eta_{N+1}^{\hat{\theta}}; \hat{\theta}) \leq Q^N$.
– If there is no such a event, it is obvious that $Q^N \geq I^N(\eta_{N+1}^{\hat{\theta}}; \hat{\theta})$.

With the basic cases and the induction step proven, we conclude our proof that Theorem 2 holds for all natural numbers N.

We apply the proposed strategy to derive upper and lower bounds for all six aforementioned contrast functions, and list them in Table 2. Note that the initial case varies for different loss functions. The globally-optimal contrast maximisation framework (GOCMF) is outlined in Algorithm 1 and Algorithm 2. We propose a nested strategy for calculating upper bounds, in which the outer layer RB evaluates the objective function, while the inner layer BB estimates the bounding box $\mathcal{P}_N^{\Theta}$ and depends on the specific motion parametrisation.

Table 2. Recursive Upper and Lower Bounds

	Upper bound $\overline{L}_N$	Lower bound $\underline{L}_N$	L_0
SoS	$\overline{L}_{N-1} + 1 + 2Q$	$\underline{L}_{N-1} + 1 + 2I^{N-1}(\eta_N^{\theta_0}; \theta_0)$	0
Var	$\overline{L}_{N-1} + \frac{1}{N_p} - \frac{2\mu_I}{N_p} + \frac{2}{N_p}Q$	$\underline{L}_{N-1} + \frac{1}{N_p} - \frac{2\mu_I}{N_p} + \frac{2}{N_p}I^{N-1}(\eta_N^{\theta_0}; \theta_0)$	μ_I^2
SoE	$\overline{L}_{N-1} + (e-1)e^Q$	$\underline{L}_{N-1} + (e-1)e^{I^{N-1}(\eta_N^{\theta_0};\theta_0)}$	N_p
SoSA	$\overline{L}_{N-1} + (e^{-\delta} - 1)e^{-\delta \cdot Q}$	$\underline{L}_{N-1} + (e^{-\delta} - 1)e^{-\delta \cdot I^{N-1}(\eta_N^{\theta_0};\theta_0)}$	N_p
SoEaS	$\overline{L}_{N-1} + 1 + 2Q + (e-1)e^Q$	$\underline{L}_{N-1} + 1 + 2I^{N-1}(\eta_N^{\theta_0};\theta_0) + (e-1)e^{I^{N-1}(\eta_N^{\theta_0};\theta_0)}$	N_p
SoSAaS	$\overline{L}_{N-1} + 1 + 2Q + (e^{-\delta} - 1)e^{-\delta Q}$	$\underline{L}_{N-1} + 1 + 2I^{N-1}(\eta_N^{\theta_0};\theta_0) + (e^{-\delta} - 1)e^{-\delta I^{N-1}(\eta_N^{\theta_0};\theta_0)}$	N_p

Algorithm 1. GOCMF: globally optimal contrast maximisation framework

Input: event set $\mathcal{E}$, initial search space Θ, branching limit N_b

Output: optimal warping parameters $\hat{\theta}$

1: Initialize $\hat{\theta}$ with the center of Θ,
2: $L^* \leftarrow 0$, $S \leftarrow \{RB(\mathcal{E}, \Theta), \Theta\}$
3: Push S into queue Q, $S^* \leftarrow S$
4: **while** $i < N_b$ **do**
5:     $L^* \leftarrow 0$
6:     **if** $S^*.\underline{L}, == S^*.\overline{L}$ **then**
7:         $\hat{\theta} \leftarrow$ Center of $S^*.\Theta$, break
8:     **for** each node $S \in Q$ **do**
9:         Pop S, split into subspaces S_j
10:        **for** all subspaces S_j **do**
11:            $\{S_j.\underline{L}, S_j.\overline{L}\} \leftarrow RB(\mathcal{E}, \Theta_j)$
12:            **if** $S_j.\underline{L} > L^*$ **then**
13:                $L^* \leftarrow S_j.\underline{L}$, $S^* \leftarrow S_j$
14:            Push S_j into Q
15:        Prune branches in Q
16:    $i \leftarrow i + 1$
17: **return** $\hat{\theta}$

Algorithm 2. RB: recursive bounds calculation

Input: event set $\mathcal{E}$, search space Θ

Output: lower bound $\underline{L}$, upper bound $\overline{L}$

1: Initialize accumulator images $\overline{I}$ and I with zeros
2: Initialize $\underline{L}$, $\overline{L}$ according to Table 2
3: $\theta_0 \leftarrow$ center of Θ
4: **for** each event $e_k \in \mathcal{E}$ **do**
5:     $\mathcal{P}_k^{\Theta} \leftarrow BB(W(\cdot), \Theta, e_k)$
6:     $Q \leftarrow \max_{\mathbf{p}_{ij} \in \mathcal{P}_k^{\Theta}} \overline{I}(\mathbf{p}_{ij})$
7:     $\eta_k^{\theta_0} \leftarrow$ round$(W(\mathbf{x}_k, t_k; \theta_0))$
8:     Update $\underline{L}$, $\overline{L}$ (cf. Table 2)
9:     $\nu_k \leftarrow$ argmax$_{\mathbf{p}_{ij} \in \mathcal{P}_k^{\Theta}} \overline{I}(\mathbf{p}_{ij})$
10:    $\overline{I}(\nu_k) \leftarrow \overline{I}(\nu_k) + 1$
11:    $I(\eta_k^{\theta_0}) \leftarrow I(\eta_k^{\theta_0}) + 1$
12: **return** $\underline{L}, \overline{L}$

4   Application to Visual Odometry with a Downward-Facing Event Camera

Motion estimation for planar Autonomous Ground Vehicles (AGVs) is an important problem in intelligent transportation [17,24,30]. An interesting alternative is given by employing a downward instead of a forward facing camera, thus permitting direct observation of the ground plane with known depth. This largely simplifies the geometry of the problem and notably turns the image-to-image warping into a homographic mapping that is linear in homogeneous space. The strategy is widely used in relevant applications such as sweeping robots and factory AGVs, and a good review is presented in [1]. However, the method is affected by potentially severe challenges given by the image appearance: a) reliable feature matching or even extraction may be difficult for certain noisy ground textures, b) fast motion may easily lead to motion blur, and c) stable appearance may require artificial illumination. Many existing methods therefore do not employ feature correspondences but aim at a correspondence-less alignment or even a full photometric image alignment. Besides more classical RANSAC-based hypothesise-and-test schemes [7], the community therefore has also developed appearance-based template matching approaches [8,15,22,23,33], solvers based on efficient second-order minimisation [18,20,38], and methods exploiting the Fast Fourier Transform [2,25], the Fourier-Mellin Transform [16,19], or the Improved Fourier Mellin Invariant [4,31]. In an attempt to tackle highly self-similar ground textures, Dille et al. [8] propose to use an optical flow sensor instead of a regular CMOS camera.

A critical question is given by the position of the camera. The camera may hang in the front or rear of the vehicle, which gives increased distance to the ground plane and in turn reduces motion blur. However, it also causes moving shadows in the image, and generally complicates the stabilisation of the image appearance and thus repeatable feature detection or region-based matching. A common alternative therefore is given by installing the camera underneath the vehicle paired with an artificial light source (e.g. [2,8]). However, the short distance to the ground plane may easily lead to unwanted motion blur. We therefore consider an event camera as a highly interesting and much more dynamic alternative visual sensor for this particular scenario.

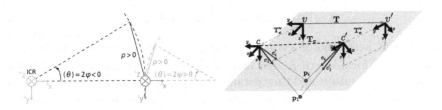

Fig. 4. Left: *The Ackermann steering model* with the ICR [14]. Both a left and a right turn are illustrated. Right: Connections between vehicle displacement, extrinsic transformation, and relative camera pose.

4.1 Homographic Mapping and Bounding Box Extraction

We rely the globally-optimal BnB solver for correspondence-less AGV motion presented in [14], which also employs a normal, downward facing camera. We employ the two-dimensional Ackermann steering model describing the commonly non-holonomic motion of an AGV. Employing this 2-DoF model leads to benefits in BnB, the complexity of which strongly depends on the dimensionality of the solution space. As illustrated in Fig. 4, the Ackermann model constrains the motion of the vehicle to follow a circular-arc trajectory about an Instantaneous Centre of Rotation (ICR). The motion between successive frames can be conveniently described at the hand of two parameters: the half-angle of the relative rotation angle ϕ, and the baseline between the two views ρ. However, the alignment of the events requires a temporal parametrisation of the relative pose, which is why we employ the angular velocity $\omega = \frac{\theta}{t} = \frac{2\phi}{t}$ as well as the translational velocity $v = \omega r = \omega\rho\frac{1}{2\sin(\phi)}$ in our model. The relative transformation from vehicle frame v' back to v is therefore given by

$$\mathbf{R}_v = \begin{bmatrix} \cos(\omega t) & -\sin(\omega t) & 0 \\ \sin(\omega t) & \cos(\omega t) & 0 \\ 0 & 0 & 1 \end{bmatrix} \text{ and } \mathbf{t}_v = \frac{v}{\omega}\begin{bmatrix} 1-\cos(\omega t) \\ \sin(\omega t) \\ 0 \end{bmatrix}. \tag{8}$$

Further details about the derivation are given in the supplementary material.

In practice the vehicle frame hardly coincides with the camera frame. The orientation and the height of the origin can be chosen to be identical, and the camera may be laterally mounted in the centre of the vehicle. However, there is likely to be a displacement along the forward direction, which we denote by the signed variable s. In other words, $\mathbf{R}_v^c = \mathbf{I}_{3\times 3}$ and $\mathbf{t}_v^c = \begin{bmatrix} 0 & s & 0 \end{bmatrix}^T$. As illustrated in Fig. 4, the transformation from camera pose c' (at an arbitrary future timestamp) to c (at the initial timestamp t_{ref}) is therefore given by

$$\begin{aligned} \mathbf{R}_c &= \mathbf{R}_v^{cT}\mathbf{R}_v\mathbf{R}_v^c, \\ \mathbf{t}_c &= -\mathbf{R}_v^{cT}\mathbf{t}_v^c + \mathbf{R}_v^{cT}\mathbf{t}_v + \mathbf{R}_v^{cT}\mathbf{R}_v\mathbf{t}_v^c. \end{aligned} \tag{9}$$

Using the known plane normal vector $\mathbf{n} = \begin{bmatrix} 0 & 0 & -1 \end{bmatrix}^T$ and depth-of-plane d, the image warping function $W(\mathbf{x}_k, t_k; [\omega\ v]^T)$ that permits the transfer of an event $e_k = \{\mathbf{x}_k, t_k, s_k\}$ into the reference view at t_{ref} is finally given by the planar homography equation

$$\mathbf{H}\begin{bmatrix} \mathbf{x}_k^T & 1 \end{bmatrix}^T = \mathbf{K}(\mathbf{R}_c - \frac{\mathbf{t}_c\mathbf{n}^T}{d})\mathbf{K}^{-1}\begin{bmatrix} \mathbf{x}_k^T & 1 \end{bmatrix}^T. \tag{10}$$

Note that $\mathbf{K}$ here denotes a regular perspective camera calibration matrix with homogeneous focal length f, zero skew, and a principal point at $\begin{bmatrix} u_0 & v_0 \end{bmatrix}^T$. Note further that the substituted time parameter needs to be equal to $t = t_k - t_{\text{ref}}$, and that the result needs to be dehomogenised. After expansion, we easily obtain

$$\begin{aligned} \mathbf{x}_k' &= W(\mathbf{x}_k, t_k; [\omega\ v]^T) = \begin{bmatrix} x_k' & y_k' \end{bmatrix}^T \\ &= \begin{bmatrix} -[y_k - v_0 + s\frac{f}{d}]\sin(\omega t) + [x_k - u_0 - \frac{f}{d}(\frac{v}{w})]\cos(\omega t) + \frac{f}{d}(\frac{v}{w}) + u_0 \\ [x_k - u_0 - \frac{f}{d}(\frac{v}{w})]\sin(\omega t) + [y_k - v_0 + s\frac{f}{d}]\cos(\omega t) - s\frac{f}{d} + v_0 \end{bmatrix}. \end{aligned} \tag{11}$$

Finally, the bounding box $\mathcal{P}_k^{\Theta}$ is found by bounding the values of x_k' and y_k' over the intervals $\omega \in \mathcal{W} = [\omega_{\min}; \omega_{\max}]$ and $v \in \mathcal{V} = [v_{\min}; v_{\max}]$. The bounding is easily achieved if simply considering monotonicity of functions over given sub-branches. For example, if $\omega_{\min} \geq 0$, $v_{\min} \geq 0$, $x_k \geq u_0$, and $y_k \geq v_0 - s\frac{f}{d}$, we obtain

$$\underline{x_k'} = -[y_k - v_0 + s\frac{f}{d}]\sin(\omega_{\max}t) + [x_k - u_0 - \frac{f}{d}(\frac{v_{\min}}{\omega_{\max}})]\cos(\omega_{\max}t) + \frac{f}{d}(\frac{v_{\min}}{\omega_{\max}}) + u_0,$$

$$\overline{x_k'} = -[y_k - v_0 + s\frac{f}{d}]\sin(\omega_{\min}t) + [x_k - u_0 - \frac{f}{d}(\frac{v_{\max}}{\omega_{\min}})]\cos(\omega_{\min}t) + \frac{f}{d}(\frac{v_{\max}}{\omega_{\min}}) + u_0,$$

$$\underline{y_k'} = [x_k - u_0 - \frac{f}{d}(\frac{v_{\max}}{\omega_{\min}})]\sin(\omega_{\min}t) + [y_k - v_0 + s\frac{f}{d}]\cos(\omega_{\max}t) - s\frac{f}{d} + v_0, \text{ and}$$

$$\overline{y_k'} = [x_k - u_0 - \frac{f}{d}(\frac{v_{\min}}{\omega_{\max}})]\sin(\omega_{\max}t) + [y_k - v_0 + s\frac{f}{d}]\cos(\omega_{\min}t) - s\frac{f}{d} + v_0. \quad (12)$$

We kindly refer the reader to the supplementary material for all further cases.

5   Experimental Evaluation

We present two suites of experiments. The first one validates the global optimality, accuracy and robustness of our solver on simulated data. The second one then applies it to the real-world scenario of AGV motion estimation.

5.1   Accuracy and Robustness of Globally Optimal Motion Estimation

We start by evaluating the accuracy of the motion estimation with contrast maximisation function L_{SoS} over synthetic data. As already implied in [11], L_{SoS} can be considered as a solid starting point for the evaluation. Our synthetic data consists of randomly generated horizontal and vertical line segments on a plane at a depth of 2.0 m. We consider Ackermann motion with an angular velocity $\omega = 28.6479°/\text{s}$ (0.5 rad/s) and a linear velocity $v = 0.5\,\text{m/s}$. Events are generated by randomly choosing a 3D point on a line, and reprojecting it into a random camera pose sampled by a random timestamp within the interval $[0, 0.1\,\text{s}]$. The result of our method is finally evaluated by running BnB over the search space $\mathcal{W} = [0.4, 0.6]$ and $\mathcal{V} = [0.4, 0.6]$, and comparing the retrieved solution against the result of an exhaustive search with sampling points every $\delta\omega = 0.001\,\text{rad/s}$ and $\delta v = 0.001\,\text{m/s}$. BnB is furthermore configured to terminate the search if $|\omega_{max} - \omega_{min}| \leq 0.00078\,\text{rad/s}$ or $|v_{max} - v_{min}| \leq 0.00078\,\text{m/s}$. The experiment is repeated 1000 times.

Figures 5(a) and 5(b) illustrate the distribution of the errors for both methods in the noise-free case. The standard deviation of the exhaustive search and BnB are $\sigma_\omega = 1.0645°/\text{s}$, $\sigma_v = 0.0151\text{m/s}$ and $\sigma_\omega = 1.305°/\text{s}$, $\sigma_v = 0.0150\text{m/s}$, respectively. While this result suggests that BnB works well and sustainably returns a result very close to the optimum found by exhaustive search, we still note that the optimum identified by both methods has a bias with respect to ground truth, even in the noise-free case. Note however that this is related to

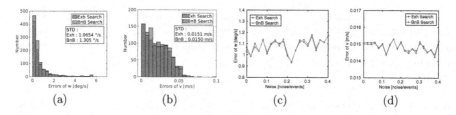

Fig. 5. Simulation results. (a) and (b) indicate the error distribution for ω and v over all experiments for both our proposed method as well as an exhaustive search. (c) and (d) visualise the average error of the estimated parameters caused by additional salt and pepper noise on the event stream. Results are averaged over 1000 random experiments. Note that our proposed method has excellent robustness even for N/E ratios up to 40%.

the nature of the contrast maximisation function, and not our globally optimal solution strategy.

In order to analyse robustness, we randomly add salt and pepper noise to the event stream with noise-to-event (N/E) ratios between 0 and 0.4 (Example objective functions for different N/E ratios have already been illustrated in Fig. 2). Figure 5(c) and 5(d) show the error for each noise level again averaged over 1000 experiments. As can be observed, the errors are very similar and behave more or less independently of the amount of added noise. The latter result underlines the high robustness of our approach.

5.2   Application to Real Data and Comparison Against Alternatives

We apply our method to real data collected by a DAVIS346 event camera, which outputs events streams with a maximum time resolution of $1\mu s$ as well as regular frames at a frame rate of 30 Hz. Images have a resolution of 346×260. We mount the camera on the front of a XQ-4 Pro robot and let it face downward. The displacement from the non-steering axis to the camera is $s = -0.45$ m, and the height difference between camera and ground is $d = 0.23$ m. We recorded several motion sequences on a wood grain foam which has highly self-similar texture and poses a challenge to reliably extract and match features. Ground truth is obtained via an Optitrack optical motion tracking system. Our algorithm is working in undistorted coordinates, which is why normalisation and undistortion are computed in advance. The following aspects are evaluated:

Different objective functions: We test the algorithm with all aforementioned six contrast functions over various types of motions, including a straight line, a circle, and an arbitrarily curved trajectory. Table 3 shows the RMS errors of the estimated dynamic parameters, and compares the accuracy of all six alternatives. We furthermore apply two state-of-the-art approaches for regular images, namely the correspondence-less globally optimal feature-based approach (GOVO) from [14], as well as the Improved Fourier Mellin Invariant transform (IFMI) in [4,31]. Even though these alternatives use the same non-holonomic or planar motion models, event-based motion estimation methods significantly outperform the intensity-camera-based alternatives (L_{SoSAaS} on top, and L_{SoS} and L_{Var} also have good performance).

Table 3. RMS errors for different datasets and methods.

Method	Line w[°/s]	Line v[m/s]	Circle w[°/s]	Circle v[m/s]	Curve w[°/s]	Curve v[m/s]
SoE	2.4089	0.0158	2.2121	0.0252	3.6282	0.0263
SoEaS	2.4057	0.0158	2.0178	0.0242	3.6282	0.0263
SoS	**0.5127**	**0.0086**	1.0884	0.0083	3.0091	0.0208
SoSA	1.9606	0.0287	4.2496	0.0734	9.2904	0.0727
SoSAaS	**0.5175**	**0.0086**	**0.5294**	**0.0046**	**0.5546**	**0.0189**
Var	**0.5127**	**0.0086**	1.0884	0.0083	3.0091	0.0208
IFMI	145.3741	1.0594	8.1092	0.0243	12.8047	0.0192
GOVO	6.9705	0.2409	4.5506	0.0642	9.8652	0.0590

Event-Based vs Frame-Based: GOVO [14] and IFMI [31] are frame-based algorithms specifically designed for planar AGV motion estimation under featureless conditions. Figure 1 shows an example frame of the wood grain foam texture, and Fig. 7 the results obtained for all methods. As can be observed, GOVO finds as little as three corner features for some of the images, thus making it difficult to accurately recover the vehicle displacement despite the globally-optimal correspondence-less nature of the algorithm. Both IFMI and GOVO occasionally lose tracking (especially for linear motion), which leaves our proposed globally-optimal event-based method using L_{SoSAaS} as the best method.

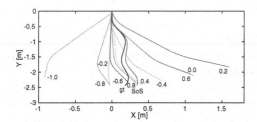

Method	w[°/s]	v[m/s]
SoS	3.0091	0.0208
GA	11.5023	0.0379

Fig. 6. Estimated trajectories by our method (SoS), gradient ascent with various initializations, and ground truth (gt). The table indicates the RMS errors for the best performing gradient ascent run and SoS.

BnB vs Gradient Ascent: We apply both gradient descent as well as BnB to the *Foam* dataset with curved motion. For the first temporal interval and the local search method, we vary the initial angular velocity ω and linear velocity v between -1 and 0.8 with steps of 0.2 (rad/s or m/s, respectively). For later intervals, we use the previous local optimum. Figure 6 illustrates the estimated trajectories for all initial values, compared against ground truth and a BnB search using L_{SoS}. RMS errors are also indicated. As clearly shown, even the best initial guess eventually diverges under a local search strategy, thus leading to clearly inferior results compared to our globally optimal search.

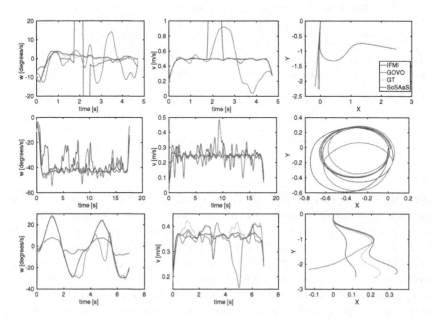

Fig. 7. Results for all methods over different datasets. The first two columns are errors over time for ω and v, and the third column illustrates a bird's eye view onto the integrated trajectories.

Various Textures: More results over datasets with other ground floor textures can be found in the supplementary material.

6   Discussion

We have introduced the first globally optimal solution to contrast maximisation for un-warped event streams. To the best of our knowledge, we are also the first to apply the idea of homography estimation via contrast maximisation to the real-world case of non-holonomic motion estimation with a downward facing camera mounted on an AGV. The challenging conditions in this scenario favorise dynamic vision sensors over regular frame-based cameras, a claim that is supported by our experimental results. The latter furthermore prove that global solutions are important and significantly outperform incremental local refinement. The recursive formulation of our bounds lets us find the global optimum over event streams of 0.04 s within less than one minute, a respectable achievement given the typically low computational efficiency of BnB solvers.

Acknowledgments. The authors would like to thank the fundings sponsored by Natural Science Foundation of Shanghai (grant number: 19ZR1434000) and Natural Science Foundation of China (grant number: 61950410612).

References

1. Aqel, M.O., Marhaban, M.H., Saripan, M.I., Ismail, N.B.: Review of visual odometry: types, approaches, challenges, and applications. SpringerPlus **5**(1), 1897 (2016)
2. Birem, M., Kleihorst, R., El-Ghouti, N.: Visual odometry based on the fourier transform using a monocular ground-facing camera. J. Real-Time Image Proc. **14**(3), 637–646 (2018)
3. Brandli, C., Berner, R., Yang, M., Liu, S.C., Delbruck, T.: A 240× 180 130 db 3 μs latency global shutter spatiotemporal vision sensor. IEEE J. Solid-State Circ. **49**(10), 2333–2341 (2014)
4. Bülow, H., Birk, A.: Fast and robust photomapping with an unmanned aerial vehicle (UAV). In: 2009 IEEE/RSJ International Conference on Intelligent Robots and Systems, pp. 3368–3373. IEEE (2009)
5. Cadena, C., Carlone, L., Carrillo, H., Latif, Y., Scaramuzza, D., Neira, J., Reid, I., Leonard, J.J.: Past, present, and future of simultaneous localization and mapping: toward the robust-perception age. IEEE Trans. Rob. **32**(6), 1309–1332 (2016)
6. Campbell, D., Petersson, L., Kneip, L., Li, H.: Globally-optimal inlier set maximisation for simultaneous camera pose and feature correspondence. In: Proceedings of the IEEE International Conference on Computer Vision, pp. 1–10 (2017)
7. Chen, X., Vempati, A.S., Beardsley, P.: Streetmap-mapping and localization on ground planes using a downward facing camera. In: 2018 IEEE/RSJ International Conference on Intelligent Robots and Systems (IROS), pp. 1672–1679. IEEE (2018)
8. Dille, M., Grocholsky, B., Singh, S.: Outdoor downward-facing optical flow odometry with commodity sensors. In: Howard, A., Iagnemma, K., Kelly, A. (eds.) Field and Service Robotics. Springer Tracts in Advanced Robotics, vol. 62, pp. 183–193. Springer, Heidelberg (2010). https://doi.org/10.1007/978-3-642-13408-1_17
9. Fuentes-Pacheco, J., Ruiz-Ascencio, J., Rendón-Mancha, J.M.: Visual simultaneous localization and mapping: a survey. Artif. Intell. Rev. **43**(1), 55–81 (2015)
10. Gallego, G., et al.: Event-basedvision: a survey. IEEE Trans. Pattern Anal. Mach. Intell. (2020)
11. Gallego, G., Gehrig, M., Scaramuzza, D.: Focus is all you need: loss functions for event-based vision. In: Proceedings of the IEEE Conference on Computer Vision and Pattern Recognition, pp. 12280–12289 (2019)
12. Gallego, G., Rebecq, H., Scaramuzza, D.: A unifying contrast maximization framework for event cameras, with applications to motion, depth, and optical flow estimation. In: Proceedings of the IEEE Conference on Computer Vision and Pattern Recognition, pp. 3867–3876 (2018)
13. Gallego, G., Scaramuzza, D.: Accurate angular velocity estimation with an event camera. IEEE Robot. Autom. Lett. **2**(2), 632–639 (2017)
14. Gao, L., Su, J., Cui, J., Zeng, X., Peng, X., Kneip, L.: Efficient globally-optimal correspondence-less visual odometry for planar ground vehicles. In: 2020 International Conference on Robotics and Automation (ICRA), pp. 2696–2702. IEEE (2020)

15. Gonzalez, R., Rodriguez, F., Guzman, J.L., Pradalier, C., Siegwart, R.: Combined visual odometry and visual compass for off-road mobile robots localization. Robotica **30**(6), 865–878 (2012)
16. Guo, X., Xu, Z., Lu, Y., Pang, Y.: An application of Fourier-Mellin transform in image registration. In: The Fifth International Conference on Computer and Information Technology (CIT 2005), pp. 619–623. IEEE (2005)
17. Huang, K., Wang, Y., Kneip, L.: Motion estimation of non-holonomic ground vehicles from a single. In: Proceedings of the IEEE Conference on Computer Vision and Pattern Recognition, pp. 12706–12715. IEEE (2019)
18. Jordan, J., Zell, A.: Ground plane based visual odometry for RGBD-cameras using orthogonal projection. IFAC-PapersOnLine **49**(15), 108–113 (2016)
19. Kazik, T., Göktoğan, A.H.: Visual odometry based on the Fourier-Mellin transform for a rover using a monocular ground-facing camera. In: 2011 IEEE International Conference on Mechatronics, pp. 469–474. IEEE (2011)
20. Lovegrove, S., Davison, A.J., Ibanez-Guzmán, J.: Accurate visual odometry from a rear parking camera. In: 2011 IEEE Intelligent Vehicles Symposium (IV), pp. 788–793. IEEE (2011)
21. Mitrokhin, A., Fermüller, C., Parameshwara, C., Aloimonos, Y.: Event-based moving object detection and tracking. In: 2018 IEEE RSJ International Conference on Intelligent Robots and Systems (IROS), pp. 1–9 (2018)
22. Nourani-Vatani, N., Borges, P.V.K.: Correlation-based visual odometry for ground vehicles. J. Field Robot. **28**(5), 742–768 (2011)
23. Nourani-Vatani, N., Roberts, J., Srinivasan, M.V.: Practical visual odometry for car-like vehicles. In: 2009 IEEE International Conference on Robotics and Automation, pp. 3551–3557. IEEE (2009)
24. Peng, X., Cui, J., Kneip, L.: Articulated multi-perspective cameras and their application to truck motion estimation. In: 2019 IEEE/RSJ International Conference on Intelligent Robots and Systems (IROS), pp. 2052–2059. IEEE (2019)
25. Piyathilaka, L., Munasinghe, R.: An experimental study on using visual odometry for short-run self localization of field robot. In: 2010 Fifth International Conference on Information and Automation for Sustainability, pp. 150–155. IEEE (2010)
26. Rebecq, H., Gallego, G., Mueggler, E., Scaramuzza, D.: EMVS: event-based multi-view stereo–3D reconstruction with an event camera in real-time. Int. J. Comput. Vis. **126**(12), 1394–1414 (2018)
27. Stoffregen, T., Gallego, G., Drummond, T., Kleeman, L., Scaramuzza, D.: Event-based motion segmentation by motion compensation. In: Proceedings of the IEEE International Conference on Computer Vision, pp. 7244–7253 (2019)
28. Stoffregen, T., Kleeman, L.: Simultaneous optical flow and segmentation (SOFAS) using dynamic vision sensor. In: 2017 Australasian Conference on Robotics and Automation (ACRA), pp. 52–61 (2017)
29. Stoffregen, T., Kleeman, L.: Event cameras, contrast maximization and reward functions: an analysis. In: Proceedings of the IEEE Conference on Computer Vision and Pattern Recognition, pp. 12300–12308 (2019)
30. Wang, Y., Huang, K., Peng, X., Li, H., Kneip, L.: Reliable frame-to-frame motion estimation for vehicle-mounted surround-view camera systems. In: 2020 IEEE International Conference on Robotics and Automation (ICRA), pp. 1660–1666. IEEE (2020)
31. Xu, Q., Chavez, A.G., Bülow, H., Birk, A., Schwertfeger, S.: Improved Fourier Mellin invariant for robust rotation estimation with omni-cameras. In: 2019 IEEE International Conference on Image Processing (ICIP), pp. 320–324. IEEE (2019)

32. Ye, C., Mitrokhin, A., Parameshwara, C., Fermüller, C., Yorke, J.A., Aloimonos, Y.: Unsupervised learning of dense optical flow and depth from sparse event data. CoRR abs/1809.08625 (2018). http://arxiv.org/abs/1809.08625
33. Yu, Y., Pradalier, C., Zong, G.: Appearance-based monocular visual odometry for ground vehicles. In: 2011 IEEE/ASME International Conference on Advanced Intelligent Mechatronics (AIM), pp. 862–867. IEEE (2011)
34. Zhu, A.Z., Atanasov, N., Daniilidis, K.: Event-based feature tracking with probabilistic data association. In: 2017 IEEE International Conference on Robotics and Automation (ICRA), pp. 4465–4470. IEEE (2017)
35. Zhu, A.Z., Chen, Y., Daniilidis, K.: Realtime time synchronized event-based stereo. In: Ferrari, V., Hebert, M., Sminchisescu, C., Weiss, Y. (eds.) ECCV 2018. LNCS, vol. 11210, pp. 438–452. Springer, Cham (2018). https://doi.org/10.1007/978-3-030-01231-1_27
36. Zhu, A.Z., Yuan, L., Chaney, K., Daniilidis, K.: EV-FlowNet: self-supervised optical flow estimation for event-based cameras. arXiv preprint arXiv:1802.06898 (2018)
37. Zhu, A.Z., Yuan, L., Chaney, K., Daniilidis, K.: Unsupervised event-based learning of optical flow, depth, and egomotion. In: Proceedings of the IEEE Conference on Computer Vision and Pattern Recognition, pp. 989–997 (2019)
38. Zienkiewicz, J., Davison, A.: Extrinsics autocalibration for dense planar visual odometry. J. Field Robot. 32(5), 803–825 (2015)

Weakly-Supervised Learning of Human Dynamics

Petrissa Zell[(✉)], Bodo Rosenhahn, and Bastian Wandt

Leibniz University Hannover, 30167 Hannover, Germany
`zell@tnt.uni-hannover.de`

Abstract. This paper proposes a weakly-supervised learning framework for dynamics estimation from human motion. Although there are many solutions to capture pure human motion readily available, their data is not sufficient to analyze quality and efficiency of movements. Instead, the forces and moments driving human motion (*the dynamics*) need to be considered. Since recording dynamics is a laborious task that requires expensive sensors and complex, time-consuming optimization, dynamics data sets are small compared to human motion data sets and are rarely made public. The proposed approach takes advantage of easily obtainable motion data which enables weakly-supervised learning on small dynamics sets and weakly-supervised domain transfer. Our method includes novel neural network (NN) layers for forward and inverse dynamics during end-to-end training. On this basis, a cyclic loss between pure motion data can be minimized, i.e. no ground truth forces and moments are required during training. The proposed method achieves state-of-the-art results in terms of ground reaction force, ground reaction moment and joint torque regression and is able to maintain good performance on substantially reduced sets.

Keywords: Artificial neural networks · Human motion · Forward dynamics · Inverse dynamics · Weakly-supervised learning · Domain transfer

1 Introduction

Inverse dynamics describes the process of estimating net moments of force acting across skeletal joints from the three dimensional motion of the human skeleton and a set of exterior contact forces and moments. The obtained net moments are generally called joint torques (JT) and are of central interest in important fields, such as diagnostics of locomotor disorders, rehabilitation and prostheses design [10,12,23]. The JT cannot be measured non-intrusively and therefore need to be derived using computationally expensive optimization techniques. The

Electronic supplementary material The online version of this chapter (https://doi.org/10.1007/978-3-030-58574-7_5) contains supplementary material, which is available to authorized users.

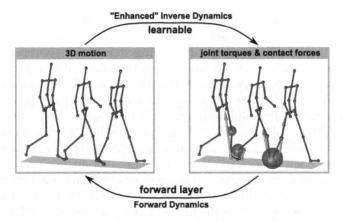

Fig. 1. An *Inverse Dynamics* method calculates joint torques based on an observed motion and contact forces. The enhanced task, that is implemented as a NN in this work, infers both, the joint torques and the exterior forces. The *Forward Dynamics* step yields a simulated motion based on the acting forces and moments. With our forward layer this step can now be integrated into NN training.

common approaches are inverse and forward dynamics optimization. In inverse dynamics optimization, the kinematics of a model are optimized to match the target motion, while JT are inversely calculated based on the interaction with the ground and the model kinematics. For this step, 2nd order time derivatives are necessary, making the approach sensitive to noisy motion capture data.

Forward dynamics optimization considers the reverse problem: The applied forces drive the motion of the human body. The equations of motion and the current motion state define an initial value problem, that can be solved by numerical integration, yielding a simulated motion. Included into an optimization framework, the forward dynamics step is utilized to find the optimal JT that generate a simulated motion with minimal distance to the captured motion. The necessary integration during each optimization step causes high computational complexity. Furthermore, both approaches, inverse and forward dynamics, require the measurement of exterior forces. In the case of locomotion, these exterior influences are the ground reaction forces and moments (GRF/M) acting at both feet. Hence, the analysis of human dynamics using conventional optimization techniques is restricted to a controlled laboratory setting with force plates to measure the GRF/M. To avoid the described problems and to achieve motion analysis in the wild, the exterior forces and the interior JT can be estimated directly from observed motions using machine learning techniques, e.g. neural networks (NN).

Deep learning of human dynamics requires large data sets of human kinematics (3D motion of a kinematic model), exterior GRF/M and the driving JT. Unfortunately, corresponding data sets are few and often very restricted in terms of size and included motion types. To solve this problem, we propose a weakly-supervised deep learning method, that realizes NN training on small dynamics sets and domain transfer to new motion types, even without any ground truth of the acting forces. More precisely, our goal is to design a training process that is less depending on a large amount of dynamics data than a supervised baseline NN that learns to regress forces and moments from motion input. The proposed approach is called **Dynamics Network** and includes two novel dynamics layers: The forward (dynamics) layer and the inverse (dynamics) layer. The network replaces the traditional inverse dynamics task and enhances it by not only inferring the JT but also the GRF/M, as illustrated in Fig. 1. Subsequently, the forward layer solves the initial value problem given by the initial motion state and the network output. This results in a simulated motion that can be compared to the input motion, which gives rise to a loss purely defined on motion data. A full cycle, as illustrated in Fig. 1 is executed. For further control over the learned forces and moments we include the inverse layer, that penalizes GRF/M which do not match the observed accelerations. In contrast to the forward layer, it considers the ground reaction independently from JT, which allows for a decoupled control of both variables during training.

We demonstrate the benefits of our Dynamics Network by reducing the part of the used training sets, that include dynamical information, relying on the networks' own dynamics layers. Furthermore, we use our method to realize weakly- and unsupervised transfer learning between the related motion types, walking and running. We focus on locomotion since it represents the most important form of movement.

In summary, the contributions of this work are:

1. A data set of 3D human kinematics with force plate measurements including various motion types.
2. A novel forward dynamics layer that integrates the equations of motion and enables the minimization of a pure motion loss.
3. A novel inverse dynamics layer that propagates forces and moments along the kinematic chain to measure the match between GRF/M and segment accelerations.
4. Since the dynamics layers allow for training on pure motion samples without force information, we use this capacity in weakly-supervised learning and domain transfer between locomotion types.

2   Related Work

A laboratory setting with embedded force plates enforces strong restrictions on captured motions. Therefore, researchers increasingly exploit artificial NN to estimate ground reactions. The exterior forces are predicted based on 3D motions [3,5,15,22], accelerometer data [16,17] or pressure insoles [25,28]. The seminal work by Oh et al. [22] includes a fully connected feed forward NN to solve the GRF ambiguity during double support. Based on the complete ground reaction information, the JT are inferred using a standard inverse dynamics method. An interesting approach proposed by Johnson et al. [15] encodes marker trajectories as RGB-images to make use of pre-trained CNNs for image classification.

Compared to GRF/M regression, relatively few works dealt with machine learning for the estimation of JT in human motion [14,33]. A method by Lv et al. [18] utilizes Gaussian mixture models to learn contact and torque priors that are included in a maximum a-posteriori framework. The priors help to lead the inverse dynamics optimization to realistic force and torque profiles. In a previous work [34], different machine learning algorithms are compared for the GRF/M and JT regression. The focus lies on contrasting end-to-end models to a hierarchical approach that subdivides the task into gait phase classification and regression.

It is worth mentioning, that machine learning for the inverse dynamics problem is also part of robotics research. Here, the common goal is to learn robotic control, such as JT, for trajectory planning. The latest works predominantly rely on recurrent NN and reinforcement learning [8,11,21,29].

In 2018, a differentiable physics engine for the inclusion into deep learning has been introduced and tested on simple simulated systems [2]. A related work proposes a comparable physics engine and includes it in an RNN for learning of robotics control [7]. These models, however, are not sufficient to represent the human kinematic chain. While robotics research focuses on the efficient execution of movement, the interaction with the environment and real-time application, the inverse dynamics problem for human motion is characterized by the complexity of the human locomotor system, which results in high data variability. Therefore, the focus primarily lies on the accurate estimation of forces and moments, in spite of the complex nature of the system, which makes regressors for human motion analysis highly dependent on large data sets.

The usage of cycle-consistency has already benefited visual correspondence tasks like temporal video alignment and cross-domain mapping of images, etc. [9, 13,26,31,36]. The success of these methods has motivated us to apply cycle-consistency to human dynamics learning.

To the best of our knowledge, this work is the first to present differentiable NN layers for forward, as well as inverse dynamics of human motion. In contrast to all prior works, the proposed method can learn human dynamics in a weakly-supervised setting, without depending on complete dynamics ground truth. Our cycle consistent approach allows for the formulation of a pure motion loss, and thus drastically enlarges the usable data pool, even allowing for domain transfer between motion types.

3   Human Motion Data Sets

Deep learning of human dynamics demands data of the observed 3D motion, the acting GRF/M and the driving JT. We recorded 195 walking and 75 running sequences performed by 22 subjects of different gender and body proportions (demographic information can be found in the supplementary material). The data was recorded using a Vicon motion capture system with synchronized AMTI force plates, embedded in the ground. An inverse kinematics algorithm was conducted to fit the skeleton of our physical model to the captured marker trajectories. In order to simplify the calculations of the forward layer, we apply a leg model with one torso segment to approximate the motion and the inertial properties of the whole upper body. This kind of model is typically used in locomotion analysis [32]. It's kinematics are completely represented by the generalized model coordinates q that consist of 6 global coordinates and 18 joint angles.

The GRF f_c and GRM m_c are calculated from the measured force plate data. Together they build the GRF/M vector

$$F_c = [f_{c_l}, f_{c_r}, m_{c_l}, m_{c_r}]^T \,, \tag{1}$$
$$m_{c_i} = d_{cop_i} \times f_{c_i} + t_{z_i} \,, \quad i = l, r$$

with the vector d_{cop} pointing from the foot center of mass to the center of pressure of the applied reaction force and the torsional torque t_z. The index $i = l, r$ indicates the foot segment, where the respective part of F_c is applied.

Based on the kinematics and GRF/M we execute a forward dynamics optimization to receive the non-measurable JT τ. The applied forward dynamics step is equivalent to our forward layer, so that the resulting JT conform with the layer dynamics during training. We employ a sliding window approach for this pre-processing step, as well as for the network training and application. This way, the parameter space is decreased and the convergence is accelerated.

To further reduce the number of parameters, we apply polynomial fits to all relevant data types. This approximation also facilitates the learning of inverse dynamics, since the networks are not required to explicitly model temporal context. Without the polynomials, additional smoothness losses would be necessary to achieve continuous forces and moments during forward dynamics optimization, as well as NN training. The kinematics q and the GRF/M F_c are approximated by 3rd order polynomials. For the JT τ we find, that linear approximations yield the best optimization results in a forward dynamics setting. The resulting polynomial coefficients are denoted by γ_q, γ_f and γ_τ, respectively. Apart from these coefficients, each forward dynamics simulation is depending on the subject specific segment dimensions l_{sub}. Together these parameters build a sample in our human motion data set:

$$[\gamma_q, l_{sub}, \gamma_f, \gamma_\tau] \,. \tag{2}$$

Using these approximations, we still achieve a representation of non-continuous contact by means of an overlapping window approach, that allows a discretization below window length.

Due to the restrictions introduced by the localized force plate measurements, approximately a third of the data set contains GRF/M. If the forward dynamics optimization converges to an insufficient minimum the corresponding torques cannot be included, so that even a smaller part of the data includes JT. We divide our data set accordingly into a pure motion subset, a motion and GRF/M subset and a subset with the complete data. These subsets are referred to as *motion-set*, *ground-reaction-set* and *torque-set*, respectively. To investigate a further scenario, that requires less supervision and measurements, we define a *contact-set*, which contains motion states and binary information about the ground contact, i.e. which foot is in contact with the ground. The presented data sets are used in different training modes that represent various levels of supervision.

4 Dynamics Network

The structure of our Dynamics Network is presented in Fig. 2. A fully connected NN executes the extended inverse dynamics task from motion to JT and GRF/M. The network has a bottle-neck structure with 5 fully connected layers, containing about 5800 parameters in total and Leaky-ReLu activations [19]. The forward dynamics step is implemented as a NN layer (forward layer) and yields simulated motion states based on the network output. A detailed description is given in Sect. 4.1. Combined, the NN and the forward layer build a cycle that enables the minimization of a loss between motion states. The additional inverse layer measures the consistency of the input motion with the predicted GRF/M by propagating forces and moments along the kinematic chain and calculating the residuals at the last segment. A complete description follows in Sect. 4.2. Furthermore, the network can be trained in a supervised manner, using a mean squared error (MSE) on the predicted GRF/M and JT. This approach will be used as a baseline. Since the corresponding ground truth data is not always available, our dynamics layers can be used to simulate and control it in a weakly-supervised setting. To gradually reduce the level of supervision, we implement a contact-loss, that penalizes forces during time frames with no ground contact. It only requires binary information.

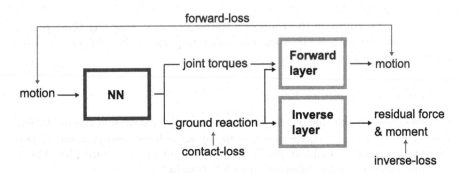

Fig. 2. Schematic structure of the Dynamics Network. The output of the NN is processed using forward and inverse layer to accomplish training without GRF/M and JT ground truth.

Our methods operate with four different loss functions, that can be activated separately or in combination. On this basis, we define and compare different training modes that realize various levels of supervision and operate on different subsets of the data: Starting with full supervision, the baseline method uses the

MSE of the predicted parameters γ_f^{pred} and $\gamma_\tau^{\text{pred}}$ for GRF/M and JT, respectively:

$$L_{\text{mse}} = \|\gamma_f^{\text{pred}} - \gamma_f^{\text{true}}\|_2^2 + \|\gamma_\tau^{\text{pred}} - \gamma_\tau^{\text{true}}\|_2^2. \tag{3}$$

The baseline network is exclusively trained on the torque-set and the ground-reaction-set.

In the next training mode, the network is additionally trained using the contact-set with a reduced level of supervision. We assume, that only binary information about the contact state is available in this subset. The corresponding training mode is referred to as *contact-forward-inverse-training* or in short *cFI-training*. During this mode, the corresponding network (*cFI-net*) is trained in an alternating procedure: If data from the contact-set is chosen as input, the procedure switches between the contact-loss, the inverse-loss and the forward-loss. Based on Eq. (2), we define the contact-loss as

$$L_{\text{contact}} = \|\boldsymbol{F}_{c_i}(c_i = 0)\|_2^2, \tag{4}$$

with the contact state $c_i = 1$ if foot i is in contact with the ground and $c_i = 0$, otherwise. If data from the torque-set or the ground-reaction-set is chosen, the MSE of Eq. (3) is minimized, similarly to the baseline method.

The third training mode is termed *forward-training* or *F-training*. In addition to supervised training on the torque-set and the ground-reaction-set, the network, *F-net*, is trained in an unsupervised setting, using the motion-set and minimizing the forward-loss.

In all training modes the included losses are minimized alternatingly. To balance the influence of different loss functions, we use adaptive weighting, that is updated after each epoch according to the ratio of the observed average values during the last epoch.

In Sect. 5 we compare the proposed training modes regarding their performance on small data sets and their capability to perform domain transfer from walking to running motions.

4.1 Forward Dynamics Layer

In this section, we describe our forward dynamics simulation and the implementation as a NN layer. We choose a simple model and a basic numerical integration technique in order to maintain relatively low computational complexity. This is necessary to facilitate the integration in NN training.

Our human body model is a leg model with one additional segment that presents the mean upper body kinematics. As mentioned before, the kinematic state of the model is fully represented by the generalized coordinates q and their derivatives $\dot{q}$. The generalized coordinates include 18 joint degrees of freedom that are effected by the JT $\boldsymbol{\tau}$. The GRF/M $\boldsymbol{F}_c$ introduced in Eq. (2) is applied at the center of mass of the respective foot segment. Each segment is associated with a mass and a tensor of inertia that are approximated from the segment shape and literature values of the population [32]. For this step, we model the segments as simple geometric shapes with constant density. The segment volume is scaled according to the length based on average scaling factors of the data set. With this assumption, the segment lengths l_{sub} completely describe the body model.

We formulate the equation of motion using the TMT-method [24] similar to [4,35]. The resulting 2nd order differential equation has the following form:

$$\mathcal{M}(q_t, l_{sub})\ddot{q}_t = \mathcal{F}(q_t, \dot{q}_t, F_{c_t}, \tau_t, l_{sub}) \tag{5}$$

Here, $\mathcal{M}$ is the generalized inertia matrix and the right hand side is the sum of all acting forces. For better readability we drop the time frame index t in the remaining part of this work. The problem is reformulated as a 1st order differential equation by introducing the state vector $x = [q^T, \dot{q}^T]^T$:

$$\dot{x} = \left[\begin{matrix} \dot{q} \\ \mathcal{M}(q, l_{sub})^{-1}\mathcal{F}(x, F_c, \tau, l_{sub}) \end{matrix} \right] \tag{6}$$

Together with an initial state vector x_0 this equation gives rise to an initial value problem, that can be solved by numerical integration.

During integration an acceleration error propagates with the squared integration time. The same applies to an error in JT and GRF/M. In order to reduce this high sensitivity for NN training, we propose to apply a damping factor to $\dot{x}$. The damping is based on the standard deviation $\sigma_{\dot{x}}$ of the absolute velocities and accelerations found in the training set and on the maximum absolute values $m_{\dot{x}}$ that occur in the current sample. For each component j the damping is set to

$$d_j = \exp\left\{ -\max\left(\frac{|\dot{x}_j| - m_{\dot{x},j} - k\sigma_{\dot{x},j}}{k\sigma_{\dot{x},j}}, 0 \right) \right\}, \tag{7}$$

where $\dot{x}_j$ is the undamped component of the current integration step. The resulting vector d is included by building the Hadamard product to result in the damped equation of motion:

$$\dot{x} = \left[\begin{matrix} \dot{q} \\ \mathcal{M}^{-1}\mathcal{F} \end{matrix} \right] \odot d. \tag{8}$$

The parameter k in Eq. (7) determines the steepness of the damping curve and the starting point of the decrease from one. In simple terms, it broadens the region of acceptable accelerations to k times of the standard deviation. The value is heuristically set to $k = 10$. We found, that this setting results in stable simulations that can still be optimized during training.

For numerical integration we apply Euler's method with constant step size to keep the computation time as small as possible. Consequently, our forward layer can be seen as a function FD, that executes $n = ($window size$ - 1)$ Euler steps. It receives the input parameters

$$p = (x_0, l_{sub}, F_{c_{1 \ldots n}}, \tau_{1 \ldots n}, m_{\dot{x}}) \tag{9}$$

and outputs the simulated motion states

$$x_{1 \ldots n}^{sim} = FD(p). \tag{10}$$

Based on this result we define the forward loss as

$$L_{\text{forward}} = \text{MSE}(x^{sim}_{1\cdots n}, x^{true}_{1\cdots n}) + \alpha\|d - 1\|_1 , \tag{11}$$

with weighting factor $\alpha = 1$ and an L_1-loss to penalize damping factors smaller than one.

For the back propagation of L_{forward} during NN training, the gradients of the output states with respect to the input of the layer need to be known. This can either be achieved using automatic differentiation included in most deep learning frameworks or by explicit calculation using sensitivity analysis. The latter approach is described in the supplementary material.

4.2   Inverse Dynamics Layer

The inverse layer receives the ground truth motion and the predicted GRF/M as input and propagates forces and moments along the kinematic chain in a bottom-up procedure. The calculation starts at the centers of mass of the model's feet, where GRF/M are applied. Each segment is considered in a free body diagram to deduce the forces and moments at the proximal joint based on the acting forces and moments at the distal joint and the linear and angular acceleration of the segment. For segment s the force F_p effecting the proximal joint is given by

$$F_p = m_s(a_s - g) - F_d , \tag{12}$$

with the distal force F_d, the segment mass m_s, the segment acceleration a_s and the gravitational acceleration g. The moment M_p acting across the proximal joint can be calculated in a related manner:

$$M_p = I_s\alpha_s - M_d - \sum_{j=p,d} r_j \times F_j , \tag{13}$$

where M_d denotes the distal moment, I_s is the tensor of inertia for the considered segment and α_s is its angular acceleration. The cross products account for moments resulting from the linear forces applied at the joints with r_j being the vector from segment center of mass to the joint coordinates.

Based on these equations, the forces and moments are propagated along the kinematic chain, resulting in a residual force F_{res} and a residual moment M_{res} at the end of the chain, in our case, the center of mass of the upper body. If the model accelerations perfectly match the GRF/M these residuals are equal to zero, so that the inverse loss is defined as

$$L_{\text{inverse}} = \|F_{\text{res}}\|_2^2 + \|M_{\text{res}}\|_2^2 . \tag{14}$$

The gradient calculation for the back propagation through the inverse layer is described in the supplementary material.

5   Experiments

In this section, the proposed methods are evaluated regarding their capability to learn exterior GRF/M and interior JT from motion. In particular, weakly-supervised learning on small training sets and domain transfer are investigated.

In the following experiments the root mean squared error (RMSE) and the relative RMSE (rRMSE), denoted by ϵ and ϵ_r, respectively, are used to quantitatively evaluate regression results. The rRMSE is normalized to average value ranges of the training set:

$$\epsilon_r = \frac{\epsilon}{\frac{1}{N} \sum_{i \in \text{train set}} [\max(v_t) - \min(v_t)]} . \tag{15}$$

Here, u is the predicted variable and v is the target variable. The number of training samples is denoted by N. All experiments are executed with three random splits into training, validation and test set. The splits are done subject wise, meaning, that sequences of the same subject are exclusively included in one set.

In addition to the experiments, presented in the following sections, an exemplary application to CMU data [6] and a noise experiment are included in the supplementary material.

5.1   Comparison to the State of the Art

In a first experiment, we compare the proposed Dynamics Network and our baseline network to state-of-the-art methods for the inference of GRF/M together with JT. For this purpose, we use the gait set including slow and fast walking. Table 1 lists the corresponding results.

Table 1. RMSE ϵ and rRMSE ϵ_r of GRF/M and JT regression results of the gait data set.

Method	ϵ_f [N/kg]	ϵ_{r_f} [%]	ϵ_m [Nm/kg]	ϵ_{r_m} [%]	ϵ_τ [Nm/kg]
Lv et al. [18]	0.700	20.3	0.077	28.1	–
Zell et al. [34]	**0.388**	**13.1**	**0.041**	**21.1**	0.055
Baseline net	0.591	14.4	0.056	21.2	0.055
F-net	0.626	14.9	0.059	22.1	**0.053**
cFI-net	0.733	14.7	0.064	22.5	0.054

While GRF/M ground truth can be calculated directly from force plate measurements and skeleton fits, the JT ground truth is a dynamics optimization result, associated with a higher uncertainty. Especially using forward dynamics, there are failure cases when the optimization does not converge to a satisfactory minimum. A comparison to these optimized sequences is not informative.

Therefore, the JT evaluation is performed sample wise and only for the learning-based approaches to allow for a fair comparison. The GRF/M are evaluated as complete sequences.

The best performing method with regards to GRF/M regression [34], uses an SVM for gait phase classification and then regresses force and moment parameters on the resulting class subsets via Random Forests. In contrast to this approach the baseline and the Dynamics Network can be trained end-to-end and yield competitive results. Regarding the JT results, the Dynamics Network slightly outperforms the other methods. Instead of minimizing a loss on the JT data directly, the forward loss regards the impact, the JT have on a simulated motion, which results in a stronger loss function. The method by Lv et al. [18] is a maximum a-posteriori inverse dynamics optimization,

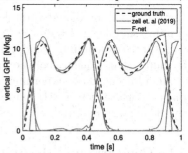

which incorporates a data-prior to guide the optimization towards realistic forces. The values were generated using our own implementation of the approach.

A qualitative comparison between F-net and [34], depicted in Fig. 3, shows that although [34] achieves low error values, the primary gait phase classification may lead to rapidly changing forces at gait phase transitions. This physically implausible behaviour is inherent to the hierarchical structure of the method and does not occur using the proposed network.

Fig. 3. Comparison of predicted vertical GRF by [34] and F-net

5.2 Learning Dynamics on Small Data Sets

The first goal of this work is to learn human locomotion dynamics on small data sets without overfitting to the training samples. In Sect. 4, we introduced two training modes with different degree of supervision to achieve this goal. These training modes are now compared to each other regarding their capability to operate on a training set with decreasing numbers of ground-reaction-set and torque-set samples. The motion-set, that only contains motion information, is always included to its full extend, so that the networks trained with forward and inverse layer, respectively, receive data of all subjects (contained in the training set). This way, we can show the effect of the higher data variability and the benefit of our dynamics layers. For cFI-training the contact-set is used, as well.

Figure 4 shows the RMSE values of predicted JT and their effect in terms of RMSE of simulated motion states. The error values are illustrated for different fractions of the used ground-reaction- and torque-set. A corresponding visualization of the mean regressed GRF/M and JT curves using only 10% of the ground-reaction- and torque-sets can be seen in Fig. 5. A percentage of 10% corresponds to one subject included in the training data, whereas the test data contains motions of 5 subjects in each validation cycle.

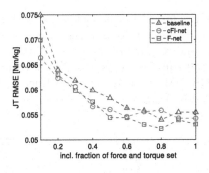 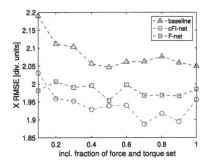

Fig. 4. Reduction of ground reaction and torque samples included in the training set. The left side shows RMSE of JT and the right side the associated RMSE of simulated motion states.

It can be seen, that compared to the baseline, the Dynamics Network yields stable results with significantly decreased training sets, which indicates that the cyclic training is able to compensate the lack of ground truth data by learning from the larger motion-set. With increasing number of ground-truth GRF/M samples (cf. Fig. 4 and Table 1), F-net performs slightly better than cFI-net. This is due to a gap between the model approximation and the measured GRF/M. While F-net mainly learns ground truth GRF/M based on the included force-samples, cFI-net relies on the modelled forces to a similar extent, using the inverse-loss.

5.3 Domain Transfer

The cyclic learning approach of the proposed method can be utilized for weakly- and unsupervised domain transfer. In the following experiment, we perform domain transfer between walking and running. For this purpose, we pre-train networks on the source motion type and apply the cyclic training modes introduced in Sect. 4 to achieve a transfer to the target motion type. During transfer learning no samples from the ground-reaction- and the torque-set are included, so that our methods operate completely independent from dynamics ground truth of the new motion type. This competence is only possible because of the novel dynamics layers. For cFI-training we use the motion-set in combination with the contact-set and minimize the corresponding loss functions alternatingly. During F-training, only the motion-set is used. For this reason, we refer to cFI-training as weakly-supervised and to F-training as unsupervised, although no ground truth data on GRF/M and JT are necessary in both cases. Table 2 lists the related results.

In this experiment, cFI-net clearly outperforms F-net, especially with respect to the GRF predictions. Most likely, the mutual dependency of GRF/M and JT is affecting the performance of F-net. The additional inverse layer, however, is able to solve this issue. In cFI-training the inverse layer is mainly responsible for the learning of realistic GRF/M, while the forward layer yields the matching JT. The contact-loss is necessary, since the minimization of the inverse-loss results in equally large gradients for the ground reaction of both feet. With the consideration of the contact state this overall equalisation is avoided. A visual comparison between the mean predicted GRF/M progressions for cFI-net and the supervised baseline network, is presented in Fig. 6.

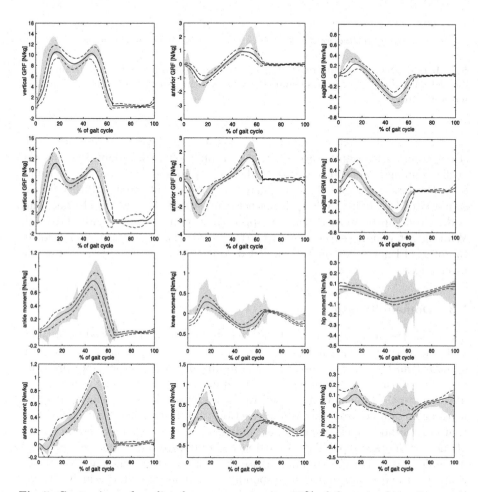

Fig. 5. Comparison of predicted mean curves using 10 % of the ground-reaction- and torque-sets. The first row shows baseline GRF/M results, the second row shows the corresponding predictions using F-net, the third row shows baseline JT results and the last row shows the corresponding results by F-net. The thick line is the mean value, the dashed lines represent standard deviations and the grey area displays the distribution of ground truth and optimized data, respectively.

Table 2. Domain transfer results for a transfer between walking and running in terms of RMSE ϵ and rRMSE ϵ_r for predicted GRF/M and JT.

Transfer	Method	ϵ_f [N/kg]	ϵ_{r_f} [%]	ϵ_m [Nm/kg]	ϵ_{r_m} [%]	ϵ_τ [Nm/kg]
Run	Supervised	1.388	23.6	0.091	21.9	0.041
Gait to Run	F-net	3.942	35.6	0.178	26.1	0.062
Gait to Run	cFI-net	1.445	23.6	0.144	27.0	0.058
Gait	Supervised	0.591	14.4	0.056	21.2	0.055
Run to Gait	F-net	3.579	37.7	0.144	34.8	0.217
Run to Gait	cFI-net	0.685	13.5	0.076	33.2	0.153

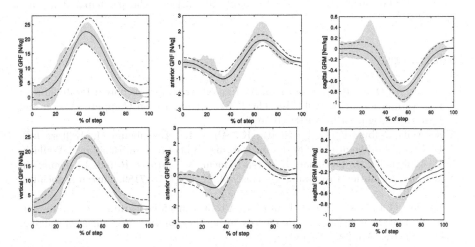

Fig. 6. Domain transfer results for the target domain *running*. The top row shows baseline results, trained from scratch with supervision and the bottom row shows the results obtained using weakly-supervised transfer with cFI-net.

6   Conclusion

This paper proposes a weakly-supervised learning approach for the inference of human dynamics. Ground reaction forces, moments and joint torques are estimated from 3D motions by means of an artificial neural network (NN), that incorporates an inverse and a forward dynamics layer to allow the minimization of a pure motion loss. The method is designed for an optimal use of currently available data of human dynamics. While there exist large public motion capture data sets, the sets that include force plate measurements are often small in comparison. In our framework, the NN estimates joint torques, as well as exterior forces and moments from motion. Together with the forward dynamics layer, that executes an integration of the equations of motion, the network performs a full cycle from motion input to the underlying forces and back to a simulated motion. This way, a pure motion loss can be minimized, allowing for weakly-supervised learning and domain transfer. The experiments show, that the proposed method achieves state-of-the-art results and performs stable, even with few ground truth samples. The domain transfer between walking and running is realized without any ground truth on contact forces and moments. This experiment demonstrates the benefit of the inverse dynamics layer. Together with a loss on the binary contact state, it reliably constrains the exterior forces. The fact that the transfer is achieved with weak-supervision offers tremendous possibilities, especially in view of recent publications in pose reconstruction [1,20,27,30] that make 3D human motion data readily available.

Acknowledgement. Research supported by the European Research Council (ERC-2013-PoC). The authors would like to thank all subjects who participated in data acquisition.

References

1. Arnab, A., Doersch, C., Zisserman, A.: Exploiting temporal context for 3D human pose estimation in the wild. In: The IEEE Conference on Computer Vision and Pattern Recognition (CVPR), June 2019
2. de Avila Belbute-Peres, F., Smith, K., Allen, K., Tenenbaum, J., Kolter, J.Z.: End-to-end differentiable physics for learning and control. In: Bengio, S., Wallach, H., Larochelle, H., Grauman, K., Cesa-Bianchi, N., Garnett, R. (eds.) Advances in Neural Information Processing Systems, vol. 31, pp. 7178–7189. Curran Associates, Inc. (2018)
3. Bastien, G.J., Gosseye, T.P., Penta, M.: A robust machine learning enabled decomposition of shear ground reaction forces during the double contact phase of walking. Gait Posture **73**, 221–227 (2019)
4. Brubaker, M.A., Fleet, D.J.: The kneed walker for human pose tracking. In: 2008 IEEE Conference on Computer Vision and Pattern Recognition, pp. 1–8, June 2008
5. Choi, A., Lee, J.M., Mun, J.H.: Ground reaction forces predicted by using artificial neural network during asymmetric movements. Int. J. Precis. Eng. Manuf. **14**(3), 475–483 (2013)
6. CMU: Human motion capture database (2014). http://mocap.cs.cmu.edu/
7. Degrave, J., Hermans, M., Dambre, J., Wyffels, F.: A differentiable physics engine for deep learning in robotics. Front. Neurorobot. **13**, 6 (2019)
8. Devin, C., Gupta, A., Darrell, T., Abbeel, P., Levine, S.: Learning modular neural network policies for multi-task and multi-robot transfer. In: 2017 IEEE International Conference on Robotics and Automation (ICRA), pp. 2169–2176, May 2017
9. Dwibedi, D., Aytar, Y., Tompson, J., Sermanet, P., Zisserman, A.: Temporal cycle-consistency learning. In: Proceedings of the IEEE/CVF Conference on Computer Vision and Pattern Recognition (CVPR), June 2019
10. Federolf, P., Boyer, K., Andriacchi, T.: Application of principal component analysis in clinical gait research: identification of systematic differences between healthy and medial knee-osteoarthritic gait. J. Biomech. **46**(13), 2173–2178 (2013)
11. Finn, C., Tan, X.Y., Duan, Y., Darrell, T., Levine, S., Abbeel, P.: Deep spatial autoencoders for visuomotor learning. In: 2016 IEEE International Conference on Robotics and Automation (ICRA), pp. 512–519, May 2016

12. Fregly, B.J., Reinbolt, J.A., Rooney, K.L., Mitchell, K.H., Chmielewski, T.L.: Design of patient-specific gait modifications for knee osteoarthritis rehabilitation. IEEE Trans. Biomed. Eng. **54**(9), 1687–1695 (2007)
13. Hoffman, J., et al.: CyCADA: cycle-consistent adversarial domain adaptation (2017)
14. Johnson, L., Ballard, D.H.: Efficient codes for inverse dynamics during walking. In: Proceedings of the Twenty-Eighth AAAI Conference on Artificial Intelligence, pp. 343–349. AAAI Press (2014)
15. Johnson, W., Alderson, J., Lloyd, D., Mian, A.: Predicting athlete ground reaction forces and moments from spatio-temporal driven CNN models. IEEE Trans. Biomed. Eng. (2018)
16. Leporace, G., Batista, L.A., Metsavaht, L., Nadal, J.: Residual analysis of ground reaction forces simulation during gait using neural networks with different configurations. In: 2015 37th Annual International Conference of the IEEE Engineering in Medicine and Biology Society (EMBC), pp. 2812–2815, August 2015
17. Leporace, G., Batista, L., Nadal, J.: Prediction of 3d ground reaction forces during gait based on accelerometer data. Res. Biomed. Eng. **34** (2018)
18. Lv, X., Chai, J., Xia, S.: Data-driven inverse dynamics for human motion. ACM Trans. Graph. **35**(6), 163:1–163:12 (2016)
19. Maas, A.L.: Rectifier nonlinearities improve neural network acoustic models (2013)
20. von Marcard, T., Henschel, R., Black, M.J., Rosenhahn, B., Pons-Moll, G.: Recovering accurate 3D human pose in the wild using IMUs and a moving camera. In: Ferrari, V., Hebert, M., Sminchisescu, C., Weiss, Y. (eds.) ECCV 2018. LNCS, vol. 11214, pp. 614–631. Springer, Cham (2018). https://doi.org/10.1007/978-3-030-01249-6_37
21. Mukhopadhyay, R., Chaki, R., Sutradhar, A., Chattopadhyay, P.: Model learning for robotic manipulators using recurrent neural networks. In: TENCON 2019–2019 IEEE Region 10 Conference (TENCON), pp. 2251–2256, October 2019
22. Oh, S.E., Choi, A., Mun, J.H.: Prediction of ground reaction forces during gait based on kinematics and a neural network model. J. Biomech. **46**(14), 2372–2380 (2013)
23. Reinbolt, J.A., Fox, M.D., Schwartz, M.H., Delp, S.L.: Predicting outcomes of rectus femoris transfer surgery. Gait Posture **30**(1), 100–105 (2009)
24. Schwab, A.L., Delhaes, G.M.J.: Lecture Notes Multibody Dynamics B, wb1413 (2009)
25. Seon Choi, H., Hee Lee, C., Shim, M., In Han, J., Su Baek, Y.: Design of an artificial neural network algorithm for a low-cost insole sensor to estimate the ground reaction force (GRF) and calibrate the center of pressure (COP). Sensors **18**, 4349 (2018)
26. Shah, M., Chen, X., Rohrbach, M., Parikh, D.: Cycle-consistency for robust visual question answering. In: Proceedings of the IEEE/CVF Conference on Computer Vision and Pattern Recognition (CVPR), June 2019
27. Sharma, S., Varigonda, P.T., Bindal, P., Sharma, A., Jain, A.: Monocular 3D human pose estimation by generation and ordinal ranking. In: The IEEE International Conference on Computer Vision (ICCV), October 2019
28. Sim, T., et al.: Predicting complete ground reaction forces and moments during gait with insole plantar pressure information using a wavelet neural network. J. Biomech. Eng. **137** (2015). 9 pages
29. Takahashi, K., Ogata, T., Nakanishi, J., Cheng, G., Sugano, S.: Dynamic motion learning for multi-DoF flexible-joint robots using active-passive motor babbling through deep learning. Adv. Robot. **31**(18), 1002–1015 (2017)

30. Wandt, B., Rosenhahn, B.: RepNet: weakly supervised training of an adversarial reprojection network for 3D human pose estimation. In: Computer Vision and Pattern Recognition (CVPR), June 2019
31. Wang, X., Jabri, A., Efros, A.A.: Learning correspondence from the cycle-consistency of time. In: Proceedings of the IEEE/CVF Conference on Computer Vision and Pattern Recognition (CVPR), June 2019
32. Winter, D.: Biomechanics and Motor Control of Human Movement. Wiley, New York (2009)
33. Xiong, B., et al.: Intelligent prediction of human lower extremity joint moment: an artificial neural network approach. IEEE Access **7**, 29973–29980 (2019)
34. Zell, P., Rosenhahn, B.: Learning inverse dynamics for human locomotion analysis. Neural Comput. Appl. **32**(15), 11729–11743 (2019). https://doi.org/10.1007/s00521-019-04658-z
35. Zell, P., Wandt, B., Rosenhahn, B.: Physics-Based Models for Human Gait Analysis. In: Müller, B., Wolf, S. (eds.) Handbook of Human Motion. Springer, Cham (2018). https://doi.org/10.1007/978-3-319-14418-4_164
36. Zhu, J., Park, T., Isola, P., Efros, A.A.: Unpaired image-to-image translation using cycle-consistent adversarial networks. In: 2017 IEEE International Conference on Computer Vision (ICCV), pp. 2242–2251 (2017)

Journey Towards Tiny Perceptual Super-Resolution

Royson Lee[1]([✉])(iD), Łukasz Dudziak[1](iD), Mohamed Abdelfattah[1](iD),
Stylianos I. Venieris[1](iD), Hyeji Kim[1](iD), Hongkai Wen[1,2](iD),
and Nicholas D. Lane[1,3](iD)

[1] Samsung AI Center, Cambridge, UK
royson.lee@samsung.com
[2] University of Warwick, Coventry, UK
[3] University of Cambridge, Cambridge, UK

Abstract. Recent works in single-image perceptual super-resolution
(SR) have demonstrated unprecedented performance in generating realistic textures by means of deep convolutional networks. However, these
convolutional models are excessively large and expensive, hindering their
effective deployment to end devices. In this work, we propose a neural
architecture search (NAS) approach that integrates NAS and generative adversarial networks (GANs) with recent advances in perceptual
SR and pushes the efficiency of small perceptual SR models to facilitate on-device execution. Specifically, we search over the architectures of
both the generator and the discriminator sequentially, highlighting the
unique challenges and key observations of searching for an SR-optimized
discriminator and comparing them with existing discriminator architectures in the literature. Our tiny perceptual SR (TPSR) models outperform SRGAN and EnhanceNet on both full-reference perceptual metric
(LPIPS) and distortion metric (PSNR) while being up to 26.4× more
memory efficient and 33.6× more compute efficient respectively.

1 Introduction

Single-image super-resolution (SR) is a low-level vision problem that entails the
upsampling of a low-resolution (LR) image to high-resolution (HR). Currently,
the highest-performing solutions to this problem are dominated by the use of convolutional networks, which leave limited space for traditional approaches [6, 26].
Nevertheless, with the SR task being inherently ill-posed, *i.e.* a given LR image
can correspond to many HR images, SR methods follow different approaches. In
this respect, existing supervised solutions can be mainly grouped into two tracks
based on the optimization target: distortion and perceptual quality.

To improve perceptual quality, Ledig *et al.* [27] first empirically showed that
the use of generative adversarial networks (GANs) [15] results in upsampled

Electronic supplementary material The online version of this chapter (https://
doi.org/10.1007/978-3-030-58574-7_6) contains supplementary material, which is available to authorized users.

A. Vedaldi et al. (Eds.): ECCV 2020, LNCS 12371, pp. 85–102, 2020.
https://doi.org/10.1007/978-3-030-58574-7_6

images that lie closer to the natural-image manifold. This observation was later backed theoretically [5] through a proof that using GANs is a principled approach to minimize the distance between the distribution of the upsampled image and that of natural images. Until today, there have been several works focusing on using GANs for perceptual SR, leading to prominent networks such as ESRGAN [48] and EnhanceNet [39].

Although these proposed perceptual SR solutions achieve promising results, they remain extremely resource-intensive in terms of computational and memory demands. Existing *efficient* SR solutions [1,8–11,21,22,28,44,47], on the other hand, are mostly optimized for distortion metrics, leading to blurry results. Hence, in this work, we pose the following question: **Can we build an efficient and constrained SR model while providing high perceptual quality?**

In order to build such SR models, we apply neural architecture search (NAS). In particular, we run NAS on both the discriminator as well as the generator architecture. To the best of our knowledge, our study is the first to search for a discriminator in SR, shedding light on the role of the discriminator in GAN-based perceptual SR. Our contributions can be summarized as follows:

- We adopt neural architecture search (NAS) to find efficient GAN-based SR models, using PSNR and LPIPS [52] as the rewards for the generator and discriminator searches respectively.
- We extensively investigate the role of the discriminator in training our GAN and we show that both existing and new discriminators of various size and compute can lead to perceptually similar results on standard benchmarks.
- We present a tiny perceptual SR (TPSR) model that yields high-performance results in both full-reference perceptual and distortion metrics against much larger full-blown perceptual-driven models.

2 Background and Related Work

In SR, there is a fundamental trade-off between distortion- and perceptual-based methods [5]; higher reconstruction accuracy results in a less visually appealing image and vice versa. Distortion-based solutions [29,46,53] aim to improve the fidelity of the upsampled image, *i.e.* reduce the dissimilarity between the upsampled image and the ground truth, but typically yield overly smooth images.

Perceptual-based methods [27,32,39,48], on the other hand, aim to improve the visual quality by reducing the distance between the distribution of natural images and that of the upsampled images, resulting in reconstructions that are usually considered more appealing. These perceptual SR models are usually commonly evaluated using full-reference methods such as LPIPS [52] or no-reference methods such as NIQE [34], BRISQUE [33], and DIIVINE [36], which are designed to quantify the deviation from natural-looking images in various domains.

Hand-Crafted Super-Resolution Models. Since the first CNN was proposed for SR [10] there has been a surge of novel methods, adapting successful ideas from other high- and low-level vision tasks. For instance, state-of-the-art distortion-driven models such as EDSR [29], RDN [54], and RCAN [53] use residual blocks [17], and attention mechanisms [2], respectively, to achieve competitive fidelity results. Independently, state-of-the-art perceptual-driven SR models have been primarily dominated by GAN-based models such as SRGAN [27] (which uses a combination of perceptual loss [24] and GANs), and ESRGAN [48] (which improves on SRGAN by employing the relativistic discriminator [25]).

Towards efficiency, Dong et al. [11] and Shi et al. [42] proposed reconstructing the upsampled image at the end of a network, rather than at its beginning, to reduce the computational complexity during feature extraction. Since then, numerous architectural changes have been introduced to obtain further efficiency gains. For instance, group convolutions [17] were adopted by Ahn et al. [1], channel splitting [30] by Hui et al. [21,22], and inverse sub-pixel convolutions by Vu et al. [47], all of which significantly reduced the computational cost.

Similar to one of our goals, Chen et al. [7] explored how the discriminator would affect performance in SR by introducing two types of attention blocks to the discriminator to boost image fidelity in both lightweight and large models. Unlike their approach, we optimize for a perceptual metric and explore a wide range of discriminators using standard popular NN operations instead.

Neural Architecture Search for Super-Resolution. Recent SR works aim to build more efficient models using NAS, which has been vastly successful in a wide range of tasks such as image classification [38,55,57], language modeling [56], and automatic speech recognition [12]. We mainly focus on previous works that adopt NAS for SR and refer the reader to Elsken et al. [13] for a detailed survey on NAS. Chu et al. [8,9] leveraged both reinforcement learning and evolutionary methods for exploitation and exploration respectively, considering PSNR, FLOPs and memory in a multi-objective optimization problem. Song et al. [44] argued that searching for arbitrary combinations of basic operations could be more time-consuming for mobile devices, a guideline that was highlighted by Ma et al. [30]. To alleviate that, they proposed searching using evolutionary methods for hand-crafted efficient residual blocks. Although we agree with their approach to utilize platform-specific optimizations, we decided to keep our approach platform-agnostic and only consider models that fit in the practical computational regime based on the models used in the current SoTA SR mobile framework [28]. Most importantly, our work differs from previous NAS with SR approaches as we focus on optimizing the perceptual quality rather than the fidelity of the upsampled images.

Neural Architecture Search for GANs. Recently, Gong et al. [14] presented a way of incorporating NAS with GANs for image generative tasks, addressing unique challenges faced by this amalgamation. Combining NAS with GANs for SR, on the other hand, presents its own set of challenges. For example, as perceptual SR only requires one visually appealing solution, mode collapse might be favorable so their proposed dynamic-resetting strategy is not desirable in our context. Another major difference is that GAN-based methods for SR usually start with a pre-trained distortion model, avoiding undesired local optima and

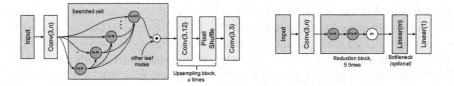

Fig. 1. Structure and search space of the generator (left) and discriminator (right). Orange nodes represent operations which are selected by the controller from the set of available candidates. In the case of the generator, the controller additionally selects only one of the incoming edges as input for each node and, after connections are selected, all leaf nodes are added together to create the cell's output. Linear(n) represents a linear layer with n output units. Operations in yellow blocks are fixed. (Color figure online)

allowing GAN training to be more stable with high-fidelity input images. Therefore, naively applying their approach is not suitable for the task. With fewer restrictions, we are able to search for a discriminator as opposed to manually tuning it to fit the generator.

3   Searching for Tiny Perceptual SR

In the proposed scheme, we extend the original REINFORCE-based NAS framework [56] in order to search for a GAN-based super-resolution model. As a first step, we split the process into two stages. First, we search only for the best generator, using a selected distortion metric to assess different architectures. Next, we utilize the best found model and search for a matching discriminator which would maximize the generator's performance on a selected perceptual metric. Although the same backbone algorithm is used in both cases to conduct the search, the differences between distortion- and GAN-based training require us to approach the two stages with a dedicated methodology, addressing the respective challenges in critical design decisions, including defining the search space and generating reward signals.

We begin with a short introduction to REINFORCE and NAS in Sect. 3.1 and continue to discuss the details related to the specific use-case of perceptual SR. The skeleton models for both the generator and the discriminator are shown in Fig. 1 and the search methodology for both of them is presented in Sects. 3.2 and 3.3 respectively, with a summary shown in Algorithm 1.

3.1   Searching Algorithm

We can formulate our NAS problem in a generic way as:

$$\mathbb{S} = \mathbb{O}_1 \times \mathbb{O}_2 \times \cdots \times \mathbb{O}_n$$
$$E : \mathbb{S} \to \mathbb{R} \tag{1}$$
$$s^\star = \operatorname*{argmax}_{s \in S} E(s)$$

Algorithm 1: A summary of the proposed two-stage approach to searching for a perceptually-good compact SR model

---

Input: search space for the generator $\mathbb{S}_G$ and discriminator $\mathbb{S}_D$, maximum number of steps when searching for generator T_G and discriminator T_D, Mult-Adds limit for the generator f

Output: trained perceptual model $\mathbf{G}^{\bullet}_{\text{best}}$

1   **Function** search($\mathbb{S}, T, E$):
2     $s^* \leftarrow$ NONE
3     $\theta \sim \mathcal{N}$
4   **for** $t \leftarrow 0$ **to** T **do**
5       $s_t \sim \pi_{\theta,\mathbb{S}}$
6       $m_t \leftarrow E(\mathbf{s}_t)$
7   **if** $m_t =$ NONE **then**
8   go back to line 5
9   **end**
10   update s^* using m_t
11      $\theta \leftarrow$ update θ using $\nabla_\theta \log \pi_{\theta,\mathbb{S}}(s_t) R(m_t)$
12   **end**
13   **return** s^*
14 **End Function**

15 **Function** $E_G(s)$:
16     $\mathbf{G} \leftarrow$ construct model according to s and initialize its weights with the cached ones
17     $f_s \leftarrow$ calc Mult-Adds required to run $\mathbf{G}$
18   **if** $f_s > f$ **then**
19   **return** NONE
20   **end**
21     $m \leftarrow$ train and evaluate $\mathbf{G}$ on the proxy distortion task
22   update cached weights according to Eq. 5
23   **return** m
24 **End Function**

25 $s^*_G \leftarrow$ search($\mathbb{S}_G, T_G, E_G$)
26 $\mathbf{G}_{\text{best}} \leftarrow$ construct model using s^*_G, initialize from cache, and train on the full dist. task
27 **Function** $E_D(\mathbf{s})$:
28     $\mathbf{D} \leftarrow$ construct discriminator according to $\mathbf{s}$
29   **return** performance of $\mathbf{G}$ on the proxy perc. task after fine-tuning using $\mathbb{D}$
30 **End Function**

31 $s^*_D \leftarrow$ search($\mathbb{S}_D, T_D, E_D$)
32 $\mathbf{D}_{\text{best}} \leftarrow$ construct discriminator according to s^*_D
33 $\mathbf{G}^{\bullet}_{\text{best}} \leftarrow$ fine-tune $\mathbf{G}_{\text{best}}$ with $\mathbf{D}_{\text{best}}$ on the full perceptual task

---

where $\mathbb{S}$ is a *search space* constructed from n independent *decisions*, $\mathbb{O}_i$ is a set of available *options* for the i-th decision, and E is a selected *evaluation function* which we aim to optimize.

Usually, E is implemented as a sequence of steps: construct a model according to the selected options s, train and evaluate it, and return its performance. In our case specifically, E represents a trained model's performance on a validation set – see the following sections for the details about training and evaluation of different models. Because training takes an excessive amount of time and it is hard to predict the performance of a model without it, brute-forcing the optimization problem in Eq. (1) quickly becomes infeasible as the number of elements in $\mathbb{S}$ increases. Therefore, a standard approach is to limit the search process to at most T models (steps), where T is usually decided based on the available time and computational resources. Given a sequence of T architectures explored during the search $\tau(T) = (s_1, s_2, \cdots, s_T)$, we can approximate the optimization problem in Eq. (1) with its equivalent over the values in $\tau(T)$:

$$s^* \approx s^* = \operatorname*{argmax}_{s \in \tau(T)} E(s) \tag{2}$$

We then use REINFORCE [50] to guide the search and ensure that, as T increases, s_T optimizes E thus providing us with a better approximation. More specifically, we include a probabilistic, trainable policy π_θ (a controller) which, at each search step $t = 1, 2, \cdots, T$, is first sampled in order to obtain a candidate structure s_t and then updated using $E(s_t)$. We use the following standard formulation to optimize this policy:

$$
\begin{aligned}
J(\theta) &= \mathbb{E}_{s \sim \pi_\theta} R(E(s)) \\
\theta_{t+1} &= \theta_t + \beta \nabla_{\theta_t} J(\theta_t) \\
\nabla_{\theta_t} J(\theta_t) &\approx \nabla_{\theta_t} \log \pi_{\theta_t}(s_t) R(E(s_t)) \\
\operatorname*{argmax}_{\theta} J(\theta) &\approx \theta_T
\end{aligned}
\tag{3}
$$

where $R : \mathbb{R} \to \mathbb{R}$ is a *reward function* used to make values of E more suitable for the learning process (*e.g.* via normalization), and β is a learning rate. Please refer to the supplementary material for further details.

3.2   Generator Search

When searching for the generator architecture, we adopt the micro-cell approach. Under this formulation, we focus the search on finding the best architecture of a single cell which is later placed within a fixed template to form a full model. In conventional works, the full model is constructed by stacking the found cell multiple times, forming in this way a deep architecture. In our case, since we aim to find highly compact models, we defined the full-model architecture to contain a single, relatively powerful cell. Furthermore, the single cell is instantiated by selecting 10 operations from the set of available candidates, Op, to assign to 10 nodes within the cell. The connectivity of each node is determined by configuring the input to its operation, selecting either the cell's input or the output of any previous node. Thus, our generator search space (Fig. 1 (left)) is defined as:

$$\mathbb{S}_G = \mathbb{S}_{\text{CELL}} = \underbrace{Op \times \mathbb{Z}_1 \times \cdots \times Op \times \mathbb{Z}_{10}}_{\text{20 elements}} \tag{4}$$

where $\mathbb{Z}_m = \{1, 2, \cdots, m\}$ is a set of indices representing possible inputs to a node. We consider the following operations when searching for the generator:

$$
\begin{aligned}
Op = \{ &\texttt{Conv}(k, n) \text{ with } k = 1, 3, 5, 7;\ \texttt{Conv}(k, n, 4), \\
&\texttt{DSep}(k, n), \text{ and } \texttt{InvBlock}(k, n, 2) \text{ with } k = 3, 5, 7; \\
&\texttt{SEBlock}(), \texttt{CABlock}(), \texttt{Identity} \}
\end{aligned}
$$

where $\mathtt{Conv}(k, n, g{=}1, s{=}1)$ is a convolution with kernel $k \times k$, n output channels, g groups and stride s; $\mathtt{DSep}(k, n)$ is depthwise-separable convolution [18]; $\mathtt{SEBlock}$ is Squeeze-and-Excitation block [19]; $\mathtt{CABlock}$ is channel attention block [53]; and $\mathtt{InvBlock}(k, n, e)$ is inverted bottleneck block [41] with kernel size $k \times k$, n output channels and expansion of e. In the case where a cell constructed from a point in the search space has more than one node which is not used as input to any other node (*i.e.* a leaf node), we add their outputs together and use the sum as the cell's output. Otherwise, the output of the last node is set as the cell's output.

We use weight sharing similar to [37]. That is, for each search step t, after evaluating an architecture $s_t \in \mathbb{S}_G$ we save trained weights and use them to initialize the weights when training a model at step $t + 1$. Because different operations will most likely require weights of different shape, for each node i we keep track of the best weights so far for each operation from the set Op independently. Let $s(i)$ be the operation assigned to the i-th node according to the cell structure s. Further, let $\mathbb{P}_{o,i,t}$ be the set of architectures explored until step t (inclusive) in which o was assigned to the i-th node, that is: $\mathbb{P}_{o,i,t} = \{s \mid s \in \tau(t) \wedge s(i) = o\}$. Finally, let $\theta_{i,o,t}$ represent weights in the cache, at the beginning of step t, for an operation o when assigned to the i-th node, and $\hat{\theta}_{i,o,t}$ represent the same weights after evaluation of s_t (which includes training). Note that $\hat{\theta}_{o,i,t} = \theta_{o,i,t}$ if $s_t(i) \neq o$ as the weights are not subject to training. We can then formally define our weight sharing strategy as:

$$\theta_{o,i,0} \sim \mathcal{N}$$

$$\theta_{o,i,t+1} = \begin{cases} \hat{\theta}_{o,i,t} & \text{if } s_t(i) = o \text{ and} \\ & E(s_t) > \max_{s_p \in \mathbb{P}_{o,i,t-1}} E(s_p) \\ \theta_{o,i,t} & \text{otherwise} \end{cases} \tag{5}$$

As SR models require at least one order of magnitude more compute than classification tasks, we employ a variety of techniques to speed up the training process when evaluating different architectures and effectively explore a larger number of candidate architectures. First, similar to previous works [57], we use lower fidelity estimates, such as fewer epochs with higher batch sizes, instead of performing full training until convergence which can be prohibitively time consuming. Moreover, we use smaller training patch sizes as previous studies [48] have shown that the performance of the model scales according to its training patch size, preserving in this manner the relative ranking of different architectures. Lastly, we leverage the small compute and memory usage of the models in our search space and dynamically assign multiple models to be trained on each GPU. We also constrain the number of Mult-Adds and discard all proposed architectures which exceed the limit before the training stage, guaranteeing the generation of small models while, indirectly, speeding up their evaluation.

After the search has finished, we take the best found design point s^* and train it on the full task to obtain the final distortion-based generator G, before proceeding to the next stage. When performing the final training, we initialize the weights with values from the cache $\theta_{o,i,T}$, as we empirically observed that it helps the generator converge to better minima. Both the proxy and full task aim to optimize the fidelity of the upsampled image and are, thus, validated using PSNR and trained on the training set $\hat{T}$ using the L1 loss, defined as:

$$L_1 = \frac{1}{|\hat{T}|} \sum_{(I^{\mathrm{LR}}, I^{\mathrm{HR}}) \in \hat{T}} |G(I^{\mathrm{LR}}) - I^{\mathrm{HR}}| \qquad (6)$$

with I^{LR} the low-resolution image and I^{HR} the high-resolution ground-truth.

3.3   Discriminator Search

After we find the distortion-based generator model G, we proceed to search for a matching discriminator D that will be used to optimize the generator towards perceptually-good solutions. The internal structure of our discriminator consists of 5 reduction blocks. Each reduction block comprises a sequence of two operations followed by a batch normalization [23] – the first operation is selected from the set of candidate operations Op which is the same as for the generator search; the second one is a reduction operation and its goal is to reduce the spatial dimensions along the x- and y-axes by a factor of 2 while increasing the number of channels by the same factor. To only choose reduction operations from the set of operations derived from Op, we only consider standard convolutions with the same hyperparameters as in Op, but with stride changed to 2 and increased number of output channels:

$$ROp = \{ \; \mathtt{Conv}(k, 2n, 1, 2) \text{ with } k = 1, 3, 5, 7 \text{ and}$$
$$\mathtt{Conv}(k, 2n, 4, 2) \text{ with } k = 3, 5, 7 \; \}$$

As a result, the search space for the discriminator can be defined as:

$$\mathbb{S}_D = \underbrace{Op \times ROp \times \cdots \times Op \times ROp}_{10 \text{ elements}} \qquad (7)$$

After the 5 reduction blocks, the extracted features are flattened to a 1-D vector and passed to a final linear layer (preceded by an optional bottleneck with m outputs), producing a single output which is then used to discriminate between the generated upsampled image, $G(I^{\mathrm{LR}})$ and the ground truth, I^{HR}. Figure 1 (right) shows the overall structure of the discriminator architecture.

To optimize for perceptual quality (Eq. (8)), we use the perceptual loss [24], L_{vgg}, and adversarial loss [15], L_{adv}, on both the proxy and full task. The discriminator is trained on the standard loss, L_D. As observed by previous works [7,39,48], optimizing solely for perceptual quality may lead to undesirable artifacts. Hence, similar to Wang et $al.$ [48], we incorporate L_1 into the generator loss, L_G. Additionally, we validate the training using a full-reference perceptual metric, Learned Perceptual Image Patch Similarity [52] (LPIPS), as we find no-reference metrics such as NIQE to be more unstable since they do not take into account the ground truth. Our generator loss and discriminator loss are as follows:

$$L_{vgg} = \frac{1}{|\hat{T}|} \sum_{(I^{LR}, I^{HR}) \in \hat{T}} (\phi(G(I^{LR})) - \phi(I^{HR}))^2$$

$$L_{adv} = -\log(D(G(I^{LR})))$$

$$L_G = \alpha L_1 + \lambda L_{vgg} + \gamma L_{adv}$$

$$L_D = -\log(D(I^{HR})) - \log(1 - D(G(I^{LR})))$$

(8)

Unlike the generator search we do not use weight sharing when searching for the discriminator. The reason behind this is that we do not want the discriminator to be too good at the beginning of training to avoid a potential situation where the generator is unable to learn anything because of the disproportion between its own and a discriminator's performance. Similar to the generator search stage, we used a lower patch size, fewer epochs, and a bigger batch size to speed up the training. Additionally, from empirical observations in previous works [24,27], the perceptual quality of the upsampled image scales accordingly with the depth of the network layer used. Therefore, we use an earlier layer of the pre-trained VGG network (ϕ) as a fidelity estimate to save additional computations. In contrast to the generator search, we do not impose a Mult-Adds limit to the discriminator as its computational cost is a secondary objective for us, since it does not affect the inference latency upon deployment.

After the search finishes, we collect a set of promising discriminator architectures and use them to train the generator on the full task. At the beginning of training, we initialize the generator with the pre-trained model found in the first stage (Sect. 3.2) to reduce artifacts and produce better visual results.

4   Evaluation

In this section, we present the effectiveness of the proposed methodology. For all experiments, the target models were trained and validated on the DIV2K [45] dataset and tested on the commonly-used SR benchmarks, namely Set5 [3], Set14 [51], B100 [31], and Urban100 [20]. For distortion (PSNR/Structural Similarity index (SSIM) [49]) and perceptual metrics (Natural Image Quality Evaluator [34] (NIQE)/Perceptual Index [4] (PI)), we shaved the upsampled image by its scaling factor before evaluation. For LPIPS, we passed the whole upsampled image and evaluated it on version 0.1 with linear calibration on top of intermediate features in the VGG [43] network[1]. For the exhaustive list of all hyperparameters and system details, please refer to the supplementary material.

---

[1] Provided by https://github.com/richzhang/PerceptualSimilarity.

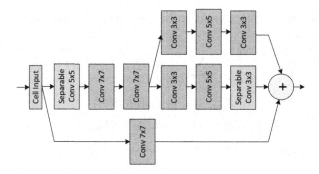

Fig. 2. Discovered cell architecture for the TPSR generator. Each operation is followed by a PReLU [16] activation.

4.1 TPSR Generator

Following Algorithm 1, we began by running the first search stage for the generator architecture to obtain a distortion-driven tiny SR model. During the search, we trained candidate models to perform ×2 upscaling (*i.e.* with one upsampling block) and we set the number of feature maps (n) to 16. Each model was evaluated using PSNR as the target metric and the final reward for the controller was calculated by normalizing the average PSNR of a model.

To obtain the final generator model, we run the generator search for 2,500 steps and stored the highest-performing cell architecture as evaluated on the proxy task. Figure 2 illustrates the obtained cell structure. We refer to this model as TPSR (Tiny Perceptual Super Resolution). For the rest of this section, we use the notation TPSR-X to refer to TPSR when trained with discriminator X and TPSR-NOGAN when TPSR is distortion-driven.

After the end of the first search stage, we trained the discovered TPSR model on the full task for ×2 upscaling and ×4 upscaling, starting from the pre-trained ×2 model, to obtain TPSR-NOGAN. Our NAS-based methodology was able to yield the most efficient architecture of only 3.6G Mult-Adds on ×4 upscaling with performance that is comparable with the existing state-of-the-art distortion-driven models that lie within the same computational regime. Given that our goal was to build a perceptual-based model, we did not optimize our base model further, considering it to be a good basis for the subsequent search for a discriminator. The distortion-based results can be found in the supplementary material.

4.2 Discriminator Analysis

To obtain a discriminator architecture, we utilized the TPSR-NOGAN variant trained on the ×4 upscaling task and searched for a suitable discriminator to minimize the perceptual LPIPS metric. To minimize the instability of the perceptual metric, we evaluated each model by considering the last three epochs and returning the best as the reward for the controller. We also incorporated spectral

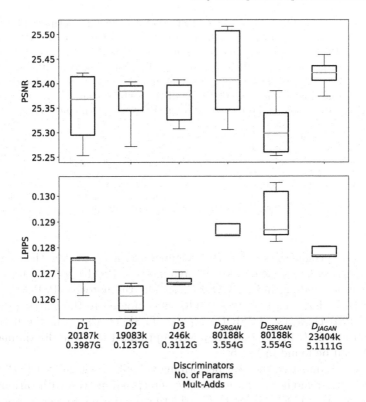

Fig. 3. Performance of TPSR after adversarial training using different discriminators found via NAS (D1, D2, D3) vs. existing discriminators designed for (SRGAN, ESRGAN, JAGAN). TPSR trained on searched discriminators, which are optimized for LPIPS, outperform fixed discriminators in the literature for the targeted metric (LPIPS). Each GAN training was performed 5 times

normalization [35] for the discriminator on both the proxy and the full task. We have found that discriminators of varying size and compute can lead to perceptually similar results (LPIPS). Upon further examinations, we have also found that these upsampled images look perceptually sharper than TPSR-NOGAN's.

In order to evaluate the fidelity of the proxy task, we took the three best performing discriminator candidates based on their performance on the proxy task. We then evaluated our TPSR model when trained with these discriminators on the full task. To compare to models from the literature, we also considered the discriminators that were used in SRGAN [27], ESRGAN [48], and the recently proposed Joint-Attention GAN [7] (JAGAN). Note that the discriminator's architecture in SRGAN and ESRGAN is the same but the latter is trained using the relativistic GAN (RGAN) loss [25]. For more details on how RGAN is adopted for SR, please refer to Wang *et al.* [48].

Each GAN training was performed 5 times and the best performing model, based on the achieved LPIPS on the validation set, was evaluated on the test

Table 1. We compare our ×4 upscaling TPSR models, which are optimized for LPIPS, with perceptual-driven models in the literature. Higher is better for PSNR and lower is better for LPIPS and PI. red/blue represents best/second best respectively. On the optimization target metric, LPIPS, our model (TPSR-D2) achieves the *second best* result while it is the *smallest* among all. Our model outperforms EnhanceNet and SRGAN in visual quality metrics (PSNR & LPIPS) while being 26.4× more memory efficient and 33.6× more compute efficient than SRGAN and EnhanceNet, respectively

Model	Params (K)	Mult-Adds (G)	Set5 PSNR/LPIPS/PI	Set14 PSNR/LPIPS/PI	B100 PSNR/LPIPS/PI	Urban100 PSNR/LPIPS/PI
ESRGAN	16,697	1034.1	30.40/0.0745/3.755	26.17/0.1074/2.926	25.34/0.1083/2.478	24.36/0.1082/3.770
SRGAN	1,513	113.2	29.40/0.0878/3.355	26.05/0.1168/2.881	25.19/0.1224/2.351	23.67/0.1653/3.323
EnhanceNet	852	121.0	28.51/0.1039/2.926	25.68/0.1305/3.017	24.95/0.1291/2.907	23.55/0.1513/3.471
FEQE	96	5.64	31.29/0.0912/5.935	27.98/0.1429/5.400	27.25/0.1455/5.636	25.26/0.1503/5.499
TPSR-D2	61	3.6	29.60/0.076/4.454	26.88/0.110/4.055	26.23/0.116/3.680	24.12/0.141/4.516

benchmarks. Specifically, we took the weighted average (based on the number of images) over the test benchmarks of three metrics: PSNR, NIQE, and LPIPS, and present our findings in Fig. 3. Our chosen discriminators (TPSR-D1, TPSR-D2, TPSR-D3) have led to better results as compared to the existing discriminators (TPSR-D_{SRGAN}, TPSR-D_{ESRGAN}, TPSR-D_{JAGAN}) in the particular perceptual metric (LPIPS) that they were optimized for. The discriminator of TPSR-D2 can be found in Fig. 5.

Finally, we compared the best performing GAN-based generator (TPSR-D2) on common full-reference and no-reference perceptual metrics with various well-known perceptual models (Table 1). Considering our optimized metric, our model outperforms SRGAN and EnhanceNet while being up to 26.4× more memory efficient when compared to EnhanceNet and 33.6× more compute efficient compared to SRGAN. Additionally, our model also achieves higher performance in distortion metrics, indicating higher image fidelity and, therefore, constitutes a dominant solution for full-reference metrics (PSNR & LPIPS) especially with our tiny computational budget. Visual comparisons can be found in Fig. 4.

5   Limitations and Discussion

In this paper, we have presented a NAS-driven framework for generating GAN-based SR models that combine high perceptual quality with limited resource requirements. Despite introducing the unique challenges of our target problem and showcasing the effectiveness of the proposed approach by finding high-performing tiny perceptual SR models, we are still faced with a few open challenges.

The usefulness of NAS approaches which utilize a proxy task to obtain feedback on candidate architectures naturally depends on the faithfulness of the proxy task with regards to the full task. As GANs are known to be unstable and hard to train [40], providing the search with a representative proxy task is even more challenging for them than for other workloads. We were able to partially mitigate this instability by smoothing out accuracy of a trained network, as

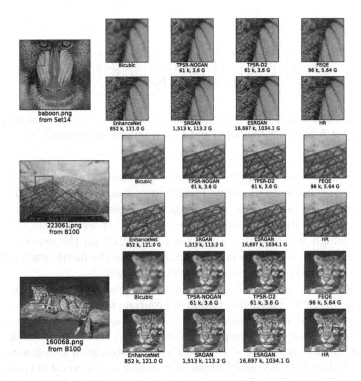

Fig. 4. Visual comparisons among SoTA perceptual-driven networks and TPSR models, with their no. of parameters (left) and mult-add operations (right). Despite the quantitative results that show that TPSR-D2 is better than e.g. SRGAN (Table 1), the qualitative results are arguably worse-off in some images, highlighting a limitation and the need for a better perceptual metric. However, TPSR-D2 still produces better reconstructions than FEQE - the current SoTA for constrained perceptual models.

mentioned in Sect. 4.2. Nevertheless, we still observed that the informativeness of results obtained on the proxy task for GAN-training is visibly worse than *e.g.* results on the proxy task when searching for a generator in the first phase of our method. This instability is reinforced even more when using no-reference perceptual metrics such as NIQE [34] and PI [4] - in which case we observed that training a single model multiple times on our proxy task can result in a set of final accuracies with variance close to the variance of all accuracies of all models explored during the search - rendering it close to useless in the context of searching. In this respect, we adopted LPIPS which, being a full-reference metric, was able to provide the search with a more robust evaluation of proposed architectures. While the strategies we used to improve the stability of the search were adequate for us to obtain decent-performing models, the challenge still remains open and we strongly suspect that overcoming it would be a main step towards improving the quality of NAS with GAN-based perceptual training.

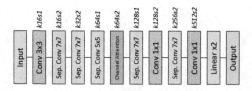

Fig. 5. Discovered architecture of the TPSR discriminator (*D*2). Convolutions are followed by batch normalization and PReLU. k = output tensor depth, s = stride

Another important challenge comprises the selection of a metric that adequately captures perceptual quality. Identifying a metric that closely aligns with human-opinion scores across a wide range of images still constitutes an open research problem with significant invested research effort [4,34,36,52]. In this respect, although we show that optimizing for LPIPS on the average leads to better quantitative results, the inherent limitations of the metric itself might not result to qualitatively better results on certain images.

With our work targeting highly compact models optimized for perceptual quality, it is currently challenging to find appropriate baselines that lie within the same computational and memory footprint regime, as FEQE [47] is, to the best of our knowledge, the only perceptual SR model that meets these specifications. As a result, in this paper, we also present comparisons with significantly larger models, including SRGAN and EnhanceNet, which our method outperforms in our optimized metric. We also compare with ESRGAN which is more than an order of magnitude more expensive than all examined models. Although our design did not outperform ESRGAN, we could extend our method to explore relaxed constraints to allow a slightly larger generator and employ a relativistic discriminator [25]. As our focus is on pushing the limits of building a constrained and perceptual SR model that can be deployed in a mobile SR framework [28], we leave the trade-off between model size and perceptual quality as future work.

Lastly, our method resulted in discriminators that are slightly better than existing discriminators in terms of perceptual performance. Nevertheless, even though the performance gains on LPIPS are marginal, our resulted discriminators are orders of magnitude smaller in terms of model size and computational cost and the obtained gains are consistently better across multiple runs.

6   Conclusion

In this paper, we investigated the role of the discriminator in GAN-based SR and the limits to which we can push perceptual quality when targeting extremely constrained deployment scenarios. In this context, we adopted the use of NAS to extensively explore a wide range of discriminators, making the following key observations on NAS for GAN-based SR: 1) Discriminators of drastically varying sizes and compute can lead to similar perceptually good images; possible solutions for the ill-posed super-resolution problem. 2) Due to this phenomenon and the high variance in the results of popular perceptual metrics, designing a faithful proxy task for NAS is extremely challenging. Nevertheless, we are able to find discriminators that are consistently better than existing discriminators on our chosen metric, generating a tiny perceptual model that outperforms the state-of-the-art SRGAN and EnhanceNet in both full-reference perceptual and distortion metrics with substantially lower memory and compute requirements.

References

1. Ahn, N., Kang, B., Sohn, K.-A.: Fast, accurate, and lightweight super-resolution with cascading residual network. In: Ferrari, V., Hebert, M., Sminchisescu, C., Weiss, Y. (eds.) ECCV 2018. LNCS, vol. 11214, pp. 256–272. Springer, Cham (2018). https://doi.org/10.1007/978-3-030-01249-6_16

2. Bahdanau, D., Cho, K., Bengio, Y.: Neural machine translation by jointly learning to align and translate (2015)

3. Bevilacqua, M., Roumy, A., Guillemot, C., line Alberi Morel, M.: Low-complexity single-image super-resolution based on nonnegative neighbor embedding. In: British Machine Vision Conference (BMVC) (2012)

4. Blau, Y., Mechrez, R., Timofte, R., Michaeli, T., Zelnik-Manor, L.: The 2018 PIRM challenge on perceptual image super-resolution. In: Leal-Taixé, L., Roth, S. (eds.) ECCV 2018. LNCS, vol. 11133, pp. 334–355. Springer, Cham (2019). https://doi.org/10.1007/978-3-030-11021-5_21

5. Blau, Y., Michaeli, T.: The perception-distortion tradeoff. In: IEEE Conference on Computer Vision and Pattern Recognition (CVPR) (2018)

6. Chang, H., Yeung, D.Y., Xiong, Y.: Super-resolution through neighbor embedding. In: Proceedings of the 2004 IEEE Computer Society Conference on Computer Vision and Pattern Recognition (CVPR) (2004)

7. Chen, R., Xie, Y., Luo, X., Qu, Y., Li, C.: Joint-attention discriminator for accurate super-resolution via adversarial training. In: Proceedings of the 27th ACM International Conference on Multimedia (ACM MM), pp. 711–719 (2019)

8. Chu, X., Zhang, B., Ma, H., Xu, R., Li, J., Li, Q.: Fast, accurate and lightweight super-resolution with neural architecture search. ArXiv abs/1901.07261 (2019)

9. Chu, X., Zhang, B., Xu, R., Ma, H.: Multi-objective reinforced evolution in mobile neural architecture search. ArXiv abs/1901.01074 (2019)

10. Dong, C., Loy, C.C., He, K., Tang, X.: Image super-resolution using deep convolutional networks. IEEE Trans. Pattern Anal. Mach. Intell. **38**, 295–307 (2016)

11. Dong, C., Loy, C.C., Tang, X.: Accelerating the super-resolution convolutional neural network. In: Leibe, B., Matas, J., Sebe, N., Welling, M. (eds.) ECCV 2016. LNCS, vol. 9906, pp. 391–407. Springer, Cham (2016). https://doi.org/10.1007/978-3-319-46475-6_25

12. Dudziak, Ł., Abdelfattah, M.S., Vipperla, R., Laskaridis, S., Lane, N.D.: ShrinkML: end-to-end ASR model compression using reinforcement learning. In: Proceedings of Interspeech 2019, pp. 2235–2239 (2019). https://doi.org/10.21437/Interspeech.2019-2811

13. Elsken, T., Metzen, J.H., Hutter, F.: Neural architecture search: a survey. J. Mach. Learn. Res. **20**, 55:1–55:21 (2018)

14. Gong, X., Chang, S., Jiang, Y., Wang, Z.: Autogan: Neural architecture search for generative adversarial networks. In: The IEEE International Conference on Computer Vision (ICCV), October 2019

15. Goodfellow, I., et al.: Generative adversarial nets. In: Advances in Neural Processing Systems (2014)
16. He, K., Zhang, X., Ren, S., Sun, J.: Delving deep into rectifiers: surpassing human-level performance on ImageNet classification. In: 2015 IEEE International Conference on Computer Vision (ICCV), pp. 1026–1034 (2015)
17. He, K., Zhang, X., Ren, S., Sun, J.: Deep Residual Learning for Image Recognition, pp. 770–778 (2016)
18. Howard, A.G., et al.: MobileNets: efficient convolutional neural networks for mobile vision applications. ArXiv abs/1704.04861 (2017)
19. Hu, J., Shen, L., Sun, G.: Squeeze-and-excitation networks. In: 2018 IEEE/CVF Conference on Computer Vision and Pattern Recognition, pp. 7132–7141 (2017)
20. Huang, J., Singh, A., Ahuja, N.: Single image super-resolution from transformed self-exemplars. In: IEEE Conference on Computer Vision and Pattern Recognition (CVPR) (2015)
21. Hui, Z., Gao, X., Yang, Y., Wang, X.: Lightweight image super-resolution with information multi-distillation network. In: Proceedings of the 27th ACM International Conference on Multimedia (ACM MM), pp. 2024–2032 (2019)
22. Hui, Z., Wang, X., Gao, X.: Fast and accurate single image super-resolution via information distillation network. In: CVPR, pp. 723–731 (2018)
23. Ioffe, S., Szegedy, C.: Batch normalization: accelerating deep network training by reducing internal covariate shift. ArXiv abs/1502.03167 (2015)
24. Johnson, J., Alahi, A., Fei-Fei, L.: Perceptual losses for real-time style transfer and super-resolution. In: Leibe, B., Matas, J., Sebe, N., Welling, M. (eds.) ECCV 2016. LNCS, vol. 9906, pp. 694–711. Springer, Cham (2016). https://doi.org/10.1007/978-3-319-46475-6_43
25. Jolicoeur-Martineau, A.: The relativistic discriminator: a key element missing from standard GAN (2018)
26. Kim, K.I., Kwon, Y.: Single-image super-resolution using sparse regression and natural image prior. IEEE Trans. Pattern Anal. Mach. Intell. (TPAMI) **32**, 1127–1133 (2010)
27. Ledig, C., et al.: Photo-realistic single image super-resolution using a generative adversarial network. In: IEEE Conference on Computer Vision and Pattern Recognition (CVPR) (2017)
28. Lee, R., Venieris, S.I., Dudziak, L., Bhattacharya, S., Lane, N.D.: MobiSR: efficient on-device super-resolution through heterogeneous mobile processors. In: The 25th Annual International Conference on Mobile Computing and Networking, MobiCom 2019 (2019). http://doi.acm.org/10.1145/3300061.3345455
29. Lim, B., Son, S., Kim, H., Nah, S., Lee, K.M.: Enhanced deep residual networks for single image super-resolution. In: IEEE Conference on Computer Vision and Pattern Recognition (CVPR) Workshops (2017)
30. Ma, N., Zhang, X., Zheng, H.-T., Sun, J.: ShuffleNet V2: practical guidelines for efficient CNN architecture design. In: Ferrari, V., Hebert, M., Sminchisescu, C., Weiss, Y. (eds.) Computer Vision – ECCV 2018. LNCS, vol. 11218, pp. 122–138. Springer, Cham (2018). https://doi.org/10.1007/978-3-030-01264-9_8
31. Martin, D., Fowlkes, C., Tal, D., Malik, J.: A database of human segmented natural images and its application to evaluating segmentation algorithms and measuring ecological statistics. In: IEEE International Conference on Computer Vision (ICCV) (2001)
32. Mechrez, R., Talmi, I., Shama, F., Zelnik-Manor, L.: Learning to maintain natural image statistics, [arxiv](https://arxiv.org/abs/1803.04626). arXiv preprint arXiv:1803.04626 (2018)

33. Mittal, A., Moorthy, A.K., Bovik, A.C.: No-reference image quality assessment in the spatial domain. IEEE Trans. Image Process. **21**, 4695–4708 (2012)
34. Mittal, A., Soundararajan, R., Bovik, A.C.: Making a "Completely Blind" image quality analyzer. IEEE Signal Process. Lett. **20**, 209–212 (2013)
35. Miyato, T., Kataoka, T., Koyama, M., Yoshida, Y.: Spectral normalization for generative adversarial networks. ArXiv abs/1802.05957 (2018)
36. Moorthy, A.K., Bovik, A.C.: Blind image quality assessment: from natural scene statistics to perceptual quality. IEEE Trans. Image Process. **20**, 3350–3364 (2011)
37. Pham, H.Q., Guan, M.Y., Zoph, B., Le, Q.V., Dean, J.: Efficient neural architecture search via parameter sharing. In: International Conference on Machine Learning (2018)
38. Real, E., Aggarwal, A., Huang, Y., Le, Q.V.: Regularized evolution for image classifier architecture search. CoRR abs/1802.01548 (2018)
39. Sajjadi, M.S.M., Schölkopf, B., Hirsch, M.: EnhanceNet: single image super-resolution through automated texture synthesis. In: 2017 IEEE International Conference on Computer Vision (ICCV), pp. 4501–4510 (2016)
40. Salimans, T., et al.: Improved Techniques for Training GANs. In: Advances in Neural Information Processing Systems (NeurIPS), pp. 2234–2242 (2016)
41. Sandler, M., Howard, A., Zhu, M., Zhmoginov, A., Chen, L.C.: MobileNetV2: inverted residuals and linear bottlenecks. In: IEEE Conference on Computer Vision and Pattern Recognition (CVPR) (2018)
42. Shi, W., et al.: Real-time single image and video super-resolution using an efficient sub-pixel convolutional neural network. In: 2016 IEEE Conference on Computer Vision and Pattern Recognition (CVPR), pp. 1874–1883 (2016)
43. Simonyan, K., Zisserman, A.: Very deep convolutional networks for large-scale image recognition. In: International Conference on Learning Representations (2015)
44. Song, D., Xu, C., Jia, X., Chen, Y., Xu, C., Wang, Y.: Efficient residual dense block search for image super-resolution. In: Thirty-Fourth AAAI Conference on Artificial Intelligence (2020)
45. Timofte, R., et al.: NTIRE 2017 challenge on single image super-resolution: methods and results. In: IEEE Conference on Computer Vision and Pattern Recognition Workshops (CVPRW) (2017)
46. Tong, T., Li, G., Liu, X., Gao, Q.: Image super-resolution using dense skip connections. In: IEEE International Conference on Computer Vision (ICCV) (2017)
47. Vu, T., Nguyen, C.V., Pham, T.X., Luu, T.M., Yoo, C.D.: Fast and efficient image quality enhancement via desubpixel convolutional neural networks. In: Leal-Taixé, L., Roth, S. (eds.) ECCV 2018. LNCS, vol. 11133, pp. 243–259. Springer, Cham (2019). https://doi.org/10.1007/978-3-030-11021-5_16
48. Wang, X., et al.: ESRGAN: enhanced super-resolution generative adversarial networks. In: Leal-Taixé, L., Roth, S. (eds.) ECCV 2018. LNCS, vol. 11133, pp. 63–79. Springer, Cham (2019). https://doi.org/10.1007/978-3-030-11021-5_5
49. Wang, Z., Bovik, A.C., Sheikh, H.R., Simoncelli, E.P.: Image quality assessment: from error visibility to structural similarity. IEEE Trans. Image Process. **13**, 600–612 (2004)
50. Williams, R.J.: Simple statistical gradient-following algorithms for connectionist reinforcement learning. Mach. Learn. **8**, 229–256 (1992)
51. Yang, J., Wright, J., Huang, T.S., Ma, Y.: Image super-resolution via sparse representation. Trans. Img. Proc. **19**(11), 2861–2873 (2010)

52. Zhang, R., Isola, P., Efros, A.A., Shechtman, E., Wang, O.: The unreasonable effectiveness of deep features as a perceptual metric. In: IEEE Conference on Computer Vision and Pattern Recognition (CVPR) (2018)

53. Zhang, Y., Li, K., Li, K., Wang, L., Zhong, B., Fu, Y.: Image super-resolution using very deep residual channel attention networks. In: Ferrari, V., Hebert, M., Sminchisescu, C., Weiss, Y. (eds.) ECCV 2018. LNCS, vol. 11211, pp. 294–310. Springer, Cham (2018). https://doi.org/10.1007/978-3-030-01234-2_18

54. Zhang, Y., Tian, Y., Kong, Y., Zhong, B., Fu, Y.: Residual dense network for image super-resolution. In: The IEEE Conference on Computer Vision and Pattern Recognition (CVPR) (2018)

55. Zhong, Z., Yan, J., Wu, W., Shao, J., Liu, C.L.: Practical block-wise neural network architecture generation. In: 2018 IEEE/CVF Conference on Computer Vision and Pattern Recognition, pp. 2423–2432 (2018)

56. Zoph, B., Le, Q.V.: Neural architecture search with reinforcement learning. In: International Conference on Learning Representations (2017). https://openreview.net/forum?id=r1Ue8Hcxg

57. Zoph, B., Vasudevan, V., Shlens, J., Le, Q.V.: Learning transferable architectures for scalable image recognition. In: 2018 IEEE/CVF Conference on Computer Vision and Pattern Recognition, pp. 8697–8710 (2018)

What Makes Fake Images Detectable? Understanding Properties that Generalize

Lucy Chai$^{(\boxtimes)}$, David Bau, Ser-Nam Lim, and Phillip Isola

MIT CSAIL, Cambridge, MA 02139, USA
{lrchai,davidbau,phillipi}@csail.mit.edu, sernam@gmail.com

Abstract. The quality of image generation and manipulation is reaching impressive levels, making it increasingly difficult for a human to distinguish between what is real and what is fake. However, deep networks can still pick up on the subtle artifacts in these doctored images. We seek to understand what properties of fake images make them detectable and identify what generalizes across different model architectures, datasets, and variations in training. We use a patch-based classifier with limited receptive fields to visualize which regions of fake images are more easily detectable. We further show a technique to exaggerate these detectable properties and demonstrate that, even when the image generator is adversarially finetuned against a fake image classifier, it is still imperfect and leaves detectable artifacts in certain image patches. Code is available at https://github.com/chail/patch-forensics.

Keywords: Image forensics · Generative models · Image manipulation · Visualization · Generalization

1 Introduction

State-of-the-art image synthesis algorithms are constantly evolving, creating a challenge for fake image detection methods to match the pace of content creation. It is straightforward to train a deep network to classify real and fake images, but of particular interest is the ability of fake image detectors to generalize to unseen fake images. What artifacts do these fake image detectors look at, and which properties can allow a detector released today to work on novel fake images?

Generalization is highly desired in machine learning, with the hope that models work not only on training data, but also on related held-out examples as well. For tasks like object detection and classification, this has been accomplished with successively deeper and deeper networks that incorporate the context of the entire image to learn about global semantics and object characteristics. On the other hand, to learn image manipulation artifacts that are shared across various image generation pipelines, global content is not the only signal that matters. In

Electronic supplementary material The online version of this chapter (https://doi.org/10.1007/978-3-030-58574-7_7) contains supplementary material, which is available to authorized users.

fact, two identical generators trained on the same training data, differing only in the random initialization seed, can create differences in content detectable by a deep network classifier [35]. Instead of these differences, we seek to identify what image generators have *in common*, so that training on examples generated from one model can help us identify fake images from another model.

Across different facial image generators, we hypothesize that global errors can differ but local errors may transfer: the global facial structure can vary among different generators and datasets, but local patches of a generated face are more stereotyped and may share redundant artifacts. Therefore, these local errors can be captured by a classifier focusing on textures [9] in small patches. We investigate a fully convolutional approach to training classifiers, allowing us to limit the receptive field of the model to focus on image patches. Furthermore, these patch-based predictions offer us a natural way to visualize patterns that are indicative of a real or fake image.

Using a suite of synthetic face datasets that span fully generative models [16,17,19,31] and facial manipulation methods [32], we find that more complex patches, such as hair, are detectable across various synthetic image sources when training on images from a single source. In one of our early experiments, however, we observed that we could obtain misleadingly high generalization simply due to subtle differences in image preprocessing – therefore, we introduce careful preprocessing to avoid simply learning differences in image formatting.

With a fixed classifier, an attacker can simply modify the generator to create adversarial examples of fake images, forcing them to become misclassified. Accordingly, we finetune a GAN to create these adversarial examples. We then show that a newly trained classifier can still detect images from this modified GAN, and we investigate properties of these detected patches. Our results here suggest that creating a coherent fake image without any traces of local artifacts is difficult: the modified generator is still unable to faithfully model certain regions of a fake image in a way that is indistinguishable from real ones.

Detecting fake images is a constant adversarial game with a number of ethical considerations. As of today, no method is completely bulletproof. Better generators, out-of-distribution images, or adversarial attacks [5,11] can defeat a fake-image detector, and our approach remains vulnerable to many of these same shortcomings. Furthermore, we train on widely used standard face datasets, but these are still images of real individuals. To protect the privacy of people in the dataset, we blur all real faces and manipulated real faces used in our figures. Our contributions are summarized as follows:

- To avoid learning image formatting artifacts, we preprocess our images to reduce formatting differences between real and fake images.
- We use a fully-convolutional patch-based classifier to focus on local patches rather than global structure, and test on different model resolutions, initialization seeds, network architectures, and image datasets.
- We visualize and categorize the patches that are most indicative of real or fake images across various test datasets.

- To visualize detectable properties of fake images, we manipulate the generated images to exaggerate characteristic attributes of fake images.
- Finetuned generators are able to overcome a fake-image detector, but a subsequent classifier shows that detectable mistakes still occur in certain image patches.

2   Related Work

Image Manipulation. Verifying image authenticity is not just a modern problem – historical instances of photo manipulation include a well-known portrait of Abraham Lincoln[1] and instances of image censorship in the former Soviet Union[2]. However, recent developments in graphics and deep learning make creating forged images easier than ever. One of these manipulation techniques is image splicing, which combines multiple images to form a composite [12]. This approach is directly relevant to face swapping, where a source face is swapped and blended onto a target background to make a person appear in a falsified setting. The deep learning analogue of face swapping, Deepfakes [1], has been the focus of much recent media attention. In parallel, improvements in generative adversarial networks (GANs) form another threat, as they are now able to create shockingly realistic images of faces simply from random Gaussian noise [16,17].

Automating Detection of Manipulated Images. Given the ease in creating manipulated images nowadays and the potential to use them for malicious purposes, a number of efforts have focused on automating detection of manipulated images. A possible solution involves checking for consistency throughout the image – examples include predicting metadata [14] or other low-level artifacts [27–29], learning similar embeddings for nearby patches [38], or learning similarity graphs from image patches [25]. Other works have focused on training classifiers for the detection task, using a deep network either directly on RGB images [2,4,32] or alternative image representations [7,26]. [30] uses a combination of both: a CNN to extract features over image patches and a separate classifier for prediction. Here we also take a patch-wise approach, and we use these patches to visualize the network decisions.

Can Detectors Generalize? The class of potential manipulations is so large that it is infeasible to cover all possible cases. Can a detector learn to distinguish real and fake images from one source and transfer that knowledge to a different source? Preprocessing is one way to encourage generalization, such as using spectral features [37] or adding blur and random noise [34]. [33] generalizes across a wide variety of datasets simply by adding various levels of augmentation. Specialized architectures also help generalization: for example [8] uses an

---

[1] https://www.bbc.com/future/article/20170629-the-hidden-signs-that-can-reveal-if-a-photo-is-fake.

[2] https://en.wikipedia.org/wiki/Censorship_of_images_in_the_Soviet_Union.

autoencoder with a bottleneck that encourages different embeddings for real and fake images. A challenge with generalization is that the classifiers are not explicitly trained on the domain they are tested on. [22] demonstrates that it is possible to simulate the domain of manipulated images; by applying warping to source images, they can detect deepfake images without using manipulated images in classifier training. [21] further studies generalization across different facial manipulation techniques also using a simulated domain of blended real images. However, a remaining question is what features do these models rely on to transfer knowledge among different domains, which we seek to investigate here.

Classification with Local Receptive Fields. We use patch-based classification to visualize properties that generalize. Small receptive fields encourage the classifier to focus on local artifacts rather than global semantics, which is also an approach taken in GAN discriminators to encourage synthesis of realistic detailed textures [15]. A related concept is the Markovian generative adversarial network for texture synthesis [20]; the limited receptive field makes the assumption that only pixels within a certain radius affect the output, and the pixels outside that radius are independent from the output. [24] demonstrate a method for converting deep neural classifiers to fully convolutional networks and use patch-wise training, allowing the model to scale efficiently to arbitrarily-sized inputs, used for the task of semantic segmentation.

3   Using Patches for Image Forensics

Rather than training a network to predict a global "real" or "fake" decisions for an image, we use shallow networks with limited receptive fields that focus on small patches of the image. This approach allows us to localize regions of the image that are detected to be manipulated and ensemble the patch-wise decisions to obtain the overall prediction.

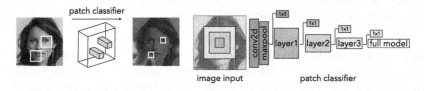

Fig. 1. We use a classifier with small receptive fields to obtain a heatmap over the patch-wise output. To obtain this patch classifier, we truncate various deep learning models after an initial sequence of layers.

3.1   Models for Patch-Based Classification

Modern deep learning architectures typically consist of a series of modular blocks. By truncating the models after an intermediate block, we can obtain model predictions based on a local region of the image, where truncating earlier in the layer sequence results in a smaller receptive field, while truncating after more layers results in a larger receptive field. We then add a 1×1 convolution layer after this truncated backbone to convert the feature representation into a binary real-or-fake prediction. We experiment with Resnet and Xception as our model backbones – generally we observe that Xception blocks perform better than Resnet blocks, however we also report results of the top performing Resnet block. We provide additional details on the model architecture and receptive field calculations in Supplementary Material Sect. 2.3.

The truncation operation reduces the size of the model's receptive field, and yields a prediction for a receptive-field-sized patch of the input, rather than the entire image at once. This forces the models to learn local properties that distinguish between real and fake images, where the same model weights are applied in a sliding fashion over the entire image, and each output prediction is only a function of a small localized patch of the image. We apply a cross entropy loss to each patch; i.e. every real patch should be considered real, and every fake image patch should be considered fake:

$$\mathcal{L}(\mathbf{x}) = \frac{1}{|P|} \sum_{i,j} \sum_{t} t \log f^t(x_{i,j}) \tag{1}$$

where f is the model output after a softmax operation to normalize the logits, t indexes over the real and fake output for binary classification, (i,j) indexes over the receptive field patches, and $|P|$ is the total number of patches per image. We train these models with the Adam optimizer with default learning rate, and terminate training when validation accuracy does not improve for a predetermined number of epochs.

By learning to classify patches, we increase the ratio of data points to model parameters: each patch of the image is treated independently, and the truncated models are smaller. The final classification output is an ensemble of the individual patch decisions rather than a single output probability. To aggregate patches at inference time, we take a simple average after applying a softmax operation to the patch-wise predictions:

$$t^* = \arg \max_{t} \left(\frac{1}{|P|} \sum_{i,j} f^t(x_{i,j}) \right) \tag{2}$$

The averaging approach can be applied in both cases where the image is wholly generated, or when only part of the image is manipulated. For example, when a generated face is spliced onto a real background, the background patches may not be predicted as fake; in this case, because the same background is present in both real and fake examples, the model remains uncertain in these locations.

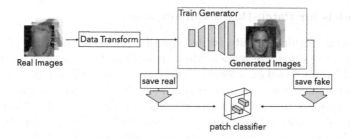

Fig. 2. To minimize the effect of image preprocessing artifacts - in which real and fake images undergo different preprocessing operations – we pass real images through the same data transform as used to train the generator. We then save the real and fake images using identical pipelines.

3.2   Dataset Preparation

Image Preprocessing. A challenge with fully generative images, such as those created by GANs, is that fake images can be saved with arbitrary codecs, e.g., we decide whether we want to save the image in JPG or PNG format. However, the set of real images is saved with a fixed codec when the original dataset is created. When training a classifier on real and fake images with subtly different preprocessing pipelines, the classifier can simply learn to detect the differences in preprocessing. If the test images also have this inconsistency, we would appear to obtain high accuracy on the test set, even though the classifier is really only detecting formatting artifacts. One way to mitigate this disparity is to apply data augmentation to reduce the effect of these differences [33,34].

We preprocess the images to make our real and fake dataset as similar as possible, in an effort to isolate fake image artifacts and minimize the possibility of learning differences in preprocessing. We create the "real" dataset by passing the real images through the generator's data loading pipeline (e.g. resizing) and saving the real images *after* this step in lossless PNG format (Fig. 2). We save the fake images in PNG format from the generator output, so the remaining differences between real and fake images are due to artifacts of the generator. We then resize all images to the same size using Lanczos interpolation before saving to file. Additional details are provided in Supplementary Material Sect. 2.1.

We take these precautions because any minor difference in preprocessing is easily learnt by the fake-image classifier and leads to an illusion of increased generalization capacity (for example, differences in the image codec leads to perfect average precision across various test datasets; see Supplementary Material Sect. 2.1). This approach allows us to focus on the inherent differences between real images and generated ones to minimize any potential confounders due to preprocessing. In the remainder of this section, we briefly detail the image generation and manipulation methods that we investigate in our experiments.

Fully Generative Models. The first class of models we consider are fully generative models which map a random sample from a known distribution (e.g. a multivariate Gaussian) to an image. *Progressive GAN* (PGAN) [16] is one recent example, which uses a progressive training schedule to increase the output resolution of images during training. We use the publicly available PGAN model trained on the CelebA-HQ face dataset. We also train several other PGANs to various smaller resolutions and on the more diverse FFHQ face dataset. *StyleGAN* (SGAN) [17] introduces an alternative generator architecture which incorporates the latent code into intermediate layers of the generator, resulting in unsupervised disentanglement of high-level attributes, e.g., hair and skin tone. We use the public versions of StyleGAN on the CelebA-HQ and FFHQ datasets, and StyleGAN2 [18] on the FFHQ dataset. In additional to PGAN and SGAN, we also consider the *Glow* generator [19], a flow-based model using modified 1×1 invertible convolutions that optimizes directly for log-likelihood rather than adversarial loss. We use the public Glow generator trained on CelebA-HQ faces. Finally, we also include a face generator based on a *Gaussian Mixture Model* (GMM) rather than convolutional layers [31]; the GMM uses low-rank plus diagonal Gaussians to efficiently model covariance in high-dimensional outputs such as images. We train the GMM model on the CelebA [23] dataset using default parameters.

Facial Manipulation Models. We use the FaceForensics++ dataset [32], which includes methods for identity manipulation and expression transfer. Identity manipulation approaches, such as *FaceSwap*, paste a source face onto a target background; specifically, FaceSwap fits detected facial landmarks to 3D model and then projects the face onto the target scene. The deep learning analogue to FaceSwap is the *Deepfake* technique, which uses a pair of autoencoders with a shared encoder to swap the source and target faces. On the other hand, expression transfer maps the expression of a source actor onto the face of a target. *Face2Face* achieves this by tracking expression parameters of the face in a source video and applying them to a target sequence. *Neural Textures* uses deep networks to learn a texture map and a neural renderer to modify the expression of the target face.

3.3 Baseline Models

We train and evaluate full MesoInception4 [2], Resnet [13], and Xception [6] models on the same datasets that we use to train the truncated classifiers. Following [2], we train MesoInception4 using squared error loss. For the Resnet model and the Xception model, also used in [32], we train with standard two-class cross entropy loss. We train these models from scratch as they are not initially trained for this classification task. Finally, we also compare to a model trained to detect CNN artifacts via blurring and compression augmentations [33]. For this model, we finetune at a learning rate of 1e-6 using similar augmentation parameters as the original paper to improve its performance specifically on face datasets. We use the same stopping criteria based on validation accuracy for all baseline models as we use for the truncated models.

4 Experiments

4.1 Classification via Patches

Nowadays with access to public source code, it becomes easy for anyone to train their own image generators with slight modifications. We conduct two experiments to test generalization across simple changes in (1) generator size and (2) the weight initialization seed. In addition to the public 1024px PGAN, we train PGANs for 512, 256, and 128px resolutions on the CelebA-HQ dataset and sample images from each generator. We then train a classifier using only images from the 128px generator.

We test the classifier on generated images from the remaining resolutions, using average precision (AP) as a metric (Table 1; left). Here, the full-model baselines tend to perform worse on the unseen test resolutions compared to the truncated models. However, adding blur and JPEG augmentations in [33] helps to overcome the full-model limitations, likely hiding the resizing artifacts. Of the truncated models, the AP tends to decrease on the unseen test images as the receptive field increases, although there is a slight decline when the receptive field is too small with the Xception Block 1 model. On average across all resolutions, the Xception Block 2 model obtains highest AP.

Table 1. Average precision across PGANs trained to different resolutions or with different random initialization seeds. The classifier is trained on a fake images from a 128px GAN and real images at 128px resolution. AP on the test set corresponding to training images is colored in gray.

Model depth	Resolution				Model seed			
	128	256	512	1024	0	1	2	3
Resnet Layer 1	100.0	99.99	99.60	96.95	100.0	100.0	100.0	100.0
Xception Block 1	100.0	100.0	99.87	98.53	100.0	100.0	100.0	100.0
Xception Block 2	100.0	100.0	100.0	99.98	100.0	100.0	100.0	100.0
Xception Block 3	100.0	100.0	100.0	99.92	100.0	100.0	100.0	100.0
Xception Block 4	100.0	100.0	99.92	99.34	100.0	100.0	100.0	100.0
Xception Block 5	100.0	100.0	98.90	91.18	100.0	100.0	100.0	100.0
[2] MesoInception4	100.0	99.59	98.15	87.00	100.0	99.99	99.82	99.95
[13] Resnet-18	99.99	96.85	91.75	80.17	99.99	98.41	95.20	95.02
[6] Xception	100.0	99.94	99.84	97.28	100.0	100.0	99.99	100.0
[33] CNN (p = 0.1)	100.0	99.99	99.97	99.78	100.0	100.0	100.0	100.0
[33] CNN (p = 0.5)	100.0	100.0	99.99	99.83	100.0	100.0	100.0	100.0

Next, we train four PGANs to 128px resolution with different weight initialization seeds. We train the classifier using fake images drawn from one of the generators, and test on the remaining generators (Table 1; right). Surprisingly, even when the only difference between generators is the random seed, the full Resnet-18 model makes errors when classifying fake images generated by the three other GANs. This suggests that fake images generated by different PGANs differ slightly between the different initialization seeds (as also noted in [35]). The MesoInception4 and Xception architectures are more robust to model seed, and so is blur/JPG augmentation. The truncated models with reduced receptive field are also robust to model seed differences.

Table 2. Average precision on different model architectures and an alternative dataset (FFHQ). The classifier is trained on 1024px PGAN random samples and reprojected PGAN images on the CelebA-HQ dataset. For the Glow model (*) we observe better performance when classifier training does not include reprojected images for the truncated models; additional results in Supplementary Material Sect. 2.4. AP on the test set corresponding to training images is colored in gray.

Model	PGAN	Architectures			FFHQ dataset		
		SGAN	Glow*	GMM	PGAN	SGAN	SGAN2
Resnet Layer 1	100.0	97.22	72.80	80.69	99.81	72.91	71.81
Xception Block 1	100.0	98.68	95.48	76.21	99.68	81.35	77.40
Xception Block 2	100.0	99.99	67.49	**91.38**	**100.0**	90.12	90.85
Xception Block 3	100.0	**100.0**	74.98	80.96	100.0	92.91	**91.45**
Xception Block 4	100.0	99.99	66.79	42.82	100.0	**95.85**	90.62
Xception Block 5	100.0	100.0	60.44	48.92	100.0	93.09	89.08
[2] MesoInception4	100.0	97.90	49.72	45.98	98.71	80.57	71.27
[13] Resnet-18	100.0	64.80	47.06	54.69	79.20	51.15	52.37
[6] Xception	100.0	99.75	55.85	40.98	99.94	85.69	74.33
[33] CNN (p = 0.1)	100.0	98.41	90.46	50.65	99.95	90.48	85.27
[33] CNN (p = 0.5)	100.0	97.34	**97.32**	73.33	99.93	88.98	84.58

We then test the ability of patch classifiers to generalize to different generator architectures (Table 2; left). To create a training set of PGAN fake images, we combine two datasets – random samples from the generator, as well as images obtained by reprojecting the real images into the GAN following [3]. Intuitively, this reprojection step creates fake images generated by the GAN that are as close as possible to their corresponding real images, forcing the classifier to focus on the remaining differences (also see Supplementary Material Sects. 1.2 and 2.4). We then test the classifier on SGAN, Glow, and GMM face generators. We show additional results training on only PGAN fake samples, as well as only on reprojected images as the fake dataset in Supplementary Material Sect. 2.4 (on the Glow model, AP is substantially better when trained without the reprojected images). Generalizing to the SGAN architecture is easiest, due to the many similarities between the PGAN and SGAN generators. With the exception of the Glow generator, the truncated models obtain higher AP compared to the larger classifiers with a fraction of the number of parameters.

Lastly, we test the classifiers' ability to generalize to a different face dataset (Table 2; right). Using the same classifiers trained on CelebA-HQ faces and PGAN samples and reprojections, we measure AP on real images from the FFHQ dataset and fake images from PGAN, SGAN, and SGAN2 trained on FFHQ faces. The truncated classifiers improve AP, particularly on the Style-based generators. The FFHQ dataset has greater diversity in faces than CelebA-HQ; however, small patches, such as hair, are likely similar between the two datasets. Using small receptive fields allows models to ignore global differences between images from different generators and datasets and focus on shared generator artifacts, perhaps explaining why truncated classifiers perform better than full models.

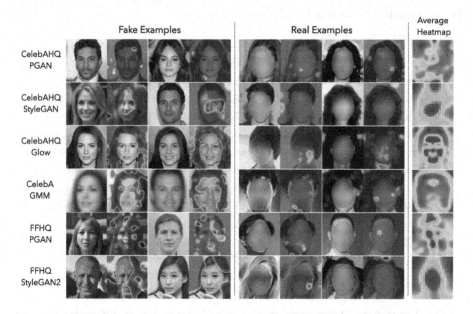

Fig. 3. Heatmaps based on the patch-wise predictions on real and fake examples from each dataset and fake image generator. We normalize all heatmaps between 0 and 1 and show fake values in blue and real values in red. We also show the average heatmap over the 100 easiest and fake examples, where red is most indicative of the correct class.

4.2   What Properties of Fake Images Generalize?

What artifacts do classifiers learn that allow them to detect fake images generated from different models? Since the patch-based classifiers output real-or-fake

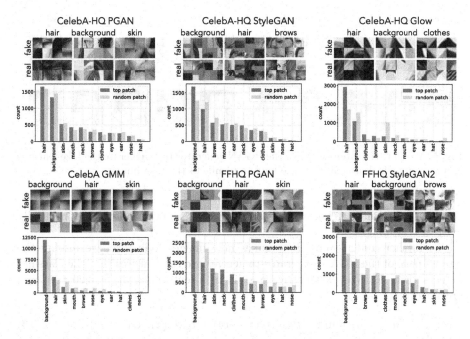

Fig. 4. We take a pretrained segmentation network to assign the most predictive patch in real and fake images to a semantic cluster. We find that the fake-image classifier (which was only trained on the CelebA-HQ dataset with PGAN fake images) relies on patches such as hair, background, clothing, and mouths to make decisions.

predictions over sliding patches of a query image, we use these patch-wise predictions to draw heatmaps over the images and visualize what parts of an image are predicted as more real or more fake (Fig. 3). Using the classifiers trained on CelebA-HQ PGAN images, we show examples of the prediction heatmaps for the other face generators and on the FFHQ dataset, using the best performing patch model for each column in Table 2. We also show an averaged heatmap over the 100 most real and most fake images, where the red areas indicate regions most indicative of the correct class (Fig. 3; right). The average heatmaps highlight predominately hair and background areas, indicating that these are the regions that patch-wise models rely on when classifying images from unseen test sources.

Next, we take a pretrained facial segmentation network to partition each image into semantic classes. For the most predictive patch in each image, we assign the patch to a cluster from the segmentation map, and plot the distribution of these semantic clusters (Fig. 4). We also sample a random patch in each image and assign it to a semantic cluster for comparison. Using the segmentation model, the predominant category of patches tends to be hair or background, with clothes, skin, or brows comprising the third-largest category. Qualitatively, many of the fake patches contain boundary edges such as those between hair and background or hair and skin, suggesting that creating a realistic boundary

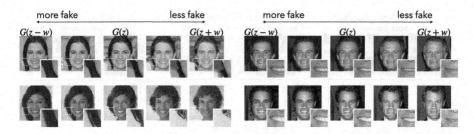

Fig. 5. We shift the latent space of the PGAN generator to exaggerate the fake features of an image, which accentuates the hair and smile of the fake images.

is difficult for image generators to imitate, whereas crisp boundaries naturally exist in real images.

To further understand what makes fake images look fake, we modify the latent space of the PGAN generator to accentuate the features that the classifier detects (Fig. 5). We parametrize a shift in latent space by a vector w, and optimize:

$$w^* = \arg\min_w \mathbb{E}_z \left[L_{\text{fake}}(G(z - w)) + L_p(G(z), \ G(z - w)) \right] \tag{3}$$

where L_{fake} refers to the classifier loss on fake images [10], and L_p is a perceptual loss regularizer [36] to ensure that the modified image does not deviate too far from the original. Applying this vector to latent space samples accentuates hair and smiling with teeth, which are both complex textures and likely difficult for generators to recreate perfectly (Fig. 5). By applying the shift in the opposite direction, $G(z + w)$, we see a reduction these textures, in effect minimizing the presence of textures that are more challenging for the generator to imitate.

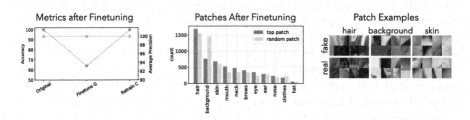

Fig. 6. We finetune the PGAN generator to evade detection by the fakeness classifier. When we subsequently train a new classifier, we find that the finetuned generator still has detectable artifacts, but now predominantely less in background patches.

4.3   Finetuning the Generator

With access to gradients from the classifier, an easy adversarial attack is to modify the generator to evade detection by the classifier. Will this now make the previously identified fake patches undetectable? To investigate this, we finetune a PGAN to create adversarial fake samples that are classified as real. To ensure that the images remain realistic, we jointly optimize the classifier loss and GAN loss on the CelebA-HQ dataset:

$$\mathcal{L} = \min_G \max_D \left[\mathcal{L}_{GAN}(G, D) + \mathcal{L}_{real}(G, C) \right]; \qquad (4)$$

i.e., we optimize both the generator and discriminator with the added constraint that the generator output should be predicted as real by the classifier C. Fine-tuning the generator does not drastically change the generated output (see Supplementary Material Sect. 2.7), but it decreases the classifier's accuracy from 100% to below 65% (Fig. 6). Using a variable threshold (AP) is less sensitive to this adversarial finetuning. We train a second classifier using images from the finetuned generator, which is able to recover in accuracy. We then compute the most predictive image patches for the retrained classifier and cluster them according to semantic category. Compared to the patches captured by the first classifier, this retrained classifier relies less on background patches and more on facial features, suggesting that artifacts in typically solid background patches are easiest for the generator to hide, while artifacts in more textured regions such as hair still remain detectable.

4.4   Facial Manipulation

Unlike the fully-generative scenario, facial manipulation methods blend content from two images, hence only a portion of the image is manipulated. Here, we train on each of the four FaceForensics++ datasets [32], and test generalization to the remaining three datasets (Table 3). We compare the effect of different receptive fields using truncated models, and investigate which patches are localized.

In these experiments, training on Face2Face images yields the best generalization to remaining datasets. On the other hand, generalization to FaceSwap images is the hardest – training on the other manipulation methods does not generalize well to FaceSwap images, and training on FaceSwap does not generalize well to other manipulation methods. Compared to the full-model baselines, we find that truncated patch classifiers tend to generalize when trained on the Face2Face or Deepfakes domains. Adding augmentations to training [33] can also boost results in some domains. While we do not use mask supervision during training, [21] notes that using this additional supervision signal improves generalization.

Next, we seek to investigate which patches are identified as predictive using the truncated classifiers in the facial manipulation setting. Unlike the fully generative scenario in which the classifiers tend to focus on the background, these classifiers trained on facial manipulation focus on the face region (without explicit supervision of the face location). In particular, when trained on the Face2Face manipulation method, the classifiers use predominately the mouth region to classify Deepfakes and NeuralTextures manipulation, with eyes or nose as a secondary feature depending on the manipulation method (Fig. 7). We show additional visualizations in Supplementary Material.

Table 3. Average precision on FaceForensics++ [32] datasets. Each model is trained on one dataset and evaluated on the remaining datasets.

Model depth	Train on Deepfakes				Train on Neural Tex.			
	DF	NT	F2F	FS	DF	NT	F2F	FS
Resnet Layer 1	98.97	**74.99**	**71.74**	57.15	**70.32**	86.93	65.04	52.37
Xception Block 1	92.95	70.52	65.94	52.83	66.30	80.72	62.65	52.05
Xception Block 2	98.04	70.28	67.48	56.04	69.61	85.75	64.27	52.70
Xception Block 3	99.41	67.58	63.62	57.97	67.62	85.44	60.71	52.07
Xception Block 4	99.14	68.91	70.36	**58.74**	73.65	90.97	60.72	52.79
Xception Block 5	99.27	68.25	66.68	43.20	83.52	92.23	63.75	49.94
[2] MesoInception4	97.28	59.27	60.17	47.24	65.75	83.27	62.92	**54.03**
[13] Resnet-18	93.90	53.22	53.45	53.69	69.98	85.40	54.77	50.89
[32] Xception	98.60	60.15	56.84	46.12	70.07	93.61	56.79	48.55
[33] CNN (p = 0.1)	97.78	60.08	59.73	50.87	68.67	95.16	68.15	47.43
[33] CNN (p = 0.5)	98.16	54.02	56.06	55.99	66.98	95.03	**71.50**	51.93
Model depth	Train on Face2Face				Train on FaceSwap			
	DF	NT	F2F	FS	DF	NT	F2F	FS
Resnet Layer 1	**84.39**	79.72	97.66	60.53	59.49	52.56	62.00	97.13
Xception Block 1	77.65	**80.88**	93.84	61.62	53.14	49.24	56.89	82.89
Xception Block 2	84.04	79.51	97.40	63.21	58.39	51.65	61.73	92.58
Xception Block 3	76.10	74.77	97.33	63.10	**61.77**	53.44	61.34	96.06
Xception Block 4	67.18	61.72	97.19	63.04	61.33	52.02	59.45	96.56
Xception Block 5	81.25	61.91	96.45	55.15	57.14	47.39	54.68	95.57
[2] MesoInception4	67.53	55.17	92.27	54.06	50.64	48.87	56.15	93.81
[13] Resnet-18	55.43	52.57	93.27	53.39	61.03	51.66	52.56	91.49
[6] Xception	66.12	56.07	97.41	53.15	53.86	50.00	56.55	96.84
[33] CNN (p = 0.1)	65.76	64.81	98.40	59.48	59.19	**53.50**	**63.07**	99.02
[33] CNN (p = 0.5)	65.43	60.36	97.94	**63.52**	60.19	52.11	59.81	98.25

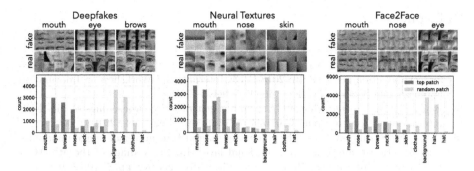

Fig. 7. Histograms of the most predictive patches from a classifier trained on Face2Face and un-manipulated images, and tested on the Neural Textures and Deepfakes manipulation methods. Unlike the fully-generative model setup, the classifier in this case localizes patches within the face.

5 Conclusion

Identifying differences between real and fake images is a constantly evolving problem and is highly sensitive to minor preprocessing details. Here, we take the approach of equalizing the preprocessing of the two classes of images to focus on the inherent differences between an image captured from a camera and a doctored image either generated entirely from a deep network, or partially manipulated in facial regions. We investigate using classifiers with limited receptive fields to focus on local artifacts, such as textures in hair, backgrounds, mouths, and eyes, rather than the global semantics of the image. Classifying these small patches allows us to generalize across different model training parameters, generator architectures, and datasets, and provides us with a heatmap to localize the potential areas of manipulation. We show a technique to exaggerate the detectable artifacts of the fake images, and demonstrate that image generators can still be imperfect in certain patches despite finetuning against a given classifier. While progress on detecting fake images inevitably creates a cat-and-mouse problem of using these results to create even better generators, we hope that understanding these detectors and visualizing what they look for can help people anticipate where manipulations may occur in a facial image and better navigate potentially falsified content in today's media.

Acknowledgements. We thank Antonio Torralba, Jonas Wulff, Jacob Huh, Tongzhou Wang, Harry Yang, and Richard Zhang for helpful discussions. This work was supported by a National Science Foundation Graduate Research Fellowship under Grant No. 1122374 to L.C. and DARPA XAI FA8750-18-C000-4 to D.B.

References

1. Deepfakes.https://github.com/deepfakes/faceswap
2. Afchar, D., Nozick, V., Yamagishi, J., Echizen, I.: MesoNet: a compact facial video forgery detection network. In: 2018 IEEE International Workshop on Information Forensics and Security (WIFS), pp. 1–7. IEEE (2018)
3. Bau, D., et al.: Seeing what a GAN cannot generate. In: Proceedings of the IEEE International Conference on Computer Vision, pp. 4502–4511 (2019)
4. Bayar, B., Stamm, M.C.: A deep learning approach to universal image manipulation detection using a new convolutional layer. In: Proceedings of the 4th ACM Workshop on Information Hiding and Multimedia Security, pp. 5–10 (2016)
5. Carlini, N., Farid, H.: Evading deepfake-image detectors with white-and black-box attacks. In: Proceedings of the IEEE/CVF Conference on Computer Vision and Pattern Recognition Workshops, pp. 658–659 (2020)
6. Chollet, F.: Xception: deep learning with depthwise separable convolutions. In: Proceedings of the IEEE Conference on Computer Vision and Pattern Recognition, pp. 1251–1258 (2017)
7. Cozzolino, D., Poggi, G., Verdoliva, L.: Recasting residual-based local descriptors as convolutional neural networks: an application to image forgery detection. In: Proceedings of the 5th ACM Workshop on Information Hiding and Multimedia Security, pp. 159–164 (2017)
8. Cozzolino, D., Thies, J., Rössler, A., Riess, C., Nießner, M., Verdoliva, L.: ForensicTransfer: weakly-supervised domain adaptation for forgery detection. arXiv preprint arXiv:1812.02510 (2018)
9. Geirhos, R., Rubisch, P., Michaelis, C., Bethge, M., Wichmann, F.A., Brendel, W.: ImageNet-trained CNNs are biased towards texture; increasing shape bias improves accuracy and robustness. arXiv preprint arXiv:1811.12231 (2018)
10. Goetschalckx, L., Andonian, A., Oliva, A., Isola, P.: GANalyze: toward visual definitions of cognitive image properties. In: Proceedings of the IEEE International Conference on Computer Vision, pp. 5744–5753 (2019)
11. Gragnaniello, D., Marra, F., Poggi, G., Verdoliva, L.: Analysis of adversarial attacks against CNN-based image forgery detectors. In: 2018 26th European Signal Processing Conference (EUSIPCO), pp. 967–971. IEEE (2018)
12. Hays, J., Efros, A.A.: Scene completion using millions of photographs. ACM Trans. Graph. (TOG) **26**(3), 4-es (2007)
13. He, K., Zhang, X., Ren, S., Sun, J.: Deep residual learning for image recognition. In: Proceedings of the IEEE conference on computer vision and pattern recognition, pp. 770–778 (2016)
14. Huh, M., Liu, A., Owens, A., Efros, A.A.: Fighting fake news: image splice detection via learned self-consistency. In: Ferrari, V., Hebert, M., Sminchisescu, C., Weiss, Y. (eds.) ECCV 2018. LNCS, vol. 11215, pp. 106–124. Springer, Cham (2018). https://doi.org/10.1007/978-3-030-01252-6_7
15. Isola, P., Zhu, J.Y., Zhou, T., Efros, A.A.: Image-to-image translation with conditional adversarial networks. In: Proceedings of the IEEE Conference on Computer Vision and Pattern Recognition, pp. 1125–1134 (2017)

16. Karras, T., Aila, T., Laine, S., Lehtinen, J.: Progressive growing of GANs for improved quality, stability, and variation. arXiv preprint arXiv:1710.10196 (2017)
17. Karras, T., Laine, S., Aila, T.: A style-based generator architecture for generative adversarial networks. In: Proceedings of the IEEE Conference on Computer Vision and Pattern Recognition, pp. 4401–4410 (2019)
18. Karras, T., Laine, S., Aittala, M., Hellsten, J., Lehtinen, J., Aila, T.: Analyzing and improving the image quality of stylegan. arXiv preprint arXiv:1912.04958 (2019)
19. Kingma, D.P., Dhariwal, P.: Glow: generative flow with invertible 1x1 convolutions. In: Advances in Neural Information Processing Systems, pp. 10215–10224 (2018)
20. Li, C., Wand, M.: Precomputed real-time texture synthesis with Markovian generative adversarial networks. In: Leibe, B., Matas, J., Sebe, N., Welling, M. (eds.) ECCV 2016. LNCS, vol. 9907, pp. 702–716. Springer, Cham (2016). https://doi.org/10.1007/978-3-319-46487-9_43
21. Li, L., Bao, J., Zhang, T., Yang, H., Chen, D., Wen, F., Guo, B.: Face x-ray for more general face forgery detection. In: Proceedings of the IEEE/CVF Conference on Computer Vision and Pattern Recognition, pp. 5001–5010 (2020)
22. Li, Y., Lyu, S.: Exposing deepfake videos by detecting face warping artifacts. arXiv preprint arXiv:1811.00656 (2018)
23. Liu, Z., Luo, P., Wang, X., Tang, X.: Deep learning face attributes in the wild. In: Proceedings of International Conference on Computer Vision (ICCV), December 2015
24. Long, J., Shelhamer, E., Darrell, T.: Fully convolutional networks for semantic segmentation. In: Proceedings of the IEEE Conference on Computer Vision and Pattern Recognition, pp. 3431–3440 (2015)
25. Mayer, O., Stamm, M.C.: Exposing fake images with forensic similarity graphs. arXiv preprint arXiv:1912.02861 (2019)
26. Mo, H., Chen, B., Luo, W.: Fake faces identification via convolutional neural network. In: Proceedings of the 6th ACM Workshop on Information Hiding and Multimedia Security, pp. 43–47 (2018)
27. Popescu, A.C., Farid, H.: Exposing digital forgeries by detecting duplicated image regions. Dept. Comput. Sci., Dartmouth College, Technical report TR2004-515 pp. 1–11 (2004)
28. Popescu, A.C., Farid, H.: Exposing digital forgeries by detecting traces of resampling. IEEE Trans. Signal Process. **53**(2), 758–767 (2005)
29. Popescu, A.C., Farid, H.: Exposing digital forgeries in color filter array interpolated images. IEEE Trans. Signal Process. **53**(10), 3948–3959 (2005)
30. Rahmouni, N., Nozick, V., Yamagishi, J., Echizen, I.: Distinguishing computer graphics from natural images using convolution neural networks. In: 2017 IEEE Workshop on Information Forensics and Security (WIFS), pp. 1–6. IEEE (2017)
31. Richardson, E., Weiss, Y.: On GANs and GMMs. In: Advances in Neural Information Processing Systems, pp. 5847–5858 (2018)
32. Rossler, A., Cozzolino, D., Verdoliva, L., Riess, C., Thies, J., Nießner, M.: Faceforensics++: learning to detect manipulated facial images. In: Proceedings of the IEEE International Conference on Computer Vision, pp. 1–11 (2019)
33. Wang, S.Y., Wang, O., Zhang, R., Owens, A., Efros, A.A.: CNN-generated images are surprisingly easy to spot... for now. arXiv preprint arXiv:1912.11035 (2019)
34. Xuan, X., Peng, B., Wang, W., Dong, J.: On the generalization of GAN image forensics. In: Sun, Z., He, R., Feng, J., Shan, S., Guo, Z. (eds.) CCBR 2019. LNCS, vol. 11818, pp. 134–141. Springer, Cham (2019). https://doi.org/10.1007/978-3-030-31456-9_15

35. Yu, N., Davis, L.S., Fritz, M.: Attributing fake images to GANs: learning and analyzing GAN fingerprints. In: Proceedings of the IEEE International Conference on Computer Vision, pp. 7556–7566 (2019)
36. Zhang, R., Isola, P., Efros, A.A., Shechtman, E., Wang, O.: The unreasonable effectiveness of deep features as a perceptual metric. In: Proceedings of the IEEE conference on computer vision and pattern recognition, pp. 586–595 (2018)
37. Zhang, X., Karaman, S., Chang, S.F.: Detecting and simulating artifacts in GAN fake images. arXiv preprint arXiv:1907.06515 (2019)
38. Zhou, P., Han, X., Morariu, V.I., Davis, L.S.: Two-stream neural networks for tampered face detection. In: 2017 IEEE Conference on Computer Vision and Pattern Recognition Workshops (CVPRW), pp. 1831–1839. IEEE (2017)

Embedding Propagation: Smoother Manifold for Few-Shot Classification

Pau Rodríguez[1(✉)], Issam Laradji[1,2], Alexandre Drouin[1],
and Alexandre Lacoste[1]

[1] Element AI, Montreal, Canada
{pau.rodriguez,issam.laradji,adrouin,allac}@elementai.com
[2] University of British Columbia, Vancouver, Canada

Abstract. Few-shot classification is challenging because the data distribution of the training set can be widely different to the test set as their classes are disjoint. This distribution shift often results in poor generalization. Manifold smoothing has been shown to address the distribution shift problem by extending the decision boundaries and reducing the noise of the class representations. Moreover, manifold smoothness is a key factor for semi-supervised learning and transductive learning algorithms. In this work, we propose to use embedding propagation as an unsupervised non-parametric regularizer for manifold smoothing in few-shot classification. Embedding propagation leverages interpolations between the extracted features of a neural network based on a similarity graph. We empirically show that embedding propagation yields a smoother embedding manifold. We also show that applying embedding propagation to a transductive classifier achieves new state-of-the-art results in *mini*Imagenet, *tiered*Imagenet, Imagenet-FS, and CUB. Furthermore, we show that embedding propagation consistently improves the accuracy of the models in multiple semi-supervised learning scenarios by up to 16% points. The proposed embedding propagation operation can be easily integrated as a non-parametric layer into a neural network. We provide the training code and usage examples at https://github.com/ElementAI/embedding-propagation.

Keywords: Few-shot · Classification · Semi-supervised learning · Metalearning

Deep learning methods have achieved state-of-the-art performance in computer vision tasks such as classification [22], semantic segmentation [30], and object detection [38]. However, these methods often need to be trained on a large amount of labeled data. Unfortunately, labeled data is scarce and its collection is expensive for most applications. This has led to the emergence of deep learning methods based on transfer learning [58], few-shot learning (FSL) [9],

Electronic supplementary material The online version of this chapter (https://doi.org/10.1007/978-3-030-58574-7_8) contains supplementary material, which is available to authorized users.

© Springer Nature Switzerland AG 2020
A. Vedaldi et al. (Eds.): ECCV 2020, LNCS 12371, pp. 121–138, 2020.
https://doi.org/10.1007/978-3-030-58574-7_8

and semi-supervised learning [5], that address the challenges of learning with limited data.

Few-shot learning methods have the potential to significantly reduce the need for human annotation. This is because such methods learn new tasks with few labeled examples by transferring the knowledge gained across several tasks. Three recent approaches have been successful for few-shot classification (FSC): metric learning, meta learning, and transfer learning. Metric learning approaches [44,52] learn an embedding space where a set of labeled examples (*support set*) is used to predict the classes for unlabeled examples (*query set*). Meta-learning approaches [10,41] learn to infer a set of parameters that can be adapted to new tasks. Transfer learning [6,31] methods aim to learn a general feature representation and then train a classifier for each new task. In this work, we use an approach between metric learning and transfer learning. During training, the model attempts to learn a general feature representation that is fine-tuned using a metric-based classifier.

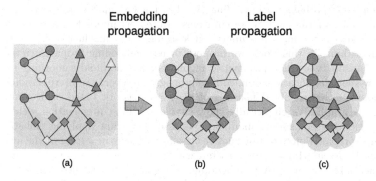

Fig. 1. Illustration of the embedding propagation (EP) method. (a) Original decision boundaries for three classes. The color of a region represents the predicted class, and the color of a node represents the node's actual class. (b) Decision boundaries after applying EP, which are smoother than in (a). (c) Predictions after propagating the labels across the graph, leveraging unlabeled points (light gray) to classify a query example (shown in dark gray). *Best viewed in color.* (Color figure online)

A key challenge in few-shot classification is training models that generalize well to unseen classes. This requires feature representations that are robust to small changes in the data distribution. This issue has been addressed outside the few-shot learning literature with a number of regularization techniques such as dropout [45], batch normalization [19], and manifold mixup [51]. However, regularization in few-shot learning remains unexplored. In this work, we show that re-framing label propagation to perform manifold smoothing improves the performance of few-shot classifiers, particularly in the transductive and semi-supervised settings. Different from manifold mixup [51], the proposed method is unsupervised and captures higher order interactions between the embedding.

We propose an embedding propagation (EP) method that outputs a set of interpolations from the network output features using their similarity in a graph. This graph is constructed with pairwise similarities of the features using the radial basis function (RBF). EP is non-parametric and can be applied on top of any feature extractor. It can be used as part of a network in order to obtain a regularized manifold for both training and testing. We refer to such network as EPNet. For few-shot classification, we empirically show that the proposed regularization improves the performance for transductive and semi-supervised learning. The hypothesis behind this improvement is based on the fact that using interpolated embeddings result in smoother decision boundaries and increased robustness to noise. These properties have been shown to be important for generalization [1,26,51] and semi-supervised learning [5].

For semi-supervised learning (SSL), EPNet takes advantage of an unlabeled set of images at test time in order to make better predictions of the query set. We adapt the SSL approach proposed by Lee et al. [24] to the few-shot classification setup. Thus, for each unlabeled image, EPNet selects the class that has the maximum predicted probability as the pseudo label. EPNet then uses these pseudo labels along with the support set to perform label propagation to predict the labels of the query set. This approach achieves significant improvement over previous state-of-the-art in the 1-shot SSL setting. We hypothesize that EPNet is effective in the SSL setting because of the properties of smoother manifolds [5].

Overall, EPNet achieves state-of-the-art results on *mini*Imagenet [52], *tiered*Imagenet [38], Imagenet-FS [15] and CUB [54] for few-shot classification, and semi-supervised learning scenarios. In our ablation experiments, we evaluate different variations of embedding propagation and their impact on the smoothness of the decision boundaries. We also show that, with EP, we also achieve a clear improvement on the SSL setup compared to the same model without EP.

Our main contributions can be summarized as follows. We show that embedding propagation:

- Regularizes the manifold in an unsupervised manner.
- Leverages embedding interpolations to capture higher order feature interactions.
- Achieves state-of-the-art few-shot classification results for the transductive and semi-supervised learning setups.

1 Related Work

Our work focuses on few-shot classification, but also intersects with manifold regularization, transductive learning, and semi-supervised learning. We describe relevant work for each of these topics and point out their relevance to our method.

Few-Shot Classification. A common practice for training models for few-shot learning is to use episodic learning [36,44,52]. This training methodology creates episodes that simulate the train and test scenarios of few-shot learning.

Meta-learning approaches make use of this episodic framework. They learn a base network capable of producing parameters for a task-specific network after observing the support set. The task-specific network is then evaluated on the query set and its gradient is used to update the base network. By doing so, the base network learns to use the support set to generate parameters that are suitable for good generalization. This was first introduced in [36]. Perhaps, the most popular meta-learning approach is MAML [10] and other algorithms that derivate from it [32,35], which learn a set of initial weights that are adapted to a specific task in a small amount of gradient steps. However, this choice of architecture, while general, offers limited performance for few-shot image classification. This lead to variants of meta-learning methods more adapted to image classification [13,33,34,41].

Most metric learning approaches are trained using episodes [29,44,52], they can also be seen as meta-learning approaches. Concretely, metric learning approaches are characterized by a classifier learned over a feature space. They focus on learning high-quality and transferable features with a neural network common to all tasks. EPNet leverages the work of Liu *et al.* [29] for learning to propagate labels, and thus falls into this category. Graph-based approaches can also be framed into this category [18,23,43,56]. Gidaris *et al.* [14] proposed to generate classification weights with a graph neural network (GNN) and apply a denoising autoencoder to regularize their representation. EP does also perform a regularization on a graph representation. Set-to-set functions have also been used for embedding adaptation [57]. However, different from GNNs and set-to-set, our graph is unsupervised and non-parametric, its purpose is manifold smoothing, and we show it improves semi-supervised learning approaches.

While metric learning offers a convenient approach to learn transferable features, it has been shown that neural networks trained with conventional supervised learning already learn transferable features [2,6,31]. Hence, to learn a classifier on a new task, it suffices to fine-tune the feature extractor to that task. Also, this approach has shown to learn more discriminative features compared to the episodic scenario. To take advantage of this transfer learning procedure, we use it in our pre-training phase. Thus, EPNet combines a metric-based classifier with the pre-training of transferable features to achieve a more general representation.

Regularization for Generalization. Regularization is a principled approach for improving the generalization performance of deep networks. Commonly used techniques such as dropout [45] and batch normalization [19] attempt to achieve robustness towards input variations. Others are based on regularizing weights [39,42]. Another line of work that is based on manifold regularization [3,49,51,61]. These works propose methods that aim to smooth the decision boundaries and flatten the class representations, which are important factors for generalization [1,26]. Similarly, we attempt to smooth the manifold by incorporating an embedding propagation operation on the extracted features during training. A concurrent work [31] and our work were the first to apply manifold regularization on few-shot classification. However, the method presented in [31] differs from ours in four ways. First, they perform smoothing in an additional training phase. Second, they train linear classifiers at inference time. Third, they use an exemplar self-supervised loss in their training procedure. Fourth, they do not show the efficacy of their method for semi-supervised learning. In the few-shot classification benchmarks, we achieve better classification accuracy on the Imagenet datasets and CUB dataset for the 1-shot, 5-shot, and 10-shot case.

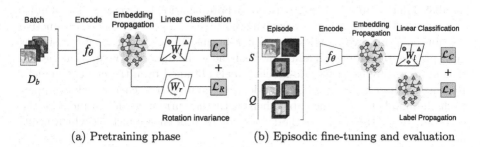

(a) Pretraining phase   (b) Episodic fine-tuning and evaluation

Fig. 2. Overview of the EPNet training procedure. EPNet is trained in two phases: a pretraining phase and an episodic fine-tuning phase. **(a)** First, the model is trained to learn general feature representations using a standard classification loss $\mathcal{L}_C$ and an auxiliar rotation loss $\mathcal{L}_R$. **(b)** Then, the model is fine-tuned using episodic learning to learn to generalize to novel classes by minimizing the standard classification loss $\mathcal{L}_C$ and a label propagation loss $\mathcal{L}_P$. In both phases the features are encoded using a feature extractor followed by our proposed embedding propagation method (Sect. 2).

There are different lines of research showing that perturbing image representations results in better generalization [19,45]. The most closely related to our work are based on feature interpolation. For instance, Zhao and Cho [7] proposed to make predictions based on the interpolation of nearest neighbors to improve adversarial robustness. In *Manifold Mixup* this idea was expanded to smooth the representations of the neural architecture and achieve better generalization [1,26]. *Manifold Mixup* has been applied to FSC architectures as a fine-tuning step to improve their performance [31]. Differently, we propose a novel procedure to smooth the manifold end-to-end. The proposed method is applied only at the output layer and achieves higher classification accuracy than previous approaches. Moreover, and also different from [31], we leverage the properties of smoother manifolds for semi-supervised learning [4], further widening the improvement margin.

Transductive Learning (TL). The idea of transduction is to perform predictions only on the test points. In contrast, the goal of inductive learning is to output a prediction function defined on an entire space [50]. Given a small set of labeled examples, transductive learning has been shown to outperform inductive learning [20,28,29]. This makes TL a desirable method for few-shot classification.

Liu *et al.* [29] presented one of the few work using TL for FSC. Similar to this work, we use label propagation [62] to predict the labels of the query set. However, they do not incorporate a manifold smoothing method such as the embedding propagation method investigated in this work.

Semi-supervised Learning. While the literature on semi-supervised learning is vast, few works leverage the use of unlabeled data in few-shot image classification. In [37], they develop a soft version of k-means to meta-learn how to use unlabeled data. Liu *et al.* [28,29] used label propagation to leverage a set of unlabeled data. Their approach works with both semi-supervised and transductive learning and improves results over soft k-means. In this work we use a similar label propagation approach and show that the semi-supervised results can be further improved by using pseudo-labels (labels obtained from the current model). Recently, Sun *et al.* [27] used a meta-learning approach to cherry-pick examples from the unlabeled set and label them with the current model to increase the label set. In contrast, our method does not require cherry-picking which needs an extra learning step.

2   Proposed Method

We propose an embedding propagation network (EPNet) that has the following pipeline. Given an input image, EPNet first extracts image features using a feature extractor. Then, we apply a novel embedding propagation method (described in Sect. 2.1) to map the features to a set of interpolated features that we refer to as embeddings. These embeddings are then used by a classifier to label the images (Sect. 2.3). The goal of embedding propagation is to increase the smoothness of the embedding manifold, which was shown to improve generalization [1,26] and the effectiveness of semi-supervised learning methods [4] (Sect. 2.5). In the following sections, we explain EPNet in more detail.

2.1   Embedding Propagation

Embedding propagation takes a set of feature vectors $\mathbf{z}_i \in \mathbb{R}^m$, obtained from applying a feature extractor (CNN) to the samples of an episode. Then, it outputs a set of embeddings $\widetilde{\mathbf{z}}_i \in \mathbb{R}^m$ through the following two steps. First, for each pair of features (i, j), the model computes the distance as $d_{ij}^2 = \|\mathbf{z}_i - \mathbf{z}_j\|_2^2$ and the adjacency as $A_{ij} = \exp\left(-d_{ij}^2/\sigma^2\right)$, where σ^2 is a scaling factor and $A_{ii} = 0$, $\forall i$, as done in TPN [29]. We chose $\sigma^2 = \mathrm{Var}\left(d_{ij}^2\right)$ which we found to stabilize training.

Next we compute the Laplacian of the adjacency matrix,

$$L = D^{-\frac{1}{2}}AD^{-\frac{1}{2}}, \quad D_{ii} = \sum_j A_{ij}. \tag{1}$$

Finally, using the label propagation formula described in [62], we obtain the propagator matrix P as,

$$P = (I - \alpha L)^{-1}, \tag{2}$$

where $\alpha \in \mathbb{R}$ is a scaling factor, and I is the identity matrix. Then, the embeddings are obtained as follows,

$$\widetilde{\mathbf{z}}_i = \sum_j P_{ij}\mathbf{z}_j. \tag{3}$$

Since the $\widetilde{\mathbf{z}}_i$ are now a weighted sum of their neighbors, embedding propagation has the effect of removing undesired noise from the feature vectors. Note that this operation is simple to implement and compatible with a wide range of feature extractors and classifiers. Further, note that the computational complexity of Eq. 2 is negligible for few-shot episodes [29] since the size of the episode is small.

2.2   Few-Shot Classification Setup

Following the common few-shot setups [37,52], we are given three datasets: a *base* dataset ($\mathcal{D}_b$), a *novel* dataset ($\mathcal{D}_n$), and a *validation* dataset ($\mathcal{D}_v$). The base dataset is composed of a large amount of labeled images $\mathcal{D}_b = \{(\mathbf{x}_i, y_i)\}_{i=1}^{N_{base}}$, where each image $\mathbf{x}_i$ is labeled with class $y_i \in \mathcal{Y}_{base}$. The novel dataset $\mathcal{D}_n = \{(\mathbf{x}_j, y_j)\}_{j=1}^{N_{novel}}$, where $\mathbf{x}_j$ comes from previously unseen classes $y_j \in \mathcal{Y}_{novel}$, such that $\mathcal{Y}_{base} \cap \mathcal{Y}_{novel} = \emptyset$, is used to evaluate the transfer learning capabilities of the model. The validation dataset $\mathcal{D}_v$ contains classes not present in $\mathcal{D}_b$ and $\mathcal{D}_n$ and is used to conduct hyperparameter search.

Furthermore, we have access to episodes. Each episode consists of n classes sampled uniformly without replacement from the set of all classes, a support set S (k examples per class) and a query set Q (q examples per class). This is referred to as n-way k-shot learning.

2.3   Inference Phase

Given an episode, we perform inference by extracting features of an input image, applying embedding propagation on those features, then applying label propagation. More formally, this is performed as follows. Let $\widetilde{Z} \in \mathbb{R}^{(k+q)\times m}$ be the matrix of propagated embeddings obtained by jointly applying Eq. 1–3 to the support and query sets. Let $P_{\widetilde{Z}}$ be the corresponding propagator matrix. Further, let $Y_S \in \mathbb{R}^{k\times n}$ be a one-hot encoding of the labels in the support set and $0 \in \mathbb{R}^{q\times n}$ a matrix of zeros. We compute the logits for the query set ($\hat{Y}_Q$) by performing label propagation as described in [62].

2.4   Training Procedure

EPNet is trained in two phases as illustrated in Fig. 2. First, the model is trained on $\mathcal{D}_b$ using the common pretraining procedure for few-shot classification [41] in order to learn a general feature representation. Second, the model is fine-tuned using episodes in order to learn to generalize to novel classes. Episodes are drawn from the same dataset $\mathcal{D}_b$. In both phases, EPNet uses the same feature extractor $f_\theta(\mathbf{x})$ parametrized by θ to obtain the features $\widetilde{\mathbf{z}}$ extracted for a given input image $\mathbf{x}$. However, each phase relies on a different objective.

Pre-training Phase. As shown in Fig. 2a, we train f_θ using two linear classifiers, which are linear layers with softmax activations parametrized by W_l and W_r, respectively. The first classifier is trained to predict the class labels of examples in $\mathcal{D}_b$. It is optimized by minimizing the cross-entropy loss,

$$\mathcal{L}_c(\mathbf{x}_i, y_i; W_l, \theta) = -\ln p(y_i|\widetilde{\mathbf{z}}_i, W_l), \tag{4}$$

where $y_i \in \mathcal{Y}_b$ and the probabilities are obtained by applying softmax to the logits provided by the neural network.

For fair comparison with recent literature, we also add a self-supervision loss [12,31] to obtain more robust feature representations. Hence, we use the second classifier to predict image rotations and use the following loss,

$$\mathcal{L}_r(\mathbf{x}_i, r_j; W_r, \theta) = -\ln p(r_j|\widetilde{\mathbf{z}}_i, W_r), \tag{5}$$

where $r_j \in \{0°, 90°, 180°, 270°\}$, and $p(r_j|\widetilde{\mathbf{z}}_i, W_r)$ is the probability of the input being rotated by r_j as predicted by a softmax classifier with weights W_r.

Overall, we use stochastic gradient descent (SGD) with batches of size 128 and 4 rotations per image to optimize the following loss,

$$\underset{\theta, W_l, W_r}{\operatorname{argmin}} \sum_{i=1}^{128} \sum_{j=1}^{4} \mathcal{L}_c(\mathbf{x}_i, y_i; W_l, \theta) + \mathcal{L}_r(\mathbf{x}_i, r_j; W_r, \theta). \tag{6}$$

Episodic Learning Phase. As shown in Fig. 2b, after the pre-training phase, we use episodic training to learn to recognize new classes. In this phase, we also optimize EPNet using two classifiers. The first classifier is based on label propagation. It computes class probabilities by applying a softmax to the query set logits $\hat{Y}_Q$ defined in Sect. 2.3, i.e.,

$$\mathcal{L}_p(\mathbf{x}_i, y_i; \theta) = -\ln p(y_i|\widetilde{\mathbf{z}}_i, \widetilde{Z}, Y_S). \tag{7}$$

The second classifier is identical to the W_l-based classifier used in pretraining. It is included to preserve a discriminative feature representation. Hence, we minimize the following loss:

$$\underset{\theta, W_l}{\operatorname{argmin}} \left[\frac{1}{|Q|} \sum_{(\mathbf{x}_i, y_i) \in Q} \mathcal{L}_p(\mathbf{x}_i, y_i; \theta) + \frac{1}{|S \cup Q|} \sum_{(\mathbf{x}_i, y_i) \in S \cup Q} \frac{1}{2} \mathcal{L}_c(\mathbf{x}_i, y_i; W_l, \theta) \right]. \tag{8}$$

2.5   Semi-supervised Learning

In the semi-supervised learning scenario, we also have access to an unlabeled set of images U. We use the unlabeled set as follows. First, we use the inference procedure described in Sect. 2.3 to predict the labels $\hat{c}_U$ for the unlabeled set as pseudo-labels. Then, we augment the support set with U using their pseudo-labels as the true labels. Finally, we use the inference procedure in Sect. 2.3 on the new support set to predict the labels for the query set.

We also consider the semi-supervised scenario proposed by Garcia and Bruna [11]. In this scenario the model is trained to perform 5-shot 5-way classification but only 20% to 60% of the support set is labeled.

As shown by Lee *et al.* [24], this procedure is equivalent to entropy regularization, an effective method for semi-supervised learning. Entropy regularization is particularly effective in cases where the decision boundary lies in low-density regions. With embedding propagation we achieve a similar decision boundary by smoothing the manifold.

3 Experiments

In this section, we present the results on three standard FSC datasets, *mini*Imagenet [52], *tiered*Imagenet [37], CUB [54], and Imagenet-FS [15]. We also provide ablation experiments to illustrate the properties of embedding propagation. As common procedure, we averaged accuracies on $\mathcal{D}_n$ over 1000 episodes [52].

3.1 Datasets

*mini*Imagenet [36]. A subset of the Imagenet dataset [40] consisting of 100 classes with 600 images per class. Classes are divided in three disjoint sets of 64 base classes, 16 for validation and 20 novel classes.

*tiered*Imagenet [37]. A more challenging subset of the Imagenet dataset [40] where class subsets are chosen from supersets of the wordnet hierarchy. The top hierarchy has 34 super-classes, which are divided into 20 base (351 classes), 6 validation (97 classes) and 8 novel (160 classes) categories.

Imagenet-FS [15]. A large-scale version of ImageNet. It is split into 389 base classes and 611 novel classes. The training set consists of 193 of the base classes. Validation consists of 193 of the base classes plus 300 novel classes. The test set consists of the remaining 196 base classes and the remaining 311 novel classes.

CUB [6,16]. A fine-grained dataset based on CUB200 [54] composed of 200 classes and 11,788 images split in 100 base, 50 validation, and 50 novel classes.

3.2 Implementation Details

For fair comparison with previous work, we used three common feature extractors: (i) a 4-layer convnet [44,52] with 64 channels per layer, (ii) a 12-layer resnet [33], and (iii) a wide residual network (WRN-28-10) [41,60]. For *mini*, *tiered*Imagenet, and CUB, images are resized to 84 × 84. For Imagenet-FS, as described in [12,13] we use a resnet-18 and images are resized to 224 × 224.

In the training stage, the models are optimized using SGD with learning rate of 0.1 for 100 epochs. The learning rate is reduced by a factor of 10 every time

Table 1. Comparison of test accuracy against state-of-the art methods for 1-shot and 5-shot classification using *mini*Imagenet and *tiered*Imagenet. The second column shows the number of parameters of each model in thousands (K). *$Robust-20$ uses an 18-layer residual network. --Net is identical to EPNet but without EP. Gray colored results are obtained using 224×224 pixels instead of the standard 84×84 pixel images.

		*mini*Imagenet		*tiered*Imagenet	
	Params	1-shot	5-shot	1-shot	5-shot
CONV-4					
Matching [52]	112K	43.56 ±0.84	55.31 ±0.73	-	-
MAML [29]	112K	48.70 ±1.84	63.11 ±0.92	51.67 ±1.81	70.30 ±0.08
ProtoNet [44]	112K	49.42 ±0.78	68.20 ±0.66	53.31 ±0.89	72.69 ±0.74
ReNet [47]	223K	50.44 ±0.82	65.32 ±0.70	54.48 ±0.92	71.32 ±0.78
GNN [11]	1619K	50.33 ±0.36	66.41 ±0.63	-	-
TPN [29]	171K	53.75 ±0.86	69.43 ±0.67	57.53 ±0.96	72.85 ±0.74
CC+rot [12]	112K	54.83 ±0.43	71.86 ±0.33	-	-
EGNN [21]	5068K	-	**76.37**	-	**80.15**
--Net (ours)	112K	57.18 ±0.83	72.57 ±0.66	57.60 ±0.93	73.30 ±0.74
EPNet (ours)	112K	**59.32** ±0.88	72.95 ±0.64	**59.97** ±0.95	73.91 ±0.75
RESNET-12					
ProtoNets++ [55]	7989K	56.52 ±0.45	74.28 ±0.20	58.47 ±0.64	78.41 ±0.41
TADAM [33]	7989K	58.50 ±0.30	76.70 ±0.30	-	-
MetaOpt-SVM [25]	12415K	62.64 ±0.61	78.60 ±0.46	65.99 ±0.72	81.56 ±0.53
TPN [29]	8284K	59.46	75.65	-	-
*Robust-20++ [8]	11174K	58.11 ±0.64	75.24 ±0.49	70.44 ±0.32	85.43 ±0.21
MTL [46]	8286K	61.20 ±1.80	75.50 ±0.80	-	-
CAN [17]	8026K	67.19 ±0.55	80.64 ±0.35	73.21 ±0.58	84.93 ±0.38
--Net (ours)	7989K	65.66 ±0.85	**81.28** ±0.62	72.60 ±0.91	85.69 ±0.65
EPNet (ours)	7989K	66.50 ±0.89	81.06 ±0.60	**76.53** ±0.87	**87.32** ±0.64
WRN-28-10					
LEO [41]	37582K	61.76 ±0.08	77.59 ±0.12	66.33 ±0.05	81.44 ±0.09
Robust-20++ [8]	37582K	62.80 ±0.62	80.85 ±0.43	-	-
wDAE-GNN [14]	48855K	62.96 ±0.15	78.85 ±0.10	68.18 ±0.16	83.09 ±0.12
CC+rot [12]	37582K	62.93 ±0.45	79.87 ±0.33	70.53 ±0.51	84.98 ±0.36
Manifold mixup [31]	37582K	64.93 ±0.48	83.18 ±0.72	-	-
--Net (ours)	37582K	65.98 ±0.85	82.22 ±0.66	74.04 ±0.93	86.03 ±0.63
EPNet (ours)	37582K	**70.74** ±0.85	**84.34** ±0.53	**78.50** ±0.91	**88.36** ±0.57

Table 2. Comparison with the state of the art on CUB-200-2011. $^*Robust-20++$ uses an 18-layer residual network, and Accuracies obtained with 224×224 images appear in gray.

	Backbone	1-shot	5-shot
*Robust-20++ [8]	RESNET-18	68.68 ±0.69	83.21 ±0.44
EPNet (ours)	RESNET-12	**82.85** ±0.81	**91.32** ±0.41
Manifold mixup [31]	WRN-28-10	80.68 ±0.81	90.85 ±0.44
EPNet (ours)	WRN-28-10	**87.75** ±0.70	**94.03** ±0.33

Table 3. Top-5 test accuracy on Imagenet-FS.

Approach	Novel Classes					All classes				
	K=1	2	5	10	20	K=1	2	5	10	20
Batch SGM [15]	-	-	-	-	-	49.3	60.5	71.4	75.8	78.5
PMN [53]	45.8	57.8	69.0	74.3	77.4	57.6	64.7	71.9	75.2	77.5
LwoF [13]	46.2	57.5	69.2	74.8	78.1	58.2	65.2	72.7	76.5	78.7
CC+ Rot [12]	46.43 ±0.24	57.80 ±0.16	69.67 ±0.09	74.64 ±0.06	77.31 ±0.05	57.88 ±0.15	64.76 ±0.10	72.29 ±0.07	75.63 ±0.04	77.40 ±0.03
wDAE-GNN [14]	48.00 ±0.21	59.70 ±0.15	70.30 ±0.08	75.00 ±0.06	77.80 ±0.05	59.10 ±0.13	66.30 ±0.10	73.20 ±0.08	76.10 ±0.04	77.50 ±0.03
wDAE-GNN + EP (ours)	**50.07** ±0.27	**62.16** ±0.16	**72.89** ±0.11	**77.25** ±0.07	**79.48** ±0.05	**60.87** ±0.16	**68.53** ±0.10	**75.56** ±0.07	**78.28** ±0.04	**78.89** ±0.03

the model reached a plateau, in which case the validation loss had not improved for 10 epochs. α is cross-validated on the 4-layer convnet.

In the episodic fine-tuning stage we randomly sample 5 classes per episode, where in each class k instances are selected for the support set and 15 for the query set. Similar to the training stage, the model is optimized with SGD with learning rate 0.001 reduced by a factor of 10 on plateau.

Table 4. SSL results with 100 unlabeled samples. --Net is identical to EPNet but without embedding propagation. *Re-implementation [59]

		*mini*Imagenet		*tiered*Imagenet	
	Backbone	1-shot	5-shot	1-shot	5-shot
TPN$_{SSL}$ [29]	CONV-4	52.78	66.42	55.74	71.01
k-Means$_{masked,soft}$ [37]	CONV-4	50.41 ±0.31	64.39 ±0.24	-	-
EPNet (ours)	CONV-4	59.32 ±0.88	72.95 ±0.64	59.97 ±0.95	73.91 ±0.75
--Net$_{SSL}$ (ours)	CONV-4	63.74 ±0.97	75.30 ±0.67	65.01 ±1.04	74.24 ±0.80
EPNet$_{SSL}$ (ours)	CONV-4	**65.13** ±0.97	**75.42** ±0.64	**66.63** ±1.04	**75.70** ±0.74
LST [27]	RESNET-12	70.10 ±1.90	78.70 ±0.80	77.70 ±1.60	85.20 ±0.80
EPNet (ours)	RESNET-12	66.50 ±0.89	81.06 ±0.60	76.53 ±0.87	87.32 ±0.64
--Net$_{SSL}$ (ours)	RESNET-12	73.42 ±0.94	83.17 ±0.58	80.26 ±0.96	88.06 ±0.59
EPNet$_{SSL}$ (ours)	RESNET-12	**75.36** ±1.01	**84.07** ±0.60	**81.79** ±0.97	**88.45** ±0.61
*k-Means$_{masked,soft}$ [37]	WRN-28-10	52.78 ±0.27	66.42 ±0.21	-	-
TransMatch [59]	WRN-28-10	63.02 ±1.07	81.19 ±0.59	-	-
EPNet (ours)	WRN-28-10	70.74 ±0.85	84.34 ±0.53	78.50 ±0.91	88.36 ±0.57
--Net$_{SSL}$ (ours)	WRN-28-10	77.70 ±0.96	86.30 ±0.50	82.03 ±1.03	88.20 ±0.61
EPNet$_{SSL}$ (ours)	WRN-28-10	**79.22** ±0.92	**88.05** ±0.51	**83.69** ±0.99	**89.34** ±0.59

For training the wide residual networks (WRN), we apply the standard data augmentation methods mentioned by Szegedy *et al.* [41,48]. For the other architectures, we do not apply data augmentation.

For Imagenet-FS, we add EP right after the denoising autoencoder of wDAE-GNN [14]. We use the original code provided by the authors[1]. Different from the other datasets, in this one evaluation is performed on the 311 test classes at the same time (*311-way*), with the number of supports $k \in \{1, 2, 5, 10, 20\}$.

We evaluate 3 variations of our method: (i) EPNet as described in Sect. 2; (ii) --Net, which is identical to EPNet but without EP; and (iii) EPNet$_{SSL}$ (semi-supervised learning) as described in Sect. 2.5.

3.3   Experimental Results

In this section we compare EPNet with previous methods in the standard few-shot classification scenario, and semi-supervised learning scenarios.

Table 5. SSL results for the 5-shot 5-way scenario with different amounts of unlabeled data. The percentages refer to the amount of supports that are labeled in a set of 5 images per class.

	Params	20%	40%	60%	100%
GNN [11]	112K	52.45	58.76	-	66.41
EGNN [21]	5068K	**63.62**	64.32	66.37	**76.37**
--Net$_{SSL}$ (ours)	112K	58.52 ±0.97	64.46 ±0.79	67.81 ±0.74	57.18 ±0.83
EPNet$_{SSL}$ (ours)	112K	60.66 ±0.97	**67.08** ±0.80	**68.74** ±0.74	59.32 ±0.88

Main Results. We first report the results for the methods that do not use an unlabeled set. As seen in Tables 1 and 2, EPNet obtains state-of-the-art accuracies on *mini*Imagenet, *tiered*Imagenet, and CUB-200-2011 for the 1-shot and 5-shot benchmarks even when compared with models that use more parameters or higher resolution images. It can also be observed the effectiveness of EP in isolation when comparing EPNet with an identical model without EP (--Net). Higher-way and 10-shot results can be found in the supplementary material. Note that EGNN [21] uses ×45 parameters. On the large-scale Imagenet-FS, EP improves all benchmarks by approximately 2% accuracy, see Table 3. These results demonstrate the scalability of our method and the orthogonality with other embedding transformations such as denoising autoencoders [14].

---

[1] github.com/gidariss/wDAE_GNN_FewShot.

Semi-supervised Learning. We evaluate EPNet on the SSL setting where 100 additional unlabeled samples are available [29, 37] (EPNet$_{SSL}$). We observe in Table 4 that including unlabeled samples increases the accuracy of EPNet for all settings, surpassing the state of the art by a wide margin of up to 16% accuracy points for the 1-shot WRN-28-10. Similar to previous experiments, removing EP to EPNet (`--Net`) is detrimental for the model, supporting our hypotheses. Following the same setting described in [11, 21], we trained our model in the 5-shot 5-way scenario where the support samples are partially labeled. In Table 5, we report the test accuracy with `conv-4` when labeling 20%, 40%, 60% and 100% of the support set. EPNet obtains up to 2.7% improvement over previous state-of-the-art when 40% of the support are labeled. Moreover, EPNet al.so outperforms EGNN [21] in the 40% and 60% scenarios, although EPNet has 45× less parameters.

3.4 Ablation Studies

In this section we investigate the different hyperparameters of our method and the properties derived from embedding propagation. Additional ablations are provided in the supplementary material.

Table 6. Algorithm ablation with conv-4 on 1-shot *mini*Imagenet. EFT: Episodic Fine-tuning, ROT: Rotation loss, LP: Label Propagation, EP: Embedding Propagation

EXP	1	2	3	4	5	6	7	8	9	10	11	12	13	14	15	16
EFT									✓	✓	✓	✓	✓	✓	✓	✓
ROT					✓	✓	✓	✓					✓	✓	✓	✓
LP			✓	✓			✓	✓			✓	✓			✓	✓
EP		✓		✓		✓		✓		✓		✓		✓		✓
ACC	49.57	52.83	53.40	55.75	50.83	53.63	53.38	55.55	54.29	56.38	56.93	58.35	54.92	56.46	57.35	58.85

Algorithm Ablation. In Table 6, we investigate the impact of the rotation loss (ROT), embedding fine-tuning (EFT), label propagation (LP), and embedding propagation (EP) on the 1-shot *mini*Imagenet accuracy. When label propagation is deactivated, we substitute it with a prototypical classifier. Interestingly, it can be seen that the improvement is larger when using LP in combination with EP (Table 6; columns 2–4, and 10–12). This finding is in accordance with the hypothesis that EP performs manifold smoothing, and this is beneficial for transductive and SSL algorithms. We included a rotation loss for fair comparison with other SotA [12, 31], however, we see that the main improvement is due to the combination of EP with LP. We also find that episodic fine-tuning successfully adapts our model to the episodic scenario (Table 6; line 2).

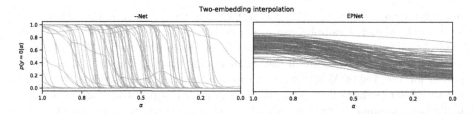

Fig. 3. Interpolation of embedding pairs of different classes vs probability of belonging to the first of these two classes. The top row shows the class probability for resnet-12 embeddings extracted from EPNet, and the second(--Net) from the same network trained without embedding propagation. The scalar α controls the weight of the first embedding in the linear interpolation.

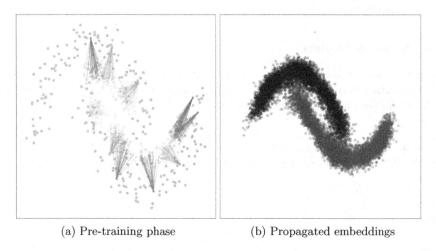

(a) Pre-training phase   (b) Propagated embeddings

Fig. 4. Visualization of embedding propagation on the two moons dataset. *The embeddings are shown on the same scale. (Color figure online)*

Embedding Propagation on Manifold Smoothness. We explore whether embedding propagation helps the classifier to attain smoother decision boundaries. We use EPNet to obtain image embeddings and select a set of random pairs $\mathbf{z}_i, \mathbf{z}_j$ that belong to different classes y_i, y_j. We then interpolate between each pair as $\widetilde{\mathbf{z}} = \alpha \cdot \mathbf{z}_i + (1 - \alpha)\mathbf{z}_j$ where $\alpha \in [0..1]$, and plot this value against $p(y_i|\widetilde{\mathbf{z}})$ (Sect. 7) in Fig. 3. We also plot $p(y_i|\hat{\mathbf{z}})$ where embeddings were obtained using EPNet without embedding propagation (--Net). We observe that EPNet has significantly smoother probability transitions than --Net as the embedding $\widetilde{\mathbf{z}}$ changes from $\mathbf{z}_i$ to $\mathbf{z}_j$. In contrast, --Net yields sudden probability transitions. This suggests that embedding propagation encourages smoother decision boundaries.

In Fig. 4, we show the effect of embedding propagation on a toy dataset. The dataset consists of embeddings that are arranged in two disjoint moons. The embeddings in the top moon belong to first class, and the other to the second class. Figure 4a) illustrates the effect of batch sampling during the pre-training phase. Gray points correspond to the extracted embeddings when no embedding propagation was applied. Each unique color shows multiple projections of the same gray point. Each projection is performed using a different batch of the data. This suggests that the projections of the same embedding fill a wide space in the manifold. As a result, the density and smoothness at the inter-class boundary increases. Figure 4b) shows the result of applying embedding propagation on all the gray points in Fig. 4a). The blue and red colors correspond to the two-moon classes. We observe that the propagated manifold is denser and more compact than the original one, possibly reducing the noise of the representations.

4   Conclusion

We have presented EPNet, an approach to address the problem of distribution shift few-shot learning. EPNet introduces a simple embedding propagation step to regularize the feature representations. Empirically, we have shown that embedding propagation smooths decision boundaries, which is an important factor for generalization. By leveraging the properties of smooth manifolds, we have shown significant improvements on the transductive, and semi-supervised learning setup compared to methods that do not use embedding propagation. As a result, EPNet achieves state-of-the-art results on *mini*Imagenet, *tiered*Imagenet, and CUB for the standard and semi-supervised scenarios. Further, we have shown that EP scales to the larger Imagenet-FS dataset, improving by more than 2% the accuracy of the state-of-the-art wDAE-GNN [14] in all setups. We have compared EPNet with a non-smooth version of the same model (--Net), showing that smoothing alone accounts for 4.8% accuracy improvement on 1-shot *mini*Imagenet with Wide Residual Networks.

References

1. Bartlett, P., Shawe-Taylor, J.: Generalization performance of support vector machines and other pattern classifiers. In: Advances in Kernel Methods–Support Vector Learning (1999)
2. Bauer, M., Rojas-Carulla, M., Światkowski, J.B., Schölkopf, B., Turner, R.E.: Discriminative k-shot learning using probabilistic models. arXiv preprint arXiv:1706.00326 (2017)
3. Belkin, M., Niyogi, P., Sindhwani, V.: Manifold regularization: a geometric framework for learning from labeled and unlabeled examples. JMLR **7**(Nov), 2399–2434 (2006)
4. Chapelle, O., Scholkopf, B., Zien, A.: Semi-supervised learning (chapelle, o. et al., eds.; 2006). IEEE Trans. Neural Netw. **20**, 542 (2009)
5. Chapelle, O., Zien, A.: Semi-supervised classification by low density separation. AISTATS **2005**, 57–64 (2005)
6. Chen, W.Y., Liu, Y.C., Kira, Z., Wang, Y.C.F., Huang, J.B.: A closer look at few-shot classification. In: ICLR (2019)

7. Cho, K., et al.: Retrieval-augmented convolutional neural networks against adversarial examples. In: Proceedings of the IEEE Conference on Computer Vision and Pattern Recognition, pp. 11563–11571 (2019)
8. Dvornik, N., Schmid, C., Mairal, J.: Diversity with cooperation: ensemble methods for few-shot classification. In: ICCV, pp. 3723–3731 (2019)
9. Fei-Fei, L., Fergus, R., Perona, P.: One-shot learning of object categories. TPAMI **28**(4), 594–611 (2006)
10. Finn, C., Abbeel, P., Levine, S.: Model-agnostic meta-learning for fast adaptation of deep networks. In: ICML, pp. 1126–1135 (2017). JMLR. org
11. Garcia, V., Bruna, J.: Few-shot learning with graph neural networks. In: ICLR (2017)
12. Gidaris, S., Bursuc, A., Komodakis, N., Pérez, P., Cord, M.: Boosting few-shot visual learning with self-supervision. In: CVPR, pp. 8059–8068 (2019)
13. Gidaris, S., Komodakis, N.: Dynamic few-shot visual learning without forgetting. In: CVPR, pp. 4367–4375 (2018)
14. Gidaris, S., Komodakis, N.: Generating classification weights with GNN denoising autoencoders for few-shot learning. In: Proceedings of the IEEE Conference on Computer Vision and Pattern Recognition, pp. 21–30 (2019)
15. Hariharan, B., Girshick, R.: Low-shot visual recognition by shrinking and hallucinating features. In: ICCV, pp. 3018–3027 (2017)
16. Hilliard, N., Phillips, L., Howland, S., Yankov, A., Corley, C.D., Hodas, N.O.: Few-shot learning with metric-agnostic conditional embeddings. arXiv preprint arXiv:1802.04376 (2018)
17. Hou, R., Chang, H., Bingpeng, M., Shan, S., Chen, X.: Cross attention network for few-shot classification. In: Advances in Neural Information Processing Systems, pp. 4005–4016 (2019)
18. Hu, Y., Gripon, V., Pateux, S.: Exploiting Unsupervised Inputs for Accurate Few-shot Classification (2020)
19. Ioffe, S., Szegedy, C.: Batch normalization: accelerating deep network training by reducing internal covariate shift. In: ICML, pp. 448–456 (2015)
20. Iscen, A., Tolias, G., Avrithis, Y., Chum, O.: Label propagation for deep semi-supervised learning. In: CVPR, pp. 5070–5079 (2019)
21. Kim, J., Kim, T., Kim, S., Yoo, C.D.: Edge-labeling graph neural network for few-shot learning. In: Proceedings of the IEEE Conference on Computer Vision and Pattern Recognition, pp. 11–20 (2019)
22. Krizhevsky, A., Sutskever, I., Hinton, G.E.: Imagenet classification with deep convolutional neural networks. In: NeurIPS, pp. 1097–1105 (2012)
23. Kye, S.M., Lee, H.B., Kim, H., Hwang, S.J.: Transductive few-shot learning with meta-learned confidence. arXiv preprint arXiv:2002.12017 (2020)
24. Lee, D.H.: Pseudo-label: the simple and efficient semi-supervised learning method for deep neural networks. In: Workshop on Challenges in Representation Learning, ICML, vol. 3, p. 2 (2013)
25. Lee, K., Maji, S., Ravichandran, A., Soatto, S.: Meta-learning with differentiable convex optimization. In: CVPR, pp. 10657–10665 (2019)
26. Lee, W.S., Bartlett, P.L., Williamson, R.C.: Lower bounds on the VC dimension of smoothly parameterized function classes. Neural Comput. **7**(5), 1040–1053 (1995)
27. Li, X., et al.: Learning to self-train for semi-supervised few-shot classification. In: NeurIPS, pp. 10276–10286 (2019)
28. Liu, B., Wu, Z., Hu, H., Lin, S.: Deep metric transfer for label propagation with limited annotated data. In: Proceedings of the IEEE International Conference on Computer Vision Workshops (2019)

29. Liu, Y., et al.: Learning to propagate labels: transductive propagation network for few-shot learning. In: ICLR (2019)
30. Long, J., Shelhamer, E., Darrell, T.: Fully convolutional networks for semantic segmentation. In: CVPR, pp. 3431–3440 (2015)
31. Mangla, P., Singh, M., Sinha, A., Kumari, N., Balasubramanian, V.N., Krishna-murthy, B.: Charting the right manifold: Manifold mixup for few-shot learning. arXiv preprint arXiv:1907.12087 (2019)
32. Nichol, A., Schulman, J.: Reptile: a scalable metalearning algorithm. arXiv preprint arXiv:1803.02999 (2018)
33. Oreshkin, B., López, P.R., Lacoste, A.: Tadam: task dependent adaptive metric for improved few-shot learning. In: NeurIPS, pp. 721–731 (2018)
34. Qiao, S., Liu, C., Shen, W., Yuille, A.L.: Few-shot image recognition by predicting parameters from activations. In: CVPR, pp. 7229–7238 (2018)
35. Rajeswaran, A., Finn, C., Kakade, S.M., Levine, S.: Meta-learning with implicit gradients. In: NeurIPS, pp. 113–124 (2019)
36. Ravi, S., Larochelle, H.: Optimization as a model for few-shot learning. In: ICLR (2016)
37. Ren, M., et al.: Meta-learning for semi-supervised few-shot classification. In: ICLR (2018)
38. Ren, S., He, K., Girshick, R., Sun, J.: Faster R-CNN: towards real-time object detection with region proposal networks. In: NeurIPS, pp. 91–99 (2015)
39. Rodríguez, P., Gonzalez, J., Cucurull, G., Gonfaus, J.M., Roca, X.: Regularizing CNNs with locally constrained decorrelations. In: ICLR (2016)
40. Russakovsky, O., et al.: ImageNet large scale visual recognition challenge. IJCC 115, 211–252 (2015). https://doi.org/10.1007/s11263-015-0816-y
41. Rusu, A.A., et al.: Meta-learning with latent embedding optimization. In: ICLR (2018)
42. Salimans, T., Kingma, D.P.: Weight normalization: a simple reparameterization to accelerate training of deep neural networks. In: NeurIPS, pp. 901–909 (2016)
43. Satorras, V.G., Estrach, J.B.: Few-shot learning with graph neural networks. In: ICLR (2018)
44. Snell, J., Swersky, K., Zemel, R.: Prototypical networks for few-shot learning. In: NeurIPS, pp. 4077–4087 (2017)
45. Srivastava, N., Hinton, G., Krizhevsky, A., Sutskever, I., Salakhutdinov, R.: Dropout: a simple way to prevent neural networks from overfitting. JMLR 15(1), 1929–1958 (2014)
46. Sun, Q., Liu, Y., Chua, T.S., Schiele, B.: Meta-transfer learning for few-shot learning. In: CVPR, pp. 403–412 (2019)
47. Sung, F., Yang, Y., Zhang, L., Xiang, T., Torr, P.H., Hospedales, T.M.: Learning to compare: Relation network for few-shot learning. In: CVPR, pp. 1199–1208 (2018)
48. Szegedy, C., et al.: Going deeper with convolutions. In: CVPR, pp. 1–9 (2015)
49. Tokozume, Y., Ushiku, Y., Harada, T.: Between-class learning for image classification. In: CVPR, pp. 5486–5494 (2018)
50. Vapnik, V.N.: An overview of statistical learning theory. IEEE Trans. Neural Netw. 10, 988–999 (1999)
51. Verma, V., et al.: Manifold mixup: better representations by interpolating hidden states. In: ICML, pp. 6438–6447 (2019)
52. Vinyals, O., Blundell, C., Lillicrap, T., Wierstra, D., et al.: Matching networks for one shot learning. In: NeurIPS, pp. 3630–3638 (2016)
53. Wang, Y.X., Girshick, R., Hebert, M., Hariharan, B.: Low-shot learning from imaginary data. In: CVPR, pp. 7278–7286 (2018)

54. Welinder, P., et al.: Caltech-UCSD Birds 200. Technical report CNS-TR-2010-001, California Institute of Technology (2010)
55. Xing, C., Rostamzadeh, N., Oreshkin, B., Pinheiro, P.O.: Adaptive cross-modal few-shot learning. In: NeurIPS, pp. 4848–4858 (2019)
56. Yang, L., Li, L., Zhang, Z., Zhou, X., Zhou, E., Liu, Y.: DPGN: distribution propagation graph network for few-shot learning. In: CVPR, pp. 13390–13399 (2020)
57. Ye, H.J., Hu, H., Zhan, D.C., Sha, F.: Few-shot learning via embedding adaptation with set-to-set functions. In: CVPR, pp. 8808–8817 (2020)
58. Yosinski, J., Clune, J., Bengio, Y., Lipson, H.: How transferable are features in deep neural networks? In: NeurIPS, pp. 3320–3328 (2014)
59. Yu, Z., Chen, L., Cheng, Z., Luo, J.: Transmatch: a transfer-learning scheme for semi-supervised few-shot learning. In: CVPR, pp. 12856–12864 (2020)
60. Zagoruyko, S., Komodakis, N.: Wide residual networks. In: BMVC, pp. 87.1-87.12. BMVA Press, September 2016. https://doi.org/10.5244/C.30.87
61. Zhang, H., Cisse, M., Dauphin, Y.N., Lopez-Paz, D.: Mixup: beyond empirical risk minimization. In: ICLR (2018)
62. Zhou, D., Bousquet, O., Lal, T.N., Weston, J., Schölkopf, B.: Learning with local and global consistency. In: NeurIPS, pp. 321–328 (2004)

Category Level Object Pose Estimation
via Neural Analysis-by-Synthesis

Xu Chen[1,3](✉), Zijian Dong[1], Jie Song[1], Andreas Geiger[2,4],
and Otmar Hilliges[1]

[1] ETH Zürich, Zürich, Switzerland
xuchen@inf.ethz.ch
[2] University of Tübingen, Tübingen, Germany
[3] Max Planck ETH Center for Learning Systems, Tübingen, Germany
[4] Max Planck Institute for Intelligent Systems, Tübingen, Germany

Abstract. Many object pose estimation algorithms rely on the analysis-by-synthesis framework which requires explicit representations of individual object instances. In this paper we combine a gradient-based fitting procedure with a parametric neural image synthesis module that is capable of implicitly representing the appearance, shape and pose of entire object categories, thus rendering the need for explicit CAD models per object instance unnecessary. The image synthesis network is designed to efficiently span the pose configuration space so that model capacity can be used to capture the shape and local appearance (i.e., texture) variations jointly. At inference time the synthesized images are compared to the target via an appearance based loss and the error signal is back-propagated through the network to the input parameters. Keeping the network parameters fixed, this allows for iterative optimization of the object pose, shape and appearance in a joint manner and we experimentally show that the method can recover orientation of objects with high accuracy from 2D images alone. When provided with depth measurements, to overcome scale ambiguities, the method can accurately recover the full 6DOF pose successfully.

Keywords: Category-level object pose · 6DoF pose estimation

1 Introduction

Estimating the 3D pose of objects from 2D images alone is a long-standing problem in computer vision and has many down-stream applications such as in robotics, autonomous driving and human-computer interaction. One popular

---

X. Chen and Z. Dong—Equal contribution.

Electronic supplementary material The online version of this chapter (https://doi.org/10.1007/978-3-030-58574-7_9) contains supplementary material, which is available to authorized users.

A. Vedaldi et al. (Eds.): ECCV 2020, LNCS 12371, pp. 139–156, 2020.
https://doi.org/10.1007/978-3-030-58574-7_9

class of solutions to this problem is based on the analysis-by-synthesis approach. The key idea of analysis-by-synthesis is to leverage a forward model (e.g., graphics pipeline) to generate different images corresponding to possible geometric and semantic states of the world. Subsequently, the candidate that best agrees with the measured visual evidence is selected. In the context of object pose estimation, the visual evidence may comprise RGB images [24,29], depth measurements [4,56] or features extracted using deep networks such as keypoints [17,29,33,39,49] or dense correspondence maps [25,38,55]. While such algorithms can successfully recover the object pose, a major limiting factor is the requirement to i) know which object is processed and ii) to have access to an explicit representation of the object for example, in the form of a 3D CAD model.

Embracing this challenge, in this paper we propose an algorithm that can be categorized as analysis-by-synthesis but overcomes the requirement of a known, explicit instance representation. At the core of our method lies a synthesis module that is based on recent advancements in the area of deep learning based image synthesis. More specifically, we train a pose-aware neural network to predict 2D images of objects with desired poses, shapes and appearances. In contrast to traditional static object representations, neural representations are able to jointly describe a large variety of instances, thereby extrapolating beyond the training set and allowing for continuous manipulation of object appearance and shape. In addition, our network is designed to efficiently span the space of 3D transformations, thus enabling image synthesis of objects in unseen poses.

After training, the synthesis module is leveraged in a gradient-based model fitting algorithm to jointly recover pose, shape and appearance of unseen object instances from single RGB or RGB-D images. Since our neural image synthesis module takes initial pose and latent codes (e.g., extracted from an image) as input, it can be used as a drop-in replacement in existing optimization-based model fitting frameworks. Given the initial pose and latent code, we generate an image and compare it with the target RGB image via an appearance based loss. The discrepancy in appearance produces error gradients which back-propagate through the network to the pose parameters and the latent code. Note that instead of updating the network parameters as during training time, we now keep the network weights fixed and instead update the appearance, shape and pose parameters. We repeat this procedure until convergence.

We evaluate our method on a publicly available real-world dataset on the task of category-level object pose estimation. Using RGB images, our method is able to estimate the 3D object orientation with an accuracy on par with and sometimes even better than a state-of-the-art method which leverages RGB-D input. As demonstrated in previous work [53], RGB-only methods suffer strongly from inherent scale ambiguities. Therefore, we also investigate an RGB-D version of our model which faithfully recovers both 3D translation and orientation. We systematically study algorithmic design choices and the hyper-parameters involved during both image generation and model fitting. In summary:

- We integrate a neural synthesis module into an optimization based model fitting framework to simultaneously recover object pose, shape and appearance from a single RGB or RGB-D image.
- This module is implemented as a deep network that can generate images of objects with control over poses and variations in shapes and appearances.
- Experiments show that our generative model reaches parity with and sometimes outperforms a strong RGB-D baseline. Furthermore, it significantly outperforms discriminative pose regression.[1]

2 Related Work

2.1 Object Pose Estimation

Given its practical importance, there is a large body of work focusing on object pose estimation. The state-of-the-art can be broadly categorized into template matching and regression techniques. Template matching techniques align 3D CAD models to observed 3D point clouds [4,56], images [24,29], learned keypoints [17,29,33,39,49] or correspondence features [25,38,55]. In contrast, [22,41,53] tackle object pose estimation as a classification or regression problem. However, to achieve high accuracy, these methods typically require template-based refinement, e.g., using ICP [4]. While yielding impressive results, all aforementioned methods require access to an instance specific 3D CAD model of the object, both during training and test time. This greatly limits their applicability since storing and comparing to all possible 3D CAD models at test time is impractical in many situations. Moreover, capturing high-fidelity and complete 3D models is often difficult and for some applications even impossible.

Only recently, researchers started the attempt to address object pose estimation without requiring access to instance-specific 3D object models at test time. NOCS [50] proposes to tackle this problem by learning to reconstruct the 3D object model in a canonical coordinate frame from RGB images and then align the reconstruction to depth measurements. They train their reconstruction network using objects from the same categories, which is expected to generalize to unseen instances within the same category at test time. While our method also learns to solve the task from objects within the same category, our method is a fully generative approach which simultaneously recovers object pose, shape and appearance. Thus, it allows for directly synthesizing the object appearance, eliminating the intermediate step of reconstructing the object in 3D. Latent-Fusion [37] proposes a 3D latent space based object representation for unseen object pose estimation. In contrast to ours, it requires multi-view imagery of the test object to form the latent space and depth measurements at test time. In contrast to both NOCS [50] and LatentFusion [37], our model enables 3D object pose estimation from a single RGB image as input.

---

[1] Project homepage: ait.ethz.ch/projects/2020/neural-object-fitting.

2.2   Pose Dependent Image Generation

Pose or viewpoint dependent image generation has been studied in two settings. One line of work focuses on synthesizing novel views for a given source image by directly generating pixels [23,34,44,48] or by warping pixels from source to target view [9,35,40,46,57]. While such techniques can be used to render objects in different poses, the object appearance and shape is controlled by the source image which cannot be optimized.

Another line of work tackles the problem of disentangled image generation [8,16,19,27,42], considering object pose as one factor among many. Recent works [32] achieve appealing results on viewpoint/pose disentanglement using a 3D latent space. While all mentioned methods are able to generate objects in different poses, shape and appearances, the pose cannot be controlled precisely (e.g., rotation by a set amount of degrees), rendering their application to absolute object pose estimation tasks difficult. Inspired by [32], our network also adopts a 3D latent space. However, we utilize the model in a supervised fashion to integrate precise absolute pose knowledge into the latent representation during training. This is achieved by integrating the 3D latent space with a conditional VAE framework. In contrast to [44] which also utilizes a 3D latent space, our model can jointly represent multiple instances of an object category and to generalize to unseen instances. Similar and concurrent to ours, [31] uses pose-aware image generation for viewpoint estimation, but in a discriminative manner.

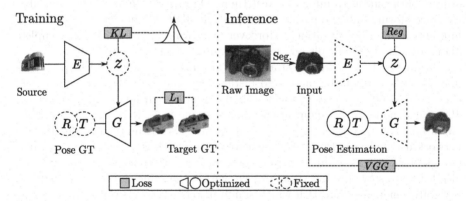

Fig. 1. Method overview. We leverage a learned pose-aware image generator G for object pose estimation. *Training:* The generator is trained in the VAE framework by leveraging multi-view images of synthetic objects. We minimize the reconstruction loss between generated and ground-truth images of known orientation together with the KL divergence. After training, the generator can produce images that faithfully reflect the (latent) appearance and desired pose. *Inference:* To estimate object pose from a segmented real image as input, our method iteratively optimizes the object pose and shape, minimizing the perceptual loss between the input and the generated image while keeping the weights of the trained networks fixed.

2.3 3D Representations for Objects

Several works have addressed the problem of generating 3D geometric representations including meshes [12,28,47], point sets [2,26,54], voxels [6,52] and implicit functions [10,30,36,45]. While these generative models are also able to represent objects at category level and could theoretically be used for category-level object fitting in combination with a differential rendering algorithm, all aforementioned techniques only consider geometry, but not the appearance. As a result depth measurements are required and the rich information underlying in the object's appearance is discarded. In contrast, our method allows for leveraging appearance information and does not require depth maps as input. While [58] is able to generate textured objects, it is limited by its reliance on 3D meshes. In contrast, we completely forego the intermediate geometry estimation task, instead focusing on pose-conditioned appearance generation.

2.4 Latent Space Optimization

The idea of updating latent representations by iterative energy minimization has been exploited for other tasks. CodeSLAM [5] learns a latent representation of depth maps, optimizing the latent representation instead of per-pixel depth values during bundle adjustment. GANFit [13] represents texture maps with GANs and jointly fits the latent code and 3DMM parameters to face images. [1,3,14,42] embeds natural images into the latent space of GANs by iteratively minimizing the image reconstruction error for image editing. Our method is inspired by these works, but targets a different application where latent appearance codes and geometric parameters such as poses must be optimized jointly.

3 Method

We propose a neural analysis-by-synthesis approach to category-level object pose estimation. Leveraging a learned image synthesis module, our approach is able to recover the 3D pose of an object from a single RGB or RGB-D image without requiring access to instance-specific 3D CAD models.

Figure 1 gives an overview of our approach. We first train a pose-aware image generator G with multi-view images of synthetic objects from the ShapeNet [7] dataset, which is able to generate object images $\hat{I} = G(R, T, z)$ that faithfully reflect the input object pose (R, T) and appearance code z. At inference time with a segmented image I as input, our method estimates object pose by iteratively optimizing the object pose and shape to minimize the discrepancy between the input image and the synthesized image $G(R, T, z)$.

3.1 Pose-Aware Image Generator

To generate images of different instances of a given category, we seek to generate images with significant but controllable shape and appearance variation.

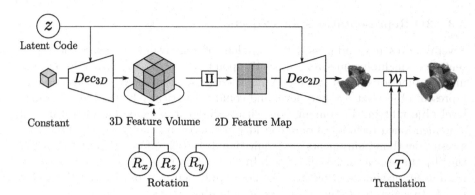

Fig. 2. Pose-aware image generator. To generate an image in the desired pose (R, T), the out-of-plane rotation $R_x R_y$ is first applied to the 3D feature volume, and then the 2D projection of the feature volume is decoded into an image. Subsequently, this image undergoes a 2D similarity transformation derived from the translation T and in-plane rotation R_z to form the final output. The latent code z is injected into the 3D feature volume generator Dec_{3D} and the 2D decoder Dec_{2D} via adaIN to control the variation in shapes and appearances.

We encode shape and appearance via latent variable z, and the desired 6 DoF object pose, comprising 3D rotation $R = R_x R_y R_z$ and 3D translation $T = [t_x \ t_y \ t_z]$, via (R, T). The z-axis is defined to align with the principal axis of the camera and the y-axis points upwards. For efficiency and to increase the capacity of our model in terms of representing the large variability of shapes and appearances, we decouple the image generation pipeline into two stages. First, we observe that 3D translations T and in-plane rotations R_z can be modeled using 2D operations and thus do not need to be learned. Therefore, we constrain our network G_{3D} to generate only images with out-of-plane rotations $\hat{I}_{rot} = G_{3D}(R_x, R_y, z)$, i.e., elevation R_x and azimuth R_y. The remaining transformations are modeled using 2D image warping operations $\mathcal{W}$ derived from 3D translations T and in-plane rotation R_z. The full generation process is defined as $G = \mathcal{W} \circ G_{3D}$.

Appearance and 3D Rotation. In order to generate images of objects in diverse appearances, shapes and poses, we adopt a 3D style-based image generation network similar to the one proposed in [32] as illustrated in Fig. 2. This network combines a 3D feature volume which faithfully captures 3D rotations with a style-based generator [21]. This enables our model to disentangle global appearance variation from geometric factors such as pose and shape. The 3D style-based image generation network consists of four main steps: i) generating the 3D feature volume, ii) transforming the feature volume based on the pose, iii) projecting the 3D volume into a 2D feature map, and iv) decoding the feature map into the predicted image $\hat{I}$. Both, the 3D generator and the 2D generator are conditioned on the latent code z via adaptive instance normalization [18] to model the variance in shape and appearance respectively. The object orientation R controls the transformation that is applied to the 3D feature volume.

Translation and 2D Rotation. While the 3D style-based decoder can in principle cover the entire space of 6 DoF poses, the resulting model would require a very large capacity and dataset to be trained on. We therefore constrain the decoder to out-of-plane rotations and handle all remaining transformation using a similarity 2D transformation. The warping field is given by:

$$\mathcal{W}(T, R_z) : \begin{bmatrix} u \\ v \end{bmatrix} \mapsto \frac{f}{t_z} \cdot \left(R_z \begin{bmatrix} u \\ v \end{bmatrix} + \begin{bmatrix} t_x \\ t_y \end{bmatrix} \right) \tag{1}$$

We use $\mathcal{W}$ to warp the generated image, yielding the final image $\hat{I}$:

$$\hat{I} = G(R, T, z) = \mathcal{W}(T, R_z) \circ G_{3D}(R_x, R_y, z) \tag{2}$$

3.2 Training

We train our image generator in a conditional VAE framework as illustrated in Fig. 1 in order to achieve precise pose control over the generated image. A VAE is an auto-encoder trained by minimizing a reconstruction term and the KL divergence between the latent space distribution and a normalized Gaussian. We use our 3D style-based image generation network as decoder and a standard CNN as encoder.

At each training iteration, the encoder first extracts the latent code from an image of a randomly chosen training object. Then the 3D image generation network takes this latent code together with the desired pose as input to generate an image $\hat{I}$ of the chosen object in the *desired* pose. The encoder and decoder are jointly trained by minimizing the reconstruction loss between the generated image and the ground-truth, regularized via the KL divergence:

$$\mathcal{L} = \|I - \hat{I}\|_1 + \lambda_{KL} \, D_{KL} \tag{3}$$

where λ_{KL} weights the regularization term and is set to $1e^{-2}$ in our experiments. The required training data, namely images of objects in difference poses and the corresponding pose label, is obtained by rendering synthetic objects from the ShapeNet dataset [7]. Since translation and 2D rotation is modelled by similarity transformation which does not require training, we only generate training samples with out-of-plane rotations for the sake of training efficiency.

3.3 Object Pose Estimation

The trained pose-aware image generator can render objects in various shapes, appearances and poses. Since the forward process is differentiable, we can solve the inverse problem of recovering its pose, shape and appearance by iteratively refining the network inputs (i.e., the pose parameters and the latent code), so that the discrepancy between the generated and the target image is minimized:

$$R^*, T^*, z^* = \underset{R,T,z}{\operatorname{argmin}} \quad E(I, R, T, z) \tag{4}$$

In the following sections, we will discuss the choice of energy function E, our initialization strategy and the optimizer in detail. Note that we assume that the object is segmented from the background which can be achieved using off-the-shelf image segmentation networks such as Mask-RCNN [15].

Energy Function. We require a distance function d that measures the discrepancy between two images. Common choices include the L_1 and L_2 per-pixel differences, the Structural Similarity Index Metric (SSIM) [51] and the perceptual loss [20] which computes the L_2 difference in deep feature space. To gain robustness with respect to domain shifts we adopt the perceptual loss as distance function and experimentally validate that it yields the best results.

Without further regularization, we found that the model may converge to degenerate solutions by pushing the latent code beyond the valid domain. To avoid such undesirable solutions, we penalize the distance to the origin of the latent space. Due to the KL divergence term used during training, codes near the origin are more likely to be useful for the decoder. Our final energy function is then given by:

$$E(I, R, T, z) = \|F_{vgg}(I) - F_{vgg}(\hat{I})\|_2 + \|z\|_2, \tag{5}$$

where F_{vgg} is a VGG network [43] pre-trained on ImageNet [11] for deep feature extraction and $\hat{I}$ is the image generated based on R, T and z according to Eq. 2.

Initialization Strategy. Since the above energy function is non-convex, gradient-based optimization techniques are prone to local minima. Therefore, we start the optimization process from multiple different initial states which we execute in parallel for efficiency. The optimal solution results in an image that aligns with the target image as well as possible, with any differences in pose or appearance leading to an increase in the reconstruction error. We thus choose the best solution by evaluating the optimization objective.

We sample the initial poses uniformly from the space of valid poses. As the latent dimension is high, random sampling can be inefficient due to the curse of dimensionality. We therefore leverage our (jointly trained) encoder to obtain mean and variance for the conditional distribution of the latent code and sample from the corresponding Gaussian distribution.

4 Evaluation

We first compare our approach with the state-of-the-art category-level object pose estimation method NOCS [50]. To validate the effectiveness of our method, we then also compare our method with several other baselines for category-level object model fitting. Furthermore, we systematically vary the architecture and hyper-parameters of our image generation network to analyze their influence on the fitting result. We also study the influence of the hyper-parameters for optimization. Finally, we evaluate the robustness of our generative model with respect to domain shifts, comparing it to a discriminative model.

4.1 Comparison with State-of-the-art

Baseline. To the best of our knowledge, NOCS [50] is the only method for category-level object pose estimation. It uses both synthetic data generated from ShapeNet CAD models, and real data to train a network that is able to reconstruct objects from a RGB image in a canonical coordinate frame. Subsequently, the object pose is recovered by aligning the reconstruction to the depth map. NOCS uses both simulated (CAMERA) and real data (REAL275) for training. Their simulated data is generated by compositing synthetic images from [7] onto real-world tables. REAL275 contains real RGB-D images (4300 for training and 2750 for testing), capturing 42 real object instances of 6 categories (camera, can, bottle, bowl, laptop and mug) in 18 different scenes.

Our method is trained with the same set of synthetic objects used in the CAMERA dataset. However our method does not require superimposing the objects onto real contexts. More importantly, in contrast to NOCS, our method does not require real images and their pose annotations for training. Note that we rely only on cheap to acquire 2D annotations of real images to fine-tune the object segmentation network (we use the REAL275 dataset for this purpose).

Since there is no public method capable of category-level object pose estimation from RGB images alone, we introduce a simple baseline consisting of a VGG16 [43] network that regresses object orientations directly from 2D images, trained on the same synthetic data as ours. Note that this is a fair comparison since the baseline and our method use the same training and test data.

Metrics. We follow the evaluation protocol defined by NOCS [50]. NOCS reports average precision which considers object detection, classification and pose estimation accuracy. They set a detection threshold of 10% bounding box overlap between prediction and ground truth to ensure that most objects are included in the evaluation. Next, they compute the average precision for different thresholds of rotation and translation error as performance indicator. Although our method assumes that the target image does not contain background and we rely on a off-the shelf 2D image segmentation network for object detection, we follow the same protocol for a fair comparison with NOCS. To remove the influence of varying detection accuracy from the comparison, we use the trained Mask-RCNN network from the NOCS Github repository.

The error in rotation e_R and translation e_t is defined by:

$$e_R = arccos\frac{Tr(\tilde{R} \cdot R^T) - 1}{2} \text{ and } e_t = \|\tilde{t} - t\|_2 \qquad (6)$$

where Tr represents the trace of the matrix. For symmetric object categories (bottle, bowl, and can), we allow the predicted 3D bounding box to freely rotate around the object's vertical axis with no penalty, as done in [50].

Results: Translation. We first evaluate the translation accuracy, summarized in Fig. 3. When using depth as input, both models perform comparable. We simply treat depth as an additional color channel during fitting and the translation parameter T_z is directly added to the generated depth map. This version is trained on synthetic RGB-D data instead of RGB data. Without using depth at training and test time, our RGB only version does not achieve the same accuracy. This is however to be expected due to the inherent scale-ambiguity of 2D observations. We remark that similar observations have been made in the instance-level pose estimation literature [53].

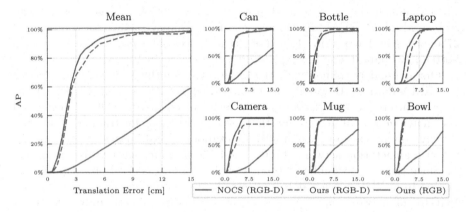

Fig. 3. Comparison with NOCS: Translation. Average precision at different translation thresholds. When using depth, our method achieves comparable results to the RGB-D method. When using RGB only, our method yields higher errors due to scale ambiguities.

Results: Orientation. The AP curve for our rotation estimation experiment is shown in Fig. 4. Despite using only RGB inputs, on average we achieve results on par or better than the privileged NOCS baseline which uses RGB and depth as well as real-images with paired pose annotations during training. Taking a closer look at each category, our method outperforms NOCS on the bottle, can and camera categories. We hypothesize that the complex textures of cans and bottles is problematic for the regression of the NOCS features, and the complex geometry of cameras poses a challenge for ICP. Figure 5 shows qualitative results. It can be seen that our method produces more accurate results than NOCS, especially for geometrically complex objects. This may also provide an explanation for the narrow performance advantage of NOCS on bowl and laptop; both object types have many planar regions which favor the point-to-plane metric used in ICP.

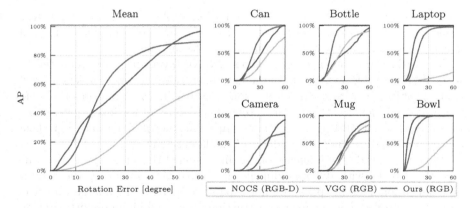

Fig. 4. Comparison with NOCS: Orientation. Average precision at different rotation error thresholds. Using only RGB as input, on average we achieve results on par or better than the NOCS baseline which uses RGB-D input and real training images with pose annotations. Our method can handle objects with complex geometry (camera) and textures (can) better than NOCS. See Fig. 5.

Fig. 5. Qualitative comparison to NOCS. Our method can handle geometrically complex objects such as cameras better. Objects in insets.

Finally, our method significantly outperforms the discriminative RGB-based baseline which directly regresses 3D orientation from images. This large gap is partially due to the sensitivity of discriminative methods towards distribution shifts and domain gaps between the training and test data (e.g., instances, lighting, occlusion and segmentation imperfections) and proves the generalization power of generative models for pose estimation.

4.2 Component Analysis

Image Generation. We evaluate the influence of our design choices in the image generation network on both the image generation and the object pose fitting task. First, we train a network in which the poses are directly concatenated to the latent code and then decoded to images with 2D convolutions only, the latter essentially being a standard conditional VAE (denoted by **w/o 3D**). Table 1a and Fig. 6 clearly show that the lack of a 3D latent space leads to poor image generation results and consequently the fitting fails.

We further train our network without the KL divergence term (denoted by **w/o VAE** in Table 1a). While the image generation network achieves a lower training objective without regularization, this results in a non-smooth latent space, i.e. only few samples in the latent space are used for image generation. In consequence, the fitting is negatively impacted since no informative gradient can be produced to guide the updates of the latent code.

Finally, we study the influence of the dimension of the latent space. We train several networks with different dimensions. Table 1b summarizes the results. Low-dimensional latent spaces are not capable of representing a large variety of objects, and inflect high image reconstruction errors and high pose fitting error. On the other extreme, we find that higher dimensionality leads to better image reconstruction quality, whereas it poses difficulty for fitting. We hypothesize that this is due the more complex structure of the latent space which is required to obtain high reconstruction fidelity. Empirically, we find that a 16-dimensional latent space leads to a good trade-off between image quality and pose accuracy.

Table 1. Effect of network design choices on object pose estimation. (a) demonstrates that both the VAE training scheme and the 3D feature volume are beneficial for object pose estimation. (b) shows that overly high- or low-dimensional latent space can negatively influence the pose estimation.

<table>
<tr><td colspan="4">(a) Network architectures.</td><td colspan="4">(b) Latent space dimension.</td></tr>
<tr><td></td><td>L1</td><td>AP_{10}</td><td>AP_{60}</td><td></td><td>L1</td><td>AP_{10}</td><td>AP_{60}</td></tr>
<tr><td>w/o 3D</td><td>0.109</td><td>1.8%</td><td>90.2%</td><td>4</td><td>0.082</td><td>9.1%</td><td>96.6%</td></tr>
<tr><td>w/o VAE</td><td>**0.049**</td><td>12.3%</td><td>92.7%</td><td>16</td><td>0.056</td><td>**16.5%**</td><td>**97.1%**</td></tr>
<tr><td>Ours</td><td>0.056</td><td>**16.5%**</td><td>**97.1%**</td><td>128</td><td>**0.041**</td><td>11.4%</td><td>96.0%</td></tr>
</table>

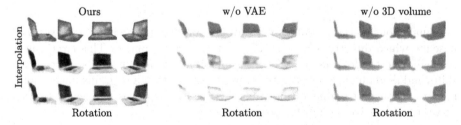

Fig. 6. Image generated with different network architectures. Our method can generate novel images in diverse shape and appearances and in desired poses. Without using KL divergence (w/o VAE) the network cannot generate novel samples. Without using 3D structure, the network struggles to faithfully reflect rotation and hence the image quality suffers.

Optimization. We study the hyper-parameters for optimization. We plot the error evolution of our energy function and the rotation error at different iterations. As evident from Table 2, with decreasing loss, the rotational error also decreases, demonstrating that our energy function provides a meaningful signal for pose estimation. In practice, our method converges in less than 50 iterations in most cases. The fitting progress is also visualized qualitatively in the figure in Table 2. The initial pose is significantly different from the target as shown in the inset. The initial appearance, which is obtained via the encoder, is close to the target appearance but still displays noticeable differences, e.g. the touchpad. Our method jointly refines both the pose and appearance. During the first few iterations, the method mainly focuses on adjusting the pose since the pose has a larger influence on the error than the appearance. In the last few iterations the method mainly focuses on fine-tuning the appearance to adapt to the image.

Table 2. Ablation study of energy functions. As shown in (a), perceptual loss outperforms other potential error functions. (b) shows that the rotational error decreases with decreasing energy value.

(a) Effect of energy functions.

	AP_{10}	AP_{60}
L1	14.3%	85.3%
L2	13.2%	88.3%
SSIM	15.8%	92.5%
w/o reg	16.2%	95.9%
Ours	**16.5%**	**97.1%**

(b) Loss and pose error along iterations.

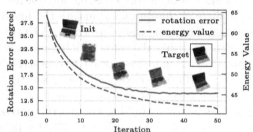

We also evaluate other potential choices for the energy function to minimize, including the mean absolute error (L1), the mean squared error (L2) and the Structural Similarity Index Metric (SSIM) [51]. These error functions do not perform as well as the perceptual loss as shown in Table 2a. This is likely due to the fact that the perceptual loss encourages semantic alignment rather than pixel-wise alignment. Thus it produces results that are globally aligned instead of focusing on local regions. We also conduct experiments in fitting without the regularization term (**w/o reg**). This leads to unrealistic samples that minimizes the loss in an undesired way, resulting in a performance decrease compared to our full model.

4.3   Robustness

In order to study the robustness of our method to varying factors causing domain shift, we evaluate our method in a controlled simulation environment. We train our network using the "laptop" category of the synthetic ShapeNet dataset and

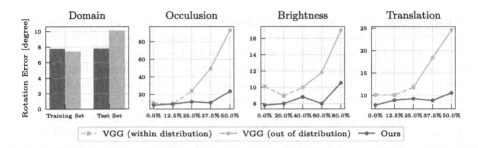

Fig. 7. Study of robustness. We study the influence of object instances, occlusion, brightness, and translation on the accuracy of rotation estimation. Compared to the VGG-based regression baseline, ours retains low error under challenging conditions even without any data augmentation at training time.

test on unseen synthetic instances. We mainly study three factors that often differ between real and simulated data, namely lighting, occlusion and offsets in bounding box detection. At test time, we vary one of these factors at a time and evaluate the average error in terms of orientation estimation. We modify the brightness of the target image for lighting, remove certain areas of the image to simulate occlusion and translate the image in 2D to emulate inaccurate 2D detection. For comparison, we train a VGG16 network to regress rotation angles from images using the same training data. It is well known that discriminative approaches are more susceptible to overfitting which often results in worse generalization performance compared to generative approaches. We verify this finding for the category-level pose estimation task. We also randomly vary the three factors already when training the discriminative approach, but only to a limited degree (up to 20% for occlusion, 40% for lighting and 25% for translation). At test time, we test the network on samples both within and beyond the training variations. Note that our method *never* sees augmented images during training.

Figure 7 illustrates the results of this experiment. First, we observe that our generative approach is less sensitive to the gap between training and test instances which is a crucial design goal of our approach in order to deal with unseen objects. When varying the three factors, the discriminative model exhibits significant performance variations especially when the factor exceeds the variations in the training distribution. In contrast, our method exhibits less performance variation which demonstrates the robustness of our method.

5   Conclusion

In this paper, we propose a novel solution to category-level object pose estimation. We combine a gradient-based fitting procedure with a parametric neural image synthesis model that is capable of implicitly representing the appearance, shape and pose of entire object categories, thus avoiding the need for instance-specific 3D CAD models at test time. We show that this approach reaches performance on par with and sometimes even outperforms a strong RGB-D baseline.

While our focus lies on rigid objects, extending our method to handle non-rigid or partially rigid objects is an interesting direction for future work.

Acknowledgement. This research was partially supported by the Max Planck ETH Center for Learning Systems and a research gift from NVIDIA.

References

1. Abdal, R., Qin, Y., Wonka, P.: Image2stylegan: how to embed images into the stylegan latent space? In: Proceedings of the IEEE International Conference on Computer Vision (ICCV) (2019)
2. Achlioptas, P., Diamanti, O., Mitliagkas, I., Guibas, L.: Learning representations and generative models for 3D point clouds. In: Proceedings of the International Conference on Machine Learning (ICML) (2018)
3. Bau, D., et al.: Semantic photo manipulation with a generative image prior. In: ACM Transactions on Graphics (TOG) (2019)
4. Besl, P.J., McKay, N.D.: Method for registration of 3-D shapes. In: Sensor Fusion IV: Control Paradigms and Data Structures (1992)
5. Bloesch, M., Czarnowski, J., Clark, R., Leutenegger, S., Davison, A.J.: Codeslam-learning a compact, optimisable representation for dense visual slam. In: Proceedings of IEEE Conference on Computer Vision and Pattern Recognition (CVPR) (2018)
6. Brock, A., Lim, T., Ritchie, J.M., Weston, N.: Generative and discriminative voxel modeling with convolutional neural networks. In: arXiv (2016)
7. Chang, A.X., et al.: Shapenet: an information-rich 3D model repository. In: arXiv (2015)
8. Chen, X., Duan, Y., Houthooft, R., Schulman, J., Sutskever, I., Abbeel, P.: Infogan: interpretable representation learning by information maximizing generative adversarial nets. In: Advances in Neural Information Processing Systems (NeurIPS) (2016)
9. Chen, X., Song, J., Hilliges, O.: Monocular neural image based rendering with continuous view control. In: Proceedings of the IEEE International Conference on Computer Vision (ICCV) (2019)
10. Chen, Z., Zhang, H.: Learning implicit fields for generative shape modeling. In: Proceedings of IEEE Conference on Computer Vision and Pattern Recognition (CVPR) (2019)
11. Deng, J., Dong, W., Socher, R., Li, L.J., Li, K., Fei-Fei, L.: Imagenet: a large-scale hierarchical image database. In: Proceedings IEEE Conference on Computer Vision and Pattern Recognition (CVPR) (2009)
12. Gao, L., et al.: SDM-net: deep generative network for structured deformable mesh. In: ACM Transactions on Graphics (TOG) (2019)
13. Gecer, B., Ploumpis, S., Kotsia, I., Zafeiriou, S.: Ganfit: generative adversarial network fitting for high fidelity 3D face reconstruction. In: Proceedings of IEEE Conference on Computer Vision and Pattern Recognition (CVPR) (2019)
14. Gu, J., Shen, Y., Zhou, B.: Image processing using multi-code GAN prior. In: Proceedings of IEEE Conference on Computer Vision and Pattern Recognition (CVPR) (2020)
15. He, K., Gkioxari, G., Dollár, P., Girshick, R.: Mask R-CNN. In: Proceedings of the IEEE International Conference on Computer Vision (ICCV) (2017)

16. Higgins, I., et al.: beta-VAE: learning basic visual concepts with a constrained variational framework. In: Proceedings of the International Conference on Learning Representations (ICLR) (2017)
17. Hu, Y., Hugonot, J., Fua, P., Salzmann, M.: Segmentation-driven 6D object pose estimation. In: Proceedings of IEEE Conference on Computer Vision and Pattern Recognition (CVPR) (2019)
18. Huang, X., Belongie, S.: Arbitrary style transfer in real-time with adaptive instance normalization. In: Proceedings of the IEEE International Conference on Computer Vision (ICCV) (2017)
19. Jahanian, A., Chai, L., Isola, P.: On the "steerability" of generative adversarial networks. In: Proceedings of the International Conference on Learning Representations (ICLR) (2020)
20. Johnson, J., Alahi, A., Fei-Fei, L.: Perceptual losses for real-time style transfer and super-resolution. In: Leibe, B., Matas, J., Sebe, N., Welling, M. (eds.) ECCV 2016. LNCS, vol. 9906, pp. 694–711. Springer, Cham (2016). https://doi.org/10.1007/978-3-319-46475-6_43
21. Karras, T., Laine, S., Aila, T.: A style-based generator architecture for generative adversarial networks. In: Proceedings of IEEE Conference on Computer Vision and Pattern Recognition (CVPR) (2019)
22. Kehl, W., Manhardt, F., Tombari, F., Ilic, S., Navab, N.: SSD-6D: Making RGB-based 3D detection and 6D pose estimation great again. In: Proceedings of the IEEE International Conference on Computer Vision (ICCV) (2017)
23. Kulkarni, T.D., Whitney, W.F., Kohli, P., Tenenbaum, J.: Deep convolutional inverse graphics network. In: Advances in Neural Information Processing Systems (NeurIPS) (2015)
24. Li, Y., Wang, G., Ji, X., Xiang, Yu., Fox, D.: DeepIM: deep iterative matching for 6D pose estimation. In: Ferrari, V., Hebert, M., Sminchisescu, C., Weiss, Y. (eds.) ECCV 2018. LNCS, vol. 11210, pp. 695–711. Springer, Cham (2018). https://doi.org/10.1007/978-3-030-01231-1_42
25. Li, Z., Wang, G., Ji, X.: CDPN: coordinates-based disentangled pose network for real-time RGB-based 6-DOF object pose estimation. In: Proceedings of the IEEE International Conference on Computer Vision (ICCV) (2019)
26. Lin, C.H., Kong, C., Lucey, S.: Learning efficient point cloud generation for dense 3D object reconstruction. In: AAAI (2018)
27. Locatello, F., et al.: Challenging common assumptions in the unsupervised learning of disentangled representations. In: Proceedings of the International Conference on Machine Learning (ICML) (2019)
28. Loper, M., Mahmood, N., Romero, J., Pons-Moll, G., Black, M.J.: SMPL: a skinned multi-person linear model. In: ACM Transactions on Graphics (TOG) (2015)
29. Manhardt, F., Kehl, W., Navab, N., Tombari, F.: Deep model-based 6D pose refinement in RGB. In: Ferrari, V., Hebert, M., Sminchisescu, C., Weiss, Y. (eds.) Computer Vision – ECCV 2018. LNCS, vol. 11218, pp. 833–849. Springer, Cham (2018). https://doi.org/10.1007/978-3-030-01264-9_49
30. Mescheder, L., Oechsle, M., Niemeyer, M., Nowozin, S., Geiger, A.: Occupancy networks: learning 3D reconstruction in function space. In: Proceedings of IEEE Conference on Computer Vision and Pattern Recognition (CVPR) (2019)
31. Mustikovela, S.K., et al.: Self-supervised viewpoint learning from image collections. In: Proceedings of IEEE Conference on Computer Vision and Pattern Recognition (CVPR) (2020)

32. Nguyen-Phuoc, T., Li, C., Theis, L., Richardt, C., Yang, Y.L.: Hologan: unsupervised learning of 3D representations from natural images. In: Proceedings of the IEEE International Conference on Computer Vision (ICCV) (2019)
33. Oberweger, M., Rad, M., Lepetit, V.: Making deep heatmaps robust to partial occlusions for 3D object pose estimation. In: Ferrari, V., Hebert, M., Sminchisescu, C., Weiss, Y. (eds.) ECCV 2018. LNCS, vol. 11219, pp. 125–141. Springer, Cham (2018). https://doi.org/10.1007/978-3-030-01267-0_8
34. Olszewski, K., Tulyakov, S., Woodford, O., Li, H., Luo, L.: Transformable bottleneck networks. In: Proceedings of the IEEE International Conference on Computer Vision (ICCV) (2019)
35. Park, E., Yang, J., Yumer, E., Ceylan, D., Berg, A.C.: Transformation-grounded image generation network for novel 3D view synthesis. In: Proceedings of IEEE Conference on Computer Vision and Pattern Recognition (CVPR) (2017)
36. Park, J.J., Florence, P., Straub, J., Newcombe, R., Lovegrove, S.: DeepSDF: learning continuous signed distance functions for shape representation. In: Proceedings of IEEE Conference on Computer Vision and Pattern Recognition (CVPR) (2019)
37. Park, K., Mousavian, A., Xiang, Y., Fox, D.: Latentfusion: end-to-end differentiable reconstruction and rendering for unseen object pose estimation. In: Proceedings of IEEE Conference on Computer Vision and Pattern Recognition (CVPR) (2020)
38. Park, K., Patten, T., Vincze, M.: Pix2pose: pixel-wise coordinate regression of objects for 6D pose estimation. In: Proceedings of the IEEE International Conference on Computer Vision (ICCV) (2019)
39. Peng, S., Liu, Y., Huang, Q., Zhou, X., Bao, H.: PVNet: pixel-wise voting network for 6D of pose estimation. In: Proceedings of IEEE Conference on Computer Vision and Pattern Recognition (CVPR) (2019)
40. Penner, E., Zhang, L.: Soft 3D reconstruction for view synthesis. In: ACM Transactions on Graphics (TOG) (2017)
41. Rad, M., Lepetit, V.: BB8: a scalable, accurate, robust to partial occlusion method for predicting the 3D poses of challenging objects without using depth. In: Proceedings of the IEEE International Conference on Computer Vision (ICCV) (2017)
42. Shen, Y., Gu, J., Tang, X., Zhou, B.: Interpreting the latent space of GANS for semantic face editing. In: Proceedings of IEEE Conference on Computer Vision and Pattern Recognition (CVPR) (2020)
43. Simonyan, K., Zisserman, A.: Very deep convolutional networks for large-scale image recognition. In: Proceedings of the International Conference on Learning Representations (ICLR) (2015)
44. Sitzmann, V., Thies, J., Heide, F., Nießner, M., Wetzstein, G., Zollhofer, M.: Deepvoxels: learning persistent 3d feature embeddings. In: Proceedings of IEEE Conference on Computer Vision and Pattern Recognition (CVPR) (2019)
45. Sitzmann, V., Zollhöfer, M., Wetzstein, G.: Scene representation networks: continuous 3D-structure-aware neural scene representations. In: Advances in Neural Information Processing Systems (NeurIPS) (2019)
46. Sun, S.-H., Huh, M., Liao, Y.-H., Zhang, N., Lim, J.J.: Multi-view to novel view: synthesizing novel views with self-learned confidence. In: Ferrari, V., Hebert, M., Sminchisescu, C., Weiss, Y. (eds.) ECCV 2018. LNCS, vol. 11207, pp. 162–178. Springer, Cham (2018). https://doi.org/10.1007/978-3-030-01219-9_10
47. Tan, Q., Gao, L., Lai, Y.K., Xia, S.: Variational autoencoders for deforming 3D mesh models. In: Proceedings of IEEE Conference on Computer Vision and Pattern Recognition (CVPR) (2018)

48. Tatarchenko, M., Dosovitskiy, A., Brox, T.: Multi-view 3D models from single images with a convolutional network. In: Leibe, B., Matas, J., Sebe, N., Welling, M. (eds.) ECCV 2016. LNCS, vol. 9911, pp. 322–337. Springer, Cham (2016). https://doi.org/10.1007/978-3-319-46478-7_20

49. Tekin, B., Sinha, S.N., Fua, P.: Real-time seamless single shot 6D object pose prediction. In: Proceedings of IEEE Conference on Computer Vision and Pattern Recognition (CVPR) (2018)

50. Wang, H., Sridhar, S., Huang, J., Valentin, J., Song, S., Guibas, L.J.: Normalized object coordinate space for category-level 6D object pose and size estimation. In: Proceedings of IEEE Conference on Computer Vision and Pattern Recognition (CVPR) (2019)

51. Wang, Z., Bovik, A.C., Sheikh, H.R., Simoncelli, E.P.: Image quality assessment: from error visibility to structural similarity. In: IEEE Transactions on Image Processing (TIP) (2004)

52. Wu, J., Zhang, C., Xue, T., Freeman, B., Tenenbaum, J.: Learning a probabilistic latent space of object shapes via 3D generative-adversarial modeling. In: Advances in Neural Information Processing Systems (NeurIPS) (2016)

53. Xiang, Y., Schmidt, T., Narayanan, V., Fox, D.: PoseCNN: a convolutional neural network for 6D object pose estimation in cluttered scenes. In: Robotics: Science and Systems (RSS) (2018)

54. Yang, G., Huang, X., Hao, Z., Liu, M.Y., Belongie, S., Hariharan, B.: Pointflow: 3D point cloud generation with continuous normalizing flows. In: Proceedings of the IEEE International Conference on Computer Vision (ICCV) (2019)

55. Zakharov, S., Shugurov, I., Ilic, S.: DPOD: 6D pose object detector and refiner. In: Proceedings of the IEEE International Conference on Computer Vision (ICCV) (2019)

56. Zeng, A., et al.: Multi-view self-supervised deep learning for 6D pose estimation in the amazon picking challenge. In: Proceedings of the International Conference on on Robotics and Automation (ICRA) (2017)

57. Zhou, T., Tulsiani, S., Sun, W., Malik, J., Efros, A.A.: View synthesis by appearance flow. In: Leibe, B., Matas, J., Sebe, N., Welling, M. (eds.) ECCV 2016. LNCS, vol. 9908, pp. 286–301. Springer, Cham (2016). https://doi.org/10.1007/978-3-319-46493-0_18

58. Zhu, J.Y., et al.: Visual object networks: image generation with disentangled 3D representations. In: Advances in Neural Information Processing Systems (NeurIPS) (2018)

High-Fidelity Synthesis with Disentangled Representation

Wonkwang Lee[1], Donggyun Kim[1], Seunghoon Hong[1(✉)], and Honglak Lee[2,3]

[1] KAIST, Daejeon, South Korea
{wonkwang.lee,kdgyun425,seunghoon.hong}@kaist.ac.kr
[2] University of Michigan, Ann Arbor, USA
honglak@umich.edu
[3] Google AI, Cambridge, USA
honglak@google.com

Abstract. Learning disentangled representation of data without supervision is an important step towards improving the interpretability of
generative models. Despite recent advances in disentangled representation learning, existing approaches often suffer from the trade-off between
representation learning and generation performance (*i.e.,* improving generation quality sacrifices disentanglement performance). We propose an
Information-Distillation Generative Adversarial Network (ID-GAN), a
simple yet generic framework that easily incorporates the existing state-
of-the-art models for both disentanglement learning and high-fidelity
synthesis. Our method learns disentangled representation using VAE-
based models, and distills the learned representation with an additional
nuisance variable to the separate GAN-based generator for high-fidelity
synthesis. To ensure that both generative models are aligned to render
the same generative factors, we further constrain the GAN generator to
maximize the mutual information between the learned latent code and
the output. Despite the simplicity, we show that the proposed method
is highly effective, achieving comparable image generation quality to the
state-of-the-art methods using the disentangled representation. We also
show that the proposed decomposition leads to an efficient and stable
model design, and we demonstrate photo-realistic high-resolution image
synthesis results (1024 × 1024 pixels) for the first time using the disentangled representations. Our code is available at https://www.github.
com/1Konny/idgan.

1 Introduction

Learning a compact and interpretable representation of data without supervision
is important to improve our understanding of data and machine learning systems.
Recently, it is suggested that a *disentangled representation* that represents data

Electronic supplementary material The online version of this chapter (https://
doi.org/10.1007/978-3-030-58574-7_10) contains supplementary material, which is
available to authorized users.

© Springer Nature Switzerland AG 2020
A. Vedaldi et al. (Eds.): ECCV 2020, LNCS 12371, pp. 157–174, 2020.
https://doi.org/10.1007/978-3-030-58574-7_10

Fig. 1. Generated images on the CelebA-HQ dataset [35]. The proposed framework allows synthesizing high-resolution images (1024 × 1204 pixels) using the disentangled representation learned by VAEs.

using independent factors of variations in data can improve the interpretability and transferability of the representation [1,5,51]. Among various use-cases of disentangled representation, we are particularly interested in its application to generative models, since it allows users to specify the desired output properties by controlling the generative factors encoded in each latent dimension. There are increasing demands on such generative models in various domains, such as image manipulation [21,28,31], drug discovery [16], ML fairness [11,36], *etc.*(Fig. 1).

Most prior works on unsupervised disentangled representation learning formulate the problem as constrained generative modeling task. Based on well-established frameworks, such as the Variational Autoencoder (VAE) or the Generative Adversarial Network (GAN), they introduce additional regularization to encourage the axes of the latent manifold to align with independent generative factors in the data. Approaches based on VAE [7,9,18,26] augment its objective function to favor a factorized latent representation by adding implicit [7,18] or explicit penalties [9,26]. On the other hand, approaches based on GAN [10] propose to regularize the generator such that it increases the mutual information between the input latent code and its output.

One major challenge in the existing approaches is the trade-off between learning disentangled representations and generating realistic data. VAE-based approaches are effective in learning useful disentangled representations in various tasks, but their generation quality is generally worse than the state-of-the-arts, which limits its applicability to the task of realistic synthesis. On the other hand, GAN-based approaches can achieve the high-quality synthesis with a more expressive decoder and without explicit likelihood estimation [10]. However, they tend to learn comparably more entangled representations than the VAE counterparts [7,9,18,26] and are notoriously difficult to train, even with recent techniques to stabilize the training [26,54].

To circumvent this trade-off, we propose a simple and generic framework to combine the benefits of disentangled representation learning and high-fidelity synthesis. Unlike the previous approaches that address both problems jointly by a single objective, we formulate two separate, but successive problems; we first learn a disentangled representation using VAE, and *distill* the learned representation to GAN for high-fidelity synthesis. The distillation is performed from VAE to GAN by transferring the inference model, which provides a meaningful latent distribution, rather than a simple Gaussian prior and ensures that both models are aligned to render the same generative factors. Such decomposition also naturally allows a layered approach to learn latent representation by first learning major disentangled factors by VAE, then learning missing (entangled) nuisance factors by GAN. We refer the proposed method as the Information Distillation Generative Adversarial Network (ID-GAN).

Despite the simplicity, the proposed ID-GAN is extremely effective in addressing the previous challenges, achieving high-fidelity synthesis using the learned disentangled representation (*e.g.*, 1024 × 1024 image). We also show that such decomposition leads to a practically efficient model design, allowing the models to learn the disentangled representation from low-resolution images and transfer it to synthesize high-resolution images.

The contributions of this paper are as follows:

- We propose ID-GAN, a simple yet effective framework that combines the benefits of disentangled representation learning and high-fidelity synthesis.
- The decomposition of the two objectives enables plug-and-play-style adoption of state-of-the-art models for both tasks, and efficient training by learning models for disentanglement and synthesis using low- and high-resolution images, respectively.
- Extensive experimental results show that the proposed method achieves state-of-the-art results in both disentangled representation learning and synthesis over a wide range of tasks from synthetic to complex datasets.

2   Related Work

Disentanglement Learning. Unsupervised disentangled representation learning aims to discover a set of generative factors, whose element encodes unique and independent factors of variation in data. To this end, most prior works based on VAE [9,18,26] and GAN [10,22,33,34] focused on designing the loss function to encourage the factorization of the latent code. Despite some encouraging results, however, these approaches have been mostly evaluated on simple and low-resolution images [37,41]. We believe that improving the generation quality of disentanglement learning is important, since it not only increases the practical impact in real-world applications, but also helps us to better assess the disentanglement quality on complex and natural images where the quantitative evaluation is difficult. Although there are increasing recent efforts to improve the generation quality with disentanglement learning [22,33,34,45], they often come with the degraded disentanglement performance [10], rely on a specific inductive bias (*e.g.*, 3D transformation [45]), or are limited to low-resolution images [22,33,34]. On the contrary, our work aims to investigate a general framework to improve the generation quality without representation learning trade-off, while being general enough to incorporate various methods and inductive biases. We emphasize that this contribution is complementary to the recent efforts for designing better inductive bias or supervision for disentanglement learning [8,38,44,48,53]. In fact, our framework is applicable to a wide variety of disentanglement learning methods and can incorporate them in a plug-and-play style as long as they have an inference model (*e.g.*, nonlinear ICA [25]).

Combined VAE/GAN Models. There have been extensive attempts in literature toward building hybrid models of VAE and GAN [4,6,20,29,55], which learn to represent and synthesize data by jointly optimizing VAE and GAN objectives. Our method is an instantiation of this model family, but is differentiated from the prior work in that (1) the training of VAE and GAN is decomposed into two separate tasks and (2) the VAE is used to learn a specific conditioning variable (*i.e.*, disentangled representation) to the generator while the previous methods assume the availability of an additional conditioning variable [4] or use VAE to learn the entire (entangled) latent distribution [6,20,29,55]. Also, extending the previous VAE-GAN methods to incorporate disentanglement constraints is not straightforward, as the VAE and GAN objectives are tightly entangled in them. In the experiment, we demonstrate that applying existing hybrid models on our task suffers from the suboptimal trade-off between the generation and disentanglement performance, and they perform much worse than our method.

3   Background: Disentanglement Learning

The objective of unsupervised disentanglement learning is to describe each data x using a set of statistically independent generative factors z. In this section, we briefly review prior works and discuss their advantages and limitations.

The state-of-the-art approaches in unsupervised disentanglement learning are largely based on the Variational Autoencoder (VAE). They rewrite their original objective and derive regularizations that encourage the disentanglement of the latent variables. For instance, β-VAE [18] proposes to optimize the following modified Evidence Lower-Bound (ELBO) of the marginal log-likelihood:

$$\mathbb{E}_{x \sim p(x)}[\log p(x)] \geq \mathbb{E}_{x \sim p(x)}[\mathbb{E}_{z \sim q_\phi(z|x)}[\log p_\theta(x|z)] - \beta \; D_{KL}(q_\phi(z|x)\|p(z))], \quad (1)$$

where setting $\beta = 1$ reduces to the original VAE. By forcing the variational posterior to be closer to the factorized prior ($\beta > 1$), the model learns a more disentangled representation, but with a sacrifice of generation quality, since it also decreases the mutual information between z and x [9,26]. To address such trade-off and improve the generation quality, recent approaches propose to gradually anneal the penalty on the KL-divergence [7], or decompose it to isolate the penalty for *total correlation* [52] that encourages the statistical independence of latent variables [1,9,26].

Approaches based on VAE have shown to be effective in learning disentangled representations over a range of tasks from synthetic [41] to complex datasets [3,35]. However, their generation performance is generally insufficient to achieve high-fidelity synthesis, even with recent techniques isolating the factorization of the latent variable [9,26]. We argue that this problem is fundamentally attributed to two reasons: First, most VAE-based approaches assume the fully-independent generative factors [9,18,26,37,40,51]. This strict assumption oversimplifies the latent manifold and may cause the loss of useful information (*e.g.*, correlated factors) for generating realistic data. Second, they typically utilize a simple generator, such as the factorized Gaussian decoder, and learn a uni-modal mapping from the latent to input space. Although this might be useful to learn meaningful representations [7] (*e.g.*, capturing a structure in local modes), such decoder makes it difficult to render complex patterns in outputs (*e.g.*, textures).

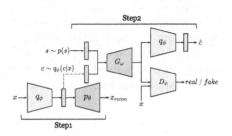

Fig. 2. Overall framework of the proposed method (ID-GAN).

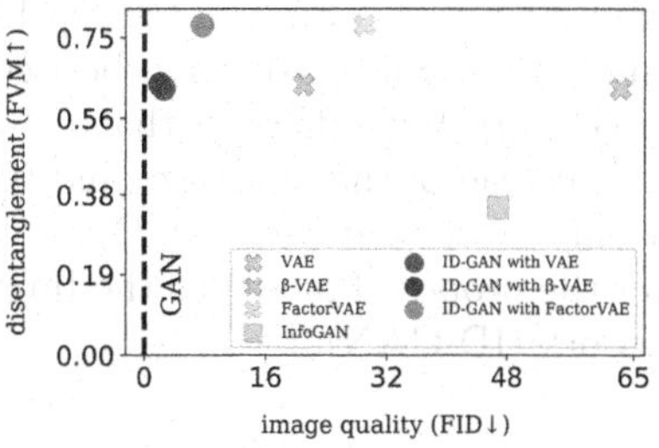

Fig. 3. Comparison of disentanglement vs. generation performance on dSprites dataset.

4 High-Fidelity Synthesis via Distillation

Our objective is to build a generative model $G_\omega : \mathcal{Z} \to \mathcal{X}$ that produces high-fidelity output $x \in \mathcal{X}$ with an interpretable latent code $z \in \mathcal{Z}$ (*i.e.*, disentangled representation). To achieve this goal, we build our framework upon VAE-based models due to their effectiveness in learning disentangled representations. However, discussions in the previous section suggest that disentanglement learning in VAE leads to the sacrifice of generation quality due to the strict constraints on fully-factorized latent variables and the utilization of simple decoders. We aim to improve the VAE-based models by enhancing generation quality while maintaining its disentanglement learning performance.

Our main idea is to decompose the objectives of learning disentangled representation and generating realistic outputs into separate but successive learning problems. Given a disentangled representation learned by VAEs, we train another network with a much higher modeling capacity (*e.g.*, GAN generator) to decode the learned representation to a realistic sample in the observation space.

Figure 2 describes the overall framework of the proposed algorithm. Formally, let $z = (s, c)$ denote the latent variable composed of the disentangled variable c

and the nuisance variable s capturing independent and correlated factors of variation, respectively. In the proposed framework, we first train VAE (*e.g.*, Eq. (1)) to learn disentangled latent representations of data, where each observation x can be projected to c by the learned encoder $q_\phi(c|x)$ after the training. Then in the second stage, we fix the encoder q_ϕ and train a generator $G_\omega(z) = G_\omega(s, c)$ for high-fidelity synthesis while *distilling* the learned disentanglement by optimizing the following objective:

$$\min_G \max_D \; \mathcal{L}_{\mathrm{GAN}}(D, G) - \lambda \mathcal{R}_{\mathrm{ID}}(G), \tag{2}$$

$$\mathcal{L}_{\mathrm{GAN}}(D, G) = \mathbb{E}_{x \sim p(x)}[\log D(x)] + \mathbb{E}_{s \sim p(s), c \sim q_\phi(c)}[\log(1 - D(G(s, c)))], \tag{3}$$

$$\mathcal{R}_{\mathrm{ID}}(G) = \mathbb{E}_{c \sim q_\phi(c), x \sim G(s,c)}[\log q_\phi(c|x)] + H_{q_\phi}(c), \tag{4}$$

where $q_\phi(c) = \frac{1}{N} \sum_i q_\phi(c|x_i)$ is the aggregated posterior [19,39,50] of the encoder network[1]. Similar to [10], Eq. (4) corresponds to the variational lower-bound of mutual information between the latent code and the generator output $I(c; G(s, c))$, but differs in that (1) c is sampled from the aggregated posterior $q_\phi(c)$ instead of the prior $p(c)$ and (2) it is optimized with respect to the generator only. Note that we treat $H_{q_\phi}(c)$ as a constant since q_ϕ is fixed in Eq.(4). We refer the proposed model as the Information Distillation Generative Adversarial Network (ID-GAN).

4.1   Analysis

In this section, we provide in-depth analysis of the proposed method and its connections to prior works.

Comparisons to β-VAEs [9,18,26]. Despite the simplicity, the proposed ID-GAN effectively addresses the problems in β-VAEs with generating high-fidelity outputs; it augments the latent representation by introducing a nuisance variable s, which complements the disentangled variable c by modeling richer generative factors. For instance, the VAE objective tends to favor representational factors that characterize as much data as possible [7] (*e.g.*, azimuth, scale, lighting, *etc.*), which are beneficial in representation learning, but incomprehensive to model the complexity of observations. Given the disentangled factors discovered by VAEs, ID-GAN learns to encode the remaining generative factors (such as high-frequency textures, face identity, *etc.*) into nuisance variable s. (Fig. 8). This process shares a similar motivation with a progressive augmentation of latent factors [32], but is used for modeling disentangled and nuisance generative factors. In addition, ID-GAN employs a much more expressive generator than a simple factorized Gaussian decoder in VAE, which is trained with adversarial loss to render realistic and convincing outputs. Combining both, our method allows the generator to synthesize various data in a local neighborhood defined by c, where the specific characteristics of each example are fully characterized by the additional nuisance variable s.

---

[1] In practice, we can easily sample c from $q_\phi(c)$ by $c \sim q_\phi(c|x)p(x)$.

Comparisons to InfoGAN [10]. The proposed method is closely related to InfoGAN, which optimizes the variational lower-bound of mutual information $I(c; G(s,c))$ for disentanglement learning. To clarify the difference between the proposed method and InfoGAN, we rewrite the regularization for both methods using the KL divergence as follows:

$$\mathcal{R}_{\text{Info}}(G, q) = -\mathbb{E}_{s \sim p(s)}[D_{\text{KL}}(p(c)\|q_\phi(c|G(s,c)))], \tag{5}$$

$$\mathcal{R}_{\text{ours}}(G, q) = \beta\mathcal{R}_{\text{VAE}}(q) + \lambda\mathcal{R}_{\text{ID}}(G), \text{ where}$$

$$\mathcal{R}_{\text{VAE}}(q) = -\mathbb{E}_{x \sim p(x)}[D_{\text{KL}}(q_\phi(c|x)\|p(c))], \tag{6}$$

$$\mathcal{R}_{\text{ID}}(G) = -\mathbb{E}_{s \sim p(s)}[D_{\text{KL}}(q_\phi(c)\|q_\phi(c|G(s,c)))], \tag{7}$$

where $\mathcal{R}_{\text{ours}}$ summarizes all regularization terms in our method[2]. See the Appendix A.1 for detailed derivations.

Equation (5) shows that InfoGAN optimizes the *forward* KL divergence between the prior $p(c)$ and the approximated posterior $q_\phi(c|G(s,c))$. Due to the zero-avoiding characteristics of forward KL [43], it forces all latent code c with non-zero prior to be covered by the posterior q_ϕ. Intuitively, it implies that InfoGAN tries to exploit every dimensions in c to encode each (unique) factor of variations. It becomes problematic when there is a mismatch between the number of true generative factors and the size of latent variable c, which is common in unsupervised disentanglement learning. On the contrary, VAE optimizes the *reverse* KL divergence (Eq. (6)), which can effectively avoid the problem by encoding only meaningful factors of variation into certain dimensions in c while collapsing the remainings to the prior. Since the encoder training in our method is only affected by Eq. (6), it allows us to discover the ambient dimension of latent generative factors robust to the choice of latent dimension $|c|$.

In addition, Eq. (5) shows that InfoGAN optimizes the encoder using the generated distributions, which can be problematic when there exists a sufficient discrepancy between the true and generated distributions (*e.g.*, mode-collapse may cause learning partial generative factors.). On the other hand, the encoder training in our method is guided by the true data (Eq. (6)) together with maximum likelihood objective, while the mutual information (Eq. (7)) is enforced only to the generator. This helps our model to discover comprehensive generative factors from data while guiding the generator to align its outputs to the learned representation.

Practical Benefits. The objective decomposition in the proposed method also offers a number of practical advantages. First, it enables plug-and-play-style adoption of the state-of-the-art models for disentangled representation learning and high-quality generation. As shown in Fig. 3, it allows our model to achieve state-of-the-art performance on both tasks. (Fig. 3). Second, such decomposition also leads to an efficient model design, where we learn disentanglement from

---

[2] In practice, we learn the encoder q_ϕ and generator G independently by Eq. (6) and (7), respectively, through two-step training.

low-resolution images and distill the learned representation to the task of high-resolution synthesis with a much higher-capacity generator. We argue that it is practically reasonable in many cases since VAEs tend to learn global structures in disentangled representation, which can be captured from low-resolution images. We demonstrate this in the high-resolution image synthesis task, where we use the disentangled representation learned with 64×64 images for the synthesis of 256×256 or 1024×1024 images.

5   Experiments

In this section, we present various results to show the effectiveness of ID-GAN. Please find the Appendix for more comprehensive results and figures.

Table 1. Quantitative comparison results on synthetic datasets.

	Color-dSprites			Scream-dSprites			Noisy-dSprites		
	FVM (↑)	MIG (↑)	FID (↓)	FVM (↑)	MIG (↑)	FID (↓)	FVM (↑)	MIG (↑)	FID (↓)
VAE [46]	.67±.12	.16±.08	21.63±4.97	.44±.03	.08±.04	7.79±2.51	**.42±.09**	.05±.04	3.27±1.94
β-VAE [18]	.67±.07	.32±.04	15.13±4.25	**.57±.01**	**.29±.00**	7.33±2.87	.32±.05	.05±.03	3.46±0.38
FactorVAE [26]	**.69±.05**	**.37±.02**	10.71±5.73	**.57±.01**	.22±.06	6.35±3.27	.40±.09	**.08±.04**	2.48±0.44
GAN [15]	N/A	N/A	.30±0.07	N/A	N/A	.11±0.03	N/A	N/A	9.74±2.18
InfoGAN [10]	.34± 00	.01±.01	30.55±21.17	.29± 00	.00±.00	5.77±3.93	.22±.02	.01±.01	5.51±4.22
OOGAN [34]	.32±.06	.01±.00	5.67±2.48	.21±.05	.00±.00	3.70±4.31	.21±.08	.01±.00	9.52±3.75
InfoGAN-CR [33]	.44±.10	.04±.02	.43±.19	.31±.08	.03±.05	6.05±5.28	.27±.02	.02±.01	48.52±57.12
ID-GAN+VAE	.67±.12	.16±.08	.32±0.10	.44±.03	.08±.04	.26±0.03	**.42±.09**	.05±.04	**1.58±0.62**
ID-GAN+β-VAE	.67±.07	.32±.04	**.25±0.23**	**.57±.01**	**.29±.00**	.18±0.02	.32±.05	.05±.03	12.42±1.13
ID-GAN+FactorVAE	**.69±.05**	**.37±.02**	.75±0.54	**.57±.01**	.22±.06	.65±0.33	.40±.09	**.08±.04**	2.07±0.87

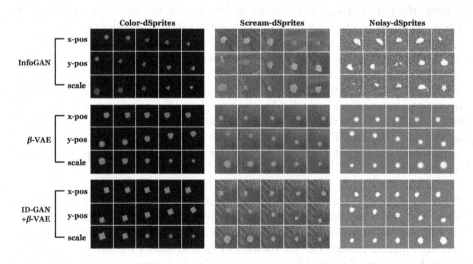

Fig. 4. Qualitative results on synthetic datasets. Both β-VAE and ID-GAN share the same latent code, but ID-GAN exhibits substantailly higher generation quality.

5.1   Implementation Details

Compared Methods. We compare our method with state-of-the-arts in disentanglement learning and generation. We choose β-VAE [18], FactorVAE [26], InfoGAN [10], OOGAN [34], and InfoGAN-CR [33] as baselines for disentanglement learning. For fair comparison, we choose the best hyperparameter for each model via extensive hyper-parameter search. We also report the performance by training each method over five different random seeds and averaging the results.

Network Architecture. For experiments on synthetic datasets, we adopt the architecture from [37] for all VAE-based methods (VAE, β-VAE, and FactorVAE). For GAN-based methods (GAN, InfoGAN, and ID-GAN), we employ the same decoder and encoder architectures in VAE as the generator and discriminator, respectively. We set the size of disentangled latent variable to 10 for all methods, and exclude the nuisance variable in GAN-based methods for a fair comparison with VAE-based methods. For experiments on complex datasets, we employ the generator and discriminator in the state-of-the-art GAN [42,47]. For VAE architectures, we utilize the same VAE architecture as in the synthetic datasets. We set the size of disentangled and nuisance variables to 20 and 256, respectively.

Evaluation Metrics. We employ three popular evaluation metrics in the literature: Factor-VAE Metric (FVM) [26], Mutual Information Gap (MIG) [9], and Fréchet Inception Distance (FID) [17]. *FVM* and *MIG* evaluate the disentanglement performance by measuring the degree of axis-alignment between each dimension of learned representations and ground-truth factors. *FID* evaluates the generation quality by measuring the distance between the true and the generated distributions.

5.2   Results on Synthetic Dataset

For quantitative evaluation of disentanglement, we employ the dSprites dataset [41], which contains synthetic images generated by randomly sampling known generative factors, such as shape, orientation, size, and x-y position. Due to the limited complexity of dSprites, we adopt three variants of dSprites, which are generated by adding color [26] (Color-dSprites) or background noise [37] (Noisy- and Scream-dSprites).

Table 1 and Fig. 4 summarize the quantitative and qualitative comparison results with existing disentanglement learning approaches, respectively. First, we observe that VAE-based approaches (*i.e.,* β-VAE and FactorVAE) achieve the state-of-the-art disentanglement performance across all datasets, outperforming the VAE baseline and InfoGAN with a non-trivial margin. The qualitative results in Fig. 4 show that the learned generative factors are well-correlated with meaningful disentanglement in the observation space. On the other hand, InfoGAN fails to discover meaningful disentanglement in most datasets. We observe that information maximization in InfoGAN often leads to undesirable factorization of generative factors, such as encoding both shape and position into one latent code, but factorizing latent dimensions by different combinations of them (*e.g.*, Color-dSprites in Fig. 4). ID-GAN achieves state-of-the-art disentanglement through the distillation of the learned latent code from the VAE-based models. Appendix B.3 also shows that ID-GAN is much more stable to train and insensitive to hyper-parameters than InfoGAN.

In terms of generation quality, VAE-based approaches generally perform much worse than GAN baseline. This performance gap is attributed to the strong constraints on the factorized latent variable and weak decoder in VAE, which limits the generation capacity. This is clearly observed in the results on the Noisy-dSprites dataset (Fig. 4), where the outputs from β-VAE fail to render the high-dimensional patterns in the data (*i.e.*, uniform noise). On the other hand, our method achieves competitive generation performance to the state-of-the-art GAN using a much more flexible generator for synthesis, which enables the modeling of complex patterns in data. As observed in Fig. 4, ID-GAN performs generation using the *same* latent code with β-VAE, but produces much more realistic outputs by capturing accurate object shapes (in Color-dSprites) and background patterns (in Scream-dSprites and Noisy-dSprites) missed by the VAE decoder. These results suggest that our method can achieve the best trade-off between disentanglement learning and high-fidelity synthesis.

Table 2. Comparison of approaches using a joint and decomposed objective for disentanglement learning and synthesis.

	dSprites		
	FVM ($\uparrow$)	MIG ($\uparrow$)	FID ($\downarrow$)
β-VAE (reference)	**0.65±0.08**	**0.28±0.09**	37.75±24.58
VAE-GAN	0.46±0.18	0.13±0.11	33.54±24.93
ID-GAN (end-to-end)	0.50±0.14	0.13±0.09	3.18±2.38
ID-GAN (two-step)	**0.65±0.08**	**0.28±0.09**	**2.00±1.74**

5.3   Ablation Study

This section provides an in-depth analysis of our method.

Is Two-Step Training Necessary? First, we study the impact of two-stage training for representation learning and synthesis. We consider two baselines: (1) VAE-GAN [29] as an extension of β-VAE with adversarial loss, and (2) end-to-end training of ID-GAN. Contrary to ID-GAN that learns to represent (q_ϕ) and synthesize (G) data via separate objectives, these baselines learn a single, entangled objective for both tasks. Table 2 summarizes the results in the dSprites dataset.

The results show that VAE-GAN improves the generation quality of β-VAE with adversarial learning. The generation quality is further improved in the end-to-end version of ID-GAN by employing a separate generator for synthesis. However, the improved generation quality in both baselines comes with the cost of degraded disentanglement performance. We observe that updating the encoder using adversarial loss hinders the discovery of disentangled factors, as the discriminator tends to exploit high-frequency details to distinguish the real images from the fake images, which motivates the encoder to learn nuisance factors. This suggests that decomposing the representation learning and generation objective is important in the proposed framework (ID-GAN two-step), which achieves the best performance in both tasks.

Is Distillation Necessary? The above ablation study justifies the importance of two-step training. Next, we compare different approaches for two-step training that perform conditional generation using the representation learned by β-VAE.

Specifically, we consider two baselines: (1) cGAN and (2) ID-GAN trained without distillation (ID-GAN w/o distill). We opt to consider cGAN as the baseline since we find that it implicitly optimizes $\mathcal{R}_{ID}$ (see Appendix A.2 for the proof). In the experiments, we train all models in the CelebA 128×128 dataset using the same β-VAE trained on the 64×64 resolution, and compare the generation quality (FID) and a degree of alignment between the disentangled code c and generator output $G(s,c)$. For comparison of the alignment, we measure $\mathcal{R}_{ID}$ (Eq. (7)) and GILBO[3] [2], both of which are valid lower-bounds of mutual information $I(c; G(s,c))$. Note that the comparison based on the lower-bound is still valid as its relative order has shown to be insensitive to the tightness of the bound [2]. Table 3 and Fig. 5 summarize the quantitative and qualitative results, respectively.

Table 3. Comparison of two-step approaches for generation (FID) and alignment ($\mathcal{R}_{ID}$ and GILBO (We report both $\mathcal{R}_{ID}$ and GILBO without $H_{q_\phi}(c)$ to avoid potential error in measuring $q_\phi(c)$ (*e.g.*, fitting a Gaussian [2]). Note that it does not affect the relative comparison since all models share the same q_ϕ)) performance.

	CelebA 128×128		
	FID ($\downarrow$)	$\mathcal{R}_{ID}$ ($\uparrow$)	GILBO [2] ($\uparrow$)
ID-GAN w/o distill	**5.75**	-65.84	-20.40
cGAN	7.07	-17.39	-7.57
ID-GAN	6.61	$\mathbf{-10.25}$	$\mathbf{-0.19}$

As shown in the table, all three models achieve comparable generation performances in terms of FID. However, we observe that their alignments to the input latent code vary across the methods. The qualitative results (Fig. 5) also show considerable mismatch between the c and the generated images. Compared

---

[3] GILBO is formulated similarly as $\mathcal{R}_{ID}$ (Eq. (4)), but optimized over another auxiliary encoder network different from the one used in $\mathcal{R}_{ID}$.

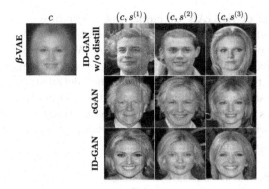

Fig. 5. Qualitative comparisons of various two-step approaches. All samples share the same disentangled code c, but different nuisance variable s. (1) First column: output of β-VAE decoder. (2) Second to fourth columns: images generated by different nuisance variables s using various methods (rows).

to this, cGAN achieves much higher degree of alignment due to the implicit optimization of $\mathcal{R}_{ID}$, but its association is much loose than our method (e.g., changes in gender and hairstyle). By explicitly constraining the generator to optimize $\mathcal{R}_{ID}$, ID-GAN achieves the best alignment.

5.4 Results on Complex Dataset

To evaluate our method with more diverse and complex factors of variation, we conduct experiments on natural image datasets, such as CelebA [35], 3D Chairs [3], and Cars [27]. We first evaluate our method on 64×64 images, and extend it to higher resolution images using the CelebA (256×256) and CelebA-HQ [24] (1024×1024) datasets.

Table 4. Quantitative results based on FID ($\downarrow$).

	3D chair	Cars	CelebA
VAE	116.46	201.29	160.06
βVAE	107.97	235.32	166.01
FactorVAE	123.64	208.60	154.48
GAN	**24.17**	14.62	**3.34**
InfoGAN	60.45	**13.67**	4.93
ID-GAN+βVAE	25.44	14.96	4.08

s

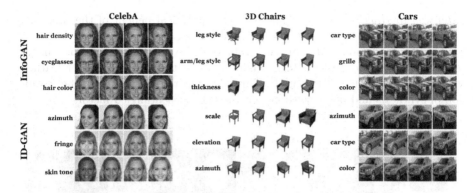

Fig. 6. Comparisons of latent traversal between GAN-based approaches. Despite the comparable generation quality, ID-GAN learns much more meaningful disentanglement.

Comparisons to Other Methods. Table 4 summarizes quantitative comparison results. Since the ground-truth factors are unknown, we report the performance based on generation quality (FID). As expected, the generation quality of VAEs is much worse in natural images. GAN-based methods, on the contrary, can generate more convincing samples although it tends to learn highly-entangled generative factors in nuisance variable. ID-GAN achieves disentanglement via disentangled factors learned by VAE, and generation performance on par with the GAN baseline. To better understand the disentanglement of GAN-based methods, we present latent traversal results in Fig. 6. We generate samples by modifying values of each dimension in the disentangled latent code c while fixing the rest. We observe that the InfoGAN fails to encode meaningful factors into c as the generation is dominated by the nuisance variable z, making all generated images almost identical. On the contrary, ID-GAN learns meaningful disentanglement with c and generates reasonable variations.

Fig. 7. Comparisons of VAE and ID-GAN outputs (top-rows: VAE, bottom-rows: ID-GAN). Note that both outputs are generated from the same latent code, but using different decoders. Both decoders are aligned well to render the same generative factors, but ID-GAN produces much more realistic outputs.

Extension to High-Resolution Synthesis. One practical benefit of the proposed two-step approach is that we can incorporate any VAE and GAN into our framework. To demonstrate this, we train ID-GAN for high-resolution images (*e.g.*, 256×256 and 1024×1024) while distilling the β-VAE encoder learned with *much smaller* 64×64 images[4]. This allows us to easily scale up the resolution of synthesis and helps us to better assess the disentangled factors.

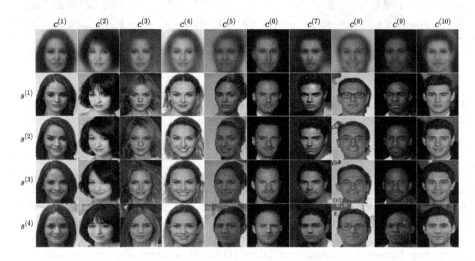

Fig. 8. Analysis on the learned disentangled variables $c^{(m)} \in \mathbb{R}^{20}$ and nuisance variables $s^{(n)} \in \mathbb{R}^{256}$ of ID-GAN on CelebA (256×256). The samples in the first row are generated by the β-VAE decoder and the rest are generated by ID-GAN. Each $c^{(m)}$ captures the most salient factors of variation (*e.g.*,azimuth) while $s^{(n)}$ contributes to the local details (*e.g.*,$s^{(2)}$ and $s^{(3)}$ for curvy and straight hair, respectively).

We first adapt ID-GAN to the 256×256 image synthesis task. To understand the impact of distillation, we visualize the outputs from the VAE decoder and the GAN generator using the same latent code as inputs. Figure 7 summarizes the results. We observe that the outputs from both networks are aligned well to render the same generative factors to similar outputs. Contrary to blurry and low-resolution (64×64) VAE outputs, however, ID-GAN produces much more realistic and convincing outputs by introducing a nuisance variable and employing more expressive decoder trained on higher-resolution (256×256). Interestingly, synthesized images by ID-GAN further clarify the disentangled factors learned by the VAE encoder. For instance, the first row in Fig. 7 shows that the ambiguous disentangled factors from the VAE decoder output is clarified by ID-GAN, which is turned out to capture the style of a cap. This suggests that ID-GAN can be useful in assessing the quality of the learned representation.

---

[4] We simply downsample the generator output by bilinear sampling to match the dimension between the generator and encoder.

To gain further insights on the learned generative factors by our method, we conduct qualitative analysis on the latent variables (c and s) by generating samples by fixing one variable while varying another (Fig. 8). We observe that varying the disentangled variable c leads to variations in the holistic structures in the outputs, such as azimuth, skin color, hair style, etc., while varying the nuisance variable s leads to changes in more fine-grained facial attributes, such as expression, skin texture, identity, etc.It shows that ID-GAN successfully distills meaningful and representative disentangled generative factors learned by the inference network in VAE, while producing diverse and high-fidelity outputs using generative factors encoded in the nuisance variable.

Finally, we further conduct experiments on the challenging task of mega-pixel image synthesis using CelebA-HQ dataset. We employ the generator architecture of VGAN [47] and adapt it to synthesize images given factors learned by β-VAE. Figure 9 presents the results, where we generate images by changing one values in one latent dimension in c. We observe that ID-GAN produces high-quality images with nice disentanglement, where it changes one factor of variation in the data (e.g., azimuth and hair-style) while preserving the others (e.g., identity).

Fig. 9. Results on the CelebA-HQ dataset (1024×1024 images).

6   Conclusion

We propose Information Distillation Generative Adversarial Network (ID-GAN), a simple framework that combines the benefits of the disentanglement representation learning and high-fidelity synthesis. It allows us to incorporate the state-of-the-art for both tasks by decomposing their objectives while constraining the generator by distilling the encoder. Extensive experiments validate that the proposed method can achieve the best trade-off between realism and disentanglement, outperforming the existing approaches with substantial margin.

Acknowledgement. This work was supported by Institute of Information & communications Technology Planning & Evaluation (IITP) grant funded by the Korea government (MSIT) (2020-0-00153 and 2016-0-00464).

References

1. Achille, A., Soatto, S.: Information dropout: learning optimal representations through noisy computation. In: TPAMI (2018)
2. Alemi, A.A., Fischer, I.: GILBO: one metric to measure them all. In: NeurIPS (2018)
3. Aubry, M., Maturana, D., Efros, A., Russell, B., Sivic, J.: Seeing 3D chairs: exemplar part-based 2D–3D alignment using a large dataset of CAD models. In: CVPR (2014)
4. Bao, J., Chen, D., Wen, F., Li, H., Hua, G.: CVAE-GAN: fine-grained image generation through asymmetric training. In: ICCV (2017)
5. Bengio, Y., Courville, A., Vincent, P.: Representation Learning: a review and new perspectives. In: PAMI (2013)
6. Brock, A., Lim, T., Ritchie, J.M., Weston, N.: Neural photo editing with introspective adversarial networks. In: ICLR (2017)
7. Burgess, C.P., et al.: Understanding disentangling in β-VAE. In: NeurIPS (2017)
8. Chen, J., Batmanghelich, K.: Weakly supervised disentanglement by pairwise similarities. In: AAAI (2020)
9. Chen, T.Q., Li, X., Grosse, R., Duvenaud, D.: Isolating sources of disentanglement in variational autoencoders. In: NeurIPS (2018)
10. Chen, X., Duan, Y., Houthooft, R., Schulman, J., Sutskever, I., Abbeel, P.: InfoGAN: interpretable representation learning by information maximizing generative adversarial nets. In: NeurIPS (2016)
11. Creager, E., et al.: Flexibly fair representation learning by disentanglement. In: ICML (2019)
12. Deng, J., Dong, W., Socher, R., Li, L.J., Li, K., Fei-Fei, L.: ImageNet: a Large-Scale Hierarchical Image Database. In: CVPR (2009)
13. Dosovitskiy, A., Brox, T.: Generating images with perceptual similarity metrics based on deep networks. In: NeurIPS (2016)
14. Fréchet, M.: Sur la distance de deux lois de probabilité. Comptes Rendus Hebdomadaires Des Seances de L'Academie Des Sciences (1957)
15. Goodfellow, I.J., et al.: Generative adversarial nets. In: NeurIPS (2014)
16. Gómez-Bombarelli, R., et al.: Automatic chemical design using a data-driven continuous representation of molecules. ACS Cent. Sci. **4**, 268–276 (2018)
17. Heusel, M., Ramsauer, H., Unterthiner, T., Nessler, B., Hochreiter, S.: GANs trained by a two time-scale update rule converge to a nash equilibrium. In: NeurIPS (2017)
18. Higgins, I., et al.: β-VAE: learning basic visual concepts with a constrained variational framework. In: ICLR (2017)
19. Hoffman, M.D., Johnson, M.J.: ELBO surgery: yet another way to carve up the variational evidence lower bound. In: NeurIPS (2016)
20. Huang, H., Li, z., He, R., Sun, Z., Tan, T.: Introvae: introspective variational autoencoders for photographic image synthesis. In: NeurIPS. Curran Associates, Inc. (2018)
21. Huang, X., Liu, M.-Y., Belongie, S., Kautz, J.: Multimodal unsupervised image-to-image translation. In: Ferrari, V., Hebert, M., Sminchisescu, C., Weiss, Y. (eds.) ECCV 2018. LNCS, vol. 11207, pp. 179–196. Springer, Cham (2018). https://doi.org/10.1007/978-3-030-01219-9_11
22. Jeon, I., Lee, W., Kim, G.: IB-GAN: disentangled representation learning with information bottleneck GAN (2019). https://openreview.net/forum?id=ryljV2A5KX

23. Johnson, J., Alahi, A., Fei-Fei, L.: Perceptual losses for real-time style transfer and super-resolution. In: Leibe, B., Matas, J., Sebe, N., Welling, M. (eds.) ECCV 2016. LNCS, vol. 9906, pp. 694–711. Springer, Cham (2016). https://doi.org/10.1007/978-3-319-46475-6_43

24. Karras, T., Aila, T., Laine, S., Lehtinen, J.: Progressive growing of GANS for improved quality, stability, and variation. In: ICLR (2018)

25. Khemakhem, I., Kingma, D., Hyvärinen, A.: Variational autoencoders and nonlinear ICA: a unifying framework. arXiv preprint arXiv:1907.04809 (2019)

26. Kim, H., Mnih, A.: Disentangling by factorising. In: ICML (2018)

27. Krause, J., Stark, M., Deng, J., Fei-Fei, L.: 3D object representations for fine-grained categorization. In: 4th International IEEE Workshop on 3D Representation and Recognition (3dRR-13) (2013)

28. Lample, G., Zeghidour, N., Usunier, N., Bordes, A., Denoyer, L., Ranzato, M.A.: Fader networks: manipulating images by sliding attributes. In: NeurIPS. Curran Associates, Inc. (2017)

29. Larsen, A.B.L., Sønderby, S.K., Larochelle, H., Winther, O.: Autoencoding beyond pixels using a learned similarity metric. In: ICML (2016)

30. Ledig, C., et al.: Photo-realistic single image super-resolution using a generative adversarial network. In: CVPR (2017)

31. Lee, H.-Y., Tseng, H.-Y., Huang, J.-B., Singh, M., Yang, M.-H.: Diverse image-to-image translation via disentangled representations. In: Ferrari, V., Hebert, M., Sminchisescu, C., Weiss, Y. (eds.) ECCV 2018. LNCS, vol. 11205, pp. 36–52. Springer, Cham (2018). https://doi.org/10.1007/978-3-030-01246-5_3

32. Lezama, J.: Overcoming the disentanglement vs reconstruction trade-off via Jacobian supervision. In: ICLR (2019)

33. d Lin, Z., Thekumparampil, K.K., Fanti, G.C., Oh, S.: InfoGAN-CR: disentangling generative adversarial networks with contrastive regularizers. In: ICML (2020)

34. Liu, B., Zhu, Y., Fu, Z., de Melo, G., Elgammal, A.: OOGAN: disentangling GAN with one-hot sampling and orthogonal regularization. In: AAAI (2020)

35. Liu, Z., Luo, P., Wang, X., Tang, X.: Deep learning face attributes in the wild. In: ICCV (2015)

36. Locatello, F., Abbati, G., Rainforth, T., Bauer, S., Schölkopf, B., Bachem, O.: On the fairness of disentangled representations. In: NeurIPS (2019)

37. Locatello, F., Bauer, S., Lucic, M., Gelly, S., Schölkopf, B., Bachem, O.: Challenging common assumptions in the unsupervised learning of disentangled representations. In: ICML (2019)

38. Locatello, F., Tschannen, M., Bauer, S., Rötsch, G., Schölkopf, B., Bachem, O.: Disentangling factors of variations using few labels. In: ICLR (2020)

39. Makhzani, A., Shlens, J., Jaitly, N., Goodfellow, I., Frey, B.: Adversarial autoencoders. In: ICLR (2016)

40. Mathieu, E., Rainforth, T., Siddharth, N., Teh, Y.W.: Disentangling disentanglement in variational auto-encoders. In: Bayesian Deep Learning Workshop, NeurIPS (2018)

41. Matthey, L., Higgins, I., Hassabis, D., Lerchner, A.: dSprites: disentanglement testing sprites dataset (2017). https://github.com/deepmind/dsprites-dataset/

42. Mescheder, L., Nowozin, S., Geiger, A.: Which training methods for GANS do actually converge? In: ICML (2018)

43. Minka, T., et al.: Divergence measures and message passing. Technical report, Technical report, Microsoft Research (2005)

44. Narayanaswamy, S., et al.: Learning disentangled representations with semi-supervised deep generative models. In: NeurIPS (2017)

45. Nguyen-Phuoc, T., Li, C., Theis, L., Richardt, C., Yang, Y.L.: Hologan: unsupervised learning of 3D representations from natural images. In: ICCV (2019)
46. Kingma, D.P., Welling, M.: Auto-encoding variational Bayes. In: ICLR (2014)
47. Peng, X.B., Kanazawa, A., Toyer, S., Abbeel, P., Levine, S.: Variational discriminator bottleneck: improving imitation learning, inverse RL, and GANs by constraining information flow. In: ICLR (2019)
48. Ruiz, A., Martínez, O., Binefa, X., Verbeek, J.: Learning disentangled representations with reference-based variational autoencoders. arXiv preprint arXiv:1901.08534 (2019)
49. Szegedy, C., Vanhoucke, V., Ioffe, S., Shlens, J., Wojna, Z.: Rethinking the inception architecture for computer vision. In: CVPR (2016)
50. Tolstikhin, I., Bousquet, O., Gelly, S., Schoelkopf, B.: Wasserstein auto-encoders. In: ICLR (2018)
51. Tschannen, M., Bachem, O.F., Lučić, M.: Recent advances in autoencoder-based representation learning. In: Bayesian Deep Learning Workshop, NeurIPS (2018)
52. Watanabe, S.: Information theoretical analysis of multivariate correlation. IBM J. Res. Dev. 4, 66–82 (1960)
53. Watters, N., Matthey, L., Burgess, C.P., Lerchner, A.: Spatial Broadcast Decoder: a simple architecture for learning disentangled representations in VAEs. arXiv preprint arXiv:1901.07017 (2019)
54. Wei, X., Liu, Z., Wang, L., Gong, B.: Improving the improved training of Wasserstein GANs. In: ICLR (2018)
55. Zhu, J.Y., et al.: Toward multimodal image-to-image translation. In: NeurIPS (2017)

PL₁P - Point-Line Minimal Problems
Under Partial Visibility in Three Views

Timothy Duff[1], Kathlén Kohn[2], Anton Leykin[1], and Tomas Pajdla[3(✉)]

[1] Georgia Tech, Atlanta, Georgia
[2] KTH Stockholm, Stockholm, Sweden
[3] CIIRC, CTU in Prague, Prague, Czechia
`pajdla@cvut.cz`

Abstract. We present a complete classification of minimal problems for generic arrangements of points and lines in space observed partially by three calibrated perspective cameras when each line is incident to at most one point. This is a large class of interesting minimal problems that allows missing observations in images due to occlusions and missed detections. There is an infinite number of such minimal problems; however, we show that they can be reduced to 140616 equivalence classes by removing superfluous features and relabeling the cameras. We also introduce camera-minimal problems, which are practical for designing minimal solvers, and show how to pick a simplest camera-minimal problem for each minimal problem. This simplification results in 74575 equivalence classes. Only 76 of these were known; the rest are new. To identify problems having potential for practical solving of image matching and 3D reconstruction, we present several natural subfamilies of camera-minimal problems as well as compute solution counts for all camera-minimal problems which have less than 300 solutions for generic data.

Keywords: Minimal problems · Calibrated cameras · 3D reconstruction

1 Introduction

Minimal problems [1,6–10,15,21,29–32,35,37,38,44–46,53,55,57,61,65] which we study, are 3D reconstruction problems recovering camera poses and world coordinates from given images such that random input instances have a finite positive number of solutions. They are important basic computational tasks in 3D reconstruction from images [58–60], image matching [54], visual odometry and localization [5,47,56,62]. Recently, a complete characterization of minimal problems for points, lines and their incidences in calibrated multi-view geometry appeared for the case of complete multi-view visibility [14]. In this paper, we extend the characterization to an important class of problems under *partial* multi-view visibility.

Electronic supplementary material The online version of this chapter (https://doi.org/10.1007/978-3-030-58574-7_11) contains supplementary material, which is available to authorized users.

A. Vedaldi et al. (Eds.): ECCV 2020, LNCS 12371, pp. 175–192, 2020.
https://doi.org/10.1007/978-3-030-58574-7_11

We provide a complete classification of minimal problems for generic arrangements of points and lines in space observed partially by three calibrated perspective cameras when each line is incident to at most one point. There is an infinite number of such minimal problems; however, we show that they can be *reduced* to 140616 equivalence classes of *reduced minimal* problems by removing superfluous features and relabeling the cameras. We compute a full description of each class in terms of the incidence structure in 3D and visibility of each 3D feature in images. All problems in every equivalence class have the same *algebraic degree*, i.e. the number of solutions over the complex numbers.

When using minimal solvers to find correct image matches by RANSAC [19, 51], we often aim to recover camera parameters only. We name such reconstruction problems *camera-minimal* and reserve "minimal" for when we aim to recover 3D structure as well. Note that minimal problems are also camera-minimal but not vice versa. For instance, 50 out of the 66 problems given in [27] are non-minimal yet they all are camera-minimal. As an example, consider the problem from [27] with 3 PPP and 1 PPL correspondences. It is camera-minimal, i.e. there are 272 (in general complex) camera solutions, but it is not minimal since the line of the PPL correspondence cannot be recovered uniquely in 3D: there is a one-dimensional pencil of lines in 3D that project to the observed line in one of the images.

For each minimal problem, we delete additional superfluous features in images that can be removed without loosing camera-minimality to obtain a simplest camera-minimal problem. Thus, we introduce *terminal camera-minimal* problems. We show that, up to relabeling cameras, there are 74575 of these. They form the comprehensive list worth studying, as a solver for any camera-minimal problem can be derived from a solver for some problem on this list. Only 76 of the 74575 terminal camera-minimal problems were known—66 problems listed in [27] plus 10 additional cases from [14]—the remaining 74499, to the best of our knowledge, are new! We find all terminal camera-minimal problems with less than 300 solutions for generic data and present other interesting cases that might be important for practical solving of image matching and 3D reconstruction.

Characterizing minimal problems under partial visibility, which allows for missing observations in images due to occlusions and missed detections, is very hard. Previous results in [14] treat the case of full visibility with no restrictions on the number of cameras and types of incidences, resulting in 30 minimal problems. By contrast, we construct a long list of interesting problems under partial visibility, even with our restrictions, i.e. having exactly three cameras and having each line incident to at most one point[1]. These restrictions make the task of enumerating problems tractable while making it still possible to account for very practical incidence cases where several existing feature detectors are applicable. For instance, SIFT [40] and LAF [42] provide quivers (points with one direction attached), which can be interpreted as lines through the points and used to compute relative camera poses [4].

---

[1] Under this restriction, in two cameras, the only reduced (camera-)minimal problem is the five-point problem; see Supplementary Material (SM) for an explanation.

2 Previous Work

A large number of minimal problems appeared in the literature. See references above and [14,27,33,39] and references therein for work on general minimal problems. Here we review the most relevant work for minimal problems in three views related to point-line incidences and their classification.

Correspondences of non-incident points and lines in three uncalibrated views are considered in early works on the trifocal tensor [23]. Point-line incidences in the uncalibrated setup are introduced in [24] as n-quivers (points incident with n lines) and minimal problems for three 1-quivers in three affine views and three 3-quivers in three perspective views are derived. General uncalibrated multi-view constraints for points, lines and their incidences are presented in [41]. Non-incident points and lines in three uncalibrated images also appear in [26,49,50]. The cases of four points and three lines, two points and six lines, and nine lines are studied; [36] constructs a solver for nine lines. Works [16–18] look at lines incident to points which arise from tangent lines to curves and [4] presents a solver for that case. Results [1–3,14,25,63,64] introduced some of the techniques that are useful for classifying classes of minimal problems.

Work [27] classifies camera-minimal problems in 3 calibrated views that can be formulated with linear constraints on the trifocal tensor [22]. It presents 66 camera-minimal problems, all covered in our classification as terminal camera-minimal problems. Among them are 16 reduced minimal problems, out of which 2 are with full visibility and 14 with partial visibility. The remaining 50 problems are not minimal.

A complete characterization of minimal problems for points, lines and their incidences in calibrated multi-view geometry for the case of complete multi-view visibility is presented in [14]. It gives 30 minimal problems. Among them, 17 problems include exactly three cameras but only 12 of them (3002_1, 3002_2, 3010_0, 2005_3, 2005_4, 2005_5, 2013_2, 2013_3, 2021_1, 1024_4, 1032_2, 1040_0 in Table 1 of [14]) meet our restrictions on incidences. These 12 cases are all terminal camera-minimal as well as reduced minimal. Notice that the remaining 5 problems (3100_0, 2103_1, 2103_2, 2103_3, 2111_1 in Table 1 of [14]) are not considered in this paper because collinearity of more than two points cannot be modeled in the setting of this paper.

This paper can be seen as an extension of [27] and [14] to a much larger class of problems in three calibrated views under partial multi-view visibility.

3 Problem Specification

Our results apply to problems in which points, lines, and point-line incidences are partially observed. We model intersecting lines by requiring that each intersection point of two lines has to be one of the points in the point-line problem.

Definition 1. A *point-line problem* is a tuple $(p, l, \mathcal{I}, \mathcal{O})$ specifying that p points and l lines in space satisfy a given incidence relation

$$\mathcal{I} \subset \{1, \ldots, p\} \times \{1, \ldots, l\},$$

where $(i, j) \in \mathcal{I}$ means that the i-th point is on the j-th line, and are projected to $m = |\mathcal{O}|$ views with

$$\mathcal{O} = ((\mathcal{P}_1, \mathcal{L}_1), \dots, (\mathcal{P}_m, \mathcal{L}_m))$$

describing which points and lines are observed by each camera—view v contains exactly the points in $\mathcal{P}_v \subset \{1, \dots, p\}$ and the lines in $\mathcal{L}_v \subset \{1, \dots, l\}$.

For $\mathcal{I}$ we assume *realizability* (the incidence relations are realizable by some point-line arrangement in $\mathbb{R}^3$) and *completeness* (every incidence which is automatically implied by the incidences in $\mathcal{I}$ must also be contained in $\mathcal{I}$).

For $\mathcal{O}$ we assume that if a camera observes two lines that meet according to $\mathcal{I}$ then it observes their point of intersection.

Note that, for instance, the realizability assumption implies that two distinct lines cannot have more than one point in common. Our assumption on $\mathcal{O}$ is natural—the set $\mathcal{I}$ of incidences describes all the knowledge about which lines intersect in space, as well as in the images. An *instance* of a point-line problem is specified by the following data:

(1) A point-line arrangement in space consisting of p points $X_1, \dots, X_p$ and l lines $L_1, \dots, L_l$ in $\mathbb{P}^3$ which are incident exactly as specified by $\mathcal{I}$. Hence, the point X_i is on the line L_j if and only if $(i, j) \in \mathcal{I}$. We write

$$\mathcal{X}_{p,l,\mathcal{I}} = \left\{ (X, L) \in (\mathbb{P}^3)^p \times (\mathbb{G}_{1,3})^l \mid \forall (i, j) \in \mathcal{I} : X_i \in L_j \right\}$$

for the associated *variety of point-line arrangements*. Note that this variety also contains degenerate arrangements, where not all points and lines have to be pairwise distinct or where there are more incidences between points and lines than those specified by $\mathcal{I}$.

(2) A list of m calibrated cameras which are represented by matrices

$$P_1 = [R_1 \mid t_1], \dots, P_m = [R_m \mid t_m]$$

with $R_1, \dots, R_m \in SO(3)$ and $t_1, \dots, t_m \in \mathbb{R}^3$.

(3) The *joint image* consisting of the projections $\{x_{v,i} \mid i \in \mathcal{P}_v\} \subset \mathbb{P}^2$ of the points $X_1, \dots, X_p$ and the projections $\{\ell_{v,j} \mid j \in \mathcal{L}_v\} \subset \mathbb{G}_{1,2}$ of the lines $L_1, \dots, L_l$ by the cameras $P_1, \dots, P_m$ to the views $v = 1, \dots, m$. We denote by $\rho = \sum_{v=1}^{m} |\mathcal{P}_v|$ and $\lambda = \sum_{v=1}^{m} |\mathcal{L}_v|$ the total numbers of observed points and lines, and write

$$\mathcal{Y}_{p,l,\mathcal{I},\mathcal{O}} = \left\{ (x, \ell) \in (\mathbb{P}^2)^\rho \times (\mathbb{G}_{1,2})^\lambda \; \middle| \; \begin{array}{l} \forall v = 1, \dots, m \; \forall i \in \mathcal{P}_v \; \forall j \in \mathcal{L}_v : \\ (i, j) \in \mathcal{I} \Rightarrow x_{v,i} \in \ell_{v,j} \end{array} \right\}$$

for the *image variety* which consists of all m-tuples of 2D-arrangements of the points and lines specified by $\mathcal{O}$ which satisfy the incidences specified by $\mathcal{I}$. We note that an m-tuple in $\mathcal{Y}_{p,l,\mathcal{I},\mathcal{O}}$ is not necessarily a joint image of a common point-line arrangement in $\mathbb{P}^3$.

Given a joint image, we want to recover an arrangement in space and cameras yielding the given joint image. We refer to a pair of such an arrangement and such a list of m cameras as a *solution* of the point-line problem for the given joint image.

To fix the arbitrary space coordinate system [22], we set $P_1 = [I \,|\, 0]$ and the first coordinate of t_2 to 1. So our *camera configurations* are parameterized by

$$
\mathcal{C}_m = \left\{ (P_1, \ldots, P_m) \in \left(\mathbb{R}^{3\times 4}\right)^m \; \middle| \; \begin{array}{l} P_i = [R_i \,|\, t_i],\, R_i \in \mathrm{SO}(3),\, t_i \in \mathbb{R}^3, \\ R_1 = I,\, t_1 = 0,\, t_{2,1} = 1 \end{array} \right\}.
$$

We will always assume that the camera positions in an instance of a point-line problem are sufficiently generic such that the points and lines in the views are in generic positions with respect to the specified incidences $\mathcal{I}$.

We say that a point-line problem is *minimal* if a generic image tuple in $\mathcal{Y}_{p,l,\mathcal{I},\mathcal{O}}$ has a nonzero finite number of solutions. We may phrase this formally:

Definition 2. Let $\Phi_{p,l,\mathcal{I},\mathcal{O}} : \mathcal{X}_{p,l,\mathcal{I}} \times \mathcal{C}_m \dashrightarrow \mathcal{Y}_{p,l,\mathcal{I},\mathcal{O}}$ denote the *joint camera map*, which sends a point-line arrangement in space and m cameras to the resulting joint image. We say that the point-line problem $(p, l, \mathcal{I}, \mathcal{O})$ is *minimal* if

- $\Phi_{p,l,\mathcal{I},\mathcal{O}}$ is a *dominant map*[2], i.e. a generic element (x, ℓ) in $\mathcal{Y}_{p,l,\mathcal{I},\mathcal{O}}$ has a solution, so $\Phi_{p,l,\mathcal{I},\mathcal{O}}^{-1}(x, \ell) \neq \emptyset$, and
- the preimage $\Phi_{p,l,\mathcal{I},\mathcal{O}}^{-1}(x, \ell)$ of a generic element (x, ℓ) in $\mathcal{Y}_{p,l,\mathcal{I},\mathcal{O}}$ is finite.

Remark 1. We require the joint camera map in Definition 2 to be dominant because we want solutions to minimal problems to be stable under perturbation of the image data that preserves the incidences $\mathcal{I}$. A classical example of a problem which is not stable under perturbation in images is the problem of four points in three calibrated views [48].

Over the complex numbers, the cardinality of the preimage $\Phi_{p,l,\mathcal{I},\mathcal{O}}^{-1}(x, \ell)$ is the same for every *generic* joint image (x, ℓ) of a minimal point-line problem $(p, l, \mathcal{I}, \mathcal{O})$. We refer to this cardinality as the *degree* of the minimal problem.

In many applications, one is only interested in recovering the camera poses, and not the points and lines in 3D. Hence, we say that a point-line problem is *camera-minimal* if, given a generic image tuple in $\mathcal{Y}_{p,l,\mathcal{I},\mathcal{O}}$, it has a nonzero finite number of possible camera poses. Formally, this means:

Definition 3. Let $\gamma : \mathcal{X}_{p,l,\mathcal{I}} \times \mathcal{C}_m \to \mathcal{C}_m$ denote the projection onto the second factor. We say that the point-line problem $(p, l, \mathcal{I}, \mathcal{O})$ is *camera-minimal* if

- its joint camera map $\Phi_{p,l,\mathcal{I},\mathcal{O}}$ is dominant, and
- $\gamma(\Phi_{p,l,\mathcal{I},\mathcal{O}}^{-1}(x, \ell))$ is finite for a generic element (x, ℓ) in $\mathcal{Y}_{p,l,\mathcal{I},\mathcal{O}}$.

The cardinality over $\mathbb{C}$ of a generic $\gamma(\Phi_{p,l,\mathcal{I},\mathcal{O}}^{-1}(x, \ell))$ is the *camera-degree* of $(p, l, \mathcal{I}, \mathcal{O})$.

---

[2] In birational geometry, dominant maps are analogs of surjective maps.

Remark 2. Every minimal point-line problem is camera-minimal, but not necessarily the other way around. In the setting of complete visibility (i.e. where every camera observes all points and all lines), both notions coincide [14, Cor. 2].

In [14], all minimal point-line problems with complete visibility are described, including their degrees. It is a natural question if one can extend the classification in [14] to all point-line problems with *partial visibility*. A first obstruction is that there are minimal point-line problems for arbitrarily many cameras[3], whereas the result in [14] shows that minimal point-line problems with complete visibility exist only for at most six views. Moreover, as we see in the following sections, deriving a classification for partial visibility seems more difficult and involves more elaborate tools. Hence, in this article, we only aim for classifying point-line problems *in three views*[4]. We also restrict our attention to point-line problems satisfying the following assumption:

Definition 4. We say that a point-line problem is a PL_1P if each line in 3D is incident to at most one point.

This assumption makes our analysis easier, since the point-line arrangement in space of a PL_1P is a collection of the following independent *local features*:

- *free line* (i.e. a line which is not incident to any point), and
- *point with k pins* where $k = 0, 1, 2, \ldots$ (i.e. a point with k incident lines).

In the following, we shortly write *pin* for a line passing through a point. We stress that a pin refers only to the line itself, rather than the incident point. A first consequence of restricting our attention to PL_1Ps is the following fact, which fails for general point-line problems[5].

Lemma 1. *The degree and camera-degree of a minimal PL_1P coincide.*

Proof. Proofs of all lemmas, theorems and justification of results are in SM.

We will see that there are *infinitely many* (camera-)minimal PL_1Ps in three views. However, we can partition them into finitely many classes such that all PL_1Ps in the same class are closely related; in particular, they have the same (camera-)degree. For this classification, we pursue the following strategy:

Step 1: We introduce *reduced* PL_1Ps as the canonical representatives of the finitely many classes of minimal PL_1Ps we aim to find (see Sect. 4).

Step 2: Basic principles from algebraic geometry brought up in [14] imply

Lemma 2. *A point-line problem* $(p, l, \mathcal{I}, \mathcal{O})$ *is minimal if and only if*

- *it is* balanced, *i.e.* $\dim(\mathcal{X}_{p,l,\mathcal{I}} \times \mathcal{C}_m) = \dim(\mathcal{Y}_{p,l,\mathcal{I},\mathcal{O}})$, *and*
- *its joint camera map* $\Phi_{p,l,\mathcal{I},\mathcal{O}}$ *is dominant.*

---

[3] See SM discussion of camera registration.

[4] See SM for a discussion on two views.

[5] See SM for an example.

We identify a *finite* list of reduced balanced PL₁Ps in three views that contains all reduced minimal PL₁Ps (see Sect. 5).

Step 3: We explicitly describe the relation of reduced camera-minimal problems to reduced minimal ones, which implies that there are only finitely many reduced camera-minimal PL₁Ps in three views (see Sect. 6).

Step 4: For each of the finitely many balanced PL₁Ps identified in Step 2, we check if its joint camera map is dominant. This provides us with a complete catalog of all reduced (camera-)minimal PL₁Ps in three views (see Sect. 7).

In addition to the classification, we compute the camera-degrees of all reduced camera-minimal PL₁Ps in three views whose camera-degree is less than 300 (see Sect. 8 for this and related results on natural subfamilies of PL₁Ps.)

4 Reduced PL₁Ps

From a given PL₁P $(p, l, \mathcal{I}, \mathcal{O})$ we can obtain a new PL₁P by forgetting some points and lines, both in space and in the views. Formally, if $\mathcal{P}' \subset \{1, \ldots, p\}$ and $\mathcal{L}' \subset \{1, \ldots, l\}$ are the sets of points and lines which are *not* forgotten, the new PL₁P is $(p', l', \mathcal{I}', \mathcal{O}')$ with $p' = |\mathcal{P}'|$, $l' = |\mathcal{L}'|$, $\mathcal{I}' = \{(i,j) \in \mathcal{I} \mid i \in \mathcal{P}', j \in \mathcal{L}'\}$, and $\mathcal{O}' = ((\mathcal{P}'_1, \mathcal{L}'_1), \ldots, (\mathcal{P}'_m, \mathcal{L}'_m))$, where $\mathcal{P}'_v = \mathcal{P}_v \cap \mathcal{P}'$ and $\mathcal{L}'_v = \mathcal{L}_v \cap \mathcal{L}'$. This induces natural projections Π and π between the domains and codomains of the joint camera maps which forget the points and lines *not* in $\mathcal{P}'$ and $\mathcal{L}'$.

$$
\begin{array}{ccc}
\mathcal{X}_{p,l,\mathcal{I}} \times \mathcal{C}_m & \xrightarrow{\;\;\Phi = \Phi_{p,l,\mathcal{I},\mathcal{O}}\;\;} & \mathcal{Y}_{p,l,\mathcal{I},\mathcal{O}} \\
\Pi \downarrow & & \downarrow \pi \\
\mathcal{X}_{p',l',\mathcal{I}'} \times \mathcal{C}_m & \xrightarrow{\;\;\Phi' = \Phi_{p',l',\mathcal{I}',\mathcal{O}'}\;\;} & \mathcal{Y}_{p',l',\mathcal{I}',\mathcal{O}'}
\end{array}
$$

In the following, we shortly write $\Phi = \Phi_{p,l,\mathcal{I},\mathcal{O}}$ and $\Phi' = \Phi_{p',l',\mathcal{I}',\mathcal{O}'}$.

Definition 5. We say that $(p, l, \mathcal{I}, \mathcal{O})$ is *reducible* to $(p', l', \mathcal{I}', \mathcal{O}')$ if

- for each forgotten point, at most one of its pins is kept, and
- a generic solution $S' = ((X', L'), P) \in \mathcal{X}_{p',l',\mathcal{I}'} \times \mathcal{C}_m$ of $(p', l', \mathcal{I}', \mathcal{O}')$ can be lifted to a solution of $(p, l, \mathcal{I}, \mathcal{O})$ for generic input images in $\pi^{-1}(\Phi'(S'))$.
  In other words, for a generic $S' = ((X', L'), P) \in \mathcal{X}_{p',l',\mathcal{I}'} \times \mathcal{C}_m$ and a generic $(x, \ell) \in \pi^{-1}(\Phi'(S'))$, there is a point-line arrangement $(X, L) \in \mathcal{X}_{p,l,\mathcal{I}}$ such that $\Phi((X, L), P) = (x, \ell)$ and $\Pi((X, L), P) = S'$.

Theorem 1. *If a PL₁P is minimal and reducible to another PL₁P, then both are minimal and have the same degree.*

We can partition *all* (infinitely many) minimal PL₁Ps in three views into finitely many classes using this reduction process. Each class is represented by a unique PL₁P that is *reduced*, i.e. not reducible to another PL₁P.

Table 1. How points with two / one / zero pins and free lines can be observed in the three views of a reduced minimal PL_1P (up to permuting the views). The rows "3D" and "2D" show the degrees of freedom of each local feature in 3-space and in the three views. The row "#" fixes notation for a signature introduced in Sect. 5.

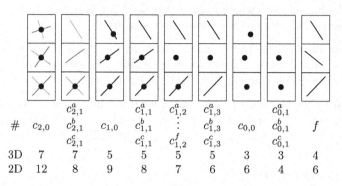

#	$c_{2,0}$	$c_{2,1}^a$ $c_{2,1}^b$ $c_{2,1}^c$	$c_{1,0}$	$c_{1,1}^a$ $c_{1,1}^b$ $c_{1,1}^c$	$c_{1,2}^a$ $:$ $c_{1,2}^f$	$c_{1,3}^a$ $c_{1,3}^b$ $c_{1,3}^c$	$c_{0,0}$	$c_{0,1}^a$ $c_{0,1}^b$ $c_{0,1}^c$	f
3D	7	7	5	5	5	5	3	3	4
2D	12	8	9	8	7	6	6	4	6

Theorem 2. *A minimal PL_1P $(p, l, \mathcal{I}, \mathcal{O})$ in three views is reducible to a unique reduced PL_1P $(p', l', \mathcal{I}', \mathcal{O}')$. The corresponding projection Π forgets:*

- *every pin that is observed in exactly two views such that both views also observe the point of the pin (it does not matter if the third view observes the point or not, but it must not see the line), e.g.* ⬚⬚⬚ *is reduced to* ⬚⬚⬚
- *every free line that is observed in exactly two views to reduce* ⬚⬚⬚ *to* ⬚⬚⬚
- *every point that has exactly one pin and is viewed like* ⬚⬚⬚ *to get* ⬚⬚⬚
- *every point together with its single pin if it is viewed like* ⬚⬚⬚ *to get* ⬚⬚⬚

In addition, applying inverses of these reductions to a minimal PL_1P in three views results in a minimal PL_1P.

Hence, it is enough to classify all reduced minimal PL_1Ps. We will see that there are finitely many reduced minimal PL_1Ps in three views. To count them, we need to understand how they look.

Theorem 3. *A reduced minimal PL_1P in three views has at most one point with three or more pins. If such a point exists,*

- *it has at most seven pins,*
- *and the point and all its pins are observed in all three views.*

All other local features are viewed as in Table 1.

5   Balanced PL1Ps

A reduced minimal PL_1P in three views is uniquely determined by a *signature*, a vector consisting of 27 numbers $(c_7, \ldots, c_3, c_{2,0}, c_{2,1}^a, \ldots, f)$, that specifies how often each local feature occurs in space and how often it is observed in a certain way by the cameras. By Theorem 3, the local features in such a PL_1P are free lines or points with at most seven pins. We denote by f the number of free lines and write $c_3, c_4, \ldots, c_7$ for the numbers of points with three, four, ..., seven pins. By Theorem 3, these local features are completely observed by the cameras. The row "#" in Table 1 shows our notation for the numbers of points with zero, one or two pins that are viewed in a certain way. For instance, $c_{2,0}$ counts how many points with two pins are completely observed by the cameras. Moreover, $c_{2,1}^a, c_{2,1}^b, c_{2,1}^c$ are the numbers of points with two pins that are partially observed like ⊡ or ⊡ or ⊡. Here the upper index a, b, c distinguishes the three different permutations of this local feature in the three views (note: as the two pins can be relabeled, there are only three and not six permutations). Similarly, upper indices distinguish different permutations of partially viewed points with at most one pin; see Table 1. We also note that assigning arbitrary 27 non-negative integers to $c_7, \ldots, f$ describes a unique PL_1P in three views, which is reduced by construction (see Theorem 2 and 3) but not necessarily minimal.

Due to Lemma 2, every minimal PL_1P $(p, l, \mathcal{I}, \mathcal{O})$ is balanced, i.e. it satisfies $\dim(\mathcal{X}_{p,l,\mathcal{I}} \times \mathcal{C}_m) = \dim(\mathcal{Y}_{p,l,\mathcal{I},\mathcal{O}})$. To compute the dimension of $\mathcal{X}_{p,l,\mathcal{I}}$, we need to know the degrees of freedom of each local feature in 3-space. For free lines and points with at most two pins, this is given in the row "3D" in Table 1. More generally, a point in space with k pins has $3 + 2k$ degrees of freedom. Hence, a reduced minimal PL_1P in three views satisfies

$$\dim(\mathcal{X}_{p,l,\mathcal{I}}) = 17c_7 + 15c_6 + 13c_5 + 11c_4 + 9c_3 + 7(c_{2,0} + c_{2,1}^a + c_{2,1}^b + c_{2,1}^c)$$
$$+ 5(c_{1,0} + c_{1,1}^a + c_{1,1}^b + c_{1,1}^c + c_{1,2}^a + \ldots + c_{1,2}^f + c_{1,3}^a + c_{1,3}^b + c_{1,3}^c)$$
$$+ 3(c_{0,0} + c_{0,1}^a + c_{0,1}^b + c_{0,1}^c) + 4f.$$

Similarly, the degrees of freedom of each local feature in the three views are shown in row "2D" in Table 1. For instance, if a point with two pins is viewed like ⊡, , then it has eight degrees of freedom in the three views: 2+1+1 in the first view, 2 in the second view, and 2 in the third view. Since a point with k pins for $k = 3, \ldots, 7$ is completely observed by the cameras, it has $3(2 + k)$ degrees of freedom in the three views. Therefore, we have

$$\dim(\mathcal{Y}_{p,l,\mathcal{I},\mathcal{O}}) = 27c_7 + 24c_6 + 21c_5 + 18c_4 + 15c_3 + 12c_{2,0} + 8(c_{2,1}^a + c_{2,1}^b + c_{2,1}^c)$$
$$+ 9c_{1,0} + 8(c_{1,1}^a + c_{1,1}^b + c_{1,1}^c) + 7(c_{1,2}^a + \ldots + c_{1,2}^f) + 6(c_{1,3}^a + c_{1,3}^b + c_{1,3}^c) \quad (1)$$
$$+ 6c_{0,0} + 4(c_{0,1}^a + c_{0,1}^b + c_{0,1}^c) + 6f.$$

As $\dim(\mathcal{C}_3) = 11$, the balanced equality $\dim(\mathcal{X}_{p,l,\mathcal{I}} \times \mathcal{C}_m) = \dim(\mathcal{Y}_{p,l,\mathcal{I},\mathcal{O}})$ for a reduced minimal PL_1P in three views is $11 = \dim(\mathcal{Y}_{p,l,\mathcal{I},\mathcal{O}}) - \dim(\mathcal{X}_{p,l,\mathcal{I}})$, i.e.

$$
\begin{aligned}
11 = {} & 10c_7 + 9c_6 + 8c_5 + 7c_4 + 6c_3 + 5c_{2,0} + (c_{2,1}^a + c_{2,1}^b + c_{2,1}^c) \\
& + 4c_{1,0} + 3(c_{1,1}^a + c_{1,1}^b + c_{1,1}^c) + 2(c_{1,2}^a + \ldots + c_{1,2}^f) + (c_{1,3}^a + c_{1,3}^b + c_{1,3}^c) \qquad (2) \\
& + 3c_{0,0} + (c_{0,1}^a + c_{0,1}^b + c_{0,1}^c) + 2f.
\end{aligned}
$$

The linear Eq. (2) has 845161 non-negative integer solutions[6]. Each of these is a signature that represents a PL_1P in three views which is reduced and balanced. Thus, it remains to check which of the 845161 signatures represent *minimal* PL_1Ps.

Some of the 845161 solutions of (2) yield *label-equivalent* PL_1Ps, i.e. PL_1Ps which are the same up to relabeling the three views. It turns out that there **143494** such label-equivalence classes of PL_1Ps given by solutions to (2)[7]. So all in all, we have to check 143494 PL_1Ps for minimality, namely one representative for each label-equivalence class.

6   Camera-Minimal PL1Ps

As in the case of minimal problems, we can understand all camera-minimal PL_1Ps from the reduced ones (see also Theorem 7).

Theorem 4. *If a PL_1P is reducible to another PL_1P, then either none of them is camera-minimal or both are camera-minimal. In the latter case, their camera-degrees are equal.*

In order to understand how reduced camera-minimal PL_1Ps look, in comparison to reduced minimal PL_1Ps as described in Theorem 3, we define a pin to be *dangling* if it is viewed by exactly one camera. Dangling pins are not determined uniquely by the camera observations, and hence they appear in PL_1Ps that are camera-minimal but not minimal.

Theorem 5. *The local features of a reduced camera-minimal PL_1P in three views are viewed as described in Theorem 3 plus as in the following three additional cases:*

Remark 3. For a dangling pin L of a reduced camera-minimal PL_1P, the point X incident to the pin L is uniquely reconstructible. Since L is viewed by exactly one camera, it belongs to the planar pencil of lines which are incident to X and have the same image as L. Thus we see that L is not uniquely reconstructible from its image.

---

[6] See SM for details on how to solve it.

[7] See SM for details on how to compute this.

The next theorem relates minimal and camera-minimal PL_1Ps. By adding more constraints to images, we make configurations in space uniquely reconstructible.

Theorem 6. *The following replacements in images lift a reduced camera-minimal PL_1P in three views to a reduced minimal PL_1P (cf. Theorem 5 and Table 1):*

$$\boxed{\cdot \diagdown \diagdown} \mapsto \boxed{\diagup \diagdown \diagdown}, \quad \boxed{\diagup \diagdown \diagdown} \mapsto \boxed{\diagup \diagdown \diagdown}, \quad \boxed{\cdot \cdot \diagup} \mapsto \boxed{\diagup \cdot \diagup} \; or \; \boxed{\cdot \cdot \diagup} \mapsto \boxed{\cdot \diagup \diagup}$$

Moreover, the camera-degrees of both PL_1Ps are the same.

This has two important implications for classifying (camera-)minimal PL_1Ps. First, reversing the replacements in Theorem 6 transforms each reduced camera-minimal PL_1P in three views into a *terminal* PL_1P of the same camera-degree.

Definition 6. We say that a camera-minimal PL_1P in three views is *terminal* if it is reduced and does not view local features like $\boxed{\diagup \diagdown \diagdown}$ or $\boxed{\diagup \diagdown \diagdown}$ or $\boxed{\diagdown \cdot \diagup}$..

Hence, to classify *all* camera-minimal PL_1Ps in three views, it is enough to find the terminal ones. Secondly, Theorem 6 implies for minimal PL_1Ps the following.

Corollary 1. *Consider a minimal PL_1P in three views. After replacing a single occurrence of $\boxed{\diagdown \cdot \diagup}$ with $\boxed{\cdot \diagdown \diagup}$ (or the other way around), the resulting PL_1P is minimal and has the same degree.*

At the end of Sect. 5, we defined two PL_1Ps to be label-equivalent if they are the same up to relabeling the views. We note that the swap described in Corollary 1 does *not* preserve the label-equivalence class of a PL_1P. Instead, we say that two PL_1Ps in three views are *swap&label-equivalent* if one can be transformed into the other by relabeling the views and applying (any number of times) the swap in Corollary 1. We conclude that either all PL_1Ps in the same swap&label-equivalence class are minimal and have the same degree, or none of them is minimal. Moreover, the lift in Theorem 6 yields the following.

Corollary 2. *The swap&label-equivalence classes of reduced minimal PL_1Ps in three views are in a camera-degree preserving one-to-one correspondence with the label-equivalence classes of terminal camera-minimal PL_1Ps in three views.*

Hence, we do not have to check minimality for all 143494 label-equivalence classes of PL_1Ps given by solutions to (2), that we found at the end of Sect. 5. Instead it is enough to consider the swap&label-equivalence classes of the solutions to (2). It turns out that there are **76446** such classes[8]. So to find *all* (camera-)minimal PL_1Ps in three views, we only have to check 76446 PL_1Ps for minimality, namely one representative for each of the swap&label-equivalence classes.

Finally, we present the analog to Theorem 2 and describe how all camera-minimal PL_1Ps are obtained from the reduced camera-minimal ones.

---

[8] See SM for details on how to compute this.

Table 2. Distribution of camera-degrees of terminal camera-minimal PL_1Ps in three calibrated views with: (a) camera-degree less than 300, (b) at most one pin per point and camera-degree less than 500.

(a)

camera-degree	64	80	144	160	216	224	240	256	264	272	288
# problems	13	9	3	547	7	2	159	2	2	11	4

(b)

camera-degree	80	160	216	240	256	264	272	288	304	312	320	352	360	368	376
# problems	9	173	4	80	2	2	2	1	5	2	213	3	9	3	1
camera-degree	384	392	400	408	416	424	432	448	456	464	472	480	488	496	
# problems	2	9	14	2	6	10	2	7	11	4	1	96	12	9	

Theorem 7. *A camera-minimal PL_1P in three views is reducible to a unique reduced PL_1P. The corresponding projection forgets:*

- *everything that is forgotten in Theorem 2*
- *every line (free or pin) that is not observed in any view*
- *every free line that is observed in exactly one view to reduce* ⬒ *to* ⬒
- *every pin that is observed in exactly one view such that the view also observes the point of the pin (it does not matter if the other two views observe the point or not, but they must not see the line), e.g.* ⬒ *is reduced to* ⬒
- *every point without pins that is observed in at most one view, e.g.* ⬒ *is reduced to* ⬒
- *every point that has exactly one pin if the point is not observed in any view, e.g. a pin viewed like* ⬒ *becomes a free line viewed like* ⬒
- *every point together with its single pin if it is viewed like* ⬒ *to get* ⬒
- *every point together with all its pins if the point has at least two pins and the point is not observed in any view, e.g.* ⬒ *is reduced to* ⬒

7   Checking Minimality

To show that a balanced point-line problem $(p, l, \mathcal{I}, \mathcal{O})$ is minimal, it is equivalent to show that the Jacobian of the joint camera map $\Phi_{p,l,\mathcal{I},\mathcal{O}}$ at some point $(X, P) \in \mathcal{X}_{p,l,\mathcal{I}} \times \mathcal{C}_m$ has full rank, i.e. rank given by the formula in Eq. (1). This follows from Lemma 2, as explained in [14]. On the implementation level, this minimality criterion requires writing down local coordinates for the various projective spaces and Grassmannians. To take advantage of fast exact arithmetic and linear algebra, we ran each test with random inputs (X, P) over a finite field $\mathbb{F}_q$ for some large prime q. We observe that *false positives*[9] for these tests are impossible. To guard against *false negatives*, we re-run the test on remaining

---

[9] Since we are testing minimality, being minimal is the positive outcome. See SM for detailed explanation why false positives cannot occur.

Table 3. Reduced minimal PL$_0$Ps and their degrees. Points not visible in a given view are indicated in grey. Five-point subproblems are indicated in red.

non-minimal candidates for different choices of q. Moreover, as a byproduct of our degree computations, we obtain yet another test of minimality, following the same procedure as [14, Algorithm 1].

The computation described above detects non-minimality for 2878 of the 143494 label-equivalence classes of PL$_1$Ps given by solutions to (2). Among the 76446 swap&label-equivalence classes, 1871 are not minimal.

Result 8. *In three calibrated views, up to relabeling cameras, there are*

- **140616** = 143494 − 2878 *reduced minimal PL$_1$Ps and*
- **74575** = 76446 − 1871 *terminal camera-minimal PL$_1$Ps.*

8   Computing Degrees

From the perspective of solving minimal problems, it is highly desirable to compute all degrees of our minimal PL$_1$Ps. In particular, we wish to identify problems with small degrees that may be of practical interest. Since some problems in this list are known from prior work [27] to have large degrees (>1000), our main technique is a monodromy approach based on numerical homotopy continuation. Our implementation in Macaulay2 [13,20] is similar to that used in prior work [14]. The next result shows that there are many interesting problems with small degrees that are solvable with existing solving technology [4,34].

Result 9. *There are 759 (up to relabeling cameras) terminal camera-minimal PL$_1$Ps in three calibrated views with camera-degree less than 300. Their camera-degree distribution is shown in Table 2(a).*

It is also interesting to look at problems with simple incidence structure, since they are easier to detect in images. This motivates the following.

Definition 7. We say that a point-line problem is a $PL_\kappa P$ if each line in 3D is incident to at most κ points.

Definition 7 generalizes Definition 4 of PL_1Ps to get a hierarchy of subfamilies of point-line problems: $PL_0P \subset PL_1P \subset PL_2P \subset \dots$

For instance, PL_0Ps consist of free points and free lines only[10]. The family of PL_1Ps contains many problems involving at most one pin per point—see Result 10 and Table 2(b). Such features are readily provided by the SIFT [40] detector. PL_1Ps can also include features with two pins per point, which are readily provided by the LAF [42] detector, which can also be used to get PL_2Ps if all 3 LAF points are used. More complex incidences (e.g. PL_3Ps) can be obtained from line t-junction detectors [66].

Result 10. *There are 9533 (up to relabeling cameras) terminal camera-minimal PL_1Ps in three calibrated views which have at most one pin per point.* **694** *of them have camera-degree less than* **500***. Their camera-degree distribution is shown in Table 2(b).*

Result 11. *There are 51 (up to relabeling cameras) reduced minimal PL_0Ps in three calibrated views. They are depicted together with their degrees in Table 3.*

Note that there are four problems in Table 3 that are *extensions* of the classical minimal problem of five points in two views. This implies that the relative pose of the two cameras can be determined from the five point correspondences (highlighted in red). As to the remaining camera, each of these four problems can be interpreted as a *camera registration* problem (the first one is known as P3P [28]): given a set of points and lines in the world and their images for a camera, find that camera pose. Note that the solution counts indicate that there are 8, 4, 8, and 8 solutions to the corresponding four camera registration problems. Similar degrees were previously reported for camera registration from 3D points and lines for perspective and generalized cameras [11,12,43,44,52].

Result 12. *We determined all PL_1Ps in three calibrated views that are extensions of the five-points minimal problem. Of them, up to relabeling cameras,*

- **6300** *are reduced minimal,*
- **61** *of the 6300 correspond to camera registration problems (see SM)*
- **3648** *are terminal camera-minimal.*

9   Conclusion

We have explicitly classified all reduced minimal and camera-minimal problems in three calibrated views for configurations of points and lines when lines contain at most one point.

---

[10] We note that reduced minimal PL_0Ps are terminal.

The number of (camera-)minimal problems in our classification is large. Apart from constructing a database of all these problems, we identify interesting subfamilies where the number of the problems is relatively small (see Tables Table 3, Table 2 in this article and Table 4 in SM.)

Another part of our computational effort focused on determining algebraic degrees of the (camera-)minimal problems. The degree of a problem provides a measure of complexity of a solver one may want to construct. The smaller the degree, the more plausible it is that a problem could be used in practice: Table 2 shows the degree distributions for problems of degree less than 300.

Our code is available at https://github.com/timduff35/PL1P.

Acknowledgements. We thank ICERM (NSF DMS-1439786 and the Simons Foundation grant 507536). We acknowledge: T. Duff and A. Leykin - NSF DMS-1719968 and the Algorithms and Randomness Center at Georgia Tech and the Max Planck Institute for Mathematics in the Sciences in Leipzig; K. Kohn - the Knut and Alice Wallenberg Foundation: WASP (Wallenberg AI, Autonomous Systems and Software Program) AI/Math initiative; T. Pajdla EU Reg. Dev. Fund IMPACT No. CZ.02.1.01/0.0/0.0/15 003/0000468, EU H2020 ARtwin No. 856994, and EU H2020 SPRING No. 871245 projects at the Czech Institute of Informatics, Robotics and Cybernetics of the Czech Technical University in Prague.

References

1. Agarwal, S., Lee, H., Sturmfels, B., Thomas, R.R.: On the existence of epipolar matrices. Int. J. Comput. Vis. **121**(3), 403–415 (2017). https://doi.org/10.1007/s11263-016-0949-7
2. Aholt, C., Oeding, L.: The ideal of the trifocal variety. Math. Comput. **83**(289), 2553–2574 (2014)
3. Aholt, C., Sturmfels, B., Thomas, R.: A hilbert scheme in computer vision. Can. J. Math **65**(5), 961–988 (2013)
4. Fabri, R., et al.: Trifocal relative pose from lines at points and its efficient solution. Preprint arXiv:1903.09755 (2019)
5. Alismail, H.S., Browning, B., Dias, M.B.: Evaluating pose estimation methods for stereo visual odometry on robots. In: the 11th International Conference on Intelligent Autonomous Systems (IAS-11) (2011)
6. Barath, D.: Five-point fundamental matrix estimation for uncalibrated cameras. In: 2018 IEEE Conference on Computer Vision and Pattern Recognition, CVPR 2018, pp. 235–243 Salt Lake City, UT, USA, June 18–22 (2018)
7. Barath, D., Hajder, L.: Efficient recovery of essential matrix from two affine correspondences. IEEE Trans. Image Process. **27**(11), 5328–5337 (2018)
8. Barath, D., Toth, T., Hajder, L.: A minimal solution for two-view focal-length estimation using two affine correspondences. In: 2017 IEEE Conference on Computer Vision and Pattern Recognition, CVPR 2017, pp. 2557–2565. Honolulu, HI, USA, July 21–26 (2017)
9. Byröd, M., Josephson, K., Åström, K.: A column-pivoting based strategy for monomial ordering in numerical gröbner basis calculations. In: Forsyth, D., Torr, P., Zisserman, A. (eds.) ECCV 2008. LNCS, vol. 5305, pp. 130–143. Springer, Heidelberg (2008). https://doi.org/10.1007/978-3-540-88693-8_10

10. Camposeco, F., Sattler, T., Pollefeys, M.: Minimal solvers for generalized pose and scale estimation from two rays and one point. In: ECCV - European Conference on Computer Vision. pp. 202–218 (2016)
11. Chen, H.H.: Pose determination from line-to-plane correspondences: existence condition and closed-form solutions. In: ICCV. pp. 374–378 (1990)
12. Dhome, M., Richetin, M., Lapreste, J., Rives, G.: Determination of the attitude of 3d objects from a single perspective view. IEEE Trans. Pattern Anal. Mach. Intell. **11**(12), 1265–1278 (1989)
13. Duff, T., Hill, C., Jensen, A., Lee, K., Leykin, A., Sommars, J.: Solving polynomial systems via homotopy continuation and monodromy. IMA J. Numer. Anal. **39**(3), 1421–1446 (2019)
14. Duff, T., Kohn, K., Leykin, A., Pajdla, T.: PLMP - Point-line minimal problems in complete multi-view visibility. In: International Conference on Computer Vision (ICCV) (2019)
15. Elqursh, A., Elgammal, A.M.: Line-based relative pose estimation. In: CVPR (2011)
16. Fabbri, R., Giblin, P., Kimia, B.: Camera pose estimation using first-order curve differential geometry. IEEE Trans. Pattern Anal. Mach. Intell. (2020)
17. Fabbri, R., Giblin, P.J., Kimia, B.B.: Camera pose estimation using first-order curve differential geometry. In: Proceedings of the European Conference in Computer Vision (2012)
18. Fabbri, R., Kimia, B.B.: Multiview differential geometry of curves. Int. J. Comput. Vision **120**(3), 324–346 (2016)
19. Fischler, M.A., Bolles, R.C.: Random sample consensus: a paradigm for model fitting with applications to image analysis and automated cartography. Commun. ACM **24**(6), 381–395 (1981)
20. Grayson, D.R., Stillman, M.E.: Macaulay2, a software system for research in algebraic geometry. http://www.math.uiuc.edu/Macaulay2/ (2002)
21. Hartley, R., Li, H.: An efficient hidden variable approach to minimal-case camera motion estimation. IEEE PAMI **34**(12), 2303–2314 (2012)
22. Hartley, R., Zisserman, A.: Multiple View Geometry in Computer Vision. Cambridge, 2nd edn. (2003)
23. Hartley, R.I.: Lines and points in three views and the trifocal tensor. Int. J. Comput. Vis. **22**(2), 125–140 (1997)
24. Johansson, B., Oskarsson, M., Åström, K.: Structure and motion estimation from complex features in three views. In: ICVGIP 2002, Proceedings of the Third Indian Conference on Computer Vision, Graphics & Image Processing, Ahmadabad, India, December 16–18, 2002 (2002)
25. Joswig, M., Kileel, J., Sturmfels, B., Wagner, A.: Rigid multiview varieties. IJAC **26**(4), 775–788 (2016). https://doi.org/10.1142/S021819671650034X
26. Kahl, F., Heyden, A., Quan, L.: Minimal projective reconstruction including missing data. IEEE Trans. Pattern Anal. Mach. Intell. **23**(4), 418–424 (2001). https://doi.org/10.1109/34.917578
27. Kileel, J.: Minimal problems for the calibrated trifocal variety. SIAM J. Appl. Algebra and Geometry **1**(1), 575–598 (2017)
28. Kneip, L., Scaramuzza, D., Siegwart, R.: A novel parametrization of the perspective-three-point problem for a direct computation of absolute camera position and orientation. In: CVPR - IEEE Conference on Computer Vision and Pattern Recognition. pp. 2969–2976 (2011)

29. Kneip, L., Siegwart, R., Pollefeys, M.: Finding the exact rotation between two images independently of the translation. In: ECCV - European Conference on Computer Vision. pp. 696–709 (2012)

30. Kuang, Y., Åström, K.: Pose estimation with unknown focal length using points, directions and lines. In: IEEE International Conference on Computer Vision, pp. 529–536, ICCV 2013, Sydney, Australia, December 1–8 (2013)

31. Kuang, Y., Åström, K.: Stratified sensor network self-calibration from tdoa measurements. In: 21st European Signal Processing Conference (2013)

32. Kukelova, Z., Bujnak, M., Pajdla, T.: Automatic generator of minimal problem solvers. In: European Conference on Computer Vision (ECCV) (2008)

33. Kukelova, Z., Kileel, J., Sturmfels, B., Pajdla, T.: A clever elimination strategy for efficient minimal solvers. In: Computer Vision and Pattern Recognition (CVPR). IEEE (2017)

34. Larsson, V., et al.: Automatic generator of minimal problems. http://www2.maths.lth.se/matematiklth/personal/viktorl/code/basis_selection.zip (2015)

35. Larsson, V., Åström, K., Oskarsson, M.: Efficient solvers for minimal problems by syzygy-based reduction. In: Computer Vision and Pattern Recognition (CVPR) (2017)

36. Larsson, V., Åström, K., Oskarsson, M.: Efficient solvers for minimal problems by syzygy-based reduction. In: 2017 IEEE Conference on Computer Vision and Pattern Recognition, pp. 2383–2392 ,CVPR 2017, Honolulu, HI, USA, July 21–26 (2017)

37. Larsson, V., Åström, K., Oskarsson, M.: Polynomial solvers for saturated ideals. In: IEEE International Conference on Computer Vision, pp. 2307–2316, CCV 2017, Venice, Italy, October 22–29 (2017)

38. Larsson, V., Kukelova, Z., Zheng, Y.: Making minimal solvers for absolute pose estimation compact and robust. In: International Conference on Computer Vision (ICCV) (2017)

39. Larsson, V., Oskarsson, M., Åström, K., Wallis, A., Kukelova, Z., Pajdla, T.: Beyond grobner bases: Basis selection for minimal solvers. In: 2018 IEEE Conference on Computer Vision and Pattern Recognition, pp. 3945–3954, CVPR 2018, Salt Lake City, UT, USA, June 18–22 (2018), http://openaccess.thecvf.com/content_cvpr_2018/html/Larsson_Beyond_Grobner_Bases_CVPR_2018_paper.html

40. Lowe, D.G.: Distinctive image features from scale-invariant keypoints. Int. J. Comput. Vis. 60(2), 91–110 (2004)

41. Ma, Y., Huang, K., Vidal, R., Kosecka, J., Sastry, S.: Rank conditions on the multiple-view matrix. Int. J. Comput. Vis. 59(2), 115–137 (2004)

42. Matas, J., Obdržálek, S., Chum, O.: Local affine frames for wide-baseline stereo. In: 16th International Conference on Pattern Recognition, pp. 363–366, ICPR 2002, Quebec, Canada, Aug. 11–15 (2002)

43. Miraldo, P., Araujo, H.: Direct solution to the minimal generalized pose. IEEE Trans. Cybernet. 45(3), 418–429 (2015)

44. Miraldo, P., Dias, T., Ramalingam, S.: A minimal closed-form solution for multi-perspective pose estimation using points and lines. In: Computer Vision - ECCV 2018–15th European Conference, pp. 490–507, Munich, Germany, September 8–14, Proceedings, Part XVI (2018)

45. Mirzaei, F.M., Roumeliotis, S.I.: Optimal estimation of vanishing points in a manhattan world. In: International Conference on Computer Vision (ICCV) (2011)

46. Nistér, D.: An efficient solution to the five-point relative pose problem. IEEE Trans. Pattern Anal. Mach. Intel. 26(6), 756–770 (2004)

47. Nistér, D., Naroditsky, O., Bergen, J.: Visual odometry. In: Computer Vision and Pattern Recognition (CVPR). pp. 652–659 (2004)
48. Nistér, D., Schaffalitzky, F.: Four points in two or three calibrated views: theory and practice. Int. J. Comput. Vis. **67**(2), 211–231 (2006)
49. Oskarsson, M., Åström, K., Overgaard, N.C.: Classifying and solving minimal structure and motion problems with missing data. In: International Conference on Computer Vision (ICCV). pp. 628–634. IEEE Computer Society (2001). https://doi.org/10.1109/ICCV.2001.10072
50. Oskarsson, M., Zisserman, A., Åström, K.: Minimal projective reconstruction for combinations of points and lines in three views. Image Vis. Comput. **22**(10), 777–785 (2004)
51. Raguram, R., Chum, O., Pollefeys, M., Matas, J., Frahm, J.: USAC: A universal framework for random sample consensus. IEEE Trans. Pattern Anal. Mach. Intell. **35**(8), 2022–2038 (2013)
52. Ramalingam, S., Bouaziz, S., Sturm, P.: Pose estimation using both points and lines for geo-localization. In: ICRA. pp. 4716–4723 (2011)
53. Ramalingam, S., Sturm, P.F.: Minimal solutions for generic imaging models. In: CVPR - IEEE Conference on Computer Vision and Pattern Recognition (2008)
54. Rocco, I., Cimpoi, M., Arandjelovic, R., Torii, A., Pajdla, T., Sivic, J.: Neighbourhood consensus networks (2018)
55. Salaün, Y., Marlet, R., Monasse, P.: Robust and accurate line- and/or point-based pose estimation without manhattan assumptions. In: European Conference on Computer Vision (ECCV) (2016)
56. Sattler, T., Leibe, B., Kobbelt, L.: Efficient & effective prioritized matching for large-scale image-based localization. IEEE Trans. Pattern Anal. Mach. Intell. **39**(9), 1744–1756 (2017)
57. Saurer, O., Pollefeys, M., Lee, G.H.: A minimal solution to the rolling shutter pose estimation problem. In: Intelligent Robots and Systems (IROS), 2015 IEEE/RSJ International Conference on. pp. 1328–1334. IEEE (2015)
58. Schönberger, J.L., Frahm, J.M.: Structure-from-motion revisited. In: Conference on Computer Vision and Pattern Recognition (CVPR) (2016)
59. Snavely, N., Seitz, S.M., Szeliski, R.: Photo tourism: exploring photo collections in 3D. In: ACM SIGGRAPH (2006)
60. Snavely, N., Seitz, S.M., Szeliski, R.: Modeling the world from internet photo collections. Int. J. Comput. Vis. (IJCV) **80**(2), 189–210 (2008)
61. Stewenius, H., Engels, C., Nistér, D.: Recent developments on direct relative orientation. ISPRS J. Photogrammetry Remote Sens. **60**, 284–294 (2006)
62. Taira, H., et al.: InLoc: Indoor visual localization with dense matching and view synthesis. In: CVPR (2018)
63. Trager, M., Ponce, J., Hebert, M.: Trinocular geometry revisited. International Journal Computer Vision pp. 1–19 (2016)
64. Trager, M.: Cameras, Shapes, and Contours: Geometric Models in Computer Vision. (Caméras, formes et contours: modèles géométriques en vision par ordinateur). Ph.D. thesis, École Normale Supérieure, Paris, France (2018)
65. Ventura, J., Arth, C., Lepetit, V.: An efficient minimal solution for multi-camera motion. In: International Conference on Computer Vision (ICCV). pp. 747–755 (2015)
66. Xia, G., Delon, J., Gousseau, Y.: Accurate junction detection and characterization in natural images. Int. J. Comput. Vis. **106**(1), 31–56 (2014)

Prediction and Recovery for Adaptive Low-Resolution Person Re-Identification

Ke Han[1,2(✉)], Yan Huang[1], Zerui Chen[1], Liang Wang[1,3,4], and Tieniu Tan[1,3]

[1] Center for Research on Intelligent Perception and Computing (CRIPAC),
National Laboratory of Pattern Recognition (NLPR), Institute of Automation,
Chinese Academy of Sciences (CASIA), Beijing, China
{ke.han,zerui.chen}@cripac.ia.ac.cn, {yhuang,wangliang,tnt}@nlpr.ia.ac.cn
[2] School of Future Technology, University of Chinese Academy of Sciences (UCAS),
Beijing, China
[3] Center for Excellence in Brain Science and Intelligence Technology (CEBSIT),
Bejing, China
[4] Chinese Academy of Sciences, Artificial Intelligence Research (CAS-AIR),
Beijing, China

Abstract. Low-resolution person re-identification (LR re-id) is a challenging task with low-resolution probes and high-resolution gallery images. To address the resolution mismatch, existing methods typically recover missing details for low-resolution probes by super-resolution. However, they usually pre-specify fixed scale factors for all images, and ignore the fact that choosing a preferable scale factor for certain image content probably greatly benefits the identification. In this paper, we propose a novel Prediction, Recovery and Identification (PRI) model for LR re-id, which adaptively recovers missing details by predicting a preferable scale factor based on the image content. To deal with the lack of ground-truth optimal scale factors, our model contains a self-supervised scale factor metric that automatically generates dynamic soft labels. The generated labels indicate probabilities that each scale factor is optimal, which are used as guidance to enhance the content-aware scale factor prediction. Consequently, our model can more accurately predict and recover the content-aware details, and achieve state-of-the-art performances on four LR re-id datasets.

Keywords: Low-resolution person re-identification · Adaptive scale factor prediction · Dynamic soft label

1 Introduction

Given a person image captured by a certain camera, person re-identification (re-id) aims to identify the same person across different cameras. With more and more video surveillance in public places, this task has attracted wider attention of both academia and industry, because of its great application potentials. Most

Electronic supplementary material The online version of this chapter (https://doi.org/10.1007/978-3-030-58574-7_12) contains supplementary material, which is available to authorized users.

researchers study this topic under the assumption that all the available person images have sufficient and similar resolutions. In real-world application scenarios, however, the resolutions of captured persons may vary greatly due to the uncontrollable distances between persons and cameras. Generally, target persons of high resolution (HR) are enrolled as the gallery set, while probe persons captured by surveillance cameras have low resolution (LR). This common problem is usually referred as the low-resolution person re-identification (LR re-id).

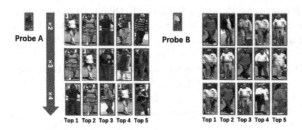

Fig. 1. Top-ranked HR gallery images of two LR probes [11] with different scale factor settings. The ground truth is indicated by a green bounding box. For the same probe, different scale factors might lead to different search results.

To deal with the resolution mismatch problem in LR re-id, existing works [17,39] typically recover missing details for LR images with super-resolution (SR) modules. In fact, performing SR has its pros and cons. We resort to it to recover details but it will inevitably bring about noise in the meanwhile. Especially when we use a larger scale factor for SR, the produced noise might greatly degenerate the image quality and identification results. Nevertheless, existing works usually ignore the problem and pre-specify a fixed scale factor for images, regardless of whether it can recover the most effective details and not incur excessive noise to degenerate the identification. We experimentally find that choosing different scale factors for the same LR probe may lead to quite different search results, as shown in Fig. 1. For example, the ground truth of the probe A drops from the first to fourth in the ranking lists, when we change the scale factor from 2 to 4. The reason probably lies in that the dazzling shadow and background of the probe A are more prone to result in noisy recovery as the scale factor increases. Intuitively, the image content should be an important cue to determine which scale factor can achieve better recovery for accurate identification.

However, how to combine the image content for choosing a preferable scale factor is seldom investigated and has many challenges. A tough one is that we have no prior annotation indicating which scale factor is optimal to identify a given person. In practice, it is also difficult and time-consuming to pre-define such an optimal scale factor. The optimal scale factor should not be consistent for different re-id modules, even for the same re-id module at different timesteps during training. This is because they have varying abilities in distinguishing the recovered details and noise. In addition, one LR image sometimes has multiple scale factors that achieve comparably good results, *e.g.*, the scale factor 3 and 4 are almost equally suitable to the probe B in Fig. 1. In view of the variability and multiplicity of optimal scale factors, realizing the content-aware scale factor prediction remains challenging.

To address the problem, we propose a novel Prediction, Recovery and Identification (PRI) model for LR re-id, which can adaptively recover details by predicting a preferable scale factor for a given image based on image content. Our model formulates the scale factor prediction as a classification problem, by choosing a preferable scale factor from a set of pre-defined ones for a given image. Unlike the typical classification setting [20,32] where an object has a one-hot label indicating its class, our scale factor prediction suffers from the mentioned problems of label variability and multiplicity. To this end, we propose a scale factor metric that automatically assigns a given LR image a dynamic soft label, *i.e.*, a normalized real-value vector. The dynamic soft label indicates the relative probabilities that each alternative scale factor is optimal, which is formulated by comparing the recovered contents by different scale factors. The *dynamic* property can dynamically evaluate and adjust the optimal scale factors during training. And the *soft* property allows multiple optimal scale factors in the form of probability and flexibly handles their variations. To enhance the content-aware scale factor prediction, the generated dynamic soft labels are exploited as supervision to guide our model to predict the preferable scale factor based on the given LR image content. Abundant experimental results show that our proposed model is effective and achieves the state-of-the-art performances on four LR re-id datasets. Besides, our proposed adaptive scale factor prediction can be used for standard re-id models to improve their performances in the LR re-id setting. The contributions of this paper are summarized as follows.

- This paper focuses on a practical but rarely investigated LR re-id problem, *i.e.*, how to choose a better scale factor for identification based on the LR image content.
- We propose a novel PRI model, which can adaptively predict the preferable scale factor, recover details for LR images, and perform the identification in an end-to-end manner.
- Without annotations of the optimal scale factors, we propose a self-supervised scale factor metric that evaluates the dynamic soft label as supervision.
- We conduct extensive experiments to demonstrate the effectiveness of our model, and achieve the state-of-the-art results on four LR re-id datasets.

2   Related Work

Standard Person Re-identification (re-id). Person re-identification [2,3,23,29,31,41] has made great progress, with the significant development of deep learning in the past years. Many approaches have been proposed to extract more discriminative identity features. For example, to align and improve local features, PCB [36] divides the deep feature maps into several stripe features, aligns each stripe and identifies them one by one. Martinel *et al.* [27] observe that body partitions should have different importances at different scales of features. They accordingly propose PyrNet that exploits pyramid features to capture image relevancy at different levels of detail. In addition, some works pay attention to addressing some challenging re-id problems, such as background bias [16,33], occlusion[13,14,28,35] and domain adaption [4,9,30,34,40].

Low-Resolution Person Re-identification (LR re-id). Among various re-id challenges, resolution mismatch is a practical but less studied problem. Super-resolving LR images by SR modules is a common approach. For example, Jiao *et al.* [17] propose a SR and re-id joint formulation, but they enlarge LR images with the preset fixed scale factors, which probably results in the suboptimal recovery to identify the person. Wang *et al.* [39] assign a scale factor for an image depending on the relative image size to acquire the super-resolved images with the uniform size. However, there seems to be no necessary relationship between the image size and the optimal scale factor, and therefore their performances are also limited. Besides, there is another kind of method aiming at learning resolution-invariant representations without requiring SR. For example, Chen *et al.* [5] exploit adversarial learning to pull the identity-related and resolution-unrelated feature maps closer. Compared with the SR-based methods, they do not take advantages of compensated details for more fine-grained analyses. Li *et al.* [25] propose to recover details while learning resolution-invariant representations. This method combines the merits of the above two kinds of methods, but recovers LR images into the same resolution, which still suffers from the problem of the suboptimal recovery level. Different from these works, we propose to adaptively predict a preferable scale factor for each image based on the image content, so that we can achieve better recovery to improve the re-id accuracy.

Image Super-Resolution (SR). Given a LR image and a scale factor, image super-resolution [8,21,26,37,42] recovers a HR image of the desired size. Although we want to employ SR modules to alleviate the resolution mismatch problem, there is a clear target difference between SR and person re-id. SR is designed for estimating low-level pixel values, which pursues the good pixel-level approximation or high visual quality, while re-id aims at learning the high-level identity discrimination. To improve the compatibility of SR and re-id modules, we integrate them into a joint-learning network. With the joint supervision of the ground-truth HR images and identity signals, our model learns the re-id oriented detail recovery to facilitate the identification.

3   Method

3.1   Overview

Given a LR image, we aim to adaptively predict and recover the content-aware details to achieve more accuracy identification. Our proposed Prediction, Recovery and Identification (PRI) model is illustrated in Fig. 2 and outlined as follows. The LR re-id dataset generally contains pairs of HR and LR images of the same identity but captured by different cameras. Inspired by [17], PRI takes as input such a pair of images along with a synthetic LR image down-sampled by the HR one. We denote such an input set composed of a HR, a LR and a synthetic LR image as $\{x_h, x_l, x_{sl}\}$ respectively for the following description.

During training, the LR image x_l is sent to the adaptive scale factor predictor P, which formulates the scale factor prediction as a N-class classification problem, and predicts the probabilities that x_l belongs to each class. N classes refer to N alternative scale factors $\{r_1, r_2, \cdots, r_N\}$, and we illustrate with $N{=}4$ as an example in Fig. 2. At the same time, x_l is also super-resolved with the SR module by all the alternative scale factors. All the super-resolved images are projected into the common feature space, where we perform the scale factor metric to acquire the dynamic soft label. The dynamic soft label is then fed back to the predictor P, and serves as the supervision guiding P to predict the desired scale factor via the prediction loss L_p. Besides, we exploit the SR loss L_{sr}, identity loss L_{id} and triplet loss L_{tri} to learn the effective detail recovery and identity discrimination. When test, we only need to super-resolve a LR image by the scale factor r_p, which has the maximum predicted probability and is more likely to achieve better recovery and identification results than the other scale factors. We will elaborate each part of our model in the following sections.

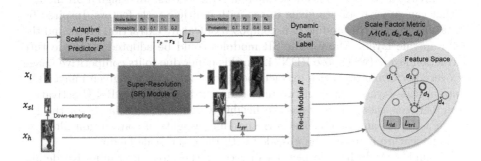

Fig. 2. The proposed Prediction, Recovery and Identification (PRI) model.

3.2 Adaptive Scale Factor Predictor

Selecting which scale factor to recover missing details is a practical problem in LR re-id. Intuitively, the optimal scale factor is probably inherently related to the image content. This inspires us to predict a preferable scale factor for a LR image based on its image content. Ideally, we want to recover helpful appearance details as much as possible, and control the undesired noise in an acceptable range that does not adversely affect the identification.

In this paper, we formulate predicting a preferable scale factor as a N-class classification problem by presetting N alternative scale factors $r_1, r_2, \cdots, r_N$. The preset scale factors should have a proper varying interval. It makes little sense to choose a better scale factor from several fairly close ones, e.g., 2.1, 2,2 and 2.3, because they have nearly the same recovery effects. Experimentally, we set the interval to 1, the number of classes N to 4, and $\{r_1, r_2, \cdots, r_N\}$ to

$\{1, 2, 3, 4\}$, respectively. We accordingly design an adaptive scale factor predictor P as a classifier. Given an image, P extracts the features and predicts the probabilities that the image belongs to each class, which are also the probabilities that each alternative scale factor is the optimal one. We choose ResNet50 [12] as the backbone of our predictor, and use $1{\times}1$ convolutional layers after global average pooling to reduce the dimension from 2048 to 512. Then, a fully-connected layer and the softmax function are used to predict the normalized probability $p_{r_i} (i = 1, 2, \cdots, N)$ that r_i is the optimal scale factor. We formulate it as

$$p_{r_1}, p_{r_2}, \cdots, p_{r_N} = P(x_l). \tag{1}$$

Thus, the predicted optimal scale factor $r_p = \arg\max_{r_i} P(x_l)$. However, unlike the common classification setting [20,32], we have no ground-truth optimal scale factors as supervision to enable the supervised learning of the predictor. To address this problem, we propose to regard the scale factor that can recover the most discriminative details as the ground-truth optimal one. To realize that, we need a SR module to perform the detail recovery.

3.3   Person Super-Resolution

To compare the recovery effects of different scale factors, we design a SR module G that can super-resolve a given image with multiple scale factors. Inspired by Meta-SR [15], the SR module G is composed of feature extraction layers and the meta-upscale layers. Many basic SR modules could be adopted as our feature extraction layers (we choose RDN [42] in this paper due to its competitive image recovery performance) which extract the feature maps for the given image. The meta-upscale layers consist of two fully-connected layers and a ReLU activation layer between them. They take the height, width and scale factor of the LR image as input, and predict the corresponding weights of convolution filters so that the feature maps can be upscaled with the given scale factor.

To find out which scale factor can recover the most discriminative details for x_l, we send x_l along with all the alternative scale factors $\{r_1, r_2, \cdots, r_N\}$ into G. Then we can acquire the recovered images by each scale factor, and denote them as $\{G_{r_1}(x_l), G_{r_2}(x_l), \cdots, G_{r_N}(x_l)\}$, respectively. Different from x_l, x_{sl} is super-resolved by one randomly chosen scale factor $r_{sl} \in \{r_1, r_2, \cdots, r_N\}$. Thus, x_{sl} and x_h constitute a pair of LR input and HR supervision to ensure that the SR module can be optimized by the SR loss L_{sr}. L_{sr} calculates the pixel-to-pixel 1-norm distance between the super-resolved image $G_{r_{sl}}(x_{sl})$ and the ground truth x^h. We formulate it as

$$L_{sr} = \frac{1}{r_{sl}^2 W H} \sum_{i=1}^{r_{sl}W} \sum_{j=1}^{r_{sl}H} |(G_{r_{sl}}(x_{sl}))_{i,j} - (x_h)_{i,j}| \tag{2}$$

where $X_{i,j}$ is the pixel value at the coordinate (i, j) of the image X, and W, H and r_{sl} are the width, height and scale factor of x_{sl}, respectively. The synthetic LR image x_{sl} contributes to the SR loss, which unites the latter identity loss to make it possible to jointly optimize the SR and re-id module. This shows the important role of x_{sl} in bridging SR and re-id two originally separate tasks.

3.4   Scale Factor Metric and Dynamic Soft Label

Scale Factor Metric. After obtaining the recovered images by all the alternative scale factors, we need to evaluate the effectiveness of the recovered contents. We regard the recovered image that contains the most discriminative details as the best recovery, and the corresponding scale factor as the optimal one. Based on this assumption, we propose a scale factor metric $\mathcal{M}$, which is a feature-based evaluation criterion by comparing which recovered image of $\{G_{r_1}(x_l), G_{r_2}(x_l), \cdots, G_{r_N}(x_l)\}$ has the most discriminative identity features. Specifically, we use a re-id module F to project all these super-resolved images into the common feature space. Similar to the adaptive scale factor predictor, we adopt ResNet50 as the re-id backbone and reduce the dimension of features. We denote the feature vectors of the above recovered images as $\{f_{r_1}, f_{r_2}, \cdots, f_{r_N}\}$, respectively. To measure which one is the most discriminative, we exploit a HR image of the same identity (*i.e.*, x_h) as an anchor, and compare the Euclidean distances among the features of the recovered images $(f_{r_1}, f_{r_2}, \cdots, f_{r_N})$ and the anchor (denoted as f_{x_h}).

Intuitively, a preferable scale factor should have a smaller relative distance to the HR anchor, due to the better detail recovery. To measure and compare the relative distances between different scale factors and the HR anchor, the proposed scale factor metric $\mathcal{M}$ is formulated as follows.

$$l_{r_i} = \mathcal{M}(d_1, \cdots, d_N) = softmax((\frac{1}{N}\sum_{j=1}^{N} d_j - d_i)^{\gamma}) \tag{3}$$

where d_i is the Euclidean distance between f_{r_i} and f_{x_h}, and γ is the regulatory factor. l_{r_i} can indicate the relative probability that r_i is the ground-truth optimal scale factor, which is normalized by the softmax function. Note that γ should be an odd number to make sure that the scale factor with a smaller feature distance than the average $(\frac{1}{N}\sum_{j=1}^{N} d_j)$ is endowed with a higher probability of being the optimal one. And the scale factor with the maximum probability is considered as the ground-truth optimal one for x_l.

Dynamic soft label. We can use the measured optimal scale factor as a one-hot label to enable the supervised learning of the predictor P via the cross-entropy classification loss. However, the optimal scale factor is often not consistent, and varies during training the re-id module, which will cause the dramatic change from a one-hot label to another. The frequent change of the one-hot label will confuse the cross-entropy loss, which typically encourages a higher probability for the only one correct class as much as possible, and make the loss function hard to converge.

To address the problem, we exploit Eq. 3 to constitute the dynamic soft label, *i.e.*, a normalized real-value vector $(l_{r_1}, l_{r_2}, \cdots, l_{r_N})$. It has the following advantages. First, the change of the optimal scale factor becomes smoother in the form of the relative probability. Second, it allows to activate multiple optimal scale factors: the scale factor with the higher probability is not necessarily optimal, but more likely to be. We set an update frequency ω to determine the frequency of updating dynamic soft labels, which indicates that we perform the scale factor metric and obtain the dynamic soft label for each LR image per ω training epochs, and keep them unchanged between two updates.

Then, we use the dynamic soft label as the ground truth to supervise the predicted results of the predictor P in Eq. 1. We accordingly exploit a soft cross-entropy prediction loss L_p, which is calculated as

$$L_p = - \sum_{i=1}^{N} l_{r_i} \log p_{r_i}. \tag{4}$$

Note that we cut off the error back-propagation from L_p to the dynamic soft label. In other words, considering the evaluated dynamic soft label as the ground truth, L_p is only used to optimize the predictor rather than the SR or re-id module. We minimize L_p to supervise the predictor to make an prediction consistent with the dynamic soft label, e.g., predicting a higher probability for the scale factor that is more likely to be evaluated as the optimal one.

3.5   Optimization

Overall loss. To learn the discriminative identity features for re-id, we send f_{r_p}, $f_{x_{sl}}$ and f_{x_h} (the feature vectors of the predicted optimal recovered image x_{r_p}, the synthetic image x_{sl} and the HR image x_h, respectively) into a classifier (i.e., a fully-connected layer) to predict the identities. This process is supervised by the cross-entropy identity loss L_{id} and triplet loss L_{tri}. L_{tri} is defined as

$$L_{tri} = \max(0, \phi + d_p - d_n) \tag{5}$$

where d_p and d_n are respectively the distances between the positive samples with the same identity and negative samples with different identities. ϕ is the margin parameter. We optimize the whole network by minimizing the weighted sum of the SR loss L_{sr}, identity loss L_{id}, triplet loss L_{tri} and prediction loss L_p. The total loss L is formulated as

$$L = L_{sr} + \alpha L_{id} + \beta L_{tri} + \lambda L_p \tag{6}$$

where α, β and λ are the weight factors of L_{id}, L_{tri} and L_p, respectively. Different from the first three losses supervising the SR and re-id module, L_p is used for the predictor separately, and therefore we set its weight λ to 1.

When test, we only need to super-resolve a LR probe by the scale factor r_p that has the maximum predicted probability. We embed the super-resolved probe and all the HR gallery images into the feature space, where we measure the similarity among their features by the Euclidean distances.

Pre-training. Experimentally, if we randomly initialize PRI for training, the dynamic soft label might vary frequently at the early training stage and degenerate the optimization process. Since the untrained SR module produces poorly recovered images, the features corresponding to different scale factors do not have relatively stable distances to the anchor, thus degenerating the effectiveness of the dynamic soft label. To alleviate the problem, we pre-train the SR and re-id module before jointly training the whole model. Specifically, we remove the prediction loss L_p, and the SR module super-resolves both x_l and x_{sl} only by a randomly chosen scale factor from the alternative ones. We only minimize the sum of L_{sr}, L_{id} and L_{tri} during pre-training, so that the SR and re-id module can learn to stably recover images and extract their features in advance, which will help to train the whole model more effectively.

4   Experiment

4.1   Datasets and Evaluation Protocol

Datasets. We evaluate our model on three synthetic and one genuine LR re-id dataset. 1) MLR-CUHK03 is built from CUHK03 [22], containing over 14,000 images of 1,467 identities captured by 5 pairs of cameras. Following [17], for a pair of images from two cameras, we down-sample one of them by randomly choosing a down-sampling factor $r \in \{2, 3, 4\}$ as a LR probe, while the other remains unchanged as a HR gallery image. Two types of images, manually cropped and automatically detected images, are both used. 2) MLR-DukeMTMC-reid [44] includes 36, 411 images of 1, 404 identities captured by 8 cameras. 3) MLR-Market1501 [43] consists of 32, 668 images of 1, 501 identities from 6 camera views. Both MLR-DukeMTMC-reid and MLR-Market1501 are synthesized by the same down-sampling operation as MLR-CUHK03. 4) CAVIAR [6] is a genuine dataset composed of 1220 images of 72 identities and two camera views. We discard 22 identities that only appear in the closer camera.

Evaluation protocol. We adopt the standard *single-shot* person re-id setting. Images of CAVIAR are randomly and evenly divided into two halves for training and test, which means that there are 25/25 identities in the training/test set. We use the 1,367/100, 702/702 and 751/750 training/test identity split on MLR-CUHK03, MLR-DukeMTMC-reid and MLRMarket1501, respectively. For test, we build the probe set with all the LR images, and the gallery set with one randomly selected HR image of each person. For test, we build the probe set with all the LR images, and the gallery set with one randomly selected HR image of each person. Above random data splits are repeated 10 times in the experiments. For the re-id performance evaluation, we use the average Cumulative Match Characteristic (CMC) and report results at ranks 1, 5 and 10.

Implementation details. Our ResNet50 backbone (for P and F) is pre-trained on ImageNet [7], and the SR module G is pre-trained on DIV2K [1]. All the images sent into ResNet50 are resized to $384 \times 128 \times 3$. A set of input images (x_l, x_{sl} and x_h) is randomly flipped horizontally at the same time. We pre-train PRI for T_1 epochs as stated in Sect. 3.5, and then further train the whole PRI model for T_2 epochs. We adopt the Adam optimizer [19] ($\beta_1 = 0.9$ and $\beta_2 = 0.999$), and set the initial learning rate of the ResNet50 backbone and the added 1×1 convolutional layers to 0.01 and 0.1, respectively. They will be respectively decayed to 0.001 and 0.01 after T_1 epochs. We set T_1/T_2 to 60/140 for CAVIAR, and 20/60 for MLR-CUHK03, MLR-DukeMTMC-re-id and MLR-Market1501. Other hyper-parameters are set as follows: the weight factor $\alpha = 1$, $\beta = 0.01$, the margin of the triplet loss $\phi = 10$, the regulatory factor $\gamma = 1$, the update frequency $\omega = 1$. We train our model on 2 NVIDIA Titan Xp GPUs with the batch size set to 16.

4.2   Comparison with State-of-the-art Models

We compare our PRI model with the state-of-the-art models on four LR re-id datasets, including CAVIAR, MLR-CUHK03, MLR-DukeMTMC-reid and MLR-Market1501 in Table 1. For a fair comparison, we do not use pre-/post-processing methods, e.g., re-ranking [45], even though they can further improve our results.

Table 1. Comparison with the state-of-the-art models on four datasets (%). Bold and underlined numbers indicate top two results, respectively.

Method	CAVIAR			MLR-CUHK03			MLR-DukeMTMC-reid			MLR-Market1501		
	Rank 1	Rank 5	Rank 10	Rank 1	Rank 5	Rank 10	Rank 1	Rank 5	Rank 10	Rank 1	Rank 5	Rank 10
JUDEA [24]	22.0	60.1	80.8	26.2	58.0	73.4	-	-	-	-	-	-
SLD^{2}L [18]	18.4	44.8	61.2	-	-	-	-	-	-	-	-	-
SDF [38]	14.3	37.5	62.5	22.2	48.0	64.0	-	-	-	-	-	-
SING [17]	33.5	72.7	89.0	67.7	90.7	94.7	65.2	80.1	84.8	74.4	87.8	91.6
CSR-GAN [39]	34.7	72.5	87.4	71.3	92.1	97.4	67.6	81.4	85.1	76.4	88.5	91.9
RAIN [5]	42.0	77.3	89.6	78.9	97.3	98.7	-	-	-	-	-	-
CAD-Net [25]	42.8	76.2	91.5	82.1	97.4	<u>98.8</u>	75.6	86.7	89.6	83.7	92.7	95.8
CamStyle [46]	32.1	72.3	85.9	69.1	89.6	93.9	64.0	78.1	84.4	74.5	88.6	93.0
FD-GAN [10]	33.5	71.4	86.5	73.4	93.8	97.9	67.5	82.0	85.3	79.6	91.6	93.5
PCB [36]	42.1	74.8	88.2	80.6	96.2	98.6	74.5	84.6	90.3	82.6	92.7	95.2
PyrNet [27]	43.6	79.2	90.4	83.9	97.1	98.5	79.6	88.1	91.2	83.8	93.3	95.6
PRI (Ours)	43.2	78.5	91.9	85.2	97.5	98.8	78.3	87.5	91.4	84.9	93.5	96.1
PCB + PRI	<u>44.3</u>	<u>83.7</u>	**94.8**	<u>86.2</u>	**97.9**	**99.1**	<u>81.6</u>	<u>89.6</u>	<u>92.4</u>	**88.1**	**94.2**	**96.5**
PyrNet + PRI	**45.2**	**84.1**	<u>94.6</u>	**86.5**	<u>97.7</u>	**99.1**	**82.1**	**91.1**	**92.8**	<u>86.9</u>	<u>93.8</u>	<u>96.4</u>

Comparison with LR re-id models. We compare our PRI model with LR re-id models, including JUDEA [24], SLD^{2}L [18], SDF [38], SING [17], CSR-GAN [39], RAIN [5] and CAD-Net [25]. Compared with the most competitive CAD-Net, PRI achieves 0.4%, 3.1%, 2.7% and 1.2% higher scores at rank 1 on CAVIAR, MLR-CUHK03, MLR-DukeMTMC-reid and MLR-Market1501, respectively. Our advantage lies in adaptively predicting and achieving better recovery that contains more discriminative details instead of noise to help identification. In contrast, CAD-Net recovers details into the fixed resolution, which might not be guaranteed to suit the images of various resolutions best. Apart from CAD-Net, there are also some notable comparisons. SING super-resolves LR probes with multiple scale factors separately and then manually fuses them, while CSR-GAN tries to depend on the image sizes to specify the scale factors. Unlike them, our model can exploit the image content to realize the adaptive scale factor prediction in an end-to-end manner.

Comparison with Standard Re-id Models. We also make a comparison between PRI and the competitive standard re-id models, including CamStyle [46], FD-GAN [10], PCB [36] and PyrNet [27]. For a fair comparison, they are trained on the LR re-id datasets in the same manner as our model. The results of CamStyle and FD-GAN are extracted from [25], and those of PCB and PyrNet are acquired by running the released codes. Among these models, only PyrNet can outperform our model at some ranks, *e.g.*, rank 1 on CAVIAR and MLR-DukeMTMC-reid. However, our method can help the standard re-id models better generalize to the LR re-id setting through a simple combination. We only need to replace our ResNet50 re-id module F with the standard re-id models, and keep the other parts (such as G and P) unchanged. For example, combining PyrNet and our method ("PyrNet + PRI" in Table 1) improves rank 1 by at most 3.1% on MLR-Market1501.

4.3   Ablation Studies

Adaptive Scale Factor Predictor. To verify the effectiveness of our adaptive scale factor predictor P, we compare different methods of predicting scale factors in Table 2. Given a well-trained PRI model on MLR-CUHK03, we replace P with the fixed, size-based and ideal predictors in turn, and compare their performances when test. We set four alternative scale factors, including 1, 2, 3 and 4. The "fixed" predictor chooses a fixed scale factor from the four alternatives for each LR probe. Similar to [39], the "size-based" predictor gives a LR probe a scale factor that is the nearest integer to the ratio of R to r. R is the average size (the product of the image height and width) of all the HR images of the training set, and r is the size of the given LR probe. The "ideal" predictor refers to traversing all the alternative scale factors and choosing the one achieving the best result. To some extent, it represents the upper bound that the given PRI model can reach, if we keep G and F unchanged, and only adjust the scale factor for each LR probe. It is not a surprise that there is a performance gap between the ideal predictor and ours, which means that ours cannot guarantee all the predictions are optimal. But it obviously outperforms the fixed and size-based predictors in

Table 2. Evaluation of different scale factor predictors on MLR-CUHK03 (%).

Predictor	Rank 1	mAP
Fixed ×1	78.6	79.2
Fixed ×2	82.3	82.9
Fixed ×3	82.1	82.5
Fixed ×4	82.7	82.8
Size-based	82.5	82.8
Ideal	86.8	87.2
Adaptive (Ours)	85.2	85.7

terms of rank 1 and mAP (mean Average Precision). Compared with the rough manual "fixed" or "size-based" predictors, our model can adaptively predict and recover the more effective details for each LR image based on its image content, which helps further improve the re-id accuracy.

Table 3. Comparison of the soft label with the one-hot label on MLR-CUHK03 (%).

Method	Rank 1	Rank 5	Rank 10
One-hot label	81.8	94.8	97.2
Soft label (Ours)	85.2	97.5	98.8

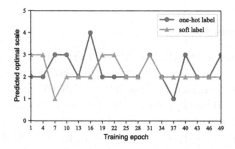

Fig. 3. A comparison between the soft label and one-hot label. This example indicates the change of the predicted optimal scale factor r_p for a LR image during training.

Soft Property. We replace the dynamic soft label of our model with the one-hot label to demonstrate the effectiveness of the soft property. The one-hot label is a binary vector where the scale factor with the maximum evaluated probability is labeled as 1, while the others are labeled as 0. We evaluate the two types of labels on MLR-CUHK03 in Table 3, which shows that the soft label outperforms the one-hot label by 3.4% at rank 1. The reason is that the variability of the optimal scale factors causes the frequent change of the one-hot label and the unstable training. In fact, we find that using the one-hot label tends to predict a same scale factor (e.g., 2) for most LR probes when test.

We visualize an example of the change of the predicted optimal scale factor r_p during training, as illustrated in Fig. 3. We can observe that the soft label stably predicts 2 after 31 epochs while the one-hot label results in a switch between 2 and 3. This indicates that the soft label can smooth the change of the predicted optimal scale factor and stabilize the optimization process.

Dynamic Property. We validate the dynamic property of the dynamic soft label by adjusting the update frequency ω. Figure 4 (a) reports the changing curve of rank 1 with ω. Note that $\omega=0$ refers to randomly determining whether to update dynamic soft labels during each training epoch. Compared with setting

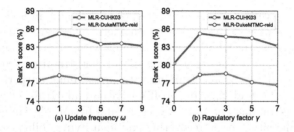

Fig. 4. Effect of the update frequency and regulatory factor.

Table 4. Rank 1 scores of three training manners (%).

Method	MLR-CUHK03	MLR-DukeMTMC-reid
Only pre-training	82.5	73.8
Without pre-training	82.8	75.1
With pre-training (Ours)	85.2	78.3

Table 5. Evaluation of losses on MLR-CUHK03 (%).

Removed loss	Rank 1	Rank 5	Rank 10
L_{id}	80.4	94.8	97.5
L_{sr}	81.5	95.4	97.9
L_{tri}	83.4	97.3	98.8
L_p	82.0	94.2	97.2
PRI (with all losses)	85.2	97.5	98.8

ω to 1, setting it to 0 slightly degenerates rank 1 on both two datasets. This is probably because randomly updating leads labels not to always timely reflect their variation. When $\omega \geq 1$, Fig. 4 (a) has a general trend that rank 1 declines as ω increases, showing that more timely updating labels can make more adaptive prediction about the optimal scale factor. Therefore, the dynamic property is effective in handling the variation of the optimal scale factors during training.

Regulatory Factor. The regulatory factor γ controls the relative importance of each scale factor in Eq. 3. Figure 4 (b) plots rank 1 scores varying with γ. We only set γ to the odd number (except 0) to make sure that the scale factor near to the HR anchor in the feature space has a higher confidence probability. As shown in Fig. 4 (b), the rank 1 reaches a peak value when γ is set to 1/3 on MLR-CUHK03/MLR-DukeMTMC-reid, respectively. Not surprisingly, setting γ to 0 degrades the performance because this considers all the scale factors as equal, and thus loses the effective supervision of the dynamic soft label.

Pre-training. To validate the effectiveness of pre-training in Sect. 3.5, we evaluate the rank 1 scores of three training manners, which are in turn: only pre-training (not training the whole model), training without pre-training and training with pre-training. As shown in Table 4, only pre-training achieves the lowest scores on two datasets, and training with pre-training outperforms without pre-training by 2.4% and 3.2% on MLR-CUHK03 and MLR-DukeMTMC-reid, respectively. Pre-training can improve our results because it can endow the SR and re-id module with a basic recovering and identifying ability, so that we can obtain more stable distributions of the features (corresponding to different scale factors) and dynamic soft labels.

Loss Functions. We train our model by minimizing the weighted sum of the identity loss L_{id}, triplet loss L_{tri}, SR loss L_{sr} and prediction loss L_p in Eq. 6. We validate each loss by removing it from the total loss. Table 5 shows that removing L_{id}, L_{tri} or L_{sr} deteriorates the performance to varying degrees. This is reasonable because L_{id} and L_{tri} are essential to learn the identity discrimination, while L_{sr} is significant to recover effective image contents. Discarding L_p makes rank 1 drop from 85.2% to 82.0%, because the predictor remains initialized and cannot be optimized for the adaptive scale factor prediction without L_p.

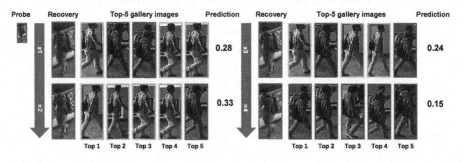

Fig. 5. Visualized examples of the recovered images (resized to the uniform size for a better comparison), top-ranked HR gallery images and predicted probabilities. Each ground truth is indicated by a green bounding box.

Example analysis. We visualize an example of the recovered images, image matching results and predicted probabilities in Fig. 5. It can be easily observed that the ground truths achieve the best ranking results and occupy the top 4 places when we super-resolve the probe by the scale factor 2. This is consistent with the fact that 2 has the highest predicted probability (0.33) of being the optimal scale factor. The recovered images could provide an intuitional explanation for the matching results. The relatively complex shirt textures make the larger scale factor (*e.g.*, 4) tend to produce the distorted or blurry recovery. Therefore, slightly super-resolving the probe with the smaller scale factor 2 is enough for better identification.

5 Conclusions

In this paper, we have proposed the PRI model to explore the potential relation between the image content and the optimal scale factor for LR person re-id. Despite lack of annotations, our proposed dynamic soft label enables us to learn the prediction of the optimal scale factors in a self-supervised manner. Given a LR image, our model can automatically make the content-aware scale factor prediction, and then recover details into the predicted level, and finally identify the recovered person image. Our method can not only predict a preferable scale factor for more effective recovery and identification, but also help the standard re-id models generalize well to the LR re-id setting.

Acknowledgements. This work is jointly supported by National Key Research and Development Program of China (2016YFB1001000), Key Research Program of Frontier Sciences, CAS (ZDBS-LY-JSC032), and National Natural Science Foundation of China (U1803261).

References

1. Agustsson, E., Timofte, R.: Ntire 2017 challenge on single image super-resolution: dataset and study. In: CVPR (2017)
2. Bai, S., Tang, P., Torr, P.H., Latecki, L.J.: Re-ranking via metric fusion for object retrieval and person re-identification. In: CVPR (2019)
3. Chen, B., Deng, W., Hu, J.: Mixed high-order attention network for person re-identification. In: ICCV (2019)
4. Chen, Y., Zhu, X., Gong, S.: Instance-guided context rendering for cross-domain person re-identification. In: ICCV (2019)
5. Chen, Y.C., Li, Y.J., Du, X., Wang, Y.C.F.: Learning resolution-invariant deep representations for person re-identification. In: AAAI (2019)
6. Cheng, D.S., Cristani, M., Stoppa, M., Bazzani, L., Murino, V.: Custom pictorial structures for re-identification. In: BMVC (2011)
7. Deng, J., Dong, W., Socher, R., Li, L.J., Li, K., Fei-Fei, L.: Imagenet: a large-scale hierarchical image database. In: CVPR (2009)
8. Dong, C., Loy, C.C., He, K., Tang, X.: Learning a deep convolutional network for image super-resolution. In: ECCV (2014)
9. Fu, Y., Wei, Y., Wang, G., Zhou, Y., Shi, H., Huang, T.S.: Self-similarity grouping: a simple unsupervised cross domain adaptation approach for person re-identification. In: ICCV (2019)
10. Ge, Y., Li, Z., Zhao, H., Yin, G., Yi, S., Wang, X., et al.: FD-GAN: Pose-guided feature distilling GAN for robust person re-identification. In: NeurIPS (2018)
11. Gray, D., Tao, H.: Viewpoint invariant pedestrian recognition with an ensemble of localized features. In: ECCV (2008)
12. He, K., Zhang, X., Ren, S., Sun, J.: Deep residual learning for image recognition. In: CVPR (2016)
13. He, L., Liang, J., Li, H., Sun, Z.: Deep spatial feature reconstruction for partial person re-identification: alignment-free approach. In: CVPR (2018)
14. He, L., Wang, Y., Liu, W., Liao, X., Zhao, H., Sun, Z., Feng, J.: Foreground-aware pyramid reconstruction for alignment-free occluded person re-identification. arXiv preprint arXiv:1904.04975 (2019)

15. Hu, X., Mu, H., Zhang, X., Wang, Z., Tan, T., Sun, J.: Meta-SR: a magnification-arbitrary network for super-resolution. In: CVPR (2019)
16. Huang, Y., Wu, Q., Xu, J., Zhong, Y.: SBSGAN: suppression of inter-domain background shift for person re-identification. In: ICCV (2019)
17. Jiao, J., Zheng, W.S., Wu, A., Zhu, X., Gong, S.: Deep low-resolution person re-identification. In: AAAI (2018)
18. Jing, X.Y., et al.: Super-resolution person re-identification with semi-coupled low-rank discriminant dictionary learning. In: CVPR (2015)
19. Kingma, D.P., Ba, J.: Adam: a method for stochastic optimization. arXiv preprint arXiv:1412.6980 (2014)
20. Krizhevsky, A., Sutskever, I., Hinton, G.E.: Imagenet classification with deep convolutional neural networks. In: NeurIPS (2012)
21. Ledig, C., et al.: Photo-realistic single image super-resolution using a generative adversarial network. In: CVPR (2017)
22. Li, W., Zhao, R., Xiao, T., Wang, X.: Deepreid: deep filter pairing neural network for person re-identification. In: CVPR (2014)
23. Li, W., Zhu, X., Gong, S.: Harmonious attention network for person re-identification. In: CVPR (2018)
24. Li, X., Zheng, W.S., Wang, X., Xiang, T., Gong, S.: Multi-scale learning for low-resolution person re-identification. In: ICCV (2015)
25. Li, Y.J., Chen, Y.C., Lin, Y.Y., Du, X., Wang, Y.C.F.: Recover and identify: a generative dual model for cross-resolution person re-identification. In: ICCV (2019)
26. Lim, B., Son, S., Kim, H., Nah, S., Mu Lee, K.: Enhanced deep residual networks for single image super-resolution. In: CVPRW (2017)
27. Martinel, N., Luca Foresti, G., Micheloni, C.: Aggregating deep pyramidal representations for person re-identification. In: CVPRW (2019)
28. Miao, J., Wu, Y., Liu, P., Ding, Y., Yang, Y.: Pose-guided feature alignment for occluded person re-identification. In: ICCV (2019)
29. Niu, K., Huang, Y., Ouyang, W., Wang, L.: Improving description-based person re-identification by multi-granularity image-text alignments. TIP (2020)
30. Niu, K., Huang, Y., Wang, L.: Fusing two directions in cross-domain adaption for real life person search by language. In: ICCVW (2019)
31. Si, J., et al.: Dual attention matching network for context-aware feature sequence based person re-identification. In: CVPR (2018)
32. Simonyan, K., Zisserman, A.: Very deep convolutional networks for large-scale image recognition. arXiv preprint arXiv:1409.1556 (2014)
33. Song, C., Huang, Y., Ouyang, W., Wang, L.: Mask-guided contrastive attention model for person re-identification. In: CVPR (2018)
34. Song, J., Yang, Y., Song, Y.Z., Xiang, T., Hospedales, T.M.: Generalizable person re-identification by domain-invariant mapping network. In: CVPR (2019)
35. Sun, Y., et al.: Perceive where to focus: learning visibility-aware part-level features for partial person re-identification. In: CVPR (2019)
36. Sun, Y., Zheng, L., Yang, Y., Tian, Q., Wang, S.: Beyond part models: person retrieval with refined part pooling (and a strong convolutional baseline). In: ECCV (2018)
37. Wang, X., et al.: ESRGAN: enhanced super-resolution generative adversarial networks. In: ECCV (2018)
38. Wang, Z., Hu, R., Yu, Y., Jiang, J., Liang, C., Wang, J.: Scale-adaptive low-resolution person re-identification via learning a discriminating surface. In: IJCAI (2016)

39. Wang, Z., Ye, M., Yang, F., Bai, X., Satoh, S.: Cascaded SR-GAN for scale-adaptive low resolution person re-identification. In: IJCAI (2018)
40. Wei, L., Zhang, S., Gao, W., Tian, Q.: Person transfer GAN to bridge domain gap for person re-identification. In: CVPR (2018)
41. Yu, T., Li, D., Yang, Y., Hospedales, T.M., Xiang, T.: Robust person re-identification by modelling feature uncertainty. In: ICCV (2019)
42. Zhang, Y., Tian, Y., Kong, Y., Zhong, B., Fu, Y.: Residual dense network for image super-resolution. In: CVPR (2018)
43. Zheng, L., Shen, L., Tian, L., Wang, S., Wang, J., Tian, Q.: Scalable person re-identification: a benchmark. In: ICCV (2015)
44. Zheng, Z., Zheng, L., Yang, Y.: Unlabeled samples generated by GAN improve the person re-identification baseline in vitro. In: ICCV (2017)
45. Zhong, Z., Zheng, L., Cao, D., Li, S.: Re-ranking person re-identification with K-reciprocal encoding. In: CVPR (2017)
46. Zhong, Z., Zheng, L., Zheng, Z., Li, S., Yang, Y.: Camera style adaptation for person re-identification. In: CVPR (2018)

Learning Canonical Representations for Scene Graph to Image Generation

Roei Herzig[1]([⊠]), Amir Bar[1], Huijuan Xu[2], Gal Chechik[3], Trevor Darrell[2], and Amir Globerson[1]

[1] Tel Aviv University, Tel Aviv-Yafo, Israel
[2] UC Berkeley, Berkeley, USA
[3] Bar-Ilan University, NVIDIA Research, Ramat Gan, Israel

Abstract. Generating realistic images of complex visual scenes becomes challenging when one wishes to control the structure of the generated images. Previous approaches showed that scenes with few entities can be controlled using scene graphs, but this approach struggles as the complexity of the graph (the number of objects and edges) increases. In this work, we show that one limitation of current methods is their inability to capture semantic equivalence in graphs. We present a novel model that addresses these issues by learning canonical graph representations from the data, resulting in improved image generation for complex visual scenes (The project page is available at https://roeiherz.github.io/CanonicalSg2Im/). Our model demonstrates improved empirical performance on large scene graphs, robustness to noise in the input scene graph, and generalization on semantically equivalent graphs. Finally, we show improved performance of the model on three different benchmarks: Visual Genome, COCO, and CLEVR.

Keywords: Scene graphs · Canonical representations · Image generation

1 Introduction

Generating realistic images is a key task in computer vision research. Recently, a series of methods were presented for creating realistic-looking images of objects and faces (e.g. [3,20,37]). Despite this impressive progress, a key challenge remains: how can one control the content of images at multiple levels to generate images that have specific desired composition and attributes. Controlling content can be particularly challenging when generating visual scenes that contain multiple interacting objects. One natural way of describing such scenes is via the structure of a *Scene Graph* (SG), which contains a set of objects as nodes and their attributes and relations as edges. Indeed, several studies addressed generating images from SGs [1,17,25]. Unfortunately, the quality of images generated

Electronic supplementary material The online version of this chapter (https://doi.org/10.1007/978-3-030-58574-7_13) contains supplementary material, which is available to authorized users.

A. Vedaldi et al. (Eds.): ECCV 2020, LNCS 12371, pp. 210–227, 2020.
https://doi.org/10.1007/978-3-030-58574-7_13

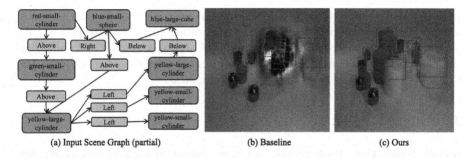

|(a) Input Scene Graph (partial)|(b) Baseline|(c) Ours|

Fig. 1. Generation of scenes with many objects. Our method achieves better performance on such scenes than previous methods. **Left:** A partial input scene graph. **Middle:** Generation using [17]. **Right:** Generation using our proposed method.

from SGs still lags far behind that of generating single objects or faces. Here we show that one problem with current models is their failure to capture logical equivalences, and we propose an approach for overcoming this limitation.

SG-to-image typically involves two steps: first, generating a layout from the SG, and then generating pixels from the layout. In the first step, the SG does not contain bounding boxes, and is used to generate a layout that contains bounding box coordinates for all objects. The transformation relies on geometric properties specified in the SG such as "(A, right, B)". Since SGs are typically generated by humans, they usually do not contain *all* correct relations in the data. For example, in an SG with relation (A, right, B) it is always true that (B, left, A), yet typically only one of these relations will appear.[1] This example illustrates that multiple SGs can describe the same physical configuration, and are thus logically equivalent. Ideally, we would like all such SGs to result in the same layout and image. As we show here, this often does not hold for existing models, resulting in low-quality generated images for large graphs (see Fig. 1).

Here we present an approach to overcome the above difficulty. We first formalize the problem as being invariant to certain logical equivalences (i.e., all equivalent SGs should generate the same image). Next, we propose to replace any SG with a "canonical SG" such that all logically equivalent SGs are replaced by the same canonical SG, and this canonical SG is the one used in the layout generation step. This approach, by definition, results in the same output for all logically equivalent graphs. We present a practical approach to learning such a canonicalization process that does not use any prior knowledge about the relations (e.g., it does not know that "right" is a transitive relation). We show how to integrate the resulting canonical SGs within a SG-to-image generation model, and how to learn it from data. Our method also learns more compact models than previous methods, because the canonicalization process distributes information across the graph with only few additional parameters.

In summary, our novel contributions are as follows: 1) We propose a model that uses canonical representations of SGs, thus obtaining stronger invariance properties. This in turn leads to generalization on semantically equivalent graphs

---

[1] We note that human raters don't typically include all logically equivalent relations. We analyzed data and found only small fraction of these are annotated in practice.

and improved robustness to graph size and noise in comparison to existing methods. 2) We show how to learn the canonicalization process from data. 3) We use our canonical representations within an SG-to-image model and show that our approach results in improved generation on Visual Genome, COCO, and CLEVR, compared to the state-of-the-art baselines.

2   Related Work

Image generation. Earlier work on image generation used autoregressive networks [35,36] to model pixel conditional distributions. Recently, GANs [11] and VAEs [21] emerged as models of choice for this task. Specifically, generation techniques based on GANs were proposed for generating sharper, more diverse and better realistic images in a series of works [5,20,26,28,32,40,44,53,60,64].

Conditional image synthesis. Multiple works have explored approaches for generating images with a given desired content. Conditioning inputs may include class labels [7,30,34], source images [15,16,27,50,66,67], model interventions [2], and text [14,38,41,42,47,57,58,61]. Other studies [9,33] focused on image manipulation using language descriptions while disentangling the semantics of both input images and text descriptions.

Structured representation. Recent models [14,65] incorporate intermediate structured representations, such as layouts or skeletons, to control the coarse structure of generated images. Several studies focused on generating images from such representations (e.g., semantic segmentation masks [6,16,37,53], layout [62], and SGs [1,17,25]). Layout and SGs are more compact representations as compared to segmentation masks. While layout [62] provides spatial information, SGs [17] provide richer information about attributes and relations. Another advantage of SGs is that they are closely related to the semantics of the image as perceived by humans, and therefore editing an SG corresponds to clear changes in semantics. SGs and visual relations have also been used in image retrieval [19,46], relationship modeling [23,39,45], image captioning [56] and action recognition [12,29]. Several works have addressed the problem of generating SGs from text [46,51], standalone objects [55] and images [13].

Scene-graph-to-image generation. Sg2Im [17] was the first to propose an end-to-end method for generating images from scene graphs. However, as we note above, the current SG-to-image models [1,8,25,31,52] show degraded performance on complex SGs with many objects. To mitigate this, the authors in [1] have utilized stronger supervision in the form of a coarse grid, where attributes of location and size are specified for each object. The focus of our work is to alleviate this difficulty by directly modeling some of the invariances in SG representation. Finally, the topic of invariance in deep architectures has also attracted considerable interest, but mostly in the context of certain permutation invariances [13,59]. Our approach focuses on a more complex notion of invariance, and addresses it via canonicalization.

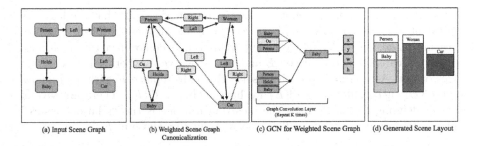

| (a) Input Scene Graph | (b) Weighted Scene Graph Canonicalization | (c) GCN for Weighted Scene Graph | (d) Generated Scene Layout |

Fig. 2. Proposed Scene Graph to Layout architecture. (a) An input scene graph. (b) The graph is first canonicalized using our WSGC method in Sect. 3.2. Dashed edges correspond to completed relations that are assigned with weights. (c) A GCN is applied to the weighted graph, resulting in bounding box coordinates. (d) The GCN outputs are used to generate the predicted layout.

3   Scene Graph Canonicalization

As mentioned above, the same image can be represented by multiple logically-equivalent SGs. Next we define this formally and propose an approach to canonicalize graphs that enforces invariance to these equivalences. In Sect. 4 we show how to use this canonical scene graph within an SG-to-image task.

Let $\mathcal{C}$ be the set of objects categories and $\mathcal{R}$ be the set of possible relations.[2] An SG over n objects is a tuple (O, E) where $O \in \mathcal{C}^n$ is the object categories and E is a set of labeled directed edges (triplets) of the form (i, r, j) where $i, j \in \{1, \ldots, n\}$ and $r \in \mathcal{R}$. Thus an edge (i, r, j) implies that the ith object (that has category o_i) should have relation r with the jth object. Alternatively the set E can be viewed as a set of $|\mathcal{R}|$ directed graphs where for each r the graph E_r contains only the edges for relation r.

Our key observation is that relations in SGs are often dependent, because they reflect properties of the physical world. This means that for a relation r, the presence of certain edges in E_r implies that other edges have to hold. For example, assume r is a **transitive relation** like "left". Then if $i, j \in E_r$ and $j, k \in E_r$, it should hold that $i, k \in E_r$. There are also dependencies between different relations. For example, if r, r' are **converse relations** (e.g., r is "left" and r' "right") then $i, j \in E_r$ implies $j, i \in E_{r'}$. Formally, all the above dependencies are first order logic formulas. For example, r, r' being converse corresponds to the formula $\forall i, j : r(i, j) \implies r'(j, i)$. Let $\mathcal{F}$ denote this set of formulas.

The fact that certain relations are implied by a graph does not mean that they are contained in its set of relations. For example, E may contain $(1, \text{left}, 2)$ but not $(2, \text{right}, 1)$.[3] However, we would like SGs that contain either or both of these relations to result in the same image. In other words, we would like all logically equivalent graphs to result in the same image, as formally stated next.

---

[2] Objects in SGs also contain attributes but we drop these for notational simplicity.

[3] This is because empirical graphs E are created by human annotators, who typically skip redundant edges that can be inferred from other edges.

Given a scene graph E denote by $Q(E)$ the set of graphs that are logically equivalent to E.[4] As mentioned above, we would like all these graphs to result in the same image. Currently, SG-to-layout architectures do not have this invariance property because they operate on E and thus sensitive to whether it has certain edges or not. A natural approach to solve this is to replace E with a *canonical form* $C(E)$ such that $\forall E' \in Q(E)$ we have $C(E') = C(E)$. There are several ways of defining $C(E)$. Perhaps the most natural one is the "relation-closure" which is the graph containing all relations implied by those in E.

Definition 1. *Given a set of formulas $\mathcal{F}$, and relations E, the closure $C(E)$ is the set of relations that are true in any SG that contains E and satisfies $\mathcal{F}$.*

We note that the above definition coincides with the standard definition for closure of relations. Our definition emphasizes the fact that $C(E)$ are relations that are necessarily true given those in E. Additionally we allow for multiple relations, whereas closure is typically defined with respect to a single property. Next we describe how to calculate $C(E)$ when $\mathcal{F}$ is known, and then explain how to learn $\mathcal{F}$ from data.

3.1 Calculating Scene Graph Canonicalization

For a general set of formulas, calculating the closure is hard as it is an instance of inference in first order logic. However, here we restrict ourselves to the following formulas for which this calculation is efficient:[5]

- Transitive Relations: We assume a set of relations $\mathcal{R}_{trans} \subset \mathcal{R}$ where all $r \in \mathcal{R}_{trans}$ satisfy the formula $\forall x, y, z : r(x,y) \wedge r(y,z) \implies r(x,z)$.
- Converse Relations: We assume a set of relations pairs $\mathcal{R}_{conv} \subset \mathcal{R} \times \mathcal{R}$ where all $(r, r') \in \mathcal{R}_{conv}$ satisfy the formula $\forall x, y : r(x,y) \implies r'(y,x)$.

Under the above set of formulas, the closure $C(E)$ can be computed via the following procedure, which we call **Scene Graph Canonicalization (SGC)**:
Initialization: Set $C(E) = E$.
Converse Completion: $\forall(r, r') \in \mathcal{R}_{conv}$, if $(i, r, j) \in E$, add (j, r', i) to $C(E)$.
Transitive Completion: For each $r \in \mathcal{R}_{trans}$ calculate the transitive closure of $C_r(E)$ (namely the r relations in $C(E)$) and add it to $C(E)$. The transitive closure can be calculated using the Floyd-Warshall algorithm [10].

It can be shown (see Supplementary) that the SGC procedure indeed produces the closure of $C(E)$.

---

[4] Equivalence of course depends on what relations are considered, but we do not specify this directly to avoid notational clutter.

[5] We note that we could have added an option for symmetric relations, but we do not include these, as they not exhibited in the datasets we consider.

3.2 Calculating Weighted Scene Graph Canonicalization

Thus far we assumed that the sets R_{trans} and R_{conv} were given. Generally, we don't expect this to be the case. We next explain how to construct a model that doesn't have access to these. In this formulation we will add edges with weights, to reflect our level of certainty in adding them. These weights will depend on parameters, which will be learned from data in an end-to-end manner (see Sect. 5). See Fig. 2 for a high level description of the architecture.

Since we don't know which relations are transitive or converses, we assign probabilities to reflect this uncertainty. In the transitive case, for each $r \in \mathcal{R}$ we use a parameter $\theta_r^{trans} \in \mathbb{R}^{|\mathcal{R}|}$ to define the probability that r is transitive:

$$p^{trans}(r) = \sigma(\theta_r^{trans}) \qquad (1)$$

where σ is the sigmoid function. For converse relations, we let $p^{conv}(r'|r)$ denote the probability that r' is the converse of r. We add another *empty* relation $r' = \phi$ such that $p^{conv}(\phi|r)$ is the probability that r has no converse in $\mathcal{R}$. This is parameterized via $\theta_{r,r'}^{conv} \in \mathbb{R}^{|\mathcal{R}| \times |\mathcal{R} \cup \phi|}$ which is used to define the distribution:

$$p^{conv}(r'|r) = \frac{e^{\theta_{r,r'}^{conv}}}{\sum_{\hat{r} \in \mathcal{R} \cup \phi} e^{\theta_{r,\hat{r}}^{conv}}} \qquad (2)$$

Finally, since converse pairs are typically symmetric (e.g.., "left" is the converse of "right" and vise-versa), for every $r, r' \in \mathcal{R} \times \mathcal{R}$ we set $\theta_{r,r'}^{conv} = \theta_{r',r}^{conv}$. Our model will use these probabilities to complete edges as explained next. In Sect. 3.1 we described the SGC method, which takes a graph E and outputs its completion $C(E)$. The method assumed knowledge of the converse and transitive relations. Here we extend this approach to the case where we have weights on the properties of relations, as per Eq. 1 and 2. Since we have weights on possible completions we will need to work with a weighted relation graph and thus from now on consider edges (i, r, j, w). Below we describe two methods *WSGC-E* and *WSGC-S* for obtaining weighted graphs. Section 4 shows how to use these weighted graphs in an SG to image model.

Exact Weighted Scene Graph Canonicalization (WSGC-E). We describe briefly a method that is a natural extension of SGC (further details are provided in the Supplementary). It begins with the user-specified graph E, with weights of one. Next two weighted completion steps are performed, corresponding to the SGC steps. **Converse Completion:** In SGC, this step adds all converse edges. In the weighted case it makes sense to add the converse edge with its corresponding converse weight. For example, if the graph E contains the edge $(i, above, j, 1)$ and $p^{conv}(below|above) = 0.7$, we add the edge $(j, below, i, 0.7)$. **Transitive Completion:** In SGC, all transitive edges are found and added. In the weighted case, a natural alternative is to set a weight of a path to be the product of weights along this path, and set the weight of a completed edge (i, r, j) to be the maximum weight of a path between i and j times the probability $p^{trans}(r)$ that the relation is transitive. This can be done in poly-time, but runtime can be substantial for large graphs. We offer a faster approach next.

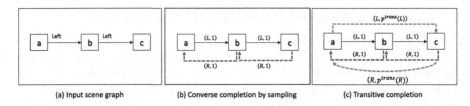

Fig. 3. Illustration of WSGC-S. (a) The input graph. (b) Converse edges (brown arrows) are sampled from p^{conv} and assigned a weight 1 (here two edges were sampled). (c) Transitive edges (green arrows) are completed and assigned a weight p^{trans}.

Sampling Based Weighted Scene Graph Canonicalization (WSGC-S). The difficulty in WSGC-E is that the transitivity step is performed on a dense graph (most weights will be non-zero). To overcome this, we propose to replace the converse completion step of WSGC-E with a sampling based approach that samples completed edges, but always gives them a weight of 1 when they are added. In this way, the transitive step is computed on a much sparser graph with weights 1. We next describe the two steps for the WSGC-S procedure.

Converse Completion: Given the original user-provided graph E, for each r and edge $(i, r, j, 1)$ we sample a random variable $Z \in \mathcal{R} \cup \phi$ from $p^{conv}(\cdot|r)$ and if $Z \neq \phi$, we add the edge $(j, Z, i, 1)$. For example, see Fig. 3b. After sampling such Z for all edges, a new graph E' is obtained, where all the weights are 1.[6]

Transitive Completion: For the graph E' and for each relation r, calculate the transitive closure of $C(E'_r)$ and add all new edges in this closure to E' with weight $p^{trans}(r)$. See illustration in Fig. 3c. Note that this can be calculated in polynomial time using the FW algorithm [10], as in the SGC case.

Finally, we note that if all assigned weights are discrete, both the WSGC-E and WSGC-S are identical to SGC.

4   Scene Graph to Image Using Canonicalization

Thus far we showed how to take the original graph E and complete it into a weighted graph E', using the WSGC-S procedure. Next, we show how to use E' to generate an image, by first mapping E' to a scene layout (see Fig. 2), and then mapping the layout to an image (see AttSPADE Figure in the Supplementary). The following two components are variants of previous SG to image models [1,17,48], and thus we describe them briefly (see Supplementary for details).

From Weighted SG to Layout: A layout is a set of bounding boxes for the nodes in the SG. A natural architecture for such graph-labeling problems is a Graph Convolutional Network (GCN) [22]. Indeed, GCNs have recently been used for the SG to layout task [1,17,25]. We also employ this approach here, but modify it to our weighted scene graph. Namely, we modify the graph convolution

---

[6] We could sample multiple times and average, but this is not necessary in practice.

layer such that the aggregation step of each node is set to be a weighted average where the weights are those in the canonical SG.

From Layout to Image: We now need to transform the obtained layout in Sect. 4 to an actual image. Several works have proposed models for this step [49,63], where the input was a set of bounding boxes and their object categories. We follow this approach, but extend it so that attributes for each object (e.g., color, shape and material, as in the CLEVR dataset) can be specified. We achieve this via a novel generative model, AttSPADE, that supports attributes. More details are in Supplementary. Figure 4 shows an example of the model trained on CLEVR and applied to several SGs. Finally, our experiments on non CLEVR datasets simply we use a pre-trained LostGAN [48] model.

5   Losses and Training

Thus far we described a model that starts with an SG and outputs an image, using the following three steps: SG to canonical weighted SG (Sect. 3.2), weighted SG to layout (Sect. 4) and finally layout to image (Sect. 4). In this section we describe how the parameters of these steps are trained in an end-to-end manner. We focus on training with the WSGC-S, since this is what we use in most of our experiments. See Supplementary for Training with WSGC-E.

Below we describe the loss for a single input scene graph E and its ground truth layout Y. The parameters of the model are as follows: θ^g are the parameters of the GCN in Sect. 4, θ^{trans} are the parameters of the transitive probability (Eq. 1), and θ^{conv} are those of the converse probability (Eq. 2). Let θ denote the set of all parameters. Recall that in the first step Sect. 3.2, we sample a set of random variables $\bar{Z}$ and use these to obtain a weighted graph $\text{WSGC}_{\bar{Z}}(E; \theta^{trans})$. Denote the GCN applied to this graph by $G_{\theta^g}(\text{WSGC}_{\bar{Z}}(E; \theta^{trans}))$.

We use the L_1 loss between the predicted and ground truth bounding boxes Y. Namely, we wish to minimize the following objective:

$$L(\theta) = \mathbb{E}_{\bar{Z} \sim q(\theta^{conv})} \left\| Y - G_{\theta^g}(\text{WSGC}_{\bar{Z}}(E; \theta^{trans})) \right\|_1 \qquad (3)$$

where $\bar{Z} = \{Z_e | e \in E\}$ is a set of independent random variables each sampled from $p^{conv}(r' | r(e); \theta^{conv})$ (see Eq. 2 and the description of WSGC-E), and $q(\theta^{conv})$ denotes this sampling distribution.

The gradient of this loss with respect to all parameters except θ^{conv} can be easily calculated. Next, we focus on the gradient with respect to θ^{conv}. Because the sampling distribution depends on θ^{conv} it is natural to use the REINFORCE algorithm [54] in this case, as explained next. Define:
$R(\bar{Z}; \theta^g, \theta^{trans}) = \left\| Y - G_{\theta^g}(\text{WSGC}_{\bar{Z}}(E; \theta^{trans})) \right\|_1$. Then Eq. 3 is:
$L(\theta^{conv}) = \mathbb{E}_{\bar{Z} \sim q(\theta^{conv})} R(\bar{Z}; \theta^g, \theta^{trans})$.

The key idea in REINFORCE is the observation that:

$$\nabla_{\theta^{conv}} L(\theta) = \mathbb{E}_{\bar{Z} \sim q(\theta^{conv})} \nabla_{\theta^{conv}} R(\bar{Z}; \theta^g, \theta^{trans}) \log p_\theta^{conv}(\bar{Z})$$

Thus, we can approximate $\nabla_{\theta^{conv}} L(\theta)$ by sampling $\bar{Z}$ and averaging the above.[7]

---

[7] We sample just one instantiation of $\bar{Z}$ per image, since this works well in practice.

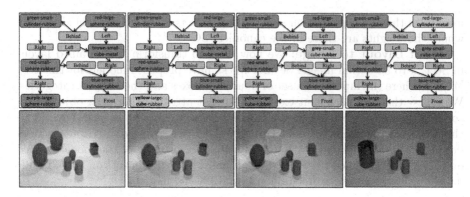

Fig. 4. Demonstration of the AttSPADE generator for scene graphs with varying attributes. Top row shows SGs where each column modifies one attribute. Bottom row is the images generated by AttSPADE.

For the layout-to-image component, most of our experiments use a pretrained LostGAN model. For CLEVR (Fig. 4) we train our AttSPADE model which is a variant of SPADE [37] and trained similarly (see Supplementary).

6   Experiments

To evaluate our proposed WSGC method, we test performance on two tasks. First, we evaluate on the SG-to-layout task (the task that WSGC is designed for. See Sect. 3.2). We then further use these layouts to generate images and demonstrate that improved layouts also yield improved generated images.

Datasets. We consider the following three datasets: COCO-stuff [4], Visual Genome (VG) [24] and CLEVR [18]. We also created a synthetic dataset to quantify the performance of WSGC in a controlled setting.

Synthetic dataset. To test the contribution of learned transitivity to layout prediction, we generate a synthetic dataset. In this dataset, every object is a square with one of two possible sizes. The set of relations includes: *Above* (transitive), Opposite Horizontally and *XNear* (non-transitive). To generate training and evaluation data, we uniformly sample coordinates of object centers and object sizes and automatically compute relations among object pairs based on their spatial locations. See Supplementary file for further visual examples.

COCO-Stuff 2017 [4]. Contains pixel-level annotations with 40K train and 5K validation images with bounding boxes and segmentation masks for 80 thing categories, and 91 stuff categories. We use the standard subset proposed in previous works [17], which contains ∼25K training, 1024 validation, and 2048 in test. We use an additional subset we call Packed COCO, containing images with at least 16 objects, resulting in 4,341 train images, 238 validation, and 238 test.

Visual Genome (VG) [24]. Contains 108,077 images with SGs. We use the standard subset [17]: 62K training, 5506 validation and 5088 test images. We

Fig. 5. Examples of image generation for CLEVR where the Sg2Im baseline and our WSGC model were trained on images with a maximum of 10 objects but tested on scenes with 16+ objects. Shown are three examples where: Top row: our WSGC generation (with boxes and without). Bottom row: Sg2Im generation (with boxes and without).

use an additional subset we call Packed VG, containing images with at least 16 objects, resulting in 6341 train images, 809 validation, and 809 test images.

CLEVR [18]. A synthetic dataset based on scene-graphs with four spatial relations: *left*, *right*, *front* and *behind*, as well as attributes *shape*, *size*, *material* and *color*. It has 70k training images and 15k for validation and test.

6.1 Scene-Graph-to-layout Generation

We evaluate the SG-to-layout task using the following metrics: 1) $mIOU$: the mean IOU value. 2) $R@0.3$ and $R@0.5$: the average recall over predictions with IOU greater than 0.3 and 0.5 respectively. We note our WSGC model is identical to the Sg2Im baseline in the SG-to-layout module in all aspects that are not related to canonicalization. This provides a well-controlled ablation showing that canonicalization improves performance.

Testing Robustness to Number of Objects. Scenes can contain a variable number of objects, and SG-to-layout models should work well across these. Here we tested how different models perform as the number of objects is changed in the synthetic dataset. We compared the following models a) A "Learned Transitivity" model that uses WSGC to learn the weights of each relation. b) A "Known Transitivity" model that is given the transitive relations in the data, and performs hard SGC completion (see Sect. 3.1). Comparison between "Learned Transitivity" and "Known Transitivity" is meant to evaluate how well WSGC can learn which relations are transitive. c) A baseline model Sg2Im [17] that does not use any relation completion, but otherwise has the same architecture.

We train these models with two and four GCN layers for up to 32 objects. Additionally, to evaluate generalization to a different number of objects at test time, we train models with eight GCN layers on 16 objects and test on up to 128 objects. Results are shown in Fig. 6a-b. First, it can be seen that the baseline performs significantly worse than transitivity based models. Second, "Learned Transitivity" closely matches "Known Transitivity" indicating that the model

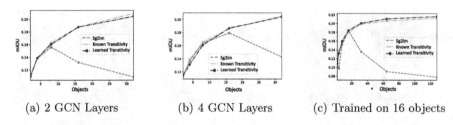

<table>
<tr><td>(a) 2 GCN Layers</td><td>(b) 4 GCN Layers</td><td>(c) Trained on 16 objects</td></tr>
</table>

Fig. 6. Synthetic dataset results. (a-b) The effect of the number of GCN layers on accuracy. Curves denote IOU performance as a function of the number of objects. Each point is a model trained and tested on a fixed number of objects given by the x axis. (c) Out of sample number of objects. The model is trained on 16 objects and evaluated on up to 128 objects.

Table 1. Accuracy of predicted bounding boxes. We consider two different data settings: "Standard" and "Packed". (a) **Standard**: Training and evaluation is on VG images with 3 to 10 objects, and COCO images with 3 to 8 objects. (b) **Packed**: Training and evaluation is on images with 16 or more objects.

Method	Standard						Packed					
	mIOU		R@0.3		R@0.5		mIOU		R@0.3		R@0.5	
	COCO	VG	COCO	VG	COCO	VG	COCO	VG	COCO	VG	COCO	VG
Sg2Im [17] 5 GCN^a	-	-	52.4	21.9	32.2	10.6	-	-	-	-	-	-
Sg2Im [17] 5 GCN^b	41.7	16.9	62.6	24.7	37.5	9.7	35.8	25.4	56.0	36.2	25.3	15.8
Sg2Im [17] 8 GCN^b	41.5	**18.3**	62.9	**26.2**	38.1	10.6	37.2	25.8	58.6	36.9	26.4	15.9
Sg2Im [17] 16 GCN^b	40.8	16.4	61.4	23.3	36.6	7.8	37.7	27.1	60.3	39.0	26.6	17.0
WSGC 5 GCN (ours)	**41.9**	18.0	**63.3**	25.9	**38.2**	10.6	**39.3**	**28.5**	**62.6**	**42.4**	**30.1**	**18.3**

[a] Results copied from manuscript.
[b] Our implementation of [17]. This is the same as our model without WSGC.

successfully learned which relations are transitive (we also manually confirmed this by inspecting θ^{trans}). Third, the baseline model requires more layers to correctly capture scenes with more objects, whereas our model performs well with two layers. This suggests that WSGC indeed improves generalization ability by capturing invariances. Figure 6c shows that our model also generalizes well when evaluated on a much larger set of objects than what it has seen at training time, whereas the accuracy of the baseline severely degrades in this case.

Layout Accuracy on Packed Scenes. Layout generation is particularly challenging in packed scenes. To quantify this, we evaluate on the Packed COCO and VG datasets. Since Sg2Im [17], PasteGAN [25], and Grid2Im [1] use the same SG-to-layout module, we compare WSGC only to Sg2Im [17]. We test Sg2Im with 5,8 and 16 GCN layers to test the effect of model capacity. The Packed setting in Table 1 shows that WSGC improves layout on all metrics.

We also evaluate on the "standard" COCO/VG setting, which contain relatively few objects, and we therefore do not expect WSGC to improve there. Results in Table 1 show comparable performance to the baselines. In addition, manual inspection revealed that the learned p^{conv} and p^{trans} are overall aligned

Table 2. Evaluating the robustness of the learned canonical representation for models which were trained on Packed COCO. For each SG, a **semantically equivalent** SG is sampled and evaluated at test time. Additionally, models are evaluated on **Noisy SGs**, for which edges contain 10% randomly chosen relations.

Method	Semantically Equivalent			Noisy SGs		
	mIOU	R@0.3	R@0.5	mIOU	R@0.3	R@0.5
Sg2Im [17] 5 GCN^b	21.8	29.5	10.7	29.4	42.9	17.8
Sg2Im [17] 8 GCN^b	23.6	33.2	11.4	29.9	43.7	18.8
Sg2Im [17] 16 GCN^b	21.6	29.0	10.1	28.7	41.8	17.7
WSGC 5 GCN (ours)	**35.3**	**53.2**	**25.7**	**31.8**	**46.6**	**21.9**

[b] Our implementation of [17]. This is the same as our model without WSGC.

Table 3. Results for SG-to-image on **Packed** datasets (16+ objects). For VG and COCO we use the layout-to-image architecture of **LostGAN** [48] and test the effect of different SG-to-layout models. For CLEVR, we use our **AttSPADE** generator.

Method	Inception		Human
	COCO	VG	CLEVR
Sg2Im [17]	5.4 ± 0.3	7.6 ± 1.0	3.2%
WSGC (ours)	$\mathbf{5.6 \pm 0.1}$	$\mathbf{8.0 \pm 1.1}$	96.8%
GT Layout	5.5 ± 0.4	8.2 ± 1.0	-

with expected values (See Supplementary). Finally, the results in the standard setting also show that increasing GCN size for Sg2Im [17] results in overfitting.

Generalization on Semantically Equivalent Graphs. A key advantage of WSGC is that it produces similar layouts for semantically equivalent graphs. This is not true for methods that do not use canonicalization. To test the effectiveness of this property, we modify the test set such that input SGs are replaced with semantically equivalent variations. For example if the original SG was $(A, right, B)$ we may change it to $(B, left, A)$. To achieve this, we generate a semantically equivalent SG by randomly choosing to include or exclude edges which do not change the semantics of the SG. We evaluate on the Packed COCO dataset. Results are shown in Table 2 and qualitative examples are shown in Fig. 7. It can be seen that WSGC significantly outperforms the baselines.

Testing Robustness to Input SGs. Here we ask what happens when input SGs are modified by adding "noisy" edges. This could happen due to noise in the annotation process or even adversarial modifications. Ideally, we would like the generation model to be robust to small SG noise. We next analyze how such modifications affect the model by randomly modifying 10% of the relations in the COCO data. As can be seen in Table 2, the WSGC model can better handle noisy SGs than the baseline. We further note that our model achieves good results on the VG dataset, which was manually annotated, suggesting it is robust to annotation noise. The results in Table 2 also show the Sg2Im generalization

222   R. Herzig et al.

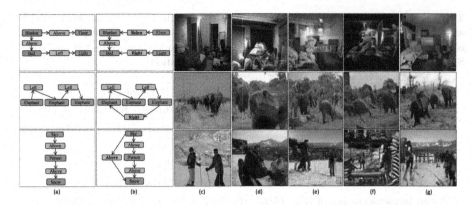

Fig. 7. Generalization from Semantically Equivalent Graphs. Each input SG is changed to a semantically equivalent SG at test time. The layout-to-image model is LostGAN [48] and different SG-to-layout models are tested. (a) Original SG (partial). (b) A modified semantically equivalent SG (partial). (c) GT image. (d-e) Sg2Im [17] and WSGC for the original SG. (f-g) Sg2Im [17] and WSGC for the modified SG.

deteriorates when growing from 8 to 16 layers, suggesting that the effect of canonicalization cannot be achieved by just increasing model complexity.

6.2   Scene-graph-to-image Generation

To test the contribution of our proposed Scene-Graph-to-layout approach to the overall task of SG-to-image generation, we further test it in an end-to-end pipeline for generating images. For Packed COCO and Packed VG, we compare our proposed approach with Sg2Im [17] using a fixed pre-trained LostGAN [49] as the layout-to-image generator. For CLEVR, we use WSGC and our own AttSPADE generator (see Sect. 4). We trained the model on images with a maximum of 10 objects and tested on larger scenes with 16+ objects.

We evaluate performance using Inception score [44] and a study where Amazon Mechanical Turk raters were asked to rank the quality of two images: one generated using our layouts, and the other using SG2Im layouts.[8] Results are provided in Table 3. For COCO and VG it can be seen that WSGC improves the overall quality of generated images. In CLEVR, Table 3, WSGC outperforms Sg2Im in terms of IOU. In 96.8% of the cases, our generated images were ranked higher than SG2Im. Finally, Figs. 5 and 8 provide qualitative examples and comparisons of images generated based on CLEVR and COCO. More generation results on COCO and VG can be seen in the Supplementary.

---

[8] We used raters only for the CLEVR data, where no GT images or bounding boxes are available for 16+ objects, and thus Inception cannot be evaluated.

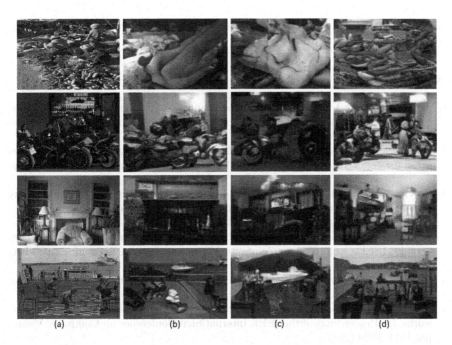

(a)   (b)   (c)   (d)

Fig. 8. Selected Scene-graph-to-image generation results on the Packed-COCO dataset. Here, we fix the layout-to-image model to LostGAN [48], while changing different scene graph-to-layout models. (a) GT image. (b) Generation from GT layout. (c) Sg2Im [17] model with LostGAN [48]. (d) Our WSGC model with LostGAN [48].

7 Conclusion

We presented a method for mapping SGs to images that is invariant to a set of logical equivalences. Our experiments show that the method results in improved layouts and image quality. We also observe that canonical representations allow one to handle packed scenes with fewer layers than non-canonical approaches. Intuitively, this is because the closure calculation effectively propagates information across the graph, and thus saves the need for propagation using neural architectures. The advantage is that this step is hard-coded and not learned, thus reducing the size of the model. Our results show the advantage of preprocessing an SG before layout generation. Here we studied this in the context of two types of relation properties. However, it can be extended to more complex ones. In this case, finding the closure will be computationally hard, and would amount to performing inference in Markov Logic Networks [43]. On the other hand, it is likely that modeling such invariances will result in further robustness of the learned models, and is thus an interesting direction for future work.

Acknowledgments. This project has received funding from the European Research Council (ERC) under the European Unions Horizon 2020 research and innovation programme (grant ERC HOLI 819080). Prof. Darrell's group was supported in part by

DoD, NSF, BAIR, and BDD. This work was completed in partial fulfillment for the Ph.D degree of the first author.

References

1. Ashual, O., Wolf, L.: Specifying object attributes and relations in interactive scene generation. In: Proceedings of the IEEE International Conference on Computer Vision. pp. 4561–4569 (2019)
2. Bau, D., et al.: Gan dissection: Visualizing and understanding generative adversarial networks. In: Proceedings of the International Conference on Learning Representations (ICLR) (2019)
3. Brock, A., Donahue, J., Simonyan, K.: Large scale GAN training for high fidelity natural image synthesis. In: International Conference on Learning Representations (2019)
4. Caesar, H., Uijlings, J.R.R., Ferrari, V.: Coco-stuff: Thing and stuff classes in context. In: IEEE Conference on Computer Vision and Pattern Recognition (CVPR) (2018)
5. Che, T., Li, Y., Jacob, A.P., Bengio, Y., Li, W.: Mode regularized generative adversarial networks. arXiv preprint arXiv:1612.02136 (2016)
6. Chen, Q., Koltun, V.: Photographic image synthesis with cascaded refinement networks. In: Proceedings of the IEEE International Conference on Computer Vision. pp. 1511–1520 (2017)
7. Chen, X., Duan, Y., Houthooft, R., Schulman, J., Sutskever, I., Abbeel, P.: Infogan: Interpretable representation learning by information maximizing generative adversarial nets. In: Advances in neural information processing systems. pp. 2172–2180 (2016)
8. Deng, Z., Chen, J., Fu, Y., Mori, G.: Probabilistic neural programmed networks for scene generation. In: Advances in Neural Information Processing Systems. pp. 4028–4038 (2018)
9. Dong, H., Yu, S., Wu, C., Guo, Y.: Semantic image synthesis via adversarial learning. In: Proceedings of the IEEE International Conference on Computer Vision. pp. 5706–5714 (2017)
10. Floyd, R.W.: Algorithm 97: shortest path. Commun. ACM 5(6), 345 (1962)
11. Goodfellow, I., Pouget-Abadie, J., Mirza, M., Xu, B., Warde-Farley, D., Ozair, S., Courville, A., Bengio, Y.: Generative adversarial nets. In: Advances in neural information processing systems. pp. 2672–2680 (2014)
12. Herzig, R., et al.: Spatio-temporal action graph networks. In: The IEEE International Conference on Computer Vision (ICCV) Workshops (2019)
13. Herzig, R., Raboh, M., Chechik, G., Berant, J., Globerson, A.: Mapping images to scene graphs with permutation-invariant structured prediction. In: Advances in Neural Information Processing Systems (NIPS) (2018)
14. Hong, S., Yang, D., Choi, J., Lee, H.: Inferring semantic layout for hierarchical text-to-image synthesis. In: Proceedings of the IEEE Conference on Computer Vision and Pattern Recognition. pp. 7986–7994 (2018)
15. Huang, X., Liu, M.Y., Belongie, S., Kautz, J.: Multimodal unsupervised image-to-image translation. In: Proceedings of the European Conference on Computer Vision (ECCV). pp. 172–189 (2018)
16. Isola, P., Zhu, J.Y., Zhou, T., Efros, A.A.: Image-to-image translation with conditional adversarial networks. In: Proceedings of the IEEE Conference on Computer Vision and Pattern Recognition. pp. 1125–1134 (2017)

17. Johnson, J., Gupta, A., Fei-Fei, L.: Image generation from scene graphs. In: IEEE Conference on Computer Vision and Pattern Recognition (CVPR) (2018)
18. Johnson, J., Hariharan, B., van der Maaten, L., Fei-Fei, L., Zitnick, C.L., Girshick, R.: Clevr: A diagnostic dataset for compositional language and elementary visual reasoning. In: CVPR (2017)
19. Johnson, J., Krishna, R., Stark, M., Li, L.J., Shamma, D., Bernstein, M., Fei-Fei, L.: Image retrieval using scene graphs. In: Proceedings of the IEEE Conference on Computer Vision and Pattern Recognition. pp. 3668–3678 (2015)
20. Karras, T., Laine, S., Aila, T.: A style-based generator architecture for generative adversarial networks. In: Proceedings of the IEEE Conference on Computer Vision and Pattern Recognition. pp. 4401–4410 (2019)
21. Kingma, D.P., Welling, M.: Auto-encoding variational bayes. arXiv preprint arXiv:1312.6114 (2013)
22. Kipf, T.N., Welling, M.: Semi-supervised classification with graph convolutional networks. arXiv preprint arXiv:1609.02907 (2016)
23. Krishna, R., Chami, I., Bernstein, M.S., Fei-Fei, L.: Referring relationships. ECCV (2018)
24. Krishna, R., et al.: Visual genome: Connecting language and vision using crowd-sourced dense image annotations. ArXiv e-prints (2016)
25. Li, Y., Ma, T., Bai, Y., Duan, N., Wei, S., Wang, X.: Pastegan: A semi-parametric method to generate image from scene graph. In: NeurIPS (2019)
26. Lim, J.H., Ye, J.C.: Geometric gan. arXiv preprint arXiv:1705.02894 (2017)
27. Liu, M.Y., Breuel, T., Kautz, J.: Unsupervised image-to-image translation networks. In: Advances in Neural Information Processing Systems. pp. 700–708 (2017)
28. Mao, X., Li, Q., Xie, H., Lau, Y.R., Wang, Z., Smolley, S.P.: Least squares generative adversarial networks. In: Proceedings of the IEEE International Conference on Computer Vision(2017)
29. Materzynska, J., Xiao, T., Herzig, R., Xu, H., Wang, X., Darrell, T.: Something-else: Compositional action recognition with spatial-temporal interaction networks. In: Proceedings of the IEEE Conference on Computer Vision and Pattern Recognition (2020)
30. Mirza, M., Osindero, S.: Conditional generative adversarial nets. arXiv preprint arXiv:1411.1784 (2014)
31. Mittal, G., Agrawal, S., Agarwal, A., Mehta, S., Marwah, T.: Interactive image generation using scene graphs. arXiv preprint arXiv:1905.03743 (2019)
32. Miyato, T., Kataoka, T., Koyama, M., Yoshida, Y.: Spectral normalization for generative adversarial networks. In: International Conference on Learning Representations (2018)
33. Nam, S., Kim, Y., Kim, S.J.: Text-adaptive generative adversarial networks: manipulating images with natural language. In: Advances in Neural Information Processing Systems. pp. 42–51 (2018)
34. Odena, A., Olah, C., Shlens, J.: Conditional image synthesis with auxiliary classifier gans. In: Proceedings of the 34th International Conference on Machine Learning-Volume 70. pp. 2642–2651. JMLR. org (2017)
35. Van den Oord, A., Kalchbrenner, N., Espeholt, L., Vinyals, O., Graves, A., et al.: Conditional image generation with pixelcnn decoders. In: Advances in Neural Information Processing Systems. pp. 4790–4798 (2016)
36. Oord, A.v.d., Kalchbrenner, N., Kavukcuoglu, K.: Pixel recurrent neural networks. arXiv preprint arXiv:1601.06759 (2016)

37. Park, T., Liu, M.Y., Wang, T.C., Zhu, J.Y.: Semantic image synthesis with spatially-adaptive normalization. In: Proceedings of the IEEE Conference on Computer Vision and Pattern Recognition. pp. 2337–2346 (2019)
38. Qiao, T., Zhang, J., Xu, D., Tao, D.: Mirrorgan: Learning text-to-image generation by redescription. In: Proceedings of the IEEE Conference on Computer Vision and Pattern Recognition. pp. 1505–1514 (2019)
39. Raboh, M., Herzig, R., Chechik, G., Berant, J., Globerson, A.: Differentiable scene graphs. In: Winter Conference on Applications of Computer Vision(2020)
40. Radford, A., Metz, L., Chintala, S.: Unsupervised representation learning with deep convolutional generative adversarial networks. arXiv preprint arXiv:1511.06434 (2015)
41. Reed, S., Akata, Z., Yan, X., Logeswaran, L., Schiele, B., Lee, H.: Generative adversarial text to image synthesis. arXiv preprint arXiv:1605.05396 (2016)
42. Reed, S.E., Akata, Z., Mohan, S., Tenka, S., Schiele, B., Lee, H.: Learning what and where to draw. In: Advances in Neural Information Processing Systems. pp. 217–225 (2016)
43. Richardson, M., Domingos, P.: Markov logic networks. Mach. Learn. 62(1–2), 107–136 (2006)
44. Salimans, T., Goodfellow, I., Zaremba, W., Cheung, V., Radford, A., Chen, X.: Improved techniques for training gans. In: Advances in Neural Information Processing Systems. pp. 2234–2242 (2016)
45. Schroeder, B., Tripathi, S., Tang, H.: Triplet-aware scene graph embeddings. In: The IEEE International Conference on Computer Vision (ICCV) Workshops (2019)
46. Schuster, S., Krishna, R., Chang, A., Fei-Fei, L., Manning, C.D.: Generating semantically precise scene graphs from textual descriptions for improved image retrieval. In: Proceedings of The Fourth Workshop on Vision and Language. pp. 70–80 (2015)
47. Sharma, S., Suhubdy, D., Michalski, V., Kahou, S.E., Bengio, Y.: Chatpainter: Improving text to image generation using dialogue. arXiv preprint arXiv:1802.08216 (2018)
48. Sun, W., Wu, T.: Image synthesis from reconfigurable layout and style. In: The IEEE International Conference on Computer Vision (ICCV) (2019)
49. Sun, W., Wu, T.: Image synthesis from reconfigurable layout and style. In: Proceedings of the IEEE International Conference on Computer Vision. pp. 10531–10540 (2019)
50. Taigman, Y., Polyak, A., Wolf, L.: Unsupervised cross-domain image generation. arXiv preprint arXiv:1611.02200 (2016)
51. Tan, F., Feng, S., Ordonez, V.: Text2scene: Generating compositional scenes from textual descriptions. In: Proceedings of the IEEE Conference on Computer Vision and Pattern Recognition. pp. 6710–6719 (2019)
52. Tripathi, S., Bhiwandiwalla, A., Bastidas, A., Tang, H.: Heuristics for image generation from scene graphs. In: ICLR LLD Workshop (2019)
53. Wang, T.C., Liu, M.Y., Zhu, J.Y., Tao, A., Kautz, J., Catanzaro, B.: High-resolution image synthesis and semantic manipulation with conditional gans. In: Proceedings of the IEEE Conference on Computer Vision and Pattern Recognition(2018)
54. Williams, R.J.: Simple statistical gradient-following algorithms for connectionist reinforcement learning. Mach. Learn. 8(3–4), 229–256 (1992)
55. Xiaotian, Q., ZHENG, Q., Ying, C., Rynson, W.: Tell me where i am: Object-level scene context prediction. In: The 32nd meeting of the IEEE/CVF Conference on Computer Vision and Pattern Recognition (CVPR 2019). IEEE (2019)

56. Xu, N., Liu, A.A., Liu, J., Nie, W., Su, Y.: Scene graph captioner: Image captioning based on structural visual representation. J. Vis. Commun. Image Represent. **58**, 477–485 (2019)
57. Xu, T., et al.: Attngan: Fine-grained text to image generation with attentional generative adversarial networks. In: Proceedings of the IEEE Conference on Computer Vision and Pattern Recognition. pp. 1316–1324 (2018)
58. Yin, G., Liu, B., Sheng, L., Yu, N., Wang, X., Shao, J.: Semantics disentangling for text-to-image generation. In: Proceedings of the IEEE Conference on Computer Vision and Pattern Recognition. pp. 2327–2336 (2019)
59. Zaheer, M., Kottur, S., Ravanbakhsh, S., Poczos, B., Salakhutdinov, R.R., Smola, A.J.: Deep sets. In: Advances in Neural Information Processing Systems 30, pp. 3394–3404. Curran Associates, Inc. (2017)
60. Zhang, H., Goodfellow, I., Metaxas, D., Odena, A.: Self-attention generative adversarial networks. In: International Conference Machine Learning (2019)
61. Zhang, H., et al.: Stackgan: Text to photo-realistic image synthesis with stacked generative adversarial networks. In: Proceedings of the IEEE International Conference on Computer Vision. pp. 5907–5915 (2017)
62. Zhao, B., Meng, L., Yin, W., Sigal, L.: Image generation from layout. In: Proceedings of the IEEE Conference on Computer Vision and Pattern Recognition. pp. 8584–8593 (2019)
63. Zhao, B., Meng, L., Yin, W., Sigal, L.: Image generation from layout. In: CVPR (2019)
64. Zhao, J., Mathieu, M., LeCun, Y.: Energy-based generative adversarial network. arXiv preprint arXiv:1609.03126 (2016)
65. Zhou, X., Huang, S., Li, B., Li, Y., Li, J., Zhang, Z.: Text guided person image synthesis. In: Proceedings of the IEEE Conference on Computer Vision and Pattern Recognition. pp. 3663–3672 (2019)
66. Zhu, J.Y., Park, T., Isola, P., Efros, A.A.: Unpaired image-to-image translation using cycle-consistent adversarial networks. In: Proceedings of the IEEE International Conference on Computer Vision. pp. 2223–2232 (2017)
67. Zhu, J.Y., et al.: Toward multimodal image-to-image translation. In: Advances in Neural Information Processing Systems. pp. 465–476 (2017)

Adversarial Robustness on In- and Out-Distribution Improves Explainability

Maximilian Augustin$^{(\boxtimes)}$, Alexander Meinke, and Matthias Hein

University of Tübingen, Tübingen, Germany
`maximilian.augustin@uni-tuebingen.de`

Abstract. Neural networks have led to major improvements in image classification but suffer from being non-robust to adversarial changes, unreliable uncertainty estimates on out-distribution samples and their inscrutable black-box decisions. In this work we propose RATIO, a training procedure for Robustness via Adversarial Training on In- and Out-distribution, which leads to robust models with reliable and robust confidence estimates on the out-distribution. RATIO has similar generative properties to adversarial training so that visual counterfactuals produce class specific features. While adversarial training comes at the price of lower clean accuracy, RATIO achieves state-of-the-art l_2-adversarial robustness on CIFAR10 and maintains better clean accuracy.

1 Introduction

Deep neural networks have shown phenomenal success in achieving high accuracy on challenging classification tasks [29]. However, they are lacking in terms of robustness against adversarial attacks [51], make overconfident predictions [20,21] especially on out-of-distribution (OOD) data [24,41] and their black box decisions are inscrutable [56]. Progress has been made with respect to all these aspects but there is currently no approach which is accurate, robust, has good confidence estimates and is explainable. Adversarial training (AT) [34] leads to models robust against adversarial attacks in a defined threat model and has recently been shown to produce classifiers with generative capabilities [46]. However, AT typically suffers from a significant drop in accuracy and is over-confident on OOD data as we show in this paper. Adversarial confidence enhanced training (ACET) [21] enforces low confidence in a neighborhood around OOD samples and can be seen as adversarial training on the out-distribution. ACET leads to models with good OOD detection performance even in an adversarial setting and suffers from a smaller loss in clean accuracy compared to AT. However, ACET models typically are significantly less robust than adversarially trained models.

In this paper we show that combining AT and ACET into RATIO, Robustness via Adversarial Training on In- and Out-distribution, inherits the good

Electronic supplementary material The online version of this chapter (https://doi.org/10.1007/978-3-030-58574-7_14) contains supplementary material, which is available to authorized users.

© Springer Nature Switzerland AG 2020
A. Vedaldi et al. (Eds.): ECCV 2020, LNCS 12371, pp. 228–245, 2020.
https://doi.org/10.1007/978-3-030-58574-7_14

properties of adversarial training and ACET without, or at least with significantly reduced, negative effects, e.g. we get SOTA l_2-robustness on CIFAR10 and have better clean accuracy than AT. On top of this we get reliable confidence estimates on the out-distribution even in a worst case scenario. In particular AT yields highly overconfident predictions on out-distribution images in the absence of class specific features whereas RATIO only yields high confident predictions if recognizable features are present. In summary, RATIO achieves high clean accuracy, is robust, calibrated and has generative properties which can be used to produce high-quality visual counterfactual explanations: see Table 1 for a summary of our results for CIFAR10 and SVHN and Table 2 for CIFAR100 and restricted ImageNet [54].

Table 1. *Summary:* We show clean and robust accuracy in an l_2-threat model with $\epsilon = 0.5$ and the expected calibration error (ECE). For OOD detection we report the mean of clean and worst case AUC over several out-distributions in an l_2-threat model with $\epsilon = 1.0$ as well as the mean maximal confidence (MMC) on the out-distributions. In light red we highlight failure cases for certain metrics. Only RATIO-0.25 ($R_{0.25}$) has good performance across all metrics.

CIFAR10	Plain	OE	ACET	$M_{0.5}$	$AT_{0.5}$	$AT_{0.25}$	JEM-0	$R_{0.5}$	$R_{0.25}$
Acc. ↑	96.2	**96.4**	94.1	90.8	90.8	94.0	92.8	91.1	93.5
R. Acc.$_{0.5}$ ↑	0.0	0.0	52.3	69.3	70.4	65.0	40.5	**73.3**	70.5
ECE (in %) ↓	**1.0**	2.9	2.8	2.6	2.2	2.2	3.9	2.8	2.7
AUC ↑	94.2	96.5	94.7	81.8	88.9	92.7	75.0	95.6	95.0
WC AUC$_{1.0}$ ↑	1.6	8.7	81.9	48.5	57.4	42.0	14.6	83.6	**84.3**
MMC ↓	62.0	**31.9**	39.1	62.7	55.8	55.2	69.7	31.9	33.9
SVHN	Plain	OE	ACET	$AT_{0.5}$	$AT_{0.25}$		$R_{0.5}$	$R_{0.25}$	
Acc. ↑	97.3	97.6	**97.8**	94.4	96.7		94.3	96.8	
R. Acc.$_{0.5}$ ↑	0.9	0.3	28.8	68.1	63.0		**68.4**	64.8	
ECE ↓	0.9	0.9	1.6	1.6	**0.8**		2.0	1.8	
AUC ↑	96.9	99.6	99.8	91.0	97.0		99.8	**99.9**	
WC AUC$_{1.0}$ ↑	8.5	18.2	96.0	51.1	48.3		**97.5**	**97.5**	
MMC ↓	61.5	16.3	11.8	67.1	49.1		12.1	**11.1**	

2   Related Work

Adversarial Robustness. Adversarial attacks are small changes of an image with respect to some distance measure, which change the decision of a classifier [51]. Many defenses have been proposed but with more powerful or adapted attacks most of them could be defeated [3,8,13,38]. Adversarial training (AT)

[34] is the most widely used approach that has not been broken. However, adversarial robustness comes at the price of a drop in accuracy [48,50]. Recent variations are using other losses [60] and boost robustness via generation of additional training data [1,9] or pre-training [26]. Another line of work are provable defenses, either deterministic [12,17,37,58] or based on randomized smoothing [11,30,33]. However, provable defenses are still not competitive with the empirical robustness of adversarial training for datasets like CIFAR10 and have even worse accuracy. We show that using AT on the in-distribution and out-distribution leads to a smaller drop in clean accuracy and similar or better robustness.

Confidence on In- and Out-Distribution. Neural networks have been shown to yield overly confident predictions far away from the training data [24,32,41] and this is even provably the case for ReLU networks [21]. Moreover, large neural networks are not calibrated on the in-distribution and have a bias to be overconfident [20]. The overconfidence on the out-distribution has been tackled in [21,25,31] by enforcing low-confidence predictions on a large out-distribution dataset e.g. using the 80 million tiny images dataset [25] leads to state-of-the-art results. However, if one maximizes the confidence in a ball around out-distribution-samples, most OOD methods are again overconfident [21,35,48,49] and only AT on the out-distribution as in ACET [21] or methods providing guaranteed worst case OOD performance [7,35] work in this worst-case setting. We show that RATIO leads to better worst case OOD performance than ACET.

Counterfactual Explanations. Counterfactual explanations have been proposed in [56] as a tool for making classifier decisions plausible, since humans also justify decisions via counterfactuals "I would have decided for X, if Y had been true" [36]. Other forms are explanations based on image features [22,23]. However, changing the decision for image classification in *image space* for non-robust models leads to adversarial samples [15] with changes that are visually not meaningful. Thus visual counterfactuals are often based on generative models or restrictions on the space of image manipulation [10,18,42,45,57,61]. Robust models wrt l_2-adversarial attacks [46,54] have been shown to change their decision when class-specific features appear in the image, which is a prerequisite for meaningful counterfactuals [6]. RATIO generates better counterfactuals, i.e. the confidence of the counterfactual images obtained by an l_2-adversarial attack tends to be high only after features of the alternative class have appeared. Especially for out-distribution images the difference to AT is pronounced.

Robust, Reliable and Explainable Classifiers. This is the holy grail of machine learning. A model which is accurate and calibrated [20] on the in-distribution, reliably has low confidence on out-distribution inputs, is robust to adversarial manipulation and has explainable decisions. Up to our knowledge there is no model which claims to have all these properties. The closest one we are aware of is the JEM-0 of [19] which is supposed to be robust, detects out-of-distribution samples and has generative properties. They state "JEM does not confidently classify nonsensical images, so instead, ... natural image properties visibly emerge". We show that RATIO gets us closer to this ultimate goal and outperforms JEM-0 in all aspects: accuracy, robustness, (worst-case) out-of-distribution detection, and visual counterfactual explanations.

3   RATIO: Robust, Reliable and Explainable Classifier

In the following we are considering multi-class (image) classification. We have the logits of a classifier $f : [0,1]^d \to \mathbb{R}^K$ where d is the input dimension and K the number of classes. With $\Delta = \{p \in [0,1]^K \mid \sum_{i=1}^{K} p_i = 1\}$ we denote the predicted probability distribution of f over the labels by $\hat{p} : \mathbb{R}^d \to \Delta$ which is obtained using the softmax function: $\hat{p}_{f,s}(x) = \frac{e^{f_s(x)}}{\sum_{j=1}^{K} e^{f_j(x)}}, s = 1, \ldots, K$. We further denote the training set by $(x_i, y_i)_{i=1}^{N}$ with $x_i \in [0,1]^d$ and $y_i \in \{1, \ldots, K\}$. As loss we always use the cross-entropy loss defined as

$$L(p, \hat{p}_f) = \sum_{j=1}^{K} p_j \log(\hat{p}_{f,j}), \tag{1}$$

where $p \in \Delta$ is the true distribution and $\hat{p}_f$ the predicted distribution.

3.1   Robustness via Adversarial Training

An adversarial sample of x with respect to some threat model $T(x) \subset \mathbb{R}^d$ is a point $z \in T(x) \cap [0,1]^d$ such that the decision of the classifier f changes for z while an oracle would unambiguously associate z with the class of x. In particular this implies that z shows no meaningful class-associated features of any other class. Formally, let y be the correct label of x, then z is an adversarial sample if

$$\arg\max_{k \neq y} f_k(z) > f_y(x), \qquad z \in [0,1]^d \cap T(x), \tag{2}$$

assuming that the threat model is small enough such that no real class change occurs. Typical threat models are l_p-balls of a given radius ϵ, that is

$$T(x) = B_p(x, \epsilon) = \{z \in \mathbb{R}^d \mid \|z - x\|_p \leq \epsilon\}. \tag{3}$$

The robust test accuracy is then defined as the lowest possible accuracy when every test image x is allowed to be changed to some $z \in T(x) \cap [0,1]^d$. Plain models have a robust test accuracy close to zero, even for "small" threat models.

Several strategies for adversarial robustness have been proposed, but adversarial training (AT) [34] has proven to produce robust classifiers across datasets and network architectures without adding significant computational overhead during inference (compared to randomized smoothing [11,30,33]).

The objective of adversarial training for a threat model $T(x) \subset \mathbb{R}^d$ is:

$$\min_{f} \mathbb{E}_{(x,y) \sim p_{\text{in}}} \left[\max_{z \in T(x)} L(\mathbf{e}_y, \hat{p}_f(z)) \right], \tag{4}$$

where $\mathbf{e}_y$ is a one-hot encoding of label y and $p_{\mathrm{in}}(x, y)$ is the training distribution. During training one approximately solves the inner maximization problem in (4) via projected gradient descent (PGD) and then computes the gradient wrt f at the approximate solution of the inner problem. The community has put emphasis on robustness wrt l_∞ but recently there is more interest in other threat models e.g. l_2-balls [44,46,53]. In particular, it has been noted [46,54] that robust models wrt an l_2-ball have the property that "adversarial" samples generated within a sufficiently large l_2-ball tend to have image features of the predicted class. Thus they are not "adversarial" samples in the sense defined above as the true class has changed or is at least ambiguous.

The main problem of AT is that robust classifiers suffer from a significant drop in accuracy compared to normal training [54]. This trade-off [47,50] can be mitigated e.g. via training 50% on clean samples and 50% on adversarial samples at the price of reduced robustness [50] or via semi-supervised learning [9,39,55].

3.2 Worst-Case OOD Detection via Adversarial Training on the Out-Distribution

While adversarial training yields robust classifiers, similarly to plain models it suffers from overconfident predictions on out-of-distribution samples. Overconfident predictions are a problem for safety-critical systems as the classifier is not reliably flagging when it operates "out of its specification" and thus its confidence in the prediction cannot be used to trigger human intervention.

In order to mitigate over-confident predictions [21,25] proposed to enforce low confidence on images from a chosen out-distribution $p_{\mathrm{out}}(x)$. A generic out-distribution would be all natural images and thus [25] suggest the 80 million tiny images dataset [52] as a proxy for this. While [25] consistently reduce confidence on different out-of-distribution datasets, similar to plain training for the in distribution one can again get overconfident predictions by maximizing the confidence in a small ball around a given out-distribution image (adversarial attacks on the out-distribution [21,35]).

Thus [21] proposed Adversarial Confidence Enhanced Training (ACET) which enforces low confidence in an entire neighborhood around the out-distribution samples which can be seen as a form of AT on the out-distribution:

$$\min_f \mathbb{E}_{(x,y)\sim p_{\mathrm{in}}}\Big[L(\mathbf{e}_y, \hat{p}_f(x))\Big] + \lambda\, \mathbb{E}_{(x,y)\sim p_{\mathrm{out}}}\Big[\max_{\|z-x\|_2\leq\epsilon} L(1/K, \hat{p}_f(z))\Big], \quad (5)$$

where $\mathbf{1}$ is the vector of all ones (outlier exposure [25] has the same objective without the inner maximization for the out-distribution). Different from [21] we use the same loss for in-and out-distribution, whereas they used the maximal log-confidence over all classes as loss for the out-distribution. In our experience the maximal log-confidence is more difficult to optimize, but both losses are minimized by the uniform distribution over the labels. Thus the difference is rather small and we also denote this version as ACET.

3.3   RATIO: Robustness via Adversarial Training on In-And Out-Distribution

We propose RATIO: adversarial training on in-and out-distribution. This combination leads to synergy effects where most positive attributes of AT and ACET are fused without having larger drawbacks. The objective of RATIO is given by:

$$\min_f \mathbb{E}_{(x,y)\sim p_{\text{in}}}\left[\max_{\|z-x\|_2\leq\epsilon_i} L(e_y,\hat{p}_f(z))\right] + \lambda\,\mathbb{E}_{(x,y)\sim p_{\text{out}}}\left[\max_{\|z-x\|_2\leq\epsilon_o} L(1/K,\hat{p}_f(z))\right],$$
(6)

where λ has the interpretation of $\frac{p_o}{p_i}$, the probability to see out-distribution p_o and in-distribution p_i samples at test time. Here we have specified an l_2-threat model for in-and out-distribution but the objective can be adapted to different threat models which could be different for in- and out-distribution. The surprising part of RATIO is that the addition of the out-distribution part can improve the results even on the in-distribution in terms of (robust) accuracy. The reason is that adversarial training on the out-distribution ensures that spurious features do not change the confidence of the classifier. This behavior generalizes to the in-distribution and thus ACET (adversarial training on the out-distribution) is also robust on the in-distribution (52.3% robust accuracy for l_2 with $\epsilon = 0.5$ on CIFAR10). One problem of adversarial training is overfitting on the training set [43]. Our RATIO has seen more images at training time and while the direct goal is distinct (keeping one-hot prediction on the in-distribution and uniform prediction on out-distribution) both aim at constant behavior of the classifier over the l_2-ball and thus the effectively increased training size improves generalization (in contrast to AT, RATIO has its peak robustness at the end of the training). Moreover, RATIO typically only shows high confidence if class-specific features have appeared which we use in the generative process described next.

4   Visual Counterfactual Explanations

The idea of a counterfactual explanation [56] is to provide the smallest change of a given input such that the decision changes into a desired target class e.g. how would this X-ray image need to look in order to change the diagnosis from X to Y. Compared to sensitivity based explanations [5,59] or explanations based on feature attributions [4] counterfactual explanations have the advantage that they have an "operational meaning" which couples the explanation directly to the decision of the classifier. On the other hand the counterfactual explanation requires us to specify a metric or a budget for the allowed change of the image which can be done directly in image space or in the latent space of a generative model. However, our goal is that the classifier directly learns what meaningful changes are and we do not want to impose that via a generative model. Thus we aim at visual counterfactual explanations directly in image space with a fixed budget for changing the image. As the decision changes, features of this class should appear in the image (see Fig. 2). Normally trained models will not achieve this since non-robust models change their prediction for non-perceptible perturbations [51], see Fig. 1. Thus robustness against (l_2-)adversarial perturbations is a necessary requirement for visual counterfactuals and indeed [46,54] have shown "generative properties" of l_2-robust models.

A *visual counterfactual* for the original point x classified as $c = \underset{k=1,...,K}{\arg\max} f_k(x)$, a target class $t \in \{1, \ldots, K\}$ and a budget ϵ is defined as

$$x^{(t)} = \underset{z \in [0,1]^d, \|x-z\|_2 \leq \epsilon}{\arg\max} \hat{p}_{f,t}(z), \tag{7}$$

where $\hat{p}_{f,t}(z)$ is the confidence for class t of our classifier for the image z. If $t \neq c$ it answers the counterfactual question of how to use the given budget to change the original input x so that the classifier is most confident in class t. Note that in our definition we include the case where $t = c$, that is we ask how to change the input x classified as c to get even more confident in class c. In Fig. 2 we illustrate both directions and show how for robust models class specific image features appear when optimizing the confidence of that class. This shows that the optimization of visual counterfactuals can be done directly in image space.

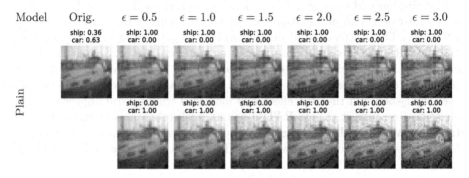

Fig. 1. Failure of a visual counterfactual for a plain model. The targeted attack immediately produces very high confidence in both classes but instead of class features only high-frequency noise appears because plain models are not robust.

5   Experiments

Comparison, Training and Attacks. We validate our approach on SVHN [40], CIFAR10/100 [28] and restricted ImageNet [46]. On CIFAR10 we compare RATIO to a pretrained JEM-0 [19] and the AT model [16] with $l_2 = 0.5$ ($M_{0.5}$) (both not available on the other datasets). As an ablation study of RATIO we train a plain model, outlier exposure (OE) [25], ACET [21] and AT with $l_2 = 0.5$ ($AT_{0.5}$) and $l_2 = 0.25$ ($AT_{0.25}$), using the same hyperparameters as for our RATIO training. On SVHN we use a ResNet18 architecture for all methods and on the other datasets we use ResNet50, both with standard input normalization. For ACET on CIFAR10 we use ResNet18 since for ResNet50 we could not obtain

Table 2. Summary for CIFAR100 and R. ImageNet (see Table 1 for details).

CIFAR100	Plain	OE	ACET	$AT_{0.5}$	$AT_{0.25}$	$R_{0.5}$	$R_{0.25}$
Acc. ↑	**81.5**	81.4	-	70.6	75.8	69.2	74.4
R. Acc.$_{0.5}$ ↑	0.0	0.0	-	43.2	37.3	**45.6**	42.4
ECE ↓	**1.2**	7.2	-	1.3	1.5	3.2	2.0
AUC ↑	84.0	**91.9**	-	75.6	79.4	87.0	86.9
WC AUC$_{1.0}$ ↑	0.4	14.6	-	29.9	24.8	**55.5**	54.5
MMC ↓	51.1	21.8	-	45.8	47.1	24.4	31.0
R.Imagenet	Plain	OE	ACET	$M_{3.5}$	$AT_{3.5}$	$AT_{1.75}$	$R_{3.5}$	$R_{1.75}$
Acc. ↑	96.6	**97.2**	96.2	90.3	93.5	95.5	93.9	95.5
R. Acc.$_{3.5}$ ↑	0.0	0.0	6.2	47.7	47.7	36.7	**49.2**	43.0
ECE ↓	0.6	1.8	0.9	0.7	0.9	0.5	**0.3**	0.7
AUC ↑	92.7	**98.9**	97.74	83.6	84.3	86.5	97.2	97.8
WC AUC$_{7.0}$ ↑	0.0	1.8	87.54	44.2	37.5	16.3	**90.9**	90.6
MMC ↓	67.9	**20.6**	34.85	69.2	75.2	81.8	33.6	32.3

a model with good worst case OOD performance as the attack seemed to fail at some point during training (on CIFAR100 this was even the case for ResNet18 and thus we omit it from comparison). In general ACET is difficult to train. For RATIO the additional adversarial training on the in-distribution seems to stabilize the training and we did not encounter any problems. As out-distribution for SVHN and CIFAR we use 80 million tiny images [52] as suggested in [25] and for restricted ImageNet the remaining ImageNet classes. For the out-distribution we always use l_2-attacks with radius $\epsilon_o = 1$ for SVHN/CIFAR and $\epsilon_o = 7$ on restricted ImageNet (both ACET and RATIO) whereas on the in-distribution we use $\epsilon_i = 0.25$ and $\epsilon_i = 0.5$ and $\epsilon_i = 1.75$ and $\epsilon_i = 3.5$, respectively (both AT and RATIO). Therefore RATIO/AT models are labeled by ϵ_i. For further training details see the Appendix. For the adversarial attacks on in- and out-distribution we use the recent Auto-Attack [13] which is an ensemble of four attacks, including the black-box Square Attack [2] and three white-box attacks (FAB-attack [14] and AUTO-PGD with different losses). For each of the white-box attacks, a budget of 100 iterations and 5 restarts is used and a query limit of 5000 for Square attack. In [13] they show that Auto-Attack consistently improves the robustness evaluation for a large number of models (including JEM-x).

Calibration on the in-Distribution. With RATIO we aim for reliable confidence estimates, in particular no overconfident predictions. In order to have comparable confidences for the different models we train, especially when we check visual counterfactuals or feature generation, we first need to "align" their confidences. We do this by minimizing the expected calibration error (ECE) via temperature rescaling [20]. Note that this rescaling does not change the classification and thus has no impact on (robust) accuracy and only a minor influence on the (worst case) AUC values for OOD-detection. For details see the Appendix.

(Robust) Accuracy on the in-Distribution. Using Auto-Attack [13] we evaluate robustness on the full test set for both CIFAR and r. Imagenet and 10000 test samples for SVHN. Tables 1 and 2 contain (robust l_2) accuracy, detailed results, including l_∞ attacks, can be found in the Appendix. On CIFAR10, RATIO achieves significantly higher robust accuracy than AT for l_2-and l_∞-attacks. Thus the additional adversarial training on the out-distribution with radius $\epsilon_o = 1$ boosts the robustness on the in-distribution. In particular, RATIO$_{0.25}$ achieves better l_2-robustness than AT$_{0.5}$ and M$_{0.5}$ at $\approx 2.7\%$ higher clean accuracy. In addition, R$_{0.5}$ yields new state-of-the-art l_2-robust accuracy at radius 0.5 (see [13] for a benchmark) while having higher test accuracy than AT$_{0.5}$, M$_{0.5}$. Moreover, the l_2-robustness at radius 1.0 and the l_∞-robustness at 8/255 is significantly better. Interestingly, although ACET is not designed to yield adversarial robustness on the in-distribution, it achieves more than 50% robust accuracy for $l_2 = 0.5$ and outperforms JEM-0 in all benchmarks. However, as our goal is to have a model which is both robust and accurate, we recommend to use $R_{0.25}$ for CIFAR10 which has a drop of only 2.6% in test accuracy compared to a plain model while having similar robustness to M$_{0.5}$ and AT$_{0.5}$. Similar observations as for CIFAR10 hold for CIFAR100 and for Restricted ImageNet, see Table 2, even though for CIFAR100 AT and RATIO suffer a higher loss in accuracy. On SVHN, RATIO outperforms AT in terms of robust accuracy trained with the same l_2-radius but the effect is less than for CIFAR10. We believe that this is due to the fact that the images obtained from the 80 million tiny image dataset (out distribution) do not reflect the specific structure of SVHN numbers which makes (worst case) outlier detection an easier task. This is supported by the fact that ACET achieves better clean accuracy on SVHN than both OE and the plain model while it has worse clean accuracy on CIFAR10.

Visual Counterfactual Generation. We use 500 step Auto-PGD [13] for a targeted attack with the objective in (7). However, note that this non-convex optimization problem has been shown to be NP-hard [27]. In Figs. 2, 3 and 4 and in the Appendix we show generated counterfactuals for all datasets. For CIFAR10 AT$_{0.5}$ performs very similar to RATIO$_{0.25}$ in terms of the emergence of class specific image features. In particular, we often see the appearance of characteristic features such as pointed ears for cats, wheels for cars and trucks, large eyes for both cats and dogs and the antlers for deers. JEM-0 and ACET perform worse but for both of them one observes the appearance of image features. However, particularly the images of JEM-0 have a lot of artefacts. For SVHN RATIO$_{0.25}$ on average performs better than AT$_{0.25}$ and ACET. It is interesting to note that for both datasets class-specific features emerge already for an l_2-radius of 1.0. Thus it seems questionable if l_2-adversarial robustness beyond a radius of 1.0 should be enforced. Due to the larger number of classes, CIFAR100 counterfactuals are of slightly lower quality. For Restricted ImageNet the visual counterfactuals show class-specific features but can often be identified as synthetic due to misaligned features.

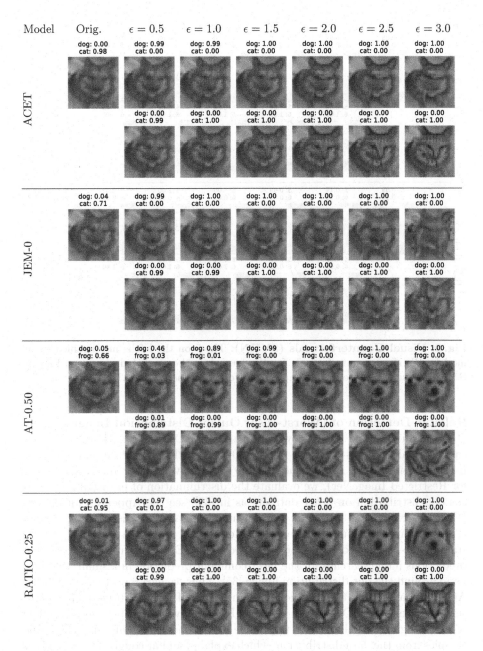

Fig. 2. Visual Counterfactuals (CIFAR10): The dog image on the left is misclassified by all models (confidence for true and predicted class are shown). The top row shows visual counterfactuals for the correct class (how to change the image so that it is classified as dog) and the bottom row shows how to change the image in order to increase the confidence in the wrong prediction for different budgets of the l_2-radius ($\epsilon = 0.5$ to $\epsilon = 3$). More examples are in the appendix.

| Model | Orig. | $\epsilon = 0.5$ | $\epsilon = 1.0$ | $\epsilon = 1.5$ | $\epsilon = 2.0$ | $\epsilon = 2.5$ | $\epsilon = 3.0$ |

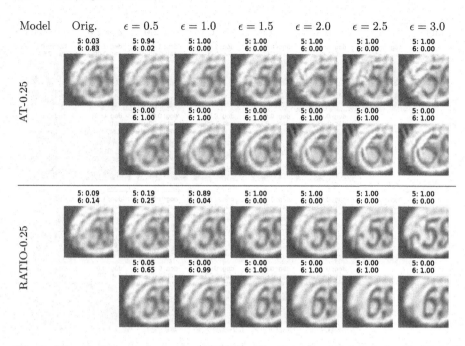

Fig. 3. Visual Counterfactuals (SVHN): The 5 on the left is misclassified by all models. We show counterfactuals for the true class the predicted class (see Fig. 2). RATIO consistently produces samples with fewer artefacts than AT.

Reliable Detection of (Worst-case) Out-of-Distribution Images. A reliable classifier should assign low confidence to OOD images. This is not the case for plain models and AT. As the 80 million tiny image dataset has been used for training for ACET and RATIO (respectively other ImageNet classes for Restricted ImageNet), we evaluate the discrimination of in-distribution versus out-distribution on other datasets as in [35], see the Appendix for details. We use $\max_k \hat{p}_{f,k}(x)$ as feature to discriminate in-and out-distribution (binary classification) and compute the AUC. However, it has been shown that even state-of-the-art methods like outlier exposure (OE) suffer from overconfident predictions if one searches for the most confident prediction in a small neighborhood around the out-distribution image [35]. Thus we also report the worst-case AUC by maximizing the confidence in an l_2-ball of radius 1.0 (resp. 7.0 for R. ImageNet) around OOD images via Auto-PGD [13] with 100 steps and 5 random restarts. Figure 5 further shows that while RATIO behaves similar to AT around samples from the data distribution, which explains similar counterfactuals, it has a flatter confidence profile around out-distribution samples on 1024 points from each out-distribution (300 points for LSUN_CR).

Using the worst case confidences of these points we find empirical upper bounds on the worst-case AUC under our threat model. We report both the average-case AUCs as well as the worst-case AUCs in the Appendix. The average

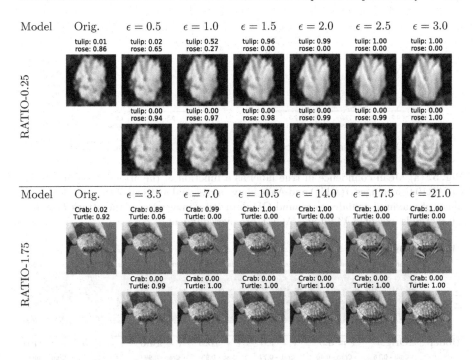

Fig. 4. Visual Counterfactuals top: RATIO-0.25 for CIFAR100 and bottom: RATIO-1.75 for RestrictedImageNet.

AUC over all OOD datasets is reported in Tables 1 and 2. The AT-model of Madry et al. ($M_{0.5}$) perform worse than the plain model even on the average case task. However, we see that with our more aggressive data augmentation this problem is somewhat alleviated ($AT_{0.5}$ and $AT_{0.25}$). As expected ACET, has good worst-case OOD performance but is similar to the plain model for the average case. JEM-0 has bad worst-case AUCs and we cannot confirm the claim that "JEM does not confidently classify nonsensical images" [19]. As expected, OE has state-of-the-art performance on the clean task but has no robustness on the out-distribution, so it fails completely in this regime. Our RATIO models show strong performance on all tasks and even outperform the ACET model which shows that adversarial robustness wrt the in-distribution also helps with adversarial robustness on the out-distribution. On SVHN the average case OOD task is simple enough that several models achieve near perfect AUCs, but again only ACET and our RATIO models manage to retain strong performance in the worst case setting. The worst-case AUC of AT models is significantly worse than that of ACET and RATIO.

Feature Generation on OOD Images. Finally, we test the abilities to generate image features with a targeted attack on OOD images (taken from 80m tiny image dataset resp. ImageNet classes not belonging to R. ImageNet). The setting is similar to the visual counterfactuals. We take some OOD image and then

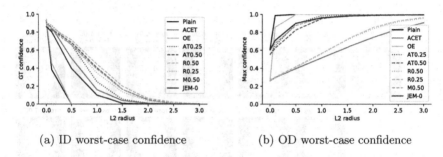

(a) ID worst-case confidence   (b) OD worst-case confidence

Fig. 5. (a) Mean confidence in true label as a function of the attack l_2-radius around CIFAR10 test images. RATIO and AT0.5 have a reasonable decay of the confidence. (b) Mean of maximal confidence around OD-data (tiny images) over the attack l_2-radius. All methods except RATIO and ACET are overconfident.

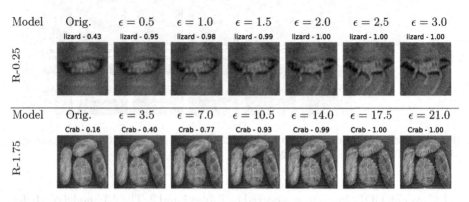

Fig. 6. Feature Generation for out-distribution images top: RATIO-0.25 for CIFAR100 and bottom: RATIO-1.75 for R.ImageNet

optimize the confidence in the class which is predicted on the OOD image. The results can be found in Fig. 7 and 6 and additional samples are attached in the Appendix. For CIFAR10 all methods are able to generate image features of the class but the predicted confidences are only reasonable for ACET and RATIO$_{0.25}$ whereas AT$_{0.5}$ and JEM-0 are overconfident when no strong class features are visible. This observation generalizes to SVHN and mostly CIFAR100 and r. Imagenet, i.e. RATIO generally has the best OOD-confidence profile.

Summary. In summary, in Table 1 and 2 we can see that RATIO$_{0.25}$ resp. RATIO$_{1.75}$ is except for CIFAR100 the only model which has no clear failure case. Here the subjective definition of a failure case (highlighted in red) is an entry which is "significantly worse" than the best possible in this metric. Thus we think that RATIO succeeds in being state-of-the-art in generating a model which is accurate, robust, has reliable confidence and is able to produce meaningful visual counterfactuals. Nevertheless RATIO is not perfect and we discuss failure cases of all models in the Appendix.

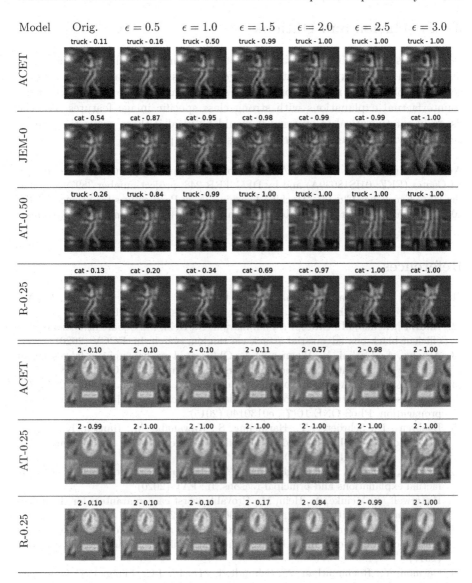

Fig. 7. Feature Generation for out-distribution images (CIFAR10 (top), SVHN (bottom)): targeted attacks towards the class achieving highest confidence on original image for different budgets of the l_2-radius ranging from $\epsilon = 0.5$ to $\epsilon = 3$. RATIO-0.25 generates the visually best images and in particular has reasonable confidence values for its decision. While AT-0.5/AT-0.25 generates also good images it is overconfident into the target class.

6   Conclusion and Outlook

We have shown that adversarial robustness on in-distribution and out-distribution (as a proxy of all natural images) gets us closer to a classifier which is accurate, robust, has reliable confidence estimates and is able to produce visual counterfactual explanations with strong class specific image features. For the usage in safety-critical in systems it would be ideal if these properties can be achieved in a provable way which remains an open problem.

Acknowledgements. M.H and A.M. acknowledge support by the BMBF Tübingen AI Center (FKZ: 01IS18039A) and by DFG TRR 248, project number 389792660 and the DFG Excellence Cluster "Machine Learning -New Perspectives for Science", EXC 2064/1, project number 390727645. A.M. thanks the IMPRS for Intelligent Systems.

References

1. Alayrac, J.B., Uesato, J., Huang, P.S., Fawzi, A., Stanforth, R., Kohli, P.: Are labels required for improving adversarial robustness? In: NeurIPS (2019)
2. Andriushchenko, M., Croce, F., Flammarion, N., Hein, M.: Square attack: a query-efficient black-box adversarial attack via random search. In: ECCV (2020)
3. Athalye, A., Carlini, N., Wagner, D.A.: Obfuscated gradients give a false sense of security: circumventing defenses to adversarial examples. In: ICML (2018)
4. Bach, S., Binder, A., Montavon, G., Klauschen, F., Müller, K.R., Samek, W.: On pixel-wise explanations for non-linear classifier decisions by layer-wise relevance propagation. PLoS ONE **10**(7), e0130140 (2015)
5. Baehrens, D., Schroeter, T., Harmeling, S., Kawanabe, M., Hansen, K., Müller, K.R.: How to explain individual classification decisions. J. Mach. Learn. Res. (JMLR) **11**, 1803–1831 (2010)
6. Barocas, S., Selbst, A.D., Raghavan, M.: The hidden assumptions behind counterfactual explanations and principal reasons. In: FAT (2020)
7. Bitterwolf, J., Meinke, A., Hein, M.: Provable worst case guarantees for the detection of out-of-distribution data. arXiv:2007.08473 (2020)
8. Carlini, N., Wagner, D.: Adversarial examples are not easily detected: bypassing ten detection methods. In: ACM Workshop on Artificial Intelligence and Security (2017)
9. Carmon, Y., Raghunathan, A., Schmidt, L., Duchi, J.C., Liang, P.S.: Unlabeled data improves adversarial robustness. In: NeurIPS (2019)
10. Chang, C.H., Creager, E., Goldenberg, A., Duvenaud, D.: Explaining image classifiers by counterfactual generation. In: ICLR (2019)
11. Cohen, J.M., Rosenfeld, E., Kolter, J.Z.: Certified adversarial robustness via randomized smoothing. In: NeurIPS (2019)
12. Croce, F., Andriushchenko, M., Hein, M.: Provable robustness of RELU networks via maximization of linear regions. In: AISTATS (2019)
13. Croce, F., Hein, M.: Reliable evaluation of adversarial robustness with an ensemble of diverse parameter-free attacks. In: ICML (2020)

14. Croce, F., Hein, M.: Minimally distorted adversarial examples with a fast adaptive boundary attack. In: ICML (2020)
15. Dong, Y., Su, H., Zhu, J., Bao, F.: Towards interpretable deep neural networks by leveraging adversarial examples (2017). arXiv preprint, arXiv:1708.05493
16. Engstrom, L., Ilyas, A., Santurkar, S., Tsipras, D.: Robustness (python library) (2019). https://github.com/MadryLab/robustness
17. Gowal, S., et al.: On the effectiveness of interval bound propagation for training verifiably robust models (2018), preprint. arXiv:1810.12715v3
18. Goyal, Y., Wu, Z., Ernst, J., Batra, D., Parikh, D., Lee, S.: Counterfactual visual explanations. In: ICML (2019)
19. Grathwohl, W., Wang, K.C., Jacobsen, J.H., Duvenaud, D., Norouzi, M., Swersky, K.: Your classifier is secretly an energy based model and you should treat it like one. In: ICLR (2020)
20. Guo, C., Pleiss, G., Sun, Y., Weinberger, K.: On calibration of modern neural networks. In: ICML (2017)
21. Hein, M., Andriushchenko, M., Bitterwolf, J.: Why ReLU networks yield high-confidence predictions far away from the training data and how to mitigate the problem. In: CVPR (2019)
22. Hendricks, L.A., Akata, Z., Rohrbach, M., Donahue, J., Schiele, B., Darrell, T.: Generating visual explanations. In: ECCV (2016)
23. Hendricks, L.A., Hu, R., Darrell, T., Akata, Z.: Grounding visual explanations. In: ECCV (2018)
24. Hendrycks, D., Gimpel, K.: A baseline for detecting misclassified and out-of-distribution examples in neural networks. In: ICLR (2017)
25. Hendrycks, D., Mazeika, M., Dietterich, T.: Deep anomaly detection with outlier exposure. In: ICLR (2019)
26. Hendrycks, D., Lee, K., Mazeika, M.: Using pre-training can improve model robustness and uncertainty. In: ICML, pp. 2712–2721 (2019)
27. Katz, G., Barrett, C., Dill, D., Julian, K., Kochenderfer, M.: Reluplex: an efficient SMT solver for verifying deep neural networks. In: CAV (2017)
28. Krizhevsky, A., Hinton, G., et al.: Learning multiple layers of features from tiny images (2009)
29. LeCun, Y., Bengio, Y., Hinton, G.: Deep learning. Nature 521, 436–444 (2015). https://doi.org/10.1038/nature14539
30. Lecuyer, M., Atlidakis, V., Geambasu, R., Hsu, D., Jana, S.: Certified robustness to adversarial examples with differential privacy. In: IEEE Symposium on Security and Privacy (SP) (2019)
31. Lee, K., Lee, H., Lee, K., Shin, J.: Training confidence-calibrated classifiers for detecting out-of-distribution samples. In: ICLR (2018)
32. Leibig, C., Allken, V., Ayhan, M.S., Berens, P., Wahl, S.: Leveraging uncertainty information from deep neural networks for disease detection. Sci. Rep. 7, 1–14 (2017)
33. Li, B., Chen, C., Wang, W., Carin, L.: Certified adversarial robustness with additive noise. In: NeurIPS (2019)
34. Madry, A., Makelov, A., Schmidt, L., Tsipras, D., Valdu, A.: Towards deep learning models resistant to adversarial attacks. In: ICLR (2018)
35. Meinke, A., Hein, M.: Towards neural networks that provably know when they don't know. In: ICLR (2020)
36. Miller, T.: Explanation in artificial intelligence: insights from the social sciences. Artif. Intell. 267, 1–38 (2019)

37. Mirman, M., Gehr, T., Vechev, M.: Differentiable abstract interpretation for provably robust neural networks. In: ICML (2018)
38. Mosbach, M., Andriushchenko, M., Trost, T., Hein, M., Klakow, D.: Logit pairing methods can fool gradient-based attacks. In: NeurIPS 2018 Workshop on Security in Machine Learning (2018)
39. Najafi, A., Maeda, S.I., Koyama, M., Miyato, T.: Robustness to adversarial perturbations in learning from incomplete data. In: NeurIPS (2019)
40. Netzer, Y., Wang, T., Coates, A., Bissacco, A., Wu, B., Ng, A.Y.: Reading digits in natural images with unsupervised feature learning. In: NeurIPS Workshop on Deep Learning and Unsupervised Feature Learning (2011)
41. Nguyen, A., Yosinski, J., Clune, J.: Deep neural networks are easily fooled: high confidence predictions for unrecognizable images. In: CVPR (2015)
42. Parafita, Á., Vitrià, J.: Explaining visual models by causal attribution. In: ICCV Workshop on XCAI (2019)
43. Rice, L., Wong, E., Kolter, J.Z.: Overfitting in adversarially robust deep learning. In: ICML (2020)
44. Rony, J., Hafemann, L.G., Oliveira, L.S., Ayed, I.B., Sabourin, R., Granger, E.: Decoupling direction and norm for efficient gradient-based L2 adversarial attacks and defenses. In: CVPR (2019)
45. Samangouei, P., Saeedi, A., Nakagawa, L., Silberman, N.: Explaingan: model explanation via decision boundary crossing transformations. In: ECCV (2018)
46. Santurkar, S., Tsipras, D., Tran, B., Ilyas, A., Engstrom, L., Madry, A.: Computer vision with a single (robust) classifier. In: NeurIPS (2019)
47. Schmidt, L., Santurkar, S., Tsipras, D., Talwar, K., Madry, A.: Adversarially robust generalization requires more data. In: NeurIPS (2018)
48. Schott, L., Rauber, J., Bethge, M., Brendel, W.: Towards the first adversarially robust neural network model on mnist. In: ICLR (2019)
49. Sehwag, V., et al.: Better the devil you know: An analysis of evasion attacks using out-of-distribution adversarial examples. preprint, arXiv:1905.01726 (2019)
50. Stutz, D., Hein, M., Schiele, B.: Disentangling adversarial robustness and generalization. In: CVPR (2019)
51. Szegedy, C., et al.: Intriguing properties of neural networks. In: ICLR, pp. 2503–2511 (2014)
52. Torralba, A., Fergus, R., Freeman, W.T.: 80 million tiny images: a large data set for nonparametric object and scene recognition. IEEE Trans. Pattern Anal. Mach. Intell. 30(11), 1958–1970 (2008)
53. Tramèr, F., Boneh, D.: Adversarial training and robustness for multiple perturbations. In: NeurIPS (2019)
54. Tsipras, D., Santurkar, S., Engstrom, L., Turner, A., Madry, A.: Robustness may be at odds with accuracy. In: ICLR (2019)
55. Uesato, J., Alayrac, J.B., Huang, P.S., Stanforth, R., Fawzi, A., Kohli, P.: Are labels required for improving adversarial robustness? In: NeurIPS (2019)
56. Wachter, S., Mittelstadt, B., Russell, C.: Counterfactual explanations without opening the black box: automated decisions and the GDPR. Harvard J. Law Technol. 31(2), 841–887 (2018)
57. Wang, T.C., Liu, M.Y., Zhu, J.Y., Tao, A., Kautz, J., Catanzaro, B.: High-resolution image synthesis and semantic manipulation with conditional gans. In: CVPR (2018)
58. Wong, E., Schmidt, F., Metzen, J.H., Kolter, J.Z.: Scaling provable adversarial defenses. In: NeurIPS (2018)

59. Zeiler, M.D., Fergus, R.: Visualizing and understanding convolutional networks. In: ECCV (2014)
60. Zhang, H., Yu, Y., Jiao, J., Xing, E.P., Ghaoui, L.E., Jordan, M.I.: Theoretically principled trade-off between robustness and accuracy. In: ICML (2019)
61. Zhu, J.Y., Krähenbühl, P., Shechtman, E., Efros, A.A.: Generative visual manipulation on the natural image manifold. In: Leibe, B., Matas, J., Sebe, N., Welling, M. (eds.) ECCV (2016)

Deformable Style Transfer

Sunnie S. Y. Kim[1]([✉]) [ID], Nicholas Kolkin[1] [ID], Jason Salavon[2] [ID],
and Gregory Shakhnarovich[1] [ID]

[1] Toyota Technological Institute at Chicago, Chicago, USA
{sunnie,nick.kolkin,greg}@ttic.edu
[2] University of Chicago, Chicago, USA
salavon@uchicago.edu

Abstract. Both geometry and texture are fundamental aspects of visual
style. Existing style transfer methods, however, primarily focus on texture, almost entirely ignoring geometry. We propose deformable style
transfer (DST), an optimization-based approach that jointly stylizes the
texture and geometry of a content image to better match a style image.
Unlike previous geometry-aware stylization methods, our approach is neither restricted to a particular domain (such as human faces), nor does it
require training sets of matching style/content pairs. We demonstrate our
method on a diverse set of content and style images including portraits,
animals, objects, scenes, and paintings. Code has been made publicly
available at https://github.com/sunniesuhyoung/DST.

Keywords: Neural style transfer · Geometric deformation ·
Differentiable image warping

1 Introduction

The goal of style transfer algorithms is to re-render the content of one image
using the style of one or several other images. Most modern approaches
[2,7–9,14,17,18,20,21] capture a definition of "style" that focuses on color and
texture. Art historians and other experts on image creation, however, define
style more broadly and almost always consider the shapes and geometric forms
present in an artwork as integral parts of its style [6,13]. Shape and form play
a vital role in recognizing the distinctive style of many artists in painting (e.g.
Picasso, Modigliani, El Greco), sculpture (e.g., Botero, Giacometti), and other
forms of media. While the results of style transfer algorithms thus far have been
impressive and have captured the public's attention, we propose a method of
extending style transfer to better match the geometry of an artist's style.

Style transfer methods that do not explicitly include geometry in their definition of style almost always keep the geometry of the content unchanged in the

Electronic supplementary material The online version of this chapter (https://
doi.org/10.1007/978-3-030-58574-7_15) contains supplementary material, which is
available to authorized users.

A. Vedaldi et al. (Eds.): ECCV 2020, LNCS 12371, pp. 246–261, 2020.
https://doi.org/10.1007/978-3-030-58574-7_15

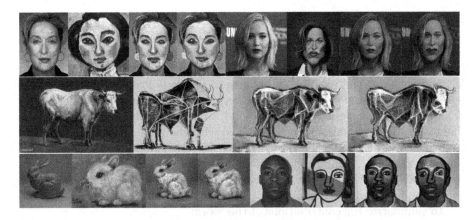

Fig. 1. Each set of four images contains (left to right) a content input, a style input, a standard style transfer output, and our proposed method's output. Sources of used images are available in the supplementary material.

final output. This results in the outputs of these algorithms being easily identified as altered or "filtered" versions of the content image, rather than novel images created using the content image as a reference. Our focus in this work is to integrate shape and geometry as important markers of style and loosen the constraints on content as a receptive canvas. We achieve this by introducing a domain-agnostic geometric deformation of the content image, optimized jointly with standard style transfer losses.

Our proposed method, deformable style transfer (DST), takes two images as the input: a content image and a style image. We assume these two images share a domain and have some approximate alignment (e.g. both are images of sitting animals). This is a general scenario likely to arise in recreational or artistic uses of style transfer, as well as in tasks such as data augmentation. The nature of this problem makes *learning* to transfer style challenging since the variation in unconstrained domains and styles can not be reasonably presumed to be captured in any feasible training set. Therefore, like other style transfer work in this setting, we develop an optimization-based method, leveraging a pretrained and fixed feature extractor derived from a convolutional network (CNN) trained for ImageNet classification.

There has been recent work on learning geometric style, using an explicit model of landmark constellations [25] or a deformation model representing a specific style [23]. These methods require a collection of images in the chosen style, and work only in a specific domain (often faces, due to their importance in culture and applications). Hence, they are not applicable to our more general scenario. Nonetheless, we compare our results to those of the aforementioned methods in their specific domain of faces in Sect. 5, and find that our method produces equally aesthetically pleasing results despite it being more general.

In this work we propose the first, to our knowledge, method for incorporating geometry into one-shot, domain-agnostic style transfer. The key idea of

DST is to find a smooth deformation, or spatial warping, of the content image that brings it into spatial alignment with the style image. This deformation is guided by a set of matching keypoints, chosen to maximize the feature similarity between paired keypoints of the two images. After roughly aligning the paired keypoints with a rigid rotation and scaling, a simple ℓ_2 loss encourages warping our output image in such a way that the keypoints become spatially aligned. This deformation loss is regularized with a total variation penalty to reduce artifacts due to drastic deformations, and combined with the more traditional style and content loss terms. DST's joint, regularized objective simultaneously encourages preserving content, minimizing the style loss, and obtaining the desired deformation, weighing these goals against each other. This objective can be solved using standard iterative techniques.

To summarize the contributions of this work:

- We propose an optimization-based framework that endows style transfer algorithms with the explicit ability to deform a content image to match the geometry of a style image. Our flexible formulation also allows explicit user guidance and control of stylization tradeoffs.
- We demonstrate, for the first time, geometry-aware style transfer in a one-shot scenario. In contrast to previous works that are limited to human faces, DST works for images in other domains, with the assumption that they share a domain and have some approximate alignment.
- We evaluate DST on a range of style transfer instances, with images of faces, animals, vehicles, and landscapes, and through a user study demonstrate that our framework can augment existing style transfer algorithms to dramatically improve the perceived stylization quality, at minimal cost to the perceived content preservation.

2 Related Work

Early style transfer methods relied on hand-crafted features and algorithms [5,10–12]. Gatys et al. [7] introduced Neural Style Transfer and dramatically improved the state-of-the-art by leveraging the features of a pretrained CNN. Neural Style Transfer represents "style" using the Gram matrix of features extracted from the shallow layers of a CNN and "content" using feature tensors extracted from the deeper layers. The pixels of a stylized output image are directly optimized to simultaneously match the style representation (of the style image) and content representation (of the content image). Subsequent works improve upon [7] with different complementary schemes, including spatial constraints [22], semantic guidance [3], and Markov Random Field priors [18]. Other work has improved upon [7] by replacing the objective function, style representation, and/or content representation [9,17,20].

Optimization-based methods produce high quality stylizations, but they can be computationally expensive as they require backpropagation at every iteration and gradually change the image, usually at a pixel level, until the desired statistics are matched. To overcome this limitation, model-based neural methods were introduced. These methods optimize a generative model offline, and at test time produce a stylized image with a single forward pass. These methods fall into two families with different tradeoffs relative to optimization-based style transfer. Some methods [21] trade flexibility for speed and quality, quickly producing excellent stylizations but only for a predetermined set of styles. Other methods [14,15] trade off quality for speed, allowing for fast transfer of arbitrary styles, but typically produce lower quality outputs than optimization-based style transfer. Each family of method excels in a different regime, and in this work we prioritize flexibility and quality over speed.

Until recently, style transfer methods could not transfer geometric style and were limited to transferring color and texture. In much work outside the domain of style transfer, however, geometric transformation has been applied to images via automatic warping. Early work required predicting a set of global transformation parameters or a dense deformation field. Cole et al. [4] enabled fine-grained local warping by proposing a method that takes a sparse set of control keypoints and warps an image with spline interpolation. The introduced warping module is differentiable and thus can be trained as part of an end-to-end system, although [4] requires pre-detected landmarks as input for its face synthesis task.

Several recent works have attempted to combine image warping with neural networks to learn both textural and geometric style of human portraits. CariGAN [19] translates a photo to a caricature by training a Generative Adversarial Network (GAN) that models geometric transformation with manually annotated facial landmarks and another GAN that translates the usual non-geometric style appearances. Face of Art (FoA) [25] trains a neural network model to automatically detect 68 canonical facial landmarks in artistic portraits and uses them to warp a photo so that the geometry of the face is closer to that of an artistic portrait. WarpGAN [23], on the other hand, adds a warping module to the generator of a GAN and trains it as part of an end-to-end system by optimizing both the locations of keypoints and their displacements, using a dataset that contains a caricature and photo pair for each identity.

The main distinction of our work from these efforts is that ours is not limited to human faces (or any other particular domain) and does not require offline training on a specially prepared dataset. In terms of methodology, FoA separates transferring "texture" and transferring geometry, while DST transfers them jointly. WarpGAN treats texture and geometry jointly, but it has to learn a warping module with paired examples in the face caricature domain while DST does not. We show in Sect. 5 that results of our more general method, even when applied to faces, are competitive with results of these two face-specific methods.

For finding correspondences between images, two recent efforts use CNN-based descriptors to identify matching points between paired images outside the domain of human faces. Fully Convolutional Self-Similarity [16] is a descriptor for dense semantic correspondence that uses local self-similarity to match keypoints among different instances within the same object class. Neural Best-Buddies (NBB) [1] is a more general method for finding a set of sparse cross-domain correspondences that leverages the hierarchical encoding of features by pre-trained CNNs. We use NBB in our method with post-processing, as described in detail in the next section.

3   Geometry Transfer via Correspondences

One path for introducing geometric style transfer is establishing spatial associations between the content and style images, and defining a *deformation* that brings the content image into (approximate) alignment with the style image. Assuming they share a domain and have similar geometry (e.g. both are images of front-facing cars), we can aim to find meaningful spatial correspondences to define the deformation. The correspondences would specify displacement "targets", derived from the style image, for keypoints in the content image. Thin-plate spline interpolation [4] can extend this sparse set of displacements to a full displacement field specifying how to deform every pixel in the output image.

Content   Style   DST Warp (Ours)   Naive Warp

Fig. 2. Illustration of our method using keypoints taken from FoA (rows 1–3) or generated manually (row 4). Keypoints are overlayed on the content and style images with matching points in the same color. Naive warp indicates output of standard style transfer warped by moving source points to target points. Figure is best viewed zoomed-in on screen.

3.1   Finding and Cleaning Keypoints

If we fix a domain and assume availability of a training set drawn from the domain, we may be able to learn a domain-specific mechanism for finding salient and meaningful correspondences. This can be done through facial landmark detection [25] or through learning a data-driven detector for relevant points [16,23]. Alternatively, we can expect a user interacting with a style transfer tool to manually select points they consider matching in the two images. If matching points are provided by such approaches, they can be used in DST as we show in Fig. 2. However, we are interested in a more general scenario, a one-shot, domain-agnostic setting where we may not have access to such points. Hence we use NBB, a generic method for point matching between images.

NBB finds a sparse set of correspondences between two images that could be from different domains or semantic categories. It utilizes the hierarchy of deep features of a pre-trained CNN, i.e. the characteristic that deeper layers extract high-level, semantically meaningful, and spatially invariant features and shallow layers encode low-level features such as edges and color features. Starting from the deepest layer, NBB searches for pairs of correspondences that are mutual nearest neighbors, filters them based on activation values, and percolates them through the hierarchy to narrow down the search region at each level. At the end of the algorithm, it clusters the set of pixel-level correspondences into k spatial clusters and returns k keypoint pairs.

The keypoint pairs returned by NBB, however, are often too noisy and not sufficiently spread out to use them as they are. To provide better guidance for geometric deformation, we modify NBB to get a cleaner and better spatially-distributed set of pairs. Specifically, we remove the final clustering step and return all pixel-level correspondences, usually on the order of hundreds of correspondence pairs. Then we use a greedy algorithm that selects a keypoint with the highest activation value (calculated by NBB) that is at least 10 pixels away from any already selected keypoint. We select up to 80 keypoint pairs and filter out keypoints with activation values smaller than 1. After the initial selection, we map the keypoints in the style image onto the content image by finding a similarity transformation that minimizes the squared distance between the two point clusters [24]. We then additionally clean up the selected keypoints by removing keypoints pairs that cross each other, to prevent a discontinuous warp field. (If keypoints are provided by FoA, manual selection, or other non-NBB methods, we skip the cleaning process and only transform the style image keypoints appropriately.) We refer to the keypoints in the content image as the "source points" and the corresponding keypoints in the style image mapped onto the content image as the "target points." This process is illustrated in Fig. 3.

3.2   Differentiable Image Warping

We specify an image deformation by a set of source keypoints $P = \{p_1, \ldots, p_k\}$ and the associated 2D displacement vectors $\theta = \{\theta_1, \ldots, \theta_k\}$. θ specify for each source keypoint p_i, the *destination* coordinates $p_i + \theta_i$. Following [23] we use thin-plate spline interpolation [4] to produce a dense flow field from the coordinates of an unwarped image I to a warped image $W(I, \theta)$. This is a closed-form procedure which finds parameters w, v, b that minimize $\sum_{i=1}^{k} ||f_\theta(p_i + \theta_i) - p_i||^2$ subject to a curvature constraint. With these parameters, we have the inverse mapping function

$$f_\theta(q) = \sum_{i=1}^{k} w_i \phi(||q - p_i - \theta_i||) + v^T q + b \qquad (1)$$

where q denotes the location of a pixel in the warped image and ϕ is a kernel function which we choose to be $\phi(r) = r^2 \log(r)$. $f_\theta(q)$ gives the inverse mapping

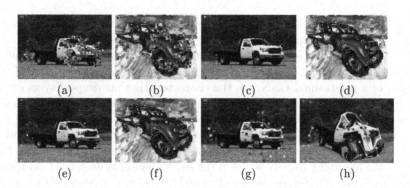

Fig. 3. An image can be spatially deformed by moving a set of source points to a set of target points. Matching keypoints are indicated by color. (a) Content image with all correspondences. (b) Style image with all correspondences. (c) Content image with original NBB keypoints. (d) Style image with original NBB keypoints. (e) Content image with our selected keypoints. (f) Style image with our selected keypoints. (g) Content image with keypoints aligned by just matching the centers. (h) Content image warped with keypoints aligned by a similarity transformation. The lines indicate where the circle source points move to (square target points). Figure is best viewed zoomed-in on screen.

of the pixel q in the original image; i.e., the pixel coordinates in the unwarped image from which we should derive the color of pixel q in the warped image. The color of each pixel can then be generated through bilinear sampling. This entire warping module is differentiable with respect to θ, allowing it to be optimized as part of an end-to-end system.

4   Spatially Guided Style Transfer

The input to DST consists of a content image I_c, a style image I_s, and aligned keypoint pairs P (source) and P' (target). Recall that these points don't have to be infused with explicit domain- or category-specific semantics. DST optimizes the stylization parameters (usually the pixels of the output image) X and the deformation parameters θ. The final output is the warped stylized image $W(X, \theta)$.

4.1   Content and Style Loss Terms

DST can be used with any one-shot, optimization-based style transfer method with a content loss and a style loss. In this work, we demonstrate our framework with two such methods: Gatys et al. [7] and Kolkin et al. [17], which we will refer to as Gatys and STROTSS, respectively. Each method defines a content loss $L_{\text{content}}(I_c, X)$ and a style loss $L_{\text{style}}(I_s, X)$. These aim to capture the visual content of I_c and the visual style of I_s in the output X. Below we briefly summarize the content/style loss of these methods. For more details, we direct the reader to [7,17].

Gatys represents "style" in terms of the Gram matrix of features extracted from multiple layers of a CNN and "content" as the feature tensors extracted from another set of layers. It defines $L_{content}$ as the squared-error between the feature representation of the content image and that of the output image. Similarly, it defines L_{style} as the weighted sum of the squared-error between the Gram matrix of the style image and that of the output image.

STROTSS, inspired by the concept of self-similarity, defines $L_{content}$ as the absolute error between the normalized pairwise cosine distance between feature vectors extracted from the content image and those of the output image. STROTSS's L_{style} is composed of three terms: the Relaxed Earth Movers Distance (EMD), the moment matching term, and the color matching term. Relaxed EMD helps transfer the structural forms of the style image to the output image. The moment matching term, which aims to match the mean and covariance of the feature vectors in the two images, combats over-or under-saturation. The color matching term, defined as the Relaxed EMD between pixel colors, encourages the output image and the style image to have a similar palette.

When using DST with a base style transfer method, we do not change anything about $L_{content}$. The style loss of DST is composed of two terms

$$L_{style}(I_s, X) + L_{style}(I_s, W(X, \theta)). \tag{2}$$

The first loss term is between the style image I_s and the *unwarped* stylized image X. The second term is between I_s and the spatially deformed stylized image $W(X, \theta)$, with θ defining the deformation as per Sect. 3. Minimizing Eq. (2) is aimed at finding a good stylization both with and without spatial deformation. This way we force the stylization parameters X and the spatial deformation parameters θ to work together to produce a harmoniously stylized and spatially deformed final output $W(X, \theta)$.

4.2   Deformation Loss Term

Given a set of k source points P and matching target points P', we define the deformation loss as

$$L_{warp}(P, P', \theta) = \frac{1}{k} \sum_{i=1}^{k} \|p'_i - (p_i + \theta_i)\|_2, \tag{3}$$

where p_i and p'_i are the i-th source and target point coordinates. Minimizing Eq. (3) with respect to θ seeks a set of displacements that move the source points to the target points. This term encourages the geometric shape of the stylized image to become closer to that of the style.

Aggressively minimizing the deformation loss may lead to significant artifacts, due to keypoint match errors or incompatibility of the content with the style geometry. To avoid these artifacts, we add a regularization term encouraging smooth deformations. Specifically, we use the (anisotropic) total variation norm of the 2D warp field f normalized by its size

$$R_{\text{TV}}(f) = \frac{1}{W \times H} \sum_{i=1}^{W} \sum_{j=1}^{H} \|f_{i+1,j} - f_{i,j}\|_1 + \|f_{i,j+1} - f_{i,j}\|_1. \tag{4}$$

This regularization term smooths the warp field by encouraging nearby pixels to move in a similar direction.

4.3   Joint Optimization

Putting everything together, the objective function of DST is

$$\begin{aligned}
L(X, \theta, I_c, I_s, P, P') =\, & \alpha L_{\text{content}}(I_c, X) \\
& + L_{\text{style}}(I_s, X) + L_{\text{style}}(I_s, W(X, \theta)) \\
& + \beta L_{\text{warp}}(P, P', \theta) \\
& + \gamma R_{\text{TV}}(f_\theta),
\end{aligned} \tag{5}$$

where X is the stylized image and θ parameterizes the spatial deformation. Hyperparameters α and β control the relative importance of content preservation and spatial deformation to stylization. Hyperparameter γ controls the amount of regularization on the spatial deformation. The effect of varying α is analyzed in [7,17]. The effect of changing β and γ is illustrated in Fig. 4. We use standard iterative techniques such as stochastic gradient descent or L-BFGS to minimize Eq. (5) with respect to X and θ. Implementation details can be found in the supplementary material and the published code.[1]

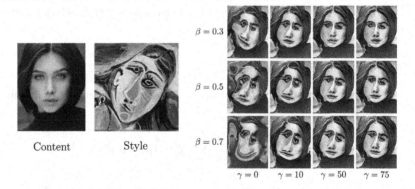

Fig. 4. DST outputs with varying β and γ using STROTSS as the base method. Image in the upper right corner (low β, high γ) has the least deformation, and the image in the bottom left corner (high β, low γ) has the most deformation.

---

[1] https://github.com/sunniesuhyoung/DST.

5   Results

We observe that DST often captures the geometric style of the target style image. One visually striking effect is that the resulting images no longer look like "filtered" versions of the original content, as they often do with standard style transfer methods. We show results of DST with Gatys and STROTSS in Figs. 5 and 6. For a pair of content and style images, we show the output of DST and the output of Gatys/STROTSS that doesn't have the spatial deformation capability. To highlight the effect of the DST-learned deformation, we also provide the content image warped by DST and the Gatys/STROTSS output naively warped with the selected keypoints without any optimization of the deformation. While naive warping produces undesirable artifacts, DST finds a warp that harmoniously improves stylization while preserving content.

As a simple quantitative evaluation, we calculated the (STROTSS) style loss on 185 pairs of DST and STROTSS outputs. Surprisingly, we found that on average this loss was 7% higher for DST outputs than STROTSS ones, even for examples we show in Fig. 6. While the loss difference is small, this is a mismatch with the human judgment of stylization quality shown in Sect. 5.2.

| Content | Style | Gatys | Gatys +
Naive Warp* | DST | Content +
DST Warp† |

Fig. 5. DST results with Gatys. *Naively warped by moving source points to target points. †Warp learned by DST applied to the content image.

5.1   Comparison with FoA and WarpGAN

While, so far as we are aware, DST is the first work to allow open-domain geometry-aware style transfer, other work has tackled this problem in the domain

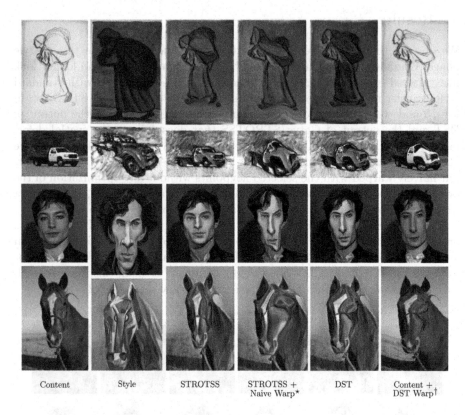

	Content	Style	STROTSS	STROTSS + Naive Warp*	DST	Content + DST Warp†

Fig. 6. DST results with STROTSS. *Naively warped by moving source points to target points. †Warp learned by DST applied to the content image.

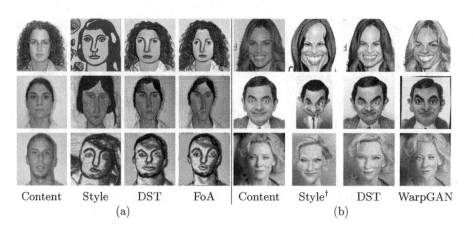

Content	Style	DST	FoA	Content	Style†	DST	WarpGAN
		(a)				(b)	

Fig. 7. Comparison of DST with (a) FoA and (b) WarpGAN. †: Note that WarpGAN's does not use a specific style image, so this style image is only used by DST; see text for details.

of human faces. To compare performance, we show results of DST and results of FoA [25] and WarpGAN [23] on the same content-style pairs in Fig. 7. Note that both of these methods require training a model on a dataset of stylized portraits or caricatures, while DST operates with access to only a single content and single style image.

DST jointly optimizes the geometric and non-geometric stylization parameters, while FoA transfers geometric style by warping the facial landmarks in the content image to a specific artist's (e.g. Modigliani) canonical facial landmark pattern (with small variations added) learned by training a model on a dataset of stylized portraits. FoA then separately transfers textural style with a standard style transfer method (e.g. Gatys, STROTSS). When we compare DST and FoA in Fig. 7, we demonstrate "one-shot FoA" since the style images used to produce the outputs in [25] are unavailable. That is, we assume that we have access to one content image, one style image, and the trained FoA landmark detector. Using the detector, we find 68 facial landmarks in the content and style images and transform the style image landmarks, as described in Sect. 3, to get the target points. Then we follow FoA's two-step style transfer and transfer the textural style by STROTSS and transfer the geometric style by warping the output image by moving the source points to the target points.

The biggest difference between WarpGAN and DST is that DST is a one-shot style transfer method that works with a single content image and a single style image. WarpGAN, on the other hand, is trained on a dataset of paired pictures and caricatures of the same identities, and generates a caricature for an input content image from its learned deformation model. To compare the performance of WarpGAN and DST, we used content/style image pairs from [23] and ran DST. In Fig. 7, we show the outputs of DST and the outputs of WarpGAN taken from [23]. Despite the lack of a *learning* component, DST results are competitive and sometimes more aesthetically pleasing than results of FoA and WarpGAN.

5.2   Human Evaluation

Quantitatively evaluating and comparing style transfer is challenging, in part because of the subjective nature of aesthetic properties defining style and visual quality, and in part due to the inherent tradeoff between content preservation and stylization [17,26]. Following the intuition developed in these papers, we conducted a human evaluation study using Amazon Mechanical Turk on a set of 75 diverse style/content pairs. The goal was to study the effect of DST on the stylization/content preservation tradeoff, in comparison to the base style transfer methods. The evaluation was conducted separately for STROTSS and Gatys-based methods. We considered three DST deformation regimes: low ($\beta = 0.3, \gamma = 75$), medium ($\beta = 0.5, \gamma = 50$), and high ($\beta = 0.7, \gamma = 10$) for STROTSS; low ($\beta = 3, \gamma = 750$), medium ($\beta = 7, \gamma = 100$), and high ($\beta = 15, \gamma = 100$) for Gatys. So for each base method, we compare four stylized output images. The effect of varying β and γ is illustrated in Fig. 4.

To measure content preservation, we asked MTurk users the question: "Does image A represent the same scene as image B", where A referred to the content image and B to the output of style transfer. The users were forced to choose one of four answers: "Yes", "Yes, with minor errors", "Yes, with major errors" and "No". Converting these answers to numerical scores (1 for "No", 4 for "Yes") and averaging across content/style pairs and users, we get a *content score* between 1 and 4 for each of the four methods.

To evaluate the effect of the proposed deformable framework, we presented the users with a pair of outputs, one from the base method (Gatys or STROTSS) and the other from DST, along with the style image. The order of the first two is randomized. We asked the users to choose which of the two output images better matches the style. The fraction of time a method is preferred in all comparisons (across methods compared to, users, content/style pairs) gives a *style score* between 0 and 1. 0.7 means that the method "wins" 70% of all comparisons it was a part of. The evaluation interfaces are provided in the supplementary material.

In total, there were 600 unique content comparisons: 4 questions × 75 images for Gatys and an equal number for STROTSS. 123 users participated in the evaluation, and each comparison was evaluated by 9.55 users on average. The standard deviation of the content choice agreement was 0.79 (over a range of 1 to 4). For stylization, there were 450 unique comparisons in total: 3 comparisons between the base method and each of the 3 DST deformation regimes×75 images for Gatys and likewise for STROTSS. 103 users participated in the stylization evaluation, and each comparison was evaluated by 8.76 users on average. For each comparison, 6.47 users agreed in their choice on average.

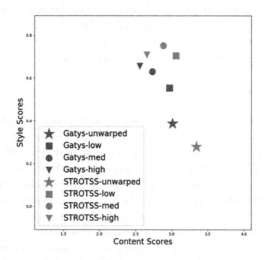

Fig. 8. Human evaluation results, comparing DST in different deformation regimes with STROTSS (green) and Gatys (blue). DST provides a much higher perceived degree of style capture without a significant sacrifice in content preservation. (Color figure online)

Results of this human evaluation are shown in Fig. 8. Across the deformation regimes (low, medium, high), for both STROTSS and Gatys, DST significantly increases the perceived stylization quality, while only minimally reducing the perceived content preservation. Note that some reduction to the content score can be expected since we intentionally alter the content more by deforming it, but our evaluation shows that this drop is small.

5.3 Limitations

In Fig. 9, we show unsuccessful examples of DST where the output image did not deform towards having a similar shape as the style image or deformed only partially. We observed that bad deformations often stem from poorly matching or too sparse set of keypoints. We expect finding better matching keypoints between images and making the method more robust to poor matches will improve results.

Content   Style   STROTSS   DST

Fig. 9. Examples of DST failures. We observed that stylization failures are often due to correspondence errors or overly complex scene layout.

6   Conclusion

Prior work on style transfer has largely ignored geometry and shape, despite the role these play in visual style. We present deformable style transfer (DST), a novel approach that combines the traditional texture and color transfer with spatial deformations. Our method incorporates deformation targets, derived from domain-agnostic point matching between content and style images, into the objective of an optimization-based style transfer framework. This is to our knowledge the first effort to develop a one-shot, domain-agnostic method for capturing and transferring geometric aspects of style.

Still many aspects of geometric style transfer remain unexplored. Narrowing this might involve developing more robust keypoint matching algorithms for highly stylized images. Furthermore, it is by no means certain that modifying geometry using warp fields driven by paired keypoints is the most effective app-roach to this problem. We hope that future work will continue to explore how to represent geometric style more flexibly, and more accurately encode the artistic extraction and abstraction of shape and form.

Acknowledgement. This work is supported by the DARPA GARD award HR00112020003 and the University of Chicago CDAC Discovery Grant. We would also like to thank Haochen Wang, Davis Gilton, Steven Basart, and members of the Perception and Learning Systems (PALS) at TTIC for their helpful comments.

References

1. Aberman, K., Liao, J., Shi, M., Lischinski, D., Chen, B., Cohen-Or, D.: Neural best-buddies: sparse cross-domain correspondence. ACM Trans. Graph. (TOG) **37**(4), 69 (2018)
2. Berger, G., Memisevic, R.: Incorporating long-range consistency in CNN-based texture generation (2016). arXiv preprint arXiv:1606.01286
3. Champandard, A.J.: Semantic style transfer and turning two-bit doodles into fine artworks (2016). CoRR abs/1603.01768, http://arxiv.org/abs/1603.01768
4. Cole, F., Belanger, D., Krishnan, D., Sarna, A., Mosseri, I., Freeman, W.T.: Synthesizing normalized faces from facial identity features. In: The IEEE Conference on Computer Vision and Pattern Recognition (CVPR), July 2017
5. Efros, A.A., Freeman, W.T.: Image quilting for texture synthesis and transfer. In: Proceedings of the 28th Annual Conference on Computer Graphics and Interactive Techniques, pp. 341–346. ACM (2001)
6. Elkins, J.: Style. The Dictionary of art, **29** (1996)
7. Gatys, L.A., Ecker, A.S., Bethge, M.: Image style transfer using convolutional neural networks. In: The IEEE Conference on Computer Vision and Pattern Recognition (CVPR), June 2016
8. Gatys, L.A., Ecker, A.S., Bethge, M., Hertzmann, A., Shechtman, E.: Controlling perceptual factors in neural style transfer. In: IEEE Conference on Computer Vision and Pattern Recognition (CVPR) (2017)
9. Gu, S., Chen, C., Liao, J., Yuan, L.: Arbitrary style transfer with deep feature reshuffle. In: CVPR (2018)
10. Haeberli, P.: Paint by numbers: abstract image representations. In: ACM SIGGRAPH Computer Graphics, vol. 24, pp. 207–214. ACM (1990)
11. Hertzmann, A.: Painterly rendering with curved brush strokes of multiple sizes. In: Proceedings of the 25th Annual Conference on Computer Graphics and Interactive Techniques, pp. 453–460. ACM (1998)
12. Hertzmann, A., Jacobs, C.E., Oliver, N., Curless, B., Salesin, D.H.: Image analogies. In: Proceedings of the 28th Annual Conference on Computer Graphics and Interactive Techniques, pp. 327–340. ACM (2001)
13. Hofstadter, D.: Metamagical themas: variations on a theme as the essence of imagination. Sci. Am. **247**(4), 14 (1983)
14. Huang, X., Belongie, S.J.: Arbitrary style transfer in real-time with adaptive instance normalization. In: ICCV (2017)
15. Johnson, J., Alahi, A., Fei-Fei, L.: Perceptual losses for real-time style transfer and super-resolution. In: Leibe, B., Matas, J., Sebe, N., Welling, M. (eds.) ECCV 2016. LNCS, vol. 9906, pp. 694–711. Springer, Cham (2016). https://doi.org/10.1007/978-3-319-46475-6_43

16. Kim, S., Min, D., Ham, B., Lin, S., Sohn, K.: Fcss: fully convolutional self-similarity for dense semantic correspondence. IEEE Trans. Pattern Anal. Mach. Intell. **41**(3), 581–595 (2019). https://doi.org/10.1109/TPAMI.2018.2803169

17. Kolkin, N., Salavon, J., Shakhnarovich, G.: Style transfer by relaxed optimal transport and self-similarity. In: The IEEE Conference on Computer Vision and Pattern Recognition (CVPR), June 2019

18. Li, C., Wand, M.: Combining Markov random fields and convolutional neural networks for image synthesis. In: The IEEE Conference on Computer Vision and Pattern Recognition (CVPR), June 2016

19. Li, W., Xiong, W., Liao, H., Huo, J., Gao, Y., Luo, J.: Carigan: caricature generation through weakly paired adversarial learning (2018). CoRR abs/1811.00445, http://arxiv.org/abs/1811.00445

20. Mechrez, R., Talmi, I., Zelnik-Manor, L.: The contextual loss for image transformation with non-aligned data (2018). arXiv preprint arXiv:1803.02077

21. Sanakoyeu, A., Kotovenko, D., Lang, S., Ommer, B.: A style-aware content loss for real-time HD style transfer. In: CVPR (2018)

22. Selim, A., Elgharib, M., Doyle, L.: Painting style transfer for head portraits using convolutional neural networks. ACM Trans. Graph. **35**(4), 129:1–129:18, July 2016. https://doi.org/10.1145/2897824.2925968, http://doi.acm.org/10.1145/2897824.2925968

23. Shi, Y., Deb, D., Jain, A.K.: Warpgan: automatic caricature generation. In: The IEEE Conference on Computer Vision and Pattern Recognition (CVPR), June 2019

24. Umeyama, S.: Least-squares estimation of transformation parameters between two point patterns. IEEE Trans. Pattern Anal. Mach. Intell. **13**(4), 376–380 (1991). https://doi.org/10.1109/34.88573

25. Yaniv, J., Newman, Y., Shamir, A.: The face of art: landmark detection and geometric style in portraits. ACM Trans. Graph. 38(4), 60:1–60:15, July 2019. https://doi.org/10.1145/3306346.3322984, http://doi.acm.org/10.1145/3306346.3322984

26. Yeh, M.C., Tang, S., Bhattad, A., Forsyth, D.A.: Quantitative evaluation of style transfer (2018). arXiv preprint arXiv:1804.00118

Aligning Videos in Space and Time

Senthil Purushwalkam[1(✉)], Tian Ye[1], Saurabh Gupta[2], and Abhinav Gupta[1,3]

[1] Carnegie Mellon University, Pittsburgh, USA
spurushw@andrew.cmu.edu
[2] University of Illinois at Urbana-Champaign, Urbana, USA
[3] Facebook AI Research, Menlo Park, USA

Abstract. In this paper, we focus on the task of extracting visual correspondences across videos. Given a query video clip from an action class, we aim to align it with training videos in space and time. Obtaining training data for such a fine-grained alignment task is challenging and often ambiguous. Hence, we propose a novel alignment procedure that learns such correspondence in space and time via cross video cycle-consistency. During training, given a pair of videos, we compute cycles that connect patches in a given frame in the first video by matching through frames in the second video. Cycles that connect overlapping patches together are encouraged to score higher than cycles that connect non-overlapping patches. Our experiments on the Penn Action and Pouring datasets demonstrate that the proposed method can successfully learn to correspond semantically similar patches across videos, and learns representations that are sensitive to object and action states.

Keywords: Understanding via association · Video alignment · Visual correspondences

1 Introduction

> Ask not "what is this?", ask "what is this like".
>
> *Moshe Bar*

What does it mean to understand a video? The most popular answer right now is labeling videos with categories such as "opening bottle". However, action categories hardly tell us anything about the process – it doesn't tell us where is the bottle or when it was opened, let all one the different other states it can exist in, and what parts are involved in what transitions. Dense semantic labeling is a non-starter because exhaustive and accurate labels for objects, their states and actions are not easy to gather.

Project webpage: http://www.cs.cmu.edu/~spurushw/publication/alignvideos/.

Electronic supplementary material The online version of this chapter (https://doi.org/10.1007/978-3-030-58574-7_16) contains supplementary material, which is available to authorized users.

A. Vedaldi et al. (Eds.): ECCV 2020, LNCS 12371, pp. 262–278, 2020.
https://doi.org/10.1007/978-3-030-58574-7_16

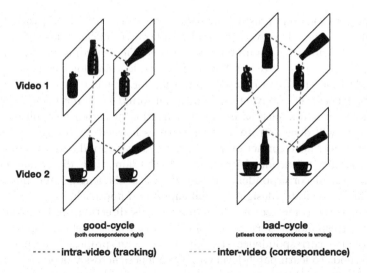

Fig. 1. Learning Correspondence via Cycle Supervision. Features that allow sequences of matches (cycles) that begin and end at the same patch are desired.

In this paper, we investigate the alternative of *understanding via association*, *i.e.* video understanding by extracting visual correspondences between training and test videos. Focusing on 'what is a given video like', rather than 'what class it belongs to', side-steps the problem of hand-defining a huge taxonomy and dense labeling. Inspired by this, in this paper, we focus on the task of creating associations or visual correspondences across training and test videos. More specifically, we try to align videos in both space and time. This poses two core and inter-related questions: (a) what is the granularity of visual correspondence? (b) what is the right distance metric or features to extract this correspondence?

Let us focus on the first issue: the granularity, *i.e.* the level at which we should establish correspondence: pixel-level, patch-level or frame-level. The trade-off here is between discriminability and the amount of data required for good correspondences. While full frames are more discriminative (and easy to match), they are also quite specific. For example, finding a frame that depicts the same relation between the bottle and the cup as shown in Fig. 1 would require large amounts of training data before a good full-frame correspondence can be found. Consequently, past work with hand-crafted descriptors focused on establishing visual correspondence by matching interest points [30, 47] and image patches [42]. However, given lack of dense supervision, recent work that tries to revisit these ideas through learning [9] seeks to correspond whole frames, through temporal consistency of frames. While this works well for full frame correspondence, it doesn't produce patch-level correspondences which is both richer, and more widely applicable. This motivates our pursuit for a method to obtain dense patch-level correspondences across videos.

The second issue at hand is of how to learn a distance metric (or equivalently an appropriate feature space) for extracting visual correspondences.

Classical work focused on using manually-defined features [30,47] with a variety of distance metrics. However, given the widespread effectiveness of supervised end-to-end learning for computer vision tasks [25] (including visual correspondence [36]), it is natural to ask how to leverage learning for this task, *i.e.* what is the right objective function and supervision for learning features for obtaining correspondences? The conventional approach would be to reuse generic features from a standard task such as image classification or action recognition. As our experiments will demonstrate, neither features learned for ImageNet classification, nor ones trained for action recognition generate good correspondences due to their inability to encode object states. At the same time, direct manual annotation for visual correspondence across videos is challenging and infeasible to scale. This necessitates design of a self-supervised approach.

Interestingly, some recent efforts pursue this direction, and exploit consistency in correspondences as supervision to learn frame-level correspondence [9], or intra-video correspondence (tracking) [52]. Our proposed method extends these methods to learn patch-level correspondences across videos via *cross video cycle-consistency*. During training, given a pair of videos, we compute matches for a patch forward in time in the first video, then match to a patch in the second video, match this patch backward in time in the second video and finally match back to a patch in the first video. This sequence of patches is referred to as a 'cycle'. Cycles that start and end at overlapping patches are encouraged to score higher than cycles that connect non-overlapping patches (see Fig. 1). This allows our approach to generate finer level correspondence across videos (as SIFT Flow [29] does for images), while also harnessing the capabilities of the modern end-to-end learning approaches. Our experiments show that features learned using our approach are more effective at corresponding objects in the same state across videos, than features trained for ImageNet classification, or for action classification.

2   Related Work

Our work learns space-time visual correspondence by use of cycle consistency. In this section, we present a survey of related literature on video understanding (datasets, tasks and techniques), correspondence techniques in videos, and use of self-supervision and cycle consistency for learning features and correspondences.

Video Datasets and Tasks. A number of past efforts have been devoted to collecting new video understanding datasets, and extending static image tasks to videos. Leading efforts in recent times include datasets like Kinetics [22], AvA [16], Charades [40], EPIC Kitchen [5], VLOG [11], MultiTHUMOS [56]. While some of these datasets focus on action classification, a number of them investigate new tasks, such as temporal action localization [56], detection of subjects, verbs and objects [16], classification in first-person videos [5], and analysis of crowd-sourced videos [15,40]. These works extend video understanding by scaling it up.

Architectures for Action Classification. Researchers have also pursued design of expressive neural network architectures for the task of action classification [4,41,45,46,48,54]. Some works investigate architectures to encourage the modelling of time flow [33,38], or long-range temporal dependencies [10,50,53], or object tracking [13]. While these models often capture useful intuitions, their focus is still on optimizing models for the task of action classification. Hence, even though the model has the right inductive biases, learning is bottle-necked by the low-entropy output space that of action class labels.

Beyond Action Recognition. Many efforts have also pursued the task of detailed video understanding in recent times. For example, video prediction tasks [7,26] have the promise to go beyond action classification, as they force the model to predict much more than what can be effectively annotated. Wang et al. [49] model actions as operators that transform states of objects, and Nagarajan et al. [34] learn about how humans interact with different objects. In contrast, we take a non-parametric approach, and understand videos by understanding what they are like, and corresponding them with other videos in space and time.

Cycle Consistency and Correspondence. Forward-backward consistency and cycle consistency have been used in computer vision for establishing correspondence in an unsupervised manner [21,39]. Zhou et al. [61] use cycle-consistency to establish dense correspondence between 3D shapes, Godard et al. [14], use cycle consistency for learning to predict depth, Zhu et al. [62] use cycle consistency to learn how to generate images, and Wang et al. [52] use cycle consistency to learn features for correspondence over time in videos. Work from Wang et al. [52] is a primary motivation for our work, and we investigate use of cycle consistency to learn cross-video correspondences. To our knowledge, ours is the first work to investigate spatio-temporal alignment across videos with cycle consistency.

Spatial Correspondence. Finding correspondences across video frames is a fundamental problem and has been actively studied for decades. Optical flow [3] seeks to establish correspondences at the pixel-level. While numerous effective approaches have been proposed [31,32,43,44], optical flow estimation is still challenging over long time periods, and fails across videos. This issue is partially alleviated by performing correspondence at a patch level. SIFT Flow[29], a seminal work in this domain, uses SIFT descriptors [30] to match patches across scene. SIFT Flow can be used to transfer labels from training data to test samples in many applications [12,28,37,57]. However, patch correspondence approaches [17,23,60], rely on the local appearance of the patches for matching. We use a similar method to obtain spatio-temporal correspondences across videos, but account for the object states and not just the local appearance.

Cross-video Spatio-Temporal Alignment. Past works have studied spatio-temporal alignment in videos. Sermanet et al. [38] learn time sensitive features in a supervised manner by collecting time aligned data for an action. Alayrac et al. [2] learn features sensitive to object states by classifying object bounding

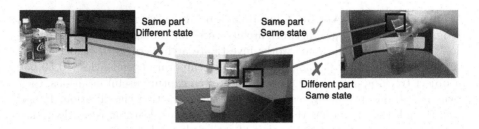

Fig. 2. What is a good correspondence? A good correspondence is a match where patches correspond to the same semantic part, and are in the same state with respect to the depicted action.

box into before or after action. Dwibedi *et al.* [9] focus on learning temporal correspondence by enforcing consistency in nearest neighbors at frame-level. This focus on frame-level modeling ignores spatial alignment. In contrast, we focus on corresponding image patches across videos in time and *space*. This leads to learning of state-sensitive *object* representations (as opposed to scene representations). We are not aware of any past work that tackles the problem of establishing spatio-temporal correspondences across videos.

Self-supervision. A number of past works employ self-supervised learning to alleviate the need for semantic supervision from humans to acquire generic image representations. Past works have employed images [8,58], videos [33,35,38,51, 52], and also motor actions [1,20]. Our alignment of videos in space and time, can also be seen as a way to learn representations in a self-supervised manner. However, we learn features that are sensitive to object state, as opposed to generic image features learned by these past methods.

3   Alignment via Cross-Video Cycle Consistency

Our goal is to learn how to spatio-temporally align two videos. We tackle this problem by extracting patch level visual correspondence across two videos. But what defines a good correspondence? A good spatio-temporal correspondence is one where two patches from different videos are linked when they depict the same objects (or their parts) and are in similar states. For example, two patches depicting rim of the cups are in correspondence as shown in Fig. 2 because the patches correspond to same part and the cups are in same state (tilted for pouring). On the other hand, the other two correspondences are bad because either the patches correspond to different object parts or the states of object do not match.

While it is easy to learn features that can correspond the same objects in various states over time by learning to track [51,52], it is far more challenging to learn features that correspond different objects in the same state. We specifically tackle this problem in our proposed approach. One of the biggest challenge here

Fig. 3. Overview: Given tracks in two video of the same class (shown by white dotted lines), we learn an embedding to correspond patches across videos. This is done by computing cycles (pair of cross-video edges) that correctly track a patch back to itself. We compute the best cycle that corresponds a patch to itself (shown in green) and encourage it to have a higher similarity than the best cycle that corresponds a patch to a different patch (shown in red) via a margin loss (Color figure online).

is the supervision. It is difficult to obtain supervision for such a dense correspondence task, thus we pursue a weakly-supervised approach. Our central idea is to employ *cross-video cycle-consistency*. Specifically, we create cycles in videos of the same action class, that track patches within a video, match it to a patch in another video, track this patch back in time, and then match back to the original video. Figure 3 illustrates the idea. Cycles that can track back to the same patch are encouraged (green cycle), while cycles that get back to a different patch in the first video are discouraged (red cycles). Enforcing this objective on a large collection of foreground patches would lead to choosing semantically aligned tracks. However, note that this could lead to some trivial cycles involving very short (or single frame) tracks in the second video. It is important to disregard such solutions in order to focus on cycles where object states vary (we disregard cycles that involve tracks of length 3 or less). We now formally describe the training objective.

3.1 Formulation

Let's assume we have a tracker $\mathcal{T}$, that given a video V, produces a set of tracks on the video. We will use $V^i_{m:n}$ to denote the sequence of patches in track i starting from frame m and ending at frame n. The image patch for track i in frame m is denoted as V^i_m (see Fig. 4). In this work, for obtaining tracks, we use the tracker proposed in [52] which is trained in an unsupervised manner. f_θ, realized via convolutional neural networks, denotes the desired feature embedding that establishes visual correspondence across *different* videos.

Consider the cycle shown in Fig. 4: $V^i_m \rightarrow V^i_n \rightarrow W^j_q \rightarrow W^j_p \rightarrow V^k_m$. This cycle has following jumps: forward-tracking in V, matching V to W, backward-tracking in W and matching back from W to V. We represent this cycle as $\{V^i_{m:n}, W^j_{p:q}, V^k_m\}$. The score of this cycle can be expressed as the sum of patch similarities of the matches involved. However, note that the first and third

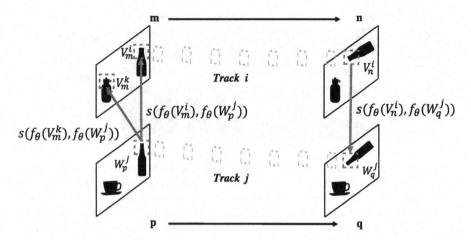

Fig. 4. Formulation: The score of a cycle is sum of the scores of two jumps as per f_θ.

matches in a cycle are extracted using off-the-shelf tracker, therefore do not depend on f_θ and can be assumed to have a constant score. Therefore, the final score of a cycle can be computed using cosine similarity s as:

$$S(\{V_{m:n}^i, W_{p:q}^j, V_m^k\}) = \underbrace{s(f_\theta(V_n^i), f_\theta(W_q^j))}_{\substack{\text{Jump from video } V \text{ (frame } n, \\ \text{patch } i) \text{ to video } W \text{ (frame } q, \\ \text{patch } j)}} + \underbrace{s(f_\theta(W_p^j), f_\theta(V_m^k))}_{\substack{\text{Jump from video } W \text{ (frame } p, \\ \text{patch } j) \text{ to video } V \text{ (frame } m, \\ \text{patch } k)}}$$

(1)

Given a starting patch V_m^i and an ending patch V_m^k, there can be numerous cycles depending on the length n considered in video V, the segment (p, q) of video W considered and the track j chosen in video W. When the patches V_m^i and V_m^k are highly overlapping, we expect the best cycle to have a high score. On the other hand, when these patches do not overlap, we want all the cycles to score low. We formulate this objective to optimize f_θ as a margin loss. First, for the pair of patches V_m^i, V_m^k, we compute the score of the best cycle as:

$$\kappa(V_m^i, V_m^k) = \max_{n,p,q,j} S(\{V_{m:n}^i, W_{p:q}^j, V_m^k\})$$

(2)

The margin loss can then be formulated as:

$$\max\left[0, -\kappa(V_m^i, V_m^{i+}) + \kappa(V_m^i, V_m^{i-}) + \delta\right]$$
$$\forall i_+, i_- : \text{IoU}(V_m^i, V_m^{i+}) \geq 0.5 \text{ and } \text{IoU}(V_m^i, V_m^{i-}) < 0.5$$

(3)

where, δ is the fixed margin. This can be optimized using stochastic gradient descent, to learn function f_θ.

We found that using a *soft version of the max function* (Γ as defined below) instead of the *max function* in Eq. 2 was important for training. Soft version of max function, Γ is defined as follows:

$$\Gamma(\mathbf{x}) = \sum_c \mathbf{x}_c \frac{e^{\mathbf{x}_c}}{\sum_{c'} e^{\mathbf{x}_{c'}}} \tag{4}$$

Here c represents a cycle and $\mathbf{x}_c$ represents the score of that cycle. This prevents the model from getting stuck in the local minima of greedily boosting the single best cycle. The soft version of max also allows computation of gradients *w.r.t* all patches that participate in score computation, thereby updating the representations of a larger number of samples.

3.2   Using Features for Spatio-Temporal Alignment

The representation f_θ trained using our approach can be used to extract cross-video correspondences at the level of patches, tracks, frames and videos:

Patch Correspondence. f_θ can be used to correspond image patches. As f_θ learns features sensitive to state of the object, it allows us to correspond and retrieve objects that are in the same state. See Sect. 4 for results.

Track Correspondence. Cycles in our formulation correspond tracks with one another. Given a set of tracks in videos V and W, we correspond each track i in video V, to the track in W that maximizes the score in Eq. 1:

$$\arg\max_j \left(\max_{n,p,q} S\left(\{ V_{m:n}^i, W_{p:q}^j, V_m^i \} \right) \right). \tag{5}$$

Temporal Alignment. We compute the similarity between a given pair of frames (V_m and W_p) in the two videos V and W by computing the total similarity between corresponding patches in the two frames:

$$T(V_m, W_p) = \sum_i \max_j s\left(f_\theta(V_m^i), f_\theta(W_p^j) \right). \tag{6}$$

These frame-level similarities can be used to obtain sub-video alignments. For example, if one wants to align K frames in video 1 to K frames in video 2 we can pick temporally-consistent top-K correspondences.

Video Retrieval. f_θ provides a natural metric for retrieving videos. Given a query video V and a set of videos $\mathcal{W}$, we retrieve the most similar video to V, by maximizing the total frame-level temporal alignment score:

$$W = \arg\max_{W \in \mathcal{W}} \sum_m \max_p T(V_m, W_p). \tag{7}$$

4   Experiments

Our goal is to demonstrate that we can align videos in space and time by leveraging f_θ learned using cross-video cycle-consistency supervision. Quantitatively measuring performance of dense spatio-temporal alignment is challenging due to the lack of ground-truth data. Therefore, in order to demonstrate the effectiveness of our approach, our experiments involve factored quantitative evaluations, and qualitative visualizations. More specifically, we study performance of our model at track correspondence, and temporal alignment.

Datasets: We perform alignment experiments on the Penn Action Dataset [59] and the Pouring Dataset [38].

Baselines: We compare our learned features to three alternate popular feature learning paradigms that focus on:

- semantics (image classification, object detection),
- local patch appearance (object trackers),
- motion and therefore object transformations (action classification models).

For models that capture semantics, we compare to ImageNet-trained ResNet-18 model `layer4` features (earlier layers do not improve results significantly), and a Mask-RCNN [18] object detection model trained on the MS-COCO [27] dataset. These models capture rich object-level semantics. For models that capture local patch appearance, we compare to features obtained via learning to track from Wang *et al.* [52]. Lastly, for models that focus on motion, we compare to features obtained via training for action classification on Kinetics [22] (ResNet-3D-18), and for frame-level action classification on Penn Action Dataset. Note, these together represent existing feature learning paradigms. Comparisons to these help us understand the extent to which our learned representations capture object state. Lastly, we also compare to recent paper from Dwibedi *et al.* [9] which only performs temporal alignment. To demonstrate the need for also modeling spatial alignment, we a consider a spatial downstream task of detecting the contact point between the thumb and a cup in the Pouring Dataset (since models from [9] are only available for the Pouring Dataset).

4.1   Experimental Settings

Tracks: We use an off-the-shelf tracker [52] to obtain tracks on videos for training and testing. Since we wish to focus on the foreground of videos for alignment, the pre-processing requires extracting tracks of foreground patches. To show robustness to patch extraction mechanism, we experiment with the following patch generation schemes (use of more sophisticated schemes is future work). For the Penn Action dataset, we track patches sampled on human detections from a Mask-RCNN detector [18]. For the Pouring dataset, we perform foreground estimation by clustering optical flow. As an ablation, we also experiment with ground-truth tracks of human keypoints in Penn Action dataset.

Fig. 5. Nearest neighbor patch correspondence. For random patches in query videos (left), we show the nearest neighbor patch across all frames (right) in a video retrieved using our method. We observe that our learned feature space is sensitive to the state of the object. Example in row 2 further highlights this point where our features match similar appearing patches differently based on the state of the person in the query. Row 3 shows an example from the Pouring dataset.

Training Details. We use a ResNet-18 [19] pre-trained on the ImageNet dataset [6] as our backbone model, and extract features from the last convolutional layer using RoI pooling. These features are further processed using 2 fully connected layers (and ReLU non-linearities) to obtain a 256-dimensional embedding for the input patch. We optimize the model using the Adam optimizer [24], with a learning rate of 0.0001, and a weight decay of 0.00001. We train the model for 30000 iterations on the Penn Action dataset and 500 iterations on the Pouring Dataset with each batch consisting of 8 pairs of videos. For computational efficiency, we divide each video into 8 temporal chunks. During training, we randomly sample one frame from each chunk to construct a sequence of 8 frames.

4.2 Qualitative Results

First we show some qualitative results of correspondences that can be extracted by our approach. Figure 5 shows some examples. We show the query frame on the left, and the corresponding nearest neighbor patch across all frames on the right. We observe that our model matches based on both the appearance and the state of the object. Next, we show that our approach can temporally align videos. Figure 6 visualizes temporal alignment on the pouring task.

Query   Retrieval   Query   Retrieval

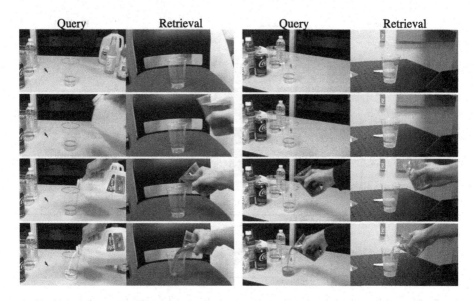

Fig. 6. Qualitative Results on Pouring Dataset: We show qualitative examples of retrieval and temporal alignment (query on left, retrieval on right) from the Pouring Dataset, based on the similarity metric learned by our model.

Finally, we qualitatively compare the correspondence using our features compared to ImageNet and action classification features. Figure 7 shows the spatio-temporal alignment on Penn-Action dataset. Given a query video, we retrieve the most similar video based on spatio-temporal alignment. We use human key-points to form tracks. The spatial alignment is shown by shape and color of keypoints, and the temporal alignment is shown in vertical (frames on top and bottom are temporally aligned). As compared to baseline methods, our approach is able to retrieve a more similar video, better align the frames in time, and more accurately correspond tracks with one other.

4.3   Quantitative Evaluation

Evaluating Temporal Alignment. Given a query video, we first obtain the closest video and then do temporal alignment as described in Sect. 3.2. For a given pair of frames V_m and W_p, we densely sample foreground patches and compute an average similarity using f_θ as the feature extractor. We can then temporally align the frames of videos V and W using the similarity measure in Eq. 6. Starting with 8 frames each, we align 4 frames from the query video to 4 frames in the retrieved video.

We evaluate the quality of the temporal alignment, by comparing the pose configuration of the human in the aligned frames (*i.e.* is the human in the same state in query and retrieved video). More specifically, we use the ground truth

Fig. 7. We show qualitative examples of retrieval and spatio-temporal alignment on the Penn Action Dataset to compare different feature spaces. The top row shows snapshots from the query video, the second row shows video retrieved from our model (trained on tracks from [52]), the third row shows retrievals using ImageNet features, and the fourth row shows retrievals using features obtained by finetuning on the dataset using the class labels. Each columns shows temporally aligned frames, while coloured markers show spatial alignment. For all methods, we use keypoint tracks at inference time in order to showcase spatial alignment.

keypoint annotations to estimate and compare the angle between the surrounding limbs at left and right knee, left and right elbow, left and right hip and the neck. We report the average absolute angle difference over all joints (lower is better) in Table 1. We observe that features learned using our proposed cross-video cycle consistency leads to better temporal alignment than features from ImageNet classification, Mask-RCNN [18], frame and video classification, and intra-video correspondence [52].

Evaluating Spatial Alignment with Patches. Our proposed model can also perform spatial alignment. Given temporally aligned video frames, we use the similarity function s with the learned features f_θ to correspond image patches in temporally aligned video frames. We measure the quality of alignment by counting how many of the corresponding keypoints lie in aligned patches. We report the average accuracy using various feature extractors in Table 2.

Evaluating Keypoint Tracks Correspondence. Given a track in query video V, a spatially aligned track in reference video W can be identified, by using the same similarity function s with the learned features f_θ. We evaluate this by

Table 1. Temporal Alignment on Penn Action Dataset [59]: We measure temporal alignment by measuring alignment in keypoint configuration at point of temporal alignment.

Method	Temporal Alignment Error ↓
ImageNet features	0.509
Features from Mask-RCNN [18]	0.504
Features from cycle-consistency based tracker [52]	0.501
Features from Kinetics [22] action classification model	0.492
Features from action classification	0.521
Our features (using tracks from [52] to train)	**0.448**

Table 2. Spatial alignment on penn action dataset [59]: We measure spatial alignment by measuring how accurately we can match keypoint by corresponding random patches between query and reference videos.

Method	Spatial alignment accuracy ↑
ImageNet features	0.153
Features from Mask-RCNN [18]	0.202
Features from cycle-consistency based tracker [52]	0.060
Features from Kinetics [22] action classification model	0.150
Features from action classification	0.157
Our features (using tracks from [52] to train)	**0.284**

aligning keypoint tracks provided in the Penn Action dataset. Given a track of a keypoint in video V, we measure the accuracy which the aligned track corresponds to the same keypoint in video W. We report this accuracy in Table 3. Note that this alignment uses keypoint tracks only for performing inference and quantitative evaluations. Model was trained using tracks from Wang $et\ al.$ [52] on foreground patches as before.

4.4 Ablations

Additionally, we also compare to 3 variants of our model, to understand the effectiveness of the different parts of our model. We discuss spatial alignment results (as measured by accuracy at keypoint track correspondence).

Impact of Quality of Tracks Used During Training. We experiment with using tracks derived from ground truth key-point labels during training. We find that this leads to better features, and achieves a keypoint track correspondence accuracy of 0.650 $vs.$ 0.551 when using tracks from Wang $et\ al.$ [52]. The next ablations also uses ground-truth tracks for training.

Not searching for temporal alignment during training. Our formulation searches over temporal alignment at training time. This is done by searching

Table 3. Track Correspondence on Penn Action Dataset [59]: We measure spatial alignment by measuring how accurately we can match keypoint tracks across videos. We compare our learned cross-video features with those obtained by pre-training on ImageNet and for action classification on the Penn Action dataset.

Method	Track correspondence accuracy ↑
ImageNet features	0.252
Features from action classification	0.110
Our features (using tracks from [52] to train)	**0.551**

for frames to jump between the two videos (max over n, p and q in Eq. 2). In this ablation, we learn features without searching for this temporal alignment, *i.e.* simply assume that the frames are aligned. The resulting features are worse at spatial alignment (keypoint track correspondence accuracy of 0.584 *vs.* 0.650).

Importance of Reference Video Retrieval. As a first step for spatio-temporal alignment, we retrieve the best video to align. In order to ablate the performance of this retrieval task, we measure the average keypoint track correspondence accuracy by aligning all the queries to all reference videos. We observe that the accuracy drops by 15% indicating that the retrieval step is effective at choosing relevant videos.

4.5 Comparison on Pouring Dataset

We now show the necessity of learning spatial alignment by considering a spatial downstream task of predicting contact locations. We annotate the Pouring Dataset [38] with locations of the contact point between the human thumb and the cup. We train a lin-

Method	Accuracy ↑
ImageNet features	27.1%
TCC [9]	32.7%
Ours	**38.6%**

ear 1×1 convolution layer on the spatial features in various models to predict the probability of the contact point. We compare features from our model that are sensitive to locations of objects, *vs.* features from Dwibedi *et al.* [9] that only focus on learning good temporal alignment. We split the data into 210 training and 116 test images. We train a linear classifier on top of different features. Table shows the Percentage of Correct Keypoint (PCK) [55] metric for the localization of this contact point within a 16px × 16px neighborhood of the ground truth. We see that our features perform better than both ImageNet features, and features from [9]. Thus, features that are sensitive to object locations are essential for obtaining a rich understanding of videos.

5 Discussion

In this work, we address the problem of video understanding in the paradigm of "understanding via associations". More specifically, we address the problem of finding dense spatial and temporal correspondences between two videos. We propose a weakly supervised cycle-consistency loss based approach to learn meaningful representations that can be used to obtain patch, track and frame level correspondences. In our experimental evaluation, we show that the features learned are more effective at encoding the states of the patches or objects involved in the videos compared to existing work. We demonstrate the efficacy of the spatio-temporal alignment through exhaustive qualitative and quantitative experiments conducted on multiple datasets.

References

1. Agrawal, P., Carreira, J., Malik, J.: Learning to see by moving. In: ICCV (2015)
2. Alayrac, J.B., Sivic, J., Laptev, I., Lacoste-Julien, S.: Joint discovery of object states and manipulation actions. In: ICCV (2017)
3. Horn, B.K, Schunck, B.G.: Determining optical flow. Artif. Intell. 17(1–3) (1981)
4. Carreira, J., Zisserman, A.: Quo vadis, action recognition? a new model and the kinetics dataset. In: CVPR (2017)
5. Damen, D., et al.: Scaling egocentric vision: The epic-kitchens dataset. In: ECCV (2018)
6. Deng, J., Dong, W., Socher, R., Li, L.J., Li, K., Fei-Fei, L.: ImageNet: a Large-Scale Hierarchical Image Database. In: CVPR (2009)
7. Denton, E., Fergus, R.: Stochastic video generation with a learned prior. In: ICML (2018)
8. Doersch, C., Gupta, A., Efros, A.A.: Unsupervised visual representation learning by context prediction. In: ICCV (2015)
9. Dwibedi, D., Aytar, Y., Tompson, J., Sermanet, P., Zisserman, A.: Temporal cycle-consistency learning. In: CVPR (2019)
10. Feichtenhofer, C., Fan, H., Malik, J., He, K.: Slowfast networks for video recognition. In: ICCV (2019)
11. Fouhey, D.F., Kuo, W., Efros, A.A., Malik, J.: From lifestyle vlogs to everyday interactions. In: CVPR (2018)
12. Garro, V., Fusiello, A., Savarese, S.: Label transfer exploiting three-dimensional structure for semantic segmentation. In: Proceedings of the 6th International Conference on Computer Vision/Computer Graphics Collaboration Techniques and Applications (2013)
13. Girdhar, R., Carreira, J., Doersch, C., Zisserman, A.: Video action transformer network. In: CVPR (2019)
14. Godard, C., Mac Aodha, O., Brostow, G.J.: Unsupervised monocular depth estimation with left-right consistency. In: CVPR (2017)
15. Goyal, R., et al.: The "something something" video database for learning and evaluating visual common sense. In: ICCV, vol. 1 (2017)
16. Gu, C., et al.: Ava: a video dataset of spatio-temporally localized atomic visual actions. In: CVPR (2018)
17. Ham, B., Cho, M., Schmid, C., Ponce, J.: Proposal flow. In: CVPR (2016)
18. He, K., Gkioxari, G., Dollár, P., Girshick, R.: Mask R-CNN. In: ICCV (2017)
19. He, K., Zhang, X., Ren, S., Sun, J.: Deep residual learning for image recognition. In: CVPR (2016)
20. Jayaraman, D., Grauman, K.: Learning image representations tied to ego-motion. In: ICCV (2015)

21. Kalal, Z., Mikolajczyk, K., Matas, J.: Forward-backward error: automatic detection of tracking failures. In: ICPR (2010)
22. Kay, W., et al.: The kinetics human action video dataset. arXiv preprint arXiv:1705.06950 (2017)
23. Kim, J., Liu, C., Sha, F., Grauman, K.: Deformable spatial pyramid matching for fast dense correspondences. In: CVPR (2013)
24. Kingma, D.P., Ba, J.: Adam: A method for stochastic optimization. arXiv preprint arXiv:1412.6980 (2014)
25. Krizhevsky, A., Sutskever, I., Hinton, G.E.: Imagenet classification with deep convolutional neural networks. In: NIPS (2012)
26. Lee, A.X., Zhang, R., Ebert, F., Abbeel, P., Finn, C., Levine, S.: Stochastic adversarial video prediction (2018)
27. Lin, T.Y., et al.: Microsoft COCO: Common objects in context. In: ECCV (2014)
28. Liu, C., Yuen, J., Torralba, A.: Nonparametric scene parsing: Label transfer via dense scene alignment. In: CVPR (2009)
29. Liu, C., Yuen, J., Torralba, A.: Sift flow: Dense correspondence across scenes and its applications. TPAMI **33**(5), 978-994 (2010)
30. Lowe, D.G.: Distinctive image features from scale-invariant keypoints. IJCV **60**(2), 91–110 (2004). https://doi.org/10.1023/B:VISI.0000029664.99615.94
31. Lucas, B.D., Kanade, T., et al.: An iterative image registration technique with an application to stereo vision (1981)
32. Mémin, E., Pérez, P.: Dense estimation and object-based segmentation of the optical flow with robust techniques. IEEE Trans. Image Process. **7**(5), 703–719 (1998)
33. Misra, I., Zitnick, C.L., Hebert, M.: Shuffle and learn: unsupervised learning using temporal order verification. In: Leibe, B., Matas, J., Sebe, N., Welling, M. (eds.) ECCV 2016. LNCS, vol. 9905, pp. 527–544. Springer, Cham (2016). https://doi.org/10.1007/978-3-319-46448-0_32
34. Nagarajan, T., Feichtenhofer, C., Grauman, K.: Grounded human-object interaction hotspots from video. In: ICCV (2019)
35. Pathak, D., Girshick, R., Dollár, P., Darrell, T., Hariharan, B.: Learning features by watching objects move. In: CVPR (2017)
36. Rocco, I., Arandjelović, R., Sivic, J.: End-to-end weakly-supervised semantic alignment. In: CVPR (2018)
37. Rubinstein, M., Joulin, A., Kopf, J., Liu, C.: Unsupervised joint object discovery and segmentation in internet images. In: CVPR (2013)
38. Sermanet, P., Lynch, C., Chebotar, Y., Hsu, J., Jang, E., Schaal, S., Levine, S., Brain, G.: Time-contrastive networks: Self-supervised learning from video. In: ICRA. Pouring dataset licensed under (CC BY 4.0) (2018)
39. Sethi, I.K., Jain, R.: Finding trajectories of feature points in a monocular image sequence. TPAMI (1) (1987)
40. Sigurdsson, G.A., Varol, G., Wang, X., Farhadi, A., Laptev, I., Gupta, A.: Hollywood in homes: crowdsourcing data collection for activity understanding. In: ECCV (2016)
41. Simonyan, K., Zisserman, A.: Two-stream convolutional networks for action recognition in videos. In: NIPS (2014)
42. Singh, S., Gupta, A., Efros, A.A.: Unsupervised discovery of mid-level discriminative patches. In: Fitzgibbon, A., Lazebnik, S., Perona, P., Sato, Y., Schmid, C. (eds.) ECCV 2012. LNCS, vol. 7573, pp. 73–86. Springer, Heidelberg (2012). https://doi.org/10.1007/978-3-642-33709-3_6
43. Sun, D., Roth, S., Black, M.J.: Secrets of optical flow estimation and their principles. In: CVPR (2010)

44. Sun, D., Yang, X., Liu, M.Y., Kautz, J.: PWC-net: CNNS for optical flow using pyramid, warping, and cost volume. In: CVPR (2018)
45. Tran, D., Bourdev, L.D., Fergus, R., Torresani, L., Paluri, M.: C3D: generic features for video analysis. CoRR, abs/1412.0767 2(7) (2014)
46. Varol, G., Laptev, I., Schmid, C.: Long-term temporal convolutions for action recognition. TPAMI **40**(6), 1510–1517 (2017)
47. Wang, H., Ullah, M.M., Klaser, A., Laptev, I., Schmid, C.: Evaluation of local spatio-temporal features for action recognition. In: BMVC (2009)
48. Wang, L., Xiong, Y., Wang, Z., Qiao, Yu., Lin, D., Tang, X., Van Gool, L.: Temporal segment networks: towards good practices for deep action recognition. In: Leibe, B., Matas, J., Sebe, N., Welling, M. (eds.) ECCV 2016. LNCS, vol. 9912, pp. 20–36. Springer, Cham (2016). https://doi.org/10.1007/978-3-319-46484-8_2
49. Wang, X., Farhadi, A., Gupta, A.: Actions transformations. In: CVPR (2016)
50. Wang, X., Girshick, R., Gupta, A., He, K.: Non-local neural networks. In: CVPR (2018)
51. Wang, X., Gupta, A.: Unsupervised learning of visual representations using videos. In: ICCV (2015)
52. Wang, X., Jabri, A., Efros, A.A.: Learning correspondence from the cycle-consistency of time. In: CVPR (2019)
53. Wu, C.Y., Feichtenhofer, C., Fan, H., He, K., Krahenbuhl, P., Girshick, R.: Long-term feature banks for detailed video understanding. In: CVPR (2019)
54. Xie, S., Sun, C., Huang, J., Tu, Z., Murphy, K.: Rethinking spatiotemporal feature learning: Speed-accuracy trade-offs in video classification. In: ECCV (2018)
55. Yang, Y., Ramanan, D.: Articulated human detection with flexible mixtures of parts. TPAMI (2012)
56. Yeung, S., Russakovsky, O., Jin, N., Andriluka, M., Mori, G., Fei-Fei, L.: Every moment counts: dense detailed labeling of actions in complex videos. Int. J. Comput. Vision **126**(2), 375–389 (2017). https://doi.org/10.1007/s11263-017-1013-y
57. Zhang, H., Xiao, J., Quan, L.: Supervised label transfer for semantic segmentation of street scenes. In: Daniilidis, K., Maragos, P., Paragios, N. (eds.) ECCV 2010. LNCS, vol. 6315, pp. 561–574. Springer, Heidelberg (2010). https://doi.org/10.1007/978-3-642-15555-0_41
58. Zhang, R., Isola, P., Efros, A.A.: Split-brain autoencoders: Unsupervised learning by cross-channel prediction. In: CVPR (2017)
59. Zhang, W., Zhu, M., Derpanis, K.G.: From actemes to action: a strongly-supervised representation for detailed action understanding. In: ICCV (2013)
60. Zhou, T., Jae Lee, Y., Yu, S.X., Efros, A.A.: Flowweb: joint image set alignment by weaving consistent, pixel-wise correspondences. In: CVPR (2015)
61. Zhou, T., Krahenbuhl, P., Aubry, M., Huang, Q., Efros, A.A.: Learning dense correspondence via 3d-guided cycle consistency. In: CVPR (2016)
62. Zhu, J.Y., Park, T., Isola, P., Efros, A.A.: Unpaired image-to-image translation using cycle-consistent adversarial networks. In: ICCV (2017)

Neural Wireframe Renderer: Learning Wireframe to Image Translations

Yuan Xue$^{(\boxtimes)}$, Zihan Zhou, and Xiaolei Huang

College of Information Sciences and Technology, The Pennsylvania State University,
University Park, PA 16802, USA
yuanxue@psu.edu123710290

Abstract. In architecture and computer-aided design, wireframes (*i.e.*, line-based models) are widely used as basic 3D models for design evaluation and fast design iterations. However, unlike a full design file, a wireframe model lacks critical information, such as detailed shape, texture, and materials, needed by a conventional renderer to produce 2D renderings of the objects or scenes. In this paper, we bridge the information gap by generating photo-realistic rendering of indoor scenes from wireframe models in an image translation framework. While existing image synthesis methods can generate visually pleasing images for common objects such as faces and birds, these methods do not explicitly model and preserve essential structural constraints in a wireframe model, such as junctions, parallel lines, and planar surfaces. To this end, we propose a novel model based on a structure-appearance joint representation learned from both images and wireframes. In our model, structural constraints are explicitly enforced by learning a joint representation in a shared encoder network that must support the generation of both images and wireframes. Experiments on a wireframe-scene dataset show that our wireframe-to-image translation model significantly outperforms the state-of-the-art methods in both visual quality and structural integrity of generated images.

1 Introduction

Recently, driven by the success of generative adversarial networks (GANs) [8] and image translation techniques [16,57], there has been a growing interest in developing data-driven methods for a variety of image synthesis applications, such as image style transfer [17,19], super-resolution [22], enhancement [53], text-to-image generation [52], domain adaption [12,34], just to name a few. In this work, we study a new image synthesis task, dubbed *wireframe-to-image translation*, in which the goal is to convert a wireframe (*i.e.*, a line-based skeletal representation) of a man-made environment to a photo-realistic rendering of the scene (Fig. 1). In the fields of visual arts, architecture, and computer-aided design, the wireframe representation is an important intermediate step for producing novel designs of man-made environments. For example, commercial

Electronic supplementary material The online version of this chapter (https://doi.org/10.1007/978-3-030-58574-7_17) contains supplementary material, which is available to authorized users.

© Springer Nature Switzerland AG 2020
A. Vedaldi et al. (Eds.): ECCV 2020, LNCS 12371, pp. 279–295, 2020.
https://doi.org/10.1007/978-3-030-58574-7_17

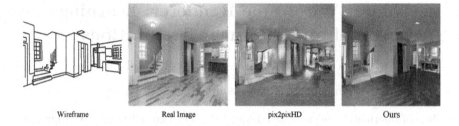

Wireframe   Real Image   pix2pixHD   Ours

Fig. 1. Wireframe-to-image translation: given the wireframe of a man-made environment, the goal is to generate a photo-realistic rendering of the scene.

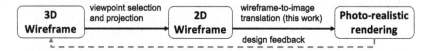

Fig. 2. Our envisioned workflow for design applications.

computer-aided design software such as AutoCAD allows designers to create 3D wireframe models as basic 3D designs for evaluation and fast design iterations.

In practice, for designers to quickly validate their design and obtain feedback from customers, it is often necessary to convert such a 3D wireframe into a photo-realistic rendering of the scene in real-time. However, compared to a full design file, a wireframe model lacks information needed by a conventional rendering engine, such as detailed shape and texture information as well as materials.

In this paper, we address the need for generating 2D renderings from wireframe models in design applications. Figure 2 illustrates our envisioned workflow, in which a 3D wireframe is first projected to the image plane given a viewpoint chosen by the user. Then, a deep network is trained to convert the 2D wireframe into a realistic scene image. Note that, compared to edge maps and sketches, wireframes contain precise information that encodes 3D geometric structure such as salient straight lines and junctions while being more sparse and ignoring lines due to planar texture. As such, an image generated given a wireframe input should respect the geometric constraints encoded in it, and should have pixel-level correspondence around straight lines and junctions where lines intersect. This requirement arises from the fact that human perception of 3D is highly dependent on recognizing structures like those encoded in a wireframe; even small violations of such constraints would make a generated image look unnatural.

State-of-the-art image translation models such as pix2pixHD [46] have difficulty in generating images that preserve structures such as straight lines and their intersections (Fig. 1). This may be due to that these models are designed for other types of input modalities, as illustrated in (Fig. 3). Inputs that are semantic segmentation maps emphasize object instance- or part-level correspondence rather than pixel-level correspondence; scribbles in free-hand sketches usually do not strictly map to lines or curves in photographic images; and edges often do not contain complete and accurate structure information and make no distinction between salient structural lines and planar texture-induced lines.

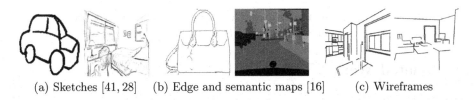

(a) Sketches [41, 28]   (b) Edge and semantic maps [16]   (c) Wireframes

Fig. 3. Comparison of different input modalities in image translation tasks. Compared with other modalities, wireframes contain more prominent structural constraints in terms of straight lines and their relationships (*e.g.*, junctions, parallelism, and orthogonality), while being sparser and containing less semantic information.

In this work, we propose a structure-appearance joint representation learning scheme that utilizes a paired wireframe-image dataset to learn to generate images with *structural integrity*. Our assumption is that there exists a shared latent space for encoding both structural and appearance constraints of a scene. Accordingly, we design our wireframe-to-image translation model to include one encoder and two decoders (see Fig. 4). The encoder encodes the input wireframe to a joint representation, the wireframe decoder reconstructs the original wireframe from the joint representation, and the scene decoder transforms the representation into a photo-realistic indoor image. Further, the jointly generated wireframe-image pairs are used to train a cGAN-like [32] discriminator, which takes the generated pairs as fake samples and groundtruth wireframe-image pairs as real samples. Such a design enables us to better preserve structural integrity and pixel-level correspondences in two ways. *First*, the encoder together with the wireframe decoder branch can be regarded as an autoencoder for wireframes, which helps enforce precise pixel-level correspondences for salient structures. *Second*, the cGAN-like discriminator provides an adversarial loss that can help train the model to adaptively learn the difference between the reconstructed wireframe-image pairs and groundtruth pairs.

We demonstrate the effectiveness of our proposed model by conducting extensive experiments on a dataset of various indoor scene images with ground truth wireframe annotations [13]. As shown in Fig. 1 and results in Sect. 4, by introducing a joint representation learning scheme combined with both adversarial loss and perceptual loss, our proposed wireframe renderer generates images that not only have higher visual realism than prior arts [1, 16, 37, 46], but also adhere much better to structural constraints encoded in the input wireframes.

To summarize, the main contributions of our work are:

– We propose a supervised image to image translation model which generates realistic image renderings from wireframe inputs. The architecture including a novel structure-appearance joint representation and multiple loss functions for the end-to-end network are carefully designed to ensure that the generated synthetic images adhere to wireframe structural constraints.
– To the best of our knowledge, we are the first to conduct wireframe-to-image translation experiments for high-fidelity indoor scene rendering using a challenging indoor scene wireframe dataset. Both quantitative and qualitative

results of our experiments indicate the superiority of our proposed method compared with previous state-of-the-art methods.

2   Related Work

Wireframe Parsing. Several methods have been developed recently to extract wireframes from images [13,50,55,56]. In this paper, we study the inverse problem of translating wireframes to photo-realistic images.

Generative Adversarial Networks. Generative adversarial networks (GANs) [8], especially the conditional GANs [32], have been widely used in image synthesis applications such as text-to-image generation [52] and image-to-image translation [16,57]. However, training GANs is known to be difficult and often requires a large training set in order to generate satisfactory results. Some attempts have be made to stabilize the GAN training [9,31], as well as use coarse-to-fine generation to get better results [18,52]. One work that explores structure information in GAN training is [47]. It utilizes RGB-D data and factorizes the image generation process into synthesis of a surface normal map and then the conditional generation of a corresponding image.

Supervised Image-to-Image Translation. The line of research that most closely relate to our work is supervised image-to-image translation, in which input-output image pairs are available during training. Prior work [1,16,46] has been focusing on leveraging different losses to generate high-quality output images. While pixel-wise losses, such as the ℓ_1 loss, are the most natural choices, using ℓ_1 loss alone has been shown to generate blurry images [16,17]. To mitigate the problem, Isola *et al.* [16] uses a combination of ℓ_1 loss and a conditional adversarial loss. To avoid the instability of adversarial training, Chen and Koltun [1] implement a cascaded refinement network trained via feature matching based on a pre-trained visual perception network. Recently, the perceptual loss [6] has been shown to be effective in measuring the perceptual similarity between images [54]. Wang *et al.* [45] integrates the perceptual adversarial loss and the generative adversarial loss to adaptively learn the discrepancy between the output and ground-truth images. Combining the merits from previous works, Wang *et al.* [46] generate high quality images with coarse-to-fine generation, multi-scale discriminators, and an improved adversarial loss.

Other works focus on improving the performance for a certain input modality. For *semantic maps*, Qi *et al.* [38] first retrieve segments from external memory, then combine the segments to synthesize a realistic image. Liu *et al.* [26] predict convolutional kernels from semantic labels and use a feature-pyramid semantics-embedding discriminator for better semantic alignment. Park *et al.* [37] modulate the normalization layer with learned parameters to avoid washing out the semantic information. For *sketches*, Sangkloy *et al.* [41] generate realistic images by augmenting the training data with multiple sketch styles; SketchyGAN [2] improves the information flow during training by injecting the input sketch at multiple scales; Lu *et al.* [28] use sketch in a joint image completion framework to handle the misalignment between sketches and photographic objects.

Joint Representation Learning. For applications that involve two or more variables, the traditional one-way mapping of GANs may be insufficient to guarantee the correspondence between the variables. Conditional GANs [3,5,32,36] learn to infer one variable from another in both directions. ALI [7], Cycle-GAN [57], and their variants (*e.g.*, [20,24,51]) learn the cross-domain joint distribution matching via bidirectional mapping of two examples.

In unsupervised image-to-image translation, several works [14,23,25] propose to map images from multiple domains to a joint latent space. To further learn instance level correspondences, DA-GAN [29] incorporate a consistency loss in the latent space between the input and output images. However, due to the lack of paired training data, it is hard for these methods to generate outputs that match all the details (*e.g.*, semantic parts) in the input images.

When paired data is available, learning a joint representation has been proved to be an effective way to capture the correspondences. To promote instance awareness in unsupervised image translation, InstaGAN [33] simultaneously translates image and the corresponding segmentation mask. Recent work on domain adaption [4] jointly predict segmentation and depth maps in order to better align the predictions of the task network for two domains.

3   Methodology

In this work, we propose to add an intermediate step in the image synthesis process to improve structural integrity and pixel-level correspondence. Specifically, we learn a structure-appearance joint representation from the input wireframe, and use the joint representation to simultaneous generate corresponding scene images and reconstructed wireframes as output. As shown in Fig. 4, The overall pipeline of our wireframe renderer consists of an encoder, a wireframe decoder, a scene image decoder, and a discriminator.

In the following, we introduce the theoretical background and architecture of our model in Sect. 3.1, and discuss implementation details in Sect. 3.2.

3.1   Learning Joint Representation for Wireframe-to-Image Translation

Formally, we measure the uncertainty of generating the correct wireframe from a joint representation of wireframe and scene image using *Conditional Entropy*. The conditional entropy of an input wireframe x conditioned on its corresponding joint representation e is defined as

$$H(x|e) = \mathbb{E}_{x \sim P(x|e)} \log P(x|e), \tag{1}$$

where $e \sim \hat{Q}(x, y)$ follows an estimated joint distribution $\hat{Q}$ of wireframe x and indoor scene image y, and is computed by an encoder network Enc. Under a supervised training scenario with paired wireframe and scene image, for simplicity, we assume that the mapping from x to e is deterministic so that $e = \text{Enc}(x)$

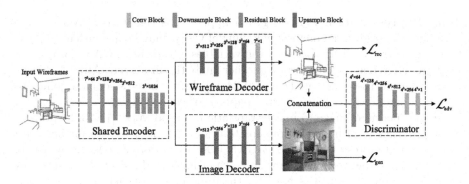

Fig. 4. Network architecture of our wireframe-to-image translation model. The numbers above each block indicate the kernel size and the output channel number.

is a joint representation of x and y. Since the mapping from e to x should also be deterministic when e contains a certain input, we have $H(x|e = \text{Enc}(x)) = 0$.

Since we do not have the ground truth distribution of $P(x|e)$, we approximate it with a decoder network Dec_w for reconstructing the wireframe from the joint representation. The conditional entropy of Dec_w is

$$
\begin{aligned}
\mathcal{L}_{ce} &= \mathbb{E}_{\hat{x} \sim P(x|e)} \log \text{Dec}_w(\hat{x}|e) \\
&= H(x|e) + \text{KL}(P(x|e)||\text{Dec}_w(\hat{x}|e)) \geq H(x|e) = 0.
\end{aligned}
\tag{2}
$$

Thus, minimizing the conditional entropy is equivalent to reducing the KL divergence between the decoder and the ground truth posterior. To approximate the $\mathcal{L}_{ce}$, given a mini-batch of N wireframes x_n, we define the wireframe reconstruction objective as

$$
\min_{\theta, \theta_w} \mathcal{L}_{\text{rec}} = \frac{1}{N} \sum_{n=1}^{N} \Big(\alpha_w ||x_n - \text{Dec}_w(\text{Enc}(x_n))||_1 + \beta_w \text{MS-SSIM}(x_n, \text{Dec}_w(\text{Enc}(x_n))) \Big),
\tag{3}
$$

where θ, θ_w are the parameters of encoder and wireframe decoder, respectively. The first term is the ℓ_1 distance between the original wireframe and the reconstructed wireframe. The second term is the Multiscale Structural Similarity (MS-SSIM) loss to compensate the ℓ_1 distance, as MS-SSIM is more perceptually preferable. More details of MS-SSIM can be found in [49]. α_w and β_w are scaling factors to balance the two loss terms.

In addition to the decoder branch that reconstructs the wireframe, we have another decoder Dec_s that generates the corresponding scene image from the learned joint representation. By having the two decoder branches share the same encoder, the encoder network is forced to learn both structure and appearance information as well as their correspondence so that the generated image can have better structural alignment with the reconstructed wireframe.

Given a mini-batch of N wireframes x_n and corresponding scene images y_n, we define the objective for scene generation as

$$\min_{\theta,\theta_s} \mathcal{L}_{\text{gen}} = \frac{1}{N} \sum_{n=1}^{N} \Big(\alpha_s ||y_n - \text{Dec}_s(\text{Enc}(x_n))||_1 + \beta_s D_{\text{perc}}(y_n, \text{Dec}_s(\text{Enc}(x_n))) \Big), \quad (4)$$

where the scene decoder network is parameterized by θ_s. The perceptual loss D_{perc} is defined as

$$D_{\text{perc}}(y, \hat{y}) = \sum_l \frac{1}{H_l W_l} ||\phi_l(y) - \phi_l(\hat{y})||_2^2, \quad (5)$$

where ϕ_l is the activations of the lth layer of a perceptual network with shape $C_l \times H_l \times W_l$. In our experiments, we use the 5 convolutional layers from VGG16 [43] pre-trained on ImageNet [40] to extract visual features, and unit-normalize the activations in the channel dimension as in [54].

Further, we propose an adversarial loss [8] to adaptively learn the difference between the reconstructed wireframe/generated image and the groundtruth. Denote $\hat{x}$ and $\hat{y}$ as the reconstructed wireframe and generated scene image, the adversarial objective is

$$\max_{\theta_d} \min_{\theta,\theta_w,\theta_s} \mathcal{L}_{\text{adv}} = \mathbb{E}_{x,y} \log \sigma(\text{Dis}(x, y)) + \mathbb{E}_{x,y} \log(1 - \sigma(\text{Dis}(\hat{x}, \hat{y}))), \quad (6)$$

where $\sigma(\cdot)$ is the sigmoid function and θ_d represents the parameters of the conditional discriminator network, Dis. For simplicity, we omit the representations such as $x \sim P_x$ in all adversarial objectives.

Therefore, the full objective for end-to-end training of our model is

$$\max_{\theta_d} \min_{\theta,\theta_w,\theta_s} \mathcal{L} = \mathcal{L}_{\text{rec}} + \mathcal{L}_{\text{gen}} + \lambda \mathcal{L}_{\text{adv}}, \quad (7)$$

where λ is another scaling factor to control the impact of the adversarial loss.

3.2   Implementation Details

In our wireframe renderer model[1], the encoder network consists of 5 convolution blocks. The first block uses 7×7 convolution kernels with stride 1 and reflection padding 3. The remaining 4 downsample blocks have kernel size 3, stride 2 and reflection padding 1. Each convolutional layer is followed by one batch normalization [15] layer and one LeakyReLU [30] activation. The last downsample block is followed by 4 residual blocks [10] with 3×3 convolution and ReLU activation.

The decoder consists of 4 upsample blocks. To avoid the characteristic artifacts introduced by the transpose convolution [35], each upsample block contains one 3×3 sub-pixel convolution [42] followed by batch normalization and ReLU activation. The last block uses a 7×7 convolution followed by a tanh activation without normalization. The two decoder networks have similar architecture except in the last layer where the outputs have different channel dimensions.

---

[1] Code available at https://github.com/YuanXue1993/WireframeRenderer.

We follow [16] and use the PatchGAN [27] discriminator for adversarial training. We use LSGAN [31] for stabilizing the adversarial training. The scaling factors in our final model are $\alpha_w = 1, \beta_w = 1, \alpha_s = 15, \beta_s = 4$ and $\lambda = 1$. These values are determined through multiple runs of experiments. The training is done using Adam optimizer [21] with initial learning rate $2e - 3$. The learning rate is decayed every 30 epochs with rate 0.5. The batch size is 16 and the maximum number of training epochs is 500.

All training images are first resized to 307×307, then randomly cropped to 256×256. A random horizontal flipping and random adjustment of brightness, contrast and saturation are applied for data augmentation. During inference, all images are re-scaled to 256×256 with no further processing.

4 Experiments

4.1 Experiment Settings

Dataset. The wireframe dataset [13] consists of 5,462 images of man-made environments, including both indoor and outdoor scenes, and manually annotated wireframes. Each wireframe is represented by a set of junctions, a set of line segments, and the relationships among them. Note that, unlike general line segments, the wireframe annotations consider structural elements of the scene only. Specifically, line segments associated with the scene structure are included, whereas line segments associated with texture (*e.g.*, carpet), irregular or curved objects (*e.g.*, humans and sofa), and shadows are ignored. Thus, to translate the wireframe into a realistic image, it is critical for a method to handle incomplete information about scene semantics and objects.

As we focus on the indoor scene image generation task in this paper, we filter out all outdoor or irrelevant images in the dataset. This results in 4,511 training images and 422 test images. The dataset contains various indoor scenes such as bedroom, living room, and kitchen. It also contains objects such as humans which are irrelevant to our task. The limited size and the scene diversity of the dataset make the task of generating interior design images even more challenging.

Baselines. We compare our image translation models with several state-of-the-art models, namely the Cascaded Refinement Network (CRN) [1], pix2pix [16], pix2pixHD [46], and SPADE [37]. For fair comparison, we adapt from the authors' original implementations wherever possible. For CRN, we use six refine modules, starting from 8×8 all the way up to 256×256. For pix2pix model, we use UNet [39] backbone model as in the original paper. We decrease the weight of pixel loss from 100 to 50 since the original weight fails to generate any meaningful results. For pix2pixHD model, we use two discriminators with different scales and the discriminator feature matching loss combined with the GAN loss. Since there is no instance map available for our problem, we train the pix2pixHD model with wireframes only. For SPADE, we use at most 256 feature channels to fit in the single GPU training.

Wireframe   CRN   pix2pix   pix2pixHD   SPADE   Ours   Real Image

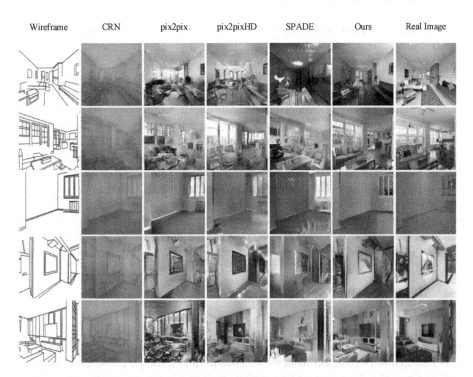

Fig. 5. Qualitative comparison for image translation models on the test set. Each row represents one wireframe/image pair and each column represents one model. The input wireframes and corresponding groundtruth images are included as references.

Besides, to verify the benefit of joint representation, we also train a variant of our method in which we remove the wireframe decoder branch. All the other components in the network are the same as our full model and we train it with the same image generation loss and adversarial loss for wireframe-to-image translation. For all baseline models involving adversarial training, since there is no wireframe predicted, the generated images are paired with their input wireframes as the input to the discriminator.

4.2   Qualitative Comparisons

The qualitative comparisons for the translation models are shown in Fig. 5. We first note that the CRN model trained on the wireframe dataset fails to generate meaningful results, despite that we have experimented with different hyperparameter settings. One possible reason is that the CRN is originally designed for image synthesis based on semantic layouts. However, the wireframe itself contains little semantic information (*e.g.*, object categories), thus the model has to infer such information from the structure information presented in the wireframe. Moreover, CRN model is the only model which does not use adversarial training. This may suggest that adversarial training is important in the wireframe-to-image translation task.

Except for the CRN, all other models are able to generate meaningful synthetic images. However, in the images generated by pix2pix and pix2pixHD, structural integrity is not always well preserved. In general, the generated images of these models cannot align well with the input wireframes, especially when structure information is complicated (*e.g.*, the furniture areas in the first and second rows of Fig. 5). Further, these methods generate noticeable artifacts in regions where structure information is sparse (*e.g.*, the white walls in the third row of Fig. 5). For SPADE [37], structural information is better preserved, but the results contain more artifacts than those of pix2pixHD and appear to be less realistic (*e.g.*, artifacts in the first, second, and fifth rows of Fig. 5). In contrast, our model generates images with best quality among all models and preserves the structure and correspondence very well. Compared with the real images in the test set, the synthetic images of our final model are almost photo-realistic.

4.3   Quantitative Evaluations

FID, LPIPS, and SSIM Scores. We first report results based on various standard metrics for image synthesis. Fréchet inception distance (FID) [11] is a popular evaluation metric for image synthesis tasks, especially for GAN models. FID features are extracted from an Inception-v3 [44] model pre-trained on ImageNet. Since the dataset contains various indoor scenes, we use the pre-trained model without fine-tuning. Lower FID score indicates a better generation result.

For our task, since we have the ground truth images associated with the input wireframes, we also calculate paired LPIPS and SSIM scores between the synthetic images and the real images. The learned perceptual image patch similarity (LPIPS) [54] is essentially a perceptual loss. It has been shown to have better agreement with human perception than traditional perceptual metrics such as SSIM [48] and PSNR. We use Eq. (5) to calculate the perceptual distance between the synthetic image and the real image. Note that in our experiments we calculate the perceptual distance instead of the similarity, thus the lower the LPIPS score, the better quality of the generated images. The feature extractor is a pre-trained VGG16 model as in our model training.

In Table 1(left), we report results of all methods except for CRN, since CRN fails to generate meaningful results. As one can see, pix2pixHD outperforms pix2pix in all metrics. Compared with the pix2pix, pix2pixHD adopts multi-scale discriminators and use the adversarial perceptual loss, leading to better performance in the image translation task. However, since the training dataset in our experiments has a limited size, a perceptual loss learned by adversarial training may not work as well as a perceptual loss computed by a pre-trained feature extractor. As shown in Table 1, our model without the joint representation learning achieves better performance than the pix2pixHD model.

Finally, our full model with the joint representation learning achieves the best performance across all metrics, as the images generated by the model better preserve the structure information encoded in the wireframes.

Table 1. Quantitative evaluation on the wireframe-to-image translation task. **Left:** Standard image synthesis metrics. For SSIM, the higher the better; For FID and LPIPS, the lower the better. **Right:** Wireframe parser scores using [55]. For sAP scores, the higher the better.

Method	FID↓	LPIPS↓	SSIM↑
pix2pix [16]	186.91	3.34	0.091
pix2pixHD [46]	153.36	3.25	0.080
SPADE [37]	93.90	2.95	0.086
Ours w/o JR	97.49	2.85	0.092
Ours	**70.73**	**2.77**	**0.102**

Method	sAP^5 ↑	sAP^{10} ↑	sAP^{15} ↑
pix2pix	7.8	10.0	11.1
pix2pixHD	10.6	13.6	15.1
SPADE	54.7	58.1	59.5
Ours w/o JR	26.7	34.4	37.5
Ours	**60.1**	**64.1**	**65.7**
Real images	58.9	62.9	64.7

Wireframe Detection Score. Since the focus of this work is to preserve structure information in the wireframe-to-image translation task, an important and more meaningful evaluation metric would be whether we can infer correct wireframes from the generated images or not.

To this end, we propose a wireframe detection score as a complimentary metric for evaluating the structural integrity in image translation systems. Specifically, we apply the state-of-the-art wireframe parser [55] to detect wireframes from the generated images. The wireframe parser outputs a vectorized wireframe that contains semantically meaningful and geometrically salient junctions and lines (Fig. 6). To evaluate the results, we follow [55] and use the *structural average precision (sAP)*, which is defined as the area under the precision-recall curve computed from a scored list of detected line segments on all test images. Here, a detected line is considered as a true positive if the distance between the predicted and ground truth end points is within a threshold θ.

Table 1(right) reports the sAP scores at $\theta = \{5, 10, 15\}$. As one can see, our full model outperforms all other methods. While SPADE also gets relatively high sAP scores by encoding wireframes in all normalization layers, their generated images contain more artifacts. In the last row of Table 1(right), we also report sAP scores obtained by applying the same wireframe parser [55] to the corresponding real images. Rather surprisingly, the images generated by our method even achieve higher sAP scores than the real images. After a close inspection of the results, we find that it is mainly because, when labeling wireframe, human annotators tend to miss some salient lines and junctions in the real images. In other words, there are often more salient lines and junctions in real images than those labelled in the ground truth. As a result, the detected wireframes from real images contain more false positives. In the meantime, the input provided to our model is just the annotated wireframes. Our model is able to faithfully preserve such information in the generated images.

Human Studies. We also conduct a human perception evaluation to compare the quality of generated images between our method and pix2pixHD, since SPADE results contain more artifacts. We show the ground truth wireframes

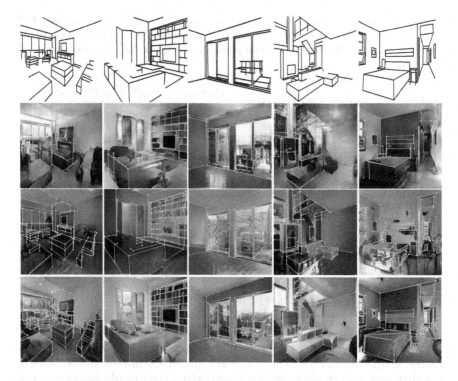

Fig. 6. Example wireframe detection results on synthesized images. **First row**: Input wireframe. **Second to fourth rows**: Detection results on images generated by pix2pixHD, SPADE, and our method, respectively. Wireframes are detected by the wireframe parser [55]. For fair comparison, no post-processing is done for the parser.

paired with images generated by our method and pix2pixHD to three workers. The workers are asked to evaluate synthetic images based on fidelity and the alignment to wireframes. They are given unlimited time to choose between our method, pix2pixHD, or "none" if both methods fail to generate realistic enough images or preserve the wireframe structure. We use all 422 test images for this evaluation. On average, the preference rates of pix2pixHD, our method, and "none" are $3.7\%, 65.1\%, 31.2\%$, respectively. The human study result further proves that our method can not only generate realistic renderings, but also respect the structure information encoded in wireframes.

4.4 Wireframe Manipulation

To provide additional insight to our model, and also to illustrate the potential use of our method in a realistic design application setting, we incrementally modify the input wireframes and check whether the generated scene images are updated in a meaningful way. As shown in Fig. 7, we manually edit some lines/junctions in the original wireframe. The results show that our model captures the changes in the wireframe and updates the generated image in a consistent fashion.

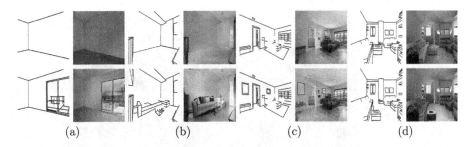

(a)   (b)   (c)   (d)

Fig. 7. Example wireframe manipulation results. **Odd columns**: Input wireframes; **Even columns**: Images generated by our model. Modifications include **(a)** adding exterior doors, **(b)** adding furniture set, **(c)** adding wall decoration, and **(d)** relocating a table in front of the sofa.

4.5 Color Guided Rendering

The previous experiments focus on using wireframes as the only input to generate color images. In this section, we introduce a color guided image generation process, which allows users to provide additional input that specifies the color theme of the rendered scene. A color guided model enables finer control of the rendering process and can be more applicable in real world design settings. Specifically, we encode a RGB color histogram (a 256×3 dimensional vector) as additional input into our joint representation. The input color histogram is first normalized to the range $[0, 1]$ then converted into the same size as the input via a linear layer. The input to our model is the concatenation of the wireframe and the transformed color histogram. On the decoder side, a linear layer and a sigmoid layer are used to reconstruct the color histogram from the synthesized image with a ℓ_1 loss. With our model, users can apply any color histogram from existing designs to an input wireframe to get a rendering result with desired color or style.

Figure 8 shows the results of the color guided generation process. Note how our model adapts to very different color schemes while maintaining consistent room layout and configuration: Even with unusual rust and emerald colors, our model responds well, for example, by replacing regular walls with crystal ones. This demonstrates the potential of our method in interactive and customized design.

4.6 Discussion

Failure Cases. While our model is able to capture structure information well, the input wireframes can be sparse and contain little semantic information such as objects. As shown in Fig. 9, when there is little wireframe information provided to the model, especially in the corner part, our model sometimes fails to generate visually meaningful results. We expect to mitigate this issue by training on a larger dataset containing more diverse images and wireframes, and providing other semantic inputs such as types of furniture to make the learning task easier.

Extensions. Our joint representation learning framework is general and may also benefit other image synthesis tasks. In fact, we have conducted preliminary

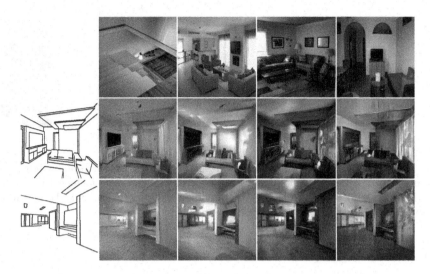

Fig. 8. Example color guided rendering results. First column shows the input wire-frames; first row shows the real images providing color guidance; the rest are images generated by our model.

Fig. 9. Failure examples generated by our model.

experiments on the noise-to-image generation task, in which we simultaneously generate paired scene image and wireframe from a noise input using the joint representation. We have obtained improved results over a baseline which generates the scene image only. Details are provided in the supplementary material.

5   Conclusion

In this paper, we study a new image synthesis task for design applications in which the input is a wireframe representation of a scene. By learning the joint representation in the shared latent space of wireframes and images, our wireframe render generates photo-realistic scene images with high structural integrity. In the future, we plan to extend our model to a wider range of design scenarios and consider semantic constraints alongside with structural constraints. We will also investigate generating image renderings directly from computer-aided design (CAD) models (in vector-graphics format) with different viewpoint projections.

Acknowledgement. This work is supported in part by NSF Award #1815491.

References

1. Chen, Q., Koltun, V.: Photographic image synthesis with cascaded refinement networks. In: ICCV, pp. 1511–1520 (2017)
2. Chen, W., Hays, J.: Sketchygan: Towards diverse and realistic sketch to image synthesis. In: CVPR, pp. 9416–9425 (2018)
3. Chen, X., Duan, Y., Houthooft, R., Schulman, J., Sutskever, I., Abbeel, P.: Infogan: interpretable representation learning by information maximizing generative adversarial nets. In: NIPS, pp. 2172–2180 (2016)
4. Chen, Y., Li, W., Chen, X., Gool, L.V.: Learning semantic segmentation from synthetic data: a geometrically guided input-output adaptation approach. In: CVPR, pp. 1841–1850 (2019)
5. Choi, Y., Choi, M., Kim, M., Ha, J.W., Kim, S., Choo, J.: Stargan: unified generative adversarial networks for multi-domain image-to-image translation. In: CVPR, pp. 8789–8797 (2018)
6. Dosovitskiy, A., Brox, T.: Generating images with perceptual similarity metrics based on deep networks. In: NIPS, pp. 658–666 (2016)
7. Dumoulin, V., et al.: Adversarially learned inference. In: ICLR (2017)
8. Goodfellow, I., et al.: Generative adversarial nets. In: NIPS, pp. 2672–2680 (2014)
9. Gulrajani, I., Ahmed, F., Arjovsky, M., Dumoulin, V., Courville, A.C.: Improved training of wasserstein gans. In: NIPS, pp. 5767–5777 (2017)
10. He, K., Zhang, X., Ren, S., Sun, J.: Deep residual learning for image recognition. In: CVPR, pp. 770–778 (2016)
11. Heusel, M., Ramsauer, H., Unterthiner, T., Nessler, B., Hochreiter, S.: Gans trained by a two time-scale update rule converge to a local nash equilibrium. In: NIPS, pp. 6626–6637 (2017)
12. Hoffman, J., et al.: Cycada: cycle-consistent adversarial domain adaptation. In: ICML, pp. 1994–2003 (2018)
13. Huang, K., Wang, Y., Zhou, Z., Ding, T., Gao, S., Ma, Y.: Learning to parse wireframes in images of man-made environments. In: CVPR, pp. 626–635 (2018)
14. Huang, X., Liu, M.Y., Belongie, S., Kautz, J.: Multimodal unsupervised image-to-image translation. In: ECCV, pp. 172–189 (2018)
15. Ioffe, S., Szegedy, C.: Batch normalization: accelerating deep network training by reducing internal covariate shift. In: ICML, pp. 448–456 (2015)
16. Isola, P., Zhu, J.Y., Zhou, T., Efros, A.A.: Image-to-image translation with conditional adversarial networks. In: CVPR, pp. 1125–1134 (2017)
17. Johnson, J., Alahi, A., Fei-Fei, L.: Perceptual losses for real-time style transfer and super-resolution. In: Leibe, B., Matas, J., Sebe, N., Welling, M. (eds.) ECCV 2016. LNCS, vol. 9906, pp. 694–711. Springer, Cham (2016). https://doi.org/10.1007/978-3-319-46475-6_43
18. Karras, T., Aila, T., Laine, S., Lehtinen, J.: Progressive growing of gans for improved quality, stability, and variation. In: ICLR (2018)
19. Karras, T., Laine, S., Aila, T.: A style-based generator architecture for generative adversarial networks. In: CVPR, pp. 4401–4410 (2019)
20. Kim, T., Cha, M., Kim, H., Lee, J.K., Kim, J.: Learning to discover cross-domain relations with generative adversarial networks. In: ICML, pp. 1857–1865. JMLR.org (2017)
21. Kingma, D.P., Ba, J.: Adam: a method for stochastic optimization. In: ICLR (2015)
22. Ledig, C., et al.: Photo-realistic single image super-resolution using a generative adversarial network. In: CVPR, pp. 4681–4690 (2017)

23. Lee, H., Tseng, H., Huang, J., Singh, M., Yang, M.: Diverse image-to-image translation via disentangled representations. In: ECCV, pp. 36–52 (2018)

24. Li, C., et al.: Alice: towards understanding adversarial learning for joint distribution matching. In: NIPS, pp. 5495–5503 (2017)

25. Liu, M.Y., Breuel, T., Kautz, J.: Unsupervised image-to-image translation networks. In: NIPS, pp. 700–708 (2017)

26. Liu, X., Yin, G., Shao, J., Wang, X., Li, H.: Learning to predict layout-to-image conditional convolutions for semantic image synthesis (2019). arXiv preprint arXiv:1910.06809

27. Long, J., Shelhamer, E., Darrell, T.: Fully convolutional networks for semantic segmentation. In: CVPR, pp. 3431–3440 (2015)

28. Lu, Y., Wu, S., Tai, Y., Tang, C.: Image generation from sketch constraint using contextual GAN. In: ECCV, pp. 213–228 (2018)

29. Ma, S., Fu, J., Wen Chen, C., Mei, T.: Da-gan: Instance-level image translation by deep attention generative adversarial networks. In: CVPR, pp. 5657–5666 (2018)

30. Maas, A.L., Hannun, A.Y., Ng, A.Y.: Rectifier nonlinearities improve neural network acoustic models. In: ICML (2013)

31. Mao, X., Li, Q., Xie, H., Lau, R.Y., Wang, Z., Paul Smolley, S.: Least squares generative adversarial networks. In: ICCV, pp. 2794–2802 (2017)

32. Mirza, M., Osindero, S.: Conditional generative adversarial nets (2014). arXiv preprint arXiv:1411.1784

33. Mo, S., Cho, M., Shin, J.: Instagan: instance-aware image-to-image translation. In: ICLR (2019)

34. Murez, Z., Kolouri, S., Kriegman, D.J., Ramamoorthi, R., Kim, K.: Image to image translation for domain adaptation. In: CVPR, pp. 4500–4509 (2018)

35. Odena, A., Dumoulin, V., Olah, C.: Deconvolution and checkerboard artifacts. Distill 1(10), e3 (2016)

36. Odena, A., Olah, C., Shlens, J.: Conditional image synthesis with auxiliary classifier gans. In: ICML, pp. 2642–2651 (2017)

37. Park, T., Liu, M.Y., Wang, T.C., Zhu, J.Y.: Semantic image synthesis with spatially-adaptive normalization. In: CVPR, pp. 2337–2346 (2019)

38. Qi, X., Chen, Q., Jia, J., Koltun, V.: Semi-parametric image synthesis. In: CVPR, pp. 8808–8816 (2018)

39. Ronneberger, O., Fischer, P., Brox, T.: U-Net: convolutional networks for biomedical image segmentation. In: Navab, N., Hornegger, J., Wells, W.M., Frangi, A.F. (eds.) MICCAI 2015. LNCS, vol. 9351, pp. 234–241. Springer, Cham (2015). https://doi.org/10.1007/978-3-319-24574-4_28

40. Russakovsky, O., et al.: Imagenet large scale visual recognition challenge. Int. J. Comput. Vis. 115(3), 211–252 (2015)

41. Sangkloy, P., Lu, J., Fang, C., Yu, F., Hays, J.: Scribbler: controlling deep image synthesis with sketch and color. In: CVPR, pp. 6836–6845 (2017)

42. Shi, W., et al.: Real-time single image and video super-resolution using an efficient sub-pixel convolutional neural network. In: CVPR, pp. 1874–1883 (2016)

43. Simonyan, K., Zisserman, A.: Very deep convolutional networks for large-scale image recognition (2014). arXiv preprint arXiv:1409.1556

44. Szegedy, C., Vanhoucke, V., Ioffe, S., Shlens, J., Wojna, Z.: Rethinking the inception architecture for computer vision. In: CVPR, pp. 2818–2826 (2016)

45. Wang, C., Xu, C., Wang, C., Tao, D.: Perceptual adversarial networks for image-to-image transformation. IEEE Trans. Image Process. 27(8), 4066–4079 (2018)

46. Wang, T.C., Liu, M.Y., Zhu, J.Y., Tao, A., Kautz, J., Catanzaro, B.: High-resolution image synthesis and semantic manipulation with conditional gans. In: CVPR, pp. 8798–8807 (2018)
47. Wang, X., Gupta, A.: Generative image modeling using style and structure adversarial networks. In: Leibe, B., Matas, J., Sebe, N., Welling, M. (eds.) ECCV 2016. LNCS, vol. 9908, pp. 318–335. Springer, Cham (2016). https://doi.org/10.1007/978-3-319-46493-0_20
48. Wang, Z., Bovik, A.C., Sheikh, H.R., Simoncelli, E.P., et al.: Image quality assessment: from error visibility to structural similarity. IEEE Trans. Image Process. **13**(4), 600–612 (2004)
49. Wang, Z., Simoncelli, E.P., Bovik, A.C.: Multiscale structural similarity for image quality assessment. In: The 37th Asilomar Conference on Signals, Systems & Computers, vol. 2, pp. 1398–1402 (2003)
50. Xue, N., Bai, S., Wang, F., Xia, G.S., Wu, T., Zhang, L.: Learning attraction field representation for robust line segment detection. In: CVPR, pp. 1595–1603 (2019)
51. Yi, Z., Zhang, H., Tan, P., Gong, M.: Dualgan: unsupervised dual learning for image-to-image translation. In: ICCV, pp. 2849–2857 (2017)
52. Zhang, H., et al.: Stackgan++: Realistic image synthesis with stacked generative adversarial networks (2017). arXiv preprint arXiv:1710.10916
53. Zhang, H., Sindagi, V., Patel, V.M.: Image de-raining using a conditional generative adversarial network (2017). arXiv preprint arXiv:1701.05957
54. Zhang, R., Isola, P., Efros, A.A., Shechtman, E., Wang, O.: The unreasonable effectiveness of deep features as a perceptual metric. In: CVPR, pp. 586–595 (2018)
55. Zhou, Y., Qi, H., Ma, Y.: End-to-end wireframe parsing. In: ICCV 2019 (2019)
56. Zhou, Y., Qi, H., Zhai, S., Sun, Q., Chen, Z., Wei, L.Y., Ma, Y.: Learning to reconstruct 3D manhattan wireframes from a single image. In: ICCV (2019)
57. Zhu, J.Y., Park, T., Isola, P., Efros, A.A.: Unpaired image-to-image translation using cycle-consistent adversarial networks. In: ICCV, pp. 2223–2232 (2017)

RBF-Softmax: Learning Deep Representative Prototypes with Radial Basis Function Softmax

Xiao Zhang[1], Rui Zhao[2], Yu Qiao[3], and Hongsheng Li[1(✉)]

[1] CUHK-SenseTime Joint Lab, The Chinese University of Hong Kong, Hong Kong, China
zhangx9411@gmail.com, hsli@ee.cuhk.edu.hk
[2] SenseTime Research, Hong Kong, China
zhaorui@sensetime.com
[3] ShenZhen Key Lab of Computer Vision and Pattern Recognition, SIAT-SenseTime Joint Lab, Shenzhen Institutes of Advanced Technology, Chinese Academy of Sciences, Shenzhen, China
yu.qiao@siat.ac.cn

Abstract. Deep neural networks have achieved remarkable successes in learning feature representations for visual classification. However, deep features learned by the softmax cross-entropy loss generally show excessive intra-class variations. We argue that, because the traditional softmax losses aim to optimize only the relative differences between intra-class and inter-class distances (**logits**), it cannot obtain representative class prototypes (class weights/centers) to regularize intra-class distances, even when the training is converged. Previous efforts mitigate this problem by introducing auxiliary regularization losses. But these modified losses mainly focus on optimizing intra-class compactness, while ignoring keeping reasonable relations between different class prototypes. These lead to weak models and eventually limit their performance. To address this problem, this paper introduces a novel Radial Basis Function (RBF) distances to replace the commonly used inner products in the softmax loss function, such that it can adaptively assign losses to regularize the intra-class and inter-class distances by reshaping the relative differences, and thus creating more representative prototypes of classes to improve optimization. The proposed RBF-Softmax loss function not only effectively reduces intra-class distances, stabilizes the training behavior, and reserves ideal relations between prototypes, but also significantly improves the testing performance. Experiments on visual recognition benchmarks including MNIST, CIFAR-10/100, and ImageNet demonstrate that the proposed RBF-Softmax achieves better results than cross-entropy and other state-of-the-art classification losses. The code is at https://github.com/2han9x1a0release/RBF-Softmax.

1 Introduction

Recent years witnessed the breakthrough of deep Convolutional Neural Networks (CNNs) on various visual recognition tasks [11,13,15,21,27]. State-of-the-art deep learning based classification methods benefit from the following

© Springer Nature Switzerland AG 2020
A. Vedaldi et al. (Eds.): ECCV 2020, LNCS 12371, pp. 296–311, 2020.
https://doi.org/10.1007/978-3-030-58574-7_18

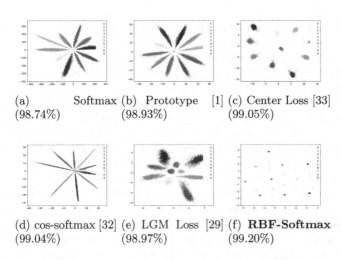

(a)   Softmax (b) Prototype   [1] (c) Center Loss [33]
(98.74%)   (98.93%)   (99.05%)

(d) cos-softmax [32] (e) LGM Loss [29] (f) **RBF-Softmax**
(99.04%)   (98.97%)   (99.20%)

Fig. 1. MNIST 2-D feature visualization of various losses. Intra-class feature distributions of sub-figure 1(a), 1(b) and 1(d) exhibit that conventional classification losses without additional regularization terms suffer from large intra-class sample-prototype distances (logits). Except proposed RBF-Softmax, class prototypes of all other losses and centers of their corresponding features have certain biases more or less.

three factors: large-scale training datasets [7,23], powerful network architectures [9,11,17,24,26], and effective training loss functions [4,20,29,33,36], which make deep neural networks the dominant model for visual classification. The cross-entropy softmax loss function and some of its variants [4,29,36] have been widely adopted for tackling the classification problem and enhancing the discriminativeness of the learned representations.

In deep classification tasks, the input image is firstly transformed into high-dimensional feature vector by Convolutional Neural Networks. To determine its class label, the similarities or distances between the feature vector and class prototypes (also called class weight vectors, class centers or class representations), namely sample-prototype distances, are calculated to get the logits. Conventionally, metrics including inner product, cosine [18] and Euclidean distance [29,36] were exploited to produce logits.

In most existing methods, the logits of an input sample are normalized across all classes by a softmax function to generate the class probabilities. Besides the softmax function, other choices include methods like RBF Network [2], Bayesian formula and Gaussian distribution [29]. During the training process, classification probabilities of each input sample are optimized towards its ground-truth by the cross-entropy loss.

Euclidean distance is often used as the similarity metric for feature vectors because it is easy to calculate, and has clear geometric meaning. The learned image feature distributions are often expected to have small intra-class distances and sufficiently large inter-class distances. However, the existing softmax loss and its variants do not directly optimize the Euclidean distances, but rather the relative differences between the intra-class logits and inter-class logits. Specifically, when the distance between a sample to its corresponding class prototype is relatively smaller than its distances to other class prototypes, the penalty from the softmax loss will be small, but the distance to its corresponding class prototype might still be large. Therefore, contrastive loss [3] and triplet loss [10] were proposed to directly optimize the Euclidean distance and yielded better performance in practice. But such losses are subject to difficulties in mining effective sample pairs and training convergence, and thus cannot completely replace the traditional softmax losses. Subsequently, DeepID2 [25], center loss [33] and range loss [37] jointly utilized the metric loss and traditional softmax loss for supervision, and achieved great success in face recognition. Along this direction, CPL [36] and LGM [29] algorithms added intra-class distance regularization terms into the softmax function to regularize the feature distributions. However, such terms still face the challenge of extra unstable regularization losses. Figure 1 shows MNIST 2-D feature distributions of some of these losses. Moreover, in Sect. 4.1 we will fully exhibit that most of these variants improve the discriminativeness of class prototypes rather than their semantic representativeness, by which we mean the reasonable relations between class prototypes.

In this paper, we propose a Radial Basis Function softmax (RBF-Softmax) loss function for visual classification. The key idea is to reshape the Euclidean distances between the sample features and class prototypes with RBF kernel, before feeding them into the softmax function for normalization. RBF-Softmax loss function can more effectively minimize intra-class Euclidean distances, and increase expansion of multi-class distribution with keeping reasonable class relations simultaneously.

On the one hand, for optimizing the intra-class Euclidean distances, the proposed RBF kernel can provide more balanced supervisions in the early training stages and distance-sensitive supervisions in the later training stages. In the early training stage, all features of the same class are likely to be scattered sparsely in the feature space due to the random initialization, leading to large intra-class variations with large logits. With the RBF kernel, the samples in the same class would have similar penalties no matter whether they have different Euclidean distances to the class prototypes, leading to stable convergence behavior. When the training is close to convergence, existing loss functions tend to provide very few supervision due to the relatively large inter-class distances. For features belonging to the same class, they still have the potential to be closer to the class prototype. The sample-to-prototype similarities by the RBF kernel have greater change rates than their original Euclidean distances or inner products to the class prototype, which are able to provide sufficient supervisions even close to convergence.

On the other hand, our proposed RBF kernel logits can effectively reshape and bound the logits, and then results in more balanced ratios between intra-class and inter-class logits. And the resulting class prototypes are more representative and, in turn, lead to better classification performance.

Extensive experiments on validating the effectiveness of the proposed RBF-Softmax loss has been tested on multiple visual recognition benchmarks, including MNIST [16], CIFAR-10/CIFAR-100 [14] and ImageNet [23]. Experiments show that the RBF-Softmax outperforms state-of-the-art loss functions on visual classification on all the tested benchmarks.

The contributions of this paper could be summarized in to three-fold: (1) We argue that the main defect caused by biased loss allocations of conventional softmax loss can lead to weak models and imperfect class prototypes; (2) We therefore proposed an effective RBF-Softmax loss to address aforementioned defect by using RBF kernel to control loss allocations; (3) We proved that RBF-Softmax can generate ideal class prototypes as well as improve classification performance through extensive experiments.

2   Related Works

Classification Losses. Visual classification is the fundamental problems in computer vision and the advances of visual classification also promote related research directions. One of its major components is how to design effective classification loss functions. The designs of classification losses are usually dependent on the classification criterion during inference. In face recognition, the testing phase requires to calculate the cosine similarity between face images. Based on this demand, a series of cosine based softmax losses [6,31] and their margin-based variants [4,30,32] were proposed and achieved great success. In prototype learning, samples need to be abstracted into feature vectors with one or more centers in a high-dimensional space. [1] and CPL [36] directly adopt the Euclidean distance as the classification score of prototype metrics.

Euclidean Distance Based Losses. Metric learning has been an important research area of machine learning and deep learning. Commonly used Euclidean distance based losses include contrastive loss [3] and triplet loss [10]. Specifically, Euclidean losses take distances among samples as optimization objectives and strive to reduce distances between samples within the same classes while enlarge distances between samples across different classes. However, such a design can cause difficulties in mining efficient sample pairs or triplets. [34] showed that the different sampling methods have significants impact on networks' training behavior as well as the final performances. Therefore, Euclidean distance based losses are often used for fine-tuning rather than training from scratch.

Regularization for Classification Based Losses. The joint supervision of classification loss and Euclidean distance based loss was adopted to train deep neural networks. Such combinations of loss terms results in more stable training behaviors. The success of Center Loss [33], Range Loss [37], Ring Loss [38], CPL [36], g-Softmax [20] and LGM [29] in face recognition and visual classification have proven that such joint supervision is a better trade-off in training deep models.

3   Radial Basis Function Softmax Loss

In this section, we will first recall the significance of class prototypes and analyze two problems in the conventional softmax cross-entorpy loss and its variants [1] (Sect. 3.1). Then we will introduce the proposed RBF-Softmax in details in Sect. 3.2. How RBF-Softmax solve defects faced by traditional softmax loss is further explained and discussed to demonstrate its effectiveness in visual classification (Sect. 3.3).

3.1   Analysis of the Softmax Cross-entropy Losses and Prototypes

Considering a classification task with C-class where the traditional softmax loss is used. x_i is the feature vector of one specific sample belonging to class $y_i \in [1, C]$, its softmax cross entropy loss is calculated as

$$\mathcal{L}_{\text{Softmax}}(x_i) = -\log P_{i,y_i} = -\log \frac{e^{f_{i,y_i}}}{\sum_{k=1}^{C} e^{f_{i,k}}}, \tag{1}$$

where P_{i,y_i} is the probability that x_i being assigned to its ground-truth class y_i, and the logit $f_{i,j}$ represents the affinity between the sample feature x_i and class prototypes W_j. Particularly, when $j = y_i$, logit f_{i,y_i} is the affinity between sample feature x_i to its corresponding class prototype W_{y_i}, which is called the *intra-class sample-prototype distance* or *intra-class logit* in this paper. Conversely, when $j \neq y_i$, logit $f_{i,j}$ is named as the *inter-class sample-prototype distance* or *inter-class logit*. To measure the similarity between a sample feature and class prototypes, inner product and Euclidean distance were widely used, for example $f_{i,j} = W_j^{\text{T}} x_i$ in Softmax loss and $f_{i,j} = -\alpha \|x_i - W_j\|_2^2$ in prototype learning [1] and CPL [36].

In these losses, a prototype can be seen as the representation of all sample features in a specified class. Intuitively, an ideal prototype should be the geometric center of all corresponding feature vectors. Therefore, prototype is required to have significant representativeness, which includes two aspects:

1. Prototypes should effectively discriminate and categorize samples from different classes. The inter-class distances are larger than intra-class distances;
2. Prototypes should demonstrate the relations among classes, which means similar classes is more closer than absolutely different classes.

These aspects can be demonstrate in Fig. 2(a). In this figure, there are three different classes: hamsters, squirrels, and tables. Hamsters and squirrels are similar, while both of them are very different from tables. Therefore, ideal sampels and prototypes distribution should ensure that every class is separable with other classes, but keep some similar classe prototypes closer.

During training, network parameters are gradually optimized to minimize the loss functions. The final feature distributions highly rely on prototypes as well as the losses used. The above mentioned existed logit calculations may lead to two defects in properly supervising the feature learning.

Biased Loss Allocation at the Beginning of Training. The class prototype vector W_j can be considered to be the mean representation of all samples in class j. Since the network in early training stages are not fully optimized, W_j as well as x_i tend to be somewhat random and do not have valid semantic information. Therefore, distances between features x_i and their corresponding class prototypes W_{y_i} cannot correctly represent their similarities. This fact indicates that samples should receive constrained training losses to avoid the negative impact of outliter (see illustration in Fig. 2(b)). Tabel 1 shows the intra-class sample-class distances in early-stage intra-class have large variances, which result in significant differences in loss for intra-class samples.

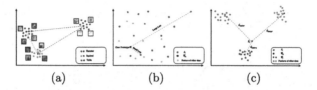

$$(a) \qquad\qquad (b) \qquad\qquad (c)$$

Fig. 2. Fig (a) is sampels and prototypes demonstration. Black spots represent proto-types of classes and solid color spots represent sample features. Sample features and prototypes of similar classes (hamster and squirrel) are separable, but have much closer distances than absolutely different class (table). Figure 2(b) is feature distribution at early training stage. Since features have not been well embedded at this stage, the loss value of each sample should be relatively similar. However, there might be large variances in different samples' loss values. Figure 2(c) is feature distribution diagram of late stage. The intra-class sample-prototype distance d_{intra} of the annotated x_i is relatively larger than other samples in its class y_i. Therefore its expected loss value should also be large. However, since d_{inter}s are much larger than d_{intra}, resulting in a rather small loss, so x_i can not be further optimized.

Eventually, such biased loss allocation may hinder the model's training behavior and cause significant bias between class prototypes and real feature distribution centers.

Table 1. Intra-class sample-prototype distance at early training stage. For different feature dimensions, the range as well as the variances of intra-class sample-prototype distances are very large at the early training stage on the MNIST dataset with a 6-layer convolutional network.

Feat. Dim.	Early Intra-class sample-prototype distance			
	Min.	Max.	Avg.	Variance
2	0.01	59.52	6.59	146.65
32	8.08	206.17	54.27	1186.8
128	15.72	271.18	69.97	2284.84

Large Intra-class Sample-Prototype Distance at Late Training Stage. During late training stage, softmax loss also leads to problematic phenomenons. As shown in Fig. 2(c), when a sample x_i's inter-class sample-prototype distances (For example its distances to other class prototypes, $f_{i,j}$ for $j \neq y_i$) are significantly larger than its intra-class logit f_{i,y_i}, this sample will receive small loss value and thus small gradients during optimization even when the intra-class logit f_{i,y_i} is large. Compared to other samples in class y_i, feature x_i needs a larger loss in order to get close to its corresponding class prototype W_{y_i}. However, since the softmax loss focuses on optimizing relative differences between intra-class and inter-class logits and cannot generate enough penalty for this case.

To further illustrate this issue, we analyze from the perspective of the sample gradient. According to Eq. (1), the gradient w.r.t. feature vector x_i is

$$\frac{\partial \mathcal{L}(x_i)}{\partial x_i} = \sum_{j=1}^{C}(P_{i,j} - \mathbb{1}(y_i = j)) \cdot \frac{\partial f_{i,j}}{\partial x_i}, \tag{2}$$

where $\mathbb{1}$ is the indicator function and $f_{i,j}$ is the logit between x_i and W_j. The classification probability $P_{i,j}$ is calculated by the softmax function. When $j = y_i$, if the relative difference between inter-class and intra-class logit of x_i is large enough, P_{i,y_i} will be very close to 1 and then the gradient of x_i will be small. At this time, the intra-class logit may still be large.

According to the above analysis, existing softmax cross-entropy loss has the problems of biased loss allocation at early training stages and large intra-class sample-prototype distance at late training stages. Therefore, we argue that solving these two defects by designing a new loss function can effectively optimize the model training.

3.2   RBF-Softmax Loss Function

To fix the above mentioned defects in existing softmax loss functions, we propose a distance named Radial Basis Function kernel distance (RBF-score) between x_i and W_j to measure the similarities between a sample feature x_i and different classes' weights W_j,

$$K_{i,j} = K_{\mathrm{RBF}}(x_i, W_j) = e^{-\frac{d_{i,j}}{\gamma}} = e^{-\frac{\|x_i - W_j\|_2^2}{\gamma}}, \tag{3}$$

where $d_{i,j}$ is the Euclidean distance between x_i and W_j, and γ is a hyperparameter. Compared to the Euclidean distance and inner product that are unbounded, RBF-score decreases as the Euclidean distance increases and its values range from 0 (when $d_{i,j} \to \infty$) to 1 (when $x_i = W_j$). Intuitively, RBF-score well measures the similarities between x_i and W_j and can be used as the logits in the softmax cross-entropy loss function.

Formally, we define the Radial Basis Function Softmax loss (RBF-Softmax) as

$$\mathcal{L}(x_i)_{\mathrm{RBF\text{-}Softmax}} = -\log P_{i,y_i} = -\log \frac{e^{s \cdot K_{\mathrm{RBF}}(x_i, W_{y_i})}}{\sum_{k=1}^{C} e^{s \cdot K_{\mathrm{RBF}}(x_i, W_k)}}$$

$$= -\log \frac{e^{s \cdot e^{-\frac{d_{i,y_i}}{\gamma}}}}{\sum_{k=1}^{C} e^{s \cdot e^{-\frac{d_{i,k}}{\gamma}}}}, \tag{4}$$

where $d_{i,j} = \|x_i - W_j\|_2^2, j \in \{1, \cdots, C\}$ and the hyperparameter s is a scale parameter in order to enlarge the range of RBF-scores. Similar hyperparameter has been extensively discussed in some cosine-based softmax losses [4,18,19,31, 32], in order to enlarge the range of RBF-scores.

3.3   Analysis of RBF-Softmax

In this subsection, we analyze two aspects of our proposed RBF-Softmax loss function: (1) the mechanism how the RBF-Softmax overcome two defects mentioned above; (2) the effects of two hyperparameters in RBF-Softmax.

Overcome the Inappropriate Penalties. RBF-Softmax essentially solves the above mentioned problems by adopting the original inner products or Euclidean distances as logits in a more reasonable way. On the one hand, it is important to balance each sample's intra-class logits at the early training stage. The initial values of intra-class logits are generally all very large. By adopting the RBF-score, the RBF kernel can map the very large Euclidean distances to very small RBF-scores as logits, thereby significantly reducing the intra-class variance. Then, due to the small variances of the intra-class RBF-score at early training stage, the loss allocation of samples belonging to the same classes is unbiased. On the other hand, at the late training stage, traditional softmax probabilities easily reach 1 on corresponding classes (gradients become 0), while RBF probabilities are much more difficult to reach 1 and can continually provide gradients for training.In this way, the proposed RBF-Softmax can better aggregate samples to their corresponding class centers, thereby improving the performance of model.

Effects of Hyperparameters. Hyperparameters (γ and s) of the proposed RBF-Softmax affect the training of model to some extent. Let $K_{i,y_i} = e^{-\frac{d_{i,y_i}}{\gamma}}$ be the RBF-score between feature x_i and its corresponding class prototype W_{y_i}, $d_{i,y_i} = \|x_i - W_{y_i}\|_2^2$ is the Euclidean distance, and P_{i,y_i} is the probability of x_i being assigned to its corresponding class y_i.

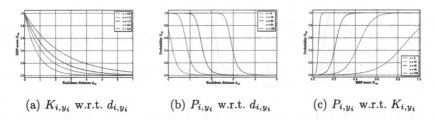

(a) K_{i,y_i} w.r.t. d_{i,y_i} (b) P_{i,y_i} w.r.t. d_{i,y_i} (c) P_{i,y_i} w.r.t. K_{i,y_i}

Fig. 3. Figure. 3(a) is curves of K_{i,y_i} w.r.t. d_{i,y_i} when choosing different γ parameters. Figure 3(b) and Fig. 3(c) are curves of P_{i,y_i} w.r.t. d_{i,y_i} and K_{i,y_i} when choosing different scale s parameters.

Figure 3(a) shows the mapping of d_{i,y_i} to K_{i,y_i} under different γ hyperparameters. When γ is larger, RBF-score K_{i,y_i} obtained by the specified d_{i,y_i} will be larger, and the similarity between the sample and their corresponding class prototypes would be higher, which means that the task becomes easier. Figure 3(b) and Fig. 3(c) shows the mapping of d_{i,y_i} and K_{i,y_i} to P_{i,y_i} under different s hyperparameters. Our experiments show that when $j \neq y_i$, $d_{i,j}$ is generally much larger, causing the value of $K_{i,j}$ to be close to 0. Moreover, s controls the range of p_{i,y_i}, and the difficulty of the classification task: for the fixed d_{i,y_i} or

K_{i,y_i}, smaller s leads to narrower range and smaller value of P_{i,y_i}, making the classification task harder.

The same conclusion can be drawn from the perspective of the gradient. The corresponding gradients of RBF-Softmax are as follows:

$$\frac{\partial \mathcal{L}_{\text{RBF-Softmax}}}{\partial \boldsymbol{x}_i} = \sum_{j=1}^{C} (P_{i,j} - \mathbb{1}(y_i = j)) \cdot s \cdot K_{i,j} \frac{\partial d_{i,j}}{\partial \boldsymbol{x}_i}, \tag{5}$$

$$\frac{\partial \mathcal{L}_{\text{RBF-Softmax}}}{\partial \boldsymbol{W}_j} = (P_{i,j} - \mathbb{1}(y_i = j)) \cdot s \cdot K_{i,j} \frac{\partial d_{i,j}}{\partial \boldsymbol{W}_j}, \tag{6}$$

where $K_{i,j} = e^{-\frac{d_{i,j}}{\gamma}}$ and $d_{i,j} = \|\boldsymbol{x}_i - \boldsymbol{W}_j\|_2^2$. In these gradients, RBF-scores are factors of gradients and determine their lengths. Therefore the change in hyperparameters can affect the norm of gradients and eventually the performance of models.

4   Experiments

In this section, we first exhibit several exploratory experiments on different prototypes, and then investigate the effectiveness and sensetiveness of different hyperparameters s and γ on the MNIST [16] dataset in Sect. 4.2. After that we evaluate the performances of proposed RBF-Softmax and compare with several state-of-the-art loss functions on CIFAR-10/100 [14] (in Sect. 4.3) and ImageNet [23] (in Sect. 4.4).

4.1   Exploratory Experiments on Prototypes

In order to analyze the prototypes of different softmax losses, here we use Word-Net [5] and CIFAR-100 [14] as demonstrations. WordNet [5] is a widely used electronic lexical database, which can calculate the similarities between different English words from the perspective of computational linguistics. CIFAR-100 [14] dataset contains 100 classes which can be grouped into 20 superclasses, such as reptiles, flowers and etc. In each superclasses, there are 5 different but similar subclasses. Therefore, we can get a similarity matrix of all 100 classes in CIFAR-100 [14] by using WordNet [5] similarities. Figure 4(a) exhibits such 100 × 100 WordNet [5] similarity matrix of CIFAR-100 [14], where the indexes of subclasses from the same superclass are continuous. Here we use WUP similarities [35] to measure the relations of classes. Paler block color means the two corresponding classes are more similar while darker color means two classes are more different. The WordNet [5] similarity matrix can be seen as the groundtruth. Then we trained ResNet-50 [9] models with conventional softmax loss and cosine based softmax loss [18] on CIFAR-100 [14], and computed their class prototype similarity matrices respectively. Figure 4(b) and Fig. 4(c) imply that the relations among classes are not reserved by prototypes in these loss functions.

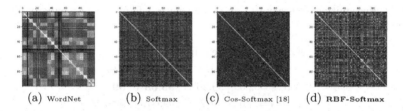

(a) WordNet   (b) Softmax   (c) Cos-Softmax [18]   (d) RBF-Softmax

Fig. 4. Prototypes similarity matrices of WordNet [5] and different losses. The color of every block represents the degree of similarity between classes. Lighter block color means higher similarity.

To further explore the representativeness of class prototypes in these losses, we introduce two indicators: comparisons between similarity matrices and Calinski-Harabaz index of all 100 subclasses. By calculating the comparisons of similarity matrices, the differences between prototype similarity matrices and WordNet [5] similarity matrices can evaluate weather trained prototypes can reserve semantic information. Calinski-Harabaz (CH) index is a widely used validation of cluster algorithm. We expect subclasses in a same superclass are compact while different superclasses are separable. Table 2 exhibits all result of these two indicators. We first measure the similarities between matrix in Fig. 4(a) and other matrices in Fig. (b), (c), and (d). Matrix of RBF-Softmax is more similar to WordNet [5] matrix. Moreover, prototypes in RBF-Softmax have significantly higher Calinski-Harabaz index. These results preliminarily tell that models trained with RBF-Softmax are more representative.

Table 2. Representativeness experiments on CIFAR-100 [14] prototypes. Similartities between WordNet matrix and others show whether prototypes keep reasonable class relations. CH indexes indicate whether classes under the same superclass is gathered.

Losses	Similarity of Simi. Mat.	Calinski-Harabaz Index
WordNet [5]	1.00	Not Appliable
Softmax	0.17 ± 0.05	2.81 ± 0.21
Cos-Softmax [18]	0.09 ± 0.04	1.68 ± 0.10
RBF-Softmax	0.36 ± 0.11	7.33 ± 0.25

4.2 Exploratory Experiments on MNIST

We first use MNIST [16] to investigate RBF-Softmax. All experiments of MNIST [16] are trained with a simple 6-layer CNN, where all convolutinal kernels are 5×5 and the activation function is PReLU [8].

Tables 3 exhibit the impacts of hyperparameter s and γ on models performance respectively. Figure 5 partly visualizes the feature distributions of different s parameters. According to these results, we find that fixing s to 2.0 and γ to 1.0 for model can outshine other configurations. Results in Table 4 compares

Table 3. Recognition accuracy (%) on MNIST with different s and γ hyperparameters and feature dimensions.

Hyperparameter		Feature Dimension		
		2-D	10-D	32-D
$\gamma = 1.0$	$s = 2.0$	99.20%	**99.68%**	**99.71%**
	$s = 4.0$	**99.29%**	99.65%	99.69%
	$s = 8.0$	99.25%	99.56%	99.61%
$s = 2.0$	$\gamma = 1.00$	**99.20%**	**99.68%**	**99.71%**
	$\gamma = 1.3$	99.15%	99.54%	99.65%
	$\gamma = 2.0$	99.03%	99.36%	99.42%

the performances of state-of-the-art loss functions on MNIST [16]. The only difference of these models is their loss functions, where RBF-Softmax follows the mentioned setting. In the MNIST [16] dataset, our RBF-Softmax outperforms all other losses. According to Sect. 3.3, both γ and s can change the constraint of RBF-Softmax. These experiments shows that too strong or too weak constraint can lead to performance degradation and RBF-Softmax is not sensitive to hyperparameters selected within a reasonable range.

Table 4. Recognition accuracy (%) on MNIST with different compared losses. The are all trained with a 6-layer CNN and different losses for three times to obtain the average accuracies. The feature dimension is 32.

Method	1st	2nd	3rd	Avg. Acc.
Softmax	99.28%	99.27%	99.25%	99.27%
RBF Networks [2]	97.42%	97.07%	97.36%	97.28%
Center Loss [33]	99.66%	99.64%	99.64%	99.65%
Ring Loss [38]	99.56%	99.59%	99.58%	99.58%
ArcFace [4]	99.60%	99.55%	99.62%	99.59%
LGM [29]	99.41%	99.35%	99.40%	99.39%
RBF-Softmax	**99.70%**	**99.73%**	**99.75%**	**99.73%**

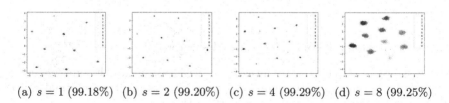

(a) $s = 1$ (99.18%) (b) $s = 2$ (99.20%) (c) $s = 4$ (99.29%) (d) $s = 8$ (99.25%)

Fig. 5. MNIST 2-D feature visualization when trained with different hyperparameters s.

4.3   Experiments on CIFAR-10/100

CIFAR-10 and CIFAR-100 [14] each contains $50,000$ training images and $10,000$ testing images, which are 32×32 color images. For the data augmentation scheme, horizon flipping (mirroring) and 32×32 random cropping after 4-pixel zero-padding on each side are adopted to all the training procedures [9].

Table 5. Recognition accuracy rates (%) on CIFAR-10 using ResNet-20 [9] and DenseNet-BC ($k = 12$) [12] models with different loss functions.

Loss Functions	Accuracy on CIFAR-10		Settings
	ResNet-20 [9]	DenseNet-BC ($k = 12$) [12]	
Softmax	91.25%	95.49%	[9,12]
G-CPL [36]	91.63%	–	[36]
Center Loss [33]	91.85%	95.77%	[33]
RBF-Softmax	92.26%	95.83%	$\gamma = 2, s = 3$
	92.42%	95.95%	$\gamma = 2, s = 4$
	92.61%	**96.13%**	$\gamma = 1.8, s = 4$
	92.77%	96.11%	$\gamma = 1.6, s = 4$

For CIFAR-10 [14], we train the ResNet-20 [9] and DenseNet-BC ($k = 12$) [12] with different loss functions. All ResNet-20 [9] models are trained with a batch size of 256 for 300 epochs. The initial learning rate is 0.1 and is then divided by 2 every 60 epochs. In DenseNet-BC ($k = 12$) [12] models, we use batch size 128 for 300 epochs, and the learning rate is set to 0.1 and then divided by 10 at the 150th epoch and the 225th epoch respectively. The recognition accuracy are exhibited in Table 5. For ResNet-20 [9] and DenseNet-BC ($k = 12$) [12], our RBF-Softmax achieves state-of-the-art 92.77% and 96.13% accuracy respectively.

Table 6. Recognition accuracy rates (%) on CIFAR-100 using VGGNet-19 [24] models with different loss functions and hyperparameter settings.

Loss Functions	Accuracy on CIFAR-100	Settings
	VGGNet-19 [24]	
Softmax	72.23%	–
Center Loss [33]	73.02%	[33]
G-CPL [36]	72.88%	[36]
RBF-Softmax	$72.72\% \pm 0.03\%$	$\gamma = 2.2, s = 10$
	$\mathbf{73.98\% \pm 0.02\%}$	$\gamma = 2.2, s = 14$
	$72.62\% \pm 0.05\%$	$\gamma = 1.0, s = 12$
	$71.77\% \pm 0.04\%$	$\gamma = 4.0, s = 12$

For CIFAR-100 [14], we train VGGNet-19 [24] with different loss functions. All RBF-softmax trainings follow the same setting: models are trained with batch size 128 for 600 epochs; the initial learning rate is 0.1, and is divided by 2 at the 100th, 300th and 500th epoch, and by 5 at 200th, 400th and 600th epoch. The results of CIFAR-100 [14] are shown in Table 6 and RBF-Softmax again shows state-of-the-art performances on VGGNet-19 [24] architectures.

4.4   Experiments on ImageNet

We investigate the performance of proposed RBF-Softmax on large-scale visual classification task using the ImageNet [23] dataset (ILSVRC2012). In order to show that the proposed RBF-Softmax is effective on various network architectures, the performed experiments using both manually designed models (like ResNet [9]) and automatically searched architectures (like EfficientNet [28]). In all ImageNet [23] experiments, models are combined with conventional softmax loss and our RBF-Softmax, respectively.

Table 7. Recognition accuracy (%) on ILSVRC2012 [23].

Networks	Methods	Single-crop Top-1 Acc.	Settings
ResNet-50 [9]	Softmax	76.8%	–
	RBF-Softmax	**77.1%**	$s = 8; \gamma = 4$
EfficientNet-B0 [28]	Softmax	75.1%	–
	RBF-Softmax	**75.3%**	$s = 35; \gamma = 16$
EfficientNet-B1 [28]	Softmax	75.9%	–
	RBF-Softmax	**76.6%**	$s = 35; \gamma = 16$
EfficientNet-B4 [28]	Softmax	78.8%	–
	RBF-Softmax	**79.0%**	$s = 35; \gamma = 16$

All models are trained on 8 NVIDIA GeForce GTX TITAN X GPUs on 1.28 million images and evaluated for both top-1 and top-5 accuracies on the 50k validation images. Most of the training processes follow settings in [22]. For training ResNet [9], the input images are single-cropped to 224×224 pixels. For EfficientNet [28], the training image size varies following its original paper. We use simple training processes without any training enhancements, like DropOut, DropConnect, AutoAugment, and etc. We apply SGD with momentum of 0.9 as optimization method and generally train for 100 epochs. During training, we use cosine schedule with 5 epoch gradual warmup as learning rate policy. The initial learning rate of ResNet [9] is 0.1, and 0.2 for EfficientNet [28]. The batch size of most models is 256 except EfficientNet-B4 [28]. Because of the limitation of GPU memory, batch size of EfficientNet-B4 is 96. The results are expressed in Table 7, where RBF-Softmax beats conventional softmax loss for both manually designed models and automatically searched models.

5   Conclusions

In this paper, we identify biased loss allocation and large intra-class logits (scores) as two primary defects prevent some conventional softmax losses from achieving ideal class prototypes and accurate classification performances. To address this problem, we propose Radial Basis Function softmax loss (RBF-Softmax) which applies RBF-kernel logits to the softmax cross-entropy loss in order to reasonably allocate losses and optimize intra-class distributions. Our RBF-Softmax is simple but highly effective and insightful. We demonstrate its effectiveness by demonstrating prototype experiments and appling it in close-set image classification tasks (MNIST [16], CIFAR-10/100 [14], and ImageNet [23]). Results shows that RBF-Softmax achieves state-of-the-art performances on all the evaluated benchmarks.

Acknowledgements. This work is supported in part by SenseTime Group Limited, in part by the General Research Fund through the Research Grants Council of Hong Kong under Grants CUHK 14202217/14203118/14205615/14207814/14213616/14208417/14239816, in part by CUHK Direct Grant and in part by the Joint Lab of CAS-HK.

References

1. Bonilla, E., Robles-Kelly, A.: Discriminative probabilistic prototype learning. arXiv preprint arXiv:1206.4686 (2012)
2. Broomhead, D.S., Lowe, D.: Radial basis functions, multi-variable functional interpolation and adaptive networks. Technical report, Royal Signals and Radar Establishment Malvern (United Kingdom) (1988)
3. Chopra, S., Hadsell, R., LeCun, Y.: Learning a similarity metric discriminatively, with application to face verification. In: 2005 IEEE Computer Society Conference on Computer Vision and Pattern Recognition (CVPR 2005), vol. 1, pp. 539–546. IEEE (2005)
4. Deng, J., Guo, J., Zafeiriou, S.: Arcface: Additive angular margin loss for deep face recognition. arXiv preprint arXiv:1801.07698 (2018)
5. Fellbaum, C., Miller, G.: WordNet: An Electronic Lexical Database. MIT press, Cambridge (1998)
6. Gopal, S., Yang, Y.: Von mises-fisher clustering models. In: International Conference on Machine Learning, pp. 154–162 (2014)
7. Guo, Y., Zhang, L., Hu, Y., He, X., Gao, J.: MS-Celeb-1M: a dataset and benchmark for large-scale face recognition. In: Leibe, B., Matas, J., Sebe, N., Welling, M. (eds.) ECCV 2016. LNCS, vol. 9907, pp. 87–102. Springer, Cham (2016). https://doi.org/10.1007/978-3-319-46487-9_6
8. He, K., Zhang, X., Ren, S., Sun, J.: Delving deep into rectifiers: surpassing human-level performance on imagenet classification. In: Proceedings of the IEEE International Conference on Computer Vision, pp. 1026–1034 (2015)
9. He, K., Zhang, X., Ren, S., Sun, J.: Deep residual learning for image recognition. In: Proceedings of the IEEE Conference on Computer Vision and Pattern Recognition, pp. 770–778 (2016)
10. Hoffer, E., Ailon, N.: Deep metric learning using triplet network. In: Feragen, A., Pelillo, M., Loog, M. (eds.) SIMBAD 2015. LNCS, vol. 9370, pp. 84–92. Springer, Cham (2015). https://doi.org/10.1007/978-3-319-24261-3_7

11. Hu, J., Shen, L., Sun, G.: Squeeze-and-excitation networks. arXiv preprint arXiv:1709.01507 (2017)
12. Huang, G., Liu, Z., Van Der Maaten, L., Weinberger, K.Q.: Densely connected convolutional networks. In: Proceedings of the IEEE Conference on Computer Vision and Pattern Recognition, pp. 4700–4708 (2017)
13. Huang, G.B., Ramesh, M., Berg, T., Learned-Miller, E.: Labeled faces in the wild: A database for studying face recognition in unconstrained environments. Technical report., Technical Report 07–49, University of Massachusetts, Amherst (2007)
14. Krizhevsky, A., Hinton, G.: Learning multiple layers of features from tiny images. Technical. report, Citeseer (2009)
15. Krizhevsky, A., Sutskever, I., Hinton, G.E.: Imagenet classification with deep convolutional neural networks. In: Advances in Neural Information Processing Systems, pp. 1097–1105 (2012)
16. LeCun, Y., Bottou, L., Bengio, Y., Haffner, P., et al.: Gradient-based learning applied to document recognition. Proc. IEEE **86**(11), 2278–2324 (1998)
17. Liu, C., et al.: Progressive neural architecture search. In: Proceedings of the European Conference on Computer Vision (ECCV), pp. 19–34 (2018)
18. Liu, Y., Li, H., Wang, X.: Learning deep features via congenerous cosine loss for person recognition. arXiv preprint arXiv:1702.06890 (2017)
19. Liu, Y., Li, H., Wang, X.: Rethinking feature discrimination and polymerization for large-scale recognition. arXiv preprint arXiv:1710.00870 (2017)
20. Luo, Y., Wong, Y., Kankanhalli, M., Zhao, Q.: g-softmax: Improving intraclass compactness and interclass separability of features. IEEE Trans. Neural Netw. Learn. Syst. **31**(2), 685–699 (2019)
21. Parkhi, O.M., Vedaldi, A., Zisserman, A., et al.: Deep face recognition. In: BMVC. vol. 1, p. 6 (2015)
22. Radosavovic, I., Kosaraju, R.P., Girshick, R., He, K., Dollár, P.: Designing network design spaces. In: Proceedings of the IEEE/CVF Conference on Computer Vision and Pattern Recognition, pp. 10428–10436 (2020)
23. Russakovsky, O., et al.: Imagenet large scale visual recognition challenge. Int. J. Comput. Vis. **115**(3), 211–252 (2015). https://doi.org/10.1007/s11263-015-0816-y
24. Simonyan, K., Zisserman, A.: Very deep convolutional networks for large-scale image recognition (2015)
25. Sun, Y., Chen, Y., Wang, X., Tang, X.: Deep learning face representation by joint identification-verification. In: Advances in Neural Information Processing Systems, pp. 1988–1996 (2014)
26. Szegedy, C., Ioffe, S., Vanhoucke, V., Alemi, A.A.: Inception-v4, inception-resnet and the impact of residual connections on learning. In: AAAI, vol. 4, p. 12 (2017)
27. Szegedy, C., et al.: Going deeper with convolutions. In: Proceedings of the IEEE Conference on Computer Vision and Pattern Recognition, pp. 1–9 (2015)
28. Tan, M., Le, Q.V.: Efficientnet: rethinking model scaling for convolutional neural networks. arXiv preprint arXiv:1905.11946 (2019)
29. Wan, W., Zhong, Y., Li, T., Chen, J.: Rethinking feature distribution for loss functions in image classification. In: Proceedings of the IEEE Conference on Computer Vision and Pattern Recognition, pp. 9117–9126 (2018)
30. Wang, F., Liu, W., Liu, H., Cheng, J.: Additive margin softmax for face verification. arXiv preprint arXiv:1801.05599 (2018)
31. Wang, F., Xiang, X., Cheng, J., Yuille, A.L.: Normface: l_2 hypersphere embedding for face verification. arXiv preprint arXiv:1704.06369 (2017)
32. Wang, H., Wang, Y., Zhou, Z., Ji, X., Li, Z., Gong, D., Zhou, J., Liu, W.: Cosface: large margin cosine loss for deep face recognition. arXiv preprint arXiv:1801.09414 (2018)

33. Wen, Y., Zhang, K., Li, Z., Qiao, Y.: A discriminative feature learning approach for deep face recognition. In: Leibe, B., Matas, J., Sebe, N., Welling, M. (eds.) ECCV 2016. LNCS, vol. 9911, pp. 499–515. Springer, Cham (2016). https://doi.org/10.1007/978-3-319-46478-7_31
34. Wu, C.Y., Manmatha, R., Smola, A.J., Krahenbuhl, P.: Sampling matters in deep embedding learning. In: Proceedings of the IEEE International Conference on Computer Vision, pp. 2840–2848 (2017)
35. Wu, Z., Palmer, M.: Verb semantics and lexical selection. arXiv preprint arXiv:cmp-lg/9406033 (1994). https://academic.microsoft.com/paper/2951798058
36. Yang, H.M., Zhang, X.Y., Yin, F., Liu, C.L.: Robust classification with convolutional prototype learning. In: Proceedings of the IEEE Conference on Computer Vision and Pattern Recognition, pp. 3474–3482 (2018)
37. Zhang, X., Fang, Z., Wen, Y., Li, Z., Qiao, Y.: Range loss for deep face recognition with long-tailed training data. In: Proceedings of the IEEE International Conference on Computer Vision, pp. 5409–5418 (2017)
38. Zheng, Y., Pal, D.K., Savvides, M.: Ring loss: Convex feature normalization for face recognition. In: Proceedings of the IEEE Conference on Computer Vision and Pattern Recognition, pp. 5089–5097 (2018)

Testing the Safety of Self-driving Vehicles by Simulating Perception and Prediction

Kelvin Wong[1,2(✉)], Qiang Zhang[1,3], Ming Liang[1], Bin Yang[1,2], Renjie Liao[1,2], Abbas Sadat[1], and Raquel Urtasun[1,2]

[1] Uber Advanced Technologies Group, Toronto, Canada
{kelvin.wong,ming.liang,byang10,rjliao,asadat,urtasun}@uber.com
[2] University of Toronto, Toronto, Canada
[3] Shanghai Jiao Tong University, Shanghai, China
zhangqiang2016@sjtu.edu.cn

Abstract. We present a novel method for testing the safety of self-driving vehicles in simulation. We propose an alternative to sensor simulation, as sensor simulation is expensive and has large domain gaps. Instead, we directly simulate the outputs of the self-driving vehicle's perception and prediction system, enabling realistic motion planning testing. Specifically, we use paired data in the form of ground truth labels and real perception and prediction outputs to train a model that predicts what the online system will produce. Importantly, the inputs to our system consists of high definition maps, bounding boxes, and trajectories, which can be easily sketched by a test engineer in a matter of minutes. This makes our approach a much more scalable solution. Quantitative results on two large-scale datasets demonstrate that we can realistically test motion planning using our simulations.

Keywords: Simulation · Perception and prediction · Self-driving vehicles

1 Introduction

Self-driving vehicles (SDVs) have the potential to become a safer, cheaper, and more scalable form of transportation. But while great progress has been achieved in the last few decades, there still remain many open challenges that impede the deployment of these vehicles at scale. One such challenge concerns how to test the safety of these vehicles and, in particular, their motion planners [13,44]. Most large-scale self-driving programs in industry use simulation for this purpose, especially in the case of testing safety-critical scenarios, which can be costly—even *unethical*—to perform in the real world. To this end, test engineers first

---

K. Wong and Q. Zhang—Indicates equal contribution. Work done during Qiang's internship at Uber ATG.

Electronic supplementary material The online version of this chapter (https://doi.org/10.1007/978-3-030-58574-7_19) contains supplementary material, which is available to authorized users.

© Springer Nature Switzerland AG 2020
A. Vedaldi et al. (Eds.): ECCV 2020, LNCS 12371, pp. 312–329, 2020.
https://doi.org/10.1007/978-3-030-58574-7_19

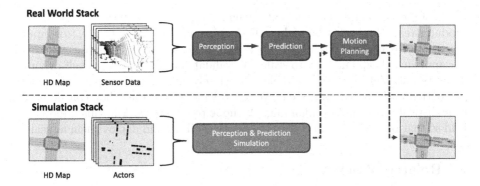

Fig. 1. Perception and prediction simulation. Our goal is to simulate the outputs of the SDV's perception and prediction system in order to realistically test its motion planner. For each timestep, our system ingests an HD map and a set of actors (bounding boxes and trajectories) and produces noisy outputs similar to those from the real system. To test the motion planner, we mock real outputs with our simulated ones.

create a large bank of test scenarios, each comprised of a high definition (HD) map and a set of actors represented by bounding boxes and trajectories. These mocked objects are then given as input to the motion planner. Finally, metrics computed on the simulation results are used to assess progress.

However, in order to provide realistic testing, the mocked objects need to reflect the noise of real perception and prediction[1] systems [7,31,33,34,50,62]. Unfortunately, existing approaches typically assume perfect perception or use simple heuristics to generate noise [18]. As a result, they yield unrealistic assessments of the motion planner's safety. For example, under this testing regime, we will never see the SDV slamming its brakes due to a false positive detection.

An alternative approach is to use sensor simulation to test the SDV's full autonomy stack, end-to-end. Sensor simulation is a popular area of research, particularly in the case of images [1,15,25,32,42,53,60]. However, most existing sensor simulators are costly and difficult to scale since they are based on virtual worlds created by teams of artists; *e.g.*, TORCS [54], CARLA [12], AirSim [46]. Rendering these virtual worlds also results in observations that have very different statistics from real sensor data. As a result, there are large domain gaps between these virtual worlds and our physical one. Recently, LiDARSim [35] leveraged real-world data to produce realistic LiDAR simulations at scale, narrowing the fidelity gap significantly. However, current autonomy stacks use a host of different sensors, including LiDAR [30,59,63], radar [8,57], cameras [10,33,51], and ultrasonics, and thus all of these sensors must be simulated consistently for this approach to be useful in testing the full autonomy stack. These challenges make sensor simulation a very exciting area of research, but also one that is potentially far from deployment in real-world systems that must meet requirements developed by safety, systems engineering, and testing teams.

In this paper, we propose to simulate the SDV's perception and prediction system instead; see Fig. 1. To this end, we provide a comprehensive study of a variety of noise models with increasing levels of sophistication. Our best model is

---

[1] We use the terms *prediction* and *motion forecasting* interchangeably.

a convolutional neural network that, given a simple representation of the scene, produces realistic perception and prediction simulations. Importantly, this input representation can be sketched by a test engineer in a matter of minutes, making our approach cheap and easy to scale. We validate our model on two self-driving datasets and show that our simulations closely match the outputs of a real perception and prediction system. We also demonstrate that they can be used to realistically test motion planning. We hope to inspire work in this important field so that one day we can certify the safety of SDVs and deploy them at scale.

2 Related Work

Sensor Simulation: The use of sensor simulation in self-driving dates back to at least the seminal work of Pomerleau [40] who used both simulated and real road images to train a neural network to drive. Since then, researchers and engineers have developed increasingly realistic sensor simulators for self-driving across various modalities. For example, [1,15,25,42,53] use photo-realistic rendering techniques to synthesize images to train neural networks and [32,60] leverage real sensor data to generate novel views. Likewise, [12,14,17,61] use physics-based ray-casting to simulate LiDAR while [35] enhances its realism with learning. And in radar, [19] propose a ray-tracing based simulator and [52] use a fully-learned approach. However, despite much progress in recent years, there remain sizeable domain gaps between simulated sensor data and real ones [35]. Moreover, developing a realistic sensor simulator requires significant effort from domain experts [25], which limits the scalability of doing so across an entire sensor suite. In this paper, we sidestep these challenges by instead simulating a much simpler scene representation: the SDV's perception and prediction outputs.

Virtual Environments: Training and testing robots in the physical world can be a slow, costly, and even dangerous affair; virtual environments are often used to circumvent these difficulties. For example, in machine learning and robotics, popular benchmarks include computer games [3,4,24,26,47], indoor environments [29,45,55,56], robotics simulators [11,28,49], and self-driving simulators [9,12,46,54]. These virtual worlds have motivated a wealth of research in fields ranging from embodied vision to self-driving. However, they also require significant effort to construct, and this has unfortunately limited the diversity of their content. For example, CARLA [12] originally had just two artist-generated towns consisting of 4.3 km of drivable roads. In this paper, we use a lightweight scene representation that simplifies the task of generating new scenarios.

Knowledge Distillation: Knowledge distillation was first popularized by Hinton et al. [22] as a way to compress neural networks by training one network with the (soft) outputs of another. Since then, researchers have found successful applications of distillation in subfields across machine learning [16,20,21,38,43]. In this paper, we also train our simulation model using outputs from an SDV's perception and prediction system. In this sense, our work is closely related with distillation. However, unlike prior work in distillation, we assume no direct knowledge of the target perception and prediction system; *i.e.*, we treat these modules as black boxes. Moreover, the inputs to our simulation model differ from the inputs to the target system. This setting is more suitable for self-driving, where perception and prediction systems can be arbitrarily complex pipelines.

3   Perception and Prediction Simulation

Our goal is to develop a framework for testing the SDV's motion planner as it will behave in the real world. One approach is to use sensor simulation to test the SDV's full autonomy stack, end-to-end. However, this can be a complex and costly endeavor that requires constructing realistic virtual worlds and developing high-fidelity sensor simulators. Moreover, there remains a large domain gap between the sensor data produced by existing simulators and our physical world.

In this work, we study an alternative approach. We observe that the autonomy stack of today's SDVs employ a cascade of interpretable modules: perception, prediction, and motion planning. Therefore, rather than simulate the raw sensor data, we simulate the SDV's intermediate perception and prediction outputs instead, thus leveraging the compositionally of its autonomy stack to bypass the challenges of sensor simulation. Testing the SDV's motion planner can then proceed by simply mocking real perception and prediction outputs with our simulated ones. We call this task *perception and prediction simulation.*

Our approach is predicated on the hypothesis that there exists systemic noise in modern perception and prediction systems that we could simulate. Indeed, our experiments show that this is the case in practice. Therefore, we study a variety of noise models with increasing levels of sophistication. Our best model is a convolutional neural network that, given a simple representation of the scene, learns to produce realistic perception and prediction simulations. This enables us to realistically test motion planning in simulation. See Fig. 1 for an overview.

In this section, we first formulate the task of perception and prediction simulation and define some useful notation. Next, we describe a number of noise models in order of increasing sophistication and highlight several key modeling choices that informs the design of our best model. Finally, we describe our best model for this task and discuss how to train it in an end-to-end fashion.

3.1   Problem Formulation

Given a sensor reading at timestep t, the SDV's perception and prediction system ingests an HD map and sensor data and produces a class label $\hat{c}_i$, a bird's eye view (BEV) bounding box $\hat{\boldsymbol{b}}_i$, and a set of future states $\hat{\boldsymbol{s}}_i = \{\hat{\boldsymbol{s}}_{i,t+\delta}\}_{\delta=1}^{H}$ for each actor i that it detects in the scene, where H is the prediction horizon. Each state $\hat{\boldsymbol{s}}_{i,t+\delta} \in \mathbb{R}^3$ consists of the actor's 2D BEV position and orientation at some timestep $t + \delta$ in the future.[2] Note that this is the typical output

---

[2] Actors' future orientations are approximated from their predicted waypoints using finite differences, and their bounding box sizes remain constant over time.

Fig. 2. Perturbation models for perception and prediction simulation.
NoNoise assumes perfect perception and prediction. GaussianNoise and Multimodal-
Noise use marginal noise distributions to perturb each actor's shape, position, and
whether it is misdetected. ActorNoise accounts for inter-actor variability by predicting
perturbations conditioned on each actor's bounding box and positions over time.

parameterization for an SDV's perception and prediction system [7,31,33,34,
50,62], as it is lightweight, interpretable, and easily ingested by existing motion
planners.

For each timestep in a test scenario, our goal is to simulate the outputs of the
SDV's perception and prediction system without using sensor data—neither real
nor simulated. Instead, we use a much simpler representation of the world such
that we can: (i) bypass the complexity of developing realistic virtual worlds and
sensor simulators; and (ii) simplify the task of constructing new test scenarios.

Our scenario representation consists of an HD map $\mathcal{M}$, a set of actors $\mathcal{A}$,
and additional meta-data for motion planning, such as the SDV's starting state
and desired route. The HD map $\mathcal{M}$ contains semantic information about the
static scene, including lane boundaries and drivable surfaces. Each actor $a_i \in \mathcal{A}$
is represented by a class label c_i, a bounding box b_i, and a set of states $s_i =
\{s_{i,t}\}_{t=0}^{T}$, where T is the scenario duration. Note that $\mathcal{A}$ is a *perfect* perception
and prediction of the world, not the (noisy) outputs of a real online system.

This simple representation can be easily sketched by a test engineer in a
matter of seconds or minutes, depending on the complexity and duration of the
scenario. The test engineer can start from scratch or from existing logs collected
in real traffic or in structured tests at a test track by adding or removing actors,
varying their speeds, changing the underlying map, *etc.*

3.2   Perturbation Models for Perception and Prediction Simulation

One family of perception and prediction simulation methods builds on the idea of
perturbing the actors $\mathcal{A}$ of the input test scenario with noise approximating that
found in real systems. In this section, we describe a number of such methods in
order of increasing sophistication; see Fig. 2. Along the way, we highlight several
key modeling considerations that will motivate the design of our best model.

NoNoise: For each timestep t of the test scenario, we can readily simulate
perfect perception and prediction by outputting the class label c_i, the bounding
box b_i, and the future states $\{s_{i,t+\delta}\}_{\delta=1}^{H}$ for each actor $a_i \in \mathcal{A}$. Indeed, most
existing methods to test motion planning similarly use perfect perception [18].
This approach gives an important signal as an upper bound on the motion
planner's performance in the real world. However, it is also unrealistic as it yields

an overly optimistic evaluation of the motion planner's safety. For example, this approach cannot simulate false negative detections; thus, the motion planner will never be tested for its ability to exercise caution in areas of high occlusion.

GaussianNoise: Due to its assumption of perfect perception and prediction, the previous method does not account for the noise present in real perception and prediction systems. As such, it suffers a sim-to-real domain gap. In domain randomization, researchers have successfully used random noise to bridge this gap during training [36,37,39,41,48]. This next approach investigates whether random noise can be similarly used to bridge the sim-to-real gap *during testing*. Specifically, we model the noise present in real perception and prediction systems with a marginal distribution p_{noise} over all actors. For each timestep t in the test scenario, we perturb each actor's bounding box b_i and future states $\{s_{i,t+\delta}\}_{\delta=1}^{H}$ with noise drawn from p_{noise}. In our experiments, we use noise drawn from a Gaussian distribution $\mathcal{N}(0, 0.1)$ to perturb each component in $b_i = (x, y, \log w, \log h, \sin \theta, \cos \theta)$, where (x, y) is the box's center, (w, h) is its width and height, and θ is its orientation. We similarly perturb each state in $\{s_{i,t+\delta}\}_{\delta=1}^{H}$. To simulate misdetections, we randomly drop boxes with probability equal to the observed rate of false negative detections in our data.[3]

MultimodalNoise: Simple noise distributions such as the one used in GaussianNoise do not adequately reflect the complexity of the noise in perception and prediction systems. For example, prediction noise is highly multi-modal since vehicles can go straight or turn at intersections. Therefore, in this next approach, we instead use a Gaussian Mixture Model, which we fit to the empirical distribution of noise in our data via expectation-maximization [5]. As before, we simulate misdetections by dropping boxes with probability equal to the observed rate of false negative detections in our data.

ActorNoise: In MultimodalNoise, we use a marginal noise distribution over all actors to model the noise present in perception and prediction systems. This, however, does not account for inter-actor variability. For example, prediction systems are usually more accurate for stationary vehicles than for ones with irregular motion. In our next approach, we relax this assumption by conditioning the noise for each actor on its bounding box b_i and past, present, and future states s_i. We implement ActorNoise as a multi-layer perceptron that learns to predict perturbations to each component of an actor's bounding box b_i and future states $\{s_{i,t+\delta}\}_{\delta=1}^{H}$. We also predict each actor's probability of misdetection. To train ActorNoise, we use a combination of a binary cross entropy loss for misdetection classification and a smooth ℓ_1 loss for box and waypoint regression.

---

[3] True positive, false positive, and false negative detections are determined by IoU following the detection AP metric. In our experiments, we use a 0.5 IoU threshold for cars and vehicles and 0.3 IoU for pedestrians and bicyclists.

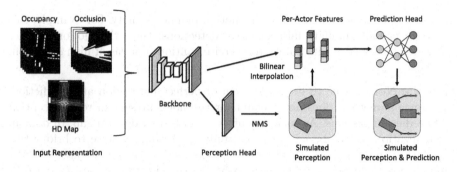

Fig. 3. ContextNoise for perception and prediction simulation. Given BEV rasterized images of the scene (drawn from bounding boxes and HD maps), our model simulates outputs similar to those from the real perception and prediction system. It consists of: (i) a shared backbone feature extractor; (ii) a perception head for simulating bounding box outputs; and (iii) a prediction head for simulating future states outputs.

3.3   A Contextual Model for Perception and Prediction Simulation

So far, we have discussed several perturbation-based models for perception and prediction simulation. However, these methods have two limitations. First, they cannot simulate false positive misdetections. More importantly, they do not use contextual information about the scene, which intuitively should correlate with the success of a perception and prediction system. For example, HD maps provide valuable contextual information to determine what actor behaviors are possible.

To address these limitations, we propose to use a convolutional neural network that takes as input BEV rasterized images of the scene (drawn from bounding boxes and HD maps) and learns to simulate dense bounding boxes and future state outputs similar to those from the real perception and prediction system. This is the native parameterization of the perception and prediction system used in our experiments. Our model architecture is composed of three components: (i) a shared backbone feature extractor; (ii) a perception head for simulating bounding box outputs; and (iii) a prediction head for simulating future states outputs. We call this model *ContextNoise*. See Fig. 3 for an overview.

Input Representation: For each timestep t of the input scenario, our model takes as input BEV raster images of the scene in ego-centric coordinates. In particular, for each class of interest, we render the actors of that class as bounding boxes in a sequence of occupancy masks [2,23] indicating their past, present, and future positions. Following [7,58], we rasterize the HD map $\mathcal{M}$ into multiple binary images. We represent lane boundaries as polylines and drivable surfaces as filled polygons. Occlusion is an important source of systemic errors for perception and prediction systems. For example, a heavily occluded pedestrian is more likely to be misdetected. To model this, we render a temporal sequence of 2D occlusion masks using a constant-horizon ray-casting algorithm [18]. By stacking these binary images along the feature channel, we obtain our final input representation.

Backbone Network: We use the backbone architecture of [33] as our shared feature extractor. Specifically, it is a convolutional neural network that computes a feature hierarchy at three scales of input resolution: 1/4, 1/8, and 1/16. These multi-scale features are then upscaled to 1/4 resolution and fused using residual connections. This yields a $C \times H/4 \times W/4$ feature map, where C is the number of output channels and H and W is the height and width of the input raster image. Note that we use this backbone to extract features from BEV raster images (drawn from bounding boxes and HD maps), *not* voxelized LiDAR point clouds as it was originally designed for. We denote the resulting feature map by:

$$\mathcal{F}_{\mathrm{bev}} = \mathrm{CNN}_{\mathrm{bev}}\left(\mathcal{A}, \mathcal{M}\right) \qquad (1)$$

Perception Head: Here, our goal is to simulate the bounding box outputs of the real perception and prediction system. To this end, we use a lightweight header to predict dense bounding box outputs for every class. Our dense output parameterization allows us to naturally handle false positive and false negative misdetections. In detail, for each class of interest, we use one convolution layer with 1×1 kernels to predict a bounding box $\tilde{\boldsymbol{b}}_i$ and detection score $\tilde{\alpha}_i$ at every BEV pixel i in $\mathcal{F}_{\mathrm{bev}}$. We parameterize $\tilde{\boldsymbol{b}}_i$ as $(\Delta x, \Delta y, \log w, \log h, \sin \theta, \cos \theta)$, where $(\Delta x, \Delta y)$ are the position offsets to the box center, (w, h) are its width and height, and θ is its orientation [59]. We use non-maximum suppression to remove duplicates. This yields a set of simulated bounding boxes $\mathcal{B}_{\mathrm{sim}} = \{\tilde{\boldsymbol{b}}_i\}_{i=1}^{N}$.

Prediction Head: Our goal now is to simulate a set of future states for each bounding box $\tilde{\boldsymbol{b}}_i \in \mathcal{B}_{\mathrm{sim}}$. To this end, for each $\tilde{\boldsymbol{b}}_i \in \mathcal{B}_{\mathrm{sim}}$, we first extract a feature vector $\boldsymbol{f}_i$ by bilinearly interpolating $\mathcal{F}_{\mathrm{bev}}$ around its box center. We then use a multi-layer perceptron to simulate its future positions:

$$\tilde{\boldsymbol{x}}_i = \mathrm{MLP}_{\mathrm{pred}}\left(\boldsymbol{f}_i\right) \qquad (2)$$

where $\tilde{\boldsymbol{x}}_i \in \mathbb{R}^{H \times 2}$ is a set of 2D BEV waypoints over the prediction horizon H. We also simulate its future orientation $\tilde{\boldsymbol{\theta}}_i$ using finite differences. Together, $\{\tilde{\boldsymbol{x}}_i\}_{i=1}^{N}$ and $\{\tilde{\boldsymbol{\theta}}_i\}_{i=1}^{N}$ yield a set of simulated future states $\mathcal{S}_{\mathrm{sim}} = \{\tilde{\boldsymbol{s}}_i\}_{i=1}^{N}$. Combining $\mathcal{S}_{\mathrm{sim}}$ with $\mathcal{B}_{\mathrm{sim}}$, we have our final perception and prediction simulation.

Learning: We train our model with a multi-task loss function:

$$\mathcal{L} = \ell_{\mathrm{perc}} + \ell_{\mathrm{pred}} \qquad (3)$$

where ℓ_{perc} is the perception loss and ℓ_{pred} is the prediction loss. Note that these losses are computed between our simulations and the outputs of the real perception and prediction system. Thus, we train our model using datasets that provide both real sensor data (to generate real perception and prediction outputs) and our input scenario representations (to give as input to our model).[4]

Our perception loss is a multi-task detection loss. For object classification, we use a binary cross-entropy loss with online negative hard-mining, where positive and negative BEV pixels are determined according to their distances to an object's center [59]. For box regression at positive pixels, we use a smooth ℓ_1 loss for box orientation and an axis-aligned IoU loss for box location and size.

Our prediction loss is a sum of smooth ℓ_1 losses over future waypoints for each true positive bounding box, where a simulated box is positive if its IoU with a box from the real system exceeds a certain threshold. In our experiments, we use a threshold of 0.5 for cars and vehicles and 0.3 for pedestrians and bicyclists.

4   Experimental Evaluation

In this section, we benchmark a variety of noise models for perception and prediction simulation on two large-scale self-driving datasets (Sect. 4.3). Our best model achieves significantly higher simulation fidelity than existing approaches that assume perfect perception and prediction. We also conduct downstream experiments with two motion planners (Sect. 4.4). Our results show that there is a strong correlation between our ability to realistically simulate perception and prediction and our ability to realistically test motion planning.

4.1   Datasets

NuScenes: nuScenes [6] consists of 1000 traffic scenarios collected in Boston and Singapore, each containing 20 s of video captured by a 32-beam LiDAR sensor at 20 Hz. In this dataset, keyframes sampled at 2 Hz are annotated with object labels within a 50 m radius. We generate additional labels at unannotated frames by linearly interpolating labels from adjacent keyframes [33]. We use the official training and validation splits and perform evaluation on the *car* class. To prevent our simulation model from overfitting to the training split, we partition the training split into two halves: one to train the perception and prediction model and the other our simulation model. Note that we do not use HD maps in our nuScenes experiments due to localization issues in some maps.[5]

ATG4D: ATG4D [59] consists of 6500 challenging traffic scenarios collected by a fleet of self-driving vehicles in cities across North America. Each scenario contains 25 seconds of video captured by a Velodyne HDL-64E at 10 Hz, resulting in 250 LiDAR sweeps per video. Each sweep is annotated with bounding boxes and trajectories for the vehicle, pedestrian, and bicyclist classes within a 100 m radius and comes with localized HD maps. We split ATG4D into two training splits of 2500 scenarios each, a validation split of 500, and a test split of 1000.

---

[4] Our representation uses bounding boxes and trajectories. Most self-driving datasets provide this as *ground truth labels* for the standard perception and prediction task. For perception and prediction simulation, we use these labels as *inputs* instead.

[5] As of nuScenes map v1.0.

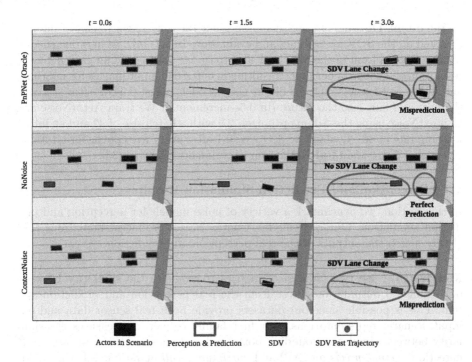

Fig. 4. Simulation results on ATG4D. We visualize PLT [44] motion planning results when given real perception and prediction (top) versus simulations from NoNoise (middle) and ContextNoise (bottom). ContextNoise faithfully simulates a misprediction due to multi-modality and induces a lane-change behavior from the motion planner.

4.2 Experiment Setup

Autonomy Stack: We simulate the outputs of PnPNet [33]—a state-of-the-art joint perception and prediction model. PnPNet takes as input an HD map and the past 0.5s of LiDAR sweeps and outputs BEV bounding boxes and 3.0s of future waypoints (in 0.5s increments) for each actor that it detects. Since our focus is on simulating perception and prediction, we use the variant of PnPNet without tracking. We configure PnPNet to use a common detection score threshold of 0. In the ATG4D validation split, this corresponds to a recall rate of 94% for vehicles, 78% for pedestrians, and 62% for bicyclists.

To gauge the usefulness of using our simulations to test motion planning, we conduct downstream experiments with two motion planners. Our first motion planner is adaptive cruise control (ACC), which implements a car-following algorithm. Our second motion planner is PLT [44]—a jointly learnable behavior and trajectory planner. PLT is pretrained on the ManualDrive dataset [44], which consists of 12,000 logs in which the drivers were instructed to drive smoothly.

Experiment Details: In nuScenes, we use a 100 m × 100 m region of interest centered on the SDV for training and evaluation. In ATG4D, we use one encompassing 70 m in front of the SDV and 40 m to its left and right. Our rasters have a resolution of 0.15625 m per pixel, resulting in 640 × 640 input images for nuScenes and 448 × 512 for ATG4D. All of our noise models ingest 0.5s of actor states in the past and 3.0s into the future (in 0.5s increments). We train ActorNoise and ContextNoise using the Adam optimizer [27] with a batch size of 32 and an initial learning rate of 4e−4, which we decay by 0.1 after every five epochs for a total of 15 epochs. We re-train PnPNet for our experiments following [33].

4.3   Perception and Prediction Simulation Results

In this section, we benchmark a variety of noise models for perception and prediction simulation. Our best model, ContextNoise, produces simulations that closely match the outputs of the real perception and prediction system.

Metrics: We use two families of metrics to evaluate the similarity between our simulated outputs and those from the real perception and prediction system. This is possible since our datasets provide both real sensor data and our input scenario representations. Our first family of metrics measures the similarity between simulated bounding boxes and real ones. To this end, we report detection *average precision* (AP) and *maximum recall* at various IoU thresholds depending on the class and dataset. Our second family of metrics measures the similarity between simulated future states and real ones. We use *average displacement error* (ADE) over 3.0s and *final displacement error* (FDE) at 3.0s for this purpose. These metrics are computed on true positive bounding boxes at 0.5 IoU for cars and vehicles and 0.3 IoU for pedestrians and bicyclists. In order to fairly compare models with different maximum recall rates, we report ADE and FDE for all methods at a common recall point, if it is attained. All metrics for GaussianNoise and MultimodalNoise are averaged over 25 sample runs. Note that we use random ordering to compute AP, ADE, and FDE for the methods that do not produce ranking scores: NoNoise, GaussianNoise, and MultimodalNoise.

Quantitative Results: Tables 1 and 2 show the results of our experiments on nuScenes and ATG4D respectively. Overall, ContextNoise attains the best performance. In contrast, simple marginal noise models such as GaussianNoise and MultimodalNoise perform worse than the method that uses no noise at all. This attests to the importance of using contextual information for simulating the noise in real perception and prediction systems. In addition, we highlight the fact that only ContextNoise improves maximum recall over NoNoise. This is at least in part due to its dense output parameterization, which can naturally model misdetections due to mislocalization, misclassification, *etc*. Finally, we note that ContextNoise's improvements in prediction metrics are most evident for the car and vehicle classes; for rarer classes, such as pedestrians and bicyclists, ContextNoise and ActorNoise perform similarly well.

Table 1. Perception and prediction simulation metrics on nuScene validation. R denotes the common recall point at which prediction metrics are computed.

	Perception metrics ↑				Prediction metrics ↓			
	AP (%)		Max recall (%)		ADE (cm)		FDE (cm)	
Car	0.5 IoU	0.7 IoU	0.5 IoU	0.7 IoU	50% R	70% R	50% R	70% R
GaussianNoise	4.9	0.9	13.0	1.7	-	-	-	-
MultimodalNoise	12.8	4.9	21.1	13.1	-	-	-	-
NoNoise	51.5	39.0	72.0	62.7	85	84	147	146
ActorNoise	65.7	55.0	72.1	63.5	64	66	97	100
ContextNoise	**72.2**	**59.1**	**80.3**	**68.9**	**54**	**61**	**81**	**90**

Table 2. Perception and prediction simulation metrics on ATG4D test.

	Perception metrics ↑				Prediction metrics ↓			
	AP (%)		Max Recall (%)		ADE (cm)		FDE (cm)	
Vehicle	0.5 IoU	0.7 IoU	0.5 IoU	0.7 IoU	70% R	90% R	70% R	90% R
GaussianNoise	16.5	0.4	34.4	5.2	-	-	-	-
MultimodalNoise	30.7	12.1	46.8	29.4	-	-	-	-
NoNoise	71.7	56.9	93.1	82.9	70	70	127	128
ActorNoise	86.6	70.4	93.2	82.9	65	57	109	93
ContextNoise	**91.8**	**82.3**	**95.7**	**87.8**	**46**	**51**	**72**	**78**
Pedestrian	0.3 IoU	0.5 IoU	0.3 IoU	0.5 IoU	60% R	80% R	60% R	80% R
GaussianNoise	13.8	3.0	30.0	13.8	-	-	-	-
MultimodalNoise	30.3	21.7	44.2	37.4	-	-	-	-
NoNoise	57.4	52.3	84.0	80.2	41	41	70	70
ActorNoise	67.1	61.6	84.0	80.0	36	35	55	54
ContextNoise	**75.1**	**66.6**	**88.2**	**80.3**	**34**	**34**	**51**	**52**
Bicyclist	0.3 IoU	0.5 IoU	0.3 IoU	0.5 IoU	50% R	70% R	50% R	70% R
GaussianNoise	4.7	0.4	17.8	5.4	-	-	-	-
MultimodalNoise	8.4	3.2	24.0	14.7	-	-	-	-
NoNoise	30.6	21.6	79.7	66.8	54	55	95	95
ActorNoise	60.4	44.1	79.7	67.8	54	**49**	88	78
ContextNoise	**66.8**	**52.8**	**89.8**	**76.5**	**52**	50	**80**	**75**

4.4 Motion Planning Evaluation Results

Our ultimate goal is to use perception and prediction simulation to test motion planning. Therefore, we conduct downstream experiments in ATG4D to quantify the efficacy of doing so for two motion planners: ACC and PLT.

Metrics: Our goal is to evaluate how similarly a motion planner will behave in simulation versus the physical world. To quantify this, we compute the ℓ_2 distance between a motion planner's trajectory given simulated perception and

Table 3. Motion planning evaluation metrics on ATG4D test.

	ℓ_2 Distance (cm) ↓			Collision Sim. (%) ↑		Driving Diff. (%) ↓		
	1.0s	2.0s	3.0s	IoU	Recall	Beh.	Jerk	Acc.
PLT								
GaussianNoise	2.6	8.4	15.9	34.5	92.7	0.30	0.10	1.05
MultimodalNoise	2.7	9.4	18.0	25.2	**93.6**	0.33	1.22	1.25
NoNoise	1.4	4.8	9.5	52.9	58.2	0.18	0.44	**0.03**
ActorNoise	1.0	3.6	7.0	57.6	63.6	0.12	0.27	0.13
ContextNoise	**0.8**	**2.9**	**5.6**	**65.1**	74.3	**0.10**	**0.05**	0.06
ACC								
GaussianNoise	6.4	32.5	79.9	36.5	**96.7**	-	5.14	**0.03**
MultimodalNoise	5.1	26.2	64.9	36.5	**96.7**	-	3.84	0.11
NoNoise	1.9	10.0	25.2	52.9	32.4	-	0.20	0.17
ActorNoise	1.6	8.1	20.0	58.6	66.3	-	0.40	0.13
ContextNoise	**1.4**	**7.2**	**17.6**	**61.3**	74.1	-	**0.14**	**0.03**

prediction outputs versus its trajectory when given real outputs instead. We report this metric for $\{1.0, 2.0, 3.0\}$ seconds into the future. In addition, we also measure their differences in terms of passenger comfort metrics; *i.e.*, jerk and lateral acceleration. Finally, we report the proportion of scenarios in which PLT chooses a different behavior when given simulated outputs instead of real ones.[6]

An especially important metric to evaluate the safety of a motion planner measures the proportion of scenarios in which the SDV will collide with an obstacle. To quantify our ability to reliably measure this in simulation, we report the intersection-over-union of collision scenarios and its recall-based variant:

$$\text{IoU}_{\text{col}} = \frac{|R_+ \cap S_+|}{|R_+ \cap S_+| + |R_+ \cap S_-| + |R_- \cap S_+|} \quad \text{Recall}_{\text{col}} = \frac{|R_+ \cap S_+|}{|R_+|} \quad (4)$$

where R_+ and S_+ are the sets of scenarios in which the SDV collides with an obstacle after 3.0s given real and simulated perception and prediction respectively, and R_- and S_- are similarly defined for scenarios with no collisions.

Quantitative Results: Table 3 shows our experiment results on ATG4D. They show that by realistically simulating the noise in real perception and prediction systems, we can induce similar motion planning behaviors in simulation as in the real world, thus making our simulation tests more realistic. For example, ContextNoise yields a 41.1% and 30.2% relative reduction in ℓ_2 distance at 3.0s over NoNoise for PLT and ACC respectively. Importantly, we can also more reliably measure a motion planner's collision rate using ContextNoise versus NoNoise.

---

[6] Note that ACC always uses the same driving behavior.

Table 4. Ablation of ContextNoise input features on ATG4D validation. We progressively add each input feature described in Sect. 3.3. **A** denotes actor occupancy images; **O** denotes occlusion masks; and **M** denotes HD maps. AP is computed using 0.7 IoU for vehicles and 0.5 IoU for pedestrians and bicyclists. FDE at 3.0s is computed at 90% recall for vehicles, 80% for pedestrians, and 70% for bicyclists.

	Inputs			AP (%) ↑			FDE (cm) ↓			ℓ_2 @ 3.0s (cm) ↓	
Variant	A	O	M	Veh.	Ped.	Bic.	Veh.	Ped.	Bic.	PLT	ACC
1	✓			85.0	64.0	59.9	87	56	**70**	4.7	15.0
2	✓	✓		85.5	63.8	61.7	86	55	72	4.7	14.4
3	✓	✓	✓	**86.9**	**68.6**	**64.1**	**76**	**52**	**70**	**4.2**	**14.2**

This is an important finding since existing methods to test motion planning in simulation typically assume perfect perception or use simple heuristics to generate noise. Our results show that more sophisticated noise modeling is necessary.

4.5 Ablation Study

To understand the usefulness of contextual information for simulation, we ablate the inputs to ContextNoise by progressively augmenting it with actor occupancy images, occlusion masks, and HD maps. From Table 4, we see that adding contextual information consistently improves simulation performance. These gains also directly translate to more realistic evaluations of motion planning.

4.6 Qualitative Results

We also visualize results from the PLT motion planner when given real perception and prediction versus simulations from NoNoise and ContextNoise. As shown in Fig. 4, ContextNoise faithfully simulates a misprediction due to multi-modality and induces a lane-change behavior from the motion planner—the same behavior as if the motion planner was given real perception and prediction. In contrast, NoNoise induces an unrealistic keep-lane behavior instead.

5   Conclusion

In this paper, we introduced the problem of perception and prediction simulation in order to realistically test motion planning. To this end, we have studied a variety of noise models. Our best model has proven to be a convolutional neural network that, given a simple representation of the scene, learns to produce realistic perception and prediction simulations. Importantly, this representation can be easily sketched by a test engineer in a matter of minutes. We have validated our model on two large-scale self-driving datasets and showed that our simulations closely match the outputs of real perception and prediction systems. We have only begun to scratch the surface of this task. We hope our findings here will inspire advances in this important field so that one day we can certify the safety of self-driving vehicles and deploy them at scale.

References

1. Alhaija, H.A., Mustikovela, S.K., Mescheder, L.M., Geiger, A., Rother, C.: Augmented reality meets computer vision: Efficient data generation for urban driving scenes. Int. J. Comput. Vis. **126**, 961 (2018). https://doi.org/10.1007/s11263-018-1070-x
2. Bansal, M., Krizhevsky, A., Ogale, A.S.: ChauffeurNet: Learning to drive by imitating the best and synthesizing the worst. In: Robotics: Science and Systems XV, University of Freiburg, Freiburg im Breisgau, Germany, June 22–26 (2019)
3. Beattie, C., et al.: Deepmind lab. CoRR (2016)
4. Bellemare, M.G., Naddaf, Y., Veness, J., Bowling, M.: The arcade learning environment: an evaluation platform for general agents. J. Artif. Intell. Res. **47**, 253 (2013)
5. Bishop, C.M.: Pattern Recognition and Machine Learning, 5th edn. Springer, New York (2007)
6. Caesar, H., et al.: nuScenes: a multimodal dataset for autonomous driving. CoRR (2019)
7. Casas, S., Luo, W., Urtasun, R.: IntentNet: learning to predict intention from raw sensor data. In: 2nd Annual Conference on Robot Learning, CoRL 2018, Zürich, Switzerland, 29–31 October 2018, Proceedings (2018)
8. Chadwick, S., Maddern, W., Newman, P.: Distant vehicle detection using radar and vision. In: International Conference on Robotics and Automation, ICRA 2019, Montreal, QC, Canada, May 20–24 (2019)
9. Chen, C., Seff, A., Kornhauser, A.L., Xiao, J.: DeepDriving: learning affordance for direct perception in autonomous driving. In: 2015 IEEE International Conference on Computer Vision, ICCV 2015, Santiago, Chile, December 7–13 (2015)
10. Chen, X., Kundu, K., Zhang, Z., Ma, H., Fidler, S., Urtasun, R.: Monocular 3D object detection for autonomous driving. In: 2016 IEEE Conference on Computer Vision and Pattern Recognition, CVPR 2016, Las Vegas, NV, USA, June 27–30 (2016)
11. Coumans, E., Bai, Y.: PyBullet, a python module for physics simulation for games, robotics and machine learning. http://www.pybullet.org (2016–2019)
12. Dosovitskiy, A., Ros, G., Codevilla, F., López, A., Koltun, V.: CARLA: an open urban driving simulator. In: 1st Annual Conference on Robot Learning, CoRL 2017, Mountain View, California, USA, November 13–15, Proceedings (2017)
13. Fan, H., et al.: Baidu apollo EM motion planner. CoRR (2018)
14. Fang, J., et al.: Simulating LIDAR point cloud for autonomous driving using real-world scenes and traffic flows. CoRR (2018)
15. Gaidon, A., Wang, Q., Cabon, Y., Vig, E.: Virtual worlds as proxy for multi-object tracking analysis. CoRR (2016)
16. Geras, K.J., et al.: Compressing LSTMs into CNNs. CoRR (2015)
17. Gschwandtner, M., Kwitt, R., Uhl, A., Pree, W.: BlenSor: blender sensor simulation toolbox. In: Advances in Visual Computing-7th International Symposium, ISVC 2011, Las Vegas, NV, USA, September 26–28. Proceedings, Part II (2011)
18. Gu, T., Dolan, J.M.: A lightweight simulator for autonomous driving motion planning development. In: ICIS (2015)

19. Gubelli, D., Krasnov, O.A., Yarovyi, O.: Ray-tracing simulator for radar signals propagation in radar networks. In: 2013 European Radar Conference (2013)
20. Guo, X., Li, H., Yi, S., Ren, J.S.J., Wang, X.: Learning monocular depth by distilling cross-domain stereo networks. In: Computer Vision-ECCV 2018–15th European Conference, Munich, Germany, September 8–14. Proceedings, Part XI (2018)
21. Gupta, S., Hoffman, J., Malik, J.: Cross modal distillation for supervision transfer. In: 2016 IEEE Conference on Computer Vision and Pattern Recognition, CVPR 2016, Las Vegas, NV, USA, June 27–30 (2016)
22. Hinton, G.E., Vinyals, O., Dean, J.: Distilling the knowledge in a neural network. CoRR (2015)
23. Jain, A., et al.: Discrete residual flow for probabilistic pedestrian behavior prediction. In: 3rd Annual Conference on Robot Learning, CoRL 2019, Osaka, Japan, October 30–November 1. Proceedings (2019)
24. Johnson, M., Hofmann, K., Hutton, T., Bignell, D.: The malmo platform for artificial intelligence experimentation. In: Proceedings of the Twenty-Fifth International Joint Conference on Artificial Intelligence, IJCAI 2016, New York, NY, USA, July 9–15 (2016)
25. Kar, A., et al.: Meta-sim: Learning to generate synthetic datasets. In: 2019 IEEE/CVF International Conference on Computer Vision, ICCV 2019, Seoul, Korea (South), October 27–November 2 (2019)
26. Kempka, M., Wydmuch, M., Runc, G., Toczek, J., Jaskowski, W.: ViZDoom: a doom-based AI research platform for visual reinforcement learning. CoRR (2016)
27. Kingma, D.P., Ba, J.: Adam: a method for stochastic optimization. In: 3rd International Conference on Learning Representations, ICLR 2015, San Diego, CA, USA, May 7–9, Conference Track Proceedings (2015)
28. Koenig, N.P., Howard, A.: Design and use paradigms for Gazebo, an open-source multi-robot simulator. In: 2004 IEEE/RSJ International Conference on Intelligent Robots and Systems, Sendai, Japan, September 28–October 2 (2004)
29. Kolve, E., Mottaghi, R., Gordon, D., Zhu, Y., Gupta, A., Farhadi, A.: AI2-THOR: an interactive 3D environment for visual AI. CoRR (2017)
30. Lang, A.H., Vora, S., Caesar, H., Zhou, L., Yang, J., Beijbom, O.: Pointpillars: Fast encoders for object detection from point clouds. In: IEEE Conference on Computer Vision and Pattern Recognition, CVPR 2019, Long Beach, CA, USA, June 16–20 (2019)
31. Li, L., et al.: End-to-end contextual perception and prediction with interaction transformer. In: 2020 IEEE/RSJ International Conference on Intelligent Robots and Systems, IROS 2020, October 25–29 (2020)
32. Li, W., et al.: AADS: augmented autonomous driving simulation using data-driven algorithms. Sci. Robot. 4, eaaw0863 (2019)
33. Liang, M., et al.: PnPNet: end-to-end perception and prediction with tracking in the loop. In: 2020 IEEE Conference on Computer Vision and Pattern Recognition, CVPR 2020, Seattle, WA, USA, June 16–18 (2020)
34. Luo, W., Yang, B., Urtasun, R.: Fast and furious: real time end-to-end 3D detection, tracking and motion forecasting with a single convolutional net. In: 2018 IEEE Conference on Computer Vision and Pattern Recognition, CVPR 2018, Salt Lake City, UT, USA, June 18–22, pp. 3569–3577 (2018)
35. Manivasagam, S., et al.: LiDARsim: realistic lidar simulation by leveraging the real world. In: 2020 IEEE Conference on Computer Vision and Pattern Recognition, CVPR 2020, Seattle, WA, USA, June 16–18 (2020)

36. Mehta, B., Diaz, M., Golemo, F., Pal, C.J., Paull, L.: Active domain randomization. In: 3rd Annual Conference on Robot Learning, CoRL 2019, Osaka, Japan, October 30–November 1, Proceedings (2019)

37. Akkaya, I., et al.: Solving rubik's cube with a robot hand. CoRR (2019)

38. Papernot, N., McDaniel, P.D., Wu, X., Jha, S., Swami, A.: Distillation as a defense to adversarial perturbations against deep neural networks. In: IEEE Symposium on Security and Privacy, SP 2016, San Jose, CA, USA, May 22–26 (2016)

39. Peng, X.B., Andrychowicz, M., Zaremba, W., Abbeel, P.: Sim-to-real transfer of robotic control with dynamics randomization. In: 2018 IEEE International Conference on Robotics and Automation, ICRA 2018, Brisbane, Australia, May 21–25 (2018)

40. Pomerleau, D.: ALVINN: an autonomous land vehicle in a neural network. In: Touretzky, D.S. (ed.) Advances in Neural Information Processing Systems, vol. 1, NIPS Conference, Denver, Colorado, USA (1988)

41. Pouyanfar, S., Saleem, M., George, N., Chen, S.: ROADS: randomization for obstacle avoidance and driving in simulation. In: IEEE Conference on Computer Vision and Pattern Recognition Workshops, CVPR Workshops 2019, Long Beach, CA, USA, June 16–20 (2019)

42. Ros, G., Sellart, L., Materzynska, J., Vázquez, D., López, A.M.: The SYNTHIA dataset: a large collection of synthetic images for semantic segmentation of urban scenes. In: 2016 IEEE Conference on Computer Vision and Pattern Recognition, CVPR 2016, Las Vegas, NV, USA, June 27–30 (2016)

43. Rusu, A.A., et al.: Policy distillation. In: 4th International Conference on Learning Representations, ICLR 2016, San Juan, Puerto Rico, May 2–4, Conference Track Proceedings (2016)

44. Sadat, A., Ren, M., Pokrovsky, A., Lin, Y., Yumer, E., Urtasun, R.: Jointly learnable behavior and trajectory planning for self-driving vehicles. In: 2019 IEEE/RSJ International Conference on Intelligent Robots and Systems, IROS 2019, Macau, SAR, China, November 3–8 (2019)

45. Savva, M., Chang, A.X., Dosovitskiy, A., Funkhouser, T.A., Koltun, V.: MINOS: multimodal indoor simulator for navigation in complex environments. CoRR (2017)

46. Shah, S., Dey, D., Lovett, C., Kapoor, A.: AirSim: high-fidelity visual and physical simulation for autonomous vehicles. CoRR (2017)

47. Tessler, C., Givony, S., Zahavy, T., Mankowitz, D.J., Mannor, S.: A deep hierarchical approach to lifelong learning in minecraft. In: Proceedings of the Thirty-First AAAI Conference on Artificial Intelligence, February 4–9, San Francisco, California, USA (2017)

48. Tobin, J., Fong, R., Ray, A., Schneider, J., Zaremba, W., Abbeel, P.: Domain randomization for transferring deep neural networks from simulation to the real world. In: 2017 IEEE/RSJ International Conference on Intelligent Robots and Systems, IROS 2017, Vancouver, BC, Canada, September 24–28 (2017)

49. Todorov, E., Erez, T., Tassa, Y.: MuJoCo: a physics engine for model-based control. In: 2012 IEEE/RSJ International Conference on Intelligent Robots and Systems, IROS 2012, Vilamoura, Algarve, Portugal, October 7–12 (2012)

50. Wang, T.H., Manivasagam, S., Liang, M., Yang, B., Zeng, W., Urtasun, R.: V2VNet: Vehicle-to-vehicle communication for joint perception and prediction. In: Computer Vision-ECCV 2020–16th European Conference, August 23–28, Proceedings (2020)

51. Wang, Y., Chao, W., Garg, D., Hariharan, B., Campbell, M.E., Weinberger, K.Q.: Pseudo-lidar from visual depth estimation: Bridging the gap in 3D object detection for autonomous driving. In: IEEE Conference on Computer Vision and Pattern Recognition, CVPR 2019, Long Beach, CA, USA, June 16–20 (2019)

52. Wheeler, T.A., Holder, M., Winner, H., Kochenderfer, M.J.: Deep stochastic radar models. CoRR (2017)

53. Wrenninge, M., Unger, J.: Synscapes: a photorealistic synthetic dataset for street scene parsing. CoRR (2018)

54. Wymann, B., Dimitrakakisy, C., Sumnery, A., Guionneauz, C.: TORCS: the open racing car simulator (2015)

55. Xia, F., et al.: Interactive Gibson benchmark: a benchmark for interactive navigation in cluttered environments. IEEE Robot. Autom. Lett. **5**, 713 (2020)

56. Xia, F., Zamir, A.R., He, Z., Sax, A., Malik, J., Savarese, S.: Gibson Env: real-world perception for embodied agents. In: 2018 IEEE Conference on Computer Vision and Pattern Recognition, CVPR 2018, Salt Lake City, UT, USA, June 18–22 (2018)

57. Yang, B., Guo, R., Liang, M., Casas, S., Urtasun, R.: Exploiting radar for robust perception of dynamic objects. In: Computer Vision-ECCV 2020–16th European Conference, August 23–28, Proceedings (2020)

58. Yang, B., Liang, M., Urtasun, R.: HDNET: exploiting HD maps for 3D object detection. In: 2nd Annual Conference on Robot Learning, CoRL 2018, Zürich, Switzerland, October 29–31, Proceedings (2018)

59. Yang, B., Luo, W., Urtasun, R.: PIXOR: real-time 3D object detection from point clouds. In: 2018 IEEE Conference on Computer Vision and Pattern Recognition, CVPR 2018, Salt Lake City, UT, USA, June 18–22 (2018)

60. Yang, Z., et al.: SurfelGAN: synthesizing realistic sensor data for autonomous driving. In: 2020 IEEE Conference on Computer Vision and Pattern Recognition, CVPR 2020, Seattle, WA, USA, June 16–18 (2020)

61. Yue, X., Wu, B., Seshia, S.A., Keutzer, K., Sangiovanni-Vincentelli, A.L.: A lidar point cloud generator: from a virtual world to autonomous driving. In: Proceedings of the 2018 ACM on International Conference on Multimedia Retrieval, ICMR 2018, Yokohama, Japan, June 11–14 (2018)

62. Zhang, Z., Gao, J., Mao, J., Liu, Y., Anguelov, D., Li, C.: STINet: Spatio-temporal-interactive network for pedestrian detection and trajectory prediction. In: 2020 IEEE Conference on Computer Vision and Pattern Recognition, CVPR 2020, Seattle, WA, USA, June 16–18 (2020)

63. Zhou, Y., Tuzel, O.: Voxelnet: end-to-end learning for point cloud based 3D object detection. In: 2018 IEEE Conference on Computer Vision and Pattern Recognition, CVPR 2018, Salt Lake City, UT, USA, June 18–22 (2018)

Determining the Relevance of Features for Deep Neural Networks

Christian Reimers[1,2](✉) ⓘ, Jakob Runge[2] ⓘ, and Joachim Denzler[1] ⓘ

[1] Computer Vision Group, Friedrich Schiller University Jena, 07743 Jena, Germany
{christian.reimers,joachim.denzler}@uni-jena.de
[2] Institute of Data Science, German Aerospace Center, 07745 Jena, Germany
jakob.runge@dlr.de

Abstract. Deep neural networks are tremendously successful in many applications, but end-to-end trained networks often result in hard to understand black-box classifiers or predictors. In this work, we present a novel method to identify whether a specific feature is relevant to a classifier's decision or not. This relevance is determined at the level of the learned mapping, instead of for a single example. The approach does neither need retraining of the network nor information on intermediate results or gradients. The key idea of our approach builds upon concepts from causal inference. We interpret machine learning in a structural causal model and use Reichenbach's common cause principle to infer whether a feature is relevant. We demonstrate empirically that the method is able to successfully evaluate the relevance of given features on three real-life data sets, namely MS COCO, CUB200 and HAM10000.

Keywords: Explainable-AI · Structural causal model · Deep learning · Causality

1 Introduction

Deep neural networks have pushed the state-of-the-art in many tasks in computer vision, for example, image classification [15], semantic image segmentation [18] and object detection [24]. Because of their success in these tasks, deep neural networks are used in many applications such as transport [11], medicine [23], legal decisions [2] and earth system science [26].

To reach these impressive results, deep neural network architectures have become more and more complex. The complex deep architectures allow the networks to perform automatic feature selection [27]. While the automatic feature selection led to better performance, the resulting neural networks are opaque, and it is difficult to understand how the network reaches its decisions and how it

Electronic supplementary material The online version of this chapter (https://doi.org/10.1007/978-3-030-58574-7_20) contains supplementary material, which is available to authorized users.

will decide on new data. One open question is, for example, whether the network uses a specific feature to reach its decision.

In many tasks, it is important to understand which features are selected by a deep neural network. It is important not just in safety- and security-critical tasks like autonomous driving or medicine, but also in responsible tasks like legal decisions. For a neural network to aid humans to come to informed decisions, it is often not enough to provide predictions, but the reasoning behind the decision is equally important. For example, in responsible decisions, like legal decisions, we need to make sure that neural networks are unbiased and do not discriminate against genders or minorities.

A simple and often used idea to decide if a feature is relevant to a response variable is correlation [14]. To determine the relevance of a feature to the prediction, we could use the output of the neural network as the response variable and calculate the correlation. Correlation is, however, for multiple reasons not well suited for deep neural networks. The first reason is that neural networks realize complicated, non-linear functions. In contrast, correlation measures only linear relationships. The second reason is that confounding of variables might lead to correlation between features and the prediction of the deep neural network, even if changes in the feature would not influence the prediction of the deep neural network and, hence, we should consider the feature to be irrelevant. An example, that demonstrates the problem of confounding can be found in Sect. 3.

To mitigate the problem of confounding, many researchers have used the gradient between the output and the input of a neural network instead of the correlation [16, 21, 29, 36]. This solves the problem of confounding but leads to new challenges. First, these methods approximate the gradient of the deep neural network on the level of single examples. While this is very useful in many situations, we are interested in explanations on the level of the learned mapping. On this level, the abovementioned methods do not provide insight. For example, in a classification system, the above methods can highlight which part of an image is relevant for the classification of this image, while our method can answer the question if some feature is, in general, relevant to the decision of the classifier. Furthermore, if we want to understand the relevance of an image region or an intermediate result of the neural network, we can use gradient information. However, we might be interested in features that are themselves function of the input. If we cannot identify a neuron that calculates this feature, we cannot calculate a gradient. Consequently, if we are interested in a feature that is a function of the input, we cannot use methods that depend on gradients.

Additionally, to calculate the gradients, we need access to the inner structure and the weights of the neural network. In the case where we have access to these values, we speak of a white-box model. Contrarily, if we do not have any access to these values, we speak of a black-box model.

In this paper, we present a novel method to determine whether a feature is relevant to a deep neural network. The key advantages of this novel method are:

- Our method is applicable to features that are functions of the input.
- It can handle non-linearity by using statistical dependence instead of corre-
  lation.
- It can handle confounding.
- Our method can be applied to black-box models, neither any retraining nor
  any information on intermediate results or gradients is necessary.

To the best of our knowledge our method is the only one that combines all of
these advantages.

We achieve this by capturing the fundamental structure of deep learning into
a structural causal model [22] (SCM). In this SCM, we calculate the statistical
dependence between the feature and the prediction of the deep neural network.
We use Reichenbach's common cause principle [25] to determine whether a feature is relevant to the decision of a deep neural network. We demonstrate that
the method can be used to validate classifiers in real-live situations. In the experiments on MS COCO we compare two classifiers on which features are relevant to
their decisions. We find that the classifier from [4] is less dependent on the position of the objects than the classifier from [5]. In an experiment on HAM10000 we
show that the symmetry of the shape is used by a classifier to identify seborrheic
keratosis but not to identify melanoma.

2   Related Work

The class of method that is used most often to understand deep neural networks
is saliency maps. Saliency maps are functions that map every pixel of the input
onto a relevance score. This relevance score highlights areas of the input. It is
calculated in one of three ways.

The first way is to use the gradient of the output of the neural network
depending on the input. Small changes in pixels with a large gradient lead to large
changes in the output of the neural network. Hence, these pixels are considered
to be more relevant. Examples can be found in [29] or [28].

The second way is to use the value of pixels and the value of activations
in intermediate layers in addition to the gradient information. The relevance is
propagated through the different layers similar to a Taylor-approximation. For
examples see [16, 20] or [21].

Both of these ways use intermediate activations or gradient information and
can, therefore, only be applied in the white-box case. Our method does not
require any information on intermediate results or gradients. Hence, our method
can be applied to black-box models and is not even restricted to neural networks.

Further, the first derivative is not an obvious measure for relevance in non-
linear function. Only little theoretical justification exists and multiple papers
advice for caution when interpreting saliency maps. For example, [1] reports
that randomly-initialized neural networks produce saliency maps that are visually and quantitatively similar to those produced by deep neural networks with
learned weights. Further, [13] reports that saliency maps fail to attribute correctly when a constant vector shift is applied. In contrast, we use the framework

of causality and Reichenbach's common cause principle to provide a rich theoretical explanation for the method proposed in this paper.

The third way is based on intervention. We start by recording the prediction for an image. Then patches of the image are replaced and the change in the prediction is taken as the relevance of the patch. Patches can be replaced by simple noise boxes [36], noisy versions of the original patch [6], by similar patches from other images [38], or by training a generative model [8].

Similar to gradients, an intervention can be performed on the input or on intermediate neurons. If we want to intervene on a feature that is a function of the input, and we cannot identify a neuron that calculates this function, it might be unclear how to intervene on it. In Sect. 4.4, we investigate the symmetry of skin lesions as a feature. To alter the symmetry of a skin lesion in a picture, one would need to replace significant parts of the image, which would naturally change the area, the mean color, the variance in color, the length of the border, the shape of the border and many more features. Further, there are infinitely many ways to change, for example, a symmetric skin lesion to a non-symmetric one. Since these ways might influence the aforementioned features differently, the outcome of the investigation will be different as well. Our method can be used in this situation. In contrast, the above way of calculating a saliency map can only be used if the feature is a part of the input or an intermediate neuron of the neural network.

Another key difference between all saliency maps and our method is that saliency maps explain decisions for individual inputs. In contrast, our method generates an explanation of the level of the learned mapping. Hence, we think that our method is a valuable addition and can be used together with saliency maps to get a more complete understanding of classifiers.

The authors of [12] present TCAV, a method to understand a neural network on the level of the learned mapping. They use images that represent a certain feature. An SVM is trained on intermediate representations extracted from the neural network. To determine whether the feature is relevant to the deep neural network's decision, they calculate whether the gradient of the deep neural network is in the same direction as the gradient of the SVM. Similar to our method, TCAV generates explanations on the level of the learned mapping, in contrast to our method that can be applied to black-box models, TCAV needs intermediate results of the neural network. Additionally, [8] reports that TCAV cannot resolve confounding.

3   Method

In this section, we explain how we use notation from the field of causal inference and Reichenbach's common cause principle to determine whether a feature is relevant to a classifier's decision. We reduce deep learning to a basic level. We identify the main elements necessary and arrange them into an SCM and subsequently into a graphical model. For each step of this process, we give a formal explanation and an illustration using an example. We will start by giving an

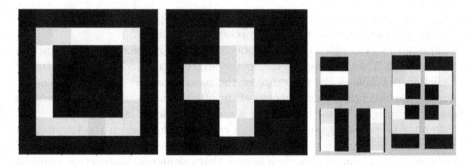

Fig. 1. From left to right, an example for the first class, an example for the second class, and all 2 × 3 patterns that appear in the first class but not in the second class are displayed.

introduction to this example. Then, first, we reduce the fundamental idea of deep learning to a pair of a training function and an inference function. Second, we explain which additional variables are needed to build this minimal formulation of deep learning into an SCM and, third, which functions connect these variables. Fourth, we explain why Reichenbach's common cause principle is applicable in this situation and how we use it to determine if a feature is relevant.

To this end, we use the notation of structural causal models (SCM) from [22]. An SCM is a model in which every variable is given as a function of other variables and independent noise. It can be built into a directed graph by using the variables as vertices and creating an edge from a variable A to a variable B if the function determining the value of B takes the variable A as an input. In this case, the authors of [22] say that A *causes* B.

The following is used as a vivid example for all definitions given in this section. The task is to distinguish between two classes of images. The images are each composed of a box for class one or a cross for class two and additive noise. Images of the base classes can be seen in Fig. 1. The dark pixels have a value of 0.0, and the light pixels have a value of 0.9, the additive noise is for each pixel independently distributed according to a uniform distribution on the interval $[0, 0.1]$. The task is to determine whether the base image is the box or the cross. We created a training set from 10000 images.

In Fig. 1, we also listed all 3 × 2 patterns that can be found in images of the first class but not in images of the second class. Note that each of these patterns alone is enough to distinguish the two classes. Since all of these patterns appear in all images of the first class and not in any image of the second class, the class is a confounding factor for the existence of these patterns and the prediction of the classifier. No matter which one of these patterns a classifier actually detects, the correlation between the existence of all of these patterns and the output of the classifier is high. Therefore, it is hard to evaluate which of these features is used by the classifier.

As the classifier, we use a convolutional neural network. The network has one convolutional layer with one kernel of size 3 × 2, followed by a global max-pooling layer. Due to this architecture, the classifier is forced to select a single discriminative pattern of size at most 3×2. A further advantage is that we can check the only kernel to verify which pattern was selected by the neural network. The classifier is trained using stochastic gradient descent for ten epochs. The accuracy on a testing set sampled from the same distribution was 1.0.

To build an SCM, we, first, reduce the basic idea of deep learning to a pair (T, F) of a training function and an inference function.

The first function T is the training function. We denote the inputs of a deep neural network by $I \in \mathcal{I}$ and the corresponding label by $Y_I \in \mathcal{Y}$. The training function takes a set of labeled inputs $\{(I, Y_I)\}$, the training set TS, as the input and maps it onto a set of weights W. Most training algorithms, like stochastic gradient descent, do not determine the weights of the deep neural networks deterministically. Therefore, we define for a probability space Ω

$$T : \mathcal{P}\left((\mathcal{I} \times \mathcal{Y})\right) \times \Omega \to \mathbb{R}^m \qquad \{(I, Y_I)\}, \omega \mapsto W. \tag{1}$$

Here $\mathcal{P}$ denotes the power set. In the example defined above, the function T is given by the stochastic gradient descent used for training. The training set TS in our example is the set of 10000 examples and the weights W are the seven weights of the convolutional layer, six for the kernel and one for the bias.

The second function F is the inference function. This function takes an unlabeled input I and the weights W calculated by the training function T as the input and maps them onto a prediction P

$$F : \mathcal{I} \times \mathbb{R}^m \to \mathbb{R}^d \qquad I, W \mapsto P. \tag{2}$$

Here d is the dimension of the output. For a classifier with d classes, the output of a deep neural network is a d-dimensional vector containing the scores for each class. In the example, the function F is given by the neural network. The prediction P is given by the output of the neural network. Note that the output of the neural network is not in $\mathcal{Y}$ but in $\mathbb{R}$. The network outputs a positive value for images of class "box" and negative values for images of class "cross."

Second, we identify all random variables that are part of the SCM. These variables are given by the training set TS, the weights W, and the prediction P, which are explained above. Additionally, we need three more variables, namely the feature of interest X, the set $\bar{X}$ of all features independent of X, and the ground truth GT. We continue with a brief explanation of these variables.

The random variable X can denote any feature of interest. It can be continuous as in Sect. 4.2 or discrete as in Sect. 4.4. It is not important whether we determine the value from the image or know it from any other source. In our example, the feature X denotes the maximum over the convolution of a pattern (light squares have value one, dark squares have value minus one) with the image. A high value can be understood as the pattern appears in the image, while a low value indicates that the pattern does not appear in the image. For this example, we decide to investigate the bottom right corner pattern that is displayed in the middle of the right graph in Fig. 2.

Since one of the advantages of deep neural networks is automatic feature selection, we are sure that the neural network bases its prediction on some features extracted from the input. We denote the set of all possible features independent of X by $\bar{X}$. Later, we will see that we never need to determine $\bar{X}$ further than this definition. We neither need the value of these features nor do we need to determine which features are part of $\bar{X}$. This restriction to orthogonal features has the following reason. Imagine a situation in which the classifier calculates $f(x^3)$. One could argue that it uses x^3 or that it uses x as the relevant feature. It is neither possible nor desirable to decline one of these options. No method can or should determine one of these as more relevant. Additionally, the method will identify features as relevant if they contain a relevant feature. This is desirable since $f(x^3)$ can be calculated from (x, y) and hence, (x, y) should be identified as relevant. However, since we want to understand which feature is the input to an unknown function, we can identify X only up to a class of features. If the function is $f(X)$, we cannot distinguish it from, for example, $f(\log(\exp(X)))$ and hence, we cannot distinguish the features X from $\exp(X)$. More specific, we cannot distinguish features that are invertible mappings of each other. In our example, the set $\bar{X}$ contains all other patterns. It also contains all other numerical features of the images, for example, its mean and its variance.

Finally, the ground truth GT describes the distribution from which X, $\bar{X}$ and TS, parameterized by the label. In our example 'box' and 'cross'.

Third, to identify the SCM, we need to find all functions that connect these variables. Besides the training function and the inference function defined above, we identify two sampling processes. On the one hand, the process that samples the training set from the ground truth distributions and provides the labeled test set, on the other hand, the process that samples single unlabeled examples from the ground truth distribution over all possible examples. Since all features are deterministically determined by the sampled example, we can understand the second sampling function as sampling the features from the ground truth instead of sampling an example. Both of these sampling processes exist in our example.

Fourth, we use the framework of causal inference to build the graphical model and use Reichenbach's common cause principle to determine whether the feature X is relevant to the prediction of the deep neural network.

The graphical model created from the SCM described in this section can be found in Fig. 2. The sampling processes sample TS, or X and $\bar{X}$ from GT. The training function maps the training set TS on the weights W, the inference function F determines the prediction P from the weights W and some features from the set $\bar{X}$. The remaining open question is, whether the inference function takes X as an input or, in other words, whether X *causes* P.

The way we identify whether a variable is causing another variable is Reichenbach's common cause principle (RCCP) [25]. This principle states that there is no correlation without causation. Since we are handling non-linear relationships, we look at statistical dependence instead of correlation. More formally, RCCP states that if two variables A and B are dependent, than there exists a variable C that *causes* A and B. In particular, C can be identical to A or B meaning that A *causes* B or B *causes* A.

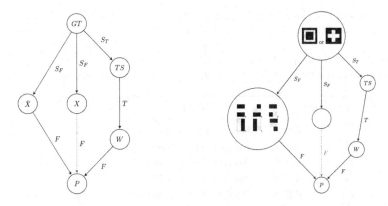

Fig. 2. On the left, the general graph of our method is displayed. On the right, we show the graph for the example.

We use RCCP to determine whether the feature X *causes* the prediction P. First, we want to rule out that a third variable *causes* X and P. From the graphical model in Fig. 2, we see that the only variable that can *cause* X and P is GT. To eliminate this possibility, we condition on GT. Second, we can rule out the possibility that the prediction P cases X because the prediction P is only calculated after the feature X is sampled. Hence, if we find a statistical dependence between X and P after conditioning on GT

$$X \not\!\perp P \,|\, GT, \tag{3}$$

we know that X *causes* P.

Note that we only need X, P, and GT for the calculations. In particular, we do not need $\bar{X}$. This allows us to handle all possible features, without ever calculating them.

To conclude, we say a feature X is relevant to the prediction P of a classifier or predictor if X is *causing* P in the sense of [22]. We use the word relevant instead of *causes* since it gives a better intuition in this exact application of the framework and to avoid confusion with the colloquial word "causes" or other definitions of causation such as the one presented by Granger in [9] or by Berkley in [3].

To illustrate further, we demonstrate the results for our example. We run the method seven times, once for each of the seven patterns illustrated in Fig. 1. The results can be found in Table 1. Since we know that the relationships in this example are linear, we use partial correlation as the independence test. The significance level is set to 0.05. We find that all features are correlated to the output with a coefficient of determination greater than 0.975. Hence, the coefficient of determination is not suited to determine which feature is used. In contrast, our method can determine the correct pattern.

Table 1. Results for the running example. The investigated feature is the maximum of the convolution of the pattern and every image. The light spots have value one and the dark spots have value minus one. We report the coefficient of determination between the feature X and the prediction P. Second, we report the significance of a partial correlation test as a measure for $X \perp\!\!\!\perp P \,|\, GT$. The significance level is set to 0.05

Pattern	$r^2(X, P)$	$X \perp\!\!\!\perp P \,|\, GT$	Equal to the kernel: ▬
▬	1.000	**Yes** (p-value = 0.000)	**Yes**
▐	0.985	No (p-value = 0.608)	No
▌	0.985	No (p-value = 0.980)	No
▬	0.979	No (p-value = 0.949)	No
▪	0.979	No (p-value = 0.384)	No
▬	0.978	No (p-value = 0.422)	No
▬	0.978	No (p-value = 0.793)	No

4   Experiments

In this section, we describe four experiments that demonstrate that our proposed method works on real-live data sets and can identify whether features are used even if the feature is a function of the input rather than part of the input directly and neither a derivative nor an intervention can be calculated. To this end, we first check whether, for images from the MS COCO data set, the area and the position of an object in the image are relevant to recognizing the object in the image. Secondly, we check whether a state-of-the-art classifier on the CUB200 bird data set uses the same discriminative characteristics of a bird species an ornithologist would use. Thirdly, we investigate a system that checks whether a skin lesion is a melanoma or a seborrheic keratosis. The feature of interest for this example is the shape symmetry, a discrete score used by dermatologists to describe how symmetric the border of a skin lesion is.

4.1   Evaluating a Classifier on MS COCO

MS COCO [17] is a multi-label dataset of real-live images. We investigate the Multi-Label Graph Convolutional Networks (ML-GCN) presented by Chen et al. in [4]. In the first experiment, we investigate whether the size of the object given by the area of the image covered by this object is relevant to the classifier.

One of the advantages of MS COCO is that the object is not always in the center but can appear anywhere in the image. This should lead to a classifier independent of the position in which the objects appear in the image. This is for the ML-GCN additionally aided by data augmentation, including random horizontal flipping of images. We, therefore, investigate if the position of the object is relevant to the prediction of the ML-GCN and if the vertical position is more relevant than the horizontal position.

For this experiment, we used the pre-trained version of the ML-GCN provided by the authors. One advantage of our method is that we can use it in combination with complex pre-trained classifiers. Neither is any retraining required nor do we need access to any weights or intermediate results of the classifier. This makes it easy and fast to apply. We conducted our experiments on the validation set of the 2014 challenge data set. As an independence test, we use the Randomized conditional Correlation Test (RCOT) [31]. Since we are testing many classes, we use a significance level of 0.001.

We run our method for the area of the object in the image and the position of the object in the image as the feature of interest. The area is calculated as its fraction of the image. If multiple instances of the object exist in the image, we consider the sum of all of their areas. We determine the area from the ground truth image segmentation. For the position, we consider the center of mass of the object. If more than one instance of the object is present in the image, we calculate the combined center of mass. For a more fine-grained analysis, we derive five features from the position of the object: The direction of the center of mass from the center of the image, the vertical position, the horizontal position, whether the object is in the right or left half and whether the object is in the top or bottom half of the image.

We expect, on the one hand, the area of the object to be relevant to the recognition score of the ML-GCN. Big objects should be easier to detect than small objects. On the other hand, we expect the position to be irrelevant to the recognition of the object. The information, whether the object is in the left or right half, should not be relevant since the images are randomly horizontally flipped during training. Further, we want an object recognition system to be independent of the position of the object.

We found that, for most of the 80 classes, the area of the object is relevant for the detection score. However, the area is irrelevant to the recognition of seven classes, namely "sheep," "elephant," "bear," "giraffe," "kite," "toaster," and "hairdryer". Further investigation sheds light on why the area of the object is irrelevant to some of these classes. On average, an object appears in 1267 images of the dataset. Instances of "hairdryer" and "toaster" appear in less than 75 images. This might lead to the network relying on context to recognize objects of these two classes. Interestingly, four of the five remaining classes are animals. Maybe, the neural network identifies only parts of the animal, e.g., the eyes, but further investigation is needed to unravel this further.

The results on the positional features can be found in the first column of Table 2. We find that despite the horizontal flipping, for one class, namely "mouse," it is relevant in which half of the image the object appears. As expected, due to the horizontal flipping, the horizontal position is much less relevant than the vertical position. The vertical half is relevant to 25 classes compared to 1 class for the horizontal half and the vertical position is relevant to 51 classes compared to 10 classes for the horizontal position. To summarize, we find that the classifier does not recognize objects independent of their position.

340   C. Reimers et al.

Table 2. The results for the experiments on the MS COCO data set for the different classifiers. For each feature and each classifier, we report, for the detection of how many out of the 80 classes, the feature was relevant. Tables with the p-value for every class can be found in the appendix

Feature	ML-GCN	SRN
Area	73/80	69/80
Half(Horizontal)	1/80	1/80
Position(Horizontal)	10/80	16/80
Half(Vertical)	25/80	32/80
Position(Vertical)	51/80	54/80
Angle	24/80	31/80

Fig. 3. From left to right: An example of a white-crowned sparrow, an example from a white-throated sparrow, the segmentation map for the white throat markings, the segmentation map for the yellow lores. (Color figure online)

Note that the position of an object is a feature that cannot be highlighted by a saliency map.

4.2 Evaluating a Classifier on CUB200

In a second experiment, we use the method proposed in this paper to investigate a classifier that discriminates birds from the CUB200 [35] data set. We use the Inception-V3 large scale fine-grained classifier (LSFGC) presented by Cui et al. [5] that is pre-trained on the iNaturalist 2017 data set and fine-tuned on CUB200. We change the LSFGC to only differentiate between two bird species, the White-crowned sparrow and the White-throated sparrow. The two main differences between these birds are two yellow lores and white throat markings [33]. Example images for both of these birds, taken from the CUB200 data set, can be found in Fig. 2. We check whether the LSFGC considers the area of the yellow lores, the area of the white throat markings, the color of the yellow lores, and the color of the white throat markings. We construct a feature out of each of these. For the area, we consider the fraction of the image that is covert by the yellow lores for the first feature and by the white throat markings for the second feature. As the color feature, we take the mean hue over the respective areas in the HSV color space. Segmentation maps for both of these features can be found in Fig. 3. We use all 120 images from the two classes in the CUB200 data set.

To determine independence, we again use the RCOT. We assume independence at a p-value below 0.05. The results can be found in Table 3.

Table 3. Results for the independence test that determine whether the yellow lores or the white throat markings are relevant to the LSFGC to distinguish white-crowned sparrows from white-throated sparrows

Feature	Area	Color
Yellow lores	No (p-value = 0.406)	No (p-value = 0.446)
white throat markings	No (p-value = 0.404)	No (p-value = 0.330)

We find that neither the size of the yellow or white throat markings nor their color is relevant to the classifier. This is not a surprising result since adversarial examples have demonstrated that neural networks often use complex, difficult to interpret features instead of the features considered relevant by human experts [7,32].

Note that a saliency map only highlight the region in the image that contains, for example, the yellow lores, while our method can distinguish between the area and the color of this region as different features.

4.3   Comparing Classifiers on MS COCO

We can also use the method presented in this work to compare classifiers beyond their performance on a test set. We compare the ML-GCN discussed above and the Spatial Regularization with Image-level Supervision classifier (SRN) presented by Zhu et al. [37]. To compare them, we use the abovementioned features. The results can be found in Table 2. We find that the ML-GCN considers the area of the actual object relevant for 73 classes, which is more often than the SRN, which considers it for only 69 classes. This indicates that the ML-GCN might be better at identifying the object while the SRN might rely more on the context to identify classes. Further, we find that the ML-GCN considers the position of the image to be relevant for fewer classes than the SRN. Since an ideal object detector would be independent of the position of the object, this analysis suggests that the ML-GCN should be preferred over the SRN.

4.4   Evaluating a Classifier on HAM10000

This fourth experiment is on the HAM10000 [34] data set, a data set of 10000 images of skin lesions. We investigate the classifier that won the best paper award at the ISIC Skin Image Analysis Workshop at the MICCAI 2018 [23]. We call this classifier SLA throughout this paper. The feature we investigate is the shape symmetry of the skin lesion.

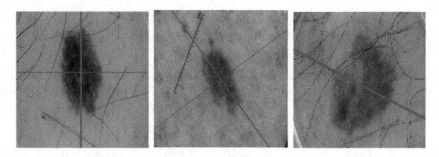

Fig. 4. Some example images for the shape symmetry feature. The red lines indicate the axes with respect to which the shape of the skin lesion is almost symmetric.

The feature describes how many orthogonal lines can be found in the image of the skin lesion such that the shape of the skin lesion is symmetric with respect to all of these lines (Fig. 4).

This feature is recognized to be important by the ABCD rule [30]. This rule is used by dermatologists and is known to be useful in distinguishing different classes of skin lesions. As discussed in Sect. 2, this feature can not be investigated using saliency maps or ablation methods.

We evaluate this feature on the ISIC 2017 Validation set. To calculate the shape symmetry, we use the implementation from [19]. The classifier outputs a score for two classes: "melanoma" and "seborrheic keratosis." For both of these classes, we determine whether the shape symmetry is relevant for the classification by the SLA. The result can be found in Table 4. We use RCOT for the independence tests. We consider the feature to be relevant if the p-value for the independence test is below 0.05.

Table 4. We test whether the shape symmetry is relevant to the classification as melanoma or seborrheic keratosis, respectively. The significance level is set to 0.05

Feature	Melanoma	Seborrheic keratosis
shape symmetry	No (p-value = 0.632)	**Yes** (p-value = 0.022)

We find that the shape symmetry is used by the classifier to determine whether a skin lesion is a seborrheic keratosis but not to determine whether a skin lesion is a melanoma.

5   Summary and Discussion

In this work, we presented a novel method to determine whether a feature is relevant to the prediction of a deep neural network. This method is built on the framework of causal-inference and has several key differences to other methods.

Firstly, it determines the global behavior of a deep neural network instead of the behavior in single examples, and it can be used to evaluate the relevance of features that are functions of the input rather than part of the input directly. Hence, it complements other methods, such as saliency maps.

Our method can be applied to a black-box classifier. Neither any retraining nor any insight into intermediate results or gradients is needed. Hence, it is easy and fast to apply the method, and it does not lead to any decrease in the performance of the classifier we want to understand. Additionally, since the only requirement to the classifier we made is that it can be formulated as a pair of two functions (T, F) our method can be applied to a vast range of classifiers. While, in this paper, we focus on deep neural networks, our method can also be applied to classical methods like kernel-SVM.

Since deep neural networks are opaque, it is difficult to evaluate the correctness of explanations for deep neural networks empirically. To this end, we presented a thorough theoretical background to our method based on structural causal models and Reichenbach's common cause principle.

A drawback of our method is that the researcher has to provide the feature of interest X prior to testing whether it is relevant. Our method does not propose features for testing. Nevertheless, in many situations either prior knowledge tells us which features might be relevant to a classifier, or we can use known methods to determine features as candidates for testing. One example of such methods are saliency maps. If we, for example, classify skin lesions, we can use a saliency map to highlight an area. If the skin lesion is highlighted in many images, we can use our method to understand which specific feature of the lesion is important. We can test the shape, the symmetry, the mean color, or others. In this way our method can be used in addition to saliency maps to understand a classifier further.

Additionally, we can evaluate the relevance of features that cannot be highlighted by saliency maps. In Sect. 4, we evaluate the position of the object as a feature. This feature cannot be evaluated using saliency maps.

As discussed in Sect. 2, our method will identify features as relevant, if they contain a relevant feature or if they are an invertible function of a relevant feature. This can lead to the method identifying multiple redundant versions of the same feature. To this end, additional feature to feature evaluations can be done using mutual information. We leave this for future work.

Whenever we apply our method, we have to select an independence test. Testing independence on finite samples is a hard problem in itself, and no single independence test is optimal for all kinds of data. When applying this method, we have to select an independence test carefully, depending on the data. For the experiments in this paper we used the RCOT [31]. To select a suitable independence test, we point the reader to [31] and [10] and the references therein.

In multiple experiments, we could demonstrate that the method can be used in relevant real-life situations. We demonstrated multiple experiments on MS COCO, CUB200, and HAM10000. In these experiments, we used the method to evaluate classifiers beyond there generalization performance on a holdout test set. We compared different classifiers beyond their generalization performance, and we evaluated whether a feature that is relevant to a human expert is relevant to a classifier. These additional evaluations can be used to generate trust in a classifier. They can help us to understand whether an existing classifier can be adapted to a new task, sharing some, but not all of the features of its old task. They can help to identify whether a neural network is biased or whether it bases its decision on meaningful features.

References

1. Adebayo, J., Gilmer, J., Goodfellow, I., Kim, B.: Local explanation methods for deep neural networks lack sensitivity to parameter values. arXiv preprint arXiv:1810.03307 (2018)
2. Barry-Jester, A.M., Casselman, B., Goldstein, D.: The new science of sentencing. In: The Marshall Project, vol. 4 (2015)
3. Berkeley, G.: A Treatise Concerning the Principles of Human Knowledge. JB Lippincott & Company, Philadelphia (1881)
4. Chen, Z.M., Wei, X.S., Wang, P., Guo, Y.: Multi-label image recognition with graph convolutional networks. In: Proceedings of the IEEE Conference on Computer Vision and Pattern Recognition. pp. 5177–5186 (2019)
5. Cui, Y., Song, Y., Sun, C., Howard, A., Belongie, S.: Large scale fine-grained categorization and domain-specific transfer learning. In: Proceedings of the IEEE Conference on Computer Vision and Pattern Recognition, pp. 4109–4118 (2018)
6. Fong, R.C., Vedaldi, A.: Interpretable explanations of black boxes by meaningful perturbation. In: Proceedings of the IEEE International Conference on Computer Vision, pp. 3429–3437 (2017)
7. Goodfellow, I.J., Shlens, J., Szegedy, C.: Explaining and harnessing adversarial examples. arXiv preprint arXiv:1412.6572 (2014)
8. Goyal, Y., Shalit, U., Kim, B.: Explaining classifiers with causal concept effect (CaCE). arXiv preprint arXiv:1907.07165 (2019)
9. Granger, C.W.: Investigating causal relations by econometric models and cross-spectral methods. Econometr. J. Econometr. Soc. **37**, 424–438 (1969)
10. Gretton, A., Bousquet, O., Smola, A., Schölkopf, B.: Measuring statistical dependence with Hilbert-Schmidt norms. In: Jain, S., Simon, H.U., Tomita, E. (eds.) ALT 2005. LNCS (LNAI), vol. 3734, pp. 63–77. Springer, Heidelberg (2005). https://doi.org/10.1007/11564089_7
11. Jarisa, W., Henze, R., Kücükay, F., Schneider, F., Denzler, J., Hartmann, B.: Fusionskonzept zur reibwertschätzung auf basis von wetter- und fahrbahnzustandsinformationen. In: VDI-Fachtagung Reifen - Fahrwerk - Fahrbahn, pp. 169–188 (2019)
12. Kim, B., Wattenberg, M., Gilmer, J., Cai, C., Wexler, J., Viegas, F., Sayres, R.: Interpretability beyond feature attribution: quantitative testing with concept activation vectors (TCAV). arXiv preprint arXiv:1711.11279 (2017)
13. Kindermans, P.-J., et al.: The (Un)reliability of saliency methods. In: Samek, W., Montavon, G., Vedaldi, A., Hansen, L.K., Müller, K.-R. (eds.) Explainable AI: Interpreting, Explaining and Visualizing Deep Learning. LNCS (LNAI), vol. 11700, pp. 267–280. Springer, Cham (2019). https://doi.org/10.1007/978-3-030-28954-6_14

14. Kretschmer, M., Runge, J., Coumou, D.: Early prediction of extreme stratospheric polar vortex states based on causal precursors. Geophys. Res. Lett. **44**(16), 8592–8600 (2017)
15. Krizhevsky, A., Sutskever, I., Hinton, G.E.: ImageNet classification with deep convolutional neural networks. In: Advances in Neural Information Processing Systems, pp. 1097–1105 (2012)
16. Lapuschkin, S., Wäldchen, S., Binder, A., Montavon, G., Samek, W., Müller, K.R.: Unmasking clever HANs predictors and assessing what machines really learn. Nat. Commun. **10**(1), 1–8 (2019)
17. Lin, T.-Y., et al.: Microsoft COCO: common objects in context. In: Fleet, D., Pajdla, T., Schiele, B., Tuytelaars, T. (eds.) ECCV 2014. LNCS, vol. 8693, pp. 740–755. Springer, Cham (2014). https://doi.org/10.1007/978-3-319-10602-1_48
18. Long, J., Shelhamer, E., Darrell, T.: Fully convolutional networks for semantic segmentation. In: Proceedings of the IEEE Conference on Computer Vision and Pattern Recognition, pp. 3431–3440 (2015)
19. Mendonça, T., Ferreira, P.M., Marques, J.S., Marcal, A.R., Rozeira, J.: PH2-a dermoscopic image database for research and benchmarking. In: 2013 35th Annual International Conference of the IEEE Engineering in Medicine and Biology Society (EMBC), pp. 5437–5440. IEEE (2013)
20. Montavon, G., Samek, W., Müller, K.R.: Methods for interpreting and understanding deep neural networks. Digit. Sig. Process. **73**, 1–15 (2018)
21. Mopuri, K.R., Garg, U., Babu, R.V.: CNN fixations: an unraveling approach to visualize the discriminative image regions. IEEE Trans. Image Process. **28**(5), 2116–2125 (2018)
22. Pearl, J.: Causality. Cambridge University Press, New York (2009)
23. Perez, F., Vasconcelos, C., Avila, S., Valle, E.: Data augmentation for skin lesion analysis. In: Stoyanov, D., et al. (eds.) CARE/CLIP/OR 2.0/ISIC -2018. LNCS, vol. 11041, pp. 303–311. Springer, Cham (2018). https://doi.org/10.1007/978-3-030-01201-4_33
24. Redmon, J., Farhadi, A.: Yolov3: an incremental improvement. arXiv preprint arXiv:1804.02767 (2018)
25. Reichenbach, H.: The Direction of Time. Dover Publications, New York (1956)
26. Reichstein, M., Camps-Valls, G., Stevens, B., Jung, M., Denzler, J., Carvalhais, N.: Prabhat: deep learning and process understanding for data-driven earth system science. Nature **566**(7743), 195–204 (2019)
27. Reimers, C., Requena-Mesa, C.: Deep learning - an opportunity and a challenge for geo- and astrophysics. In: Skoda, P., Adam, F. (eds.) Knowledge Discovery in Big Data from Astronomy and Earth Observation, chap. 13, pp. 251–266. Elsevier (2020)
28. Simon, M., Rodner, E.: Neural activation constellations: unsupervised part model discovery with convolutional networks. In: Proceedings of the IEEE International Conference on Computer Vision, pp. 1143–1151 (2015)
29. Simonyan, K., Vedaldi, A., Zisserman, A.: Deep inside convolutional networks: visualising image classification models and saliency maps. arXiv preprint arXiv:1312.6034 (2013)
30. Stolz, W., et al.: Multivariate analysis of criteria given by dermatoscopy for the recognition of melanocytic lesions. In: Book of Abstracts, Fiftieth Meeting of the American Academy of Dermatology, Dallas, Tex: Dec, pp. 7–12 (1991)
31. Strobl, E.V., Zhang, K., Visweswaran, S.: Approximate kernel-based conditional independence tests for fast non-parametric causal discovery. J. Causal Infer. **7**(1), 1–24 (2019)

32. Szegedy, C., et al.: Intriguing properties of neural networks. arXiv preprint arXiv:1312.6199 (2013)
33. The Cornell Lab of Ornithology: All about birds. https://www.allaboutbirds.org/guide/White-crowned_Sparrow/species-compare/64980371. Accessed 01 Mar 2020
34. Tschandl, P., Rosendahl, C., Kittler, H.: The ham10000 dataset, a large collection of multi-source dermatoscopic images of common pigmented skin lesions. Sci. Data **5**, 180161 (2018)
35. Welinder, P., Branson, S., Mita, T., Wah, C., Schroff, F., Belongie, S., Perona, P.: Caltech-UCSD Birds 200. Technical report CNS-TR-2010-001, California Institute of Technology (2010)
36. Zeiler, M.D., Fergus, R.: Visualizing and understanding convolutional networks. In: Fleet, D., Pajdla, T., Schiele, B., Tuytelaars, T. (eds.) Visualizing and understanding convolutional networks. LNCS, vol. 8689, pp. 818–833. Springer, Cham (2014). https://doi.org/10.1007/978-3-319-10590-1_53
37. Zhu, F., Li, H., Ouyang, W., Yu, N., Wang, X.: Learning spatial regularization with image-level supervisions for multi-label image classification. In: Proceedings of the IEEE Conference on Computer Vision and Pattern Recognition, pp. 5513–5522 (2017)
38. Zintgraf, L.M., Cohen, T.S., Adel, T., Welling, M.: Visualizing deep neural network decisions: Prediction difference analysis. arXiv preprint arXiv:1702.04595 (2017)

Weakly Supervised Semantic Segmentation with Boundary Exploration

Liyi Chen, Weiwei Wu$^{(\boxtimes)}$, Chenchen Fu$^{(\boxtimes)}$, Xiao Han, and Yuntao Zhang

School of Computer Science and Engineering, Southeast University, Nanjing, China
{lychen,weiweiwu,101012509,xiaohan}@seu.edu.cn, ytzhang01@foxmail.com

Abstract. Weakly supervised semantic segmentation with image-level labels has attracted a lot of attention recently because these labels are already available in most datasets. To obtain semantic segmentation under weak supervision, this paper presents a simple yet effective approach based on the idea of explicitly exploring object boundaries from training images to keep coincidence of segmentation and boundaries. Specifically, we synthesize boundary annotations by exploiting coarse localization maps obtained from CNN classifier, and use annotations to train the proposed network called BENet which further excavates more object boundaries to provide constraints for segmentation. Finally generated pseudo annotations of training images are used to supervise an off-the-shelf segmentation network. We evaluate the proposed method on PASCAL VOC 2012 benchmark and the final results achieve 65.7% and 66.6% mIoU scores on *val* and *test* sets respectively, which outperforms previous methods trained under image-level supervision.

Keywords: Weak supervision · Semantic segmentation · Deep learning

1 Introduction

Deep learning and Convolutional Neural Networks (CNNs) have recently achieved great success in computer vision, such as semantic segmentation. Driven by the requirement of scene recognition, various models have been proposed [5,34] to accurately segment foreground in images. However, manual annotation for training semantic segmentation network demands massive financial investments and is a time-consuming effort. To alleviate the heavy dependence on pixel-level annotations, weakly supervised learning for semantic segmentation is adopted, which uses weak annotations in semantic segmentation, including bounding boxes (*i.e.* information of instance location and dimension) [15], scribbles (*i.e.* a sparse set of pixels with a category label) [21] and image-level labels (*i.e.* information of which object classes are present/absent) [13,30]. Among all the supervisions above, image-level label is widely used as it is available in most datasets (*e.g.* VOC and MS COCO).

Even though using image-level label is common and convenient in recent years, there exists a critical issue when classifying each pixel only with image-level class labels. The classification task requires translation *invariance* but the

© Springer Nature Switzerland AG 2020
A. Vedaldi et al. (Eds.): ECCV 2020, LNCS 12371, pp. 347–362, 2020.
https://doi.org/10.1007/978-3-030-58574-7_21

semantic segmentation task is position-sensitive and requires translation *variance*. To address this issue, *Class Activation Maps* (CAM) [35] is proposed to overcome the inherent gap between classification and segmentation by adding a global average pooling (GAP) in the top of fully convolutional network to get class localization maps. However, this architecture tends to activate most discriminative object regions and obtains incomplete segmentation results. In recent works [2,13,26,30], CAM is usually taken as an initial localization technology followed by additional methods to refine it. However, most approaches focus on propagating foreground regions but do not consider the coincidence of segmentation and morphological boundary, which is as the main limitation for segmentation performance. In many cases, the segmentation might be into irrelevant regions if its propagation is not properly constrained by object boundaries.

Although object boundary is an essential factor to influence the segmentation performance, it is difficult to excavate it without boundary annotation and prior knowledge. In this paper, we propose *boundary exploration based segmentation* (BES) approach, which explicitly explores object boundaries to refine semantic segmentation of training images. More concretely, we propose a simple scheme to obtain a small amount of boundary labels by filtering given localization maps, and then the network BENet trained by synthetic boundary labels is designed to explicitly explore more object boundaries. Finally, massive explored boundary information is used to provide constraints for localization maps propagation.

The main contributions of the paper are summarized as follows:

- The proposed BES approach can explicitly explore object boundaries with only image-level annotation.
- To get reliable initial localization maps, we introduce a module called attention-pooling to improve the performance of CAM.
- We demonstrate the effectiveness of BES by training DeepLab-v2 [5] with generated training image segmentations. BES achieves the state-of-the-art performance on PASCAL VOC 2012 benchmark [8] with 65.7% mIoU on *val* set and 66.6% mIoU on *test* set.

The remainder of this paper is organized as follows. We present related work in Sect. 2. The details of BES approach are described in Sect. 3. In Sect. 4, we investigate BES efficiency and compare it to the state-of-the-art approaches. Finally, Sect. 5 concludes this work.

2 Related Work

In this section, we firstly present the previous related researches in weakly semantic segmentation, and then describe the literatures of image-level supervision learning. Additionally, we summarize and analyse the common idea of image-level supervised semantic segmentation.

Weakly-Supervised Semantic Segmentation. Weakly-supervised method for semantic segmentation attracts a large interest recently due to the simplicity and availability of its required labels compared to fully supervision segmentation learning. Various types of annotations are applied as supervision to address the data deficiency problem, including image-level label [1,20,31], bounding box [15,23], scribble [21], and so on. In particular, image-level labels as a simplest supervision are popularly used since they demand minimum costs and can be obtained from most visual datasets.

Image-Level Supervised Learning. Image-level class labels provide the multi-class classification information but no object localization cues. In early works, Graph-based models [32,33] which consider superpixels similarity of images are adopted to do segmentation task. With the development of deep learning, the problem of semantic segmentation was transferred to the task of assigning class labels for each pixel in images so that neural network framework can be conveniently employed. The work in [25] utilizes multiple instance learning (MIL) to train the segmentation model. Papandreou et al. [23] employed the Expectation-Maximization algorithm to predict object pixels. Both of them were time-consuming and their performances were not satisfactory. Recently, some new approaches are proposed which make great progress in benchmark. In [31], an iterative learning method is adopted, the network is initially trained using simple images and corresponding saliency maps as labels, and the ability of segmentation is progressively enhanced by increasing complexity of train data. [17] proposed a method to train segmentation network with joint loss function (*i.e.* seeding, expansion and constrain-to-boundary).

Even if most state-of-the-art methods of weakly semantic segmentation have different implementation details, they share a similar strategy: *coarse-to-fine*. *coarse* here means to localize object in image and allow the existence of deviation from ground truth, these mismatch prediction will be refined in *fine* step.

Coarse-to-fine. Excavating localization cues with only classification annotation available is a challenging task. Early methods like saliency detection [27] had achieved huge progress. Most recently, researchers notice that CAM [35] is a good staring-point for segmentation from image-level annotation. The bridge of classification and localization is usually accomplished by adding a global average pooling (GAP) or re-designed calculation operation [17,25] in the top of fully convolutional network. Object regions will be activated by network and these pixels contributed to classification score are regarded as foreground, Such localization technology is usually used in *coarse* step of weakly semantic segmentation.

However, CAM tends to focus on discriminative parts of object and other smooth-texture regions will not be activated or with a low response. To address this issue, additional processes to refine localization results are adopted which is called *fine* step. Incomplete object prediction and mismatch with object boundaries are two main limitations in the performance of *coarse*. In [13], coarse localization maps are regarded as initial seed and then expanded, conditional random field (CRF) is adopted to make prediction coincide with boundaries in expanding process. AffinityNet in [1,2] is used to predict semantic affinities between pixels, where the pixel-wise affinity is further transformed into transition probability matrix to direct the propagation of CAM results. [30] uses initial CAM as erasing masks to force classification network discover more relative regions, and then fuse each part to get segmentation maps.

Although object boundary is absolutely essential for semantic segmentation, it is difficult to capture precise boundary information with only image class annotations. In [30,31], authors did not take account of object boundary and just employ dCRF to make segmentation smooth. Some other approaches [1,2] implicitly exploit boundary information by calculating affinities between pixels, which is not accurate enough and usually deviate from the ground truth. In this paper, we propose BES to explicitly predict object boundary for segmentation without extra annotations. And BES do not need additional information like more training samples [12] or salience prior [13,27]. The most related work to ours is [1] which implicitly obtains boundaries by predicting affinity between pixels. However our BES can predict boundaries in a explicit way and achieves much more efficiency. Additionally, we provide experimental comparisons to above methods in Sect. 4.

3   The Proposed Approach

The BES framework for obtaining semantic segmentation for training images is illustrated in Fig. 1. As the key component in the framework, *boundary exploration* targets to predict precise boundary maps with the original training images as input. Boundary labels are manually synthesized from localization maps and used to train BENet to predict boundaries. The boundary classification ability of BENet helps to explore massive boundaries which are then used for revising localization maps. The other component in framework called *attention-pooling CAM* is an improved CAM mechanism to obtain better initial object localization maps. The details of these two components are described in the following subsections.

3.1   Boundary Exploration for Localization Maps

In this subsection, we introduce the design of *boundary exploration* and how does it used to revise localization maps. We firstly exploit localization maps to synthesize a small amount of credible boundary labels, and then these are used to explore more boundary cues through training BENet.

Synthesizing Boundary Labels. As localization maps represented by pixel-wise class probability are inconvenience for boundary label synthesis, we firstly convert probability to a certain class label for each pixel. Suppose P_i^c is the

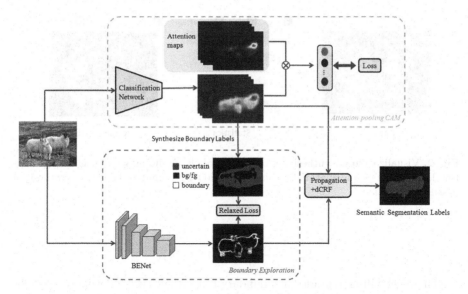

Fig. 1. The proposed BES framework. First, coarse localization maps are obtained through the attention-pooling CAM. Then, boundary labels are synthesized to train BENet which is able to excavate more object boundaries. Finally, semantic segmentation is generated by applying predicted boundary information to revise localization maps.

probability of pixel i belonging to class $c \in \mathcal{C}$. The classification result $\hat{y}_i$ for pixel i is obtained by a thresholding operation as following:

$$
\hat{y}_i = \begin{cases} \arg\max\limits_{c \in \mathcal{C}}(P_i^c) & \text{if } \max\limits_{c \in \mathcal{C}}(P_i^c) > \theta_{fg} \\ 0 & \text{if } \max\limits_{c \in \mathcal{C}}(P_i^c) < \theta_{bg} \\ 255 & \text{otherwise} \end{cases}, \tag{1}
$$

where 0 and 255 mean background label and uncertain label, respectively, while θ_{fg} and θ_{bg} are thresholds for foreground and background respectively in order to filter uncertain pixels. An additional dCRF operation is used to refine reliable foreground and background regions.

We notice that though localization maps exist some misclassified pixels, it works well in regions near the boundaries. In other words, the classification results for pixels in the border of background and foreground are much reliable. According to the definition of boundary, we assume that there exist boundaries where adjacent regions contain approximate numbers of identical foreground and background pixels. Following this idea, we use a sliding window to count numbers of local identical pixels and employ statistics information to determine whether the pixel in the center of window is boundary or not. Given a sliding window centered at pixel i with size w, we use N_i^c to denote the number of pixels assigned with label c in the window. The statistical proportion of the window for each class is denoted as S_i^c:

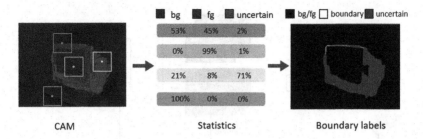

Fig. 2. Visualization of synthesizing boundary labels. A sliding window is used to capture local statistics information for each pixel, and then boundary labels are synthesized based on statistics.

$$S_i^c = \frac{N_i^c}{w \times w} \quad \forall c \in \mathcal{C} \cup \{0\}. \tag{2}$$

The pixel will be regraded as boundary if it satisfies the following two conditions. First, there should exist sufficient identical pixels in the window to support inference. Second, the area size of foreground region and background region in the window need to be close enough. Formally, the boundary label $\hat{B}_i$ for pixel i is computed as follows:

$$\hat{B}_i = \begin{cases} 0 & \text{if } \min\{\max\limits_{c \in \mathcal{C}} S_i^c, S_i^0\} > 2\,\theta_{scale} \\ & \text{and } |\max\limits_{c \in \mathcal{C}} S_i^c - S_i^0| \geq 2\,\theta_{diff} \\ 1 & \text{if } \min\{\max\limits_{c \in \mathcal{C}} S_i^c, S_i^0\} > \theta_{scale} \\ & \text{and } |\max\limits_{c \in \mathcal{C}} S_i^c - S_i^0| < \theta_{diff} \\ 255 & \text{otherwise} \end{cases} \tag{3}$$

where θ_{scale} and θ_{diff} are thresholds for two conditions, respectively. 255 means that the pixel's boundary label is uncertain.

Pixels near boundaries are usually difficult to discriminate and may cause bad influence on BENet training. Therefore, the Eq. (3) is designed as a discontinuous discriminant so that pixels near boundaries will be assigned with uncertain labels and not provide any supervision in the training phase. Figure 2 shows the process of synthesizing boundary labels. We calculate local statistics information for each pixel in the localization map and accordingly obtain boundary labels.

Relax Boundary Classification Loss for BENet Training. We employ BENet to directly predict a boundary map $\mathcal{B} \in [0,1]^{w \times h}$ for input image under the supervision of synthesized boundary labels. In training phase, the numbers of boundary, foreground and background pixels exist notable differences, and the imbalance of training samples would make the model prediction tend to suppress boundary responses. To address this issue, we divide the training data into three parts: boundary pixels, foreground pixels and background pixels.

The cross-entropy for each part is calculated respectively and aggregated into the final boundary loss function:

$$L_B = - \sum_{i \in \Phi_{bry}} \frac{W_i \log(P_i)}{|\Phi_{bry}|} - \frac{1}{2} \left(\sum_{i \in \Phi_c} \frac{\log(1 - P_i)}{|\Phi_c|} + \sum_{i \in \Phi_{bg}} \frac{\log(1 - P_i)}{|\Phi_{bg}|} \right), \quad (4)$$

where $\Phi_{bry} = \{i | \hat{B}_i = 1\}$, $\Phi_c = \{i | \hat{B}_i = 0, \max_{c \in C} S_i^c > S_i^0\}$, $\Phi_{bg} = \{i | \hat{B}_i = 0, S_i^0 > \max_{c \in C} S_i^c\}$ are pixel sets of boundary, foreground and background respectively, P_i is the boundary probability predicted by BENet for pixel i. To reduce the heavy dependence on synthetic boundary labels which may contain some misclassified samples, we relax the assumption that all boundary labels are reliable by adding a weight parameter W_i in the boundary loss term. In practice, W_i is set to $\sqrt{P_i}$ for online training. Consider a pixel labeled as boundary, i.e. $i \in \Phi_{bry}$, if its boundary probability estimated by BENet is a low value (which indicates that it is like background or foreground), its contribution weight for loss function will be decreased to reduce its influence for training.

Revising Localization Maps with Explored Boundaries. Trained BENet is able to excavate massive object boundaries. Then, we use predicted boundary maps as constraints to direct the propagation of coarse localization maps and get semantic segmentation. Compared to some flood-fill based propagation methods [13], random walk [1,3] is an elegant method to revise localization maps. We adopt the methodology used in [1] to transfer boundary maps $\mathcal{B} \in [0,1]^{w \times h}$ to semantic affinity matrix. In the matrix, the affinity between pixel i and j is denoted as a_{ij}, which depends on the maximum boundary confidences in the path from i to j. To improve the computational efficiency, affinity will be treated positive only if distance of two pixels is less than a threshold γ:

$$a_{ij} = \begin{cases} (1 - \max_{k \in \Pi_{ij}} \mathcal{B}_k)^\beta & \text{if } P(i,j) < \gamma \\ 0 & \text{otherwise} \end{cases}, \quad (5)$$

where Π_{ij} is a set of pixels in the path from i to j, $P(i,j)$ is euclidean distance between i and j, and the hyper-parameter β is a value greater than 1 to control how conservative the random walk propagation is.

To simulate random walk process, element value a_{ij} in semantic affinity matrix is regraded as transition probability. Then propagation is accomplished by multiplying matrix to the localization maps, the simulation will be performed iteratively until predefined number of iterations is reached. Finally, dense Conditional Random Field (dCRF) [18] is applied to further slightly improve the quality of segmentation.

3.2 Attention-Pooling CAM to Obtain Localization Maps

Initial localization maps play an essential role in BES approach, which is not only used as seed region for revisiting, but also used to synthesize boundary labels.

A common solution to obtain localization maps is to employ CAM technology which utilizes GAP after a fully convolutional network. However, as mentioned in [7,17,25], GAP used in CAM takes average value in the class localization map as classification score which implicitly assigns equal weights to each pixel vote. This will encourage response of irrelevant regions. Inspired by this motivation, we propose a new calculation called attention-pooling to replace GAP component in CAM.

Attention-Pooling for CAM. We preserve the fully convolutional network (FCN [22]) architecture used in CAM to capture object's spatial information, and change the calculation for obtaining classification scores by applying attention-pooling which can dynamically assign different weight for pixels. Let denote the localization map for class $c \in \mathcal{C}$ as M^c, which is embedded by convolutional layers, while M_i^c is the activation value at position i in M^c. The attention map A^c is generated for each class localization map M_i^c, the attention value in position i of A^c is denoted as A_i^c which represents the contribution weight of M_i^c to classification score s^c. s^c is the computed by summing up responses over all pixel positions, as follows:

$$s^c = \sum_i (M_i^c \times A_i^c) \quad \forall c \in \mathcal{C}. \tag{6}$$

The attention masks A^c is generated by utilizing the softmax function on relevant class localization map M^c:

$$A_i^c = \frac{\exp(kM_i^c)}{\sum_{j \in \mathcal{J}} \exp(kM_j^c)} \quad \forall c \in \mathcal{C}, \tag{7}$$

where $\mathcal{J}$ is the set of pixels in M^c, and k is a hyper-parameter to adjust the intensity of attention. When k is set as zero, the attention-pooling will assign equal weight for every pixel. As the value k increases, the attention tends to focus on pixels with high response values. Generally, attention-pooling will be similar to global average pooling if k is close to zero, and be similar to global max pooling if k is high enough.

After training, the attention-pooling will be removed and localization maps are normalized to obtain class probability P_i^c:

$$P_i^c = \frac{M_i^c}{\max_{j \in \mathcal{J}} M_j^c} \quad \forall c \in \mathcal{C}. \tag{8}$$

As described above, BES generates semantic segmentation for each training image. In Sect. 4, we demonstrate effectiveness of BES approach.

4   Experiments

In this section, we evaluate the efficacy of BES on the Pascal VOC 2012 semantic segmentation dataset [8] by training DeepLab-ASPP [5] with generated semantic segmentation of training images.

4.1 Implementation Details

Datasets. The benchmark of Pascal VOC 2012 has 21 different classes including background. The images in dataset are divided into three parts: 1464 images for training, 1449 images for validation and 1456 images for testing. Following common practice, we augment training part by adding training data from SBD [9]. In total, 10,582 images and relative image-level class labels are used for training. We use mean intersection-over-union (mIoU) as evaluation metric to measure semantic segmentation performance.

Attention-Pooling CAM Setting. In practice, we utilize ResNet50 as backbone network and replace the last fully connected layer with a 1×1 convolution layer. The stride in last stage is reduced from 2 to 1 so that more spatial information can be preserved. Therefore, resolution of output localization maps drop down to $\frac{1}{16}$ of input resolution after passing through the network.

Acceleration for Synthesizing Boundary Labels. Iteratively counting local numbers for every pixel would increase GPU memory usage and is very time-consuming. A simply way to compute statistics is to realize sliding window with the average pooling layer which has been implemented in common deep learning frameworks like PyTorch [24].

BENet Setting. BENet is based on ReNet50 [10] pretrained on ImageNet [6]. To fuse different level features of image, the features from shallow layers and deep layers are combined by concatenating resized feature maps from five stages with 1×1 convolution layers. In training phase, the parameters of network are optimized via batched stochastic gradient descent (SGD) for about 3,500 iterations, with a batch size 16. The learning rate is initially set to 0.1, and the momentum and weight decay are set to 0.9 and 0.0001 respectively. The training images are resized with a random ratio from (0.5, 1.5), and then augmented with horizontal flip after normalization, finally it is randomly cropped into size of 513×513.

Hyper Parameter Setting. Parameter k in Eq. (7) is set to 0.001. θ_{fg} and θ_{bg} in Eq. (1) are fixed to 0.30 and 0.07 respectively. To generate boundary labels, we set the size of search window w to 13, θ_{scale} to 0.35 and θ_{diff} to 0.10. For random walk parameters in revising stage, we use the setting given in [1] except setting the parameter β in Eq. (5) to 5. For dCRF, we follow the setting in [1] for CAM refinement, and θ_{α} is set to 20 for pseudo labels post-processing as shown in following equation:

$$k\left(f_{i}, f_{j}\right)=w_{g} \exp \left(-\frac{\left|p_{i}-p_{j}\right|}{2 \theta_{\alpha}^{2}}-\frac{\left|I_{i}-I_{j}\right|}{2 \theta_{\beta}^{2}}\right)+w_{rgb} \exp \left(-\frac{\left|p_{i}-p_{j}\right|^{2}}{2 \theta_{\gamma}^{2}}\right). \quad (9)$$

Table 1. Ablation study on PASCAL VOC 2012 training set.

CAM	Attention-pooling CAM	Boundary exploration	dCRF	mIoU
✓				49.6
	✓			50.4
✓		✓		65.7
	✓	✓		66.4
	✓	✓	✓	**67.2**

4.2 Analysis of the BES

In this subsection, we firstly perform an ablation study to illustrate effective of each part. Then, we evaluate the impact of various parameters values. Finally, we objectively analyse the quality of proposed BES approach.

Ablation Experiment. To demonstrate the efficiency of the BES method, we report the influence of each step in Table 1 with mIoU as the evaluation metric. Comparing to CAM baseline which achieves 49.6%, the proposed attention-pooling CAM improves mIoU by 0.8% and this improvement is remained even after revising process. Applying boundary exploration, the localization maps performance is significantly improved from 50.4% to 66.4%. Additionally, post process dCRF brings extra 0.8% improvement. In experiments, we employ setting in last line which achieves 67.2% mIoU in VOC 2012 training set.

Hyper Parameter Effects. We evaluate the impact of hyper parameters for semantic segmentation in training set and report the results in Fig. 3. For boundary label synthesis, we evaluate the influence of θ_{diff} and θ_{scale} in Eq. (3) on the segmentation performance. As shown in Fig. 3(a), BES approach is robust to various parameters values. For attention-pooling CAM, Fig. 3(b) illustrates the effect of attention intensity parameter k in Eq. (7). Compared to GAP-based CAM, the proposed attention-pooling CAM gets slightly improvement when attention intensity parameter k is set to a small value, but further increasing of k value makes performance drop down quickly.

Boundaries Evaluation. To better demonstrate the efficiency of boundary exploration, we evaluate the generated boundary maps on SBD benchmark [9], which contains semantic boundary annotations from 11355 images taken from the PASCAL VOC 2011 dataset. Since predicted boundary maps are class-agnostic and do not satisfy the semantic boundary requirement of SBD benchmark, we transform the ground-truth semantic boundary labels into class-agnostic labels. The precision, recall and maximal F-measure of the generated 11355 boundary maps are reported in Fig. 4.

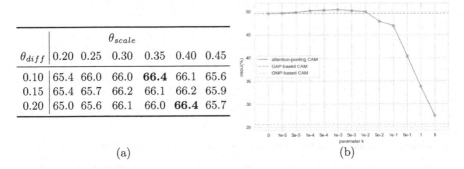

	θ_{scale}					
θ_{diff}	0.20	0.25	0.30	0.35	0.40	0.45
0.10	65.4	66.0	66.0	**66.4**	66.1	65.6
0.15	65.4	65.7	66.2	66.1	66.2	65.9
0.20	65.0	65.6	66.1	66.0	**66.4**	65.7

(a)   (b)

Fig. 3. The performance when employing different parameter values in VOC 2012 training set. (a) The performance of semantic segmentation for different values of parameter θ_{diff} and θ_{scale} in boundary exploration. (b) The performance of attention-pooling CAM with various values of parameter k.

Precision(%)	Recall(%)	MF(%)
46.4	45.5	45.9

(a)   (b)

Fig. 4. Performance of boundary exploration, evaluated on the SBD *trainval* set. (a) The sample of predicted boundary map and the corresponding boundary label. (b) The boundary evaluation result.

Quality Analysis. DeepLab-ASPP [5] trained by pseudo labels is employed to evaluate the proposed approach. Table 2 and 3 record concrete performance in VOC 2012 *val* and *test* set. We get substantial performance improvement compared to other methods, especially in large-scale object (e.g., bus and car) segmentation tasks.

We also analyse our failure cases and show it in Fig. 5. The segmentation performance of BES is not good enough when dealing some objects (e.g., bike and chair) with complicated structures. We argue that it is due to two main factors. First, the BENet makes judgement for each pixel separately, and the discrete boundary prediction is hard to output consecutive boundary to provide effective constraint for propagation. Second, as the inherent limitation of neural network, it is difficult to capture exact location of small object components like bike pedals or table legs.

Table 2. Semantic segmentation performance in PASCAL VOC 2012 *val* set.

Method	bkg	aero	bike	bird	boat	bottle	bus	car	cat	chair	cow	table	dog	horse	mbk	person	plant	sheep	sofa	train	tv	mean
EM-Adapt [23]	67.2	29.2	17.6	28.6	22.2	29.6	47.0	44.0	44.2	14.6	35.1	24.9	41.0	34.8	41.6	32.1	24.8	37.4	24.0	38.1	31.6	33.8
MIL+seg [25]	79.6	50.2	21.6	40.9	34.9	40.5	45.9	51.5	60.6	12.6	51.2	11.6	56.8	52.9	44.8	42.7	31.2	55.4	21.5	38.8	36.9	42.0
SEC [17]	82.4	62.9	26.4	61.6	27.6	38.1	66.6	62.7	75.2	22.1	53.5	28.3	65.8	57.8	62.3	52.5	32.5	62.6	32.1	45.4	45.3	50.7
TPL[16]	82.8	62.2	23.1	65.8	21.1	43.1	71.1	66.2	76.1	21.3	59.6	35.1	70.2	58.8	62.3	66.1	35.8	69.9	33.4	45.9	45.6	53.1
PSA[2]	88.2	68.2	**30.6**	81.1	49.6	61.0	77.8	66.1	75.1	29.0	66.0	40.2	80.4	62.0	70.4	**73.7**	42.5	70.7	42.6	**68.1**	51.6	61.7
SSDD[26]	**89.0**	62.5	28.9	**83.7**	52.9	59.5	77.6	73.7	**87.0**	**34.0**	**83.7**	47.6	**84.1**	**77.0**	**73.9**	69.6	29.8	**84.0**	**43.2**	68.0	**53.4**	64.9
BES (Ours):																						
DeepLab-ASPP	88.9	**74.1**	29.8	81.3	**53.3**	**69.9**	**89.4**	**79.8**	84.2	27.9	76.9	46.6	78.8	75.9	72.2	70.4	**50.8**	79.4	39.9	65.3	44.8	**65.7**

Table 3. Semantic segmentation performance in PASCAL VOC 2012 *test* set.

Method	bkg	aero	bike	bird	boat	bottle	bus	car	cat	chair	cow	table	dog	horse	mbk	person	plant	sheep	sofa	train	tv	mean
EM-Adapt [23]	76.3	37.1	21.9	41.6	26.1	38.5	50.8	44.9	48.9	16.7	40.8	29.4	47.1	45.8	54.8	28.2	30.0	44.0	29.2	34.3	46.0	39.6
MIL+seg [25]	78.7	48.0	21.2	31.1	28.4	35.1	51.4	55.5	52.8	7.8	56.2	19.9	53.8	50.3	40.0	38.6	27.8	51.8	24.7	33.3	46.3	40.6
SEC [17]	83.5	56.4	28.5	64.1	23.6	46.5	70.6	58.5	71.3	23.2	54.0	28.0	68.1	62.1	70.0	55.0	38.4	58.0	39.9	38.4	48.3	51.7
TPL [16]	83.4	62.2	26.4	71.8	18.2	49.5	66.5	63.8	73.4	19.0	56.6	35.7	69.3	61.3	71.7	69.2	39.1	66.3	44.8	35.9	45.5	53.8
PSA [2]	89.1	70.6	**31.6**	77.2	42.2	**68.9**	79.1	66.5	74.9	29.6	68.7	56.1	82.1	64.8	**78.6**	**73.5**	**50.8**	70.7	47.7	63.9	**51.1**	63.7
SSDD [26]	**89.5**	71.8	31.4	79.3	47.3	64.2	79.9	74.6	84.9	**30.8**	73.5	**58.2**	**82.7**	73.4	76.4	69.9	37.4	80.5	54.5	**65.7**	50.3	65.5
BES (Ours):																						
DeepLab-ASPP	89.0	**72.7**	30.4	**84.6**	**47.5**	63.0	**86.8**	**80.7**	**85.2**	30.1	**76.5**	56.4	81.8	**79.9**	77.0	67.8	48.6	**82.3**	**57.2**	54.0	46.7	**66.6**

Fig. 5. Examples of failure cases in semantic segmentation.

Table 4. Comparison of semantic segmentation methods on PACAL VOC 2012 *val* and *test* set. The supervision types (Sup.) indicate: B–bounding box label, S–scribble label, F–pixel-level label, and I–image-level class label.

Methods	Sup	Backbone	Training	val	test
WSSL [23]	B	VGG-16	10K	60.6	62.2
SDI [15]	B	VGG-16	10K	65.7	67.5
Scribblesup [21]	S	VGG-16	10K	63.1	-
FCN [22]	F	VGG-16	10K	-	62.2
DeepLab-v1 [4]	F	VGG-16	10K	67.6	70.3
PSPNet [34]	F	ResNet-101	10K	-	85.4
STC [31]	I	VGG-16	50k	49.8	51.2
TransferNet [11]	I	VGG-16	70K	52.1	51.2
AE_PSL [30]	I	VGG-16	10K	55.0	55.7
GAIN [20]	I	VGG-16	10K	55.3	56.8
CrawlSeg [12]	I	VGG-16	970K	58.1	58.7
MCOF [29]	I	ResNet-101	10K	60.3	61.2

(*continued*)

Table 4. (*continued*)

Methods	Sup	Backbone	Training	val	test
DSRG [13]	I	ResNet-101	10K	61.4	63.2
IRNet [1]	I	ResNet-50	10K	63.5	64.8
FickleNet [19]	I	ResNet-101	10K	64.9	65.3
SSDD [26]	I	ResNet-38	10K	64.9	65.5
OOA [14]	I	ResNet-101	10K	65.2	66.4
BES (Ours):					
DeepLab-CRF-LargeFOV	I	VGG-16	10K	60.1	61.1
DeepLab-ASPP	I	ResNet-101	10K	**65.7**	**66.6**

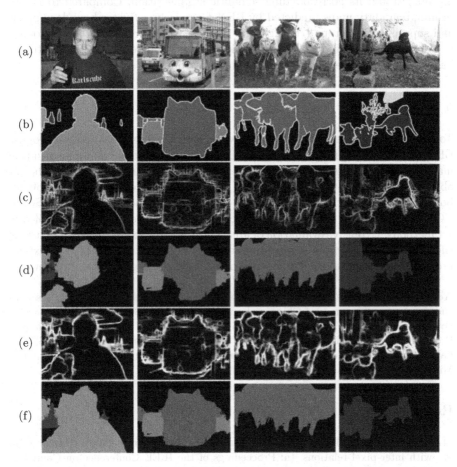

Fig. 6. Qualitative generated semantic segmentation on PASCAL VOC 2012 training set. (a) Original images. (b) Ground-truth. (c) Boundary maps of IRNet. (d) IRNet results. (e) Boundary maps of BES. (f) BES results.

4.3   Comparisons to the State-of-the-Art

In Table 4, we can observe that semantic labels generated by BES help the DepplLab-ASPP outperform all the listed image-level supervised methods both in *val* and *test* set. And even competitive with works [15] relying on bounding box. For fair comparison, we additionally provide DeepLab-CRF-LargeFOV [4] based result which uses VGG-16 [28] as backbone. We believe that other segmentation networks trained by our generated annotations can also achieve considerable performance.

Finally, we compare the BENet with IRNet, which predicts pixel affinity to implicitly capture boundary information. Figure 6 illustrates the training images and its corresponding semantic segmentation. Compared to IRNet results, boundary maps predicted by BENet precisely activates boundary pixels and suppresses foreground/background regions, which presents a better boundary discrimination ability. The semantic segmentation results demonstrate the benefit of explicitly exploring sufficient object boundaries.

5   Conclusion

To address the problem of weakly supervised semantic segmentation, we propose BES approach to explicitly explore object boundaries to refine coarse localization maps for training images. We design an attention-pooling CAM to get better object localization maps as seed region, then BENet is created to explore object boundaries and direct the propagation of semantic segmentation. On PASCAL VOC 2012 benchmark, BES performance outperforms the previous state-of-the-art methods. Extensive evaluation of ablation study and experiments validate the effectiveness and the robust of proposed BES. In the future, we plan to extend proposed approach to develop an end-to-end semantic segmentation framework.

Acknowledgments. This work was supported in part by the national key research and development program of China under grant No.2019YFB2102200,Natural Science Foundation of China under Grant No. 61902062,61672154, 61972086. and Jiangsu Provincial Natural Science Foundation of China under Grant No. BK20190332,Key Laboratory of Computer Network and Information Integration (Southeast University), Ministry of Education.

References

1. Ahn, J., Cho, S., Kwak, S.: Weakly supervised learning of instance segmentation with inter-pixel relations. In: Proceedings of the IEEE Conference on Computer Vision and Pattern Recognition, pp. 2209–2218 (2019)
2. Ahn, J., Kwak, S.: Learning pixel-level semantic affinity with image-level supervision for weakly supervised semantic segmentation. In: Proceedings of the IEEE Conference on Computer Vision and Pattern Recognition, pp. 4981–4990 (2018)

3. Bertasius, G., Torresani, L., Yu, S.X., Shi, J.: Convolutional random walk networks for semantic image segmentation. In: Proceedings of the IEEE Conference on Computer Vision and Pattern Recognition, pp. 858–866 (2017)
4. Chen, L.C., Papandreou, G., Kokkinos, I., Murphy, K., Yuille, A.L.: Semantic image segmentation with deep convolutional nets and fully connected CRFS. arXiv preprint arXiv:1412.7062 (2014)
5. Chen, L.C., Papandreou, G., Kokkinos, I., Murphy, K., Yuille, A.L.: Deeplab: semantic image segmentation with deep convolutional nets, atrous convolution, and fully connected CRFS. IEEE Trans. Pattern Anal. Mach. Intell. **40**(4), 834–848 (2017)
6. Deng, J., Dong, W., Socher, R., Li, L.J., Li, K., Fei-Fei, L.: Imagenet: a large-scale hierarchical image database. In: 2009 IEEE Conference on Computer Vision and Pattern Recognition, pp. 248–255. IEEE (2009)
7. Durand, T., Mordan, T., Thome, N., Cord, M.: Wildcat: Weakly supervised learning of deep convnets for image classification, pointwise localization and segmentation. In: Proceedings of the IEEE Conference on Computer Vision and Pattern Recognition, pp. 642–651 (2017)
8. Everingham, M., Van Gool, L., Williams, C.K., Winn, J., Zisserman, A.: The pascal visual object classes (VOC) challenge. Int. J. Comput. Vis. **88**(2), 303–338 (2010)
9. Hariharan, B., Arbeláez, P., Bourdev, L., Maji, S., Malik, J.: Semantic contours from inverse detectors. In: 2011 International Conference on Computer Vision, pp. 991–998. IEEE (2011)
10. He, K., Zhang, X., Ren, S., Sun, J.: Deep residual learning for image recognition. In: Proceedings of the IEEE Conference on Computer Vision and Pattern Recognition, pp. 770–778 (2016)
11. Hong, S., Oh, J., Lee, H., Han, B.: Learning transferrable knowledge for semantic segmentation with deep convolutional neural network. In: Proceedings of the IEEE Conference on Computer Vision and Pattern Recognition, pp. 3204–3212 (2016)
12. Hong, S., Yeo, D., Kwak, S., Lee, H., Han, B.: Weakly supervised semantic segmentation using web-crawled videos. In: Proceedings of the IEEE Conference on Computer Vision and Pattern Recognition, pp. 7322–7330 (2017)
13. Huang, Z., Wang, X., Wang, J., Liu, W., Wang, J.: Weakly-supervised semantic segmentation network with deep seeded region growing. In: Proceedings of the IEEE Conference on Computer Vision and Pattern Recognition, pp. 7014–7023 (2018)
14. Jiang, P.T., Hou, Q., Cao, Y., Cheng, M.M., Wei, Y., Xiong, H.K.: Integral object mining via online attention accumulation. In: Proceedings of the IEEE International Conference on Computer Vision, pp. 2070–2079 (2019)
15. Khoreva, A., Benenson, R., Hosang, J., Hein, M., Schiele, B.: Simple does it: weakly supervised instance and semantic segmentation. In: Proceedings of the IEEE Conference on Computer Vision and Pattern Recognition, pp. 876–885 (2017)
16. Kim, D., Cho, D., Yoo, D., So Kweon, I.: Two-phase learning for weakly supervised object localization. In: Proceedings of the IEEE International Conference on Computer Vision, pp. 3534–3543 (2017)
17. Kolesnikov, A., Lampert, C.H.: Seed, expand and constrain: three principles for weakly-supervised image segmentation. In: Leibe, B., Matas, J., Sebe, N., Welling, M. (eds.) ECCV 2016. LNCS, vol. 9908, pp. 695–711. Springer, Cham (2016). https://doi.org/10.1007/978-3-319-46493-0_42
18. Krähenbühl, P., Koltun, V.: Efficient inference in fully connected CRFS with gaussian edge potentials. In: Advances in Neural Information Processing Systems, pp. 109–117 (2011)

19. Lee, J., Kim, E., Lee, S., Lee, J., Yoon, S.: Ficklenet: weakly and semi-supervised semantic image segmentation using stochastic inference. In: Proceedings of the IEEE Conference on Computer Vision and Pattern Recognition, pp. 5267–5276 (2019)
20. Li, K., Wu, Z., Peng, K.C., Ernst, J., Fu, Y.: Tell me where to look: guided attention inference network. In: Proceedings of the IEEE Conference on Computer Vision and Pattern Recognition, pp. 9215–9223 (2018)
21. Lin, D., Dai, J., Jia, J., He, K., Sun, J.: Scribblesup: scribble-supervised convolutional networks for semantic segmentation. In: Proceedings of the IEEE Conference on Computer Vision and Pattern Recognition, pp. 3159–3167 (2016)
22. Long, J., Shelhamer, E., Darrell, T.: Fully convolutional networks for semantic segmentation. In: Proceedings of the IEEE Conference on Computer Vision and Pattern Recognition, pp. 3431–3440 (2015)
23. Papandreou, G., Chen, L.C., Murphy, K.P., Yuille, A.L.: Weakly-and semi-supervised learning of a deep convolutional network for semantic image segmentation. In: Proceedings of the IEEE International Conference on Computer Vision, pp. 1742–1750 (2015)
24. Paszke, A., et al.: Automatic Differentiation in Pytorch (2017)
25. Pinheiro, P.O., Collobert, R.: From image-level to pixel-level labeling with convolutional networks. In: Proceedings of the IEEE Conference on Computer Vision and Pattern Recognition, pp. 1713–1721 (2015)
26. Shimoda, W., Yanai, K.: Self-supervised difference detection for weakly-supervised semantic segmentation. In: Proceedings of the IEEE International Conference on Computer Vision, pp. 5208–5217 (2019)
27. Simonyan, K., Vedaldi, A., Zisserman, A.: Deep inside convolutional networks: visualising image classification models and saliency maps. arXiv preprint arXiv:1312.6034 (2013)
28. Simonyan, K., Zisserman, A.: Very deep convolutional networks for large-scale image recognition. arXiv preprint arXiv:1409.1556 (2014)
29. Wang, X., You, S., Li, X., Ma, H.: Weakly-supervised semantic segmentation by iteratively mining common object features. In: Proceedings of the IEEE Conference on Computer Vision and Pattern Recognition, pp. 1354–1362 (2018)
30. Wei, Y., Feng, J., Liang, X., Cheng, M.M., Zhao, Y., Yan, S.: Object region mining with adversarial erasing: a simple classification to semantic segmentation approach. In: Proceedings of the IEEE Conference on Computer Vision and Pattern Recognition, pp. 1568–1576 (2017)
31. Wei, Y., et al.: STC: a simple to complex framework for weakly-supervised semantic segmentation. IEEE Trans. Pattern Anal. Mach. Intell. 39(11), 2314–2320 (2016)
32. Zhang, L., Gao, Y., Xia, Y., Lu, K., Shen, J., Ji, R.: Representative discovery of structure cues for weakly-supervised image segmentation. IEEE Trans. Multimedia 16(2), 470–479 (2013)
33. Zhang, L., Yang, Y., Gao, Y., Yu, Y., Wang, C., Li, X.: A probabilistic associative model for segmenting weakly supervised images. IEEE Trans. Image Process. 23(9), 4150–4159 (2014)
34. Zhao, H., Shi, J., Qi, X., Wang, X., Jia, J.: Pyramid scene parsing network. In: Proceedings of the IEEE Conference on Computer Vision and Pattern Recognition, pp. 2881–2890 (2017)
35. Zhou, B., Khosla, A., Lapedriza, A., Oliva, A., Torralba, A.: Learning deep features for discriminative localization. In: Proceedings of the IEEE Conference on Computer Vision and Pattern Recognition, pp. 2921–2929 (2016)

GANHopper: Multi-hop GAN for Unsupervised Image-to-Image Translation

Wallace Lira[1(✉)], Johannes Merz[1], Daniel Ritchie[2], Daniel Cohen-Or[3], and Hao Zhang[1]

[1] Simon Fraser University, Burnaby, Canada
{wpintoli,johannes_merz,haoz}@sfu.ca
[2] Brown University, Providence, USA
daniel_ritchie@brown.edu
[3] Tel Aviv University, Tel Aviv, Israel
dcor@tau.ac.il

Abstract. We introduce GANHOPPER, an unsupervised image-to-image translation network that transforms images *gradually* between two domains, through multiple *hops*. Instead of executing translation directly, we steer the translation by requiring the network to produce *in-between* images that resemble *weighted hybrids* between images from the input domains. Our network is trained on *unpaired* images from the two domains only, without any in-between images. All hops are produced using a *single generator* along each direction. In addition to the standard cycle-consistency and adversarial losses, we introduce a new *hybrid discriminator*, which is trained to classify the intermediate images produced by the generator as weighted hybrids, with weights based on a predetermined hop count. We also add a smoothness term to constrain the magnitude of each hop, further regularizing the translation. Compared to previous methods, GANHOPPER excels at image translations involving domain-specific image features and geometric variations while also preserving non-domain-specific features such as general color schemes.

Keywords: Unsupervised learning · Adversarial learning · Image translation

1 Introduction

Unsupervised image-to-image translation has been one of the most intensively studied problems in computer vision, since the introduction of domain transfer network (DTN) [22], CycleGAN [28], DualGAN [25], and UNIT [15] in 2017. While these networks and many follow-ups were designed to perform general-purpose translations, it is challenging for the translator to learn transformations

Electronic supplementary material The online version of this chapter (https://doi.org/10.1007/978-3-030-58574-7_22) contains supplementary material, which is available to authorized users.

A. Vedaldi et al. (Eds.): ECCV 2020, LNCS 12371, pp. 363–379, 2020.
https://doi.org/10.1007/978-3-030-58574-7_22

Fig. 1. *What dog would look most similar to a given cat?* Our *multi-hop* image translation network, GANHopper, produces such transforms and also *in-between* transitions through "hops". Direct translation methods can "undershoot the target" by failing to produce the necessary geometry variations (middle left) or "overshoot" by significantly altering non-domain-specific features such as general color schemes (middle right).

beyond local and stylistic adjustments, such as geometry and shape variations. For example, typical dog-cat translations learned by CycleGAN do not transform the animals in terms of geometric facial features; only pixel-scale color or texture alterations take place, e.g., see Fig. 1 (middle right).

When the source and target domains exhibit sufficiently large discrepancies, any proper translation function is expected to be complex and difficult to learn. Without any paired images to supervise the learning process, the search space for the translation functions can be immense. With large image changes, there are even more degrees of freedom to account for. In such cases, a more *constrained* and *steerable* search would be desirable.

In this paper, we introduce an unsupervised image-to-image translator that is constrained to transform images *gradually* between two domains, e.g., cats and dogs. Instead of performing the transformation directly, our translator executes the task in steps, called *hops*. Our *multi-hop* network is built on CycleGAN [28]. However, we steer the translation paths by forcing the network to produce *in-between* images which resemble *weighted hybrids* between images from the two input domains. For example, a four-hop network for dog-to-cat translation produces three in-between images: the first is 25% cat-like and 75% dog-like, the second is 50/50 in terms of cat and dog likeness, and the third is 75% cat-like and 25% dog-like. The fourth and final hop is a 100% translated cat.

Our network, GANHopper, is unsupervised and trained on unpaired images from two input domains, without any in-between hybrid images in its training set. Equally important, all hops are produced using a *single generator* along each direction, hence the network capacity does not exceed that of CycleGAN. To make training possible, we introduce a new *hybrid discriminator*, which is trained exclusively on real images (e.g., dogs or cats) to evaluate the in-between images by classifying them as weighted hybrids, depending on the prescribed hop count. In addition to the original cycle-consistency and adversarial losses from CycleGAN, we introduce two new losses: a *hybrid loss* to assess the degree to which an image belongs to one of the input domains, and a *smoothness* loss which further regulates the image transitions to ensure that a generated image in the hop sequence does not deviate much from the preceding image.

GANHOPPER does not merely transform an input cat into *a* dog—many dogs can fool the discriminator. Rather, it aims to generate *the* dog which looks most similar to the given cat; see Fig. 1 (middle left). Compared to previous unsupervised image-to-image translation networks, our network excels at image translations involving domain-specific image features and geometric variations (i.e., "what makes a dog a dog?") while preserving non-domain-specific image features such as the fur color of the input cat in Fig. 1.

The ability to produce large changes, in particular, geometry transformations, via unsupervised domain translation has been a hotly-pursued problem. There appears to be a common belief that the original CycleGAN/DualGAN architecture cannot learn geometry variations. To do so, the feature representation and/or training approach must be changed. As a result, many approaches resort to latent space translations, e.g., with style-content [7] or scale [26] separation and feature disentanglement [24]. Our work challenges this assumption, as GANHOPPER follows fundamentally the same architecture as CycleGAN, working directly in image space; it merely enforces a gradual, multi-hop translation to steer and regulate the image transitions. In addition, multi-hop GANs represent a generic "meta idea" which is quite extensible, e.g., in terms of varying the number and architecture of the in-between translators. As demonstrated by Fig. 1 and more results later, even the simplest option of using *one* network can already make a significant difference for various domain translation tasks.

2   Related Work

The foundation of modern image-to-image translation is the UNet architecture, first developed for semantic image segmentation [20]. This architecture was later extended with conditional adversarial training to a variety of image-to-image translation tasks [8]. Further improvements led to the generation of higher-resolution outputs [23] and multiple possible outputs for the same image in "one-to-many" translation tasks, e.g. grayscale image colorization [29].

The above methods require paired input and output images $\{(x_i, y_i)\}$ as training data. A more recent class of image-to-image translation networks is capable of learning from only *unpaired* data in the form of two sets $\{x_i\}$ and $\{y_i\}$ of input and output images, respectively [11,25,28]. These methods jointly train a network G to map from x to y and a network F to map from y to x, enforcing at training time that $F(G(x)) = x$ and $G(F(y)) = y$. Such *cycle consistency* is thought to regularize the learned mappings to be semantically meaningful, rather than arbitrary translations.

While the above approaches succeed at domain translations involving low-level appearance shift (e.g. summer to winter, day to night), they often fail when the translation requires a significant shape deformation (e.g. cat to dog). Cycle-consistent translators have been shown to perform larger shape changes when trained with a discriminator and perceptual loss function that consider more global image context [5]. An alternative approach is to interpose a shared latent code z from which images in both domains are generated (i.e. $x = F(z)$

and $y = G(z))$ [15]. This method can also be extended to enable translation into multiple output images [7]. Another tactic is to explicitly and separately model geometry vs. appearance in the translation process. A domain-specific method for translating human faces to caricature sketches accomplishes this by detecting facial landmarks, deforming them, then using them to warp the input face [2]. More recent work has proposed a related technique that is not specific to faces [24]. Finally, it is also possible to perform domain translation via the feature hierarchy of a pre-trained image classification network [10]. This method can also produce large shape changes.

In contrast to the above, we show that direct image-to-image translation can produce large shape changes, while also preserving appearance details, if translation is performed in a sequence of smooth hops. This process can be viewed as producing an interpolation sequence between two domains. Many GANs can produce interpolations between images via linear interpolation in their latent space. These interpolations can even be along interpretable directions which are either specified in the dataset [12] or automatically inferred [4]. However, GAN latent space interpolation does not perform cross-domain interpolation. Aberman et al. [1] perform cross-domain interpolation by identifying corresponding points on images from two domains and using these points as input to drive image morphing [13]. However, this approach requires images in both the source and target domain to interpolate between, whereas our method takes just a source image and produces an interpolation to the best-matching target image. Lastly, InstaGAN [18] addresses large shape changes, e.g., pants to skirts, by using a multi-instance transfiguration network, relying on segmentation masks to translate one instance at a time. Their implementation includes a sequential minibatch inference/training option for a different purpose: to alleviate GPU overload when translating a large number of instances.

3   Method

Let X and Y denote our source and target image domains, respectively. Our goal is to learn a transformation that, given an image $x \in X$, outputs another image $y' \in Y$ such that y' is perceived to be the counterpart of the image x in the dataset Y. The same must be achieved with the analog transformation from $y \in Y$ to $x' \in X$. This task is identical to that performed by CycleGAN [28]. However, we do not translate the input image in one pass through the network. Rather, we facilitate the translation process via a sequence of intermediate images. We introduce the concept of a **hop**, which we define as the process of warping one image toward the target domain by a limited amount using a generator network. Repeated hops produce *hybrid images* as byproducts of the translation process.

Since we do not translate images in a single pass through a network, our training process must be modified from the traditional cycle-consistent learning framework. In particular, the generation of *hybrid images* during the translation is a challenge, because the training data does not include such images. Therefore, the *hybridness* of these generated images must be estimated on the fly during

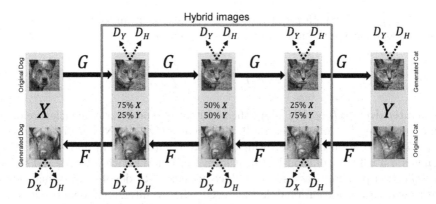

Fig. 2. Let X and Y represent two domains that we wish to translate (dogs and cats, respectively, in this figure). Our approach warps images from X to Y using the generator G and from Y to X using the generator F by applying each generator h times. The generator is trained by combining: **(a)** the adversarial loss, obtained by feeding the generated images, including the *hybrid images*, to either D_X (from X to Y) or D_Y (from Y to X); **(b)** the reconstruction loss, which is the result of comparing a generated image, including *hybrid images*, or input i with either $G(F(i))$ if i is being translated from X to Y or $F(G(i))$ if i is being translated from Y to X; **(c)** a domain *hybrid loss*, a membership score to either class determined by evaluating every generated image with the hybrid discriminator D_H, which is trained exclusively on real images to classify the input as being either a member of X or Y.

training. To this end, we introduce a new discriminator, which we call the *hybrid discriminator*, whose objective is to evaluate how similar an image is to both input domains, generating a membership score. We also add a new *smoothness term* to the loss, whose purpose is to encourage a gradual warping of the images through the hops so that the generator does not overshoot the translation. The following subsections present the multi-hop framework.

3.1 Multi-hop Framework

Our model consists of the original two generators from CycleGAN, denoted by G and F, and three discriminators, two of which are CycleGAN's original adversarial discriminators D_Y and D_X. The third discriminator is the new *hybrid discriminator* D_H. Figure 2 depicts how these different generators and discriminators work together during training time to translate images via multiple hops.

Hop Nomenclature. A **hop** is defined as using either G or F to warp an image towards the domain Y or X, respectively. A full translation is achieved by performing h hops using the same generator, where h is a user defined value. For instance, if $h = 3$, $G(G(G(x))) = y'$, where $x \in X$ and $y' \in Y$. Similarly,

$F(F(F(y))) = x'$, where $y \in Y$ and $x' \in X$. Given an image i, the translation hops are defined via the following recurrence relations:

$$G_h(i) = G(G_{h-1}(i)) \qquad G_0(i) = i$$
$$F_h(i) = F(F_{h-1}(i)) \qquad F_0(i) = i \tag{1}$$

Generator Architecture. We adopt the architecture and layer nomenclature originally proposed by Johnson et al. [9] and used in CycleGAN. Let c7s1-k denote a 7×7 Convolution-InstanceNorm-ReLU layer with k filters and stride 1. dk denotes a 3×3 Convolution-InstanceNorm-ReLU layer with k filters and stride 2. Reflection padding was used to reduce artifacts. Rk denotes a residual block with two 3×3 convolutional layers, each with k filters. uk denotes a 3×3 TransposeConvolution-InstanceNorm-ReLU layer with k filters and stride 1/2. The network takes 128×128 images as input and consists of the following layers: c7s1-64, d128, d256, R256 ($\times 12$), u128, u64, c7s1-3.

Discriminator Architecture. For the discriminator networks D_Y, D_X and D_H, we use the same 70×70 PatchGAN [8] used in CycleGAN. Let Ck denote a 4×4 Convolution-InstanceNorm-LeakyReLU layer with k filters and stride 2. Given the 128×128 input images, we produce a 16×16 feature matrix. Each of its elements is associated with one of the 70×70 patches from the input image. The discriminators consist of the following layers: C64, C128, C256, C512.

3.2 Training

The full loss function combines the reconstruction loss, adversarial loss, domain loss and smoothness loss, denoted respectively as $\mathcal{L}_{cyc}$, $\mathcal{L}_{adv}$, $\mathcal{L}_{dom}$ and $\mathcal{L}_{smooth}$:

$$\mathcal{L}(G, F, D_X, D_Y, D_H, h) = \gamma \mathcal{L}_{cyc}(G, F, h) + \epsilon [\mathcal{L}_{adv}(G, D_Y, X, Y, h)$$
$$+ \mathcal{L}_{adv}(F, D_X, Y, X, h)] + \delta \mathcal{L}_{dom}(G, F, D_H, X, Y, h) + \zeta \mathcal{L}_{smooth}(G, F, h) \tag{2}$$

We empirically define the values for the weights in the full objective function as: $\gamma = 10$, $\epsilon = 1$, $\delta = 1$, $\zeta = 2.5$.

Cycle-Consistency Loss. Rather than enforcing cycle consistency between the input and output images, as in CycleGAN, we enforce it locally along every hop of our multi-hop translation. That is, F should undo a single hop of G and vice versa. We enforce this property via a loss proportional to the difference between $F(G_n)$ and G_{n-1} for all hops n (and symmetrically between $G(F_n)$ and F_{n-1}:

$$\mathcal{L}_{cyc}(G, F, h) = \mathbb{E}_{x \sim p_{data}(X)} \left[\sum_{n=1}^{h} ||F(G_n(x)) - G_{n-1}(x)||_1 \right]$$
$$+ \mathbb{E}_{y \sim p_{data}(Y)} \left[\sum_{n=1}^{h} ||G(F_n(y)) - F_{n-1}(y)||_1 \right] \tag{3}$$

Adversarial Loss. The generator G tries to produce images $G_n(x)$ that look similar to those from domain Y, while the discriminator D_Y aims to distinguish between the generated images and real images $y \in Y$. Note that the "generated images" include both the final output images and the in-between images. The discriminators use a least squares formulation [17]:

$$
\mathcal{L}_{\mathrm{adv}}(G, D_Y, X, Y, h)
$$
$$
= \mathbb{E}_{y \sim p_{\mathrm{data}}(Y)} \left[(D_Y(y) - 1)^2 \right] + \mathbb{E}_{x \sim p_{\mathrm{data}}(X)} \left[\sum_{n=1}^{h} D_Y(G_n(x))^2 \right] \tag{4}
$$

Hybrid Loss. The *hybrid term* assesses the degree to which an image belongs to one of the two domains. For instance, if GANHOPPER is trained with 4 hops, we desire that the first hop $G_1(x)$ be judged as belonging 25% to domain Y and 75% to domain X. Thus, we define the *target hybridness score* of hop G_n to be n/h; conversely, it is defined as $(h - n)/h$ for the reverse hops F_n. To encourage each hop to achieve its target hybridness, we penalize the distance between the target hybridness and the output of the hybrid discriminator D_H on that hop. Since D_H is also trained to output 0 for ground-truth images in X and 1 for ground-truth images in Y (i.e. it is a binary domain classifier), an image i for which $D_H(i)$ produces an output of 0.25 can be interpreted as an image which the classifier is 25% confident belongs to domain Y:

$$
\mathcal{L}_{\mathrm{dom}}(G, F, D_H, X, Y, h) = \mathbb{E}_{x \sim p_{\mathrm{data}}(X)} \left[\sum_{n=1}^{h} \left(D_H(G_n(x)) - \frac{n}{h} \right)^2 \right]
$$
$$
+ \mathbb{E}_{y \sim p_{\mathrm{data}}(Y)} \left[\sum_{n=1}^{h} \left(D_H(F_n(y)) - \frac{h - n}{h} \right)^2 \right] \tag{5}
$$

Smoothness Loss. The smoothness term penalizes the image-space difference between hop n and hop $n - 1$. This term encourages the hops to be individually as small as possible while still leading to a full translation when combined, which has a regularizing effect on the training:

$$
\mathcal{L}_{\mathrm{smooth}}(G, F, h) = \mathbb{E}_{x \sim p_{\mathrm{data}}(X)} \left[\sum_{n=1}^{h} ||G_n(x) - G_{n-1}(x))||_1 \right]
$$
$$
+ \mathbb{E}_{y \sim p_{\mathrm{data}}(Y)} \left[\sum_{n=1}^{h} ||F_n(y) - F_{n-1}(y)||_1 \right] \tag{6}
$$

Training Procedure. Algorithm 1 shows how we train GANHOPPER, i.e. for each image to be translated, we perform a single hop, update the weights of the generator and discriminator networks, perform the next hop, etc. Training the network this way, rather than performing all hops and then doing a single weight update, has the advantage of requiring significantly less memory. Using one specialized generator for each specific hop would considerably increase memory usage, scaling linearly on the number of hops. The **generator_update** and **discriminator_update** procedures use a single term of the sums which define the loss $\mathcal{L}$ (i.e. the term for hop n) to compute parameter gradients.

initialize G, F, D_X, D_Y, D_H
for *each epoch* **do**
 $x, y \leftarrow$ random_batch();
 $x_{\text{real}}, y_{\text{real}} \leftarrow x, y$;
 for $n = 1$ to h **do**
  $x, y \leftarrow G(x), F(y)$;
  generator_update(G, x, n);
  generator_update(F, y, n);
  discriminator_update(D_X, y, x_{real}, n);
  discriminator_update(D_Y, x, y_{real}, n);
  classifier_update(D_H, x_{real}, y_{real});
 end
end

Algorithm 1: Training GANHOPPER

4 Results and Evaluation

Our network takes 128×128 images as input and outputs images of the same resolution. Experiments were performed on a NVIDIA GTX 1080 Ti (using batch size 6) and a NVIDIA Titan X (batch size 24). We trained GANHOPPER using Adam with a learning rate of 0.0002. With the exception of the cat/human faces experiment, we trained all experiments for 100 epochs (cat/human mode collapsed after 25 epochs, so we report the results from epoch 22).

In our experiments, we used combinations of seven datasets, translating between pairs. Some translation pairs demand both geometric and texture changes:

- 8,223 dog faces from the Columbia dataset [14]
- 47,906 cat faces from Flickr100m [19]
- 202,599 human faces from aligned CelebA [16]
- The zebra, horse, summer, and winter datasets used in CycleGAN [28]

We compare GANHOPPER with four prior approaches: CycleGAN [28], DiscoGAN [11], GANimorph [5] and UNIT [15]. All four are "unsupervised direct image-to-image translation" methods, in that they transform the input image from one domain into the output image from another domain without any prior pairing of samples between the two domains. We trained these baselines on the aforementioned datasets with their public implementation and default settings.

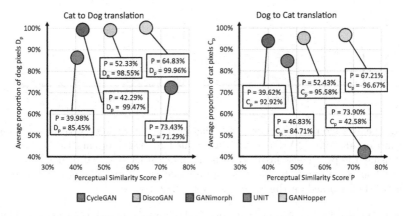

Fig. 3. Quantitative analysis of dog/cat translation. GANHOPPER was trained using 4 hops. The horizontal axis presents the average perceptual similarity [27] between all inputs and the respective outputs. The vertical axis presents the percentage of output pixels correctly labeled as the output class (e.g. dog or cat) by DeepLabV3 [3] trained on pascal PASCAL VOC 2012. Higher and to the right is better.

While FID [6] is a popular GAN evaluation metric, it is *not* a specific measure for the *translation* task. This is the reason why seminal papers that tackled this task [5,25,28] did not report FID or other similar metrics. For instance, CycleGAN performed their quantitative evaluation by quantifying the proportion of pixels in Cityscape's label-to-photo translation correctly classified by a pretrained FCN [21] (Fully Connected Networks) using the input label image as the ground truth for the metric. Similar to GANHOPPER, GANimorph proposed to evaluate image-to-image translations using two complimentary measures: DeepLabV3's pixel-wise labeling [3] and a perceptual similarity metric [27]. Therefore, we first compute the percentage of output pixels that are classified as belonging to the target domain by a pre-trained semantic segmentation network (DeepLabV3 [3], trained on PASCAL VOC 2012). Secondly, we measure how well the output preserves salient features from the input using a perceptual similarity metric [27]. We argue that the combination of these two metrics provide a better evaluation for image-to-image translation networks.

The results of this quantitative analysis can be seen in Fig. 3. CycleGAN produces outputs that best resemble the input but fails to perform domain translation. Our approach outperforms UNIT, GANimorph and DiscoGAN on both metrics. This result indicates that one need not necessarily sacrifice domain translation ability to preserve salient features of the input. Figure 4 shows how the percentage of pixels translated varies as a function of the number of hops performed. While not strictly linearly translating the pixels, it is still a smooth monotonic function, suggesting that hops successfully encourage in-between images that can be interpreted as domain hybrids.

Perceptual studies are the gold standard for assessing graphical realism [28]. Therefore, we performed a perceptual evaluation to measure (a) the extent to

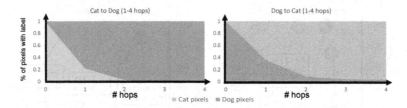

Fig. 4. The average percentage of pixels classified as cat or dog (vertical axis) on each hop (horizontal axis). GANHOPPER was trained to translate cats to dogs (and vice versa) using 4 hops. Pixels classified with any label other than cat or dog are omitted. The 0th hop corresponds to the raw inputs. The classification was performed using DeepLabV3 [3] trained on the PASCAL VOC 2012 dataset.

Table 1. Qualitative analysis of cat-to-dog and dog-to-cat translations performed using Amazon Mechanical Turk to evaluate how real the generated images are perceived to be and the extent to which GANHOPPER and the image-to-image translation baselines succeed at the translation task

Approach	Cat-to-dog		Dog-to-cat	
	Real/Fake	Translation	Real/Fake	Translation
GANHOPPER	26.98%	**38.11%**	**36.94%**	**63.76%**
UNIT	20.08%	35.19%	31.47%	16.28%
DiscoGAN	24.73%	20.61%	29.55%	12.76%
GANimporph	**36.24%**	6.07%	29.61%	7.2%

which dog and cat faces generated by our method, DiscoGAN, GANimorph, and UNIT are perceived as real; and (b) how much the generated samples from these four approaches resemble the input image. For evaluation (a), 36 participants were exposed to 128 paired random samples of cat-to-dog translations while 36 other participants were exposed to the same amount of random dog-to-cat translations. Both images of each pair were shown for one second at the same time. Also, for each given pair, one of the images was always a real sample while the other was a fake generated by one of the image translation networks. After an image pair was shown, the participant was asked which one of the two images shown looked real. A score of 50% for a given method would indicate that participants were unable to discriminate between real data and generated data on a given domain. For evaluation (b), we displayed 128 random images from our input test data to the participants, and the outputs of the translation using UNIT, DiscoGAN, GANimorph and GANHOPPER. Afterwards, the participant was asked which image better translates the input to the target domain. For (b) there was no time constraint and, as in (a), 18 participants were evaluated for each class. Therefore, the perceptual study with humans had 108 participants in total. As shown in Table 1, the perceptual experiment results indicate that our method was outperformed exclusively by GANimorph in how real the generated dogs are perceived to be. However, GANHOPPER outperforms GANimporph if one also takes into account the translation task, measure in which the later network had the worst performance compared to the other approaches. Furthermore, GANHOPPER significantly outperforms all other three methods in how real generated cats are perceived to be by humans and also on the translation task for both dog-to-cat and cat-to-dog translations.

Figure 5 compares our method to the baselines on cat to dog and dog to cat translation. Our multi-hop procedure translates the input via a sequence of hybrid images (Fig. 5(a)), allowing it to preserve key visual characteristics of the input if changing them is not necessary to achieve domain translation. For instance, fur colors and background textures are preserved in most cases (e.g. white cats map to white dogs) as is head orientation, while domain-specific features such as eyes, noses, and ears are appropriately deformed. The multi-hop procedure also allows control over how much translation to perform. The user can control the degree of "dogness" or "catness" introduced by the translation, including performing more hops than the network was trained on in order to exaggerate the characteristics of the target domain. Figure 5(b) shows the result of performing 8 hops using a network trained to perform a complete translation using 4 hops. Note that, in the fifth row of Fig. 5, the additional hops help to clarify the shape of the output dog's tongue.

By contrast, the baselines produce less desirable results. CycleGAN preserves the input features too much, leading to incomplete translations (Fig. 5(c)). Note that CycleGAN's outputs often look similar to the first hop of our network; this makes sense, since each hop uses a CycleGAN-like generator network. Our network uses multiple hops of that same architecture to overcome CycleGAN's original limitations. DiscoGAN (Fig. 5(d)) can properly translate high-level properties such as head pose and eye placement but fails to preserve lower-level appearance details such as fur patterns and color. Its results are also often geometrically malformed (lines 2, 4, 5, 7, and 8 on Fig. 5). GANimporph (Fig. 5(e)) produces images that are convincingly part of the target domain but preserve little of the input image's features (typically only head pose). Finally, while UNIT (Fig. 5(f)) produces images that normally preserve head pose, features like fur patterns are needlessly changed in the translation process. For instance, a white cat should be translated to a white dog instead of a black dog, as shown on line 5. Note that all networks besides GANHOPPER and CycleGAN tend to produce outputs with noticeably decreased saturation and contrast.

Figure 6 shows a similar comparison on human to cat translation. Again, our method preserves input features well: facial structures stay roughly the same, and cats with light fur tend to generate blonde-haired people. Our method also preserves background details better than the baselines.

We also examine the impact of the number of hops used during training. A network using too few hops must more quickly change the domain of the image; this causes the generator to "force" the translation and produce undesirable outputs. In the summer to winter translation of Fig. 7 (Top), the hiker's jacket quickly loses its blue color in the first row ($h = 2$) compared with the second

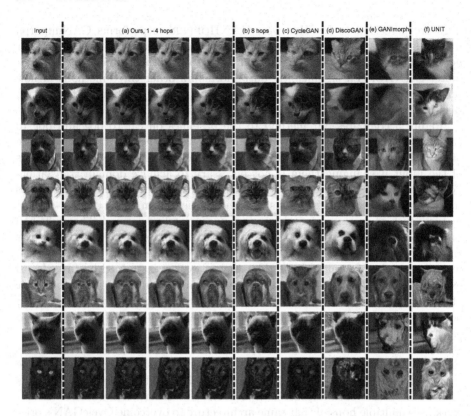

Fig. 5. Comparing different translation methods on the challenging dog/cat faces dataset. We trained GANHOPPER with four hops; (a) shows the result of hopping 1 to 4 times from the input and (b) shows the result of 8 hops from the input. We compare our results to (c) CycleGAN, (d) DiscoGAN, (e) GANimorph, and (f) UNIT.

row ($h = 4$). In the winter to summer translation of Fig. 7 (Bottom), the lake incorrectly becomes green when using a two-hop network but is preserved with four hops (while vegetation is still converted to green). The results suggest that increasing the number of hops has the added benefit of increasing image diversity and also allowing for smoother transition from one domain to another. Figure 7 and Fig. 9 also show how GANHOPPER addresses datasets with varying dominant color schemes on each domain: colors are smoothly interpolated from the input to the output on each hop until the translation process terminates.

Figure 8 demonstrates the impact of the smoothness weight ζ on training dog-to-cat translations with 4 hops. Default hyperparameters help GANHOPPER to preserve the original fur patterns while still preserving sharp local features in both translation directions, as shown in Fig. 8(a). With $\zeta = 0$, as shown in Fig. 8(b) (Left), the network collapses to producing mostly cats with gray and white fur, while generating noticeably blurrier dogs. Figure 8(b) (Right) shows

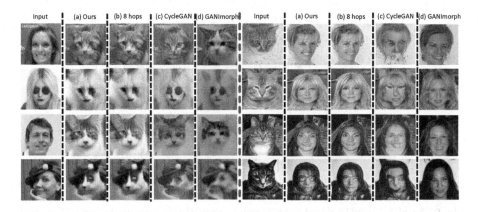

Fig. 6. Examples of human-to-cat faces translation. The approaches compared are (a) GANHOPPER, (b) 4 extra hops after the full translation, (c) CycleGAN and (d) GANimorph. GANHOPPER was trained with default hyperparameter values.

Fig. 7. Impact of training hop count. Using $h = 4$ hops (b) better preserves input features, but using $h = 2$ hops (a) allows more drastic changes. Red squares denote the hops that correspond to a full translation in each setting; images further to the right are extrapolations obtained by applying additional hops.

Fig. 8. Evaluation of the impact of the smoothness term weight ζ and hybrid term δ on the dog to cat dataset trained with 4 hops. The results using default hyperparameters are shown in (a). The value of δ at (b) is 1 and the value of ζ at (c) is 2.5.

that, as ζ increases, both issues are progressively mitigated. Further, we can observe in Fig. 8(c) (Left) that $\delta = 0$ tends to produce slightly less sharp features. This effect is more pronounced in the cat-to-dog translation than in the reverse direction. Figure 8(c)(Right) shows that increasing δ to 2.5 leads to more

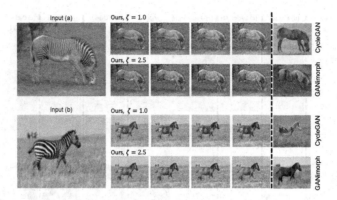

Fig. 9. As with CycleGAN and GANimorph, our method occasionally "erases" part of an object and replaces it with background, rather than correctly translating it (e.g. the zebra legs disappear). This can be mitigated by increasing the smoothness loss weight ζ. All other hyperparameters are set to default values.

artifacts in the translation process. For instance, note the asymmetry in the left and right eyes of the dog-to-cat translations.

As our method uses CycleGAN as a sub-component, it inherits some of the problems faced by that method, as well as other direct unsupervised image translators. Figure 9 shows one prominent failure mode, in which the network "cheats" by erasing part of the object to be translated and replacing it with background (e.g. zebra legs). The smoothness term in our loss function penalizes differences between hops, so increasing its weight mitigates this issue.

5   Conclusion and Future Work

Unsupervised image-to-image translation is an ill-posed problem. Different methods have chosen different regularizing assumptions to drive their solutions [7,15,24]. In this paper, we follow the cycle-consistency assumption of CycleGAN [28] and DualGAN [25], while introducing the multi-hop paradigm to exert fine-grained control over the translation using a new hybrid discriminator. As shown by both the quantitative analysis and human evaluation experiment presented in Sect. 4, GANHOPPER outperforms other baseline approaches by better preserving features of the input images while still applying the necessary transformations to create outputs which clearly belong to the target domain.

The meta idea of "transforming images in small steps" raises new and interesting questions worth exploring. For example, how many steps are ideal? The results in this paper used 2–4 hops, as more hops did not noticeably improve performance but did increase training time. However, some images in a domain X are clearly harder than others to translate into a different domain Y (e.g. translating dogs with long vs. short snouts into cats). Can we automatically learn the ideal number of hops for each input image? Taken to an extreme, can we use a very large number of tiny hops to produce a smooth interpolation sequence from source to target domain? We also want to identify domains where GANHOPPER systematically fails and explore the design space of multi-hop translation architectures in response. For instance, while GANHOPPER uses the same network for all hops, it may be better to use different networks per hop (i.e. the optimal function for translating a 25% dog to a 50% dog may not be the same as the function for translating a 75% dog to a real dog).

It would be interesting to combine GANHOPPER with ideas from MUNIT [7] or BiCycleGAN [29], so that the user can control the output of the translation via a "style" code while still preserving important input features (e.g. translating a white cat into different white-furred dog breeds). Yet another potential future work is to include the current hop information as part of the generator input (e.g. one-hot vector) to avoid the reliance on the generator to infer which hop operation should be performed based only on the input image. Finally, we would like to investigate the idea that initially spurred the development of GANHOPPER: generating meaningful *extrapolation* sequences *beyond* the boundaries of a given image domain, to produce creative and novel outputs.

References

1. Aberman, K., Liao, J., Shi, M., Lischinski, D., Chen, B., Cohen-Or, D.: Neural best-buddies: sparse cross-domain correspondence. ACM Trans. Graph. **37**(4), 1–14 (2018)
2. Cao, K., Liao, J., Yuan, L.: Carigans: unpaired photo-to-caricature translation (2018)
3. Chen, L., Papandreou, G., Schroff, F., Adam, H.: Rethinking atrous convolution for semantic image segmentation. CoRR abs/1706.05587 (2017)
4. Chen, X., Duan, Y., Houthooft, R., Schulman, J., Sutskever, I., Abbeel, P.: Infogan: interpretable representation learning by information maximizing generative adversarial nets. In: Proceedings of the 30th International Conference on Neural Information Processing Systems (2016)
5. Gokaslan, A., Ramanujan, V., Ritchie, D., Kim, K.I., Tompkin, J.: Improving shape deformation in unsupervised image-to-image translation. CoRR abs/1808.04325 (2018). http://arxiv.org/abs/1808.04325
6. Heusel, M., Ramsauer, H., Unterthiner, T., Nessler, B., Hochreiter, S.: GANs trained by a two time-scale update rule converge to a local nash equilibrium. In: Guyon, I., et al. (eds.) Advances in Neural Information Processing Systems 30, pp. 6626–6637. Curran Associates, Inc. (2017). http://papers.nips.cc/paper/7240-gans-trained-by-a-two-time-scale-update-rule-converge-to-a-local-nash-equilibrium.pdf
7. Huang, X., Liu, M.Y., Belongie, S., Kautz, J.: Multimodal unsupervised image-to-image translation. In: ECCV (2018)

8. Isola, P., Zhu, J., Zhou, T., Efros, A.A.: Image-to-image translation with conditional adversarial networks. CoRR abs/1611.07004 (2016). http://arxiv.org/abs/1611.07004

9. Johnson, J., Alahi, A., Li, F.: Perceptual losses for real-time style transfer and super-resolution. CoRR abs/1603.08155 (2016). http://arxiv.org/abs/1603.08155

10. Katzir, O., Lischinski, D., Cohen-Or, D.: Cross-domain cascaded deep feature translation. In: European Conference on Computer Vision (ECCV). Springer, Cham (2020)

11. Kim, T., Cha, M., Kim, H., Lee, J.K., Kim, J.: Learning to discover cross-domain relations with generative adversarial networks. In: ICML (2017)

12. Lample, G., Zeghidour, N., Usunier, N., Bordes, A., Denoyer, L., et al.: Fader networks: manipulating images by sliding attributes. In: Advances in Neural Information Processing Systems (2017)

13. Liao, J., Lima, R.S., Nehab, D., Hoppe, H., Sander, P.V., Yu, J.: Automating image morphing using structural similarity on a halfway domain. ACM Trans. Graph. 33(5), 1–12 (2014)

14. Liu, J., Kanazawa, A., Jacobs, D., Belhumeur, P.: Dog breed classification using part localization. In: Fitzgibbon, A., Lazebnik, S., Perona, P., Sato, Y., Schmid, C. (eds.) ECCV 2012. LNCS, vol. 7572, pp. 172–185. Springer, Heidelberg (2012). https://doi.org/10.1007/978-3-642-33718-5_13

15. Liu, M., Breuel, T., Kautz, J.: Unsupervised image-to-image translation networks. CoRR abs/1703.00848 (2017). http://arxiv.org/abs/1703.00848

16. Liu, Z., Luo, P., Wang, X., Tang, X.: Deep learning face attributes in the wild. CoRR abs/1411.7766 (2014). http://arxiv.org/abs/1411.7766

17. Mao, X., Li, Q., Xie, H., Lau, R.Y.K., Wang, Z.: Least squares generative adversarial networks. In: ICCV (2017)

18. Mo, S., Cho, M., Shin, J.: Instagan: instance-aware image-to-image translation. In: International Conference on Learning Representations (2019). https://openreview.net/forum?id=ryxwJhC9YX

19. Ni, K., et al.: Large-scale deep learning on the YFCC100M dataset. CoRR abs/1502.03409 (2015). http://arxiv.org/abs/1502.03409

20. Ronneberger, O., Fischer, P., Brox, T.: U-net: convolutional networks for biomedical image segmentation. In: MICCAI (2015)

21. Shelhamer, E., Long, J., Darrell, T.: Fully convolutional networks for semantic segmentation. IEEE Trans. Pattern Anal. Mach. Intell. 39(4), 640–651 (2017). https://doi.org/10.1109/TPAMI.2016.2572683. http://ieeexplore.ieee.org/document/7478072/

22. Taigman, Y., Polyak, A., Wolf, L.: Unsupervised cross-domain image generation. In: Proceedings of ICLR (2017)

23. Wang, T.C., Liu, M.Y., Zhu, J.Y., Tao, A., Kautz, J., Catanzaro, B.: High-resolution image synthesis and semantic manipulation with conditional GANs. In: Proceedings of the IEEE Conference on Computer Vision and Pattern Recognition (2018)

24. Wu, W., Cao, K., Li, C., Qian, C., Loy, C.C.: Transgaga: geometry-aware unsupervised image-to-image translation. In: Proceedings of CVPR (2019)

25. Yi, Z., Zhang, H., Tan, P., Gong, M.: DualGAN: unsupervised dual learning for image-to-image translation. In: Proceedings of ICCV (2017)

26. Yin, K., Chen, Z., Huang, H., Cohen-Or, D., Zhang, H.: LOGAN: unpaired shape transform in latent overcomplete space. ACM Trans. Graph. 38(6), 1–13 (2019)

27. Zhang, R., Isola, P., Efros, A.A., Shechtman, E., Wang, O.: The unreasonable effectiveness of deep features as a perceptual metric. In: 2018 IEEE/CVF Conference on Computer Vision and Pattern Recognition, pp. 586–595, June 2018. https://doi.org/10.1109/CVPR.2018.00068
28. Zhu, J., Park, T., Isola, P., Efros, A.A.: Unpaired image-to-image translation using cycle-consistent adversarial networks. In: International Conference on Computer Vision (ICCV) (2017, to appear)
29. Zhu, J.Y., et al.: Toward multimodal image-to-image translation. In: Advances in Neural Information Processing Systems (2017)

DOPE: Distillation of Part Experts for Whole-Body 3D Pose Estimation in the Wild

Philippe Weinzaepfel$^{(\boxtimes)}$, Romain Brégier, Hadrien Combaluzier,
Vincent Leroy, and Grégory Rogez

NAVER LABS Europe, Meylan, France
philippe.weinzaepfel@naverlabs.com

Abstract. We introduce DOPE, the first method to detect and estimate whole-body 3D human poses, including bodies, hands and faces, in the wild. Achieving this level of details is key for a number of applications that require understanding the interactions of the people with each other or with the environment. The main challenge is the lack of in-the-wild data with labeled whole-body 3D poses. In previous work, training data has been annotated or generated for simpler tasks focusing on bodies, hands or faces separately. In this work, we propose to take advantage of these datasets to train independent experts for each part, namely a body, a hand and a face expert, and distill their knowledge into a single deep network designed for whole-body 2D-3D pose detection. In practice, given a training image with partial or no annotation, each part expert detects its subset of keypoints in 2D and 3D and the resulting estimations are combined to obtain whole-body pseudo ground-truth poses. A distillation loss encourages the whole-body predictions to mimic the experts' outputs. Our results show that this approach significantly outperforms the same whole-body model trained without distillation while staying close to the performance of the experts. Importantly, DOPE is computationally less demanding than the ensemble of experts and can achieve real-time performance. Test code and models are available at https://europe.naverlabs.com/research/computer-vision/dope.

Keywords: Human pose estimation · Human pose detection · 3D pose estimation · 2D pose estimation · Body pose estimation · Hand pose estimation · Face landmarks estimation

1 Introduction

Understanding humans in real-world images and videos has numerous potential applications ranging from avatar animation for augmented and virtual reality [15, 46] to robotics [21,23]. To fully analyze the interactions of people with each other or with the environment, and to recognize their emotions or activities, a

© Springer Nature Switzerland AG 2020
A. Vedaldi et al. (Eds.): ECCV 2020, LNCS 12371, pp. 380–397, 2020.
https://doi.org/10.1007/978-3-030-58574-7_23

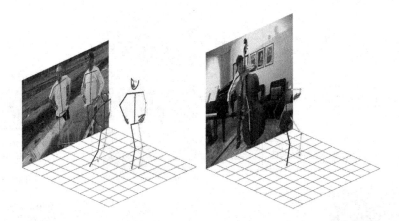

Fig. 1. Results of our DOPE approach for 2D-3D whole-body pose estimation.

detailed pose of the whole human body would be beneficial. This includes 3D body keypoints, *i.e.*, torsos, arms and legs, that give information on the global posture of the persons, but also detailed information about hands and faces to fully capture their expressiveness. The task of whole-body 3D human pose estimation has been mainly addressed part by part as indicated by the large literature on estimating 3D body pose [3,24,38,46,48,55], 3D hand pose [10,49, 67,73] or 3D face landmarks and shape [9,57] in the wild. These methods now reach outstanding performances on their specific tasks, and combining them in an efficient way is an open problem.

More recently, a few approaches have been introduced that capture body, hands and face pose jointly. Hidalgo *et al.* [29] extend OpenPose [12] to predict 2D whole-body poses in natural images. To train their multi-task learning approach, they partly rely on datasets for which adding 2D pose annotations is possible, *e.g.*, adding 2D hand pose annotations [58] to the MPII body pose dataset [1]. Such annotation scheme is not possible when dealing with 3D poses. Importantly, they observe global failure cases when a significant part of the target person is occluded or outside of the image boundaries. Some other works have leveraged expressive parametric human models composed of body, hand and face components stitched together such as Adam [37,64] or SMPL-X [51]. These optimization-based approaches remain sensitive to initialization and are usually slow to converge. Their performance highly depends on the intermediate estimation of the 3D orientations of body parts or 2D keypoint locations, and is therefore limited in cases of occlusions or truncations at the image boundary compared to more direct approaches.

In this paper, we propose the first learning-based method that, given an image, detects the people present in the scene and directly predicts the 2D and 3D poses of their bodies, hands and faces, see examples in Fig. 1. Inspired by LCR-Net++ [55], a Faster R-CNN like architecture [53] tailored for in-the-wild 2D-3D body pose estimation, we design a classification-regression network where

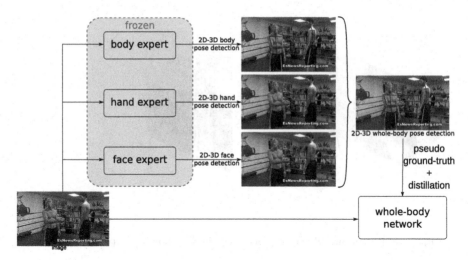

Fig. 2. Overview of our DOPE training scheme. Each training image is processed by the part experts to detect their specific parts and estimate their 2D and 3D poses. The resulting detections are combined to obtain the whole-body poses used as ground-truth for this image when training our network. We show only 2D poses for the sake of clarity but we also distill the 3D poses.

the object categories to detect are body, hand and face pose classes. In a second step, a class-specific regression is applied to refine body, hand and face pose estimates by deforming the average pose of each class both in 2D and 3D.

There exists no in-the-wild dataset to directly train our network, *i.e.*, images with 3D pose annotations for body, hand and face poses. Such data could only be obtained in specific controlled environments, *e.g.* in motion capture rooms or through computer-generation, which would not suit our purpose of whole-body pose estimation in unconstrained scenarios. However, multiple in-the-wild datasets are available for each independent task, *i.e.*, for 3D body pose estimation [38,46], 3D hand pose estimation [25,70,73] or 3D facial landmark estimation [9,18]. Task-specific methods trained on these datasets perform well in practice but our experiments show that training our single model for whole-body 3D pose estimation on the union of these datasets leads to poor performances. Each dataset being annotated with partial pose information (*i.e.*, its specific part), unannotated parts are mistakenly considered as negatives by our detection framework, burdening the performance of the network.

To handle this problem, we propose to train independent experts for each part, namely body, hand and face experts, and distill their knowledge to our whole-body pose detection network designed to perform the three tasks jointly. In practice, given a training image with partial or no annotation, each part expert detects and estimates its subset of keypoints, in 2D and 3D, and the resulting estimations are combined to obtain whole-body pseudo ground-truth poses for the whole-body network. Figure 2 illustrates this training scheme.

A distillation loss is applied on the network's output to keep it close to the experts' predictions. We name our method **DOPE** for **D**istillation **O**f **P**art **E**xperts. Our unified DOPE model performs on par with the part experts when evaluating each of the three tasks on dedicated datasets, while being computationally less demanding than the ensemble of experts and achieving real-time performances. In summary, we propose (a) a new architecture that can detect and estimate the whole-body 2D-3D pose of multiple people in the wild in real-time and (b) a novel and effective training scheme based on distillation that leverages previous data collection efforts for the individual subtasks.

This paper is organized as follows. After reviewing the related work (Sect. 2), we present our DOPE method in Sect. 3. Finally, experimental results for body, hand and face pose estimation are reported in Sect. 4.

2   Related Work

The problem of 3D human whole-body pose estimation has been mainly tackled by breaking the body into parts and focusing on the pose inference of these parts separately. In the following, we briefly review the state of the art for each of these subtasks, before summarizing the few approaches that predict the 3D pose of the entire body, and finally discussing existing distillation methods.

3D Body Pose Estimation. Two basic categories of work can be found in the recent literature: (a) approaches that directly estimate the 3D body keypoints from an input image [46,48,52,54,55] and (b) methods that leverage 2D human pose estimation [6,13,38,45]. The latter ones rely on a previous localization of the body keypoints in the image, through an off-the-shelf 2D pose detector [12,19,27], and lift them to 3D space [13,45] or, as in [6,38], use them to initialize the optimization procedure of a parametric model of the human body such as SMPL [43]. For our body expert, we employ LCR-Net++ [55] that jointly estimates 2D and 3D body poses from the image and has demonstrated robustness to challenging in-the-wild scenarios, i.e., showing multiple interacting persons, with cluttered backgrounds and/or captured under severe occlusions and truncations.

3D Hand Pose Estimation. 3D hand pose estimation from depth data has been studied for many years and state-of-the-art results on this task are now impressive as shown in a recent survey [60]. RGB-based 3D hand pose estimation is more challenging, and has gained interest in recent years. Regression-based techniques try to directly predict 3D location of hand keypoints [66] or even the vertices of a mesh [22] from an input image. Some methods incorporate priors by regressing parameters of a deformable hand model such as MANO [8,26,56], and many techniques leverage intermediate representations such as 2D keypoints heatmaps to perform 3D predictions [10,49,71,73]. However, pose estimation is often performed on an image cropped around a single hand, and hand detection is performed independently. For our hand expert, we therefore use the detector of [55] (adapted to hands) that recently achieved outstanding performances in RGB-based 3D hand pose estimation under hand-object interaction [2].

3D Face Pose Estimation. As with hands, the recovery of the pose of a face is typically performed from an image crop, by detecting particular 2D facial landmarks [63]. To better perceive the 3D pose and shape of a face, some works propose to fit a 3D Morphable Model [5,7,72] or to regress dense 3D face representations [17,20,34]. In this work, we also adopt [55] as face expert, resulting in an hybrid model-free approach that regresses 3D facial landmarks independently from their visibility, as in the approach introduced for the Menpo 3D benchmark [18].

3D Whole-Body Pose Estimation. The few existing methods [51,64] that predict the 3D pose of the whole-body all rely on parametric models of the human body, namely Adam [37] and SMPL-X [51]. These models are obtained by combining body, hand and face parametric models. Adam stitches together three different models: a simpler version of SMPL for the body, an artist-created rig for the hands, and the FaceWarehouse model [11] for the face. In the case of SMPL-X, the SMPL body model is augmented with the FLAME head model [40] and MANO [56]. A more realistic model is obtained in the case of SMPL-X by learning the shape and pose-dependent blend shapes. Both methods are based on an optimization scheme guided by 2D joint locations or 3D part orientations. Monocular Total Capture [64] remains limited to a single person while for SMPL-X [51], the optimization strategy is applied independently on each person detected by OpenPose [12]. Optimizing over the parameters of such models can be time-consuming and the performance often depends on a correct initialization. Our approach is the first one that predicts whole-body 3D pose without relying on the optimization of a parametric model and can make real-time predictions of multiple 3D whole-body poses in real-world scenes. In addition, our DOPE training scheme can leverage datasets that do not contain ground-truth for all the parts at once.

Distillation. Our learning procedure is based on the concept of distillation which was proposed in the context of efficient neural network computation by using class probabilities of a higher-capacity model as soft targets of a smaller and faster model [30]. Distillation has been successfully employed for several problems in computer vision such as object detection [14], video classification [4], action recognition [16], multi-task learning [42] or lifelong learning [32]. In addition to training a compact model [4,14], several works [16,31] have shown that distillation can be combined with privileged information [61], also called generalized distillation [44] in order to train a network while leveraging extra modalities available for training, e.g.training on RGB and depth data while only RGB is available at test time. In this paper, we propose to use distillation in order to transfer the knowledge of several body-part experts into a unified network that outputs a more complete representation of the whole human body.

3   DOPE for 2D-3D Whole-Body Pose Estimation

After introducing our architecture for multi-person whole-body pose estimation (Sect. 3.1), we detail our training procedure based on distillation (Sect. 3.2).

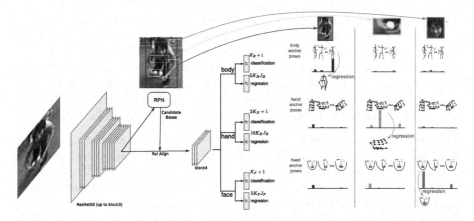

Fig. 3. Overview of our whole-body pose estimation architecture. Given an input image, convolutional features are computed and fed into a Region Proposal Network (RPN) to produce a list of candidate boxes. For each box, after RoI-Align and a few additional layers, 6 final outputs are computed (2 for each part). The first one returns a classification score for each anchor-pose corresponding to this part (including a background class not represented for clarity) while the second one returns refined 2D-3D pose estimates obtained through class-specific regression from the fitted anchor pose.

3.1 Whole-Body Pose Architecture

We propose a method that, given an image, detects the people present in the scene and directly predicts the 2D and 3D poses of their bodies, hands and faces. Our network architecture takes inspiration from [55], which extends a Faster R-CNN like architecture [53] to the problem of 2D-3D body pose estimation and has shown to be robust in the wild. We thus design a Localization-Classification-Regression network where the objects to be detected are bodies, hands and faces with respectively J_B, J_H and J_F keypoints to be estimated in 2D and 3D. Figure 3 shows an overview of this architecture.

Localization. Given an input image, convolutional features (ResNet50 [28] up to block3 in practice) are computed and fed into a Region Proposal Network (RPN) [53] to produce a list of candidate boxes containing potential body, hand or face instances. Although they might belong to the same person, we specifically treat the parts as separate objects to be robust to cases where only a face, a hand or a body is visible in the image. Our network can also output whole-body poses of multiple people at once, when their different parts are visible. The candidate boxes generated by the RPN are used to pool convolutional features using RoI Align, and after a few additional layers (block4 from ResNet50 in practice), they are fed to the classification and regression branches, 6 in total: one classification and one regression branch per part.

Classification. Classification is performed for the three sub-tasks: body, hand and face classification. As in [55], pose classes are defined by clustering the

3D pose space. This clustering is applied independently in the 3 pose spaces, corresponding to the 3 parts, obtaining respectively a set of K_B, K_H and K_F classes for bodies, hands and faces. Note that to handle left and right hands with the same detector, we actually consider $2 \times K_H$ hand classes, K_H for each side. For each classification branch, we also consider an additional background class to use the classifier as a detector. Therefore, each candidate box is classified into $K_B + 1$ labels for body classes, $2K_H + 1$ for hands and $K_F + 1$ for faces.

Regression. In a third step, a class-specific regression is applied to estimate body, hand and face poses in 2D and 3D. First, for each class of each part, we define offline the 'anchor-poses', computed as the average 2D and 3D poses over all elements in the corresponding cluster. After fitting all the 2D anchor-poses into each of the candidate boxes, we perform class-specific regressions to deform these anchor-poses and match the actual 2D and 3D pose in each box. This operation is carried out for the 3 types of parts, obtaining $5 \times J_B \times K_B$ outputs for the body part, $5 \times 2 \times J_H \times K_H$ for the hands and $5 \times J_F \times K_F$ for the face. The number 5 corresponds to the number of dimensions, *i.e.*, 2D+3D.

Postprocessing. For each body, hand or face, multiple proposals can overlap and produce valid predictions. As in [55], these pose candidates are combined, taking into account their 2D overlap, 3D similarity and classification scores. To obtain whole-body poses from the independent part detections produced by our network, we simply attach a hand to a body if their respective wrist estimations are close enough in 2D, and similarly for the face with the head body keypoint.

3.2   Distillation of Part Experts

Even if in-the-wild datasets with 3D pose annotations have been produced for bodies, hands and faces separately, there exists no dataset covering the whole-body at once. One possibility is to employ a union of these datasets to train our whole-body model. Since the datasets specifically designed for pose estimation of one part do not contain annotations for the others, *e.g.* body datasets do not have hand and face annotations and vice-versa, unannotated parts are therefore considered as negatives for their true classes in our detection architecture. In practice, this deteriorates the detector's ability to detect these parts and leads to worse overall performances (~10% drop for hands and faces, and ~2% for bodies). To leverage the multiple part-specific datasets, we therefore propose to train independent experts for each part, namely body, hand and face experts, and distill their knowledge into our whole-body pose network designed to perform the three tasks jointly.

Part Experts. To ease the distillation of the knowledge, we select our 3 experts to match the structure of the classification-regression branches of our whole-body pose estimation architecture and consider the same anchor poses as for the individual tasks. We therefore selected the Localization-Classification-Regression network from LCR-Net++ [55] as body expert and estimate $J_B = 13$ body joints with $K_B = 10$ classes. We also used the hand detection version of this architecture [2], replacing the K_B body pose classes by $K_H = 5$ hand anchor-poses for each side and using the standard number of $J_H = 21$ hand joints: 1 keypoint for the wrist plus 4 for each finger. Finally, to obtain our face expert, we adapted the same architecture to detect 2D-3D facial landmarks. We used the 84 landmarks defined in the 3D Face Tracking Menpo benchmark [69] that include eyes, eyebrows, nose, lips and facial contours. We defined $K_F = 10$ anchor-poses by applying K-means on all faces from the training set.

Training via Distillation. We propose to distill the knowledge of our three part experts to our whole-body pose detection model. Let $\mathcal{B}$, $\mathcal{H}$ and $\mathcal{F}$ be the training datasets used for the three individuals tasks, *i.e.*, body, hand, and face pose detection, respectively. They are associated with ground-truth (2D and 3D) pose annotations for bodies b, hands h and faces f, respectively. In other words, the body expert is for instance trained on $\mathcal{B} = \{I_i, b_i\}_i$, *i.e.*, a set of images I_i with body ground-truth annotations b_i, and similarly for the other parts.

To train our network, we need ground-truth annotations w for the whole body. We propose to leverage the detections made by the experts in order to augment the annotations of the part-specific datasets. We denote by $\hat{b}_i$, $\hat{h}_i$ and $\hat{f}_i$ the detections obtained when processing the images I_i with our expert for body, hands and face respectively. We train our DOPE network on:

$$\mathcal{W}_{DOPE} = \{I_i, w_i\}_{i \in \mathcal{B} \cup \mathcal{H} \cup \mathcal{F}} \text{ where } w_i = \begin{cases} \{b_i, \hat{h}_i, \hat{f}_i\} \text{ if } i \in \mathcal{B} \,, \\ \{\hat{b}_i, h_i, \hat{f}_i\} \text{ if } i \in \mathcal{H} \,, \\ \{\hat{b}_i, \hat{h}_i, f_i\} \text{ if } i \in \mathcal{F} \,. \end{cases} \tag{1}$$

The detections $\hat{b}_i$, $\hat{h}_i$ and $\hat{f}_i$ estimated by the experts are therefore considered as pseudo ground-truth for the missing keypoints in 2D and 3D. In practice, ground-truth annotations are completed using these estimations, for example when some annotations have been incorrectly labeled or are simply missing. Note that training images with no annotation at all could also be used to train our network, using only pseudo ground-truth annotations [39], *i.e.*, $w_i = \{\hat{b}_i, \hat{h}_i, \hat{f}_i\}$. The training scheme is illustrated in Fig. 2.

Loss. Our loss $\mathcal{L}$ to train the network combines the RPN loss $\mathcal{L}_{RPN}$ as well as the sum of three terms for each part $p \in \{$body,hand,face$\}$: (a) a classification loss $\mathcal{L}^p_{cls}$, (b) a regression loss $\mathcal{L}^p_{reg}$, (c) a distillation loss $\mathcal{L}^p_{dist}$:

$$\mathcal{L} = \mathcal{L}_{RPN} + \sum_{p \in \{\text{body,hand,face}\}} \mathcal{L}^p_{cls} + \mathcal{L}^p_{reg} + \mathcal{L}^p_{dist}, \tag{2}$$

where $\mathcal{L}_{RPN}$ is the RPN loss from Faster R-CNN [53]. The classification loss $\mathcal{L}^p_{cls}$ for each part p is a standard softmax averaged over all boxes. If a box sufficiently overlaps with a ground-truth box, its ground-truth label is obtained by finding the closest anchor-pose from the ground-truth pose. Otherwise it is assigned a background label, *i.e.*, 0.

The regression loss $\mathcal{L}^p_{reg}$ is a standard L1 loss on the offset between ground-truth 2D-3D poses and their ground-truth anchor-poses, averaged over all boxes.

Note that the regression is class-specific, and the loss is only applied on the output of the regressor specific to the ground-truth class for each positive box.

The distillation loss $\mathcal{L}_{dist}^p$ is composed of two elements, one for the distillation of the classification scores $\mathcal{L}_{dist\_cls}^p$ and another one, $\mathcal{L}_{dist\_reg}^p$, for the regression:

$$\mathcal{L}_{dist}^p = \mathcal{L}_{dist\_cls}^p + \mathcal{L}_{dist\_reg}^p. \tag{3}$$

Given a box, the goal of the distillation loss is to make the output of the whole-body network as close as possible to the output of the part expert p. The classification component $\mathcal{L}_{dist\_cls}^p$ is a standard distillation loss between the predictions produced by the corresponding part expert and those estimated by the whole-body model for part p. In other words, $\mathcal{L}_{dist\_cls}^p$ is the soft version of hard label loss $\mathcal{L}_{cls}^p$. The regression component $\mathcal{L}_{dist\_reg}^p$ is a L1 loss between the pose predicted by the part expert and the one estimated by the whole-body model for the ground-truth class. Note that the pseudo ground-truth pose is obtained by averaging all overlapping estimates made by the part expert. While $\mathcal{L}_{reg}^p$ is designed to enforce regression of this pseudo ground-truth pose, $\mathcal{L}_{dist\_reg}^p$ favors regression of the exact same pose predicted by the part expert for a given box.

In practice, proposals generated by the RPNs of part experts and whole-body model are different but computing distillation losses requires some proposals to coincide. At training, we thus augment the proposals of the whole-body model with positive boxes from the part experts to compute these losses. In summary, given a training image, we: (a) run each part expert, keeping the positive boxes with classification scores and regression outputs, (b) run the whole-body model, adding the positive boxes from the experts to the list of proposals. Losses based on pseudo ground-truths are then averaged over all boxes while distillation losses are averaged only over positive boxes from the part experts.

3.3   Training Details

Data. We train our body expert on the same combination of the MPII [1], COCO [41], LSP [35], LSPE [36], Human3.6M [33] and Surreal [62] datasets augmented with pseudo 3D ground-truth annotations as in [55]. We applied random horizontal flips while training for 50 epochs. We train our hand expert on the RenderedHand (RH) dataset [73] for 100 epochs, with color jittering, random horizontal flipping and perspective transforms. $K_H = 5$ anchor poses are obtained by clustering the 3D poses of right and flipped left hands from the training set. Finally, we train the face expert for 50 epochs on the Menpo dataset [69] with random horizontal flips and color jittering during training.

Implementation. We implement DOPE in Pytorch [50], following the Faster R-CNN implementation from Torchvision. We consider a ResNet50 backbone [28]. We train it for 50 epochs, using the union of the datasets of each part expert, simply doubling the RH dataset used for hands as the number of images is significantly lower than for the other parts. The same data augmentation strategy used for training each part expert is employed for the whole-body network. We use Stochastic Gradient Descent (SGD) with a momentum of 0.9, a weight decay of 0.0001 and an initial learning rate of 0.02, which is divided by 10 after 30 and 45 epochs. All images are resized such that the smallest image dimension is 800 pixels during training and testing and 1000 proposals are kept at test time.

Runtime. DOPE runs at 100ms on a single NVIDIA T4 GPU. When reducing the smallest image size to 400px and the number of box proposals to 50, and using half precision, it runs at 28 ms per image, *i.e.*, in real-time at 35 fps, with a 2–3% decrease of performance. For comparison, each of our experts runs at a similar framerate as our whole-body model since only the last layers change. Optimization-based 3D whole-body estimation methods [51,64] take up to a minute to process each person.

4 Experiments

Given that there is no dataset to evaluate whole-body 3D pose estimation in the wild, we evaluate our method on each task separately. After presenting datasets and metrics (Sect. 4.1), we compare the performance of our whole-body model to the experts (Sect. 4.2) and to the state of the art (Sect. 4.3).

4.1 Evaluation Datasets and Metrics

MPII for 2D Body Pose Estimation. As in [55], we remove 1000 images from the MPII [1] training set and use them to evaluate our 2D body pose estimation results. We follow the standard evaluation protocol and report the PCKh@0.5 which is the percentage of correct keypoints with a keypoint being considered as correctly predicted if the error is smaller than half the size of the head.

MuPoTs for 3D Body Pose Estimation. MuPoTs-3D [46] (Multi-person Pose estimation Test Set in 3D) is composed of more than 8,000 frames from 20 real-world scenes with up to three subjects. The ground-truth 3D poses, obtained using a multi-view MoCap system, have a slightly different format than the one estimated by our body expert and whole-body model. To better fit their 14-joint skeleton model, we modified the regression layer of our networks to output 14 keypoints instead of 13 while freezing the rest of the network. We finetuned this last layer only on the MuCo-3DHP dataset [46], the standard training set when testing on MuPoTs. We report the 3D-PCK, *i.e.*, the percentage of joint predictions with less than 15 cm error, per sequence, and averaged over the subjects for which ground truth is available.

RenderedHand for 3D Hand Pose Estimation. RenderedHand (RH) test set [73] consists of 2,728 images showing the hands of a single person. We report the standard AUC (Area Under the Curve) metric when plotting the 3D-PCK after normalizing the scale and relative translation between the ground-truth and the prediction. Note that while state-of-the-art methods evaluate hand pose estimation given ground-truth crops around the hands, we instead perform an automatic detection but miss around 2% of the hands.

Table 1. Comparison between our part experts and our whole-body model

	MPII (PCKh@0.5)	MuPoTs (PCK3D)	RH test (AUC)	Menpo (AUC)
Body expert	**89.6**	66.8	–	–
Hand expert	–	–	**87.1**	–
Face expert	–	–	–	73.9
Whole-body trained on gt	88.3	66.6	81.1	61.7
DOPE without $\mathcal{L}^p_{dist}$	88.3	66.4	83.5	**75.2**
DOPE with $\mathcal{L}^p_{dist}$	88.8	**67.2**	84.9	75.0

Menpo for Facial Landmark Estimation. We report results for facial land-mark evaluation using the standard 3D-aware 2D metric [18] on the 30 videos from the test set of the ICCV'17 challenge [69]. Given a ground truth-matrix $s \in \mathcal{M}_{N,2}(\mathbb{R})$ representing the 2D coordinates in the image of the $N = 84$ landmarks of a face, and a facial landmark prediction $\hat{s} \in \mathcal{M}_{N,2}(\mathbb{R})$, this 2D normalized point-to-point RMS error is defined as:

$$\epsilon(s, \hat{s}) = \frac{\|s - \hat{s}\|_2}{\sqrt{N} d_{scale}}, \tag{4}$$

where d_{scale} is the length of the diagonal of the minimal 2D bounding box of s.

4.2   Comparison to the Experts

Table 1 presents a comparison of the performances obtained by the part experts and our DOPE model, for body, hand and face pose estimation tasks.

We first compare the part experts to a baseline where our whole-body net-work is trained on the partial ground-truth available for each dataset, e.g.only body annotations are available on images from body datasets, etc.. The per-formance degrades quite significantly compared to those of the hand and face experts (−6% AUC for hand on the RH dataset and −12% for face landmarks). This is explained by a lower detection rate of the detector due to the fact that, for instance, unannotated faces present in the body datasets are considered as negatives during training. The performance of this model on body pose estima-tion is quite similar to the one of the body expert: as bodies are not observed too much in hand and face datasets, there are almost no missing body annotations.

We then compare the experts to a first version of our DOPE model without the distillation loss $\mathcal{L}^p_{dist}$. The performance on body pose estimation remains similar but, for hands and faces, a significant gain is obtained, in particular for faces, where the whole-body network performs even better than the expert. This might be explained by the fact that the whole-body network is trained on a larger variety of data, including images from body and hands datasets with many additional faces. In contrast, the hand component performs slightly lower

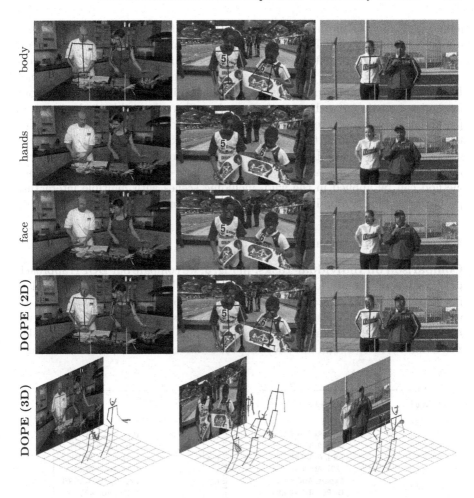

Fig. 4. Each column shows an example with the results of the 3 experts on the first three rows (we show only the 2D for clarity). The last two rows show the results obtained by our proposed DOPE approach in 2D and in 3D respectively.

than the expert. One hypothesis is that many hands in the body datasets are too small to be accurately estimated, leading to noisy pseudo ground-truth poses. However, the performance remains close to that of the hand expert.

With the addition of the distillation loss, the accuracy increases for hand pose estimation (+1.4%) and slightly for body pose estimation (+0.5% on MPII, +0.8% on MuPoTs), bringing the performance of the whole-body network even closer to the experts' results. Sometimes, DOPE even outperforms the part expert as observed on MuPoTs for multi-person 3D pose estimation or on Menpo for facial landmark detection. Figure 4 presents some qualitative results for the part experts and our proposed DOPE model trained with distillation loss. Two additional examples of our model's results can be found in Fig. 1. DOPE produces high-quality whole-body detections that include bodies, hands and faces. In the example on the left in Fig. 4, our whole-body network correctly detects and estimates the pose of three hands, misdetecting only the lady's right hand. By contrast, the hand expert only finds one hand in this image. Note that our method is holistic for each part: if a part is sufficiently visible in the image, a prediction is made for every keypoint of the part despite partial occlusions or truncations, as shown for the bodies in this same example. However, if a part is not visible, no prediction is made. This is the case for the occluded hands in the middle and right examples in Fig. 4. Overall, these examples illustrate that our method can be applied in the wild, including scenes with multiple interacting people, varied background, severe occlusions or truncations.

4.3 Comparison to the State of the Art

Comparison on Individual Tasks. In Fig. 5, we compare our DOPE approach to the state of the art for each individual task. Note that our main goal is not to outperform the state of the art on each of these tasks but rather to unify 3 individual models into a single one while still achieving a competitive performance. DOPE is among the top performing methods for all three tasks, *i.e.*, hand (a), face (b) and body (c) 3D pose estimation, while being the first and

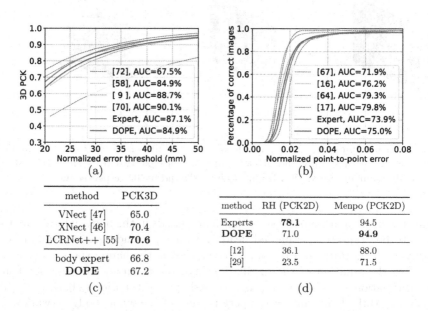

Fig. 5. Comparison to the state of the art: (a) PCK3D on RH for varying error threshold (hand). (b) Percentage of images with correct face detections for varying 3DA-2D thresholds on Menpo (face). (c) PCK3D on MuPoTs (body). (d) 2D PCK at a threshold of 10% of the tight bounding box's largest size on RH (hand) and 5% on Menpo (face). The higher the better.

only method to report on these three tasks together. Additionally, our detection network tackles a more difficult task than most of our competitors who assume that a bounding box around the ground-truth hands [10,59,71,73] or faces [17, 18,65,68] is given at test time. We also compare with existing whole-body 2D pose estimation methods (d).

Qualitative Comparison to [51,64]. Since there is no dataset to numerically compare the performances of our learning-based approach in the wild against the optimization-based pipelines such as [51,64], we show some qualitative examples in Fig. 6. We find that Monocular Total Capture [64] performs quite poorly on static images (second row), in particular due to occlusions. It greatly benefits from temporal information when processing the sequences from which the images

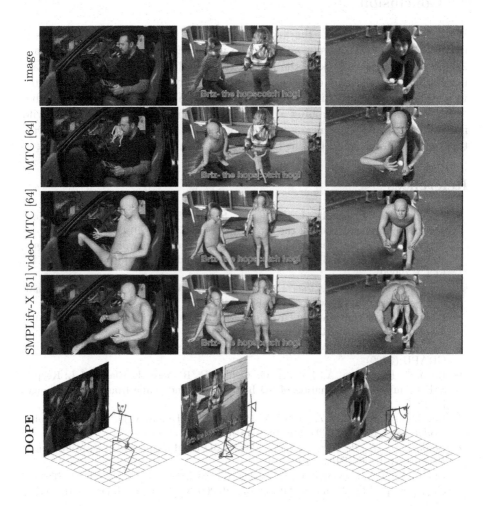

Fig. 6. Three examples with from top to bottom the original image, the results from MTC [64] from static image or the video, SMPLify-X [51] and ours.

are extracted (third row). However, there are still some errors, especially in case of occlusions (*e.g.*legs in the left column image). For [51] (fourth row), in the first example, OpenPose [12] does not estimate the 2D location of the feet that fall out of the field of view, impacting the optimization of the model's legs. In our case, the pose of the legs is correctly estimated. The same phenomenon happens in the second example where a little girl is kneeling and the self-occlusions prevent her feet from being detected. Finally, in the third example, the optimization gets stuck in a local minimum while our estimation is more robust. In addition of its robustness in the wild, our learning-based approach is also about 1000 times faster than [51] which takes about a minute per person in an image.

5   Conclusion

We have proposed DOPE, the first learning-based method to detect and estimate whole-body 3D human poses in the wild, including body, hand and face 2D-3D keypoints. We tackled the lack of training data for this task by leveraging distillation from part experts to our whole-body network. Our experiments validated this approach showing performances close to the part experts' results.

Our method allows training a network on a more diverse set of in-the-wild images, potentially without any pose annotations. In future work, we will investigate if our model could benefit from additional unlabeled training data.

References

1. Andriluka, M., Pishchulin, L., Gehler, P., Schiele, B.: 2D human pose estimation: new benchmark and state of the art analysis. In: CVPR (2014)
2. Armagan, A., et al.: Measuring generalisation to unseen viewpoints, articulations, shapes and objects for 3D hand pose estimation under hand-object interaction. In: ECCV (2020)
3. Arnab, A., Doersch, C., Zisserman, A.: Exploiting temporal context for 3D human pose estimation in the wild. In: CVPR (2019)
4. Bhardwaj, S., Srinivasan, M., Khapra, M.M.: Efficient video classification using fewer frames. In: CVPR (2019)
5. Blanz, V., Vetter, T.: A morphable model for the synthesis of 3D faces. In: SIGGRAPH (1999)
6. Bogo, F., Kanazawa, A., Lassner, C., Gehler, P., Romero, J., Black, M.J.: Keep it SMPL: automatic estimation of 3D human pose and shape from a single image. In: ECCV (2016)
7. Booth, J., Roussos, A., Zafeiriou, S., Ponniahy, A., Dunaway, D.: A 3D morphable model learnt from 10,000 faces. In: CVPR (2016)
8. Boukhayma, A., de Bem, R., Torr, P.H.S.: 3D hand shape and pose from images in the wild. In: CVPR (2019)
9. Bulat, A., Tzimiropoulos, G.: How far are we from solving the 2D & 3D face alignment problem? (and a dataset of 230,000 3D facial landmarks). In: ICCV (2017)
10. Cai, Y., Ge, L., Cai, J., Yuan, J.: Weakly-supervised 3D hand pose estimation from monocular RGB images. In: ECCV (2018)

11. Cao, C., Weng, Y., Zhou, S., Tong, Y., Zhou, K.: FaceWarehouse: a 3D facial expression database for visual computing. IEEE Trans. Vis. Comput. Graph. **20**(3), 413–425 (2013)
12. Cao, Z., Hidalgo, G., Simon, T., Wei, S.E., Sheikh, Y.: OpenPose: realtime multi-person 2D pose estimation using Part Affinity Fields. In: arXiv preprint arXiv:1812.08008 (2018)
13. Chen, C.H., Ramanan, D.: 3D human pose estimation = 2D pose estimation + matching. In: CVPR (2017)
14. Chen, G., Choi, W., Yu, X., Han, T., Chandraker, M.: Learning efficient object detection models with knowledge distillation. In: NeurIPS (2017)
15. Cimen, G., Maurhofer, C., Sumner, B., Guay, M.: AR poser: automatically augmenting mobile pictures with digital avatars imitating poses. In: CGVCVIP (2018)
16. Crasto, N., Weinzaepfel, P., Alahari, K., Schmid, C.: MARS: motion-augmented RGB stream for action recognition. In: CVPR (2019)
17. Crispell, D., Bazik, M.: Pix2Face: direct 3D face model estimation. In: ICCV Workshop (2017)
18. Deng, J., et al.: The Menpo benchmark for multi-pose 2D and 3D facial landmark localisation and tracking. IJCV **127**(6–7), 599–624 (2019)
19. Fang, H.S., Xie, S., Tai, Y.W., Lu, C.: RMPE: regional multi-person pose estimation. In: ICCV (2017)
20. Feng, Y., Wu, F., Shao, X., Wang, Y., Zhou, X.: Joint 3D face reconstruction and dense alignment with position map regression network. In: ECCV (2020)
21. Garcia-Salguero, M., Gonzalez-Jimenez, J., Moreno, F.A.: Human 3D pose estimation with a tilting camera for social mobile robot interaction. Sensors **19**(22), 4943 (2019)
22. Ge, L., et al.: 3D hand shape and pose estimation from a single RGB image. In: CVPR (2019)
23. Gui, L.Y., Zhang, K., Wang, Y.X., Liang, X., Moura, J.M., Veloso, M.: Teaching robots to predict human motion. In: IROS (2018)
24. Habibie, I., Xu, W., Mehta, D., Pons-Moll, G., Theobalt, C.: In the wild human pose estimation using explicit 2D features and intermediate 3D representations. In: CVPR (2019)
25. Hampali, S., Rad, M., Oberweger, M., Lepetit, V.: Honnotate: a method for 3D annotation of hand and objects poses. In: CVPR (2020)
26. Hasson, Y., et al.: Learning joint reconstruction of hands and manipulated objects. In: CVPR (2019)
27. He, K., Gkioxari, G., Dollár, P., Girshick, R.: Mask R-CNN. In: ICCV (2017)
28. He, K., Zhang, X., Ren, S., Sun, J.: Deep residual learning for image recognition. In: CVPR (2016)
29. Hidalgo, G., et al.: Single-network whole-body pose estimation. In: ICCV (2019)
30. Hinton, G., Vinyals, O., Dean, J.: Distilling the knowledge in a neural network. In: NIPS Workshop (2014)
31. Hoffman, J., Gupta, S., Darrell, T.: Learning with side information through modality hallucination. In: CVPR (2016)
32. Hou, S., Pan, X., Change Loy, C., Wang, Z., Lin, D.: Lifelong learning via progressive distillation and retrospection. In: ECCV (2018)
33. Ionescu, C., Papava, D., Olaru, V., Sminchisescu, C.: Human3.6M: large scale datasets and predictive methods for 3D human sensing in natural environments. IEEE Trans. PAMI **36**(7), 1325–1339 (2013)

34. Jackson, A.S., Bulat, A., Argyriou, V., Tzimiropoulos, G.: Large pose 3D face reconstruction from a single image via direct volumetric CNN regression. In: ICCV (2017)
35. Johnson, S., Everingham, M.: Clustered pose and nonlinear appearance models for human pose estimation. In: BMVC (2010)
36. Johnson, S., Everingham, M.: Learning effective human pose estimation from inaccurate annotation. In: CVPR (2011)
37. Joo, H., Simon, T., Sheikh, Y.: Total capture: a 3D deformation model for tracking faces, hands, and bodies. In: CVPR (2018)
38. Lassner, C., Romero, J., Kiefel, M., Bogo, F., Black, M.J., Gehler, P.V.: Unite the people: closing the loop between 3D and 2D human representations. In: CVPR (2017)
39. Lee, D.H.: Pseudo-label: the simple and efficient semi-supervised learning method for deep neural networks. In: ICML Workshop (2013)
40. Li, T., Bolkart, T., Black, M.J., Li, H., Romero, J.: Learning a model of facial shape and expression from 4D scans. ACM Trans. Graph. (ToG) **36**(6), 194 (2017)
41. Lin, T.Y., et al.: Microsoft coco: common objects in context. In: ECCV (2014)
42. Liu, X., He, P., Chen, W., Gao, J.: Improving multi-task deep neural networks via knowledge distillation for natural language understanding. arXiv preprint arXiv:1904.09482 (2019)
43. Loper, M., Mahmood, N., Romero, J., Pons-Moll, G., Black, M.J.: SMPL: a skinned multi-person linear model. ACM Trans. Graph. **34**(6), 1–16 (2015)
44. Lopez-Paz, D., Bottou, L., Schölkopf, B., Vapnik, V.: Unifying distillation and privileged information. In: ICLR (2016)
45. Martinez, J., Hossain, R., Romero, J., Little, J.J.: A simple yet effective baseline for 3D human pose estimation. In: ICCV (2017)
46. Mehta, D., et al.: Single-shot multi-person 3D pose estimation from monocular RGB. In: 3DV (2018)
47. Mehta, D., et al.: VNect: real-time 3D human pose estimation with a single RGB camera. ACM Trans. Graph. **36**(4), 1–14 (2017)
48. Moon, G., Chang, J.Y., Lee, K.M.: Camera distance-aware top-down approach for 3D multi-person pose estimation from a single RGB image. In: ICCV (2019)
49. Mueller, F., et al.: GANerated hands for real-time 3D hand tracking from monocular RGB. In: CVPR (2018)
50. Paszke, A., et al.: Pytorch: an imperative style, high-performance deep learning library. In: NeurIPS (2019)
51. Pavlakos, G., et al.: Expressive body capture: 3D hands, face, and body from a single image. In: CVPR (2019)
52. Pavlakos, G., Zhou, X., Derpanis, K.G., Daniilidis, K.: Coarse-to-fine volumetric prediction for single-image 3D human pose. In: CVPR (2017)
53. Ren, S., He, K., Girshick, R., Sun, J.: Faster R-CNN: towards real-time object detection with region proposal networks. In: NIPS (2015)
54. Rogez, G., Schmid, C.: Mocap-guided data augmentation for 3D pose estimation in the wild. In: NIPS (2016)
55. Rogez, G., Weinzaepfel, P., Schmid, C.: LCR-Net++: multi-person 2D and 3D pose detection in natural images. IEEE Trans. PAMI **42**(5), 1146–1161 (2019)
56. Romero, J., Tzionas, D., Black, M.J.: Embodied hands: modeling and capturing hands and bodies together. ACM Trans. Graph. **36**(6), 245 (2017)
57. Sanyal, S., Bolkart, T., Feng, H., Black, M.J.: Learning to regress 3D face shape and expression from an image without 3D supervision. In: CVPR (2019)

58. Simon, T., Joo, H., Matthews, I., Sheikh, Y.: Hand keypoint detection in single images using multiview bootstrapping. In: CVPR (2017)
59. Spurr, A., Song, J., Park, S., Hilliges, O.: Cross-modal deep variational hand pose estimation. In: CVPR (2018)
60. Supančič, J.S., Rogez, G., Yang, Y., Shotton, J., Ramanan, D.: Depth-based hand pose estimation: methods, data, and challenges. IJCV **126**(11), 1180–1198 (2018)
61. Vapnik, V., Izmailov, R.: Learning using privileged information: similarity control and knowledge transfer. JMLR **16**(1), 2023–2049 (2015)
62. Varol, G., et al.: Learning from synthetic humans. In: CVPR (2017)
63. Wu, Y., Ji, Q.: Facial landmark detection: a literature survey. IJCV **127**(2), 115–142 (2019)
64. Xiang, D., Joo, H., Sheikh, Y.: Monocular total capture: Posing face, body, and hands in the wild. In: CVPR (2019)
65. Xiong, P., Li, G., Sun, Y.: Combining local and global features for 3D face tracking. In: ICCV Workshops (2017)
66. Yang, L., Li, S., Lee, D., Yao, A.: Aligning latent spaces for 3D hand pose estimation. In: ICCV (2019)
67. Yuan, S., Stenger, B., Kim, T.K.: RGB-based 3D hand pose estimation via privileged learning with depth images. arXiv preprint arXiv:1811.07376 (2018)
68. Zadeh, A., Baltrusaitis, T., Morency, L.P.: Convolutional experts constrained local model for facial landmark detection. In: CVPR Workshop (2017)
69. Zafeiriou, S., Chrysos, G., Roussos, A., Ververas, E., Deng, J., Trigeorgis, G.: The 3D menpo facial landmark tracking challenge. In: ICCV Workshops (2017)
70. Zhang, J., Jiao, J., Chen, M., Qu, L., Xu, X., Yang, Q.: A hand pose tracking benchmark from stereo matching. In: ICIP (2017)
71. Zhang, X., Li, Q., Mo, H., Zhang, W., Zheng, W.: End-to-end hand mesh recovery from a monocular RGB image. In: ICCV (2019)
72. Zhu, X., Liu, X., Lei, Z., Li, S.Z.: Face alignment in full pose range: a 3D total solution. IEEE Trans. PAMI **41**(1), 78–92 (2017)
73. Zimmermann, C., Brox, T.: Learning to estimate 3D hand pose from single RGB images. In: ICCV (2017)

Multi-view Adaptive Graph Convolutions for Graph Classification

Nikolas Adaloglou, Nicholas Vretos$^{(\boxtimes)}$, and Petros Daras

The Visual Computing Lab - Information Technologies Institute,
Centre for Research and Technology Hellas, 57001 Thessaloniki, Greece
{adaloglou,vretos,daras}@iti.gr

Abstract. In this paper, a novel multi-view methodology for graph-based neural networks is proposed. A systematic and methodological adaptation of the key concepts of classical deep learning methods such as convolution, pooling and multi-view architectures is developed for the context of non-Euclidean manifolds. The aim of the proposed work is to present a novel multi-view graph convolution layer, as well as a new view pooling layer making use of: a) a new hybrid Laplacian that is adjusted based on feature distance metric learning, b) multiple trainable representations of a feature matrix of a graph, using trainable distance matrices, adapting the notion of views to graphs and c) a multi-view graph aggregation scheme called graph view pooling, in order to synthesise information from the multiple generated "views". The aforementioned layers are used in an end-to-end graph neural network architecture for graph classification and show competitive results to other state-of-the-art methods.

Keywords: Distance metric learning · Graph neural networks · Graph classification · Multi-view · View pooling · Adaptive graph convolution

1 Introduction

Graph theory enabled us, among other things, to powerfully represent relationships between data. Due to their avast application field, ranging from biological structures to modern social networks, graph representations, along with the recently exploding field of Graph Neural Networks (GNNs), assisted us to re-address challenging graph related tasks under the prism of neural networks. To that end, the task of adapting operations from classical convolutional neural networks (CNNs), such as convolution and pooling, to non-Euclidean domains (e.g., graphs and manifolds), gave rise to the emerging field of geometric deep learning [4].

A typical CNN consists of different layers of convolutions and pooling that are usually combined in a sequential manner [13,24,26]. The idea of adapting these key operations of CNNs to irregular grids is not new. Until recently, a considerable amount of research effort has been invested to adapt the classical convolution layers in many different ways towards graph-based convolutions [5–12]

© Springer Nature Switzerland AG 2020
A. Vedaldi et al. (Eds.): ECCV 2020, LNCS 12371, pp. 398–414, 2020.
https://doi.org/10.1007/978-3-030-58574-7_24

giving birth to the Graph-based Neural networks. GNNs have shown promising results on representation learning mainly due to the graphs' ability to encode the structure of the data, in contrast to regular grids [39], by encapsulating information in the graph's vertices [28].

Many different graph theoretical domains have made use of the above ideas to this point. Among them, graph classification has attracted a lot of attention lately due to its wide application areas [15,42,49]. Graph classification is considered as the task to find a mapping $f : G \rightarrow T$ that maps each graph in G to a label from a set of target labels T. Nonetheless, in graph classification, the continuous-valued vertex attributes, such as the ones that can be found in biological measurements [11], are rarely exploited.

In this paper, a flexible multi-view GNN architecture for the task of graph classification is proposed, which propagates both structural and signal information throughout the network. To that end, a novel multi-view graph convolutional layer is presented making use of a hybrid Laplacian, which combines information of the feature space with the structure of the input graph. Subsequently, the use of multiple trainable distance metrics is proposed to cope with training instabilities and overfitting, since it has been proven that single distance metric learning can be prone to overfitting [17]. Finally, by applying a spectral filtering on the graph's signal with different hybrid Laplacians associated to each "view", a per "view" projected signal is calculated. Similar to [41], a batch normalized max view pooling layer is proposed to aggregate the different per "view" projected signals. This leads our model to learn from compact generalized representations.

The remainder of this paper is organized as follows: in Sect. 2, related work is briefly described. In Sect. 3, the different components of the proposed methodology are outlined as well as their application to a GNN architecture is detailed. In Sect. 4, the performed experimental results in several and diverse datasets are reported. Finally, conclusions are drawn in Sect. 5.

2   Related Work

Graph convolutional filters can be divided in two main approaches: a) the spatial and b) the spectral ones. Spatial approaches operate directly in the vertices' neighborhoods while spectral approaches operate on the graph's Laplacian eigenspace [56]. In PSCN [34], the authors presented a generalized spatial approach in order to generate local normalized neighborhood regions while in DGCNN [53] an end-to-end architecture is proposed that keeps extra vertex information through sorted graph representations from spatial graph convolutions. In order to process graph data with classical CNNs, KGCNN [35] uses a 2-step approach, starting from extracting patches from graphs via common community detection algorithms, embedding them with graph kernels and finally feed them in a classical CNN. Furthermore, another approach proposed in GIN [47] developed an architecture based on Weisfeiler-Lehman test [38], stating that its discriminating power is equal to the power of the Weisfeiler-Lehman isomorphism test. Finally, in DGK [50] the authors proposed to leverage the dependency information between sub-structures used in graph kernels by learning their latent representations.

A major breakthrough in graph spectral convolutions was proposed in [10]. Therein, the authors showed the ability of the spectral GNN to extract local features through graph convolutional layers. Moreover, they proposed an efficient pooling strategy on graphs, based on a binary tree structure of the rearranged vertices. Several recently developed graph pooling methods attempt to reduce the number of vertices [6,10,14,52], producing coarser and sparser representations of a graph. However, for graph classification, where the number of vertices is relatively small, it is difficult to design such models, while sometimes it could lead to unstable training behaviour [52]. Furthermore, the coarsened vertices are not always arranged in a meaningful way. Moreover, graph coarsening processes are usually keeping a fixed number of vertices, which results in training and inference bias [10].

There exist various attempts that define pooling operation on graphs. In Graph U-Nets [14], the authors propose a max pooling scheme using a trainable projection vector of the graph signal and then assign the corresponding indices to the adjacency matrix. In DIFFPOOL [52], the authors try to learn the hierarchical structure through a trainable cluster assignment matrix, providing a flexible architecture that can be applied in a plethora of GNNs. In the same direction, CLIQUEPOOL [30] also attempts to coarsen the vertices of graph by aggregating maximal cliques. In another recent work called SAGPool [27], the authors define an alternative graph pooling method based on self-attention that considers both the vertex features and the graph structure. Finally, in HO-GNN [32], a GNN architecture is used that takes into account higher-order graph structures at multiple scales.

Some recent approaches have attempted to design architectures that explore different graph structures. In this direction, MGCN [22] is developed to capture multi-relational graph relationships through multi-dimensional Chebyshev polynominals. In GCAPS-CNN [45], the authors introduced the notion of capsules in spectral GNNs, in order to encapsulate local higher order statistical information per vertex feature. In a proximal work, CAPS-GNN [46] explores additional vertex information by computing hand-crafted statistics. However, both approaches compute extra vertex information explicitly, while they do not involve any trainable components.

Moreover, one of the first works that introduced single supervised metric learning on graph related tasks is [29], which is closer to our approach. Nonetheless, this work explores only one graph structure through the graph's Laplacian as opposed to our work where multiple graphs are used. Besides, distance metric learning has also been applied in [25] to resolve the irregular graph matching task, using spectral graph convolutional networks in the field of biomedical applications. Finally, WKPI [55] employ a metric learning scheme, which learns a positive semi-definite weighted-kernel for persistence summaries from labelled data.

In [41] the notion of "view" was introduced, where each "view" represents a $2D$ projection of a $3D$ object from a different angle, in order to produce informative representations for the tasks of object recognition and retrieval. In [54], the authors used the idea of "views" to construct different brain graphs, where structure was determined by a structural MRI scan and the feature matrices were calculated from multiple tractography algorithms based on diffusion MRI acquisition, to fuse information scattered in different medical imaging modalities for pairwise similarity prediction. However, none of the above view-based approaches introduced a trainable task-driven generation of views, as is the case in our approach.

The majority of graph convolution methods are based on projected graph features into a single graph structure. The motivation behind our approach is that "views" are artificially created from a common input. These, can extract different learning representations, the same way 3D objects are projected onto 2D images and processed independently. Nevertheless, the fact that the generated "views" are trainable, as opposed to previous approaches, is a novel and unexplored domain.

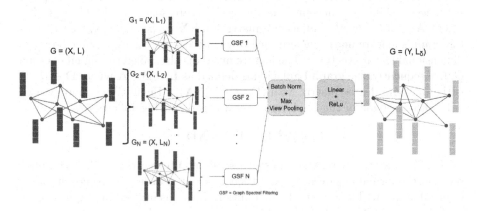

Fig. 1. An overview of the proposed layers (multi-view graph convolution and view pooling)

3   Proposed Method

The proposed work is inspired from [41] and [54] in using the notion of "views" produced by a shared input (i.e. human vision). The key idea of the proposed multi-view graph convolution (MV-GC) layer is that in each "view" a different n complete graph (K_n) is constructed from the pairwise Mahalanobis distances [8] of the vertices in the feature space. Each "view" is thus encapsulating a different relation between vertices in a distance metric learning context. This information is encoded in the MV-GC layer via the so-called hybrid Laplacian.

The hybrid Laplacian is a linear combination of the input graph's Laplacian and a non-Euclidean distance-based Laplacian term, called from now on the "view" Laplacian, derived from the aforementioned K_n graph. As a result, the spectral graph convolution is approximated by a different hybrid Laplacian eigenspace, producing multiple learnable projections of the same graph signal. Therefore, applying batch normalization as in [19] and a view-wise max pooling operation, called from now on "view pooling layer (VPOOL)", an aggregated graph output signal is produced. In contrast to other existing methods [21] that keep the structure of the graph constant throughout the network, in the proposed approach the intrinsic graph's structure is altered during the learning process of the GNN. The whole process can be illustrated in Fig. 1.

3.1 Notations and Prerequisites

To ameliorate the readability of this paper, a summary of the notations and some initial background theory to be used is provided. A graph G is defined as $G = (\mathbf{V}, \mathbf{E})$, where $\mathbf{V}$ is a set of vertices and $\mathbf{E}$ a set of edges, with $e_{ij} \in \mathbf{E}$ defined as (v_i, v_j) and $v_i, v_j \in \mathbf{V}$. An alternative representation of a graph of n vertices, taking into account the vertices' feature space can be $G = (\mathbf{A}, \mathbf{X})$, where $\mathbf{A} \in \mathbb{R}^{n \times n}$ is the adjacency matrix and $\mathbf{X} = [\mathbf{x}_1, \mathbf{x}_2, .., \mathbf{x}_n] \in \mathbb{R}^{n \times d}$ is the graph's feature matrix where each row contains the corresponding vertex d-dimensional feature vector $\mathbf{x}$. The feature matrix is also called the signal of graph G. Consequently, the graph Laplacian is defined as $\mathbf{L} = \mathbf{D} - \mathbf{A}$ where $\mathbf{D} \in R^{n \times n}$ is the diagonal degree matrix with $(\mathbf{D})_{ii} = \sum_j (\mathbf{A})_{ij}$. Finally, a commonly used normalized version of the Laplacian operator is defined as follows [7]:

$$\mathbf{L}_{norm} \triangleq \mathbf{I}_n - \mathbf{D}^{-1/2} \mathbf{A} \mathbf{D}^{-1/2}. \tag{1}$$

$\mathbf{L}_{norm}$ is a real symmetric, positive semi-definite matrix, with a complete set of orthonormal eigenvectors and their associated ordered real non-negative eigenvalues λ_i, with $i = [0, n-1]$. In addition, $\mathbf{L}_{norm}$ is utilized in graph spectral convolution, due to the fact that its eigenvalues lie in the range $[0, \lambda_{max}]$, with $\lambda_{max} \leq 2$ and is widely adopted in most spectral GNN architectures.

The generalized Mahalanobis distance, with transformation matrix $\mathbf{M}$, for any positive semi-definite matrix and vectors $\mathbf{x}, \mathbf{y}$, is defined as:

$$d(\mathbf{x}, \mathbf{y}) = \sqrt{(\mathbf{x} - \mathbf{y})^T \mathbf{M} (\mathbf{x} - \mathbf{y})} \quad \forall \mathbf{x}, \mathbf{y}, \tag{2}$$

where ^{T} denotes the transpose operation. The above equation can represent a quantitative measure of dissimilarity between vectors $\mathbf{x}$ and $\mathbf{y}$, which are drawn from the same distribution with covariance matrix $\mathbf{C} = \mathbf{M}^{-1}$. For $\mathbf{M} = \mathbf{I}$, Eq. 2 reduces to the Euclidean distance. The latter assumes that the variances among different dimensions to be one and covariances to be zero, which is rarely the case in real life applications.

Furthermore, let *diag* be the operator that maps the main diagonal of an $c \times c$ matrix into a vector $\in \mathbb{R}^c$ and $\mathbf{1}_d$ be a d element vector of ones. A useful equation, derived from the properties of the Hadamard product [18], denoted as $\odot$, is that for given matrices $\mathbf{A}, \mathbf{B} \in R^{c \times d}$:

$$diag(\mathbf{A}\mathbf{B}^T) = (\mathbf{A} \odot \mathbf{B})\mathbf{1}_d \in \mathbb{R}^c. \tag{3}$$

Batch normalization across a set of N representations (or views) of X_v, where $\mathbf{X}_v \in R^{n \times d}$, can be defined as an element-wise operation as:

$$BN(x_v) = \gamma_v \left(\frac{x_v - \mu(\mathbf{X}_v)}{\sigma(\mathbf{X}_v)} \right) + \beta_v, \tag{4}$$

where x_v denotes the elements of $\mathbf{X}_v$, while γ_v and β_v are trainable scalars that correspond to a single view. $\mu_v(\mathbf{X}_v)$ is the mean value of the elements of matrix $\mathbf{X}_v$ and σ their standard deviation.

Similarly, given N representations $\mathbf{Z} = [\mathbf{X}_1, \mathbf{X}_2, .., \mathbf{X}_N]$ that may correspond to "views", max view-wise pooling [41] can be computed by simply taking the maximum across the different views:

$$(\mathbf{Z})_{i,j} = \max((\mathbf{X}_1)_{i,j}, (\mathbf{X}_2)_{i,j}, .., (\mathbf{X}_N)_{i,j}) \tag{5}$$

3.2 Construction of the Hybrid Laplacian

For each graph $G = (\mathbf{A}, \mathbf{X})$, N "views" are initially created. Each "view" is associated to a feature transformation matrix $\mathbf{M}_v \in \mathbb{R}^{d \times d}$ with $v \in [1, .., N]$. Each $\mathbf{M}_v$ is a positive semi-definite matrix defined as $\mathbf{M}_v = \mathbf{Q}_v \mathbf{Q}_v^T \in \mathbb{R}^{d \times d}$, where $\mathbf{Q}_v$ is randomly initialized at the beginning of the learning process. In particular, taking the generalized Mahalanobis distance between feature vectors $\mathbf{x}_i$ and $\mathbf{x}_j$ of the i_{th} and j_{th} vertices respectively, it follows that:

$$d(\mathbf{x}_i, \mathbf{x}_j) = \sqrt{(\mathbf{x}_i - \mathbf{x}_j)^T \mathbf{M}_v (\mathbf{x}_i - \mathbf{x}_j)} \quad \forall \mathbf{x}_i, \mathbf{x}_j. \tag{6}$$

Moreover, a feature difference matrix $\mathbf{F} \in \mathbb{R}^{c \times d}$, with $c = \frac{1}{2}n(n-1)$, is defined as the matrix of all feature differences between unique pairs of vertices $(v_i, v_j) \in \mathbf{V}$, without taking into account their connectivity in $\mathbf{E}$. Based on all the above, Eq. 6 can be written, using Eq. 3 as:

$$\mathbf{d}_v = diag(((\mathbf{F}\mathbf{M}_v\mathbf{F}^T) \odot \mathbf{I}_c)^{1/2}) = ((\mathbf{F}\mathbf{M}_v \odot \mathbf{F})\mathbf{1}_d)^{1/2} \quad \in \mathbb{R}^c \tag{7}$$

The above step is necessary as it significantly reduces the required memory (see Sect. 3.4), and allows the network to be trained in a end-to-end way. During the learning process, it is attempted to learn optimized supervised distance metrics, from the given data, that minimize the GNN's graph classification loss, through backpropagation. The unique distance pairs of $\mathbf{d}_v$ are placed back in a "view distance matrix $\mathbf{H}_v \in \mathbb{R}^{n \times n}$. The per "view" similarity matrix, using the Gaussian kernel, is defined as:

$$\mathbf{S}_v = exp\left(-\mathbf{H}_v/2\sigma^2\right), \tag{8}$$

where σ is the standard deviation and the hybrid Laplacian, $\mathbf{L}_h$ with $h \in [1, .., N]$, is calculated as:

$$\mathbf{L}_h = \mathbf{L}_{in} + \alpha \mathbf{L}_v, \tag{9}$$

with $\mathbf{L}_v = \mathbf{I}_n - \mathbf{D}^{-1/2}\mathbf{S}_v\mathbf{D}^{-1/2}$ and $\mathbf{L}_{in}$ being the input graph's Laplacian. The contribution of each "view" is controlled by the scalar value α, which is set to 1, to avoid extra hyperpameter tuning. $\mathbf{L}_v$ represents a n complete graph (K_n) with $c = \frac{1}{2}n(n-1)$ weighted edges based on the feature differences and the trainable distance matrix $\mathbf{M}_v$. Thus, a dense hybrid Laplacian is produced for each "view", encoding different relation types between vertices.

For each view v, we compute L_v by taking into account the different trainable Q_v, based only on the features of the graph; thus computing different distances. However, since we want to maintain the original graph's structure, we propagate input-graphs' connectivity by adding L_{in} to L_v. Doing so, we also imitate the successful Res-Net architecture that propagates previous layer outputs to subsequent layers (the so-called "identity connection shortcut"). All the above contribute to faster convergence and encounter for the vanishing gradient problem in the early layers.

3.3   Construction of the Graph Output Signal

As it is described in [10], convolution of graph signal $\mathbf{X}$ can be defined in the spectral domain and can therefore be approximated by applying a filter g_θ in the eigenvalues of the Laplacian of a graph as:

$$\mathbf{Y} = g_\theta(\mathbf{L})\mathbf{X} = g_\theta(\mathbf{U}\Lambda\mathbf{U}^T)\mathbf{X} = \mathbf{U}g_\theta(\Lambda)\mathbf{U}^T\mathbf{X}, \tag{10}$$

where $\mathbf{U}$ represents the eigenvectors of $\mathbf{L}$ and Λ is a diagonal matrix whose elements are the corresponding eigenvalues. In order to make the spectral filter independent of the graph size and also restrict it in a local graph's region (simulating the CNNs' localization property), the filter is usually modeled as a polynomial function of powers of Λ. This expansion can be approximated by using the recurrent Chebyshev expansion to speed up the computations as:

$$g_\theta(\Lambda) = \sum_{p=0}^{K-1} \theta_p \Lambda^p = \sum_{p=0}^{K-1} \theta_p \mathbf{T}_p(\tilde{\Lambda}) \tag{11}$$

with $\mathbf{T}_p(\tilde{\Lambda}) = 2\tilde{\Lambda}\mathbf{T}_{p-1}(\tilde{\Lambda}) - \mathbf{T}_{p-2}(\tilde{\Lambda})$, $\tilde{\Lambda} = \frac{2}{\lambda_{max}}\Lambda - \mathbf{I}$ and $\theta \in \mathbb{R}^K$ is the vector of the spectral coefficients. Given a decomposition, $\mathbf{L}^p = (\mathbf{U}\Lambda\mathbf{U}^T)^p = \mathbf{U}\Lambda^p\mathbf{U}^T$, g_θ can be parametrized as a polynomial function of $\mathbf{L}$, that can be calculated from a recurrent Chebyshev expansion of order K. Using the re-scaled Laplacian $\tilde{\mathbf{L}}_h = \frac{2}{\lambda_{max}}\mathbf{L}_h - \mathbf{I}_n$ the computation of decomposition is avoided. Each Laplacian power can be interpreted as expressing the graph constructed from the p-hops thus providing the desired localization property. In our approach, such a spectral filter is created for each "view", thus, for each hybrid Laplacian. For graph signal

$\mathbf{X} \in \mathbb{R}^{n \times d}$ the projected features $\mathbf{X}_v \in \mathbb{R}^{n \times K \cdot d}$, where each $\mathbf{X}_v$ represents a different "view" signal, are calculated as:

$$\mathbf{X}_v = g_\theta(\tilde{\mathbf{L}}_h)\mathbf{X} = [\tilde{\mathbf{X}}_0, \tilde{\mathbf{X}}_1, .., \tilde{\mathbf{X}}_{K-1}]\boldsymbol{\theta}_v, \qquad (12)$$

with $\boldsymbol{\theta}_v = [\theta_0, \theta_1, .., \theta_{K-1}]$ are the learnable coefficients shared across vertices in the same "view" and $\tilde{\mathbf{X}}_p = \mathbf{T}_p(\tilde{\mathbf{L}}_h)\mathbf{X} = 2\tilde{\mathbf{L}}_h\tilde{\mathbf{X}}_{p-1} - \tilde{\mathbf{X}}_{p-2}$. The first two recurrent terms of the polynominal expansion are calculated as: $\tilde{\mathbf{X}}_0 = \mathbf{X}$ and $\tilde{\mathbf{X}}_1 = \tilde{\mathbf{L}}_h\mathbf{X}$. Thus, the graph signal $\mathbf{X}$ is projected onto the Chebyshev basis $\mathbf{T}_p(\tilde{\mathbf{L}}_h)$ and concatenated for all orders $p \in [0, K-1]$, similar to [22].

As a result, multiple complex relationships between neighboring vertices from different "views" are gradually captured. The receptive field is controlled by K and the trainable parameters $\boldsymbol{\theta}_v$ adjust the contribution of each Chebyshev basis. The majority of spectral convolution methods are based on projected graph features into a single graph structure, including but not limited to Chebyshev approximation. The usage of several trainable hybrid Laplacians, enables spectral filters to capture information in different projected domains.

For an input graph G, N graph signals $\mathbf{Z}_s = [\mathbf{X}_1, \mathbf{X}_2, .., \mathbf{X}_N]$ are stacked, as well as N hybrid Laplacians $\mathbf{L}_s = [\mathbf{L}_1, \mathbf{L}_2, .., \mathbf{L}_N]$. Then, batch normalization is applied to $\mathbf{Z}_s$, followed by a view-wise max aggregation step (VPOOL). This way, the VPOOL layer becomes invariant to random initialization of $\mathbf{Q}_v$ thanks to the batch normalization and also fuses information captured from different "views" due to the aggregation step. The aggregated view-pooled signal has a shared feature matrix, which is then passed to a linear layer followed by a non-linear activation function σ and a Dropout layer (DROP) [40]. It has to be noted that applying batch normalization to $\mathbf{Z}_s$ the graph signals from the different views have zero-mean and an activation function in the aggregated output can be meaningfully applied. Less literally, all the above procedure can be summarized in the following equation:

$$\mathbf{Y} = DROP(\sigma(VPOOL(\mathbf{Z}_s)\mathbf{W} + \mathbf{b})), \qquad (13)$$

where $\mathbf{Y} \in \mathbb{R}^{n \times m}$ is the graph output signal, with m being the number of the output features. The linear layer parameters are $\mathbf{W} \in \mathbb{R}^{K \cdot d \times m}$, $\mathbf{b} \in \mathbb{R}^m$. Based on the above, the proposed method can handle a varying number of input vertices, given that the features space is of constant dimension between different graphs (i.e., d is constant between different graphs of the same dataset). In other words, in Eq. 13 the model parameters are only dependent to the Chebyshev degree K and the feature vector; thus independent of the vertices of the graph. In addition, the linear layer learns to process aggregated compact signals from multiple views which results in better generalization properties. Furthermore, based on the indices of VPOOL, the corresponding most frequent hybrid Laplacian is passed to the next layer, which we call "dominant" hybrid Laplacian, defined as $\mathbf{L}_\delta$. Max and mean view pooling have also been tested on $\mathbf{L}_s$, giving slightly inferior results.

Finally, the overall multi-view GNN architecture consists of three MV-GC layers, each one followed by a VPOOL and a linear layer as depicted in Eq. 13.

In the first MV-GC layer the input Laplacian is calculated from the adjacency matrix as in Eq. 1, which we call intrinsic Laplacian. In the rest layers, the "dominant" Laplacian $\mathbf{L}_\delta$ of the previous VPOOL layer is the input Laplacian of the next. The choice of m provides the flexibility to adjust the number of trainable parameters and model complexity. For $m > K \cdot d$ the linear layer behaves as an encoding layer (usually the first layer of our architecture), while for $m < K \cdot d$ acts as a decoding layer. In the last layer, mean and max operators are applied in the graph output signal across the vertex dimension, similar to [6] and [48], which are further concatenated. This step further aggregates the learned features, while concurrently reduces complexity. The concatenated output features are then fed to a 2 fully connected layers. For the prediction, a softmax function is used to produce the final output $\bar{\mathbf{y}}_{pred}$. The whole network architecture is trained end-to-end. As loss function the cross entropy is used with q classes, given that $\mathbf{y}_T$ is the target one-hot vector, defined as:

$$l_s = -\sum_1^q \mathbf{y}_T \log(\bar{\mathbf{y}}_{pred}). \tag{14}$$

3.4 Computational Complexity Analysis

The proposed method produces dense graph representations. The proposed MV-GC layer requires the calculation of all the differences between vertex features, which is of $O(n^2)$. As shown in Eq. 7, exploiting distance matrix symmetry, we only used the feature differences between unique pairs of vertices. As a consequence, the time complexity of dense non-square matrix multiplications was reduced from $O(n^2 d^2)$ to $0.5O(n^2 d^2)$ and Hadamard element-wise multiplication from $O(n^2 d)$ to $0.5O(n^2 d)$ per view. Although time complexity remains quadratic, we were able to scale it down by a factor of 4. With the current implementation, the time complexity of the MV-GC layer is linearly dependent to the number of views. Nonetheless, the required operations for each view are completely independent and can be implemented in a parallel way. In addition, space complexity required for Eq. 7 is reduced from $O(n^4)$ to $0.5O(n^2 d)$ per view, using Eq. 3. As mentioned in [29], the required learning space complexity is $O(d^2)$ per view and $O(K \cdot d \cdot m)$ per linear layer, which are independent of the number of vertices. Still, it remains a challenging task to scale our layers for big graph data analysis and further performance optimization is left for future work.

4   Experimental Evaluation

4.1   Dataset Description and Modifications

The proposed model (MV-AGC) is evaluated on four biological datasets and four social network datasets, available at [20]. Each dataset has an arbitrary undirected set of graphs with number of n vertices and binary edges, as well as

Table 1. Graph classification datasets

Datasets	Graphs	Classes	Mean number of vertices	Mean number of edges	Vertex labels	Vertex attributes dim
MUTAG	188	2	17.93	19.79	Yes	–
PTC-MR	344	2	14.29	14.69	Yes	–
SYNTHIE	400	4	95.00	172.93	No	15
ENZYMES	600	6	32.63	62.14	Yes	18
PROTEINS	1113	2	39.06	72.82	Yes	29
IMDB-B	1000	2	19.77	96.53	No	–
IMDB-M	1500	3	13.00	65.94	No	–

a categorical graph label T. A summary description can be found on Table 1. In MUTAG [9], edges correspond to atom bonds and vertices to atom properties. PTC-MR [43] is a dataset of 344 molecules graphs, where classes indicate carcinogenicity in rats. In ENZYMES [37], each enzyme is a member of one of the Enzyme Commission top level enzyme classes. PROTEINS [2] consists of 1113 graphs modeled with vertices being their secondary structure elements and edges between two vertices exists if they are neighbors in the $3D$ space. COLLAB [51] is a scientific collaboration dataset with $5K$ graphs of different researchers from three fields of Physics. IMDB-B and IMDB-M [50] consist of ego-networks of actors that have appeared together in a movie and the goal is to find the movies genre. SYNTHIE [31] is a synthetic dataset which consists of 400 graphs with four classes and each vertex has 15 continuous-valued attributes. All datasets are publicly available[1] [20].

Some biological datasets had both discrete vertex labels and continuous-valued vertex attributes. For a fair comparison between other approaches we used the discrete vertex labels in Table 2. However, classification accuracy can be further improved using the continuous-valued attributes, as shown in Table 4. The proposed model is also tested in the aforementioned social network datasets, where vertex information is not provided, using the one hot encoding of the degree of each vertex as feature vector up to a certain degree, in our case from 30 to 50, as in [52]. Using the one hot encoding of the discrete vertex labels usually falls into the case of all the vertices in the graph to have the same label, which renders the computation of $\mathbf{L}_v$ to be infeasible. We included the mentioned data to train the model apart from the "view" transformation matrices $\mathbf{M}_v$. An experimental evaluation was conducted, following the conventional approach of 10 fold cross-validation, similar to [22,50,52] and mean classification accuracy

---

[1] https://ls11-www.cs.tu-dortmund.de/staff/morris/graphkerneldatasets.

Table 2. Mean accuracies with standard deviations using discrete vertex labels - biological datasets. The reported methods are sorted in chronological order.

Method	Datasets			
	MUTAG	PTC-MR	ENZYMES	PROTEINS
WL [38]	86.0 ± 1.7	61.3 ± 1.4	59.05 ± 1.05	75.6 ± 0.4
WL-OA [23]	84.5 ± 1.7	63.6 ± 1.5	59.9 ± 1.1	76.4 ± 0.4
DGK [50]	87.44 ± 2.72	60.08 ± 2.55	53.43 ± 0.91	75.68 ± 0.54
PSCN [34]	92.63 ± 4.21	62.29 ± 5.68	–	75.89 ± 2.76
KGCNN [35]	–	62.94 ± 1.69	46.35 ± 0.23	75.76 ± 0.28
DGCNN [53]	85.83 ± 1.66	58.59 ± 2.47	–	76.26 ± 0.24
DIFFPOOL [52]	–	–	62.53	76.25
GIN [47]	90.0 ± 8.8	66.6 ± 6.9	–	76.2 ± 2.6
GCAPS-CNN[45]	–	66.01 ± 5.91	61.83 ± 5.39	76.40 ± 4.17
MGCN [22]	89.1 ± 1.4	–	61.7 ± 1.3	76.5 ± 0.4
Graph U-Nets [14]	–	–	–	77.68
SAGPool [27]	–	–	–	71.86 ± 0.97
CLIQUEPOOL [30]	–	–	60.71	72.59
WKPI [55]	88.3 ± 2.6	–	–	78.5 ± 0.4
MV-AGC (Ours)	$\mathbf{92.98 \pm 5.12}$	$\mathbf{74.45 \pm 3.42}$	$\mathbf{64.57 \pm 5.27}$	$\mathbf{78.81 \pm 3.31}$

across folds with standard deviation are reported in Tables 2, 3, 4 and 5. The continuous-valued attributes were preprocessed with mean/std normalization before plugged in the network. The datasets are presented in ascending order with respect to their containing number of graphs.

4.2 Implementation Details

The described multi-view GNN architecture is implemented in the PyTorch [36] framework. Training is achieved using the stochastic gradient descent optimizer [3] with a constant learning rate ranging from $4 \cdot e^{-4}$ to $8 \cdot e^{-3}$ and single batch size. As non-linear activation function ReLU is used. Dropout was used to avoid overfitting, mostly on the small data sets, similar to [34]. Chebyshev degree K was set to 6 for all conducted experiments. The hidden fully connected layer has 128 units. $\mathbf{Q}_v$ is initialized with a random uniform distribution in range $(0, 1)$. $\mathbf{M}_v$ is regularized in each iteration divided with it's maximum element, although preserving it's desired properties. The number of views per MV-GC layer is set to 8 for the first layer and 6 for the others. The epochs per dataset vary from 30, in COLLAB, to 80, in the ENZYMES dataset. The number of output features m of each linear layer was set to 80, 128 and 256 for the bioinformatics datasets. For the COLLAB dataset, a smaller number of views per MV-GC layer was used, due to high computational demands. For all datasets the experiments were

Table 3. Mean accuracies with standard deviations using vertex degrees - social network datasets

Method	Datasets		
	IMDB-B	IMDB-M	COLLAB
DGK [50]	66.96 ± 0.56	44.55 ± 0.52	73.09 ± 0.25
KGCNN [35]	71.45 ± 0.15	47.46 ± 0.21	74.93 ± 0.14
DGCNN [53]	70.03 ± 0.86	47.83 ± 0.85	73.76 ± 0.5
PSCN [34]	71.00 ± 2.29	45.23 ± 2.84	72.60 ± 2.15
DIFFPOOL [52]	–	–	82.13
GIN [47]	75.1 ± 5.1	52.3 ± 2.8	80.6 ± 1.9
Graph U-Nets [14]	–	–	77.56
CLIQUEPOOL [30]	–	–	74.50
GCAPS-CNN[45]	71.69 ± 3.40	48.50 ± 4.10	77.71 ± 2.51
CAPS-GNN [46]	73.10 ± 4.83	50.27 ± 2.65	79.62 ± 0.91
HO-GNN [32]	74.2	49.5	–
WKPI [55]	75.1 ± 1.1	49.05 ± 0.4	–
MV-AGC (Ours)	$\mathbf{78.20 \pm 3.05}$	$\mathbf{53.47 \pm 3.62}$	$\mathbf{82.41 \pm 1.09}$

Table 4. Mean accuracies with standard deviations using only the continuous-valued vertex attributes

Method	Datasets		
	SYNTHIE	ENZYMES	PROTEINS
HGK [31]	86.27 ± 0.72	66.73 ± 0.91	75.14 ± 0.47
GraphHopper [11]	–	69.60 ± 1.30	–
SP [1]	–	71.30 ± 1.30	75.50 ± 0.80
FGW [44]	–	71.00 ± 6.76	74.55 ± 2.74
PROPAK [33]	–	71.67 ± 5.63	61.34 ± 4.38
MV-AGC (Ours)	$\mathbf{90.02 \pm 3.87}$	$\mathbf{72.62 \pm 2.63}$	$\mathbf{77.66 \pm 2.51}$

conducted in a NVIDIA GeForce GTX-1080 GPU with 12 GB of memory and 16 GB of RAM.

An incremental training strategy was adopted to choose the model hyperparameters e.g. number of views. First, we used a single MV-GC layer and we observed that multiple views helped significantly in graph classification. As a sanity check, we inspected the gradients of Q_v that roughly started from a mean value of 10^{-3} and reached a mean value of 10^{-8} at the end of the training. Then, due to complexity we could not fit more than three layers, which provided the best results. We made hyperparameter tuning and trained the network on two datasets and used the same model and hyperparameters in the other datasets.

Table 5. Model (MV-AGC) comparison with varying number of views per layer

# Views	Datasets		
	MUTAG	ENZYMES	PROTEINS
2	87.71 ± 6.3	56.02 ± 6.3	75.36 ± 3.9
3	88.88 ± 5.4	57.61 ± 3.7	$\mathbf{78.08 \pm 3.4}$
6	90.43 ± 5.1	$\mathbf{62.27 \pm 4.3}$	77.83 ± 3.7
9	$\mathbf{90.52 \pm 5.4}$	61.10 ± 4.6	77.81 ± 3.4

4.3   Experimental Results

We evaluate our model compared to other graph deep learning approaches, as well as classical graph kernel methods. As presented in Table 2, superior results in 4 biological datasets are reported, using vertex labels as one hot encodings. A significant gain of 7.85 was reached in PTC-MR dataset, which is justified in the fact that the provided vertex labels of the dataset are of critical importance for classification. In social network datasets, as shown in Table 3, using vertices degrees as input features, we report state-of-the-art results in 3 social network datasets. Our method surpasses all previous approaches in the datasets that contain continuous-valued feature attributes as depicted in Table 4. As show in Table 5, where we vary the number of "views" per MV-GC layer without any hyperparameter tuning, there is a significant increase in generalization as the number of views per layer increases up to a certain value. Having only one trainable transformation matrix per layer would reduce the model close to [29], which is usually unstable to train and does not produce generalized representations. There is also a trade-off in the choice of views between training time and accuracy. Nevertheless, Table 5 clearly proves that the idea of multi-view metric learning for graph classification is non-trivial.

4.4   Discussion

Some limitations that have to be taken account that influence the model's standard deviation and accuracy, based on our experimental study, are the following: a) the number of samples per dataset, b) the variability in the number of vertices, c) how informative is the graph signal for the prediction, and d) the choice of α in Eq. 9. It is observed that it is more difficult to estimate optimal global affine transformations as the number of samples increase and as the graphs have a wider range of vertices. On the other hand, in PTC-MR we observed a huge gain, because the graph signal is a significant feature for classification and the vertex variability is low. The choice of α to be equal to 1 introduces some extra standard deviation, but it still yields better accuracy for the majority of datasets. The reason behind this choice is to not scale down the gradient values on the affine transformation matrices. Moreover, large-scale graphs (with more than 3000 vertices) cannot be process in the referenced hardware. In a future work, we aim to encounter this limitation.

We claim that MV-AGC best fits continuous-valued datasets, due to the multi-view representation of the feature space. This is demonstrated in Table 4 by the higher gains in the continuous-valued datasets. As a future work, the convergence of the network with respect to the views will be further investigated.

5 Conclusions

In the present work, a graph analog of multi-view operations in CNNs was developed. We propose a novel multi-view GNN architecture able to exploit vertices information in an adaptive manner. The proposed MV-GC layer generates "views" representing multiple graph structures, based on a trainable non-Euclidean distance metric learning process. We explore pairwise feature relationships inside a graph via the newly introduced hybrid Laplacian. Spectral filtering is applied to the input graph signal with a different hybrid Laplacian per "view", producing multiple projected signals and, thus, encapsulating different relations between the data. A new view pooling layer is also introduced, able to fuse information from different views. The proposed multi-view graph distance metric learning methodology can also be applied in other graph convolutional schemes, which is out of the scope of this paper and left as a future research direction. Our model (MV-AGC) provides state-of-the-art results in 4 bioinformatics datasets with discrete vertices labels, as well as in 3 social network datasets. Finally, the proposed method outperforms previous approaches in all datasets with continuous-valued vertex attributes.

Acknowledgement. The work presented in this paper was supported by the European Commission under contract H2020-822601 NADINE.

References

1. Borgwardt, K.M., Kriegel, H.P.: Shortest-path kernels on graphs. In: Fifth IEEE International Conference on Data Mining (ICDM 2005), p. 8. IEEE (2005)
2. Borgwardt, K.M., Ong, C.S., Schönauer, S., Vishwanathan, S., Smola, A.J., Kriegel, H.P.: Protein function prediction via graph kernels. Bioinformatics **21**(Suppl. 1), i47–i56 (2005)
3. Bottou, L.: Large-scale machine learning with stochastic gradient descent. In: Lechevallier, Y., Saporta, G. (eds.) COMPSTAT, pp. 177–186. Springer, Heidelberg (2010). https://doi.org/10.1007/978-3-7908-2604-3_16
4. Bronstein, M.M., Bruna, J., LeCun, Y., Szlam, A., Vandergheynst, P.: Geometric deep learning: going beyond Euclidean data. IEEE Signal Process. Mag. **34**(4), 18–42 (2017)
5. Bruna, J., Zaremba, W., Szlam, A., LeCun, Y.: Spectral networks and locally connected networks on graphs. arXiv preprint arXiv:1312.6203 (2013)
6. Cangea, C., Veličković, P., Jovanović, N., Kipf, T., Liò, P.: Towards sparse hierarchical graph classifiers. arXiv preprint arXiv:1811.01287 (2018)
7. Chung, F.R., Graham, F.C.: Spectral graph theory. No. 92, American Mathematical Society (1997)

8. De Maesschalck, R., Jouan-Rimbaud, D., Massart, D.L.: The mahalanobis distance. Chemometr. Intell. Lab. Syst. **50**(1), 1–18 (2000)
9. Debnath, A.K., Lopez de Compadre, R.L., Debnath, G., Shusterman, A.J., Hansch, C.: Structure-activity relationship of mutagenic aromatic and heteroaromatic nitro compounds. correlation with molecular orbital energies and hydrophobicity. J. Med. Chem. **34**(2), 786–797 (1991)
10. Defferrard, M., Bresson, X., Vandergheynst, P.: Convolutional neural networks on graphs with fast localized spectral filtering. In: Advances in Neural Information Processing Systems, pp. 3844–3852 (2016)
11. Feragen, A., Kasenburg, N., Petersen, J., de Bruijne, M., Borgwardt, K.: Scalable kernels for graphs with continuous attributes. In: Advances in Neural Information Processing Systems, pp. 216–224 (2013)
12. Fey, M., Eric Lenssen, J., Weichert, F., Müller, H.: Splinecnn: fast geometric deep learning with continuous b-spline kernels. In: Proceedings of the IEEE Conference on Computer Vision and Pattern Recognition, pp. 869–877 (2018)
13. Fukushima, K.: Neocognitron: a self-organizing neural network model for a mechanism of pattern recognition unaffected by shift in position. Biol. Cybern. **36**(4), 193–202 (1980)
14. Gao, H., Ji, S.: Graph u-net (2019). https://openreview.net/forum?id=HJe-PRoAct7
15. Gomez, L.G., Chiem, B., Delvenne, J.C.: Dynamics based features for graph classification. arXiv preprint arXiv:1705.10817 (2017)
16. Henaff, M., Bruna, J., LeCun, Y.: Deep convolutional networks on graph-structured data. arXiv preprint arXiv:1506.05163 (2015)
17. Hoi, S.C., Liu, W., Chang, S.F.: Semi-supervised distance metric learning for collaborative image retrieval and clustering. ACM Trans. Multimedia Comput. Communi. Appli. (TOMM) **6**(3), 18 (2010)
18. Horadam, K.J.: Hadamard Matrices and Their Applications. Princeton University Press, Princeton (2012)
19. Ioffe, S., Szegedy, C.: Batch normalization: accelerating deep network training by reducing internal covariate shift. arXiv preprint arXiv:1502.03167 (2015)
20. Kersting, K., Kriege, N.M., Morris, C., Mutzel, P., Neumann, M.: Benchmark data sets for graph kernels (2016). http://graphkernels.cs.tu-dortmund.de
21. Kipf, T.N., Welling, M.: Semi-supervised classification with graph convolutional networks. arXiv preprint arXiv:1609.02907 (2016)
22. Knyazev, B., Lin, X., Amer, M.R., Taylor, G.W.: Spectral multigraph networks for discovering and fusing relationships in molecules. arXiv preprint arXiv:1811.09595 (2018)
23. Kriege, N.M., Giscard, P.L., Wilson, R.: On valid optimal assignment kernels and applications to graph classification. In: Advances in Neural Information Processing Systems, pp. 1623–1631 (2016)
24. Krizhevsky, A., Sutskever, I., Hinton, G.E.: Imagenet classification with deep convolutional neural networks. In: Advances in Neural Information Processing Systems, pp. 1097–1105 (2012)
25. Ktena, S.I., et al.: distance metric learning using graph convolutional networks: application to functional brain networks. In: Descoteaux, M., Maier-Hein, L., Franz, A., Jannin, P., Collins, D.L., Duchesne, S. (eds.) MICCAI 2017. LNCS, vol. 10433, pp. 469–477. Springer, Cham (2017). https://doi.org/10.1007/978-3-319-66182-7_54

26. LeCun, Y., Haffner, P., Bottou, L., Bengio, Y.: Object recognition with gradient-based learning. Shape, Contour and Grouping in Computer Vision. LNCS, vol. 1681, pp. 319–345. Springer, Heidelberg (1999). https://doi.org/10.1007/3-540-46805-6_19
27. Lee, J., Lee, I., Kang, J.: Self-attention graph pooling. arXiv preprint arXiv:1904.08082 (2019)
28. Li, Q., Han, Z., Wu, X.M.: Deeper insights into graph convolutional networks for semi-supervised learning. In: Thirty-Second AAAI Conference on Artificial Intelligence (2018)
29. Li, R., Wang, S., Zhu, F., Huang, J.: Adaptive graph convolutional neural networks. In: Thirty-Second AAAI Conference on Artificial Intelligence (2018)
30. Luzhnica, E., Day, B., Lio, P.: Clique pooling for graph classification. arXiv preprint arXiv:1904.00374 (2019)
31. Morris, C., Kriege, N.M., Kersting, K., Mutzel, P.: Faster kernels for graphs with continuous attributes via hashing. In: 2016 IEEE 16th International Conference on Data Mining (ICDM), pp. 1095–1100. IEEE (2016)
32. Morris, C., et al.: Weisfeiler and leman go neural: higher-order graph neural networks. In: Proceedings of the AAAI Conference on Artificial Intelligence, vol. 33, pp. 4602–4609 (2019)
33. Neumann, M., Garnett, R., Bauckhage, C., Kersting, K.: Propagation kernels: efficient graph kernels from propagated information. Mach. Learn. **102**(2), 209–245 (2016)
34. Niepert, M., Ahmed, M., Kutzkov, K.: Learning convolutional neural networks for graphs. In: International Conference on Machine Learning, pp. 2014–2023 (2016)
35. Nikolentzos, G., Meladianos, P., Jean-Pierre Tixier, A., Skianis, K., Vazirgiannis, M.: Kernel Graph Convolutional Neural Networks. arXiv e-prints arXiv:1710.10689 (2017)
36. Paszke, A., et al.: Automatic differentiation in pytorch (2017)
37. Schomburg, I., et al.: Brenda, the enzyme database: updates and major new developments. Nucleic Acids Res. **32**(Suppl. 1), D431–D433 (2004)
38. Shervashidze, N., Schweitzer, P., Leeuwen, E.J.V., Mehlhorn, K., Borgwardt, K.M.: Weisfeiler-Lehman graph kernels. J. Mach. Learn. Res. **12**(Sep), 2539–2561 (2011)
39. Shuman, D.I., Narang, S.K., Frossard, P., Ortega, A., Vandergheynst, P.: The emerging field of signal processing on graphs: Extending high-dimensional data analysis to networks and other irregular domains. arXiv preprint arXiv:1211.0053 (2012)
40. Srivastava, N., Hinton, G., Krizhevsky, A., Sutskever, I., Salakhutdinov, R.: Dropout: a simple way to prevent neural networks from overfitting. J. Mach. Learn. Res. **15**(1), 1929–1958 (2014)
41. Su, H., Maji, S., Kalogerakis, E., Learned-Miller, E.G.: Multi-view convolutional neural networks for 3D shape recognition. In: Proceedings of ICCV (2015)
42. Takerkart, S., Auzias, G., Thirion, B., Schön, D., Ralaivola, L.: Graph-based inter-subject classification of local fMRI patterns. In: Wang, F., Shen, D., Yan, P., Suzuki, K. (eds.) MLMI 2012. LNCS, vol. 7588, pp. 184–192. Springer, Heidelberg (2012). https://doi.org/10.1007/978-3-642-35428-1_23
43. Toivonen, H., Srinivasan, A., King, R.D., Kramer, S., Helma, C.: Statistical evaluation of the predictive toxicology challenge 2000–2001. Bioinformatics **19**(10), 1183–1193 (2003)
44. Vayer, T., Chapel, L., Flamary, R., Tavenard, R., Courty, N.: Optimal transport for structured data with application on graphs. arXiv preprint arXiv:1805.09114 (2018)

45. Verma, S., Zhang, Z.L.: Graph capsule convolutional neural networks. arXiv preprint arXiv:1805.08090 (2018)
46. Xinyi, Z., Chen, L.: Capsule graph neural network. In: International Conference on Learning Representations (2019). https://openreview.net/forum?id=Byl8BnRcYm
47. Xu, K., Hu, W., Leskovec, J., Jegelka, S.: How powerful are graph neural networks? arXiv preprint arXiv:1810.00826 (2018)
48. Xu, K., Li, C., Tian, Y., Sonobe, T., Kawarabayashi, K.i., Jegelka, S.: Representation learning on graphs with jumping knowledge networks. arXiv preprint arXiv:1806.03536 (2018)
49. Yan, S., Xiong, Y., Lin, D.: Spatial temporal graph convolutional networks for skeleton-based action recognition. In: Thirty-Second AAAI Conference on Artificial Intelligence (2018)
50. Yanardag, P., Vishwanathan, S.: Deep graph kernels. In: Proceedings of the 21th ACM SIGKDD International Conference on Knowledge Discovery and Data Mining, pp. 1365–1374. ACM (2015)
51. Yanardag, P., Vishwanathan, S.: A structural smoothing framework for robust graph comparison. In: Advances in Neural Information Processing Systems, pp. 2134–2142 (2015)
52. Ying, Z., You, J., Morris, C., Ren, X., Hamilton, W., Leskovec, J.: Hierarchical graph representation learning with differentiable pooling. In: Advances in Neural Information Processing Systems, pp. 4805–4815 (2018)
53. Zhang, M., Cui, Z., Neumann, M., Chen, Y.: An end-to-end deep learning architecture for graph classification. In: Thirty-Second AAAI Conference on Artificial Intelligence (2018)
54. Zhang, X., He, L., Chen, K., Luo, Y., Zhou, J., Wang, F.: Multi-view graph convolutional network and its applications on neuroimage analysis for Parkinson's disease. In: AMIA Annual Symposium Proceedings, vol. 2018, p. 1147. American Medical Informatics Association (2018)
55. Zhao, Q., Wang, Y.: Learning metrics for persistence-based summaries and applications for graph classification. In: Advances in Neural Information Processing Systems, pp. 9855–9866 (2019)
56. Zhou, J., Cui, G., Zhang, Z., Yang, C., Liu, Z., Sun, M.: Graph neural networks: a review of methods and applications. arXiv preprint arXiv:1812.08434 (2018)

Instance Adaptive Self-training
for Unsupervised Domain Adaptation

Ke Mei[1], Chuang Zhu[1(✉)], Jiaqi Zou[1], and Shanghang Zhang[2]

[1] School of Information and Communication Engineering,
Beijing University of Posts and Telecommunications, Beijing, China
{raykoo,czhu,jqzou}@bupt.edu.cn
[2] EECS, University of California, Berkeley, Berkeley, CA 94720, USA
shz@eecs.berkeley.edu

Abstract. The divergence between labeled training data and unlabeled testing data is a significant challenge for recent deep learning models. Unsupervised domain adaptation (UDA) attempts to solve such a problem. Recent works show that self-training is a powerful approach to UDA. However, existing methods have difficulty in balancing scalability and performance. In this paper, we propose an instance adaptive self-training framework for UDA on the task of semantic segmentation. To effectively improve the quality of pseudo-labels, we develop a novel pseudo-label generation strategy with an instance adaptive selector. Besides, we propose the region-guided regularization to smooth the pseudo-label region and sharpen the non-pseudo-label region. Our method is so concise and efficient that it is easy to be generalized to other unsupervised domain adaptation methods. Experiments on 'GTA5 to Cityscapes' and 'SYNTHIA to Cityscapes' demonstrate the superior performance of our approach compared with the state-of-the-art methods.

Keywords: Domain adaptation · Semantic segmentation ·
Self-training · Regularization

1 Introduction

Domain shifts refer to the divergence between the training data (source domain) and the testing data (target domain), induced by factors such as the variance in illumination, object viewpoints, and image background [4,27]. Such domain shifts often lead to the phenomenon that the trained model suffers from a significant performance drop in the unlabeled target domain. The unsupervised domain adaptation (UDA) methods aim to improve the model generalization performance by transferring knowledge from labeled source domain to unlabeled target domain.

Recently, the adversarial training (AT) methods have received significant attention for semantic segmentation [6,9,10,21,27,29]. These methods aim to

Electronic supplementary material The online version of this chapter (https://doi.org/10.1007/978-3-030-58574-7_25) contains supplementary material, which is available to authorized users.

© Springer Nature Switzerland AG 2020
A. Vedaldi et al. (Eds.): ECCV 2020, LNCS 12371, pp. 415–430, 2020.
https://doi.org/10.1007/978-3-030-58574-7_25

minimize a series of adversarial losses to align source and target feature distributions. More recently, an alternative research line to reduce domain shift focuses on building schemes based on the self-training (ST) framework [2,20,31,34–36]. These works iteratively train the model by using both the labeled source domain data and the generated pseudo-labels for the target domain and thus achieve the alignment between source and target domains. Besides, several works [19,28,34] have explored to combine AT and ST methods, which shows great potential on semantic segmentation UDA. Through carefully designed network structure, these methods achieve state-of-the-art performance on the benchmark.

Table 1. Performance comparison of AT and ST. *AT*: adversarial training based methods; *ST*: self-training based methods; *AT + ST*: the mixed methods

Method	BLF [19]	AdaptMR [34]	AdaptSeg [27]	AdvEnt [29]	PyCDA [20]	CRST [35]	Ours	Mean
AT	44.3	42.7	42.4	45.5	–	–	43.8	43.7
ST	–	–	–	–	47.4	47.1	48.8	47.8
AT+ST	48.5	48.3	–	–	–	–	**50.2**	**49.0**

Despite the success of these AT and ST methods, a natural question comes up: what is the most effective one among these methods? AT or ST? Table 1 lists some of the above representative methods performance on the GTA5 to Cityscapes benchmark. All these methods use the same segmentation network for a fair comparison. In terms of performance, an explicit conclusion is: AT + ST (49.0) [19,34] > ST (47.8) [20,35] > AT (43.7) [27,29]. The mixed methods, such as BLF [19] and AdaptMR [34], both have achieved great performance gains (+ 4.2, + 5.6) after using ST. However, in order to achieve better performance, these mixed methods generally have serious coupling between sub-modules (such as network structure dependency), thus losing scalability and flexibility.

This paper aims to propose a self-training framework for semantic segmentation UDA, which has good scalability that can be easily applied to other non-self-training methods and achieves state-of-the-art performance. To achieve this, we locate the main obstacle of existing self-training methods is how to generate high-quality pseudo-labels. This paper designs a new pseudo-label generation strategy and model regularization to solve this obstacle.

Fig. 1. Pseudo-label results. Columns correspond to original images with ground truth labels, class-balanced method, and our method

The pseudo-label generation suffers from information redundancy and noise. The generator tends to keep pixels with high confidence as pseudo-labels and ignore pixels with low confidence. Because of this conservative threshold selection, they are inefficient when more similar samples with high confidence are applied to training. The existing class-balanced self-training (CBST) [36] utilized rank-based reference confidence for each class among all related images. This results in the ignorance of key information from the hard images with most of the pixels having low prediction scores. For example, in Fig. 1, the pseudo-labels generated by CBST are concentrated on the road, while pedestrians and trucks are ignored, which loses much learnable information. Therefore, we try to design a pseudo-label generation that can be adjusted adaptively according to the instance strategy to reduce data redundancy and increase the diversity of pseudo-labels.

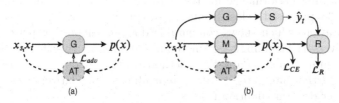

Fig. 2. IAST framework. (a) Warm-up phase, an initial model G is trained using any existing non-self-training method (e.g. AT). (b) Self-training phase, the selector S filters the pseudo-labels generated by G, and R is the regularization

In this work, we propose an instance adaptive self-training framework (IAST) for semantic segmentation UDA, as shown in Fig. 2. We employ an instance adaptive selector in considering pseudo-label diversity during the training process. Besides, we design region-guided regularization in our framework, which has different roles in the pseudo-label region and the non-pseudo-label region. The main contributions of our work are summarized as follows:

- We propose a new self-training framework. Our methods significantly outperform the current state-of-the-art methods on the public semantic segmentation UDA benchmark.
- We design an instance adaptive selector to involve more useful information for training. It effectively improves the quality of pseudo-labels. Besides, region-based regularization is designed to smooth the prediction of the pseudo-label region and sharpen the prediction of the non-pseudo-label region.
- We propose a general approach that makes it easy to apply other non-self-training methods to our framework. Moreover, our framework can also be extended to semi-supervised semantic segmentation tasks.

2   Related Works

Adversarial Training for UDA: A large number of UDA schemes [1,13,16,17] are proposed to reduce the domain gap by building shared embedding space to both the source and target domain. Following the same idea, many adversarial training based UDA methods are proposed by adding a domain discriminator in recent years [6,10,21,27,29,32,33]. With adversarial training, the domain adversarial loss can be minimized to directly align features between two domains. Motivated by the recent image-to-image translation works, some works [9,19] regard the mapping from the source domain to the target domain as the image synthesis problem that reduce the domain discrepancy before training.

Self-training: Self-training schemes are commonly used in semi-supervised learning (SSL) areas [18]. These works iteratively train the model by using both the labeled source domain data and the generated pseudo-labels in the target domain and thus achieve the alignment between the source and target domain [26]. However, these methods directly choose pseudo-labels with high prediction confidence, which will result in the model bias towards easy classes and thus ruin the transforming performance for the hard classes. To solve this problem, the authors in [36] proposed a class-balanced self-training (CBST) scheme for semantic segmentation, which shows comparable domain adaptation performance to the best adversarial training based methods. [20] proposed a self-motivated pyramid curriculum domain adaptation method using self-training. More recently, CRST [35] further integrated a variety of confidence regularizers to CBST, producing better domain adaption results.

Regularization: Regularization refers to schemes that are intended to reduce the testing error and thus make the trained model generalize well to unseen data [7,15]. For deep neural network learning, different kinds of regularization schemes such as weight decay [14] and label smoothing [25] are proposed. The recent work [35] designed labels and model regularization under self-training architecture for UDA. However, the proposed regularization scheme is just applied to the pseudo-label region.

3   Preliminary

3.1   UDA for Semantic Segmentation

It is assumed that there are two domains: source domain S and target domain T. The source domain includes image $\mathbb{X}_S = \{x_s\}$, semantic mask $\mathbb{Y}_S = \{y_s\}$, and the target domain only has image $\mathbb{X}_T = \{x_t\}$. In UDA, the semantic segmentation model is trained only from the ground truth $\mathbb{Y}_S$ as the supervisory signal. UDA semantic segmentation model can be defined as follows:

$$\{\mathbb{X}_S, \mathbb{Y}_S, \mathbb{X}_T\} \Rightarrow \mathbf{M}_{UDA}$$

$\mathbf{M}_{UDA}$ uses some special losses and domain adaptation methods to align the distribution of two domains to learn domain-invariant feature representation.

3.2   Self-training for UDA

Because the ground truth labels of target domain are not available, we can treat the target domain as an extra unlabeled dataset. In this case, the UDA task can be transformed into a semi-supervised learning (SSL) task. Self-training is an effective method for SSL. The problem can be described as the following forms:

$$
\min_{\mathbf{w}} \mathcal{L}_{CE} = - \frac{1}{|\mathbb{X}_S|} \sum_{\mathbf{x}_s \in \mathbb{X}_S} \sum_{c=1}^{C} y_s^{(c)} \log p(c|\mathbf{x}_s, \mathbf{w})
$$
$$
- \frac{1}{|\mathbb{X}_T|} \sum_{\mathbf{x}_t \in \mathbb{X}_T} \sum_{c=1}^{C} \hat{y}_t^{(c)} \log p(c|\mathbf{x}_t, \mathbf{w}) \tag{1}
$$

where C is the number of classes, $y_s^{(c)}$ indicates the label of class c in source domain, and $\hat{y}_t^{(c)}$ indicates the pseudo-label of class c in target domain. $\mathbf{x}_s$ and $\mathbf{x}_t$ are input images, $\mathbf{w}$ indicates weights of $\mathbf{M}$, $p(c|\mathbf{x}, \mathbf{w})$ is the probability of class c in softmax output, and $|\mathbb{X}|$ indicates the number of images.

In particular, $\hat{\mathbb{Y}}_T = \{\hat{y}_t\}$ are the "pseudo-labels" generated according to the existing model, which is limited to a one-hot vector (only single 1 and all the others 0) or an all-zero vector. The pseudo-labels can be used as approximate target ground truth labels.

3.3   Adversarial Training for UDA

Adversarial training uses an additional discriminator to align feature distributions. The discriminator $\mathbf{D}$ attempts to distinguish the feature distribution in the output space of the source and target. The segmentation model $\mathbf{M}$ attempts to fool the discriminator to confuse the feature distributions of the source and target, thereby aligning the feature distributions. The optimization process is as follows:

$$
\min_{\mathbf{w}} \max_{\mathbf{D}} \mathcal{L}_{AT} = - \frac{1}{|\mathbb{X}_S|} \sum_{\mathbf{x}_s \in \mathbb{X}_S} \sum_{c=1}^{C} y_s^{(c)} \log p(c|\mathbf{x}_s, \mathbf{w})
$$
$$
+ \frac{\lambda_{adv}}{|\mathbb{X}_T|} \sum_{\mathbf{x}_t \in \mathbb{X}_T} [\mathbf{D}(\mathbf{M}(\mathbf{x}_t, \mathbf{w})) - 1]^2 \tag{2}
$$

The first term is the cross-entropy loss of source, and the second term uses a mean squared error as the adversarial loss, where λ_{adv} is the weight of the adversarial loss. Equation (2) is used to optimize $\mathbf{M}$ and $\mathbf{D}$ alternately.

4   Proposed Method

An overview of our framework is shown in Fig. 3. We propose an instance adaptive self-training framework (IAST) with instance adaptive selector (IAS) and region-guided regularization. IAS selects an adaptive pseudo-label threshold for each semantic category in units of images and dynamically reduces the proportion of "hard" classes, to eliminate noise in the pseudo-labels. Besides, region-guided regularization is designed to smooth the prediction of the confident region and sharpen the prediction of the ignored region. Our overall objective function is as follows:

$$\min_{\mathbf{w}} \mathcal{L}_{CE}(\mathbf{w}, \hat{\mathbb{Y}}_T) + \mathcal{L}_R(\mathbf{w})$$
$$= \mathcal{L}_{CE}(\mathbf{w}, \hat{\mathbb{Y}}_T) + (\lambda_i \mathcal{R}_i(\mathbf{w}) + \lambda_c \mathcal{R}_c(\mathbf{w})) \tag{3}$$

where $\mathcal{L}_{CE}$ is the cross-entropy loss, which is different from Eq. (1) and only calculates the cross-entropy loss of the target domain images. $\hat{\mathbb{Y}}_T$ is the set of pseudo-labels, and the detailed generation process is described in Sect. 4.1. $\mathcal{R}_i$ and $\mathcal{R}_c$ are regularization of the ignored and confidence regions, which is described in Sect. 4.2. And λ_i, λ_c are regularization weights.

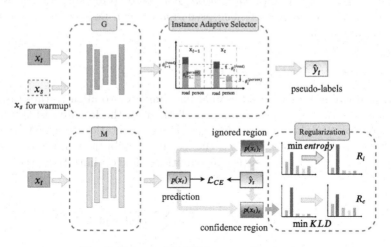

Fig. 3. Proposed IAST framework overview

The IAST training process consists of three phases.

- (a) In the *warm-up phase*, a non-self-training method uses both the source data and the target data to train an initial segmentation model $\mathbf{M}_0$ as the initial pseudo-label generator $\mathbf{G}_0$.
- (b) In the *pseudo-label generation phase*, $\mathbf{G}$ is used to obtain the prediction result of the target data, and a pseudo-label is generated by an instance adaptive selector.

- (c) In the *self-training phase*, according to Eq. (3), the segmentation model **M** is trained using the target data.

Why Warm-up? Before self-training, we expect to have a stable pre-trained model so that IAST can be trained in the right direction and avoid disturbances caused by constant fitting the noise of pseudo-labels. We use the adversarial training method described in Sect. 3.3 to obtain a stable model by roughly aligning the output of the source and target. In addition, in the warm-up phase, we can optionally apply any other semantic segmentation UDA method as the basic method, and it can be retained even in the (c) phase. In fact, we can use IAST as a decorator to decorate other basic methods.

Multi-round Self-training. Performing (b) phase and (c) phase once counts as one round. As with other self-training tasks, in this experiment we performed a total of three rounds. At the end of each round, the parameters of model **M** will be copied into model **G** to generate better target domain prediction results in the next round.

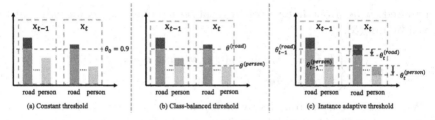

Fig. 4. Illustration of three different thresholding methods. $\mathbf{x}_{t-1}$ and $\mathbf{x}_t$ represent two consecutive instances, the bars approximately represent the probabilities of each class. (a) A constant threshold is used for all instances. (b) class-balanced thresholds are used for all instances. (c) Our method adaptively adjusts the threshold of each class based on the instance

4.1 Pseudo-Label Generation Strategy with an Instance Adaptive Selector

Pseudo-labels $\hat{\mathbb{Y}}_T$ have a decisive effect on the quality of self-training. The generic pseudo-label generation strategy can be simplified to the following form when segmentation model parameter $\mathbf{w}$ is fixed:

$$\min_{\hat{\mathbb{Y}}_T} -\frac{1}{|\mathbb{X}_T|} \sum_{\mathbf{x}_t \in \mathbb{X}_T} \sum_{c=1}^{C} \hat{y}_t^{(c)} \log \frac{p(c|\mathbf{x}_t, \mathbf{w})}{\theta_t^{(c)}} \tag{4}$$

$$s.t. \ \hat{\mathbf{y}}_t \in \{[onehot]^C\} \cup \mathbf{0} \ , \ \forall \hat{\mathbf{y}}_t \in \hat{\mathbb{Y}}_T$$

Algorithm 1. pseudo-labels generation

Input: Model $\mathbf{M}$, target instance $\{\mathbf{x}_t\}^T$,
Parameter: proportion α, momentum β, weight decay γ,
Output: target pseudo-labels

1: **init** $\theta_0 = 0.9$
2: **for** $t = 1$ **to** T **do**
3:     $\mathbf{P}_{index} = \arg\max(\mathbf{M}(\mathbf{x}_t))$
4:     $\mathbf{P}_{value} = \max(\mathbf{M}(\mathbf{x}_t))$
5:     **for** $c = 1$ **to** C **do**
6:         $\mathbb{P}^{(c)}_{\mathbf{x}_t} = \mathrm{sort}(\mathbf{P}_{value}[\mathbf{P}_{index} = c], \mathrm{descending})$
7:         $\theta^{(c)}_{\mathbf{x}_t} = \Psi(\mathbf{x}_t, \theta^{(c)}_{t-1})$ Eq.(7)
8:     **end for**
9:     $\theta_t = \beta\theta_{t-1} + (1 - \beta)\theta_{\mathbf{x}_t}$ Eq.(6)
10:     $\hat{\mathbf{y}}_t = \mathrm{onehot}(\mathbf{P}_{index}[\mathbf{P}_{value} > \theta_t])$
11: **end for**
12: **return** $\{\hat{\mathbf{y}}_t\}^T$

---

where $\theta^{(c)}$ indicates the confidence threshold for class c, and $\hat{\mathbf{y}}_\mathbf{t} = [\hat{y}^{(1)}_t, ..., \hat{y}^{(C)}_t]$ is required to be a one-hot vector or a all-zero vector. Therefore, $\hat{y}^{(c)}_t$ can be solved by Eq. (5).

$$\hat{y}^{(c)}_t = \begin{cases} 1, \; if \; c = \arg\max_c p(c|\mathbf{x}_t, \mathbf{w}) \; and \; p(c|\mathbf{x}_t, \mathbf{w}) > \theta^{(c)} \\ 0, \; otherwise \end{cases} \tag{5}$$

When class c output probability $p(c|\mathbf{x}_t, \mathbf{w}) > \theta^{(c)}$, these pixels are regarded as confidence region (pseudo-label region), and the rest are ignored regions (non-pseudo-label region). Therefore, $\theta^{(c)}$ become the key to the pseudo-labels generation process. As shown in Fig. 4: (a) the traditional pseudo-labels generation strategy based on a constant confidence threshold; (b) the generation strategy which uses the same class-balanced θ for all target images; (c) we propose a data diversity-driven pseudo-labels generation strategy with an instant adaptive selector (IAS).

IAS maintains two thresholds $\{\theta_t, \theta_{\mathbf{x}_t}\}$, where θ_t indicates the historical threshold and $\theta_{\mathbf{x}_t}$ indicates the threshold of current instance $\mathbf{x}_t$. During the generation process, IAS dynamically updates θ_t based on $\theta_{\mathbf{x}_t}$ of the current instance $\mathbf{x}_t$, so each instance gets an adaptive threshold, combining global and local information. Specifically, for each instance $\mathbf{x}_t$, we sort the confidence probability of each class in descending order, and then take the $\alpha \times 100\%$ confidence probability as the **local** threshold $\theta^{(c)}_{\mathbf{x}_t}$ for each class in instance $\mathbf{x}_t$. Finally, we use the exponentially weighted moving average to update the threshold θ_t containing historical information as the **global** threshold. The details are summarized in Algorithm 1.

Exponential Moving Average (EMA) Threshold. When generating pseudo-labels one by one, we use an exponential moving average method, denoted as Eq. (6), which can smooth the threshold of each instance, introduce past historical information, and avoid noise interference. Equation (7) $\Psi(\mathbf{x}_t, \theta_{t-1}^{(c)})$ represents the threshold for acquiring the current instance $\mathbf{x}_t$. β is a momentum factor used to preserve past threshold information. As β increases, the threshold $\theta_t^{(c)}$ becomes smoother.

$$\theta_t^{(c)} = \beta\theta_{t-1}^{(c)} + (1 - \beta)\Psi(\mathbf{x}_t, \theta_{t-1}^{(c)}) \tag{6}$$

$$\Psi(\mathbf{x}_t, \theta_{t-1}^{(c)}) = \mathbb{P}_{\mathbf{x}_t}^{(c)}\left[\alpha\theta_{t-1}^{(c)}{}^{\gamma}|\mathbb{P}_{\mathbf{x}_t}^{(c)}|\right] \tag{7}$$

"Hard" Classes Weight Decay (HWD). For "hard" classes, pseudo-labels tend to bring more noise labels. In Eq. (7), we design $\theta_{t-1}^{(c)}{}^{\gamma}$ to modify the proportion of pseudo-labels α. γ is a weight decay parameter, which is used to control the decay degree. The thresholds $\theta_{t-1}^{(c)}$ of the "hard" classes are usually smaller, so HWD reduces more pseudo-labels of "hard" classes. On the contrary the thresholds $\theta_{t-1}^{(c)}$ of easy classes is usually larger, so HWD has a weaker impact. It is easy to prove that when $\Psi(\mathbf{x}_t, \theta_{t-1}^{(c)}) = \theta_{t-1}^{(c)}$, θ will converge to a larger value, thereby reduce the amount of the "hard" classes.

4.2   Region-Guided Regularization

Confident Region KLD Minimization. During training, the model is prone to overfit pseudo-labels, which will damage the model. For the confidence region $\mathbb{I}_{\mathbf{x}_t} = \{1 \mid \hat{\mathbf{y}}_t^{(h,w)} > 0\}$, there are pseudo labels as supervising signals to supervise the model for learning. However, as shown in Table 4, although a series of techniques for generating high-confidence pseudo labels have been used, the quality of the pseudo labels is still not as good as the ground truth labels, which means that there are some noise labels in the pseudo-labels. How to reduce the impact of noise labels is a key issue. Zou et al. [35] has proposed various regularization for this. We use the KLD which works best in [35] to smooth the prediction results of the confidence region, so that the prediction results do not overfit the pseudo-labels.

$$\mathcal{R}_c = -\frac{1}{|\mathbb{X}_T|}\sum_{\mathbf{x}_t \in \mathbb{X}_T} \mathbb{I}_{\mathbf{x}_t} \sum_{c=1}^{C} \frac{1}{C} \log p(c|\mathbf{x}_t, \mathbf{w}) \tag{8}$$

As shown in Eq. (8), when the prediction result $\log p(c|\mathbf{x}_t, \mathbf{w})$ is approximately close to the uniform distribution (the probability of each class is $\frac{1}{C}$), $\mathcal{R}_c$ gets smaller. KLD minimization promotes smoothing of confidence regionsand avoid the model blindly trusting false labels.

Ignored Region Entropy Minimization. On the other hand, for the ignored region $\mathbb{I}_{\mathbf{x}_t}^{\mathbf{C}} = \{1 \mid \hat{\mathbf{y}}_t^{(h,w)} = \mathbf{0}\}$, there is no supervision signal during the training process. Because the prediction result of the region $\mathbb{I}_{\mathbf{x}_t}^{\mathbf{C}}$ is smooth and has low confidence, we use the minimized entropy of the ignored region to prompt the model to predict the low entropy result, which makes the prediction result look more "sharper".

$$\mathcal{R}_i = -\frac{1}{|\mathbb{X}_T|} \sum_{\mathbf{x}_t \in \mathbb{X}_T} \mathbb{I}_{\mathbf{x}_t}^{\mathbf{C}} \sum_{c=1}^{C} p(c|\mathbf{x}_t, \mathbf{w}) \log p(c|\mathbf{x}_t, \mathbf{w}) \tag{9}$$

As shown in Eq. (9), sharpening the prediction result of the ignored region by minimizing $\mathcal{R}_i$ can promote the model to learn more useful features from the ignored region without any supervised signal, which has also been proved to be effective for UDA in the work [29].

5   Experiment

5.1   Experimental Settings

Network Architecture and Datasets. We adapt Deeplab-v2 [3], which is widely used in the semantic segmentation UDA problem, as our basic network architecture. ResNet-101 [8] is selected as the backbone network of the model. All experiments in this work are carried out under this network architecture. We evaluate our UDA methods for semantic segmentation on the popular synthetic-to-real adaptation scenarios: (a) GTA5 [23] to Cityscapes [5], (b) SYNTHIA [24] to Cityscapes. The GTA5 dataset has 24966 images that are rendered from the GTA5 game and 19 classes with Cityscapes. SYNTHIA dataset includes 9400 images and 16 common classes with Cityscapes. Cityscapes is split into training set, validation set, and testing set. Following the standard protocols in [27], we use the training set which has 2975 images as the target dataset and use the validation dataset to evaluate our models with mIoU.

Implementation Details. In our experiments, we implement IAST using PyTorch on an NVIDIA Tesla V100. The training images are randomly cropped and resized to 1024×512, the aspect ratio of the crop window is 2.0, and the window height is randomly selected from $[341 \sim 950]$ for GTA5 and $[341 \sim 640]$ for SYNTHIA. All weights of batch normalization layers were frozen. Deeplab-v2 is pre-trained on ImageNet. In IAST, we adopt Adam with learning rate 2.5×10^{-5}, batch size 6 for 4 epochs. The pseud-label parameters α, β, γ are set to 0.2, 0.9 and 8.0. The regularization weights λ_i and λ_c are set to 3.0 and 0.1. Our code and pre-trained molels are available at: https://github.com/Raykoooo/IAST.

5.2   Discussion and Ablation Study

Why IAS Works? Table 2 shows a sensitivity analysis on the parameter α and β. When we set $\alpha = 0.2$ and $\beta = 0$, it means IAS takes 20% of each image as the

Fig. 5. Visualization of pseudo-labels. Columns correspond to original images with ground truth labels, our method, and class-balanced method [36]

confidence region. As a comparison, the class-balanced method [36] takes 20% of pixels in the whole target set as the confidence region. As shown in Fig. 5, pseudo-labels of class-balanced method miss some pixels for persons, cars and bikes. In contrast, the pseudo-labels of our method are more diverse, especially for some "hard" classes. When we set $\alpha = 0.2$ and $\beta = 0.9$, IAS combines global and local information to get more diverse content so that the model achieve the best performance.

Table 2. α and β sensitivity analysis (GTA5 to Cityscapes)

α	β	Proportion (%)	mIoU (%)
.20	.0	20.0	49.8
.20	.50	31.2	50.3
.20	.90	36.5	**50.5**
.20	.99	40.1	50.0
.30	.90	42.5	49.7
.50	.90	48.6	48.2
Constant (Fig. 4 a)		38.6	45.1
Class-balanced (Fig. 4 b)		20.0	47.9

Table 3. λ_i and λ_c sensitivity analysis (GTA5 to Cityscapes)

λ_i	λ_c	mIoU (%)
.5	.10	50.6
1.0	.10	51.1
2.0	.10	50.9
3.0	.10	**51.5**
4.0	.10	51.2
5.0	.10	51.3
3.0	.05	50.6
3.0	.15	51.0

Figure 6 shows that as the γ increases, the proportion of some easy classes (sky, car) that have a high prediction score does not decrease significantly, while the proportion of some "hard" classes (motor, wall, fence and pole) that have a low prediction score decreases sharply. This proves that Eq. (7) can effectively reduce the pseudo-labels of "hard" classes and suppress noise interference in the pseudo-labels. Table 4 shows a sensitivity analysis on the parameter γ. We find that as the γ increases, pseudo-labels have smaller proportions but have better quality. Therefore, we let $\gamma = 8$ as the trade-off between the proportion and the quality of pseudo-labels. On the contrary, moderate regularization helps the model to improve the prediction accuracy and avoid overfitting the noise labels.

Table 3 shows a sensitivity analysis of the parameter λ_i and λ_c. We performed multiple sets of experiments with fixed λ_i and λ_c, respectively. When $\lambda_c = 0.1$ is fixed and λ_i is gradually increased, the overall model performance tends to improve until $\lambda_i = 4$. It can be expected that when the low entropy prediction is excessively performed in the non-pseudo-label region, the influence of noise will be amplified and the model will be damaged.

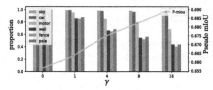

Fig. 6. Relationship between the pseudo-labels proportion and γ

Table 4. γ sensitivity analysis ($\alpha = 0.2, \beta = 1.0$). *P-mIoU* means mIoU of pseudo-labels

γ	0	1	4	8	16
Proportion	0.36	0.34	0.30	0.28	0.25
P-mIoU (%)	65.6	66.3	67.4	68.2	69.0
mIoU (%)	50.5	50.8	51.2	**51.5**	50.9

Ablation Studies. The results of the ablation studies are reported in Table 5. We attempt the methods proposed in Sect. 4.1 and Sect. 4.2 one by one to study their performance in the test set. From the data in Table 5, after using self-training (Fig. 4 a) without using any other techniques, the model performance has a gain of 1.3%. After adding IAST modules (IAS, $\mathcal{R}_i$, $\mathcal{R}_c$), the performance of the model is gradually and steadily improved, and finally, 51.5% mIoU is achieved. In addition, we also try multi-scale testing and the combined result achieved the best 52.2% mIoU.

Table 5. Results of ablation study (GTA5 to Cityscapes)

Method	ST	IAS	$\mathcal{R}_c$	$\mathcal{R}_i$	mIoU	Δ
Source	–	–	–	–	35.6	0
Warm-up	–	–	–	–	43.8	+8.2
+ Constant ST (Fig. 4 a)	✓				45.1	+1.3
+ Instance adaptive selector	✓	✓			49.8	+4.7
+ Confidence region R	✓	✓	✓		50.7	+0.9
+ Ignored region R	✓	✓	✓	✓	51.5	+0.8

5.3   Experimental Results

Comparison with the State-of-the-Art Methods: The results of IAST and some other state-of-the-art methods on GTA5 to Cityscapes are present in

Table 6. Results of our proposed method IAST and other state-of-the-art methods (GTA5 to Cityscapes). A&S means a mixed method of AT and ST

Method	Arch.	Road	SW	Build	Wall	Fence	Pole	TL	TS	Veg.	Terrain	Sky	PR	Rider	Car	Truck	Bus	Train	Motor	Bike	mIoU
Source [27]		75.8	16.8	77.2	12.5	21.0	25.5	30.1	20.1	81.3	24.6	70.3	53.8	26.4	49.9	17.2	25.9	6.5	25.3	36.0	36.6
AdaptSegNet [27]		86.5	36.0	79.9	23.4	23.3	23.9	35.2	14.8	83.4	33.3	75.6	58.5	27.6	73.7	32.5	35.4	3.9	30.1	28.1	42.4
SIBAN [22]	AT	88.5	35.4	79.5	26.3	24.3	28.5	32.5	18.3	81.2	40.0	76.5	58.1	25.8	82.6	30.3	34.3	3.4	21.6	21.5	42.6
SSF-DAN [6]		90.3	38.9	81.7	24.8	22.9	30.5	37.0	21.2	84.8	38.8	76.9	58.8	30.7	85.7	30.6	38.1	5.9	28.3	36.9	45.4
AdvEnt [29]		89.4	33.1	81.0	26.6	26.8	27.2	33.5	24.7	83.9	36.7	78.8	58.7	30.5	84.8	38.5	44.5	1.7	31.6	32.4	45.4
APODA [30]		85.6	32.8	79.0	29.5	25.5	26.8	34.6	19.9	83.7	40.6	77.9	59.2	28.3	84.6	34.6	49.2	8.0	32.6	39.6	45.9
Source [36]		71.3	19.2	69.1	18.4	10.0	35.7	27.3	6.8	79.6	24.8	72.1	57.6	19.5	55.5	15.5	15.1	11.7	21.1	12.0	33.8
CBST [36]	ST	91.8	53.5	80.5	32.7	21.0	34.0	28.9	20.4	83.9	34.2	80.9	53.1	24.0	82.7	30.3	35.9	16.0	25.9	42.8	45.9
PyCDA[20]		90.5	36.3	84.4	32.4	28.7	34.6	36.4	31.5	**86.8**	37.9	78.5	62.3	21.5	85.6	27.9	34.8	18.0	22.9	**49.3**	47.4
MRKLD [35]		91.0	55.4	80.0	33.7	21.4	**37.3**	32.9	24.5	85.0	34.1	80.8	57.7	24.6	84.1	27.8	30.1	**26.9**	26.0	42.3	47.1
BLF [19]		91.0	44.7	84.2	34.6	27.6	30.2	36.0	36.0	85.0	**43.6**	83.0	58.6	31.6	83.3	35.3	49.7	3.3	28.8	35.6	48.5
AdaptMR [34]	A&S	90.5	35.0	84.6	34.3	24.0	36.8	44.2	**42.7**	84.5	33.6	82.5	**63.1**	34.4	85.8	32.9	38.2	2.0	27.1	41.8	48.3
PatchAlign [28]		92.3	51.9	82.1	29.2	25.1	24.5	33.8	33.0	82.4	32.8	82.2	58.6	27.2	84.3	33.4	26.3	2.2	29.5	32.3	46.5
Source(ours)		64.8	21.7	74.3	15.4	21.2	18.2	30.7	13.0	80.9	33.7	76.3	55.6	20.0	43.9	27.0	35.5	4.4	24.9	14.3	35.6
IAST(ours)	A&S	93.8	57.8	85.1	39.5	26.7	26.2	43.1	34.7	84.9	32.9	88.0	62.6	29.0	87.3	39.2	49.6	23.2	34.7	39.6	51.5
IAST-MST(ours)		**94.1**	**58.8**	**85.4**	**39.7**	**29.2**	25.1	43.1	34.2	84.8	34.6	**88.7**	62.7	30.3	**87.6**	**42.3**	**50.3**	24.7	**35.2**	40.2	**52.2**

Table 7. Results of our proposed method IAST and other state-of-the-art methods (SYNTHIA to Cityscapes)

Method	Arch.	Road	SW	Build	Wall*	Fence*	Pole*	TL	TS	Veg.	Sky	PR	Rider	Car	Bus	Motor	Bike	mIoU	mIoU*
Source [27]		55.6	23.8	74.6	-	-	-	6.1	12.1	74.8	79.0	55.3	19.1	39.6	23.3	13.7	25.0	-	38.6
AdaptSegNet [27]		84.3	42.7	77.5	-	-	-	4.7	7.0	77.9	82.5	54.3	21.0	72.3	32.2	18.9	32.3	-	46.7
SIBAN [22]	AT	82.5	24.0	79.4	-	-	-	16.5	12.7	79.2	82.8	58.3	18.0	79.3	25.3	17.6	25.9	-	46.3
SSF-DAN [6]		84.6	41.7	80.8	-	-	-	11.5	14.7	80.8	**85.3**	57.5	21.6	82.0	36.0	19.3	34.5	-	50.0
AdvEnt [29]		85.6	42.2	79.7	8.7	0.4	25.9	5.4	8.1	80.4	84.1	57.9	23.8	73.3	36.4	14.2	33.0	41.2	48.0
APODA [30]		**86.4**	41.3	79.3	-	-	-	22.6	17.3	80.3	81.6	56.9	21.0	84.1	**49.1**	24.6	45.7	-	53.1
Source [36]		64.3	21.3	73.1	2.4	1.1	31.4	7.0	27.7	63.1	67.6	42.2	19.9	73.1	15.3	10.5	38.9	34.9	40.3
CBST [36]	ST	68.0	29.9	76.3	10.8	1.4	33.9	22.8	29.5	77.6	78.3	60.6	28.3	81.6	23.5	18.8	39.8	42.6	48.9
PyCDA [20]		75.5	30.9	83.3	**20.8**	0.7	32.7	27.3	33.5	**84.7**	85.0	64.1	25.4	85.0	45.2	21.2	32.0	46.7	53.3
MRKLD [35]		67.7	32.2	73.9	10.7	1.6	**37.4**	22.2	**31.2**	80.8	80.5	60.8	29.1	82.8	25.0	19.4	45.3	43.8	50.1
BLF [19]		86.0	**46.7**	80.3	-	-	-	14.1	11.6	79.2	81.3	54.1	27.9	73.7	42.2	25.7	45.3	-	51.4
AdaptMR [34]	A&S	83.1	38.2	81.7	9.3	1.0	35.1	30.3	19.9	82.0	80.1	62.8	21.1	84.4	37.8	24.5	**53.3**	46.5	53.8
PatchAlign [28]		82.4	38.0	78.6	8.7	0.6	26.0	3.9	11.1	75.5	84.6	53.5	21.6	71.4	32.6	19.3	31.7	40.0	46.5
Source(ours)		63.4	24.1	66.7	7.1	0.1	28.4	11.6	16.8	77.0	74.6	60.4	20.5	75.6	22.0	14.4	21.2	36.5	42.2
IAST(ours)	A&S	81.9	41.5	**83.3**	17.7	**4.6**	32.3	**30.9**	28.8	83.4	85.0	**65.5**	**30.8**	**86.5**	38.2	**33.1**	52.7	**49.8**	**57.0**

Table 6. From the overall results, IAST has the best mIoU 52.2% and has obvious advantages over other methods. Compared with some adversarial training methods AdaptSegNet [27] and SIBAN [22], IAST improves by 9.6% mIoU and have significant gains in almost all classes. Compared with the same self-training methods such as MRKLD [35], IAST improves by 4.8% mIoU. In addition, BLF [19] is a method that combines adversarial training and self-training, which has

the second-best 48.5% mIoU. Compared to BLF, IAST still has a significant improvement.

Table 7 is the results of the SYNTHIA to Cityscapes dataset. For a comprehensive comparison, as in the previous work, we also report two mIoU metrics: 13 classes of mIoU* and 16 classes of mIoU. The domain gap between SYNTHIA and Cityscapes is much larger than the domain gap between GTA5 and Cityscapes. Many of the methods that performed well on GTA5 to Cityscapes have experienced a significant performance degradation on this dataset. Correspondingly, the performance gap between different methods is becoming more apparent. IAST also achieves the best results, which are 49.8% mIoU and 57.0% mIoU* and significantly higher than all recent state-of-the-art methods.

Table 8. Semi-supervised learning results on the Cityscapes val set. 1/8, 1/4 and 1/2 mean the proportion of labeled images

Method	Data Amount			
	1/8	1/4	1/2	Full
Baseline	57.3	59.0	61.2	70.2
Univ-full [12]	55.9	–	–	–
AdvSemi [11]	58.8	62.3	65.7	67.7
IAST (ours)	64.6	66.7	69.8	70.2

Table 9. Extension analysis, applying IAST to non-self-learning UDA methods [27,29] (test on Cityscapes), and *Source* means training IAST without warmup

Method	GTA5			SYNTHIA		
	Base	+IAST	Δ	Base	+IAST	Δ
AdaptSeg [27]	42.4	50.2	+7.8	46.7	54.7	+8.0
AdvEnt [29]	45.4	49.8	+4.4	48.0	55.1	+7.1
Source	35.6	48.8	+13.2	42.2	54.2	+12.0

Apply to Other UDA Methods. Because IAST has no special structure or model dependencies, it can be directly used to decorate other UDA methods. We chose two typical adversarial training methods, AdaptSeg [27] and AdvEnt [29] for experiments. As shown in Table 9, these two methods have significantly improved performance under the IAST framework.

Extension: Other Tasks. The self-training method can also be applied to semi-supervised semantic segmentation task. We use the same configuration as [11] in Cityscapes for semi-supervised training with different proportions of data as labeled data. As shown in Table 8, we have significantly better performance than [11] and [12].

6   Conclusions

In this paper, we propose an instance adaptive self-training framework for semantic segmentation UDA. Compared with other popular UDA methods, IAST still has a significant improvement in performance. Moreover, IAST is a method with no model or special structure dependency, which means that it can be easily applied to other UDA methods with almost no additional cost to improve performance. In addition, IAST can also be applied to semi-supervised semantic segmentation tasks, which also achieves state-of-the-art performance. We hope this work will prompt people to rethink the potential of self-training on UDA or semi-supervised learning tasks.

Acknowledgement. This work was supported in part by the Natural Science Foundation of Beijing Municipality under Grant 4182044.

References

1. Baktashmotlagh, M., Harandi, M.T., Lovell, B.C., Salzmann, M.: Unsupervised domain adaptation by domain invariant projection. In: ICCV, pp. 769–776 (2013)
2. Chen, C., et al.: Progressive feature alignment for unsupervised domain adaptation. In: CVPR, pp. 627–636 (2019)
3. Chen, L.C., Papandreou, G., Kokkinos, I., Murphy, K., Yuille, A.L.: DeepLab: semantic image segmentation with deep convolutional nets, atrous convolution, and fully connected CRFs. TPAMI **40**(4), 834–848 (2017)
4. Chen, Y., Li, W., Sakaridis, C., Dai, D., Van Gool, L.: Domain adaptive faster R-CNN for object detection in the wild. In: CVPR, pp. 3339–3348 (2018)
5. Cordts, M., et al.: The cityscapes dataset for semantic urban scene understanding. In: CVPR, pp. 3213–3223 (2016)
6. Du, L., et al.: SSF-DAN: separated semantic feature based domain adaptation network for semantic segmentation. In: ICCV (2019)
7. Goodfellow, I., Bengio, Y., Courville, A.: Deep Learning. MIT Press, Cambridge (2016)
8. He, K., Zhang, X., Ren, S., Sun, J.: Deep residual learning for image recognition. In: CVPR, pp. 770–778 (2016)
9. Hoffman, J., et al.: Cycada: cycle-consistent adversarial domain adaptation. In: ICML (2018)
10. Huang, X., Liu, M.Y., Belongie, S., Kautz, J.: Multimodal unsupervised image-to-image translation. In: ECCV, pp. 172–189 (2018)
11. Hung, W.C., Tsai, Y.H., Liou, Y.T., Lin, Y.Y., Yang, M.H.: Adversarial learning for semi-supervised semantic segmentation. In: BMVC (2019)
12. Kalluri, T., Varma, G., Chandraker, M., Jawahar, C.: Universal semi-supervised semantic segmentation. In: Proceedings of the IEEE International Conference on Computer Vision, pp. 5259–5270 (2019)
13. Kan, M., Shan, S., Chen, X.: Bi-shifting auto-encoder for unsupervised domain adaptation. In: ICCV, pp. 3846–3854 (2015)
14. Krizhevsky, A., Sutskever, I., Hinton, G.E.: Imagenet classification with deep convolutional neural networks. In: NIPS, pp. 1097–1105 (2012)
15. Kukačka, J., Golkov, V., Cremers, D.: Regularization for deep learning: a taxonomy. arXiv preprint arXiv:1710.10686 (2017)
16. Lee, C.Y., Batra, T., Baig, M.H., Ulbricht, D.: Sliced wasserstein discrepancy for unsupervised domain adaptation. In: CVPR, pp. 10285–10295 (2019)
17. Li, J., et al.: Multi-human parsing machines. In: ACM Multimedia, pp. 45–53 (2018)
18. Li, M., Zhou, Z.-H.: SETRED: self-training with editing. In: Ho, T.B., Cheung, D., Liu, H. (eds.) PAKDD 2005. LNCS (LNAI), vol. 3518, pp. 611–621. Springer, Heidelberg (2005). https://doi.org/10.1007/11430919_71

19. Li, Y., Yuan, L., Vasconcelos, N.: Bidirectional learning for domain adaptation of semantic segmentation. In: CVPR (2019)
20. Lian, Q., Lv, F., Duan, L., Gong, B.: Constructing self-motivated pyramid curriculums for cross-domain semantic segmentation: a non-adversarial approach. In: CVPR, pp. 6758–6767 (2019)
21. Long, M., Cao, Z., Wang, J., Jordan, M.I.: Conditional adversarial domain adaptation. In: NIPS, pp. 1640–1650 (2018)
22. Luo, Y., Liu, P., Guan, T., Yu, J., Yang, Y.: Significance-aware information bottleneck for domain adaptive semantic segmentation. In: ICCV (2019)
23. Richter, S.R., Vineet, V., Roth, S., Koltun, V.: Playing for data: ground truth from computer games. In: Leibe, B., Matas, J., Sebe, N., Welling, M. (eds.) ECCV 2016. LNCS, vol. 9906, pp. 102–118. Springer, Cham (2016). https://doi.org/10.1007/978-3-319-46475-6_7
24. Ros, G., Sellart, L., Materzynska, J., Vazquez, D., Lopez, A.M.: The synthia dataset: a large collection of synthetic images for semantic segmentation of urban scenes. In: CVPR, pp. 3234–3243 (2016)
25. Szegedy, C., Vanhoucke, V., Ioffe, S., Shlens, J., Wojna, Z.: Rethinking the inception architecture for computer vision. In: CVPR, pp. 2818–2826 (2016)
26. Triguero, I., García, S., Herrera, F.: Self-labeled techniques for semi-supervised learning: taxonomy, software and empirical study. KAIS 42(2), 245–284 (2015)
27. Tsai, Y.H., Hung, W.C., Schulter, S., Sohn, K., Yang, M.H., Chandraker, M.: Learning to adapt structured output space for semantic segmentation. In: CVPR, pp. 7472–7481 (2018)
28. Tsai, Y.H., Sohn, K., Schulter, S., Chandraker, M.: Domain adaptation for structured output via discriminative patch representations. In: CVPR (2019)
29. Vu, T.H., Jain, H., Bucher, M., Cord, M., Pérez, P.: Advent: adversarial entropy minimization for domain adaptation in semantic segmentation. In: CVPR (2019)
30. Yang, J., Xu, R., Li, R., Qi, X., Shen, X., Li, G., Lin, L.: An adversarial perturbation oriented domain adaptation approach for semantic segmentation. In: AAAI (2020)
31. Zhang, Q., Zhang, J., Liu, W., Tao, D.: Category anchor-guided unsupervised domain adaptation for semantic segmentation. In: NeurIPS, pp. 433–443 (2019)
32. Zhao, J., et al.: Towards pose invariant face recognition in the wild. In: CVPR, pp. 2207–2216 (2018)
33. Zhao, J., et al.: Self-supervised neural aggregation networks for human parsing. In: CVPRW, pp. 7–15 (2017)
34. Zheng, Z., Yang, Y.: Unsupervised scene adaptation with memory regularization in vivo. arXiv preprint arXiv:1912.11164 (2019)
35. Zou, Y., Yu, Z., Liu, X., Kumar, B., Wang, J.: Confidence regularized self-training. In: ICCV, pp. 5982–5991 (2019)
36. Zou, Y., Yu, Z., Vijaya Kumar, B., Wang, J.: Unsupervised domain adaptation for semantic segmentation via class-balanced self-training. In: ECCV, pp. 289–305 (2018)

Weight Decay Scheduling and Knowledge Distillation for Active Learning

Juseung Yun, Byungjoo Kim, and Junmo Kim[✉]

KAIST, Daejeon, South Korea
{juseung_yun,junmo.kim}@kaist.ac.kr, byungjoo.kim92@gmail.com

Abstract. Although convolutional neural networks perform extremely well for numerous computer vision tasks, a considerably large amount of labeled data is required to ensure a good outcome. Data labeling is labor-intensive, and in some cases, the labeling budget may be limited. Active learning is a technique that can reduce the labeling required. With this technique, the neural network selects on its own the unlabeled data most helpful for learning, and then requests the human annotator for the labels. Most existing active learning methods have focused on acquisition functions for an effective selection of the informative samples. However, in this paper, we focus on the data-incremental nature of active learning, and propose a method for properly tuning the weight decay as the amount of data increases. We also demonstrate that the performance can be improved by knowledge distillation using a low-performance teacher model trained from the previous acquisition step. In addition, we present a novel perspective of the weight decay, which provides a regularization effect by limiting the number of effective parameters and channels in the convolutional filter. We validate our methods on the MNIST, CIFAR-10, and CIFAR-100 datasets using convolutional neural networks of various sizes.

Keywords: Active learning · Weight decay · Knowledge distillation

1 Introduction

Deep convolutional neural networks (CNNs) have shown a significant in several computer vision tasks [9,29,34]. However, a large amount of data is needed to ensure the desirable performance of such networks. Unfortunately, because the process requires considerable manual effort, it is occasionally difficult to collect a sufficient amount of labeled data. In certain cases, the budget allowed for labeling may be limited. Active learning can be used to mitigate the aforementioned problem. The goal of active learning is to minimize the labeling budget, while achieving maximum performance. In this paper, we focus on pool-based active learning. The process of pool-based active learning starts with completely unlabeled data. While training, the neural network selects a set of data and requests the human annotator for their labels. The network is then trained using these

© Springer Nature Switzerland AG 2020
A. Vedaldi et al. (Eds.): ECCV 2020, LNCS 12371, pp. 431–447, 2020.
https://doi.org/10.1007/978-3-030-58574-7_26

labels. Iterative training proceeds until it meets certain constraints, such as the labeling budget, or the desired performance. Because the selection of data notably affects the performance, it is important to select those *informative* samples that are most helpful for training a model from unlabeled pools.

In the existing literature, there are three major approaches used to determine an informative sample, namely, uncertainty-based methods [6,18,26,27], distribution-based methods [37], and expected model change methods [5,19,49]. Because it is infeasible and redundant to train neural networks from scratch every time we obtain additional labels, a rounding setting or batch mode setting is widely used, where the neural network requests labels for multiple data at the same time.

The majority of existing active learning methods focus on sampling the *most informative* samples by finding the acquisition functions. However, in our approach, we address the problem by considering the data incremental nature of active learning. Few annotations are accessible during the early stage of training, and the network is easily over-fitted to the annotated data; this degrades the generalization performance. Therefore, a strong regularization is necessary at the beginning of the training to prevent over-fitting. As the training progresses, we obtain additional data, and the total amount of annotated data increases. If we maintain the strong regularization of the first round during the subsequent rounds, the performance decreases because the network cannot learn new information in an efficient manner. The more data we have, the weaker the regularizer needed to ensure that the model can learn sufficient information. Thus, in active learning, the number of data continues to increase and regularization must be performed in a planned manner.

To this end, we propose a novel method for active learning. We control the regularization effect by scheduling the weight decay as the amount of data increases. We show that reducing the weight decay inversely proportional to the amount of data is simple but extremely effective. We also demonstrate that initializing the network parameters randomly and learning from scratch during every round is better than initializing the model trained during the previous round. However, if we re-initialize the network during each round, we are unable to use any information previously trained by the model. As an alternative, we use the method of distilling knowledge to a new model, in which the model from the previous round acts as a teacher. We show that the proposed method is effective in various CNN architectures and datasets.

Contribution. The three main contributions of our study are as follows.

1. We propose a weight decay scheduling method for CNNs with batch normalization during active learning to reduce the weight decay inversely proportional to the number of training data. We also verified that the weight decay method is effective in batch normalization because it regulates the model complexity by adjusting the number of effective parameters and convolutional channels.
2. We show that a network with a low performance and effective capacity can distill useful knowledge to networks with a higher performance and

effective capacity. When training a new model after an acquisition, even distilling knowledge from a previous model shows a better performance than the training alone.

3. We also verified that our method shows an improved performance on the MNIST, CIFAR-10, and CIFAR-100 datasets when using various CNN architectures with batch normalization.

2   Related Work

Active Learning. Classic active learning methods can be categorized into the following three types: an uncertainty-based approach [18,26,27], a diversity-based approach [4,8,33], and expected model change-based methods [5,19,39]. In an uncertainty-based approach, entropy [18,30,38], max margin [36], or distance to the decision boundary [43,45] are used as a proxy for the uncertainty. With diversity-based approaches, diverse samples are selected that represent the distribution of an unlabeled data space [33]. The method of an expected model change estimates an expected gradient length or optimal model improvement [5,19]. In addition, active learning methods have been applied in deep neural networks. Through an uncertainty-based approach, Wang et al. [46] used entropy in deep neural networks, and demonstrated its effectiveness. Gal et al. [6] estimated the uncertainty through a Monte Carlo dropout. Beluch et al. [2] used an ensemble of CNNs for estimating uncertainty. Sener et al. [37] proposed a distribution-based approach, in which the core-set covering the feature space of the entire unlabeled pool is selected. Finally, Yoo et al. [49] proposed a loss prediction module and selected samples that are expected to have the highest loss.

However, in most studies, the incremental data characteristics of active learning are not considered and the model is trained using the same hyper-parameters regardless of the increase in the amount of data [2,13,37,46,49]. Some studies have used a method to reduce the weight decay as the amount of data increases [6,21]. However, rather than adjusting the weight decay with the rules, the authors heuristically identified an appropriate weight decay during each round and used CNN without batch normalization.

Weight Decay. Weight decay is a regularization method that prevents overfitting by limiting the complexity of parametric models in machine learning [24]. It is also used in modern deep neural networks and acts as a good regularizer [9,14,41]. However, when weight decay is used with batch normalization [16], the output of each layer is re-scaled, and the weights can be scaled using a small factor without changing the network's prediction. Therefore, Van et al. [44] suggested that the weight decay does not effectively limit the complexity of the network. Furthermore, Zhang et al. [51] indicated that the increase in the effective learning rate leads to a larger gradient noise, which in turn acts as a stochastic regularizer [17,20,32], which the authors argue is reason why a weight decay leads to performance gains even when batch normalization is used.

Knowledge Distillation. Knowledge distillation is a method for transferring knowledge to a small student network using a high-capacity model or an ensemble of multiple models as the teacher. The student is trained to imitate the teacher model in the form of class probabilities [11], feature representation [1,10,22,35], attention map [50] or inter-layer flow [48]. Most existing methods use highly complex or high capacity models as the teacher and aim at obtaining small and fast models. Rometo *et al.* [35] used a student network deeper than that of the teacher. However, the numbers of channels and parameters in the student model are smaller than those of the teacher.

Recently, Xie *et al.* [47] successfully distilled knowledge to a larger student model. However, when training the student model, they used strong regularizers such as RandAugment data augmentation [3], a dropout [42], and stochastic depth [15]. Therefore, the performance gain was predictable to a certain extent. By contrast, our method has a large weight decay for the teacher and a small weight decay for the student. In other words, in our study, we analyze a case in which the student has a more effective capacity and is trained with no additional regularizers such as RandAugment [3].

3   Method

In this section, we describe the active learning problem, along with our proposed method. In Sect. 3.1, we present an overview of the entire active learning procedure. Next, we introduce our weight decay scheduling method in Sect. 3.2, and knowledge distillation in Sect. 3.3.

3.1   Entropy-Based Active Learning

We consider a C-class classification problem. In addition, following previous studies [2,31,37,49], we consider active learning in a batch setting, i.e, the neural network requests labels for multiple data at the same time. During initial round, we randomly sample K data points from an unlabeled data pool $\mathcal{D}$, and ask a human oracle to annotate them to create an initial labeled dataset $\mathcal{D}_0^L = \{(\boldsymbol{x}, y)\}^K$, where $\boldsymbol{x} \in \mathcal{X}$ is an input, and $y \in \mathcal{Y} = \{1, 2, ..., C\}$ is its label. The subscript 0 denotes the initial round. Let $\mathcal{D}_0^U = \mathcal{D} \setminus \mathcal{D}_0^L$ be the rest of the unlabeled pool. Subsequently, we train the initial CNN, $f_0(\boldsymbol{x}; \boldsymbol{\theta})$, using the labeled dataset $\mathcal{D}_0^L$ with a weight decay λ_0. After the initial training, we evaluate all data points in the unlabeled pool $\mathcal{D}_0^U$ using an acquisition function $a\left(\mathcal{D}^U, f\right)$. Finding a good acquisition function was not the focus of our study, however, and we therefore used entropy as $a\left(\mathcal{D}^U, f\right)$, which is simple but achieves a good performance [46]. Once the network f outputs a probabilistic class posterior $p(c|\boldsymbol{x}, \boldsymbol{\theta})$ for a sample $\boldsymbol{x}$ over a class c, the entropy $H(p)$ can be calculated as follows:

$$H(p) = -\sum_{c=1}^{C} p(c|\boldsymbol{x}, \boldsymbol{\theta}) log\left(p(c|\boldsymbol{x}, \boldsymbol{\theta})\right). \tag{1}$$

Subsequently, we select K samples with the largest entropy from $\mathcal{D}_0^U$ and request the human annotator for labels. The labeled dataset is then updated and $\mathcal{D}_1^L$

is obtained. Next, we train the CNN $f_1(\boldsymbol{x}; \boldsymbol{\theta})$ over $\mathcal{D}_1^L$, and select K samples with the largest entropy from the $\mathcal{D}_1^U = \mathcal{D} \backslash \mathcal{D}_1^L$. We repeat this process until the desired performance is achieved or the labeling budget is exhausted.

3.2 Weight Decay Scheduling

With active learning, the amount of training data in the first round is small and increases as the learning progresses. An over-fitting is likely to occur as the amount of data is initially small, and therefore, a strong regularizer is needed in the initial stages of training. By contrast, the more data we have, the weaker the regularizer needed to ensure that the model can learn sufficient information. If we keep using a strong regularizer through the training, the network suffers during the learning. We propose a method for controlling the degree of regularization by scheduling a weight decay in the network, which contains a batch normalization layer [16].

Assume that we train a neural network with N_1 labeled samples to minimize the cross-entropy loss, $\mathcal{L}_{CE}$, and L_2 weight decay. The total loss, $\mathcal{L}$, is then expressed as follows:

$$\mathcal{L} = \mathcal{L}_{CE} + \frac{1}{2}\lambda_1 \|\boldsymbol{\theta}\|_2^2, \tag{2}$$

where λ denotes the weight decay parameter. Because we train the network with a mini-batch, kN_1 iterations are required for the entire training process. Here, k is a proportional constant, which is determined by the size of the mini-batch and the total number of epochs. The optimizations over $\mathcal{L}_{CE}$ and $\|\boldsymbol{\theta}\|_2^2$ are closely related. In general, reducing the L_2 norm to a significant extent will not effectively reduce the cross-entropy loss, and vice versa. However, when the network contains a batch normalization layer, it is shown that the weights can be scaled by a small factor without changing the prediction of the network [12,28,44,51]. Formally, let $\boldsymbol{\theta}_l$ be the learnable weights for a convolutional layer. Assume that the output of the layer feeds in to a batch norm layer, and let $\mathbf{BN}(\boldsymbol{x}; \boldsymbol{\theta}_l)$ denote the output of that batch norm layer. Suppose that, as a result of a L_2 penalty term, we scale $\boldsymbol{\theta}_l$ by a factor of $0 < \kappa < 1$. Then, the new output of the batch norm layer is as follows:

$$\mathbf{BN}(\boldsymbol{x}; \kappa\boldsymbol{\theta}_l) = \mathbf{BN}(\boldsymbol{x}; \boldsymbol{\theta}_l). \tag{3}$$

This implies that scaling the weights by κ has a negligible effect on the output. Therefore, we can consider the effect of the weight decay term, $\frac{1}{2}\lambda_1 \|\boldsymbol{\theta}\|_2^2$, independent of the cross-entropy loss. Because we are using the stochastic gradient descent (SGD) optimizer with an initial parameter θ_0, and learning rate η, the update by the weight decay proceeds as follows:

$$\theta_1 = \theta_0 - \eta\lambda_1\theta_0 = (1 - \eta\lambda_1)\theta_0 \tag{4}$$

$$\theta_2 = (1 - \eta\lambda_1)\theta_1 = (1 - \eta\lambda_1)^2\theta_0 \tag{5}$$

$$\vdots$$

$$\theta_{kN_1} = (1 - \eta\lambda_1)^{kN_1}\theta_0. \tag{6}$$

If we train another network with N_2 labeled samples, the weight θ_{kN_2} becomes $\theta_{kN_2} = (1 - \eta\lambda_2)^{kN_2}\theta_0$. For an identical effect of the weight decay regularization on the networks, we have the following:

$$(1 - \eta\lambda_2)^{kN_2}\theta_0 = (1 - \eta\lambda_1)^{kN_1}\theta_0 \tag{7}$$

$$\lambda_2 = \frac{1}{\eta}\left\{1 - (1 - \eta\lambda_1)^{\frac{N_1}{N_2}}\right\} \tag{8}$$

$$\approx \frac{1}{\eta}\left\{1 - \left(1 - \frac{N_1}{N_2}\eta\lambda_1\right)\right\} \tag{9}$$

$$= \frac{N_1}{N_2}\lambda_1. \tag{10}$$

In Eq. (9), we only approximate the first two terms from the binomial expansion, because η and λ are much smaller than 1. This result shows that when training a CNN with batch normalization, reducing the weight decay inversely proportional to the number of data can approximately have the same effect on the weight. Therefore, we set λ_0 during the initial round and reduce it to a value inversely proportional to the number of data from the second round onward. In addition, because the initial parameters are assumed to be the same when deriving the equation, the model should be randomly initialized during every round. Note that the weight values do not have to be exactly the same, but they only need to be initialized to a distribution of equal size. If we initialize the model using the model trained in the previous round, the effect of the weight decay will be more significant than desired because the weight is already reduced by the weight decay during the previous round.

3.3   Knowledge Distillation

If we re-initialize the model during every round and train from scratch, the information learned by the previous model f_{t-1} is only used to select a new sample and form $\mathcal{D}_t^L$; it is not applied to train the new model f_t. Some previous studies have initialized f_t with f_{t-1} to employ previously learned information[21, 31,40,46,49]. However, we found that, without re-initialization, the effect of the weight decay will be so large that the performance will decrease, even if the same weight decay scheduling is used. This is consistent with the findings of Hu *et al.* [13]. We discuss this in more detail in Sect. 5.1.

As an alternative to initializing f_t to f_{t-1}, we propose a transfer of knowledge of f_{t-1} to f_t using a knowledge distillation technique. We follow the knowledge distillation proposed by Hinton *et al.* [11]. In the first round, we train the model without a teacher network. From the second round onward, we train the student model f_t by distilling knowledge from the teacher model f_{t-1}. We experimented using two cases: distilling all $\mathcal{D}_t^L$ and distilling only $\mathcal{D}_{t-1}^L$ that the teacher model previously used for training. For the former, the total loss $\mathcal{L}_t$ used to train the student model, f_t, is as follows:

$$\mathcal{L}_t^{KD1} = \frac{1-\alpha}{|\mathcal{D}_t^L|} \sum_{x \in \mathcal{D}_t^L} \mathcal{L}_{CE}\left(y, \sigma\left(z_t(x)\right)\right)$$

$$+ \frac{\alpha T^2}{|\mathcal{D}_t^L|} \sum_{x \in \mathcal{D}_t^L} \mathcal{L}_{KL}\left(\sigma\left(\frac{z_{t-1}(x)}{T}\right), \sigma\left(\frac{z_t(x)}{T}\right)\right) + \frac{1}{2}\lambda_t \|\theta\|_2^2$$

(11)

where z_t is the logits output by the network f_t, T is the temperature, σ is the softmax function, $\mathcal{L}_{KL}$ is the Kullback Leibler (KL) divergence, and $|\cdot|$ represents the cardinality, the latter of which is as follows:

$$\mathcal{L}_t^{KD2} = \frac{1-\alpha}{|\mathcal{D}_t^L|} \sum_{x \in \mathcal{D}_t^L} \mathcal{L}_{CE}\left(y, \sigma\left(z_t(x)\right)\right)$$

$$+ \frac{\alpha T^2}{|\mathcal{D}_{t-1}^L|} \sum_{x \in \mathcal{D}_{t-1}^L} \mathcal{L}_{KL}\left(\sigma\left(\frac{z_{t-1}(x)}{T}\right), \sigma\left(\frac{z_t(x)}{T}\right)\right) + \frac{1}{2}\lambda_t \|\theta\|_2^2.$$

(12)

The overall framework for knowledge distillation is the same as that of [11]. However, Hinton *et al.* [11] focused on compressing and speeding up the model by transferring knowledge of a larger model to a smaller model. By contrast, our goal was to identify knowledge distillation from the teacher model, which shows a reduced performance and has a low effective complexity. Note that reducing the KL divergence with a lower performing teacher can interfere with the training and cause a performance degradation as compared to when training alone without teacher.

4 Experiments

In this section, we first verify the method of adjusting a weight decay inversely proportional to the number of training data (Sect. 4.1). We also evaluated the proposed active learning method on the MNIST [25], CIFAR-10, and CIFAR-100 [23] datasets using CNNs of various architectures (Sect. 4.2–4.4).

Comparison Targets. We initialize a labeled dataset $\mathcal{D}_0^L$ through random sampling. For each method, we repeat the same experiment five times with different initially labeled images. In addition, for a fair comparison, all methods use the same random seed for each of the five experiments. We consider three acquisition methods for comparison:

- Random indicates a random sampling regardless of the active learning method.
- Entropy is the most frequently compared method in active learning [2,6,37, 49]. We use entropy for all of our methods because the acquisition function is not our focus.

Table 1. Accuracy (%) of (a) 5-layer CNN with various fixed weight decays on the MNIST dataset where the number of training data varies from 200 to 10,000 and (b) Resnet18 with various fixed weight decays on the CIFAR-10 dataset where the number of training data varies from 1,000 to 50,000.

(a) MNIST

WD	\multicolumn{6}{c}{Number of labeled images}
	200	500	1k	2k	5k	10k
0.2	92.37	94.86	95.64	95.81	93.84	94.50
0.1	**92.46**	95.75	96.75	96.94	96.67	96.82
0.04	91.82	**96.30**	97.12	97.68	98.17	98.26
0.02	91.00	96.03	**97.29**	97.96	98.54	98.71
0.01	89.97	95.06	97.25	**98.03**	98.58	98.94
0.004	89.94	94.50	96.70	97.91	**98.70**	98.97
0.002	89.25	94.25	96.42	97.63	98.60	**98.98**
0.001	89.67	94.18	96.17	97.45	98.54	98.90

(b) CIFAR-10

WD	\multicolumn{6}{c}{Number of labeled images}
	1k	2k	5k	10k	20k	50k
0.02	52.44	54.25	33.03	19.58	17.66	10.00
0.01	**62.84**	71.80	75.83	74.60	71.91	61.75
0.005	58.46	**73.93**	81.50	84.06	83.47	83.37
0.002	54.12	70.83	**83.15**	87.54	90.42	92.05
0.001	53.30	67.63	83.05	**88.26**	92.00	94.48
0.0005	52.1	65.34	81.37	88.13	**92.23**	95.18
0.0002	49.47	63.56	79.23	86.56	91.39	**95.26**
0.0001	50.18	64.06	78.50	85.76	90.91	94.84

- In LL [49], samples that are expected to have the highest loss are selected using the loss prediction module. To the best of our knowledge, this method achieves a state-of-the-art performance on the CIFAR-10 dataset.

We also consider distilling all $\mathcal{D}_t^L$ and distilling only $\mathcal{D}_{t-1}^L$ learned by the teacher, which we denote as KD1 and KD2, respectively.

4.1 Results for Weight Decay vs the Number of Data

Table 1 shows the test accuracy (%) of the networks according to the fixed weight decay at each number of labeled training data. We use a 5-layer CNN for MNIST, and Resnet18 for the CIFAR-10 dataset. The implementation details are described in Sects. 4.2 and 4.3. For each number of data, bold values represent the highest accuracy; the corresponding weight decay decreases inversely proportional to the number of data. The more data we have, the weaker the regularizer we need to ensure that the model can learn a sufficient amount of information. If the strong weight decay of the first round is maintained in the subsequent rounds, the performance deteriorates. The optimal weight decay changes depending on the number of data. Thus, to reach the target performance with the minimum number of data, it is necessary to continuously adjust the optimal weight decay. For this reason, we propose a scheduling weight decay; a fixed weight decay is unsuitable for active learning.

4.2 Results for Active Learning on MNIST

Implementation Details. For the MNIST dataset, we use a 5-layer CNN, which is composed of four convolutional layers followed by stride-2 max pooling and the last fully connected layer. Each convolutional layer has 32, 64, 64, and 64 channels. Following [9], we used three consecutive operations for the convolutional layers: a 3×3 convolution with a stride of 1 without padding, batch

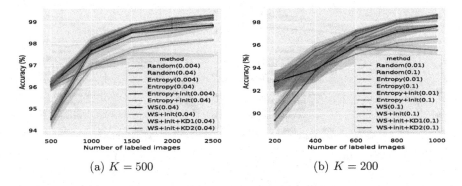

(a) $K = 500$ (b) $K = 200$

Fig. 1. Performance comparison on MNIST

normalization [16], and a rectified linear unit (ReLU) [7]. For all methods, we train models for 100 epochs with the initial learning rate 0.01 decayed by a factor of 0.1 at 50 epochs and use no data augmentation. The batch size is set to 32. For distillation, we use an α of 0.5 and T of 6. We test five rounds and sample K images every round. The CNN is trained using $5K$ data during the final round. We use two budget settings, i.e., $K = 500$ and $K = 200$, for the experiments.

Results. Figure 1 shows the results. For a fixed weight decay, the value in parentheses for each method represents the weight decay value. For the weight decay scheduling method, which we note as WS, the number in parentheses represents the initial value. The method of random re-initialization in each round is denoted by init. Shaded areas represent 95% confidence intervals by performing 1000 bootstrap resampling. During the initial round, the methods with WS show outstanding performance because of their well-tuned weight decay. As the weight decay decreases, the performance gap is reduced. When the number of labeled images is 2,500, Entorpy(0.004) and Entorpy+init(0.004) show 99.12% and 99.17% respectively. WS+init+KD1 and WS+init+KD2 show 99.27% and 99.29% respectively, and they outperform all the other methods regardless of labeling budget. The two distillation methods show similar performance and there is no significant difference in trend.

4.3   Results for Active Learning on CIFAR-10

Implementation Details. For the CIFAR-10 dataset, we use Resnet18 [9] and Densenet100 [14]. For Resnet18, we train the models for 350 epochs with an initial learning rate 0.1 decayed by factor of 0.1 at epochs 150 and 250. The batch size is set to 128. For Densenet100, we train for 300 epochs with an initial learning rate 0.1 decayed by factor 0.1 at epochs 150 and 225. The batch size is set to 64. We use the standard augmentation setting such as resizing, cropping, and flipping for both architectures. For distillation, we use an α of 0.5 and T of 6. We test ten rounds and sample K images every round. The CNN is trained

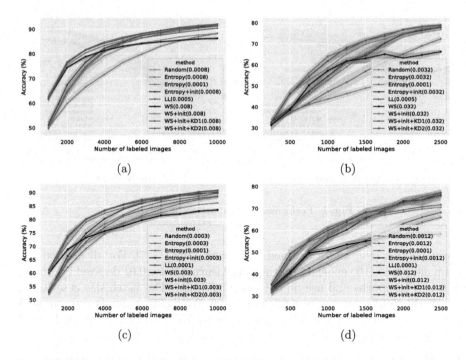

Fig. 2. Performance comparison on CIFAR-10: (a) Resnet18, $K = 1000$, (b) Resnet18, $K = 250$, (c) Densenet100, $K = 1000$, and (d) Densenet100, $K = 250$

with $10K$ data during the final round. We experiment on two budget settings, i.e., $K = 1000$ and $K = 250$.

Results. Except for Entropy(0.0001) and LL, the methods are set to have the same weight decay during the last round. If we set the weight decay of Entropy to the same initial value of the WS method, the CNN does not converge as the round proceeds. This occurs because an excessive weight decay interferes with the model training. Here, 0.0001 is the value used in the original paper on both Resnet [9] and Densenet [14]. For the LL method [49], we also follow the weight decay value from the original paper.

Figure 2 shows the results. In Fig. 2 (a), WS+init (0.008) and Entropy+init (0.0008) are 91.68% and 91.51%, respectively, during the last round. In addition, in Fig. 2 (c), WS+init (0.003) and Entropy+init (0.0003) are 89.96% and 90.43% respectively during the last round. Note that the WS+init and Entropy+init methods have the same weight decay value during the last round. Nevertheless, the performance of WS+init is better than that of Entropy+init for all four cases. This shows that, although the same acquisition function is used, a well-tuned CNN can select more informative samples. Therefore, appropriately scheduling the weight decay in each round seems important for the sampling, as well as for the performance of the current model. In addition, by simply adjusting the weight

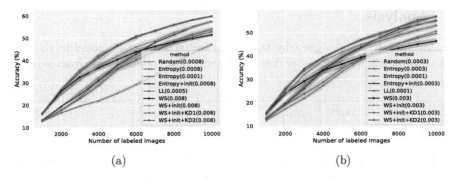

Fig. 3. Performance comparison on CIFAR-100 for $K = 1000$: (a) Resnet18, and (b) Densenet100

decay and applying a random initialization on each round, Entropy+init(0.0008) shows a better performance than LL(0.0005).

In Fig. 2 (d), Random achieves a better performance than Entropy during the early stage. During the third round, Random (0.0012) and Entropy (0.0012) achieve rates of 51.37% and 49.31% respectively. However, during the last round, Entropy (0.0012) shows a better performance. It appears that, if the number of training data is too small, applying only difficult samples hinders the training.

In most cases, initializing with a pre-trained model from the previous round degrades the performance. In particular, WS suffers from a significant degradation in the performance. We discuss this phenomenon in Sect. 5.1.

4.4   Results for Active Learning on CIFAR-100

Implementation Details. For the CIFAR-100 dataset, we also use Resnet18 [9] and Densenet100 [14]. All settings are the same as with CIFAR-10, except for K. If we set K to 250, there might be some classes that are not selected during the initial round, and thus we only experiment using $K = 1000$.

Results. Figure 3 shows the result. There is an inconsistency in the behaviors of the methods when switching from CIFAR-10 to CIFAR-100. During the last round, WS+init (0.008) and Entropy+init (0.0008) achieve results of 57.38% and 57.43%, respectively (Fig. 3 (a)). In addition, WS+init (0.003) and Entropy+init (0.0003) achieve rates of 54.88% and 55.23%, respectively (Fig. 3 (b)). The accuracy of WS+init is worse than that of Entropy+init during the last round. Even Random shows a better result than Entropy. For the CIFAR-100 dataset, the accuracy of the CNN is low and the number of training data per class is smaller than that of CIFAR-10; and thus it seems that applying only difficult samples hinders the training. However, the best performance is shown when WD scheduling and knowledge distillation methods are used together (WD+init+KD).

5   Analysis

In this section, we analyze why the model initialized to the model in the previous round shows a worse performance than the model trained from scratch.

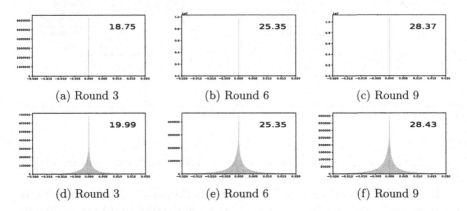

Fig. 4. Histogram of convolutional weights in Resnet18 during the active learning process. The number in each sub-figure represents the L2-norm of the weights: (a)–(c) WS(0.008), and (d)–(f) WS+init(0.008)

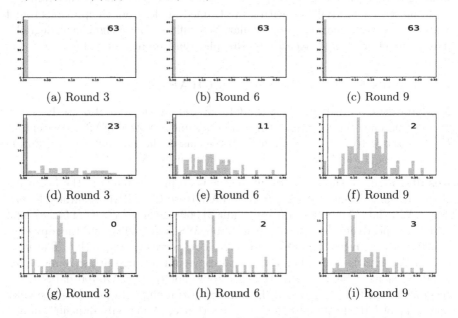

Fig. 5. Histogram of batch norm weights in ResNet18 during the active learning process. We show only the first batch norm weights of the first residual block. The red vertical line represents the average divided by 10 and the number in each sub-figure represent the number of weights that are less than the average divided by 10: (a)–(c) WS(0.008), (d)–(f) WS+init(0.008), and (g)–(i) Entropy+init(0.0008)

(Sect. 5.1). We also analyze how the distillation parameter α affects the distillation performance (Sect. 5.2).

5.1 Effect of Weight Decay

Figure 4 shows a histogram of the weights in convolutional layers of ResNet18. The number in each sub-figure represents the L2-norm of the weights. The experimental setting is the same as that in Sect. 4.3 where the labeling budget K is 1000. The upper column represents the result when the model is initialized to the model trained in the previous round (WD(0.008)), and the lower column represents the results when the model is randomly initialized during every round (WD+init(0.008)). The norm of WS(0.008) is similar to the norm of WS+init(0.008) even though most of the weights are distributed close to 0. In other words, the norm of the weight is very unevenly distributed, and a small number of weights with large norms have much more influence in determining the overall prediction. This implies that the actual network capacity is smaller than the actual number of parameters. This may cause the performance degradation.

With a similar analysis, we found that another reason for the performance degradation is the weight decay causing the weight of the batch norm to be sparse, resulting in a reduced number of effective convolutional channels.[1] In other words, although the weight of the convolution is re-scaled at the batch norm layer, the weight decay can still limit the complexity by reducing the number of actual filters. Figure 5 shows a histogram of batch the norm weights for the following three cases: WS(0.008), WS+init(0.008), and Entropy+init(0.0008). The figure shows the absolute value of the weights and we show only the first batch norm weights of the first residual block. The red vertical line in each sub-figure represents the average divided by 10 and the number in each sub-figure are the number of weights that are smaller than the mean of the weights divided by 10. In the case of WS(0.008), the impact of the weight decay is great, thereby causing most of the weight of the batch norm to be close to zero (Fig. 5 (a)–(c)), as well as causing a reduction in the weight of the convolutional filter. Weight values that are much smaller than the average value refer to the corresponding filter, which has little impact on the prediction, thereby reducing the actual complexity of the model. Therefore, a model without random re-initialization is significantly affected by the weight decay, and the poor performance appears to be due to the low complexity. By contrast, in the case of WS+init(0.008), the number of batch norm weights at near zero decreases (Fig. 5 (d)–(f)) as the round proceeds and the number of training data increases. Through weight decay scheduling, the model is trained to have a small number of effective channels when the number of training data is small, and to have a large number of effective channels when the number of training data is large. If random initialization is applied during every round but weight decay scheduling is not applied, we can

---

[1] This analysis is applicable when weight decay is applied to the batch norm weight. Pytorch implementation of several CNN models also gives weight decay to the weight of the batch norm.

Table 2. Performance comparison according to knowledge distillation parameter α on CIFAR-10 using Resnet18

Method	α	Number of labeled images									
		1000	2000	3000	4000	5000	6000	7000	8000	9000	10000
WS+init	·	62.17	75.40	80.40	83.33	85.45	87.60	88.93	90.03	91.07	91.68
WS+init+KD1	0.1	**62.57**	75.49	80.74	83.72	85.71	87.70	89.46	90.26	91.28	91.90
WS+init+KD1	0.5	61.27	**76.24**	**81.85**	**84.77**	86.91	88.07	89.52	90.57	91.53	91.96
WS+init+KD1	0.9	62.55	74.18	80.88	84.59	**86.99**	**88.60**	**89.81**	**90.86**	**91.66**	**92.18**

see that the number of effective channels does not increase in proportion to the number of data (Fig. 5 (g)–(i)). In other words, regardless of the round, the effective capacity is similar, which means that an over-fitting can occur during the early rounds.

5.2   Effect of Knowledge Distillation Parameter

In this section, we analyze how the knowledge distillation parameter affects the performance. In our experiments, the temperature T does not show a significant difference in performance. We compare the performance when α changes. Table 2 shows the result. A small α gives more weight to the cross-entropy loss and a large α gives more weight to the distillation loss. In the early rounds during which the difference in performance between the teacher and student is large, it is better to provide similar weights to the cross-entropy and distillation loss. However, because the training proceeds and the performances of the teacher and student are similar, a large α value shows a better performance. For a small α, there is no significant performance improvement even after knowledge distillation.

6   Conclusion

We showed that reducing the weight decay inversely proportional to the number of data is simple but effective, and we that even a low-performance teacher can distill knowledge in an active learning setting. The experimental results show that our method outperforms the baseline methods. In addition, we presented a new perspective of how the weight decay regularizes a convolutional neural network, which contains a batch normalization layer. The weight decay provides a regularization effect by limiting the number of parameters and effective channels of the convolutional layers.

References

1. Ba, J., Caruana, R.: Do deep nets really need to be deep? In: Advances in Neural Information Processing Systems, pp. 2654–2662 (2014)

2. Beluch, W.H., Genewein, T., Nürnberger, A., Köhler, J.M.: The power of ensembles for active learning in image classification. In: Proceedings of the IEEE Conference on Computer Vision and Pattern Recognition, pp. 9368–9377 (2018)
3. Cubuk, E.D., Zoph, B., Shlens, J., Le, Q.V.: Randaugment: practical automated data augmentation with a reduced search space. arXiv preprint arXiv:1909.13719 (2019)
4. Elhamifar, E., Sapiro, G., Yang, A., Shankar Sasrty, S.: A convex optimization framework for active learning. In: Proceedings of the IEEE International Conference on Computer Vision, pp. 209–216 (2013)
5. Freytag, A., Rodner, E., Denzler, J.: Selecting influential examples: active learning with expected model output changes. In: Fleet, D., Pajdla, T., Schiele, B., Tuytelaars, T. (eds.) ECCV 2014. LNCS, vol. 8692, pp. 562–577. Springer, Cham (2014). https://doi.org/10.1007/978-3-319-10593-2_37
6. Gal, Y., Islam, R., Ghahramani, Z.: Deep Bayesian active learning with image data. In: Proceedings of the 34th International Conference on Machine Learning, vol. 70, pp. 1183–1192. JMLR.org (2017)
7. Glorot, X., Bordes, A., Bengio, Y.: Deep sparse rectifier neural networks. In: Proceedings of the Fourteenth International Conference on Artificial Intelligence and Statistics, pp. 315–323 (2011)
8. Guo, Y.: Active instance sampling via matrix partition. In: Advances in Neural Information Processing Systems, pp. 802–810 (2010)
9. He, K., Zhang, X., Ren, S., Sun, J.: Deep residual learning for image recognition. In: Proceedings of the IEEE Conference on Computer Vision and Pattern Recognition, pp. 770–778 (2016)
10. Heo, B., Kim, J., Yun, S., Park, H., Kwak, N., Choi, J.Y.: A comprehensive overhaul of feature distillation. In: Proceedings of the IEEE International Conference on Computer Vision, pp. 1921–1930 (2019)
11. Hinton, G., Vinyals, O., Dean, J.: Distilling the knowledge in a neural network. arXiv preprint arXiv:1503.02531 (2015)
12. Hoffer, E., Banner, R., Golan, I., Soudry, D.: Norm matters: efficient and accurate normalization schemes in deep networks. In: Advances in Neural Information Processing Systems, pp. 2160–2170 (2018)
13. Hu, P., Lipton, Z.C., Anandkumar, A., Ramanan, D.: Active learning with partial feedback. arXiv preprint arXiv:1802.07427 (2018)
14. Huang, G., Liu, Z., Van Der Maaten, L., Weinberger, K.Q.: Densely connected convolutional networks. In: Proceedings of the IEEE Conference on Computer Vision and Pattern Recognition, pp. 4700–4708 (2017)
15. Huang, G., Sun, Yu., Liu, Z., Sedra, D., Weinberger, K.Q.: Deep networks with stochastic depth. In: Leibe, B., Matas, J., Sebe, N., Welling, M. (eds.) ECCV 2016. LNCS, vol. 9908, pp. 646–661. Springer, Cham (2016). https://doi.org/10.1007/978-3-319-46493-0_39
16. Ioffe, S., Szegedy, C.: Batch normalization: accelerating deep network training by reducing internal covariate shift. arXiv preprint arXiv:1502.03167 (2015)
17. Jastrzębski, S., et al.: Three factors influencing minima in SGD. arXiv preprint arXiv:1711.04623 (2017)
18. Joshi, A.J., Porikli, F., Papanikolopoulos, N.: Multi-class active learning for image classification. In: 2009 IEEE Conference on Computer Vision and Pattern Recognition, pp. 2372–2379. IEEE (2009)
19. Käding, C., Rodner, E., Freytag, A., Denzler, J.: Active and continuous exploration with deep neural networks and expected model output changes. arXiv preprint arXiv:1612.06129 (2016)

20. Keskar, N.S., Mudigere, D., Nocedal, J., Smelyanskiy, M., Tang, P.T.P.: On large-batch training for deep learning: generalization gap and sharp minima. arXiv preprint arXiv:1609.04836 (2016)
21. Khodabandeh, M., Deng, Z., Ibrahim, M.S., Satoh, S., Mori, G.: Active learning for structured prediction from partially labeled data. arXiv preprint arXiv:1706.02342 (2017)
22. Kim, J., Park, S., Kwak, N.: Paraphrasing complex network: network compression via factor transfer. In: Advances in Neural Information Processing Systems, pp. 2760–2769 (2018)
23. Krizhevsky, A., Hinton, G., et al.: Learning multiple layers of features from tiny images (2009)
24. Krogh, A., Hertz, J.A.: A simple weight decay can improve generalization. In: Advances in Neural Information Processing Systems, pp. 950–957 (1992)
25. LeCun, Y., Bottou, L., Bengio, Y., Haffner, P.: Gradient-based learning applied to document recognition. Proc. IEEE **86**(11), 2278–2324 (1998)
26. Lewis, D.D., Catlett, J.: Heterogeneous uncertainty sampling for supervised learning. In: Machine Learning Proceedings 1994, pp. 148–156. Elsevier (1994)
27. Lewis, D.D., Gale, W.A.: A sequential algorithm for training text classifiers. In: Croft, B.W., van Rijsbergen, C.J. (eds.) SIGIR 1994, pp. 3–12. Springer, London (1994). https://doi.org/10.1007/978-1-4471-2099-5_1
28. Li, H., Xu, Z., Taylor, G., Studer, C., Goldstein, T.: Visualizing the loss landscape of neural nets. In: Advances in Neural Information Processing Systems, pp. 6389–6399 (2018)
29. Long, J., Shelhamer, E., Darrell, T.: Fully convolutional networks for semantic segmentation. In: Proceedings of the IEEE Conference on Computer Vision and Pattern Recognition, pp. 3431–3440 (2015)
30. Luo, W., Schwing, A., Urtasun, R.: Latent structured active learning. In: Advances in Neural Information Processing Systems, pp. 728–736 (2013)
31. Meyer, B.J., Drummond, T.: The importance of metric learning for robotic vision: open set recognition and active learning. In: 2019 International Conference on Robotics and Automation (ICRA), pp. 2924–2931. IEEE (2019)
32. Neelakantan, A., et al.: Adding gradient noise improves learning for very deep networks. arXiv preprint arXiv:1511.06807 (2015)
33. Nguyen, H.T., Smeulders, A.: Active learning using pre-clustering. In: Proceedings of the Twenty-First International Conference on Machine Learning, p. 79 (2004)
34. Ren, S., He, K., Girshick, R., Sun, J.: Faster R-CNN: towards real-time object detection with region proposal networks. In: Advances in Neural Information Processing Systems, pp. 91–99 (2015)
35. Romero, A., Ballas, N., Kahou, S.E., Chassang, A., Gatta, C., Bengio, Y.: Fitnets: hints for thin deep nets. arXiv preprint arXiv:1412.6550 (2014)
36. Roth, D., Small, K.: Margin-based active learning for structured output spaces. In: Fürnkranz, J., Scheffer, T., Spiliopoulou, M. (eds.) ECML 2006. LNCS (LNAI), vol. 4212, pp. 413–424. Springer, Heidelberg (2006). https://doi.org/10.1007/11871842_40
37. Sener, O., Savarese, S.: Active learning for convolutional neural networks: a core-set approach. arXiv preprint arXiv:1708.00489 (2017)
38. Settles, B., Craven, M.: An analysis of active learning strategies for sequence labeling tasks. In: Proceedings of the 2008 Conference on Empirical Methods in Natural Language Processing, pp. 1070–1079 (2008)
39. Settles, B., Craven, M., Ray, S.: Multiple-instance active learning. In: Advances in Neural Information Processing Systems, pp. 1289–1296 (2008)

40. Shen, Y., Yun, H., Lipton, Z.C., Kronrod, Y., Anandkumar, A.: Deep active learning for named entity recognition. arXiv preprint arXiv:1707.05928 (2017)
41. Simonyan, K., Zisserman, A.: Very deep convolutional networks for large-scale image recognition. arXiv preprint arXiv:1409.1556 (2014)
42. Srivastava, N., Hinton, G., Krizhevsky, A., Sutskever, I., Salakhutdinov, R.: Dropout: a simple way to prevent neural networks from overfitting. J. Mach. Learn. Res. **15**(1), 1929–1958 (2014)
43. Tong, S., Koller, D.: Support vector machine active learning with applications to text classification. J. Mach. Learn. Res. **2**(Nov), 45–66 (2001)
44. Van Laarhoven, T.: L2 regularization versus batch and weight normalization. arXiv preprint arXiv:1706.05350 (2017)
45. Vijayanarasimhan, S., Grauman, K.: Large-scale live active learning: Training object detectors with crawled data and crowds. Int. J. Comput. Vision **108**(1–2), 97–114 (2014)
46. Wang, K., Zhang, D., Li, Y., Zhang, R., Lin, L.: Cost-effective active learning for deep image classification. IEEE Trans. Circuits Syst. Video Technol. **27**(12), 2591–2600 (2016)
47. Xie, Q., Hovy, E., Luong, M.T., Le, Q.V.: Self-training with noisy student improves imagenet classification. arXiv preprint arXiv:1911.04252 (2019)
48. Yim, J., Joo, D., Bae, J., Kim, J.: A gift from knowledge distillation: fast optimization, network minimization and transfer learning. In: Proceedings of the IEEE Conference on Computer Vision and Pattern Recognition, pp. 4133–4141 (2017)
49. Yoo, D., Kweon, I.S.: Learning loss for active learning. In: Proceedings of the IEEE Conference on Computer Vision and Pattern Recognition, pp. 93–102 (2019)
50. Zagoruyko, S., Komodakis, N.: Paying more attention to attention: Improving the performance of convolutional neural networks via attention transfer. arXiv preprint arXiv:1612.03928 (2016)
51. Zhang, G., Wang, C., Xu, B., Grosse, R.: Three mechanisms of weight decay regularization. arXiv preprint arXiv:1810.12281 (2018)

HMQ: Hardware Friendly Mixed Precision Quantization Block for CNNs

Hai Victor Habi, Roy H. Jennings$^{(\boxtimes)}$, and Arnon Netzer

Sony Semiconductor Israel, Hod HaSharon, Israel
{hai.habi,roy.jennings,arnon.netzer}@sony.com

Abstract. Recent work in network quantization produced state-of-the-art results using mixed precision quantization. An imperative requirement for many efficient edge device hardware implementations is that their quantizers are uniform and with power-of-two thresholds. In this work, we introduce the Hardware Friendly Mixed Precision Quantization Block (HMQ) in order to meet this requirement. The HMQ is a mixed precision quantization block that repurposes the Gumbel-Softmax estimator into a smooth estimator of a pair of quantization parameters, namely, bit-width and threshold. HMQs use this to search over a finite space of quantization schemes. Empirically, we apply HMQs to quantize classification models trained on CIFAR10 and ImageNet. For ImageNet, we quantize four different architectures and show that, in spite of the added restrictions to our quantization scheme, we achieve competitive and, in some cases, state-of-the-art results.

Keywords: Deep neural networks · Model compression · Quantization

1 Introduction

In recent years, convolutional neural networks (CNNs) produced state-of-the-art results in many computer vision tasks including image classification [14,17,21,22, 38,39], object detection [29,36,40], semantic segmentation [31,37], etc. Deploying these models on embedded devices is a challenging task due to limitations on available memory, computational power and power consumption. Many works address these issues using different methods. These include pruning [16,45,47], efficient neural architecture design [14,21,24,38], hardware and CNN co-design [14,20,43] and quantization [6,13,15,23,24,46].

In this work, we focus on quantization, an approach in which the model is compressed by reducing the bit-widths of weights and activations. Besides reduction in memory requirements, depending on the specific hardware, quantization usually also results in the reduction of both latency and power consumption. The challenge of quantization is to reduce the model size without compromising its performance. For high compression rates, this is usually achieved by *fine-tuning*

The code of this work is available in https://github.com/sony-si/ai-research.

© Springer Nature Switzerland AG 2020
A. Vedaldi et al. (Eds.): ECCV 2020, LNCS 12371, pp. 448–463, 2020.
https://doi.org/10.1007/978-3-030-58574-7_27

a pre-trained model for quantization. In addition, recent work in quantization focused on making quantizers more *hardware friendly* (amenable to deployment on embedded devices) by restricting quantization schemes to be: per-tensor, uniform, symmetric and with thresholds that are powers of two [24,41].

Recently, *mixed-precision* quantization was studied in [12,41,42,44]. In these works, the bit-widths of weights and activations are not equal across the model and are learned during some optimization process. In [42], reinforcement learning is used, which requires the training of an agent that decides the bit-width of each layer. In [44], neural architecture search is used, which implies duplication of nodes in the network and that the size of the model grows proportionally to the size of the search space of bit-widths. Both of these methods limit the bit-width search space because of their computational cost. In [12], the bit-widths are not searched during training, but rather, this method relies on the relationship between the layer's Hessian and its sensitivity to quantization.

An imperative requirement for many efficient edge device hardware implementations is that their quantizers are symmetric, uniform and with power-of-two thresholds (see [24]). This removes the cost of special handling of zero points and real value scale factors. In this work, we introduce a novel quantization block we call the *Hardware Friendly Mixed Precision Quantization Block* (HMQ) that is designed to search over a finite set of quantization schemes that meet this requirement. HMQs utilize the Gumbel-Softmax estimator [25] in order to optimize over a categorical distribution whose samples correspond to quantization scheme parameters.

We propose a method, based on HMQs, in which both the bit-width and the quantizer's threshold are searched simultaneously. We present state-of-the-art results on MobileNetV1, MobileNetV2 and ResNet-50 in most cases, in spite of the hardware friendly restriction applied to the quantization schemes. Additionally, we present the first (that we know of) mixed precision quantization results of EfficientNet-B0. In particular, our contributions are the following:

- We introduce HMQ, a novel, hardware friendly, mixed precision quantization block which enables a simple and efficient search for quantization parameters.
- We present an optimization method, based on HMQs, for mixed precision quantization in which we search simultaneously for both the bit-width and the threshold of each quantizer.
- We present competitive and, in most cases, state-of-the-art results using our method to quantize ResNet-50, EfficientNet-B0, MobileNetV1 and MobileNetV2 classification models on ImageNet.

2   Related Work

Quantization lies within an active area of research that tries to reduce memory requirements, power consumption and inference latencies of neural networks. These works use techniques such as pruning, efficient network architectures and distillation (see e.g. [7,14,15,18,19,21,30,34,35,38,39,48]). Quantization is a key method in this area of research which compresses and accelerates the model by reducing the number of bits used to represent model weights and activations.

Quantization. Quantization techniques can be roughly divided into two families: post-training quantization techniques and quantization-aware training techniques. In post-training quantization techniques, a trained model is quantized without retraining the model (see e.g. [1,5]). In quantization-aware training techniques, a model undergoes an optimization process during which the model is quantized. A key challenge in this area of research, is to compress the model without significant degradation to its accuracy. Post-training techniques suffer from a higher degradation to accuracy, especially for high compression rates.

Since the gradient of quantization functions is zero almost everywhere, most quantization-aware training techniques use the straight through estimator (STE) [4] for the estimation of the gradients of quantization functions. These techniques mostly differ in their choice of quantizers, the quantizers' parametrization (thresholds, bit-widths, step size, etc.) and their training procedure. During training, the network weights are usually stored in full-precision and are quantized before they are used in feed-forward. The full-precision weights are then updated via back-propagation. Uniform quantizers are an important family of quantizers that have several benefits from a hardware point-of-view (see e.g. [13,24,41]). Non-uniform quantizers include clustering, logarithmic quantization and others (see e.g. [3,33,46,49]).

Mixed Precision. Recent works on quantization produced state-of-the-art results using mixed precision quantization, that is, quantization in which the bit-widths are not constant across the model (weights and activations). In [42], reinforcement learning is used to determine bit-widths. In [12], second order gradient information is used to determine bit-widths. More precisely, the bit-widths are selected by ordering the network layers using this information. In [41], bit-widths are determined by learnable parameters whose gradients are estimated using STE. This work focuses on the choice of parametrization of the quantizers and shows that the threshold (dynamic range) and step size are preferable over parametrizations that use bit-widths explicitly.

In [44], a mixed precision quantization-aware training technique is proposed where the bit-widths search is converted into a network architecture search (based on [27]). More precisely, in this solution, the search space of all possible quantization schemes is, in fact, a search for a sub-graph in a super-net. The disadvantage of this approach, is that the size of the super net grows substantially with every optional quantization edge/path that is added to the super net. In practice, this limits, the architecture search space. Moreover, this work deals with bit-widths and thresholds as two separate problems where thresholds follow the solution in [8].

3   The HMQ Block

The *Hardware Friendly Mixed Precision Quantization Block* (HMQ) is a network block that learns, via standard SGD, a uniform and symmetric quantization scheme. The scheme is parametrized by a pair (t, b) of threshold t and bit-width b. During training, an HMQ searches for (t, b) over a finite space $T \times B \subseteq \mathbb{R}^+ \times \mathbb{N}$. In this work, we make HMQs "hardware friendly" by also forcing their thresholds to be powers of two. We do this by restricting

$$T = \{2^M, 2^{M-1}, \dots, 2^{M-8}\} \tag{1}$$

where $M \in \mathbb{Z}$ is an integer we configure per HMQ (see Sect. 4).

The step size Δ of a uniform quantization scheme is the (constant) gap between any two adjacent quantization points. Δ is parametrized by (t, b) differently for a signed quantizer, where $\Delta = \frac{2t}{2^b}$, and an unsigned one, where $\Delta = \frac{t}{2^b}$. Note that Δ ties the bit-width and threshold values into a single parameter but Δ is not uniquely defined by them. The definition of the quantizer that we use in this work is similar to the one in [24]. The signed version Q^s of a quantizer of an HMQ is defined as follows:

$$Q^s(x, \Delta, t) = \text{clip}\left(\Delta \cdot \left\lceil \frac{x}{\Delta} \right\rfloor, -(t - \Delta), t\right) \tag{2}$$

where $\text{clip}(x, a, b) = \min(\max(x, a), b)$ and $\lceil x \rfloor$ is the rounding function. Similarly, the unsigned version Q^{us} is defined as follows:

$$Q^{us}(x, \Delta, t) = \text{clip}\left(\Delta \cdot \left\lceil \frac{x}{\Delta} \right\rfloor, 0, t - \Delta\right). \tag{3}$$

In the rest of this section we assume that the quantizer Q of an HMQ is signed, but it applies to both signed and unsigned quantizers.

In order to search over a discrete set, the HMQ represents each pair in $T \times B$ as a sample of a categorical random variable of the Gumbel-Softmax estimator (see [25,32]). This enables the HMQ to search for a pair of threshold and bit-width. The Gumbel-Softmax is a continuous distribution on the simplex that approximates categorical samples. In our case, we use this approximation as a joint discreet probability distribution of thresholds and bit-widths $P_{T,B}(T=t, B=b|g_{t,b})$ on $T \times B$:

$$P_{T,B}(T = t, B = b|g_{t,b}) = \frac{\exp(\frac{\log(\hat{\pi}_{t,b}) + g_{t,b}}{\tau})}{\sum_{t' \in T} \sum_{b' \in B} \exp(\frac{\log(\hat{\pi}_{t',b'}) + g_{t',b'}}{\tau})} \tag{4}$$

where $\hat{\pi}$ is a matrix of class probabilities whose entries $\hat{\pi}_{t,b}$ correspond to pairs in $T \times B$, $g_{t,b}$ are random i.i.d. variables drawn from Gumbel$(0, 1)$ and $\tau > 0$ is a softmax temperature value. We define $\hat{\pi} = \text{softmax}(\pi)$ where π is a matrix of trainable parameters $\pi_{t,b}$. This guarantees that the matrix $\hat{\pi}$ forms a categorical distribution.

The quantizers in Eqs. 2 and 3 are well defined for any two real numbers $\Delta > 0$ and $t > 0$. During training, in feed forward, we sample $g_{t,b}$ and use these samples in the approximation $P_{T,B}$ of a categorical choice. The HMQ parametrizes its quantizer $Q(x, \hat{\Delta}, \hat{t})$ using an **expected step size** $\hat{\Delta}$ and an **expected threshold** $\hat{t}$ that are defined as follows:

$$\hat{\Delta} = \sum_{t \in T} \sum_{b \in B} P_{T,B}(T = t, B = b|g_{t,b}) \cdot \Delta_{t,b}, \tag{5}$$

$$\hat{t} = \sum_{t \in \mathrm{T}} P_{\mathrm{T}}(\mathrm{T} = t) \cdot t \qquad (6)$$

where $P_{\mathrm{T}}(\mathrm{T} = t) = \sum_{b' \in \mathrm{B}} P_{\mathrm{T},\mathrm{B}}(\mathrm{T} = t, \mathrm{B} = b'|g_{t,b'})$ is the marginal distribution of thresholds and $\Delta_{t,b} = \frac{2t}{2^b}$.

In back-propagation, the gradients of rounding operations are estimated using the STE and the rest of the module, i.e. Eqs. 4, 5 and 6, are differentiable. This implies that the HMQ smoothly updates the parameters $\pi_{t,b}$ which, in turn, smoothly updates the estimated bit-width and threshold values of the quantization scheme. Figure 1 shows examples of HMQ quantization schemes during training. During inference, the HMQ's quantizer is parametrized by the pair (t, b) that corresponds to the maximal parameter $\pi_{t,b}$.

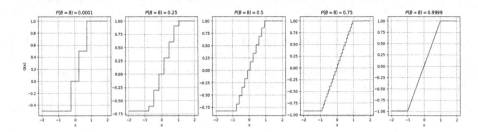

Fig. 1. The quantization scheme of an HMQ with $\mathrm{T} = \{1\}$ and $\mathrm{B} = \{2, 8\}$ for different approximations of the Gumbel-Softmax. Transition from 2-bit quantization $P(\mathrm{B} = 8) \approx 0$ (left) to 8-bit quantization $P(\mathrm{B} = 8) \approx 1$ (right)

Note that the temperature parameter τ of the Gumbel-Softmax estimator in Eq. 4 has a dual effect during training. As it approaches zero, in addition to approximating a categorical choice of a unique pair $(t, b) \in \mathrm{T} \times \mathrm{B}$, smaller values of τ also incur a larger variance of gradients which adds instability to the optimization process. This problem is mitigated by annealing τ (see Sect. 4).

4   Optimization Process

In this section, we present a fine-tuning optimization process that is applied to a full precision, 32-bit floating point, pre-trained model after adding HMQs. Throughout this work, we use the term model weights (or simply weights) to refer to all of the trainable model weights, *not including* the HMQ parameters. We denote by Θ, the set of weight tensors to be quantized; by $\mathcal{X}$, the set of activation tensors to be quantized and by Π, the set of HMQ parameters. Given a tensor T, we use the notation $|T|$ to denote the number of entries in T.

From a high level view, our optimization process consists of two phases. In the first phase, we simultaneously train both the model weights and the HMQ parameters. We take different approaches for quantization of weights and activations. These are described in Sects. 4.1 and 4.2. We split the first phase into cycles with an equal number of epochs each. In each cycle of the first phase, we reset the Gumbel-Softmax temperature τ in Eq. 4 and anneal it till the end of the cycle. In the second phase of the optimization process, we fine-tune only the model weights. During this phase, similarly to HMQs behaviour during inference, the quantizer of every HMQ is parametrized by the pair (t, b) that corresponds to the maximal parameter $\pi_{t,b}$ that was learnt in the first phase.

4.1 Weight Compression

Let θ be an input tensor of weights to be quantized by some HMQ. We define the set of thresholds T in the search space T × B of the HMQ by setting M in Eq. 1 to be $\min\{M : 2^M \geq \max(\text{abs}(\theta)), i \in \mathbb{Z}\}$. The values in B are different per experiment (see Sect. 5).

Denote by Π_w the subset of Π containing all of the parameters of HMQs quantizing weights. The expected weight compression rate, induced by the values of Π_w is defined as follows:

$$\tilde{R}(\Pi_w) = \frac{32 \sum_{\theta_i \in \Theta} |\theta_i|}{\sum_{\theta_i \in \Theta} \mathbb{E}[b_i] |\theta_i|} \tag{7}$$

where θ_i is a tensor of weights and $\mathbb{E}[b_i] = \sum_{b \in B} b \cdot P_B^i(B = b)$ is the expected bit-width of θ_i, where P_B^i is the bit-width marginal distribution in the Gumbel-Softmax estimation of the corresponding HMQ. In other words, assuming that all of the model weights are quantized by HMQs, the numerator is the memory requirement of the weights of the model before compression and the denominator is the expected memory requirement during training.

During the first phase of the optimization process, we optimize the model with respect to a target weight compression rate $R_w \in \mathbb{R}^+$, by minimizing (via standard SGD) the following loss function:

$$J(\Theta, \Pi) = J_{task}(\Theta, \Pi) + \lambda (J_w(\Pi_w))^2 \tag{8}$$

where $J_{task}(\Theta, \Pi)$ is the original, task specific loss, e.g. the standard cross entropy loss, $J_w(\Pi_w)$ is a loss with respect to the target compression rate R_w and λ is a hyper-parameter that control the trade-off between the two. We define $J_w(\Pi_w)$ as follows:

$$J_w(\Pi_w) = \frac{\max(0, R_w - \tilde{R}(\Pi_w))}{R_w}. \tag{9}$$

In practice, we gradually increase the target compression rate R_w during the first few cycles in the first phase of our optimization process. This approach of gradual training of quantization is widely used, see e.g. [2,10,12,49]. In most cases, layers are gradually added to the training process whereas in our process we gradually decrease the bit-width across the whole model, albeit, with mixed precision.

By the definition of $J_w(\Pi_w)$, if the target weight compression rate is met during training, i.e. $\tilde{R}(\Pi_w) > R_w$, then the gradients of $J_w(\Pi_w)$ with respect to the parameters in Π_w are zero and the task specific loss function determines the gradients alone. In our experiments, the actual compression obtained by using a specific target compression R_w depends on the hyper-parameter λ and the sensitivity of the architecture to quantization.

4.2   Activations Compression

We define T in the search space T × B of an HMQ that quantizes a tensor of activations similarly to HMQs quantizing weights. We set $M \in \mathbb{Z}$ in Eq. 1 to be minimum such that 2^M is greater or equal than the maximum absolute value of an activation of the pre-trained model over the entire training set.

The objective of activations compression is to fit any single activations tensor, after quantization, into a given size of memory $\overline{U} \in \mathbb{N}$ (number of bits). This objective is inspired by the one in [41] and is especially useful for DNNs in which the operators in the computational graph induce a path graph, i.e. the operators are executed sequentially. We define the target activations compression rate R_a to be

$$R_a = \frac{32 \cdot \max_{X_i \in \mathcal{X}} |X_i|}{\overline{U}} \tag{10}$$

where X_i are the activation tensors to be quantized. Note that $\overline{U}$ implies the precise (maximum) number of bits $b(X)$ of every feature map $X \in \mathcal{X}$:

$$b(X) = \left\lfloor \frac{\overline{U}}{|X|} \right\rfloor. \tag{11}$$

We assume that $b(X) \geq 1$ for every feature map $X \in \mathcal{X}$ (otherwise, the requirement cannot be met and $\overline{U}$ should be increased) and fix B = $\{\min(b(X), 8)\}$ in the search space of the HMQ that corresponds to X. Note that this method can also be applied to models with a more complex computational graph, such as ResNet, by applying Eq. 11 to blocks instead of single feature maps. Note also, that by definition, the maximum bit-width of *every activation* is 8. We can therefore assume that $R_a \geq 4$.

Here, the bit-widths of every feature map is determined by Eq. 11. This is in contrast to the approach in [41] (for activations compression) and our approach for weight compression in Sect. 4.1, where the choice of bit-widths is a result of an SGD minimization process. This allows a more direct approach for the quantization of activations in which we gradually increase R_a, during the first few cycles in the first phase of the optimization process. In this approach, while activation HMQs learn the thresholds, their bit-widths are implied by R_a. This, in contrast to adding a target activations compression component to the loss, both guarantees that the target compression of activations is obtained and simplifies the loss function of the optimization process.

5   Experimental Results

In this section, we present results using HMQs to quantize various classification models. As proof of concept, we first quantize ResNet-18 [17] trained on CIFAR-10 [26]. For the more challenging ImageNet [9] classification task, we present results quantizing ResNet-50 [17], EfficientNet-B0 [39], MobileNetV1 [21] and MobileNetV2 [38].

In all of our experiments, we perform our fine-tuning process on a full precision, 32-bit floating point, pre-trained model in which an HMQ is added after every weight and every activation tensor per layer, *including the first and last layers*, namely the input convolutional layer and the fully connected layer. The parameters $\pi_{t,b}$ of every HMQ are initialized as a categorical distribution in which the parameter that corresponds to the pair of the maximum threshold with the maximum bit-width is initialized to 0.9 and 0.1 is uniformly distributed between the rest of the parameters. The bit-width set B in the search space of HMQs is set differently for CIFAR-10 and ImageNet (see Sects. 5.1 and 5.2).

Note that in all of the experiments, in all of the weight HMQs, the maximal bit-width is 8 (similarly to activation HMQs). This implies that $\tilde{R}(\Pi_w) \geq 4$ throughout the fine-tuning process. The optimizer that we use in all of our experiments is RAdam [28] with $\beta_1 = 0.9$ and $\beta_2 = 0.999$. We use different learning rates for the model weights and the HMQ parameters. The data augmentation that we use during fine-tuning is the same as the one used to train the base models.

The entire process is split into two phases, as described in Sect. 4. The first phase consists of 30 epochs split into 6 cycles of 5 epochs each. In each cycle, the temperature τ in Eq. 4, is reset and annealed till the end of the cycle. We update the temperature every N steps within a cycle, where $25 \cdot N$ is the number of steps in a single epoch. The annealing function that we use is similar to the one in [25]:

$$\tau(i) = \max(e^{-ir}, 0.5) \tag{12}$$

where i is the training step (within the cycle) and $r = e^{-2}$. The second phase, in which only weights are fine-tuned, consists of 20 epochs.

As mentioned in Sect. 4, during the first phase, we gradually increase both the weight and activation target compression rates R_w and R_a, respectively. Both target compression rates are initialized to a minimum compression of 4 (implying 8-bit quantization) and are increased, in equally sized steps, at the beginning of each cycle, during the first 4 cycles.

Figure 2 shows an example of the behaviour of the expected weight compression rate $\tilde{R}(\Pi_w)$ and the actual weight compression rate (implied by the quantization schemes corresponding to the maximum parameters $\pi_{t,b}$) during training, as the value of the target weight compression rate R_w is increased and the temperature τ of the Gumbel-Softmax is annealed in every cycle. Note how the difference between the expected and the actual compression rate values decreases with τ, in every cycle (as to be expected by the Gumbel-Softmax estimator's behaviour).

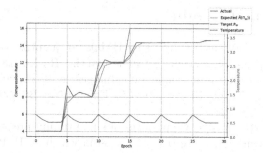

Fig. 2. Expected and actual weight compression rates during fine-tuning of MobileNetV2 on ImageNet as the target compression rate and τ are updated

We compare our results with those of other quantization methods based on top1 accuracy vs. compression metrics. We use weight compression rate (WCR) to denote the ratio between the total size (number of bits) of the weights in the original model and the total size of the weights in the compressed model. Activation compression rate (ACR) denotes the ratio between the size (number of bits) of the largest activation tensor in the original model and its size in the compressed model. As explained in Sect. 4.2, our method guarantees that the size of every single activation tensor in the compressed model is bounded from above by a predetermined value $\overline{U}$.

5.1 ResNet-18 on CIFAR-10

As proof of concept, we use HMQs to quantize a ResNet-18 model that is trained on CIFAR-10 with standard data-augmentation from [17]. Our baseline model has top-1 accuracy of 92.45%. We set $B = \{1, 2, 3, 4, 5, 6, 7, 8\}$ in the search space of HMQs quantizing weights. For activations, B is set according to our method in Sect. 4.2. In all of the experiments in this section, we set $\lambda = 32$ in the loss function in Eq. 8. The learning rate that we use for model weights is 1e-5. For HMQ parameters the learning rate is 1e3. The batch-size that we use is 256.

Figure 3 presents the Pareto frontier of weight compression rate vs. top-1 accuracy for different quantization methods of ResNet-18 on CIFAR-10. In this figure, we show that our method is effective, in comparison to other methods, namely DNAS [44], UNIQ [3], LQ-Nets [46] and HAWQ [12], using different activation compression rates.

We explain our better results, compared to LQ-Nets and UNIQ, in-spite of the higher activation and weight compression rates, by the fact that HMQs take advantage of mixed precision quantization. Compared to DNAS, our method has a much larger search space, since in their method, each quantization scheme is translated into a sub-graph in a super net. Moreover, HMQs tie the bit-width and threshold into a single parameter using Eq. 5. Comparing our method to HAWQ, HAWQ only uses the Hessian information whereas we perform an optimization over the bit-width.

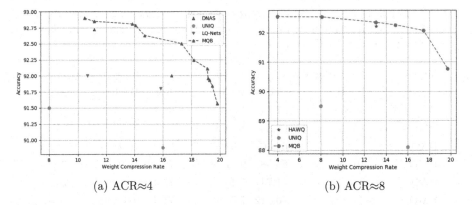

(a) ACR≈4   (b) ACR≈8

Fig. 3. Pareto frontier of weight compression rate vs. top-1 accuracy of ResNet-18 on CIFAR-10 for two Activation Compression Rate (ACR) groups: 4 (Fig. 3a) and 8 (Fig. 3b) compared with different quantization methods

5.2 ImageNet

In this section, we present results using HMQs to quantize several model architectures, namely MobileNetV1 [21], MobileNetV2 [38], ResNet-50 [17] and EfficientNet-B0 [39] trained on the ImageNet [9] classification dataset. In each of these cases, we use the same data augmentation as the one reported in the corresponding paper. Our baseline models have the following top-1 accuracies: MobileNetV1 (70.6), MobileNetV2 (71.88[1]), ResNet-50 (76.15 (see footnote 1)) and EfficientNet-B0 (76.8[2]). In all of the experiments in this section, we set $B = \{2, 3, 4, 5, 6, 7, 8\}$ in the search space of HMQs quantizing weights. For activations, B is set according to our method in Sect. 4.2.

As mentioned above, we use the RAdam optimizer in all of our experiments and we use different learning rates for the model weights and the HMQ parameters. For model weights, we use the following learning rates: MobileNetV1 (5e-6), MobileNetV2 (2.5e-6), ResNet-50 (2.5e-6) and EfficientNet-B0 (2.5e-6). For HMQ parameters, the learning rate is equal to the learning rate of the weights multiplied by 1e3. The batch-sizes that we use are: MobileNetV1 (256), MobileNetV2 (128), ResNet-50 (64) and EfficientNet-B0 (128).

Weight Quantization. In Table 1, we present our results using HMQs to quantize MobileNetV1, MobileNetV2 and ResNet-50. In all of our experiments in this table, we set $R_a = 4$ in Eq. 10, implying (single precision) 8-bit quantization of all of the activations. We split the comparison in this table into three compression rate groups: ∼16, ∼10 and ∼8 in rows 1–2, 3–4 and 5–6, respectively.

Note that our method excels in very high compression rates. Moreover, this is in spite of the fact that an HMQ uses uniform quantization and its thresholds are

---

[1] Torchvision models (https://pytorch.org/docs/stable/torchvision/models.html).
[2] https://github.com/tensorflow/tpu/tree/master/models/official/efficientnet.

Table 1. Weight Compression Rate (WCR) vs. top-1 accuracy (Acc) of MobileNetV1, MobileNetV2 and ResNet-50 on ImageNet. R_w is the target weight compression rate in Eq. 9 that was used for fine-tuning

Method	MobileNetV1		MobileNetV2		ResNet-50	
	WCR	Acc	WCR	Acc	WCR	Acc
HAQ [42]	14.8	57.14	14.07	66.75	15.47	70.63
HMQ (ours)	14.15 $(R_w = 16)$	68.36	14.4$(R_w = 16)$	65.7	15.7 $(R_w = 16)$	75
HAQ	10.22	67.66	9.68	70.9	10.41	75.30
HMQ	10.68 $(R_w = 11)$	69.88	9.71 $(R_w = 10)$	70.12	10.9 $(R_w = 11)$	76.1
HAQ	7.8	71.74	7.46	71.47	8	76.14
HMQ	7.6 $(R_w = 8)$	70.912	7.7 $(R_w = 8)$	71.4	9.01 $(R_w = 9)$	76.3

Table 2. Comparing Activation Compression Rate (ACR), Weight Compression Rate (WCR) and top-1 accuracy (Acc) of MobileNetV2 and ResNet-50 on ImageNet using different mixed precision quantization techniques. Under ACR: for HAWQ and HAWQ-V2, 8 means that the maximum compression obtained for a single activation tensor is 8. For DQ and HMQ, 8 means that the compression of the largest activation tensor is 8

(a) MobileNetV2

Method	ACR	WCR	Acc
DQ [41]	8.05	8.53	69.74
HMQ$(R_w = 8)$ (ours)	8	8.05	70.9

(b) ResNet-50

Method	ACR	WCR	Acc
HAWQ [42]	8	12.28	75.3
HAWQ-V2 [11]	8	12.24	75.7
HMQ$(R_w = 13)$ (ours)	8	13.1	75.45

limited to powers of two whereas HAQ uses k-means quantization. We explain our better results by the fact that in HAQ, the bit-widths are the product of a reinforcement learning agent and the thresholds are determined by the statistics, opposed to HMQs, where they are the product of SGD optimization.

Weight and Activation Quantization. In Table 2, we compare mixed precision quantization methods in which both weights and activations are quantized. In all of the experiments in this table, the activation compression rate is equal to 8. This means (with some variation between methods) that the smallest number of bits used to quantize activations is equal to 4. This table shows that our method achieves on par results with other mixed precision methods, in spite of the restrictions on the quantization schemes of HMQs. We believe that this is due to the fact that, during training, there is no gradient mismatch for HMQ parameters (see Eqs. 5 and 6). In other words, HMQs allow smooth propagation of gradients. Additionally, HMQs tie each pair of bit-width and threshold in their search space with a single trainable parameter (opposed to determining the two separately).

Table 3. Weight Compression Rate (WCR) vs. top-1 accuracy (Acc) of EfficientNetB0 on ImageNet using HMQ quantization. An Activation Compression Rate (ACR) of 4 means single precision 8-bit quantization of activation tensors. R_w is the target weight compression rate that was used during fine-tuning

ACR	R_w	WCR	Acc
4	4	4	76.4
	8	8.05	76
	12	11.97	74.6
	16	14.87	71.54

EfficientNet. In Table 3, we present results quantizing EfficientNet-B0 using HMQs and in Fig. 4, we use the Pareto frontier of accuracy vs model size to summarize our results on all four of the models that were mentioned in this section.

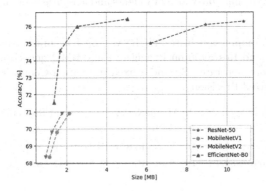

Fig. 4. Pareto frontier of top-1 accuracy vs. model size of MobileNetV1, MobileNetV2, ResNet-50 and EfficientNet-B0 quantization by HMQ

Additional Results. In Fig. 5, we present an example of the final bit-widths of weights and activations in MobileNetV1 quantized by HMQ. This figure implies that point-wise convolutions are less sensitive to quantization, compared to their corresponding depth-wise convolutions. Moreover, it seems that deeper layers are also less sensitive to quantization. Note that the bit-widths of activations in Fig. 5b are not a result of fine-tuning but are pre-determined by the target activation compression, as described in Sect. 4.2. In Table 4, we present additional results using HMQs to quantize models trained on ImageNet. This table extends the results in Table 1, here, both weights and activations are quantized using HMQs.

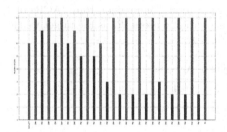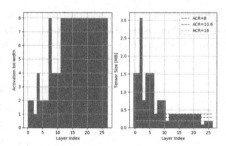

(a) Weight bit-widths. The red bars correspond to the first and last layers of the network. The green bars correspond to depth-wise convolution layers and the blue bars correspond to point-wise convolution layers

(b) Activation bit-widths. The right figure shows the sizes, per layer, of 32-bit activation tensors. The dashed horizontal lines show the maximal tensor size implied by three target activation compression rates. The left figure shows the bit-widths, per layer (corresponding the right figure), at compression rate equal to 16

Fig. 5. Example of the final bit-width of weights and activations in MobileNetV1 quantized by HMQ

Table 4. Weight Compression Rate (WCR) vs. top-1 accuracy (Acc) of MobileNet-V1, MobileNet-V2 and ResNet50 on ImageNet using HMQ quantization with various target weight compression rates R_w and a fixed Activation Compression Rate (ACR) of 8. MP means Mixed Precision

(a) MobileNetV1

R_w	ACR	WCR	Acc
16	8MP	14.638MP	67.9
11	8MP	10.709MP	69.3

(b) MobileNetV2

R_w	ACR	WCR	Acc
16	8MP	14.8MP	64.47
10	8MP	10MP	69.9

(c) ResNet50

R_w	ACR	WCR	Acc
16	8MP	15.45MP	74.5
11	8MP	11.1MP	75.73

6   Conclusions

In this work, we introduced the HMQ, a novel quantization block that can be applied to weights and activations. The HMQ repurposes the Gumbel-Softmax estimator in order to smoothly search over a finite set of uniform and symmetric activation schemes. We presented a standard SGD fine-tuning process, based on HMQs, for mixed precision quantization that achieves state-of-the-art results in accuracy vs. compression for various networks. Both the model weights and the quantization parameters are trained during this process. This method can facilitate different hardware requirements, including memory, power and inference speed by configuring the HMQ's search space and the loss function. Empirically, we experimented with two image classification datasets: CIFAR-10 and ImageNet. For ImageNet, we presented state-of-the-art results on MobileNetV1, MobileNetV2 and ResNet-50 in most cases. Additionally, we presented the first (that we know of) quantization results of EfficientNet-B0.

Acknowledgments. We would like to thank Idit Diamant and Oranit Dror for many helpful discussions and suggestions.

References

1. Banner, R., Nahshan, Y., Soudry, D.: Post training 4-bit quantization of convolutional networks for rapid-deployment. In: Advances in Neural Information Processing Systems, pp. 7948–7956 (2019)
2. Baskin, C., et al.: Nice: noise injection and clamping estimation for neural network quantization. arXiv preprint arXiv:1810.00162 (2018)
3. Baskin, C., et al.: Uniq: uniform noise injection for non-uniform quantization of neural networks. arXiv preprint arXiv:1804.10969 (2018)
4. Bengio, Y., Léonard, N., Courville, A.: Estimating or propagating gradients through stochastic neurons for conditional computation. arXiv preprint arXiv:1308.3432 (2013)
5. Cai, Y., et al.: Zeroq: a novel zero shot quantization framework. In: Proceedings of the IEEE/CVF Conference on Computer Vision and Pattern Recognition, pp. 13169–13178 (2020)
6. Cai, Z., He, X., Sun, J., Vasconcelos, N.: Deep learning with low precision by half-wave gaussian quantization. In: Proceedings of the IEEE Conference on Computer Vision and Pattern Recognition, pp. 5918–5926 (2017)
7. Chen, G., Choi, W., Yu, X., Han, T., Chandraker, M.: Learning efficient object detection models with knowledge distillation. In: Advances in Neural Information Processing Systems, pp. 742–751 (2017)
8. Choi, J., Wang, Z., Venkataramani, S., Chuang, P.I.J., Srinivasan, V., Gopalakrishnan, K.: Pact: parameterized clipping activation for quantized neural networks. arXiv preprint arXiv:1805.06085 (2018)
9. Deng, J., Dong, W., Socher, R., Li, L.J., Li, K., Fei-Fei, L.: Imagenet: a large-scale hierarchical image database. In: 2009 IEEE Conference on Computer Vision and Pattern Recognition, pp. 248–255. IEEE (2009)
10. Dong, Y., Ni, R., Li, J., Chen, Y., Zhu, J., Su, H.: Learning accurate low-bit deep neural networks with stochastic quantization. arXiv preprint arXiv:1708.01001 (2017)
11. Dong, Z., et al.: Hawq-v2: hessian aware trace-weighted quantization of neural networks. arXiv preprint arXiv:1911.03852 (2019)
12. Dong, Z., Yao, Z., Gholami, A., Mahoney, M.W., Keutzer, K.: Hawq: hessian aware quantization of neural networks with mixed-precision. In: Proceedings of the IEEE International Conference on Computer Vision, pp. 293–302 (2019)
13. Esser, S.K., McKinstry, J.L., Bablani, D., Appuswamy, R., Modha, D.S.: Learned step size quantization. arXiv preprint arXiv:1902.08153 (2019)
14. Gholami, A., et al.: Squeezenext: hardware-aware neural network design. In: Proceedings of the IEEE Conference on Computer Vision and Pattern Recognition Workshops, pp. 1638–1647 (2018)
15. Han, S., Mao, H., Dally, W.J.: Deep compression: compressing deep neural networks with pruning, trained quantization and Huffman coding. arXiv preprint arXiv:1510.00149 (2015)
16. Han, S., Pool, J., Tran, J., Dally, W.: Learning both weights and connections for efficient neural network. In: Advances in Neural Information Processing Systems, pp. 1135–1143 (2015)

17. He, K., Zhang, X., Ren, S., Sun, J.: Deep residual learning for image recognition. In: Proceedings of the IEEE Conference on Computer Vision and Pattern Recognition, pp. 770–778 (2016)
18. He, Y., Liu, P., Wang, Z., Hu, Z., Yang, Y.: Filter pruning via geometric median for deep convolutional neural networks acceleration. In: Proceedings of the IEEE Conference on Computer Vision and Pattern Recognition, pp. 4340–4349 (2019)
19. He, Y., Zhang, X., Sun, J.: Channel pruning for accelerating very deep neural networks. In: Proceedings of the IEEE International Conference on Computer Vision, pp. 1389–1397 (2017)
20. Howard, A., et al.: Searching for mobilenetv3. In: Proceedings of the IEEE International Conference on Computer Vision, pp. 1314–1324 (2019)
21. Howard, A.G., et al.: Mobilenets: efficient convolutional neural networks for mobile vision applications. arXiv preprint arXiv:1704.04861 (2017)
22. Hu, J., Shen, L., Sun, G.: Squeeze-and-excitation networks. In: Proceedings of the IEEE Conference on Computer Vision and Pattern Recognition, pp. 7132–7141 (2018)
23. Jacob, B., et al.: Quantization and training of neural networks for efficient integer-arithmetic-only inference. In: Proceedings of the IEEE Conference on Computer Vision and Pattern Recognition, pp. 2704–2713 (2018)
24. Jain, S.R., Gural, A., Wu, M., Dick, C.: Trained quantization thresholds for accurate and efficient fixed-point inference of deep neural networks. arXiv preprint arXiv:1903.08066 (2019)
25. Jang, E., Gu, S., Poole, B.: Categorical reparametrization with gumble-softmax. In: International Conference on Learning Representations (ICLR 2017). OpenReview.net (2017)
26. Krizhevsky, A., Hinton, G., et al.: Learning multiple layers of features from tiny images. Technical report, Citeseer (2009)
27. Liu, H., Simonyan, K., Yang, Y.: DARTS: differentiable architecture search. In: International Conference on Learning Representations (2019). https://openreview.net/forum?id=S1eYHoC5FX
28. Liu, L., et al.: On the variance of the adaptive learning rate and beyond. In: International Conference on Learning Representations (2020). https://openreview.net/forum?id=rkgz2aEKDr
29. Liu, W., et al.: SSD: single shot MultiBox detector. In: Leibe, B., Matas, J., Sebe, N., Welling, M. (eds.) ECCV 2016. LNCS, vol. 9905, pp. 21–37. Springer, Cham (2016). https://doi.org/10.1007/978-3-319-46448-0_2
30. Liu, Z., Li, J., Shen, Z., Huang, G., Yan, S., Zhang, C.: Learning efficient convolutional networks through network slimming. In: Proceedings of the IEEE International Conference on Computer Vision, pp. 2736–2744 (2017)
31. Long, J., Shelhamer, E., Darrell, T.: Fully convolutional networks for semantic segmentation. In: Proceedings of the IEEE Conference on Computer Vision and Pattern Recognition, pp. 3431–3440 (2015)
32. Maddison, C.J., Mnih, A., Teh, Y.W.: The concrete distribution: a continuous relaxation of discrete random variables. In: International Conference on Learning Representations (2017). https://openreview.net/forum?id=S1jE5L5gl
33. Miyashita, D., Lee, E.H., Murmann, B.: Convolutional neural networks using logarithmic data representation. arXiv preprint arXiv:1603.01025 (2016)
34. Molchanov, P., Tyree, S., Karras, T., Aila, T., Kautz, J.: Pruning convolutional neural networks for resource efficient inference. In: International Conference on Learning Representations (2017). https://openreview.net/forum?id=SJGCiw5gl

35. Polino, A., Pascanu, R., Alistarh, D.: Model compression via distillation and quantization. In: International Conference on Learning Representations (2018). https://openreview.net/forum?id=S1XolQbRW

36. Ren, S., He, K., Girshick, R., Sun, J.: Faster R-CNN: towards real-time object detection with region proposal networks. In: Advances in Neural Information Processing Systems, pp. 91–99 (2015)

37. Ronneberger, O., Fischer, P., Brox, T.: U-Net: convolutional networks for biomedical image segmentation. In: Navab, N., Hornegger, J., Wells, W.M., Frangi, A.F. (eds.) MICCAI 2015. LNCS, vol. 9351, pp. 234–241. Springer, Cham (2015). https://doi.org/10.1007/978-3-319-24574-4_28

38. Sandler, M., Howard, A., Zhu, M., Zhmoginov, A., Chen, L.C.: Mobilenetv 2: inverted residuals and linear bottlenecks. In: Proceedings of the IEEE Conference on Computer Vision and Pattern Recognition, pp. 4510–4520 (2018)

39. Tan, M., Le, Q.: Efficientnet: rethinking model scaling for convolutional neural networks. In: International Conference on Machine Learning, pp. 6105–6114 (2019)

40. Tan, M., Pang, R., Le, Q.V.: Efficientdet: scalable and efficient object detection. arXiv preprint arXiv:1911.09070 (2019)

41. Uhlich, S., et al.: Mixed precision DNNS: all you need is a good parametrization. In: International Conference on Learning Representations (2020). https://openreview.net/forum?id=Hyx0slrFvH

42. Wang, K., Liu, Z., Lin, Y., Lin, J., Han, S.: HAQ: hardware-aware automated quantization with mixed precision. In: Proceedings of the IEEE Conference on Computer Vision and Pattern Recognition, pp. 8612–8620 (2019)

43. Wu, B., et al.: Fbnet: hardware-aware efficient convnet design via differentiable neural architecture search. In: Proceedings of the IEEE Conference on Computer Vision and Pattern Recognition, pp. 10734–10742 (2019)

44. Wu, B., Wang, Y., Zhang, P., Tian, Y., Vajda, P., Keutzer, K.: Mixed precision quantization of convnets via differentiable neural architecture search. arXiv preprint arXiv:1812.00090 (2018)

45. Yu, R., et al.: NISP: pruning networks using neuron importance score propagation. In: Proceedings of the IEEE Conference on Computer Vision and Pattern Recognition, pp. 9194–9203 (2018)

46. Zhang, D., Yang, J., Ye, D., Hua, G.: LQ-nets: learned quantization for highly accurate and compact deep neural networks. In: Proceedings of the European Conference on Computer Vision (ECCV), pp. 365–382 (2018)

47. Zhang, T., et al.: A systematic DNN weight pruning framework using alternating direction method of multipliers. In: Proceedings of the European Conference on Computer Vision (ECCV), pp. 184–199 (2018)

48. Zhang, X., Zhou, X., Lin, M., Sun, J.: Shufflenet: an extremely efficient convolutional neural network for mobile devices. In: Proceedings of the IEEE Conference on Computer Vision and Pattern Recognition, pp. 6848–6856 (2018)

49. Zhou, A., Yao, A., Guo, Y., Xu, L., Chen, Y.: Incremental network quantization: towards lossless CNNs with low-precision weights. In: International Conference on Learning Representations (2017). https://openreview.net/forum?id=HyQJ-mclg

Truncated Inference for Latent Variable Optimization Problems: Application to Robust Estimation and Learning

Christopher Zach$^{(\boxtimes)}$ [iD] and Huu Le [iD]

Chalmers University of Technology, Gothenburg, Sweden
{zach,huul}@chalmers.se

Abstract. Optimization problems with an auxiliary latent variable structure in addition to the main model parameters occur frequently in computer vision and machine learning. The additional latent variables make the underlying optimization task expensive, either in terms of memory (by maintaining the latent variables), or in terms of run-time (repeated exact inference of latent variables). We aim to remove the need to maintain the latent variables and propose two formally justified methods, that dynamically adapt the required accuracy of latent variable inference. These methods have applications in large scale robust estimation and in learning energy-based models from labeled data.

Keywords: Majorization-minimization · Latent variable models · Stochastic gradient methods

1 Introduction

In this work[1] we are interested in optimization problems that involve additional latent variables and therefore have the general form,

$$\min_{\theta} \min_{\overline{\mathbf{u}}} \overline{J}(\theta, \overline{\mathbf{u}}) =: \min_{\theta} J(\theta), \tag{1}$$

where θ are the main parameters of interest and $\overline{\mathbf{u}}$ denote the complete set of latent variables. By construction $\overline{J}(\theta, \overline{\mathbf{u}})$ is always an upper bound to the "ideal" objective J. In typical computer vision and machine learning settings the objective function in Eq. 1 has a more explicit structure as follows,

$$\overline{J}(\theta, \overline{\mathbf{u}}) = \frac{1}{N} \sum_{i=1}^{N} \overline{J}_i(\theta, \overline{u}_i), \tag{2}$$

---

[1] This work was partially supported by the Wallenberg AI, Autonomous Systems and Software Program (WASP) funded by the Knut and Alice Wallenberg Foundation.

Electronic supplementary material The online version of this chapter (https://doi.org/10.1007/978-3-030-58574-7_28) contains supplementary material, which is available to authorized users.

© Springer Nature Switzerland AG 2020
A. Vedaldi et al. (Eds.): ECCV 2020, LNCS 12371, pp. 464–480, 2020.
https://doi.org/10.1007/978-3-030-58574-7_28

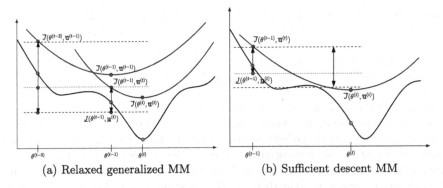

(a) Relaxed generalized MM   (b) Sufficient descent MM

Fig. 1. Illustration of the principle behind our proposed majorization-minimization variants. Left: relaxed generalized MM requires that the current duality gap at $\theta^{(t-1)}$ (between dotted and lower dashed lines) is at most a given fraction of the gap induced by the previous upper bound (between dashed lines). Right: sufficient descent MM requires that the current duality gap (between upper dashed and dotted lines) is at most a given fraction of a guaranteed decrease (between dashed lines).

where the index i ranges over e.g. training samples or over observed measurements. Each $\bar{u}_i$ corresponds to the inferred (optimized) latent variable for each term, and $\bar{u}$ is the entire collection of latent variables, i.e. $\bar{u} = (\bar{u}_1, \ldots, \bar{u}_N)$. Examples for this problem class are models for (structured) prediction with latent variables [10,32], supervised learning of energy-based models [20,30] (in both scenarios N labeled training samples are provided), and robust estimation using explicit confidence weights [11,35] (where N corresponds to the number of sensor measurements).

We focus on the setting when N is very large, and maintaining the values of $\bar{u}_i$ for all N terms in memory is intractable. In particular, storing the entire vector $\bar{u}$ is undesirable when the dimensionality of each $\bar{u}_i$ is large. In one of our applications $\bar{u}_i$ represents the entire set of unit activations in a deep neural network, and therefore $\bar{u}_i$ is high-dimensional in such cases.

Observe that neither $J(\theta)$ nor $\nabla J(\theta)$ are easy to evaluate directly. By using a variable projection approach, the loss J in Eq. 2 can in principle be optimized using a "state-less" gradient method,

$$\nabla J(\theta) = \frac{1}{N} \sum_{i=1}^{N} \nabla_\theta \bar{J}_i(\theta; \bar{u}_i^*(\theta)) \tag{3}$$

where $\bar{u}_i^*(\theta) = \arg\min_{\bar{u}_i} \bar{J}_i(\theta; \bar{u}_i)$. Usually determining $\bar{u}_i^*(\theta)$ requires itself an iterative minimization method, hence exactly solving $\arg\min_{\bar{u}_i} \bar{J}_i(\theta; \bar{u}_i)$ renders the computation of $\nabla J(\theta)$ expensive in terms of run-time (e.g. it requires solving a quadratic program in the application presented in Sect. 6.2). On the other hand, by using Eq. 3 there is no need to explicitly keep track of the values $\bar{u}_i^*(\theta)$ (as long as determining the minimizer $\bar{u}_i^*(\theta)$ is "cold-started", i.e. run from scratch). Note that Eq. 3 is only correct for stationary points $\overline{u}_i^*(\theta)$. For inexact minimizers $\overline{u}_i'(\theta) \approx \overline{u}_i^*(\theta)$ the second term in the total derivative,

$$\frac{d\overline{J}_i(\theta; \overline{u}_i'(\theta))}{d\theta} = \frac{\partial \overline{J}_i(\theta; \overline{u}_i)}{\partial \theta}\bigg|_{\overline{u}_i = \overline{u}_i'(\theta)} + \frac{\partial \overline{J}_i(\theta; \overline{u}_i)}{\partial \overline{u}_i}\bigg|_{\overline{u}_i = \overline{u}_i'(\theta)} \cdot \frac{\partial \overline{u}_i'(\theta)}{\partial \theta} \qquad (4)$$

does not vanish, and the often complicated dependence of $\overline{u}_i'(\theta)$ on θ must be explicitly modeled (e.g. by "un-rolling" the iterations of a chosen minimization method yielding $\overline{u}_i'(\theta)$). Otherwise, the estimate for $\nabla_\theta J$ will be biased, and minimization of J will be eventually hindered. Nevertheless, we are interested in such inexact solutions $\overline{u}_i'(\theta)$, that can be obtained in finite time (without warm-starting from a previous estimate), and the question is how close $\overline{u}_i'(\theta)$ has to be to $\overline{u}_i^*(\theta)$ in order to still successfully minimize Eq. 2. Hence, we are interested in algorithms that have the following properties:

1. returns a minimizer (or in general a stationary point) of Eq. 2,
2. does not require storing $\overline{\mathbf{u}} = (\overline{u}_1, \dots, \overline{u}_N)$ between updates of θ,
3. and is optionally applicable in a stochastic or incremental setting.

We propose two algorithms to minimize Eq. 2, that leverage inexact minimization for the latent variables $\overline{u}_i$ (described in Sects. 4 and 5). Our analysis applies to the setting, when each $\overline{J}_i(\theta; \overline{u}_i)$ is convex in $\overline{u}_i$. The basic principle is illustrated in Fig. 1: in iteration t of each of the proposed algorithms, a new upper bound parametrized by $\overline{u}^{(t)}$ is found, that guarantees a sufficient improvement over the previous upper bound according to a respective criterion. This criterion either uses past objective values (Fig. 1(a)) or current gradient information (Fig. 1(b)). In Sect. 6 we demonstrate the proposed algorithms for large scale robust estimation instances and for training a layered energy-based model.

2   Related Work

Our proposed methods are based on the majorization-minimization (MM) principle [12,14], which generalizes methods such as expectation-maximization [7,21,28] and the convex-concave procedure [33]. A large number of variants and extensions of MM exist. The notion of a (global) majorizer is relaxed in [17,19], where also a stochastic variant termed MISO (Minimization by Incremental Surrogate Optimization) is proposed. The memory consumption of MISO is $O(ND)$, as sufficient information about each term in Eq. 2 has to be maintained. Here D is the size of the data necessary to represent a surrogate function (i.e. $D = \dim(\overline{u}_i)$). The first-order surrogates introduced in [17] are required to agree with the gradient at the current solution, which is relaxed to asymptotic agreement in [31].

The first of our proposed methods is based on the "generalized MM" method presented in [22], which relaxes the "touching condition" in MM by a looser diminishing gap criterion. Our second method is also a variant of MM, but it is stated such that it easily transfers to a stochastic optimization setting. Since our surrogate functions are only upper bounds of the true objective, the gradient induced by a mini-batch will be biased even at the current solution. This is different from e.g. [37], where noisy surrogate functions are considered, which have unbiased function values and gradients at the current solution. The *stochastic majorization-minimization* [18] and the *stochastic successive upper-bound minimization* (SSUM, [24]) algorithms average information from the surrogate functions gathered during the iterations. Thus, for Lipschitz gradient (quadratic) surrogates, the memory requirements reduce to $O(D)$ (compared to $O(ND)$ for the original MISO). Several gradient-based methods that are able to cope with noisy gradient oracles are presented in [3,8,9] with different assumptions on the objective function and on the gradient oracle,

Majorization-minimization is strongly connected to minimization by alternation (AM). In [6] a "5-point" property is proposed, that is a sufficient condition for AM to converge to a global minimum. Byrne [4] points out that AM (and therefore MM) fall into a larger class of algorithms termed "sequential unconstrained minimization algorithm" (SUMMA).

Contrastive losses such as the one employed in Sect. 6.2 occur often when model parameters of latent variable models are estimated from training data (e.g. [20,32]). Such losses can be interpreted either as finite-difference approximations to implicit differentiation [26,30,36], as surrogates for the misclassification loss [32], or as approximations to the cross-entropy loss [36]. Thus, contrastive losses are an alternative to the exact gradient computation in bilevel optimization problems (e.g. using the Pineda-Almeida method [2,23,25]).

3   Minimization Using Families of Upper Bounds

General Setting. Let $J : \mathbb{R}^d \to \mathbb{R}_{\geq 0}$ be a differentiable objective function, that is bounded from below (we choose w.l.o.g. $J(\theta) \geq 0$ for all θ). The task is to determine a minimizer θ^* of J (or stationary point in general).[2] We assume that J is difficult to evaluate directly (e.g. J has the form of Eq. 2), but a differentiable function $\overline{J}(\theta; \overline{u})$ taking an additional argument $\overline{u} \in \mathcal{U} \subseteq \mathbb{R}^D$ is available that has the following properties:

1. $\overline{J}(\theta, \overline{u}) \geq J(\theta)$ for all $\theta \in \mathbb{R}^d$ and $\overline{u} \in \mathcal{U}$,
2. $\overline{J}(\theta, \overline{u})$ is convex in $\overline{u}$ and satisfies strong duality,
3. $J(\theta) = \min_{\overline{u} \in \mathcal{U}} \overline{J}(\theta, \overline{u})$.

This means that $\overline{J}(\theta, \overline{u})$ is a family of upper bounds of J parametrized by $\overline{u} \in \mathcal{U}$, and the target objective $J(\theta)$ is given as the lower envelope of $\{\overline{J}(\theta, \overline{u}) : \overline{u} \in \mathcal{U}\}$. The second condition implies that optimizing the upper bound for a given θ is relatively easy (but in general it still will require an iterative algorithm). As pointed out in Sect. 1, $\overline{u}$ may be very high-dimensional and expensive to maintain in memory. We will absorb the constraint $\overline{u} \in \mathcal{U}$ into $\overline{J}$ and therefore drop this condition in the following.

---

[2] By convergence to a stationary point we mean that the gradient converges to 0. Convergence of solution is difficult to obtain in the general non-convex setting.

The Baseline Algorithm: Minimization by Alternation. The straightforward method to minimize J in Eq. 1/Eq. 2 is by alternating minimization (AM) w.r.t. θ and $\bar{u}$. The downside of AM is, that the entire set of latent variables represented by $\bar{u}$ has to be stored while updating θ. This can be intractable in machine learning applications when $N \gg 1$ and $D \gg 1$.

4   Relaxed Generalized Majorization-Minimization

Our first proposed method extends the generalized majorization-minimization method [22] to the case when computation of J is expensive. Majorization-minimzation (MM, [12,14]) maintains a sequence of solutions $(\theta^{(t)})_{t=1}^{T}$ and latent variables $(\bar{u}^{(t)})_{t=1}^{T}$ such that

$$\theta^{(t-1)} \leftarrow \arg\min_{\theta} \bar{J}(\theta, \bar{u}^{(t-1)}) \qquad \bar{u}^{(t)} \leftarrow \arg\min_{\bar{u}} \bar{J}(\theta^{(t-1)}, \bar{u}). \qquad (5)$$

Standard MM requires the following "touching condition" to be satisfied,

$$\bar{J}(\theta^{(t-1)}, \bar{u}^{(t)}) = J(\theta^{(t-1)}). \qquad (6)$$

It should be clear that a standard MM approach is equivalent to the alternating minimization baseline algorithm. In most applications of MM, the domain of the latent variables defining the upper bound is identical to the domain for θ.

Generalized MM relaxes the touching condition to the following one,

$$\bar{J}(\theta^{(t-1)}, \bar{u}^{(t)}) \leq \eta J(\theta^{(t-1)}) + (1-\eta)\bar{J}(\theta^{(t-1)}, \bar{u}^{(t-1)})$$
$$= \bar{J}(\theta^{(t-1)}, \bar{u}^{(t-1)}) - \eta\left(\bar{J}(\theta^{(t-1)}, \bar{u}^{(t-1)}) - J(\theta^{(t-1)})\right), \qquad (7)$$

where $\eta \in (0,1)$ is a user-specified parameter. By construction the gap $d_t := \bar{J}(\theta^{(t-1)}, \bar{u}^{(t-1)}) - J(\theta^{(t-1)})$ is non-negative. The above condition means that $\bar{u}^{(t)}$ has to be chosen such that the new objective value $\bar{J}(\theta^{(t)}, \bar{u}^{(t)})$ is guaranteed to sufficiently improve over the current upper bound $\bar{J}(\theta^{(t-1)}, \bar{u}^{(t-1)})$,

$$\bar{J}(\theta^{(t)}, \bar{u}^{(t)}) \leq \bar{J}(\theta^{(t-1)}, \bar{u}^{(t)}) \leq \bar{J}(\theta^{(t-1)}, \bar{u}^{(t-1)}) - \eta d_t.$$

It is shown that the sequence $\lim_{t\to\infty} d_t \to 0$, i.e. asymptotically the true cost J is optimized. Since generalized MM decreases the upper bound less aggressively than standard MM, it has an improved empirical ability to reach better local minima in highly non-convex problems [22].

Generalized MM is not directly applicable in our setting, as J is assumed not to be available (or at least expensive to compute, which is exactly we aim to avoid). By leveraging convex duality we have a lower bound for $\underline{J}(\theta, \underline{u}) \leq J(\theta)$ available. Hence, we modify the generalized MM approach by replacing $J(\theta^{(t-1)})$ with a lower bound $\underline{J}(\theta^{(t-1)}, \underline{u}^{(t)})$ for a suitable dual parameter $\underline{u}^{(t)}$, leading to a condition on $\bar{u}^{(t)}$ and $\underline{u}^{(t)}$ of the form

$$\bar{J}(\theta^{(t-1)}, \bar{u}^{(t)}) \leq \eta\underline{J}(\theta^{(t-1)}, \underline{u}^{(t)}) + (1-\eta)\bar{J}(\theta^{(t-1)}, \bar{u}^{(t-1)}).$$

Algorithm 1. ReGeMM: Relaxed Generalized Majorization-Minimization

---

Require: Initial $\theta^{(0)} = \theta^{(-1)}$ and $\overline{\mathbf{u}}^{(0)}$, number of rounds T

1: **for** $t = 1, \ldots, T$ **do**
2:     Determine $\overline{\mathbf{u}}^{(t)}$ and $\underline{\mathbf{u}}^{(t)}$ that satisfy Eq. 8
3:     Set $\theta^{(t)} \leftarrow \arg\min_\theta \overline{J}(\theta, \overline{\mathbf{u}}^{(t)})$
4: **end for**
5: **return** $\theta^{(T)}$

This condition still has the significant shortcoming, that both $\overline{J}(\theta^{(t-1)}, \overline{\mathbf{u}}^{(t)})$ and $\overline{J}(\theta^{(t-1)}, \overline{\mathbf{u}}^{(t-1)})$ need to be evaluated. While computation of the first quantity is firmly required, evaluation of the second value is unnecessary as we will see in the following. Not needing to compute $\overline{J}(\theta^{(t-1)}, \overline{\mathbf{u}}^{(t-1)})$ also means that the memory associated with $\overline{\mathbf{u}}^{(t-1)}$ can be immediately reused. Our proposed condition on $\overline{\mathbf{u}}^{(t)}$ and $\underline{\mathbf{u}}^{(t)}$ for a *relaxed generalized* MM (or *ReGeMM*) method is given by

$$\overline{J}(\theta^{(t-1)}, \overline{\mathbf{u}}^{(t)}) \leq \eta \underline{J}(\theta^{(t-1)}, \underline{\mathbf{u}}^{(t)}) + (1 - \eta)\overline{J}(\theta^{(t-2)}, \overline{\mathbf{u}}^{(t-1)}), \tag{8}$$

where $\eta \in (0,1)$, e.g. $\eta = 1/2$ in our implementation. The resulting algorithm is given in Algorithm 1. The existence of a pair $(\overline{\mathbf{u}}^{(t)}, \underline{\mathbf{u}}^{(t)})$ is guaranteed, since both $\underline{J}(\theta^{(t-1)}; \underline{\mathbf{u}}^{(t)})$ and $\overline{J}(\theta^{(t-1)}; \overline{\mathbf{u}}^{(t)})$ can be made arbitrarily close to $J(\theta^{(t-1)})$ by our assumption of strong duality. We introduce c_t,

$$c_t := \overline{J}(\theta^{(t-2)}, \overline{\mathbf{u}}^{(t-1)}) - \underline{J}(\theta^{(t-1)}, \underline{\mathbf{u}}^{(t)}) \geq 0, \tag{9}$$

and Eq. 8 can therefore be restated as

$$\overline{J}(\theta^{(t-1)}, \overline{\mathbf{u}}^{(t)}) \leq \overline{J}(\theta^{(t-2)}, \overline{\mathbf{u}}^{(t-1)}) - \eta c_t. \tag{10}$$

Proposition 1. *We have* $\lim_{t \to \infty} c_t = 0$.

Proof. We define $v_t := \overline{J}(\theta^{(t-2)}, \overline{\mathbf{u}}^{(t-1)}) - \eta c_t$. First, observe that

$$c_t = \overline{J}(\theta^{(t-2)}; \overline{\mathbf{u}}^{(t-1)}) - \underline{J}(\theta^{(t-1)}; \underline{\mathbf{u}}^{(t)}) \geq \overline{J}(\theta^{(t-1)}; \overline{\mathbf{u}}^{(t-1)}) - \underline{J}(\theta^{(t-1)}; \underline{\mathbf{u}}^{(t)})$$

$$\geq \overline{J}(\theta^{(t-1)}; \overline{\mathbf{u}}^{(t-1)}) - J(\theta^{(t-1)}) \geq 0$$

(using the relations $\overline{J}(\theta^{(t-1)}; \overline{\mathbf{u}}^{(t-1)}) \leq \overline{J}(\theta^{(t-2)}; \overline{\mathbf{u}}^{(t-1)})$ and $\underline{J}(\theta^{(t-1)}; \underline{\mathbf{u}}) \leq J(\theta^{(t-1)}) \leq \overline{J}(\theta^{(t-1)}; \overline{\mathbf{u}})$ for any $\underline{\mathbf{u}}$ and $\overline{\mathbf{u}}$). We further have

$$\sum\nolimits_{t=1}^{T} c_t = \eta^{-1} \sum\nolimits_{t=1}^{T} \left(\overline{J}(\theta^{(t-2)}; \overline{\mathbf{u}}^{(t-1)}) - v_t \right)$$

$$\leq \eta^{-1} \sum\nolimits_{t=1}^{T} \left(\overline{J}(\theta^{(t-2)}; \overline{\mathbf{u}}^{(t-1)}) - \overline{J}(\theta^{(t-1)}; \overline{\mathbf{u}}^{(t)}) \right)$$

$$= \eta^{-1} \left(\overline{J}(\theta^{(-1)}; \overline{\mathbf{u}}^{(0)}) - \overline{J}(\theta^{(T-1)}; \overline{\mathbf{u}}^{(T)}) \right) < \infty,$$

since $\overline{J}$ is bounded from below. In the first line we used the definition of d_t and in the second line we utilized that $\overline{J}(\theta^{(t-1)}; \overline{\mathbf{u}}^{(t)}) \leq v_t$. The last line follows from the telescopic sum. Overall, we have that

$$\lim_{T \to \infty} \sum\nolimits_{t=1}^{T} c_t = \eta^{-1} \left(\overline{J}(\theta^{(-1)}; \overline{\mathbf{u}}^{(0)}) - \lim_{T \to \infty} \overline{J}(\theta^{(T-1)}; \overline{\mathbf{u}}^{(T)}) \right),$$

which is finite, since J (and therefore $\overline{J}$) is bounded from below. From $c_t \geq 0$ and $\lim_{T \to \infty} \sum_{t=1}^{T} c_t < \infty$ we deduce that $\lim_{T \to \infty} c_t = 0$.

Hence, in analogy with the generalized MM method [22], the upper bound $\overline{J}(\theta^{(t)}, \overline{\mathbf{u}}^{(t)})$ approaches the target objective value $J(\theta^{(t)})$ in the proposed relaxed scheme. This result also implies that finding $\overline{\mathbf{u}}^{(t)}$ will be increasingly harder. This is expected, since one ultimately aims to minimize J. If we additionally assume that the mapping $\theta \mapsto \nabla_\theta \overline{J}(\theta, \overline{\mathbf{u}})$ has Lipschitz gradient for all $\overline{\mathbf{u}}$, then it can be also shown that $\nabla_\theta \overline{J}(\theta^{(t)}, \overline{\mathbf{u}}^{(t)}) \to 0$ (we refer to the supplementary material).

The relaxed generalized MM approach is therefore a well-understood method when applied in a full batch scenario (recall Eq. 2). Since the condition in Eq. 8 is based on all terms in the objectives, it is not clear how it generalizes to an incremental or stochastic setting, when θ is updated using small mini-batches. This is the motivation for developing an alternative criterion to Eq. 8 in the next section, that is based on "local" quantities.

Using Constant Memory. Naive implementations of Algorithm 1 require $O(N)$ memory to store $\overline{\mathbf{u}} = (\overline{u}_1, \dots, \overline{u}_N)$. In many applications the number of terms N is large, but the latent variables $(\overline{u}_i)_i$ have the same structure for all i (e.g. $\overline{u}_i$ represent pixel-level predictions for training images of the same dimensions). If we use a gradient method to update θ, then the required quantities can be accumulated in-place, as shown in the supplementary material. The constant memory algorithm is not limited to first order methods for θ, but any method that accumulates the information needed to determine $\theta^{(t)}$ from $\theta^{(t-1)}$ in-place is feasible (such as the Newton or the Gauss-Newton method).

5   Sufficient Descent Majorization-Minimization

The ReGeMM method proposed above has two disadvantages: (i) the underlying condition is somewhat technical and it is also a global condition, and (ii) the resulting algorithm does not straightforwardly generalize to incremental or stochastic methods, that have proven to be far superior compared to full-batch approaches, especially in machine learning scenarios.

In this section we make the additional assumption on $\overline{J}$, that

$$\overline{J}(\theta', \overline{\mathbf{u}}) \leq \overline{J}(\theta, \overline{\mathbf{u}}) + \nabla_\theta \overline{J}(\theta, \overline{\mathbf{u}})^T (\theta' - \theta) + \frac{L}{2} \|\theta' - \theta\|^2, \tag{11}$$

for a constant $L > 0$ and all $\overline{\mathbf{u}}$. This essentially means, that the mapping $\theta \mapsto \overline{J}(\theta, \overline{\mathbf{u}})$ has a Lipschitz gradient with Lipschitz constant L. This assumption is frequent in many gradient-based minimization methods. Note that the minimizer of the r.h.s. in Eq. 11 w.r.t. θ' is given by $\theta' = \theta - \frac{1}{L} \nabla_\theta \overline{J}(\theta, \overline{\mathbf{u}})$. Hence, we focus on gradient-based updates of θ in the following, i.e. $\theta^{(t)}$ is given by

$$\theta^{(t)} = \theta^{(t-1)} - \frac{1}{L} \nabla_\theta \overline{J}(\theta^{(t-1)}, \overline{\mathbf{u}}^{(t)}). \tag{12}$$

Combining this with Eq. 11 yields

$$\overline{J}(\theta^{(t)}, \overline{\mathbf{u}}^{(t)}) \le \overline{J}(\theta^{(t-1)}, \overline{\mathbf{u}}^{(t)}) - \frac{1}{2L}\|\nabla_\theta \overline{J}(\theta^{(t-1)}, \overline{\mathbf{u}}^{(t)})\|^2,$$

hence the update from $\theta^{(t-1)}$ to $\theta^{(t)}$ yields a guaranteed reduction of $\overline{J}(\cdot, \overline{\mathbf{u}}^{(t)})$ in terms of the respective gradient magnitude.

We therefore propose the following condition on $(\overline{\mathbf{u}}^{(t)}, \underline{\mathbf{u}}^{(t)})$ based on the current iterate $\theta^{(t-1)}$: for a $\rho \in (0,1)$ (which is set to $\rho = 1/2$ in our implementation) determine $\overline{\mathbf{u}}^{(t)}$ and $\underline{\mathbf{u}}^{(t)}$ such that

$$\overline{J}(\theta^{(t-1)}; \overline{\mathbf{u}}^{(t)}) - \underline{J}(\theta^{(t-1)}; \underline{\mathbf{u}}^{(t)}) \le \frac{\rho}{2L}\|\nabla \overline{J}(\theta^{(t-1)}; \overline{\mathbf{u}}^{(t)})\|^2 \tag{13}$$

This condition requires intuitively, that the duality gap $\overline{J}(\theta^{(t-1)}; \overline{\mathbf{u}}^{(t)}) - \underline{J}(\theta^{(t-1)}; \underline{\mathbf{u}}^{(t)})$ is sufficiently smaller than the reduction of $\overline{J}(\cdot; \overline{\mathbf{u}}^{(t)})$ guaranteed by a gradient descent step. Convexity and strong duality of $\overline{J}(\theta; \cdot)$ for each θ allows to determine such a pair $(\overline{\mathbf{u}}^{(t)}, \underline{\mathbf{u}}^{(t)})$ using convex optimization methods. Rearranging the above condition (and using that $\theta^{(t)} = \theta^{(t-1)} - \nabla \overline{J}(\theta^{(t-1)}, \overline{\mathbf{u}}^{(t)})/L$) yields

$$\overline{J}(\theta^{(t)}; \overline{\mathbf{u}}^{(t)}) \le \overline{J}(\theta^{(t-1)}; \overline{\mathbf{u}}^{(t)}) - \frac{1}{2L}\|\nabla \overline{J}(\theta^{(t-1)}; \overline{\mathbf{u}}^{(t)})\|^2$$

$$\le \underline{J}(\theta^{(t-1)}; \underline{\mathbf{u}}^{(t)}) - \frac{1-\rho}{2L}\|\nabla \overline{J}(\theta^{(t-1)}; \overline{\mathbf{u}}^{(t)})\|^2$$

$$\le J(\theta^{(t-1)}) - \frac{1-\rho}{2L}\|\nabla \overline{J}(\theta^{(t-1)}; \overline{\mathbf{u}}^{(t)})\|^2,$$

i.e. the upper bound at the new solution $\theta^{(t)}$ is sufficiently below the lower bound (and the true function value) at the current solution $\theta^{(t-1)}$. This can be stated compactly,

$$J(\theta^{(t)}) \le \overline{J}(\theta^{(t)}; \overline{\mathbf{u}}^{(t)}) \le J(\theta^{(t-1)}) - \frac{1-\rho}{2L}\|\nabla \overline{J}(\theta^{(t-1)}; \overline{\mathbf{u}}^{(t)})\|^2, \tag{14}$$

and the sequence $(J(\theta^{(t)})_{t=1}^\infty$ is therefore non-increasing. Since we are always asking for a sufficient decrease (in analogy with the Armijo condition), we expect convergence to a stationary solution θ^*. This is the case:

Proposition 2. $\lim_{t\to\infty} \nabla_\theta \overline{J}(\theta^{(t-1)}; \overline{\mathbf{u}}^{(t)}) = 0.$

Proof. By rearranging Eq. 14 we have

$$\sum_t \|\nabla \overline{J}(\theta^{(t-1)}; \overline{\mathbf{u}}^{(t)})\|^2 \le \frac{2L}{1-\rho}\sum_t \left(J(\theta^{(t-1)}) - J(\theta^{(t)})\right)$$

$$= \frac{2L}{1-\rho}\left(J(\theta^{(0)}) - J(\theta^*)\right) < \infty,$$

and therefore $\|\nabla \overline{J}(\theta^{(t-1)}; \overline{\mathbf{u}}^{(t)})\| \to 0$, which implies that $\nabla \overline{J}(\theta^{(t-1)}; \overline{\mathbf{u}}^{(t)}) \to 0$.

Algorithm 2. SuDeMM: Sufficient-Descent Majorization-Minimization

---

Require: Initial $\theta^{(0)}$, number of rounds T
1: **for** $t = 1, \ldots, T$ **do**
2:     Determine $\overline{\mathbf{u}}^{(t)}$ and $\underline{\mathbf{u}}^{(t)}$ that satisfy Eq. 13
3:     Set $\theta^{(t)} \leftarrow \theta^{(t-1)} - \frac{1}{L}\nabla_\theta \overline{J}(\theta^{(t-1)}, \overline{u}^{(t)})$
4: **end for**
5: **return** $\theta^{(T)}$

We summarize the resulting *sufficient descent MM* (or *SuDeMM*) method in Algorithm 2. As with the ReGeMM approach, determining $\overline{u}$ is more difficult when closing in on a stationary point (as $\nabla_\theta \overline{J}(\theta^{(t)}, \overline{u}) \to 0$). The gradient step indicated in line 3 in Algorithm 2 can be replaced by any update that guarantees sufficient descent. Finally, in analogy with the ReGeMM approach discussed in the previous section, it is straightforward to obtain a constant memory variant of Algorithm 2. The stochastic method described below incorporates both immediate memory reduction from $O(N)$ to $O(B)$, where B is the size of the mini-batch, and faster minimization due to the use of mini-batches.

5.1 Extension to the Stochastic Setting

In many machine learning applications J will be of the form of Eq. 2 with $N \gg 1$ being the number of training samples. It is well known that in such settings methods levering the full gradient accumulated over all training samples are hugely outperformed by stochastic gradient methods, which operate on a single training sample (i.e. term in Eq. 2) or, alternatively, on a small mini-batch of size B randomly drawn from the range $\{1, \ldots, N\}$.

It is straightforward to extend Algorithm 2 to a stochastic setting working on single data points (or mini-batches) by replacing the objective values $\overline{J}(\theta^{(t-1)}; \overline{\mathbf{u}}^{(t)})$, $\underline{J}(\theta^{(t-1)}; \underline{\mathbf{u}}^{(t)}))$ and the full gradient $\nabla_\theta \overline{J}(\theta^{(t-1)}, \overline{\mathbf{u}}^{(t)})$ with the respective mini-batch counter-parts. The resulting algorithm is depicted in Algorithm 3 (for mini-batches of size one). Due to the stochastic nature of the gradient estimate $\nabla_\theta \overline{J}_i(\theta^{(t-1)}, \overline{\mathbf{u}}^{(t)})$, both the step sizes $\alpha_t > 0$ and the reduction parameter $\rho_t > 0$ are time-dependent and need to satisfy the following conditions,

$$\sum_{t=1}^{\infty} \alpha_t = \infty \qquad \sum_{t=1}^{\infty} \alpha_t^2 < \infty \qquad \sum_{t=1}^{\infty} \rho_t < \infty. \qquad (15)$$

The first two conditions on the step sizes $(\alpha_t)_t$ are standard in stochastic gradient methods, and the last condition on the sequence $(\rho_t)_t$ ensures that the added noise by using time-dependent upper bounds $\overline{J}(\cdot, \overline{\mathbf{u}}^{(t)})$ (instead of the time-independent function $J(\cdot)$) has bounded variance. The constraint on ρ_t is therefore stronger than the intuitively necessary condition $\rho_t \overset{t \to \infty}{\to} 0$. We refer to the supplementary material for a detailed discussion. Due to the small size B of a mini-batch, the values of $\overline{\mathbf{u}}_i^{(t)}$ and $\underline{\mathbf{u}}_i^{(t)}$ in the mini-batch can be maintained, and the restarting strategy outlined in Sect. 4 is not necessary.

Algorithm 3. Stochastic Sufficient Descent Majorization-Minimization

Require: Initial $\theta^{(0)}$, number of rounds T
1: **for** $t = 1, \ldots, T$ **do**
2:     Uniformly sample i from $\{1, \ldots, N\}$
3:     Determine $\overline{u}_i$ and $\underline{u}_i$ that satisfy

$$\overline{J}_i(\theta^{(t-1)}, \overline{u}_i) - \underline{J}_i(\theta^{(t-1)}, \underline{u}_i) \leq \frac{\rho_t}{2} \|\nabla_\theta \overline{J}_i(\theta^{(t-1)}, \overline{u}_i)\|^2 \qquad (16)$$

4:     Set $\theta^{(t)} \leftarrow \theta^{(t-1)} - \alpha_t \nabla_\theta \overline{J}_i(\theta^{(t-1)}, \overline{u}^{(t)})$
5: **end for**
6: **return** $\theta^{(T)}$

6 Applications

6.1 Robust Bundle Adjustment

In this experiment we first demonstrate the applicability of our proposed ReGeMM schemes to a large scale robust fitting task. The aim is to determine whether ReGeMM is also able to avoid poor local minima (in analogy with the k-means experiment in [22]). The hypothesis is, that optimizing the latent variables just enough to meet the ReGeMM condition (Eq. 8) corresponds to a particular variant of graduated optimization, and therefore will (empirically) return better local minima for highly non-convex problems.

Robust bundle adjustment aims to refine the camera poses and 3D point structure to maximize a log-likelihood given image observations and established correspondences. The unknowns are $\theta = (P_1, \ldots, P_n, X_1, \ldots, X_m)$, where $P_k \in \mathbb{R}^6$ refers to the k-th camera pose and $X_j \in \mathbb{R}^3$ is the position of the j-th 3D point. The cost J is given by

$$J(\theta) = \sum_i \psi(f_i(\theta) - m_i), \qquad (17)$$

where $m_i \in \mathbb{R}^2$ is the i-th image observation and f_i projects the respective 3D point to the image plane of the corresponding camera. ψ is a so called robust kernel, which generally turns J into a highly non-convex objective functions with a large number of local minima. Following [35] an upper bound $\overline{J}$ is given via half-quadratic (HQ) minimization [11],

$$\overline{J}(\theta, \overline{\mathbf{u}}) = \sum_i \left(\frac{\overline{u}_i}{2} \|f_i(\theta) - m_i\|^2 + \kappa(\overline{u}_i) \right), \qquad (18)$$

where $\kappa : \mathbb{R}_{\geq 0} \to \mathbb{R}_{\geq 0}$ depends on the choice for ψ, and $\overline{u}_i$ is identified as the (confidence) weight on the i-th observation. The standard MM approach corresponds essentially to the iteratively reweighted least squares method (IRLS), which is prone to yield poor local minima if θ is not well initialized. For given θ the optimal latent variables $\overline{u}_i^*(\theta)$ are given by $\overline{u}_i^*(\theta) = \omega(\|f_i(\theta) - m_i\|)$, where $\omega(\cdot)$ is the weight function associated with the robust kernel ψ. Joint HQ minimization of $\overline{J}$ w.r.t. θ and $\overline{u}$ is suggested and evaluated in [35], which empirically

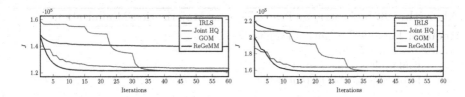

Fig. 2. Objective value w.r.t. number of iterations of a NNLS solver for the Dubrovnik-356 (left) and Venice-427 (right) datasets.

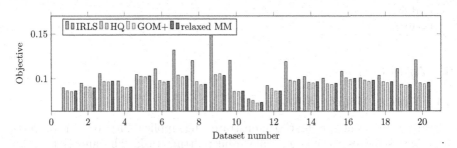

Fig. 3. Final objective values reached by different methods for 20 metric bundle adjustment instances after 100 NNLS solver iterations.

yields significantly better local minima of J than IRLS. We compare this joint-HQ method (as well as IRLS and an explicit graduated method GOM [34]) with our ReGeMM condition (Eq. 8), where the confidence weights $\overline{\mathbf{u}}$ are optimized to meet but not substantially surpass this criterion: a scale parameter $\sigma \geq 1$ is determined such that $\overline{u}_i^{(t)}$ is set to $\omega(\|f_i(\theta^{(t-1)}) - m_i\|/\sigma)$, and $\overline{\mathbf{u}}$ satisfies the ReGeMM condition (Eq. 8) and

$$\eta' J(\theta^{(t-1)}) + (1 - \eta')\overline{J}(\theta^{(t-2)}, \overline{\mathbf{u}}^{(t-1)}) \leq \overline{J}(\theta^{(t-1)}, \overline{\mathbf{u}}^{(t)}) \qquad (19)$$

for an $\eta' \in (\eta, 1)$. In our implementation we determine σ using bisection search and choose $\eta' = 3/4$. In this application the evaluation of J is inexpensive, and therefore we use $J(\theta^{(t-1)})$ instead of a lower bound $\underline{J}(\theta^{(t-1)}, \mathbf{u}^{(t)})$ in the r.h.s. The model parameters θ are updated for given $\overline{\mathbf{u}}$ using a Levenberg-Marquardt solver. Our choice of ψ is the smooth truncated quadratic cost [35].

In Fig. 2 we depict the evolution of the target objective Eq. 17 for two metric bundle adjustment instances from [1]. The proposed ReGeMM approach (with the initial confidence weights $\overline{\mathbf{u}}$ all set to 1) compares favorably against IRLS, joint HQ [35] and even graduated optimization [34] (that leads only to a slightly better minimum). This observation is supported by comparing the methods using a larger database of 20 problem instances [1] (listed in the supplementary material) in Fig. 3, where the final objective values reached after 100 NNLS iterations by different methods are depicted. ReGeMM is again highly competitive. In terms of run-time, ReGeMM is between 5% and 25% slower per iteration than IRLS in our implementation.

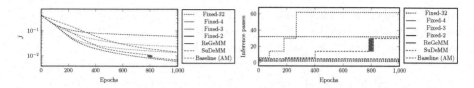

Fig. 4. Objective value w.r.t. number of epochs (left) and the (accumulated) number of inference steps needed to meet the respective criterion (right) in the full-batch setting.

6.2 Contrastive Hebbian Learning

Contrastive Hebbian learning uses an energy model over latent variables to explicitly infer (i.e. minimize over) the network activations (instead of using a predefined rule such as in feed-forward DNNs). Feed-forward DNNs using certain activation functions can be identified as limit case of suitable energy-based models [26,30,36]. We use the formulation proposed in [36] due to the underlying convexity of the energy model. In the following we outline that the corresponding supervised learning task is an instance of Eq. 2. In contrastive Hebbian learning the activations for the network are inferred in two phases: the *clamped phase* uses information from the target label (via a loss function ℓ that is convex in its first argument) to steer the output layer, and the *free phase* does not put any constraint on the output. The input layer is always clamped to the provided training input. The clamped network energy is given by[3]

$$\hat{E}(z;\theta) = \ell(a_L; y) + \frac{1}{2} \|z_1 - W_0 x - b_0\|^2 + \frac{1}{2} \sum_{k=1}^{L-2} \|z_{k+1} - W_k z_k - b_k\|^2 \quad (20)$$

subject to $z_k \in \mathcal{C}_k$, where $\mathcal{C}_k$ is a convex set and θ contains all network weights W_k and biases b_k. In order to mimic DNNs with ReLU activations, we choose $\mathcal{C}_k = \mathbb{R}_{\geq 0}^{n_k}$. The loss function is chosen to be the Euclidean loss, $\ell(a_L; y) = \|a_L - y\|^2/2$. The dual network energy can be derived as

$$\hat{E}^*(\lambda; \theta) = -\ell^*(-\lambda_L; y) - \frac{1}{2} \sum_{k=1}^{L-1} \|\lambda_k\|^2 - \lambda_1^T W_0 x + \sum_{k=1}^{L} \lambda_k^T b_{k-1} \quad (21)$$

subject to $\lambda_k \geq W_k^T \lambda_{k+1}$ for $k = 1, \ldots, L-1$. If $\ell \equiv 0$, i.e. there is no loss on the final layer output, then we denote the corresponding *free* primal and dual energies by $\check{E}$ and $\check{E}^*$, respectively. Observe that $\hat{E}/\check{E}$ are convex w.r.t. the network activations z, and $\hat{E}^*/\check{E}^*$ are concave w.r.t. the dual variables λ.

---

[3] We omit the explicit feedback parameter used in [30,36], since it can be absorbed into the activations and network weights.

Training Using Contrastive Learning. Let $\{(x_i, y_i)\}_i$ be a labeled dataset containing N training samples, and the task for the network is to predict y_i from given x_i. The utilized contrastive training loss is given by

$$J(\theta) := \sum_i \left(\min_{\hat{z}} \hat{E}(\hat{z}; x_i, y_i, \theta) - \min_{\check{z}} \check{E}(\check{z}; x_i, \theta) \right)$$

$$= \sum_i \min_{\hat{z}} \max_{\check{z}} \left(\hat{E}(\hat{z}; x_i, y_i, \theta) - \check{E}(\check{z}; x_i, \theta) \right), \qquad (22)$$

which is minimized w.r.t. the network parameters θ. Using duality this saddle-point problem can be restated as pure minimization and maximization tasks [36],

$$\overline{J}(\theta, (\hat{z}_i, \check{\lambda}_i)_{i=1}^N) = \sum_i \left(\hat{E}(\hat{z}_i; x_i, y_i, \theta) - \check{E}^*(\check{\lambda}_i; x_i, \theta) \right) \qquad (23)$$

and

$$\underline{J}(\theta, (\hat{\lambda}_i, \check{z}_i)_{i=1}^N) = \sum_i \left(\hat{E}^*(\hat{\lambda}_i; x_i, y_i, \theta) - \check{E}(\check{z}_i; x_i, \theta) \right). \qquad (24)$$

Thus, the latent variables $\overline{u}_i = (\hat{z}_i, \check{\lambda}_i)$ and $\underline{u}_i = (\hat{\lambda}_i, \check{z}_i)$ correspond to primal-dual pairs representing the network activations, and therefore the entire set of latent variables $\overline{\mathbf{u}}$ is very high-dimensional. In this scenario the true cost J is not accessible, since it requires solving a inner minimization problem w.r.t. $\overline{u}_i$ not having a closed form solution (it requires solving a convex QP). Inference (minimization) w.r.t. $\overline{u}_i$ is conducted by coordinate descent, which is guaranteed to converge to a global solution as both $\hat{E}$ and $-\check{E}^*$ are strongly convex [16,27].

Full Batch Methods. In Fig. 4 we illustrate the evolution of J on a subset of MNIST [15] using a fully connected 784-64(×4)-10 architecture for 4 methods: (i) inferring $\overline{u}_i$ with a fixed number of 2, 3, 4 and 32 passes of an iterative method, respectively, (ii) using the ReGeMM condition Eq. 8, and (iii) using the SuDeMM criterion Eq. 13. Inference for $\overline{u}_i$ is continued until the respective criterion is met. Both ReGeMM and SuDeMM use the respective constant memory variants. In this scenario 32 passes are considered sufficient to perform inference, and the ReGeMM and SuDeMM methods track the best curve well. We chose to use the number of epochs (i.e. the number of updates of θ) on the x-axis to align the curves. Clearly, using a fixed number of 2 passes is significantly faster than using 32 or an adaptive but growing number of inference steps. Interestingly, the necessary inference steps grow much quicker (to the allowed maximum of 40 passes) for the ReGeMM condition compared to the SuDeMM test. The baseline method alternates between gradient updates w.r.t. $\overline{\mathbf{u}}$ (using line search) and θ. In all methods the gradient update for θ uses the same fixed learning rate.

Stochastic Methods. For the stochastic method in Algorithm 3 we illustrate the evolution of the objectives values $\overline{J}$ and the number of inference passes in Fig. 5. For MNIST and its drop-in replacements Fashion-MNIST [29] and KMNIST [5] we again use the same 784-64(×4)-10 architecture as above. For a

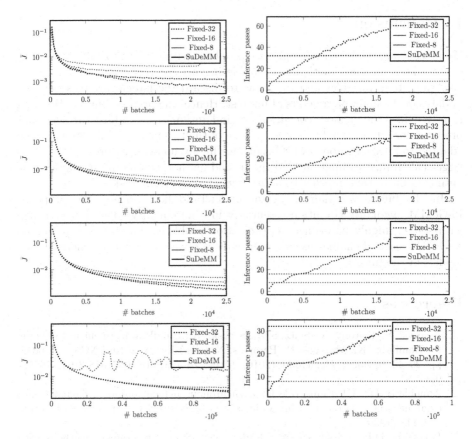

Fig. 5. Objective value w.r.t. number of processed mini-batches (left column) and the number of inference steps needed to meet the respective criterion (right column) for MNIST (1st row), Fashion-MNIST (2nd row), KMNIST (3rd row) and CIFAR-10 (bottom row) using the stochastic gradient method.

greyscale version of CIFAR-10 [13] we employ a 1024-128($\times$3)-10 network. The batch size is 10, and a constant step size is employed. The overall conclusions from Fig. 5 are as follows: using an insufficient number of inference passes yields poor surrogates for the true objective J and it can lead to numerical instabilities due to the biasedness of the gradient estimates. Further, the proposed SuDeMM algorithm yields the lowest estimates for the true objective by gradually adapting the necessary inference precision.[4]

---

[4] We refer to the supplementary material for results corresponding to sparse coding as the underlying network model.

7 Conclusion

We present two approaches to optimize problems with a latent variable structure. Our formally justified methods (i) enable inexact (or truncated) minimization over the latent variables and (ii) allow to discard the latent variables between updates of the main parameters of interest. Hence, the proposed methods significantly reduce the memory consumption, and automatically adjust the necessary precision for latent variable inference. One of the two presented methods can be adapted to return competitive solutions for highly non-convex problems such as large-scale robust estimation, and the second method can be run in a stochastic optimization setting in order to address machine learning tasks.

In the future we plan to better understand how turning the proposed ReGeMM inequality condition essentially into an equality constraint can help with solving highly non-convex optimization problems. Further, the presented SuDeMM method enables us to better explore a variety of convex energy-based models in the future.

References

1. Agarwal, S., Snavely, N., Seitz, S.M., Szeliski, R.: Bundle adjustment in the large. In: Daniilidis, K., Maragos, P., Paragios, N. (eds.) ECCV 2010. LNCS, vol. 6312, pp. 29–42. Springer, Heidelberg (2010). https://doi.org/10.1007/978-3-642-15552-9_3

2. Almeida, L.B.: A learning rule for asynchronous perceptrons with feedback in a combinatorial environment. In: Artificial Neural Networks: Concept Learning, pp. 102–111 (1990)

3. Bertsekas, D.P., Tsitsiklis, J.N.: Gradient convergence in gradient methods with errors. SIAM J. Optim. **10**(3), 627–642 (2000)

4. Byrne, C.L.: Alternating minimization as sequential unconstrained minimization: a survey. J. Optim. Theory Appl. **156**(3), 554–566 (2013)

5. Clanuwat, T., Bober-Irizar, M., Kitamoto, A., Lamb, A., Yamamoto, K., Ha, D.: Deep learning for classical japanese literature. arXiv preprint arXiv:1812.01718 (2018)

6. Csiszár, I., Tusnády, G.E.: Information geometry and alternating minimization procedures. In: Statistics and Decisions (1984)

7. Dempster, A.P., Laird, N.M., Rubin, D.B.: Maximum likelihood from incomplete data via the EM algorithm. J. Roy. Stat. Soc.: Ser. B (Methodol.) **39**(1), 1–22 (1977)

8. Devolder, O., Glineur, F., Nesterov, Y.: First-order methods of smooth convex optimization with inexact oracle. Math. Program. **146**, 37–75 (2013). https://doi.org/10.1007/s10107-013-0677-5

9. Dvurechensky, P., Gasnikov, A.: Stochastic intermediate gradient method for convex problems with stochastic inexact oracle. J. Optim. Theory Appl. **171**(1), 121–145 (2016)

10. Felzenszwalb, P.F., Girshick, R.B., McAllester, D., Ramanan, D.: Object detection with discriminatively trained part-based models. IEEE Trans. Pattern Anal. Mach. Intell. **32**(9), 1627–1645 (2009)

11. Geman, D., Reynolds, G.: Constrained restoration and the recovery of discontinuities. IEEE Trans. Pattern Anal. Mach. Intell. **14**(3), 367–383 (1992)
12. Hunter, D.R., Lange, K.: A tutorial on MM algorithms. Am. Stat. **58**(1), 30–37 (2004)
13. Krizhevsky, A., Hinton, G.: Learning multiple layers of features from tiny images. Technical report, Citeseer (2009)
14. Lange, K., Hunter, D.R., Yang, I.: Optimization transfer using surrogate objective functions. J. Comput. Graph. Stat. **9**(1), 1–20 (2000)
15. LeCun, Y., Bottou, L., Bengio, Y., Haffner, P., et al.: Gradient-based learning applied to document recognition. Proc. IEEE **86**(11), 2278–2324 (1998)
16. Luo, Z.Q., Tseng, P.: On the convergence of the coordinate descent method for convex differentiable minimization. J. Optim. Theory Appl. **72**(1), 7–35 (1992)
17. Mairal, J.: Optimization with first-order surrogate functions. In: International Conference on Machine Learning, pp. 783–791 (2013)
18. Mairal, J.: Stochastic majorization-minimization algorithms for large-scale optimization. In: Advances in Neural Information Processing Systems, pp. 2283–2291 (2013)
19. Mairal, J.: Incremental majorization-minimization optimization with application to large-scale machine learning. SIAM J. Optim. **25**(2), 829–855 (2015)
20. Movellan, J.R.: Contrastive Hebbian learning in the continuous hopfield model. In: Connectionist Models, pp. 10–17. Elsevier (1991)
21. Neal, R.M., Hinton, G.E.: A view of the EM algorithm that justifies incremental, sparse, and other variants. In: Jordan, M.I. (ed.) Learning in Graphical Models, pp. 355–368. Springer, Dordrecht (1998). https://doi.org/10.1007/978-94-011-5014-9_12
22. Parizi, S.N., He, K., Aghajani, R., Sclaroff, S., Felzenszwalb, P.: Generalized majorization-minimization. In: International Conference on Machine Learning, pp. 5022–5031 (2019)
23. Pineda, F.J.: Generalization of back-propagation to recurrent neural networks. Phys. Rev. Lett. **59**(19), 2229 (1987)
24. Razaviyayn, M., Sanjabi, M., Luo, Z.Q.: A stochastic successive minimization method for nonsmooth nonconvex optimization with applications to transceiver design in wireless communication networks. Math. Program. **157**(2), 515–545 (2016)
25. Scarselli, F., Gori, M., Tsoi, A.C., Hagenbuchner, M., Monfardini, G.: The graph neural network model. IEEE Trans. Neural Netw. **20**(1), 61–80 (2008)
26. Scellier, B., Bengio, Y.: Equilibrium propagation: bridging the gap between energy-based models and backpropagation. Front. Comput. Neurosci. **11**, 24 (2017)
27. Wright, S.J.: Coordinate descent algorithms. Math. Program. **151**(1), 3–34 (2015). https://doi.org/10.1007/s10107-015-0892-3
28. Wu, C.J.: On the convergence properties of the EM algorithm. Ann. Stat. **11**, 95–103 (1983)
29. Xiao, H., Rasul, K., Vollgraf, R.: Fashion-MNIST: a novel image dataset for benchmarking machine learning algorithms. arXiv preprint arXiv:1708.07747 (2017)
30. Xie, X., Seung, H.S.: Equivalence of backpropagation and contrastive Hebbian learning in a layered network. Neural Comput. **15**(2), 441–454 (2003)
31. Xu, C., Lin, Z., Zhao, Z., Zha, H.: Relaxed majorization-minimization for nonsmooth and non-convex optimization. In: Thirtieth AAAI Conference on Artificial Intelligence (2016)

32. Yu, C.N.J., Joachims, T.: Learning structural SVMs with latent variables. In: Proceedings of the 26th Annual International Conference on Machine Learning, pp. 1169–1176 (2009)
33. Yuille, A.L., Rangarajan, A.: The concave-convex procedure. Neural Comput. **15**(4), 915–936 (2003)
34. Zach, C., Bourmaud, G.: Descending, lifting or smoothing: secrets of robust cost optimization. In: Proceedings of ECCV (2018)
35. Zach, C.: Robust bundle adjustment revisited. In: Fleet, D., Pajdla, T., Schiele, B., Tuytelaars, T. (eds.) ECCV 2014. LNCS, vol. 8693, pp. 772–787. Springer, Cham (2014). https://doi.org/10.1007/978-3-319-10602-1_50
36. Zach, C., Estellers, V.: Contrastive learning for lifted networks. In: British Machine Vision Conference (2019)
37. Zhang, H., Zhou, P., Yang, Y., Feng, J.: Generalized majorization-minimization for non-convex optimization. In: Proceedings of the 28th International Joint Conference on Artificial Intelligence, pp. 4257–4263. AAAI Press (2019)

Geometry Constrained Weakly Supervised Object Localization

Weizeng Lu[1,2], Xi Jia[3], Weicheng Xie[1,2], Linlin Shen[1,2(✉)], Yicong Zhou[4], and Jinming Duan[3(✉)]

[1] Computer Vision Institute, School of Computer Science and Software Engineering, Shenzhen University, Shenzhen, China
luweizeng2018@email.szu.edu.cn
{wcxie,llshen}@szu.edu.cn
[2] Shenzhen Institute of Artificial Intelligence and Robotics for Society, Shenzhen, China
[3] School of Computer Science, University of Birmingham, Birmingham, UK
{x.jia.1,j.duan}@cs.bham.ac.uk
[4] Department of Computer and Information Science, University of Macau, Zhuhai, China
yicongzhou@um.edu.mo

Abstract. We propose a geometry constrained network, termed GC-Net, for weakly supervised object localization (WSOL). GC-Net consists of three modules: a detector, a generator and a classifier. The detector predicts the object location defined by a set of coefficients describing a geometric shape (i.e. ellipse or rectangle), which is geometrically constrained by the mask produced by the generator. The classifier takes the resulting masked images as input and performs two complementary classification tasks for the object and background. To make the mask more compact and more complete, we propose a novel multi-task loss function that takes into account area of the geometric shape, the categorical cross-entropy and the negative entropy. In contrast to previous approaches, GC-Net is trained end-to-end and predict object location without any post-processing (e.g. thresholding) that may require additional tuning. Extensive experiments on the CUB-200-2011 and ILSVRC2012 datasets show that GC-Net outperforms state-of-the-art methods by a large margin. Our source code is available at https://github.com/lwzeng/GC-Net.

1 Introduction

In a supervised setting, convoluational neural network (CNN) has showed an unprecedented success in localizing objects under complicated scenes [6,10,11]. However, such a success is relying on large-scale, manually annotated bounding boxes (bboxes), which are expensive to acquire and may not be always accessible. Recently, researchers start to shift their interests to weakly supervised object localization (WSOL) [1,13,15,21–24]. Such methods predict both object class

Electronic supplementary material The online version of this chapter (https://doi.org/10.1007/978-3-030-58574-7_29) contains supplementary material, which is available to authorized users.

© Springer Nature Switzerland AG 2020
A. Vedaldi et al. (Eds.): ECCV 2020, LNCS 12371, pp. 481–496, 2020.
https://doi.org/10.1007/978-3-030-58574-7_29

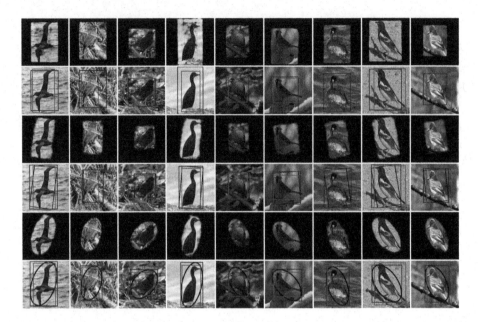

Fig. 1. Weakly supervised object localization results of examples from CUB-200-2011 dataset using GC-Net. 1st-2nd rows: predictions using a normal rectangle geometry constraint. 3rd-4th rows: predictions using a rotated rectangle geometry constraint. 5th-6th rows: predictions using a rotated ellipse geometry constraint. Predicted and ground truth bboxes are in blue and red, respectively. Rotated rectangles and ellipses are in black, which induced the predicted bboxes.

and location by using only classification labels. However, since loss functions widely used in fully supervised settings are not directly generalizable to weakly supervised counterparts, it remains a challenging problem as to how to develop an effective supervision for object localization using only image-level information.

Up to update, two types of learning-based approaches are commonly used for the WSOL task, including self-taught learning [1] and methods that take advantage of class activation maps (CAMs) [21–24]. Unfortunately, the former method is not end-to-end. While the latter CAM-based approaches being able to learn end-to-end, they are suffering two obvious issues. First, the use of activated regions which sometimes are ambiguous may not be able to reflect the exact location of object of interest. As such, supervision signal produced by these methods is not strong enough to train a deep network for precise object localization. The second issue is that in these approaches a threshold value needs to be tuned manually and carefully so as to extract good bboxes from the respective activation map.

To overcome the existing limitations above, we propose the geometry constrained network for WSOL, which we term GC-Net. It has three modules: a detector, a generator and a classifier. The detector takes responsibility for regressing the coefficients of a specific geometric shape. The generator, which can be either learning-driven or model-driven, converts these coefficients to a binary mask conforming to that shape, applied then to masking out the object of interest in the input image. This can be seen in the 1st, 3rd and 5th rows of Fig. 1.

The classifier takes the masked images (both object and background) as inputs and performs two complementary image classification tasks. To train GC-Net effectively, we propose a novel multi-task loss function, including the area loss, the object loss and the background loss. The area loss constrains the predicted geometric shape to be tight and compact, and the object and background losses together guarantee that the masked region contains only the object. Once the network is trained using image class label information, the detector is deployed to produce object class and bbox directly and accurately. Collectively, the main contributions of the paper can be summarized as:

- We propose a novel GC-Net for WSOL in the absence of bbox annotations. Different from the currently most popular CAM-based approaches, GC-Net is trained end-to-end and does not need any post-processing step (e.g. thresholding) that may need a careful hyperparameter tuning. It is easy and accurate and therefore paves a new way to solve this challenging task.
- We propose a generator by learning or using knowledge about mathematical modeling. In both methods, the generator allows backpropagation of network errors. The generator also imposes a hard, explicit geometry constraint on GC-Net. In contrast to previous methods where no constraint was considered, supervision signal induced by such a geometry constraint is strong and can be used to supervise and train GC-Net effectively.
- We propose three novel losses (i.e. object loss, background loss, and area loss) to supervise the training of detector. While the object loss tells the detector where the object locates, the background loss ensures the completeness of the object location. Moreover, the area loss computes the geometric shape area by imposing tightness on the resulting mask used to highlight the object for classification. These three losses work together effectively to deliver highly accurate localization.
- We evaluate our method on a fine-grained classification dataset, CUB-200-2011 and a large-scale dataset, ILSVRC2012. The method outperforms existing state-of-the-art WSOL methods by a large margin.

2   Related Work

[1] proposed a self-taught learning-based method for WSOL, which determines the object location by masking out different regions in the image and then observes the changes of resulting classification performance. When the selected region shifts from object to background, the classification score drops significantly. This method was embedded in a agglomerative cluster to generate self-taught localization hypotheses, from which the bbox was obtained. While the changes of the classifier score indicated the location of the object, the approach was not end-to-end. Instead, localization was carried out by a follow-up clustering step.

In [24], the authors proposed the global average pooling (GAP) layer to compute CAMs for object localization. Specifically, after the forward pass of a trained CNN classifier, the feature maps generated by the classifier were multiplied by the weights from the fully connected layer that uses the GAP layer outputs as the inputs. The resulting weighted feature map formed the final CAM, from which a bbox was extracted. Later on, researchers [3,8] found that the last fully connected layer used in the classifier in [24] is removable and GAP itself has the capability of classifying images. They also found that the feature maps before the GAP layer can be directly used as CAMs. As a result, these findings drastically simplified the process of generating distinctive CAMs. Although these methods are end-to-end, the use of CAMs only identifies the most distinguishing parts of the object. It is non-trivial to learn an accurate CAM that contains the compact and complete object.

Since then, different extensions have been proposed to improve the generation process of CAMs such that they can catch more complete regions belonging to the object. A self-produced guidance (SPG) approach [23] used a classification network to learn high confident regions, under the guidance of which they then leveraged attention maps to progressively learn the SPG masks. Object regions were separated from background regions with these masks. ACoL [22] improved localization accuracy through two adversarial classification branches. In this method, different regions of the object were activated by the adversarial learning and the network inter-layer connections. The resulting CAMs from the two branches were concatenated to predict more complete regions of the object. Similarly, DA-Net [21] used a discrepant divergent activation (DDA) to minimize the cosine similarity between CAMs obtained from different branches. Each branch can thus activate different regions of the object. For classification, DA-Net employed a hierarchical divergent activation (HDA) to predict hierarchical categories, and the prediction of a parent class enabled the activation of similar regions in its child classes.

3   The Proposed Method

Different from the methods above, Our GC-Net consists of three modules: a detector, a generator, and a classifier. The detector predicts a set of coefficients representing some geometric shape enclosing the object. The generator transforms the coefficients into a binary mask. The classifier then classifies the resulting masked images. During training, only classification labels are needed and during inference the detector is used to predict the geometry coefficients, from which object location can be computed. An overview of the proposed GC-Net is given in Fig. 2. In the following, we provide more details about each module, as well as define the loss functions for training these modules.

3.1   Detector

The detector can be a state-of-the-art CNN architecture for image classification, such as VGG16, GoogLeNet, etc. However, for different geometric shapes, we need to change the output number of the last fully connected layer in the detector. For example, for a normal rectangle, the detector has 4 outputs (i.e. coefficients): namely the center (c_x, c_y), the width h, and the height w. For a rotated rectangle, the detector regresses 5 coefficients: the center (c_x, c_y), the

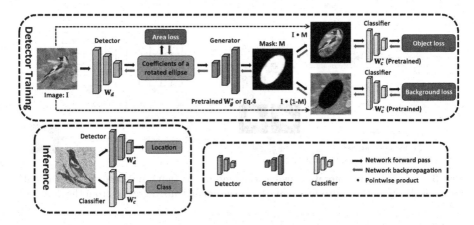

Fig. 2. The architecture of our GC-Net including the detector, generator and classifier. In this figure, the geometry constraint is imposed by a rotated ellipse. The network is trained end-to-end and during inference the classifier and detector respectively predict the object category and location. No post-processing, such as thresholding, is required.

width a, the height b, and the rotation angle θ. For an ellipse, the detector regresses 5 coefficients: the center (c_x, c_y), the axis a, the axis b, and the rotation angle θ. In our experiments, we will compare object localization accuracy using these shape designs. Using one set of coefficients, one can easily compute a respective geometric shape, which can form a binary mask in that image. However, it is non-trivial if one wants to backpropagate network errors during training. To tackle this, next we propose two methods to generate the object mask.

3.2 Generator

In this section, we propose a learning-driven method and a model-driven method to generate the object mask, The accuracy of each method will be compared in Sect. 4.4. Figure 3 left shows the learning-driven mask generator, which uses a network to learn the conversion between the coefficients from the detector and the object binary mask. Figure 3 right shows the model-driven mask generator. In this method, the conversion is done by using mathematical models (knowledge) without learning. Both methods impose a hard constraint on the detector such that the predicted shape satisfy some specific geometric constraints. Such a constraint improves localization accuracy and makes our method different from previous methods based on CAMs.

Learning-Driven Generator: The mask generator can be a neural network, such as the one defined in Fig. 3 left, where we showed an example about how to generate a mask from the 5 coefficients of an ellipse. In the generator, the input was a 5-dimensional vector (representing the 5 coefficients), which was fed to a

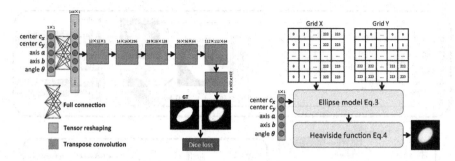

Fig. 3. Object mask generation using learning-driven (left) and model-driven (right) methods. Both methods produce a mask via the coefficients regressed from the detector.

fully connected layer resulting in a 144-dimensional vector. The new vector was reshaped to a two-dimensional tensor (excluding the last dimension), which was then upsampled all the way to the size of the original image. The upsampling was carried out through the transpose convolution operation. The network architecture was inspired by the AUTOMAP [25] for image reconstruction. Here, we have modified it to improve computational efficiency.

It is necessary to pretrain the mask generator before we use it to optimize the weights in the detector. To do so, we need to generate lots of paired data for training. Using ellipse as an example, the paired data is defined as the 5 coefficients versus the ground truth binary mask corresponding to these coefficients. To generate such paired data, we randomly sampled the coefficients following a Gaussian distribution. With the Dice loss and synthesized paired data, we are able to train the mask generator. The training process and details have been given in Sect. 4.2.

Once the generator is trained, we freeze its weights and connect it to the detector. By doing this, the generator has the capability of mapping the coefficients predicted from the detector to a binary mask, which can be employed to identify the object region as well as the background region. On the other hand, the errors produced by the classifier (introduced next) can propagate back to the detector, so the training process of the detector is effectively supervised.

Model-Driven Generator: Instead of learning, the mask generation process can be also realized by a mathematical approach. The illustration is given in Fig. 3 right. Again let us use ellipse as an example. Similar deviations for other geometric shapes have been given in the supplementary. Given the coefficients (c_x, c_y, θ, a, b) of a general ellipse, we have the following mathematical model to represent it

$$\frac{((x - c_x)cos\theta + (y - c_y)sin\theta)^2}{a^2} + \frac{((x - c_x)sin\theta - (y - c_y)cos\theta)^2}{b^2} = 1, \quad (1)$$

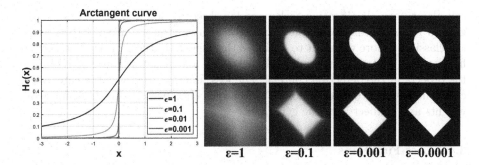

Fig. 4. Impact of ϵ on the approximated Heaviside function for 1D (left) and 2D (right) cases. The smaller ϵ is, the closer the function is approaching to the true binary function.

where $x, y : \Omega \subset \mathbb{R}^2$. To generate the mask induced by the ellipse, we can use the following Heaviside (binary) function

$$H(\phi(x,y)) = \begin{cases} 0 & \phi(x,y) > 0 \\ 1 & \phi(x,y) \le 0 \end{cases}, \tag{2}$$

with $\phi(x,y)$ defined as

$$\phi(x,y) = \frac{((x-c_x)cos\theta + (y-c_y)sin\theta)^2}{a^2} + \frac{((x-c_x)sin\theta - (y-c_y)cos\theta)^2}{b^2} - 1. \tag{3}$$

However, it is difficult to backpropagate network errors using such a representation due to its non-differentiability. To tackle this difficulty, we propose to use the inverse of a tangent function to approximate the Heaviside function [2,5]

$$H_\epsilon(\phi(x,y)) = \frac{1}{2}\left(1 + \frac{2}{\pi}arctan\left(\frac{\phi(x,y)}{\epsilon}\right)\right). \tag{4}$$

With this equation, the pixel indices falling in the ellipse region are 1, otherwise 0. Note that there is a hyperparameter ϵ which controls the smoothness of the Heaviside function. The bigger its value is, the smoother H_ϵ will be. When ϵ is infinitely close to zero, (4) is equivalent to (2). In Fig. 4, we illustrate the results of using different ϵ in this approximation for 1D and 2D cases. In our implementation, we made the parameter learnable in our network in order to avoid manual tuning of this hyperparameter. Of note, if the generator is chosen model-driven, we can use it directly in GC-Net in Fig. 2 without pretraining.

3.3 Classifier

The classifier is a common image classification neural network. In inference phase, the classifier is responsible for predicting the image category. In detector training phase, it takes the resulting masked images as inputs and performs two complementary classification tasks: one for object region and another for background region. Similarly to the learning-driven generator, we need to pretrain the classifier before we use it to optimize the weights in the detector. The classifier could be pretrained using ILSVRC2012 [12] and then fine tuned to recognize the objects in the detection context. The loss function used was the categorical cross-entropy loss, defined in loss (7). Once the classifier is trained, we freeze its weights and connect it to the generator.

3.4   Loss Functions

After both the object mask generator and classifier are pretrained (if the generator mode is learning-driven), we can start to optimize the weights in the detector. Three loss functions were developed to supervise the detector training: the area loss $\mathcal{L}_a$, the object loss $\mathcal{L}_o$, and the background loss $\mathcal{L}_b$. In Fig. 2, we have illustrated where they should be used. The final loss is a sum of the three, given as

$$\mathcal{L}(\mathbf{W}_d) = \alpha\mathcal{L}_a(\mathbf{W}_d) + \beta\mathcal{L}_o(\mathbf{W}_d, \mathbf{W}_g^*, \mathbf{W}_c^*) + \gamma\mathcal{L}_b(\mathbf{W}_d, \mathbf{W}_g^*, \mathbf{W}_c^*), \tag{5}$$

where α, β and γ are three hyperparameters balancing the three losses. $\mathbf{W}_d$ denotes the network weights in the detector; $\mathbf{W}_g^*$ denotes the fixed, pretrained network weights in the mask generator; $\mathbf{W}_c^*$ denotes the fixed, pretrained network weights in the classifier. The aim is to find the optimal $\mathbf{W}_d^*$ such that the combined loss is minimized. Here the area loss is imposed on the object mask. This loss ensures the tightness/compactness of the mask, without which the mask size is not constrained and therefore can be very big sometimes. The area of a geometrical shape can be simply approximated by

$$\mathcal{L}_a = a \cdot b, \tag{6}$$

where $\cdot$ denotes the pointwise product; a and b can represent the two axes of an ellipse or the width and height of a rectangle, which are two output coefficients from the detector.

Next, the object loss is defined as the following categorical cross-entropy

$$\mathcal{L}_o = -\sum_{j}^{m}\sum_{i}^{n} q_{i,j}\log\left(\frac{e^{p_{i,j}^o}}{\sum_{k}^{n} e^{p_{k,j}^o}}\right), \tag{7}$$

where m and n denote the number of training samples and the number of class labels, respectively; q stands for the ground truth class label; p^o represents the output of the classifier fed with the masked image enclosing only object region, and it is of the form

$$p^o = \mathbf{CNN}(M \cdot I, \{\mathbf{W}_d, \mathbf{W}_g^*, \mathbf{W}_c^*\}).$$

$\mathbf{CNN}$ above represents the whole network with the weights $\{\mathbf{W}_d, \mathbf{W}_g^*, \mathbf{W}_c^*\}$ and it takes as input the original image I multiplied by the mask M.

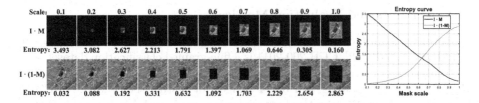

Fig. 5. Statistical analysis of entropy. Left: masked object regions (top) and background regions (bottom). Right: entropy values versus mask scales. The entropy increases when there are more uncertainties. Oppositely, it decreases when more certainties are present.

The value of the object loss (7) is small if the object is enclosed correctly inside the mask M. However, using this loss alone, we found in experiments that the masked region sometimes contains the object partially, such as head or body of a bird. This observation motives us to consider how to use background region. As such, we propose the following background loss

$$\mathcal{L}_b = \sum_j^m \sum_i^n \frac{e^{p_{i,j}^b}}{\sum_k^n e^{p_{k,j}^b}} \log \left(\frac{e^{p_{i,j}^b}}{\sum_k^n e^{p_{k,j}^b}} \right), \tag{8}$$

where p^b represents the output of the classifier fed with the masked image enclosing only background region, and it is of the form

$$p^b = \mathbf{CNN}(I \cdot (1 - M), \{\mathbf{W}_d, \mathbf{W}_g^*, \mathbf{W}_c^*\}).$$

We note that the proposed loss (8) is known as the negative entropy. In information theory, entropy is the measure of uncertainty in a system or an event. In our case, we want the classifier to produce the maximum uncertainty on the background region, which is the situation that only pure background remains (i.e. the object is completely enclosed by the mask, as shown in Fig. 5). The negative sign is to reverse the maximum entropy to the minimum. By minimizing the three loss functions simultaneously, we are able to classify the object accurately and meanwhile produce compact and complete bbox around the object of interest using only classification labels. Our method is end-to-end without using any post-processing step and therefore is very accurate, as can be confirmed from our experiments next.

4 Experiments

In this section, we first introduce datasets and quantitative metrics used for experiments. This is followed by implementation details of the proposed method as well as ablation studies of different loss functions. Next, learning- and model-driven methods are compared and different geometry constraints are evaluated. Extensive comparisons with state-of-the-art methods are given in the end.

4.1 Datasets and Evaluation Metrics

We evaluated our GC-Net using two large-scale datasets, i.e., CUB-200-2011 [19] and ILSVRC2012 [12]. CUB-200-2011 is a fine-grained classification dataset with 200 categories of birds. There are a total of 11,788 images, which were split into 5,994 images for training and 5,794 images for testing. For the ILSVRC2012 dataset, we chose the subset[1] where we have ground truth labels for this WSOL task. The subset contains 1000 object categories, which have already been split into training and validation. We used 1.2 million images in the training set to train our model and 50,000 images in the validation set for testing.

For evaluation metrics, we follow [4] and [12], where they defined the location error [4] and the correct localization [12] for performance evaluation. The location error (LocErr) is calculated based on both classification and localization accuracy. More specifically, LocErr is 0 if both classification and localization are correct, otherwise 1. Classification is correct if the predicted category is the same to ground truth, and localization is correct if the value of intersection over union (IoU) between the predicted bbox and the ground truth bbox is greater than 0.5. The smaller the LocErr is, the better the network performs. The correct location (CorLoc) is computed solely based on localization accuracy. For example, it is 1 if IoU> 0.5. The higher the CorLoc is, the better the method is. In some experiments, we also reported the classification error (ClaErr) for performance evaluation.

4.2 Implementation Details

We need to pretrain the generator and classifier prior to training the detector. We first provide implementation details of training the classifier. For ILSVRC2012, we directly used the pretrained weights provided by PyTorch for the classifier. For CUB-200-2011, we changed the output size of the classifier from 1000 to 200 and initialized remaining weights using those pretrained from ILSVRC2012. We then fine tuned the weights on CUB-200-2011 using SGD [16] with a learning rate of 0.001 and a batch size of 32.

For the learning-driven generator, we used SGD with a learning rate of 0.1 and a batch size of 128. We used Dice as the loss function as it is able to ease the class imbalance problem in segmentation. We randomly sampled many sets of coefficients, each being a 5×1 vector and representing the center (c_x, c_y), the axis a, the axis b and the rotation angle θ (ranging from $-90°$ to $90°$). These vectors and their respective masks were then fed to the generator for training. We optimized the generator for 0.12 million iterations and within each iteration we used a batch size of 128. By the end of training the generator has seen 15 million paired data and therefore is generalizable enough to unseen coefficients.

To train the detector, we freezed the weights of the pretrained generator and classifier and updated the weights only in the detector. We used Adam [9] optimizer with a learning rate of 0.0001, as we found that it is difficult for SGD

---

[1] This subset has not been changed or modified since 2012.

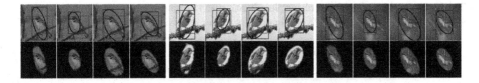

Fig. 6. Three examples showing the impact of using different losses. The predicted (blue) and ground truth (red) bboxes are shown in top row. For each example, from left to right the losses used are $\mathcal{L}_o$, $\mathcal{L}_o+\mathcal{L}_a$, $\mathcal{L}_o+\mathcal{L}_b$ and $\mathcal{L}_a+\mathcal{L}_o+\mathcal{L}_b$, respectively.

to optimize the detector effectively. For CUB-200-2011, we used a batch size of 32. For ILSVRC2012, we used a batch size of 256. The detector outputs were activated by the sigmoid nonlinearity before they were passed to the generator. We tested several commonly used backbone network architectures, including VGG16 [14], GoogLeNet [17] and Inception-V3 [18]. Of note, we used the same backbone for both the classifier and detector.

4.3 Ablation Studies

The ablation studies on CUB-200-2011 were performed to evaluate the contribution of each loss (i.e. the area loss $\mathcal{L}_a$, the object loss $\mathcal{L}_o$ and the background loss $\mathcal{L}_b$ in Sect. 3.4) for localization. For this experiment, we trained CG-Net using VGG16 as backbone and the learning-driven generator constrained by the rotated ellipse. Table 1 reported the localization accuracy measured by LocErr and CorLoc. When only $\mathcal{L}_o$ was used, there are two obvious issues: (1) CG-Net could not guarantee the mask is tight and compact to get rid of irrelevant background regions; and (2) CG-Net fails to detect some regions belonging to the object, These issues can be clearly observed in the 1st column of each example in Fig. 6.

To address the first issue, we added $\mathcal{L}_a$ to penalize area such that irrelevant background can be removed. However, using $\mathcal{L}_o+\mathcal{L}_a$ made the network focus on the most discriminate regions, as shown in the 2nd column of each example in Fig. 6. This side effect led to a sharp decreasing in localization accuracy, suggested by both LocErr and CorLoc (39.89%) in Table 1. This is because in many cases GC-

Table 1. Comparison of the object localization performance on CUB-200-2011 using different losses.

Loss functions	LocErr		CorLoc
	Top1	Top5	
$\mathcal{L}_o$	59.22	51.75	51.69
$\mathcal{L}_o+\mathcal{L}_a$	69.89	63.12	39.89
$\mathcal{L}_o+\mathcal{L}_b$	47.03	37.69	66.52
$\mathcal{L}_a+\mathcal{L}_o+\mathcal{L}_b$	**41.15**	**30.10**	**74.89**

Net detected only very small regions such as upper bodies of birds, reducing the IoU value and hence resulting in a big accuracy drop. As such, it is necessary to address the second issue. For this, we further added $\mathcal{L}_b$. This loss maximizes the uncertainty for background classification and therefore compensates the incomplete localization problem. As shown in the last column of each example in Fig. 6 and the last row in Table 1, such a combination delivered the most accurate performance. From the figure, we can also see that the localization contains more

Table 2. Comparison of the object localization performance on CUB-200-2011, using learning-driven and model-driven generators under different geometry constraints.

Strategies	Geometries	LocErr		CorLoc	Rotation
		Top1	Top5		
Learning-driven	Rectangle	44.35	34.25	70.06	×
	Rotated rectangle	**36.76**	**24.46**	**81.05**	✓
	Rotated ellipse	41.15	30.10	74.89	✓
Model-driven	Rectangle	44.10	33.28	71.56	×
	Rotated rectangle	44.25	33.62	71.13	✓
	Rotated ellipse	41.73	30.60	74.61	✓

irrelevant background if only $\mathcal{L}_o + \mathcal{L}_b$ is used without the area constraint. This experiment proved that all three loss functions are useful and necessary.

4.4 Learning-Driven Versus Model-Driven Geometry Constraints

In this section, we want to test which generator is better: model-driven or learning-driven? Also, we intend to see the performance of using different geometry constraints. As such, we performed experiments on CUB-200-211 using VGG16 as backbone for the detector. For each geometry, we implemented both learning- and model-driven strategies.

Table 2 reported location errors using both generators under different geometry constraints. The LocErr from the learning-driven generator was higher than that from the model-driven generator. During experiments, we found that the model-driven approach was more sensitive to hyperparameter tuning (i.e. α, β and γ in the loss). In addition, different initializations of learnable ϵ in Eq. (4) also affected localization accuracy a lot. Through many attempts, ϵ was initialized to 0.1, and α, β and γ were set to 1, 2.5 and 1 respectively. In contrast, the learning-driven method was robust to hyperparameter tuning. We were able to get a decent performance by setting both α, β and γ to 1. As such, we think that the inferior performance of the model-driven method may be due to the difficulty of hyperparameter tuning. Its performance may be further boosted by a more careful hyperparamter search. Although the learning-driven method has the advantage of a better localization performance, the model-driven method does not need training in advance.

Table 2 also reported location errors using three masks with different geometrical shapes. The least accurate geometry was rectangle, because it can easily include irrelevant background regions, thus decreasing the overall performance of the detector. Moreover, normal rectangles were unable to capture rotations, which seemed to be crucial to compute a high IOU value. In contrast, rotated rectangles were able to filter out noisy background regions and achieved the best localization performance among all three geometries. Although the localization accuracy from rotated ellipses was between rectangles and its rotated

Table 3. Comparison of the performance between GC-Net and the state-of-the-art on the CUB-200-2011 test set. Our method outperforms all other methods by a large margin for object localization. Here 'ClsErr', 'LocErr' and 'CorLoc' are short for classification error, location error and correct location, respectively.

Methods compared	ClsErr		LocErr		CorLoc
	Top1	Top5	Top1	Top5	
CAM-VGG [24]	23.4	**7.5**	55.85	47.84	56.0
ACoL-VGG [22]	28.1	–	54.08	43.49	54.1
SPG-VGG [23]	24.5	7.9	51.07	42.15	58.9
TSC-VGG [7]	–	–	–	–	65.5
DA-Net-VGG [21]	24.6	7.7	47.48	38.04	67.7
GC-Net-Elli-VGG (ours)	**23.2**	7.7	41.15	30.10	74.9
GC-Net-Rect-VGG (ours)	**23.2**	7.7	**36.76**	**24.46**	**81.1**
CAM-GoogLeNet [24]	26.2	8.5	58.94	49.34	55.1
Friend or Foe-GoogLeNet [20]	–	–	–	–	56.5
SPG-GoogLeNet [23]	–	–	53.36	42.28	–
DA-Net-Inception-V3 [21]	28.8	9.4	50.55	39.54	67.0
GC-Net-Elli-GoogLeNet (ours)	**23.2**	**6.6**	43.46	31.58	72.6
GC-Net-Rect-GoogLeNet (ours)	**23.2**	**6.6**	**41.42**	**29.00**	**75.3**

versions, they achieved the best performance in predicting rotations, which can be confirmed in the last two rows of Fig. 1. As is evident, rotations predicted by ellipses have a better match with true rotations of the objects. In contrast, rotations predicted by rotated rectangles were less accurate, as shown in the 3th and 4th rows of Fig. 1. Due to the lack of ground truth rotation labels, we could not study rotation quantitatively.

4.5   Comparison with the State-of-the-Art

In this section, we compared our GC-Net and its variants with the existing state-of-the-art on CUB-200-2011 and ILSVRC2012. We used VGG16, GoogLeNet and Inception-V3 as three backbones. Table 3 and 4 reported the performance of different methods.

Table 3 reported the performance of our GC-Net and other methods on CUB-200-2011. We used an average result from 10 crops to compute ClsErr and the center crop to compute LocErr, which is in line with what DA-Net [21] has done. When VGG16 was used as backbone, GC-Net constrained by the rotated rectangle (GC-Net-Rect-VGG) was the most accurate method among all compared. For top 1 LocErr, GC-Net-Rect-VGG was about 11% lower than DA-Net-VGG. For top 5 LocErr, it was about 14% lower than DA-Net-VGG. When GoogLeNet was used as backbone, GC-Net-rect-GoogLeNet achieved 41.42% top 1 LocErr and 29.00% top 5 LocErr, outperforming DA-Net-Inception-V3 by

Table 4. Comparison of the performance between GC-Net and the state-of-the-art on the ILSVRC2012 validation set. Our methods again perform the best.

Methods compared	ClsErr		LocErr	
	Top1	Top5	Top1	Top5
Backprop-VGG [13]	–	–	61.12	51.46
CAM-VGG [24]	33.4	12.2	57.20	45.14
ACol-VGG [22]	32.5	12.0	54.17	40.57
Backprop-GoogLeNet [13]	–	–	61.31	50.55
GMP-GoogLeNet [24]	35.6	13.9	57.78	45.26
CAM-GoogLeNet [24]	35.0	13.2	56.40	43.00
HaS-32-GoogLeNet [15]	–	–	54.53	–
ACol-GoogLeNet [22]	29.0	11.8	53.28	42.58
SPG-GoogLeNet [23]	–	–	51.40	40.00
DA-Net-InceptionV3 [21]	27.5	8.6	52.47	41.72
GC-Net-Elli-Inception-V3 (ours)	**22.6**	**6.4**	51.47	42.58
GC-Net-Rect-Inception-V3 (ours)	**22.6**	**6.4**	**50.94**	41.91

Fig. 7. Localization results on some images from the ILSRC2012 dataset using GC-Net. Top: single object localization. Bottom: multiple object localization. GC-Net tends to predict a bbox that contains all target objects. Ground truth bboxes are in red, predictions are in blue. Rotated rectangles and ellipses are in black, which induced the predicted bboxes.

9% and 11%, respectively. In terms of ClsErr, GC-Nets achieved comparable performance with CAM-based methods when VGG16 was concerned. However, GC-Net became significantly better when GoogLeNet was used.

As LocErr was calculated based on both classification and localization accuracy, a wrong classification could turn a correct localization to a wrong one. As such, in order to exclude the effect of classification, we also computed CorLoc, which is determined by only localization accuracy. In Table 3, we reported the performance of different methods using the CorLoc metric. One can clearly see that our approach has a significantly higher CorLoc value than that of runner-up DA-Nets. The accuracy (81.1%) of our GC-Net-Rect-VGG was about 13% higher than that of DA-Net-VGG, and the accuracy (75.3%) of GC-Net-rect-GoogLeNet was about 8% higher than that of DA-Net-Inception-V3.

For ILSVRC2012, we used inception-V3 as our backbone, which is the same for DA-Net. In order to directly use the pretrained model for our classifier, the input size of each image was resized to 299 × 299. Table 4 reported the performance of GC-Nets. First, our approach obtained a much lower ClsErr than that of DA-Net, i.e., about 5% improvement in top 1 accuracy has been achieved. However, the LocErr values of our GC-Nets were close to those of DA-Nets. Notice that on CUB-200-2011 each image contains only a single object, a large number of images in ILSVRC2012 contain multiple objects, as shown in Fig. 7 bottom. Overall, our methods achieved much better performance than CAM-based approaches.

5   Conclusion

In this study, we proposed a geometry constrained network for the challenging task of weakly supervised object localization. We have provided technical details about the proposed method and extensive numerical experiments have been carried out to evaluate and prove the effectiveness of the method. We believe that our new method will open a new door for researches in this area.

Acknowledgement. The work is supported by the National Natural Science Foundation of China under Grant 91959108, 61672357 and 61602315, and by the Ramsay Research Fund from the School of Computer Science at the University of Birmingham.

References

1. Bazzani, L., Bergamo, A., Anguelov, D., Torresani, L.: Self-taught object localization with deep networks. In: 2016 IEEE Winter Conference on Applications of Computer Vision (WACV), pp. 1–9 (2016)
2. Chan, T.F., Vese, L.A.: Active contours without edges. IEEE Trans. Image Process. **10**(2), 266–277 (2001)
3. Chaudhry, A., Dokania, P.K., Torr, P.H.: Discovering class-specific pixels for weakly-supervised semantic segmentation. arXiv preprint arXiv:1707.05821 (2017)
4. Deselaers, T., Alexe, B., Ferrari, V.: Weakly supervised localization and learning with generic knowledge. Int. J. Comput. Vis. **100**(3), 275–293 (2012). https://doi.org/10.1007/s11263-012-0538-3
5. Duan, J., Pan, Z., Yin, X., Wei, W., Wang, G.: Some fast projection methods based on Chan-Vese model for image segmentation. EURASIP J. Image Video Process. **2014**(1), 1–16 (2014). https://doi.org/10.1186/1687-5281-2014-7
6. Girshick, R., Donahue, J., Darrell, T., Malik, J.: Rich feature hierarchies for accurate object detection and semantic segmentation. In: The IEEE Conference on Computer Vision and Pattern Recognition (CVPR), pp. 580–587 (2014)

7. He, X., Peng, Y.: Weakly supervised learning of part selection model with spatial constraints for fine-grained image classification. In: Thirty-First AAAI Conference on Artificial Intelligence (AAAI) (2017)

8. Hwang, S., Kim, H.E.: Self-transfer learning for weakly supervised lesion localization. In: Medical Image Computing and Computer-Assisted Intervention (MICCAI), pp. 239–246 (2016)

9. Kingma, D.P., Ba, J.: Adam: a method for stochastic optimization. arXiv preprint arXiv:1412.6980 (2014)

10. Liu, W., et al.: SSD: single shot MultiBox detector. In: Leibe, B., Matas, J., Sebe, N., Welling, M. (eds.) ECCV 2016. LNCS, vol. 9905, pp. 21–37. Springer, Cham (2016). https://doi.org/10.1007/978-3-319-46448-0_2

11. Redmon, J., Divvala, S., Girshick, R., Farhadi, A.: You only look once: unified, real-time object detection. In: The IEEE Conference on Computer Vision and Pattern Recognition (CVPR), pp. 779–788 (2016)

12. Russakovsky, O., et al.: ImageNet large scale visual recognition challenge. Int. J. Comput. Vis. **115**(3), 211–252 (2015). https://doi.org/10.1007/s11263-015-0816-y

13. Simonyan, K., Vedaldi, A., Zisserman, A.: Deep inside convolutional networks: Visualising image classification models and saliency maps. arXiv preprint arXiv:1312.6034 (2013)

14. Simonyan, K., Zisserman, A.: Very deep convolutional networks for large-scale image recognition. arXiv preprint arXiv:1409.1556 (2014)

15. Singh, K.K., Lee, Y.J.: Hide-and-seek: forcing a network to be meticulous for weakly-supervised object and action localization. In: The IEEE International Conference on Computer Vision (ICCV), pp. 3544–3553 (2017)

16. Sutskever, I., Martens, J., Dahl, G., Hinton, G.: On the importance of initialization and momentum in deep learning. In: The International Conference on Machine Learning (ICML), pp. 1139–1147 (2013)

17. Szegedy, C., et al.: Going deeper with convolutions. In: The IEEE Conference on Computer Vision and Pattern Recognition (CVPR), pp. 1–9 (2015)

18. Szegedy, C., Vanhoucke, V., Ioffe, S., Shlens, J., Wojna, Z.: Rethinking the inception architecture for computer vision. In: The IEEE Conference on Computer Vision and Pattern Recognition (CVPR), pp. 2818–2826 (2016)

19. Wah, C., Branson, S., Welinder, P., Perona, P., Belongie, S.: The Caltech-UCSD Birds-200-2011 Dataset (2011)

20. Xu, Z., Tao, D., Huang, S., Zhang, Y.: Friend or foe: fine-grained categorization with weak supervision. IEEE Trans. Image Process. **26**(1), 135–146 (2016)

21. Xue, H., Liu, C., Wan, F., Jiao, J., Ji, X., Ye, Q.: Danet: Divergent activation for weakly supervised object localization. In: The IEEE International Conference on Computer Vision (ICCV), pp. 6589–6598 (2019)

22. Zhang, X., Wei, Y., Feng, J., Yang, Y., Huang, T.S.: Adversarial complementary learning for weakly supervised object localization. In: The IEEE Conference on Computer Vision and Pattern Recognition (CVPR), pp. 1325–1334 (2018)

23. Zhang, X., Wei, Y., Kang, G., Yang, Y., Huang, T.: Self-produced guidance for weakly-supervised object localization. In: The European Conference on Computer Vision (ECCV), pp. 597–613 (2018)

24. Zhou, B., Khosla, A., Lapedriza, A., Oliva, A., Torralba, A.: Learning deep features for discriminative localization. In: The IEEE Conference on Computer Vision and Pattern Recognition (CVPR), pp. 2921–2929 (2016)

25. Zhu, B., Liu, J.Z., Cauley, S.F., Rosen, B.R., Rosen, M.S.: Image reconstruction by domain-transform manifold learning. Nature **555**(7697), 487–492 (2018)

Duality Diagram Similarity: A Generic Framework for Initialization Selection in Task Transfer Learning

Kshitij Dwivedi[1,3] , Jiahui Huang[2] , Radoslaw Martin Cichy[3] ,
and Gemma Roig[1(✉)]

[1] Department of Computer Science, Goethe University Frankfurt,
Frankfurt, Germany
dwivedi@em.uni-frankfurt.de, roig@cs.uni-frankfurt.de
[2] ISTD, Singapore University of Technology and Design, Singapore, Singapore
jiahui_huang@sutd.edu.sg
[3] Department of Education and Psychology, Freie Universität Berlin,
Berlin, Germany
rmcichy@zedat.fu-berlin.de

Abstract. In this paper, we tackle an open research question in transfer learning, which is selecting a model initialization to achieve high performance on a new task, given several pre-trained models. We propose a new highly efficient and accurate approach based on duality diagram similarity (DDS) between deep neural networks (DNNs). DDS is a generic framework to represent and compare data of different feature dimensions. We validate our approach on the Taskonomy dataset by measuring the correspondence between actual transfer learning performance rankings on 17 taskonomy tasks and predicted rankings. Computing DDS based ranking for 17×17 transfers requires less than 2 min and shows a high correlation (0.86) with actual transfer learning rankings, outperforming state-of-the-art methods by a large margin (10%) on the Taskonomy benchmark. We also demonstrate the robustness of our model selection approach to a new task, namely Pascal VOC semantic segmentation. Additionally, we show that our method can be applied to select the best layer locations within a DNN for transfer learning on 2D, 3D and semantic tasks on NYUv2 and Pascal VOC datasets.

Keywords: Transfer learning · Deep neural network similarity · Duality diagram similarity · Representational similarity analysis

1 Introduction

Deep Neural Networks (DNNs) are state-of-the-art models to solve different visual tasks, *c.f.* [18,42]. Yet, when the number of training examples with labeled data is small, the models tend to overfit during training. To tackle this issue, a common approach is to use transfer learning by selecting a pre-trained network

Electronic supplementary material The online version of this chapter (https://doi.org/10.1007/978-3-030-58574-7_30) contains supplementary material, which is available to authorized users.

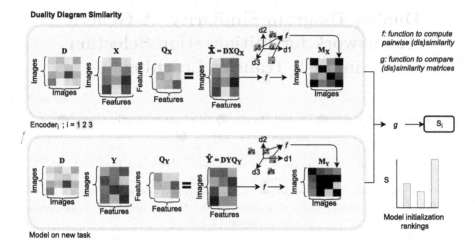

Fig. 1. *Duality Diagram Similarity (DDS):* We apply DDS to compare features of a set of initialization options (encoders) with features of a new task to get model initialization rankings to select the encoder initialization for learning a new task. The task feature for an image is obtained by doing a feedforward pass through a model trained on that task. $\mathbf{D}$ is the matrix that weights the images, $\mathbf{X}$ ($\mathbf{Y}$) is the matrix that stores the features from the encoder for all images, $\mathbf{Q_X}$ ($\mathbf{Q_Y}$) is a matrix that stores relations between features dimensions, $\mathbf{M_X}$ ($\mathbf{M_Y}$) contains the pairwise (dis)similarity distances between images, and S_i is the score for the ranking.

on a large-scale dataset and use it as initialization [19,28]. But how does one choose the model initialization that yields the highest accuracy performance when learning a new task?

Nowadays, there are a plethora of online available pre-trained models on different tasks. However, there are only a few methods [8,35] that automatically assist in selecting an initialization given a large set of options. Due to lack of a standard benchmark with standard evaluation metrics, comparing and building upon these methods is not trivial. Recently, Dwivedi and Roig [8] and Song *et al.* [35] used the transfer learning performance on the Taskonomy dataset [42] as groundtruth to develop methods for model selection. Both aforementioned methods for model selection are efficient compared to the bruteforce approach of obtaining transfer performance from all the models and selecting the best one. Yet, they used different metrics to evaluate against the groundtruth, and hence, they are not comparable in terms of accuracy. Although different, both of them used metrics that evaluate how many models in top-K ranked model initializations according to transfer learning performance were present in the top-K ranked models obtained using their method. We argue that such a metric doesn't provide a complete picture as it ignores the ranking within the top-K models as well as the ranking of models not in the top-K.

In this work, we first introduce a benchmark with a standard evaluation metric using Taskonomy [42] transfer learning dataset to compare different model initialization selection methods. We use Spearman's correlation between the rankings of different initialization options according to transfer learning performance and the rankings based on a model initialization selection method as our metric for comparison. We argue that our proposed benchmark will facilitate the comparison of existing and new works on model selection for transfer learning. We then introduce a duality diagram [6,9,12] based generic framework to compare DNN features which we refer to as duality diagram similarity (DDS). Duality diagram expresses the data taking into account the contribution of individual observations and individual feature dimensions, and the interdependence between observations as well as feature dimensions (see Fig. 1). Due to its generic nature, it can be shown that recently introduced similarity functions [8,17] for comparing DNN features are special cases of the general DDS framework.

We find that model initialization rankings using DDS show very high correlation (>0.84) with transfer learning rankings on Taskonomy tasks and outperform state-of-the-art methods [8,35] by a 10% margin. We also demonstrate the reliability of our method on a new dataset and task (PASCAL VOC semantic segmentation) in the experiments section.

Previous works [22,41] have shown the importance of selecting which layer in the network to transfer from. In this paper, we also explore if the proposed method could be used to interpret representations at different depths in a pre-trained model, and hence, it could be used to select from which layer the initialization of the model should be taken to maximize transfer learning performance. We first show that the representation at different blocks of pre-trained ResNet [11] model on ImageNet [7] varies from 2D in block1, to 3D in block 3 and semantic in block 4. These observations suggest that representation at different depths of the network is suitable for transferring to different tasks. Transfer learning experiments using different blocks in a ResNet-50 trained on ImageNet as initialization for 2D, 3D, and semantic tasks on both, NYUv2 [23] and Pascal VOC [10] datasets, reveal that it is indeed the case.

2   Related Works

Our work relies on comparing DNN features to select pre-trained models as initialization for transfer learning. Here, we first briefly discuss related literature in transfer learning, and then, different methods to compare DNN features.

Transfer Learning. In transfer learning [25] the representations from a source tasks are re-used and adapted to a new target task. While transfer learning in general may refer to task transfer[19,28,40,42], or domain adaptation[30,37], in this work we focus specifically on task transfer learning. Razavian et al. [32] showed that features extracted from Overfeat [31] network trained on ImageNet [7] dataset can serve as a generic image representation to tackle a wide variety of recognition tasks. ImageNet pre-trained models also have been used to transfer to a diverse range of other vision related tasks [5,19,28,40]. Other works [14,17] have investigated why ImageNet trained models are good for transfer learning. In contrast, we are interested in improving the transfer performance by finding a better initialization that is more related to the target task.

Azizpour *et al.* [1] investigated different transferability factors. They empirically verified that the effectiveness of a factor is highly correlated with the distance between the source and target task distance obtained with a predefined categorical task grouping. Zamir *et al.* [42] showed in a fully computational manner that initialization matters in transfer learning. Based on transfer performance they obtained underlying task structure that showed clusters of 2D, 3D, and semantic tasks. They introduced the Taskonomy dataset [42], which provides pre-trained models on over 20 single image tasks with transfer learning performance on each of these tasks with every pre-trained model trained on other tasks as the initialization, and thus, providing groundtruth for a large number of transfers. Recent works [8,35] have used the Taskonomy transfer performance as groundtruth to evaluate methods of estimating task transferabilities. Those works use different evaluation metrics, which makes the comparison between those methods difficult. Following those works, we use Taskonomy transfer performance as a benchmark, and propose a unified evaluation framework to facilitate comparison between existing and future methods.

Yosinski *et al.* [41] explored transferability at different layers of a pre-trained network, and Zhuo *et al.* [44] showed the importance of focusing on convolutional layers of the model in domain adaptation. We also investigate if the similarity between DNN representations can be applied to both model and layer selection for transfer learning, which indeed is the case, as we show in the results section.

Similarity Measures for Transfer Learning Performance. Our approach is built under the assumption that the higher the similarity between representations is, the higher will be the transfer learning performance. Some previous works used similarity measures to understand the properties of DNNs. Raghu *et al.* [26] proposed affine transform invariant measure called Singular Vector Canonical Correlation Analysis (SVCCA) to compare two representations. They applied SVCCA to probe the learning dynamics of neural networks. Kornblith *et al.* [16] introduced centered kernel alignment (CKA) that shows high reliability in identifying correspondences between representations in networks trained using different initializations. However, in the above works, the relation between similarity measures and transfer learning was not explored.

Dwivedi and Roig [8] showed that Representational Similarity Analysis (RSA) can be used to compare DNN representations. They argued that using the model parameters from a model that has a similar representation to the new task's representation as initialization, should give higher transfer learning performance compared to an initialization from a model with a lower similarity score. Recently, Song *et al.* [35] used attribution maps [2,33,34] to compare two models and showed that it also reflects transfer learning performance. Our work goes beyond the aforementioned ones. Besides proposing an evaluation metric to set up a benchmark for comparison of these methods, we introduce a general framework using duality diagrams for similarity measures. We show that similarity measures, such as RSA and CKA, can be posed as a particular case in our general formulation. It also allows to use other more powerful similarities that are more highly correlated to transfer learning performance.

There is evidence in the deep learning literature, that normalization plays a crucial role. For instance, batch normalization allows training of deeper networks [15], efficient domain adaptation [3,20] and parameter sharing across multiple domains [27]. Instance normalization improves the generated image quality in fast stylization [13,38], and group normalization stabilizes small batch training [39]. In our DDS generic framework, it is straightforward to incorporate feature normalization. Thus, we further take into account the normalization of features before assessing the similarity between two DNN features and compare it to transfer learning performance.

3   Duality Diagram Similarity (DDS)

The term duality diagram was introduced by Escoufier [9] to derive a general formula of Principal Component Analysis that takes into account change of scale, variables, weighing of feature dimensions and elimination of dependence between samples. With similar motivation, we investigate the application of duality diagrams in comparing two DNNs. Let $\mathbf{X} \in \mathbb{R}^{n \times d_1}$ refer to a matrix of features with dimensionality d_1 obtained from feedforwarding n images through a DNN. The duality diagram of matrix $\mathbf{X} \in \mathbb{R}^{n \times d_1}$ is a triplet $(\mathbf{X},\mathbf{Q},\mathbf{D})$ consisting of a matrix $\mathbf{Q} \in \mathbb{R}^{d_1 \times d_1}$ that quantifies dependencies between the individual feature dimensions, and a matrix $\mathbf{D} \in \mathbb{R}^{n \times n}$ that assigns weights on the observations, i.e., images in our case. Hence, a DNN representation for a set of n examples can be expressed by its duality diagram. By comparing duality diagrams of two DNNs we can obtain a similarity score. We denote the two DNN duality diagrams as $(\mathbf{X},\mathbf{Q_X},\mathbf{D})$ and $(\mathbf{Y},\mathbf{Q_Y},\mathbf{D})$, in which the subindices in the matrix $\mathbf{Q}$ denote that they are computed from the set of features and images in $\mathbf{X}$ and $\mathbf{Y}$.

Table 1. *Distance and Kernel functions used in DDS.* Notation: $\mathbf{x}_i \in \mathbb{R}^{d_1}$ and $\mathbf{x}_j \in \mathbb{R}^{d_1}$ refer to the features corresponding to i^{th} and j^{th} image (i^{th} and j^{th} row of feature matrix $\mathbf{X}$), respectively. Here, γ_1 and γ_2 refer to the bandwidth of Laplacian and RBF kernel.

Distances	Pearson's: $1 - \frac{(\mathbf{x}_i - \overline{\mathbf{x}_i}) \cdot (\mathbf{x}_j - \overline{\mathbf{x}_j})}{\|\mathbf{x}_i - \overline{\mathbf{x}_i}\| \cdot \|\mathbf{x}_j - \overline{\mathbf{x}_j}\|}$	Euclidean: $\sqrt{\mathbf{x}_i^T \cdot \mathbf{x}_i + \mathbf{x}_j^T \cdot \mathbf{x}_j - 2 * \mathbf{x}_i^T \cdot \mathbf{x}_j}$	Cosine: $1 - \frac{\mathbf{x}_i \cdot \mathbf{x}_j}{\|\mathbf{x}_i\| \cdot \|\mathbf{x}_j\|}$
Kernels	linear: $\mathbf{x}_i^T \mathbf{x}_j$	Laplacian: $\exp(-\gamma_1 \|\mathbf{x}_i - \mathbf{x}_j\|_1)$	RBF: $\exp(-\gamma_2 \|\mathbf{x}_i - \mathbf{x}_j\|^2)$

To compare two duality diagrams, Robert and Escoufier [29] introduced the RV coefficient. The motivation behind RV coefficient was to map n observations of $\mathbf{X}$ in the d_1-dimensional space and $\mathbf{Y}$ in the d_2-dimensional space. Then, the similarity between $\mathbf{X}$ and $\mathbf{Y}$ can be assessed by comparing the pattern of obtained maps or, equivalently, by comparing the set of distances between all pairwise observations of both maps. To estimate the distances between pairwise observation, Robert and Escoufier [29] used dot product and compared two (dis)similarity matrices using the cosine distance.

In a nutshell, to compare two sets of DNN features $\mathbf{X}$ and $\mathbf{Y}$, we require three steps (Fig. 1): first, transforming the data using $\mathbf{Q_X}$ and $\mathbf{D}$ to $\hat{\mathbf{X}}$, using $\hat{\mathbf{X}} = \mathbf{DXQ_X}$, and $\hat{\mathbf{Y}}$ with $\hat{\mathbf{Y}} = \mathbf{DYQ_Y}$. Second, using a function, which we denote as f, to measure (dis)similarity between each pair of data points to generate pairwise distance maps. Let $\mathbf{M_X}$ be the matrix that stores the (dis)similarity between pairwise distance maps for $\hat{\mathbf{X}}$, also referred to as representational (dis)similarity matrices. It is computed as $\mathbf{M_X}(i,j) = f(\hat{\mathbf{X}}(i,:), \hat{\mathbf{X}}(j,:))$, in which i and j denote the indices of the matrices. Analogously, $\mathbf{M_Y}$ is the matrix that stores the (dis)similarity between pairwise distance maps of $\hat{\mathbf{Y}}$. Third, a function g to compare $\mathbf{M_X}$ and $\mathbf{M_Y}$ to obtain a final similarity score, denoted as S, and computed as $S = g(\mathbf{M_X}, \mathbf{M_Y})$ is applied. The above formulation using duality diagrams provides a general formulation that allows us to investigate empirically which combination of $\mathbf{Q}, \mathbf{D}$, f and g is suitable for a given application, which in our case is estimating transferability rankings to select the best model (or layer in a model) to transfer given a new dataset and/or task.

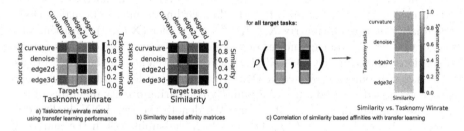

a) Taskonomy winrate matrix using transfer learning performance   b) Similarity based affinity matrices   c) Correlation of similarity based affinities with transfer learning

Fig. 2. *Transfer learning vs. similarity measures.* We consider a) Taskonomy winrate matrix, b) an affinity matrix obtained by measuring similarity between DNNs trained on different tasks. c) the Spearman's correlation (denoted by ρ) between the columns of two matrices. The resulting vector shows the correlation of the similarity based rankings with transfer learning performance based rankings for 4 Taskonomy tasks. Here we illustrate the results using DDS ($f = Laplacian$), and the procedure remains the same using any similarity measure.

Interestingly, using the above DDS framework, we can easily show that recently used similarity measures, e.g., CKA and RSA, can be formulated as special cases of DDS. For RSA [8], $\mathbf{Q}$ is an identity matrix, $\mathbf{I} \in \mathbb{R}^{d_1 \times d_1}$, and $\mathbf{D}$ is a centering matrix, *i.e.*, $\mathbf{C} = \mathbf{I_n} - \frac{1}{n}\mathbf{1_n}$. f is Pearson's distance and g is Spearman's correlation between lower/upper triangular part of $\mathbf{M_X}$ and $\mathbf{M_Y}$. For CKA [17], $\mathbf{Q}$ and $\mathbf{D}$ are identity matrices $\mathbf{I} \in \mathbb{R}^{d_1 \times d_1}$ and $\mathbf{I} \in \mathbb{R}^{n \times n}$ respectively, f used is linear or RBF kernel and g is cosine distance between unbiased centered (dis)similarity matrices. In the supplementary section S1, we derive RSA and CKA as particular cases of the DDS framework.

In this work, we focus on exploring different instantiations of $\mathbf{Q}$, $\mathbf{D}$, f and g from our DDS framework that are most suitable for estimating transfer learning performance. We consider different formulations of $\mathbf{Q}$ and $\mathbf{D}$, resulting in z-scoring, batch normalization, instance normalization, layer normalization and group normalization (details in Supplementary S2). For function f we explore cosine, Euclidean, and Pearson's distance, as well as kernel based similarities, namely linear, RBF, and Laplacian. Mathematical equations for all functions are in Table 1. For function g, we consider Pearson's correlation to compare (dis)similarity matrices with and without unbiased centering [17,36].

4   Our Approach

4.1   Which DDS Combination ($\mathbf{Q}$, $\mathbf{D}$, f,g) Best Predicts Transferability?

After having defined the general formulation for using similarity measures for transfer learning, we can instantiate each of the parameters ($\mathbf{Q}$, $\mathbf{D}$, f and g) to obtain different similarity measures. To evaluate which combination of $\mathbf{Q}$, $\mathbf{D}$, f and g best predicts transferability and compare it to state-of-the-art methods, we consider transfer learning performance based winrate matrix (Fig. 2a) and affinity matrix proposed in Taskonomy dataset [42], as a transferability benchmark. The affinity matrix is calculated by using actual transfer learning performance on the target task given multiple source models pre-trained on different tasks. The winrate matrix is calculated using a pairwise competition between all feasible sources for transferring to a target task. Both these matrices represent transfer learning performance obtained by bruteforce, and hence, can be considered as an upper bound for benchmarking transferability. We use the Taskonomy dataset as a benchmark as it consists of pre-trained models on over 20 single image tasks with transfer learning performance on each of these tasks with every pre-trained model trained on other tasks as the initialization, thus, providing groundtruth for a large number of task transfers.

We use DDS to quantify the similarity between two models trained on different Taskonomy tasks and use that value to compute the DDS based affinity matrix (Fig. 2b). A column vector corresponding to a specific task in the Taskonomy affinity matrix shows the transfer learning performance on the target task when different source tasks were used for initialization. To evaluate how well a DDS based affinity matrix represents transferability, we calculate the Spearman's correlation between columns of the Taskonomy winrate/affinity matrix and DDS based affinity matrix. Using the rank-based Spearman's correlation for comparison between two rankings allows comparing the source tasks ranking on the basis of transfer learning performance with DDS based ranking. The resulting vector (Fig. 2c) represents the per task correlation of DDS with transferability.

We further evaluate if the best combination(s) we obtained from the above proposed evaluation benchmark using Taskonomy are robust to a new dataset and task. For this, we consider a new task, Pascal VOC semantic segmentation, following [8]. For the benchmark, we use the transfer learning performance on Pascal VOC semantic segmentation task given all Taskonomy models as sources.

We also investigate if the images selected to compute DDS have any effect on Spearman's correlation with transfer learning. For this purpose, we select images from NYUv2, Taskonomy, and Pascal VOC dataset and evaluate the proposed methods on both, Taskonomy and Pascal VOC benchmark. We further compute the variance performing bootstrap by randomly sampling 200 images from the same dataset 100 times to compute similarity. The bootstrap sampling generates a bootstrap distribution of correlation between transfer performance and similarity measures, which allows measuring the variance in Spearman's correlation with transfer performance when selecting different images from the same dataset.

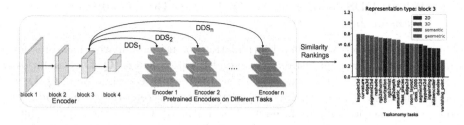

Fig. 3. *DNN Layer Selection.* Given a pre-trained encoder and a set of pre-trained models trained on diverse tasks, we can assess the representation type at different depth of the network by comparing the similarity between features at a given depth and pre-trained models.

4.2 Does DDS Find Best Layer Representation Within a Model to Transfer From?

In previous works [8,35,42], a major focus was to select a model to initialize from. However, once the model is selected as an encoder for initialization, the new layers of decoder usually branch out from the last layer of the pre-trained encoder. Such an approach is based on the *a priori* assumption that, for any new task, the output from the last layer of the pre-trained encoder is the best representation for transfer learning. We argue that this is task-type dependent. For instance, it has been shown that earlier layers of DNNs trained on ImageNet object recognition learn low-level visual features while deeper layers learn high-level categorical features [24]. Therefore, one would expect for low-level visual task, the representation in earlier layers of DNN might be better for transfer learning. Based on this intuition, we investigate if layers at different depths of the network are better suited to transfer to different types of tasks. We compute DDS of a pre-trained model at different depths with Taskonomy models to assess representation types at different depths (Fig. 3). To validate it, we select 3 task types (2D, 3D, and semantic) from NYUv2 and Pascal VOC dataset and perform transfer learning by attaching the decoder to different encoder layers.

5   Experimental Setup

We implemented the DDS general framework in python[1], in which new parameters and functions (Q, D, f, g) can be incorporated in the future. Below, we first provide details of datasets and models used for comparing the DDS combinations for model selection. Then, we describe the datasets and models used for layer selection from a pre-trained encoder.

5.1   Dataset and Models for Model Selection

Datasets. To compare different DDS combinations against the Taskonomy affinity and winrate matrix, we randomly select 200 images from the Taskonomy dataset. We use 200 images based on an analysis that shows that the correlation of DDS with transfer learning performance saturates at around 200 images (see Supplementary S3). To perform the bootstrap based comparison on a new semantic segmentation task on the Pascal VOC dataset, we randomly select 5000 images from Taskonomy, 5000 images from Pascal VOC, and all (1449) images from NYUv2 dataset.

Models. We use the selected 200 images to generate features from the last layer of the encoder of 17 models trained on 17 different tasks on the Taskonomy dataset. The Taskonomy models have an encoder/decoder architecture. The encoder architecture for all the tasks is a fully convolutional Resnet-50 without pooling to preserve high-resolution feature maps. The decoder architecture varies depending on the task. The models were trained on different tasks independently using the same input images but different labels corresponding to different tasks. For comparing two models, we use the features of the last layer of the encoder following [8,42]. The Pascal VOC semantic segmentation model that we use also has the same encoder architecture as Taskonomy models, and the decoder is based on the spatial pyramid pooling module, which is suitable for semantic segmentation tasks [5]. For comparison with the Pascal VOC model, we use the features of the last layer of the encoder of 17 Taskonomy models and the one Pascal VOC semantic segmentation model trained from scratch. We also report comparison with a small Pascal VOC model from [8] in Supplementary S4 to show that model selection can be performed even using small models.

5.2   Dataset and Models for Layer Selection

Datasets. To validate whether the proposed layer selection using similarity measures reflects transferability, we perform training on different datasets and tasks by branching the decoders from different layers of the encoder. Specifically, we evaluate on 3 tasks (Edge Detection, Surface Normal Prediction and Semantics Segmentation) on Pascal VOC [10] dataset, and 3 tasks (Edge Detection, Depth

---

[1] Code available at https://github.com/cvai-repo/duality-diagram-similarity.

Prediction and Semantic Segmentation) on NYUv2 [23] dataset. Following Zamir
et al. [42], we use Canny Edge Detector [4] to generate groundtruth edge maps
while other labels were downloaded from Maninis et al. [21].

Models. We describe the models' encoder and decoder.

Encoder: We use a ResNet-50 [11] pre-trained on ImageNet [7] as our encoder,
which has four blocks, each of the block consist of several convolution layers
with skip connections, followed by a pooling layer. The branching locations that
we explore are after each of the four pooling layers. We also consider Resnet-50
pre-trained on Places [43] using the same experimental set-up, and report the
results in Supplementary S5.

Decoder: Following the success of DeepLabV3 [5] model, we use their decoder
architecture in all our experiments. Since the output channels of the ResNet-50
encoder varies at different branching locations, we stack the output feature maps
to keep the number of parameters in the downstream constant. More specifically,
the encoder outputs 256, 512, 1024, 2048 channels for location 1, 2, 3 and 4
respectively, we stack the output of early branchings multiple times (8× for
location 1, 4× for location 2 and 2× for location 3) to achieve a constant 2048
output channels to input to the decoder.

Training. ImageNet [7] pre-trained encoder is fine-tuned for the specific tasks,
while the decoder is trained from scratch. In all the performed experiments, we
use synchronized SGD with momentum of 0.9 and weight decay of 1e-4. The
initial learning rate was set to 0.001 and updated with the "poly" learning rate
policy [5]. The total number of epochs for the training was set to 60 and 200,
for Pascal VOC [10] and NYUv2 [23], respectively as in Maninis et al. [21].

6   Results

In this section, we first report the comparison results of different similarity measures. After selecting the best similarity measure we apply it for identifying the
representation type at different depth of the pre-trained encoder. Finally, we
validate if the branching selection suggested using similarity measures gives the
best transfer performance, by training models with different branching locations
on NYUv2 and Pascal VOC datasets.

6.1   Finding Best DDS Combination (Q, D, f ,g) for Transferability

We perform a thorough analysis to investigate which combinations of (Q, D,
f, and g) of the DDS lead to higher correlation with transferability rankings.
We focus on how to assign weights to different feature dimensions using Q,
D and distance functions f to compute the pairwise similarity between observations. In Table 2, we report results on the correlation with transferability
rankings showing the effect of applying combination of Q and D instantiated as
identity, z-score, batch/instance/group/layer normalization, and using different

Table 2. *Finding best DDS combination (**Q**, **D**, f ,g).* We report the results of comparison with transferability for differents sets of **Q**, **D** and f. Top 3 scores are shown in green, blue, brown, respectively. Best **Q**, **D** for each f is shown in bold.

Q,D	f					
	Kernels			Distances		
	Linear	Laplacian	RBF	Pearson	Euclidean	Cosine
Identity	0.632	0.815	0. 800	0.823	0.688	0.742
Z-score	0.842	**0.860**	**0.841**	0.856	**0.850**	0.864
Batch norm	0.729	0.852	0.840	0.857	0.807	0.850
Instance norm	**0.849**	0.835	0.838	0.850	0.847	0.850
Layer norm	0.823	0.806	0.786	0.823	0.813	0.823
Group norm	0.829	0.813	0.790	0.829	0.814	0.829

distance/kernel function as f. For g we use Pearson's correlation on unbiased centered dissimilarity matrices because it consistently showed a higher correlation with transfer learning performance (Supplementary Section S6). We observed a similar trend in results using Spearman's correlation for g (Supplementary Section S7).

In Table 2 we report the mean correlation of all the columns of the Taskonomy winrate matrix with the corresponding columns of a DDS based affinity matrix, which serve as the measure for computing how each of the similarity measures best predicts the transferability performance for each model. We first observe the results when **Q** and **D** are identity matrices. Laplacian and RBF kernels outperform linear kernel. For distance functions, Pearson outperforms euclidean and cosine. A possible reason for the better performance of Pearson's could be due to its invariance to translation and scale.

We next observe the effect of normalization using appropriate **Q** and **D**. We observe that the correlation with transferability rankings improves for all distance and kernel functions especially for low-performance distance and kernel functions. The gain in improvement is highest using z-scoring in most of the cases. A possible reason for overall performance improvement is that applying z-scoring reduces the bias in distance computation due to feature dimensions having high magnitude but low variance. Hence, for our next experiments, we choose z-scoring and select the top performing f: Laplacian and cosine.

6.2   Comparison with State-of-the-art on Taskonomy

We first compare the DDS based affinity matrices on the Taskonomy transferability benchmark. To quantify in terms of mean correlation across all the tasks, we report mean correlation with Taskonomy affinity and winrate matrix in Table 3. In Table 3 (also Supplementary Section S8), we observe that all the proposed DDS based methods outperform the state-of-the-art methods [8,35] by a large margin. DDS (f = cosine) improves [8] and [35] by 10.9% (12.6%) and 26.3%

Table 3. *Correlation of DDS based affinity matrices with Taskonomy affinity and win-rate matrix, averaged for 17 Taskonomy tasks, and comparison to state-of-the-art.* Top 2 scores are shown in green, and blue respectively. For this experiment, **Q** and **D** are selected to perform z-scoring, in all DDS tested frameworks.

Method	Affinity	Winrate	Total time(s)
Taskonomy Winrate[42]	0.988	1	1.6×10^7
Taskonomy affinity[42]	1	0.988	1.6×10^7
saliency[35]	0.605	0.600	3.2×10^3
DeepLIFT[35]	0.681	0.682	3.3×10^3
ϵ-LRP[35]	0.682	0.682	5.6×10^3
RSA[8]	0.777	0.767	78.2
DDS ($f = cosine$)	0.862	0.864	84.14
DDS ($f = Laplacian$)	0.860	0.860	103.36

(26.6%) on affinity (winrate), respectively. We report the correlation of different DDS based rankings with the rankings based on winrate and task affinities for 17 Taskonomy tasks in Supplementary S9 and find that proposed DDS based methods outperform state-of-the-art methods for almost all the tasks. We also report comparison using PR curve following [35] in Supplementary S10.

To compare the efficiency of different methods with respect to bruteforce approach, we report the computational budget required for different methods. A single forward pass of Taskonomy models on Tesla V100 GPU takes 0.022 s. Thus, for 17 tasks and 200 feedforward passes for each task, the total time for feedforward pass is 74.8 sec. Hence, the DDS based methods are several orders of magnitude faster than bruteforce approach, used in the Taskonomy approach [42], that requires several GPU hours to perform transfer learning on all the models. The number reported in Table 3 for Taskonomy was calculated by taking the fraction of the total transfer time (47,886 h for 3000 transfers) for 17^2 transfers used for comparison in this work. Further, the time for obtaining DDS based rankings takes only a few seconds on CPU and is an order of magnitude faster than attribution maps based methods.

6.3 Evaluating Robustness on a New Task and Dataset

In the evaluation benchmark that we proposed, which was used in the above reported experiments, we considered models that were trained using images from the Taskonomy dataset, and the images used to compute the DDS were also from the same dataset. To evaluate the robustness of DDS against a new task and images used to compute DDS, we consider a new task, namely Pascal VOC semantic segmentation, and use images from different datasets to compute DDS. To evaluate effect of selecting different images within the same dataset, we perform bootstrap to estimate the variance in correlation with transferability.

Table 4. *DDS correlation with transfer learning for Pascal VOC Semantic Segmentation.* Here each row represents a particular distance/kernel function as f, and each column represents a dataset. The values in the table are bootstrap mean correlation and standard deviation of a particular similarity measure computed using the image from a particular dataset. Top score is shown in green.

Method	Taskonomy	Pascal VOC	NYUv2
DDS ($f = cosine$)	0.525 ±0.057	0.722 ±0.049	0.518 ±0.034
DDS ($f = Laplacian$)	0.5779 ±0.050	0.765 ±0.038	0.521 ±0.029

In Table 4, we report the bootstrap mean and standard deviation of correlation of different similarity measures with transfer learning performance on the Pascal VOC semantic segmentation task. We observe that the similarity measures show a high correlation (>0.70 for $f = cosine$ and >0.75 for $f = Laplacian$) when using images from Pascal VOC, but low correlation when using images from another dataset (Taskonomy and NYUv2). We also observed a similar trend in Taskonomy benchmark (Supplementary Section S11). Thus, the similarity measure is effective when using images from the same distribution as the training images for the model of the new task. We believe that using images from the same data distribution in DDS as the ones used to train the model on the new task for selecting the best initialization is important because the model in the new task is trained using data sampled from this distribution. Since high correlation of DDS ($f = Laplacian$) with transferability is obtained in all the investigated scenarios using the images from the dataset of the new task that we want to transfer to, we argue that this is the most suitable choice for estimating transferability as compared to other similarity measures and set-ups.

6.4   Finding Representation Type at Different Depth of a Model

In the previous experiments, we demonstrated DDS ability to select models for transfer learning to a new task, given a set of source models. Here, we use DDS to interpret the representation type at different depths of the model, which would allow us to select which model layer to transfer from for a given type of task. For this purpose, we generate the features of the last layer of the encoder of 20 Taskonomy models to get the representation of each task type. We then compute the DDS ($f = Laplacian$) of Taskonomy features with each output block of the pre-trained ImageNet model. We use images from the same data distribution (Taskonomy) as used in the trained models to reveal the correlation with each layer and task type, as suggested in the previous experiment.

As shown in Fig. 4, we observe that the representation of block 1 is more similar to 2D models, block 3 is more similar to 3D and block 4 to semantic models. These results suggest that the representation of block 1 is better suited to transfer for 2D tasks, block 3 for 3D tasks and block 4 for semantic tasks. There is no clear preference for block 2. We observe a similar pattern with the pre-trained Places model (see Supplementary S5).

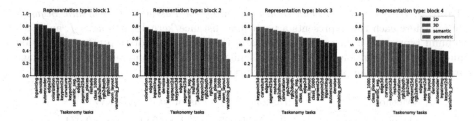

Fig. 4. *Block selection using DDS* on pre-trained encoder on Imagenet, and with DNNs trained on Taskonomy dataset on different tasks.

6.5   Does DDS Predict Best Branching Location from an Encoder?

Here we report the results of transfer learning performances of 4 tasks: surface normal prediction on Pascal VOC [10], Depth Prediction on NYU Depth V2 [23], and edge detection and semantic segmentation on both datasets. These 4 tasks cover the 3 task clusters we observed in the previous section. The results are shown on Table 5. We report the qualitative comparison of different block outputs in Supplementary S5. We observe that branching out from block 3 gives the best performance on depth and surface normal, branching out from block 1 provides the best result on edge detection, and branching out from block 4 is best for semantic segmentation. The transfer learning results are consistent with the similarity results in Fig. 4, which suggests that DDS ($f = Laplacian$) is a robust method for encoder block selection for different tasks.

Table 5. *Transfer learning performance of branching ImageNet pre-trained encoder on different tasks on Pascal VOC and NYUv2. Results show that branching out from block 1, 3, 4 of the encoder have better performances on edge, normals (depth) and semantic tasks, respectively. This is consistent with the diagram similarity in Fig. 4.*

	Task					
	Pascal VOC			NYUv2		
Block	Edge (MAE)	Normals (mDEG_DIFF)	Semantic (mIOU)	Edge (MAE)	Depth (log RMSE)	Semantic (mIOU)
1	**0.658**	18.09	0.257	**0.823**	0.322	0.124
2	0.686	15.59	0.392	0.857	0.290	0.165
3	0.918	**14.39**	0.627	1.297	**0.207**	0.219
4	0.900	15.11	**0.670**	1.283	0.208	**0.285**

7   Conclusion

In this work, we investigated duality diagram similarity as a general framework to select model initialization for transfer learning. We found that after taking into account the weighing of feature dimension, DDS (for all distance functions) show a high correlation (>0.84) with transfer learning performance. We demonstrated on Taskonomy models that the DDS ($f = Laplacian, f = cosine$) shows 10% improvement in correlation with transfer learning performance over state-of-the-art methods. DDS ($f = Laplacian$) is highly efficient and robust to novel tasks to create a duality diagram. We further show the DDS ($f = Laplacian$) effectiveness in layer selection within a model to transfer from.

Acknowledgments. G.R. thanks the support of the Alfons and Gertrud Kassel Foundation. R.M.C. is supported by DFG grants (CI241/1-1, CI241/3-1) and the ERC Starting Grant (ERC-2018-StG 803370).

References

1. Azizpour, H., Razavian, A.S., Sullivan, J., Maki, A., Carlsson, S.: Factors of transferability for a generic convnet representation. IEEE Trans. Pattern Anal. Mach. Intell. **38**(9), 1790–1802 (2015)
2. Bach, S., Binder, A., Montavon, G., Klauschen, F., Müller, K.R., Samek, W.: On pixel-wise explanations for non-linear classifier decisions by layer-wise relevance propagation. PLoS ONE **10**(7), e0130140 (2015)
3. Balaji, Y., Chellappa, R., Feizi, S.: Normalized wasserstein for mixture distributions with applications in adversarial learning and domain adaptation. In: 2019 IEEE/CVF International Conference on Computer Vision (ICCV), pp. 6499–6507 (2019)
4. Canny, J.: A computational approach to edge detection. In: Readings in computer vision, pp. 184–203. Elsevier (1987)
5. Chen, L.C., Papandreou, G., Schroff, F., Adam, H.: Rethinking atrous convolution for semantic image segmentation. ArXiv abs/1706.05587 (2017)
6. De la Cruz, O., Holmes, S.: The duality diagram in data analysis: examples of modern applications. Ann. Appl. Statist. **5**(4), 2266 (2011)
7. Deng, J., Dong, W., Socher, R., Li, L.J., Li, K., Fei-Fei, L.: Imagenet: a large-scale hierarchical image database. In: 2009 IEEE Conference on Computer Vision and Pattern Recognition, pp. 248–255 (2009)
8. Dwivedi, K., Roig, G.: Representation similarity analysis for efficient task taxonomy & transfer learning. In: Proceedings of the IEEE Conference on Computer Vision and Pattern Recognition, pp. 12387–12396 (2019)
9. Escoufier, Y.: The duality diagram: a means for better practical applications. In: Developments in Numerical Ecology, pp. 139–156. Springer, Heidelberg (1987). https://doi.org/10.1007/978-3-642-70880-0_3
10. Everingham, M., Van Gool, L., Williams, C.K., Winn, J., Zisserman, A.: The pascal visual object classes (voc) challenge. Int. J. Comput. Vision **88**(2), 303–338 (2010). https://doi.org/10.1007/s11263-009-0275-4
11. He, K., Zhang, X., Ren, S., Sun, J.: Deep residual learning for image recognition. In: 2016 IEEE Conference on Computer Vision and Pattern Recognition (CVPR), pp. 770–778 (2016)
12. Holmes, S., et al.: Multivariate data analysis: the french way. In: Probability and statistics: essays in honor of David A. Freedman, pp. 219–233. Institute of Mathematical Statistics (2008)

13. Huang, X., Belongie, S.: Arbitrary style transfer in real-time with adaptive instance normalization. In: Proceedings of the IEEE International Conference on Computer Vision, pp. 1501–1510 (2017)

14. Huh, M., Agrawal, P., Efros, A.A.: What makes imagenet good for transfer learning? arXiv preprint arXiv:1608.08614 (2016)

15. Ioffe, S., Szegedy, C.: Batch normalization: accelerating deep network training by reducing internal covariate shift. In: International Conference on Machine Learning, pp. 448–456 (2015)

16. Kornblith, S., Norouzi, M., Lee, H., Hinton, G.: Similarity of neural network representations revisited. In: International Conference on Machine Learning, pp. 3519–3529 (2019)

17. Kornblith, S., Shlens, J., Le, Q.V.: Do better imagenet models transfer better? In: Proceedings of the IEEE Conference on Computer Vision and Pattern Recognition, pp. 2661–2671 (2019)

18. Krizhevsky, A., Sutskever, I., Hinton, G.E.: Imagenet classification with deep convolutional neural networks. Commun. ACM **60**, 84–90 (2012)

19. Laina, I., Rupprecht, C., Belagiannis, V., Tombari, F., Navab, N.: Deeper depth prediction with fully convolutional residual networks. In: 2016 Fourth International Conference on 3D Vision (3DV), pp. 239–248 (2016)

20. Li, Y., Wang, N., Shi, J., Liu, J., Hou, X.: Revisiting batch normalization for practical domain adaptation. ArXiv abs/1603.04779 (2016)

21. Maninis, K.K., Radosavovic, I., Kokkinos, I.: Attentive single-tasking of multiple tasks. In: Proceedings of the IEEE Conference on Computer Vision and Pattern Recognition, pp. 1851–1860 (2019)

22. Misra, I., Shrivastava, A., Gupta, A., Hebert, M.: Cross-stitch networks for multitask learning. In: Proceedings of the IEEE Conference on Computer Vision and Pattern Recognition, pp. 3994–4003 (2016)

23. Silberman, N., Hoiem, D., P.K., Fergus, R.: Indoor segmentation and support inference from RGBD images. In: ECCV (2012)

24. Olah, C., Mordvintsev, A., Schubert, L.: Feature visualization. Distill (2017). https://doi.org/10.23915/distill.00007, https://distill.pub/2017/feature-visualization

25. Pan, S.J., Yang, Q.: A survey on transfer learning. IEEE Trans. Knowl. Data Eng. **22**(10), 1345–1359 (2009)

26. Raghu, M., Gilmer, J., Yosinski, J., Sohl-Dickstein, J.: Svcca: singular vector canonical correlation analysis for deep learning dynamics and interpretability. In: Advances in Neural Information Processing Systems, pp. 6076–6085 (2017)

27. Rebuffi, S.A., Bilen, H., Vedaldi, A.: Efficient parametrization of multi-domain deep neural networks. In: Proceedings of the IEEE Conference on Computer Vision and Pattern Recognition, pp. 8119–8127 (2018)

28. Ren, S., He, K., Girshick, R., Sun, J.: Faster r-cnn: Towards real-time object detection with region proposal networks. In: Advances in Neural Information Processing Systems, pp. 91–99 (2015)

29. Robert, P., Escoufier, Y.: A unifying tool for linear multivariate statistical methods: the RV-coefficient. J. Roy. Stat. Soc.: Ser. C (Appl. Stat.) **25**(3), 257–265 (1976)

30. Rozantsev, A., Salzmann, M., Fua, P.: Beyond sharing weights for deep domain adaptation. IEEE Trans. Pattern Anal. Mach. Intell. **41**(4), 801–814 (2018)

31. Sermanet, P., Eigen, D., Zhang, X., Mathieu, M., Fergus, R., LeCun, Y.: Overfeat: integrated recognition, localization and detection using convolutional networks. arXiv preprint arXiv:1312.6229 (2013)

32. Sharif Razavian, A., Azizpour, H., Sullivan, J., Carlsson, S.: CNN features off-the-shelf: an astounding baseline for recognition. In: Proceedings of the IEEE Conference on Computer Vision and Pattern Recognition Workshops, pp. 806–813 (2014)

33. Shrikumar, A., Greenside, P., Shcherbina, A., Kundaje, A.: Not just a black box: learning important features through propagating activation differences. arXiv preprint arXiv:1605.01713 (2016)

34. Simonyan, K., Zisserman, A.: Very deep convolutional networks for large-scale image recognition. CoRR abs/1409.1556 (2015)

35. Song, J., Chen, Y., Wang, X., Shen, C., Song, M.: Deep model transferability from attribution maps. In: Advances in Neural Information Processing Systems (2019)

36. Székely, G.J., Rizzo, M.L., et al.: Partial distance correlation with methods for dissimilarities. Ann. Statist. **42**(6), 2382–2412 (2014)

37. Tzeng, E., Hoffman, J., Saenko, K., Darrell, T.: Adversarial discriminative domain adaptation. In: Proceedings of the IEEE Conference on Computer Vision and Pattern Recognition, pp. 7167–7176 (2017)

38. Ulyanov, D., Vedaldi, A., Lempitsky, V.: Instance normalization: the missing ingredient for fast stylization. arXiv preprint arXiv:1607.08022 (2016)

39. Wu, Y., He, K.: Group normalization. In: Proceedings of the European Conference on Computer Vision (ECCV), pp. 3–19 (2018)

40. Xie, S., Tu, Z.: Holistically-nested edge detection. In: Proceedings of the IEEE International Conference on Computer Vision, pp. 1395–1403 (2015)

41. Yosinski, J., Clune, J., Bengio, Y., Lipson, H.: How transferable are features in deep neural networks? In: Advances in Neural Information Processing Systems, pp. 3320–3328 (2014)

42. Zamir, A.R., Sax, A., Shen, W.: Taskonomy: disentangling task transfer learning. In: Proceedings of IEEE Conference on Computer Vision and Pattern Recognition (CVPR) (2018)

43. Zhou, B., Khosla, A., Lapedriza, À., Torralba, A., Oliva, A.: Places: an image database for deep scene understanding. CoRR abs/1610.02055 (2017)

44. Zhuo, J., Wang, S., Zhang, W., Huang, Q.: Deep unsupervised convolutional domain adaptation. In: MM 2017 (2017)

OneGAN: Simultaneous Unsupervised Learning of Conditional Image Generation, Foreground Segmentation, and Fine-Grained Clustering

Yaniv Benny$^{(\boxtimes)}$ and Lior Wolf

Tel-Aviv University, Tel Aviv, Israel
`yanivbenny@mail.tau.ac.il`

Abstract. We present a method for simultaneously learning, in an unsupervised manner, (i) a conditional image generator, (ii) foreground extraction and segmentation, (iii) clustering into a two-level class hierarchy, and (iv) object removal and background completion, all done without any use of annotation. The method combines a Generative Adversarial Network and a Variational Auto-Encoder, with multiple encoders, generators and discriminators, and benefits from solving all tasks at once. The input to the training scheme is a varied collection of unlabeled images from the same domain, as well as a set of background images without a foreground object. In addition, the image generator can mix the background from one image, with a foreground that is conditioned either on that of a second image or on the index of a desired cluster. The method obtains state of the art results in comparison to the literature methods, when compared to the current state of the art in each of the tasks.

1 Introduction

We hypothesize that solving multiple unsupervised tasks together, enables one to improve on the performance of the best methods that solve each individually. The underlying motivation is that in unsupervised learning, the structure of the data is a key source of knowledge and each task exposes a different aspect of it. We advocate for solving the various tasks in phases, where easier tasks are addressed first, and the other tasks are introduced gradually, while constantly updating the solutions of the previous sets of tasks. The method consists of multiple networks that are trained end-to-end and side-by-side to solve multiple tasks. The method starts from learning background image synthesis and image generation of objects from a particular domain. It then advances to more complex tasks, such as clustering, semantic segmentation and object removal. Finally,

Electronic supplementary material The online version of this chapter (https://doi.org/10.1007/978-3-030-58574-7_31) contains supplementary material, which is available to authorized users.

© Springer Nature Switzerland AG 2020
A. Vedaldi et al. (Eds.): ECCV 2020, LNCS 12371, pp. 514–530, 2020.
https://doi.org/10.1007/978-3-030-58574-7_31

we show the model's ability to perform image-to-image translation. The entire learning process is unsupervised, meaning that no annotated information is used. In particular, the method does not employ class labels, segmentation masks, bounding boxes, etc. However, it does require a separate set of clean background images, which are easy to obtain in many cases.

Contributions. Beyond the conceptual novelty of a method that treats single-handedly multiple unsupervised tasks, which were previously solved by individual methods, the method displays a host of technical novelties, including: (i) a novel architecture that supports multiple paths addressing multiple tasks, (ii) employing bypass paths that allow a smooth transition between autoencoding and generation based on a random seed, (iii) backpropagation through three paths in each iteration, (iv) mixup module, which applies interpolation between latent representations of the generation and reconstruction paths, and more. Due to each of these novelties, backed by the ablation studies, we obtain state of the art results compared to the literature methods in each of the individual tasks.

2 Related Work

Since our work touches on many tasks, we focus the literature review on general concepts and on the most relevant work. **Generative models** are typically based on Generative Adversarial Networks [11] or Variational Auto-Encoders [18]. In addition, these two can be combined [21]. **Conditional image generation** conditions the output on an initial variable, most commonly, the target class. CGAN [23] and InfoGAN [7] proposed different methods to apply the condition on the discriminator. Our work is more similar to InfoGAN, since we do not use labeled data and the label is not linked to any real image and no conditional discriminator can be applied. The condition is maintained by a classifier that tries to predict the conditioned label and, as a result, forces the generator to condition the result on that label. **Semantic Segmentation** deals with the classification of the image pixels based on their class labels. For the supervised setting Unet [24], DeepLab [4], DeepLabV3 [5], HRNet [30] have shown great performance leaps using a regression loss. For the unsupervised case, more creative solutions are considered. In [3,6,8,14,16,27,31,32] a variety of methods have been used including inpainting, learning feature representation, clustering or video frames comparison. In **Clustering,** deep learning methods are the current state of the art. JULE [33] and DEPICT [10], cluster based on a learned feature representation. IIC [14] trains a classifier directly.

The most similar approach to ours is FineGAN [26], which our generators and discriminators are based upon. However, there are many significant differences and additions: (i) We added a set of encoders, which are trained to support new tasks. (ii) While FineGAN employs one-hot input, our generators use coded input, which is important for our autoencoding path. (iii) We added a skip connection, followed by a mixup module that combines the bypass tensor with the pre-image tensor. The mixup also allows passing only one of the tensors, making either the bypass or the pre-image optional in each flow. (iv) We employ single foreground generator instead of FineGAN's double hierarchical design, where we have found one generator to be dominant and the second one redundant. (v) Our model uses layer normalization [1] instead of batch normalization, which better performs for large number of classes, small batch size, and alternating paths. (vi) We define a new normalization method for the generators, where GLU [9] activation layers were used as non-linear activations. (vii) We add many losses and training techniques. Many of which are completely novel, as far as we can ascertain. As a result, our work outperforms FineGAN in all tasks and is capable of performing new tasks that its predecessor could not handle.

Mixup [35] is a technique for applying a weighted sum between two latent variables in order to synthesize a new latent variable. We use it to merge different paths in the model by mixing latent variables that are part coded by the encoder and part produced by the lower levels of the generation. As far as we can ascertain, this is the first usage of mixup to merge information from different paths. Our mixup is applied to image reconstruction in four different locations.

3   Method

To solve the tasks of clustering, foreground segmentation, and conditional generation, our method trains multiple neural networks side-by-side. Each task is solved by applying the networks in a specific order. Similarly, the model is trained by applying the networks in two different paths, with a specific set of losses.

Architecture. The compound network consists of two generators, three encoders and two discriminators. Figure 1,2 illustrate the two training paths. In the generation path, the generators produce a synthetic image conditioned on selected code, the encoders then retrieve the latent code from the generated images. In the reconstruction path, the encoders code an input image into latent code which is used by the generators to reconstruct the image. The reconstruction path is applied twice in each iteration, once on real images and once on fake images from the generation path. The reconstruction of fake images adds multiple capabilities of self-supervision such as reconstructing the background and mask, which is not applicable with real images without additional supervision.

Generators. The generation is performed by merging the results of two separate generators that run in parallel to produce the output image. One generator is dedicated for generating the background and the other for the foreground. The generators are conditioned on a two-level hierarchical categorization. Each category has a unique child class ϕ_c and a parent class ϕ_p shared by multiple child classes. These classes are represented by the one-hot vectors (e_c, e_p).

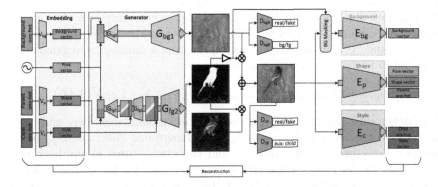

Fig. 1. Flow of the generation path. The generators decode the four priors (e_{bg}, e_p, e_c, z) and produce three separate images (foreground, background, mask) that are combined into the final image. The generated image is then coded by three encoders to retrieve the latent variables and priors.

An additional background one-hot vector e_{bg} affects the generation of the background images. Since there is a tight coupling between the class of the object (water bird, tropical bird, etc.) and the expected background, the typology of the background follows the coarse hierarchy, i.e. the parent class. The generator architecture is influenced by.

$$e_c[i] = \delta_{i,\phi_c}, \quad e_p[i] = \delta_{i,\phi_p}, \quad e_{bg} = e_p \tag{1}$$

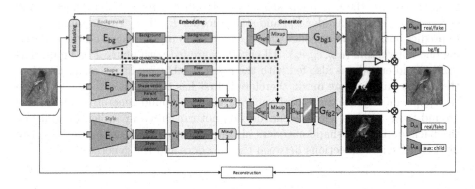

Fig. 2. Flow of the reconstruction path. The same sub-networks are rearranged to perform image reconstruction. The image is coded with the shape and style encoders and then decoded by the foreground generator to produce the foreground image and mask. Then the background encoder and generator code the masked image and produces a background image. The output image combines the foreground and background images. The mixup modules, placed in four different locations, merge the encoders' predicted codes with intermediate stages of the generation, acting as a robust skip connection.

The generation starts by converting the one-hot vectors into code vectors using learned embeddings. Such an embedding is often used when working with categorical values. A fourth vector z is sampled from a multi-variate gaussian distribution to represent non-categorical features.

$$v_{bg} = V_{bg}(e_{bg}), \quad v_p = V_p(e_p), \quad v_c = V_c(e_c), \quad z \sim \mathcal{N}(0,1)^{d_z} \qquad (2)$$

The background generator G_{bg} receives the background vector v_{bg} and noise z and produces a background image I_{bg}. The foreground generator G_{fg} receives the parent vector e_p, child vector e_c and the same z used in the background generation and produces a foreground image I_{fg} and a foreground mask I_m. The generator is optimized such that all foreground images with the same e_p will have the same object shape and all images with the same e_c will have a similar object appearance. The latent vector z is implicitly conditioned to represent all non-categorical information, such as pose, orientation, size, etc. It is used in both the background and foreground generation, so that the images produced by both networks will merge into a coherent image. Each generator is a composition of sub-modules applied back to back, with intermediate pre-images (A_{bg}, A_{fg}):

$$I_{bg} = G_{bg_1}(A_{bg}), \qquad\qquad A_{bg} = G_{bg_0}(v_{bg}, z) \qquad (3)$$
$$(I_{fg}, I_m) = G_{fg_2}(G_{fg_1}(A_{fg}, v_p), v_c), \qquad A_{fg} = G_{fg_0}(v_p, z) \qquad (4)$$

The final generated image is: (where $\circ$ denotes element-wise multiplication)

$$I = I_{bg} \circ (1 - I_m) + I_{fg} \circ I_m \qquad (5)$$

Encoders. Unlike FineGAN, which performs only the generation task, our method requires the use of encoders. We introduce three encoders: background encoder E_{bg}, shape encoder E_p, and style encoder E_c. They run in semi-parallel to predict both the latent codes (v_{bg}, v_p, v_c, z) of an input image and the underlying one-hot vectors (e_{bg}, e_p, e_c). All encoders are fed with image I as input. The background encoder is also fed with the mask I_m. During image reconstruction, there is no initial image mask, therefore it first has to be generated by encoding the shape and style features and applying the foreground generator. The lack of ground-truth mask is why the encoders do not run fully in parallel. In addition, the background and shape encoders also produce bypass tensors (B_{bg}, B_{fg}) to be used as skip connections between the encoders and the generators.

$$(B_{bg}) = E_{bg}(I, I_m) \qquad (6)$$
$$(\hat{e}_p, \mu_p, \sigma_p, B_{fg}, \mu_z, \sigma_z) = E_p(I) \qquad (7)$$
$$(\hat{e}_c, \mu_c, \sigma_c) = E_c(I) \qquad (8)$$

where (μ, σ) are three paired vectors of sizes (d_z, d_p, d_c) defining the mean and variance to sample each element of $(\hat{z}, \hat{v}_p, \hat{v}_c)$ from a gaussian distribution.

Mixup. At the intersection between the encoders and generators, we introduce a novel method to merge information coded by the encoders and information produced by the embeddings and lower levels of the generators. The mixup module [35], mixes two input variables with a weight parameter β. The rationale behind this application is that during generation there is no data coming from the encoders, so the mixup is turned off and only information from the embeddings and lower levels of the generators are passed forward. During reconstruction, we want our method to utilize the skip connections to improve performance and also use the predicted embeddings (v_p, v_c) to represent the object's shape and style. The contrast between the two paths leads to a difficulty in optimizing them simultaneously. The introduction of the mixup simplifies this by having both paths active during forward path and back-propagation. In contrast to regular residual connections, the ever changing β used in the mixup forces both inputs to be independent representations and not complement each other.

The mixup modules at the vector embeddings level (mixup1 and mixup2 in Fig. 2) mix the vectors (v_p, v_c) given by the embeddings (V_p, V_c), Eq. 2, with the predicted vectors $(\hat{v}_p, \hat{v}_c)$ produced by the encoders (E_p, E_c), Eq. 7,8. The mixture of features leads to both the embeddings and the encoders being optimized for reconstructing the object. This has two benefits. First, it trains the encoders to properly code the images, which improves clustering and learns image-to-image translation implicitly. Second, it trains the embeddings to represent the real object classes, which improves the generation task.

The mixup modules at the skip connections (mixup3 and mixup4 in Fig. 2) mix the pre-image tensors (A_{bg}, A_{fg}), Eq. 3,4, with the bypass tensors (B_{bg}, B_{fg}), Eq. 6,7. It serves to create the condition where the reconstruction path will be simultaneously dependent on the bypass and on the lower stage of the generators. This way, at any time we can choose any β or even pass only the bypass or only the pre-image and result in an almost identical image.

Given two inputs and a parameter β, the mixup is defined as follows:

$$v_{p_{mix}} = v_p \circ (1 - \beta_1) + \hat{v}_p \circ \beta_1, \quad v_{c_{mix}} = v_c \circ (1 - \beta_2) + \hat{v}_c \circ \beta_2$$
$$A_{fg_{mix}} = A_{fg} \circ (1 - \beta_3) + B_{fg} \circ \beta_3, \quad A_{bg_{mix}} = A_{bg} \circ (1 - \beta_4) + B_{bg} \circ \beta_4 \tag{9}$$

In our implementation, $\beta_1, \beta_2 \in [0, 1]$ and $\beta_3, \beta_4 \in [0.5, 1]$, are sampled in each iteration for each instance in the batch. At reconstruction, the mixed features $(v_{p_{mix}}, v_{c_{mix}}, A_{fg_{mix}}, A_{bg_{mix}})$ replace the features $(v_p, v_c, A_{fg}, A_{bg})$ in Eq. 3,4 as input to the generators. For illustration, please refer to Fig. 2.

GLU Layer Normalization. Following StackGANv2 and FineGAN architecture, we apply GLU [9] activation in the generators. Due to the multiple paths, the large scale and high complexity of our method, batch normalization was unstable for our low batch size, and, increasing the batch size was not an option. As a solution, we switched to layer normalization, which is not affected by the batch size. We fused the normalization and activation into a single module termed "GLU Layer Normalization". Given an input x with x_L, x_R representing an equal split in the channel axis (left/right): $GLU(x_L, x_R) = x_L \circ Sigmoid(x_R)$, $GLU\text{-}LNorm(x_L, x_R) = GLU(LNorm(x_L), x_R)$. In this method, the normalization is only applied on x_L. The input to the sigmoid, x_R, is not normalized. This is favorable, because x_R serves as a mask on x_L, and normalizing it across the channels contradicts this goal.

Discriminators. Following FineGAN, the two discriminators are adversarial opponents on the outputs I_{bg}, I. The background discriminator D_{bg} has two tasks, with a separate output for each. The tasks are as follows: (i) patch-wise prediction if the input image is real or fake when presented with either a real or fake background image, annotated as D_{bg_A}. (ii) patch-wise prediction if the input image is a background image or not when presented with either a real background image or a real object image, annotated as D_{bg_B}. The background generator is hereby optimized to generate images that look like real images and do not contain object features. In addition, when performing the reconstruction path on fake images, we also extract a hidden layer output and apply perceptual loss between generated and reconstructed backgrounds, annotated as D_{bg_C}, to reduce the perceptual distance between the original and the reconstructed image.

The image discriminator D_c receives real images from X_c or generated fake images, and also has two tasks: (i) predict if the input image is real or fake, annotated as D_{c_A}. (ii) predict the child class ϕ_c of the image, annotated as D_{c_B}, as in all InfoGAN-influenced methods. This trains the foreground generator to generate images that look real and represent the conditioned child class. In addition, we also extract a hidden layer output and apply perceptual loss between generated and reconstructed foreground images, annotated as D_{c_C}.

4   Training

To train to solve various tasks, we perform in each iteration two different paths through the model, by connecting the various sub-networks in a specific order.

4.1   Generation Path

The generation path is described in Fig. 1, Eq. 2–5. For illustrations, see Fig. 3. The inputs for this path are e_{bg}, e_p, e_c, z. During generation, the model learns to generate image I in a way that relies on generating a background I_{bg}, foreground I_{fg}, and mask I_m images. The discriminators are trained along with the generators and produce an adversarial training signal. In addition, the encoders are also trained to retrieve the latent variables from the generated images, as a self-supervised task.

The losses in this path can be put into four groups: adversarial losses, classification losses, distance losses, and regularizations. For brevity, e represents the dependence on all prior codes (e_{bg}, e_p, e_c). Similarly, $G(e, z)$ represents the full generation of the final image, Eq. 3–5.

Adversarial losses. These involve the two discriminators and are derived from the minimax equation: $\min_G \max_D \mathbb{E}_x[\log(D(x))] + \mathbb{E}_z[\log(1 - D(G(z)))]$, for a generic generator G and discriminator D. The concrete GAN loss is the sum of the losses for the separation between real/fake background, the separation between background/object and the separation between real/fake object.

For the discriminators, where X_{bg}, X_c are the sets of real background images and real object images, the losses are:

$$
\begin{aligned}
\mathcal{L}_{D_{bg_A}} &= \mathbb{E}_{x \sim X_{bg}}[\log(D_{bg_A}(x))] + \mathbb{E}_{e_{bg},z}[\log(1 - D_{bg_A}(G_{bg}(e_{bg},z)))] \\
\mathcal{L}_{D_{bg_B}} &= \mathbb{E}_{x \sim X_{bg}}[\log(D_{bg_B}(x))] + \mathbb{E}_{x \sim X_c}[\log(1 - D_{bg_B}(x))] \\
\mathcal{L}_{D_{c_A}} &= \mathbb{E}_{x \sim X_c}[\log(D_{c_A}(x))] + \mathbb{E}_{e,z}[\log(1 - D_{c_A}(G(e,z)))] \\
\mathcal{L}_D &= 10 \cdot \mathcal{L}_{D_{bg_A}} + \mathcal{L}_{D_{bg_B}} + \mathcal{L}_{D_{c_A}}
\end{aligned}
\tag{10}
$$

For the generators, the losses are:

$$
\begin{aligned}
\mathcal{L}_{G_{bg_A}} &= \mathbb{E}_{e_{bg},z}[\log(D_{bg_A}(G_{bg}(e_{bg},z)))], \mathcal{L}_{G_{bg_B}} = \mathbb{E}_{e_{bg},z}[\log(D_{bg_B}(G_{bg}(e_{bg},z)))] \\
\mathcal{L}_{G_{c_A}} &= \mathbb{E}_{e,z}[\log(D_{c_A}(G(e,z)))], \mathcal{L}_G = 10 \cdot \mathcal{L}_{G_{bg_A}} + \mathcal{L}_{G_{bg_B}} + \mathcal{L}_{G_{c_A}}
\end{aligned}
\tag{11}
$$

Classification losses. These losses optimize the generators to generate distinguished images for each style and shape priors and optimize the encoders to retrieve the prior classes. We use the cross entropy loss between the conditioned classes (ϕ_p, ϕ_c) and the encoders' predictions $(\hat{e}_p, \hat{e}_c)$ form Eq.7,8. In addition, we use the auxiliary task D_{C_B}.

$$
\mathcal{L}_E = \text{CE}(\hat{e}_p, \phi_p) + \text{CE}(\hat{e}_c, \phi_c) + \text{CE}(D_{c_B}(I), \phi_c)
\tag{12}
$$

Distance Losses. We train the encoders to minimize the mean squared error between the vectors in the latent space produced during generation and their predicted counterparts. These vectors are used in the reconstruction path, thus this self-supervised task assists in this regard. We minimize the distance between the pre-images and bypasses $(A_{bg}, A_{fg}, B_{bg}, B_{fg})$, and between the latent vectors (v_p, v_c) and the mean vectors μ_p, μ_c used to sample the latent code $(\hat{v}_p, \hat{v}_c)$.

$$
\mathcal{L}_{\text{MSE}} = \text{MSE}(v_c, \mu_c) + \text{MSE}(v_p, \mu_p) + \text{MSE}(A_{fg}, B_{fg}) + \text{MSE}(A_{bg}, B_{bg})
\tag{13}
$$

Regularization Losses. For regularization, a loss term is applied on the latent codes (v_{bg}, v_p, v_c), annotated as $\mathcal{L}_{R_v}$, and on the foreground mask I_m, annotated as $\mathcal{L}_{R_M}$. They are detailed in the supplementary.

All the losses are summed together to the total loss:

$$
\mathcal{L}_{\text{GEN}} = \mathcal{L}_G + \mathcal{L}_E + \mathcal{L}_{\text{MSE}} + 0.1 \cdot \mathcal{L}_{R_v} + 2 \cdot \mathcal{L}_{R_M}
\tag{14}
$$

4.2   Reconstruction Path

The reconstruction path is described in Fig. 2. For illustrations, see Fig. 4. The input is an image I. The precise flow is: (1) encode the foreground through the shape and style encoders (E_p, E_c), Eq. 7,8, (2) generate a foreground image and mask with the foreground generator (G_{fg}), Eq. 4, (3) encode the image and mask through the background encoder (E_{bg}), Eq. 6, (4) generate the background image with the background generator (G_{bg}), Eq. 3, and (5) compose the final image with I_{fg}, I_{bg}, I_m, Eq. 5. In addition, the mixup is applied as in Eq. 9 between encoding and generation. This path optimizes the clustering and segmentation tasks directly and also implicitly optimizes the generation task by reconstruction real images. We perform the reconstruction path on both real images and generated images from the generation path. This fully utilizes the information available to learn all tasks with minimal supervision.

The losses in this path can be put in three groups: statistical losses, reconstruction losses, and perceptual losses.

Statistical Losses. As in Variational Auto-Encoders [18], we compare the Kullback-Leiber Divergence between the latent variables encoded by the encoders $(\hat{v}_p, \hat{v}_c, \hat{z})$ to a multivariate gaussian distribution. For the pose vector z, we used the standard normal distribution with covariance matrix equal to the identity matrix ($\Sigma = I_{d_z}$) and a zero mean vector ($\mu = \mathbf{0}$). For the shape and style vectors $(\hat{v}_p, \hat{v}_c)$ we still use identity Σ, but since they should match their latent code (v_p, v_c), we use these latent codes as the target mean.

$$
\begin{aligned}
\mathcal{L}_{\mathrm{VAE}_p} &= D_{\mathrm{KL}}(\mathcal{N}(\mu_p, \mathrm{diag}(\sigma_p)) \| \mathcal{N}(v_p, I_{d_p})) \\
\mathcal{L}_{\mathrm{VAE}_c} &= D_{\mathrm{KL}}(\mathcal{N}(\mu_c, \mathrm{diag}(\sigma_c)) \| \mathcal{N}(v_c, I_{d_c})) \\
\mathcal{L}_{\mathrm{VAE}_z} &= D_{\mathrm{KL}}(\mathcal{N}(\mu_z, \mathrm{diag}(\sigma_z)) \| \mathcal{N}(\mathbf{0}, \quad I_{d_z})) \\
\mathcal{L}_{\mathrm{VAE}} &= \mathcal{L}_{\mathrm{VAE}_p} + \mathcal{L}_{\mathrm{VAE}_c} + \mathcal{L}_{\mathrm{VAE}_z}
\end{aligned}
\tag{15}
$$

Reconstruction Losses. The reconstruction losses are a set of L1 losses that compare the difference between the input image to the output. The network trains at reconstructing both real and fake images. For fake images, we have the extra self-supervision to also compare reconstruction of the background image and foreground mask.

$$
\mathcal{L}_{\mathrm{REC}} = \begin{cases} \mathrm{L1}(I, \hat{I}) & , \text{real} \\ \mathrm{L1}(I, \hat{I}) + \mathrm{L1}(I_{bg}, \hat{I}_{bg}) + \mathrm{L1}(I_m, \hat{I}_m) & , \text{fake} \end{cases}
\tag{16}
$$

Perceptual Losses. Comparing images to their ground-truth counterpart is known to produce blurred images; Perceptual loss [15] is known to aid in producing sharper images with more visible context [36] by comparing the images on the feature level as well. The perceptual loss is often used along with a pre-trained network, but this relies on added supervision. In our case, we use the discriminators as feature extractors. We use the notation D_{bg_C}, D_{c_C} from Sect. 3 to describe the extraction of the hidden layers used for this comparison.

$$
\mathcal{L}_{\mathrm{PER}} = \begin{cases} \mathrm{L2}_{D_{c_C}}(I, \hat{I}) & , \text{real} \\ \mathrm{L2}_{D_{c_C}}(I, \hat{I}) + \| D(D_{bg_C}) - D(\hat{I}_{bg}) \|^2 & , \text{fake} \end{cases}
\tag{17}
$$

All the losses are summed together to the total loss:

$$
\mathcal{L}_{\mathrm{AE}} = \mathcal{L}_{\mathrm{GEN}} + \mathcal{L}_{\mathrm{VAE}} + \mathcal{L}_{\mathrm{REC}} + \mathcal{L}_{\mathrm{PER}}
\tag{18}
$$

4.3   Multi-phase Training

In order to simplify training, instead of training both paths at once, we schedule the training process by phases. The phases are designed to train the network for a gradually increasing subset of tasks, starting from image-level tasks (generating images) to semantic tasks (semantic segmentation of the foreground, and semantic clustering) that benefit from the capabilities obtained in the generation path. In the first phase we only perform the generation path 4.1 and in the second phase we add the reconstruction path 4.2.

Without multi-phase training, the networks would be trained to generate and reconstruct images simultaneously. While the generation flow encourages a separation between the background and foreground components, the reconstruction flow resists this separation due to the trivial solution of encoding and decoding the image in one of the paths (foreground or background) and applying an all-zero or all-one mask. In the experiments, in Table 1, 2, we show that without multi-phase the model is incapable of learning any task.

In this controlled environment, the generators are much more likely to converge to the required setting. After a decent amount of iterations, determined in advance by a hyper-parameter, the second phase kicks in, where the model is also trained to reconstruct images, which will train the encoders on top of the generator instead of breaking it.

When entering Phase II, the fake images for both discriminators can be a result of either (i) generation path, (ii) fake image reconstruction, or (iii) real image reconstruction. We noticed that images from the reconstruction paths fail to converge to real-looking images when the discriminators were only trained by the generation path outputs. We hypothesized that this is probably due to each path producing images from a different source domain and these paths can generate very different images during training and the discriminators get overwhelmed by the different tasks and are not able to optimize them simultaneously. To solve this, upon entering Phase II, we clone each discriminator (D_c, D_{bg}) twice and associate one separate clone for each path, resulting in a total of three background discriminators and another three for the foreground. In this setting, each path receives the adversarial signal that is concentrated only at improving that path.

5   Experiments

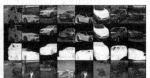

Fig. 3. Image Generation for each dataset. From top to bottom: (i) final image, (ii) foreground, (iii) foreground mask, (iv) background.

Fig. 4. Image reconstruction for each dataset. From top to bottom: (i) real image, (ii) reconstructed image, (iii) reconstructed foreground, (iv) reconstructed background, (v) ground-truth foreground mask, (vi) predicted foreground mask.

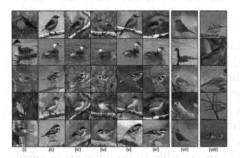 

Fig. 5. Conditional Generation. From left to right: (i) real images, (ii-vi) generation of images with the encoded parent and child codes and a different vector z per column, (vii) FineGAN [26] + our encoders, (viii) StackGANv2 [34] + our encoders.

Fig. 6. Style Transfer. From left to right: (i) real images. (ii-vi) reconstructed images when the child code e_c is switched with a code from a selected category, (vii) FineGAN [26] + our encoders, (viii) StackGANv2 [34] + our encoders.

Table 1. Quantitative generation results. FID↓, IS↑, CFID↓, CIS↑

Model	Birds				Dogs				Cars			
	FID	IS	CFID	CIS	FID	IS	CFID	CIS	FID	IS	CFID	CIS
Dataset	0	163.6	0	47.9	0	114.2	0	77.1	0	163.1	0	55.4
StackGANv2	21.4	67.0	96.8	15.0	56.7	82.4	184.7	10.2	25.0	88.1	190.3	13.3
FineGAN	23.0	66.4	65.3	24.7	54.9	83.1	100.4	15.7	24.8	86.2	126.0	13.6
OneGAN	**20.5**	**67.4**	**55.2**	**30.7**	**48.7**	**89.7**	**92.0**	**19.6**	**24.2**	**90.3**	**100.7**	**18.7**
No real recon	22.3	65.6	58.6	25.6	55.4	84.2	95.3	17.0	25.1	88.2	104.3	15.5
Phase I only	23.9	63.2	59.1	21.6	56.1	82.0	97.8	16.8	25.4	87.7	106.1	13.4
No multi-phase	196.5	11.0	356.1	2.3	217.8	16.9	543.2	1.7	264.7	23.4	767.9	3.9

Table 2. Segmentation and clustering results. §unfair upper bound results, obtained by selecting the best result out of many. †provided by [26]. *model performed task by using our encoders. ✗ model cannot perform task. Higher is better in all scores.

	Segmentation						Clustering					
	Birds		Dogs		Cars		Birds		Dogs		Cars	
Model	IOU	DICE	IOU	DICE	IOU	DICE	ACC	NMI	ACC	NMI	ACC	NMI
ReDO	46.5	60.2	38.4	52.8	16.2	26.2	✗	✗	✗	✗	✗	✗
WNet	24.8	38.9	47.7	62.1	52.8	67.6	✗	✗	✗	✗	✗	✗
UISB§	44.2	60.1	62.7	75.5	64.7	77.5	✗	✗	✗	✗	✗	✗
IIC-seg stf-3§	36.5	50.2	58.5	71.5	58.5	71.5	✗	✗	✗	✗	✗	✗
IIC-seg stf§	35.2	50.4	56.6	70.2	58.8	71.7	✗	✗	✗	✗	✗	✗
JULE†	✗	✗	✗	✗	✗	✗	.045	.204	.043	.142	.046	.232
DEPICT†	✗	✗	✗	✗	✗	✗	.061	.290	.052	.182	**.063**	**.329**
IIC-cluster	✗	✗	✗	✗	✗	✗	.084	.345	.060	.200	.056	.254
StackGANv2	✗	✗	✗	✗	✗	✗	.057*	.253*	.040*	.139*	.039*	.174*
FineGAN	44.5*	56.9*	48.7*	59.3*	53.2*	60.3*	.086*	.349*	.059*	.194*	.051*	.233*
OneGAN	**55.5**	**69.2**	**71.0**	**81.7**	**71.2**	**82.6**	.101	**.391**	**.073**	**.211**	.060	.272
No real recon	53.5	67.7	67.1	78.6	69.8	81.1	.095	.389	.062	.194	.057	.250
Phase I only	45.7	60.6	65.1	77.3	64.8	75.9	.084	.352	.058	.175	.052	.244
No multi-phase	28.2	43.2	7.4	13.6	45.9	60.5	.050	.216	.019	.082	.041	.208

Table 3. Ablation studies on CUB: (a) normalization methods, (b) modules' behaviour, and (c) losses. Measuring FID and C-IS for generation and IOU for segmentation.

Model	FID	C-IS	IOU	Model	FID	C-IS	IOU	Model	FID	C-IS	IOU
OneGAN	20.5	30.7	55.5	OneGAN	20.5	30.7	55.5	OneGAN	20.5	30.7	55.5
GLU-INorm	122.0	10.2	31.3	No bypass	21.2	22.8	53.3	No loss $\mathcal{L}_{R_M}$	97.2	19.5	35.3
LNorm	87.5	14.5	45.4	No mixup(1,2)	22.6	17.5	54.1	No loss $\mathcal{L}_{VAE}$	44.1	18.5	39.6
INorm	103.4	9.8	30.1	No mixup(3,4)	20.9	22.2	53.8	No loss $\mathcal{L}_{PER}$	25.5	24.1	53.0
(a)				(b)				(c)			

We train the network for 600,000 iterations, with batch size 20. All sub-networks are optimized using Adam [19], with lr=2e-4. Phase I duration is 200,000 iterations and Phase II 400,000. Within Phase II, we start with training only on fake images and real image reconstruction starts after another 200,000 iterations.

We evaluate our model on various tasks against the state of the art methods. Since no other model can solve all these tasks, we evaluate against different methods in each task. Depending on availability, some baselines were pre-trained models released by the authors and some were trained from scratch with the authors' official code and instructions.

Datasets. We evaluate our model with three datasets of fine-grained categorization. **Caltech-UCSD Birds-200-2011 (Birds)** [29]: This dataset consists of 11,788 images of 200 classes of birds, annotated with bounding boxes and segmentation masks. **Stanford Dogs (Dogs)** [20]: This dataset consists of 20,580 images of 120 classes of dogs, annotated with bounding boxes. For evaluation, target segmentation masks were generated by a pre-trained DeepLabV3 [5] model on the COCO [22] dataset. The pre-trained model was acquired from the gluoncv toolkit [12]. **Stanford Cars (Cars)** [17]: This dataset consists of 16,185 images of 196 classes of cars, annotated with bounding boxes. Segmentation masks were generated as above with the pre-trained DeepLabV3 model.

Similarly to FineGAN, before training the model, we produced a background subset by cutting background patches with the bounding boxes. In addition to FineGAN, the bounding boxes were not used in any other way to train our method and we made sure that no image was used for both foreground and background examples. This was done by splitting the dataset in a 80/20 ratio, and use the larger subset as foreground X_c and only the smaller subset for background X_{bg}.

Due to the different size of classes in each dataset, there is also a different size of child and parent classes in the design for each dataset. Birds: $N_C = 200, N_P = 20$, Dogs: $N_C = 120, N_P = 12$, Cars: $N_C = 196, N_P = 14$.

Image Generation. We compare our image generation results to FineGAN [26] and StackGANv2 [34], by relying on an InceptionV3 fine-tuned on each dataset. We evaluate our method in both IS [25] and FID [13]. In addition, we measure the conditional variants of these metrics (CIS, CFID), as presented in [2]. The conditional metrics measure the similarity between real and fake images within each class, which cannot be measured by the unconditional metrics.

Our results, reported in Table 1 show that OneGAN outperforms in both conditional and unconditional image generation. In unconditional generation, our method and the baselines performed roughly the same, since the generators are very similar. In conditional generation, our method improves on the baseline by a large margin. StackGANv2 was the worst performing model. This suggest that the mask-based generation, that FineGAN and our method rely on, generates a stronger conditioning on the object in the image. In addition, our multi-path training method improves conditional generation further, as is shown in the ablation tests. For illustration of conditional generation, see Fig. 5.

Unsupervised Foreground Segmentation. We compare our mask prediction from the reconstruction path to the real foreground mask. We evaluate according to IOU and DICE scores. We compare against three baselines, ReDO [6], WNet [32] and UISB [16] which are trained for each dataset separately, and a third one, IIC-seg [14], which was trained on coco-stuff and coco-stuff-3 (a subset). While coco-stuff is a different dataset than the ones we used, it contains all the relevant classes. ReDO and WNet produce a foreground mask which we compare to the ground-truth similarly to how we evaluate our model. UISB is an iterative method that produces a final segmentation with a varying number of classes between 2 and 100. We iterated UISB on each image 50 times. The output was usually between 4–20 classes. Since there is no labeling of the foreground or background classes, this method cannot be immediately used for this task. In order to get an evaluation, we look for each image for the class that has the highest IOU with the ground-truth foreground. The rest of the classes are merged to a single background class. We then repeat with a single background class and the rest merged into foreground. Finally, taking the best out of the two options, each obtained by using an oracle to select out of many options, which provides a liberal upper bound on the performance of UISB. IIC also produces a multi-class segmentation map, we use it in the same way we use UISB by taking the best class for either background or foreground in respect to IOU. IIC has 2-headed output, one for the main task and one for over-clustering. For coco-stuff trained IIC, we look for the best mask in one of the 15 classes of the main head. For coco-stuff-3 trained IIC, the main head is trained to cluster sky/ground/plants, so we look for the best mask in one of the 15 classes of the over-clustering head. Fine-GAN cannot perform segmentation, since it does not have a reconstruction path. But we added an additional baseline by training FineGAN with our encoders to allow such path. The results in Table. 2 show that our method outperforms all the baselines. The ablation show that the biggest contribution comes from the reconstruction path and the multi-phase scheduling.

Unsupervised Clustering. We compare our method against JULE [33], DEPICT [10] and IIC-cluster [14]. In addition, we added the baselines of Stack-GANv2 and FineGAN trained with our encoders. We evaluate how well the encoders cluster the real images. OneGAN outperforms the other methods for both Birds and Dogs. For Cars, our model was second after DEPICT. By looking at the generated images, this can be explained by the fact our method clusters the cars based more on color and less on car model. This aligns with the lower conditional generation score for Cars than for the other datasets.

Image to Image Translation. To further evaluate our model, we show its capability to transfer an input image to a target category. The results can be seen in Fig. 6. Even though our model was never trained on this task, the disentanglement between the shape and the texture enables this translation simply by passing a different child code during reconstruction. In contrast, FineGAN and StackGANv2 are unable to perform this task correctly as there is no learned disentanglement in StackGANv2 and no bypass connection in FineGAN.

Object Removal and Inpainting. Our model is also capable of performing automatic object removal and background reconstruction, see Fig. 4. Due to the lack of perfect ground-truth mask, our model does not only fill the missing pixels but fully reconstructs the background image. As a result, the background image is not identical to the original background, but it is semantically similar to it. We compare our method with previous work in the supplementary.

Ablation Study. In Table 1,2, we provide multiple versions of our method for ablation. In the version without real reconstruction, we only add fake image reconstruction in Phase II, meaning that real images did not pass through the network during training. Another variant employs only the first phase of training. Finally, a third variant trains without multi-phase scheduling. These tests show the contribution of the multiple paths and the multi-phase scheduling. In Table 3, we provide an extensive ablation study on three aspects. In (a), we compared layer and instance normalization [28] methods in the generators. Our "GLU layer normalization" outperformed all other options. In (b), we turned of intersection modules between encoders and generators. The experiment shows that these models strongly improve the CIS, which explains why our method outperformed FineGAN and StackGANv2 in conditional generation. In (c), we evaluated the contribution of selected novel losses, which affected all scores. Together, all these experiments show the contribution of the proposed novelties in our method.

6   Conclusions

By building a single model to handle multiple unsupervised tasks at once, we convincingly demonstrate the power of co-training, by surpassing the performance of the best in class methods for each task. This capability is enabled by a complex architecture with many sub-networks. However, supporting this complexity during training is challenging. We introduce a mixup module that integrates multiple pathways in a homogenized manner and a multi-phase training, which helps to avoid some tasks dominating over the others.

Acknowledgement. This project has received funding from the European Research Council (ERC) under the European Unions Horizon 2020 research and innovation programme (grant ERC CoG 725974).

References

1. Ba, J.L., Kiros, J.R., Hinton, G.E.: Layer normalization. arXiv preprint arXiv:1607.06450 (2016)
2. Benny, Y., Galanti, T., Benaim, S., Wolf, L.: Evaluation metrics for conditional image generation. arXiv preprint arXiv:2004.12361 (2020)
3. Bielski, A., Favaro, P.: Emergence of object segmentation in perturbed generative models. In: Advances in Neural Information Processing Systems, pp. 7256–7266 (2019)
4. Chen, L.C., Papandreou, G., Kokkinos, I., Murphy, K., Yuille, A.L.: Deeplab: Semantic image segmentation with deep convolutional nets, atrous convolution, and fully connected crfs. IEEE Trans. Pattern Anal. Mach. Intell. **40**(4), 834–848 (2017)
5. Chen, L.C., Papandreou, G., Schroff, F., Adam, H.: Rethinking atrous convolution for semantic image segmentation. arXiv preprint arXiv:1706.05587 (2017)
6. Chen, M., Artières, T., Denoyer, L.: Unsupervised object segmentation by redrawing. arXiv preprint arXiv:1905.13539 (2019)
7. Chen, X., Duan, Y., Houthooft, R., Schulman, J., Sutskever, I., Abbeel, P.: Infogan: interpretable representation learning by information maximizing generative adversarial nets. In: Advances in neural information processing systems, pp. 2172–2180 (2016)
8. Croitoru, I., Bogolin, S.V., Leordeanu, M.: Unsupervised learning of foreground object detection. arXiv preprint arXiv:1808.04593 (2018)
9. Dauphin, Y.N., Fan, A., Auli, M., Grangier, D.: Language modeling with gated convolutional networks. In: Proceedings of the 34th International Conference on Machine Learning-Volume 70. pp. 933–941. JMLR. org (2017)
10. Ghasedi Dizaji, K., Herandi, A., Deng, C., Cai, W., Huang, H.: Deep clustering via joint convolutional autoencoder embedding and relative entropy minimization. In: Proceedings of the IEEE International Conference on Computer Vision, pp. 5736–5745 (2017)

11. Goodfellow, I., Pouget-Abadie, J., Mirza, M., Xu, B., Warde-Farley, D., Ozair, S., Courville, A., Bengio, Y.: Generative adversarial nets. In: Advances in neural information processing systems, pp. 2672–2680 (2014)
12. Guo, J., et al.: Gluoncv and gluonnlp: Deep learning in computer vision and natural language processing. arXiv preprint arXiv:1907.04433 (2019)
13. Heusel, M., Ramsauer, H., Unterthiner, T., Nessler, B., Hochreiter, S.: Gans trained by a two time-scale update rule converge to a local nash equilibrium. In: Advances in Neural Information Processing Systems, pp. 6626–6637 (2017)
14. Ji, X., Henriques, J.F., Vedaldi, A.: Invariant information clustering for unsupervised image classification and segmentation. In: Proceedings of the IEEE International Conference on Computer Vision, pp. 9865–9874 (2019)
15. Johnson, J., Alahi, A., Fei-Fei, L.: Perceptual losses for real-time style transfer and super-resolution. In: Leibe, B., Matas, J., Sebe, N., Welling, M. (eds.) ECCV 2016. LNCS, vol. 9906, pp. 694–711. Springer, Cham (2016). https://doi.org/10.1007/978-3-319-46475-6_43
16. Kanezaki, A.: Unsupervised image segmentation by backpropagation. In: 2018 IEEE International Conference on Acoustics, Speech and Signal Processing (ICASSP), pp. 1543–1547. IEEE (2018)
17. Khosla, A., Jayadevaprakash, N., Yao, B., Fei-Fei, L.: Novel dataset for fine-grained image categorization. In: First Workshop on Fine-Grained Visual Categorization, IEEE Conference on Computer Vision and Pattern Recognition. Colorado Springs, CO, June 2011
18. Kingma, D.P., Welling, M.: Auto-encoding variational bayes. Stat **1050**, 1 (2014)
19. Kingma, D., Ba, J.: Adam: A method for stochastic optimization. In: The International Conference on Learning Representations (ICLR) (2016)
20. Krause, J., Stark, M., Deng, J., Fei-Fei, L.: 3d object representations for fine-grained categorization. In: 4th International IEEE Workshop on 3D Representation and Recognition (3dRR-13). Sydney, Australia (2013)
21. Larsen, A.B.L., Sønderby, S.K., Larochelle, H., Winther, O.: Autoencoding beyond pixels using a learned similarity metric. arXiv preprint arXiv:1512.09300 (2015)
22. Lin, T.-Y., et al.: Microsoft COCO: common objects in context. In: Fleet, D., Pajdla, T., Schiele, B., Tuytelaars, T. (eds.) ECCV 2014. LNCS, vol. 8693, pp. 740–755. Springer, Cham (2014). https://doi.org/10.1007/978-3-319-10602-1_48
23. Mirza, M., Osindero, S.: Conditional generative adversarial nets. arXiv preprint arXiv:1411.1784 (2014)
24. Ronneberger, O., P.Fischer, Brox, T.: U-net: Convolutional networks for biomedical image segmentation. In: Medical Image Computing and Computer-Assisted Intervention (MICCAI). LNCS, vol. 9351, pp. 234–241. Springer (2015), http://lmb.informatik.uni-freiburg.de//Publications/2015/RFB15a, (available on arXiv:1505.04597 [cs.CV])
25. Salimans, T., Goodfellow, I.J., Zaremba, W., Cheung, V., Radford, A., Chen, X.: Improved techniques for training gans. arXiv preprint arXiv:1606.03498 (2016)
26. Singh, K.K., Ojha, U., Lee, Y.J.: Finegan: Unsupervised hierarchical disentanglement for fine-grained object generation and discovery. arXiv preprint arXiv:1811.11155 (2018)
27. Sultana, M., Mahmood, A., Javed, S., Jung, S.K.: Unsupervised deep context prediction for background estimation and foreground segmentation. Mach. Vis. Appl. **30**(3), 375–395 (2019)
28. Ulyanov, D., Vedaldi, A., Lempitsky, V.: Instance normalization: The missing ingredient for fast stylization. arXiv preprint arXiv:1607.08022 (2016)

29. Wah, C., Branson, S., Welinder, P., Perona, P., Belongie, S.: The Caltech-UCSD Birds-200-2011 Dataset. Technical Report CNS-TR-2011-001, California Institute of Technology (2011)
30. Wang, J., et al.: Deep high-resolution representation learning for visual recognition. arXiv preprint arXiv:1908.07919 (2019)
31. Wang, Y., et al.: Unsupervised video object segmentation with distractor-aware online adaptation. arXiv preprint arXiv:1812.07712 (2018)
32. Xia, X., Kulis, B.: W-net: A deep model for fully unsupervised image segmentation. arXiv preprint arXiv:1711.08506 (2017)
33. Yang, J., Parikh, D., Batra, D.: Joint unsupervised learning of deep representations and image clusters. In: Proceedings of the IEEE Conference on Computer Vision and Pattern Recognition, pp. 5147–5156 (2016)
34. Zhang, H., Xu, T., Li, H., Zhang, S., Wang, X., Huang, X., Metaxas, D.N.: Stackgan++: realistic image synthesis with stacked generative adversarial networks. IEEE Trans. Pattern Anal. Mach. Intell. **41**(8), 1947–1962 (2018)
35. Zhang, H., Cisse, M., Dauphin, Y.N., Lopez-Paz, D.: mixup: Beyond empirical risk minimization. arXiv preprint arXiv:1710.09412 (2017)
36. Zhang, R., Isola, P., Efros, A.A., Shechtman, E., Wang, O.: The unreasonable effectiveness of deep features as a perceptual metric. In: Proceedings of the IEEE Conference on Computer Vision and Pattern Recognition, pp. 586–595 (2018)

Mining Self-similarity: Label Super-Resolution with Epitomic Representations

Nikolay Malkin[1]([✉]), Anthony Ortiz[2], and Nebojsa Jojic[3]

[1] Yale University, 06520 New Haven, CT, USA
kolya.malkin@yale.edu
[2] Microsoft AI for Good Research Lab, 98052 Redmond, WA, USA
anthony.ortiz@microsoft.com
[3] Microsoft Research, 98052 Redmond, WA, USA
jojic@microsoft.com

Abstract. We show that simple patch-based models, such as epitomes (Jojic et al., 2003), can have superior performance to the current state of the art in semantic segmentation and label super-resolution, which uses deep convolutional neural networks. We derive a new training algorithm for epitomes which allows, for the first time, learning from very large data sets and derive a label super-resolution algorithm as a statistical inference over epitomic representations. We illustrate our methods on land cover mapping and medical image analysis tasks.

Keywords: Label super-resolution · Semantic segmentation · Self-similarity

1 Introduction

Deep convolutional neural networks (CNNs) have become a tool of choice in computer vision. They typically outperform other approaches in core tasks such as object recognition and segmentation, but suffer from several drawbacks. First, CNNs are hard to interpret, which makes them difficult to improve by adding common-sense priors or invariances into the architecture. Second, they are usually trained in a supervised fashion on large amounts of labeled data, yet in most applications labels are sparse, leading to various domain adaptation challenges. Third, there is evidence of failure of the architecture choices that were meant to promote CNNs' reasoning over large distances in images. The *effective* receptive field [17] of CNNs – the distance at which faraway pixels stop contributing to the activity of deeper neurons – is often a small fraction of the theoretical one.

With the third point in mind, we ask a simple question, the answer to which can inform an agenda in building models which are interpretable, can be pretrained in an unsupervised manner, adopt priors with ease, and are amenable to well-understood statistical inference techniques: *If deep CNNs effectively use only small image patches for vision tasks, and learn from billions of pixels, then how*

Electronic supplementary material The online version of this chapter (https://doi.org/10.1007/978-3-030-58574-7_32) contains supplementary material, which is available to authorized users.

© Springer Nature Switzerland AG 2020
A. Vedaldi et al. (Eds.): ECCV 2020, LNCS 12371, pp. 531–547, 2020.
https://doi.org/10.1007/978-3-030-58574-7_32

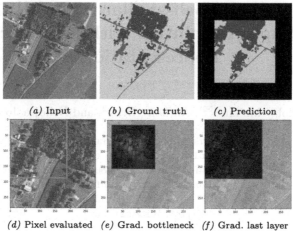

(a) Input   (b) Ground truth   (c) Prediction

(d) Pixel evaluated   (e) Grad. bottleneck   (f) Grad. last layer

Fig. 1. Gradient-based effective receptive field estimation: We use the gradients from selected intermediate layers to the input image to estimate the size of the effective receptive field. In *(e)*, we visualize the normalized gradient map (at a single coordinate shown on green in *(d)*) of the U-Net's bottleneck (highest downsampling) layer with respect to the input image; *(f)* shows gradients of the *final* layer for the same pixel. The dark squares show the theoretical receptive field of the layers in question (139×139 for the bottleneck and 183×183 for the final layer). However, the gradient map *(f)* suggests that the effective receptive field is only about 13×13 pixels on average

would simple exemplar-like approaches perform, and can they be made practical computationally? We show that models based on epitomic representations [14], illustrated in Fig. 2, match and surpass deep CNNs on several weakly supervised segmentation and domain transfer tasks.

For example, in Fig. 1 we show a patch of aerial imagery and the output of a U-Net [29] trained to predict land cover. The network misclassifies as vegetation the road pixels that appear in tree shadows. The model was trained on a large land cover map [3,27] that presents many opportunities to learn that roads are long and uninterrupted. The land cover data contains many more patterns that would help see rivers through a forest, recognize houses based on their proximity to roads, etc., but the U-Nets do not seem to learn such long-range patterns. This myopic behavior has been observed in other architectures as well [2,9,17].

In contrast, our algorithms directly model small image patches, forgoing long-range relationships. As generative models of images, epitomes are highly interpretable: they look like the images they were trained on (Fig. 2). Our generative formulation of image segmentation allows the inference of labels in the latent variable space, with or without high-resolution supervision (Fig. 4). They achieve comparable performance to the state-of-the-art CNNs on semantic segmentation tasks, and surpass the CNNs' performance in domain transfer and weakly supervised (label super-resolution) settings.

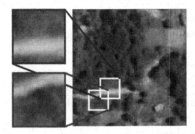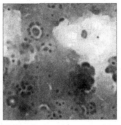

Fig. 2. A quarter of an epitome (μ parameters shown) trained on aerial imagery (*left*) and an epitome trained on pathology slides (*right*). Any 31×31 training data patch is generated by, and likely similar to, some 31×31 window in the epitome. Note the two overlapping windows: the patches are distant in color space, but their corresponding mixture components share parameters on the intersection. The epitomes are $200\times$ and $30000\times$ smaller, respectively, than their total training data

In summary, our contributions are as follows:

(1) As previous training algorithms fail to fit large epitomes well, we develop new algorithms that are suitable for mining self-similarity in very large datasets.

(2) We develop a new label super-resolution formulation that mines image self-similarity using epitomes or directly in a single (small) image.

(3) We show how these models surpass the recent (neural network) state of the art in aerial and pathology image analysis.

(4) We illustrate that our approaches allow and even benefit from unsupervised pre-training (separation of feature learning from label embedding).

(5) We show that our models deal with data size gracefully: We can train an epitome on a large fully labeled aerial imagery/land cover map and obtain better transfer in a new geography than CNNs [18,27], but we get even better results by analyzing one 512×512 tile at a time, with only low-resolution labels.

2   Epitomes as Segmentation Models

Epitomes [14] are an upgraded version of a Gaussian mixture model of image patches. In this section we present, for completeness, the definition of these models. We then explain how they can be turned into segmentation models.

Consider a training set consisting of image patches x^t unwrapped as vectors $x^t = \{x_{i,j,k}^t\}$, where i, j are coordinates in the patch and k is the spectral channel (R, G, B,...), and the corresponding vector of one-hot label embeddings $y_t = \{y_{i,j,\ell}^t\}$, $\ell \in \{1,\ldots,L\}$. In a mixture model, the distribution over the (image, label) data is represented with the aid of a latent variable $s \in \{1,\ldots,S\}$ as

$$p(x^t, y^t) = \sum_{s=1}^{S} p(x^t|s)p(y^t|s)p(s), \tag{1}$$

where $p(s)$ is the frequency of a mixture component s, while the conditional probability $p(x^t|s)$ describes the allowed variation in the image patch that s

generates and $p(y^t|s)$ describes the likely labels for it. Under this model, the estimate for $\hat{y}$, the expected segmentation of a new image x, is

$$p(y|x) = \sum_s p(s|x)p(y|s). \tag{2}$$

A natural choice for $p(x|s)$ is a diagonal Gaussian distribution,

$$p(x|s) = \prod_{i,j,k} \frac{\exp\left(-\frac{1}{2}(x_{i,j,k} - \mu_{s,i,j,k})^2/\sigma^2_{s,i,j,k}\right)}{(2\pi\sigma^2_{s,i,j,k})^{\frac{1}{2}}} \tag{3}$$

and for $p(y|s)$ a product of categorical distributions over labels at each pixel position. The mean of the mixture component s contains pixel values $\mu_{s,i,j,k}$, while the covariance matrix is expressed in terms of its diagonal elements $\sigma^2_{s,i,j,k}$, the variances of different color channels k for individual pixels i, j.

Epitomic representations [14] compress this parametrization by recognizing that patches of interest come from *overlapping* regions and that different components s should share parameters. The component index $s = (s_1, s_2)$ lives on a $N \times N$ grid, so $0 \leq s_1, s_2 \leq N - 1$, and the parameters are shared:

$$\mu_{s,i,j,k} = \boldsymbol{\mu}_{s_1+i,s_2+j,k} \qquad \sigma^2_{s,i,j,k} = \boldsymbol{\sigma}^2_{s_1+i,s_2+j,k} \tag{4}$$

(Indices are to be interpreted modulo N, i.e., with toroidal wrap-around.) Thus, the epitome is a large grid of parameters $\boldsymbol{\mu}_{m,n,k}, \boldsymbol{\sigma}_{m,n,k}$, so that the parameters for the mixture component $s = (s_1, s_2)$ start at position s_1, s_2 and extend to the left and down by the size of the patch, as shown in Fig. 2. Modeling $K \times K$ patches will take K^2 times fewer parameters for the similar expressiveness as a regular mixture model trained on $K \times K$ patches. The posterior $p(s|x) \propto p(x|s)p(s)$ is efficiently computed using convolutions/correlations, e.g.,

$$p(s_1, s_2|x) \propto \exp \sum_{i,j,k} \frac{-1}{2} \left(\frac{x^2_{i,j,k}}{\sigma^2_{s_1+i,s_2+j,k}} - \frac{2x_{i,j,k}\boldsymbol{\mu}_{s_1+i,s_2+j,k}}{\sigma^2_{s_1+i,s_2+j,k}} \right.$$
$$\left. + \frac{\boldsymbol{\mu}^2_{s_1+i,s_2+j,k}}{\sigma^2_{s_1+i,s_2+j,k}} + \log \boldsymbol{\sigma}^2_{s_1+i,s_2+j,k} \right) \cdot p(s_1, s_2). \tag{5}$$

Epitomes are a summary of self-similarity in the images on which they are trained. They should thus contain a much smaller number of pixels than the training imagery, but be much larger than the patches with which they are trained. Each pixel in the epitome is contained in K^2 patches of size $K \times K$ and can be tracked back to many different positions in many images.

Conversely, this mapping of images enables embedding of *labels* into the epitome after the epitome of the images x has been trained. Every location in the epitome m, n will have (soft) label indicators $z_{m,n,\ell}$, computed as

$$p(\ell|m,n) \propto z_{m,n,\ell} = \sum_t \sum_{s_1,s_2:(m,n)\in W_{s_1,s_2}} p(s_1, s_2|x^t)y^t_{m-s_1,n-s_2,\ell}, \tag{6}$$

Fig. 3. Numerical near-fixed points of naïve epitome training by SGD without location promotion, caused by vanishing posteriors, and a 399×399 epitome trained with location promotion (*left*); non-diversifying and self-diversifying 499×499 epitomes trained on imagery of forests (*right*)

where W_{s_1,s_2} is the epitome window starting at (s_1, s_2), i.e. the set of K^2 coordinates (m, n) in the epitome that belong to the mixture component (s_1, s_2). The posterior tells us the strength of the mapping of the patch x^t to each component s that overlaps the position (m, n). The corresponding location in the patch of labels y^t is $(m - s_1, n - s_2)$, so $y^t_{m-s_1,n-s_2,\ell}$ is added to the count $z_{m,n,l}$ of label ℓ at location (m, n). Finally, we declare $p(y_{i,j,\ell}|s_1, s_2) \propto z_{s_1+i,s_2+j,\ell}$, allowing inference of ℓ for a new image patch by (2).

3   A Large-Scale Epitome Training Algorithm

Epitomes have been used in recognition and segmentation tasks, e.g. [1,20,21,23, 24,30,34,35]. However, the standard EM training algorithm [14] that maximizes the data log-likelihood $\sum_t \log \sum_s p(x^t|s)p(s)$ is not suitable to building *large* epitomes of *large* data sets due to the problem of "vanishing posterior". As training advances, the dynamic range of the posterior $p(s|x^t)$ becomes too big for machine precision, and the small probabilities are set to zero. Further parameter updates discourage mapping to these unlikely positions, leading to a die-off of chunks of "real estate" in the epitome. The problem is exacerbated by the size of the data (and of the epitome). Due to stability issues or computational cost, previous solutions to this [15] do not allow the models to be trained on the scale on which neural networks are trained. The analogous problem exists in estimating the prior $p(s)$ over epitome positions, which also needs to have a large dynamic range. If the range is flatter (e.g., if we use a uniform prior) then maximization of likelihood requires that the epitome learn only the most frequent patterns in the data, replicating slight variations of them everywhere. As imagery is mostly uniform and smooth, this creates blurry epitomes devoid of rarer features with higher variances, like various edges and corners.

Instead of EM, we develop a large-scale epitome learning algorithm combining three important ingredients: stochastic gradient descent, location promotion techniques, and the diversity-promoting optimization criterion:

Stochastic gradient descent. Instead of changing the parameters of the model based on all data at once, we update them incrementally in the direction of the gradient of the log-likelihood of a batch of individual data points

$\frac{d}{d\theta} \log \sum_t \sum_s p(x^t|s)p(s)$, where $\theta = \{\boldsymbol{\mu}_{m,n,k}, \boldsymbol{\sigma}^2_{m,n,k}, p(s_1, s_2)\}$. Note that gradient descent alone does not solve the vanishing posterior problem, as the posterior also factors into the expression for the gradient (see the SI). In fact, SGD makes the situation worse (Fig. 3): the model parameters evolve before all of the data is seen, thus speeding up the extinction of the epitome's "real estate".

Location promotion. To maintain the relatively uniform evolution of all parts of the epitome, we directly constrain the learning procedure to hit all areas of the epitome through a form of posterior regularization [8]. Within an SGD framework, this can be accomplished simply by keeping counters R_{s_1,s_2} at each position s_1, s_2 and incrementing them by the posterior $p(s_1, s_2|x^t)$ upon every sample x^t, then disallowing mapping to the windows s_1, s_2 which contain the *most frequently* mapped pixels. In particular, we compute a mask $M = \{R_{s_1,s_2} < c/N^2\}$, where $N \times N$ is the size of the epitome, for some small constant $c < 1$, and optimize only $\log \sum_{(s_1,s_2) \in M} p(x^t|s_1, s_2)p(s_1, s_2)$ at each gradient descent step. When $|M| > (1 - \delta)|N|^2$ for some small δ, all counters are reset to 0.

Diversification training. As illustrated in Fig. 3 (right), standard SGD tends to learn uniform patterns, especially when trained on large datasets. Just like EM, it has to rely on the prior $p(s)$ to avoid learning blurry epitomes, but the dynamic range needed to control this is too high. Additionally, through location promotion, we in fact encourage more uniform coverage of locations. Thus, we change the optimization criterion from log-likelihood of *all* data to log-likelihood of the worst modeled subset of each batch, $\sum_{t \in L_p} \sum_s p(x^t|s)$, were L_p is the set of data in the worst-modeled quantile p (the lowest quarter, in our experiments) in terms of data likelihood, either under a previously trained model or under the model being trained (*self-diversification*). This version of a max-min criterion avoids focusing on outliers while ensuring that the data is uniformly well modeled. The resulting epitomes capture a greater variety of features, as seen in the right panel of Fig. 3. The diversification criterion also helps the model generalize better on the test set, as we show in the experiments.

In the SI, we provide the details of the training parameters and analysis of execution time. The simple and runnable example training code[1] illustrates all three features of the algorithm.

4   Label Super-Resolution by Self-similarity

Labeling images at a pixel level is costly and time-consuming, so a number of semi-supervised approaches to segmentation have been studied, e.g., [5,12,22,25]. Recently, [18] proposed a "label super-resolution" (LSR) technique which uses statistics of occurrence of high-resolution labels within coarse blocks of pixels labeled with a different set of low-resolution classes. (For clarity, we refer to low-res information as *classes* and high-res information as *labels*.) Each class, indexed by c, has a different composition of high-resolution labels, indexed by ℓ.

---

[1] https://github.com/anthonymlortiz/epitomes_lsr.

The label super-resolution technique in [18] assumes prior knowledge of the compositions $p(\ell|c)$ of high-res labels in low-res classes and uses them to define an alternative optimization cost at the top of a core segmentation network that predicts the high-res labels. Training the network end-to-end with coarse classes results in a model capable of directly predicting the high-res labels of the individual pixels. Backpropagation through such alternative cost criteria is prone to collapse, and [18] reports best results when the data with high-res labels (HR) is mixed with data with low-res labels (LR). Furthermore, the problem is inherently ill-posed: given an expressive enough model and a perfect learning algorithm, many solutions are possible. For example, the model could learn to recognize an individual low-res block and then choose an arbitrary pattern of high-res labels within it that satisfies the counts $p(\ell|c)$. Thus the technique depends on the inductive biases of the learning algorithm and the network architecture to lead to the desirable solutions.

On the other hand, following statistical models we discuss here, we can develop a statistical LSR inference technique from first principles. The data x is modeled by a mixture indexed by the latent index s. Using this index to also model the structure in the joint distribution over labels ℓ inside the patches generated by component s and classes c to which the patches belong, the known distribution of labels given the classes should satisfy $p(\ell|c) = \sum_s p(\ell|s)p(s|c)$. Thus, we find the label embedding $p(\ell|s)$ by minimizing the KL distance between the known $p(\ell|c)$ and the model's prediction $\sum_s p(\ell|s)p(s|c)$, i.e, by solving

$$p(\ell|s) = \arg \max_{p(\ell|s)} \sum_c p(c) \sum_\ell p(\ell|c) \log \sum_s p(\ell|s)p(s|c), \qquad (7)$$

where $p(c)$ are the observed proportions of low-res classes in the data and $p(s|c)$ is obtained as the posterior over s for data of label c, as we will discuss in a moment. First, we derive an EM algorithm for solving the problem in Eq. 7 using auxiliary distributions $q_{\ell,c}(s)$ to repeatedly bound $\log \sum_s p(\ell|s)p(s|c)$ and reestimate $p(\ell|s)$. To derive the E step, we observe that

$$\log \sum_s p(\ell|s)p(s|c) = \log \sum_s q_{\ell,c}(s) \frac{p(\ell|s)p(s|c)}{q_{\ell,c}(s)} \geq \sum_s q_{\ell,c}(s) \log \frac{p(\ell|s)p(s|c)}{q_{\ell,c}(s)}.$$

The bound holds for all distributions $q_{\ell,c}$ and is made tight for

$$q_{\ell,c}(s) \propto p(\ell|s)p(s|c). \qquad (8)$$

Optimizing for $p(\ell|s)$, we get

$$p(\ell|s) \propto \sum_c p(c)p(\ell|c)q_{\ell,c}(s). \qquad (9)$$

Coordinate ascent on the $q_{l,c}(s)$ and $p(\ell|s)$ by iterating (8) and (9) converges to a local maximum of the optimization criterion.

Therefore, all that is needed for label super-resolution are the distributions $p(s|c)$ that tell us how often each mixture component is seen within the class c.

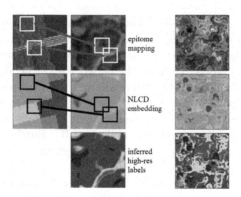

Fig. 4. Two image patches are shown mapped to a piece of an epitome (*left*). Below the source image, we show class labels for 30×30 m blocks. Below the epitome we show a piece of the class embedding $p(m, n|c)$ at a pixel level (Eqn. 11) using the same color scheme, with colors weighted by the inferred class probabilities. Below the class embedding we show the piece of the output of the label super-resolution algorithm in Sect. 4. We also show the full epitome and its embeddings (*right*)

Given low-res labeled data, i.e., pairs (x^t, c^t) and a trained mixture model for image patches x^t, the answer is

$$p(s|c) \propto \sum_{t:c^t=c} p(s|x^t). \tag{10}$$

In other words, we go through all patches, look at the posterior of their assignment to prototypes s, and count how many times each prototype was associated with each of the classes.

The epitomic representation with its parameter sharing has an additional advantage here. With standard Gaussian mixtures of patches, the level of the super-resolution we can accomplish is defined by the size of the patch x we use in the analysis, because all of the reasoning is performed on the level of the patch index s, not at individual pixels. Thus, to get super-resolution at the level of a single pixel, our mixture model would have to be over individual pixels, i.e., a simple color clustering model (see the SI for examples). With epitomes, however, instead of using whole patch statistics, we can assign statistics $p(m, n|c)$ to individual positions in the epitome,

$$p(m, n|c) \propto \sum_{t} \sum_{i,j} p((s_1, s_2) = (m - i, n - j)|x^t)[c^t = c], \tag{11}$$

where $p(\cdot, \cdot|x^t)$ is the posterior over positions. This equation represents counting how many times each *pixel* in the epitome was mapped to by a patch that was inside a block of class c, as illustrated in Fig. 4: While the two patches map close to each other into the epitome, the all-forest patch is unlikely to cover any piece of the road. Considering all patches in a larger spatial context, the individual

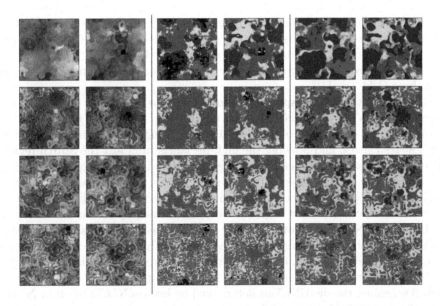

Fig. 5. Epitomes (total area $2 \cdot 10^6$ pixels) trained on $5 \cdot 10^9$ pixels of **South** imagery (*left*); land cover embeddings (argmax label shown) derived from high-resolution **South** ground truth (*middle*), land cover embeddings derived by epitomic LSR from **North** 30m-resolution NLCD data (*right*)

pixels in the epitome can get statistics that differ from their neighbors'. This allows the inference of high-res labels ℓ for the entire epitome, shown with its embedding of low-res classes c and super-resolved high-res labels ℓ on the right.

In summary, our LSR algorithm first uses the epitome model of $K \times K$ patches to embed class labels on an individual pixel level using Eq. 11. This then allows us to run the EM algorithm that iterates Eqs. 8 and 9 on positions m, n associated with the shared parameters in the epitome instead of mixture components s, using $p(m, n|c)$ in Eq. 11 in place of $p(s|c)$. Once the estimate of the high-res labels $p(\ell|m, n)$ is computed for each position in the epitome, we can predict labels in imagery using Eq. 2. This procedure performs probabilistic reasoning over the frequencies of repeating patterns in imagery labeled with low-resolution classes to reason over individual pixels in these patterns.

5 Experiments

5.1 Land Cover Segmentation and Super-Resolution

Our first example is the problem of land cover segmentation from aerial imagery. We work with the data studied by [27], available for 160,000km^2 of land in the Chesapeake Bay watershed (Northeast US):

(1) 1m-resolution 4-band aerial imagery (NAIP) taken in the years 2013-4;

(2) High-resolution (1m) land cover segmentation in four classes (water, forest, field/low vegetation, built/impervious) produced by [3];

(3) Low-resolution (30m) land cover labels from the National Land Cover Database (NLCD) [11].

As in [27], the data is split into **South** and **North** regions, comprising the states of MD, VA, WV, DE (S) and NY and PA (N). Our task is to produce 1m-resolution land cover maps of the **North** region, using only the imagery, possibly the low-res classes, and possibly the high-res labels from just the **South** region. The predictions are evaluated against high-res ground truth in the **North** region.

Despite the massive scale of the data, differences such as imaging conditions and frequency of occurrence of vegetation patterns make it difficult for neural networks trained to predict high-res labels from imagery in the **South** region to transfer to **North**. However, in their study of this problem using data fusion methods, [27] obtained a large improvement in **North** performance by multi-task training: the networks were trained to predict high-res labels with the objectives of (1) cross-entropy loss against high-res labels in **South** and (2) super-resolution loss [18] against the distributions determined by low-res NLCD labels in **North** (see the first and third rows of Table 1).

Epitome training. We fit eight 499×499 epitomes to all available **South** imagery. To encourage a diversity of represented land types, for each of the four high-res labels ℓ (water, forest, field, built), we trained a self-diversifying epitome $E_0^{(\ell)}$ on patches of size 11×11 to 31×31 containing at least one pixel labeled with label ℓ. We then trained a model $E_1^{(\ell)}$ on the quarter of such patches with lowest likelihood under $E_0^{(\ell)}$ and a model $E_2^{(\ell)}$ on the quarter with lowest likelihood under $E_1^{(\ell)}$. The first epitome $E_0^{(\ell)}$ was then discarded.[2] The final model is a uniform mixture of the $E_i^{(\ell)}$ ($i = 1, 2$). The $\mu_{m,n}$ parameters of its components can be seen in the left column of Fig. 5. (Notice that while the epitomes in each row were trained on patches containing pixels of a given label ℓ, other label appear in them as well. For example, we see roads in the forest epitome (second row), since roads are sometimes found next to trees, and indeed are poorly modeled by a model of only trees, cf. Fig. 3.)

High-resolution label embedding. We derive high-resolution soft label embeddings $p(\ell|m, n)$ from high-res **South** labels by the following procedure: for 10 million iterations, we uniformly sample a 31×31 patch of **South** imagery x^t and associated high-res labels y^t and evaluate the posterior over positions $p(s_1, s_2|x^t)$, then embed the center 11×11 patch of labels y^t weighted by the posterior (sped up by sampling; see the SI for details). The label embeddings $p(\ell|m, n) \propto z_{m,n,\ell}$ are proportional to the sum of these embeddings over all patches; these quantities estimate the probability that a patch generated by an epitome window with center near (s_1, s_2) would generate label ℓ at the corresponding position. These embeddings are shown in the middle column of Fig. 5.

---

[2] $E_2^{(\ell)}$ is trained to model the patches poorly modeled by the self-diversifying $E_1^{(\ell)}$. Hence, $E_2^{(\ell)}$ simply has much higher posteriors and more diversity of texture.

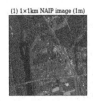
(1) 1×1km NAIP image (1m)

(2) 20-class NLCD (30m)

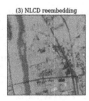
(3) NLCD reembedding

(4) LSR to 4 classes

(5) 4-class ground truth (1m)

Fig. 6. Self-epitomic LSR on a 1024×1024 patch of land (1). The low-res classes (2) are embedded at locations similar in appearance, yielding (3). The inference procedure described in Sect. 4 produces (4), which closely resembles the ground truth (5)

Low-resolution NLCD embedding. Using the same set of epitomes trained on **South**, we derive the posteriors $p(m, n|c)$ given a low-resolution class c: we sample 11×11 patches x^t from **North** with center pixel labeled with low-res class c^t and embed the label c^t weighted by the posterior $p(s_1, s_2|x^t)$. By (11), $p(m, n|c)$ is then proportional to the sum of these embeddings. An example of the embeddings in one epitome component is shown in Fig. 4.

Epitomic label super-resolution. The joint distribution of high-res and low-res classes, $p(\ell|c)$, can be estimated on a small subset of jointly labeled data; we use the statistics reported by [18]. We apply our LSR algorithm to the low-res embeddings $p(m, n|c)$, the joint $p(c, \ell)$, and the known distribution $p(c)$ to arrive at high-res label probabilities at each epitome position, $p(\ell|m, n)$. They are shown in the right column of Fig. 5.

We evaluate the two epitome embeddings $p(\ell|m, n)$, derived from high-res labels in **South** or from low-res classes in **North**, on a sample of 1600km^2 of imagery in the **North** region in the following fashion: we select 31×31 patches x^t and reconstruct the labels in the center 11×11 blocks as the posterior-weighted mean of the $p(\ell|m, n)$. At the large scale of data, this requires an approximation by sampling, see the SI for details. The results are shown in the second and last rows of Table 1.

When the area to be super-resolved is small, we can perform epitomic LSR *using the imagery itself as an epitome*. We experiment with small tiles from **North** (256×256 up to 2048×2048 pixels). For a given tile, we initialize an epitome with the same size as the tile, with uniform prior, mean equal to the true pixel intensities, and fixed variance $\sigma^2 = 0.01$. We then embed low-res NLCD labels from the tile into this epitome just as described above and run the LSR inference algorithm. The probabilities $p(\ell|m, n)$ are then the predicted land cover labels[3]. An example appears in Fig. 6, and more in the SI. The results of this *self-epitomic* LSR, performed on a large evaluation set dissected into tiles of different sizes, can be seen in Table 1.

Results. From Table 1, we draw the following conclusions:

---

[3] We found it helpful to work with $2\times$ downsampled images and use 7×7 patches for embedding, with approximately $0.05|W|^2$ patches sampled for tiles of size $W \times W$.

Table 1. Performance of various methods on land cover segmentation in the **North** region. We report overall accuracy and mean intersection/union (Jaccard) index

Model	Label training set	Acc.	IoU
U-Net [27]	HR (S)	59.4%	40.5%
Epitome (S imagery)	HR (S)	79.5	59.3
U-Net neural LSR [18,27]	HR (S), LR (N)	86.9	62.5
U-Net neural LSR [18]	LR (N)	80.1	41.3
256^2 self-epitomic LSR	LR (N)	85.9	63.3
512^2 self-epitomic LSR	LR (N)	87.0	65.3
1024^2 self-epitomic LSR	LR (N)	87.8	66.9
2048^2 self-epitomic LSR	LR (N)	88.0	67.8
All-tile epitomic LSR	LR (N)	83.9	58.5

*Epitomes trained only on imagery and high-res labels in **South** transfer better to **North** than U-Nets that use the same data.* The U-Nets trained only on imagery and high-res labels in the **South** region transfer poorly to **North**: patterns associated, for example, with forests in the **North** are more frequently associated with fields in **South**, and the discriminatively trained models couple the high-frequency patterns in **South** with their associated land cover labels. Most surprisingly, even the U-Nets trained on the LR **North** imagery perform worse than any of the epitome models trained on the same data.[4]

There is evidence that the far better transfer performance of the epitomes is due to generative training. First, it is nearly unsupervised: no labels are seen in training, except to weakly guide the sampling of patches. Second, diversification training ensures, for example, that forests resembling those found in **North**, while rare, still appear in the epitomes trained on **South** imagery and receive somewhat accurate label embeddings. The posterior on those areas of the epitomes is then much higher in the **North**. (In the SI we show the mean posteriors over epitome positions illustrating this point.)

The self-similarity in images that defines the repetition of patterns in certain classes is highly local. If we were to study self-similarity in a large region, we would be bound to find that some imagery patterns that are associated with a particular high-res label in one area are less so in another. Therefore, the size of the area on which to perform LSR reasoning is an important design parameter. If the area is too small, then we may not get enough observations of coarse classes to unambiguously assign high-res patterns to them: indeed, self-epitomic LSR accuracy increases with the size of the tile. It is remarkable that we can get better high-res segmentation results than the state of the art by studying one

---

[4] We used training settings identical to those of [18]. The training collapsed to a minimum in which the "water" class was not predicted, but the accuracy would be lower than that of all-tile epitomic LSR even if all water were predicted correctly.

512×512 patch at a time, together with low-res classes for 30×30 blocks, and no other training data or high-res labels.

On the other hand, when the area is too large, then the pattern diversity increases and ambiguity may reduce the effectiveness of the method. Furthermore, when the area is too large, self-epitomic LSR is not computationally practicable – the imagery must be compressed in an epitome to mine self-similarity. All-tile epitomic LSR improves over the baseline models although *no high-res labels are seen*, while the best-performing U-Nets required high-res labels in **South**, low-res classes in **North**, and imagery from both **South** and **North** in training.

5.2 Lymphocyte Segmentation in Pathology Images

Our second example is the task of identifying tumor-infiltrating lymphocytes (TILs) in pathology imagery. We work with a set of 50000 240×240 crops of 0.5μm-resolution H&E-stained tumor imagery [31]. There is no high-res *segmentation* data available for this task. However, [13] produced a set of 1786 images centered on single cells, labeled with whether the center cell is a TIL, on which our methods can be evaluated.

The best results for this task that used high-resolution supervision required either a manually tuned feature extraction pipeline and SVM classifier [13,36] or, in the case of CNNs, a sparse autoencoder pretraining mechanism [13]. More recently, [18] nearly matched the supervised CNN results using the neural label super-resolution technique: the only guidance available to the segmentation model in training was low-resolution estimates of the probability of TIL infiltration in 100×100 regions for the entire dataset derived by [31], as well as weak pixel-level rules (masking regions below certain thresholds of hematoxylin level).

We address the same problem as [18], using the low-res probability maps as the only supervision in epitomic LSR:

Epitome training. We train 299×299 epitomes on patches of size 11×11 to 31×31 intersecting the center pixels of the images to be segmented. The resulting models trained with and without self-diversification are shown in Fig. 7.

Low-resolution embedding. Following [18], we define 10 classes c, for each range of density estimates $[0.1 \cdot n, 0.1 \cdot (n+1)]$. We find the posteriors $p(m,n|c)$ by embedding 1 million 11×11 patches from the entire dataset.

Epitomic label super-resolution. We estimate the mean TIL densities in each probability range, $p(\ell|c)$ and set a uniform prior $p(c)$. We then produce the probabilities of TIL presence per position $p(\ell|m,n)$ by the LSR algorithm.

We then evaluate our models on the data for which high-res labels exist by sampling 11×11 patches x containing the center pixel – 100 for each test image – and computing the mean probability of TIL presence $\sum_s p(\ell|s)p(s|x)$ as the final prediction score. We obtained better results when we instead averaged the probability of TIL presence *anywhere* in an embedded patch in the epitome, that is, convolved $p(\ell|s)$ with a 11×11 uniform filter before computing this sum.

Table 2. Performance of various methods on the TIL segmentation task. We report the area under the ROC curve

Model	Label training set	AUC
Manual features SVM [13,36]	HR	0.713
CNN [13]	HR	0.494
CNN with pretraining [13]	HR	0.786
U-Net neural LSR [18]	LR + color masks	0.783
Non-div. epitomic LSR	LR	0.794
Div. epitomic LSR	LR	0.801

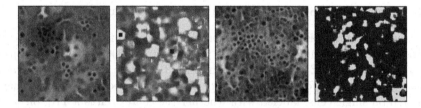

Fig. 7. Epitomes trained on tumor imagery and the embedding of the tumor-infiltrating lymphocyte label. The model on the right was trained with self-diversification

Results. As summarized in Table 2, our epitomic LSR outperforms all previous methods, including both the supervised models and the neural LSR, with self-diversifying epitomes providing the greatest improvement. The results suggest that TIL identification is a highly local problem. Deep CNNs, with their large receptive fields, require hand-engineered features or unsupervised pretraining to reach even comparable performance. In addition, epitomes are entirely unsupervised and thus amenable to adaptation to new tasks, such as classifying other types of cells: given coarse label data, we may simply embed it into the pretrained epitomes and perform LSR.

6   Conclusion

Motivated by the observation that deep convolutional networks usually have a small effective receptive field, we revisit simple patch mixture models, in particular, epitomes. As generative models that allow addition of latent variables, these approaches have several advantages. They are interpretable: an epitome looks like the imagery on which it was trained (Fig. 2), and examining the posteriors over epitome positions is akin to understanding weights for many neurons at once. The desired invariances can be directly modeled with additional hidden variables, just as [7] modeled illumination. They can be combined with other statistical procedures, as we show with our novel label super-resolution formulation (Sect. 4). They can be pretrained on a large amount of unlabeled data so that a small number of labeled points are needed to train prediction models, and they can be a base of hierarchical or pyramidal models that reason over long ranges, e.g., [4,6,16,26,33]. Using epitome-derived features in tasks that require long-range reasoning, such as common benchmarks for segmentation or classification of large images, is an interesting subject for future work.

Just as deep neural networks suffered from the vanishing gradient problem for years, before such innovations as stagewise pretraining [10], dropout [32], and the recognition of the numerical advantages of ReLU units [19], epitomic representations had suffered from their own numerical problems stemming from the large dynamic range of the posterior distributions. As a remedy, we designed a new large-scale learning algorithm that allowed us to run experiments on hundreds of billions of pixels. We showed that simply through mining patch self-similarity, epitomic representations outperform the neural state of the art in domain transfer and label super-resolution in two important application domains.

We direct the reader to the SI for more examples, code, results on another competition dataset (in which epitomes were the basis for the winning method [28]), and discussion on future research.

Acknowledgments. The authors thank Caleb Robinson for valuable help with experiments [28] and the reviewers for comments on earlier versions of the paper.

References

1. Bazzani, L., Cristani, M., Perina, A., Murino, V.: Multiple-shot person re-identification by chromatic and epitomic analyses. Pattern Recogn. Lett. **33**(7), 898–903 (2012)
2. Brendel, W., Bethge, M.: Approximating CNNs with bag-of-local-features models works surprisingly well on imagenet. In: International Conference on Learning Representations (ICLR) (2019)
3. Chesapeake Conservancy: Land cover data project (2017). https://chesapeakeconservancy.org/wp-content/uploads/2017/01/LandCover101Guide.pdf
4. Cheung, V., Jojic, N., Samaras, D.: Capturing long-range correlations with patch models. In: 2007 IEEE Conference on Computer Vision and Pattern Recognition. pp. 1–8. IEEE (2007)
5. Dai, J., He, K., Sun, J.: Boxsup: Exploiting bounding boxes to supervise convolutional networks for semantic segmentation. In: Proceedings of the IEEE International Conference on Computer Vision. pp. 1635–1643 (2015)
6. Fergus, R., Fei-Fei, L., Perona, P., Zisserman, A.: Learning object categories from google's image search. In: Tenth IEEE International Conference on Computer Vision (ICCV 2005). vol. 2, pp. 1816–1823. IEEE (2005)
7. Frey, B.J., Jojic, N.: Transformed component analysis: Joint estimation of spatial transformations and image components. In: Proceedings of the Seventh IEEE International Conference on Computer Vision. vol. 2, pp. 1190–1196. IEEE (1999)
8. Ganchev, K., Gillenwater, J., Taskar, B., et al.: Posterior regularization for structured latent variable models. J. Mach. Learn. Res. **11**, 2001–2049 (2010)
9. Geirhos, R., Rubisch, P., Michaelis, C., Bethge, M., Wichmann, F.A., Brendel, W.: Imagenet-trained CNNs are biased towards texture; increasing shape bias improves accuracy and robustness. In: International Conference on Learning Representations (ICLR) (2019)

10. Hinton, G.E., Salakhutdinov, R.R.: Reducing the dimensionality of data with neural networks. Science **313**(5786), 504–507 (2006)
11. Homer, C., et al.: Completion of the 2011 national land cover database for the conterminous united states-representing a decade of land cover change information. Photogramm. Eng. Remote Sens. **81**(5), 345–354 (2015)
12. Hong, S., Noh, H., Han, B.: Decoupled deep neural network for semi-supervised semantic segmentation. In: Advances in Neural Information Processing Systems. pp. 1495–1503 (2015)
13. Hou, L., et al.: Sparse autoencoder for unsupervised nucleus detection and representation in histopathology images. Pattern Recogn. **86**, 188–200 (2019)
14. Jojic, N., Frey, B.J., Kannan, A.: Epitomic analysis of appearance and shape. In: ICCV. vol. 3, p. 34 (2003)
15. Jojic, N., Perina, A., Murino, V.: Structural epitome: a way to summarize one's visual experience. In: Advances in Neural Information Processing Systems. pp. 1027–1035 (2010)
16. Lazebnik, S., Schmid, C., Ponce, J.: Beyond bags of features: Spatial pyramid matching for recognizing natural scene categories. In: 2006 IEEE Computer Society Conference on Computer Vision and Pattern Recognition (CVPR 2006). vol. 2, pp. 2169–2178. IEEE (2006)
17. Luo, W., Li, Y., Urtasun, R., Zemel, R.: Understanding the effective receptive field in deep convolutional neural networks. In: Lee, D.D., Sugiyama, M., Luxburg, U.V., Guyon, I., Garnett, R. (eds.) Advances in Neural Information Processing Systems 29, pp. 4898–4906. Curran Associates, Inc. (2016). http://papers.nips.cc/paper/6203-understanding-the-effective-receptive-field-in-deep-convolutional-neural-networks.pdf
18. Malkin, K., et al.: Label super-resolution networks. In: International Conference on Learning Representations (2019)
19. Nair, V., Hinton, G.E.: Rectified linear units improve restricted boltzmann machines. In: Proceedings of the 27th International Conference on Machine Learning (ICML-2010). pp. 807–814 (2010)
20. Ni, K., Kannan, A., Criminisi, A., Winn, J.: Epitomic location recognition. IEEE Trans. Pattern Anal. Mach. Intell. **31**(12), 2158–2167 (2009)
21. Nilsback, M.E., Zisserman, A.: A visual vocabulary for flower classification. In: 2006 IEEE Computer Society Conference on Computer Vision and Pattern Recognition (CVPR2 006). vol. 2, pp. 1447–1454. IEEE (2006)
22. Papandreou, G., Chen, L.C., Murphy, K.P., Yuille, A.L.: Weakly-and semi-supervised learning of a deep convolutional network for semantic image segmentation. In: Proceedings of the IEEE International Conference on Computer Vision. pp. 1742–1750 (2015)
23. Papandreou, G., Chen, L.C., Yuille, A.L.: Modeling image patches with a generic dictionary of mini-epitomes. In: Proceedings of the IEEE Conference on Computer Vision and Pattern Recognition. pp. 2051–2058 (2014)
24. Papandreou, G., Kokkinos, I., Savalle, P.A.: Modeling local and global deformations in deep learning: Epitomic convolution, multiple instance learning, and sliding window detection. In: Proceedings of the IEEE Conference on Computer Vision and Pattern Recognition. pp. 390–399 (2015)
25. Pathak, D., Krahenbuhl, P., Darrell, T.: Constrained convolutional neural networks for weakly supervised segmentation. In: Proceedings of the IEEE International Conference on Computer Vision. pp. 1796–1804 (2015)

26. Perina, A., Jojic, N.: Spring lattice counting grids: scene recognition using deformable positional constraints. In: Fitzgibbon, A., Lazebnik, S., Perona, P., Sato, Y., Schmid, C. (eds.) ECCV 2012. LNCS, vol. 7577, pp. 837–851. Springer, Heidelberg (2012). https://doi.org/10.1007/978-3-642-33783-3_60

27. Robinson, C., et al.: Large scale high-resolution land cover mapping with multi-resolution data. In: Proceedings of the IEEE Conference on Computer Vision and Pattern Recognition. pp. 12726–12735 (2019)

28. Robinson, C., Malkin, K., Hu, L., Dilkina, B., Jojic, N.: Weakly supervised semantic segmentation in the 2020 IEEE GRSS Data Fusion Contest. In: Proceedings of the International Geoscience and Remote Sensing Symposium (2020)

29. Ronneberger, O., Fischer, P., Brox, T.: U-Net: convolutional networks for biomedical image segmentation. In: Navab, N., Hornegger, J., Wells, W.M., Frangi, A.F. (eds.) MICCAI 2015. LNCS, vol. 9351, pp. 234–241. Springer, Cham (2015). https://doi.org/10.1007/978-3-319-24574-4_28

30. Russakovsky, O., Deng, J., Su, H., Krause, J., Satheesh, S., Ma, S., Huang, Z., Karpathy, A., Khosla, A., Bernstein, M., et al.: Imagenet large scale visual recognition challenge. Int. J. Comput. Vis. **115**(3), 211–252 (2015)

31. Saltz, J., Gupta, R., Hou, L., Kurc, T., Singh, P., Nguyen, V., Samaras, D., Shroyer, K.R., Zhao, T., Batiste, R., et al.: Spatial organization and molecular correlation of tumor-infiltrating lymphocytes using deep learning on pathology images. Cell reports **23**(1), 181 (2018)

32. Srivastava, N., Hinton, G., Krizhevsky, A., Sutskever, I., Salakhutdinov, R.: Dropout: a simple way to prevent neural networks from overfitting. J. Mach. Learn. Res. **15**(1), 1929–1958 (2014)

33. Weber, M., Welling, M., Perona, P.: Unsupervised learning of models for recognition. In: Vernon, D. (ed.) ECCV 2000. LNCS, vol. 1842, pp. 18–32. Springer, Heidelberg (2000). https://doi.org/10.1007/3-540-45054-8_2

34. Yeung, S., Kannan, A., Dauphin, Y., Fei-Fei, L.: Epitomic variational autoencoders (2016)

35. Zhang, H., Fritts, J.E., Goldman, S.A.: Image segmentation evaluation: a survey of unsupervised methods. Comput. Vis. Image Underst. **110**(2), 260–280 (2008)

36. Zhou, N., et al.: Evaluation of nucleus segmentation in digital pathology images through large scale image synthesis. In: Medical Imaging 2017: Digital Pathology. vol. 10140, p. 101400K. International Society for Optics and Photonics (2017)

AE-OT-GAN: Training GANs from Data Specific Latent Distribution

Dongsheng An[1], Yang Guo[1], Min Zhang[2], Xin Qi[1], Na Lei[3(✉)],
and Xianfang Gu[1]

[1] Stony Brook University, Stony Brook, USA
{doan,yangguo,xinqi,gu}@cs.stonybrook.edu
[2] Harvard Medical School, Boston, USA
mzhang@bwh.harvard.edu
[3] Dalian University of Technology, Dalian, China
nalei@dlut.edu.cn

Abstract. Though generative adversarial networks (GANs) are prominent models to generate realistic and crisp images, they are unstable to train and suffer from the mode collapse problem. The problems of GANs come from approximating the intrinsic discontinuous distribution transform map with continuous DNNs. The recently proposed AE-OT model addresses the discontinuity problem by explicitly computing the discontinuous optimal transform map in the latent space of the autoencoder. Though have no mode collapse, the generated images by AE-OT are blurry. In this paper, we propose the AE-OT-GAN model to utilize the advantages of the both models: generate high quality images and at the same time overcome the mode collapse problems. Specifically, we firstly embed the low dimensional image manifold into the latent space by autoencoder (AE). Then the extended semi-discrete optimal transport (SDOT) map is used to generate new latent codes. Finally, our GAN model is trained to generate high quality images from the latent distribution induced by the extended SDOT map. The distribution transform map from this dataset related latent distribution to the data distribution will be continuous, and thus can be well approximated by the continuous DNNs. Additionally, the paired data between the latent codes and the real images gives us further restriction about the generator and stabilizes the training process. Experiments on simple MNIST dataset and complex datasets like CIFAR10 and CelebA show the advantages of the proposed method.

Keywords: Generative model · Optimal transport · GAN · Continuity

1 Introduction

Image generation has been one of the core topics in the area of computer vision for a long time. Thanks to the quick development of deep learning, numerous

Electronic supplementary material The online version of this chapter (https://doi.org/10.1007/978-3-030-58574-7_33) contains supplementary material, which is available to authorized users.

generative models are proposed, including encoder-decoder based models [2,16, 37], generative adversarial networks (GANs) [3,5,11,12,31,40], density estimator based models [7,8,17,29] and energy based models [19,28,41,44]. The encoder-decoder based models and GANs are the most prominent ones due to their capability to generate high quality images.

Intrinsically, the generator in a generative model aims to learn the real data distribution supported on the data manifold [36]. Suppose the distribution of a specific class of natural data ν_{gt} is concentrated on a low dimensional manifold χ embedded in the high dimensional data space. The encoder-decoder methods first attempt to embed the data into the latent space Ω through the encoder f_θ, then samples from the latent distribution are mapped back to the manifold to generate new data by decoder g_ξ. While GANs, which have no encoder, directly learn a map (generator) that transports a given prior low dimensional distribution to ν_{gt}.

Usually, GANs are unstable to train and suffer from mode collapse [10,25]. The difficulties come from the fact that the generator of a GAN model is trained to approximate the discontinuous distribution transport map from the *unimodal Gaussian distribution* to the *real data distribution* by the continuous neural networks [2,15,40]. In fact, when the supporting manifolds of the source and target distributions differ in topology or convexity, the OT map between them will be discontinuous [38]. Distribution transport maps can have complicated singularities, even when the ambient dimension is low [9]. This poses a great challenge for the generator training in standard GAN models.

To tackle the mode collapse problem caused by discontinuous transport maps, the authors of [2] proposed the AE-OT model. In this model, an autoencoder is used to map the image manifold χ into the latent manifold Ω. Then, the semi-discrete optimal transport (SDOT) map T from the uniform distribution $Uni([0,1]^d)$ to the empirical latent distribution is explicitly computed via convex optimization approach. Then a piece-wise linear extension map of the SDOT, denoted by $\tilde{T}$, pushes forward the uniform distribution to a continuous latent distribution μ, which in turn gives a good approximation of the latent distribution $\mu_{gt} = f_{\theta\#}\nu_{gt}$ ($f_{\theta\#}$ means the push forward map induced by f_θ). Composing the continuous decoder g_ξ and discontinuous $\tilde{T}$ together, i.e. $g_\xi \circ \tilde{T}(w)$, where w is sampled from uniform distribution, this model can generate new images. Though have no mode collapse, the generated images look blurry.

In this work we propose the AE-OT-GAN framework to combine the advantages of the both models and generate high quality images without mode collapse. Specifically, after the training of the autoencoder and the computation of the extended SDOT map, we can directly sample from the latent distribution μ by applying $\tilde{T}(w)$ on the uniform distribution to train the GAN model. In contrast to the conventional GAN models, whose generators are trained to transport the latent Gaussian distribution to the data manifold distribution, our GAN model sample from the data inferred latent distribution μ. The distribution transport map from μ to the data distribution ν_{gt} is continuous and thus can be well approximated by the generator (parameterized by CNNs). Moreover, the decoder of the pre-trained autoencoder gives a warm start of the generator, so that the Kullback–Leibler divergence can be directly applied in the discriminator because the real and fake batches of images have non-vanishing overlap in their supports during the training phase. Furthermore, the content loss and feature loss between the paired latent codes and real input images regularize the adversarial loss, stabilize the GAN training and help get rid of mode collapse problem. Experiments have shown efficacy and efficiency of our proposed model.

The contributions of the current work can be summarized as follows: **(1)** This paper proposes a novel AE-OT-GAN model that combines the strengths of AE-OT model and GAN model. The proposed model removes the blurriness of the images generated by AE-OT, and at the same time keep the good properties of the latter in eliminating the mode collapse problems. **(2)** The decoder of the autoencoder provides a good initialization of the generator of GAN, which makes the supports of the real and fake image distributions overlap and thus the KL divergence can be used in the discriminator. **(3)** In addition to the adversarial loss, the explicit correspondence between the latent codes and the real images provide auxiliary constraints, namely the content loss and feature loss, to the generator. The both losses make sure that there is no mode collapse in our model. **(4)** The experiments demonstrate that our model can generate images consistently better than the results of state-of-the-art methods.

2   Related Work

The proposed method in this paper is highly related to encoder-decoder based generation models, the generative adversarial networks (GANs), conditional GANs and the hybrid models that take the advantages of above.

Encoder-decoder Architecture. A breakthrough for image generating comes from the scheme of Variational Autoencoders (VAEs) (e.g. [16]), where the decoders approximate real data distributions from a Gaussian distribution in a variational approach (e.g [16] and [33]). Latter Yuri Burda et al. [4] lower the requirement of latent distribution and propose the importance weighted autoencoder (IWAE) model through a different lower bound. Bin and David [6] propose that the latent distribution of VAE may not be Gaussian and improve it by firstly training the original model and then generating new latent code through the extended ancestral process. Another improvement of the VAE is the VQ-VAE model [30], which requires the encoder to output discrete latent codes by vector quantisation, then the posterior collapse of VAEs can be overcome. By multiscale hierarchical organization, this idea is further used to generate high quality images in VQ-VAE-2 [32]. In [37], the authors adopt the Wasserstein distance in the latent space to measure the distance between the distribution of the latent code and the given one and generate images with better quality. Different from the VAEs, the AE-OT model [2] firstly embed the images into the latent space by autoencoder, then an extended semi-discrete OT map is computed to generate new latent code based on the fixed ones. Decoded by the decoder, new images can be generated. Although the encoder-decoder based methods are relatively simple to train, the generated images tend to be blurry.

Generative Adversarial Networks. The GAN model [11] tries to alternatively update the generator, which maps the noise sampled from a given distribution to real images, and the discriminator differentiates between the generated images and the real ones. If the generated images successfully fool the discriminator, the model is well trained. Later, [31] proposes a deep convolutions neural network (DCGAN) to generate images with better quality. While being a powerful tool in generating realistic samples, GANs can be hard to train and suffer from mode collapse problem [10]. After delicate analysis, [3] points out that it is the KL divergence the original GAN used causes these problems. Then the authors introduced the celebrated WGAN, which makes the whole framework easy to converge. To satisfy the Lipschitz continuity required by WGAN, a lot of methods are proposed, including clipping [3], gradient penalty [12], spectral normalization [27] and so on. Later, Wu et al. [39] use the Wasserstein divergence objective, which get rid of the Lipschitz approximation problem and get a better result. Differently, the OT-GAN [35] uses the Sinkhorn algorithm to approximate the Wasserstein distance in the image space. Instead of L_1 cost adopted by WGAN, Liu et.al [24] propose the WGAN-QC by taking the L_2 cost into consideration. Though various GANs can generate sharp images, they will theoretically encounter the mode collapse problem [2,10].

Note that no mode collapse in the AE-OT model cannot directly guarantee that there is no mode collapse of the AE-OT-GAN model. For the AE-OT model, the pre-trained decoder of the AE is used as generator, thus if there is no mode collapse in the latent space, there will be no mode collapse in the image space. For the AE-OT-GAN model, the decoder is changed. The elimination of the mode collapse is thus guaranteed by the paired content loss between the latent codes and the real images.

3   The Proposed Method

In this section, we explain our proposed AE-OT-GAN model in detail. There are mainly three modules, an autoencoder (AE), an optimal transport mapper (OT) and a GAN model. Firstly, an AE model is trained to embed the data manifold χ into the latent space. At the same time, the encoder f_θ pushes forward the ground-truth data distribution ν_{gt} supported on χ to the ground-truth latent distribution μ_{gt} supported on Ω in the latent space. Secondly, we compute the semi-discrete OT map from the uniform distribution to the discrete empirical latent distribution $\hat{\mu}_{gt}$. By the extended SDOT map $\tilde{T}$, we can construct the continuous distribution μ that approximates the ground-truth latent distribution μ_{gt} well. Finally, starting from μ as the latent distribution, our GAN model is trained to generate both realistic and crisp images. The pipeline of our proposed model is illustrated in Fig. 1. In the following, we will explain the three modules one by one.

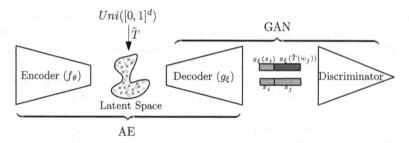

Fig. 1. The framework of the proposed method. Firstly, the autoencoder is trained to embed the images into the latent space, the real latent codes are shown as the orange circles. Then we compute the extended semi-discrete OT map $\tilde{T}$ to generate new latent codes in the latent space (the purple crosses). Finally, our GAN model is trained from the latent distribution $\mu = \tilde{T}_{\#}Uni([0,1]^d)$ to the image distribution. Here the generator is just the decoder of the autoencoder. The fake batch (the bar with orange and purple colors) to train the discriminator is composed of two parts: the reconstructed images $g_\xi(z_i)$ of the real latent codes and the generated images $g_\xi(\tilde{T}(w))$ from the randomly generated latent codes with w sampled from uniform distribution. The real batch (the bar with only orange color) is also composed of two parts: the real images x_i corresponding to z_i, and the randomly selected images x_j. (Color figure online)

3.1   Data Embedding with Autoencoder

We model the real data distribution as a probability measure ν_{gt} supported on an r dimensional manifold χ embedded in the D dimensional Euclidean space $\mathbb{R}^D$ (ambient space) with $r \ll D$. In the first step of our AE-OT-GAN model, we train an autoencoder (AE) to embed the real data manifold χ to be the latent manifold Ω. In particular, training the AE model is equivalent to compute the encoding map f_θ and decoding map g_ξ

$$(\nu_{gt}, \chi) \xrightarrow{f_\theta} (\mu_{gt}, \Omega) \xrightarrow{g_\xi} (\nu_{gt}, \chi)$$

by minimizing the loss function:

$$\mathcal{L}(\theta, \xi) := \sum_{i=1}^{n} \|x_i - g_\xi \circ f_\theta(x_i)\|^2,$$

with f_θ and g_ξ parameterized by standard CNNs (θ and ξ are the parameters of the networks, respectively). Given a dense sampling from the image manifold (detailed explanation is included in the supplementary) and ideal optimization (namely the loss function goes to 0), $f_\theta \circ g_\xi$ coincides with the identity map. After training, f_θ is a continuous, convertible map, namely a *homeomorphism*, and g_ξ is the inverse homeomorphism. This means $f_\theta : \chi \to \Omega$ is an embedding, and pushes forward ν_{gt} to the latent data distribution $\mu_{gt} := f_{\theta\#}\nu_{gt}$. In practice, we only have the empirical data distribution given by $\hat{\nu}_{gt} = \frac{1}{n}\sum_{i=1}^{n}\delta(x - x_i)$, which is pushed forward to be the empirical latent distribution $\hat{\mu}_{gt} = \frac{1}{n}\sum_{i=1}^{n}\delta(z - z_i)$, where n is the number of samples.

3.2 Constructing μ with Semi-Discrete OT Map

In this section, from the empirical latent distribution $\hat{\mu}_{gt}$, we construct a continuous latent distribution μ following [2] such that (i) it generalizes $\hat{\mu}_{gt}$ well, so that all of the modes in the latent space are covered by the support of μ (ii) the support of μ has similar topology to that of μ_{gt}, which ensures that the transport map from μ to ν_{gt} has less discontinuities and (iii) it is efficient to sample from μ.

To obtain μ, the semi-discrete OT map T from the uniform distribution $Uni([0,1]^d)$ to the empirical latent distribution $\hat{\mu}_{gt}$ is firstly computed. Here d is the dimension of the latent space. By extending T to be a piece-wise linear map $\tilde{T}$, we can construct μ as the push forward distribution of $Uni([0,1]^d)$ under $\tilde{T}$:

$$(Uni([0,1]^d), [0,1]^d) \xrightarrow{\tilde{T}} (\mu, \Omega)$$

Theorem 1. *The 2-Wasserstein distance between μ and $\hat{\mu}_{gt}$ satisfies $W_2(\mu, \hat{\mu}_{gt}) \leq \varepsilon$, where ε is a given constant to build μ. Moreover, if the latent codes are densely sampled from the latent manifold Ω, we have $W_2(\mu, \mu_{gt}) \leq 2\varepsilon$, μ-almost surely.*

The construction details of μ can be found in [2] and the supplementary, and we also give the proof of the above theorem in the supplementary. This theorem tells us that as a continuous generalization of $\hat{\mu}_{gt}$, μ is a good approximation of μ_{gt}. Also, we want to mention that $\tilde{T}$ is a piece-wise linear map that pushes forward $Uni([0,1]^d)$ to μ, which makes the sampling from μ efficient and accurate. Based on the construction of $\tilde{T}$, the sampling from μ is equivalent to the locally piecewise linear interpolation of z_is in the latent space, which guarantees that there is no mode collapse in μ.

3.3 GAN Training from μ

The GAN model computes the transport map from the continuous latent distribution μ to the data distribution on the manifold.

$$(\mu, \Omega) \xrightarrow{g_\xi} (\nu_{gt}, \chi).$$

Our GAN model is based on the vanilla GAN model proposed by Ian Goodfellow et.al [11]. The generator g_ξ is used to generate new images by sampling from the latent distributin μ, while the discriminator d_η is used to discriminate if the distribution of the generated images are the same with that of the real images. The training process is formalized to be a min-max optimization problem:

$$\min_\xi \max_\eta \mathcal{L}(\xi, \eta),$$

where the loss function is given by

$$\mathcal{L}(\xi, \eta) = \mathcal{L}_{adv} + \mathcal{L}_{feat} + \beta \mathcal{L}_{img} \tag{1}$$

In our model, the loss function consists of three terms, the adversarial loss $\mathcal{L}_{adv}$, the image content loss $\mathcal{L}_{img}$ and the feature loss $\mathcal{L}_{feat}$. Here $\beta > 0$ is the weight of the content loss.

Adversarial Loss. We adopt the vanilla GAN model [11] based on the Kullback–Leibler (KL) divergence. The key difference between our model and the original GAN is that our latent samples are drawn from the data related latent distribution μ, instead of the Gaussian distribution. The adversarial loss is given by:

$$\mathcal{L}_{adv} = \min_{\xi} \max_{\zeta} E_{x \sim \nu_{gt}}[log\ d_{\zeta}(x)] + E_{z \sim \mu}[log(1 - d_{\zeta}(g_{\xi}(z)))]$$

According to [3], vanilla GAN is hard to converge because the supports of the distributions of the real images and fake images may not intersect each other, which makes the KL divergence between them infinity. This issue is solved in our case, because (1) the training of AE gives a warm start to the generator, so at the beginning of the training, the support of the generated distribution $g_{\xi\#}\mu$ is close to that of the real data distribution ν_{gt}; (2) by delicate settings of the fake and real batches used to train the discriminator, we can keep the KL divergence between them converge well. In detail, as shown in Fig. 1, the fake batch is composed of both the reconstructed images from the real latent codes (the orange circles) and the generated images from the generated latent codes (the purple crosses), and the real batch includes both the real images corresponding to the real latent codes and some randomly selected real images.

Content Loss. Recall that the generator can produce two types of images: images reconstructed by real latent codes and images from generated latent codes. Given a real sample x_i, its latent code is $z_i = f_{\theta}(x_i)$, the reconstructed image is $g_{\xi}(z_i)$. Each reconstructed image is represented as a triple $(x_i, z_i, g_{\xi}(z_i))$. Suppose there are n reconstructed images in total, the content loss is given by

$$\mathcal{L}_{img} = \frac{1}{n} \sum_{i=1}^{n} \|g_{\xi}(z_i) - x_i\|_2^2 \tag{2}$$

Where g_{ξ} is the generator parameterized by ξ.

Feature Loss. We adopt the feature loss similar to that in [21]. Given a reconstructed image triple $(x_i, z_i, g_{\xi}(z_i))$, we encode $g_{\xi}(z_i)$ by the encoder of AE. Ideally, the real image x_i and the generated image $g_{\xi}(z_i)$ should be the same, therefore their latent codes should be similar. We measure the difference between their latent codes by the feature loss. Furthermore, we can measure the difference between their intermediate features from different layers of the encoder.

Suppose the encoder is a network with L layers, the output of the lth layer is denoted as $f_{\theta}^{(l)}$. The feature loss is given by

$$\mathcal{L}_{feat} := \frac{1}{n} \sum_{i=1}^{n} \sum_{l=1}^{L} \alpha^{(l)} \|f_{\theta}^{(l)}(x_i) - f_{\theta}^{(l)} \circ g_{\xi}(z_i)\|_2^2,$$

Where $\alpha^{(l)}$ is the weight of the feature loss of the l-th layer.

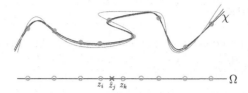

Fig. 2. Manifold fitting result of the decoder/GAN. The blue curve is the original manifold. The green one shows the fitting result of the AE-OT model. By the AE-OT-GAN framework, we can not only draw $g_\xi(z_i)$ much closer to x_i, the whole manifold (the red curve) also fit the original one (blue curve) better. The orange circles on Ω represent the real latent codes, and the purple one represents the generated latent code. The orange disks on the manifold represent real data. (Color figure online)

For reconstructed images $(x_i, z_i, g_\xi(z_i))$, the content loss and the feature loss force the generated image $g_\xi(z_i)$ to be the same with the real image x_i. Therefore the eliminating of mode collapse in the latent space means that there is no mode collapse in the image space.

3.4 Geometric Perspective of AE-OT-GAN

Another perspective of the proposed model is that it can be treated as a manifold fitting framework. Ideally, if given an embedding map $f : \chi \to \Omega$ and a dense dataset X sampled from a distribution ν_{gt} supported on χ, the purpose of the generation model is to generate new samples following the distribution of ν_{gt} and locating on the manifold χ. For the AE-OT model [2], it only requires that the reconstructed images should be similar to the real ones under L_2 distance. As a result, the support of the generated image distribution may only fit the real manifold χ well near the given samples. As shown in Fig. 2, the orange circles represent the latent codes, and the green curve represents the support of the generated distribution of AE-OT model, which only fits the real manifold χ well nearby the given samples. For the AE-OT-GAN model, on one hand, the feature loss and content loss require that the reconstructed manifold (the red curve of Fig. 2) should approach to the real manifold χ on the given samples; on the other hand, the discriminator is used to regularize the fitting performance of the generated manifold on both the given samples and new generated samples, namely both the reconstructed images $g_\xi(z_i)$ and the generated images $g_\xi(\hat{z}_j)$ should fit the real manifold well. Here z_i and $\hat{z}_j$ represent the real latent codes and the generated latent codes. Therefore, the generated manifold by the AE-OT-GAN model fits the real manifold χ far more better than the AE-OT model. Moreover, according to Sect. 3.2, generating a new latent code from μ is essentially equivalent to locally linear interpolation by the real latent codes. As a result, the generated images can actually be treated as the non-linear interpolation by the nearby real images. For example, $\hat{z}_j$ is generated by linear interpolation between z_i and z_k, then the location of $g_\xi(z_i)$ should be between x_i and x_k.

4 Experiments

To evaluate the proposed method, experiments are conducted on various datasets including MNIST [20], stack MNIST [23], Cifar10 [18], CelebA [43] and CelebA-HQ [22].

Evaluation Metrics. To illustrate the performance of the proposed method, we adopt the commonly used Frechet Inception distance (FID) [13] as our main evaluation metrics. When the images are embedded into the feature space by inception network, two high dimensional Gaussian distributions are used to approximate the empirical distributions of the generated and real features, respectively. The FID is given by the difference between the two Gaussian distributions. Lower FID means better quality of the generated dataset. For the Cifar10 dataset, another popular metric is the Inception Score (IS) [34], which can be used to measure the quality of each single image. Higher IS means better quality of the generated image.

Training Details. To get rid of the vanishing gradient problem and make the model converge better, we use the following three strategies:

(i) Train the discriminator using Batch Composition There are two types of latent codes in our method: *the real latent codes* coming from encoding the real images by the encoder, and the generated latent codes coming from the extended SDOT map. Correspondingly, there are two types of generated images, *the reconstructed images* from the real latent codes and *the generated images* from the generated latent codes.

To train the discriminator, both the fake batch and real batch are used. *The fake batch* consists of both randomly selected reconstructed images and generated images, and *the real batch* only includes real images, in which the first part has a one-to-one correspondence with the reconstructed images in the fake batch, as shown in Fig. 1. In all the experiments, the ratio between the number of generated images and reconstructed images in the fake batch is 3. This strategy ensures that there is an overlap between the supports of the fake and real batches, so that the KL divergence is not infinity.

(ii) Different learning rate For better training, we use different learning rates for the generator and the discriminator as suggested by Heusel et al. in [13]. Specifically, we set the learning rate of the generator to be $lr_G = 2e - 5$ and that of the discriminator to be $lr_D = lr_G/R$, where $R > 1$. This improves the stability of the training process.

(iii) Different inner steps Another way to improve the training consistency of the whole framework is to set different update steps for the generator and discriminator. Namely, when the discriminator updates once, the generator updates S times correspondingly. This strategy is opposite to the training of vanilla GANs, which typically require multiple discriminator update steps per generator update step.

By setting R and S, we can keep the discriminator output of the real images slightly large than that of the generated ones, which can better guide the training of the generator. For the MNIST and stack MNIST datasets, $R = 15$ and $S = 3$; for the Cifar10 dataset, $R = 25$ and $S = 10$; and for the CelebA and CelebA-HQ

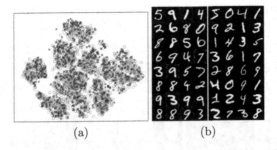

(a)   (b)

Fig. 3. (a) Latent code distribution. The orange circles represent the fixed latent code and the purple crosses are the generated ones. (b) Comparison between the generated digits (left) and the real digits (right). (Color figure online)

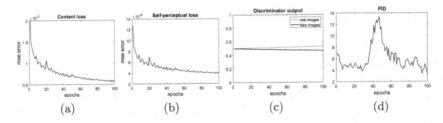

(a)   (b)   (c)   (d)

Fig. 4. The curves for training on MNIST dataset [20] of each epoch, including the results of content loss (a) and self-perceptual loss (b), the discriminator output (c) and FIDs (d).

datasets, $R = 15$ and $S = 5$. In Eq. 1, $\beta = 2000$ and $\alpha^{(l)} = 0.06$ with $l < L$, where L denotes the last layer of the encoder. $\alpha^L = 2.0/\|Z\|_2$ is used to regularize the loss of the latent codes.

With the above settings and the warm initialization of the generator from the pre-trained decoder, for each dataset, the total epochs will be less than 1000.

4.1 Convergence Analysis on MNIST

In this experiment, we evaluate the performance of our proposed model on MNIST dataset [20], which can be well embedded into the 64 dimensional latent space with the architecture of InfoGAN [5]. In Fig. 3(a), we visualize the real latent codes (orange circles) and the generated latent codes (purple crosses) by t-SNE [26]. It is obvious that the support of the real latent distribution and that of the generated latent distribution align well. Frame (b) of Fig. 3 shows the comparison between the generated handwritten digits (left) and the real digits (right), which is very difficult for humans to distinguish.

To show the convergent property of the proposed method, we plot the related curves in Fig. 4. The frame (a) and (b) show the changes of the content loss and the feature loss, and both of them decrease monotonously. The frame (c) shows that the output of the discriminator for real images is only slightly larger than

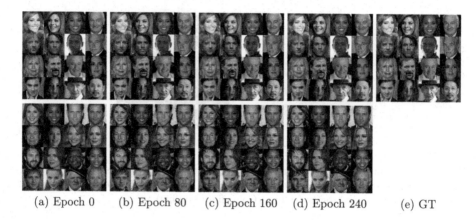

(a) Epoch 0   (b) Epoch 80   (c) Epoch 160   (d) Epoch 240   (e) GT

Fig. 5. Evolution of the generator during training on the CelebA dataset [43].

that for the fake images during the training process, which can help the generator generate more realistic digits. The frame (d) gives the evolution of FID and the final value is 3.2. For MNIST dataset, the best known FIDs with the same InfoGAN architecture are 6.7 and 6.4, reported in [25] and [2] respectively. This shows our model outperforms the state-of-the-art.

4.2 Mode Collapse Analysis on Stack MNIST

In this section, we test the diversity of the generated samples for the proposed AE-OT-GAN model on stack MNIST dataset [23], which includes 1,000 modes in total. The AE module of the AE-OT-GAN is consistent with [2] and the architecture of the discriminator is set to be the same as the encoder with the final output to be a scalar. The number of modes and the reverse KL divergence are used as the metrics to test the mode collapse performance. In Table 1, we show the results of the proposed method and the comparisons including DCGAN [31], VEEGAN [1], PacGAN [23], WGAN [3] and AE-OT [2]. It is obvious that the AE-OT-GAN model keeps the 'no-mode-collapse' property of the AE-OT model and has no mode miss in the generated images.

Table 1. Experiments on stacked MNIST.

	Stacked MNIST	
	Modes	KL
DCGAN	99.0	3.40
VEEGAN	150.0	2.95
PacDCGAN4	1000.0 ± 0.00	0.07 ± 0.005
WGAN	314.3 ± 38.54	2.44 ± 0.170
AE-OT	1000.0 ± 0.00	0.03 ± 0.0008
AE-OT-GAN	1000.0 ± 0.0	0.05 ± 0.006

4.3   Quality Evaluation on Complex Dataset

In this section, we compare with the SOTA methods both quantitatively and qualitatively. The standard and ResNet models used to train the Cifar10 dataset are the same with those used by SNGAN [27], and the architectures of WGAN-div [39] are used to train the CelebA dataset. The architecture used to train the CelebA-HQ dataset is illustrated in the supplementary. The frameworks of the encoders are just set to be the mirror of the corresponding generators/decoders.

Table 2. The FID and IS between the AE-OT-GAN and the state of the arts on Cifar10 and CelebA.

	CIFAR10				CelebA	
	Standard		Resnet		Standard	Resnet
	FID	IS	FID	IS	FID	FID
WGAN-GP [12]	40.2	6.68	19.6	7.86	21.2	18.4
PGGAN [14]	–	–	18.8	8.80	–	16.3
SNGAN [27]	25.5	7.58	21.7	8.22	–	–
WGAN-div [39]	–	–	18.1	–	17.5	15.2
WGAN-QC [24]	–	–	–	–	–	12.9
AE-OT [2]	34.2	6.62	28.5	7.67	24.3	28.6
AE-OT-GAN	25.2	7.62	17.1	8.24	11.2	7.6

Progressive Quality Improvement. Firstly, we show the evolution results of the proposed method in Fig. 5 during the GAN's training process. Quality of the generated images increases monotonously during the process. Images in the first four frames of the first row illustrates the results reconstructed from the real latent codes by the generator, with the last frame showing the corresponding ground-truth input images. By examining the frames carefully, it is obvious that as the increase of the epochs, the reconstructed images become sharper and sharper, and eventually they are very close to the ground truth. The second row shows the generated images from some generated latent codes (therefore, no corresponding real images). Similarly. the images become sharper as the increase of epochs. Here we need to state that the 0 epoch stage means the images are generated by the original decoder, which are equivalent to the outputs of an AE-OT model [2]. Thus we can conclude that the proposed AE-OT-GAN does improve the performance of AE-OT prominently.

Comparison on CelebA and CIFAR 10. Secondly, we compare with the state-of-the-arts including WGAN-GP [12], PGGAN [14], SNGAN [27], CTGAN [42], WGAN-div [39], WGAN-QC [24] and the recently proposed AE-OT model [2] on Cifar10 [18] and CelebA [43]. Table 2 shows the FIDs (lower is better) of our method and the comparisons trained under both the standard and ResNet

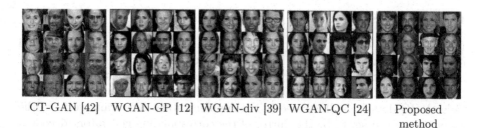

CT-GAN [42]   WGAN-GP [12]   WGAN-div [39]   WGAN-QC [24]   Proposed
                                                                 method

Fig. 6. The visual comparison between the proposed method and the state-of-the-arts on CelebA dataset [43] with ResNet architecture.

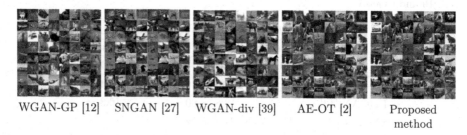

WGAN-GP [12]   SNGAN [27]   WGAN-div [39]   AE-OT [2]   Proposed
                                                            method

Fig. 7. The visual comparison between the proposed method and the state-of-the-arts on Cifar10 dataset [18] with ResNet architecture.

architectures. The FIDs of other methods come from the listed papers except those of the AE-OT, which are directly computed by our model (the results of epoch 0). From the table we can see that our method gets much better results than others on both the Cifar10 and the CelebA datasets, under both the standard and the ResNet architectures. Also, the generated images of the proposed methods have less flaws compared to other GANs, as shown on Fig. 6 and Fig. 7. The convergence curves of the FIDs for the both datasets can be found in Fig. 8. For the Cifar10 dataset, another popular metric is the Inception score (IS, higher is better), which is also reported on Table 2.

Table 3. The FIDs of the proposed method and the state-of-the-arts on CelebA-HQ.

PGGAN	WGAN-div	WGAN-QC	AE-OT-GAN
14.7	13.5	7.7	7.4

Experiment on CelebA-HQ. Furthermore, we also test the proposed method on images with high resolution, namely the CelebA-HQ dataset with image size to be 256 × 256. In our method, the generated images can be treated as locally interpolation among the nearby given real images. In Fig. 9, the left column shows the generated images and the right 5 columns show the top-5 images used

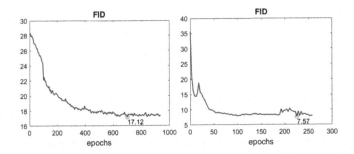

Fig. 8. The FID curves for Cifar10 and CelebA.

Fig. 9. The interpolation of the AE-OT-GAN model. The left column shows the generated images, and the right 5 images are the ones used to generate the left images in the latent space.

to generate them. From Table 3, we can see that the performance of the AE-OT-GAN model is better than the comparisons. We also display several generated images in the supplementary, which are crisp and visually realistic.

5   Conclusion and Future Work

In this paper, we propose the AE-OT-GAN model which composes the AE-OT model and vanilla GAN together. By utilizing the merits of the both models, our method can generate high quality images without mode collapse. Firstly, the images are embedded into the latent space by the autoencoder, then the SDOT map from the uniform distribution to the empirical latent distribution is computed. Sampling from the generated latent distribution by applying the extended SDOT map, we can train our GAN model steady and efficiently. Moreover, the paired latent codes and images give us additional constraints about the generator and help get rid of the mode collapse problem. Using the FID as the metric, we show that the proposed model is able to generate images comparable or better than the state of the arts.

Acknowledgements. The project is partially supported by NSF CMMI-1762287, NSF DMS-1737812 and Ford URP and NSFC (61936002, 61772105, 61720106005).

References

1. Akash, S., Lazar, V., Chris, R., Gutmann, M.U., Charles, S.: Veegan: reducing mode collapse in gans using implicit variational learning. In: Neural Information Processing Systems (2017)
2. An, D., Guo, Y., Lei, N., Luo, Z., Yau, S.T., Gu, X.: Ae-ot: a new generative model based on extended semi-discrete optimal transport. In: International Conference on Learning Representations (2020)
3. Arjovsky, M., Chintala, S., Bottou, L.: Wasserstein generative adversarial networks. In: ICML. pp. 214–223 (2017)
4. Burda, Y., Grosse, R., Salakhutdinov, R.: Importance weighted autoencoders. In: ICML (2015)
5. Chen, X., Duan, Y., Houthooft, R., Schulman, J., Sutskever, I., Abbeel, P.: Info-gan: interpretable representation learning by information maximizing generative adversarial nets. In: Advances in Neural Information Processing Systems (2016)
6. Dai, B., Wipf, D.: Diagnosing and enhancing VAE models. In: International Conference on Learning Representations (2019)
7. Dinh, L., Krueger, D., Bengio, Y.: Nice: Non-linear independent components estimation (2014). arXiv preprint arXiv:1410.8516
8. Dinh, L., Sohl-Dickstein, J., Bengio, S.: Density estimation using real nvp. In: ICLR (2017)
9. Figalli, A.: Regularity properties of optimal maps between nonconvex domains in the plane. Commun. Partial Diff. Equat. **35**(3), 465–479 (2010)
10. Goodfellow, I.: Nips 2016 tutorial: Generative adversarial networks (2016). arXiv preprint arXiv:1701.00160
11. Goodfellow, I.J., et al.: Generative adversarial nets. In: Advances in neural information processing systems (2014)
12. Gulrajani, I., Ahmed, F., Arjovsky, M., Dumoulin, V., Courville, A.C.: Improved training of wasserstein gans. In: NIPS, pp. 5769–5779 (2017)
13. Heusel, M., Ramsauer, H., Unterthiner, T., Nessler, B., Klambauer, G., Hochreiter, S.: Gans trained by a two time-scale update rule converge to a nash equilibrium. In: Advances in neural information processing systems (2017)
14. Karras, T., Aila, T., Laine, S., Lehtinen, J.: Progressive growing of gans for improved quality, stability, and variation. In: ICLR (2018)
15. Khayatkhoei, M., Singh, M.K., Elgammal, A.: Disconnected manifold learning for generative adversarial networks. In: Advances in Neural Information Processing Systems (2018)
16. Kingma, D.P., Welling, M.: Auto-encoding variational bayes (2013). arXiv preprint arXiv:1312.6114
17. Kingma, D.P., Dhariwal, P.: Glow: Generative flow with invertible 1 x 1 convolutions. In: NeurIPS (2018)
18. Krizhevsky, A.: Learning multiple layers of features from tiny images. Technical report (2009)
19. Lecun, Y., Chopra, S., Hadsell, R.: A tutorial on energy-based learning. Predict. Struct. Data (2006)
20. LeCun, Y., Cortes, C.: MNIST handwritten digit database (2010). http://yann.lecun.com/exdb/mnist/

21. Ledig, C., et al.: Photo-realistic single image super-resolution using a generative adversarial network. In: Proceedings of the IEEE Conference on Computer Vision and Pattern Recognition (2017)

22. Lee, C.H., Liu, Z., Wu, L., Luo, P.: Maskgan: towards diverse and interactive facial image manipulation (2019). arXiv preprint arXiv:1907.11922

23. Lin, Z., Khetan, A., Fanti, G., Oh, S.: Pacgan: the power of two samples in generative adversarial networks. In: Advances in Neural Information Processing Systems, pp. 1505–1514 (2018)

24. Liu, H., Gu, X., Samaras, D.: Wasserstein gan with quadratic transport cost. In: ICCV (2019)

25. Lucic, M., Kurach, K., Michalski, M., Gelly, S., Bousquet, O.: Are gans created equal? a large-scale study. In: Advances in neural information processing systems, pp. 698–707 (2018)

26. van der Maaten, L., Hinton, G.: Visualizing data using t-SNE. J. Mach. Learn. Res. **9**, 2579–2605 (2008)

27. Miyato, T., Kataoka, T., Koyama, M., Yoshida, Y.: Spectral normalization for generative adversarial networks. In: ICLR (2018)

28. Nijkamp, E., Hill, M., Zhu, S.C., Wu, Y.N.: On learning non-convergent non-persistent short-run MCMC toward energy-based model (2019). arXiv preprint arXiv:1904.09770

29. van den Oord, A., Kalchbrenner, N., Espeholt, L., kavukcuoglu, k., Vinyals, O., Graves, A.: Conditional image generation with pixelcnn decoders. In: Advances in Neural Information Processing Systems (2016)

30. van den Oord, A., Vinyals, O., Kavukcuoglu, K.: Neural discrete representation learning. In: NeurIPS (2017)

31. Radford, A., Metz, L., Chintala, S.: Unsupervised representation learning with deep convolutional generative adversarial networks. In: ICLR (2016)

32. Razavi, A., Oord, A., Vinyals, O.: Generating diverse high-fidelity images with vq-vae-2. In: Advances in Neural Information Processing Systems (2019)

33. Rezende, D.J., Mohamed, S., Wierstra, D.: Stochastic backpropagation and approximate inference in deep generative models (2014). arXiv preprint arXiv:1401.4082

34. Salimans, T., Goodfellow, I., Zaremba, W., Cheung, V., Radford, A., Chen, X.: Improved techniques for training gans. In: Advances in neural information processing systems (2016)

35. Salimans, T., Zhang, H., Radford, A., Metaxas, D.: Improving GANs using optimal transport. In: International Conference on Learning Representations (2018)

36. Tenenbaum, J.B., Silva, V., Langford, J.C.: A global geometric framework for nonlinear dimensionality reduction. Science **290**(5500), 2391–232 (2000)

37. Tolstikhin, I., Bousquet, O., Gelly, S., Schoelkopf, B.: Wasserstein auto-encoders. In: ICLR (2018)

38. Villani, C.: Optimal Transport: Old and New, vol. 338. Springer Science & Business Media, Berlin (2008)

39. Wu, J., Huang, Z., Thoma, J., Acharya, D., Gool, L.V.: Wasserstein divergence for gans. In: ECCV (2018)

40. Xiao, C., Zhong, P., Zheng, C.: Bourgan: Generative networks with metric embeddings. In: NeurIPS (2018)

41. Xie, J., Lu, Y., Zhu, S., Wu, Y.: Cooperative training of descriptor and generator networks. IEEE Trans. Pattern Anal. Mach. Intell. **42**(1), 27–45 (2016)

42. Xu, L., Skoularidou, M., Cuesta-Infante, A., Veeramachaneni, K.: Modeling tabular data using conditional gan. In: Advances in Neural Information Processing Systems (2019)

43. Zhang, Z., Luo, P., Loy, C.C., Tang, X.: From facial expression recognition to interpersonal relation prediction. Int. J. Comput. Vis. **126**(5), 550–569 (2017). https://doi.org/10.1007/s11263-017-1055-1
44. Zhu, S., Wu, Y., Mumford, D.: Filters, random fields and maximum entropy (frame): towards a unified theory for texture modeling. Int. J. Comput. Vis. **27**(2), 107–126 (1998)

Null-Sampling for Interpretable and Fair Representations

Thomas Kehrenberg, Myles Bartlett$^{(\boxtimes)}$, Oliver Thomas, and Novi Quadrianto

Predictive Analytics Lab (PAL), University of Sussex, Brighton, UK
{t.kehrenberg,m.bartlett,ot44,n.quadrianto}@sussex.ac.uk

Abstract. We propose to learn invariant representations, in the data domain, to achieve interpretability in algorithmic fairness. Invariance implies a selectivity for high level, relevant correlations w.r.t. class label annotations, and a robustness to irrelevant correlations with protected characteristics such as race or gender. We introduce a non-trivial setup in which the training set exhibits a strong bias such that class label annotations are irrelevant and spurious correlations cannot be distinguished. To address this problem, we introduce an adversarially trained model with a *null-sampling* procedure to produce invariant representations in the data domain. To enable disentanglement, a partially-labelled *representative* set is used. By placing the representations into the data domain, the changes made by the model are easily examinable by human auditors. We show the effectiveness of our method on both image and tabular datasets: Coloured MNIST, the CelebA and the Adult dataset. (The code can be found at https://github.com/predictive-analytics-lab/nifr).

Keywords: Fairness · Interpretability · Adversarial learning · Normalising flows · Invertible neural networks · Variational autoencoders

1 Introduction

Without due consideration for the data collection process, machine learning algorithms can exacerbate biases, or even introduce new ones if proper control is not exerted over their learning [10]. While most of these issues can be solved by controlling and curating data collection in a fairness-conscious fashion, doing so is not always an option, such as when working with historical data. Efforts to address this problem algorithmically have been centred on developing statistical definitions of fairness and learning models that satisfy these definitions. One popular definition of fairness used to guide the training of fair classifiers, for example, is *demographic parity*, stating that positive outcome rates should be equalised (or *invariant*) across protected groups.

Electronic supplementary material The online version of this chapter (https://doi.org/10.1007/978-3-030-58574-7_34) contains supplementary material, which is available to authorized users.

In the typical setup, we have an input x, a sensitive attribute s that represents some non-admissible information like gender and a class label y which is the prediction target. The idea of fair *representation* learning [6,24,29] is then to transform the input x to a representation z which is invariant to s. Thus, learning from z will not introduce a forbidden dependence on s. A good fair representation is one that preserves most of the information from x while satisfying the aforementioned constraints.

As unlabelled data is much more freely available than labelled data, it is of interest to learn the representation in an unsupervised manner. This will allow us to draw on a much more diverse pool of data to learn from. While annotations for y are often hard to come by (and often noisy [16]), annotations for the sensitive attribute s are usually less so, as s can often be obtained from demographic information provided by census data. We thus consider the setting where the representation is learned from data that is only labelled with s and not y. This is in contrast to most other representation learning methods. We call the set used to learn the representation the *representative* set, because its distribution is meant to match the distribution of the deployment setting (and is thus representative).

Once we have learnt the mapping from x to z, we can transform the *training* set which, in contrast to the representative set, has the y labels (and s labels). In order to make our method more widely applicable, we allow the case in which the training set contains a strong spurious correlation between s and y, which makes it impossible to learn from it a representation which is invariant to s but not invariant to y. Non-invariance to y is important in order to be able to predict y. The training set thus does *not* match the deployment setting, thereby rendering the representative set essential for learning the right invariance. From hereon, we will use the terms *spurious* and *sensitive* interchangeably, depending on the context, to refer to an attribute of the data we seek invariance to. We can draw a connection between learning in the presence of spurious correlations and what [15] call *residual unfairness*. Consider the Stop, Question and Frisk (SQF) dataset for example: the data was collected in New York City, but the demographics of the recorded cases do not represent the true demographics of NYC well. The demographic attributes of the recorded individuals might correlate so strongly with the prediction target that the two are nearly indistinguishable. This is the scenario that we are investigating: s and y are so closely correlated in the labelled dataset that they cannot be distinguished, but the learning of s is favoured due to being the "path of least resistance". The deployment setting (i.e. the test set) does not possess this strong correlation and thus a naïve approach will lead to very unfair predictions. In this case, a disentangled representation is insufficient; the representation needs to be explicitly invariant solely with respect to s. In our approach, we make use of the (partially labelled) representative set to learn this invariant representation.

While there is a substantial body of literature devoted to the problems of fair representation-learning, exactly how the invariance in question is achieved is often overlooked. When critical decisions, such as who should receive bail or be released from jail, are being deferred to an automated decision making system, it is critical that people be able to trust the logic of the model underlying it, whether it be via semantic or visual explanations. We build on the work of [26] and learn a decomposition ($f^{-1} : Z_s \times Z_{\neg s} \to X$) of the *data domain* ($X$) into independent subspaces *invariant to s* ($Z_{\neg s}$) and *indicative of s* (Z_s), which lends an interpretability that is absent from most representation-learning methods. While model interpretability has no strict definition [30], we follow the intuition of [1] – *a simple relationship to something we can understand*, a definition which representations in the data domain naturally fulfil.

Whether as a result of the aforementioned sampling bias or simply because the features necessarily co-occur, it is not rare for features to correlate with one another in real-world datasets. Lipstick and gender for example, are two attributes that we expect to be highly correlated and to enforce invariance to gender can implicitly enforce invariance to makeup. This is arguably the desired behaviour. However, unforeseen biases in the data may engender cases which are less justifiable. By baking interpretability into our model (by having representations in the data domain), though we still have no better control over what is learned, we can at least diagnose such pathologies.

To render our representations interpretable, we rely on a simple transformation we call *null-sampling* to map invariant representations in the data domain. Previous approaches to fair representation learning [3,6,23,24] predominantly rely upon autoencoder models to jointly minimise reconstruction loss and invariance. We discuss first how this can be done with such a model that we refer to as cVAE (conditional VAE), before arguing that the bijectivity of invertible neural networks (INNs) [5] makes them better suited to this task. We refer to the variant of our method based on these as cFlow (conditional Flow). INNs have several properties that make them appealing for unsupervised representation learning. The focus of our approach is on creating invariant representations that preserve the non-sensitive information maximally, with only knowledge of s and not of the target y, while at the same time having the ability to easily probe what has been learnt.

Our contribution is thus two-fold: 1) We propose a simple approach to generating representations that are invariant to a feature s, while having the benefit of interpretability that comes with being in the data domain (see Figs. 1 and 2). 2) We explore a setting where the labelled training set suffers from varying levels of sampling bias, which we expect to be common not only in fairness problems but machine learning problems more broadly, demonstrating an approach based on transferring information from a more diverse representative set, with guarantees of the non-spurious information being preserved.

2 Background

Learning Fair Representations. Given a sensitive attribute s (for example, gender or race) and inputs $\boldsymbol{x}$, a fair representation $\boldsymbol{z}$ of $\boldsymbol{x}$ is then one for which $\boldsymbol{z} \perp s$ holds, while ideally also being predictive of the class label y. [29] was the first to propose the learning of fair representations which allow for transfer to new classification tasks. More recent methods are often based on variational autoencoders (VAEs) [3,6,20,23]. The achieved fairness of the representation can be measured with various fairness metrics. These measure, however, usually how fair the predictions of a classifier are and not how fair a representation is.

The appropriate measure of fairness for a given task is domain-specific [21] and there is often not a universally accepted measure. However, *Demographic Parity* is the most widely used [3,6,23]. Demographic Parity demands $\hat{y} \perp s$ where $\hat{y}$ refers to the predictions of the classifier. In the context of fair representations, we measure the Demographic Parity of a downstream classifier, $f(\cdot)$, which is trained on the representation z i.e. $f : Z \to \hat{Y}$.

A core principle of all fairness methods is the *accuracy-fairness trade-off*. As previously stated, the fair representation should be invariant to s ($\to$ fairness) but still be predictive of y ($\to$ accuracy). These desiderata cannot, in general, be simultaneously satisfied if s and y are correlated.

(a) Original images. (b) x_u null-samples from the cFlow model. (c) x_b null-samples from the cFlow model.

Fig. 1. CelebA null-samples learned by our cFlow model, with gender as the sensitive attribute. (a) The original, untransformed samples from the CelebA dataset (b) Reconstructions using only information unrelated to s. (c) Reconstruction using only information related to $\neg s$. The model learns to disentangle gender from the non-gender related information. Note that some attributes like skin tone seem to change along with gender due to the correlation between the attributes. This is especially visible in images (1, 1) and (3, 2). Only because our representations are produced in the data-domain can we easily spot such instances of entanglement.

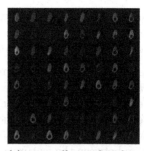

(a) Samples from the cM-NIST training set, $\sigma = 0$.

(b) x_u null-samples from the cFlow model.

(c) x_b null-samples from the cFlow model.

Fig. 2. Sample images from the coloured MNIST dataset problem with 10 predefined mean colours. (a): Images from the spuriously correlated subpopulation where colour is a reliable signal of the digit class-label. (b-c): Results of running our approach realised with cFlow on the cMNIST dataset. The model learns to retain the shape of the digit shape while removing the relationship with colour. A downstream classifier is now less prone to exploiting correlations between colour and the digit label class.

The majority of existing methods for fair representations also make use of y labels during training, in order to ensure that z remains predictive of y. This aspect can, in theory, be removed from the methods, but then there is no guarantee that information about y is preserved [23].

Learning Fair, Transferrable Representations. In addition to producing fair representations, [24] want to ensure the representations are transferrable. Here, an adversary is used to remove sensitive information from a representation z. Auxiliary prediction and reconstruction networks, to predict class label y and reconstruct the input x respectively, are trained on top of z, with s being ancillary input to the reconstruction.

Also related is [4] who employ a FactorVAE [18] regularised for fairness. The idea is to learn a representation that is both disentangled and invariant to multiple sensitive attributes. This factorisation makes the latent space easily manipulable such that the different subspaces can be freely removed and composed at test time. Zeroing out the dimensions or replacing them with independent noise imparts invariance to the corresponding sensitive attribute. This method closely resembles ours when we use an invertible encoder. However, the emphasis of our approach is on interpretability, information-preservation, and coping with sampling bias - especially extreme cases where $|\operatorname{supp}(S_{tr} \times Y_{tr})| < |\operatorname{supp}(S_{te} \times Y_{te})|$.

Attempts were made by [26] prior to this work to learn fair representations in the data domain in order to make it interpretable and transferable. In their work, the input is assumed to be additively decomposable in the feature space into a *fair* and *unfair* component, which together can be used by the decoder to recover the original input. This allows us to examine representations in a human-interpretable space and confirm that the model is not learning a relationship reliant on a sensitive attribute. Though a first step in this direction, we believe such a linear decomposition is not sufficiently expressive to fully capture the relationship between the sensitive and non-sensitive attributes. Our approach allows for the modelling of more complex relationships.

Learning in the Presence of Spurious Correlations. Strong spurious correlations make the task of learning a robust classifier challenging: the classifier may learn to exploit correlations unrelated to the true causal relationship between the features and label, and thereby fail to generalise to novel settings. This problem was recently tackled by [17] who apply a penalty based on the mutual information between the feature embedding and the spurious variable. While the method is effective under mild biasing, we show experimentally that it is not robust to the range of settings we consider.

Jacobsen et al. [11] explore the vulnerability of traditional neural networks to spurious variables – e.g., textures, in the case of ImageNet [8] – and propose a INN-based solution akin to ours. The INN's encoding is split such that one partition, z_b is encouraged to be predictive of the spurious variable while the other serves as the logits for classification of the semantic label. Information related to the nuisance variable is "pulled out" of the logits as a result of maximising $\log p(s|z_n)$. This specific approach, however, is incompatible with the settings we consider, due to its requirement that both s and y be available at training time.

Viewing the problem from a causal perspective, [2] develop a variant of empirical risk minimisation called invariant risk minimisation (IRM). The goal of IRM is to train a predictor that generalises across a large set of unseen environments; because variables with spurious correlations do not represent a stable causal mechanism, the predictor learns to be invariant to them. IRM assumes that the training data is not *i.i.d.* but is partitioned into distinct environments, $e \in E$. The optimal predictor is then defined as the minimiser of the sum of the empirical risk R_e over this set. In contrast, we assume possession of only a single source of *labelled*, albeit spuriously-correlated, data, but that we have a second source of data that is free of spurious correlations, with the benefit being that it only needs to be labelled *with respect to s*.

3   Interpretable Invariances by Null-Sampling

3.1   Problem Statement

We assume we are given inputs $x \in \mathcal{X}$ and corresponding labels $y \in \mathcal{Y}$. Furthermore, there is some spurious variable $s \in \mathcal{S}$ associated with each input x which we do *not* want to predict. Let X, S and Y be random variables that take on the values x, s and y, respectively. The fact that both y and s are predictive of x implies that $\mathcal{I}(X;Y), \mathcal{I}(X;S) > 0$, where $\mathcal{I}(\cdot;\cdot)$ is the mutual information. Note, however, that the conditional entropy is non-zero: $H(S|X) \neq 0$, i.e., S is not completely determined by X.

The difficulty of this setup emerges in the training set: there is a close correspondence between S and Y, such that for a model that sees the data through

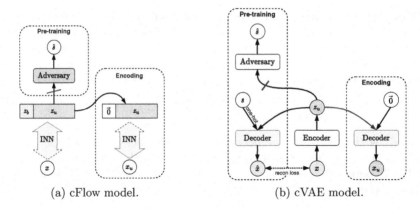

Fig. 3. Training procedure for our models. x: input, s: sensitive attribute, z_u: de-biased representation, x_u: de-biased version of the input in the data domain. The red bar indicates a gradient reversal layer, and $\vec{0}$ the null-sampling operation. (Color figure online)

the lens of the loss function, the two are indistinguishable. Furthermore, we assume that this is *not* the case in the test set, meaning the model cannot rely on shortcuts provided by S if it is to generalise from the training set.

Such scenarios where we only have access to the labels of a biasedly-sampled subpopulation are not uncommon in the real-world. For instance, in long-feedback systems such as mortgage-approval where the demographics of the subpopulation with observed outcomes is *not* representative of the subpopulation on which the model has been deployed. In this case, s has the potential to act as a false (or *spurious*) indicator of the class label and training a model with such a dataset would limit generalisability. Let (X^{tr}, S^{tr}, Y^{tr}) then be the random variables sampled for the training set and (X^{te}, S^{te}, Y^{te}) be the random variables for the test set. The training and test sets thus induce the following inequality for their mutual information: $\mathcal{I}(S^{tr}; Y^{tr}) \gg \mathcal{I}(S^{te}; Y^{te}) \approx 0$.

Our goal is to learn a representation z_u that is independent of s and transferable between downstream tasks. Complementary to z_u, we refer to some abstract component of the model that absorbs the unwanted information related to s as $\mathcal{B}$, the realisation of which we define with respect to each of the two models to be described. The requirement for z_u can be expressed via mutual information:

$$I(z_u; s) \overset{!}{=} 0 . \tag{1}$$

However, for the representation to be useful, we need to capture as much relevant information in the data as possible. Thus, the combined objective function:

$$\min_{\theta} \mathbb{E}_{x \sim X}[-\log p_\theta(x)] + \lambda I(f_\theta(x); s) \tag{2}$$

where θ refers to the trainable parameters of our model f_θ and $p_\theta(x)$ is the likelihood it assigns to the data.

We optimise this loss in an adversarial fashion by playing a min-max game, in which our encoder acts as the generative component. The adversary is an auxiliary classifier g, which receives z_u as input and attempts to predict the spurious variable s. We denote the parameters of the adversary as ϕ; for the parameters of the encoder we use θ, as before. The objective from Eq. (2) is then

$$\min_{\theta \in \Theta} \max_{\phi \in \Phi} \mathbb{E}_{x \sim X}[\log p_\theta(x) - \lambda \mathcal{L}_c(g_\phi(f_\theta(x))); s)] \tag{3}$$

where $\mathcal{L}_c$ is the cross-entropy between the predictions for s and the provided labels. In practice, this adversarial term is realised with a gradient reversal layer (GRL) [7] between z_u and g as is common in adversarial approaches to fair representation learning [6].

3.2   The Disentanglement Dilemma

The objective in Eq. (3) balances the two desiderata: predicting y and being invariant to s. However, in the training set (X^{tr}, S^{tr}, Y^{tr}), y and s are so strongly correlated that removing information about s inevitably removes information about y. This strong correlation makes existing methods fail under this setting. In order to even define the right learning goal, we require another source of information that allows us to disentangle s and y. For this, we assume the existence of another set of samples that follow a similar distribution to the test set, but whilst the sensitive attribute is available, the class labels are not. In reality, this is not an unreasonable assumption, as, while properly annotated data is scarce, unlabelled data can be obtained in abundance (with demographic information from census data, electoral rolls, etc.). Previous work has also considered treated "unlabelled data" as still having s labels [27]. We are restricted only in the sense that the spurious correlations we want to sever are indicated in the features. We call this the *representative set*, consisting of X^{rep} and S^{rep}. It fulfils $\mathcal{I}(S^{rep}; Y^{rep}) \approx 0$ (or rather, it would, if the class labels Y^{rep} were available).

We now summarise the training procedure; an outline for the invertible network model (cFlow) can be seen in Fig. 3a. First, the encoder network f is trained on (X^{rep}, S^{rep}), during the first phase. The trained network is then used to encode the training set, taking in x and producing the representation, z_u, decorrelated from the spurious variable. The encoded dataset can then be used to train any off-the-shelf classifier safely, with information about the spurious variable having been absorbed by some auxiliary component $\mathcal{B}$. In the case of the conditional VAE (cVAE) model, $\mathcal{B}$ takes the form of the decoder subnetwork, which reconstructs the data conditional on a one-hot encoding of s, while for the invertible network $\mathcal{B}$ is realised as a partition of the feature map z (such that $z = [z_u, z_b]$), given the bijective constraint. Thus, the classifier cannot take the shortcut of learning s and instead must learn how to predict y directly. Obtaining the s-invariant representations, x_u, in the data domain is simply a matter of replacing the $\mathcal{B}$ component of the decoder's input for the cVAE, and z_b for cFlow, with a zero vector of equivalent size. We refer to this procedure used to generate x_u as *null-sampling* (here, with respect to z_b).

Null-sampling resembles the *annihilation* operation described in [28], however we note that the two serve very different roles. Whereas the annihilation operation serves as a regulariser to prevent trivial solutions (similar to [13]), null-sampling is used to generate the invariant representations post-training.

3.3 Conditional Decoding

We first describe a VAE-based model similar to that proposed in [24], before highlighting some of its shortcomings that motivate the choice of an invertible representation learner.

The model takes the form of a class conditional β-VAE [9], in which the decoder is conditioned on the spurious attribute. We use $\theta_{enc}, \theta_{dec} \in \theta$ to denote the parameters of the encoder and decoder sub-networks, respectively. Concretely, the encoder component performs the mapping $x \rightarrow z_u$, while $\mathcal{B}$ is instantiated as the decoder, $\mathcal{B} := p_{\theta_{dec}}(x|z_u, s)$, which takes in a concatenation of the learned non-spurious latent vector z_u and a one-hot encoding of the spurious label s to produce a reconstruction of the input $\hat{x}$. Conditioning on a one-hot encoding of s, rather than a single value, as done in [24] is the key to visualising invariant representations in the data domain. If $\mathcal{I}(z_u; s)$ is properly minimised, the decoder can only derive its information about s from the label, thereby freeing up z_u from encoding the unwanted information while still allowing for reconstruction of the input. Thus, by feeding a zero-vector to the decoder we achieve $\hat{x} \perp s$. The full learning objective for the cVAE is given as

$$\mathcal{L}_{\text{cVAE}} = \mathbb{E}_{q_{\theta_{enc}}(z_u, b|x)}[\log p_{\theta_{dec}}(x|z, b) - \log p_{\theta_{dec}}(s|z_u)] \\ - \beta D_{KL}(q_{\theta_{enc}}(z_u|x)\|p(z_u)) \tag{4}$$

where β is a hyperparameter that determines the trade-off between reconstruction accuracy and independence constraints, and $p(z_u)$ is the prior imposed on the variational posterior. For all our experiments, $p(z_u)$ is realised as an Isotropic Gaussian. Figure 3b summarises the procedure as a diagram.

While we show this setup can indeed work for simple problems, as [24] before us have, we show that it lacks scalability due to disagreement between the components of the loss. Since information about s is only available to the decoder as a binary encoding, if the relationship between s and x is highly non-linear and cannot be summarised by a simple on/off mechanism, as is the case if s is an attribute such as gender, off-loading information to the decoder by conditioning is no longer possible. As a result, z_u is forced to carry information about s in order to minimise the reconstruction error.

The obvious solution to this is to allow the encoder to store information about s in a partition of the latent space as in [4]. However, we question whether an autoencoder is the best choice for this setup, with the view that an invertible model is the better tool for the task. Using an invertible model has several guarantees, namely complete information-preservation and freedom from a reconstruction loss, the importance of which we elaborate on below.

3.4   Conditional Flow

Invertible Neural Networks. Invertible neural networks are a class of neural network architecture characterised by a bijective mapping between their inputs and output [5]. The transformations are designed such that their inverses and Jacobians are efficiently computable. These flow-based models permit *exact* likelihood estimation [14] through the warping of a base density with a series of invertible transformations and computing the resulting, highly multi-modal, but still normalised, density, using the change of variable theorem:

$$\log p(x) = \log p(z) + \sum \log \left| \det \left(\frac{dh_i}{h_{i-1}} \right) \right|, \quad p(z) = \mathcal{N}(z; 0, \mathbb{I}) \tag{5}$$

where h_i refers to the outputs of the layers of the network and $p(z)$ is the base density, specifically an Isotropic Gaussian in our case. Training of the invertible neural network is then reduced to maximising $\log p(x)$ over the training set, i.e. maximising the probability the network assigns to samples in the training set.

The Benefits of Bijectivity. Using an invertible network to generate our encoding, z_u, carries a number of advantages over other approaches. Ordinarily, the main benefit of flow-based models is that they permit exact density estimation. However, since we are not interested in sampling from the model's distribution, in our case the likelihood term serves as a regulariser, as it does for [12]. Critically, this forces the mean of each latent dimension to zero enabling null-sampling. The invertible property of the network guarantees the preservation of all information relevant to y which is independent of s, regardless of how it is allocated in the output space. Secondly, we conjecture that the encodings are more robust to out-of-distribution data. Whereas an autoencoder could map a previously seen input and a previously unseen input to the same representation, an invertible network sidesteps this due to the network's bijective property, ensuring all relevant information is stored somewhere. This opens up the possibility of transfer learning between datasets with a similar manifestation of s, as we demonstrate in the Appendix G.

Under our framework, the invertible network f maps the inputs x to a representation z_u: $f(x) = z$. We interpret the embedding z as being the concatenation of two smaller embeddings: $z = [z_u, z_b]$. The dimensionality of z_b, and z_u, by complement, is a free parameter (see Appendix C for tuning strategies). As f is invertible, x can be recovered like so:

$$x = f^{-1}([z_u, z_b]) \tag{6}$$

where z_b is required for equality of the output dimension and input dimension to satisfy the bijectivity of the network – we cannot output z_u alone, but have to output z_b as well. In order to generate the pre-image of z_u, we perform null-sampling with respect to z_b by zeroing-out the elements of z_b (such that $x_u = f^{-1}([z_u, \vec{0}]))$, i.e. setting them to the mean of the prior density, $\mathcal{N}(z; 0, I)$.

How can we be sure that z_u contains enough information about y? The importance of the invertible architecture bears out from this consideration. As long as z_b does not contain the information about y, z_u necessarily must. We can raise or lower the information capacity of z_b by adjusting its size; this should be set to the smallest size sufficient to capture all information about s, so as not to sacrifice class-relevant information.

4 Experiments

We present experiments to demonstrate that the null-sampled representations are in fact invariant to s while still allowing a classifier to predict y from them. We run our cVAE and cFlow models on the coloured MNIST (cMNIST) and CelebA dataset, which we artificially bias, first describing the sampling procedure we follow to do so for non-synthetic datasets. As baselines we have the model of [17] (Ln2L) and the same CNN used to evaluate the cFlow and cVAE models but with the unmodified images as input (CNN). For the cFlow model we adopt a Glow-like architecture [19], while both subnetworks of the cVAE model comprise gated convolutions [25], where the encoding size is 256. For cMNIST, we construct the Ln2L baseline according to its original description, for CelebA, we treat it as an augmentation of the baseline CNN's objective function. Detailed information regarding model architectures and the code can be found in Appendix A.

Synthesising Dataset Bias. For our experiments, we require a training set that exhibits a strong spurious correlation, together with a test set that does not. For cMNIST, this is easily satisfied as we have complete control over the data generation process. For CelebA and UCI Adult, on the other hand, we have to generate the split from the existing data. To this end, we first set aside a randomly selected portion of the dataset from which to sample the biased dataset The portion itself is then split further into two parts: one in which $(s = -1 \wedge y = -1) \vee (s = +1 \wedge y = +1)$ holds true for all samples, call this part $\mathcal{D}_{eq}$, and the other part, call it $\mathcal{D}_{opp}$, which contains the remaining samples. To investigate the behaviour at different levels of correlation, we mix these two subsets according to a mixing factor η. For $\eta \leq \frac{1}{2}$, we combine (all of) $\mathcal{D}_{eq}$ with a fraction of 2η from $\mathcal{D}_{opp}$. For $\eta > \frac{1}{2}$, we combine (all of) $\mathcal{D}_{opp}$ and a fraction of $2(1 - \eta)$ from $\mathcal{D}_{eq}$. Thus, for $\eta = 0$, the biased dataset is just $\mathcal{D}_{eq}$, for $\eta = 1$ it is just $\mathcal{D}_{opp}$ and for $\eta = \frac{1}{2}$ the biased dataset is an ordinary subset of the whole data. The test set is simply the data remaining from the initial split.

Evaluation Protocol. We evaluate our results in terms of accuracy and fairness. A model that perfectly decouples its predictions from s will achieve near-uniform accuracy across all biasing-levels. For binary s/y we quantify the fairness of a classifier's predictions using *demographic parity* (DP): the absolute difference in the probability of a positive prediction for each sensitive group.

4.1 Experimental Results

In this section, we report the results from two image datasets: cMNIST, as a synthetic dataset, provides a good starting point for characterising our model

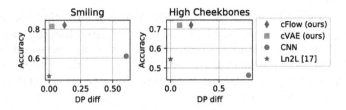

Fig. 4. Accuracy of our approach in comparison with other baseline models on the cMNIST dataset, for different standard deviations (σ) for the colour sampling.

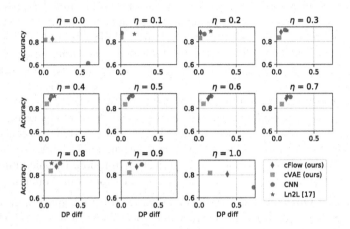

Fig. 5. Performance of our model for different targets (mixing factor $\eta = 0$). Left: *Smiling* as target, right: *high cheekbones*. *DP diff* measures fairness with respect to demographic parity. A perfectly fair model has a *DP diff* of 0.

due to the direct control it affords us over the biasing. CelebA, on the other hand, offers a more practical and challenging example. We also test our method on a tabular dataset, the UCI Adult dataset.

cMNIST. The coloured MNIST (cMNIST) dataset is a variant of the MNIST dataset in which the digits are coloured. In the training set, the colours have a one-to-one correspondence with the digit class. In the test set (and the representative set), colours are assigned randomly. The colours are drawn from Gaussians with 10 different means. We follow the colourisation procedure outlined by [17], with the mean colour values selected so as to be maximally dispersed. The full list of such values can be found in Appendix D. We produce multiple variants of the cMNIST dataset corresponding to different standard deviations σ for the colour sampling: $\sigma \in \{0.00, 0.01, ..., 0.05\}$.

Since the data-generation process is known, we can establish a baseline an additional by following the simple heuristic of grey-scaling the dataset which only leaves the luminosity as spurious information. We also evaluate the model, with all the associated hyperparameters, from [17]. The only difference between the setups is on the side of dataset creation, including the range of σ values

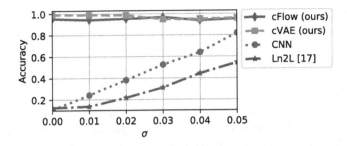

Fig. 6. Performance of our model for the target "smiling" for different mixing factors η. *DP diff* measures fairness with respect to demographic parity. A perfectly fair model has a *DP diff* of 0, thus the closer to top-left the better it is in terms of we accuracy-fairness trade-off. Only values $\eta = 0$ and $\eta = 1$ correspond to the scenario of a strongly biased training set. The results for $0.1 \leq \eta \leq 0.9$ are to confirm that our model does not harm performance for non-biased training sets.

we consider. Our versions of the dataset, on the whole, exhibit much stronger colour bias, to the point of the mapping the digit's colour and class being bijective. Figure 4 shows that the model significantly underperforms even the naïve baseline, aside from at $\sigma = 0$, where they are on par.

Inspection of the null-samples shows that both the cVAE and cFlow model succeed in removing almost all colour information, which is supported quantitatively by Fig. 4. While the cVAE outperforms cFlow marginally at low σ values, performance degrades as this increases. This highlights the problems with the conditional decoder we anticipated in Sect. 3.3. The lower σ, and therefore the variation in sampled colour, is, the more reliably the s label, corresponding to the mean of RGB distribution, encodes information about the colour. For higher σ values, the sampled colours can deviate far from the mean and so the encoder must incorporate information about s into its representation if it is to minimise the reconstruction loss. cFlow, on the other hand, is consistent across σ values.

CelebA. To evaluate the effectiveness of our framework on real-world image data we use the CelebA dataset [22], consisting of 202,599 celebrity images. These images are annotated with various binary physical attributes, including "gender", "hair color", "young", etc., from which we select our sensitive and target attributes. The images are centre cropped and resized to 64×64, as is standard practice. For our experiments, we designate "gender" as the sensitive attribute, and "smiling" and "high cheekbones" as target attributes. We chose gender as the sensitive attribute as it a common sensitive attribute in the fairness literature. For the target attributes, we chose attributes that are harder to learn than gender and which do not correlate too strongly with gender in the dataset ("wearing lipstick" for example being an attribute too closely correlated with gender). The model is trained on the representative set (normal subset of CelebA) and is then used to encode the artificially biased training set and the test set. The results for the most strongly biased training set ($\eta = 0$) can be found in Fig. 5. Our method outperforms the baselines in accuracy and fairness.

We also assess performance for different mixing factors (η) which correspond to varying degrees of bias in the training set (see Fig. 6). This is to verify that the model does not *harm* performance when there is not much bias in the training set. For these experiments, the model is trained once on the representative set and is then used to encode different training sets. The results show that for the intermediate values of η, our model incurs a small penalty in terms of accuracy, but at the same time makes the results *fairer* (corresponding to an accuracy-fairness trade-off). Qualitative results can be found in Fig. 5 (images from the cVAE model can be found in Appendix F).

To show that our method can handle multinomial, as well as binary, sensitive attributes, we also conduct experiments with $s = $ hair color as a ternary attribute ("Blonde" "Black", "Brown"), excluding "Red" because of the paucity of samples and the noisiness of their labels. The results for these experiments can be found in Appendix B.

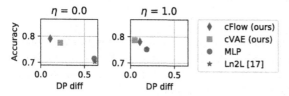

Fig. 7. Results for the **Adult** dataset. The x-axis corresponds to the difference in positive rates. An ideal result would occupy the **top-left**.

Results for the UCI Adult Dataset. The UCI Adult dataset consists of census data and is commonly used to evaluate models focused on algorithmic fairness. Following convention, we designate "gender" as the sensitive attribute s and whether an individual's salary is $50,000 or greater as y. We show the performance of our approach in comparison to baseline approaches in Fig. 7. We evaluate the performance of all models for mixing factors (η) 0 and 1. Results shown in Fig. 7 show that we match or exceed the baseline. In terms of fairness metrics, our approach generally outperforms the baseline models for both of η. Detailed results can be found in the Appendix B.

5   Conclusion

We have proposed a general and straightforward framework for producing invariant representations, under the assumption that a representative but partially-labelled *representative* set is available. Training consists of two stages: an encoder is first trained on the representative set to produce a representation that is invariant to a designated spurious feature. This is then used as input for a downstream task-classifier, the training data for which might exhibit extreme bias with respect to that feature. We train both a VAE- and INN-based model according to this procedure, and show that the latter is particularly well-suited to this setting due to its losslessness. The design of the models allows for representations that are in the data domain and therefore exhibit meaningful invariances. We characterise this for synthetic as well as real-world datasets for which we develop a method for simulating sampling bias.

Acknowledgements. This work was in part funded by the European Research Council under the ERC grant agreement no. 851538. We are grateful to NVIDIA for donating GPUs.

References

1. Adel, T., Ghahramani, Z., Weller, A.: Discovering interpretable representations for both deep generative and discriminative models. In: International Conference on Machine Learning (ICML), pp. 50–59 (2018)
2. Arjovsky, M., Bottou, L., Gulrajani, I., Lopez-Paz, D.: Invariant risk minimization. arXiv preprint arXiv:1907.02893 (2019)
3. Beutel, A., Chen, J., Zhao, Z., Chi, E.H.: Data decisions and theoretical implications when adversarially learning fair representations. In: Workshop on Fairness, Accountability, and Transparency in Machine Learning (FAT/ML) (2017)
4. Creager, E., et al.: Flexibly fair representation learning by disentanglement. In: Proceedings of the 36th International Conference on Machine Learning (ICML), pp. 1436–1445 (2019)
5. Dinh, L., Krueger, D., Bengio, Y.: Nice: non-linear independent components estimation. In: International Conference on Learning Representations (ICLR) (2014)
6. Edwards, H., Storkey, A.: Censoring representations with an adversary. In: International Conference on Learning Representations (ICLR) (2016)
7. Ganin, Y., et al.: Domain-adversarial training of neural networks. J. Mach. Learn. Res. **17**(1), 2030–2096 (2016)
8. Geirhos, R., Rubisch, P., Michaelis, C., Bethge, M., Wichmann, F.A., Brendel, W.: ImageNet-trained CNNs are biased towards texture; increasing shape bias improves accuracy and robustness. In: International Conference on Learning Representations (ICLR) (2019)
9. Higgins, I., et al.: β-VAE: learning basic visual concepts with a constrained variational framework. In: International Conference on Learning Representations (ICLR) (2017)
10. Holstein, K., Wortman Vaughan, J., Daumé III, H., Dudik, M., Wallach, H.: Improving fairness in machine learning systems: what do industry practitioners need? In: CHI Conference on Human Factors in Computing Systems, pp. 1–16 (2019)
11. Jacobsen, J.H., Behrmann, J., Zemel, R., Bethge, M.: Excessive invariance causes adversarial vulnerability. In: International Conference on Learning Representations (ICLR) (2019)
12. Jacobsen, J., Smeulders, A.W.M., Oyallon, E.: i-RevNet: deep invertible networks. In: International Conference on Learning Representations (ICLR) (2018)
13. Jaiswal, A., Wu, R.Y., Abd-Almageed, W., Natarajan, P.: Unsupervised adversarial invariance. In: Advances in Neural Information Processing Systems, pp. 5092–5102 (2018)
14. Jimenez Rezende, D., Mohamed, S.: Variational Inference with Normalizing Flows. In: International Conference on Machine Learning (ICML) (2015)
15. Kallus, N., Zhou, A.: Residual unfairness in fair machine learning from prejudiced data. In: International Conference on Machine Learning (ICML). pp. 2444–2453 (2018)
16. Kehrenberg, T., Chen, Z., Quadrianto, N.: Tuning fairness by balancing target labels. Front. Artif. Intell. **3**, 33 (2020)

17. Kim, B., Kim, H., Kim, K., Kim, S., Kim, J.: Learning not to learn: training deep neural networks with biased data. In: Computer vision and pattern recognition (CVPR) (2019)
18. Kim, H., Mnih, A.: Disentangling by factorising. In: International Conference on Machine Learning (ICML), pp. 2654–2663 (2018)
19. Kingma, D.P., Dhariwal, P.: Glow: Generative flow with Invertible 1x1 convolutions. In: Advances in Neural Information Processing Systems (NeurIPS). pp. 10236–10245 (2018)
20. Kingma, D.P., Welling, M.: Auto-encoding variational bayes. In: International Conference on Learning Representations (ICLR) (2014)
21. Liu, L., Dean, S., Rolf, E., Simchowitz, M., Hardt, M.: Delayed impact of fair machine learning. In: International Conference on Machine Learning (ICML), pp. 3156–3164 (2018)
22. Liu, Z., Luo, P., Wang, X., Tang, X.: Deep learning face attributes in the wild. In: International Conference on Computer Vision (ICCV) (2015)
23. Louizos, C., Swersky, K., Li, Y., Welling, M., Zemel, R.: The variational fair autoencoder. In: International Conference on Learning Representations (ICLR) (2016)
24. Madras, D., Creager, E., Pitassi, T., Zemel, R.S.: Learning adversarially fair and transferable representations. In: International Conference on Machine Learning (ICML), pp. 3381–3390 (2018)
25. Van den Oord, A., Kalchbrenner, N., Espeholt, L., Vinyals, O., Graves, A., et al.: Conditional image generation with pixel CNN decoders. In: Advances in Neural Information Processing Systems, pp. 4790–4798 (2016)
26. Quadrianto, N., Sharmanska, V., Thomas, O.: Discovering fair representations in the data domain. In: Computer Vision and Pattern Recognition (CVPR) (2019)
27. Wick, M., Tristan, J.B., et al.: Unlocking fairness: a trade-off revisited. In: Advances in Neural Information Processing Systems, pp. 8783–8792 (2019)
28. Xiao, T., Hong, J., Ma, J.: DNA-GAN: learning disentangled representations from multi-attribute images. In: ICLR Workshop (2018)
29. Zemel, R.S., Wu, Y., Swersky, K., Pitassi, T., Dwork, C.: Learning fair representations. In: International Conference on Machine Learning (ICML) (2013)
30. Zhang, Q.S., Zhu, S.C.: Visual interpretability for deep learning: a survey. Front. Inf. Technol. Electron. Eng. **19**(1), 27–39 (2018)

Guiding Monocular Depth Estimation Using Depth-Attention Volume

Lam Huynh[1]([✉]) [ID], Phong Nguyen-Ha[1] [ID], Jiri Matas[2] [ID], Esa Rahtu[3] [ID], and Janne Heikkilä[1] [ID]

[1] Center for Machine Vision and Signal Analysis, University of Oulu, Oulu, Finland
{lam.huynh,phong.nguyen,janne.heikkila}@oulu.fi
[2] Center for Machine Perception, Czech Technical University,
Prague, Czech Republic
matas@fel.cvut.cz
[3] Computer Vision Group, Tampere University, Tampere, Finland
esa.rahtu@tuni.fi

Abstract. Recovering the scene depth from a single image is an ill-posed problem that requires additional priors, often referred to as monocular depth cues, to disambiguate different 3D interpretations. In recent works, those priors have been learned in an end-to-end manner from large datasets by using deep neural networks. In this paper, we propose guiding depth estimation to favor planar structures that are ubiquitous especially in indoor environments. This is achieved by incorporating a non-local coplanarity constraint to the network with a novel attention mechanism called depth-attention volume (DAV). Experiments on two popular indoor datasets, namely NYU-Depth-v2 and ScanNet, show that our method achieves state-of-the-art depth estimation results while using only a fraction of the number of parameters needed by the competing methods. Code is available at: https://github.com/HuynhLam/DAV.

Keywords: Monocular depth · Attention mechanism · Depth estimation

1 Introduction

Depth estimation is a fundamental problem in computer vision due to its wide variety of applications including 3D modeling, augmented reality and autonomous vehicles. Conventionally it has been tackled by using stereo and structure from motion techniques based on multiple view geometry [11,32]. In recent years, the advances in deep learning have made monocular depth estimation a compelling alternative [2,5,8,10,13,19,20,24,26–28,40,44].

In learning-based monocular depth estimation, the basic idea is simply to train a model to predict a depth map for a given input image, and to hope that the model can learn those monocular cues that enable inferring the depth

---

Electronic supplementary material The online version of this chapter (https://doi.org/10.1007/978-3-030-58574-7_35) contains supplementary material, which is available to authorized users.

© Springer Nature Switzerland AG 2020
A. Vedaldi et al. (Eds.): ECCV 2020, LNCS 12371, pp. 581–597, 2020.
https://doi.org/10.1007/978-3-030-58574-7_35

directly from the pixel values. This kind of a brute-force approach requires a huge amount of training data and leads to large network architectures. It has been a common practice to use a deep encoder such as VGG-16 [5], ResNet-50 [19,26,27], ResNet-101 [8], ResNext-101 [40], SeNet-154 [2,13] followed by some upsampling and fusion strategy including the up-projection module [19], multi-scale feature fusion [13] or adaptive dense feature fusion [2] that all result in bulky networks with a large number of parameters. Because high computational complexity and memory requirements limit the use of these networks in practical applications, also fast monocular depth estimation models such as FastDepth [36] have been proposed, but their speed increase comes with the price of reduced accuracy. Moreover, despite of good results achieved with standard benchmark datasets such as NYU-Depth-v2, it still remains questionable if these networks are able to generalize well to unseen scenes and poses that are not present in the training data.

Instead of trying to learn all the monocular cues blindly from the data, in this paper, we investigate an approach where the learning is guided by exploiting a simple coplanarity constraint for scene points that are located on the same planar surfaces. Coplanarity is an important constraint especially in indoor environments that are composed of several non-parallel planar surfaces such as walls, floor, ceiling, tables, etc. We introduce a concept of depth-attention volume (DAV) to aggregate spatial information non-locally from those coplanar structures. We use both fronto-parallel and non-fronto-parallel constraints to learn the DAV in an end-to-end manner.

It should be noticed that plane approximations have already been used previously in monocular depth estimation, for example, in PlaneNet [24], where 3D planes were explicitly segmented and estimated from the images, but in contrast to these works, we embed the coplanarity constraint *implicitly* to the model by using the DAV, which is a building block inspired by the non-local neural networks [35]. Unlike the convolutional operation, it operates non-locally and produces a weighted average of the features across the whole image paying attention on planar structures, and favoring depth values that are originating from those planes. By using the DAV we not only incorporate an efficient and important geometric constraint to the model, but also enable shrinking the size of the network considerably without sacrificing the accuracy. To summarize, our key contributions include:

- A novel attention mechanism called depth-attention volume that captures non-local depth dependencies between coplanar points.
- An end-to-end neural network architecture that implicitly learns to recognize planar structures from the scene and use them as priors in monocular depth estimation.
- State-of-the-art depth estimation results on NYU-Depth-v2 and ScanNet datasets with a model that uses considerably less parameters than previous methods achieving similar performance.

Fig. 1. Visualization of depth-attention maps. The input image with four query points is shown on the left. The corresponding ground-truth and predicted depth maps are in the middle. Because of the coplanarity prior the depth of the textureless white wall can be accurately recovered. The ground-truth and predicted depth-attention maps for the query points are on the right. Warm colour indicates strong depth prediction ability for the query point.

2   Related Work

Learning-Based Monocular Depth Estimation: Saxena et al. [29] is one of the first studies using Markov Random Field (MRF) to predict depth from a single image. Later on Eigen et al. proposed method to estimate depth using multi-scale deep network [6] and a multi-task learning model [5]. Since then, various studies using deep neural networks (DNNs) have been introduced. Laina et al. [19] employed a fully convolutional residual network (FCRN) as the encoder and four up-projection modules as the decoder to up-sample the depth map resolution. Fu et al. [8] successfully formulated monocular depth estimation as an ordinal regression problem. Qi et al. [26] proposed a network called GeoNet that investigate the duality between depth map and surface normal. The DNNs from Ren et al. [28] classified input images as indoor or outdoor before estimating the depth values. Lee et al. [20] suggested an idea of using a DNNs to estimate the relative depth between pairs of pixels. The proposed method from Jiao et al. [15] incorporated object segmentation into the training to increase depth estimation accuracy. Hu et al. [13] introduced an architecture that included an encoder, a decoder, a multi-scale feature fusion (MFF), and a new loss term for preserving edge structures. Inspired by [13], Chen et al. [2] used adaptive dense feature fusion (ADFF), and residual pyramid decoder in their network. The study by Facil et al. [7] proposed a DNNs that aims to learn calibration-aware patterns to improve the generalization capabilities of monocular depth prediction. Recently, Ramamonjisoa et al. [27] presented SharpNet that exploits occluding contours as an additional driving factor to optimize the depth estimation model besides the depth and the surface normal.

Plane-Based Approaches: Liu et al. [24] was the first study to consider using the planar constraint to predict depth maps from single images. Later the same authors published an incremental study to refine the quality of plane segmentation [23]. Yin et al. [40] formed a geometric constraint called virtual normal to predict the depth map as well as a point cloud and surface normals. Note that methods by Liu et al. focused explicitly on estimating a set of plane parameters

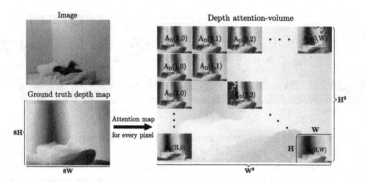

Fig. 2. Depth-attention volume (DAV) is a collection of depth-attention maps (Eq. 3, Fig. 1) obtained using each image location as a query point at a time. Therefore, the DAV for an image of size $8H \times 8W$ is a 4D tensor of size $H \times W \times H \times W$.

and planar segmentation masks, while Yin et al. calculated a large virtual plane to train a DNNs that is robust to noise in the ground truth depth.

Attention Mechanism: Attention was initially used in machine translation and it was brought to computer vision by Xu et al. [39]. Since then, attention mechanism has evolved and branched into channel-wise attention [12,33], spatial-wise attention [1,35] and mix attention [34] in order to tackle object detection and image classification problems. Some recent monocular depth estimation studies also followed this line of work. Xu et al. [38] proposed multi-scale spatial-wise attention to guide a Conditional Random Fields (CRFs) model. Li et al. [22] proposed a discriminative depth estimation model using channel-wise attention. Kong et al. [18] embedded a discrete binary mask, namely the pixel-wise attentional gating unit, into a residual block to modulate learned features.

In this paper, we propose using depth-attention volume (DAV) to encode non-local geometric dependencies. It can be seen as an attention mechanism that guides depth estimation to favor depth values originating from planar surfaces that are ubiquitous in man-made scenes. In contrast to previous plane-based approaches, we do not train the network to segment the planes explicitly, but instead, we let the network to learn the coplanarity constraint implicitly.

3   Proposed Method

This section describes the proposed depth estimation method. The first subsection defines the depth-attention volume and the following two subsections outline the network architecture and the loss functions. Further details are provided in the supplementary material.

3.1   Depth-Attention Volume

Given two image points $P_0 = (x_0, y_0)$ and $P_1 = (x_1, y_1)$ with corresponding depth values d_0 and d_1, we define that the depth-attention $A(P_0, P_1)$ is the ability of P_1 to predict the depth of P_0. This ability is quantified as a confidence in the range $[0, 1]$ so that 0 means no ability and 1 represents maximum certainty of being a good *predictor*.

To estimate A we make the assumption that the scene contains multiple non-parallel planes, which is common particularly in indoor environments. The depth values of all points belonging to the same plane are linearly dependent. Hence, they are good depth predictors of each other. To exploit this property, we detect N prominent planes from the training images and parameterize each plane with $S = (n_x, n_y, n_d, c)$, where (n_x, n_y, n_d) is the plane normal and c is the orthogonal distance from the origin. We construct the first-order depth-attention volumes for all N planes:

$$A_i(P_0, P_1) = 1 - \sigma(|S_i \cdot X_0| + |S_i \cdot X_1|), \quad i = 1, \ldots, N \tag{1}$$

where σ is the sigmoid function, $X_0 = (x_0, y_0, d_0, 1)$ and $X_1 = (x_1, y_1, d_1, 1)$. These volumes are represented as 4-D tensors of size $H \times W \times H \times W$, where H and W are the vertical and horizontal sizes, respectively. In practice, one needs to subsample the volumes to keep the memory requirements reasonable. In all our experiments, we used a subsampling factor of 8.

In addition, we assume that all points located on the same fronto-parallel plane are good depth predictors of each other, because they share the same depth value. We use the ground-truth depths, and create a zero-order depth-attention volume (DAV) for every training image

$$A_0(P_0, P_1) = 1 - \sigma(|d_0 - d_1|). \tag{2}$$

Finally, we combine these volumes by taking the maximum attention value of all volumes:

$$A_D(P_0, P_1) = \max(A_i(P_0, P_1)), \quad i = 0, \ldots, N \tag{3}$$

It is easy to observe that DAV is a symmetric function, i.e. $A_D(P_0, P_1) = A_D(P_1, P_0)$.

If we consider P_0 to be a query point in the image as illustrated in Fig. 1 (left), we can visualize the DAV as a two-dimensional *attention map* shown in Fig. 1 (right). Figure 2 provides an example of a depth-attention volume generated from the ground truth depth map.

3.2   Network Architecture

Figure 3 gives an overview of our model that includes three main modules: an encoder, a non-local depth-attention module, and a decoder.

We opt to use a simplified dilated residual networks (DRN) with 22 layers (DRN-D-22) [41,42] as our encoder, which extracts high-resolution features and downsamples the input image only 8 times. The DRN-D-22 is a variation of DRN that completely removes max-pooling layers as well as smoothly distributes the dilation to minimize the gridding artifacts. This is crucial to our network, because to make training feasible, the non-local depth-attention module needs to operate on a sub-sampled feature space. However, to capture meaningful spatial relationships this feature space also needs to be large enough.

The decoder part of our network contains a straightforward up-scaling scheme that increases the spatial dimension from 29×38 to 57×76 and then to 114×152. Upsampling consists of two bilinear interpolation layers followed by convolutional layers with a kernel size of 3×3. Two convolutional layers with a kernel size of 5×5 are then used to estimate the final depth map.

The non-local depth-attention module is located between the encoder and the decoder. It maps the input features $\mathbf{X}$ to the output features $\mathbf{Y}$ of the same size. The primary purpose of the module is to add the non-local information embedded in the depth-attention volume (DAV) to $\mathbf{Y}$, but it is also used to predict and learn the DAV based on the ground-truth data. The structure of the module is presented in Fig. 4.

We implement the DAV-predictor by first transforming $\mathbf{X}$ into green and blue embeddings using 1×1 convolution. We exploit the symmetry of DAV, and maximize the correlation between these two spaces by applying cross-denormalization on both green and blue embeddings. Cross-denormalization is a conditional normalization technique [4] that is used to learn an affine transformation from the data. Specifically, the green embedding is first normalized to zero mean and unit standard deviation using batch-normalization (BN). Then, the blue embedding is convolved to create two tensors that are multiplied and added the normalized features from the green branch, and vise versa. The denormalized representations are then activated with ReLUs and transformed by another 1×1 convolution before multiplying with each others. Finally, the DAV is activated using the sigmoid function to ensure that the output values are in range $[0, 1]$. We empirically verified that applying cross-modulation in two embedding spaces is superior than using a single embedding with double the number of features.

Furthermore, $\mathbf{X}$ is fed into the orange branch and multiplied with the estimated DAV to amplify the effect of the input features. Finally, we add a residual connection (red) to prevent the vanishing gradient problem when training our network.

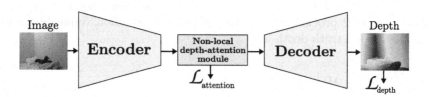

Fig. 3. The pipeline of our proposed network. An image is passed through the encoder, then the non-local depth-attention module, and finally the decoder to produce the estimated depth map. The model is trained using $\mathcal{L}_{attention}$ and $\mathcal{L}_{depth}$ losses, which are described in Subsect. 3.3.

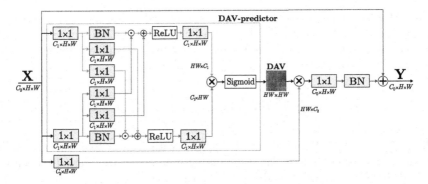

Fig. 4. Structure of the non-local depth-attention module. "$\odot$" presents element-wise multiplication, "$\oplus$" presents element-wise sum, and "$\otimes$" is the outer product.

3.3 Loss Function

As illustrated in Fig. 3 our loss function consists of two main components: attention loss and depth loss.

Attention Loss: The primary goal of this term is to minimize the error between the estimated (output of the DAV-predictor in Fig. 4) and the ground-truth DAV. The $\mathcal{L}_{mae}$ is defined as the mean absolute error between the predicted and the ground truth depth-attention values:

$$\mathcal{L}_{mae} = \frac{1}{(HW)^2} \sum_i \sum_j |\hat{A}_{i,j} - A_{i,j}| \tag{4}$$

where $\hat{A}_{i,j} \equiv \hat{A}_D(P_i, P_j)$ and $A_{i,j} \equiv A_D(P_i, P_j)$ are the predicted and ground truth depth-attention volumes.

In addition, we minimize the angle between the predicted and the ground truth depth-attention maps for all query positions i and j:

$$\mathcal{L}_{ang} = \frac{1}{HW} \left(\sum_i \left| 1 - \frac{\sum_j \hat{A}_{i,j} A_{i,j}}{\sqrt{\sum_j \hat{A}_{i,j}^2 \sum_j A_{i,j}^2}} \right| + \sum_j \left| 1 - \frac{\sum_i \hat{A}_{i,j} A_{i,j}}{\sqrt{\sum_i \hat{A}_{i,j}^2 \sum_i A_{i,j}^2}} \right| \right) \tag{5}$$

The full attention loss is defined by

$$\mathcal{L}_{attention} = \mathcal{L}_{mae} + \lambda \mathcal{L}_{ang} \tag{6}$$

where $\lambda \in \mathbb{R}^+$ is the weight loss coefficient.

Depth Loss: Moreover, we define depth loss as a combination of three terms $\mathcal{L}_{log}$, $\mathcal{L}_{grad}$ and $\mathcal{L}_{norm}$ that were originally introduced in [13]. The $\mathcal{L}_{log}$ loss is a variation of the L_1 norm that is calculated in the logarithm space and defined as

$$\mathcal{L}_{log} = \frac{1}{M} \sum_{i=1}^{M} F(|\hat{d}_i - d_i|) \tag{7}$$

where M is the number of valid depth values, d_i is the ground truth depth, $\hat{d}_i$ is the predicted depth, and $F(x) = \log(x+\alpha)$ with α set to 0.5 in our experiments.

Another loss term is $\mathcal{L}_{grad}$, which is used to penalize sudden changes of edge structures in both x and y directions. It is defined by

$$\mathcal{L}_{grad} = \frac{1}{M} \sum_{i=1}^{M} F(\Delta_x(|\hat{d}_i - d_i|)) + F(\Delta_y(|\hat{d}_i - d_i|)) \tag{8}$$

where Δ_x and Δ_y is the gradient of the error with respect to x and y. Finally, we use $\mathcal{L}_{norm}$ to emphasize small details by minimizing the angle between the ground truth (n_i) and the predicted $(\hat{n}_i)$ surface normals:

$$\mathcal{L}_{norm} = \frac{1}{M} \sum_{i=1}^{M} |1 - \hat{n}_i \cdot n_i|. \tag{9}$$

where surface normals are estimated as $n \equiv (-\nabla_x(d), -\nabla_y(d), 1)$ using Sobel filter, like [13]. The depth loss is then defined by

$$\mathcal{L}_{depth} = \mathcal{L}_{log} + \mu\mathcal{L}_{grad} + \theta\mathcal{L}_{norm} \tag{10}$$

where $\mu, \theta \in \mathbb{R}^+$ are weight loss coefficients. Our full loss is

$$\mathcal{L} = \mathcal{L}_{attention} + \gamma\mathcal{L}_{depth} \tag{11}$$

where $\gamma \in \mathbb{R}^+$ is a weight loss coefficient. Subsection 4.2 describes in detail how the network is trained using these loss functions.

4   Experiments

In this section, we evaluate the performance of the proposed method by comparing it against several baselines. We start by introducing datasets, evaluation metrics, and implementation details. The last three subsections contain the comparison to the state-of-the-art, ablation studies, and a cross-dataset evaluation. Further results are available in the supplementary material.

4.1   Datasets and Evaluation Metrics

Datasets: We assess the proposed method using NYU-Depth-v2 [30] and Scan-Net [3] datasets. NYU-Depth-v2 contains ~120K RGB-D images obtained from 464 indoor scenes. From the entire dataset, we use 50K images for training and the official test set of 654 images for evaluation. ScanNet dataset comprises of 2.5 million RGB-D images acquired from 1517 scenes. For this dataset, we use the training subset of ~20K images provided by the Robust Vision Challenge 2018 [9] (ROB). Unfortunately, the ROB test set is not available, so we report the results on the Scannet official test set of 5310 images instead. SUN-RGBD is yet another indoor dataset consisting of ~10K images collected with four different sensors. We do not use it for training, but only for cross-evaluating the pre-trained models on the test set of 5050 images.

Evaluation Metrics: The performance is assessed using the standard metrics provided for each dataset. That is, for NYU-Depth-v2 [30] we calculate the mean absolute relative error (REL), root mean square error (RMS), and thresholded accuracy (δ_i). For the ScanNet and SUN-RGBD dataset, we provide the mean absolute relative error (REL), mean square relative error (sqREL), scale-invariant mean squared error (SI), mean absolute error (iMAE), and root mean square error (iRMSE) of the inverse depth values. For iBims-1 benchmark [17], we compute 5 similar metrics as for NYU-Depth-v2 plus the root mean square error in log-space (log10), planarity errors $(\epsilon^{plan}, \epsilon^{orie})$, depth boundary errors $(\epsilon^{acc}, \epsilon^{comp})$, and directed depth error $(\epsilon^0, \epsilon^-, \epsilon^+)$. Detailed definitions of the metrics are provided in the supplementary material.

4.2   Implementation Details

The proposed model is implemented with the Pytorch [25] framework, and trained using a single Tesla-V100, batch size of 32 images, and Adam optimizer [16] with $(\beta_1, \beta_2, \epsilon) = (0.9, 0.999, 10^{-8})$. The training process is split into three parts. During the first phase, we replace the DAV-predictor (Fig. 4) with the DAVs computed from the ground truth depth maps. We train the model for 200 epochs using only the depth loss (Eq. 10) and the learning rate of 10^{-4}. In the second phase, we add the DAV-predictor to the model, freeze the weights of other parts of the model, and train for 200 epochs with the learning rate of 7.0×10^{-5}. In the last phase, we train the entire model for 300 epochs using the learning rate of 7.0×10^{-5} for the first 100 epochs and then reduce it at the rate of 5% per 25 epochs. The last two stages employ the full loss function defined in Eq. (11). We set all the weight loss coefficients λ, μ, θ, and γ as 1.

We augment the training data using random scaling ($[0.875, 1.25]$), rotation ($[-5.0, +5.0]°$), horizontal flip, rectangular window droppings, and colorization. Planes, required for training, are obtained by fitting a parametric model to the back-projected 3D point cloud using RANSAC with the inlier threshold of 1 cm. We select at most the best N-planes in terms of the inlier count with a maximum of 100 iterations. Furthermore, we keep only planes that cover more than 7% of the image area.

4.3   Comparison with the State-of-the-Art

In this section, we compare the proposed approach with the current state-of-the-art monocular depth estimation methods.

NYU-Depth-v2: Table 1 contains the performance metrics on the official NYU-Depth-v2 test set for our method and for [2,5,8,10,13,19,20,24,26–28,40,44]. In addition, the table shows the number of model parameters for each method. The performance figures for the baselines are obtained using the pre-trained models provided by the authors [2,8,13,24,27,40] or from the original papers if the model was not available [5,10,19,20,26,28,44]. Methods indicated with ** and ‡ are trained using the entire training set of 120K images or with external data, respectively. For instance, Ramamonjisoa et al. [27] trained the method using synthetic dataset PBRS [43] before fine-tuning on NYU-Depth-v2. The

Table 1. Evaluation results on the NYU-Depth-v2 dataset. Metrics with ↓ mean lower is better and ↑ mean higher is better. Timing is the average over 1000 images using a NVIDIA GTX-1080 GPU, in frames-per-second (FPS).

Methods	#params	Memory	FPS	REL↓	RMS↓	δ_1↑	δ_2↑	δ_3↑
Eigen'15 [5]**	141.1M	–	–	0.215	0.907	0.611	0.887	0.971
Laina'16 [19]**	63.4M	–	–	0.127	0.573	0.811	0.953	0.988
Liu'18 [24]‡	47.5M	124.6MB	93	0.142	0.514	0.812	0.957	0.989
Fu'18 [8] **	110.0M	489.1MB	42	0.115	0.509	0.828	0.965	0.992
Qi'18 [26]	67.2M	–	–	0.128	0.569	0.834	0.960	0.990
Hao'18 [10]	60.0M	–	–	0.127	0.555	0.841	0.966	0.991
Lee'19 [20]	118.6M	–	–	0.131	0.538	0.837	0.971	0.994
Ren'19 [28] **	49.8M	–	–	0.113	0.501	0.833	0.968	0.993
Zhang'19 [44]	95.4M	–	–	0.121	0.497	0.846	0.968	0.994
Ramam.'19 [27]‡	80.4M	336.6MB	47	0.139	0.502	0.836	0.966	0.993
Hu'19 [13]	157.0M	679.7MB	15	0.115	0.530	0.866	0.975	0.993
Chen'19 [2]	210.3M	1250.9MB	12	0.111	0.514	0.878	0.977	0.994
Yin'19 [40]	114.2M	437.6MB	37	**0.108**	0.416	0.875	0.976	0.994
Ours	**25.1M**	**96.1MB**	**218**	**0.108**	**0.412**	**0.882**	**0.980**	**0.996**

best performance is achieved by the proposed model that also contains the least amount of parameters. The best performing baselines, Yin et al. [40], Hu et al. [13], and Chen et al. [2], have 4.5, 6.2, and 8.3 times more parameters compared to ours, respectively. Figure 5 provides an additional illustration of the model parameters with respect to the performance.

Figure 6 shows qualitative examples of the obtained depth maps. In this case, the maps for the baseline methods are produced using the pre-trained models provided by the authors. The method by Eigen and Fergus [5] performs well on uniform regions, but has difficulties in detailed structures. Laina et al. [19] produces overly smoothed depth maps losing many small details. In contrast, Fu et al. [8] returns many details, but with the expense of discontinuities inside

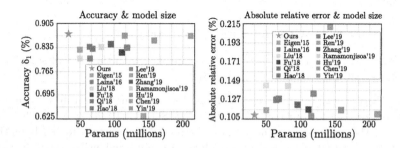

Fig. 5. Analyzing the accuracy δ_1(%) and mean absolute relative error (%) with respect to the number of parameters (*millions*) for recent monocular depth estimation methods on NYU-Depth-v2. The left picture presents the thresholded accuracy where higher values are better, while the right picture shows the absolute relative error where lower values are better.

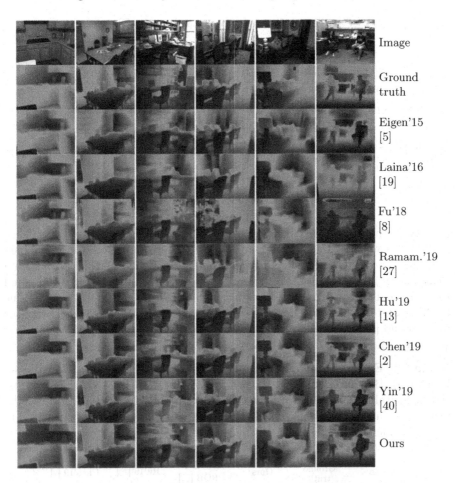

	Image
	Ground truth
	Eigen'15 [5]
	Laina'16 [19]
	Fu'18 [8]
	Ramam.'19 [27]
	Hu'19 [13]
	Chen'19 [2]
	Yin'19 [40]
	Ours

Fig. 6. Qualitative results on the official NYU-Depth-v2 [30] test set from different methods. The color indicates the distance where red is far and blue is close. Our estimated depth maps are closer to the ground truth depth when comparing with state-of-art methods. (Color figure online)

objects or smooth areas. The depth images by Ramamonjisoa et al. [27] contain noise and are prone to miss fine details. Yin et al. [40], Hu et al. [13], and Chen et al. [2] provide the best results among the baselines. However, they have difficulties e.g.. on the third (near the desk and table) and the fourth examples from the left (wall area). We provide further qualitative examples in the supplementary material.

ScanNet: Table 2 contains the performance figures on the official ScanNet test set for our method, Ren et al. [28] (taken from the original paper), Hu et al. [13] and Chen et al. [2]. We use the public code from [2,13] to train their models. Unfortunately, the other baselines do not provide the results for ScanNet official test set. Moreover, the test set used in the Robust Vision Challenge (ROB) is not available at the moment and we are unable to report our performance on

Table 2. Evaluation result on ScanNet [3].

Architecture	#params	REL	sqREL	SI	iMAE	iRMSE	Test set
CSWS_E_ROB [21]	65.8M	0.150	0.060	0.020	0.100	0.130	ROB
DORN_ROB [8]	110.0M	0.140	0.060	0.020	0.100	0.130	
DABC_ROB [22]	56.6M	0.140	0.060	0.020	0.100	0.130	
Hu'19 [13]	157.0M	0.139	0.081	0.016	0.100	0.105	Official
Chen'19 [2]	210.3M	0.134	0.077	**0.015**	0.093	0.100	
Ren'19 [28]	49.8M	0.138	**0.057**	–	–	–	
Ours	**25.1M**	**0.118**	**0.057**	**0.015**	**0.089**	**0.097**	

that. Nevertheless, we have included the best methods from the ROB challenge in Table 2 to provide indicative comparison. Note that all methods are trained with the same ROB training split. The proposed model outperforms [28] with a clear margin in terms of REL. The results are also substantially better compared to ROB challenge methods, although the comparison is not strictly fair due to different test splits. Figure 7 provides qualitative comparison between our method and [2,13,22], using the sample images provided in [22]. The geometric structures and details are clearly better extracted by our method.

Planarity Error Analysis: We also evaluated our method on the iBims-1 benchmark [17] and compared it with two recent works [24,27]. The results, shown in Table 3, indicate that we outperform the baselines in most of the metrics, including plane related ones. Extensive planarity analysis is provided in the supplementary material.

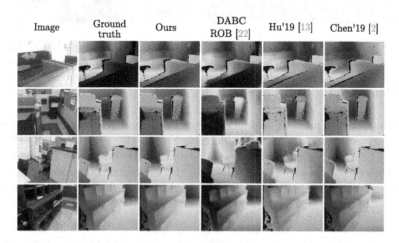

Fig. 7. Predicted depth maps from our model with baselines on the official ScanNet [3] test set.

Table 3. The iBims-1 benchmark

Method	REL↓	log10↓	RMS↓	$\delta_1\uparrow$	$\delta_2\uparrow$	$\delta_3\uparrow$	$\epsilon^{plan}\downarrow$	$\epsilon^{orie}\downarrow$	$\epsilon^{acc}\downarrow$	$\epsilon^{comp}\downarrow$	$\epsilon^0\uparrow$	$\epsilon^-\downarrow$	$\epsilon^+\downarrow$
Liu'18 [24]	0.29	0.17	1.45	0.41	0.70	0.86	7.26	**17.24**	4.84	8.86	71.24	28.36	**0.40**
Ramam.'19 [27]	0.26	0.11	1.07	**0.59**	**0.84**	**0.94**	9.95	25.67	3.52	7.61	84.03	9.48	6.49
Ours	**0.24**	**0.10**	**1.06**	**0.59**	**0.84**	**0.94**	7.21	18.45	**3.46**	**7.43**	**84.36**	**6.84**	6.27

4.4 Ablation Studies

Firstly, we assess how the number of prominent planes, used to estimate the ground truth DAVs in the training phase, affects the performance (see Sect. 3.1). To this end, we train our model using the fronto-parallel planes (see Eq. 2) plus three, five, and seven non-fronto-parallel planes (N in Eq. 1). The corresponding results for the NYU-Depth-v2 test set are provided in Table 4. One can observe that the results improve by increasing the number of planes up to five and decrease after that. Possible explanation for this could be that the images used in the experiments do not typically contain more than five significant planes that can predict the depth values reliably. We also re-trained our model without the non-local depth attention (DAV) module (and any planes) and the performance degraded substantially as shown in Table 4.

Secondly, we study the impact of the attention loss term (Eq. 6). For this purpose, we first train our model with and without the attention loss, and then continue training by dropping the attention loss after convergence. We report the results in Table 5. The model without the attention loss has clearly inferior performance indicating the importance of this loss term. Furthermore, continuing training by dropping the attention loss also degrades the performance.

4.5 Cross-dataset Evaluation

To assess the generalisation properties of the model, we perform a cross-dataset evaluation, where we train the network using NYU-Depth-v2 and test with SUN-RGBD [14,31,37] without any fine-tuning. We also evaluate the baseline methods from [2,13] and report the results in Table 6. As can be seen our model performs favourably compared to the other methods. Figure 8 contains a few examples of the results with the SUN-RGBD dataset. One can observe that our model is able to well estimate the geometric structures and details of the scene despite the differences in data distributions between the training and testing sets. Moreover, we evaluated our model without the DAV-module in the same cross-dataset

Table 4. Performance of our model using different types of depth-attention volume.

DAV-types	REL↓	RMS↓	$\delta_1\uparrow$	$\delta_2\uparrow$	$\delta_3\uparrow$
w/o DAV-module	0.140	0.577	0.827	0.960	0.989
‖-Plane-DAV	0.116	0.442	0.867	0.976	0.995
3-Plane-DAV	0.110	0.421	0.879	0.978	0.995
5-Plane-DAV	**0.108**	**0.412**	**0.882**	**0.980**	**0.996**
7-Plane-DAV	0.111	0.447	0.851	0.970	0.993

Table 5. Ablation studies of models without and with the attention loss on the NYU-Depth-v2. This shows the importance of the DAV in guiding the monocular depth model.

Training	REL↓	RMS↓	δ_1↑	δ_2↑	δ_3↑
w/o $\mathcal{L}_{attention}$	0.126	0.540	0.841	0.967	0.992
w/ full loss	**0.108**	**0.412**	**0.882**	**0.980**	**0.996**
Continue w/o $\mathcal{L}_{attention}$	0.109	0.415	0.882	0.979	0.995

Table 6. Cross-dataset evaluation with training on NYU-Depth-v2 and testing on SUN-RGBD.

Models	#params	REL	sqREL	SI	iMAE	iRMSE
w/o DAV-module	**17.5M**	0.254	0.416	0.035	0.111	0.091
Hu'19 [13]	157.0M	0.245	0.389	0.031	0.108	0.087
Chen'19 [2]	210.3M	0.243	0.393	0.031	**0.102**	**0.069**
Ours	**25.1M**	**0.238**	**0.387**	**0.030**	0.104	0.075

| Image | Ground truth | Ours | Hu'19 | Chen'19 |

Fig. 8. Direct results on SUN RGB-D dataset [31] without fine-tuning. Some regions in the white boxes show missing or incorrect depth values from the ground truth data.

setup. The results, shown in Table 6, clearly demonstrates that the DAV-module improves the generalization.

5 Conclusions

This paper proposed a novel monocular depth estimation method that incorporates a non-local coplanarity constraint with a novel attention mechanism called depth-attention volume (DAV). The proposed attention mechanism encourages depth estimation to favor planar structures, which are common especially in indoor environments. The DAV enables more efficient learning of the necessary priors, which results in considerable reduction in the number of model parameters. The performance of the proposed solution is state-of-the-art on two popular benchmark datasets while using 2–8 times less parameters than competing methods. Finally, the generalisation ability of the method was further demonstrated in cross dataset experiments.

References

1. Bello, I., Zoph, B., Vaswani, A., Shlens, J., Le, Q.V.: Attention augmented convolutional networks. In: Proceedings of the IEEE International Conference on Computer Vision, pp. 3286–3295 (2019)
2. Chen, X., Chen, X., Zha, Z.J.: Structure-aware residual pyramid network for monocular depth estimation. In: Proceedings of the 28th International Joint Conference on Artificial Intelligence, pp. 694–700. AAAI Press (2019)
3. Dai, A., Chang, A.X., Savva, M., Halber, M., Funkhouser, T., Nießner, M.: ScanNet: richly-annotated 3D reconstructions of indoor scenes. In: Proceedings of the IEEE Conference on Computer Vision and Pattern Recognition, pp. 5828–5839 (2017)
4. Dumoulin, V., Shlens, J., Kudlur, M.: A learned representation for artistic style. In: International Conference on Learning Representations ICLR (2017)
5. Eigen, D., Fergus, R.: Predicting depth, surface normals and semantic labels with a common multi-scale convolutional architecture. In: Proceedings of the IEEE International Conference on Computer Vision, pp. 2650–2658 (2015)
6. Eigen, D., Puhrsch, C., Fergus, R.: Depth map prediction from a single image using a multi-scale deep network. In: Advances in Neural Information Processing Systems, pp. 2366–2374 (2014)
7. Facil, J.M., Ummenhofer, B., Zhou, H., Montesano, L., Brox, T., Civera, J.: CAM-convs: camera-aware multi-scale convolutions for single-view depth. In: Proceedings of the IEEE Conference on Computer Vision and Pattern Recognition, pp. 11826–11835 (2019)
8. Fu, H., Gong, M., Wang, C., Batmanghelich, K., Tao, D.: Deep ordinal regression network for monocular depth estimation. In: Proceedings of the IEEE Conference on Computer Vision and Pattern Recognition, pp. 2002–2011 (2018)
9. Geiger, A., Nießner, M., Dai, A.: Robust vision challenge. In: CVPR Workshop (2018)
10. Hao, Z., Li, Y., You, S., Lu, F.: Detail preserving depth estimation from a single image using attention guided networks. In: 2018 International Conference on 3D Vision (3DV), pp. 304–313. IEEE (2018)
11. Hartley, R., Zisserman, A.: Multiple View Geometry in Computer Vision. Cambridge University Press, Cambridge (2003)
12. Hu, J., Shen, L., Sun, G.: Squeeze-and-excitation networks. In: Proceedings of the IEEE Conference on Computer Vision and Pattern Recognition, pp. 7132–7141 (2018)
13. Hu, J., Ozay, M., Zhang, Y., Okatani, T.: Revisiting single image depth estimation: toward higher resolution maps with accurate object boundaries. In: IEEE Winter Conference on Applications of Computer Vision (WACV) (2019)
14. Janoch, A., et al.: A category-level 3D object dataset: putting the kinect to work. In: Fossati, A., Gall, J., Grabner, H., Ren, X., Konolige, K. (eds.) Consumer Depth Cameras for Computer Vision. Advances in Computer Vision and Pattern Recognition. Springer, London (2013). https://doi.org/10.1007/978-1-4471-4640-7_8
15. Jiao, J., Cao, Y., Song, Y., Lau, R.: Look deeper into depth: monocular depth estimation with semantic booster and attention-driven loss. In: Ferrari, V., Hebert, M., Sminchisescu, C., Weiss, Y. (eds.) ECCV 2018. LNCS, vol. 11219, pp. 55–71. Springer, Cham (2018). https://doi.org/10.1007/978-3-030-01267-0_4
16. Kingma, D.P., Ba, J.: Adam: a method for stochastic optimization. arXiv preprint arXiv:1412.6980 (2014)

17. Koch, T., Liebel, L., Fraundorfer, F., Körner, M.: Evaluation of CNN-based single-image depth estimation methods. In: Leal-Taixé, L., Roth, S. (eds.) ECCV 2018. LNCS, vol. 11131, pp. 331–348. Springer, Cham (2019). https://doi.org/10.1007/978-3-030-11015-4_25

18. Kong, S., Fowlkes, C.: Pixel-wise attentional gating for scene parsing. In: 2019 IEEE Winter Conference on Applications of Computer Vision (WACV), pp. 1024–1033. IEEE (2019)

19. Laina, I., Rupprecht, C., Belagiannis, V., Tombari, F., Navab, N.: Deeper depth prediction with fully convolutional residual networks. In: 2016 Fourth International Conference on 3D Vision (3DV), pp. 239–248. IEEE (2016)

20. Lee, J.H., Kim, C.S.: Monocular depth estimation using relative depth maps. In: Proceedings of the IEEE Conference on Computer Vision and Pattern Recognition, pp. 9729–9738 (2019)

21. Li, B., Dai, Y., He, M.: Monocular depth estimation with hierarchical fusion of dilated CNNs and soft-weighted-sum inference. Pattern Recogn. **83**, 328–339 (2018)

22. Li, R., Xian, K., Shen, C., Cao, Z., Lu, H., Hang, L.: Deep attention-based classification network for robust depth prediction. In: Jawahar, C.V., Li, H., Mori, G., Schindler, K. (eds.) ACCV 2018. LNCS, vol. 11364, pp. 663–678. Springer, Cham (2019). https://doi.org/10.1007/978-3-030-20870-7_41

23. Liu, C., Kim, K., Gu, J., Furukawa, Y., Kautz, J.: PlanerCNN: 3D plane detection and reconstruction from a single image. In: Proceedings of the IEEE Conference on Computer Vision and Pattern Recognition, pp. 4450–4459 (2019)

24. Liu, C., Yang, J., Ceylan, D., Yumer, E., Furukawa, Y.: PlaneNet: piece-wise planar reconstruction from a single RGB image. In: Proceedings of the IEEE Conference on Computer Vision and Pattern Recognition, pp. 2579–2588 (2018)

25. Paszke, A., et al.: Pytorch: an imperative style, high-performance deep learning library. In: Advances in Neural Information Processing Systems, vol. 32, pp. 8024–8035. Curran Associates, Inc. (2019). http://papers.neurips.cc/paper/9015-pytorch-an-imperative-style-high-performance-deep-learning-library.pdf

26. Qi, X., Liao, R., Liu, Z., Urtasun, R., Jia, J.: GeoNet: geometric neural network for joint depth and surface normal estimation. In: Proceedings of the IEEE Conference on Computer Vision and Pattern Recognition, pp. 283–291 (2018)

27. Ramamonjisoa, M., Lepetit, V.: SharpNet: fast and accurate recovery of occluding contours in monocular depth estimation. In: The IEEE International Conference on Computer Vision (ICCV) Workshops (2019)

28. Ren, H., El-khamy, M., Lee, J.: Deep robust single image depth estimation neural network using scene understanding. In: Proceedings of the IEEE Conference on Computer Vision and Pattern Recognition Workshops, pp. 37–45 (2019)

29. Saxena, A., Chung, S.H., Ng, A.Y.: Learning depth from single monocular images. In: Advances in Neural Information Processing Systems, pp. 1161–1168 (2006)

30. Silberman, N., Hoiem, D., Kohli, P., Fergus, R.: Indoor segmentation and support inference from RGBD images. In: Fitzgibbon, A., Lazebnik, S., Perona, P., Sato, Y., Schmid, C. (eds.) ECCV 2012. LNCS, vol. 7576, pp. 746–760. Springer, Heidelberg (2012). https://doi.org/10.1007/978-3-642-33715-4_54

31. Song, S., Lichtenberg, S.P., Xiao, J.: Sun RGB-D: A RGB-D scene understanding benchmark suite. In: Proceedings of the IEEE Conference on Computer Vision and Pattern Recognition, pp. 567–576 (2015)

32. Szeliski, R.: Structure from motion. In: Computer Vision. Texts in Computer Science, pp. 303–334. Springer, London (2011). https://doi.org/10.1007/978-1-84882-935-0_7

33. Tan, M., et al.: MnasNet: platform-aware neural architecture search for mobile. In: Proceedings of the IEEE Conference on Computer Vision and Pattern Recognition, pp. 2820–2828 (2019)
34. Wang, F., et al.: Residual attention network for image classification. In: Proceedings of the IEEE Conference on Computer Vision and Pattern Recognition, pp. 3156–3164 (2017)
35. Wang, X., Girshick, R., Gupta, A., He, K.: Non-local neural networks. In: Proceedings of the IEEE Conference on Computer Vision and Pattern Recognition. pp. 7794–7803 (2018)
36. Wofk, D., Ma, F., Yang, T.J., Karaman, S., Sze, V.: FastDepth: fast monocular depth estimation on embedded systems. In: 2019 International Conference on Robotics and Automation (ICRA), pp. 6101–6108. IEEE (2019)
37. Xiao, J., Owens, A., Torralba, A.: Sun3D: a database of big spaces reconstructed using SFM and object labels. In: Proceedings of the IEEE International Conference on Computer Vision, pp. 1625–1632 (2013)
38. Xu, D., Wang, W., Tang, H., Liu, H., Sebe, N., Ricci, E.: Structured attention guided convolutional neural fields for monocular depth estimation. In: Proceedings of the IEEE Conference on Computer Vision and Pattern Recognition, pp. 3917–3925 (2018)
39. Xu, K., et al.: Show, attend and tell: Neural image caption generation with visual attention. In: International Conference on Machine Learning, pp. 2048–2057 (2015)
40. Yin, W., Liu, Y., Shen, C., Yan, Y.: Enforcing geometric constraints of virtual normal for depth prediction. In: The IEEE International Conference on Computer Vision (ICCV) (2019)
41. Yu, F., Koltun, V.: Multi-scale context aggregation by dilated convolutions. In: International Conference on Learning Representations (ICLR) (2016)
42. Yu, F., Koltun, V., Funkhouser, T.: Dilated residual networks. In: Proceedings of the IEEE Conference on Computer Vision and Pattern Recognition, pp. 472–480 (2017)
43. Zhang, Y., et al.: Physically-based rendering for indoor scene understanding using convolutional neural networks. In: The IEEE Conference on Computer Vision and Pattern Recognition (CVPR) (2017)
44. Zhang, Z., Cui, Z., Xu, C., Yan, Y., Sebe, N., Yang, J.: Pattern-affinitive propagation across depth, surface normal and semantic segmentation. In: Proceedings of the IEEE Conference on Computer Vision and Pattern Recognition, pp. 4106–4115 (2019)

Tracking Emerges by Looking Around Static Scenes, with Neural 3D Mapping

Adam W. Harley[✉], Shrinidhi Kowshika Lakshmikanth, Paul Schydlo, and Katerina Fragkiadaki

Carnegie Mellon University, Pittsburgh, PA 15213, USA
{aharley,kowshika,pschydlo,katef}@cs.cmu.edu

Abstract. We hypothesize that an agent that can look around in static scenes can learn rich visual representations applicable to 3D object tracking in complex dynamic scenes. We are motivated in this pursuit by the fact that the physical world itself is mostly static, and multiview correspondence labels are relatively cheap to collect in static scenes, e.g., by triangulation. We propose to leverage multiview data of *static points* in arbitrary scenes (static or dynamic), to learn a neural 3D mapping module which produces features that are correspondable across time. The neural 3D mapper consumes RGB-D data as input, and produces a 3D voxel grid of deep features as output. We train the voxel features to be correspondable across viewpoints, using a contrastive loss, and correspondability across time emerges automatically. At test time, given an RGB-D video with approximate camera poses, and given the 3D box of an object to track, we track the target object by generating a map of each timestep and locating the object's features within each map. In contrast to models that represent video streams in 2D or 2.5D, our model's 3D scene representation is disentangled from projection artifacts, is stable under camera motion, and is robust to partial occlusions. We test the proposed architectures in challenging simulated and real data, and show that our unsupervised 3D object trackers outperform prior unsupervised 2D and 2.5D trackers, and approach the accuracy of supervised trackers. This work demonstrates that 3D object trackers can emerge without tracking labels, through multiview self-supervision on static data.

1 Introduction

A large part of the real world almost never moves. This may be surprising, since moving entities easily attract our attention [13], and because we ourselves spend most of our waking hours continuously in motion. Objects like roads and buildings, however, stay put. Can we leverage this property of the world to learn visual features suitable for interpreting complex scenes with many moving objects?

In this paper, we hypothesize that a correspondence module learned in static scenes will also work well in dynamic scenes. This is motivated by the fact that

Electronic supplementary material The online version of this chapter (https://doi.org/10.1007/978-3-030-58574-7_36) contains supplementary material, which is available to authorized users.

© Springer Nature Switzerland AG 2020
A. Vedaldi et al. (Eds.): ECCV 2020, LNCS 12371, pp. 598–614, 2020.
https://doi.org/10.1007/978-3-030-58574-7_36

the content of dynamic scenes is the same as the content of static scenes. We would like our hypothesis to be true, because correspondences are far cheaper to obtain in static scenes than in dynamic ones. In static scenes, one can simply deploy a Simultaneous Localization and Mapping (SLAM) module to obtain a 3D reconstruction of the scene, and then project reconstructed points back into the input imagery to obtain multiview correspondence labels. Obtaining correspondences in dynamic scenes would require taking into account the motion of the objects (i.e., tracking).

We propose to leverage multiview data of static points in arbitrary scenes (static or dynamic), to learn a neural 3D mapping module which produces features that are correspondable across viewpoints *and* timesteps. The neural 3D mapper consumes RGB-D (color and depth) data as input, and produces a 3D voxel grid of deep features as output. We train the voxel features to be correspondable across viewpoints, using a contrastive loss. At test time, given an RGB-D video with approximate camera poses, and given the 3D box of an object to track, we track the target object by generating a map of each timestep and locating the object's features within each map.

In contrast to models that represent video streams in 2D [46,48,49], our model's 3D scene representation is disentangled from camera motion and projection artifacts. This provides an inductive bias that scene elements maintain their size and shape across changes in camera viewpoint, and reduces the need for scale invariance in the model's parameters. Additionally, the stability of the 3D map under camera motion allows the model to constrain correspondence searches to the 3D area where the target was last seen, which is a far more reliable cue than 2D pixel coordinates. In contrast to models that use 2.5D representations (e.g., scene flow [27]), our neural 3D maps additionally provide features for partially occluded areas of the scene, since the model can infer their features from context. This provides an abundance of additional 3D correspondence candidates at test time, as opposed to being limited to the points observed by a depth sensor.

Our work builds on geometry-aware recurrent neural networks (GRNNs) [43]. GRNNs are modular differentiable neural architectures that take as input RGB-D streams of a static scene under a moving camera and infer 3D feature maps of the scene, estimating and stabilizing against camera motion. The work of Harley et al. [17] showed that training GRNNs for contrastive view prediction in static scenes helps semi-supervised 3D object detection, as well as moving object discovery. In this paper, we extend those works to learn from dynamic scenes with independently moving objects, and simplify the GRNN model by reducing the number of losses and modules. Our work also builds on the work of Vondrick et al. [46], which showed that 2D pixel trackers can emerge without any tracking labels, through self-supervision on a colorization task. In this work, we show that 3D voxel trackers can emerge without tracking labels, through contrastive self-supervision on static data. In the fact that we learn features from correspondences established through triangulation, our work is similar to Dense Object Nets [11], though that work used object-centric data, and used background subtraction to apply loss on static objects, whereas in our work we do moving-object subtraction to apply loss on *anything* static. We do not assume a priori that we know which objects to focus on.

We test the proposed architectures in simulated and real datasets of urban driving scenes (CARLA [9] and KITTI [15]). We evaluate the learned 3D visual feature representations on their ability to track objects over time in 3D. We show that the learned visual feature representations can accurately track objects in 3D, simply supervised by observing static data. Furthermore, our method outperforms 2D and 2.5D baselines, demonstrating the utility of learning a 3D representation for this task instead of a 2D one.

The main contribution of this paper is to show that learning feature correspondences from static 3D points causes 3D object tracking to emerge. We additionally introduce a neural 3D mapping module which simplifies prior works on 3D inverse graphics, and learns from a simpler objective than considered in prior works. Our code and data are publicly available[1].

2 Related Work

2.1 Learning to See by Moving

Both cognitive psychology and computational vision have realised the importance of motion for the development of visual perception [16,50]. Predictive coding theories [14,36] suggest that the brain predicts observations at various levels of abstraction; temporal prediction is thus of central interest. These theories currently have extensive empirical support: stimuli are processed more quickly if they are predictable [26,33], prediction error is reflected in increased neural activity [4,36], and disproven expectations lead to learning [38]. Several computational models of frame predictions have been proposed [10,31,36,40,43]. Alongside future frame prediction, predicting some form of contextual or missing information has also been explored, such as predicting frame ordering [23], temporal instance-level associations [48] color from grayscale [46], egomotion [1,19] and motion trajectory forecasting [47]. Most of these unsupervised methods are evaluated as pre-training mechanisms for object detection or classification [17,28,47,48].

Video motion segmentation literature explores the use of videos in unsupervised moving object discovery [34]. Most motion segmentation methods operate in 2D image space, and cluster 2D optical flow vectors or 2D flow trajectories to segment moving objects [5,12,29], or use low-rank trajectory constraints [7,8,41]. Our work differs in that we address object detection and segmentation in 3D as opposed to 2D, by estimating 3D motion of the "imagined" (complete) scene, as opposed to 2D motion of the pixel observation stream.

2.2 Vision as Inverse Graphics

Earlier works in Computer Vision proposed casting visual recognition as inverse rendering [30,53], as opposed to feedforward labelling. The "blocks world" of

---

[1] https://github.com/aharley/neural_3d_tracking.

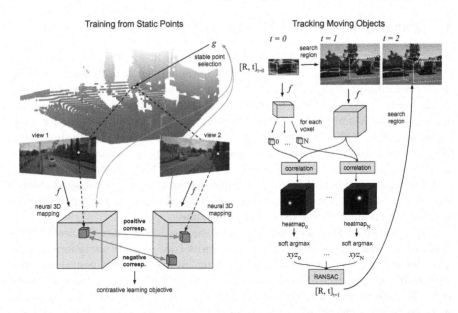

Fig. 1. Tracking emerges by looking around in static scenes, with neural 3D mapping. *Left: Training regime.* Our learned 3D neural mapper f maps RGB-D inputs into featurized 3D scene maps. Points that correspond across multiple views, provided by static data or selected by a reliability network g, provide labels for a contrastive learning objective. *Right: Testing regime.* Given an object box in the zeroth frame, our encoder creates features for the object, and searches for re-occurences of those features in the 3D scene maps of future time steps. The model then explains the full-object motion via a robust estimate of the rigid transformation across frames. Each estimated transformation is used to initialize the search region in the next timestep. Our model does not use any human supervision, and never trains explicitly for tracking; instead, it is supervised only by observing static points in 3D scenes.

Roberts [37] had the goal of reconstructing the 3D scene depicted in the image in terms of 3D solids found in a database. A key question to be addressed is: what representations should we use for the intermediate latent 3D structures? Most works seek to map images to explicit 3D representations, such as 3D pointclouds [44,45,51,54], 3D meshes [21,24], or binary 3D voxel occupancies [20,42,52]. The aforementioned manually designed 3D representations, e.g., 3D meshes, 3D keypoints, 3D pointclouds, 3D voxel grids, may not be general enough to express the rich 3D world, which contains liquids, deformable objects, clutter, dirt, wind, etc., and at the same time may be over descriptive when detail is unnecessary. In this work, we opt for *learning-based 3D feature representations* extracted end-to-end from the RGB-D input stream as proposed by Tung et al. [43] and Harley et al. [17]. We extend the architectures of those works to handle and learn from videos of dynamic scenes, as opposed to only videos of static scenes.

3   Learning to Track with Neural 3D Mapping

We consider a mobile agent that can move around in a 3D scene, and observe it from multiple viewpoints. The scene can optionally contain dynamic (moving and/or deforming) objects. The agent has an RGB camera with known intrinsics, and a depth sensor registered to the camera's coordinate frame. It is reasonable to assume that a mobile agent who moves at will has access to its approximate egomotion, since it chooses where to move and what to look at [32]. In simulation, we use ground truth camera poses; in real data, we use approximate camera poses provided by an inertial navigation system (GPS and IMU). In simulation, we use random viewpoints; in real data, we use just one forward-facing camera (which is all that is available). Note that a more sophisticated mobile agent might attempt to select viewpoints intelligently at training time.

Given the RGB-D and egomotion data, our goal is to learn 3D feature representations that can correspond entities across time, despite variations in pose and appearance. We achieve this by training inverse graphics neural architectures that consume RGB-D videos and infer 3D feature maps of the full scenes, as we describe in Sect. 3.1. To make use of data where some parts are static and other parts are moving, we learn to identify static 3D points by estimating a reliability mask over the 3D scene, as we describe in Sect. 3.2. Finally, we track in 3D, by re-locating the object within each timestep's 3D map, as described in Sect. 3.3. Figure 1 shows an overview of the training and testing setups.

3.1   Neural 3D Mapping

Our model learns to map an RGB-D (RGB and depth) image to a 3D feature map of the scene in an end-to-end differentiable manner. The basic architecture is based on prior works [17,43], which proposed view prediction architectures with a 3D bottleneck. In our case, the 3D feature map is the *output* of the model, rather than an intermediate representation.

Let $\mathcal{M} \in \mathbb{R}^{W \times H \times D \times C}$ denote the 3D feature map representation, where W, H, D, C denote the width, height, depth and number of feature channels, respectively. The map corresponds to a large cuboid of world space, placed at some pose of interest (e.g., surrounding a target object). Every (x, y, z) location in the 3D feature map $\mathcal{M}$ holds a C-length feature vector that describes the semantic and geometric content of the corresponding location of the world scene. To denote the feature map of timestep i, we write $\mathcal{M}^{(i)}$. We denote the function that maps RGB-D inputs to 3D feature maps as $f : (I, D) \mapsto \mathcal{M}$. To implement this function, we voxelize the inputs into a 3D grid, then pass this grid through a 3D convolutional network, and L_2-normalize the outputs.

Tung et al. [43] learned the parameters of f by predicting RGB images of unseen viewpoints, and applying a regression loss; Harley et al. [17] demonstrated that this can be outperformed by contrastive prediction objectives, in 2D and 3D. Here, we drop the view prediction task altogether, and focus entirely on a 3D correspondence objective: if a static point (x, y, z) is observed in two views i and j, the corresponding features $m_i = \mathcal{M}^{(i)}_{x,y,z}, m_j = \mathcal{M}^{(j)}_{x,y,z}$ should be similar to each other, and distinct from other features. We achieve this with a cross entropy loss [6,18,31,39]:

$$\mathcal{L}_{i,j} = -\log \frac{\exp(m_i^\top m_j/\tau)}{\sum_{k\neq i}\exp(m_i^\top m_k/\tau)}, \tag{1}$$

where τ is a temperature parameter, which we set to 0.07, and the sum over $k \neq i$ iterates over non-corresponding features. Note that indexing correctly into the 3D scene maps to obtain the correspondence pair m_i, m_j requires knowledge of the relative camera transformation across the input viewpoints; we encapsulate this registration and indexing in the notation $\mathcal{M}_{x,y,z}$. Following He et al. [18], we obtain a large pool of negative correspondences through the use of an offline dictionary, and stabilize training with a "slow" copy of the encoder, f_{slow}, which is learned via high-momentum updates from the main encoder parameters.

Since the neural mapper (a) does not know a priori which voxels will be indexed for a loss, and (b) is fully convolutional, it learns to generate view-invariant features densely in its output space, even though the supervision is sparse. Furthermore, since (a) the model is encouraged to generate correspondable features invariant to viewpoint, and (b) varying viewpoints provide varying contextual support for 3D locations, the model learns to *infer* correspondable features from limited context, which gives it robustness to partial occlusions.

3.2   Inferring Static Points for Self-supervision in Dynamic Scenes

The training objective in the previous subsection requires the location of a static point observed in two or more views. In a scenario where the data is made up entirely of static scenes, as can be achieved in simulation or in controlled environments, obtaining these static points is straightforward: any point on the surface of the scene will suffice, provided that it projects into at least two camera views.

To make use of data where some parts are static and other parts are moving, we propose to simply discard data that appears to be moving. We achieve this by training a neural module to take the difference of two scene features $\mathcal{M}^{(i)}, \mathcal{M}^{(j)}$ as input, and output a "reliability" mask indicating a per-voxel confidence that the scene cube within the voxel is static: $g : (\text{sg}(\mathcal{M}^{(i)} - \mathcal{M}^{(j)})) \mapsto \mathcal{R}^{W,H,D}$, where **sg** stops gradients from flowing from g into the function f which produces $\mathcal{M}^{(i)}, \mathcal{M}^{(j)}$. We implement g as a per-voxel classifier, with 2-layer fully-connected network applied fully convolutionally. We do not assume to have true labels of moving/static voxels, so we generate synthetic labels using static data: given two maps of the *same* scene $\mathcal{M}^{(i)}, \mathcal{M}^{(j)}$, we generate positive-label inputs with $\mathcal{M}^{(i)} - \mathcal{M}^{(j)}$ (as normal), and generate negative-label inputs with $\mathcal{M}^{(i)} - \text{shuffle}(\mathcal{M}^{(j)})$, where the shuffle operation ruins the correspondence between the two tensors. After this training, we deploy this network on pairs of frames from dynamic scenes, and use it to select high-confidence static data to further train the encoder f.

Our training procedure is then: (1) learn the encoder f on static data; (2) learn the reliability function g; (3) in dynamic data, finetune f on data selected by g. Steps 2–3 can be repeated a number of times. In practice we find that results do not change substantially after the first pass.

3.3   Tracking via Point Correspondences

Using the learned neural 3D mapper, we track an object of interest over long temporal horizons by re-locating it in a map produced at each time step. Specifically, we re-locate each voxel of the object, and use these new locations to form a motion field. We convert these voxel motions into an estimate for the entire object by fitting a rigid transformation to the correspondences, via RANSAC.

We assume we are given the target object's 3D box on the zeroth frame of a test video. Using the zeroth RGB-D input, we generate a 3D scene map centered on the object. We then convert the 3D box into a set of coordinates X_0, Y_0, Z_0 which index into the map. Let $m_i = \mathcal{M}^{(0)}_{x_i \in X_0, y_i \in Y_0, z_i \in Z_0}$ denote a voxel feature that belongs to the object. On any subsequent frame t, our goal is to locate the new coordinate of this feature, denoted x_i^t, y_i^t, z_i^t. We do so via a soft spatial argmax, using the learned feature space to provide correspondence confidences:

$$(x_i^t, y_i^t, z_i^t) = \sum_{x \in X, y \in Y, z \in Z} \left(\frac{\exp(m_i^\top \mathcal{M}^{(t)}_{x,y,z})}{\sum_{x_2 \in X, y_2 \in Y, z_2 \in Z} \exp(m_i^\top \mathcal{M}^{(t)}_{x_2, y_2, z_2})} (x, y, z) \right), \quad (2)$$

where X, Y, Z denote the set of coordinates in the search region. We then compute the motion of the voxel as $(\delta_{x_i}^t, \delta_{y_i}^t, \delta_{z_i}^t) = (x_i^t, y_i^t, z_i^t) - (x_i, y_i, z_i)$. After computing the motion of every object voxel in this way, we use RANSAC to find a rigid transformation that explains the majority of the correspondences. We apply this rigid transform to the input box, yielding the object's location in the next frame.

Vondrick et al. [46] computed a similar attention map during tracking (in 2D), but did not compute its soft argmax, nor explain the object's motion with a single transformation, but rather propagated a "soft mask" to the target frame, which is liable to grow or shrink. Our method takes advantage of the fact that all coordinates are 3D, and makes the assumption that the objects are rigid, and propagates a fixed-size box from frame to frame.

We empirically found that it is critical to constrain the search region of the tracker in 3D. In particular, on each time step we create a search region centered on the object's last known position. The search region is 16 m × 2 m × 16 m large, which is half of the typical full-scene resolution. This serves three purposes. The first is: it limits the number of spurious correspondences that the model can make, since it puts a cap on the metric range of the correspondence field, and thereby reduces errors. Second: it "re-centers" the model's field of view onto the target, which allows the model to incorporate maximal contextual information surrounding the target. Even if the bounds were sufficiently narrow to reduce spurious correspondences, an object at the *edge* of the field of view will have less-informed features than an object at the middle, due to the model's convolutional

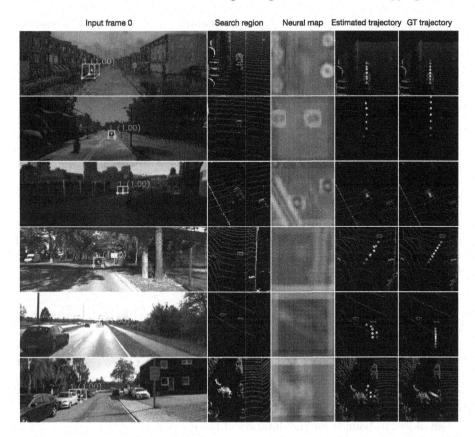

Input frame 0   Search region   Neural map   Estimated trajectory   GT trajectory

Fig. 2. Visualization of tracking inputs, inferred 3D scene features, and tracking outputs. Given the input frame on the left, along with a 3D box specifying the object to track, the model (1) creates a search region for the object centered on the object's position (bird's eye view of occupancy shown), (2) encodes this region into a 3D neural map (bird's eye view of PCA compression shown), and (3) finds correspondences for the object's features. The top three rows show CARLA results; the bottom three rows show KITTI results.

architecture. The third reason is computational: even 2D works [46] struggle with the computational expense of the large matrix multiplications involved in this type of soft attention, and in 3D the expense is higher. Searching locally instead of globally makes Eq. 2 tractable.

4   Experiments

We test our model in the following two datasets:

1. **Synthetic RGB-D Videos of Urban Scenes Rendered in the CARLA Simulator** [9]. CARLA is an open-source photorealistic simulator of urban

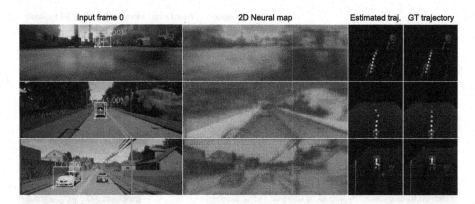

Fig. 3. Visualization of tracking inputs, inferred 2D scene features, and tracking outputs, for our adaptation of Dense Object Nets [11]. This model operates in the same way as our full 3D one, but creates features in 2D, and unprojects them to a sparse 3D grid for tracking.

driving scenes. It permits moving the camera to any desired viewpoint in the scene. We obtain data from the simulator as follows. We begin by generating 10000 autopilot episodes of 16 frames each, at 10 FPS. We define 18 viewpoints along a 40m-radius hemisphere anchored to the ego-car (i.e., it moves with the car). In each episode, we sample 6 random viewpoints from the 18 and randomly perturb their pose, and then capture each timestep of the episode from these 6 viewpoints. We discard episodes that do not have an object in-bounds for the duration of the episode.

We treat the Town1 data as the "training" set, and the Town2 data as the "test" set, so there is no overlap between the train and test sets. This yields 4313 training videos, and 2124 test videos.

2. **Real RGB-D Videos of Urban Scenes, from the KITTI Dataset [15].** This data was collected with a sensor platform mounted on a moving vehicle, with a human driver navigating through a variety of areas in Germany. We use the "left" color camera, and LiDAR sweeps synced to the RGB images.

For training, we use the "odometry" subset of KITTI; it includes egomotion information accurate to within 10 cm. The odometry data includes ten sequences, totalling 23201 frames.

We test our model in the validation set of the "tracking" subset of KITTI, which has twenty labelled sequences, totalling 8008 frames. For supervised baselines, we split this data into 12 training sequences and 8 test sequences. For evaluation, we create 8-frame subsequences of this data, in which a target object has a valid label for all eight frames. This subsequencing is necessary since objects are only labelled when they are within image bounds. The egomotion information in the "tracking" data is only approximate.

We evaluate our model on its ability to track objects in 3D. On the zeroth frame, we receive the 3D box of an object to track. On each subsequent frame, we estimate the object's new 3D box, and measure the intersection over union (IOU) of the estimated box with the ground truth box. We report IOUs as a function of timesteps.

4.1 Baselines

We evaluate the following baselines. We provide additional implementation details for each baseline (and for our own model) in the supplementary file.

- **Unsupervised 3D Flow** [17]. This model uses an unsupervised architecture similar to ours, but with a 2-stage training procedure, in which features are learned first from static scenes and frozen, then a 3D flow module is learned over these features in dynamic scenes. We extend this into a 3D tracker by "chaining" the flows across time, and by converting the trajectories into rigid motions via RANSAC.
- **2.5D Dense Object Nets** [11]. This model learns to map input images into dense 2D feature maps, and uses a contrastive objective at known correspondences across views. We train this model using static points for correspondence labels (like our own model). We extend this model into a 3D tracker by "unprojecting" the learned embeddings into sparse 3D scene maps, then applying the *same tracking pipeline* as our own model.
- **2.5D Tracking by Colorization** [22,46]. This model learns to map input images into dense 2D feature maps, using an RGB reconstruction objective. The model trains as follows: given two RGB frames, the model computes a feature map for each frame; for each pixel of the first frame's feature map, we compute that feature's similarity with all features of the second frame, and then use that similarity matrix to take a weighted combination of the second frame's colors; this color combination at every pixel is used as the reconstruction of the first frame, which yields an error signal for learning. We extend this model into a 3D tracker in the same way that we extended the "dense object nets" baseline.
- **3D Neural Mapping with Random Features.** This model is equivalent to our proposed model but with randomly-initialized network parameters. This model may be expected to perform at better-than-chance levels due to the power of random features [35] and due to the domain knowledge encoded in the architecture design.
- **3D Fully Convolutional Siamese Tracker (supervised)** [3]. This is a straightforward 3D upgrade of a fully convolutional 2D siamese tracker, which uses the object's feature map as a cross correlation template, and tracks the object by taking an argmax of the correlation heatmap at each step. It is necessary to supervise this model with ground-truth box trajectories. We also evaluate a "cosine windowing" variant of this model, which suppresses correlations far from the search region's centroid [3].
- **3D Siamese Tracker with Random Features.** This model is equivalent to the 3D siamese supervised tracker, but with randomly-initialized network parameters. Similar to the random version of 3D neural mapping, this model

measures whether random features and the implicit biases are sufficient to track in this domain.

– **Zero Motion.** This baseline simply uses the input box as its final estimate for every time step. This baseline provides a measure for how quickly objects tend to move in the data, and serves as a lower bound for performance.

All of these are fairly simple trackers. A more sophisticated approach might incrementally update the object template [25], but we leave that for future work.

Ablations. We compare our own model against the following ablated versions. First, we consider a model without search regions, which attempts to find correspondences for each object point in the *entire* 3D map at test time. This model is far more computationally expensive, since it requires taking the dot product of each object feature with the entire scene. Second, we consider a similar "no search region" model but at half resolution, which brings the computation into the range of the proposed model. This ablation is intended to reveal the effect of resolution on accuracy. Third, we omit the "static point selection" (via the function g). This is intended to evaluate how correspondence errors caused by moving objects (violating the static scene assumption) can weaken the model.

4.2 Quantitative Results

We evaluate the mean 3D IOU of our trackers over time. Figure 4-left shows the results of this evaluation in CARLA. As might be expected, the supervised 3D trackers perform best, and cosine windowing improves results.

Our model outperforms all other unsupervised models, and nearly matches the supervised performance. The 2.5D dense object net performs well also, but its accuracy is likely hurt by the fact that it is limited exclusively to points observed in the depth map. Our own model, in contrast, can match against both observed and unobserved (i.e., hallucinated or inpainted) 3D scene features. The colorization model performs under the 2.5D dense object net approach, likely because this model only indirectly encourages correspondence via the colorization task, and therefore is a weaker supervision than the multi-view correspondence objectives used in the other methods.

Random features perform worse than the zero-motion baseline, both with a neural mapping architecture and a siamese tracking architecture. Inspecting the results qualitatively, it appears that these models quickly propagate the 3D box off of the object and onto other scene elements. This suggests that random features and the domain knowledge encoded in these architectures are not enough to yield 3D trackers in this data.

We perform the same evaluation in KITTI, and show the results in Fig. 4-right. On this benchmark, accuracies are lower for all models, indicating that the task here is more challenging. This is likely related to the fact that (1) the egomotion is imperfect in this data, and (2) the tracking targets are frequently farther away than they are in CARLA. Nonetheless, the ranking of methods is the same, with our 3D neural mapping model performing best. One difference is

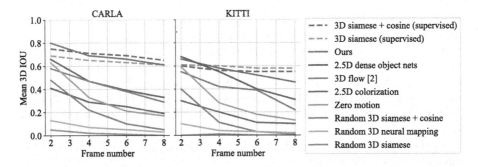

Fig. 4. Single-object tracking accuracy, in mean IOU across time, in CARLA (left) and KITTI (right). Methods are sorted in the legend in decreasing order of mean IOU.

that cosine windowing actually worsens siamese tracking results in KITTI. This is likely related to the fact that egomotion stabilization is imperfect in KITTI: a zero-motion prior is only helpful in frames where the target is stationary *and* camera motion is perfectly accounted for; otherwise it is detrimental.

We additionally split the evaluation on stationary vs. moving objects in CARLA. We use a threshold of 1 m total distance (in world coordinates) across the 8-frame trajectories to split these categories. At the last timestep, the mean 3D IOU for all objects together it is 0.61 (as shown in Fig. 4-left); for static objects only, the value is 0.64; for moving objects only, it is 0.56. This suggests that the model tracks stationary objects more accurately than moving objects, likely because their appearance changes less with respect to the camera and the background.

Finally, we evaluate the top two models in CARLA using the standard 2D tracking metrics, multi-object tracking accuracy (MOTA) and multi-object tracking precision (MOTP) [2], though we note that our task only has one target object per video. We find that the 3D siamese + cosine model (supervised) achieves a MOTA of 0.9578 and MOTP of 0.7407, while our model achieves MOTA 0.9125 and MOTP 0.8384. This suggests that the supervised tracker makes fewer misses, but our method delivers slightly better precision.

4.3   Qualitative Results

We visualize our tracking results, along with inputs and colorized visualizations of our neural 3D scene maps, in Fig. 2. To visualize the neural 3D maps, we take a mean along the vertical axis of the grid (yielding a "bird's eye view" 2D grid), compress the deep features in each grid cell to 3 channels via principal component analysis, normalize, and treat these values as RGB intensities. Comparing the 3D features learned in CARLA vs those learned in KITTI reveals a very obvious difference: the KITTI features appear blurred and imprecise in comparison with the CARLA features. This is likely due to the imperfect egomotion information, which leads to slightly inaccurate correspondence data at training time (i.e., occasional failures by the static point selector g).

In Fig. 3, we visualize the features learned by Dense Object Nets in this data. From the PCA colorization it appears that objects are typically colored differently from their surroundings, which is encouraging, but the embeddings are not as clear as those in the original work [11], likely because this domain does not have the benefit of background image subtraction and object-centric losses.

In the supplementary file, we include video visualizations of the learned features and 3D tracking results.

4.4   Ablations

We evaluate ablated versions of our model, to reveal the effect of (1) search regions, (2) resolution, and (3) static point selection in dynamic scenes. Results are summarized in Table 1.

Without search regions, the accuracy of our model drops by 20 IOU points, which is a strong impact. We believe this drop in performance comes from the fact that search regions take advantage of 3D scene constancy, by reducing spurious correspondences in far-away regions of the scene.

Resolution seems to have a strong effect as well: halving the resolution of the wide-search model reduces its performance by 15 IOU points. This may be related to the fact that fewer points are then available for RANSAC to find a robust estimate of the object's rigid motion.

Since static point selection is only relevant in data with moving objects, we perform this experiment in KITTI (as opposed to CARLA, where the training domain is all static by design). The results show that performance degrades substantially without the static point selection. This result is to be expected, since this ablation causes erroneous correspondences to enter the training objective, and thereby weakens the utility of the self-supervision.

Table 1. Ablations of our model.

Method	Mean IOU
Ours in CARLA	0.61
... without search regions	0.40
... without search regions, at half resolution	0.25
Ours in KITTI	0.46
... without static point selection	0.39

4.5   Limitations

The proposed model has three important limitations. First, our work assumes access to RGB-D data with accurate egomotion data at training time, with a wide variety of viewpoints. This is easy to obtain in simulators, but real-world data of this sort typically lies along straight trajectories (as it does in KITTI), which limits the richness of the data. Second, our model architecture requires a lot of GPU memory, due to its third spatial dimension. This severely limits either the resolution or the metric span of the latent map $\mathcal{M}$. On 12G Titan X GPUs we encode a space sized 32 m $\times$ 4 m $\times$ 32 m at a resolution of $128 \times 32 \times 128$, with a batch size of 4; iteration time is 0.2 s/iter. Sparsifying our feature grid, or using points instead of voxels, are clear areas for future work. Third, our test-time tracking algorithm makes two strong assumptions: (1) a tight box is provided in the zeroth frame, and (2) the object is rigid. For non-rigid objects, merely propagating the box with the RANSAC solution would be insufficient, but the voxel-based correspondences might still be helpful.

5   Conclusion

We propose a model which learns to track objects in dynamic scenes just from observing static scenes. We show that a multi-view contrastive loss allows us to learn rich visual representations that are correspondable not only across views, but across time. We demonstrate the robustness of the learned representation by benchmarking the learned features on a tracking task in real and simulated data. Our approach outperforms prior unsupervised 2D and 2.5D trackers, and approaches the accuracy of supervised trackers. Our 3D representation benefits from denser correspondence fields than 2.5D methods, and is invariant to the artifacts of camera projection, such as apparent scale changes of objects. Our approach opens new avenues for learning trackers in arbitrary environments, without requiring explicit tracking supervision: if we can obtain an accurate pointcloud reconstruction of an environment, then we can learn a tracker for that environment too.

Acknowledgements. This material is based upon work funded and supported by the Department of Defense under Contract No. FA8702-15-D-0002 with Carnegie Mellon University for the operation of the Software Engineering Institute, a federally funded research and development center. We also acknowledge the support of the Natural Sciences and Engineering Research Council of Canada (NSERC), AiDTR, the DARPA Machine Common Sense program, and the AWS Cloud Credits for Research program.

References

1. Agrawal, P., Carreira, J., Malik, J.: Learning to see by moving. In: ICCV (2015)
2. Bernardin, K., Elbs, A., Stiefelhagen, R.: Multiple object tracking performance metrics and evaluation in a smart room environment. In: Sixth IEEE International Workshop on Visual Surveillance, in Conjunction with ECCV, vol. 90, p. 91. Citeseer (2006)

3. Bertinetto, L., Valmadre, J., Henriques, J.F., Vedaldi, A., Torr, P.H.S.: Fully-convolutional siamese networks for object tracking. In: Hua, G., Jégou, H. (eds.) ECCV 2016. LNCS, vol. 9914, pp. 850–865. Springer, Cham (2016). https://doi.org/10.1007/978-3-319-48881-3_56

4. Brodski, A., Paasch, G.F., Helbling, S., Wibral, M.: The faces of predictive coding. J. Neurosci. **35**(24), 8997–9006 (2015)

5. Brox, T., Malik, J.: Object segmentation by long term analysis of point trajectories. In: Daniilidis, K., Maragos, P., Paragios, N. (eds.) ECCV 2010. LNCS, vol. 6315, pp. 282–295. Springer, Heidelberg (2010). https://doi.org/10.1007/978-3-642-15555-0_21

6. Chen, T., Kornblith, S., Norouzi, M., Hinton, G.: A simple framework for contrastive learning of visual representations. arXiv preprint arXiv:2002.05709 (2020)

7. Cheriyadat, A., Radke, R.J.: Non-negative matrix factorization of partial track data for motion segmentation. In: ICCV (2009)

8. Costeira, J., Kanade, T.: A multi-body factorization method for motion analysis. In: ICCV (1995)

9. Dosovitskiy, A., Ros, G., Codevilla, F., Lopez, A., Koltun, V.: CARLA: an open urban driving simulator. In: CORL, pp. 1–16 (2017)

10. Eslami, S.M.A., et al.: Neural scene representation and rendering. Science **360**(6394), 1204–1210 (2018). https://doi.org/10.1126/science.aar6170

11. Florence, P.R., Manuelli, L., Tedrake, R.: Dense object nets: learning dense visual object descriptors by and for robotic manipulation. In: CoRL (2018)

12. Fragkiadaki, K., Shi, J.: Exploiting motion and topology for segmenting and tracking under entanglement. In: CVPR (2011)

13. Franconeri, S.L., Simons, D.J.: Moving and looming stimuli capture attention. Perception & psychophysics **65**(7), 999–1010 (2003). https://doi.org/10.3758/BF03194829

14. Friston, K.: Learning and inference in the brain. Neural Netw. **16**(9), 1325–1352 (2003)

15. Geiger, A., Lenz, P., Stiller, C., Urtasun, R.: Vision meets robotics: the kitti dataset. Int. J. Robot. Res. (IJRR) **32**, 1231–1237 (2013)

16. Gibson, J.J.: The Ecological Approach to Visual Perception. Houghton Mifflin, Boston (1979)

17. Harley, A.W., Lakshmikanth, S.K., Li, F., Zhou, X., Tung, H.Y.F., Fragkiadaki, K.: Learning from unlabelled videos using contrastive predictive neural 3D mapping. In: ICLR (2020)

18. He, K., Fan, H., Wu, Y., Xie, S., Girshick, R.: Momentum contrast for unsupervised visual representation learning. In: CVPR (2020)

19. Jayaraman, D., Grauman, K.: Learning image representations tied to ego-motion. In: ICCV (2015)

20. Kar, A., Häne, C., Malik, J.: Learning a multi-view stereo machine. In: NIPS (2017)

21. Kato, H., Ushiku, Y., Harada, T.: Neural 3D mesh renderer. In: CVPR (2018)

22. Lai, Z., Lu, E., Xie, W.: MAST: a memory-augmented self-supervised tracker. In: CVPR (2020)

23. Lee, H.Y., Huang, J.B., Singh, M., Yang, M.H.: Unsupervised representation learning by sorting sequences. In: Proceedings of the IEEE International Conference on Computer Vision, pp. 667–676 (2017)

24. Loper, M., Mahmood, N., Romero, J., Pons-Moll, G., Black, M.J.: SMPL: a skinned multi-person linear model. ACM Trans. Graph. **34**(6), 248:1–248:16 (2015). https://doi.org/10.1145/2816795.2818013, http://doi.acm.org/10.1145/2816795.2818013

25. Matthews, L., Ishikawa, T., Baker, S.: The template update problem. IEEE Trans. Pattern Anal. Mach. Intell. **26**(6), 810–815 (2004)
26. McClelland, J.L., Rumelhart, D.E.: An interactive activation model of context effects in letter perception: I. an account of basic findings. Psychol. Rev. **88**(5), 375 (1981)
27. Menze, M., Geiger, A.: Object scene flow for autonomous vehicles. In: CVPR (2015)
28. Misra, I., Zitnick, C.L., Hebert, M.: Unsupervised learning using sequential verification for action recognition. In: ECCV (2016)
29. Ochs, P., Brox, T.: Object segmentation in video: a hierarchical variational approach for turning point trajectories into dense regions. In: ICCV (2011)
30. Olshausen, B.: Perception as an inference problem. In: Gazzaniga, M.S. (ed.) The Cognitive Neurosciences. MIT Press, Cambridge (2013)
31. Oord, A.v.d., Li, Y., Vinyals, O.: Representation learning with contrastive predictive coding. arXiv:1807.03748 (2018)
32. Patla, A.E.: Visual control of human locomotion. Adv. Psychol. **78**, 55–97 (1991). Elsevier
33. Pinto, Y., van Gaal, S., de Lange, F.P., Lamme, V.A., Seth, A.K.: Expectations accelerate entry of visual stimuli into awareness. J. Vis. **15**(8), 13–13 (2015)
34. Pont-Tuset, J., Perazzi, F., Caelles, S., Arbeláez, P., Sorkine-Hornung, A., Van Gool, L.: The 2017 davis challenge on video object segmentation. arXiv:1704.00675 (2017)
35. Rahimi, A., Recht, B.: Random features for large-scale kernel machines. In: Advances in Neural Information Processing Systems, pp. 1177–1184 (2008)
36. Rao, R.P., Ballard, D.H.: Predictive coding in the visual cortex: a functional interpretation of some extra-classical receptive-field effects. Nat. Neurosci. **2**(1), 79 (1999)
37. Roberts, L.: Machine perception of three-dimensional solids. Ph.D. thesis, MIT (1965)
38. Schultz, W., Dayan, P., Montague, P.R.: A neural substrate of prediction and reward. Science **275**(5306), 1593–1599 (1997)
39. Sohn, K.: Improved deep metric learning with multi-class N-pair loss objective. In: NIPS, pp. 1857–1865 (2016)
40. Tatarchenko, M., Dosovitskiy, A., Brox, T.: Single-view to multi-view: reconstructing unseen views with a convolutional network. In: ECCV (2016)
41. Tomasi, C., Kanade, T.: Shape and motion from image streams under orthography: a factorization method. Int. J. Comput. Vis. **9**(2), 137–154 (Nov 1992). https://doi.org/10.1007/BF00129684
42. Tulsiani, S., Zhou, T., Efros, A.A., Malik, J.: Multi-view supervision for single-view reconstruction via differentiable ray consistency. In: CVPR (2017)
43. Tung, H.Y.F., Cheng, R., Fragkiadaki, K.: Learning spatial common sense with geometry-aware recurrent networks. In: CVPR (2019)
44. Tung, H.F., Harley, A.W., Seto, W., Fragkiadaki, K.: Adversarial inverse graphics networks: Learning 2d-to-3d lifting and image-to-image translation with unpaired supervision. In: ICCV (2017)
45. Vijayanarasimhan, S., Ricco, S., Schmid, C., Sukthankar, R., Fragkiadaki, K.: SFM-net: learning of structure and motion from video. arXiv:1704.07804 (2017)
46. Vondrick, C., Shrivastava, A., Fathi, A., Guadarrama, S., Murphy, K.: Tracking emerges by colorizing videos. In: Proceedings of the European Conference on Computer Vision (ECCV), pp. 391–408 (2018)

47. Walker, J., Doersch, C., Gupta, A., Hebert, M.: An uncertain future: forecasting from static images using variational autoencoders. In: Leibe, B., Matas, J., Sebe, N., Welling, M. (eds.) ECCV 2016. LNCS, vol. 9911, pp. 835–851. Springer, Cham (2016). https://doi.org/10.1007/978-3-319-46478-7_51

48. Wang, X., Gupta, A.: Unsupervised learning of visual representations using videos. In: ICCV (2015)

49. Wang, X., Jabri, A., Efros, A.A.: Learning correspondence from the cycle-consistency of time. In: CVPR (2019)

50. Wiskott, L., Sejnowski, T.J.: Slow feature analysis: unsupervised learning of invariances. Neural Comput. **14**(4), 715–770 (2002)

51. Wu, J., et al.: Single image 3D interpreter network. In: Leibe, B., Matas, J., Sebe, N., Welling, M. (eds.) ECCV 2016. LNCS, vol. 9910, pp. 365–382. Springer, Cham (2016). https://doi.org/10.1007/978-3-319-46466-4_22

52. Wu, Z., et al.: 3D shapenets: a deep representation for volumetric shapes. In: CVPR, pp. 1912–1920. IEEE Computer Society (2015)

53. Yuille, A., Kersten, D.: Vision as Bayesian inference: analysis by synthesis? Trends Cogn. Sci. **10**, 301–308 (2006)

54. Zhou, T., Brown, M., Snavely, N., Lowe, D.G.: Unsupervised learning of depth and ego-motion from video. In: CVPR (2017)

Boosting Weakly Supervised Object Detection with Progressive Knowledge Transfer

Yuanyi Zhong[1]([✉]), Jianfeng Wang[2], Jian Peng[1], and Lei Zhang[2]

[1] University of Illinois at Urbana-Champaign, Champaign, USA
{yuanyiz2,jianpeng}@illinois.edu
[2] Microsoft, Redmond, USA
{jianfw,leizhang}@microsoft.com

Abstract. In this paper, we propose an effective knowledge transfer framework to boost the weakly supervised object detection accuracy with the help of an external fully-annotated source dataset, whose categories may not overlap with the target domain. This setting is of great practical value due to the existence of many off-the-shelf detection datasets. To more effectively utilize the source dataset, we propose to iteratively transfer the knowledge from the source domain by a one-class universal detector and learn the target-domain detector. The box-level pseudo ground truths mined by the target-domain detector in each iteration effectively improve the one-class universal detector. Therefore, the knowledge in the source dataset is more thoroughly exploited and leveraged. Extensive experiments are conducted with Pascal VOC 2007 as the target weakly-annotated dataset and COCO/ImageNet as the source fully-annotated dataset. With the proposed solution, we achieved an mAP of 59.7% detection performance on the VOC test set and an mAP of 60.2% after retraining a fully supervised Faster RCNN with the mined pseudo ground truths. This is significantly better than any previously known results in related literature and sets a new state-of-the-art of weakly supervised object detection under the knowledge transfer setting. Code: https://github.com/mikuhatsune/wsod_transfer.

Keywords: Weakly supervised · Object detection · Transfer learning · Semi-supervised

1 Introduction

Thanks to the development of powerful CNNs and novel architectures, the performance of object detectors has been dramatically improved in recent years [7,9,21,37]. However, such successes heavily rely on supervised learning with

---

Y. Zhong—Part of this work was done when the author was an intern at Microsoft.

Electronic supplementary material The online version of this chapter (https://doi.org/10.1007/978-3-030-58574-7_37) contains supplementary material, which is available to authorized users.

© Springer Nature Switzerland AG 2020
A. Vedaldi et al. (Eds.): ECCV 2020, LNCS 12371, pp. 615–631, 2020.
https://doi.org/10.1007/978-3-030-58574-7_37

fully annotated detection datasets which can be costly to obtain, since annotating locations and category labels of all object instances is time-consuming and sometimes prohibitively expensive. This issue has motivated many prior works on weakly supervised object detection (WSOD), where only image-level labels are available and normally much cheaper to obtain than box-level labels.

Existing WSOD methods [2,25–27] are mostly based on multiple instance learning (MIL), in which an image is represented as a bag of regions, e.g., generated by selective search [31]. The training algorithm needs to infer which instances in a bag are positive for a positive image-level class. Thus, the problem of learning a detector is converted into training an MIL classifier.

Compared to fully supervised detectors, a large performance gap exists for weakly supervised detectors. For example, on the Pascal VOC 2007 dataset [6], a fully supervised Faster RCNN can achieve an mAP of 69.9% [21], while the state-of-the-art weakly supervised detector, to the best of our knowledge, can only reach to an mAP of 53.6% [33].

One direction to bridge the performance gap is to utilize in a domain transfer learning setting the well-annotated external source datasets, many of which are publicly available on the web, e.g., COCO [18], ImageNet [4], Open Images [15], and Object 365 [23]. Due to the existence of these off-the-shelf detection datasets, this domain transfer setting is of great practical value and has motivated many prior works, under the name transfer learning [5,14,16,24,29,34], domain adaptation [3,10–12,17], and mixed supervised detection [35]. For example, [30] proposes to train a generic proposal generator on the source domain and an MIL classifier on the target domain in a one-step transfer manner. In [16], a universal bounding box regressor is trained on the source domain and used to refine bounding boxes for a weakly supervised detector. In [35], a domain-invariant objectness predictor is utilized to filter distracting regions before applying the MIL classifier. Other related works include [3,5,12,14,17,24,29,34].

Although the domain transfer idea is very promising, it is worth noting that the top pure weakly supervised detector [33] actually outperforms the best transfer-learned weakly supervised detector [16,35] on VOC in the literature. Despite many challenges in domain transfer, one technical deficiency particularly related to object detection lies in imperfect annotations, where the source images may contain objects of the target domain categories but unannotated. In such cases, the object instances will be treated as background regions (or false negatives) in the source data, which is known as the incomplete label problem in object detection [32]. As a result, detectors trained with the source data will likely have a low recall of objects of interest in the target domain.

To address this problem, we propose to transfer progressively so that the knowledge can be extracted more thoroughly by taking into account the target domain. Specifically, we iterate between extracting knowledge by a one-class universal detector (OCUD) and learning a target domain object detector through MIL. The target domain detector is used to mine the pseudo ground truth annotations in both the source and target datasets to refine the OCUD. Compared with existing works, the key novelty is to extract knowledge in multi-steps rather than one-step. Technically, by adding pseudo ground truths in the source data, we effectively alleviate the problem of false negatives as aforementioned. By adding pseudo ground truths in and including the target dataset in fine-tuning, the refined OCUD is more adapted to the target domain data distribution. Empirically, we observe significant gains, e.g., from 54.93% mAP with one-step transfer to 59.71% with multi-step transfer (5 refinements) on Pascal VOC 2007 test data by leveraging COCO-60 as source (removing the VOC 20 categories). By retraining a fully supervised Faster RCNN with the mined pseudo ground truths, we can achieve 60.24% mAP, which again surpasses the pure WSOD method [33] remarkably and sets a new state of the art under the transfer setting. Finally, as a reference, the detection performance also surpasses the original fully supervised Faster RCNN with the ZF net backbone (59.9% mAP) [21].

2   Related Work

Weakly Supervised Object Detection (WSOD). WSOD is extensively studied in the literature [2, 25–27]. The problem is often formulated as an image classification with multi-instance learning. Typically, candidate bounding boxes are first generated by independent proposal methods such as Edge Boxes [39] and Selective Search [31]. Then the proposals on one image are treated as a bag with the image labels as bag-level labels. WSDDN [2] utilizes a two-stream architecture that separates the detection and classification scores, which are then aggregated through softmax pooling to predict the image labels. OICR [27] and the subsequent PCL [26] transform the image-level labels into instance-level labels by multiple online classifier refinement steps. Class activation maps can also be used to localize objects [38]. WSOD2 [33] exploits the bottom-up and top-down objectness to improve performance. Among existing works, pseudo ground truth mining is heavily used as a tool for iterative refinement [26,28,36].

Classifier refinement methods such as OICR [27] and PCL [26] are related in that they conduct refinement steps. Our method is similar to them when restricted to operating on the target data only. However, there are several notable differences. We study the WSOD-with-transfer rather than the pure WSOD setting. Our pseudo ground truth mining is conducted on both the source and target data. We refine both the classifier and the box proposals by retraining the OCUD rather than the instance classifier only.

WSOD with Knowledge Transfer. One way to improve the accuracy is to utilize a source dataset and transfer the knowledge to the target domain through semi-supervised or transfer learning. Visual or semantic information in the category labels or images is often exploited to help solve the problem. For example, the word embeddings of category texts are employed in [1,29] to represent class semantic relationships. The appearance model learned on the source classes are transferred to the target classes in [17,22,24]. Many methods leverage weight prediction to effectively turn a novel category classifier into a detector [10,14,29]. For example, LSDA [10] and [29] transfer the classifier-to-detector weight differences. Recent works [5,16,30,35] share with us in spirit learning general object knowledge from the source data. The knowledge can either be the objectness predictor [5,35], the object proposals [30] or the universal bounding box regressor [16]. In particular, [30] also trains a universal detector (in their case, SSD

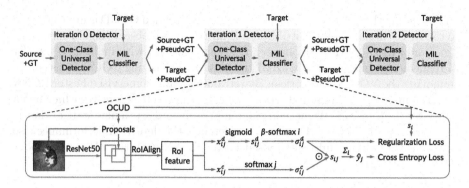

Fig. 1. An illustration of the proposed progressive knowledge transfer framework. One-class universal detector (OCUD) is initially trained with fully annotated source data and iteratively refined on source and target data with pseudo ground truths (GT). OCUD acts as the proposal generator during the subsequent training of target domain MIL classifiers. OCUD and MIL classifier together form the target domain detector.

[19]) on the source dataset, and uses the detection results from this detector as proposals during MIL on the target dataset. The process can be seen as a special case of our algorithm with a single-step transfer and a different instantiation of network and MIL method. Comparatively, we differentiate our approach from them by progressively exploiting the knowledge in the source dataset in a multi-step way, such that the accuracy can improve gradually. Empirically, we observed non-trivial performance gain with progressive knowledge transfer.

3   Proposed Approach

Given source dataset $\mathcal{S}$ with bounding box annotations and target dataset $\mathcal{T}$ with only image-level labels, the goal is to train an object detector for object categories in $\mathcal{T}$. The categories of $\mathcal{S}$ and $\mathcal{T}$ can be non-overlapping, which differentiates our setting from a typical semi-supervised setting.

The proposed training framework and workflow are outlined in Fig. 1 and Algorithm 1. The basic flow is to first train a target domain detector as a seed based on the existing labels, and then mine the pseudo ground truth boxes, which are then used to refine the detector. The process is repeated to improve the target domain detector gradually since more target domain boxes can be found in both $\mathcal{S}$ and $\mathcal{T}$ through the process. The architecture design of the detector is versatile. Here we present a simple solution consisting of a one-class universal detector (OCUD) and a MIL classifier.

3.1   One-Class Universal Detector (OCUD)

The one-class universal detector, which we refer to as OCUD for convenience, treats all categories as a single generic category. While we employ Faster RCNN [21] with ResNet50 [9] backbone, any modern object detector can be used.

Algorithm 1: WSOD with Progressive Knowledge Transfer.

Input: Max number of refinements N, source dataset $\mathcal{S}$, target dataset $\mathcal{T}$;

1 Train the one-class universal detector (OCUD) on the source dataset $\mathcal{S}$;

2 Train the MIL classifier based on the OCUD and the target dataset $\mathcal{T}$;

3 **for** $K = 1, 2, \ldots N$ **do**

4   Mine pseudo ground truths in $\mathcal{S}$ and $\mathcal{T}$ with OCUD and the MIL classifier;

5   Refine the OCUD with the mined boxes and original source annotations;

6   Refine the MIL classifier based on the OCUD and the target dataset $\mathcal{T}$;

7 **return** The OCUD and MIL classifier as the target domain detector;

Initially, the OCUD is trained on source data only, which is similar to [30]. Although the categories can be non-overlapping between the source domain and the target domain, the objects may be visually similar to some extent, which gives the detector certain capability to detect the target domain objects. For example, a detector trained on *cat* might be able to detect *dog*.

3.2 MIL Classifier

With the OCUD, we extract multiple proposals in the target dataset image and perform multiple instance learning (MIL) with the proposals. Our MIL classifier is based on WSDDN [2], but adapted to incorporate knowledge from the OCUD.

The MIL classifier has a two-stage Faster-RCNN-like architecture sketched in Fig. 1. Assume that the OCUD gives R proposals in a target dataset image: $\{b_i, s_i\}_{i=1}^{R}$. We run RoIAlign [8] to extract a feature map for each proposal, and feed the feature into two branches as in [2]: the detection branch and the classification branch. Each branch consists of 2 linear layers with ReLU. The last linear layer's output has the same dimension as the number of target domain categories. Let $x_{ij}^{d} \in \mathbb{R}$ and $x_{ij}^{c} \in \mathbb{R}$ be the output for the i-th proposal and the j-th category from the detection branch and the classification branch, respectively. The predicted score s_{ij} is calculated as follows,

$$
\begin{aligned}
s_{ij}^{d} = \mathrm{sigmoid}(x_{ij}^{d}), \quad & \sigma_{ij}^{d} = \mathrm{softmax}_i(\beta s_{ij}^{d}), \\
\sigma_{ij}^{c} = \mathrm{softmax}_j(x_{ij}^{c}), \quad & s_{ij} = \sigma_{ij}^{d}\sigma_{ij}^{c}.
\end{aligned}
\tag{1}
$$

The softmax is computed along the i and j dimensions respectively. Different from [2], we squash the detection scores s_{ij}^{d} to $(0, 1)$ by sigmoid. This has two benefits: (1) It allows multiple proposals to belong to the same category: s_{ij}^{d} represents how likely each proposal individually belongs to category j, and σ_{ij}^{d} is a normalization; (2) It makes it easier to enforce the objectness regularization as we shall see below. To make σ_{ij}^{d} amenable to train, we introduce a scaling factor β to adjust the input range from $(0, 1)$ to $(0, \beta)$. With a larger β, the range of the scaled softmax is wider, and the value is easier to be spiked.

Let $\{y_j\}_{j=1}^{C} \in \{0, 1\}^{C}$ be the image-level label, and C be the number of categories. Given the scores of all proposals, an image-level classification prediction

$\hat{y}_j$ is calculated and used in an image-level binary classification loss L_{wsddn},

$$\hat{y}_j = \sum_{i=1}^{R} s_{ij}, \quad L_{\text{wsddn}} = -\frac{1}{C} \sum_{j=1}^{C} y_j \log \hat{y}_j + (1 - y_j) \log(1 - \hat{y}_j). \quad (2)$$

To further exploit the knowledge present in OCUD, we introduce the following L_2 regularization loss on the detection branch scores s_{ij}^{d}. The intuition behind is that the objectness score s_i predicted by the OCUD could guide MIL by promoting the object candidates' confidence. It should match the target domain detector's objectness of region i defined as the max over classes. The overall training loss for each image is the weighted sum with coefficient λ as in Eq. 4.

$$L_{\text{guide}} = \frac{1}{R} \sum_{i=1}^{R} \left(\max_{1 \leq j \leq C} s_{ij}^{\text{d}} - s_i \right)^2. \quad (3)$$

$$\mathcal{L} = L_{\text{wsddn}} + \lambda L_{\text{guide}}. \quad (4)$$

During inference, the final detection score is the linear interpolation of s_i from the OCUD and s_{ij} from the MIL classifier. This scheme is shown to be robust [30]. Specifically, with a coefficient $\eta \in [0, 1]$, we compute the final score by Eq. 5. The model trusts the MIL classifier more with a larger η.

$$s_{ij}^{\text{final}} = \eta s_{ij} + (1 - \eta) s_i. \quad (5)$$

3.3   Pseudo Ground Truth Mining

Given the OCUD and the MIL classifier, we mine the pseudo ground truth on both the source and the target dataset based on the latest target domain detector (OCUD + MIL classifier). Following [13,27,33], we adopt the simple heuristic to pick the most confident predictions, as summarized in Algorithm 2.

In the source dataset, the predictions with high confidence (thresholded by τ) and low overlap ratio (thresholded by o) with the nearest ground truth bounding box are taken as a pseudo ground truth. Here we use the intersection over the predicted bounding box area as the overlap ratio, to conservatively mine the box in the source data and avoid mining object parts. Empirically, this simple scheme is effective to locate target domain objects in the source dataset.

In the target dataset, the image-level labels are used to filter the predictions in addition to the confidence scores. For each positive class, we select as pseudo ground truth the top one box and any detection result with a confidence score higher than the threshold τ. In this way, any misclassified bounding box is filtered out, and each positive class is guaranteed to have at least one box.

3.4   Refinement of OCUD and MIL Classifier

Pseudo ground truth augmented source and target datasets are used to refine the OCUD. The fine-tuning is the same as the initial OCUD training, except

---

Algorithm 2: Pseudo Ground Truth Mining.

Input: Detector D_T, source S, target T, score threshold τ, overlap threshold o

1   $S^+ \leftarrow \emptyset$, $T^+ \leftarrow \emptyset$;

2   **for** (image I, boxes B) in S **do**

3   predictions $P \leftarrow D_T(I)$; annotations $anno \leftarrow B$;

4   **for** predicted box p in P **do**

5   **if** $p.score > \tau$ **then**

6            $overlaps \leftarrow \text{overlap}(p.box, B) / \text{area}(p.box)$;

7   **if** $\max overlaps < o$ **then** add p to $anno$

8   add $(I, anno)$ to S^+;

9   **for** (image I, image label Y) in T **do**

10   predictions $P \leftarrow D_T(I)$; annotations $anno \leftarrow \emptyset$;

11   **for** category y in Y **do**

12   find subset predictions $P_y \leftarrow \{p \in P : p.category = y\}$;

13   **for** box p in P_y **do**

14   **if** $p.score > \tau$ or $p.score = \max P_y.scores$ **then** add p to $anno$

15   add $(I, anno)$ to T^+;

16   **return** S^+, T^+;

---

that the two domain images are now mixed together, and the model is initialized from the last OCUD. More advanced techniques can be leveraged, e.g., assigning different weights for the pseudo ground truth in the target dataset, the source dataset, and the original source annotations. We leave it as future work.

In the experiments, we find this simple refinement approach is effective. Through the last target domain detector, the mined pseudo ground truth boxes are better aligned towards the target domain categories. In the target dataset, the objects could be correctly localized, and the boxes become the pseudo ground truths to improve the OCUD. In the source dataset, the pseudo ground truth can improve the recall rate, especially when the image content contains the target category (not in the source domain category). Without refinement, those regions will be treated as the background, which is detrimental.

With the improved OCUD, the MIL classifier is also fine-tuned by the improved object proposals detected by the OCUD. Before the refinements, the OCUD contains little information on the target domain categories, and the proposals are generated by solely relying on the similarity of the categories across domains (e.g., being able to detect *horse* might help detect *sheep*). Afterwards, the OCUD is improved to incorporate more information about the target domain, and the proposals will also likely be aligned to improve the MIL classifier.

4   Experiments

4.1   Experiment Settings

Target Dataset. Following [16,35], we use Pascal VOC 2007 dataset [6] as the target dataset, which has 2501 training images with 6301 box-level annotations,

2510 validation images with 6,307 annotations and 4,952 testing images with 12,032 annotations. As in [2,16,26,33,35], we combine the training and validation sets into one trainval set for training, and evaluate the accuracy on the test set. The bounding boxes are removed in the trainval set, and only the image-level labels are kept for the weakly supervised training. There are 20 categories.

Source Dataset. Similar to [16], we use COCO [18] 2017 detection dataset as the source dataset, which contains 118,287 training images with 860,001 box-level annotations and 5,000 validation images with 36,781 annotations. The number of categories is 80, and all the 20 categories of VOC are covered. As in [16], we remove all the images that have overlapped categories with VOC, resulting in a train set of 21,987 images with 70,549 annotations, and a validation set of 921 images with 2,914 annotations. The resulting train and validation sets are merged as the source dataset, which we denote as COCO-60. We aim to transfer the knowledge through the one-class universal detector from the COCO-60 dataset to the weakly labeled VOC dataset with no overlapping classes.

Another source dataset we investigate is ILSVRC 2013 detection dataset, which contains 395,909 train images (345,854 box annotations) and 20,121 validation images (55,502 box annotations) of 200 classes. After removing images of the 21^1 categories overlapping with VOC, we arrive at 143,095 train images and 6,229 val images of 179 classes. The train and validation images are combined as the source dataset, denoted as ILSVRC-179 in the ablation study. Without an explicit description, we use COCO-60 as the source dataset.

Evaluation Metrics. We adopt two evaluation metrics frequently used in weakly supervised detection literature, namely mean average precision (mAP) and Correct Localization (CorLoc). Average precision (AP) is the area under the precision/recall curve for each category, and mAP averages the APs of all categories. CorLoc [5] measures the localization accuracy on the training dataset. It is defined as the percentage of images of a certain class that the top one prediction of the algorithm correctly localizes one object. A prediction is correct if the intersection-over-union (IoU) with ground truth is larger than 0.5.

Network. We use the Faster RCNN as the one-class universal detector (OCUD), where the RPN network is based on the first 4 conv stages of ResNet, and the RoI CNN is based on the 5th conv stage. It is worth noting that any detector can be used here. Up to 100 detected boxes are fed from the OCUD to the MIL classifier. ResNet50 is used as the backbone for both OCUD and the MIL classifier. Our implementation is based on maskrcnn-benchmark [20].

Training and Inference. The training is distributed over 4 GPUs, with a batch size of 8 images. The OCUD is initialized with the ImageNet pre-trained model and trained with 17,500 steps. Afterwards, the OCUD is fine-tuned with 5000 steps in the refinements. The MIL classifier is trained for 5000 steps initially and then fine-tuned similarly for 2000 steps in each following refinement. The base learning rate is set to 0.008 for all experiments and all models and is reduced by 0.1 after finishing roughly 70% of the training progress.

---

[1] ILSVRC has 2 classes *water bottle* and *wine bottle* while COCO and VOC have *bottle*.

Table 1. mAP performance on VOC 2007 test set. 'Ours' are trained with COCO-60 as source. Superscript '+' indicates multi-scale testing. 'Distill' means to re-train a Faster RCNN based on the mined boxes. 'Ens' indicates ensemble methods.

Method	aero	bike	bird	boat	bottl	bus	car	cat	chair	cow	table	dog	horse	mbik	pers.	plant	sheep	sofa	train	tv	mAP
Pure WSOD:																					
WSDDN-Ens [2]	46.4	58.3	35.5	25.9	14.0	66.7	53.0	39.2	8.9	41.8	26.6	38.6	44.7	59.0	10.8	17.3	40.7	49.6	56.9	50.8	39.3
OICR-Ens+FR [27]	65.5	67.2	47.2	21.6	22.1	68.0	68.5	35.9	5.7	63.1	49.5	30.3	64.7	66.1	13.0	25.6	50.0	57.1	60.2	59.0	47.0
PCL-Ens+FR [26]	63.2	69.9	47.9	22.6	27.3	71.0	69.1	49.6	12.0	60.1	51.5	37.3	63.3	63.9	15.8	23.6	48.8	55.3	61.2	62.1	48.8
WSOD2+ [33]	65.1	64.8	57.2	39.2	24.3	69.8	66.2	61.0	29.8	64.6	42.5	60.1	71.2	70.7	21.9	28.1	58.6	59.7	52.2	64.8	53.6
With transfer:																					
MSD-Ens+ [35]	70.5	69.2	53.3	43.7	25.4	68.9	68.7	56.9	18.4	64.2	15.3	72.0	74.4	65.2	15.4	25.1	53.6	54.4	45.6	61.4	51.08
OICR+UBBR [16]	59.7	44.8	54.0	36.1	29.3	72.1	67.4	70.7	23.5	63.8	31.5	61.5	63.7	61.9	37.9	15.4	55.1	57.4	69.9	63.6	52.0
Ours:																					
Ours(single scale)	64.4	45.0	62.1	42.8	42.4	73.1	73.2	76.0	28.2	78.6	28.5	75.1	74.6	67.7	57.5	11.6	65.6	55.4	72.2	61.3	57.77
Ours+	64.8	50.7	65.5	45.3	46.4	75.7	74.0	80.1	31.3	77.0	26.2	79.3	74.8	66.5	57.9	11.5	68.2	59.0	74.7	65.5	59.71
Ours(distill,vgg16)+	62.6	56.1	64.5	40.9	44.5	74.4	76.8	80.5	30.6	75.4	25.5	80.9	73.4	71.0	59.1	16.7	64.1	59.5	72.4	68.0	59.84
Ours(distill)+	65.5	57.7	65.1	41.3	43.0	73.6	75.7	80.4	33.4	72.2	33.8	81.3	79.6	63.0	59.4	10.9	65.1	64.2	72.7	67.2	60.24
Upper bounds:																					
Fully Supervised	75.9	83.0	74.4	60.8	56.5	79.0	83.8	83.6	54.9	81.6	66.8	85.3	84.3	77.4	82.6	47.3	74.0	72.2	78.0	74.8	73.82
Ideal OCUD	70.0	72.4	72.6	51.7	57.5	76.1	80.7	86.8	45.8	81.3	50.6	81.6	78.4	72.5	74.4	45.4	70.1	61.5	76.0	72.9	68.92

It is worth noting that the overhead training time of K refinements is less than K times the usual training time, due to the shortened training schedule for the refinements. For example, in the COCO-60-to-VOC experiments, the initial OCUD and MIL training cost 190 min and 23 min, but the OCUD and MIL refinements only took 50 min and 8 min. The testing time of the final distilled detector is similar to the usual detector. The details are in the supplementary.

Without explicit description, the parameter β in Eq. 1 is 5, the λ in Eq. 4 is 0.2, the η in Eq. 5 is 0.5, and the number of refinements is 5. In the phase of pseudo ground truth mining, the confidence threshold τ is 0.8, and the IoU threshold o is 0.1. We also studied the sensitivity of these parameters.

The training images are resized to have a short edge of 640 pixels. During testing, we study both the single-scale no-augmentation configuration, and the multi-scale (two: 320, 640 pixels) setting with horizontal flipping as adopted in prior work [26,33,35]. The non-maximum suppression IoU is 0.4 during testing.

4.2   Comparison with SOTA

Table 1 and Table 2 compare our approach with previous state-of-the-art approaches in terms of mAP and CorLoc, respectively. We compare to pure WSOD methods: (1) WSDDN-Ens [2], the ensemble of 3 Weakly Supervised Detection Networks. Our two branch MIL is modified from WSDDN. (2) OICR-Ens+FR [27], a Fast RCNN [7] retrained from a VGG ensemble of the Online Instance Classifier Refinement models. (3) PCL-Ens+FR [26], an improvement over OICR [27] which leverages proposal clusters to refine classifiers. (4) WSOD2+ [33], one of the best-performing WSODs on VOC which combines bottom-up and top-down objectness cues. We also compare with two WSOD-with-transfer methods: (1) MSD-Ens+ [35] which transfers the objectness learned from source, (2) OICR+UBBR [16] which learns a universal box regressor on source data.

From the tables, we have the following observations.

Table 2. CorLoc performance on VOC 2007 trainval set. 'Ours' are trained with COCO-60 as source. Superscript '+' indicates multi-scale testing. 'Distill' means to re-train a Faster RCNN based on the mined boxes. 'Ens' indicates ensemble methods.

Method	aero	bike	bird	boat	bottl	bus	car	cat	chair	cow	table	dog	horse	mbik	pers.	plant	sheep	sofa	train	tv	Cor.
Pure WSOD:																					
WSDDN-Ens [2]	68.9	68.7	65.2	42.5	40.6	72.6	75.2	53.7	29.7	68.1	33.5	45.6	65.9	86.1	27.5	44.9	76.0	62.4	66.3	66.8	58.0
OICR-Ens+FR [27]	85.8	82.7	62.8	45.2	43.5	84.8	87.0	46.8	15.7	82.2	51.0	45.6	83.7	91.2	22.2	59.7	75.3	65.1	76.8	78.1	64.3
PCL-Ens+FR [26]	83.8	85.1	65.5	43.1	50.8	83.2	85.3	59.3	28.5	82.2	57.4	50.7	85.0	92.0	27.9	54.2	72.2	65.9	77.6	82.1	66.6
WSOD2+ [33]	87.1	80.0	74.8	60.1	36.6	79.2	83.8	70.6	43.5	88.4	46.0	74.7	87.4	90.8	44.2	52.4	81.4	61.8	67.7	79.9	69.5
With transfer:																					
WSLAT-Ens [22]	78.6	63.4	66.4	56.4	19.7	82.3	74.8	69.1	22.5	72.3	31.0	63.0	74.9	78.4	48.6	29.4	64.6	36.2	75.9	69.5	58.8
MSD-Ens+ [35]	80.2	75.7	75.1	66.5	58.8	78.2	88.9	66.9	28.2	86.3	29.7	83.5	83.3	92.8	23.7	40.3	85.6	48.9	70.3	68.1	66.8
OICR+UBBR [16]	47.9	18.9	63.1	39.7	10.2	62.3	69.3	61.0	27.0	79.0	24.5	67.9	79.1	49.7	28.6	12.8	79.4	40.6	61.6	28.4	47.5
Ours:																					
Ours(single scale)	86.7	62.4	87.1	70.2	66.4	85.3	87.6	88.1	42.3	94.5	32.3	87.7	91.2	88.8	71.2	20.5	93.8	51.6	87.5	76.7	73.6
Ours+	87.5	64.7	87.4	69.7	67.9	86.3	88.8	88.1	44.4	93.8	31.9	89.1	92.9	86.3	71.5	22.7	94.8	56.5	88.2	76.3	74.4
Ours(distill,vgg16)+	87.9	66.7	87.7	67.6	70.2	85.8	89.9	89.2	47.9	94.5	30.8	91.6	91.8	87.6	72.2	23.8	91.8	67.2	88.6	81.7	75.7
Ours(distill)+	85.8	67.5	87.1	68.6	68.3	85.8	90.4	88.7	43.5	95.2	31.6	90.9	94.2	88.8	72.4	23.8	88.7	66.1	89.7	76.7	75.2
Upper bounds:																					
Fully Supervised	99.6	96.1	99.1	95.7	91.6	94.9	94.7	98.3	78.7	98.6	85.6	98.4	98.3	98.8	96.6	90.1	99.0	80.1	99.6	93.2	94.3
Ideal OCUD	97.5	85.1	96.7	83.5	84.4	91.9	92.5	94.5	65.4	95.2	70.0	94.2	94.6	91.6	90.6	81.3	96.9	61.3	96.6	88.2	87.6

1. Our approach without multi-scale testing and model retraining (distilling) achieves significantly higher accuracy than any pure WSOD. In terms of mAP, the gain is more than 4 points from 53.6% [33] to 57.77% (ours). For CorLoc, it is from 59.5% [33] to 73.6%. This demonstrates the superior advantage of leveraging existing detection source dataset to help the novel or unseen weakly supervised training task.

2. Compared with the approaches using external data, our approach performs consistently higher than the top related approach both in mAP and CorLoc. The best previous mAP is 52.0% [16], and the best CorLoc is 66.8% [35]. Both numbers are behind the best pure WSOD approach, and the reason might be the insufficient utilization of the external data. Instead, we utilize the external data more thoroughly with multiple progressive refinements, which significantly boosts the final accuracy.

3. For our approach, the multi-scale testing gives around 2 points' gain in mAP and 1 point's gain in CorLoc.

4. Similar to [13, 17, 26], we retrain a Faster RCNN detector on the VOC trainval images with the pseudo box annotations from our OCUD and MIL classifier. With VGG16 as the backbone, the accuracy (shown with distill) is 59.84% in mAP and 75.7% in CorLoc. With a more powerful backbone of ResNet50, mAP is 60.24% and CorLoc is 75.2%. Though the backbones are notably different, we observe the accuracy does not change accordingly, and the bottleneck may still be the quality of the mined pseudo ground truth. With 60.24% mAP, our approach surpasses the Faster RCNN fully supervised detector with the ZF network backbone (59.9% mAP) [21].

5. Two numbers are reported as upper bounds in Table 1. The first one is a fully supervised Faster RCNN (ResNet50) based on the true box annotations, which achieves 73.82% mAP. The other upper bound is estimated based on our training pipeline but with the fully annotated VOC as the source dataset. That is, the true ground truth bounding boxes of VOC trainval are used to

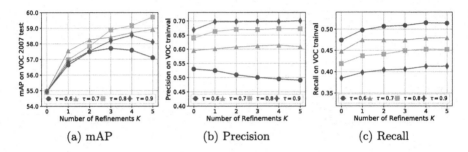

Fig. 2. Accuracy with different pseudo ground truth mining thresholds. (a) mAP on VOC test; (b)/(c): precision/recall of the mined pseudo ground truth on VOC trainval.

train the OCUD, which yields 68.92% mAP. Thus, the gap from 60.24% (our best result) to 68.92% mAP may mainly come from data disparity between the source and the target, signifying room for further improvement. Investigating a more advanced pseudo ground truth mining approach and resorting to more source data could help close the gap in the future.

4.3 Ablation Study

τ **and** K. Figure 2(a) shows the mAP with multi-scale testing under different thresholds of τ (0.6,0.7,0.8,0.9) and the number of refinements K. Figure 2(b) and (c) shows the corresponding precision and recall of the pseudo ground truth on the target dataset. The threshold τ is used in the pseudo ground truth mining in Algorithm 2. From (b) and (c), we can see a higher threshold leads to higher precision but lower recall and vice versa. The threshold of 0.8 achieves the best trade-off mAP with $K \geq 3$. When $K \leq 2$, a smaller threshold is better. This is reasonable because more boxes can be leveraged.

Along the dimension of K, the precision and recall improve in general, except for $\tau = 0.6$ where the precision deteriorates when $K \geq 3$. For $\tau = 0.8$, the accuracy improves significantly from 55.0% to 59.7% when the number of refinements is increased from 0 to 5. The gradual accuracy improvement indicates that one-step knowledge transfer is sub-optimal, and the final accuracy benefits a lot from more iterations of knowledge transfer.

β. The β parameter in Eq. 3 scales the detection score $s_{ij}^d \in (0,1)$ before softmax. When $\beta = 0$, it is equivalent to remove the detection branch. When $\beta \to +\infty$, all the non-maximum values are zero after softmax, which reduces the importance of the classification branch. The best accuracy locates at $\beta = 5$ in Fig. 3(a).

λ. Coefficient λ balances the image classification loss L_{wsddn} and detection score regularization L_{guide} in Eq. 4. A larger λ means stronger regularization. The result is shown in Fig. 3(b), and $\lambda = 0.2$ delivers the best performance. A non-zero λ performing well suggests that the OCUD can provide valuable information to guide the MIL classifier learning, which is overlooked in previous work [30].

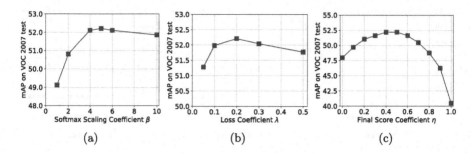

Fig. 3. Ablation study of the scaling factor β in Eq. 1, λ in Eq. 4 and η in Eq. 5. The accuracy is based on the initial OCUD and MIL classifier with single-scale inference.

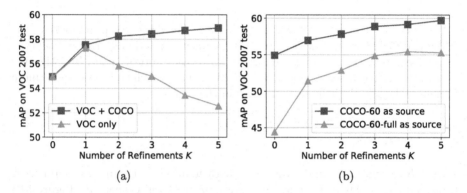

Fig. 4. Accuracy with different configurations of the source datasets: (a) VOC+COCO vs VOC, (b) COCO-60 vs COCO-60-full. The accuracy is based on multi-scale testing.

η. Linear coefficient η in Eq. 5 balances the score from the MIL classifier and the OCUD during inference. As illustrated in Fig. 3(c), the accuracy is worse if we rely on either MIL classifier ($\eta = 1$) or the OCUD ($\eta = 0$) alone. The best accuracy is located at $\eta = 0.4 \sim 0.5$.

VOC vs VOC+COCO. After we have the initial OCUD, one alternative is to remove the source dataset afterwards. Figure 4(a) shows the experiment results with $\tau = 0.7$. As we can see, without the source dataset, the performance drops dramatically after one refinement. The reason might be that the error of the mined box annotation can be accumulated and the OCUD becomes unstable without the guidance of the manually-labeled boxes. This ablation is similar to pure WSOD methods such as OICR [27], where the detector is refined only on the target data. The inferior result suggests that transferring knowledge from the source is indeed critical in the success of our method.

COCO-60 vs COCO-60-Full. Following [16,35], we removed all images in the source dataset (COCO) which has overlapping categories with the target VOC dataset. Instead of removing the images, we also conduct the experiments by keeping the images but removing the annotations of overlapping categories,

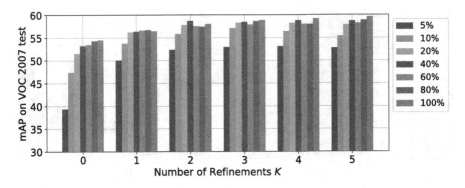

Fig. 5. Ablation study on the size of the source dataset (subsets of COCO-60).

and denote this source set by COCO-60-full. Figure 4(b) shows the experiment results. Obviously, the accuracy with COCO-60 is higher than that with COCO-60-full. The reason is that the regions with the annotation removed are treated as background in OCUD, which will reduce the recall rate for COCO-60-full. Another observation is that even with this challenging source dataset, we can still boost the accuracy from less than 45% to more than 55%, with a gain of more than 10 points with our progressive transfer learning. Comparatively, the gain on COCO-60 is much less at around 5 points. The reason is that the propagation on the COCO-60-full can provide more positive pseudo ground truth boxes.

Figure 6(a) and 6(b) visualize the mined pseudo ground truth boxes (in red) of a few example images in the VOC trainval data and COCO-60-full after 2 refinements. From the results, we can see that some missing box-level annotations in VOC are successfully recovered, which helps the OCUD align with the target domain. The mined boxes in the COCO-60-full can also reduce the impact of the missing labels and improve the recall.

Size of the Source Data. We study the effect of varying the source dataset's size to explore the boundary of the amount of data necessary for a successful transfer. Specifically, we randomly sample 5%, 10%, ..., 80% of the COCO-60 as the source dataset. The smaller percentage subset is subsequently included in the larger percentage subset. Figure 5 shows the experiment results. We can observe that as few as 20% of COCO-60 (4396 train + 194 val images) brings accuracy to more than 58% mAP on VOC.

COCO vs ILSVRC. We replace COCO-60 by ILSVRC-179 and run our algorithm for 4 refinements with the same hyper-parameters as in the COCO-60 experiment. The OCUD is trained with 4 times more gradient steps, because of the larger data size. The final accuracy is 56.46%, which is higher than COCO-60-full, but worse than COCO-60. Compared with COCO-60-full, the superiority might come from the larger dataset. Compared with COCO-60, we believe the inferiority is from the data quality and consistency with the target dataset. Although ILSVRC-179 contains more images than COCO-60, the quality is not

(a)   (b)

Fig. 6. (a) Mined pseudo ground truth boxes (in red) in VOC trainval. (b) Original ground truth (in green) and pseudo ground truth boxes (in red) in COCO-60-full. (Color figure online)

as good, and we observed more images with missing labels. Visual images are shown in the supplementary materials. This introduces more regions that are target domain objects but are taken as negative regions for OCUD.

4.4 ILSVRC Transfer Setting

Following the setting in [10,29,30,35], we also conduct experiments with the 200 classes in the ILSVRC 2013 detection dataset [4]. The setting uses the first 100 classes sorted in alphabetic order as the source classes, and the last 100 classes as the target weak classes. We were able to achieve 37.0% mAP on the weak 100 categories of val2 set with our algorithm and the ResNet50 backbone, which is comparable to the 36.9% mAP reported in [30] with the stronger Inception-ResNet and is much better than any earlier results under the same setting [10, 29,35]. Note that our method without any refinement is 33.5%, and iterative knowledge transfer boosts the performance by 3.5 points after two refinements. This again confirms our argument that the multi-step transfer is more effective than one-step. The detail is provided in the supplementary material.

5 Conclusion

We have studied the weakly supervised object detection problem by transfer learning from a fully annotated source dataset. A simple yet effective progressive knowledge transfer algorithm is developed to learn a one-class universal detector and a MIL classifier iteratively. As such, the source dataset's knowledge can be thoroughly exploited and leveraged, leading to a new state-of-the-art on VOC 2007 with COCO-60 as the source dataset. The results suggest that knowledge transfer from an existing well-annotated dataset could be a fruitful future direction towards mitigating the annotation effort problem for novel domains.

References

1. Bansal, A., Sikka, K., Sharma, G., Chellappa, R., Divakaran, A.: Zero-shot object detection. In: Proceedings of the European Conference on Computer Vision (ECCV), pp. 384–400 (2018)
2. Bilen, H., Vedaldi, A.: Weakly supervised deep detection networks. In: Proceedings of the IEEE Conference on Computer Vision and Pattern Recognition, pp. 2846–2854 (2016)
3. Chen, H., Wang, Y., Wang, G., Qiao, Y.: LSTD: a low-shot transfer detector for object detection. In: Thirty-Second AAAI Conference on Artificial Intelligence (2018)
4. Deng, J., Dong, W., Socher, R., Li, L.J., Li, K., Fei-Fei, L.: ImageNet: a large-Scale Hierarchical Image Database. In: CVPR (2009)
5. Deselaers, T., Alexe, B., Ferrari, V.: Weakly supervised localization and learning with generic knowledge. Int. J. Comput. Vis. **100**(3), 275–293 (2012)
6. Everingham, M., Van Gool, L., Williams, C.K., Winn, J., Zisserman, A.: The pascal visual object classes (VOC) challenge. Int. J. Comput. Vis. **88**(2), 303–338 (2010)
7. Girshick, R.: Fast R-CNN. In: Proceedings of the IEEE International Conference on Computer Vision, pp. 1440–1448 (2015)
8. He, K., Gkioxari, G., Dollár, P., Girshick, R.: Mask R-CNN. In: Proceedings of the IEEE International Conference on Computer Vision, pp. 2961–2969 (2017)
9. He, K., Zhang, X., Ren, S., Sun, J.: Deep residual learning for image recognition. In: Proceedings of the IEEE Conference on Computer Vision and Pattern Recognition, pp. 770–778 (2016)
10. Hoffman, J., et al.: LSDA: large scale detection through adaptation. In: Advances in Neural Information Processing Systems, pp. 3536–3544 (2014)
11. Hoffman, J., Pathak, D., Darrell, T., Saenko, K.: Detector discovery in the wild: joint multiple instance and representation learning. In: Proceedings of the IEEE Conference on Computer Vision and Pattern Recognition, pp. 2883–2891 (2015)
12. Hoffman, J., et al.: Large scale visual recognition through adaptation using joint representation and multiple instance learning. J. Mach. Learn. Res. **17**(1), 4954–4984 (2016)
13. Jie, Z., Wei, Y., Jin, X., Feng, J., Liu, W.: Deep self-taught learning for weakly supervised object localization. In: Proceedings of the IEEE Conference on Computer Vision and Pattern Recognition, pp. 1377–1385 (2017)
14. Kuen, J., Perazzi, F., Lin, Z., Zhang, J., Tan, Y.P.: Scaling object detection by transferring classification weights. In: Proceedings of the IEEE International Conference on Computer Vision, pp. 6044–6053 (2019)
15. Kuznetsova, A., et al.: The open images dataset V4: unified image classification, object detection, and visual relationship detection at scale. arXiv preprint arXiv:1811.00982 (2018)
16. Lee, S., Kwak, S., Cho, M.: Universal bounding box regression and its applications. In: Jawahar, C.V., Li, H., Mori, G., Schindler, K. (eds.) ACCV 2018. LNCS, vol. 11366, pp. 373–387. Springer, Cham (2019). https://doi.org/10.1007/978-3-030-20876-9_24
17. Li, D., Huang, J.B., Li, Y., Wang, S., Yang, M.H.: Weakly supervised object localization with progressive domain adaptation. In: Proceedings of the IEEE Conference on Computer Vision and Pattern Recognition, pp. 3512–3520 (2016)
18. Lin, T.-Y., et al.: Microsoft COCO: common objects in context. In: Fleet, D., Pajdla, T., Schiele, B., Tuytelaars, T. (eds.) ECCV 2014. LNCS, vol. 8693, pp. 740–755. Springer, Cham (2014). https://doi.org/10.1007/978-3-319-10602-1_48

19. Liu, W., et al.: SSD: single shot multibox detector. In: Leibe, B., Matas, J., Sebe, N., Welling, M. (eds.) ECCV 2016. LNCS, vol. 9905, pp. 21–37. Springer, Cham (2016). https://doi.org/10.1007/978-3-319-46448-0_2

20. Massa, F., Girshick, R.: MaskRCNN-benchmark: fast, modular reference implementation of instance segmentation and object detection algorithms in PyTorch (2018)

21. Ren, S., He, K., Girshick, R., Sun, J.: Faster R-CNN: towards real-time object detection with region proposal networks. In: Advances in Neural Information Processing Systems, pp. 91–99 (2015)

22. Rochan, M., Wang, Y.: Weakly supervised localization of novel objects using appearance transfer. In: Proceedings of the IEEE Conference on Computer Vision and Pattern Recognition, pp. 4315–4324 (2015)

23. Shao, S., et al.: Objects365: a large-scale, high-quality dataset for object detection. In: Proceedings of the IEEE International Conference on Computer Vision, pp. 8430–8439 (2019)

24. Shi, M., Caesar, H., Ferrari, V.: Weakly supervised object localization using things and stuff transfer. In: Proceedings of the IEEE International Conference on Computer Vision, pp. 3381–3390 (2017)

25. Song, H.O., Girshick, R., Jegelka, S., Mairal, J., Harchaoui, Z., Darrell, T.: On learning to localize objects with minimal supervision. In: International Conference on Machine Learning, pp. 1611–1619 (2014)

26. Tang, P., et al.: PCL: proposal cluster learning for weakly supervised object detection. IEEE Trans. Pattern Anal. Mach. Intell. **42**, 176–191 (2018)

27. Tang, P., Wang, X., Bai, X., Liu, W.: Multiple instance detection network with online instance classifier refinement. In: Proceedings of the IEEE Conference on Computer Vision and Pattern Recognition, pp. 2843–2851 (2017)

28. Tang, P., et al.: Weakly supervised region proposal network and object detection. In: Proceedings of the European Conference on Computer Vision (ECCV), pp. 352–368 (2018)

29. Tang, Y., et al.: Visual and semantic knowledge transfer for large scale semi-supervised object detection. IEEE Trans. Pattern Anal. Mach. Intell. **40**(12), 3045–3058 (2017)

30. Uijlings, J., Popov, S., Ferrari, V.: Revisiting knowledge transfer for training object class detectors. In: Proceedings of the IEEE Conference on Computer Vision and Pattern Recognition, pp. 1101–1110 (2018)

31. Uijlings, J.R., Van De Sande, K.E., Gevers, T., Smeulders, A.W.: Selective search for object recognition. Int. J. Comput. Vis. **104**(2), 154–171 (2013)

32. Wu, Z., Bodla, N., Singh, B., Najibi, M., Chellappa, R., Davis, L.S.: Soft sampling for robust object detection. In: BMVC, p. 225. BMVA Press (2019)

33. Zeng, Z., Liu, B., Fu, J., Chao, H., Zhang, L.: WSOD2: learning bottom-up and top-down objectness distillation for weakly-supervised object detection. In: Proceedings of the IEEE International Conference on Computer Vision, pp. 8292–8300 (2019)

34. Zhang, D., Han, J., Zhao, L., Meng, D.: Leveraging prior-knowledge for weakly supervised object detection under a collaborative self-paced curriculum learning framework. Int. J. Comput. Vis. **127**(4), 363–380 (2019)

35. Huang, K., Zhang, J., Zhang, J., et al.: Mixed supervised object detection with robust objectness transfer. IEEE Trans. Pattern Anal. Mach. Intell. **41**(3), 639–653 (2018)

36. Zhang, Y., Bai, Y., Ding, M., Li, Y., Ghanem, B.: W2F: a weakly-supervised to fully-supervised framework for object detection. In: Proceedings of the IEEE Conference on Computer Vision and Pattern Recognition, pp. 928–936 (2018)

37. Zhong, Y., Wang, J., Peng, J., Zhang, L.: Anchor box optimization for object detection. In: The IEEE Winter Conference on Applications of Computer Vision, pp. 1286–1294 (2020)

38. Zhu, Y., Zhou, Y., Ye, Q., Qiu, Q., Jiao, J.: Soft proposal networks for weakly supervised object localization. In: Proceedings of the IEEE International Conference on Computer Vision, pp. 1841–1850 (2017)

39. Zitnick, C.L., Dollár, P.: Edge boxes: locating object proposals from edges. In: Fleet, D., Pajdla, T., Schiele, B., Tuytelaars, T. (eds.) ECCV 2014. LNCS, vol. 8693, pp. 391–405. Springer, Cham (2014). https://doi.org/10.1007/978-3-319-10602-1_26

BézierSketch: A Generative Model for Scalable Vector Sketches

Ayan Das[1,2(✉)], Yongxin Yang[1,2], Timothy Hospedales[1,3], Tao Xiang[1,2], and Yi-Zhe Song[1,2]

[1] SketchX, CVSSP, University of Surrey, Guildford, UK
{a.das,yongxin.yang,t.xiang,y.song}@surrey.ac.uk
[2] iFlyTek-Surrey Joint Research Centre on Artificial Intelligence, Guildford, UK
[3] University of Edinburgh, Edinburgh, UK
t.hospedales@ed.ac.uk

Abstract. The study of neural generative models of human sketches is a fascinating contemporary modeling problem due to the links between sketch image generation and the human drawing process. The landmark SketchRNN provided breakthrough by sequentially generating sketches as a sequence of waypoints. However this leads to low-resolution image generation, and failure to model long sketches. In this paper we present BézierSketch, a novel generative model for fully *vector* sketches that are automatically scalable and high-resolution. To this end, we first introduce a novel inverse graphics approach to stroke embedding that trains an encoder to embed each stroke to its best fit Bézier curve. This enables us to treat sketches as short sequences of paramaterized strokes and thus train a recurrent sketch generator with greater capacity for longer sketches, while producing scalable high-resolution results. We report qualitative and quantitative results on the *Quick, Draw!* benchmark.

Keywords: Sketch generation · Scalable graphics · Bézier curve

1 Introduction

Generative neural modeling of images [6,12] is now an established research area in contemporary machine learning and computer vision. Rapid progress has been made in generating photos [11,24], with effort being focused on fidelity, diversity, and resolution of image generation, along with stability of training; as well as sequential models for text and video [2,31]. Generative modeling of human *sketches* in particular has recently gained interest, along with other applications of sketch analysis such as recognition [33,34], retrieval [4,21,28] and forensics [13] – all facilitated by the growth of large scale sketch datasets [8,28].

Electronic supplementary material The online version of this chapter (https://doi.org/10.1007/978-3-030-58574-7_38) contains supplementary material, which is available to authorized users.

Fig. 1. Left: SketchRNN [8] generates sketches by sampling waypoints (red dots) which lead to coarse images upon zoom. Right: our BézierSketch samples smooth curves (green control points) thus providing scalable *vector* graphic generation. (Color figure online)

Sketch generation provides an excellent opportunity to study sequential generative models, and is particularly fascinating due to the potential to establish links between learned generative models and human sketching – a communication modality that comes innately to children, and has existed for millennia. Recent breakthroughs in this area include SketchRNN [8], which provided the first neural generative sequential model for sketch images, and Learn2Sketch [30] which provided the first conditional image to sequential sketch model. While conventional image generation models focus on producing ever-larger pixel arrays in high fidelity, these methods aim to model sketches using a more human-like representation consisting of a collection of strokes.

SketchRNN [8], the landmark neural sketch generation algorithm, treats sketches as a digitized sequence of 2D points on a drawing canvas sampled along the trajectory of the ink-flow. This model of sketches has several issues, however: It is inefficient, due to the dense representation of redundant information like highly correlated temporal samples; and as sketches are ultimately pixels on a grid, it is prone to sampling noise. Crucially it provides limited graphical scalability: SketchRNN sets out to achieve vector graphic generation (and claims to achieve this). However it does not generate truly scalable vector graphs as required by applications such as digital art. Since generated sketches are composed of dense line segments, its samples are only somewhat smoother than raster graphics (Fig. 1). Finally, it suffers from limited capacity. Because it models sketches as a sequence of pixels, it is limited in the length of sketch it can model before the underlying recurrent neural network begins to run out of capacity.

In this paper we propose a fundamental paradigm change in the representation of sketches that enables the above issues to be addressed. Specifically, we aim to represent sketches in terms of parameterized smooth curves [27]. These provide a scalable representation of a finite length curve using few *Control Points*. From a large family of parametric curves, we choose Bézier curves due to their simple structure. In order to train a generative model of human sketches with this representation, the key question is how to encode human sketches as parameterized curves. To this end, a key technical contribution is a vision-as-inverse-graphics [5,14,26] approach, that learns to embed human sketch strokes as interpretable parameterized Bézier curves. We train BézierEncoder in an inverse-graphics manner by learning to reconstruct strokes through a white-box graphics (Bézier) decoder. Given this new low-dimensional stroke representation, we then train BézierSketch to generate sketches. Our stroke-level generative model requires many fewer iterations than the segment-level SketchRNN, and thus provides better generation of longer sketches, while providing high-resolution scalable vector-graphic sketch generation (Fig. 1).

In summary, the contributions of our work are: (1) BézierEncoder, a novel inverse-graphics approach for mapping strokes to parameterized Béziers, (2) BézierSketch, a sequential generative model for sketches that produces high-resolution and low-noise vector graphic samples with improved scalability to longer sketches compared to the previous state of the art SketchRNN.

2 Related Work

Parameterized Curves. Bézier curves are a powerful tool in the field of computer graphics and are extensively used in interactive curve and surface design [27], as are a more general family of curves known as *Splines* [3]. Optimization algorithms to fit Bézier curves and Splines from data have been studied. Few specially crafted algorithms do exist specifically for cubic Bézier curves [20,29]. However the challenge for most curve and spline-fitting methods is the existence of latent variables t that correspond training points and the location of their projection onto the curve. This leads to two-stage alternating algorithms for separately optimizing the curve parameters (control points) and latent parameter t [17,22]. Importantly, such methods [17,22] including few promising ones [35] require expensive *per-sample* alternating optimization, or iterative inference in expensive generative models [15,25] which make them unsuitable for large scale or online applications. In contrast, we uniquely take the approach of learning a neural network that maps strokes to Bézier curves in a single shot. This neural encoder is a model that needs to be trained, but unlike per-sample optimization approaches, it is inductive. So once trained it can provide one-shot estimation of curve parameters and point association from an input stroke.

Generative Models. Generative models have been studied extensively in the machine learning literature, often in terms of density estimation with directed [1,23] or undirected [10] graphical models. Research in this field accelerated after the emergence of Generative adversarial networks (GAN) [6], Variational Autoencoder (VAE) [12] and their derivatives. Handling sequences are of particular importance and hence specialized algorithms [2,31] were developed. Although RNNs have been successfully used for generating handwriting [7] without variational training, these methods lacked flexibility in terms of generation quality. The emergence of VAE and variational training methods allows the fusion of RNNs with variational objective led to the first successful generative sequence model [2] in the domain of Natural Language Processing (NLP). It was quickly adapted by SketchRNN [8] in order to extend [7] to free-hand sketches.

Inverse Graphics. "Inverse Graphics" is line of work that aims to estimate 3D scene parameters from raster images without supervision. Instead it predicts the input parameters of a computer graphics pipeline that can reconstruct the image. Several attempts were made [14, 26] to estimate explicit model parameters of 3D objects from raw images. A specialized case of the generic Inverse Graphics idea is to estimate parameters of 2D objects such as curves. As a recent example, an RNN based agent named SPIRAL [5] learned to draw characters in terms of pen an brush curves. SPIRAL, however, is extremely costly due to its reliance on Policy Gradient [32] reinforcement learning training and black-box renderer.

Learning for Curves. Few works have studied learning for curve generation. The recent SVG Font Generator [18] trains an excellent font embedding with a recurrent vector font image generator. However it is trained with supervision rather than inverse graphics, and limited to the more structured domain of font images. Other attempts [16] also use supervised learning on synthetic data, rather than unsupervised learning on real human sketches as we consider here.

3   Methodology

Background: Conventional Sketch Representation and Generation. A common format [8] for a digitally acquired sketch $\mathcal{S}$ is as a sequence of 2-tuples, each containing a $2D$ coordinate on the canvas sampled from a continuous drawing flow and a pen-state bit denoting whether the pen touches the canvas or not.

$$\mathcal{S} = \left[(\mathbf{X}_i, q_i) \right]_{i=1}^{L} \tag{1}$$

where $\mathbf{X}_i \triangleq \begin{bmatrix} x & y \end{bmatrix}_i^T \in \mathbb{R}^2$, $q_i \in \{\text{PenUp}, \text{PenDown}\}$ and L is the cardinality of $\mathcal{S}$ representing the length of the sketch. The state-of-the-art sketch generator SketchRNN [8] learns a parametric Recurrent Neural Network (RNN) to model the joint distribution of coordinates and pen state as a product of conditionals, i.e. $p_{sketchrnn}(\mathcal{S}; \theta) = \prod_{i=1}^{L} p(\mathbf{X}_i, q_i | \mathbf{X}_{<i}, q_{<i}; \theta)$, where θ is the set of parameters of the model and $\mathbf{X}_{<i}$ and $q_{<i}$ denote the list of locations and pen-state bits respectively before $\mathbf{X}_i$ and q_i.

Towards a Stroke-Level Representation. We are interested in moving from such a segment-level representation toward stroke-level. To this end we modify the structure of our input data to $\bar{\mathcal{S}} \triangleq \left[\mathbf{T}_j \right]_{j=1}^{N}$, with $\mathbf{T}_j \triangleq \left[\mathbf{X}_i^{(j)} \right]_{i=1}^{N_j}$ where $\mathbf{T}_j$ is the jth stroke of length $N_j \triangleq |\mathbf{T}_j|$ segregated from the sketch by following the pen-state bit, and consequently $\sum_{j=1}^{N} N_j = L$.

Towards a Stroke-Level Generative Model. Existing generative sketch models [8, 30] generate a segment at each iteration. Given a stroke-segmented training set $\bar{\mathcal{S}}$, we would like to train a generative model analogous to SketchRNN. That is, to model the distribution over possible sketches with a parametric model $p_{model}(\bar{\mathcal{S}}; \theta)$ and that approximates the original data distribution $p_{data}(\bar{\mathcal{S}})$. Different sketches having different lengths N makes this problem suitable for Recurrent Neural Networks (RNN). One could model the probability of a sketch as a product of the probabilities of individual strokes $\mathbf{T}_j$ conditioned on all its previously seen strokes $\mathbf{T}_{<j}$ and parameterized by set of parameters θ as $p_{model}(\bar{\mathcal{S}}; \theta) = \prod_j p(\mathbf{T}_j | \mathbf{T}_{<j}; \theta)$. However, a problem with such an approach is that the individual strokes $\mathbf{T}_j$ are of varying length which would require a hierarchical model where $p(\mathbf{T}_j | \cdot)$ is again modeled as a sequence. So we instead propose to learn fixed length embedding $\mathbf{e}_j \triangleq \mathbf{e}(\mathbf{T}_j) \in \mathbb{R}^d$ for any stroke $\mathbf{T}_j$ and corresponding non-parametric decoder $\mathbf{d}(\cdot)$ such that $\mathbf{T}_j \approx \mathbf{d}(\mathbf{e}_j)$. We then model the encoded sketch $\mathbf{e}(\bar{\mathcal{S}}) \triangleq \{\mathbf{e}_j\}_{j=1}^N$ as

$$p_{model}(\mathbf{e}(\bar{\mathcal{S}}); \theta) = \prod_{j=1}^N p(\mathbf{e}_j | \mathbf{e}_{<j}; \theta) \tag{2}$$

where the individual conditionals are typically one or more mixtures of Gaussians (GMMs) and where the raw sketch can be rendered at any point by the decoder. In order to sample a new sketch from the model, we sample each jth stroke from $p(\mathbf{e}_j | \mathbf{e}_{<j}; \theta)$ and render it as $\mathbf{d}(\mathbf{e}_j)$.

A natural choice for the embedding $\mathbf{e}(\cdot)$ could be an encoder RNN trained as part of a Sequence-to-Sequence autoencoder [31]. However, We take a different approach and propose a novel inverse-graphics based encoder-decoder framework $\mathbf{T} \approx \mathbf{d}(\mathbf{e}(\mathbf{T}))$ where our neural encoder $\mathbf{e}(\cdot)$ produces an *interpretable* representation because it must decode through a white-box Bézier renderer $\mathbf{d}(\cdot)$.

3.1   Stroke Embedding: BézierEncoder

To train our parametric stroke embedding with an inverse graphics strategy, we must first define a differentiable 'graphics decoder' which will be later used to train our neural encoder to map human strokes to Bézier curves.

Inverse Graphics Decoder. Bézier curves, used heavily in computer graphics, are smooth curves representable in a closed functional form parameterized by a sequence of $n+1$ anchor coordinates $\mathbf{P} \triangleq \begin{bmatrix} P_x & P_y \end{bmatrix}^T \in \mathbb{R}^2$ termed *control points*. A degree n Bézier curve with control points $\begin{bmatrix} \mathbf{P}_0, \mathbf{P}_1, \cdots \mathbf{P}_n \end{bmatrix}$ is represented as

$$\mathbf{C}(t; \{\mathbf{P}_i\}) = \sum_{i=0}^n \mathcal{B}_{i,n}(t) \cdot \mathbf{P}_i \tag{3}$$

where $t \in [0,1]$ is the *parameter* of the curve, $\mathcal{B}_{i,n}(t) \triangleq \binom{n}{i} t^i (1-t)^{n-i}$ is the Bernstein Basis Polynomial in t and $\mathbf{C}(t) \triangleq \begin{bmatrix} C_x(t) & C_y(t) \end{bmatrix}^T \in \mathbb{R}^2$ denotes a point on the curve at $t = t$. As t assumes values $0 \to 1$, the curve starts from $\mathbf{P}_0$ and ends at $\mathbf{P}_n$ and the control points $\begin{bmatrix} \mathbf{P}_1, \cdots, \mathbf{P}_{n-1} \end{bmatrix}$ control the trajectory of the curve, as illustrated in Fig. 2(a). We further use $\mathcal{P}^n \triangleq \begin{bmatrix} P_{x0}, P_{y0}, \cdots, P_{xn}, P_{yn} \end{bmatrix} \in \mathbb{R}^{2(n+1)}$ to denote elements (curves) in the continuous space of $n+1$ control points. The decoder function $\mathbf{d} : \mathcal{P} \to \mathbf{T}$ can be trivially realized by Eq. 3 with the set of t-values chosen as per resolution requirement.

We now denote $(\mathbf{T}, \mathcal{P})$ as an arbitrary stroke and its Bézier representation, where we have dropped the subscript j and superscript n for notational brevity.

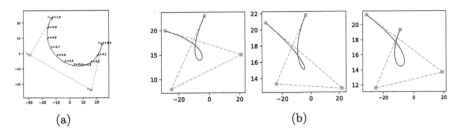

Fig. 2. (a) An example of Bézier curve of degree $n = 3$ with $n + 1$ control points. (b) Bézier curves with Gaussian noise ($\mu = 0, \Sigma = 5I_2$) added to control points produce similar curves in image space.

Using $\mathcal{P}$ as an embedding space for $\mathbf{T}$ leads to an extremely useful and key property: Given a choice of n, two similar points in $\mathcal{P}$ space correspond to similar strokes in $\mathbf{T}$ space. As a consequence, we can sample from the conditionals in Eq. 2 to generate variations of a stroke.

Property 1. Given a $(\mathbf{T}, \mathcal{P})$ pair where $\mathbf{T} = \mathbf{d}(\mathcal{P})$ and sample $\widehat{\mathcal{P}} \sim \mathcal{N}(\mathcal{P}, \sigma)$, then the decoded $\widehat{\mathbf{T}} = \mathbf{d}(\widehat{\mathcal{P}})$ is distributed as $\mathcal{N}(\mathbf{T}, \sigma')$.

Proof. Refer to Appendix A in the supplementary document for the proof. Illustrative examples are given in Fig. 2(b).

A Stroke to Bézier Encoder. We wish to learn an embedding function $\mathbf{e}(\cdot)$ that will map a given stroke $\mathbf{T}$ to its best fit Bézier representation $\mathcal{P}$. Due to the variable length of strokes $\mathbf{T}$, we model BézierEncoder with a bi-directional RNN, with forward and backward states $\overrightarrow{\mathbf{s}_i}, \overleftarrow{\mathbf{s}_i} \in \mathbb{R}^h$ at time-step i as

$$\left[\overrightarrow{\mathbf{s}_i}, \overleftarrow{\mathbf{s}_i}\right] = \mathrm{BiRNN}(\mathbf{X}_{i-1}, \mathbf{s}_{i-1}; \theta) \tag{4}$$

However, unlike regular encoder RNNs, we further transform the last hidden state to get a Bézier curve representation

$$\mathcal{P} = \mathbf{W}_{\mathcal{P}} \left[\overrightarrow{\mathbf{s}}_{end}; \overleftarrow{\mathbf{s}}_{end}\right] \tag{5}$$

where the '*end*' subscript denotes the state of the RNN at last time-step, $[\ ;\ ]$ denotes the concatenation operator and $\mathbf{W}_{\mathcal{P}} \in \mathbb{R}^{2(n+1) \times 2h}$.

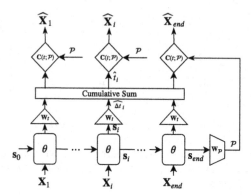

Fig. 3. Inverse graphics training of our BézierEncoder architecture for model-based single-pass stroke $[\mathbf{X}_i]$ to Bézier $\mathcal{P}$ mapping.

The formulation so far enables extracting a curve $\mathcal{P}$ from data $\mathbf{T}$. However, while $\mathcal{P}$ is now a sufficient representation to decode the Bézier by means of Eq. 3, we do not have sufficient information to compute a reconstruction loss like $\|\mathbf{T} - \mathbf{d}(\mathbf{e}(\mathbf{T}))\|$ because we lack the association between input coordinates $\mathbf{X}_i$ and interpolation parameters t_i. This is where many classic Bézier fitting techniques [17,35] resort to slow alternating optimization techniques.

We take a different approach and ask our encoder to also predict the corresponding interpolation parameter t_i for each input point $\mathbf{X}_i$. In order to make valid predictions for t we note the properties it requires due to its role in Bézier curves generation: **1.** $0 \leqslant \widehat{t}_i \leqslant 1$ (by definition of Bézier curve). **2.** $\widehat{t}_i \leqslant \widehat{t}_{i+1}$ (due to sequential nature of $\mathbf{X}_i$). Apart from these, we impose another property without any lose of generality: **3.** $t_1 = 0$ and $t_{end} = 1$ (this will make $\mathbf{X}_1$ and $\mathbf{X}_{end}$ coincide with $\mathbf{P}_0$ and $\mathbf{P}_n$ respectively). Please refer to the experiment section for an implementation trick to do so.

To enable our encoder to meet these requirements above, we do not compute t_is directly, but instead compute increments $\Delta t_i \triangleq t_i - t_{i-1}$ (with $t_0 \triangleq 0$) from $[\vec{\mathbf{s}}_i; \overleftarrow{\mathbf{s}}_i]$ at every step i. The t_i-values can then be easily computed as a cumulative sum of all Δt_i up to i. Thus, the second path of our encoder predicts

$$\widehat{t}_i = \sum_{i'=1}^{i} \widehat{\Delta t}_{i'}, \text{ with } \widehat{\Delta t}_i = \text{SOFTMAX}_i(\mathbf{W}_t \cdot [\vec{\mathbf{s}}_i; \overleftarrow{\mathbf{s}}_i]). \tag{6}$$

The usage of SOFTMAX() enforces all three requirements stated above.

To summarize: Our full architecture, as shown in Fig. 3 thus has two pathways: A Bézier embedding pathway that predicts the curve $\mathcal{P}$ for the entire stroke input $\mathbf{T}$ and an interpolation parameter pathway that further predicts the estimated curve parameter $\widehat{t}_i$ for each input point $\mathbf{X}_i$ in $\mathbf{T}$. Given the $(\mathbf{X}_i, \widehat{t}_i)$ pairs and $\mathcal{P}$ predicted by our encoder, we can now train our model with the following reconstruction loss:

$$\mathcal{L}(\theta, \mathbf{W}_\mathcal{P}, \mathbf{W}_t) \triangleq \sum_i \left\| \mathcal{C}(\widehat{t}_i, \mathcal{P}) - \mathbf{X}_i \right\|^2 \tag{7}$$

which is optimized w.r.t. encoder parameters $\{\theta, \mathbf{W}_{\mathcal{P}}, \mathbf{W}_t\}$ by SGD. Once trained, we can compute the best-fit Bézier for any stroke using Eq. 5, which provides a feed-forward single pass solution to a typically alternating optimization.

A Multi-degree Representation Extension. To add more flexibility, we can extend this basic building block to learn a multi-degree representation of a given stroke $\mathbf{T}$. In order to do so, we encode the stroke using the the same RNN in Eq. 4 parameterized by θ but use a set of different $\mathbf{W}_{\mathcal{P}^n}$ and $\mathbf{W}_t^n$ for a predefined range of degree $n \in [n_{min}, \cdots, n_{max}]$ to predict Bézier representations of different degrees along with their corresponding t_i^n-values.

$$\widehat{t}_i^n = \sum_{i'=1}^i \widehat{\Delta t}_{i'}^n, \text{ with } \widehat{\Delta t}_i^n = \text{SOFTMAX}_i(\mathbf{W}_t^n \cdot [\overrightarrow{\mathbf{s}}_i; \overleftarrow{\mathbf{s}}_i]) \text{ and} \tag{8}$$

$$\mathcal{P}^n = \mathbf{W}_{\mathcal{P}^n} [\overrightarrow{\mathbf{s}}_{end}; \overleftarrow{\mathbf{s}}_{end}]$$

The total loss is now the sum of losses at every order n:

$$\mathcal{L}_{total} \triangleq \sum_{n=n_{min}}^{n_{max}} \mathcal{L}_n, \text{ with } \mathcal{L}_n(\theta, \mathbf{W}_{\mathcal{P}^n}, \mathbf{W}_t^n) \triangleq \sum_i \left\| \mathcal{C}(\widehat{t}_i^n, \mathcal{P}^n) - \mathbf{X}_i \right\|^2 \tag{9}$$

Inference in this model can now predict a *set* of Bézier representations for different degrees, where higher order curves fit the data better at the cost of more control points. The preferred order can then be chosen manually according to user requirement, or automatically by heuristic. An effective heuristics is to evaluate the loss $\mathcal{L}_n$ for all n and choose the smallest n for which $\mathcal{L}^n \leq L_{tolerance}$.

Smoothness Regularizer. Our training objectives Eq. 7 or Eq. 9 may lead to overfitting in the domain of Bézier curves during encoder learning. To avoid this we add a smoothness regularizer (with regularization strength β) that prefers sequential control points to be nearby. Specifically, we add $\beta \cdot \mathcal{R}_n$ with $\mathcal{L}_n$ for each n, where $\mathcal{R}_n(\mathcal{P}^n) \triangleq \sum_{i=1}^n \|\mathbf{P}_{i+1} - \mathbf{P}_i\|_2^2$.

3.2   Sketch Generation: BézierSketch

We next leverage our choice of Bézier representation space, and encoding model $\mathcal{P} = \mathbf{e}(\cdot)$ to define two alternative vector graphic generative models for sketches.

Control Point Mode. Given a sketch as a sequence of stroke embeddings $\{\mathcal{P}_j\}_{i=1}^N$ obtained from the raw input strokes as $\mathcal{P} = \mathbf{e}(\mathbf{T})$, we can modify the original data structure in Eq. 1 and substitute the set of absolute co-ordinates of every stroke by the set of control points of its Bézier representation. The modified sketch $\mathcal{S}_{cp}$ would be

$$\mathcal{S}_{cp} = \left[\left(\mathbf{P}_0^{(j)}, q_0^{(j)} \right), \cdots, \left(\mathbf{P}_i^{(j)}, q_i^{(j)} \right), \cdots, \left(\mathbf{P}_{n_j}^{(j)}, q_{n_j}^{(j)} \right) \right]_{j=1}^N \tag{10}$$

When encoded this way by our Bézier encoder, each sketch is represented by a relatively shorter (mostly) list of parametric control points rather than the original long list of coordinates. In this format, different strokes can have different degrees, as indicated by the use of n_j above.

Given this sequential representation of a sketch dataset, we can now train a generative sketch model. Since $\mathcal{S}_{cp}$ is structurally same as original $\mathcal{S}$ apart from its length and the interpretation of its co-ordinates, we can re-use exactly the same architecture and training procedure as SketchRNN [8]. We use a variational sequence-to-sequence autoencoder [31] with a latent vector encoding the whole sketch. Thus one sketch is encoded first to a list of Bézier curves, and then to a latent vector in SketchRNN architecture; and decoded first to a list of curve parameters, and then rendered by the Bézier renderer. Please refer to Appendix B for a brief review of the SketchRNN architecture in the context of our problem.

Stroke Mode. Given a sketch $\mathcal{S}$ as set of strokes $\{\mathbf{T}_j\}_{j=1}^N$, we transform it as $\mathcal{S}_{st} = \{\mathcal{P}_j\}_{j=1}^N$ where $\mathcal{P}_j = \mathbf{e}(\mathbf{T}_j)$. We model the whole sketch using a sequence-to-sequence autoencoder, where each time-step processes one stroke represented as a fixed order Bézier curve. We use a bi-directional RNN to encode the whole sketch stroke-by-stroke. The hidden states (forward and backward) of the encoder $\overrightarrow{\mathbf{h}}_j, \overleftarrow{\mathbf{h}}_j$ at time-step j is given as

$$\left[\overrightarrow{\mathbf{h}}_j, \overleftarrow{\mathbf{h}}_j\right] = \text{BiRNN}(\mathcal{P}_{j-1}, \mathbf{h}_{i-1}; \Theta)$$

A latent vector $\mathbf{z} \in \mathbb{R}^{N_z}$ encoding the whole sketch is sampled using the parameters of a Gaussian distribution computed from the last hidden states

$$\mathbf{z} \sim \mathcal{N}(\mu_{\mathbf{z}}, \text{diag}(\sigma_{\mathbf{z}})), \text{ with } [\mu_{\mathbf{z}}, \sigma_{\mathbf{z}}] = f\left(\left[\overrightarrow{\mathbf{h}}_N; \overleftarrow{\mathbf{h}}_N\right]; \Theta\right)$$

An unidirectional decoder RNN is initialized using $\mathbf{z}$ and models the probability of jth stroke embedding conditioned on the hidden state $\mathbf{g}_j \in \mathbb{R}^{H^d}$

$$p(\mathcal{P}_j|\mathbf{g}_j; \Theta) = \text{GMM}\left(\mathcal{P}_j; \{\mu_j^m(\mathbf{g}_j), \Sigma_j^m(\mathbf{g}_j), \pi_j^m(\mathbf{g}_j)\}_{m=1}^M\right)$$
$$\mathbf{g}_j = \text{DecoderRNN}([\mathcal{P}_{j-1}; \mathbf{z}], \mathbf{g}_{j-1}; \Theta)$$
(11)

where $\{\mu_j^m, \Sigma_j^m, \pi_j^m\}$ are the parameters of the M-component GMM for the jth stroke. For computational efficiency, we consider diagonal Σ_j^m and by definition $\sum_m \pi_j^m = 1$. Given a trained model, we can sample from this distribution to generate similar $\mathcal{P}_j$ which will resemble its original domain data $\mathbf{T}_j$ as guaranteed by Property 1. Along with $\mathcal{P}_j$ at every step j, we also predict a stop bit $\widehat{b}_j \in [0, 1]$ denoting end of sketch which is compared against the ground-truth stop bit $b_j \triangleq \mathbb{1}_{j=N}$. The sketch generator is trained with the following objective function

$$\mathcal{L}(\{\mathcal{P}_j\}_{i=1}^{N}; \Theta) = \left[-\frac{1}{N_{max}} \sum_{j=1}^{N} \log \mathrm{GMM}\left(\mathcal{P}_j | \{\mu_j^m, \Sigma_j^m, \pi_j^m\}_{m=1}^{M}; \Theta \right) \right.$$

$$\left. -\frac{1}{N_{max}} \sum_{j=1}^{N} b_j \log \widehat{b}_j \right] - \frac{1}{2N_z} \sum_{i=1}^{N_z} \left(1 + \sigma_{\mathbf{z}}^i - \mu_{\mathbf{z}}^i - exp(\sigma_{\mathbf{z}}^i) \right) \tag{12}$$

The first two terms of $\mathcal{L}$ are the log-likelihood of a sequence $\{\mathcal{P}_j\}_{i=1}^{N}$ under the model and the loss due to the stop bit respectively. The third term denotes the KL-divergence loss for imposing a Gaussian prior on the latent code $\mathbf{z}$. The diagonal entries of Σ_j^m have been raised by $exp(\cdot)$ to make them non-negative and SOFTMAX$(\cdot)$ has been used to ensure $\sum_m \pi_j^m = 1$.

4   Experiments and Results

Dataset. *Quick, Draw!* is a large sketch dataset [8] collected as a part of an online game to draw a given category within a time-limit, in which thousands of people around the world participated. Due to the problem definition and structure of data used by our framework (see Eq. 1), *Quick, Draw!* is the most suitable dataset to validate it. Different versions of the dataset use different sampling rates at which the sketches are stored as point sequences. SketchRNN is known to work well only on data with lower sampling rate (i.e., $\mathbb{E}_\mathbf{T}[|\mathbf{T}|]$ is lower) than the raw data ($\mathbb{E}_\mathbf{T}[|\mathbf{T}|]$ is higher) recorded. Due to fixed length of Bézier representations, our framework can adapt to data with both high and low sampling rates without any modification. Although our method is generalizable across all categories, we experimented with few categories to validate our claims.

Our framework has two main components: **1.** Embedding each stroke into its Bézier representation. **2.** Training a generative model with the encoded sketches either in *control point mode* or *stroke mode*. As our BézierEncoder is a key contribution, we validate this in isolation, before comparing our whole BézierSketch framework to SketchRNN [8].

4.1   Stroke Embedding Experiments

Implementation Details. We created a dataset of all strokes from all sketches in a category of *Quick, Draw!* in order to train the stroke embedding model described in Sect. 3.1. We adopted some tricks that made the training and representation more efficient in practice. We normalized all strokes to start from the origin (i.e., $\mathbf{X}_1 = [0,0]^T$). Furthermore, we assumed that the first control point $\mathbf{P}_0$ of a Bézier representation is always aligned to the first absolute coordinate of the stroke (i.e., $\mathbf{X}_1 = \mathbf{P}_0$). Given these design choices, we can ignore the first control point (fixing it to origin) and only predict successive differences of control points (i.e., $\Delta\mathbf{P}_1 \triangleq \mathbf{P}_1 - \mathbf{P}_0$, $\Delta\mathbf{P}_2 \triangleq \mathbf{P}_2 - \mathbf{P}_1$ and so on) and then decode $\mathbf{P}_i$ as $\mathbf{P}_i = \sum_{i'=1}^{i} \Delta\mathbf{P}_{i'}$ while evaluating the loss in Eq. 7. We chose the hidden state dimension to be $h = 256$ and $n_{min} = 3, n_{max} = 9$ for learning multi-degree Bézier representation. To exclude over complicated strokes, we apply some heuristics to split a stroke into two or more. Specifically, we split a stroke into multiple parts based on two criteria: 1. Every part is within a maximum length and 2. Every part has only one sharp bend (determined by computing its curvature at a given point). We set the regularizer weight $\beta = 10^{-3}$.

Results. We first qualitatively demonstrate the results of inferring Bézier representations of input strokes. Figure 4(top left) shows fitting results for various curve orders (columns) – showing variable amounts of detail being captured at different orders. It also shows fitting examples at both low (above) and high (below) sampling rates – confirming that our encoder can adapt to both.

We next qualitatively illustrate the training dynamics of our model via the fit estimated as training progresses. The results in Fig. 4(middle) show the estimated fit during training in terms of Bézier curve (red) and control points (green) for a stroke defined by (blue) points. Recall that our encoder also predicts the interpolation parameters t that match each input point to a location on the curve. These correspondences are indicated in (cyan). Clearly both the fit and the estimated correspondences improve with training iterations. Refer to Appendix C in the supplementary document for similar visualization of more samples.

Given that our training data is grouped into categories, we next verify that our encoder indeed learns a generic Bèzier embedding, and is not overfitted to a specific category. Specifically, we compare the test loss for reconstructing data of each category when the encoder is trained on the same category as testing vs trained vs a disjoint category to testing. The results in Fig. 4(top right) shows that the embedding generalizes quite well to categories it is not trained on.

Finally, Fig. 4(bottom) shows examples of full sketches encoded by our encoder, and then decoded as Béziers. We can see that the encoded sketches reflect the input, but are smoother and cleaner.

4.2 Sketch Generation Experiments

Setup. In control point mode, a fully trained multi-degree embedding model is used to restructure all sketches in our dataset as $\mathcal{S}_{cp}$. We set $\mathcal{L}_{tolerance} = 10^{-3}$ to select the best n. We then train a SketchRNN-like model [8] using the restructured data. As data augmentation, we added 2D standard normal noise at all control points. Sampling from the latent space and decoding it by the decoder will generate sequence of control points and stroke/sketch ending bits. Treating one entire stroke as a set of control points, we can then draw it on a canvas using Eq. 3 with any required level of granularity.

In stroke mode, we encode each stroke with a fixed degree of $n = 9$. Very similar to *control point mode*, we use a Bi-LSTM to encode the whole sketch stroke-by-stroke and extract N_z dimensional latent vector. By conditioning on the latent vector, the decoder produces Bézier representation $\mathcal{P}$ of one stroke at each time-step. Thus, the length of a sketch coincides with the number of strokes present in the sketch. At each step of the decoder, we sample one stroke from

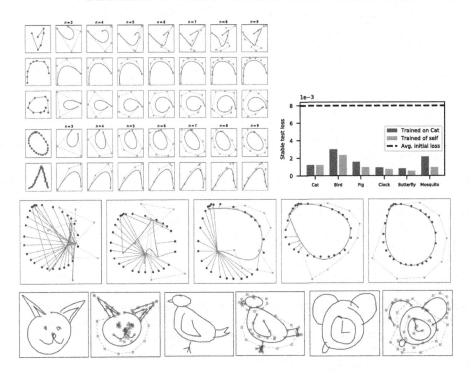

Fig. 4. Evaluating our BézierEncoder. (Top left) Learned representations of multi-degree Bézier stroke embedding. Top and bottom rows contain moderate and high-sampling rate respectively. (Top right) test loss for various categories when trained on same category vs "Cat", demonstrating transferability of the encoder. (Middle) visualising training dynamics. Blue: stroke to fit. Red and Green: Bézier curve and control points. Cyan: estimated point correspondence. (Bottom) examples of full sketches and their learned Bézier representation. (Color figure online)

$p(\mathcal{P}_j|\mathbf{g}_j, \Theta)$ which is modeled as a GMM with $M = 10$ mixture components. However, unlike the control point mode and its corresponding SketchRNN-like architecture, we do not use correlation parameter in the constituent Gaussians. This design choice makes the individual dimensions of the Gaussians independent, sampling from which is justified given Property. 1. Apart from $\mathcal{P}_j$, we predict one more quantity in practice: the start location $\mathbf{v}_j \triangleq (v_x, v_y)_j^T$ of the stroke w.r.t the whole sketch. The need for $\mathbf{v}_j$ arises due to the practical consideration of relocating the start of each individual stroke at the origin while encoding them.

Results. Qualitative results of generated unconditional sketch samples from both our model variants are shown in Fig. 5(a). We can see that, similarly to SketchRNN, BézierSketch generates diverse and plausible samples. However, uniquely our samples are high-resolution vector graphic sketches. Figure 5(b) also

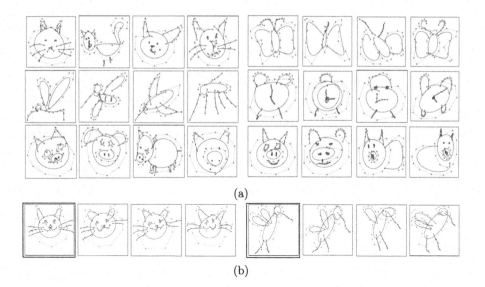

(a)

(b)

Fig. 5. Qualitatively evaluating BézierSketch. (a) Samples drawn unconditionally in control point mode (left half) and stroke mode (right half). (b) Sketch samples generated by conditioning on the first sketch (double bordered) in each set.

shows examples of conditional samples where the right group of three images are samples conditioned on the left sketch encoding.

The use of Bézier curves as stroke representation reduces the average length of a given stroke's representation significantly and as a direct consequence, the description length for whole sketches as well. In Fig. 6, we compare the length histograms of original data and its Bézier representation both on stroke and sketch level, confirming that Béziers are systematically shorter (left). This is the same for strokes and sketches sampled by vanilla and SketchRNN and BézierSketch respectively (right).

This property of shorter representations for any given sketch means that our generator should have an advantage modeling longer sketches compared to vanilla SketchRNN since it only needs to model shorter sequences. To evaluate this, we use a modified Fréchet Inception Distance (FID) [9] score to compare the generated samples from both models. We first trained both our generator model and SketchRNN on the entire dataset (of each category). We then create a subset of sketches whose original length is $l \pm 20$ and use them to generate samples. All original and generated samples are rendered on a canvas and projected down to a concise feature vector using pre-trained Sketch-a-Net 2.0 [33] classifier. We compute the empirical mean and covariance of both real samples and generated samples as (μ_r, Σ_r) and (μ_g, Σ_g) and then estimate modified FID as:

$$\text{FID} = \|\mu_r - \mu_g\|^2 + \text{Tr}(\Sigma_r + \Sigma_g - 2(\Sigma_r \Sigma_g)^{1/2})$$

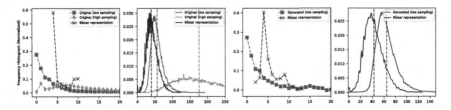

Fig. 6. Stroke/Sketch length histogram for original data (left) and generated samples (right). Bézier encodings are shorter sequences than the raw data.

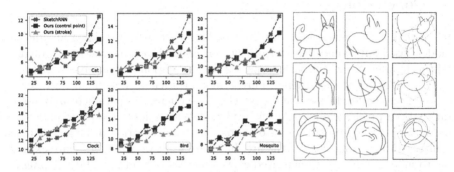

Fig. 7. Left: FID score (↓) vs length of sketch shows the effectiveness of our generative model on longer sketches. Right: Qualitative samples of long sketches. Three columns denote the original sketch, SketchRNN and our BézierSketch.

The results in Fig. 7 plots the modified FID score with increasing length value l for both SketchRNN and our model on each category of sketches. We can see that our model leads to improved (lower) FID score, especially for longer sketches. This is illustrated qualitatively in Fig. 7, where we can see that for longer sketches, our framework produces much more reliable reconstruction than QuickDraw, which fails to make reasonable reconstruction in these cases.

Other Applications. Although crafted with sketches in mind, our framework can be adapted to other applications like handwriting generation (in line with the work of [7]) with little to no modification. In fact, any 2D sequence data with two-level hierarchical representation (e.g., stroke and sketch) can be modeled using the same framework. Online handwritten characters are composed of relatively short strokes which we model with Bézier curves. We use the online handwritten sentences from the IAM handwriting database [19], embed the constituent strokes with our Bézier representation and train our generative model for words. Figure 8 shows qualitative samples from our resulting word generator.

Fig. 8. Unconditionally generating handwritten words from the IAM database.

5 Conclusions

In this paper we presented an inverse graphics approach to training an efficient model-based single-pass stroke-to-Bézier encoder via reconstruction through a Bézier decoder. Such approach surpasses the conventional fitting-based methods in terms of quality and efficiency. Furthermore, this enabled us to advance generative sketch models by generating sketches as sequences of parameterized curves rather than pixels, leading to arbitrary-resolution scalable vector graphic samples. This new representation also enables better generation of longer sketches compared to existing state of the art. In future work we will investigate extending to more complex parameterized curves such as B-splines, and developing an encoder to predict curves from rasterized images directly.

References

1. Bishop, C.M.: Mixture density networks. Technical report, Aston University (1994)
2. Bowman, S.R., Vilnis, L., Vinyals, O., Dai, A., Jozefowicz, R., Bengio, S.: Generating sentences from a continuous space. In: CoNLL (2016)
3. De Boor, C., De Boor, C., Mathématicien, E.U., De Boor, C., De Boor, C.: A Practical Guide to Splines, vol. 27. Springer, New York (1978)
4. Dey, S., Riba, P., Dutta, A., Llados, J., Song, Y.Z.: Doodle to search: practical zero-shot sketch-based image retrieval. In: CVPR (2019)
5. Ganin, Y., Kulkarni, T., Babuschkin, I., Eslami, S.M.A., Vinyals, O.: Synthesizing programs for images using reinforced adversarial learning. In: ICML (2018)
6. Goodfellow, I., et al.: Generative adversarial nets. In: NIPS (2014)
7. Graves, A.: Generating sequences with recurrent neural networks. CoRR abs/1308.0850 (2013)
8. Ha, D., Eck, D.: A neural representation of sketch drawings. In: ICLR (2018)
9. Heusel, M., Ramsauer, H., Unterthiner, T., Nessler, B., Hochreiter, S.: GANs trained by a two time-scale update rule converge to a local nash equilibrium. In: NIPS (2017)
10. Hinton, G.E., Salakhutdinov, R.R.: Reducing the dimensionality of data with neural networks. Science **313**(5786), 504–507 (2006)
11. Isola, P., Zhu, J.Y., Zhou, T., Efros, A.A.: Image-to-image translation with conditional adversarial networks. In: CVPR (2017)
12. Kingma, D.P., Welling, M.: Auto-encoding variational bayes. ICLR (2014)
13. Klare, B., Li, Z., Jain, A.: Matching forensic sketches to mug shot photos. IEEE Trans. Pattern Anal. Mach. Intell. **33**(3), 639–646 (2011)

14. Kulkarni, T.D., Whitney, W., Kohli, P., Tenenbaum, J.B.: Deep convolutional inverse graphics network. In: NIPS (2015)
15. Lake, B.M., Salakhutdinov, R., Tenenbaum, J.B.: Human-level concept learning through probabilistic program induction. Science **350**(6266), 1332–1338 (2015)
16. Laube, P., Franz, M.O., Umlauf, G.: Deep learning parametrization for B-spline curve approximation. In: 2018 International Conference on 3D Vision (3DV) (2018)
17. Liu, Y., Wang, W.: A revisit to least squares orthogonal distance fitting of parametric curves and surfaces. In: Chen, F., Jüttler, B. (eds.) GMP 2008. LNCS, vol. 4975, pp. 384–397. Springer, Heidelberg (2008). https://doi.org/10.1007/978-3-540-79246-8_29
18. Lopes, R.G., Ha, D., Eck, D., Shlens, J.: A learned representation for scalable vector graphics. In: ICCV (2019)
19. Marti, U.V., Bunke, H.: A full English sentence database for off-line handwriting recognition. In: ICDAR (1999)
20. Masood, A., Ejaz, S.: An efficient algorithm for robust curve fitting using cubic Bezier curves. In: Huang, D.-S., Zhang, X., Reyes García, C.A., Zhang, L. (eds.) ICIC 2010. LNCS (LNAI), vol. 6216, pp. 255–262. Springer, Heidelberg (2010). https://doi.org/10.1007/978-3-642-14932-0_32
21. Pang, K., et al.: Generalising fine-grained sketch-based image retrieval. In: CVPR (2019)
22. Plass, M., Stone, M.: Curve-fitting with piecewise parametric cubics. In: SIGGRAPH (1983)
23. Rabiner, L., Juang, B.: An introduction to hidden Markov models. IEEE ASSP Mag. **3**(1), 4–16 (1986)
24. Radford, A., Metz, L., Chintala, S.: Unsupervised representation learning with deep convolutional generative adversarial networks. In: ICLR (2016)
25. Revow, M., Williams, C.K.I., Hinton, G.E.: Using generative models for handwritten digit recognition. IEEE Trans. Pattern Anal. Mach. Intell. **18**(6), 592–606 (1996)
26. Romaszko, L., Williams, C.K.I., Moreno, P., Kohli, P.: Vision-as-inverse-graphics: obtaining a rich 3D explanation of a scene from a single image. In: ICCVW (2017)
27. Salomon, D.: Curves and Surfaces for Computer Graphics. Springer, Heidelberg (2007). https://doi.org/10.1007/0-387-28452-4
28. Sangkloy, P., Burnell, N., Ham, C., Hays, J.: The sketchy database: learning to retrieve badly drawn bunnies. In: SIGGRAPH (2016)
29. Shao, L., Zhou, H.: Curve fitting with Bezier cubics. Graphical Models Image Process. **58**(3), 223–232 (1996)
30. Song, J., Pang, K., Song, Y., Xiang, T., Hospedales, T.M.: Learning to sketch with shortcut cycle consistency. In: CVPR (2018)
31. Srivastava, N., Mansimov, E., Salakhudinov, R.: Unsupervised learning of video representations using LSTMs. In: ICML (2015)
32. Sutton, R.S., McAllester, D.A., Singh, S.P., Mansour, Y.: Policy gradient methods for reinforcement learning with function approximation. In: NIPS (1999)
33. Yu, Q., Yang, Y., Liu, F., Song, Y.Z., Xiang, T., Hospedales, T.: Sketch-a-net: a deep neural network that beats humans. Int. J. Comput. Vis. **122**, 411–425 (2017)
34. Yu, Q., Yang, Y., Song, Y.Z., Xiang, T., Hospedales, T.: Sketch-a-net that beats humans. In: BMVC (2015)
35. Zheng, W., Bo, P., Liu, Y., Wang, W.: Fast B-spline curve fitting by L-BFGS. Comput. Aided Geometr. Design **29**(7), 448–462 (2012)

Semantic Relation Preserving Knowledge Distillation for Image-to-Image Translation

Zeqi Li$^{(\boxtimes)}$, Ruowei Jiang, and Parham Aarabi

ModiFace, Toronto, Canada
{lizeqi,irene,parham}@modiface.com

Abstract. Generative adversarial networks (GANs) have shown significant potential in modeling high dimensional distributions of image data, especially on image-to-image translation tasks. However, due to the complexity of these tasks, state-of-the-art models often contain a tremendous amount of parameters, which results in large model size and long inference time. In this work, we propose a novel method to address this problem by applying knowledge distillation together with distillation of a semantic relation preserving matrix. This matrix, derived from the teacher's feature encoding, helps the student model learn better semantic relations. In contrast to existing compression methods designed for classification tasks, our proposed method adapts well to the image-to-image translation task on GANs. Experiments conducted on 5 different datasets and 3 different pairs of teacher and student models provide strong evidence that our methods achieve impressive results both qualitatively and quantitatively.

Keywords: Knowledge distillation · Generative adversarial networks · Image-to-image translation · Model compression

1 Introduction

Generative adversarial networks (GANs) [9] have presented significant potential in modeling high dimensional distributions of image data, on a variety of visual tasks. Many of these tasks, such as style-transfer [16,32] and super-resolution [18], are considered to be image-to-image translation tasks, in which we train a model to map images from one domain to another. The community has shown success in researching solutions to generate high fidelity images [2,27] and dealing with unpaired data [32]. The success in these works has also led to a popular

---

Z. Li and R. Jiang—Equal contribution.

Electronic supplementary material The online version of this chapter (https://doi.org/10.1007/978-3-030-58574-7_39) contains supplementary material, which is available to authorized users.

© Springer Nature Switzerland AG 2020
A. Vedaldi et al. (Eds.): ECCV 2020, LNCS 12371, pp. 648–663, 2020.
https://doi.org/10.1007/978-3-030-58574-7_39

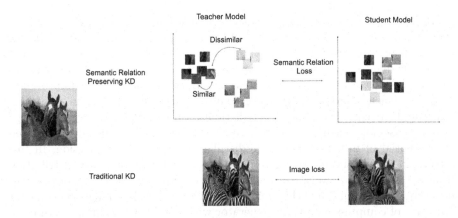

Fig. 1. A visualization of our proposed idea. In the top row, we show that our proposed method transfers the semantic relations learned in a teacher model to a student model. In high dimensional space, feature encoding for pixels of the same semantic class may locate closer. The bottom row shows how traditional knowledge distillation would work on image-to-image translation tasks

trend of developing mobile applications based on generative models. However, little work has been done in making these models efficient on mobile devices. As a result, the state-of-the-art GAN models are often large and slow on resource-limited edge devices. For instance, a CycleGAN [32] model needs 2.69 s to process one image of resolution 256 × 256 on a single CPU core of Intel(R) Xeon(R) E5-2686, with the model being 44M large.

With achievements of convolutional neural networks (CNNs), many works [10,11,14,15,26] for model compression have been proposed to improve model efficiency in a variety of computer vision tasks including classification, object detection and semantic segmentation. In 2016, Han et al. [10] proposed a three-stage pipeline that first prunes the model by cutting down less important connections and then quantizes the weights and applies Huffman encoding. They successfully reduced AlexNet [17] and VGG-16 [29] by 35× to 49× on the ImageNet dataset [8]. This method, with a complex training pipeline, requires a great amount of manual efforts in each stage. In [15,26], efforts have been dedicated to improving model efficiency by redesigning convolutional layers into separable convolutional layers. Redesigning network architecture often requires domain experts to explore the large design space and conduct a significant amount of experiments. Later works such as [11,14], have leveraged techniques in neural architectural search and reinforcement learning to efficiently reduce the amount of such manual efforts by performing pruning and network designing based on a trained agent's predictions. Upon successful results in compressing networks for classification tasks, research works [4,20,25] have further extended the aforementioned techniques to object detection and semantic segmentation.

However, the aforementioned solutions do not adapt well to GANs, as GANs typically demand excessive amounts of training processes and manual design efforts. The training of generative adversarial networks is usually harder and less stable due to the design of alternating training strategy for the discriminator and the generator. Therefore, we explore methods that not only improve the model's efficiency but also provide guidance while training. Hinton et al. [13] reinvented the concept of knowledge distillation to transfer the dark knowledge from an ensemble teacher model to a single student model, which demonstrated the potential of utilizing knowledge distillation in model compression. In this setting, inexplicit and intermediate information such as probability distribution from the teacher's network can be leveraged at training time to guide the student. Given the intuition of this concept, knowledge distillation naturally fits our objective of compressing a GAN generator with a guided training procedure.

In this work, we apply knowledge distillation on image-to-image translation tasks and further propose a novel approach to distill information of semantic relationships from teacher to student. Our hypothesis is that, given a feature tensor, feature pixels of the same semantic class may have similar activation patterns while feature pixels of different semantic classes may be dissimilar. To better illustrate our idea, we provide a visualization in Fig. 1. For example, on the horse-to-zebra task, feature tensors of horses may locate closer but far from other background pixels such as sky and grass in high dimensional space. A well-trained teacher model is able to capture these correlations better among different semantic pixels at both dataset and image level. We will also demonstrate evidence to support this intuition in Methods.

Our main contributions of this work are:

- We present a novel method of applying knowledge distillation in compressing GAN generators on image-to-image translation task by distilling the semantic relations. The student's pairwise similarities among feature pixels are trained in a supervised setting by the teacher's.
- We experimentally demonstrate the potential of this method on 5 different image-to-image translation benchmark datasets. Our results, both qualitatively and quantitatively, evidently show that our method trains the student model to be on par with and sometimes better than the original teacher model.

2   Related Work

2.1   GANs for Image-to-Image Translation

Along with the success of GANs in modeling high dimensional data, image-to-image translation tasks are dominated by GANs nowadays due to GANs' superiority in generating images of high fidelity and extendibility on different data domains. In [16], authors proposed a model known as Pix2Pix applying conditional GANs on paired image-to-image translation tasks such as transferring from sketches/semantic labels to photos. A subsequent work CycleGAN

[32], tackling unpaired image-to-image translation tasks between two domains, proposed to construct two generators transferring images in both directions and enforce an additional cycle consistency loss during the training. StarGAN [6] has further extended the capability of CycleGAN to the multi-domain translation by adding a domain-specific attribute vector in the input while training the generators.

2.2 Semantic Relation Preserving Knowledge Distillation

There has been a long line of efforts dedicated to transferring knowledge from a teacher model to a student model. Hinton et al. [13] reinvented the concept of knowledge distillation in which a single student model learns the knowledge from an ensemble of separately trained models. Comparing to one-hot output, the information contained within a teacher's soft logits provides more concrete knowledge and helps guide the training of a student model. In addition to classification tasks, this idea has also been widely adopted in numerous computer vision tasks such as object detection and semantic segmentation [3,21].

Recently, it is observed that learning class relationship enhances model performance non-trivially in various problems. Many works [5,23,24,30] have shown progress in applying similarity and relational learning in a knowledge distillation setting. In [23] and [24], they both demonstrated that correlation among instances can be transferred and well learned in a student model through geometric similarity learning of multiple instances. In [30], they demonstrated empirically that similar activation patterns would appear on images of the same class (e.g. dog). Based on this observation, they proposed to guide the student with a similarity matrix of image instances calculated as the outer product of the teacher's feature encoding of certain layers. However, on the image-to-image translation tasks, image-wise relationships do not give comprehensive information as they are typically images from the same class (e.g. horses, zebras). Might similar correlation patterns exist among semantic pixels? In this work, we explore the idea to retain pixel-wise semantic relation in the student model, by transferring this knowledge from the teacher.

2.3 Model Compression on GANs

Image-to-image translation tasks using generative models are essentially different from classification tasks with discriminative models. Traditional model compression approaches are designed for classification tasks, which do not adapt well to GANs trivially. Work [1] applied KD to compress the GAN generator by enforcing a joint loss of pixel-wise loss and adversarial loss with a shared discriminator, with a focus on the unconditional image generation task. Another work [28] devoted effort to compressing GAN models through a co-evolutionary strategy of the two generators in CycleGAN [32], resulting in a method that efficiently eliminates redundant convolutional filters. However, it requires external effort to maintain the quality of generated images by controlling the model compression ratio and other hyper-parameters.

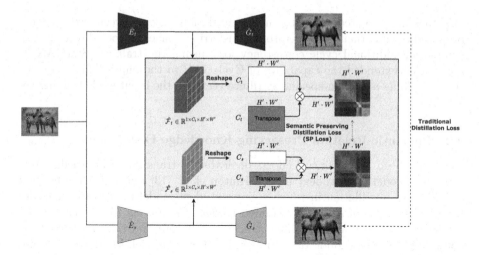

Fig. 2. An overview of our training pipeline. The semantic relation activation matrix is calculated as the outer product of the feature encoding. A distillation loss is used to compare the teacher's activation matrix and the student's

In this work, we aim to tackle the GAN compression problem on the image-to-image translation task. Our proposed KD method inspired by [30] from the classification task significantly reduces the amount of effort needed for hyper-parameter tuning and achieves better image fidelity while realizing effective compression by leveraging the semantic relation similarity between feature pixels of images from a well-trained teacher model.

3   Methods

The goal of this work is to improve GANs efficiency by utilizing knowledge distillation in compressing the generator. As discussed in the Introduction, the training of GANs is challenging. In addition to the vanilla knowledge distillation loss, we separate each generator into one encoder and one decoder and formulate a semantic preserving loss based on the feature encoding produced by the encoder. In Fig. 2, we present an overview of our distillation strategies in preserving semantic relationships. At an intermediate layer, we represent semantic relations by calculating pairwise activation similarities on pixels of the feature encoding and transfer the knowledge via a distillation loss on the similarity matrices. This loss can be added in addition to traditional distillation loss on the final generated images. In this section, we will discuss details about how we apply vanilla knowledge distillation and semantic preserving distillation on GANs.

3.1   Vanilla Knowledge Distillation on GANs

In traditional knowledge distillation, the task is formulated as:

$$\theta_s = \operatorname*{argmin}_{\theta} \mathbb{E}_{x_i, y_i} \Big[(1 - \alpha) \mathcal{L}(y_i, f_\theta(x_i)) + \alpha \mathcal{L}(f_t(x_i), f_\theta(x_i)) \Big], \qquad (1)$$

where y_i denotes the ground truth for input x_i, $f_\theta(x_i)$ and $f_t(x_i)$ denote the student model output and teacher model output respectively. n is the number of inputs and α is a hyper-parameter to balance between teacher's output and the ground truth. Equation (1) encourages the network to minimize two terms: 1) the loss between ground truth and student's output, and 2) the loss between the teacher's output and the student's output. The second part of the objective function is designed to help the student learn inexplicit knowledge on different tasks. For example, on a classification task, soft logits with temperature control are matched between the student and the teacher to encourage the student to mimic the teacher.

In the setting of generative adversarial training, an example approach to applying knowledge distillation would be introducing another minimax game between the teacher's generated images $G_t(x)$ and the student's $G_s(x)$:

$$\min_{G_s} \max_{\mathcal{D}_s} V(G_s, \mathcal{D}_s) = \alpha \Big(\mathbb{E}_{y \sim \mathcal{P}_{data}(y)} [\log \mathcal{D}_s(y)] + \mathbb{E}_{x \sim \mathcal{P}_{data}(x)} [\log(1 - \mathcal{D}_s(G_s(x)))] \Big)$$
$$+ (1 - \alpha) \mathcal{L}_{KD}, \qquad (2)$$

where

$$\mathcal{L}_{KD} = \mathbb{E}_{y \sim \mathcal{P}_{data}(G_t(x))} [\log \mathcal{D}'_s(y)] + \mathbb{E}_{x \sim \mathcal{P}_{data}(x)} [\log(1 - \mathcal{D}'_s(G_s(x)))], \qquad (3)$$

Subscript t and s indicate components of the teacher and the student. $\mathcal{D}_s$ is the discriminator for the student's output and real images while $\mathcal{D}'_s$ differentiate student's output and teacher's. x and y are real images from its respective class.

In our preliminary experiments, we tried using such adversarial loss between teacher and student's output, but we found this strategy is unstable and difficult to train. Besides, we did not observe improved performance on converged experiments. Previous works [16,32] have shown the benefits of mixing GAN objective with other traditional losses such as L1. Therefore, we apply vanilla knowledge distillation by computing a traditional reconstruction loss comparing teacher's and student's output. For example in CycleGAN [32], the original loss is weighted among two GAN losses and one cycle consistency loss. We add the distillation loss only on cycle consistency loss which is an L1 norm loss. Our vanilla knowledge distillation setting has the following objective:

$$\mathcal{L}(G_s, F_s, D_X, D_Y) = \mathcal{L}_{adv}(G_s, D_Y, X, Y) + \mathcal{L}_{adv}(F_s, D_X, Y, X)$$
$$+ \lambda(\alpha \mathcal{L}_{cyc}(G_s, F_s, X, Y) + (1 - \alpha)\mathcal{L}_{cyc}(G_s, F_s, X_t, Y_t)), \qquad (4)$$

where $\mathcal{L}_{adv}$ is the adversarial loss and $\mathcal{L}_{cyc}$ is the reconstruction loss. Also, G_s and F_s denote generators transferring from style class X to Y and Y to X respectively. Accordingly, X_t and Y_t are teacher generated reconstruction

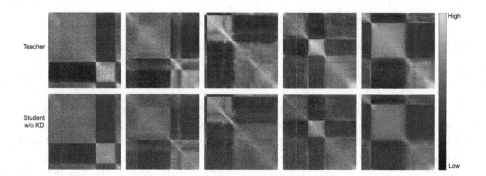

Fig. 3. To enhance the interpretability of this semantic similarity mapping, pixels are grouped and aligned together based on their semantic class. Brighter colors indicate a higher correlation. The teacher model exhibits similarity for semantic pixels within the same semantic class (diagonal block matrices) and dissimilarity across different semantic classes (off-diagonal block matrices). This matches with our hypothesis, where the teacher model displays clearer semantic relationship than the student model

images. λ is the balancing coefficient. Notations are adapted from [32]. We also apply similar settings in Pix2Pix [16] training. The detailed objective function is described in Supplementary.

3.2 Semantic Preserving Loss

Notation. We consider a generator G to be composed by two parts: an encoder $\hat{E}$ that encodes the input images and a generator $\hat{G}$ that decodes and generates the output images. We note y_i to be the output image of i-*th* input x_i where $y_i = G(x) = \hat{G}(\hat{E}(x_i))$.

Semantic Relation Activation Matrix. Tung and Mori [30] demonstrated interestingly distinct activation patterns among image instances of different classes versus image instances of the same class. However, on the image-to-image translation tasks, less information is contained in instances' correlation as they are typically from the same class (e.g. horses, oranges). Our hypothesis is that similarity and dissimilarity might likewise present in the feature encoding of different semantic pixels, which is also more informative on the image-to-image translation tasks. A distillation loss can be introduced to penalize the difference between a teacher and a student's encoded similarity. We represent this activation matrix by the outer product of feature encoding $\mathcal{F}$, similar to [30,31]. Here, we define the feature encoding $\mathcal{F}^{(i)}$ to be the output matrix of the i-th image example at the last layer of encoder $\hat{E}$:

$$\hat{\mathcal{F}}_t^{(i)} = \hat{E}_t(x_i); \hat{\mathcal{F}}_s^{(i)} = \hat{E}_s(x_i), \tag{5}$$

$$\hat{\mathcal{F}}_t^{(i)} \in \mathbb{R}^{1 \times C_t \times H' \times W'} \rightarrow \mathcal{F}_t^{(i)} \in \mathbb{R}^{C_t \times (H' \cdot W')},$$
$$\hat{\mathcal{F}}_s^{(i)} \in \mathbb{R}^{1 \times C_s \times H' \times W'} \rightarrow \mathcal{F}_s^{(i)} \in \mathbb{R}^{C_s \times (H' \cdot W')}, \tag{6}$$

where H' and W' indicate the feature encoding height and width while C_t/C_s are number of channels respectively. We use a batch size of 1. We then calculate semantic relation activation matrices $\mathcal{A} \in \mathbb{R}^{(H' \cdot W') \times (H' \cdot W')}$ as the outer product of $\mathcal{F}$, followed by a row-wise L2 normalization.

$$
\hat{A}_t = \mathcal{F}_t^{(i)} \cdot \mathcal{F}_t^{(i)^T}; \hat{A}_s = \mathcal{F}_s^{(i)} \cdot \mathcal{F}_s^{(i)^T},
$$
$$
\mathcal{A}_{t[k,:]} = \frac{\hat{A}_t}{\sqrt{\sum_j \hat{A}_{t[k,j]}^2}}; \mathcal{A}_{s[k,:]} = \frac{\hat{A}_s}{\sqrt{\sum_j \hat{A}_{s[k,j]}^2}}, \tag{7}
$$

We show some evidence to support our intuition of semantic relation activation matrices in Fig. 3. We sample 5 horse and zebra images from COCO dataset [19] which provides ground truth segmentation masks, and generate all corresponding teacher's and student's activation matrices $\mathcal{A}$ by Eq. 7. We group the values by pixels of the same semantic class to clearly show different activation patterns. The clear blockwise patterns in the teacher model indicate that pixels of the same semantic class are much more similar compared to pixels of different classes. On the other hand, this pattern is less observable in the student model learned without distillation. This empirical finding strongly supports our hypothesis that there exists certain relation patterns which can be explicitly transferred from a teacher network to a student network. Secondly, the activation matrix $\mathcal{A}$ is independent of the number of channels in feature $\mathcal{F}$, which avoids the difficulty of introducing a handcrafted feature loss to match $\mathcal{F}_t$ and $\mathcal{F}_s$ in different feature space.

We define our semantic preserving distillation loss $\mathcal{L}_{SP}$ to be the L1 loss between two activation matrices:

$$
\mathcal{L}_{SP} = \mathbb{E}_{x \sim \mathcal{P}_{data}(x)} \big[\|\mathcal{A}_t - \mathcal{A}_s\|_1 \big], \tag{8}
$$

In preliminary experiments, we also tried L2 loss in enforcing the matching of two matrices but didn't obtain better results. Our full objective is then,

$$
\mathcal{L} = \mathcal{L}_{adv_A} + \mathcal{L}_{adv_B} + \gamma_1 \cdot \mathcal{L}_{SP_A} + \gamma_2 \cdot \mathcal{L}_{SP_B}
$$
$$
+ \lambda \Big(\alpha \mathcal{L}_{cyc}(G_s, F_s, X, Y) + (1 - \alpha) \mathcal{L}_{cyc}(G_s, F_s, X_t, Y_t) \Big). \tag{9}
$$

where A and B indicate the generators of each direction respectively. γ_1, γ_2 and α are hyper-parameters. λ is the balancing coefficient.

4   Experiments

4.1   Different Image-to-Image Translation Datasets

Setup. To illustrate the effectiveness of our method on GAN compression, we qualitatively and quantitatively evaluated it on 5 benchmark image-to-image translation datasets including horse $\leftrightarrow$ zebra, summer $\leftrightarrow$ winter, apple $\leftrightarrow$ orange, tiger $\leftrightarrow$ leopard and Cityscapes label $\leftrightarrow$ photo.

We followed CycleGAN implementation and setup from the official PyTorch implementation[1] for a fair comparison. Specifically, the teacher generator stacks one 7×7 stride-1 convolutional layer, two 3×3 stride-2 convolutional layers, six or nine residual blocks, two 3×3 stride-2 transposed convolutional layers and one final 7×7 stride-1 convolutional layer sequentially. The student generator has the same architecture as the teacher generator but is narrower for each layer by a factor of 2 or 4 depending on the datasets trained on. Since all generators share the same structure in downsampling and upsampling parts, we use the number of residual blocks and the number of filters in the first convolutional layer to specify the generator architecture. This convention defines both depth and width of the model. Specifically, we used Resnet9, ngf64 and Resnet9, ngf16 as our major teacher student model pair for all datasets except horse ↔ zebra dataset, where Resnet9, ngf32 is used for the student model. As the Cityscapes dataset is inherently a paired dataset of the street view photo images and their corresponding semantic segmentation labels, we also conducted experiments in a Pix2Pix setting. The teacher and the student generators in our Pix2Pix experiments have a UNet structure [16]. The discriminator network follows the PatchGAN discriminator [16] structure. For all datasets, we trained and evaluated all models on images of resolution 256×256.

Quantitative Evaluation Metrics. We adopt *Fréchet Inception Distance* (FID) [12] on horse ↔ zebra, summer ↔ winter, apple ↔ orange and tiger ↔ leopard datasets. FID calculates the Wasserstein-2 distance between feature

Table 1. The FID values for references/baselines (top) and variations of our methods (bottom). We conducted experiments on datasets horse-to-zebra ($h \rightarrow z$, $z \rightarrow h$), summer-to-winter ($s \rightarrow w$, $w \rightarrow s$), apple-to-orange ($a \rightarrow o$, $o \rightarrow a$), tiger-to-leopard ($t \rightarrow l$, $l \rightarrow t$). Lower is better. Both Co-evolutionary [28] and ThiNet [22] apply pruning while Co-evolutionary is specifically designed for compressing CycleGAN and ThiNet is a pruning method adapted from the classification task. For a fair comparison to Co-evolutionary and ThiNet, the models compared above have similar model size and computation requirement. (see Table 2) In all cases except $t \rightarrow l$, our method further improves over 50% relatively compared to the baseline method (vanilla KD). FID trade off curve for varying ngf is in Supplementary

	$h \rightarrow z$	$z \rightarrow h$	$s \rightarrow w$	$w \rightarrow s$	$a \rightarrow o$	$o \rightarrow a$	$t \rightarrow l$	$l \rightarrow t$
Teacher	84.01	136.85	76.99	74.39	132.37	130.72	76.68	77.60
Student	94.95	141.64	**76.47**	74.90	132.99	137.10	93.98	89.37
ThiNet [22]	189.28	184.88	81.06	80.17	–	–	–	–
Co-evolutionary [28]	96.15	157.90	79.16	78.58	–	–	–	–
Vanilla KD	106.10	144.52	80.10	79.33	127.21	135.82	82.04	87.29
Intermediate KD	97.20	143.43	77.75	**74.67**	126.90	133.16	86.82	92.99
+ SP	90.65	143.03	78.75	76.21	125.90	132.83	81.53	86.52
+ 2 direction SP (**Ours**)	**86.31**	**140.15**	76.59	75.69	**121.17**	**132.83**	**81.17**	**80.75**

---

[1] CycleGAN official PyTorch implementation: https://github.com/junyanz/pytorch-CycleGAN-and-pix2pix .

Table 2. Computation and storage results for models on major experiments. T: teacher, S1, S2: student. Our models achieve superior performance in all tasks with a smaller/similar model size and computation compared to Co-evolutionary and ThiNet. We choose S1 on h ↔ z and S2 on the rest of the datasets. The choice is made based on the gap between teacher and student baseline performance. Latency measurement plot for varying ngf is in Supplementary

Model	Size (MB)	# Params	Memory (MB)	FLOPs
ResNet 9blocks, ngf 64 (T)	44	11.38M	431.61	47.22G
ThiNet [22]	11 (75%↓)	–	–	–
Co-evolutionary [28] h ↔ z	10 (77%↓)	–	–	13.06G (72%↓)
Co-evolutionary [28] s ↔ w	7.6 (83%↓)	–	–	10.99G (77%↓)
Co-evolutionary [28] cityscapes	12 (73%↓)	–	–	16.45G (65%↓)
ResNet 9blocks, ngf 32 (S1)	11 (75%↓)	2.85M (75%↓)	216.95 (50%↓)	12.14G (74%↓)
ResNet 9blocks, ngf 16 (S2)	2.8 (94%↓)	0.72M (94%↓)	109.62 (75%↓)	3.20G (93%↓)

maps extracted by Inception network from fake and real images. As a distance measure, a lower score is preferred for a higher correlation between synthetic and real images. On Cityscapes label → photo dataset [7], we use FCN-score following the evaluation method used by Isola et al. [16]. The method uses FCN-8s network, a pretrained semantic classifier, to score on synthetic photos with standard segmentation evaluation metrics from the Cityscapes benchmark including mean pixel accuracy, mean class accuracy and mean class Intersection over Union (IoU).

Quantitative Comparison. In Table 1, we list our experiments conducted on 4 unpaired datasets trained on CycleGAN. We compare our results with two previous works [22,28] on pruning and different settings of our design. As a reference to the compression ratio, we show a table of computed model size, the number of parameters, memory usage and the number of FLOPs in Table 2.

We explore variations of our methods on CycleGAN by conducting the following experiments: 1) We introduce an intermediate distillation loss on the fake image generated by the first generator in the cycle, computing an L1 norm difference between the teacher's generated image and the student's. We note this as **intermediate KD**. 2) We experiment with semantic relation preserving loss in two parts of the cycle. Semantic Preserving (**SP**) indicates that we only apply the semantic distillation loss on the first generator of the cycle (i.e. $\gamma_2 = 0$ in Eq. (9)). **2 direction SP** denotes that we applied the semantic distillation loss on both generators in the cycle. '+' means it was added in addition to **Vanilla KD**.

Though all compared models reach a similar performance on the $s \leftrightarrow w$ dataset, our method accomplishes critically better performance than other methods on the rest of the datasets. Adding our proposed distillation losses on both generators boosts the performance significantly from vanilla knowledge distillation, with the possibility to outperform the original teacher model on some tasks. We will further demonstrate visual evidence in later discussions. On the summer-

Table 3. FCN-score for different models on the Cityscapes through CycleGAN training

	Mean pixel acc.	Mean class acc.	Mean class IoU
Teacher	0.592	0.179	0.138
Student	0.584	0.182	0.129
ThiNet [22]	0.218	0.089	0.054
Co-evolutionary [28]	0.542	**0.212**	0.131
Ours	**0.704**	0.205	**0.154**

to-winter task ($s \leftrightarrow w$), however, we do not observe performance gain and we suspect the reason is that the baseline student model barely differs from the teacher model numerically. There is limited space and knowledge for improvement to take place. Additionally, we run experiments on Cityscapes dataset and show FCN-score in Table 3. Interestingly, we notice a dramatic increase on FCN-score in applying the proposed method but only a similar or slightly better quality of image compared to the original model is observed (See Supplementary). Our proposed semantic preserving loss strongly reacts to this semantic segmentation dataset, by making pixels more recognizable in a semantic way.

Fig. 4. Images generated by the teacher model, prior work [28] and our proposed method on their selected examples. The top row displays input horse image and generated zebra; the bottom row displays input zebra image and generated horse images

Qualitative Results. In this section, we present visual observations on the generated images from our models and reference models. To compare our results to [28], we also generated images using our models on their selected input images displayed in Fig. 4. Evidently, our generated images contain a more realistic horse/zebra and reduce the artifacts to a minimum in the background. In the earlier discussion, we mention the potential of the student model to outperform

Input   Teacher   Student   Ours

Fig. 5. Two examples of the apple-to-orange task. Clear and realistic texture is generated using our method, even outperforming the teacher

Input   Teacher   Student   Ours

Fig. 6. SP method translated more zebras than the teacher and the student.

Input   Teacher   Student   Ours

Fig. 7. An example on the horse-to-zebra task. A more detailed and realistic eye is preserved from horse to generated zebra image in our model

the teacher by adding our proposed semantic preserving loss, with the numerical evidence in Table 1. The extra guidance signal from the teacher's pairwise semantic preserving activations not only encourages the student to learn more intra-pixel relationships within a specific image but also semantic understanding of the entire training population. Furthermore, this method accelerates the learning of discriminators towards catching more details in the early stage. Incorporating both effects empowers the student model to even outperform the teacher model in certain cases. In Fig. 5, we show 2 examples where our proposed method achieves exceptionally better results.

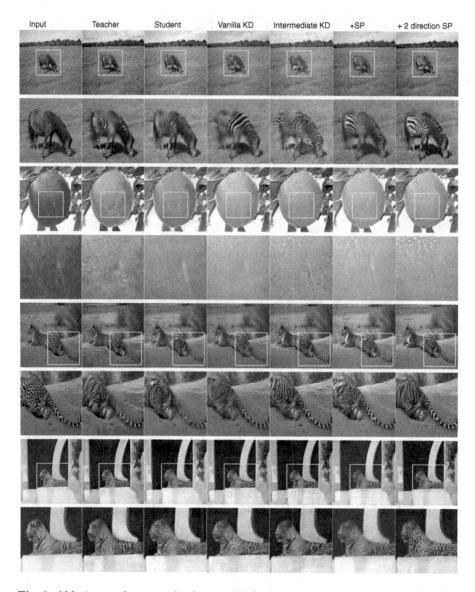

Fig. 8. Ablation study: examples from multiple datasets comparing results in baseline models and variation of our methods. More images can be seen in Supplementary.

An intriguing failure (Fig. 6) case shows that CycleGAN fails to transfer multiple objects while our method succeeds. We also observe significantly better details and textures preserving in different tasks. In Fig. 7, a more detailed and realistic eye is preserved. In addition, we provide examples from different datasets in Fig. 8 in an ablation study manner.

Table 4. FID value for Resnet6 generators on Horse ↔ Zebra dataset

	Teacher	Student	Intermediate KD	Vanilla KD	+ SP	+ 2 direction SP
$h \rightarrow z$	88.27	109.93	107.04	105.49	108.71	**105.51**
$z \rightarrow h$	143.08	144.01	142.63	146.26	**141.50**	141.90

Table 5. FCN-score on Cityscapes. Feature encoding extracted from Unet256 has a spatial resolution of 64×64 and 32×32 at layer 2 and layer 3 respectively

	Mean pixel acc.	Mean class acc.	Mean class IoU
Teacher	0.757	0.235	0.191
Student	0.710	0.219	0.169
Vanilla KD	0.742	0.224	0.182
+ SP layer 2	0.743	**0.230**	**0.183**
+ SP layer 3	**0.770**	0.229	**0.183**

4.2 Different Architectures

We also demonstrate that our method is extensible to other types of network structure. On the horse-to-zebra task, we test Resnet6 generator for both the teacher and the student models. The FID evaluation is shown in Table 4. Our method gains the most performance over others but it is less significant as in the Resnet9 case. We conjecture that the teacher model of 6 blocks contains less semantic relationships, which limits the amount of knowledge to be transferred. We also conducted additional experiments using UNet [16] on the Cityscapes dataset translate from semantic mask to street view photos. As UNet's encoder downsamples the input to 1×1 resolution at the bottleneck layer, the desired spatial semantic information is lacking at the bottleneck layer. Therefore, we distill the semantic relation activation matrix at layer 2 or layer 3. We show FCN-score results in Table 5. We find the highest mean pixel accuracy with distilling at layer 3 but similar mIoU at both layers. Compression ratio and visual results can be found in Supplementary.

5 Conclusions

We approach model compression of GANs via a novel proposed method extended on traditional knowledge distillation. Our strategy, which transfers semantic relation knowledge from a teacher model to a selected student model, shows strong potential in generating images with better details and texture after explicitly leaning the semantic relationships while using knowledge distillation to significantly reduce the model size and computation requirement. Our experiments conducted on 5 different datasets and 3 different architectures have demonstrated quantitatively and qualitatively that our proposed method helps bring a previously incompetent student network to the level of its teacher, with the capability to generate images at a significantly higher level of quality.

Acknowledgement. Authors thank Brendan Duke, Soheil Seyfaie, Zhi Yu, Yuze Zhang for their comments and suggestions.

References

1. Aguinaldo, A., Chiang, P.Y., Gain, A., Patil, A., Pearson, K., Feizi, S.: Compressing GANs using knowledge distillation. arXiv preprint arXiv:1902.00159 (2019)
2. Brock, A., Donahue, J., Simonyan, K.: Large scale GAN training for high fidelity natural image synthesis. In: International Conference on Learning Representations (2019)
3. Chen, G., Choi, W., Yu, X., Han, T., Chandraker, M.: Learning efficient object detection models with knowledge distillation. In: Guyon, I., et al. (eds.) Advances in Neural Information Processing Systems, vol. 30, pp. 742–751. Curran Associates, Inc. (2017). http://papers.nips.cc/paper/6676-learning-efficient-object-detection-models-with-knowledge-distillation.pdf
4. Chen, Y., Yang, T., Zhang, X., Meng, G., Pan, C., Sun, J.: DetNAS: backbone search for object detection (2019)
5. Chen, Y., Wang, N., Zhang, Z.: DarkRank: accelerating deep metric learning via cross sample similarities transfer. In: Thirty-Second AAAI Conference on Artificial Intelligence (2018)
6. Choi, Y., Choi, M., Kim, M., Ha, J.W., Kim, S., Choo, J.: StarGAN: unified generative adversarial networks for multi-domain image-to-image translation. In: Proceedings of the IEEE Conference on Computer Vision and Pattern Recognition, pp. 8789–8797 (2018)
7. Cordts, M., et al.: The cityscapes dataset for semantic urban scene understanding. In: Proceedings of the IEEE Conference on Computer Vision and Pattern Recognition, pp. 3213–3223 (2016)
8. Deng, J., Dong, W., Socher, R., Li, L.J., Li, K., Fei-Fei, L.: ImageNet: a large-scale hierarchical image database. In: 2009 IEEE Conference on Computer Vision and Pattern Recognition, pp. 248–255. IEEE (2009)
9. Goodfellow, I., et al.: Generative adversarial nets. In: Advances in Neural Information Processing Systems, pp. 2672–2680 (2014)
10. Han, S., Mao, H., Dally, W.J.: Deep compression: compressing deep neural network with pruning, trained quantization and huffman coding. In: Bengio, Y., LeCun, Y. (eds.) 4th International Conference on Learning Representations, ICLR 2016, San Juan, Puerto Rico, 2–4 May 2016, Conference Track Proceedings (2016). http://arxiv.org/abs/1510.00149
11. He, Y., Lin, J., Liu, Z., Wang, H., Li, L.J., Han, S.: AMC: AutoML for model compression and acceleration on mobile devices. In: Proceedings of the European Conference on Computer Vision (ECCV), pp. 784–800 (2018)
12. Heusel, M., Ramsauer, H., Unterthiner, T., Nessler, B., Hochreiter, S.: GANs trained by a two time-scale update rule converge to a local nash equilibrium. In: Advances in Neural Information Processing Systems, pp. 6626–6637 (2017)
13. Hinton, G., Vinyals, O., Dean, J.: Distilling the knowledge in a neural network. arXiv preprint arXiv:1503.02531 (2015)
14. Howard, A., et al.: Searching for MobileNetV3. In: Proceedings of the IEEE International Conference on Computer Vision, pp. 1314–1324 (2019)
15. Howard, A.G., et al.: MobileNets: efficient convolutional neural networks for mobile vision applications. arXiv preprint arXiv:1704.04861 (2017)

16. Isola, P., Zhu, J.Y., Zhou, T., Efros, A.A.: Image-to-image translation with conditional adversarial networks. In: Proceedings of the IEEE Conference on Computer Vision and Pattern Recognition, pp. 1125–1134 (2017)
17. Krizhevsky, A., Sutskever, I., Hinton, G.E.: ImageNet classification with deep convolutional neural networks. In: Advances in Neural Information Processing Systems, pp. 1097–1105 (2012)
18. Ledig, C., et al.: Photo-realistic single image super-resolution using a generative adversarial network. In: Proceedings of the IEEE Conference on Computer Vision and Pattern Recognition, pp. 4681–4690 (2017)
19. Lin, T.-Y., et al.: Microsoft COCO: common objects in context. In: Fleet, D., Pajdla, T., Schiele, B., Tuytelaars, T. (eds.) ECCV 2014. LNCS, vol. 8693, pp. 740–755. Springer, Cham (2014). https://doi.org/10.1007/978-3-319-10602-1_48
20. Liu, C., et al.: Auto-deeplab: hierarchical neural architecture search for semantic image segmentation. In: The IEEE Conference on Computer Vision and Pattern Recognition (CVPR), June 2019
21. Liu, Y., Chen, K., Liu, C., Qin, Z., Luo, Z., Wang, J.: Structured knowledge distillation for semantic segmentation. In: Proceedings of the IEEE Conference on Computer Vision and Pattern Recognition, pp. 2604–2613 (2019)
22. Luo, J.H., Wu, J., Lin, W.: Thinet: A filter level pruning method for deep neural network compression. In: Proceedings of the IEEE International Conference on Computer Vision, pp. 5058–5066 (2017)
23. Park, W., Kim, D., Lu, Y., Cho, M.: Relational knowledge distillation. In: Proceedings of the IEEE Conference on Computer Vision and Pattern Recognition, pp. 3967–3976 (2019)
24. Peng, B., et al.: Correlation congruence for knowledge distillation. In: Proceedings of the IEEE International Conference on Computer Vision, pp. 5007–5016 (2019)
25. Redmon, J., Farhadi, A.: YOLOV3: an incremental improvement. arXiv preprint arXiv:1804.02767 (2018)
26. Sandler, M., Howard, A., Zhu, M., Zhmoginov, A., Chen, L.C.: MobileNetV2: inverted residuals and linear bottlenecks. In: Proceedings of the IEEE Conference on Computer Vision and Pattern Recognition, pp. 4510–4520 (2018)
27. Shaham, T.R., Dekel, T., Michaeli, T.: SinGAN: learning a generative model from a single natural image. In: Proceedings of the IEEE International Conference on Computer Vision, pp. 4570–4580 (2019)
28. Shu, H., et al.: Co-evolutionary compression for unpaired image translation. In: Proceedings of the IEEE International Conference on Computer Vision, pp. 3235–3244 (2019)
29. Simonyan, K., Zisserman, A.: Very deep convolutional networks for large-scale image recognition. In: International Conference on Learning Representations (2015)
30. Tung, F., Mori, G.: Similarity-preserving knowledge distillation. In: Proceedings of the IEEE International Conference on Computer Vision, pp. 1365–1374 (2019)
31. Zagoruyko, S., Komodakis, N.: Paying more attention to attention: improving the performance of convolutional neural networks via attention transfer. arXiv preprint arXiv:1612.03928 (2016)
32. Zhu, J.Y., Park, T., Isola, P., Efros, A.A.: Unpaired image-to-image translation using cycle-consistent adversarial networks. In: Proceedings of the IEEE International Conference on Computer Vision, pp. 2223–2232 (2017)

Domain Adaptation Through Task Distillation

Brady Zhou$^{(\boxtimes)}$, Nimit Kalra , and Philipp Krähenbühl

The University of Texas at Austin, Austin, TX, USA
{bzhou,nimit,philkr}@cs.utexas.edu

Abstract. Deep networks devour millions of precisely annotated images to build their complex and powerful representations. Unfortunately, tasks like autonomous driving have virtually no real-world training data. Repeatedly crashing a car into a tree is simply too expensive. The commonly prescribed solution is simple: learn a representation in simulation and transfer it to the real world. However, this transfer is challenging since simulated and real-world visual experiences vary dramatically. Our core observation is that for certain tasks, such as image recognition, datasets are plentiful. They exist in any interesting domain, simulated or real, and are easy to label and extend. We use these recognition datasets to link up a source and target domain to transfer models between them in a task distillation framework. Our method can successfully transfer navigation policies between drastically different simulators: ViZDoom, SuperTuxKart, and CARLA. Furthermore, it shows promising results on standard domain adaptation benchmarks.

Keywords: Domain adaptation · Autonomous driving · Sim-to-real

1 Introduction

Labeled data has been the main driving force behind the rise of deep learning [7]. Tasks with an abundance of labeled data flourished [3,6,7,14,29], whereas tasks short on data saw only limited progress [31,45]. Over the past decade, deep networks have cut the error rate for image recognition by a factor of four [16, 26,40], doubled object detection performance [13,15,29], and allow for a near-perfect pixel-wise segmentation of an image [5,58]. Yet, these same networks do not yet drive real-world autonomous vehicles, pilot a drone, or control a robot from the same diverse real-world visual inputs [3]. In simulation [10,24,43], these tasks are not necessarily much harder to learn than recognition [4]—they simply have little to no labeled real-world data. Unfortunately, models born and raised purely in simulation often fail to perform well in the real world [41,42]. This

---

B. Zhou and N. Kalra—Indicates equal contribution.

Electronic supplementary material The online version of this chapter (https://doi.org/10.1007/978-3-030-58574-7_40) contains supplementary material, which is available to authorized users.

© Springer Nature Switzerland AG 2020
A. Vedaldi et al. (Eds.): ECCV 2020, LNCS 12371, pp. 664–680, 2020.
https://doi.org/10.1007/978-3-030-58574-7_40

Fig. 1. Raw visual inputs (a) may significantly vary across different domains, yet they often share common recognition labels (b). In this work, we use these recognition labels to transfer tasks between different domains.

problem is not unique to simulated and real domains—even models trained on one specific dataset often fail to generalize to other datasets [51].

Our core observation is that the gap between many datasets is much smaller in the output labels than the input images, as shown in Fig. 1. This is no accident. Recognition tasks are carefully hand-designed to infer a compact, general, and abstract representation of the world [7,12,27,29,47]. Datasets often share largely overlapping label sets, and task definitions are compatible. Most recognition tasks were designed as a first stepping stone to the rich world of visual reasoning tasks [57,59]. Why not solve recognition in all domains, and then build downstream tasks on top of recognition models [2,33,49,56]? Since the gap between label spaces is small, representations will generalize. As it turns out, "solving recognition" turns out to be quite hard [3,11,29,40]. Current recognition systems mislabel objects, detect an object where there is none, or worse, fail to recognize objects altogether. If recognition is not solved in its entirety, errors will compound to downstream tasks, and a domain gap will persist between domains with good recognition systems and those with poor ones.

In this paper, we take a different approach. We use the ground truth recognition labels directly to transfer downstream tasks from a source to target domain through task distillation. First, we learn a proxy model that maps ground-truth recognition labels to outputs of the source model, through distillation [18]. This proxy model generalizes much better to the target domain, as it operates on a more compact and abstract input. Next, we perform a second step of distillation to recover an image-based target model that imitates the proxy. This target model, no longer uses any ground truth supervision and learns the task in an end-to-end manner. We call this procedure *task distillation* as it distills a source task to operate in a target domain with the help of an auxiliary recognition task.

This procedure may seem counterintuitive, but it has several advantages over other domain adaptation methods. Firstly, recognition labels from different domains exhibit a smaller domain shift than their raw image counterparts. Secondly, we do not need to solve recognition in either source or target domain—we simply need a recognition dataset in each domain with a compatible label space. Finally, task distillation results in an end-to-end model in the target domain, and does not suffer from compounding errors in deployment.

We investigate how our task transfer framework performs under two distinct domain adaptation applications: 1) driving policy transfer for visual navigation, and 2) simulation-to-reality transfer for semantic segmentation prediction. We first show that our framework is able to transfer a lane-following driving policy from a simple racing game to a fully-fledged driving simulator. Furthermore, our framework is even able to transfer an obstacle-avoidance policy from a maze-navigation video game to driving among other moving vehicles. In the target domain, both of our transferred policies drive twice as far as the closest baselines.

Next, we apply our proposed framework to the standard domain adaptation task of transferring semantic segmentation models from simulated to real-world datasets. Here, task distillation again significantly outperforms prior work. Our framework is conceptually simple and easy to implement. All code and data is publicly available at https://github.com/bradyz/task-distillation.

2   Related Work

Dataset bias is likely as old as machine learning itself [51]—models trained on one dataset tend to generalize poorly out-of-the-box to related ones. The rise of deep learning ushered in a wave of massive datasets [3,6,7,14,29]. While these diverse datasets have significantly improved the general proclivity of state-of-the-art models to generalize to other datasets, a domain gap still exists. One popular and direct method to close this domain gap is to pre-train on a source domain and then fine-tune on a target domain [21,30]. In the same spirit, our work leverages a large amount of ground-truth labels to provide supervision for vision tasks in a different domain. However, rather than rely on final task labels in the target domain, as they may be difficult or impossible to collect, we use generic recognition labels in both domains.

Domain adaptation aims to bridge the source and target domain by adapting the weights of a model to increase its performance in a target domain. Domain adaptation techniques include domain-specific normalization techniques [28], statistical matching on input [34,53,60], output [19,52], and intermediate activation [20] distributions between source and target domains. While most techniques rely only on the statistical distributions of the input data and the transferred model, recent works have introduced auxiliary labels and tasks to aid adaptation [48,54]. Ramirez et al. [37] learn a common representation for an auxiliary task in both the source and target domain, then use this representation to link the two domains and aid transfer between them. Our approach is significantly simpler and does not require training any models for the auxiliary task.

Simulation-to-reality transfer has received a lot of attention in recent years, as simulators effortlessly produce massive amounts of labeled data [25,38]. Transfer via modular pipelines is a promising simulation-to-reality method, wherein the observation space in both domains is mapped to a shared intermediate proxy task to ease generalization. Doersch et al. [8] use motion to transfer 3D human pose labels. Müller et al. [33] use a semantic segmentation proxy task to transfer a driving policy, whereas Mousavian et al. [32] use it as input to learned visual navigation policies. Zhou et al. [59] explore the impact of various high-level intermediate visual representations on learning to act, whereas Sax et al. [44] explore how mid-level visual priors assist learning to navigate.

While modular systems all greatly outperform using unsupervised domain adaptation techniques, they still suffer from compounding errors. If the intermediate auxiliary tasks is not solved perfectly, different error patterns between source and target domain will persist and lead to weaker transfer. Our framework, on the other hand directly uses the error-free ground truth annotations for transfer, and thus does not suffer from compounding errors.

Another popular avenue for simulation-to-reality transfer is through the use of domain randomization. In an effort to capture and generalize to the target domain distribution, these techniques randomize visual and dynamical properties of the simulation during training, similar to data augmentation in general deep learning. Domain randomization requires no real-world labels and are especially popular in transferring robotic manipulation tasks [1,22,35,50]. James et al.successfully use this technique to reduce the amount of real world training data for robot grasping by two orders of magnitude [22]. While domain randomization works well in simple closed environments, it is not yet clear how to randomize more complex simulators to enable transfer to real-world visual domains.

3   Method

Our framework makes heavy use of model distillation [18]. Let $f_\theta(x)$ be a deep network with parameters θ. Let $g(x)$ be a second function, possibly another deep network. Distillation trains f_θ to produce the same output as g on a dataset D:

$$\text{minimize}_\theta E_{x \sim D} \left[\ell(f_\theta(x), g(x)) \right]$$

Distillation learns to imitate more than just the ground truth labels. It gets to see and imitate all outputs from a target function g, and thus captures some of its inner workings and representation, also known as dark knowledge [18]. The original distillation work [18] learns classification tasks using a smooth cross entropy loss ℓ. However, a large family of loss functions generally work. For simplicity, we use an L_1 loss $\ell(f_\theta(x), g(x)) = |f_\theta(x) - g(x)|$ for both categorical and regression tasks.

Distillation is easily extended to a pair of models that use different inputs x and y, as long as there exists a dataset with paired input modalities (x, y).

$$\text{minimize}_\theta E_{(x,y) \sim D} \left[\ell(f_\theta(x), g(y)) \right]$$

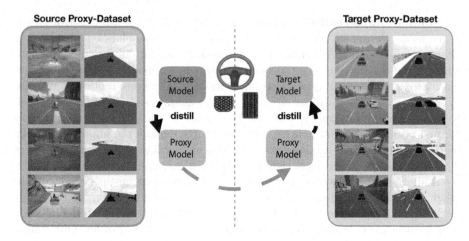

Fig. 2. Our method first distills a source model to a proxy model that uses labels as inputs. As proxy labels generalize to the target domain, a second stage of distillation is performed to produce a target model.

For notational simplicity, we call this process $f := \mathcal{D}_D(g)$ in later sections. Distillation is the cornerstone of our domain adaptation algorithm, and the generalized process is also pervasive in policy optimization under the term behavior cloning or imitation learning [36]. In previous works, it has been successfully used to replace a privileged driving policy with a pure sensorimotor policy [4].

3.1 Task Distillation

Let $\mathcal{S}$ be the source domain and $\mathcal{T}$ be the target domain. We denote images from source and target domains as I^S and I^T, respectively. Let L^S and L^T be labels for a proxy task in both domains (e.g., image recognition). Our goal is to transfer a model $f^S : I^S \to o$ producing outputs o from the source domain to the target domain. In our formulation, this output represents the desired prediction we aim to transfer to the target domain; hence, we assume o is only available in the source domain. We want to learn an adapted model $f^T : I^T \to o$ that performs the same task as f^S in the target domain.

We propose a two-stage approach, as shown in Fig. 2. First, we learn a proxy model $f^P : L^S \to o$ using model distillation on a source dataset; i.e: $f^P := \mathcal{D}_S(f^S)$. Next, we distill the target model $f^T : I^T \to o$ from the proxy model on a target dataset, yielding $f^T := \mathcal{D}_T(f^P)$. If the label sets do not perfectly align between source and target domains, we bring them closer using simple hand designed transformations, such as remapping semantic labels, or different forms of data augmentation, as described in Sect. 4.

3.2 Comparison with Modular Approach

Under which conditions does task distillation confer benefits over previous domain adaptation approaches? Which scenarios will likely cause it to fail? Both task distillation and the modular approach derive stronger generalization in the target domain through the use of an abstract, yet rich and informative, proxy task and proxy model. However, whereas task distillation queries the proxy model at train-time with *ground-truth* proxy labels, a modular pipeline queries this proxy model at deploy-time with *predicted* proxy labels, thereby incurring the cost of an imperfect recognition system.

We denote the accuracy of the recognition system in the target domain as a^l, the proxy model accuracy in the source domain as a^P, and the *similarity* between the two domains as $G^I = |I^S \cap I^T|/|I^T|$ in image space and $G^L = |L^S \cap L^T|/|L^T|$ in label space. Suppose a failure at any stage causes the entire system to fail. Then, the final accuracy is

$$a^T_{\text{modular}} = a^P a^l G^L; \qquad (1)$$

that is, the system succeeds only if proxy, recognition, and label transfer succeed.

Similarly, let a^d be the accuracy of the second distillation stage in our proposed framework. Then, task distillation succeeds at a rate of

$$a^T_{\text{distill}} = a^P G^L a^d; \qquad (2)$$

that is, when the labels transfer and the second distillation succeeds.

Finally, direct transfer ignores the issue of domain shift altogether, and simply evaluates the source model f^S in the target image domain. If f^S has accuracy a^S, this approach succeeds at a rate of

$$a^T_{\text{direct}} = a^S G^I. \qquad (3)$$

These accuracy estimations can be difficult to compare without references or experiments. However, note that experimentally distillation commonly does not lose any accuracy—Hinton et al. [18] observe an increase in accuracy through distillation, while Chen et al. [4] show equivalent accuracies. It is thus safe to assume that $a^S \approx a^P$ in most cases.

With these estimates, we can reason about the relationships between domain adaptation approaches and develop some intuition. Firstly, if the domain gap in the image domain is not significantly larger than the domain gap in the label domain $(G^I \approx G^L)$, then direct transfer is likely to work quite well. Moreover, task distillation and the modular approach differ by a single term—the recognition accuracy a^l versus the distillation accuracy a^d. If recognition is easier to learn in the target domain, a modular approach likely yields a higher accuracy. However, if the target task is easier to learn through distillation, a task distillation approach likely works better.

We find that, for many applications, modular pipelines must infer a proxy recognition task that is often far richer than needed for the end task. Target tasks

Source Input	Ground-Truth	Ground-Truth	Predicted	Target Input

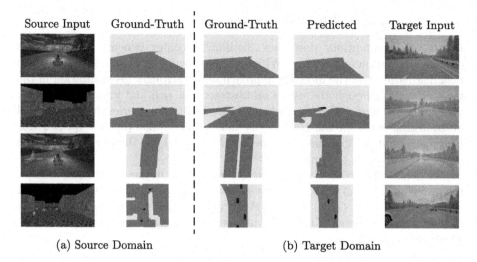

| (a) Source Domain | (b) Target Domain |

Fig. 3. We compare visual domains by their raw monocular images and corresponding semantic representations. While the domains vary significantly in their raw images, they are quite similar in their semantic modalities. However, note that the predicted modalities used by a modular pipeline are not perfect. For example, in the bottom-most row, the map-view prediction fails to capture the yellow car in view directly left of the agent. When supplied to the downstream driving policy, this vision failure can result in unintended behavior. (Color figure online)

are empirically easier to learn than recognition, as they can often be inferred from a subset of recognition. Although recognition is easier to supervise, with ground-truth labels in abundance, solving recognition pixel-perfect is very difficult. In contrast, the target task of driving from pixels, for example, only relies on inferring a subset of recognition. Intuitively, imperfect recognition 100 m down the road, or on the opposite lane of a separated freeway, does not impact downstream driving performance.

We note that our task distillation framework and the modular approach both rely on a^P and G^L—their success depends on the performance of the proxy model in solving the final task and the ability of the proxy task to generalize between domains. Hence, the choice of proxy task is a careful trade-off between expressiveness and abstractness.

Although this analysis provides some intuition, our assumptions do ignore several practical aspects of modular approaches and distillation. Firstly, not all mistakes are equally bad—models are generally able to recover from partial failures and degrade slowly. Moreover, while the second stage of our task distillation framework may introduce some mislabeled training data if the label spaces are too dissimilar, deep learning algorithms (namely stochastic gradient descent with data augmentation) gracefully generalize and can withstand some erroneous supervision. Hence, these accuracy estimations may be overly pessimistic.

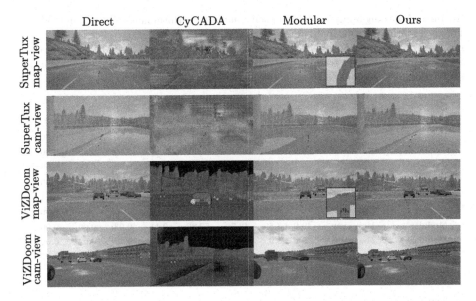

Fig. 4. We qualitatively examine how four different driving policies transfer to CARLA. Each policy is evaluated at the same state over four transfer methods, with predicted waypoints shown in red. Inferred modality is displayed for CyCADA and Modular. As shown, an inaccurate modality is used by a modular driving policy when transferring from SuperTuxKart via camera-view semantic segmentation. The median is misclassified as drivable road and the predicted waypoints direct the agent off of the road. (Best viewed on screen). (Color figure online)

4   Experiments and Results

We demonstrate our task distillation framework in two domain adaptation scenarios: 1) policy transfer of a navigation policy, and 2) general domain adaptation for semantic segmentation prediction.

4.1   Policy Transfer

Evaluating real-world navigational policies in a controlled and reproducible fashion can be tricky, requiring a physical vehicle and a reusable testbed environment. We sidestep these issues and instead transfer a navigation policy between three simulators of drastically different input fidelity, physical accuracy, and complexity: 1) SuperTuxKart, a simplistic open-source racing game, 2) ViZDoom [23], a professionally-developed maze-based shooting game, and 3) CARLA [10], a photorealistic driving simulator. As shown in Fig. 3, the visual domain shift between these simulators is significant. We train our policies in the relatively low-fidelity ViZDoom and SuperTuxKart video games and transfer these agents to drive in the realistic CARLA driving simulator.

Table 1. Adapting a SuperTuxKart racing agent to perform lane-following in CARLA. For each method, we evaluate 25 episodes using five fixed PID controller parameters. † denotes transferring raw low-level steering and throttle control to CARLA, as opposed to waypoints. § denotes training the driving policy using proxy task predictions in the source domain, as opposed to ground-truth labels.

Method	Proxy task	Distance traveled (m)			Completion rate			
		avg.	min	max	100 m	250 m	500 m	1000 m
Direct	—	22.4 ±3.2	16.6	26.0	0.00	0.00	0.00	0.00
CyCADA [19]	—	24.0 ±1.3	22.4	26.0	0.00	0.00	0.00	0.00
CyCADA†	—	26.7 ±2.0	23.6	28.7	0.02	0.00	0.00	0.00
Modular§	Cam-view	89.9 ±9.8	81.4	108.6	0.24	0.08	0.00	0.00
Modular [33]	Cam-view	110.4 ±17.1	95.7	138.2	0.38	0.06	0.02	0.01
Ours	Cam-view	164.6 ±14.9	147.5	191.6	0.59	0.18	0.03	0.00
Modular§	Map-view	49.9 ±3.8	42.7	52.82	0.11	0.03	0.00	0.00
Modular	Map-view	135.3 ±8.0	126.0	147.3	0.44	0.12	0.04	0.00
Ours	Map-view	**260.5 ±15.2**	**244.5**	**281.3**	**0.66**	**0.26**	**0.20**	**0.03**

We build our policies on the network architecture of Chen et al. [4], a ResNet-18 backbone that regresses to a trajectory plan of waypoints, which provide a domain-agnostic abstraction for control [33]. During deployment, a low-level PID controller converts waypoints to steering, throttle, and brake controls in CARLA.

We chose semantic segmentation in either camera-view [33] or map-view [2, 4,55] (also known as bird's-eye view in the literature) as the proxy recognition representation. Semantic segmentation is a particularly useful proxy task since it is extremely prevalent in most datasets and domains. Moreover, it allows us to easily enforce relationships between domains simply by mapping source classes to target classes. In doing so, we can easily frame the desired behavior of the target CARLA vehicle in terms of the source agent we wish to transfer.

We build our policies on the network architecture of Chen et al. [4], wherein each policy outputs a trajectory plan using waypoints. This representation provides a domain-agnostic abstraction for control [33]. During deployment in the target domain, waypoints are fed into a low-level PID controller to obtain steering, throttle, and brake controls in CARLA.

Evaluation. For each transferred policy, we evaluate how far the agent travels until a driving infraction (i.e: collision) in an unseen test town in CARLA. We force all agents to travel at 20km/h, as traveling speed greatly impacts the agent's performance. For waypoint-based agents, we hand-tune five PID controllers on a reference planner in a training town, and use these controllers to obtain low-level driving commands. We then evaluate all agents for 25 episodes under each controller, selecting the weather configuration and spawn points at random. Our experimental setup follows the official evaluation protocol of CARLA [10], except we do not have a fixed goal, and thus do not use high-level commands. Instead, agents can chose to follow any route through the test town.

Table 2. Results from transferring a ViZDoom maze-navigation agent to perform lane-following and vehicle-avoidance in CARLA.

Method	Proxy task	Distance traveled (m)			Completion rate			
		avg.	min	max	100 m	250 m	500 m	1000 m
Direct	—	17.4 ±2.4	13.6	21.0	0.02	0.00	0.00	0.00
CyCADA	—	24.4 ±5.1	20.7	33.9	0.02	0.00	0.00	0.00
Modular[§]	Cam-view	148.6 ±40.3	92.6	211.2	0.42	0.20	0.01	0.00
Modular	Cam-view	140.4 ±18.6	120.2	173.7	0.51	0.16	0.02	0.00
Ours	Cam-view	166.9 ±33.6	125.2	223.8	0.62	0.17	0.06	0.00
Modular[§]	Map-view	89.5 ±7.8	78.3	100.9	0.31	0.06	0.00	0.00
Modular	Map-view	145.3 ±15.5	125.2	170.9	0.55	0.18	0.02	0.00
Ours	Map-view	**277.3 ±56.6**	**204.2**	**353.3**	**0.63**	**0.35**	**0.20**	**0.05**

Baselines. We evaluate our method against direct transfer, image-to-image translation via CyCADA [19], and modular transfer [33]. Direct transfer ignores the issue of domain shift—we simply evaluate the source model in the target domain. Different baselines rely on varying proxy supervision during training, but the final model for each method maps raw input images to waypoints.

SuperTuxKart → CARLA. SuperTuxKart is a simple racing game, wherein players are expected to race on winding tracks—which can be quite challenging to traverse—by controlling the steering angle and throttle. Compared to the two-way traffic and major intersections found in CARLA environments, each SuperTuxKart map has a single non-overlapping one-way track. We train our source policy in SuperTuxKart using proximal policy optimization (PPO) [46] to maximize the distance traveled down the track. Our goal is to transfer this source policy to drive in CARLA. Following the setup of Müller et al. [33], we disable other traffic participants in CARLA, and focus solely navigating the road. We report our results in Table 1.

Ignoring the issue of visual domain shift and simply deploying our source policy in CARLA results in predictably poor results—the agent drives 100 m without infraction only 2% of the time. Attempting to translate the target visual inputs to emulate the style of the source domain (as done in unsupervised domain adaptation approaches such as CyCADA) yields a poor and inconsistent inferred modality, as shown in Fig. 4. Using this faulty input representation results in an agent with similarly low driving performance. As highlighted in Fig. 3, these two visual domains are simply too far from each other.

By leveraging the compact semantic segmentation representation, the modular pipeline approach and our task distillation method both achieve an order of magnitude improvement in driving performance. For both sets of experiments, we align the "track" class in SuperTuxKart with the "road" class in CARLA to preserve the original source task's semantic relationship with the navigable track region (i.e: to stay on the track).

We observe that the map-view proxy task works better for both methods. As Wang et al. [55] show, this representation is more informative than the camera-view, but it is also harder to infer due to perspective distortion. Task distillation enables us to transfer a policy that is able to navigate twice as far as a modular approach using the same map-view proxy task. Moreover, the map-view results in a 66.2% increase in distance traveled over semantic camera-view under task distillation; however, it provides almost no improvement in a modular pipeline. Finally, unlike with a modular pipeline, our agent can exploit a stronger signal with being distracted by distortions, as they do not exist in the ground truth maps. See Fig. 3 for visual examples.

Finally, we evaluate the performance of our transferred agent as the target-domain proxy-task dataset size changes (see Fig. 5). By default, we use ten thousand labeled target images to both train the second stage of task distillation and to train the target recognition model in our modular pipelines. We find that even when training on only *half* of the target-domain samples, task distillation outperforms the modular approach.

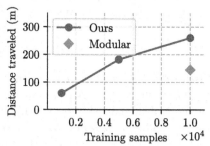

Fig. 5. Performance at different amounts of target-domain training data.

ViZDoom → CARLA. In ViZDoom, we train an agent using direct future prediction (DFP) [9] to navigate and explore complex maze environments while searching for health-kits and avoiding poison. Unlike the winding SuperTuxKart tracks, ViZDoom maze corridors resemble the road intersections of an urban driving environment. We aim to transfer this policy to a crowded street scenario in CARLA, wherein the agent must avoid other traffic participants while also navigating the road. To this end, we semantically align the two domains by mapping the "poison" class in ViZDoom with the "car" class in CARLA, in addition to aligning the "road" and "floor" classes. Hence, we frame the agent's tendency to avoid poison in the context of our target domain; i.e: the transferred policy avoids cars while staying on the road. We report our results in Table 2.

Direct transfer and CyCADA fail to yield a strong target policy and crash within a few meters. Despite facing a more difficult CARLA evaluation with traffic participants, both the modular approach and task distillation outperform their counterpart experiments in SuperTuxKart. We attribute these improvements to the inherent similarity between ViZDoom corridors and urban roads. Task distillation significantly exceeds the performance of a modular pipeline, especially when using the expressive, but difficult to infer, map-view proxy task.

Our policy transfer experiments concern a very specific domain adaptation application. However, task distillation is not limited to transferring sequential decision-making policies between domains. We can apply our framework to transfer general computer vision tasks from simulated to real-world datasets.

Input	Depth	Ours	Ground-Truth

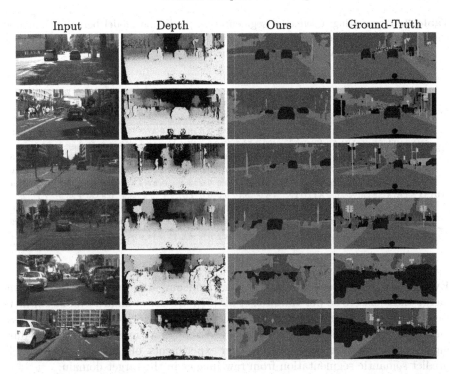

Fig. 6. Transferring the semantic segmentation task from the simulated SYNTHIA-SF dataset to the real-world Cityscapes dataset using task distillation with a depth estimation proxy task. We display representative samples near the reported mIoU in the top four rows. When depth estimation from stereo vision is too noisy, performance drops substantially, as shown in the bottom two rows. This highlights the importance of proxy task performance. Our final adapted model predicts semantic segmentation using only raw monocular images—we simply display the proxy depth labels for illustration.

4.2   General Domain Adaptation

We transfer the semantic segmentation task between a variety of datasets: 1) SYNTHIA [17,39], a collection of synthetic scenes in a virtual city, 2) Cityscapes [6], an assortment of video sequences recorded on real-world urban streets, and 3) a hand-collected set of frames rendered in the CARLA driving simulator. All three datasets consist of raw monocular images with semantic and depth annotations. We train a semantic segmentation prediction model on the SYNTHIA-SF dataset and adapt the model on both the Cityscapes and CARLA datasets.

In our task distillation setup, we use the low-level visual signal of depth estimation as a proxy task. Our experimental setup mimics that of Ramirez et al. [37], who use depth as an auxiliary supervisory signal to link domains in their AT/DT framework. However, we utilize a different semantic segmentation network architecture, building upon the simple DeepLabv3 model [5].

Table 3. Transferring a semantic segmentation prediction model between simulated and real-world datasets. ¶ denotes using the AT/DT architecture for direct transfer. * denotes evaluating our proxy model on the target dataset.

	Source	Target	Method	Road	Sidewalk	Walls	Fence	Person	Poles	Vegetation	Vehicles	Tr. Signs	Building	Sky	mIoU	Acc
(a)	SYNTHIA-SF	CARLA	Direct	9.1	30.9	0.1	0.0	13.7	14.9	57.3	15.5	4.5	22.8	64.6	21.2	48.0
	SYNTHIA-SF	CARLA	AT/DT¶	63.9	54.9	15.2	0.0	13.6	12.8	52.7	27.3	4.9	50.2	79.7	34.1	73.4
	SYNTHIA-SF	CARLA	AT/DT [37]	73.6	62.6	**26.9**	0.0	17.8	37.3	35.3	52.9	17.8	**63.0**	87.5	43.1	80.0
	SYNTHIA-SF	CARLA	Ours	**95.4**	**90.2**	10.4	0.0	**26.6**	**52.1**	**66.1**	**60.5**	**53.1**	57.3	**95.5**	**55.2**	**87.0**
(b)	SYNTHIA-SF	Cityscapes	Direct	0.7	1.6	0.0	0.0	13.4	6.0	**57.4**	21.6	**2.0**	<u>42.7</u>	19.7	15.0	41.3
	SYNTHIA-SF	Cityscapes	AT/DT¶	6.9	0.7	0.0	0.0	2.5	9.1	3.2	8.9	0.8	25.9	26.9	7.7	28.5
	SYNTHIA-SF	Cityscapes	AT/DT	85.8	29.4	1.2	0.0	3.7	14.6	1.9	8.9	0.4	**42.8**	**67.1**	23.2	<u>64.0</u>
	SYNTHIA-SF	Cityscapes	Ours	**86.8**	**46.3**	**8.1**	0.0	**34.9**	**19.2**	12.9	**52.4**	0.3	40.9	6.4	**28.0**	**64.3**
	SYNTHIA-SF	Cityscapes	Proxy*	84.9	37.5	8.2	0.0	26.6	23.0	16.8	43.1	19.3	43.3	19.7	29.3	64.4

Evaluation. As these datasets may have incompatible semantic classes, we merge these classes as per Ramirez et al. [37]. We use standard evaluation metrics for semantic segmentation, and report the intersection-over-union per class, mean IoU, and global pixel-wise accuracy. Although we rely on proxy labels during training, just as in our policy transfer experiments, our final adapted models predict semantic segmentation from raw images in the target domain.

SYNTHIA-SF → CARLA. As shown in Table 3, the AT/DT direct baseline (denoted by ¶) outperforms our direct baseline. As their baseline uses no auxiliary tasks for aiding transfer, this seems to suggest that our model architecture is inferior. However, task distillation is able to easily bridge this difference without any architectural changes. Using the same additional depth supervision, our simple DeepLabv3 model yields significant improvement in mIoU over the complex AT/DT architecture. In particular, we observe increase in the IoU of several pervasive semantic classes: "roads", "sidewalk", "vegetation", and "traffic sign."

SYNTHIA-SF → Cityscapes. Since the Cityscapes dataset contains noisy depth estimations from stereo images, whereas the SYNTHIA-SF dataset provides depth labels directly from the rendering engine, there is a non-negligible domain gap in label space. Moreover, stereo matching failures produce gaps in the Cityscapes depth estimation. Hence, we must carefully align the proxy labels to ensure strong transfer. To this end, we apply various data augmentations to make the SYNTHIA-SF depth maps more similar to the noisy Cityscapes labels. During training, we simulate this noise by randomly sampling Cityscapes masks and applying stereo-matching failure regions to the perfect depth maps in the source datasets. Furthermore, to encourage invariance to slight scale changes, we add per-pixel multiplicative noise to each image.

Despite this proxy label mismatch between the two datasets, our adapted model achieves an absolute improvement of 4.8 mIoU over Ramirez et al. [37], yielding improved accuracy in the "sidewalk", "person", and "vehicle" semantic classes, as shown in Fig. 6. However, we struggle with the "sky" class, likely due to noisy depth labels. This result is quite exciting, as we do not depend on any specialized real-world sensors. Using simple stereo images, we can transfer a semantic segmentation model trained in simulation for use in the real world.

Our adapted model performs well on scenes with high-quality depth estimation and struggles otherwise. As our method thrives when the domain gap between label spaces is small, and hence better depth estimates would likely further improve final performance. Moreover, our final model performs similarly to the proxy model in the target domain, thereby indicating that 1) the final distillation is successful, and 2) our final model's performance is constrained by the inability of our proxy model to generalize to the noisy proxy labels.

Limitations. Task distillation, like the modular approach, relies heavily on the proxy task being transferable. For example, adapting a model from SYNTHIA-RAND, in which the camera poses vary drastically, to Cityscapes results in an mIoU of 11.5. Transfer via the depth estimation proxy task fails due to the inconsistent appearance induced by changes in camera pose.

5   Conclusion

In this work, we propose a simple and effective framework for transferring knowledge from a source to target domain. Our method doesn't require any end-task labels in the target domain. Instead, we choose a proxy task with ample annotations in both simulation and the real world, e.g., depth or semantics, to tie both domains together. Task distillation outperforms competing alternatives for simulation-to-reality navigation policy transfer and domain adaptation for semantic segmentation.

Acknowledgments. This work has been supported in part by the National Science Foundation under grant IIS-1845485.

References

1. Akkaya, I., et al.: Solving Rubik's cube with a robot hand. arXiv preprint arXiv:1910.07113 (2019)
2. Bansal, M., Krizhevsky, A., Ogale, A.: ChauffeurNet: learning to drive by imitating the best and synthesizing the worst. In: RSS (2019)
3. Caesar, H., et al.: nuScenes: a multimodal dataset for autonomous driving. arXiv preprint arXiv:1903.11027 (2019)
4. Chen, D., Zhou, B., Koltun, V., Krähenbühl, P.: Learning by cheating. In: CoRL (2019)
5. Chen, L.C., Papandreou, G., Schroff, F., Adam, H.: Rethinking atrous convolution for semantic image segmentation. arXiv preprint arXiv:1706.05587 (2017)
6. Cordts, M., et al.: The Cityscapes dataset for semantic urban scene understanding. In: CVPR (2016)
7. Deng, J., Dong, W., Socher, R., Li, L.J., Li, K., Fei-Fei, L.: ImageNet: a large-scale hierarchical image database. In: CVPR (2009)

8. Doersch, C., Zisserman, A.: Sim2real transfer learning for 3D human pose estimation: motion to the rescue. In: NeurIPS (2019)
9. Dosovitskiy, A., Koltun, V.: Learning to act by predicting the future. In: ICLR (2017)
10. Dosovitskiy, A., Ros, G., Codevilla, F., Lopez, A., Koltun, V.: CARLA: an open urban driving simulator. In: CoRL (2017)
11. Everingham, M., Eslami, S.A., Van Gool, L., Williams, C.K., Winn, J., Zisserman, A.: The PASCAL visual object classes challenge: a retrospective. IJCV **111**, 98–136 (2015)
12. Everingham, M., Van Gool, L., Williams, C.K., Winn, J., Zisserman, A.: The PASCAL visual object classes (VOC) challenge. IJCV **88**, 303–338 (2010)
13. Felzenszwalb, P.F., Girshick, R.B., McAllester, D., Ramanan, D.: Object detection with discriminatively trained part-based models. TPAMI **32**, 1627–1645 (2009)
14. Geiger, A., Lenz, P., Stiller, C., Urtasun, R.: Vision meets robotics: the KITTI dataset. IJRR **32**, 1231–1237 (2013)
15. He, K., Gkioxari, G., Dollár, P., Girshick, R.: Mask R-CNN. In: ICCV (2017)
16. He, K., Zhang, X., Ren, S., Sun, J.: Deep residual learning for image recognition. In: CVPR (2016)
17. Hernandez-Juarez, D., et al.: Slanted stixels: representing San Francisco's steepest streets. In: BMVC (2017)
18. Hinton, G., Vinyals, O., Dean, J.: Distilling the knowledge in a neural network. arXiv preprint arXiv:1503.02531 (2015)
19. Hoffman, J., et al.: CyCADA: cycle-consistent adversarial domain adaptation. In: ICML (2018)
20. Huang, H., Huang, Q., Krähenbühl, P.: Domain transfer through deep activation matching. In: ECCV (2018)
21. Huh, M., Agrawal, P., Efros, A.A.: What makes ImageNet good for transfer learning? arXiv preprint arXiv:1608.08614 (2016)
22. James, S., et al.: Sim-to-real via sim-to-sim: data-efficient robotic grasping via randomized-to-canonical adaptation networks. In: CVPR (2019)
23. Kempka, M., Wydmuch, M., Runc, G., Toczek, J., Jaśkowski, W.: ViZDoom: a doom-based AI research platform for visual reinforcement learning. In: CIG (2016)
24. Kolve, E., et al.: AI2-THOR: an interactive 3D environment for visual AI. arXiv preprint arXiv:1712.05474 (2017)
25. Krähenbühl, P.: Free supervision from video games. In: CVPR (2018)
26. Krizhevsky, A., Sutskever, I., Hinton, G.E.: ImageNet classification with deep convolutional neural networks. In: NeurIPS (2012)
27. Kuznetsova, A., et al.: The open images dataset V4: unified image classification, object detection, and visual relationship detection at scale. arXiv preprint arXiv:1811.00982 (2018)
28. Li, Y., Wang, N., Shi, J., Liu, J., Hou, X.: Revisiting batch normalization for practical domain adaptation. In: ICLR (2017)
29. Lin, T.-Y., et al.: Microsoft COCO: common objects in context. In: Fleet, D., Pajdla, T., Schiele, B., Tuytelaars, T. (eds.) ECCV 2014. LNCS, vol. 8693, pp. 740–755. Springer, Cham (2014). https://doi.org/10.1007/978-3-319-10602-1_48
30. Long, J., Shelhamer, E., Darrell, T.: Fully convolutional networks for semantic segmentation. In: CVPR (2015)
31. Martin, D., Fowlkes, C., Tal, D., Malik, J.: A database of human segmented natural images and its application to evaluating segmentation algorithms and measuring ecological statistics. In: ICCV (2001)

32. Mousavian, A., Toshev, A., Fišer, M., Košecká, J., Wahid, A., Davidson, J.: Visual representations for semantic target driven navigation. In: ICRA (2019)
33. Müller, M., Dosovitskiy, A., Ghanem, B., Koltun, V.: Driving policy transfer via modularity and abstraction. In: CoRL (2018)
34. Murez, Z., Kolouri, S., Kriegman, D., Ramamoorthi, R., Kim, K.: Image to image translation for domain adaptation. In: CVPR (2018)
35. Peng, X.B., Andrychowicz, M., Zaremba, W., Abbeel, P.: Sim-to-real transfer of robotic control with dynamics randomization. In: ICRA (2018)
36. Pomerleau, D.A.: ALVINN: an autonomous land vehicle in a neural network. In: NeurIPS (1989)
37. Ramirez, P.Z., Tonioni, A., Salti, S., Stefano, L.D.: Learning across tasks and domains. In: ICCV (2019)
38. Richter, S.R., Hayder, Z., Koltun, V.: Playing for benchmarks. In: ICCV (2017)
39. Ros, G., Sellart, L., Materzynska, J., Vazquez, D., Lopez, A.M.: The SYNTHIA dataset: a large collection of synthetic images for semantic segmentation of urban scenes. In: CVPR (2016)
40. Russakovsky, O., et al.: ImageNet large scale visual recognition challenge. IJCV 115, 211–252 (2015)
41. Rusu, A.A., Vecerik, M., Rothörl, T., Heess, N., Pascanu, R., Hadsell, R.: Sim-to-real robot learning from pixels with progressive nets. In: CoRL (2017)
42. Sadeghi, F., Levine, S.: CAD2RL: real single-image flight without a single real image. In: RSS (2017)
43. Savva, M., et al.: Habitat: a platform for embodied AI research. In: ICCV (2019)
44. Sax, A., et al.: Learning to navigate using mid-level visual priors. In: CoRL (2020)
45. Saxena, A., Sun, M., Ng, A.Y.: Make3D: learning 3D scene structure from a single still image. TPAMI 31, 824–840 (2008)
46. Schulman, J., Wolski, F., Dhariwal, P., Radford, A., Klimov, O.: Proximal policy optimization algorithms. arXiv preprint arXiv:1707.06347 (2017)
47. Shao, S., et al.: Objects365: a large-scale, high-quality dataset for object detection. In: ICCV (2019)
48. Sun, Y., Tzeng, E., Darrell, T., Efros, A.A.: Unsupervised domain adaptation through self-supervision. In: ICLR (2019)
49. Teichmann, M., Weber, M., Zoellner, M., Cipolla, R., Urtasun, R.: MultiNet: real-time joint semantic reasoning for autonomous driving. In: Intelligent Vehicles (2018)
50. Tobin, J., Fong, R., Ray, A., Schneider, J., Zaremba, W., Abbeel, P.: Domain randomization for transferring deep neural networks from simulation to the real world. In: IROS (2017)
51. Torralba, A., Efros, A.A.: Unbiased look at dataset bias. In: CVPR (2011)
52. Tsai, Y.H., Hung, W.C., Schulter, S., Sohn, K., Yang, M.H., Chandraker, M.: Learning to adapt structured output space for semantic segmentation. In: CVPR (2018)
53. Vu, T.H., Jain, H., Bucher, M., Cord, M., Pérez, P.: ADVENT: adversarial entropy minimization for domain adaptation in semantic segmentation. In: CVPR (2019)
54. Vu, T.H., Jain, H., Bucher, M., Cord, M., Pérez, P.: DADA: depth-aware domain adaptation in semantic segmentation. In: ICCV (2019)
55. Wang, D., Devin, C., Cai, Q.Z., Krähenbühl, P., Darrell, T.: Monocular plan view networks for autonomous driving. In: ICRA (2019)
56. Wong, K., Wang, S., Ren, M., Liang, M., Urtasun, R.: Identifying unknown instances for autonomous driving. In: CoRL (2019)

57. Zamir, A.R., Sax, A., Shen, W., Guibas, L.J., Malik, J., Savarese, S.: Taskonomy: Disentangling task transfer learning. In: CVPR (2018)
58. Zhao, H., Shi, J., Qi, X., Wang, X., Jia, J.: Pyramid scene parsing network. In: CVPR (2017)
59. Zhou, B., Krähenbühl, P., Koltun, V.: Does computer vision matter for action? Sci. Robot. (2019)
60. Zhu, J.Y., Park, T., Isola, P., Efros, A.A.: Unpaired image-to-image translation using cycle-consistent adversarial networks. In: ICCV (2017)

PatchAttack: A Black-Box Texture-Based Attack with Reinforcement Learning

Chenglin Yang$^{(\boxtimes)}$, Adam Kortylewski, Cihang Xie, Yinzhi Cao, and Alan Yuille

Johns Hopkins University, Baltimore, USA
chenglin.yangw@gmail.com, {akortyl1,yinzhi.cao}@jhu.edu,
cihangxie306@gmail.com, alan.l.yuille@gmail.com

Abstract. Patch-based attacks introduce a perceptible but localized change to the input that induces misclassification. A limitation of current patch-based black-box attacks is that they perform poorly for targeted attacks, and even for the less challenging non-targeted scenarios, they require a large number of queries. Our proposed *PatchAttack* is query efficient and can break models for both targeted and non-targeted attacks. PatchAttack induces misclassifications by superimposing small textured patches on the input image. We parametrize the appearance of these patches by a dictionary of class-specific textures. This texture dictionary is learned by clustering Gram matrices of feature activations from a VGG backbone. *PatchAttack* optimizes the position and texture parameters of each patch using reinforcement learning. Our experiments show that PatchAttack achieves >99% success rate on ImageNet for a wide range of architectures, while only manipulating 3% of the image for non-targeted attacks and 10% on average for targeted attacks. Furthermore, we show that PatchAttack circumvents state-of-the-art adversarial defense methods successfully. The code is publicly available here.

Keywords: Adversarial machine learning · Black-box attack

1 Introduction

Computer vision models have achieved strong performance on image recognition tasks, however, they are known to be vulnerable against adversarial examples [49]. Adversarial examples are modifications of images crafted to induce misclassification. Understanding the vulnerability of computer vision models to adversarial attacks has emerged as an important research area, providing opportunities for understanding and improving computer vision models.

Recent works have introduced very successful attacks in the white-box setting [9,20,34], where both the network architecture and parameters are available

Electronic supplementary material The online version of this chapter (https://doi.org/10.1007/978-3-030-58574-7_41) contains supplementary material, which is available to authorized users.

© Springer Nature Switzerland AG 2020
A. Vedaldi et al. (Eds.): ECCV 2020, LNCS 12371, pp. 681–698, 2020.
https://doi.org/10.1007/978-3-030-58574-7_41

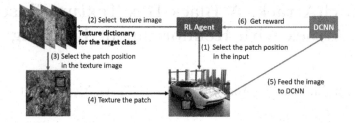

Fig. 1. Illustration of our black-box texture-based patch attack via reinforcement learning (RL): (1) The RL agent selects the patch position in the input image and (2) selects a texture image for the target category (lionfish in this example) from our learned texture dictionary. (3) The agent selects a patch position in the texture image to extract a texture patch, (4) which is then superimposed on the input image. (5) The adversarial image is fed into the deep convolutional network (DCNN). (6) The output scores of the DCNN is used to calculate the reward for the optimization of the agent. This six step process is repeated until the DCNN is attacked successfully. (Color figure online)

to the attacker. In real-world applications, a more common attacking scenario is that the attacker only has access to the model's input and the predicted output, e.g., attacking popular image analysis APIs [1,2,21,22,25,26] or self-driving cars [6,12,15,28,39,40,48,50]. This *black-box* scenario is challenging because adversarial modification of the input must be computed without access to the loss gradient of the model (Fig. 1).

Two paradigms have emerged for black-box attacks. *Perturbation-based* methods introduce imperceptible changes to the image that are constrained to have a small norm but are typically applied to the whole input image [4,5,10,37, 38,51]. Recently, several defense methods have shown that perturbation-based attacks can be successfully defended [20,31,34,53].

In this paper, we study a complementary type of adversary, *Patch-based black-box attacks*, introducing a perceptible (large norm) but localized change to the input. In their pioneering work, Fawzi et al. [16] show that superimposing monochrome black patches onto images generated by random search can successfully induce misclassificataions. However, a major limitation of current patch-based black box attacks is that they perform poorly on targeted attacks and require large amounts of queries for non-targeted attacks (Experiments 4.2).

In this work, we introduce *PatchAttack*, a patch-based black-box attack that is query efficient and achieves very high success rates for both targeted and non-targeted attacks. Our main contributions are two fold: 1) We formulate the search over the position and shape of adversarial patches as a reinforcement learning problem. Hence, we define the attack as a decision-making process of an agent that interacts with its' environment (the model) by taking actions (placing patches in the image) and observing rewards (misclassification rates). In this way, the parameter search is formulated as an optimization problem that is much more effective compared to random search strategies in terms of query efficiency. 2) Our experiments show that attacks with monochrome patches do not succeed as targeted attacks. The intuition is that monochrome patches can remove information from the image, but do not add any information, which is critical to confuse a model in a targeted manner. We overcome this limitation by introducing texture to the adversarial patches. To parameterize the texture efficiently, we learn a dictionary of class-specific textures by clustering Gram matrices of feature activations from a VGG backbone. The texture dictionary enables a query-efficient search over the patch appearance and leads to very high success rates at targeted and non-targeted attacks, while also strongly reducing the image area that needs to be corrupted for a successful attack.

Our results on ImageNet [42] show that PatchAttack achieves considerably higher success rates for targeted and non-targeted attacks compared to related work, while being more efficient in terms of the number of queries and the size of the attacked image area (on average only 3% of the image needs to be modified for non-targeted and <10% for targeted attacks respectively). Furthermore, we show that PatchAttack can successfully overcome Feature Denoising [53], a state-of-the-art defense for perturbation based attacks. Finally, we perform experiments with shape-based DCNNs [19] which were designed to overcome the texture bias of DCNNs trained on ImageNet, and hence should be more robust to PatchAttack. Interestingly, we cannot observe any increased robustness of shape-based DCNNs, although PatchAttack is texture-based and the object shape is largely preserved in the adversarial images.

2   Related Work

Sparked by the seminal works of Szegedy et al. [49] adversarial machine learning has emerged as an important research area for understanding and improving deep neural networks. In recent years, two complementary paradigms have emerged for black-box attacks, perturbation-based and patch-based attacks. In this paper, we focus on patch-based black-box attacks, but we also provide a short review of perturbation-based black-box attacks as the search strategies for both attack types are related.

Perturbation-Based Black Box Attacks. While we focus on black-box attacks with access to model output scores, attacks with even more limited access to model decisions only have been explored [7,11,29]. Such approaches often require lots of queries and are therefore difficult to apply in real-world applications. Early work on perturbation-based black box attacks with access to prediction scores proposed to estimate model gradients with finite differences [5,10,29,30,51,52]. In particular, these iterative attacks estimate gradients via sampling from a noise distribution around the feature point. While this approach is successful it requires large amounts of model queries. Other approaches use evolutionary algorithms [3,30] or random search strategies [4,23], but still often require many queries to be successful. A complementary approach is to compute transferable adversarial examples based on the gradient of substitute networks, [14,32,33,35,37,38,45,54,56].

The success of perturbation-based attacks has sparked an arms race between adversarial attacks and corresponding defense mechanisms [20,31,34,53]. A particularly successful defense method is feature denoising [53], where the features in a neural network are denoised using non-local means during adversarial training. To the best of our knowledge, this defense mechanism has not been successfully broken yet. In our experiments, we show that our patch-based attack can defeat this defense successfully.

Patch-Based White Box Attacks. Tom et al. [8] proposed adversarial patch as a white-box attack to cause classification errors. They craft adversarial examples by superimposing a patch onto the input image. Given a deep network, the pattern of the patch is optimized using gradient descent. The trained patch performs well but overfits to the network architecture. As shown in their experiments, the patches trained from four different networks are still not able to confuse a fifth network with a high success rate when the patch area is less than 10%. We perform transferability experiments in Appendix E.

Patch-Based Black Box Attacks. The seminal work of Fawzi et al. [16] introduced patch-based black box attacks. They don't optimize the pattern of the patches, and instead use the monochrome patches. The position and shape of the rectangular patches was searched using Metropolis-Hastings sampling. We refer their attack as Hastings Patch Attack (HPA). While their approach is successful, the random search strategy requires many queries. Furthermore, our experimental results show that using monochrome patches only to craft adversarial examples leads to very low success rates and even then requires to cover more than 70% of the image (see Experiments 4.2).

We introduce a patch-based black-box attack using textured patches that is optimized with reinforcement learning. Our approach is significantly more query efficient, achieves >99% success rates on targeted and non-targeted attacks and modifies only very small areas of the input image.

3   Methods

In this section, we first discuss the mathematical framework for patch-based adversarial attacks (Sect. 3.1). In Sect. 3.2 we introduce our reinforcement learning (RL) framework for patch-based black-box attacks. Finally, we discuss how the texture of adversarial patches can be optimized efficiently using RL by parametrizing the appearance of the patch with a class-specific texture dictionary learned by clustering Gram matrices of feature activations from a DCNN backbone (Sect. 3.3).

3.1   Mathematical Framework

We denote a deep neural network as a function $y = f(x; \theta)$, where x, θ and y denote the input image, model parameters, and output score of the model after softmax. To perform an adversarial attack we optimize an objective function:

$$\mathcal{L}(\mathbf{y}, y'), \quad \text{where} \quad \mathbf{y} = \mathbf{f}(\mathbf{g}(\mathbf{x}); \boldsymbol{\theta}), \tag{1}$$

where $\mathcal{L}$ is the loss between the output of the neural network $\mathbf{y}$ and a target class y' with y denoting the ground truth label. $\mathbf{g}(\mathbf{x})$ denotes the adversarial example obtained by perturbing $\mathbf{x}$. For targeted attacks, the goal is to induce a high confidence score for the class y' while non-targeted attacks, it is only to induce misclassifications. In perturbation-based attacks, $\mathbf{g}(\cdot)$ modifies $\mathbf{x}$ at every pixel and the perturbation is constrained to have a small norm. In contrast, the only constraint for patch-based attacks is that the perturbation must be localized in a small region $\mathcal{E}$:

$$\mathbf{g}\left(\mathbf{x}\right): \begin{cases} x_{u,v} = \mathbf{T}\left(x_{u,v}\right), & \text{if} \quad (u,v) \in \mathcal{E} \\ x_{u,v} = x_{u,v}, & \text{otherwise} \end{cases} \tag{2}$$

$$\mathcal{E} = \mathbf{s}\left(\mathbf{x}, \mathbf{f}(\cdot, \theta), \mathcal{S}\right) \subseteq \{(u,v) \,|\, u \in [0, H)\,, v \in [0, W)\} \tag{3}$$

H, W are the height and width of a image, u, v are the pixel coordinates. $\mathbf{T}(\cdot)$ is the transformation function applied to pixels inside $\mathcal{E}$. To determine $\mathcal{E}$, a search mechanism $\mathbf{s}(\cdot)$ is defined over a search space $\mathcal{S}$ of potential image areas. The optimal region $\mathcal{E}^*$ depends on the input image $\mathbf{x}$ and the neural network $\mathbf{f}(\cdot, \theta)$. HPA uses Metropolis Hastings sampling to search the space $\mathcal{S}$ defined in Eq. 4.

3.2 Patch Search with Reinforcement Learning

In this section, we propose our Monochrome Patch Attack (MPA). In general, this black-box attack uses monochrome rectangular patches which do not have patterns but have variable sizes and positions. We formulate the search over the position and size of adversarial patches as a reinforcement learning problem. The environment consists of $\mathbf{x}$ and $\mathbf{f}(\cdot, \theta)$, and an agent $\mathbb{A}$ is trained to sequentially place monochrome patches in the input image. The search space is defined as:

$$\mathcal{S} = \{(u_1^1, v_1^2, u_1^3, v_1^4, \cdots, u_C^1, v_C^2, u_C^3, v_C^4)\} \tag{4}$$

where C is the number of patches and each element in this set represents the coordinates of C pair of opposite corner points with each pair determining one rectangular region. $\mathcal{S}$ has $4C$ dimensions therefore we set the agent to take $4C$ actions in sequence to generate $\mathbf{a} \in \mathcal{S}$. We formulate the attack in the following:

$$\mathbb{A}(\theta_\mathbb{A}) : P(a_t | (a_1, \cdots, a_{t-1}), \mathbf{f}(\cdot; \theta), \mathbf{x}) \qquad t = \{1, \cdots, 4C\} \tag{5}$$

$$\mathbf{r} = \begin{cases} \ln y' - \mathbf{A}\left(\mathbf{a}\right) / \sigma^2, & \text{target attack} \\ \ln(1-y) - \mathbf{A}\left(\mathbf{a}\right) / \sigma^2, & \text{non-target attack} \end{cases} \tag{6}$$

$$\text{MPA} : \begin{cases} \mathcal{E} = \mathbf{J}\left(\mathbf{a}\right) \\ \mathbf{T}\left(x_{u,v}\right) = 0 \\ \mathcal{L} = -\mathbf{r} \cdot \ln \mathbf{P} \end{cases} \tag{7}$$

Similar to [41,46], we define $\mathbb{A}$ to be a combination of an LSTM and a fully connected layer which represents a policy network with $\theta_\mathbb{A}$ being its parameters.

At step t, the environment state is determined by previous actions, the deep network and the input. The agent outputs the probability distribution over the possible actions for step t as shown in Eq. 5. Then it samples one action and records the probability of the sampled action. In the end, this agent generates an action sequence $\mathbf{a}$ and the probability sequence $\mathbf{P}$ recording sampling these actions at each step. $\mathbf{J}(\cdot) : \mathbf{a} \rightarrow \mathcal{E}$ is the function transferring $\mathbf{a}$ to the areas formed by the C patches. The values of pixels in $\mathcal{E}$ are changed to 0 as shown in Eq. 6. Since $\mathbf{x}$ is normalized, the patch color is gray. The reward $\mathbf{r}$ for the agent is defined in Eq. 6, where $\mathbf{A}(\cdot)$ calculates the area of $\mathcal{E}$ and σ controls the penalty on this area. The loss function to optimize $\boldsymbol{\theta}_A$ is shown in Eq. 7.

Based on this framework, we further extend the search space to

$$\mathcal{S} = \{(u_1^1, v_1^2, u_1^3, v_1^4, R_1^5, G_1^6, B_1^7, \cdots, u_C^1, v_C^2, u_C^3, v_C^4, R_C^5, G_C^6, B_C^7)\} \tag{8}$$

where R, G, B represent the values of the RGB channels of the patches, splitting MPA into two variants MPA_Gray and MPA_RGB.

3.3   Texture-Based Patch Attacks

Monochrome Patch Attacks (MPAs) are powerful in non-targeted setting, however, in targeted setting their performance is not satisfying (Experiments 4.2), because MPAs only remove information at some parts of the image. The lack of additional input signals prevents MPAs from performing targeted attacks. However, we observe that MPA_RGB achieves superior performance compared to MPA_Gray (Table 1), motivating our texture-based patch attacks.

A Class-Specific Dictionary of Adversarial Textures. A major challenge when adding texture to patches is to find an efficient parameterization of the texture to retain fast and query efficient attacks. Our solution is to build a class-specific texture dictionary, where the patch patterns can be searched from. Each dictionary element represents a prototypical adversarial texture of a target class. Hence, to attack models trained on ImageNet, we build a dictionary with 1000 different categories, corresponding to the 1000 object classes in ImageNet. Each category has 30 different texture images whose contents are extracted from the ImageNet training set (see Fig. 2 for examples of dictionary elements).

We generate the texture dictionary using a four step process: First, we extract class-specific textures from a set of images of the target class. Inspired by style transfer [17,18], we use VGG19 [47] as the backbone for extracting texture information from images. Let $\mathbb{D}$ be the fully convolutional part of VGG19 pre-trained on ImageNet and it consists of 5 blocks. Let $\mathbf{F}_i^j$ be the feature maps from the jth convolution layer in the ith block of $\mathbb{D}$, and $\mathbf{G}_i^j$ be the corresponding Gram matrix of the feature activations. Following the approach of style transfer, we feed each image into $\mathbb{D}$ and compute the following gram matrices: $\mathbf{G}_1^2, \mathbf{G}_2^2, \mathbf{G}_3^2$ and $\mathbf{G}_4^2$. Subsequently, we flatten all gram matrices and concatenate them into one vector $\bar{\mathbf{G}}$ that encodes the texture information.

In a natural image, not all the regions are equally important for the final classification. Often the backgrounds or other objects are not of interest. Therefore,

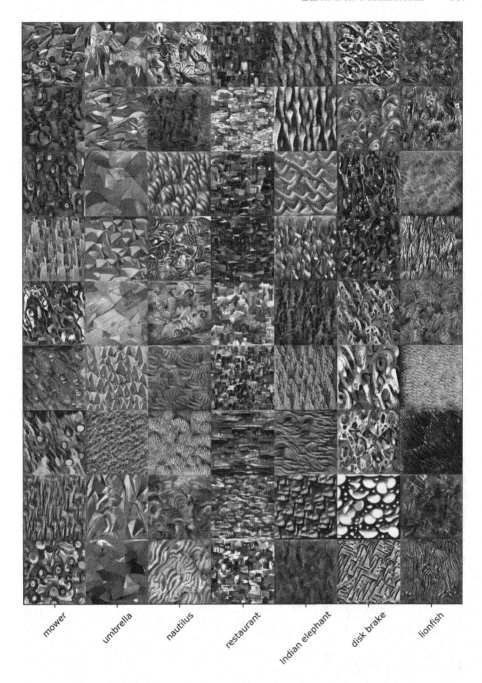

mower   umbrella   nautilus   restaurant   Indian elephant   disk brake   lionfish

Fig. 2. Examples in our designed texture dictionary.

we need to extract only the texture of relevant objects in images and hence make the extracted $\bar{\mathbf{G}}$ more semantically meaningful and increase the transferability among different deep networks. In order to locate the relevant information in each image, we perform Grad-CAM [44] on VGG19 for each image and mask out irrelevant regions of the image before texture extractions.

The third step is to generate the texture embedding. For each category, we conduct k-means algorithms on $\bar{\mathbf{G}}$s and use the 30 calculated clusters as the texture embedding for that category $\{\bar{\mathbf{G}}_c^1, \dots, \bar{\mathbf{G}}_c^{30}\}$, in order to increase the generalization property while maintaining the diversity of the embedding. The fourth part is to generate texture images from the $30 \times 1000\bar{\mathbf{G}}$s to build the dictionary. For each $\bar{\mathbf{G}}$, we optimize a texture image $\mathbf{t}$ starting from random noise according to the objective function $\mathcal{L}_{\text{texture}} = \lambda(\bar{\mathbf{G}} - \mathbf{G_t})^2$, where $\mathbf{G_t}$ and λ denote the feature embedding of $\mathbf{t}$ and the weight. See details in Sect. 4.1.

Integrating the Texture Dictionary into Patch Attack. Combining the generated texture dictionary, we propose Texture-based Patch Attack (TPA). Compared with MPA, the patches with the optimized locations in TPA are textured and provide more additional information, making TPA a powerful attack in both the non-targeted and targeted setting.

There are two updates from MPA to TPA. First, the search space is updated:

$$\mathcal{S} = \{(u_1^1, v_1^2, i_1^3, u_1^4, v_1^5, \cdots, u_C^1, v_C^2, i_C^3, u_C^4, v_C^5)\} \tag{9}$$

where i_c^3 indexes the texture image in category y' used to texture the cth patch. u_c^1, v_c^2 determines the patch position in $\mathbf{x}$, represented by $\mathbf{J}(\cdot)_t^1$ in Eq. 10. While u_c^4, v_c^5 denote the patch position in the i_c^3th texture image where we crop the patterns as the texture of the attacking patches, represented by $\mathbf{J}(\cdot)_t^2$. Note that in TPA, C instead of 1 agents are trained one after another. The cth agent's task is to find a position to put one more textured patch onto the image with $(c-1)$ patches already superimposed by the previous agents. The number of agents required to perform an successful attack C varies for different $\mathbf{x}$. We set a maximum number of the patches allowed to place and stop training new agents if the attack is already successful or C reaches the limit. The second update is that there is no penalty term on the patch area in Eq. 7, since the size of each patch an agent can place and texture is pre-fixed. Different from MPA, the total area of the attacking regions is well controlled.

$$\text{TPA}: \begin{cases} \mathcal{E} = \mathbf{J}_t^1(u_1^1, v_1^2, \cdots, u_C^1, v_C^2) \\ \mathbf{T}(x_{u,v}) = \mathbf{J}_t^2((i_1^3, u_1^4, v_1^5, \cdots, i_C^3, u_C^4, v_C^5)) \end{cases} \tag{10}$$

4 Experiments

We conduct experiments on a challenging dataset, ILSVRC2012 [42], a popular subset of the ImageNet database [13]. It consists of 1.3M training images and 50k testing images with high resolution. There are 1000 object categories in total, which are distributed approximately uniformly in the training set and strictly

Fig. 3. Adversarial examples generated by TPA_N1_4%. The first blue row shows the ground truth labels while the second row the predictions of ResNet50. Each attacking patch is textured by the texture dictionary, taking 4% of the overall area.

uniformly in the testing set. The networks against which we perform the attacks include ResNet [24], DenseNet [27], ResNeXt [55] and MobileNetV2 [43]. Since our texture dictionary are built through VGG [47] backbone, we do not involve this network to demonstrate the transferability of the texture images in the dictionary. For MPA and TPA, we conduct baseline subtraction on the rewards for the agents, and adopt early stopping when the difference of $\ln r$ averaged on 3 consecutive iterations is less than 1×10^{-4}, where r is reward.

4.1 Texture Dictionary Setting

The texture dictionary is built upon the training set in ILSVRC2012. All max pooling layers in the extractor $\mathbb{D}$ are replaced by average pooling layers with the kernel and stride sizes both being 2. The Grad-CAM is applied, using the feature map responses of the 5th convolution block of VGG19 to generate a attention map whose values are then normalized between 0 and 1. We consider the region with attention scores larger than the threshold 0.8 as useful. In the generation of texture images, the Adam optimizer is used with the starting learning rate 0.01. The total iteration number is 10000 and the weight λ in $\mathcal{L}_{\text{texture}}$ is 1×10^6. The texture dictionary is constructed with a two-level index structure with first-level key indexing the categories and sub-level indexing 30 texture images of a category. Figure 2 and Fig. 3 shows some example texture images and how the texture dictionary is utilized to perform attacks.

4.2 Attack Performance

In this section, we demonstrate the effectiveness of our proposed attacks, Monochrome Patch Attack (MPA) and Texture-based Patch Attack (TPA). The baseline

Table 1. Experimental results of the non-targeted attacks on a 1000 images randomly selected from the ILSVRC2012 validation set. The maximum allowed query number is 10000. Acc., Avg_area, Avg_qry denotes the classification accuracy, average area percentage occluded by the patches, average queries, respectively

Network	Attack	Acc. (%)	Avg_area (%)	Avg_qry
ResNet50	–	72.80	–	–
	HPA	0.40	18.05	10000
	MPA_Gray	0.00	6.57	9659
	MPA_RGB	0.00	5.41	9681
	TPA_N4_4%	0.30	5.06	1137
	TPA_N8_2%	0.30	3.10	983
DenseNet121	–	74.10	–	–
	HPA	0.10	19.82	10000
	MPA_Gray	0.00	6.87	9624
	MPA_RGB	0.00	5.73	9696
	TPA_N4_4%	0.50	5.13	1195
	TPA_N8_2%	0.30	3.13	1001
ResNeXt50	–	76.20	–	–
	HPA	0.80	19.22	10000
	MPA_Gray	0.00	7.88	9748
	MPA_RGB	0.00	6.23	9752
	TPA_N4_4%	0.70	5.21	1280
	TPA_N8_2%	0.50	3.25	1088
MobileNet-V2	–	68.80	–	–
	HPA	0.20	16.61	10000
	MPA_Gray	0.00	5.35	9578
	MPA_RGB	0.00	4.11	9603
	TPA_N4_4%	0.30	4.63	862
	TPA_N8_2%	0.30	2.74	756

is Hastings Patch Attack (HPA) [16]. Both HPA and MPA_Gray superimpose three gray rectangular patches onto the image. Each patch can take an arbitrary aspect ratio and an arbitrary scale. The updates of MPA_RGB is that the patch color is optimized. In TPA, we adopt the square patches and fix their sizes. We set a maximum number of the patches which the algorithm can superimpose. Therefore, the actual number for each image varies. For example, TPA_N4_4% indicates that each patch occupies 4% of the image and the maximum patch number is 4. This means TPA is able to control the maximum allowed area of an image to be occluded by the patches. There is no such limit on HPA and MPA, which means TPA attacks are better controllable. Additionally, we provide comparisons between Hastings sampling and reinforcement learning in Appendix D.

The experimental results in non-targeted setting are summarized in Table 1. In terms of accuracy drops, all the attacks achieve good performances against all the networks, decreasing their classification accuracy down to less than 1%. However, in terms of the average attacked area, HPA occludes 18.05%, 19.82%, 19.22% and 16.61% of the original images against the 4 architectures, while our MPA_RGB only occludes 5.41%, 5.73%, 6.23% and 4.11% respectively. Comparing MPA_RGB with MPA_Gray, we find that optimizing the RGB channel of the patches in MPA decreases the occluded area averaged over all the cases, from 6.67% to 5.37%. This proves that increasing the optimization dimensions and improving the complexity of the patches is beneficial, motivating us to texture these patches. TPA occludes the least area of the image with 3.10%, 3.13%, 3.25% and 2.74% against the different networks. TPA_N8_8% works better than TPA_N4_4%. In terms of query numbers, HPA is inefficient and always uses the whole query budget since it takes 10000 samples and chooses the best one. From MPA to TPA, the algorithm becomes more and more efficient with the query times dropping from 9652 to 957.

For the more challenging targeted setting the experimental results are reported in Table 2. Before performing the attacks, all the networks have a target accuracy not larger than 0.1%. It is observed that although HPA increases target accuracy to 23.05% on average, it occluded 71.54%, 71.68%, 72.57% and 69.45% of the image in the four attacking cases, failing to be considered a successful attack algorithm. For MPA, we use the RGB version since it has been proved to be superior than the gray version in Table 1. Although the MPA can only increase the target accuracy to 26.53%, it occludes much less areas than HPA with an average proportion 17.08%. On the contrary, our TPA achieves high performances. TPA_N10_4% is able to increase the target accuracy to 99.70%, 99.90%, 99.70% and 99.90% against the different architectures. The other 2 variant TPA_N10_2% and TPA_N10_10% corresponds to two different requirements for the attack. The first one provides the smaller occlusion area as it uses 7.80%, 7.87%, 7.59% and 7.78% of the areas respectively to increase the target accuracy to 97.70% on average. The second one is more query-efficient as it takes 3747, 3970, 3538 and 4422 queries and obtain an average target accuracy 100%.

In both the non-targeted and non-targeted settings, MPA and TPA are superior to HPA to a large margin. TPA is the best attack among all the perspectives including the accuracy/target_accuracy, occluded areas and query efficiency.

4.3   Texture-Based Patch Attacks Against Defenses

This section evaluates our attacks against popular defenses. As our MPA and TPA are new types of attacks, we first test them on traditional SOTA defense methods [53]. Another direction is to defend our attack with shape-biased network [19], which is expected to be a good defense against our texture-based patch attack. Additionally, we perform evaluation against the Local Gradients Smoothing (LGS) [36] specifically designed to defend against the patch-based attack in Appendix C.

Table 2. Experimental results of the targeted attacks on a 1000 images randomly selected from the ILSVRC2012 validation set. The maximum allowed query number is 50000. The target label for each image is difference from its ground truth label. T_acc., Avg_area, Avg_qry denotes the classification accuracy on target labels, average area percentage occluded by the patches, average queries, respectively

Network	Attack	T_acc. (%)	Avg_area (%)	Avg_qry
ResNet50	–	0.10	–	–
	HPA	23.20	71.54	50000
	MPA_RGB	25.90	18.45	28361
	TPA_N10_2%	97.60	7.80	15728
	TPA_N10_4%	99.70	9.97	8643
	TPA_N10_10%	100.00	15.36	3747
DenseNet121	–	0.10	–	–
	HPA	21.50	71.68	50000
	MPA_RGB	24.90	19.38	28088
	TPA_N10_2%	97.10	7.87	15920
	TPA_N10_4%	99.90	10.19	8953
	TPA_N10_10%	100.00	15.84	3970
ResNeXt50	–	0.00	–	–
	HPA	25.40	72.57	50000
	MPA_RGB	27.60	13.86	24738
	TPA_N10_2%	97.60	7.59	15189
	TPA_N10_4%	99.70	9.60	8223
	TPA_N10_10%	100.00	15.04	3538
MobileNet-V2	–	0.10	–	–
	HPA	22.10	69.45	50000
	MPA_RGB	27.70	16.64	28294
	TPA_N10_2%	98.50	7.78	15479
	TPA_N10_4%	99.90	10.39	8948
	TPA_N10_10%	100.00	16.85	4422

Defense 1: Feature Denoising. In this experimental part, we choose Denoise-ResNet152 [53] to perform MPA and TPA against. It is the SOTA defense against traditional perturbation-based adversarial attacks in a white-box setting. In this scenario, the attacker has access to the architecture and weights of the deep network. This is a strictly easier setting than a black-box one. PGD [34] can only decrease the accuracy to 55.7% and 45.5% after 10 and 100 iterations, respectively. Our experimental results are summarized in Table 3. For non-targeted attacks, both MPA and TPA successfully attack Denoise-ResNet152. MPA reduces the accuracy from 61.6% to 0.00% with the occluded area only being 0.48%, which is even smaller than those of any our previous non-targeted

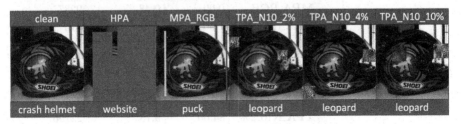

Fig. 4. Visualization of patch-attacked examples on ResNet50. The first row corresponds to non-targeted attacks and the second targeted attacks with the target class being leopard. More examples and their attention maps are provided in Appendix A and B.

attack on normal networks in Table 1. The two versions of TPA decrease the accuracy to 1.6% and 1.3%, respectively, both with the taken queries less than 1000. For targeted attacks, the target accuracy for the network is 0.1%. Although MPA only increases this to 38.3%, it is higher than that of any our previous MPA attacks in targeted settings in Table 2. TPA_N10_4% is able to improve the target accuracy to 94.60%, reflecting the vulnerability of this defense against TPA (Fig. 4).

Defense 2: Against Shape-Biased Network. The textures of the patch play a significant role in magnifying the power of our patch attack, as shown in the comparisons between MPA and TPA in Sect. 4.2. According to this dependence on the texture, the best defense against TPA is the model making predictions primarily based on the shapes of objects in the images instead of being largely influenced by their textures. Therefore, we consider the Shape-Network in [19] as the current best potential defense against TPA. The Shape-Network is trained on the Stylized-ImageNet, which is created by conducting style transfer on the whole training and validation sets of ImageNet, randomly changing object textures while maintaining object shapes in each image. By this design, the Shape-Network is supposed to be insensitive to textures but rely more on shapes to make inferences. Note that the construction of our texture dictionary used by TPA is also inspired by the style transfer dealing with object textures, as illustrated in Sect. 3.3. So in principle, the Shape-Network is a very strong defense against our attacks. However, the experimental results in Table 4 show that TPAs easily confuse the Shape-Network with basically no difference as against a

Table 3. Experimental results of the defenses on 1000 images randomly selected from the ILSVRC2012 validation set. The maximum allowed query number is 10000 and 50000 for the non-targeted and targeted settings. Acc., T_acc., Avg_area, and Avg_qry denote the classification accuracy on ground truth and target labels, average area percentage occluded by the patches, average query number, respectively

Non-target	Attack	Acc. (%)	Avg_area (%)	Avg_qry
Denoise_ResNet152	–	61.60	–	–
	MPA_RGB	0.00	0.48	9287
	TPA_N4_4%	1.60	4.71	919
	TPA_N8_10%	1.30	2.91	867
Target	Attack	T_acc. (%)	Avg_area (%)	Avg_qry
Denoise_ResNet152	–	0.10	–	–
	MPA_RGB	38.30	6.39	27464
	TPA_N10_2%	84.00	9.73	22196
	TPA_N10_4%	94.60	13.40	13932
	TPA_N10_10%	99.30	20.90	6920

Table 4. Experimental results of the defenses on 1000 images randomly selected from the ILSVRC2012 validation set. The maximum allowed query number is 10000 and 50000 for the non-targeted and targeted settings. Acc., T_acc., Avg_area, and Avg_qry denote the classification accuracy on ground truth and target labels, average area percentage occluded by the patches, average query number, respectively

Non-target	Attack	Acc. (%)	Avg_area (%)	Avg_qry
Shape-Network	–	73.70	–	–
	TPA_N4_4%	0.50	5.19	1242
	TPA_N8_10%	0.20	3.17	1031
Target	Attack	T_acc. (%)	Avg_area (%)	Avg_qry
Shape-Network	–	0.10	–	–
	TPA_N10_2%	96.30	8.36	17443
	TPA_N10_4%	100.00	10.31	9229
	TPA_N10_10%	100.00	15.52	3822

normal deep network. In the non-targeted setting, TPAs decrease the network's accuracy from 77.70% to 0.50% and 0.20% with the occluded area being 5.19% and 3.17% for the two variants respectively. The average taken queries is 1137. For the targeted setting, the three variants of TPAs increase the target accuracy from 0.10% to 96.30%, 100.00% and 100.00%, respectively. TPA_N10_2% provides the smallest occluded area 8.36%. TPA_N10_10% is the most query-efficient with only 3822 taken queries but high occluded area 15.52%. TPA_N10_4% is the moderate choice with small occluded area 10.31% and small taken queries 9229.

5   Conclusion

In this work, we propose *PatchAttack*, a powerful black-box texture-based patch attack. Our attack shows that even small textured patches are able to break deep neural networks. We model the attacking process as a reinforcement learning problem with an agent that is trained to superimpose patches onto the images in order to induce misclassification. Using monochrome patches only, we achieve a strong performance on non-targeted attack, surpassing previous work by a large margin using less queries and smaller patch areas. After enabling the reinforcement learning agent to also use texture from an adversarial texture dictionary, PatchAttack achieves exceptional performances in both non-targeted and targeted settings. Furthermore, we show that PatchAttack breaks traditional SOTA defenses and shape-based networks.

Acknowledgements. This work was supported in part by the Johns Hopkins University Institute for Assured Autonomy with grant IAA 80052272, National Science Foundation (NSF) grant BCS-1827427 and NSF grant CNS-18-54000.

References

1. Clarifai API (2020). https://clarifai.com/
2. Google vision API (2020). https://cloud.google.com/vision/
3. Alzantot, M., Sharma, Y., Chakraborty, S., Zhang, H., Hsieh, C.J., Srivastava, M.B.: Genattack: practical black-box attacks with gradient-free optimization. In: Proceedings of the Genetic and Evolutionary Computation Conference (2019)
4. Andriushchenko, M., Croce, F., Flammarion, N., Hein, M.: Square attack: a query-efficient black-box adversarial attack via random search. arXiv preprint arXiv:1912.00049 (2019)
5. Bhagoji, A.N., He, W., Li, B., Song, D.: Practical black-box attacks on deep neural networks using efficient query mechanisms. In: Ferrari, V., Hebert, M., Sminchisescu, C., Weiss, Y. (eds.) ECCV 2018. LNCS, vol. 11216, pp. 158–174. Springer, Cham (2018). https://doi.org/10.1007/978-3-030-01258-8_10
6. Bojarski, M., et al.: End to end learning for self-driving cars. arXiv preprint arXiv:1604.07316 (2016)
7. Brendel, W., Rauber, J., Bethge, M.: Decision-based adversarial attacks: reliable attacks against black-box machine learning models. arXiv preprint arXiv:1712.04248 (2017)
8. Brown, T.B., Mané, D., Roy, A., Abadi, M., Gilmer, J.: Adversarial patch. arXiv preprint arXiv:1712.09665 (2017)
9. Carlini, N., Wagner, D.: Towards evaluating the robustness of neural networks. In: 2017 IEEE Symposium on Security and Privacy (2017)
10. Chen, P.Y., Zhang, H., Sharma, Y., Yi, J., Hsieh, C.J.: Zoo: zeroth order optimization based black-box attacks to deep neural networks without training substitute models. In: Proceedings of the 10th ACM Workshop on Artificial Intelligence and Security (2017)
11. Cheng, M., Le, T., Chen, P.Y., Yi, J., Zhang, H., Hsieh, C.J.: Query-efficient hard-label black-box attack: An optimization-based approach. arXiv preprint arXiv:1807.04457 (2018)

12. Chernikova, A., Oprea, A., Nita-Rotaru, C., Kim, B.: Are self-driving cars secure? Evasion attacks against deep neural networks for steering angle prediction. In: 2019 IEEE Security and Privacy Workshops (2019)

13. Deng, J., Dong, W., Socher, R., Li, L.J., Li, K., Fei-Fei, L.: Imagenet: a large-scale hierarchical image database. In: Proceedings of the IEEE Conference on Computer Vision and Pattern Recognition (2009)

14. Dong, Y., et al.: Boosting adversarial attacks with momentum. In: Proceedings of the IEEE Conference on Computer Vision and Pattern Recognition (2018)

15. Eykholt, K., et al.: Robust physical-world attacks on deep learning visual classification. In: Proceedings of the IEEE Conference on Computer Vision and Pattern Recognition (2018)

16. Fawzi, A., Frossard, P.: Measuring the effect of nuisance variables on classifiers. In: British Machine Vision Conference (2016)

17. Gatys, L., Ecker, A.S., Bethge, M.: Texture synthesis using convolutional neural networks. In: Advances in Neural Information Processing Systems (2015)

18. Gatys, L.A., Ecker, A.S., Bethge, M.: Image style transfer using convolutional neural networks. In: Proceedings of the IEEE Conference on Computer Vision and Pattern Recognition (2016)

19. Geirhos, R., Rubisch, P., Michaelis, C., Bethge, M., Wichmann, F.A., Brendel, W.: Imagenet-trained CNNs are biased towards texture; increasing shape bias improves accuracy and robustness. arXiv preprint arXiv:1811.12231 (2018)

20. Goodfellow, I.J., Shlens, J., Szegedy, C.: Explaining and harnessing adversarial examples. arXiv preprint arXiv:1412.6572 (2014)

21. Goodman, D.: Transferability of adversarial examples to attack cloud-based image classifier service. arXiv pp. arXiv-2001 (2020)

22. Goodman, D., Wei, T.: Cloud-based image classification service is not robust to simple transformations: A forgotten battlefield. arXiv preprint arXiv:1906.07997 (2019)

23. Guo, C., Gardner, J.R., You, Y., Wilson, A.G., Weinberger, K.Q.: Simple black-box adversarial attacks. arXiv preprint arXiv:1905.07121 (2019)

24. He, K., Zhang, X., Ren, S., Sun, J.: Deep residual learning for image recognition. In: Proceedings of the IEEE Conference on Computer Vision and Pattern Recognition (2016)

25. Hosseini, H., Kannan, S., Zhang, B., Poovendran, R.: Deceiving Google's perspective API built for detecting toxic comments. arXiv preprint arXiv:1702.08138 (2017)

26. Hosseini, H., Xiao, B., Poovendran, R.: Google's cloud vision API is not robust to noise. In: 2017 16th IEEE International Conference on Machine Learning and Applications (2017)

27. Huang, G., Liu, Z., Van Der Maaten, L., Weinberger, K.Q.: Densely connected convolutional networks. In: Proceedings of the IEEE Conference on Computer Vision and Pattern Recognition (2017)

28. Huang, L., et al.: Universal physical camouflage attacks on object detectors. In: Proceedings of the IEEE Conference on Computer Vision and Pattern Recognition (2020)

29. Ilyas, A., Engstrom, L., Athalye, A., Lin, J.: Black-box adversarial attacks with limited queries and information. arXiv preprint arXiv:1804.08598 (2018)

30. Ilyas, A., Engstrom, L., Madry, A.: Prior convictions: black-box adversarial attacks with bandits and priors. arXiv preprint arXiv:1807.07978 (2018)

31. Kannan, H., Kurakin, A., Goodfellow, I.: Adversarial logit pairing. arXiv preprint arXiv:1803.06373 (2018)

32. Li, Y., Bai, S., Zhou, Y., Xie, C., Zhang, Z., Yuille, A.: Learning transferable adversarial examples via ghost networks. In: Proceedings of the AAAI Conference on Artificial Intelligence (2020)
33. Liu, Y., Chen, X., Liu, C., Song, D.: Delving into transferable adversarial examples and black-box attacks. arXiv preprint arXiv:1611.02770 (2016)
34. Madry, A., Makelov, A., Schmidt, L., Tsipras, D., Vladu, A.: Towards deep learning models resistant to adversarial attacks. arXiv preprint arXiv:1706.06083 (2017)
35. Naseer, M.M., Khan, S.H., Khan, M.H., Khan, F.S., Porikli, F.: Cross-domain transferability of adversarial perturbations. In: Advances in Neural Information Processing Systems (2019)
36. Naseer, M., Khan, S., Porikli, F.: Local gradients smoothing: defense against localized adversarial attacks. In: 2019 IEEE Winter Conference on Applications of Computer Vision (2019)
37. Papernot, N., McDaniel, P., Goodfellow, I.: Transferability in machine learning: from phenomena to black-box attacks using adversarial samples. arXiv preprint arXiv:1605.07277 (2016)
38. Papernot, N., McDaniel, P., Goodfellow, I., Jha, S., Celik, Z.B., Swami, A.: Practical black-box attacks against machine learning. In: Proceedings of the 2017 ACM on Asia Conference on Computer and Communications Security (2017)
39. Pei, K., Cao, Y., Yang, J., Jana, S.: Deepxplore: automated whitebox testing of deep learning systems. In: Proceedings of the 26th Symposium on Operating Systems Principles (2017)
40. Ranjan, A., Janai, J., Geiger, A., Black, M.J.: Attacking optical flow. In: Proceedings of the IEEE International Conference on Computer Vision (2019)
41. Ren, Z., Wang, X., Zhang, N., Lv, X., Li, L.J.: Deep reinforcement learning-based image captioning with embedding reward. In: Proceedings of the IEEE Conference on Computer Vision and Pattern Recognition (2017)
42. Russakovsky, O., et al.: Imagenet large scale visual recognition challenge. Int. J. Comput. Vision 115(3), 211–252 (2015)
43. Sandler, M., Howard, A., Zhu, M., Zhmoginov, A., Chen, L.C.: Mobilenetv2: inverted residuals and linear bottlenecks. In: Proceedings of the IEEE Conference on Computer Vision and Pattern Recognition (2018)
44. Selvaraju, R.R., Cogswell, M., Das, A., Vedantam, R., Parikh, D., Batra, D.: Gradcam: visual explanations from deep networks via gradient-based localization. In: Proceedings of the IEEE International Conference on Computer Vision (2017)
45. Shi, Y., Wang, S., Han, Y.: Curls & whey: boosting black-box adversarial attacks. In: Proceedings of the IEEE Conference on Computer Vision and Pattern Recognition (2019)
46. Shu, M., Liu, C., Qiu, W., Yuille, A.: Identifying model weakness with adversarial examiner. arXiv preprint arXiv:1911.11230 (2019)
47. Simonyan, K., Zisserman, A.: Very deep convolutional networks for large-scale image recognition. arXiv preprint arXiv:1409.1556 (2014)
48. Sitawarin, C., Bhagoji, A.N., Mosenia, A., Chiang, M., Mittal, P.: Darts: deceiving autonomous cars with toxic signs. arXiv preprint arXiv:1802.06430 (2018)
49. Szegedy, C., et al.: Intriguing properties of neural networks. arXiv preprint arXiv:1312.6199 (2013)
50. Tian, Y., Pei, K., Jana, S., Ray, B.: Deeptest: automated testing of deep-neural-network-driven autonomous cars. In: Proceedings of the 40th International Conference on Software Engineering (2018)

51. Tu, C.C., et al.: Autozoom: autoencoder-based zeroth order optimization method for attacking black-box neural networks. In: Proceedings of the AAAI Conference on Artificial Intelligence (2019)

52. Uesato, J., O'Donoghue, B., Oord, A.V.D., Kohli, P.: Adversarial risk and the dangers of evaluating against weak attacks. arXiv preprint arXiv:1802.05666 (2018)

53. Xie, C., Wu, Y., Maaten, L.V.D., Yuille, A.L., He, K.: Feature denoising for improving adversarial robustness. In: Proceedings of the IEEE Conference on Computer Vision and Pattern Recognition (2019)

54. Xie, C., et al.: Improving transferability of adversarial examples with input diversity. In: Proceedings of the IEEE Conference on Computer Vision and Pattern Recognition (2019)

55. Xie, S., Girshick, R., Dollár, P., Tu, Z., He, K.: Aggregated residual transformations for deep neural networks. In: Proceedings of the IEEE Conference on Computer Vision and Pattern Recognition (2017)

56. Zhou, W., et al.: Transferable adversarial perturbations. In: Proceedings of the European Conference on Computer Vision (2018)

More Classifiers, Less Forgetting: A Generic Multi-classifier Paradigm for Incremental Learning

Yu Liu[1]([✉]), Sarah Parisot[2,3], Gregory Slabaugh[2], Xu Jia[2], Ales Leonardis[2], and Tinne Tuytelaars[1]

[1] KU Leuven, Leuven, Belgium
{yu.liu,tinne.tuytelaars}@kuleuven.be
[2] Huawei Noah's Ark Lab, Shatin, Hong Kong
{sarah.parisot,gregory.slabaugh,xu.jia,ales.leonardis}@huawei.com
[3] Mila, Montreal, Canada

Abstract. Overcoming catastrophic forgetting in neural networks is a long-standing and core research objective for incremental learning. Notable studies have shown regularization strategies enable the network to remember previously acquired knowledge devoid of heavy forgetting. Since those regularization strategies are mostly associated with classifier outputs, we propose a MUlti-Classifier (MUC) incremental learning paradigm that integrates an ensemble of auxiliary classifiers to estimate more effective regularization constraints. Additionally, we extend two common methods, focusing on parameter and activation regularization, from the conventional single-classifier paradigm to MUC. Our classifier ensemble promotes regularizing network parameters or activations when moving to learn the next task. Under the setting of task-agnostic evaluation, our experimental results on CIFAR-100 and Tiny ImageNet incremental benchmarks show that our method outperforms other baselines. Specifically, MUC obtains 3%–5% accuracy boost and 4%–5% decline of forgetting ratio, compared with MAS and LwF. Our code is available at https://github.com/Liuy8/MUC.

Keywords: Incremental learning · Regularization · Classifier ensemble

1 Introduction

Incremental learning dates back decades, but has recently shown an increased popularity due to the renewed interest in deep neural networks [20,33]. Unlike standard multi-task learning, the tasks during incremental learning arrive sequentially, and the data of previous tasks is not accessible anymore (*e.g.* , due to memory limits or privacy issues). Here, we consider the *class-incremental*

Electronic supplementary material The online version of this chapter (https://doi.org/10.1007/978-3-030-58574-7_42) contains supplementary material, which is available to authorized users.

© Springer Nature Switzerland AG 2020
A. Vedaldi et al. (Eds.): ECCV 2020, LNCS 12371, pp. 699–716, 2020.
https://doi.org/10.1007/978-3-030-58574-7_42

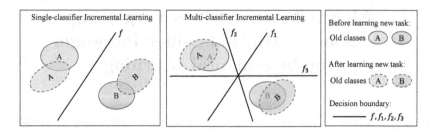

Fig. 1. Conceptual comparison between single-classifier and multi-classifier incremental learning. Our multi-classifier paradigm is better at regularizing the feature distributions of old classes than the single-classifier paradigm.

learning setup [16,35], in which each new task learns a set of classes disjoint from the old tasks. The network needs to learn feature representations for classifying the images of old and new classes. Besides, we adopt a *task-agnostic* evaluation: at test time it is unknown which task an image sample belongs to.

The major challenge in incremental learning is the so-called *catastrophic forgetting* [29], a phenomenon where previously acquired knowledge is lost from the network after it is trained on the newly incoming task. To reduce forgetting, a large set of methods exploit *regularization strategies* to constrain changes of network parameters or activations. When learning a new task, the network is updated by combining the regularization loss with the standard classification loss. The objective is to find the optimal trade-off between the *adaptation* to new tasks and the *preservation* on previous tasks. Most regularization strategies are closely associated with *classifier outputs*: (1) *parameter regularization* methods such as EWC [18] and MAS [1] estimate an importance weight for each parameter in the network and penalize changes to important parameters. The computation of those importance weights is based on the loss or output of the classifier. (2) *activation regularization* methods like LwF [24] introduce a knowledge distillation based regularization that enforces the classifier outputs of the new model to be close to those of the old model. In both regularization methods, the classifier is crucial not only for classifying new tasks, but also for regularizing old ones. However, these existing methods learn a single classifier only for each task and their regularization strategies are heavily limited by the output of one single classifier. Motivated by the above finding, our work aims to address the question: *How to exploit more classifiers to improve the effectiveness of the regularization strategies for incremental learning?*

To this end, we propose a MUlti-Classifier (MUC) paradigm that integrate *classifiers ensemble* to estimate more effective regularization constraints. First, we train a standard neural network with in-distribution data of current task. Then, we construct upon the network a set of new and auxiliary classifiers which are trained on out-of-distribution data irrelevant to current task. To enhance the discrepancy among those classifiers, we train a *classifier discrepancy loss* to maximize prediction disagreement on the out-of-distribution data and agreement on the in-distribution data. Despite that those classifiers make different decision boundaries for the same classification objective, they help to produce complementary and robust information to regularize forgetting of previously learned classes. We show in Fig. 1 how MUC work differently from conventional single-classifier paradigm. MUC is a generic method and can be integrated with most pre-existing regularization strategies. Additionally, we show MUC leverages multiple classifiers for improving two common incremental learning methods, focusing on parameter and activation regularization, respectively.

The contributions of this paper are summarized below:

- We propose a novel and generic multi-classifier incremental learning paradigm, coined MUC. which demonstrates the effectiveness of taking into account the role of the classifier for reducing forgetting. This work is the first to exploit the classifier discrepancy for incremental learning.
- We introduce two instantiations based on MUC, by extending parameter and activation regularization, respectively. It suggests improving existing regularization strategies is also important for incremental learning.
- In the setting of class-incremental learning, we experiment with CIFAR-100 and Tiny ImageNet incremental benchmarks, where MUC achieves considerable and promising improvements over the single-classifier paradigm. Extensive analysis additionally verifies the strengths of MUC.

2   Related Work

In recent years, incremental learning has become one of the most critical yet challenging directions in a broad spectrum of application domains, including image classification [24,35], object detection [10,39] and semantic segmentation [5,30]. Due to the "*stability-plasticity*" dilemma in neural networks [3,29], incremental learners perform well on the latest task but witness a dramatic degradation of performance on previous tasks. To alleviate such a forgetting issue, extensive regularization strategies have been proposed in the literature, which can be grouped into two main categories below.

The first category is normally called *parameter regularization* [1,6,18,23,25, 48] that penalizes drastic updates of important parameters when the network is learning a new task. The intuition is that keeping the important parameters for old tasks intact can reduce forgetting while the remaining parameters learn to adapt to the incoming new task. Being one of the most representative approaches, Elastic Weight Consolidation (EWC) [18] estimated the parameters' importance to the change in loss function by the diagonal of the Fisher information matrix (FIM). Memory Aware Synapses (MAS) [1] presented a new importance weight through the gradient of the L2-normalization outputs *w.r.t.* the parameter. Nevertheless, devising a robust manner to formulate importance weights is still an open and challenging problem. The second category is *activation regularization* that imposes regularization constraints on the feature activations in the network rather than on the parameters themselves. Learning without Forgetting (LwF) [24], being a fundamental approach in this category, fed the data of the new task into the stored model and recorded the output probabilities as soft targets. Then a knowledge distillation loss [13] was used to encourage the newly updated model to produce similar predictions as the soft labels. Upon LwF, many approaches have been proposed to improve the regularization based on knowledge distillation [7,22,43,49,50]. For instance, LwM [7] considered adding knowledge distillation on the feature activations of intermediate layers. Instead of designing a specific regularization strategy, our work presents a generic paradigm in which existing strategies can be improved to further reduce forgetting.

Next to the above regularization, other rehearsal based methods [2,15,17,26, 35] store some old data to make the network remember previous tasks, albeit violating the motivation of incremental learning to some extent. iCaRL [35] used an external memory to store a subset of data samples (*a.k.a.* exemplars) for old classes. It also employed a knowledge distillation loss to help regularize the update of the network. Additionally, some research efforts are made to address the data imbalance between a large amount of new classes samples and a small budget of old classes samples [4,14,44]. Inspired by the success of Generative Adversarial Networks (GANs), a few works [11,38,45] proposed training generative networks to produce pseudo-rehearsal samples instead of storing the original and real data. Unlike these works, our MUC is not limited by the need of storing and re-using old data. Nevertheless, we empirically in the experiment show its effectiveness under the rehearsal-based scenario.

Multi-classifier learners have been studied in several vision tasks [21,42,46]. On the one hand, the research objective is to maximize the *consensus* of outputs from multiple classifiers, to consolidate the transfer learning from source domain to target domain [8,27]. On the other hand, the objective is to maximize the *discrepancy* of the classifiers' predictions. For example, the approach in [47] enlarged the discrepancy between two classifiers to separate in-distribution samples from out-of-distribution samples. Focusing on unsupervised domain adaptation, the work in [36] combined the above two objectives in an adversarial learning manner. It first maximized the discrepancy for the target samples and then minimized the discrepancy for feature generation. However, our work aims to exploit the classifier discrepancy for incremental learning.

3   Proposed Method

Overall Idea. We focus on the class-incremental learning (CIL) setup, in which the model continually learns more classes from new tasks while retaining the recognition of old classes from previous tasks. Note that, we mainly follow the standard setting, without re-using the image samples from previous tasks. First of all, we introduce how the MUC paradigm is trained in a two-stage fashion (in Sect. 3.1). In the first stage, we add a main classifier (*i.e.* the last layer of the network) on top of the feature extractor (*i.e.* the earlier layers of the network) and update the entire network to correctly classify the newly incremental classes. During the second stage, we freeze the feature extractor and train a set of additional side classifiers (*i.e.* newly auxiliary layers) in parallel to the main

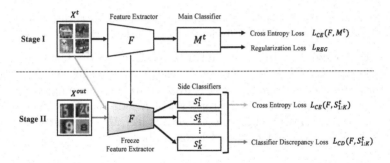

Fig. 2. Pipeline of training MUC in a two-stage fashion. The two stages optimize the cross-entropy loss $\mathcal{L}_{CE}$ for a main classifier M^t and a set of K side classifiers $S^t_{1:K}$, respectively. The regularization term $\mathcal{L}_{REG}$ in **Stage I** is used to reduce forgetting for previous tasks. The classifier discrepancy loss $\mathcal{L}_{CD}$ in **Stage II** aims to diversify the side classifiers.

classifier. Since most CIL methods heavily rely on a single classifier, we then extend two instantiations based on MUC (Sect. 3.2 and Sect. 3.3), by utilizing multiple classifiers for more robust and effective regularization.

Problem Notation. Suppose that there are T of sequential tasks together with their data $\{X^t, Y^t\}^T_{t=1}$. $X^t = \{x^t_i\}^{N^t}_{i=1}$ and $Y^t = \{y^t_i\}^{N^t}_{i=1}$ are the input images and their ground-truth labels, where N^t denotes the number of image samples in task t. Task t contains a number of C^t classes, and the classes from different tasks should be disjoint. The feature extractor F is shared across all tasks, but is updated continually by the data. The main classifier M^t and K side classifiers $S^t_{1:K} = \{S^t_k\}^K_{k=1}$ are associated with task t. After training all tasks, the sets of main classifiers and side classifiers are denoted as $\{M^t\}^T_{t=1}$ and $\{S^t_{1:K}\}^T_{t=1}$.

3.1 Multi-classifier Incremental Learning

Our MUC for incrementally learning tasks is performed in two stages (Fig. 2).

Stage I: Train Feature Extractor and Main Classifier. During incremental learning, the feature extractor is trained from scratch for the first task and is then updated continually by subsequent tasks. For each task, its main classifier is randomly initialized and newly trained. Given the training data $\{X^t, Y^t\}$ for the new task t, we minimize the standard cross-entropy (CE) loss and optimize the feature extractor F and the main classifier M^t simultaneously. Additionally, it is crucially necessary for incremental learning to impose a regularization loss $\mathcal{L}_{REG}$ that is used to constrain the updates of important parameters associated with previous tasks. The objective in this stage becomes

$$\mathcal{L}_{\text{stageI}} = \mathcal{L}_{CE}(F, M^t) + \lambda \mathcal{L}_{REG} = \sum_{i=1}^{N^t} -\log[p(y^t_i | x^t_i)] + \lambda \mathcal{L}_{REG}, \qquad (1)$$

where $p(y_i^t|x_i^t)$ is the Softmax probability for the ground-truth label y_i^t. λ is a trade-off hyper-parameter. We will detail $\mathcal{L}_{REG}$ in later subsections.

Stage II: Freeze Feature Extractor and Train Side Classifiers. This stage seeks to learn new side classifiers for task t. Specifically, the same feature extractor F transferred from `Stage I` is frozen during the training of `Stage II`. We develop upon the feature extractor a set of K side classifiers, each of which learns to correctly classify the same C^t classes like M^t. To jointly train these side classifiers, we accumulate their CE loss to be

$$\mathcal{L}_{CE}(F, S_{1:K}^t) = \sum_{i=1}^{N^t} \sum_{k=1}^{K} -\log[p_k(y_i^t|x_i^t)], \qquad (2)$$

where $p_k(y_i^t|x_i^t)$ is the prediction probability from the k-th side classifier S_k^t.

However, training only with a classification objective leads to nearly identical side classifiers. The side classifiers learn similar parameters including weights and bias. Consequently, the identical classifiers produce the same regularization terms that have no benefit for further reducing the forgetting ratio on the old tasks. To make the side classifiers learn different parameters, we additionally maximize the *classifier discrepancy* (or *disagreement*) when training the side classifiers $S_{1:K}^t$. Maximum classifier discrepancy (MCD) has been used in other areas [36,47], but this work is the first to exploit it for incremental learning. First, we need to choose an *out-of-distribution* (OOD) dataset X^{out}, which contains N^{out} samples that are totally different from the in-distribution classes in the tasks. The OOD samples can be unlabeled, as the classifier discrepancy loss does not need to use their labels. Given any OOD sample $x^{out} \in X^{out}$, we compute the classifier discrepancy with the side classifiers' probabilistic vectors. The classifier discrepancy between any two probabilistic vectors is the L1-norm distance of their absolute difference

$$d(\mathbf{p}_m(y|x^{out}), \mathbf{p}_n(y|x^{out})) = |\mathbf{p}_m(y|x^{out}) - \mathbf{p}_n(y|x^{out})|, \qquad (3)$$

where $\mathbf{p}_m(y|x^{out})$ and $\mathbf{p}_n(y|x^{out})$ represent the C^t-dimensional probabilistic vectors predicted by S_m^t and S_n^t, respectively. For K side classifiers, there are $\binom{K}{2}$ many possible pairs. The total classifier discrepancy loss is denoted by

$$\mathcal{L}_{CD}(F, S_{1:K}^t) = \sum_{i=1}^{N^{out}} \sum_{m=1}^{K} \sum_{n=m+1}^{K} d(\mathbf{p}_m(y|x_i^{out}), \mathbf{p}_n(y|x_i^{out})). \qquad (4)$$

Finally, the objective of `Stage II` is to minimize the classification cost and at the same time maximize the classifier discrepancy

$$\mathcal{L}_{\text{stageII}} = \mathcal{L}_{CE}(F, S^t) - \mathcal{L}_{CD}(F, S_{1:K}^t). \qquad (5)$$

Consequently, these side classifiers become distinct by learning different parameters for the same task. In addition, they retain the *agreement* on the samples of task t while increasing the *disagreement* on the samples of OOD dataset. The core in incremental learning is how to impose an extra regularization term to consolidate previous knowledge when learning the next task. In the following two subsections, we extend pre-existing regularization strategies from the single-classifier paradigm to the MUC paradigm.

3.2 MUC with Parameter Regularization

Here, we present how to perform the parameter regularization (PR) methods in our MUC paradigm. Without loss of generality, we employ the importance weight defined in Memory aware synapses (MAS) [1], while MUC can also handle with the importance weights in other PR methods. Our method, namely MUC-MAS, enables to estimate importance weights from not only the main classifier, but also additional side classifiers. To be specific, after training the task $t-1$ in Stage I, the importance weight per parameter is denoted by

$$\alpha_j^{t-1} = \frac{1}{N^{t-1}} \sum_{i=1}^{N^{t-1}} \left|\left| \frac{\partial [l_2^2(M^{t-1}(F(x_i^{t-1})))]}{\partial \theta_j} \right|\right|, \tag{6}$$

where $\theta_j \in \boldsymbol{\theta}$ are the parameters in the feature extractor, and $M^{t-1}(F(\cdot))$ is the output before the Softmax function. We do not compute importance weights for the parameters of the classifiers, because they will be fixed once the network starts to learn the next task. Likewise, the side classifiers learned in Stage II are also used to estimate more importance weights. The feature extractor is fixed during Stage II, the side classifiers, however, are able to provide diverse outputs due to their different parameters. Thereby, the importance weight $\delta_{j,k}^{t-1}$ based on the k-th side classifier S_k^{t-1} becomes

$$\delta_{j,k}^{t-1} = \frac{1}{N^{t-1}} \sum_{i=1}^{N^{t-1}} \left|\left| \frac{\partial [l_2^2(S_k^{t-1}(F(x_i^{t-1})))]}{\partial \theta_j} \right|\right|. \tag{7}$$

We further average the importance weights from K side classifiers by

$$\delta_j^{t-1} = \frac{1}{K} \sum_{k=1}^{K} \delta_{j,k}^{t-1}. \tag{8}$$

Moreover, we propose a new property called *stability factor*, which allows us to assess how stable the parameters in the network are. For each parameter, if its importance weights from the side classifiers are close with that from the main classifier, it shows that this parameter is robust and stable to different classifiers. In this case, we assign this parameter with a larger stability factor. To be specific, we compute the standard deviation *w.r.t.* the importance weights

$$\text{std}(\theta_j) = \frac{1}{\alpha_j^{t-1}} \sqrt{\frac{\sum_{k=1}^{K}(\delta_{j,k}^{t-1} - \alpha_j^{t-1})^2}{K}}. \tag{9}$$

This standard deviation $\text{std}(\theta_j)$ quantifies the differences of the importance weights between the main classifier and the side classifiers. Based on the standard deviation, we define the *stability factor* with

$$\gamma_j^{t-1} = e^{1-\text{std}(\theta_j)} \in (0, e]. \tag{10}$$

The stability factor will be multiplied with δ_j^{t-1}, to adjust the impact of the importance weights. Finally, the parameter regularization loss in MUC-MAS for learning the t task is formulated by

$$\mathcal{L}_{REG}^{PR} = \underbrace{\sum_j^{|\theta|} \alpha_j^{t-1}(\theta_j - \tilde{\theta}_j)^2}_{\text{main classifier}} + \underbrace{\sum_j^{|\theta|} \gamma_j^{t-1}\delta_j^{t-1}(\theta_j - \tilde{\theta}_j)^2}_{\text{side classifiers}}, \tag{11}$$

where $\tilde{\theta}_j$ is the corresponding parameter weight stored in the old network.

3.3   MUC with Activation Regularization

Activation regularization (AR), which aims to compare the activations between old and new networks, is driven by the idea of knowledge distillation [13]. In LwF [24], the activations refer to the probability predictions, which act as soft labels to constrain the updates of the network. Here, we demonstrate MUC-LwF by extending LwF to the MUC paradigm. First, we compute the AR loss based on the main classifier as follows

$$\mathcal{L}_{AR}(F, M^{1:t-1}) = \frac{1}{N^t} \sum_{i=1}^{N^t} \text{KD}\left(\log\left[\sigma\left(\frac{Q(x_i^t)}{ts}\right)\right], \sigma\left(\frac{\tilde{Q}(x_i^t)}{ts}\right)\right), \tag{12}$$

where KD is the function for computing the knowledge distillation term; σ is the Softmax function; the temperature scalar ts is normally fixed with 2. Taking as input a sample x_i^t into the network, $Q(x_i^t) = M^{1:t-1}(F(x_i^t))$ represents a concatenation vector output from the main classifiers corresponding to the previous $t-1$ tasks. Likewise, $\tilde{Q}(x_i^t) = \tilde{M}^{1:t-1}(\tilde{F}(x_i^t))$ is the vector derived from the old network. Accordingly, we further accumulate the AR loss for K side classifiers by

$$\mathcal{L}_{AR}(F, S_{1:K}^{1:t-1}) = \frac{1}{N^t}\frac{1}{K} \sum_{i=1}^{N^t}\sum_{k=1}^{K} \text{KD}\left(\log\left[\sigma\left(\frac{Q_k(x_i^t)}{ts}\right)\right], \sigma\left(\frac{\tilde{Q}_k(x_i^t)}{ts}\right)\right), \tag{13}$$

where $Q_k(x_i^t) = S_k^{1:t-1}(F(x_i^t))$ is the concatenation vector of the k-th side classifier towards task 1 to task $t-1$. $\tilde{Q}_k(x_i^t) = \tilde{S}_k^{1:t-1}(\tilde{F}(x_i^t))$ is the corresponding vector extracted from the old model. Lastly, the total activation regularization loss in MUC-LwF when the network learns the t-th task becomes

$$\mathcal{L}_{REG}^{AR} = \underbrace{\mathcal{L}_{AR}(F, M^{1:t-1})}_{\text{main classifier}} + \underbrace{\mathcal{L}_{AR}(F, S_{1:K}^{1:t-1})}_{\text{side classifiers}}. \tag{14}$$

It is worthy mentioning that our MUC is a generic framework for many incremental learning methods, but is not limited to MAS and LwF. Particularly, in the experiment we empirically demonstrate its effectiveness under the rehearsal based scenario (Sect. 4.5).

4 Experiments

4.1 Datasets and Evaluation Metrics

We conducted the experiments on two widely-used benchmarks, CIFAR-100 [19] and Tiny ImageNet [41]. CIFAR-100 contains 100 classes, each of which has 500 training images and 100 test images of size 32×32. In Tiny ImageNet, there are 200 classes and each class contains 500 training images, 50 validation images and 50 test images of size 64×64. Since the class labels of test images in Tiny ImageNet are not available, the performance is generally evaluated on the validation set. Regarding the out-of-distribution dataset, we use the SVHN dataset [31] that contains only digits classes and is different from CIFAR-100 and Tiny ImageNet. In the setting of class-incremental learning, we split the classes with $g = 10$ or 20 for CIFAR-100, and $g = 20$ or 40 for Tiny ImageNet, where g indicates the number of classes in each task. This setting results in $T = 10$ or 5 tasks for both datasets. The first evaluation metric we use is the standard top-1 classification accuracy. In addition, we report the forgetting ratio which was defined in [37]. The ratio belongs to $[-1, 0]$ and less negative ratios mean less forgetting. Normally, it is unnecessary to compare the performance of the first task, as it has no incremental learning yet.

4.2 Implementation Details

For a fair comparison with previous works, the network architecture we use is ResNet-32 [12]. We train the network from scratch for the first task and then update it continually for subsequent tasks. We downsample images of Tiny ImageNet to 32×32, so that they can use the same network as CIFAR-100. During each incremental session, we train the network with 200 epochs. The learning rate starts from 0.1 and decays with a factor of 10 after 120, 160 and 180 epochs. We optimize the network using SGD with a momentum of 0.9 and a weight decay of 5e-4. We use a batch size of 128 for all experiments. We use the same hyper-parameters to train Stage II but terminate the training after 80 epochs. Like iCaRL [35], we run the experiments several times and report the average performance. At test time, we use the predictions from the main classifier to compute the performance. We also test the predictions from the side classifiers, and they have the similar performance as the main classifier. We employ the '*single-head*' (*i.e.* task-agnostic) evaluation which is more practical than the '*multi-head*' (*i.e.* task-conditioned) evaluation [9].

Notably, the parameter λ in Eq. 1 is significant for balancing the two loss terms during incremental learning. After learning more tasks, it is needed to

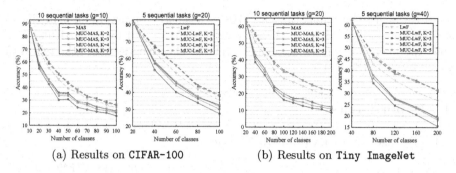

(a) Results on CIFAR-100   (b) Results on Tiny ImageNet

Fig. 3. Results of classification accuracy on two datasets, each of which contains 10 or 5 sequential tasks. Our methods (MUC-MAS and MUC-LwF) outperform the corresponding baselines (MAS and LwF) across tasks and datasets.

Table 1. Results of forgetting ratio (less negative indicates less forgetting) on CIFAR-100 (top table) and Tiny ImageNet (bottom table). The average forgetting ratio (Avg.) excludes the first task as it has no incremental learning. MUC methods exhibit less forgetting than the baselines.

CIFAR-100	Number of classes (10 tasks)											Number of classes (5 tasks)					
Method	10	20	30	40	50	60	70	80	90	100	Avg.	20	40	60	80	100	Avg.
MAS	–	−0.36	−0.47	−0.62	−0.61	−0.68	−0.69	−0.75	−0.75	−0.77	−0.55	–	−0.21	−0.45	−0.53	−0.57	−0.44
MUC-MAS	–	−0.31	−0.42	−0.55	−0.56	−0.61	−0.62	−0.71	−0.70	−0.72	**−0.50**	–	−0.17	−0.39	−0.48	−0.54	**−0.39**
LwF	–	−0.10	−0.35	−0.29	−0.34	−0.39	−0.44	−0.51	−0.56	−0.61	−0.33	–	−0.10	−0.26	−0.33	−0.41	−0.28
MUC-LwF	–	−0.08	−0.31	−0.24	−0.29	−0.32	−0.39	−0.45	−0.51	−0.55	**−0.29**	–	−0.07	−0.22	−0.30	−0.38	**−0.24**

Tiny ImageNet	Number of classes (10 tasks)											Number of classes (5 tasks)					
Method	20	40	60	80	100	120	140	160	180	200	Avg.	40	80	120	160	200	Avg.
MAS	–	−0.43	−0.53	−0.65	−0.72	−0.75	−0.79	−0.80	−0.82	−0.85	−0.71	–	−0.44	−0.58	−0.63	−0.70	−0.59
MUC-MAS	–	−0.40	−0.48	−0.60	−0.67	−0.71	−0.75	−0.76	−0.78	−0.81	**−0.66**	–	−0.41	−0.53	−0.58	−0.66	**−0.54**
LwF	–	−0.21	−0.31	−0.44	−0.48	−0.53	−0.62	−0.63	−0.65	−0.68	−0.51	–	−0.34	−0.41	−0.50	−0.52	−0.44
MUC-LwF	–	−0.17	−0.28	−0.40	−0.44	−0.49	−0.58	−0.60	−0.61	−0.65	**−0.47**	–	−0.28	−0.37	−0.45	−0.49	**−0.40**

increase the importance of the regularization loss, so as to avoid incessant forgetting on old tasks. Specifically, we set $\lambda = t - 1$ for MUC-LwF, similar with the setting in BiC [44]. However, λ is fixed for MUC-MAS, because its regularization loss has already accumulated new and old importance weights, as suggested in MAS [1]. We set λ to be 0.01 for CIFAR-100 and 0.005 for Tiny ImageNet.

4.3   Comparison and Discussion

We implement two baseline methods, including MAS [1] and LwF [24], because our MUC-MAS and MUC-LwF are build with their regularization. The same hyper-parameters are used to train our methods and the baselines for a fair comparison. In addition, we assess our methods with varying numbers (*i.e.* K) of side classifiers. Figure 3 presents the accuracy results on the two datasets.

Results of Parameter Regularization. Compared with the baseline MAS, the best accuracy from MUC-MAS achieves about 4%–5% gains on CIFAR-100

Table 2. Euclidean distances among the parameter vectors of three side classifiers. By using the classifier discrepancy loss, the parameters of the classifiers become dissimilar.

Side classifiers	w/o $\mathcal{L}_{CD}$	with $\mathcal{L}_{CD}$
S_1 v.s. S_2	0.057	5.284
S_1 v.s. S_3	0.059	5.110
S_2 v.s. S_3	0.054	5.662

Table 3. Accuracy results of one-stage and two-stage training on CIFAR-100. The one-stage training has higher accuracy at the beginning, while largely underperforms the two-stage training for subsequent tasks.

Method	Training	20	40	60	80	100
MUC-MAS	One-stage	**83.5**	**58.9**	44.8	35.2	28.8
MUC-MAS	Two-stage	82.6	58.4	**46.3**	**37.9**	**31.7**
MUC-LwF	One-stage	**83.5**	**70.8**	58.0	47.6	38.4
MUC-LwF	Two-stage	82.6	69.6	**59.4**	**49.5**	**41.6**

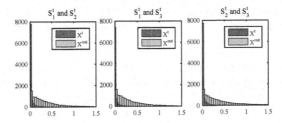

Fig. 4. Histogram statistics of prediction disagreements for X^t and X^{out}. X axis indicates the L1-norm discrepancy distance and Y axis counts the number of samples.

and 3%–4% gains on Tiny ImageNet. The comparison demonstrates the benefit of exploiting side classifiers for parameter regularization. In terms of the number of side classifiers, the MUC-MAS variant with $K = 3$ has about **1.5%** improvement over that with $K = 2$. When K reaches to 4 or 5, the accuracy results are close with those when $K = 3$. This finding is consistent with prior works [36,47], where they used only two classifiers and achieved promising performance. To maintain the efficiency, we use the MUC-MAS variant with $K = 3$.

Results of Activation Regularization. It suggests in prior works [34,49] that LwF performs better than MAS in the context of class-incremental learning. Nevertheless, MUC-LwF surpasses LwF with a margin of **3%–5%** gains on both datasets. Likewise, we also evaluate MUC-LwF with different numbers of side classifiers. By comparing those MUC-MAS variants, the one with $K = 3$ is slightly better than others. For consistency and generalization, we also use three side classifiers for MUC-LwF.

Results of Forgetting Ratio. We further report the forgetting ratio results in Table 1. It shows that our methods outperform the baselines with an average decline of 4%–5% forgetting ratios. The results support our motivation: *using more classifiers leads to less forgetting.*

Complexity Analysis. Despite the fact that the side classifiers impose extra computational cost, however, the number of their parameters is a small fraction with respect to the number of all the parameters in the network. For the case

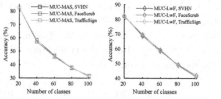 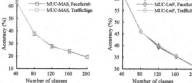

(a) 5 sequential tasks on `CIFAR-100`   (b) 5 sequential tasks on `Tiny ImageNet`

Fig. 5. Performance of MUC-MAS and MUC-LwF by using different OOD datasets. Our results are consistent across three OOD datasets.

Table 4. Effect of increasing the trade-off parameter λ for incrementally learning 5 tasks on `CIFAR-100`.

Method	Parameter	20	40	60	80	100
MAS	$\lambda = 0.01$	82.6	53.2	41.2	33.9	27.5
MAS	$\lambda = 0.02$	82.6	57.6	45.4	36.7	30.8
MUC-MAS	$\lambda = 0.01$	82.6	58.4	46.3	37.9	31.7
MUC-MAS	$\lambda = 0.02$	82.6	59.5	48.2	40.8	34.4

Table 5. Analyzing the stability factor in MUC-MAS. This comparison is performed on the five tasks of `CIFAR-100`. The fixed factor is 1.5.

MUC-MAS	20	40	60	80	100
w/o stability factor	82.6	57.6	45.4	36.7	30.8
with fixed factor	82.6	57.0	45.6	37.0	31.0
with stability factor	82.6	58.4	46.3	37.9	31.7

when $K = 3$ and $g = 20$ on `CIFAR-100`, the final network consumes about 20,000 extra parameters due to adding the side classifiers, while they are only **4%** of the total parameters. It suggests that MUC is a practical and efficient method for incremental learning, without violating the memory limit much.

4.4   Component Analysis

Analysis of classifier discrepancy. This study is to show how the the classifier discrepancy loss $\mathcal{L}_{CD}$ in `Stage II` diversify the side classifiers. Specifically, we reshape the parameters (weights and bias) of each side classifier into a one-dimensional vector, and then compute the Euclidean distance between a pair of those parameter vectors. Table 2 reports the distances with or without using the classifier discrepancy loss, in terms of $K = 3$ on `CIFAR-100`. Notably, this loss succeeds in increasing the disagreement among the side classifiers in case that they learn nearly identical parameters.

Comparison Between In-distribution and OOD Samples. Recall that the objective of `Stage II` is to make the side classifiers produce consistent predictions for in-distribution samples but distinct predictions for OOD samples. We use the L1-norm distance in Eq. 3 to quantify the discrepancy among the predictions (Fig. 4). It can be seen that the disagreements for most in-distribution samples are close to 0, while the OOD samples has much larger disagreements. In this example, we show the results when $t = 1$ on `CIFAR-100`, while similar behavior is observed as well for subsequent tasks.

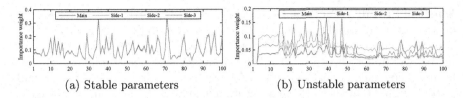

(a) Stable parameters   (b) Unstable parameters

Fig. 6. Importance weights derived from the main classifier (Main) and three side classifiers (Side-1, Side-2 and Side-3). Based on the stability factors, we choose to show (a) 100 stable parameters and (b) 100 unstable parameters.

Evaluation of Different OOD Datasets. This experiment shows the performance when we choose OOD samples from different datasets. Apart from the SVHN dataset, we additionally use another two datasets including Face-Scrub [32] and TrafficSign [40]. The results in Fig. 5 depict that our MUC is robust to different OOD datasets. We choose to use SVHN due to its popularity in the field.

Two-Stage *versus* One-Stage. We aim to show the advantage of the two-stage fashion for training MUC. To this end, we also implement a one-stage training fashion, in which the main and side classifiers are trained simultaneously. As such, the total objective is composed of three terms: cross-entropy loss, classifier discrepancy loss and regularization loss. We report the comparison results in Table 3, where the two-stage training performs better than the one-stage training for a larger number of tasks. The main reason is that the classifier discrepancy loss has a negative effect on the regularization loss in the one-stage training. Hence, we decouple these two loss terms in two stages.

Effect of the Trade-Off Parameter λ. We fix λ to be 0.01 for MAS and MUC-MAS, while it is encouraged to test the performance by increasing λ. In Table 4, we compare the results when $\lambda = 0.01$ and $\lambda = 0.02$. First, both MAS and MUC-MAS yield considerable gains due to a larger λ. Importantly, the results of MUC-MAS with $\lambda = 0.01$ are even better than those of MAS with $\lambda = 0.02$. The reason is that MUC-MAS learns complementary regularization terms derived from the side classifiers, rather than simply increasing λ for the regularization term from the main classifier. However, when $\lambda = 0.02$, we find an impractical trend that the accuracy of new tasks is lower than that of old tasks. In other words, the method tends to trade new tasks accuracy for higher accuracy of old tasks. To avoid this issue, we instead choose to use $\lambda = 0.01$.

Effect of Stability Factors. Regarding MUC-MAS, we discuss the results with or without using stability factors (Table 5). Using stability factors brings about 1% gains across the tasks. In addition, we consider using a fixed factor for all parameters and compare it with our parameter-adaptive stability factor. For fairness, The fixed factor is set with 1.5 which is the average value of all stability factors. We see that the performance with fixed factors has no considerable gains. It suggests the advantage of our stability factor that adapts to each individual parameter. Although the performance gains are not significant, our stability factor provides a new degree to analyze the parameters in the network.

Comparison of Importance Weights. For MUC-MAS, we investigate important weights captured from the main classifier and side classifiers. Instead of choosing the parameters randomly or manually, we provide a robust selection based on the stability factors. To be specific, we rank all the parameters by their stability factors, and choose 100 stable parameters that have the largest factors and 100 unstable parameters being with the smallest factors. Figure 6 visually compares the importance weights from the main classifier and side classifiers. For 100 stable parameters, the importance weights from the side classifiers are almost the same as those from the main classifier. On the other hand, regarding 100 unstable parameters, each classifier produces a different importance weight. Our method allows to quantify the stability of the parameters and help to discover potentially stable parameters.

Visualization of Soft Labels. Regarding MUC-LwF, this experiment is to study the soft labels from the classifiers. Specifically, we pick up one class from task $t = 5$ and feed its data into four old models when $t = 1$ to $t = 4$. Then, we extract the soft labels from each old model and visualize the distributions with t-SNE [28] (Fig. 7). First, the distributions with three side classifiers are different from that with the main classifier. In addition, the distributions associated with three side classifiers tend to differ more largely from $t = 1$ to $t = 4$.

4.5   Learning with Exemplars

It is feasible to extend MUC to the scenario of storing some exemplars for old classes, even though it is not the core of our work. Following iCaRL [35], we store a fixed budget of 2000 exemplars. Instead of using the herding algorithm in iCaRL, we select an equal number of samples for new and old classes, and additionally run a balanced fine-tuning stage. As suggested in recent work [4,49], this simple fine-tuning stage achieves competitive performance with iCaRL. We adapt exemplars to the methods including MAS, LwF, MUC-MAS and MUC-LwF (Fig. 8). In the case of using exemplars, MUC-LwF* yields 3% gains against LwF* and 1.5% gains against iCaRL*. Despite the fact that the performance gap becomes slight due to using exemplars, it will be a promising direction about how to fully leverage exemplars in the MUC paradigm.

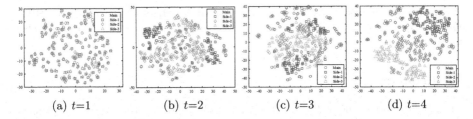

(a) $t=1$ (b) $t=2$ (c) $t=3$ (d) $t=4$

Fig. 7. Visualization of soft labels extracted from the main classifier (M) and three side classifiers (Side-1, Side-2 and Side-3). Given the image samples from one class, it visually shows how their soft labels from each classifier change over a sequence of tasks (more details when zoomed in).

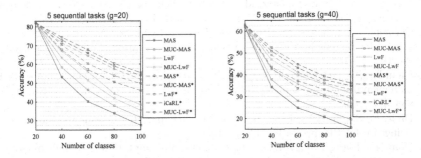

Fig. 8. Results of incrementally learning 5 tasks in the setting of using exemplars for (Left) CIFAR-100 and (Right) Tiny ImageNet. The methods with '*' store a fixed budget of 2000 exemplars for old tasks; otherwise are exemplar-free.

5   Conclusion

We have proposed a generic multi-classifier incremental learning paradigm, based on which we further develop two instantiations to improve the effectiveness of parameter and activation regularization, respectively. Compared with the single-classifier methods, our MUC has achieved higher accuracy and less forgetting across tasks and datasets. Through additional component analysis, MUC demonstrated more insights which were not shown in the single-classifier paradigm. This work makes us realize that the classifiers play a crucial role in the scenario of incrementally learning tasks. In the future, it is promising to exploit MUC for other vision applications in the context of incremental learning, such as object detection and semantic segmentation.

Acknowledgements. This research was funded by Huawei as part of an HIRP Open project and by the FWO project "Structure from Semantics" (grant number G086617N).

References

1. Aljundi, R., Babiloni, F., Elhoseiny, M., Rohrbach, M., Tuytelaars, T.: Memory aware synapses: learning what (not) to forget. In: ECCV, pp. 144–161 (2018)
2. Belouadah, E., Popescu, A.: IL2M: class incremental learning with dual memory. In: ICCV, pp. 583–592 (2019)
3. Carpenter, G.A., Grossberg, S.: Art 2: self-organization of stable category recognition codes for analog input patterns. Appl. Opt. **26**(23), 4919–4930 (1987)
4. Castro, F.M., Marín-Jiménez, M.J., Guil, N., Schmid, C., Alahari, K.: End-to-end incremental learning. In: ECCV, pp. 241–257 (2018)
5. Cermelli, F., Mancini, M., Bulò, S.R., Ricci, E., Caputo, B.: Modeling the background for incremental learning in semantic segmentation. CoRR abs/2002.00718 (2020)
6. Chaudhry, A., Dokania, P.K., Ajanthan, T., Torr, P.H.S.: Riemannian walk for incremental learning: understanding forgetting and intransigence. In: ECCV, pp. 556–572 (2018)
7. Dhar, P., Singh, R.V., Peng, K., Wu, Z., Chellappa, R.: Learning without memorizing. In: CVPR, pp. 5138–5146 (2019)
8. Duan, L., Tsang, I.W., Xu, D., Chua, T.: Domain adaptation from multiple sources via auxiliary classifiers. In: ICML, pp. 289–296 (2009)
9. Farquhar, S., Gal, Y.: Towards robust evaluations of continual learning. CoRR abs/1805.09733 (2018)
10. Hao, Y., Fu, Y., Jiang, Y., Tian, Q.: An end-to-end architecture for class-incremental object detection with knowledge distillation. In: ICME, pp. 1–6 (2019)
11. He, C., Wang, R., Shan, S., Chen, X.: Exemplar-supported generative reproduction for class incremental learning. In: BMVC, p. 98 (2018)
12. He, K., Zhang, X., Ren, S., Sun, J.: Deep residual learning for image recognition. In: CVPR, pp. 770–778 (2016)
13. Hinton, G., Vinyals, O., Dean, J.: Distilling the knowledge in a neural network. In: NIPS Deep Learning and Representation Learning Workshop (2015)
14. Hou, S., Pan, X., Loy, C.C., Wang, Z., Lin, D.: Lifelong learning via progressive distillation and retrospection. In: ECCV, pp. 452–467 (2018)
15. Hou, S., Pan, X., Loy, C.C., Wang, Z., Lin, D.: Learning a unified classifier incrementally via rebalancing. In: CVPR, pp. 831–839 (2019)
16. Hsu, Y., Liu, Y., Kira, Z.: Re-evaluating continual learning scenarios: A categorization and case for strong baselines. CoRR abs/1810.12488 (2018)
17. Kemker, R., Kanan, C.: Fearnet: brain-inspired model for incremental learning. In: ICLR (2018)
18. Kirkpatrick, J., et al.: Overcoming catastrophic forgetting in neural networks. PNAS **114**(13), 3521–3526 (2016)
19. Krizhevsky, A.: Learning multiple layers of features from tiny images. Master's thesis, Department of Computer Science, University of Toronto (2009)
20. Lange, M.D., et al.: Continual learning: a comparative study on how to defy forgetting in classification tasks. CoRR abs/1909.08383 (2019)
21. Lee, C., Xie, S., Gallagher, P., Zhang, Z., Tu, Z.: Deeply-supervised nets. In: AISTATS (2015)

22. Lee, K., Lee, K., Shin, J., Lee, H.: Overcoming catastrophic forgetting with unlabeled data in the wild. In: ICCV, pp. 312–321 (2019)
23. Lee, S., Kim, J., Jun, J., Ha, J., Zhang, B.: Overcoming catastrophic forgetting by incremental moment matching. In: NIPS, pp. 4652–4662 (2017)
24. Li, Z., Hoiem, D.: Learning without forgetting. In: ECCV, pp. 614–629 (2016)
25. Liu, X., Masana, M., Herranz, L., van de Weijer, J., López, A.M., Bagdanov, A.D.: Rotate your networks: Better weight consolidation and less catastrophic forgetting. In: ICPR, pp. 2262–2268 (2018)
26. Lopez-Paz, D., Ranzato, M.: Gradient episodic memory for continual learning. In: NIPS, pp. 6467–6476 (2017)
27. Luo, P., Zhuang, F., Xiong, H., Xiong, Y., He, Q.: Transfer learning from multiple source domains via consensus regularization. In: CIKM, pp. 103–112 (2008)
28. van der Maaten, L., Hinton, G.: Visualizing high-dimensional data using t-SNE. JMLR **9**, 2579–2605 (2008)
29. McCloskey, M., Cohen, N.J.: Catastrophic interference in connectionist networks: the sequential learning problem. In: Psychology of Learning and Motivation, vol. 24, pp. 109–165. Academic Press (1989)
30. Michieli, U., Zanuttigh, P.: Incremental learning techniques for semantic segmentation. In: ICCV, Workshop on TASK-CV (2019)
31. Netzer, Y., Wang, T., Coates, A., Bissacco, A., Wu, B., Ng, A.Y.: Reading digits in natural images with unsupervised feature learning. In: NIPS Workshop on Deep Learning and Unsupervised Feature Learning (2011)
32. Ng, H., Winkler, S.: A data-driven approach to cleaning large face datasets. In: International Conference on Image Processing, pp. 343–347 (2014)
33. Parisi, G.I., Kemker, R., Part, J.L., Kanan, C., Wermter, S.: Continual lifelong learning with neural networks: a review. Neural Netw. **113**, 54–71 (2019)
34. Rajasegaran, J., Hayat, M., Khan, S., Khan, F.S., Shao, L.: Random path selection for incremental learning. In: Advances in Neural Information Processing Systems (2019)
35. Rebuffi, S., Kolesnikov, A., Sperl, G., Lampert, C.H.: iCaRL: incremental classifier and representation learning. In: CVPR, pp. 5533–5542 (2017)
36. Saito, K., Watanabe, K., Ushiku, Y., Harada, T.: Maximum classifier discrepancy for unsupervised domain adaptation. In: CVPR, pp. 3723–3732 (2018)
37. Serrà, J., Suris, D., Miron, M., Karatzoglou, A.: Overcoming catastrophic forgetting with hard attention to the task. In: ICML, pp. 4555–4564 (2018)
38. Shin, H., Lee, J.K., Kim, J., Kim, J.: Continual learning with deep generative replay. In: NIPS, pp. 2990–2999 (2017)
39. Shmelkov, K., Schmid, C., Alahari, K.: Incremental learning of object detectors without catastrophic forgetting. In: ICCV, pp. 3420–3429 (2017)
40. Stallkamp, J., Schlipsing, M., Salmen, J., Igel, C.: The German traffic sign recognition benchmark: a multi-class classification competition. In: IEEE International Joint Conference on Neural Networks, pp. 1453–1460 (2011)
41. Stanford: Tiny imagenet challenge, cs231n course. https://tiny-imagenet.herokuapp.com/
42. Szegedy, C., et al.: Going deeper with convolutions. In: CVPR, pp. 1–9 (2015)
43. Triki, A.R., Aljundi, R., Blaschko, M.B., Tuytelaars, T.: Encoder based lifelong learning. In: ICCV, pp. 1329–1337 (2017)
44. Wu, Y., et al.: Large scale incremental learning. In: CVPR, pp. 374–382 (2019)
45. Xiang, Y., Fu, Y., Ji, P., Huang, H.: Incremental learning using conditional adversarial networks. In: ICCV, pp. 6618–6627 (2019)

46. Xie, S., Tu, Z.: Holistically-nested edge detection. In: ICCV, pp. 1395–1403 (2015)
47. Yu, Q., Aizawa, K.: Unsupervised out-of-distribution detection by maximum classifier discrepancy. In: ICCV, pp. 9517–9525 (2019)
48. Zenke, F., Poole, B., Ganguli, S.: Continual learning through synaptic intelligence. In: ICML, pp. 3987–3995 (2017)
49. Zhang, J., et al.: Class-incremental learning via deep model consolidation. CoRR abs/1903.07864 (2019)
50. Zhou, P., Mai, L., Zhang, J., Xu, N., Wu, Z., Davis, L.S.: M2KD: multi-model and multi-level knowledge distillation for incremental learning. CoRR abs/1904.01769 (2019)

Extending and Analyzing Self-supervised Learning Across Domains

Bram Wallace$^{(\boxtimes)}$ and Bharath Hariharan

Cornell University, Ithaca, USA
bw462@cornell.edu, bharathh@cs.cornell.edu

Abstract. Self-supervised representation learning has achieved impressive results in recent years, with experiments primarily coming on ImageNet or other similarly large internet imagery datasets. There has been little to no work with these methods on other smaller domains, such as satellite, textural, or biological imagery. We experiment with several popular methods on an unprecedented variety of domains. We discover, among other findings, that Rotation is the most semantically meaningful task, while much of the performance of Jigsaw is attributable to the nature of its induced distribution rather than semantic understanding. Additionally, there are several areas, such as fine-grain classification, where all tasks underperform. We quantitatively and qualitatively diagnose the reasons for these failures and successes via novel experiments studying pretext generalization, random labelings, and implicit dimensionality. Code and models are available at https://github.com/BramSW/Extending_SSRL_Across_Domains/.

1 Introduction

A good visual representation is key to all visual recognition tasks. However, in current practice, one needs large labeled training sets to train such a representation. Unfortunately, such datasets can be hard to acquire in many domains, such as satellite imagery or the medical domain. This is often either because annotations require expertise and experts have limited time, or the images themselves are limited (as in medicine). To bring the benefits of visual recognition to these disparate domains, we need powerful representation learning techniques that do not require large labeled datasets.

A promising direction is to use self-supervised representation learning (SSRL), which has gained increasing interest over the last few years [15,18, 23,34,58,59]. However, past work has primarily evaluated these techniques on general category object recognition in internet imagery (e.g. ImageNet classification) [42]. There has been very little attention on how (and if) these techniques extend to other domains, be they fine-grained classification problems or datasets in biology and medicine. Paradoxically, these domains are often most in need of such techniques precisely because of the lack of labeled training data.

Electronic supplementary material The online version of this chapter (https://doi.org/10.1007/978-3-030-58574-7_43) contains supplementary material, which is available to authorized users.

© Springer Nature Switzerland AG 2020
A. Vedaldi et al. (Eds.): ECCV 2020, LNCS 12371, pp. 717–734, 2020.
https://doi.org/10.1007/978-3-030-58574-7_43

As such, a key question is whether conclusions from benchmarks on self-supervised learning [18,23] which focused on internet imagery, carry over to this broader universe of recognition problems. In particular, does one technique dominate, or are different pretext tasks useful for different types of domains (**Sect.** 5.1)? Are representations from an ImageNet classifier still the best we can do (**Sect.** 5.1)? Do these answers change when labels are limited (**Sect.** 5.1)? Are there problem domains where all proposed techniques currently fail (**Sect.** 5.2)?

A barrier to answering these questions is our limited understanding of self-supervised techniques themselves. We have seen their *empirical* success on ImageNet, but when they do succeed, what is it that drives their success (**Sect.** 5.3)? Furthermore, what does the space of learned representations look like, for instance in terms of the dimensionality (**Sect.** 6.1) or nearest neighbors (**Sect.** 6.2)?

In this work, we take the first steps towards answering these questions. We evaluate and analyze multiple self-supervised learning techniques (Rotation [15], Instance Discrimination [54] and Jigsaw [34]) on the broadest benchmark yet of 16 domains spanning internet, biological, satellite, and symbolic imagery. We find that Rotation has the best overall accuracy (reflective of rankings on ImageNet), but is outperformed by Instance Discrimination on biological domains (**Sect.** 5.1). When labels are scarce, pretext methods outperform ImageNet initialization and even full supervision on numerous tasks (**Sect.** 5.1). A prominent failure case for SSRL is fine-grained classification problems, due to important cues such as color being discarded during training (**Sect.** 5.2). Finally, when SSRL techniques do succeed, their reason for success varies: Rotation relies more on the semantic nature of the pretext task, compared to Jigsaw and Instance Discrimination (**Sect.** 5.3). Perhaps as a consequence, the representations of Rotation having comparatively higher implicit dimensionality (**Sect.** 6.1).

2   Datasets

We include 16 datasets in our experiments, significantly more than all prior work. Dataset samples are shown in Fig. 1. We group these datasets into 4 categories: **Internet, Symbolic, Scenes & Textures**, and **Biological**. A summary is shown in Table 1. Some of the datasets in the first three groups are also in the Visual Domain Decathlon (VDD) [40], a multi-task learning benchmark.

Internet Object Recognition: This group consists of object recognition problems on internet imagery. We include both coarse-grained (CIFAR100, Daimler Pedestrians) and fine-grained (FGVC-Aircraft, CUB, VGG Flowers) object classification tasks. Finally, we include the "dynamic images" of UCF101, a dataset that possesses many of the same qualitative attributes of the group.

Symbolic: We include three well-known symbolic tasks: Omniglot, German Traffic Signs (GTSRB), and Street View House Numbers (SVHN). Though the classification problems might be deemed simple, these offer domains where classification is very different from natural internet imagery: texture is not generally a useful cue and classes follow strict explainable rules.

Fig. 1. Samples from all datasets. Top rows: Daimler Pedestrians, CIFAR100, FGVC-Aircraft, CU Birds, VGG-Flowers, UCF101, BACH, Protein Atlas. Bottom rows: GTSRB, SVHN, Omniglot, UC Merced Land Use, Describable Textures, Indoor Scenes, Kather, ISIC. Color coding is by group: Internet Symbolic Scenes & Textures Biological

Table 1. Summary of the 16 datasets included in our experiments: encompassing fine-grain, symbolic, scene, textural, and biological domains. This is the first work exploring self-supervised representation learning on almost all of these tasks

Name	Type	Size (Train)	Coarse/Fine	Abbreviation
Daimler Pedestrians [31]	Road Object	20k	Coarse	PED
CIFAR100 [24]	Internet Object	40k	Coarse	C100
FGVC-Aircraft [28]	Internet Object	3.3k	Fine	AIR
Caltech-UCSD Birds [53]	Internet Object	8.3k	Fine	CUB
VGG-Flowers [33]	Internet Object	1k	Fine	FLO
UCF101 [3,45]	Pseudo-Internet Action	9.3k	Coarse	UCF
German Traffic Signs [46]	Symbolic	21k	Coarse	GTS
Street View House Numbers [32]	Symbolic	59k	Coarse	SVHN
Omniglot [25]	Symbolic	19k	Fine	OMN
UC Merced Land Use [55]	Aerial Scene	1.5k	Coarse	MER
Describable Textures [9]	Texture	1.9k	Fine	DTD
Indoor Scene Recognition [39]	Natural Scene	11k	Coarse	SCE
ICIAR BACH [1]	Biological	240	Coarse	BACH
Kather [22]	Biological	3k	Coarse	KATH
Protein Atlas [35]	Biological	9k	Fine	PA
ISIC [10,49]	Biological	17k	Coarse	ISIC

Scenes & Textures: These domains, UC Merced Land Use (satellite imagery), Describable Textures, and Indoor Scenes, all require holistic understandings, none having an overarching definition of object/symbol. Indoor Scenes does contain internet imagery as in our first group, but is not object-focused.

Biological: BACH and Kather consist of histological (microscopic tissue) images of breast and colon cancer respectively, with the classes being the condition/type of cancer. Protein Atlas is microscopy images of human cells, with the goal being

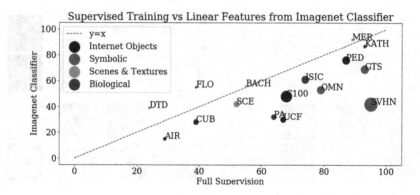

Fig. 2. Test accuracy of a fully supervised network vs. a linear classifier on top of an ImageNet-classification frozen feature extractor. Marker area indicates dataset size

classification of the cell part/structure shown. Finally, ISIC is a dermatology dataset consisting of photographs of different types of skin lesions.

Before evaluating self-supervision, we study the datasets themselves in terms of difficulty and similarity to ImageNet. To do so, we compare the accuracy of a network trained from scratch with that of a linear classifier operating on an ImageNet-pretrained network (Fig. 2). The higher of the two numbers measures the difficulty, while their relationship quantifies the similarity to ImageNet.

We find that small datasets in the Internet domain tend to be the hardest, while large Symbolic datasets are the simplest. The symbolic tasks also have the largest gap between supervision and feature extraction, suggesting that these are the farthest from ImageNet. Overall, the ImageNet feature extractor performance is strongly linearly correlated to that of the fully supervised model ($p = 0.004$). This is expected for the Internet domain, but the similar utility of the feature extractor for the Biological domains is surprising. Dataset size also plays a role, with the pretrained feature extractor working well for smaller datasets.

For fine-grained classification (AIR, CUB, FLO), the supervised models perform comparably, while the ImageNet classifier's performance varies widely. In addition to the small size of VGG-Flowers, this case is also partly explainable by how these datasets overlap with ImageNet. Almost half of the classes in ImageNet are animals or plants, including flowers, making pretraining especially useful.

3 Methods

3.1 Self-supervised Learning Techniques

In this paper we look at three popular methods, Rotation, Jigsaw, and Instance Discrimination. We also look at the classical technique of Autoencoders as a baseline for the large variety of autoencoder-based pretexts [38,58,59]. We briefly describe each method below, please view the cited works for detailed information.

Learning by Rotation: A network is trained to classify the angle of a rotated image among the four choices of 0, 90, 180, or 270° [15].

Learning by Solving Jigsaw Puzzles: The image is separated into a 3×3 grid of patches, which are then permuted and fed through a siamese network which must identify the original layout [5,34]. We use 2000 training permutations in our experiments, finding this offered superior performance to 100 or 10,000 under our hyperparameters.

Instance Discrimination: Instance Discrimination (ID) maps images to features on the unit sphere with each image being considered as a separate class under a non-parametric softmax classifier [54].

Autoencoders: Autoencoders were one of the earliest methods of self-supervised learning [2,20,38,50,59]. An autoencoder learns an encoder-decoder pair of networks that reconstruct the input image.

3.2 Architecture and Evaluation

We resize inputs to 64×64 and use a ResNet26, as in Rebuffi et al. [40,41]. The lower resolution eases computational burden as well as comparison and future adaptation to the VDD. For Autoencoding, a simple convolutional decoder is used. Features maps of size $256 \times 8 \times 8$ are extracted before the final pooling layer and average pooled to 256, 4096 ($256 \times 4 \times 4$), or 9216 ($256 \times 6 \times 6$), with 256 being the default. A linear classifier is trained on these features. Training/architecture details are in the Supplementary.

4 Related Work

There are three pertinent recent surveys of self-supervision. The first is by Kolesnikov et al. who evaluate several methods on ImageNet and Places205 classification across network architectures [23]. We focus on many domains, an order of magnitude more than their work. The second relevant survey is by Goyal et al., who introduce a benchmark suite of tasks on which to test models as feature extractors. While they scale on a variety of downstream tasks, the pretraining datasets are all internet imagery, either ImageNet or YFCC variants [18,48]. Our work includes a much wider variety of both pretraining and downstream datasets. VTAB tests *pretrained feature extractors* on a variety of datasets, performing self-supervised learning only on ImageNet [57]. Finally, a concurrent paper evaluates these self-supervised techniques as an auxilliary loss for few-shot learning [47].

One trend of inquiry concerns classifiers that perform well on multiple domains while sharing most of the parameters across datasets [40,41,52]. The pre-eminent examples of this are by Rebuffi et al. [40,41] who present approaches on the VDD across 10 different domains. We use these datasets (and more) in our training, but evaluate *self-supervised approaches* in *single-domain* settings.

There has also been prior work using problem/domain-specific SSRL methods, such as [7,14,21,27] in the biological and medical fields or [44] for aerial imagery. Many of these approaches use variations of autoencoding as the pretext task; we include autoencoding in our evaluation. In contrast to these, our focus is on the cross-dataset applicability of these pretexts.

Other SSRL methods include generative models [12,13,16], colorization [26,58], video-based techniques [17,30,36,37,43,51], or generic techiques [4,6, 8,19,29]. It is very possible that a subset of these methods could offer improved performance on some of the domains we work with, however in this work we focus on the popular fundamental methods of Rotation, Jigsaw, and Instance Discrimination as well as Autoencoding as a representative set. Doersch and Zisserman use multiple pretexts simultaneously to improve representation quality [11]. This approach could be complementary to the work featured here. Semi-supervised approaches such as S4L [56] are relevant to Sect. 5.1.

5   Downstream Task Performance Analysis

5.1   Downstream Task Accuracy

A summary of downstream testing accuracies is shown in Fig. 3. The obvious question to ask in this investigation is "which pretext is best"? On ImageNet, per the respective original works, the ordering (best to worst) was Rotation, Instance Discrimination, Jigsaw, Autoencoding. We see that this ranking is not universal: while Rotation is the best pretext on the first three groups, it lags behind even random initialization on the Biological domains. Furthermore, the relative rankings of ID and Jigsaw vary between groups. We investigate what powers the performance of each of these methods in Sect. 5.3.

Limited Label Training. Self-supervised learning has made an impact in the field of *semi*-supervised learning, where only a subset of the dataset given is labeled, as in the work of Zhai et al. [56]. In that work on ImageNet, a self-supervised feature extractor followed by a supervised linear head falls well short of the purely supervised baseline (40% accuracy compared to 80% when 10% of labels are available). We find that this conclusion does not hold on our domains when 10% of labels are used, with a pretext + linear setup outperforming the fully supervised models on some datasets/groups (Fig. 4).[1]

On the Internet and Scenes & Textures groups, Rotation matches/outperforms full supervision. On ISIC, both Instance Discrimination and Jigsaw match Supervision. Interestingly, Autoencoding performs well in the Biological domains. Given the difficulty of expert annotation in the medical field, this is a valuable finding to encourage Autoencoder-based methods in these label-scarce domains, vindicating choices in past work [7,14,21,27]. The unlabeled 90% of the data being available for SSRL methods is critical: when only the labeled subset is used for pretraining the performance drops an average of approximately 10%.

5.2   Inspecting Failure Modes

We call specific attention to the problems where self-supervised techniques do not achieve even *half* of the supervised accuracy (Aircraft, CUB, Textures and Protein Atlas). These seem to involve two kinds of problems.

---

[1] Note that [56] performs extensive hyperparameter tuning for the supervised baseline.

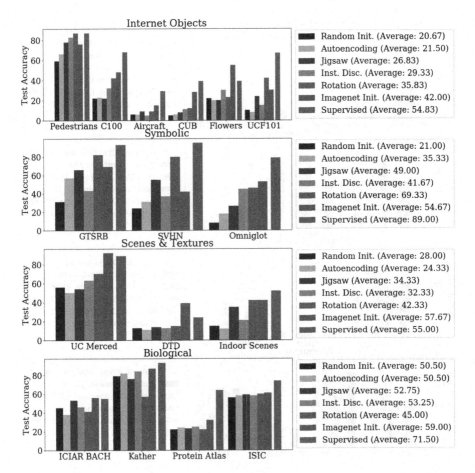

Fig. 3. Downstream classification accuracies for each pretext, as well as a randomly initialized feature extractor, a frozen ImageNet classifier, and fully supervised training. Rotation achieves the highest accuracies on the first three groups, but fails on the Biological domain, where Instance Discrimination performs best. The relative rankings of Jigsaw and ID vary between groups and are practically equal in overall average

Textures and Protein Atlas: In both these datasets, the entities being classified are not objects of recognizable shape, which is true of most *object recognition* datasets where the self-supervised techniques were developed. The images also do not have a canonical orientation, unlike in internet imagery where gravity and photographers' biases provide such an orientation. We hypothesize that the lack of orientability hobbles Rotation, and the textural nature of both problems results in there being little to distinguish a patch in the Jigsaw pretext from a complete image, meaning Jigsaw can do little besides cue off of low-level properties (such as chromatic aberrations [34]) As such, modulo low-level dataset biases, the Rotation and Jigsaw pretext tasks *cannot even be solved in these domains.*

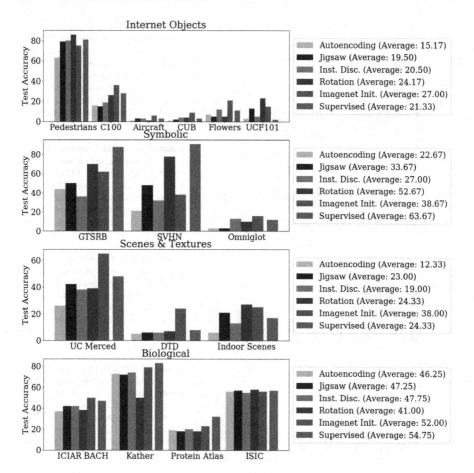

Fig. 4. Pretext feature extractors trained on the entire dataset, then a linear head trained on 10% of the labels. The fully supervised method simply trains on 10% of the dataset. We observe Rotation matching/outperforming Supervision for Internet and Scenes & Textures imagery. Autoencoding performs very well on the Biological domains in the semi-supervised setting, a novel result that indicates the potential for future development (given that this Autoencoder implementation is the simplest possible)

Fine-Grained Classification on Aircraft and CUB: In these datasets, the Rotation and Jigsaw pretexts are solvable, involving objects captured in a canonical orientation. Even so, neither pretext learns a good representation. While the *domains* are favorable to the pretexts, the *tasks* are not: both tasks involve fine-grained distinctions in color or texture, and subtle differences in shape. One hypothesis is that modeling these subtle differences is not necessary for solving the pretext task, causing the learnt representation to be *invariant* to these vital distinctions. Indeed, when we look at nearest neighbors in CUB for

Fig. 5. The 10 nearest neighbors (in order) of the far-left image in the CUB validation set measure by the unpooled feature space of the Rotation pretext model. We see that coloring plays almost no role in determining neighbors, but pose is a very strong signal

our Rotation model, we see birds of completely different colors but in the same pose, suggesting that the representation has captured pose, but ignored color (Fig. 5). We quantitatively evaluate this hypothesis further in Sect. 5.3.

Note that we have not discussed the failures of Instance Discrimination in both domains. Instance Discrimination must learn to distinguish between individual images, which should be solvable in any domain as long as the images are distinct. As such, its failure and general performance is much more unpredictable and less interpretable, as we elaborate on in the next section.

5.3   Reasons for Success

The flip side of why they fail is why they succeed. In prior work on the domain of internet imagery, this has mostly been answered by intuition. Rotation and Jigsaw were engineered as tasks that ostensibly require semantic understanding to solve. Instance Discrimination's success is similarly intuitive: spreading points in a constrained space will naturally cluster similar images. Given the failures above, neither of these intuitions endure without modification in the varied domains of our work, and a more nuanced reasoning is necessary.

Semantic Understanding: As discussed above, for some domains such as Aircraft or CUB, the pretexts do not produce a good semantic representation perhaps because they do not require a semantic understanding to solve. As an additional example, Jigsaw classifies permutations on Omniglot with 77% accuracy, but performs poorly on the classification task: line-matching is not understanding. Another example is Kather, where Rotation picks up on some hidden cue to fully solve the pretext problem without attaining any semantic knowledge. On the other side of the spectrum, we observe on the Symbolic domains in Fig. 6 that Rotation *is* implicitly performing semantic classification, making it a near-optimal pretext task. *When* is semantic understanding a prerequisite for a pretext task, and how can we test this?

We propose that semantic understanding is a prerequisite for a pretext *when the solution method is class-dependent*: in this case, the network must necessarily implicitly classify the image to perform the pretext well. For example, in the fine-grained classification of airplanes and birds, determining the orientation of the object is class-*in*dependent, so a network trained on the Rotation pretext does not need to learn features indicative of class. One way of testing if the pretext solution is class independent is to see if a network trained to solve the pretext

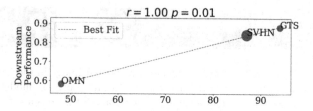

Fig. 6. Rotation pretext testing accuracy vs. unnormalized downstream performance. Almost perfect correlation is evident

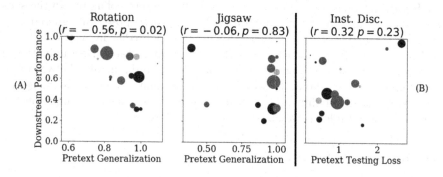

Fig. 7. **(A)** Generalization of the pretexts to novel classes is plotted on the x-axis, calculated as $\frac{PretextAcc_{Test}}{PretextAcc_{Val0.5}}$, where Train/Val0.5 contain only half the classes of their usual counterparts. On the y-axis is downstream accuracy normalized by Supervision accuracy *for the regularly trained model*, e.g. $\frac{ClassAcc_{Rot}}{ClassAcc_{Sup}}$. We see a strong correlation for Rotation, but none for Jigsaw. **(B)** Instance Discrimination pretext loss vs. downstream classification accuracy, no significant correlations. Marker area indicates dataset size and color the domain grouping.

on one set of classes solves the pretext on *unseen* classes. We call this test *pretext generalization* (Fig. 7): we train and validate pretexts on only half of the available classes, and then evaluate the pretext on the entire test set. We predict that worse pretext generalization should imply better downstream performance.

Our prediction is correct for Rotation, affirming our hypothesis, but Jigsaw models seem to show high pretext generalization in almost all cases. This lack of correlation might be because Jigsaw is relying on low-level cues that do generalize *in addition to* the semantic information. We contrast these findings with a concurrent paper [47] which speculates that Rotation is not as useful for few-shot learning on FGVC-Aircraft or VGG-Flowers due to the relative difficulty of the pretext task.

For Instance Discrimination, counterintuitively, downstream accuracy is *not* correlated with pretext loss (Fig. 7B). Our proposal is thus not the complete picture.

Table 2. Pearson correlations and p-values for training accuracy with random labels vs. normal. Jigsaw and ID have significant correlations, while Rotation trails substantially

	Jigsaw		Inst. Disc.		Rotation.	
(r, p)	0.59	0.02	0.46	0.07	0.45	0.08

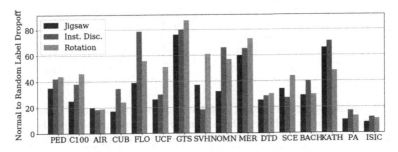

Fig. 8. Difference between normal and random label training accuracy. Note that even though Instance Discrimination had lower average *validation* accuracy than Rotation across all datasets, they actually had similar (normal label) average *training* accuracy at 56% (Jigsaw had 47%).

Linear Separability: The above discussion assumes that the relationship between the pretext task and the downstream task is the key. But what if the downstream task is immaterial? Pretext tasks might be succeeding by simply enabling *all* tasks, by creating a feature space where *many* labelings of the data points are expressible as linear classifiers. To test this hypothesis, we retrain linear classifiers with randomly shuffled training labels and compare this (training) accuracy to the training accuracy with correct labels. We find that these quantities are more correlated for Jigsaw than Instance Discrimination or Rotation (Table 2), per task decreased are shown in Fig. 8. This means that Jigsaw succeeds more by learning generic feature descriptors of images rather than by capturing semantics specific to the downstream task, while this is less true for Rotation or Instance Discrimination. Note that here we are talking of the training accuracy, or the empirical risk; this experiment does not reveal how or why pretext methods generalize to data not in the training set.

6 Feature Space Exploration

The discussion above suggests the virtue of analyzing the learnt representations independent of the downstream task. Below, we look at the *intrinsic dimensionality* of the learned representations, and the resulting notions of similarity.

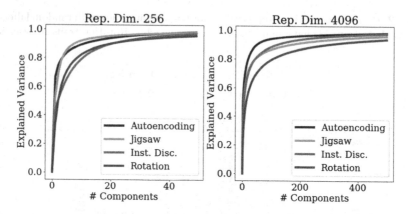

Fig. 9. Plot of the average fraction of explained variance vs. number of principal components (validation sets); a higher number means greater explanation, and thus relatively *lower* implicit dimension. Bach is omitted due to its extremely small size

6.1 Implicit Dimensionality of the Representations

The dimensionality of the representation is largely regarded as a hyperparameter to be tuned. Kolesnikov et al. show that a larger representation is always more useful when operating on large datasets, but this comes with a tradeoff of memory/storage [23]. What has not been studied is the *implicit* dimensionality of the representations, such as via Principal Component Analyis (PCA). Intuitively, one would expect the 4-way Rotation task to produce compact representations, with Instance Discrimination using all available dimensions to spread out the points as the loss demands. We find that this is *not* the case, via performing PCA on the representations and summing the explained variance of the first n values averaged across all datasets (Fig. 9). We also find that the implicit dimensionality induced by each pretext varies considerably across domains (Fig. 10).

Surprisingly, Instance Discrimination and Rotation have extremely similar implicit dimensionality in the 256-dimensional case. Also note that Instance Discrimination clearly is not fully utilizing the available latent space, as the first 40 components explain over 95% of the variance. In the higher-dimensional example, Rotation has by far the largest implicit dimensionality.

We next investigate the effect of dataset size on implicit dimensionality. Intuition says that a larger dataset would demand a more expressive representation on every task, and we see in Fig. 10 that this indeed holds true for *all* tasks except for Jigsaw. We hypothesize the lack of dimensionality increase for Jigsaw is because it exploits relatively low-level attributes instead of semantic knowledge.

6.2 Nearest Neighbors

As seen in Fig. 5, the nearest neighbors in feature space can yield great insight into the inner workings of our models. We repeat this experiment for all of our

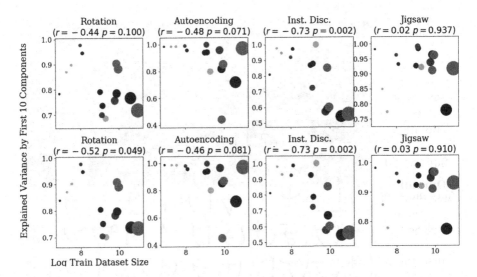

Fig. 10. The fraction of variance explained by the first 10 components vs. the log of the training set size. Top row is training PCA, bottom row is validation PCA. Moderate to strong correlations exists for all pretext tasks besides Jigsaw. Marker area indicates dataset size and the colors are domain groupings.

main methods on three datasets (CUB, Omniglot, Kather) in Fig. 11 (additional examples in the supplementary).

CUB: The strong pose-capturing of Rotation is again observed. Jigsaw exhibits similar phenomenon slightly more weakly, and also favors similarly cluttered edge-heavy backgrounds as in the base image. Instance Discrimination appears to have reasonably matched the species in the first and tenth neighbor, but in between has many unrelated birds.

Omniglot: The poor performance of Autoencoding is reflected in its matching ability. Rotation exhibits strong retrieval, with Jigsaw offering similar but weaker results. Instance Discrimination is a similar case to CUB, where a discernable trend is hard to spot, but several correct characters are matched.

Kather: No method improved much on random initialization (79% accuracy). Reflectively, Autoencoding, Jigsaw, and ID all simply match reasonably visually similar results. Rotation, however, failed catastrophically (<60% accuracy), despite high pretext accuracy (95% testing). We hypothesized that the pretext was exploiting a spurious cue, which is affirmed by radically varying neighbors.

Fig. 11. Each block of images comes from a single dataset, with each row corresponding to the pretext method. The farthest left image is the base image from which the distance in feature space is calculated to all the others in the validation set. Left-to-right is increasing distance in feature space among the 10 nearest neighbors

7   Conclusion

In this work, we have for the first time explored the notion of self-supervised learning in small-scale images in novel domains, identifying three domains where all current self-supervised methods have need of development: fine-grained, textural, and biological domains. In addition, we have revealed intriguing properties of the pretexts and the corresponding learnt representations, whose impact deserves further study. We hope that the release of our codes, models, and formatted dataset splits will help aid progress on all of these fronts.

Acknowledgements. This work was funded by a DARPA LwLL grant.

References

1. Aresta, G., et al.: Bach: grand challenge on breast cancer histology images. Med. Image Anal. **56**, 122–139 (2019)
2. Bengio, Y.: Learning deep architectures for AI. Found. Trends Mach. Learn. **2**(1), 1–127 (2009)
3. Bilen, H., Fernando, B., Gavves, E., Vedaldi, A., Gould, S.: Dynamic image networks for action recognition. In: Proceedings of the IEEE Conference on Computer Vision and Pattern Recognition. pp. 3034–3042 (2016)
4. Bojanowski, P., Joulin, A.: Unsupervised learning by predicting noise. In: Proceedings of the 34th International Conference on Machine Learning-Volume 70. pp. 517–526. JMLR. org (2017)
5. Bromley, J., Guyon, I., LeCun, Y., Säckinger, E., Shah, R.: Signature verification using a "siamese" time delay neural network. In: Advances in Neural Information Processing Systems. pp. 737–744 (1994)
6. Caron, M., Bojanowski, P., Joulin, A., Douze, M.: Deep clustering for unsupervised learning of visual features. In: European Conference on Computer Vision (2018)
7. Chen, L., Bentley, P., Mori, K., Misawa, K., Fujiwara, M., Rueckert, D.: Self-supervised learning for medical image analysis using image context restoration. Med. Image Anal. **58**, 101539 (2019)
8. Chen, T., Kornblith, S., Norouzi, M., Hinton, G.: A simple framework for contrastive learning of visual representations. arXiv preprint arXiv:2002.05709 (2020)
9. Cimpoi, M., Maji, S., Kokkinos, I., Mohamed, S., Vedaldi, A.: Describing textures in the wild. In: Proceedings of the IEEE Conference on Computer Vision and Pattern Recognition. pp. 3606–3613 (2014)
10. Codella, N., et al.: Skin lesion analysis toward melanoma detection 2018: A challenge hosted by the international skin imaging collaboration (isic). arXiv preprint arXiv:1902.03368 (2019)
11. Doersch, C., Zisserman, A.: Multi-task self-supervised visual learning. In: The IEEE International Conference on Computer Vision (ICCV) October 2017
12. Donahue, J., Krähenbühl, P., Darrell, T.: Adversarial feature learning. arXiv preprint arXiv:1605.09782 (2016)
13. Dumoulin, V., et al.: Adversarially learned inference. arXiv preprint arXiv:1606.00704 (2016)
14. Esser, P., Sutter, E., Ommer, B.: A variational u-net for conditional appearance and shape generation. In: Proceedings of the IEEE Conference on Computer Vision and Pattern Recognition. pp. 8857–8866 (2018)
15. Gidaris, S., Singh, P., Komodakis, N.: Unsupervised representation learning by predicting image rotations. In: International Conference on Learning Representations (2018), https://openreview.net/forum?id=S1v4N2l0-
16. Goodfellow, I., et al.: Generative adversarial nets. In: Advances in Neural Information Processing Systems. pp. 2672–2680 (2014)
17. Goroshin, R., Mathieu, M.F., LeCun, Y.: Learning to linearize under uncertainty. In: Advances in Neural Information Processing Systems. pp. 1234–1242 (2015)
18. Goyal, P., Mahajan, D., Gupta, A., Misra, I.: Scaling and benchmarking self-supervised visual representation learning. In: The IEEE International Conference on Computer Vision (ICCV) October 2019

19. He, K., Fan, H., Wu, Y., Xie, S., Girshick, R.: Momentum contrast for unsupervised visual representation learning. arXiv preprint arXiv:1911.05722 (2019)
20. Hinton, G.E., Salakhutdinov, R.R.: Reducing the dimensionality of data with neural networks. Science **313**(5786), 504–507 (2006)
21. Kallenberg, M., et al.: Unsupervised deep learning applied to breast density segmentation and mammographic risk scoring. IEEE Trans. Med. Imaging **35**(5), 1322–1331 (2016)
22. Kather, J.N., et al.: Multi-class texture analysis in colorectal cancer histology. Scientific Reports **6**, 27988 (2016)
23. Kolesnikov, A., Zhai, X., Beyer, L.: Revisiting self-supervised visual representation learning. In: The IEEE Conference on Computer Vision and Pattern Recognition (CVPR) June 2019
24. Krizhevsky, A., et al.: Learning multiple layers of features from tiny images. Technical Report, Citeseer (2009)
25. Lake, B.M., Salakhutdinov, R., Tenenbaum, J.B.: Human-level concept learning through probabilistic program induction. Science **350**(6266), 1332–1338 (2015)
26. Larsson, G., Maire, M., Shakhnarovich, G.: Learning representations for automatic colorization. In: Leibe, B., Matas, J., Sebe, N., Welling, M. (eds.) ECCV 2016. LNCS, vol. 9908, pp. 577–593. Springer, Cham (2016). https://doi.org/10.1007/978-3-319-46493-0_35
27. Lu, A.X., Kraus, O.Z., Cooper, S., Moses, A.M.: Learning unsupervised feature representations for single cell microscopy images with paired cell inpainting. PLoS Comput. Biol. **15**(9), e1007348 (2019)
28. Maji, S., Rahtu, E., Kannala, J., Blaschko, M., Vedaldi, A.: Fine-grained visual classification of aircraft. arXiv preprint arXiv:1306.5151 (2013)
29. Misra, I., van der Maaten, L.: Self-supervised learning of pretext-invariant representations. arXiv preprint arXiv:1912.01991 (2019)
30. Misra, I., Zitnick, C.L., Hebert, M.: Shuffle and learn: unsupervised learning using temporal order verification. In: Leibe, B., Matas, J., Sebe, N., Welling, M. (eds.) ECCV 2016. LNCS, vol. 9905, pp. 527–544. Springer, Cham (2016). https://doi.org/10.1007/978-3-319-46448-0_32
31. Munder, S., Gavrila, D.M.: An experimental study on pedestrian classification. IEEE Trans. Pattern Anal. Mach. Intell. **28**(11), 1863–1868 (2006)
32. Netzer, Y., Wang, T., Coates, A., Bissacco, A., Wu, B., Ng, A.Y.: Reading digits in natural images with unsupervised feature learning (2011)
33. Nilsback, M.E., Zisserman, A.: Automated flower classification over a large number of classes. In: 2008 Sixth Indian Conference on Computer Vision, Graphics & Image Processing. pp. 722–729. IEEE (2008)
34. Noroozi, M., Favaro, P.: Unsupervised learning of visual representations by solving jigsaw puzzles. In: ECCV (2016)
35. Ouyang, W., et al.: Analysis of the human protein atlas image classification competition. Nat. Methods **16**, 1254–1261 (2019). https://doi.org/10.1038/s41592-019-0658-6
36. Owens, A., Wu, J., McDermott, J.H., Freeman, W.T., Torralba, A.: Ambient sound provides supervision for visual learning. In: Leibe, B., Matas, J., Sebe, N., Welling, M. (eds.) ECCV 2016. LNCS, vol. 9905, pp. 801–816. Springer, Cham (2016). https://doi.org/10.1007/978-3-319-46448-0_48
37. Pathak, D., Girshick, R., Dollár, P., Darrell, T., Hariharan, B.: Learning features by watching objects move. In: Proceedings of the IEEE Conference on Computer Vision and Pattern Recognition. pp. 2701–2710 (2017)

38. Pathak, D., Krahenbuhl, P., Donahue, J., Darrell, T., Efros, A.A.: Context encoders: Feature learning by inpainting. In: Proceedings of the IEEE Conference on Computer Vision and Pattern Recognition. pp. 2536–2544 (2016)
39. Quattoni, A., Torralba, A.: Recognizing indoor scenes. In: 2009 IEEE Conference on Computer Vision and Pattern Recognition. pp. 413–420. IEEE (2009)
40. Rebuffi, S.A., Bilen, H., Vedaldi, A.: Learning multiple visual domains with residual adapters. In: Advances in Neural Information Processing Systems (2017)
41. Rebuffi, S.A., Bilen, H., Vedaldi, A.: Efficient parametrization of multi-domain deep neural networks. In: The IEEE Conference on Computer Vision and Pattern Recognition (CVPR) June 2018
42. Russakovsky, O., et al.: Imagenet large scale visual recognition challenge. Int. J. Comput. Vis. **115**(3), 211–252 (2015)
43. de Sa, V.R.: Learning classification with unlabeled data. In: Advances in Neural Information Processing Systems. pp. 112–119 (1994)
44. Saha, S., Bandyopadhyay, S.: Unsupervised pixel classification in satellite imagery using a new multiobjective symmetry based clustering approach. In: TENCON 2008–2008 IEEE Region 10 Conference. pp. 1–6 (2008)
45. Soomro, K., Zamir, A.R., Shah, M.: Ucf101: A dataset of 101 human actions classes from videos in the wild. arXiv preprint arXiv:1212.0402 (2012)
46. Stallkamp, J., Schlipsing, M., Salmen, J., Igel, C.: Man vs computer: benchmarking machine learning algorithms for traffic sign recognition. Neural Networks **32**, 323–332 (2012)
47. Su, J.C., Maji, S., Hariharan, B.: When does self-supervision improve few-shot learning? arXiv preprint arXiv:1910.03560 (2019)
48. Thomee, B., et al.: Yfcc100m: the new data in multimedia research. Commun. ACM **59**(2), 64–73 (2016)
49. Tschandl, P., Rosendahl, C., Kittler, H.: The ham10000 dataset, a large collection of multi-source dermatoscopic images of common pigmented skin lesions. Scientific Data **5**, 180161 (2018)
50. Vincent, P., Larochelle, H., Bengio, Y., Manzagol, P.A.: Extracting and composing robust features with denoising autoencoders. In: Proceedings of the 25th International Conference on Machine learning. pp. 1096–1103. ACM (2008)
51. Walker, J., Doersch, C., Gupta, A., Hebert, M.: An uncertain future: forecasting from static images using variational autoencoders. In: Leibe, B., Matas, J., Sebe, N., Welling, M. (eds.) ECCV 2016. LNCS, vol. 9911, pp. 835–851. Springer, Cham (2016). https://doi.org/10.1007/978-3-319-46478-7_51
52. Wang, X., Cai, Z., Gao, D., Vasconcelos, N.: Towards universal object detection by domain attention. In: The IEEE Conference on Computer Vision and Pattern Recognition (CVPR) June 2019
53. Welinder, P., et al.: Caltech-ucsd birds 200 (2010)
54. Wu, Z., Xiong, Y., Yu, S.X., Lin, D.: Unsupervised feature learning via non-parametric instance discrimination. In: Proceedings of the IEEE Conference on Computer Vision and Pattern Recognition. pp. 3733–3742 (2018)
55. Yang, Y., Newsam, S.: Bag-of-visual-words and spatial extensions for land-use classification. In: Proceedings of the 18th SIGSPATIAL International Conference on Advances in Geographic Information Systems. pp. 270–279. ACM (2010)
56. Zhai, X., Oliver, A., Kolesnikov, A., Beyer, L.: S4l: Self-supervised semi-supervised learning. In: Proceedings of the IEEE International Conference Computer Vision. pp. 1476–1485 (2019)
57. Zhai, X., et al.: The visual task adaptation benchmark. arXiv preprint arXiv:1910.04867 (2019)

58. Zhang, R., Isola, P., Efros, A.A.: Colorful image colorization. In: Leibe, B., Matas, J., Sebe, N., Welling, M. (eds.) ECCV 2016. LNCS, vol. 9907, pp. 649–666. Springer, Cham (2016). https://doi.org/10.1007/978-3-319-46487-9_40
59. Zhang, R., Isola, P., Efros, A.A.: Split-brain autoencoders: Unsupervised learning by cross-channel prediction. In: Proceedings of the IEEE Conference on Computer Vision and Pattern Recognition. pp. 1058–1067 (2017)

Multi-source Open-Set Deep Adversarial Domain Adaptation

Sayan Rakshit[1]($\boxtimes$)(iD), Dipesh Tamboli[1], Pragati Shuddhodhan Meshram[1],
Biplab Banerjee[1](iD), Gemma Roig[2](iD), and Subhasis Chaudhuri[1]

[1] Indian Institute of Technology Bombay, Mumbai, India
sayan1by2@gmail.com, dipeshtamboli1@gmail.com, pragatimeshram30@gmail.com,
getbiplab@gmail.com, sc@iitb.ac.in
[2] Goethe University Frankfurt, Frankfurt, Germany
roig@cs.uni-frankfurt.de

Abstract. We introduce a novel learning paradigm of multi-source open-set unsupervised domain adaptation (MS-OSDA). Recently, the notion of single-source open-set domain adaptation (SS-OSDA) which considers the presence of previously unseen open-set (unknown) classes in the target-domain in addition to the source-domain closed-set (known) classes has drawn attention. In the SS-OSDA setting, the labeled samples are assumed to be drawn from the same source. Yet, it is more plausible to assume that the labeled samples are distributed over multiple source-domains, but the existing SS-OSDA techniques cannot directly handle this more realistic scenario considering the diversities among multiple source-domains. As a remedy, we propose a novel adversarial learning-driven approach to deal with MS-OSDA. Precisely, we model a shared feature space for all the domains which explicitly mitigates the domain-gap among the source-domains. The adversarial learning strategy is introduced to align the known-class samples from the target-domain with the source data while making the unknown-classes more separable. We validate our method on the Office-31, Office-Home, Office-CalTech, and Digits datasets and find that the proposed model consistently outperforms the baseline and benchmark SS-OSDA approaches.

Keywords: Domain adaptation · Multi-source · Open-set

1 Introduction

Deep learning techniques are attested to be highly successful over a wide variety of visual inference tasks, thanks to their data-driven feature learning capabilities [13,16]. However, their performance is heavily dependent on the availability of voluminous labeled training samples to achieve a reliable level of generalization. Ideally, a supervised learning algorithm trained on a certain distribution

Electronic supplementary material The online version of this chapter (https://doi.org/10.1007/978-3-030-58574-7_44) contains supplementary material, which is available to authorized users.

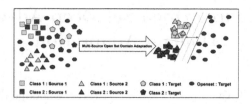

Fig. 1. Given an MS-OSDA setup, our goal is to obtain a discriminative feature space for the known-class samples from all the source and target domains while pushing the unknown-class samples from the target domain far from the known-class support.

of labeled samples (source-domain) often fails to generalize convincingly when deployed on a new environment (target-domain) in the presence of distributions-shift. In this regard, unsupervised domain adaptation (DA) [22] algorithms seek to combat the domain-shift problem by aligning the data distributions of the source and target domains by learning a domain-invariant feature space using statistical or adversarial learning approaches, preferably in the absence of label information in the target-domain [3,29]. In this paper, we tackle the completely novel paradigm of multi-source open-set domain adaptation (MS-OSDA), illustrated in Fig. 1.

In general, the notion of multi-source DA (MSDA) [28] is regarded more practical as well as challenging than the single-source DA (SSDA) setup considering that labeled samples may come from diverse sources. In MSDA, we note that the source-domains have different data distributions among themselves in addition to the usual domain-gap between the source and the target domains. One of the straight-forward solutions to MSDA is based on the idea of combining all the source-domains into a single auxiliary source-domain and subsequently deploying any SSDA method. Clearly, such a naive approach may lead to sub-optimal classification results if proper care is not taken in mitigating the gaps among all the domains exclusively.

The paradigm of closed-set DA has mostly been practiced in the literature for both SSDA and MSDA where the same set of classes is shared across the domains [22]. In contrast, the recently introduced single-source open-set DA (SS-OSDA) [21] setting allows the presence of domain-specific classes in addition to the classes shared by the domains. There exists two possibilities in this regard. While the SS-OSDA setup by [21] considers that both source and target specific open-set classes may be available, the setup followed in [15,25] permits the presence of target specific open-set samples only. Such an SS-OSDA arrangement of [15, 25] is extremely challenging given the unavailability of any prior information regarding the open-set distribution. The closed-set DA techniques cannot be directly applied in this case since these target specific open-set samples, in turn, may jeopardize the domain alignment process. In order to tackle such a situation, accurate discrimination between the known and unknown target-domain classes is advocated during adaptation so that only the shared classes can be aligned.

The existing MSDA techniques contemplate the presence of the same set of classes in all the source and the target domains [34]. This is a strict scenario as far as the unsupervised DA setup is considered where the target-domain is assumed to be completely unlabeled. Hence, it is highly likely that the target-domain may contain samples from novel classes different from those already in the source-domains. Inspired by these arguments, we propose a novel learning scenario in this paper for multi-source open-set unsupervised DA (MS-OSDA) where there exists multiple labeled source-domains each containing samples from the same set of semantic classes, and the unlabeled target-domain contains two types of data items: either from the source-domain known-classes or from novel unknown-classes. Under this setup, the task is to classify the target-domain samples either in one of the known categories or they are assigned a common unknown-class label. Such an MS-OSDA setup invariably holds huge applications in fields relating to on-the-fly real-world visual perception like medical imaging, remote sensing, where acquisition of multi-domain data is perennial and novel categories may turn up abruptly. Nonetheless, we note that the MS-OSDA problem cannot be effectively solved by directly utilizing the SS-OSDA paradigm of [15,25] mainly because of the following factors: i) the presence of multiple diverse source-domains hinders the effectiveness of a traditional SS-OSDA technique, and ii) design of the known/unknown class discriminator for target samples may become non-trivial since the target-domain may have varied degrees of relatedness with different source-domains.

To solve these problems, we propose a new framework which aims at learning a shared feature space for all the source and target domains where i) the source-domains are purposefully aligned among themselves, and ii) a target-domain pseudo-classifier is designed to accomplish two tasks: a) to align the target-domain known-class samples with those of the source-domains, and b) to maximize the gap between the known and unknown target-domain samples (Fig. 1). To this end, our proposed model: Multi-source Open-Set DA NETwork (MOSDANET) consists of a shared feature encoder for the source and target domains and separate multi-class classifiers for the source-domains, respectively. The classifiers are augmented with an extra unknown-class label for all the open-set samples in addition to the known-class labels. The pseudo-classifier for the target-domain is subsequently designed using an ensemble of these source classifiers.

Recently, [23] argued that reducing the domain-gap among the source-domains explicitly leads to a more robust and effective MSDA model. We find this idea to be particularly relevant to MS-OSDA since aligning the source-domains among themselves inherently helps in better discrimination of the target-domain samples into known and unknown categories. Otherwise, the domain-shift among the source-domains may mislead the pseudo-classifier to wrongly identify an unknown-class sample to be originated from a known-class or vice-versa. In the same line, we propose to perform fine-grained alignment among the source-domains in the shared space to induce the notion of discriminativeness among the known-class data. On the other hand, a novel adversarial loss function is proposed to train the large-margin pseudo-classifier for the target-domain samples.

We consider to use adversarial strategy in this case given their recent success in implicit distributions matching for cross-domain inference tasks [32]. Imposing the large-margin constraint helps in dealing with different openness factors (fraction of classes present in the open-set) in an efficient manner since the margin idea offers more separability for the unknown-class data. Our major contributions can be summarized as follows:

- We introduce the problem setting for multi-source open-set DA and propose an adversarial learning based framework termed as MOSDANET.
- We highlight some of the important aspects of MOSDANET as: a) aligning the source-domains explicitly at class-level, b) design of an intuitive large-margin discriminator for the target-domain known/unknown classes through a newly developed adversarial training strategy, and c) consideration of target-domain samples with pseudo-labels corresponding to the known-classes to explicitly aid in the fine-grained domain alignment process.
- We establish the efficacy of MOSDANET through extensive experiments on four benchmark datasets where we perform thorough robustness analysis.

2   Related Works

Closed-Set and Open-Set Single-Source DA: The existing literature is rich in methods relating both to closed-set and open-set DA involving a single source-domain. For SSDA, several ad-hoc techniques existed prior to the deep learning era where the goal was to either project both the domains onto a shared latent space or to align the data distribution of a given domain to match the properties of the other [2,5,20]. These techniques were subsequently replaced by more accurate deep CNN based approaches which reduce the domain-gap in the learned CNN representations through an end-to-end training [1,17,27]. Nowadays, there exist a plethora of models influenced by the adversarial training strategy which have showcased superlative performance [29,31]. Typically, these approaches pose the DA problem as learning a domain-confused feature space through an adversarial training between two players: a feature generator and a domain discriminator, respectively. For example, domain adversarial neural network (DANN) [4] introduces the *gradient-reversal* layer to accomplish the task. A few methods in this respect resort to the notion of ensemble learning and exploit the outcomes of the committee of source-domain classifiers to define the adversary [18,25].

The SS-OSDA problem, on the other hand, was first coined in assign and transform iterative (ATI-λ) [21] which considers the distance between the target samples and the source clusters to decide on the potential known/unknown class labels for the target data. Note that ATI-λ utilizes some of the open-set classes from the source-domain during training. The open-set DA by back-propagation (OSDA-BP) [25] trains the feature generator within a typical generator and discriminator based adversarial learning framework to lead the discriminator to predict the class-label of a target sample to be unknown if the likelihood exceeds a predefined threshold. The improved OSDA-BP [3] replaces the cross-entropy based adversarial loss of [25] by a symmetric version of Kullback-Leibler (KL) divergence and showcases improved SS-OSDA performance. While these approaches are based on aligning the source and the target domains at one go, an alternate approach proposed in [15] progressively builds the alignment given the domains.

Closed-Set Multi-source DA: MSDA techniques assume that the labeled training samples are distributed over multiple source-domains. One of the first MSDA approaches (A-SVM) [33] in this respect distills the capacity of all the source classifiers to better model a target classifier. Following [33], there have been several endeavors towards MSDA for different application areas like language processing, sentiment analysis etc. [11]. As far as the adversarial approaches are concerned, [23] proposes a moment-matching network for MSDA which is based on aligning higher-order moments between the domain-specific features. On the other hand, [34] proposes a multi-source domain adversarial network (MDAN) which models separate mapping functions for each of the source-target pairs. [6] introduces the idea of deploying a mixture of source experts for MSDA for cross-domain sentiment analysis.

MS-OSDA is a completely new paradigm that we introduce with an adversarial training strategy followed for the target-domain pseudo-classifier, which is loosely inspired by [25]. Since the adversarial training of [25] is based on the standard cross-entropy based classification loss, it is susceptible to severe misclassification if the known and unknown-class samples have some similarities. Furthermore, this restricts the ability of the model to deal with different openness. In MOSDANET, we solve these bottlenecks of [25] by introducing a margin-based loss-term along with the classification loss. In addition, our target-domain pseudo-classifier is essentially a committee of classifiers since we are dealing with multiple source-domains. Finally, as opposed to the existing MSDA methods [6,23,34], we are interested in diminishing any domain-shift among the source-domains in the shared space.

3   Proposed Methodology

3.1   Problem Definition and Notation

Let us consider the availability of L different source-domains $\mathcal{S} = \{\mathcal{S}_1, \mathcal{S}_2, \cdots, \mathcal{S}_L\}$ each equipped with the domain-specific training set $\mathbb{X}_l = \{x_l^i, y_l^i\}_{i=1}^{n_l}$, ($l \in \{1, 2, \cdots, L\}$ and n_l defines the number of training samples of $\mathcal{S}_l$). Further we note that $(x_l, y_l) \in \mathcal{X}_l \otimes \mathcal{Y}_s$ given the domain-specific feature space $\mathcal{X}_l$ while the label space $\mathcal{Y}_s = \{1, 2, 3, \cdots, K\}$ is shared among all the source-domains. On the other hand, there exists a target-domain $\mathcal{T}$ consisting of n_t unlabeled test samples $\mathbb{X}_t = \{x_t^j\}_{j=1}^{n_t}$ arising from $\mathcal{Y}_t$ categories where $x_t \in \mathcal{X}_t$ given the target-domain feature space $\mathcal{X}_t$. According to our setup, $\mathcal{Y}_s \subset \mathcal{Y}_t$ and $\mathcal{Y}_{t/s}$ denotes the open-set classes of $\mathcal{T}$ which are not part of $\mathcal{S}$. In a typical closed-set MSDA setup, it is assumed that the marginal data distributions of all the source and the target domains are mutually different: $P_l(\mathcal{X}_l) \neq P_m(\mathcal{X}_m)$ and $P_l(\mathcal{X}_l) \neq P_t(\mathcal{X}_t)$, $\mathcal{S}_l, \mathcal{S}_m \in \mathcal{S}$. For MS-OSDA, the distribution of the known classes from $\mathcal{T}$ differs from that of a given $\mathcal{S}_l$: $P_l(\mathcal{X}_l) \neq P_t(\mathcal{X}_t^{1:K})$ where $\mathcal{X}_t^{1:K}$ represents the target-domain samples with known class-labels. Also let $\mathcal{X}_t^{K+1}$ be the samples from unknown classes in $\mathcal{T}$.

Under this setup, the task is to classify the data from $\mathbb{X}_t$ into $K+1$ categories where the first K indices correspond to classes in $\mathcal{Y}_s$ and the $(K+1)^{th}$ index denotes a common label for all the classes in $\mathcal{Y}_{t/s}$. In order to accomplish the task, we propose a deep neural network with a shared feature encoder $\mathcal{E}(;,\theta_\mathcal{E})$ having parameters $\theta_\mathcal{E}$, L source-domains specific $(K+1)$-class classifiers $\{\mathcal{F}_l(;,\theta_\mathcal{F}^l)\}_{l=1}^L$ each with its own set of parameters $\theta_\mathcal{F}^l$ (an illustration is provided in Fig. 2). We use $\theta_\mathcal{F}$ to define all the classifier's parameters $\{\theta_\mathcal{F}^l\}_{l=1}^L$ together. Finally, the classifier model for $\mathcal{T}$: $\mathcal{F}_t(;,\theta_\mathcal{F})$ is essentially an ensemble-classifiers system which is defined by average-pooling the responses of the $\{\mathcal{F}_l\}_{l=1}^L$ for each sample from $\mathcal{X}_t$. In particular, we average-pool the unnormalized logit-scores and apply the softmax function on the pooled responses for obtaining the posterior class-distributions. For a given x_t, let us denote $\mathbf{q}_t = [q_t^1, q_t^2, \cdots, q_t^{K+1}]$ to be the final logit vector obtained in this way. The posterior probability for the kth class $(k \in \{1, 2, \cdots, K+1\})$ is mentioned as: $p(y_t = k|x_t) = \frac{\exp(q_t^k)}{\sum\limits_{c=1}^{K+1} \exp(q_t^c)}$.

3.2   Training and Inference

Overview of the Training Process: Following the aforementioned setup, we focus on three objectives for training MOSDANET in order to obtain the domain-independent and discriminative shared feature encoder $\mathcal{E}$: i) align the L source-domains in $\mathcal{S}$ at a fine-scale, ii) align known-class target-domain samples in $\mathcal{X}_t^{1:K}$ with $\mathcal{S}$, and iii) widen the margin between $\mathcal{X}_t^{1:K}$ and the unknown-class samples in $\mathcal{X}_t^{K+1}$. Apparently, Objective-(i) is easy to achieve given the availability of labeled training samples for the source-domains. On the other hand, Objectives (ii) and (iii) are non-trivial to attain since $\mathcal{T}$ is unlabeled. We follow an adversarial game between $\mathcal{E}$ and $\mathcal{F}_t$ for approximating the labels for the target-domain samples and thus realizing Objectives (ii) and (iii) simultaneously. To ensure a fine-grained alignment between $\mathcal{S}$ and $\mathcal{T}$, we furthermore propose to re-use some of the potential samples from $\mathcal{X}_t$ with pseudo-labels corresponding to one of the K known-classes in Objective-(i) pretending that they belong to $\mathcal{S}$. The loss functions are detailed in the following.

i) Alignment of the Source-Domains: We propose to maximize the pairwise similarities among the samples from different source-domains but sharing identical class-labels in the shared space, thus reducing the domain-shift among the source-domains. It leads us to obtain a unified feature space for the known-class samples from different source-domains, which subsequently helps in the better alignment of $\mathcal{X}_t^{1:K}$ with samples from $\mathcal{S}$. Precisely, for each of the known-class labels $k \in \mathcal{Y}_s$, we separately select samples from all of the L source-domains. Let $\mathcal{X}_l^k \subset \mathcal{X}_l$ define the set of samples with class label k obtained from the lth

source-domain. Given that, we define the source alignment loss $\mathcal{L}_{SA}$ as:

$$\mathcal{L}_{SA} = \frac{1}{K}\sum_{k\in\mathcal{Y}_s}\frac{1}{L}\sum_{l,m=1,l\neq m}^{L}\mathbb{E}||\mathcal{E}(\mathcal{X}_l^k) - \mathcal{E}(\mathcal{X}_m^k)||_2^2 + \frac{1}{L}\sum_{l=1}^{L}\mathcal{L}_{CE}(\mathcal{F}_l(\mathcal{E}(\mathcal{X}_l)),\mathcal{Y}_s) \quad (1)$$

The first term of Eq. 1 accomplishes two goals: a) maximizing the pairwise cosine similarities among the encoded features of the samples originating from different source-domains but sharing identical class-labels: $\min |\mathcal{E}(\boldsymbol{x}_i) - \mathcal{E}(\boldsymbol{x}_j)|_2 \approx \max \mathcal{E}(\boldsymbol{x}_i)\mathcal{E}(\boldsymbol{x}_j)^T$ for a pair of unit-norm vectors $\boldsymbol{x}_i$ $\boldsymbol{x}_j$ (note that the $\mathcal{E}$ is designed to ensure the norm constraint), and b) bringing the centroids of the feature samples for each of the class-labels from different source-domains closer. Together, the L source classifiers $\{\mathcal{F}_l\}_{l=1}^L$ are trained using separate instances of cross-entropy loss $\mathcal{L}_{CE}$. Hence, the shared space becomes class-wise discriminative taking all the source samples into account.

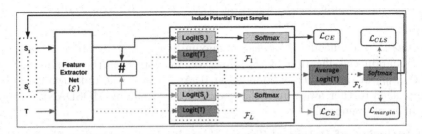

Fig. 2. A depiction of MOSDANET. It majorly consists of a shared feature encoder $\mathcal{E}$ and separate $K + 1$-class classifiers $\mathcal{F}_l$s for each of the source domains. $\mathcal{F}_t$ denotes the classifier for $\mathcal{T}$. The figure also depicts the loss terms to be evaluated. # in the figure refers to the first term of Eq. 1. Logit(S) means the unnormalized logit vectors.

ii) **Alignment Between $\mathcal{S}$ and $\mathcal{T}$:** For samples in $\mathcal{T}$, we intend to i) correctly classify the known-class samples in one of the K categories by ensuring proper alignment with the source data in the shared space, and ii) classify any unknown-class data with label $K + 1$. In addition, we also constrain that the known/unknown separation should be carried out with a high confidence. By confidence, we aim at imposing a large-margin between the known and unknown-class supports as produced by $\mathcal{F}_t$.

Ideally, we need to construct a decision boundary for the open-set, but we are devoid of any prior information in this respect. Alternately, it is intuitive to initially construct a pseudo decision boundary for the unknown-classes in $\mathcal{T}$ using $\mathcal{F}_t$ and to subsequently train $\mathcal{E}$ to deceive the classifier. This refers to the adversarial game between $\mathcal{E}$ and $\mathcal{F}_t$. We deduce a binary cross-entropy based classification loss ($\mathcal{L}_{CLS}$) for defining the pseudo- unknown-class boundary for $\mathcal{T}$ which considers the probability of a given $x_t \in \mathcal{X}_t$ to belong to the $(K + 1)^{th}$-class or the cumulative probability to belong to the K known categories as yielded by $\mathcal{F}_t$ (Eq. 2):

$$\mathcal{L}_{CLS} = \mathbb{E}[-0.5\log(p(y_t = K + 1|\mathcal{E}(x_t)) - 0.5\log(1 - p(y_t = K + 1|\mathcal{E}(x_t)))] \quad (2)$$

Following [25], the ground-truth probability for $\mathcal{L}_{CLS}$ is set to 0.5 in order to avoid any trivial solution where all the samples from $\mathcal{T}$ may be wrongly labeled with only known or unknown class labels. We find that the adversarial training using $\mathcal{L}_{CLS}$ produces good alignment between $\mathcal{S}$ and $\mathcal{T}$ if the known and unknown classes are quite distinct but fails if they are find-grained in nature. This is due to the fact that $\mathcal{F}_t$ becomes uncertain in estimating the class-labels if the classes are overlapping in the feature space. In order to tackle the situation, we propose to maximize the margin between the supports of the known and the unknown class boundaries. Ideally for a given x_t, if $|p(y_t = K + 1|\mathcal{E}(x_t) - (1 - p(y_t = K + 1|\mathcal{E}(x_t))| \geq \tau$ for some predefined threshold τ ($\tau \in [0,1]$, $\tau \approx 1$), then we can claim that the classification is confident. We introduce a margin loss $\mathcal{L}_{margin}$ given the softmax predictions of $\mathcal{F}_t$ as a solution that penalizes samples for which the known and unknown class predictions are closer than τ as follows,

$$\mathcal{L}_{margin} = \mathbb{E}[\min (0, |\sum_{k=1}^{K} p(y_t = k|\mathcal{E}(x_t)) - p(y_t = K + 1|\mathcal{E}(x_t))|_1 - \tau)] \quad (3)$$

Ideally, the encoder $\mathcal{E}$ seeks to maximize $\mathcal{L}_{margin}$ in order to ensure a large-margin classification by $\mathcal{F}_t$. However, we note that the maximum value of $\mathcal{L}_{margin}$ at optimality is bounded at 0. As a result, the unknown-class data are pushed further away from the known-classes, making MOSDANET robust to different openness.

iii) Inclusion of Potential Target Samples in $\mathcal{L}_{SA}$ During Training: In order to further encourage fine-grained alignment between $\mathcal{S}$ and $\mathcal{T}$, we propose to incorporate potential samples from $\mathcal{T}$ with pseudo-labels corresponding to one of the K known classes in the evaluation of $\mathcal{L}_{SA}$ professing that these samples are part of one of the source-domains. We initiate the process of identifying such samples at least after one training epoch is over to ensure reliability.

However, we cannot blindly rely on such pseudo-labels considering the implicit domain differences. A possible solution could be to threshold the predicted class probabilities to decide on the reliability of the pseudo-labels obtained. If the predicted probability for a certain class is extremely high (≈ 1), then the chance of the sample to actually belong to that particular class automatically increases. Given a threshold hyper-parameter α, we use the following rule to decide whether a given x_t qualifies for consideration in this regard:

– If only

$$p(y_t = k|\mathcal{E}(x_t)) \geq \alpha, \alpha \in [0,1], k \in \mathcal{Y}_s \quad (4)$$

(x_t, k) can be included in the augmented training set.

Network Optimization: We follow an alternate optimization strategy for training MOSDANET end-to-end. The following three stages are iterated until convergence:

Stage-1: For a fixed encoder, $\mathcal{E}$, the source-domain classifiers are trained to minimize the following cost:

$$\min_{\theta_{\mathcal{F}}} \frac{1}{L}\sum_{l=1}^{L}\mathcal{L}_{CE}(\mathcal{F}_l(\mathcal{E}(\mathcal{X}_l)), \mathcal{Y}_s) + \mathcal{L}_{CLS} \tag{5}$$

Equation 5 signifies that the parameters of the classifiers are simultaneously optimized for correctly classifying the respective source-domain samples in one of the K classes (second term of Eq. 1) while preserving the pseudo unknown-class boundary given samples from $\mathcal{T}$ (Eq. 2). Please note that the first term of Eq. 1 deals with optimizing the encoder parameters, which in this case are fixed.

Stage-2: On the second step, $\mathcal{E}$ is assigned the job of minimizing $\mathcal{L}_{SA}$ (Eq. 1), thus classwise aligning the source domains together with optimizing the source classifiers and, ii) maximizing $\mathcal{L}_{CLS} + \mathcal{L}_{margin}$ (Eq. 2 and 3, respectively) in order to classify the target samples in known or unknown classes with a high confidence. In particular, $\mathcal{E}$ is updated by optimizing the following cost given a fixed $\theta_{\mathcal{F}}$:

$$\min_{\theta_{\mathcal{E}}} \mathcal{L}_{SA} - (\mathcal{L}_{CLS} + \mathcal{L}_{margin}) \tag{6}$$

Stage-3: We investigate the occurrence of potential target-domain samples with pseudo known-class labels (Eq. 4). Once we obtain such samples, they are used in evaluating Eq. 2 along with samples from $\mathcal{S}$ from subsequent iteration.

Inference: During inference, the target samples in $\mathbb{X}_t$ are propagated through the encoder $\mathcal{E}$ followed by the classifiers-ensemble $\mathcal{F}_t$ and the class with maximum softmax score is selected.

Table 1. The performance comparison for MOSDANET with 20 shared and 11 unknown-classes for Office-31 dataset (in %). † = single best, ‡ = source combine and * = best member classifier.

Method	AD - W		AW - D		WD - A		AVG	
	OS*	OS	OS*	OS	OS*	OS	OS*	OS
OSVM [26](†)	73.3	70.2	95.1	94.4	40.2	39.1	69.5 ± 0.3	67.9 ± 0.4
OSVM [26](‡)	71.2	51.2	84.9	56.2	58.2	61.4	71.4 ± 0.5	56.3 ± 0.7
OSVM+DANN [4](‡)	65.0	83.3	68.0	91.9	51.2	37.5	61.4 ± 0.3	70.9 ± 0.4
OSVM+ [23]	88.3	58.8	95.5	59.5	82.3	52.7	88.7 ± 0.6	57.0 ± 0.4
OSDA-BP [25](†)	98.1	93.0	99.0	94.1	77.1	75.0	91.4 ± 0.5	87.4 ± 0.4
OSDA-BP [25](‡)	94.0	90.0	93.0	89.0	79.0	75.0	88.7 ± 0.7	84.7 ± 0.4
IOSDA-BP [3](†)	98.7	67.0	98.1	62.1	74.7	74.1	90.5 ± 0.5	67.7 ± 0.3
IOSDA-BP [3](‡)	91.1	88.0	87.8	87.1	75.0	74.5	84.6 ± 0.6	83.2 ± 0.5
MOSDANET(*)	95.2	91.4	94.4	90.3	77.5	73.1	89.0 ± 0.3	84.9 ± 0.2
MOSDANET	**99.0**	**98.2**	**99.4**	**98.3**	81.0	**79.3**	**93.1±0.4**	**91.9 ± 0.2**

Table 2. The performance comparison for MOSDANET for 5 shared and 5 unknown classes for Office-caltech dataset and 45 shared 20 unknown classes for the Office-Home dataset (in %). † = single best, ‡ = source combine and * = best member classifier.

Method	Office-Caltech					Office-Home				
	ADW-C	ADC-W	AWC-D	DCW-A	AVG	ACP - R	APR - C	PCR - A	ACR - P	AVG
	OS	OS	OS	OS	OS	OS	OS	OS	OS	OS
OSVM [26](†)	43.1	36.5	42.6	44.6	41.7	67.1	59.7	59.3	75.1	65.3
OSVM [26](‡)	45.3	35.3	34.4	45.5	40.1	60.2	46.3	48.6	57.0	53.0
OSVM+DANN [4](‡)	46.2	42.5	42.3	47.1	44.5	54.5	31.6	40.9	53.8	45.2
OSVM+ [23]	18.6	39.5	40.3	21.9	30.1	60.2	51.5	69.9	59.8	60.3
OSDA-BP [25](†)	86.4	91.2	92.4	88.4	89.6	73.0	57.0	58.1	70.4	64.6
OSDA-BP [25](‡)	80.4	87.4	91.7	90.4	87.4	53.6	38.0	46.9	54.9	48.3
IOSDA-BP [3](†)	78.6	91.5	93.0	87.0	87.5	58.6	31.4	46.2	64.0	50.0
IOSDA-BP [3](‡)	58.6	57.9	61.6	62.7	60.2	64.5	46.2	54.9	66.4	58.1
MOSDANET(*)	86.1	96.8	96.7	94.1	92.9	78.0	66.0	62.0	76.3	70.5
MOSDANET	90.6	99.2	98.9	94.8	95.8	80.3	67.5	60.6	80.0	72.1

4   Experimental Evaluations

Datasets: We evaluate the MOSDANET on four benchmark datasets: Office-31 [24], Office-Home [30], and Office-CalTech [24], and Digits, respectively. The three domains of Office-31 are: Amazon (**A**), Web (**W**), and DSLR (**D**) each consisting of images from 31 categories. A total of 4652 images are present in this dataset. We consider all possible combinations with two source and one target domains. Besides, 20 shared classes and 11 open-set classes are considered based on the alphabetic order. Office-CalTech is an extension of the Office-31 and consists of the 10 shared classes of Amazon (**A**), CalTech (**C**), Webcam (**W**), and DSLR (**D**), respectively. We consider all the setups having three source-domains and one target-domain with 5 known and 5 open-set classes. The Office-Home dataset contains four domains: Art (**A**), Clipart (**C**), Real-world (**R**), and Product (**P**) where each of the domains is equipped with 65 object categories. In total, there are 15, 500 images present in this dataset. We consider all four possible combinations with three source-domains and one target-domain with 45 shared and 20 open-set classes. Finally, the Digits dataset consists of three domains of hand-written digits: MNIST (**M**) [14], USPS (**U**) [8], and SVHN (**S**) [19] and we consider the combined available training and test samples per domain for this dataset with a total of 1, 78, 589 images together for all the domains. 5 known (digits 0−4) and 5 unknown-classes (digits 5−9) are considered for comparative analysis. For completeness, we report results on the subset of the DomainNet challenge [23] in the supplementary along with some more analysis.

Model Architecture and Experimental Protocols: For Office-31, Office-CalTech, and Office-Home, our feature encoder $\mathcal{E}$ is constructed from the Imagenet pre-trained Resnet-50 model [7]. However, we replace all the layers after the final 2048-dimensional fully-connected (fc) layer by three new fc-layers with 1000, 512, and 128 nodes, respectively. Batch-norm [9] and Leaky-ReLU non-linearity are considered after each of the new layers for stable training. The parameters of the original network layers remain fixed during training and only the newly considered layers are trained. For Digits, we consider the LeNet [14] architecture as the feature encoder $\mathcal{E}$ and the network is trained from the scratch in contrast to the previous case. The classifiers are further constructed in terms of a small neural network that project the features onto the $K + 1$-dimensional class scores.

Table 3. The performance analysis of MOSDANET for the Digits dataset with 5 known and 5 open-set classes (in %). † = single best, ‡ = source combine.

Method	M+U - S			S+M - U			S+U - M			AVG OS
	OS	OS*	UNK	OS	OS*	UNK	OS	OS*	UNK	
OSVM [26](†)	65.8	62.6	71.3	74.8	76.9	87.0	50.3	61.1	11.5	63.6 ± 0.4
OSVM [26](‡)	66.9	65.4	69.4	72.8	74.9	85.6	60.2	68.0	17.1	66.6 ± 0.3
OSVM+ [23]	58.4	87.9	10.9	59.1	96.9	6.5	10.7	20.7	0.3	42.7 ± 0.4
IOSDA-BP [3](†)	76.5	74.6	89.9	85.6	88.6	90.5	82.9	83.4	80.4	81.6 ± 0.8
IOSDA-BP [3](‡)	78.6	75.8	92.7	82.9	79.7	91.1	82.1	82.3	90.5	81.2 ± 0.5
MOSDANET	**79.1**	**88.2**	**93.8**	**86.6**	**98.8**	**98.9**	**95.2**	**98.2**	**99.1**	**87.1 ± 0.3**

The network is trained using the Adam optimizer [12] with an initial learning rate of 0.001 and a batch size of 64 (for Office datasets) and of size 100 for Digits. Regarding fixing the hyper-parameters, we are convinced that the a higher value for the margin parameter τ (Eq. 3) indeed helps in attaining better separation between the known and the unknown classes in $\mathcal{T}$ and we set $\tau = 0.6$ for all the experiments in Table 1, 2 and 3 as the performance mostly saturates for $\tau \geq 0.6$. The α parameter (Eq. 4) which is entitled to decide on the pseudo-labels for the target-domain samples is set to 0.9 since a high α helps in producing more confident pseudo-labels.

4.1   Comparison to the Literature and Baselines

We compare our method with three different experimental settings in Table 1, 2 and 3 considering the absence of any prior MS-OSDA literature: i) **source-combine**: here the source-domains are combined to construct an auxiliary source-domain and the single-source and single-target DA setup is followed. In the source-domain, only the known-class samples are considered whereas both known and unknown-class samples are used in the target-domain during training. In this regard, we use three situations: a) Baseline case where the open-set multi-class support vector machines (OSVM) [10] is trained on the auxiliary source-domain and is then directly evaluated on the target-domain samples. b) We perform domain alignment between the auxiliary source and the target domains using the benchmark closed-set DA method of DANN [4]. Once the training is over, we consider the generated features and use the OSVM for open-set classification. c) We consider two existing SS-OSDA techniques: OSDA-BP [25] and improved OSDA-BP (IOSDA-BP) [3] to be trained and evaluated on the

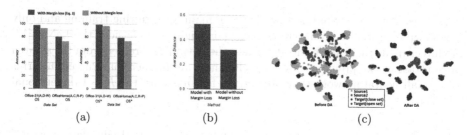

Fig. 3. (a) Effect of $\mathcal{L}_{margin}$ in terms of OS value for two combinations of Office-31 (A,D-W) and Office-Home (ACR-P), (b) Effect of $\mathcal{L}_{margin}$ in maximizing the difference between the known and unknown-class probabilities for the correctly classified target samples for A,D-W (Office-31), (c) t-SNE plot for the case A,D-W (Office-31) before and after adaptation.

auxiliary source and the target domains, respectively. ii) **single-best**: For baseline OSVM, OSDA-BP, and IOSDA-BP, we also report the best results obtained for the single-source and single-target setup, e.g., for $\mathbf{A,D} \mapsto \mathbf{W}$, the best result between $\mathbf{A} \mapsto \mathbf{W}$ and $\mathbf{D} \mapsto \mathbf{W}$ is reported, and iii) **multi-source**: In this regard, we consider the very recent benchmark MSDA method of [23] and train the model using known-classes in the source-domains and known + unknown classes in the target and then use OSVM for classification. For the single-best and source-combine cases, we follow similar architecture for the feature encoder as of MOSDANET (Sect. 4). For baseline OSVM, we train the feature encoder on the (auxiliary) source domain and subsequently utilize the same as the feature generator for the target samples. We report the OS and OS^* [21] scores to signify the average classwise accuracy for known + unknown classes and only for known-classes, respectively. For Digits, we also report the performance on the unknown-classes (UNK).

We note that all the considered DA techniques except OSDA-BP and IOSDA-BP are basically designed for closed-set DA. Hence, their performances on the known-classes are good while they fail to detect the unknown-classes properly (Table 1, 2 and 3). Similar trends can be observed when the benchmark multi-source DA method [23] is used for the domain alignment. On the other hand, the source combine versions of OSDA-BP and IOSDA-BP produce better average OS values than DANN + OSVM. Finally, our method produces the best average OS for all the datasets. In particular, Digits is extremely large-scale in terms of the number of samples and Office-Home has complex class-distributions with several fine-grained categories. Still, the performance of MOSDANET on these datasets are comparatively high. We also report the OS values for the best-performing member-classifier within the ensemble. It can be observed that the decision fusion used in $\mathcal{F}_l$ sharply enhances the performance over each member.

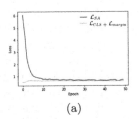 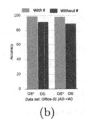 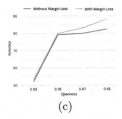

(a)	(b)	(c)

Fig. 4. (a) The training graphs showcasing the evolution of $\mathcal{L}_{SA}$ and $\mathcal{L}_{CLS} + \mathcal{L}_{margin}$ for $\mathbf{A},\mathbf{D} \mapsto \mathbf{W}$ (Office-31) for 50 epochs, (b) Effects of explicit source alignment on OS and OS^* for $\mathbf{A},\mathbf{D} \mapsto \mathbf{W}$ (Office-31). # in the figure refers to the first term of Eq. 1. (c) Openness analysis of full model and model without $\mathcal{L}_{margin}$ for $\mathbf{D},\mathbf{W} \mapsto \mathbf{A}$ (Office-31).

4.2   Critical Analysis

The Effect of the Margin-Loss ($\mathcal{L}_{margin}$) and the Margin Parameter τ: We showcase the effectiveness of $\mathcal{L}_{margin}$ on two cases: $\mathbf{A},\mathbf{D} \mapsto \mathbf{W}$ (Office-31) and $\mathbf{A},\mathbf{C},\mathbf{R} \mapsto \mathbf{P}$ (Office-Home) (Fig. 3(a)) in terms of the OS and OS^* values for our full model and the model without $\mathcal{L}_{margin}$. It can be observed that the inclusion of $\mathcal{L}_{margin}$ in Eq. 6 causes an enhancement in the OS values at least by 4%. Furthermore, $\mathcal{L}_{margin}$ depends on the choice of the τ hyper-parameter for controlling the confidence of the classifier. In Table 4(a), we showcase an ablation analysis on the τ parameter. As deserved, a large τ is preferred as it maximizes the margin between the known and unknown class samples. Increasing trends for both the OS and OS^* can be seen as τ is increased, however, τ is found to get saturated after 0.6. In Fig. 3(b), we show the difference between the known and unknown class probabilities for the full model and the model trained without $\mathcal{L}_{margin}$ in Eq. 6 for $\tau = 0.6$. In this regard, the full model has average difference score of ≈ 0.55 which is superior to the model without $\mathcal{L}_{margin}$ (≈ 0.3).

Sensitivity to Different Openness: Openness is defined as $\mathcal{O} = 1 - \frac{|\mathcal{Y}_s|}{|\mathcal{Y}_t|}$ [15] where $|\mathcal{Y}_s|$ denotes the number of classes in $\mathcal{S}$ whereas $|\mathcal{Y}_t|$ is the number of known and unknown classes present in $\mathcal{T}$. A large $\mathcal{O}$ signifies that the number of unknown classes is much higher than the number of shared classes.

Table 4. (a)Sensitivity to the margin term τ for two cases of Office-31 and Office-Home, (b) Accuracy assessment for different openness values for different combinations of Office-31.

	AD - W		ACR - P	
	OS*	OS	OS*	OS
$\tau = 0.2$	98.1	95.8	66.5	66.4
$\tau = 0.4$	98.2	96.8	76.1	75.3
$\tau = 0.6$	99.0	98.2	79.0	80.0

	AD - W		AW - D		WD - A	
	OS*	OS	OS*	OS	OS*	OS
$\mathcal{O} = 0.83$	99.2	97.6	100.0	97.3	89.3	88.2
$\mathcal{O} = 0.67$	100.0	97.4	99.6	97.1	81.3	83.0
$\mathcal{O} = 0.35$	99.0	98.2	99.4	98.3	81.0	79.3
$\mathcal{O} = 0.03$	89.7	89.4	91.9	91.1	56.5	53.3

(a)	(b)

The source-combine or single-best versions of [25] and [3] show poor performance when $\mathcal{O} \approx 1$ whereas they show high accuracy for $\mathcal{O} \approx 0.5$. This is due to the fact that methods like [3, 25] are prone to confound the known with unknown classes. From Table 4(b), we observe that MOSDANET produces promising results even when $\mathcal{O} \to 1$. This guarantees the invariance of MOSDANET to varied openness which is majorly attributed to the efficacy of $\mathcal{L}_{margin}$ in separating the unknown classes. To establish this, we mention a comparison of the OS scores for different $\mathcal{O}$ values between the models with and without the margin-loss in Fig. 4(c) for $\mathbf{D,W} \mapsto \mathbf{A}$ (a challenging scenario of Office-31). The full model in this case consistently produces superior OS scores.

Effects of Aligning the Source-Domains: In order to assess the importance of the source alignment term (first term in Eq. 1), we train two separate models with and without the first term of Eq. 1 for $\mathbf{A,D} \mapsto \mathbf{W}$ (Office-31). As can be observed in Fig. 4(b), we observe sharp improvements of more than 10% both in OS and OS^* when source-domains are explicitly aligned.

Visualization: In Fig. 3(c), we depict the t-SNE plot to highlight the discriminating nature of the shared feature space as provided by our full MOSDANET model for $\mathbf{A,D} \mapsto \mathbf{W}$ (Office-31). It can be seen that the open-set target-domain classes are mostly clustered around the center while the known-class samples of all the domains are properly overlapped with clear discrimination among the different categories. Besides, the evolution of different loss terms for the full model during training can be found in Fig. 4(a) which shows early convergence.

5   Conclusions

We formally introduce the learning paradigm of multi-source open-set domain adaptation in this paper and propose a novel framework which seeks to learn a shared feature space for all the source and target domains under consideration. In the process, we explicitly align the source-domains using class information while an improved adversarial learning paradigm is introduced to map the known-class samples from the target-domain with the source-domains. We judiciously incorporate target-domain samples with pseudo known-class labels during training to encourage fine-grained domain alignment. We believe that the proposed problem paradigm opens a new set of possibilities that can be expanded. For instance, in the future, we would be interested to explore the inclusion of open-set categories in the different source domains.

Acknowledgment. B. Banerjee was partially supported by grant ECR-2017-000365 from SERB, DST.

References

1. Bousmalis, K., Trigeorgis, G., Silberman, N., Krishnan, D., Erhan, D.: Domain separation networks. In: Advances in Neural Information Processing Systems, pp. 343–351 (2016)
2. Fernando, B., Habrard, A., Sebban, M., Tuytelaars, T.: Unsupervised visual domain adaptation using subspace alignment. In: Proceedings of the IEEE International Conference on Computer Vision, pp. 2960–2967 (2013)
3. Fu, J., Wu, X., Zhang, S., Yan, J.: Improved open set domain adaptation with backpropagation. In: 2019 IEEE International Conference on Image Processing (ICIP), pp. 2506–2510. IEEE (2019)
4. Ganin, Y., Lempitsky, V.: Unsupervised domain adaptation by backpropagation. arXiv preprint arXiv:1409.7495 (2014)
5. Gong, B., Shi, Y., Sha, F., Grauman, K.: Geodesic flow kernel for unsupervised domain adaptation. In: 2012 IEEE Conference on Computer Vision and Pattern Recognition (CVPR), pp. 2066–2073. IEEE (2012)
6. Guo, J., Shah, D.J., Barzilay, R.: Multi-source domain adaptation with mixture of experts. arXiv preprint arXiv:1809.02256 (2018)
7. He, K., Zhang, X., Ren, S., Sun, J.: Deep residual learning for image recognition. In: Proceedings of the IEEE Conference on Computer Vision and Pattern Recognition, pp. 770–778 (2016)
8. Hull, J.J.: A database for handwritten text recognition research. IEEE Trans. Pattern Anal. Mach. Intell. **16**(5), 550–554 (1994)
9. Ioffe, S., Szegedy, C.: Batch normalization: accelerating deep network training by reducing internal covariate shift. arXiv preprint arXiv:1502.03167 (2015)
10. Jain, L.P., Scheirer, W.J., Boult, T.E.: Multi-class open set recognition using probability of inclusion. In: Fleet, D., Pajdla, T., Schiele, B., Tuytelaars, T. (eds.) ECCV 2014. LNCS, vol. 8691, pp. 393–409. Springer, Cham (2014). https://doi.org/10.1007/978-3-319-10578-9_26
11. Jhuo, I.H., Liu, D., Lee, D., Chang, S.F.: Robust visual domain adaptation with low-rank reconstruction. In: 2012 IEEE Conference on Computer Vision and Pattern Recognition (CVPR), pp. 2168–2175. IEEE (2012)
12. Kingma, D.P., Ba, J.: Adam: a method for stochastic optimization. arXiv preprint arXiv:1412.6980 (2014)
13. Krizhevsky, A., Sutskever, I., Hinton, G.E.: ImageNet classification with deep convolutional neural networks. In: Advances in Neural Information Processing Systems, pp. 1097–1105 (2012)
14. LeCun, Y., Bottou, L., Bengio, Y., Haffner, P.: Gradient-based learning applied to document recognition. Proc. IEEE **86**(11), 2278–2324 (1998)
15. Liu, H., Cao, Z., Long, M., Wang, J., Yang, Q.: Separate to adapt: open set domain adaptation via progressive separation. In: Proceedings of the IEEE Conference on Computer Vision and Pattern Recognition, pp. 2927–2936 (2019)
16. Liu, W., Wang, Z., Liu, X., Zeng, N., Liu, Y., Alsaadi, F.E.: A survey of deep neural network architectures and their applications. Neurocomputing **234**, 11–26 (2017)
17. Long, M., Cao, Y., Wang, J., Jordan, M.I.: Learning transferable features with deep adaptation networks. arXiv preprint arXiv:1502.02791 (2015)
18. Luo, Y., Zheng, L., Guan, T., Yu, J., Yang, Y.: Taking a closer look at domain shift: category-level adversaries for semantics consistent domain adaptation. In: Proceedings of the IEEE Conference on Computer Vision and Pattern Recognition, pp. 2507–2516 (2019)

19. Netzer, Y., Wang, T., Coates, A., Bissacco, A., Wu, B., Ng, A.Y.: Reading digits in natural images with unsupervised feature learning. In: NIPS Workshop on Deep Learning and Unsupervised Feature Learning (2011)

20. Pan, S.J., Tsang, I.W., Kwok, J.T., Yang, Q.: Domain adaptation via transfer component analysis. IEEE Trans. Neural Netw. **22**(2), 199–210 (2011)

21. Panareda Busto, P., Gall, J.: Open set domain adaptation. In: Proceedings of the IEEE International Conference on Computer Vision, pp. 754–763 (2017)

22. Patel, V.M., Gopalan, R., Li, R., Chellappa, R.: Visual domain adaptation: a survey of recent advances. IEEE Signal Process. Mag. **32**(3), 53–69 (2015)

23. Peng, X., Bai, Q., Xia, X., Huang, Z., Saenko, K., Wang, B.: Moment matching for multi-source domain adaptation. arXiv preprint arXiv:1812.01754 (2018)

24. Saenko, K., Kulis, B., Fritz, M., Darrell, T.: Adapting visual category models to new domains. In: Daniilidis, K., Maragos, P., Paragios, N. (eds.) ECCV 2010. LNCS, vol. 6314, pp. 213–226. Springer, Heidelberg (2010). https://doi.org/10.1007/978-3-642-15561-1_16

25. Saito, K., Yamamoto, S., Ushiku, Y., Harada, T.: Open set domain adaptation by backpropagation. In: Ferrari, V., Hebert, M., Sminchisescu, C., Weiss, Y. (eds.) ECCV 2018. LNCS, vol. 11209, pp. 156–171. Springer, Cham (2018). https://doi.org/10.1007/978-3-030-01228-1_10

26. Scheirer, W.J., Jain, L.P., Boult, T.E.: Probability models for open set recognition. IEEE Trans. Pattern Anal. Mach. Intell. **36**(11), 2317–2324 (2014)

27. Sun, B., Saenko, K.: Deep CORAL: correlation alignment for deep domain adaptation. In: Hua, G., Jégou, H. (eds.) ECCV 2016. LNCS, vol. 9915, pp. 443–450. Springer, Cham (2016). https://doi.org/10.1007/978-3-319-49409-8_35

28. Sun, S., Shi, H., Wu, Y.: A survey of multi-source domain adaptation. Inf. Fus. **24**, 84–92 (2015)

29. Tzeng, E., Hoffman, J., Saenko, K., Darrell, T.: Adversarial discriminative domain adaptation. In: Proceedings of the IEEE Conference on Computer Vision and Pattern Recognition, pp. 7167–7176 (2017)

30. Venkateswara, H., Eusebio, J., Chakraborty, S., Panchanathan, S.: Deep hashing network for unsupervised domain adaptation. In: Proceedings of the IEEE Conference on Computer Vision and Pattern Recognition, pp. 5018–5027 (2017)

31. Wang, M., Deng, W.: Deep visual domain adaptation: a survey. Neurocomputing **312**, 135–153 (2018)

32. Wang, Z., She, Q., Ward, T.E.: Generative adversarial networks: a survey and taxonomy. arXiv preprint arXiv:1906.01529 (2019)

33. Yang, J., Yan, R., Hauptmann, A.G.: Cross-domain video concept detection using adaptive SVMs. In: Proceedings of the 15th ACM international conference on Multimedia, pp. 188–197. ACM (2007)

34. Zhao, H., Zhang, S., Wu, G., Moura, J.M., Costeira, J.P., Gordon, G.J.: Adversarial multiple source domain adaptation. In: Advances in Neural Information Processing Systems, pp. 8559–8570 (2018)

Neural Batch Sampling
with Reinforcement Learning
for Semi-supervised Anomaly Detection

Wen-Hsuan Chu$^{(\boxtimes)}$ and Kris M. Kitani

Carnegie Mellon University, Pittsburgh, USA
{chuwenhsuan,kmkitani}@cmu.edu

Abstract. We are interested in the detection and segmentation of anomalies in images where the anomalies are typically small (i.e., a small tear in woven fabric, broken pin of an IC chip). From a statistical learning point of view, anomalies have low occurrence probability and are not from the main modes of a data distribution. Learning a generative model of anomalous data from a natural distribution of data can be difficult because the data distribution is heavily skewed towards a large amount of non-anomalous data. When training a generative model on such imbalanced data using an iterative learning algorithm like stochastic gradient descent (SGD), we observe an expected yet interesting trend in the loss values (a measure of the learned models performance) after each gradient update across data samples. Naturally, as the model sees more non-anomalous data during training, the loss values over a non-anomalous data sample decreases, while the loss values on an anomalous data sample fluctuates. In this work, our key hypothesis is that this change in loss values during training can be used as a feature to identify anomalous data. In particular, we propose a novel semi-supervised learning algorithm for anomaly detection and segmentation using an anomaly classifier that uses as input the *loss profile* of a data sample processed through an autoencoder. The loss profile is defined as a sequence of reconstruction loss values produced during iterative training. To amplify the difference in loss profiles between anomalous and non-anomalous data, we also introduce a Reinforcement Learning based meta-algorithm, which we call the neural batch sampler, to strategically sample training batches during autoencoder training. Experimental results on multiple datasets with a high diversity of textures and objects, often with multiple modes of defects within them, demonstrate the capabilities and effectiveness of our method when compared with existing state-of-the-art baselines.

Keywords: Anomaly detection · Semi-supervised learning

Electronic supplementary material The online version of this chapter (https://doi.org/10.1007/978-3-030-58574-7_45) contains supplementary material, which is available to authorized users.

© Springer Nature Switzerland AG 2020
A. Vedaldi et al. (Eds.): ECCV 2020, LNCS 12371, pp. 751–766, 2020.
https://doi.org/10.1007/978-3-030-58574-7_45

1   Introduction

Given a small set of labeled images along with a set of unlabeled images, our goal is to utilize the limited labeled data efficiently to detect and segment the anomalies in the unlabeled set. Anomaly detection and segmentation is useful for applications manufacturing industry, optical inspection tasks are concerned with picking out defective products such that they are not sold to the consumers. Meanwhile, in safety inspection tasks such as in construction sites, cracks in concrete or rust on metal may indicate that the structure or the foundation of the building is unsafe, and would require workers to reinforce the problematic sections such that it does not pose as safety risks.

Although supervised segmentation algorithms have seen significant advances in recent years [7,17,22], they are difficult to apply directly to such tasks due to the rare occurrence of anomalies during data collection. This results in an extremely imbalanced dataset, with non-anomalous images dominating the data while the anomalous images only making up a small fraction of the dataset. Furthermore, the collected anomalies are usually underrepresented, as it is difficult to capture all possible modes of anomalies during data collection.

Due to these challenges, it is unsurprising that the majority of the work has been directed towards novelty detection in images using little to no supervision from anomalous data. A family of work is interested in detecting if a new input is out-of-distribution when compared with the training data (i.e., from different classes), which is commonly referred to as one-class-classification or outlier detection [10,13,15,19,27,28]. While this type of classification on the *class* or *image* level is important, we are concerned with a different type of "novelty" (or anomaly), where they usually occur only in small areas in the object or image (i.e., crack on a surface). Some works have investigated this problem with the prior assumption that there exists a large set of anomaly-free images to be used as training data, often referred to as unsupervised anomaly detection [1,3,6].

In our work, we wish to explore semi-supervised methods for anomaly detection and segmentation in images. To put more generally, this can be framed as a binary semi-supervised segmentation task with significant skew in its data distribution. We observe that while training a generative model on the imbalanced data using an iterative learning algorithm like SGD, the majority of the gradient updates are dominated by the more frequently occurring non-anomalous data, resulting in unstable and possibly non-converging behaviors for the anomalous data. This suggests that we can use *loss profiles* as an informative cue for detecting anomalies. Thus, we introduce an anomaly classifier to detect and segment anomalies using the loss profiles of the data from training an autoencoder. By periodically re-initializing and re-training the autoencoder, the resulting loss profiles change due to differences in both the initial weights and sampled training batches, which provides diversified inputs to the classifier, preventing overfitting.

One question to consider is what the optimal way of sampling training batches for the autoencoder is, such that it produces the most discriminative loss profiles. Conventionally, heuristics-based methods such as random sampling are used to train neural networks with the intention of providing stable gradient estimates, but that is different from what we desire. Another heuristics-based method is to sample on non-anomalous regions only, but this can only be done on the small amount of labeled data as the majority of data is unlabeled. Instead of using heuristics, we introduce a Reinforcement Learning (RL) based neural batch sampler that is trained to produce training batches from the data for the autoencoder to maximize the difference of the loss profiles between the anomalies and non-anomalies. Under this formulation, the neural batch sampler and the classifier work together such that it achieves satisfactory prediction error on the small labeled set of images, while the autoencoder acts as a "proxy" with the sole purpose of providing loss profiles as input to the classifier.

In summary, the contributions of our paper is as follows:

- We propose a semi-supervised learning framework for a binary segmentation task with significant data imbalance, with the application to anomaly detection and segmentation.
- We introduce an anomaly classifier that takes as input the reconstruction loss profiles from an autoencoder. The autoencoder is periodically re-initialized and re-trained, producing diversified loss profiles as input.
- We train a RL-based neural batch sampler that supplies the autoencoder with training batches. It aims to maximize the difference of the loss profiles between anomalous and non-anomalous regions.
- Empirical results on multiple datasets spanning a large variety of objects and textures show our superiority over existing works.

2 Related Work

2.1 Anomaly Detection and Segmentation

Existing literature on anomaly detection and segmentation are mostly focused on what is so called "unsupervised" anomaly detection, where it is assumed that a known set of non-anomalous images is available as training data. Note that this is strictly different from the formal definition of unsupervised learning, where no knowledge on the labels are available. The goal is to then detect and segment anomalous regions that appears differently (i.e., defects on a surface) from the training data. Carrera et al. [6] takes inspiration from traditional reconstruction-based unsupervised anomaly detection algorithms and trains an autoencoder on the non-anomalous images such that it overfits and uses the magnitude of reconstruction loss on test images to determine anomalous regions. There has also been works that builds upon this, proposing to use structural losses instead of per-pixel MSE losses [4] or to replace autoencoders with VAE [1] and GANs [21].

The aforementioned methods tries to learn features directly from the giving training data. An alternate approach [14] uses pretrained ResNet [11] features from ImageNet [9], but their method is restricted to per-image predictions instead of spatial anomaly maps. There are also methods that apply hand-crafted features from non-anomalous images using GMMs [5] or variational models [24], but they have been shown to achieve subpar performance compared to the previously mentioned methods [3].

There has also been some works on applying supervised learning based approaches to tasks like crack detection in roads [8,23]. While supervised segmentation algorithms have seen significant advances in recent years [7,17,22], it is generally difficult to apply to anomaly detection tasks as argued earlier due to the difficulty in collecting a large amount of anomalous data. In contrast to unsupervised and fully-supervised method which are arguably at the two ends of the spectrum, we consider a semi-supervised setting which only uses a handful of labeled anomalous data to train a classifier. This allows us to combine the advantages of the precision found in supervised methods and the substantially reduced need for large amounts of data in unsupervised methods.

2.2 One-Class Classification

One-class classification, sometimes referred to as outlier detection, is concerned about detecting out-of-distribution samples relative to the training set. While this sounds similar to anomaly detection and can also be broadly encompassed under *novelty detection*, the definition of "novelty" is extremely different for the two tasks. One-class classification is concerned about outliers on a *class-level* or *image-level*, where the anomalies and non-anomalies in anomaly detection tasks generally belong to the same class. For example, while anomaly detection tasks may be concerned about finding rust on metal, one-class classification may be interested in distinguishing cats from a dataset of dogs.

One line of work for one-class classification focuses on using statistical modeling to detect out-of-distribution samples. For example, some works fit distributions on features that are extracted from samples in the training set and denote samples far from this distribution as outliers [10,13,28]. Other works [15,27] are based on PCA and assumes that inlier samples have high correlations and can be spanned in low dimensional subspaces, often forming large clusters. As a result, samples that don't accord well in the low dimension subspace or forming small individual clusters are denoted as outliers.

Another line of work uses deep adversarial learning for one-class classification. Ravanbakhsh et al. [16] proposed to learn the generator as a reconstructor of normal events, and labels chunks of events that are not reconstructed well as anomalies. The work by Sabokrou et al. [20] takes a similar approach, but learns a generator that refines and reconstructs noisy inlier images and distorts noisy outlier images. This amplifies the difference in reconstruction even further and leads to an increase in performance.

Recently, there has been work on semi-supervised one-class classification using information theoretic approaches [19]. They formulate a training objective to model the latent distribution of the normal data to have low entropy, and the latent distribution of anomalies to have high entropy.

3   Method

Here we introduce our algorithm for semi-supervised anomaly detection and segmentation. Our data $\mathcal{D}$ is split into two sets: $\mathcal{D}_l$, which contains a small

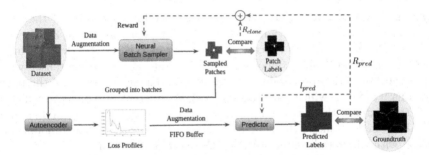

Fig. 1. High-level overview of our algorithm. The solid lines represent the pipeline of the forward pass and the red dashed lines represent the flow of the loss and reward terms to train the predictor and the neural batch sampler. Note that we do not perform any data augmentation nor use the FIFO buffer during inference. (Color figure online)

amount of image-label pairs with some collected anomalous data, and $\mathcal{D}_u$, which is a large unlabeled set of images. Our goal is to leverage the entire dataset $(\mathcal{D}_l \cup \mathcal{D}_u)$ to predict the corresponding labels of the images in $\mathcal{D}_u$.

3.1 Overview

On a high level, our framework contains 3 modules, a neural batch sampler, a convolutional autoencoder, and an anomaly predictor, as depicted in Fig. 1. First, consider what happens when we train an autoencoder (AE) over the highly imbalanced data we have. When we calculate the reconstruction loss for the AE and update its weights, most of the loss is contributed by the non-anomalous regions. As a result, the AE mostly optimizes for the reconstruction of the non-anomalous regions, leading to highly fluctuating loss profiles in the anomalous regions and more converging loss profiles in the non-anomalous regions. Based on this observation, we train a CNN-based predictor to classify anomalies based on the produced loss profiles. To amplify the difference between the loss profiles of the anomalous and non-anomalous regions, and make classification easier for the predictor, a neural batch sampler is trained using Reinforcement Learning to supply training batches to the AE.

Having gone over the high level concepts, we now elaborate on the specific designs of the 3 modules. Implementation details such as network architectures and hyperparameter choices can be found in the supplementary materials.

Neural Batch Sampler. The neural batch sampler is introduced to produce training batches for the AE such that the difference between the loss profiles of anomalous and non-anomalous regions are maximized. There are two possible sources where this information can be inferred from: the RGB information x_i and the current pixel-wise reconstruction loss l_i of an image. Intuitively, the neural batch sampler may realize that specific patterns may lead to less discriminative loss profiles (i.e., patches that contain anomalies), while larger loss values may correspond to anomalies due to them being harder to train. To give the sampler an idea of what has already been sampled, we additionally supply the binary sampling history h_i as input, which are binary values indicating if the pixels in an image have been previously sampled in the episode. These 3 sources of information (x_i, l_i, h_i) are concatenated to represent the state, then fed into 5 convolutional and 2 fully-connected layers, producing an output tensor which represents the action probabilities of the policy. The action space of the policy contains 9 actions, which corresponds to eight different directions in which to shift the center of the extracted patch in (by a pre-specified value) and an additional action that allows the neural batch sampler to switch to a (random) new image, with the initial center of the patch selected at random.

Autoencoder. The AE is used solely to produce loss profiles for the predictor. As a result, the design of the AE is fairly standard: it takes the input patch and compresses it spatially into a $1 \times 1 \times K$ bottleneck tensor using convolutional layers, then decodes it back into the original input with transpose convolution layers. Additionally, we add some shortcut connections between the encoder and decoder to speed up the training. A problem here is that as the AE trains and converges, the updates become smaller, leading to decreased variety in the loss profiles. To combat this issue, we periodically re-initialize and re-train the AE. This is crucial to producing diversified loss profiles for training the predictor, as every time the AE is re-trained it starts from a different set of weights and is optimized towards different local minimas. To store the loss profiles for training the predictor, we add them to a FIFO buffer of fixed size.

Predictor. Intuitively, the predictor is a classifier performing object segmentation in the "loss space" instead of the RGB space. As such, we draw many inspirations from existing object segmentation works [7,17,22]. The predictor is implemented with a fully convolutional network using dilated convolutions, which scales up the receptive field exponentially w.r.t. the number of layers. It takes as input loss history profiles of size $W \times H \times T$, where W and H corresponds to the width and height of the image, and outputs binary segmentation masks of size $W \times H \times 1$. We perform normalization on the raw loss history profiles as a form of pre-processing via dividing the loss history profiles by its mean. This allows the predictor to focus on the relative differences between the loss profiles at individual pixels instead of their absolute values, which changes dramatically throughout the training of the autoencoder.

3.2   Training

There are 3 modules that require training: the neural batch sampler, the AE, and the predictor. At the high level, training steps for the three components are repeated in an alternating fashion until convergence. First, the neural batch sampler samples training batches for the AE, which the AE uses to performs an update and then re-evaluates its reconstruction loss l. The reconstruction loss is appended to the loss profile h, with the oldest element popped off ($h \leftarrow h[1:] \frown l$), and saved to a FIFO buffer. The predictor then samples loss profiles from the buffer and updates itself, while producing a prediction loss for computing the reward of the neural batch sampler. The neural batch sampler then uses the reward to perform an update, and the whole process repeats. As reference, the pseudocode of the training algorithm is provided in Algorithm 1. Note that the AE is periodically re-initialized every K update steps and we skip the first M updates for the neural batch sampler after re-initializing the AE as the starting reconstruction loss values are too noisy.

Algorithm 1: Training

Input: Labeled data $\{(x_l, y_l)\} \in \mathcal{D}_l$, unlabeled data $\{x_u\} \in \mathcal{D}_u$, hyperparameters K, M
Output: Neural batch sampler θ_s, predictor θ_p, best loss history profile h^*
begin

Initialize neural batch sampler θ_s, autoencoder θ_e, predictor θ_p, buffer $\mathcal{B}$

Perform data augmentation on $\mathcal{D}_l$, $\mathcal{D}_u$, giving $\mathcal{D}_l'$, $\mathcal{D}_u'$
$j \leftarrow 0$, $h_u \leftarrow 0$, $h_l \leftarrow 0$, $lowest\_loss \leftarrow \infty$
while *not converged* **do**

Sample patches $\{p_{l,i}\} \sim \mathcal{D}_l'$ with θ_s, compute R_{clone}, R_{cover}
Sample patches $\{p_i\} \sim (\mathcal{D}_l' \cup \mathcal{D}_u')$ with θ_s
Group $\{p_i\}$ into mini-batches and train θ_e
Evaluate reconstruction loss l_u and l_l on $\mathcal{D}_u$ and $\mathcal{D}_l$ with θ_e
$h_l \leftarrow h_l[1:] \frown l_l$, $h_u \leftarrow h_u[1:] \frown l_u$
Perform data augmentation on (h_l, y_l) and append to $\mathcal{B}$
Sample $(h_l, y_l) \sim \mathcal{B}$, normalize h_l, calculate l_{pred} and update θ_p
if $j \% K > M$ **then** Calculate R_{pred} and update θ_s using Eq. 1, 3, 4
if $l_{pred} < lowest\_loss$ **then** $h_* \leftarrow h_u$
if $j \% K = 0$ **then** Reinitialize θ_e, h_u, h_l
$j \leftarrow j + 1$
Update β according to Eq. 3

Neural Batch Sampler. The neural batch sampler aims to sample a sequence of patches $\{p_1, p_2, ..., p_N\}$ from the dataset $\mathcal{D}$ to train the autoencoder such that it produces the most discriminative loss profiles between the anomalies and non-anomalies for the predictor. To achieve this, we invoke the Reinforcement Learning framework [25], which assigns credit to the actions (in this case, how the patches are sampled) taken based on the obtained reward at the end of the sequence of actions. Since we wish to enhance the contrast of the loss profiles and aid the predictor by selecting the right training batches, we define the reward function R_{pred}[1] to be the negative of the prediction loss:

$$R_{pred} = \begin{cases} -l_{pred}, & t = N \\ 0, & \text{otherwise} \end{cases} \tag{1}$$

where the prediction loss l_{pred} is defined as the weighted binary cross entropy loss to account of the inherent imbalance in the data.

$$l_{pred} = -\frac{1}{K} \sum_K \frac{1}{WH} \sum_{W,H} y \log \hat{y} + \alpha(1 - y) \log(1 - \hat{y}). \tag{2}$$

---

[1] To be more precise, this should be written as $R_{pred,t}$, but we omit the subscript t in the paper for simplicity.

Here K represents the batch size, α is the empirically calculated re-weighting factor between the anomalous and non-anomalous pixels, y represents the ground truth annotations in the small labeled subset $\mathcal{D}_l$, and $\hat{y}$ is the predicted labels obtained from the predictor at the end of the framework. To prevent images with larger anomalies from dominating the loss signal, we first take the average over individual images with dimensionality $W \times H$ in Eq. 2.

While we can directly use standard RL algorithms like Policy Gradient methods to optimize for a batch sampling strategy from scratch by maximizing the obtained reward, empirical experiments show that such a naive method is extremely inefficient and makes it hard for the network to train. This is due to the sparse nature of the rewards, which only occurs at the end of each episode as defined in Eq. 1. To alleviate this issue, we make the observation that we do know of a good but perhaps sub-optimal heuristics-based strategy that allows us to bootstrap the exploration phase by assigning dense rewards for every patch sampled via behavior cloning [18]. This allows the neural batch sampler to start from a meaningful strategy instead of trying to learn everything from scratch. The heuristics-based strategy is simple: only sample from locations that are non-anomalous. Intuitively, if the autoencoder has never seen anomalies before, then it should not have any knowledge on how to encode and decode anomalies, leading to high loss on anomalies. Thus, we can perform behavior cloning by running the neural batch sampler on our small labeled subset, $\mathcal{D}_l$, and assign a reward R_{clone} for every sampled patch by checking if the corresponding label y_{patch} contains any anomalies.

In R_{clone}, the neural batch sampler is not concerned about the ultimate goal of improving the contrast between the loss profiles of anomalous and non-anomalous regions. This results in a peculiar strategy: the batch sampler will repeatedly sample on regions near the first non-anomalous patch to minimize the risk of sampling an anomaly. To prevent this, we encourage the neural batch sampler to cover different portion of the data by including a small coverage bonus R_{cover}. This also preserves incentive for exploration and prevents the policy from collapsing to a single mode of action prematurely.

Naively, the training can be done in a stage-wise manner by first optimizing for R_{clone} and R_{cover} for a good initial policy then switch over to optimizing for R_{pred} for the goal of obtaining discriminative loss profiles between anomalies and non-anomalies. However, this rough transition between the two objectives can cause instability, so we take inspiration from scheduled sampling [2] approaches for a smoother transition:

$$R = \beta \left(R_{clone} + R_{cover} \right) + (1 - \beta)R_{pred}, \quad \beta = \max \left(0, \ 1 - \frac{j}{L} \right) \quad (3)$$

where L is a hyperparameter and β controls the weighting between the behavior cloning reward and the true optimization goal by putting more emphasis on R_{pred} as the number of training steps j increases. In contrast, R is dominated by the behavior cloning term when the network has just started training. This achieves the effect of using the dense rewards from behavior cloning to bootstrap the neural batch sampler while ensuring a smooth transition to the desired goal of finding a sampling strategy that improves the prediction results.

Having defined the reward function, we now apply a standard Policy Gradient algorithm named REINFORCE [26] to update our neural batch sampler. The update rule for REINFORCE can be written as

$$\nabla_\theta J(\theta) = \mathbb{E}_{\tau \sim \pi_\theta(\tau)} \left[\nabla_\theta \log \pi_\theta(\tau) r(\tau) \right], \tag{4}$$

where the sampling strategy $\pi_\theta(\tau)$ is parameterized by the neural batch sampler and $r(\tau)$ is the discounted sum of rewards. The expectation is approximated using Monte Carlo sampling, and we found empirically that using 1 rollout sequence of actions to approximate the gradient works out well and allows us to use standard backpropagation to update the neural batch sampler.

We would like to note that a common trick aimed to increase the stability of the algorithm by normalizing the rewards actually *harms* the training in our scenario, where the reward is only observed during the final timestep (as defined in Eq. 1). While this trick can normalize the size of the gradient steps between different rollouts and stabilize training, the normalization step actually removes the reward signal during training in our scenario. A short proof of this behavior is given in the supplementary materials.

Autoencoder. Since the AE's sole purpose is to provide a large variety of loss profiles, its training is fairly standard. After the neural batch sampler produces a sequence of patches, the patches are grouped into multiples of minibatches of size N and fed into the AE. We evaluate the reconstruction loss l_{ae} between the reconstructed patches $\hat{p}_i$ and the input patches p_i and backpropagate the loss into the AE. To generate a diverse amount of loss profiles for training the predictor, the AE is re-initialized with random weights and re-trained periodically. Empirically this is done after a fixed number (K) of update steps, where the weights updates become small as the AE converges.

After each update step, we evaluate the new reconstruction loss of the dataset $\mathcal{D}$ and update the loss profiles. The new reconstruction loss values are used as input to the neural batch sampler, while the updated loss profiles of the labeled subset $\mathcal{D}_l$ in a FIFO buffer for training the predictor. The best performing loss profiles of the unlabeled subset $\mathcal{D}_u$ is saved to disc for inference.

Predictor. Fundamentally, the predictor is just a classifier that makes prediction based on loss profiles, and thus is trained similarly to normal classifiers. While we can directly train on the loss profiles produced by the autoencoder, this causes problems in the mini-batch gradient estimation as loss profiles produced within a similar time period are highly correlated and dependent on each other, which induces significant bias in the gradient estimation and leads to training instability. Thus, we save the loss profiles in a FIFO buffer then sample randomly from it, which remedies the issue as the samples in a mini-batch are no longer grouped together temporally and are more likely to be independent. After the predictor outputs the predicted labels, the weighted binary cross entropy loss is calculated as described in Eq. 2 to update the predictor. Note that the same calculated loss is used for computing the reward term in Eq. 1 for updating the neural batch sampler.

3.3   Inference

Recall that after training, we have the saved weights of the most promising neural batch sampler and the predictor in addition to the loss profiles of the unlabeled set $\mathcal{D}_u$. The inference step is very simple: we take the loss profiles and run it through the predictor again, producing the raw prediction results of $\mathcal{D}_u$. A fully connected CRF [12] is applied to the raw predictions to smooth out the prediction results, producing the final prediction labels. The kernel of the CRF assumes that nearby regions with similar RGB values are likely to belong to the same class while removing small isolated regions in the raw predictions.

3.4   Interpretations

Here we would like to draw some interesting connections and analyze our algorithm in the viewpoints of traditional CV models and RL models.

The CV Viewpoint. One way to interpret the algorithm is to adopt the traditional image/object classification or segmentation view and treat everything before the predictor as a special operator (i.e., the augmentations, the neural batch sampler, and the AE) that transforms the input of the predictor from RGB space to "loss profile space". In this case, there exists two sources of stochasticity in the transformation: the periodic re-initialization of the autoencoder, which randomly sets the starting point in the loss space; and the randomness that arises from the sampling strategy of the neural batch sampler, which moves the starting point towards local minimas in the loss space. Combined together with data augmentations on the RGB space and the loss space, this results in a diverse one-to-many relationship between RGB images and loss profiles. This is what enables the successful training of a parametric model under the scarcity of labeled data.

The RL Viewpoint. Another way to interpret the algorithm is to adopt the Reinforcement Learning view and consider everything other than the neural batch sampler to be part of the environment in which a task is defined. In this case, the environment is dynamically changing, as the reward evaluation requires evaluating the actions of the neural batch sampler (i.e., the sampled patches) on an ever-changing AE and a slowly converging predictor. Thus, the neural batch sampler must find a sampling strategy that not only leads to discriminative loss profiles between the anomalous and non-anomalous regions, but it also must work on different training phases of AE. This is also one of the reasons that the neural batch sampler receives the current reconstruction loss as input as described previously.

4 Results

We conduct a thorough evaluation on multiple datasets and compare with other methods to demonstrate the effectiveness of our algorithm. For the baselines, we consider two state-of-the-art algorithms that can been applied to anomaly detection works. The first baseline is the best performing unsupervised anomaly detection algorithm in the MVTec AD dataset paper [3], which makes predictions based on the final pixel-wise reconstruction loss after training an autoencoder only on non-anomalous data. Since their code is not made available publicly, we carefully re-implemented the algorithm as described in their paper and tried our best to reproduce the results given in the paper. The second baseline is the U-Net [17], a state-of-the-art supervised learning method originally for binary object segmentation, and has since been generalized to many other semantic segmentation tasks. We also apply standard data augmentation techniques with the baselines to help them generalize better under the scarcity of data.

Since many of these datasets were originally collected for unsupervised anomaly detection tasks, we create our own data splits for training and testing (i.e., labeled and unlabeled set) as detailed in the next section.

4.1 Datasets

MVTec AD. MVTec AD [3] is a dataset originally created for unsupervised anomaly detection, where the training set consists of only non-anomalous images and the testing set being a mix of anomalous and non-anomalous images. The dataset includes image samples from 5 texture classes and 10 object classes, with around 200 to 300 non-anomalous images in the original training set and around 100 images in the testing set for the majority of classes. The anomalies in the testing set are also grouped by difference modes for analysis.

For our semi-supervised method and the supervised baseline U-Net, we first resize all images to 256×256 and randomly sample 5 images from the original testing set in each class so that we get some anomalous samples in the labeled set (i.e. $|\mathcal{D}_l| = 5$). The remainder of the original testing set is reserved for performance evaluation. Since the training set is randomly sampled, it is possible that the training set lacks certain anomaly modes. The unsupervised baseline is preprocessed, trained, and evaluated exactly as in the original MVTec AD dataset paper, which uses the original training sets with 200 to 300 non-anomalous images for training and the entirety of the testing set for performance evaluation. The experiments were run separately for each class as in the original paper.

NanoTWICE. The NanoTWICE dataset [6] is also originally a dataset collected for unsupervised anomaly detection. The image samples in NanoTWICE are close-up views of nanofibres, while the anomalies are manufacturing defects such as unnatural arrangements or clumps in the fibre. As such, the anomalies in NanoTWICE are often small, consisting only of a handful of pixels (refer to

Fig. 3 for examples). The dataset consists of 45 images, in which 5 images are anomaly-free and is originally used for training the unsupervised methods, with the remaining 40 all containing some form of anomalies. Note that unlike the MVTec AD dataset where some testing data are anomaly-free, **all** testing data in the NanoTWICE dataset contain some form of anomaly.

For the semi-supervised approach, we create a data split similar to what we did for the MVTec AD dataset. All images are first resized to 256×256, then we randomly sample 5 images for use as our labeled set $\mathcal{D}_l$. All the remaining images are placed in the unlabeled set $\mathcal{D}_u$. For training the U-Net, we use $\mathcal{D}_l$ and reserve $\mathcal{D}_u$ for performance evaluation. For the unsupervised method, we follow the recommended data split, using the 5 anomaly-free images for training and evaluate on the remainder of the image samples.

CrackForest. CrackForest [23] is originally created for a supervised learning task with 118 images total. It contains many road images with cracks and is reflective of urban road surfaces. Being a dataset intended for supervised learning, all 118 images in the dataset contain some kind of anomaly.

Like with the other datasets, we resize images to 256×256 and randomly sample 5 images from the whole dataset as the labeled set $\mathcal{D}_l$ for our semi-supervised method and U-Net, and reserve the remainder of the dataset as the unlabeled set $\mathcal{D}_u$ or for evaluation. Unlike the MVTec AD dataset, the anomalies are not grouped by type, so we do not know if the sampled data covers all anomaly modes, but it is highly likely that some modes are not represented in the training set due to the low number of samples. Since the dataset does not contain any image samples that are anomaly-free, we do not evaluate the unsupervised method on this dataset.

4.2   Experimental Results

We report the precision, recall, and F1 measure in Table 1 for the different classes in MVTec AD and in Table 2 for NanoTWICE and CrackForest.

While the unsupervised method has achieves good recall, the precision score is extremely low, which impacts its overall F1 score. This happens due to a large number of false positives being predicted from thresholding over a single point of reconstruction loss. Such results suggests that while anomalies tend to have higher reconstruction loss, it is not necessary that only the anomalous regions incur higher reconstruction loss, which is why simple thresholding leads to subpar precision. Interestingly, even with just 5 labeled samples, U-Net serves as a strong baseline, achieving higher F1 scores when compared to the unsupervised method, due to a higher precision in many of the categories, even if it scores a lower recall score than the unsupervised method. On the other hand, our proposed method consistently scores the highest on MVTec and CrackForest, boasting the highest score in almost all performance metrics. On NanoTWICE, the proposed method scores an extremely high recall score, but the precision falls behind of U-Net, bringing down its F1 score.

Table 1. Performance of the evaluated methods on MVTec AD. The top 10 classes are object classes and the lower 5 are texture classes. For each class, the precision, recall, and F1 measure are given. The best performing method for each class is **bolded**.

	Unsupervised [3]			U-Net [17]			Proposed		
	Precision	Recall	F1	Precision	Recall	F1	Precision	Recall	F1
Bottle	0.24	0.54	0.34	0.25	0.41	0.31	**0.79**	**0.81**	**0.80**
Cable	0.08	0.17	0.10	0.16	0.53	0.25	**0.20**	**0.66**	**0.31**
Capsule	0.05	0.25	0.08	0.04	0.08	0.05	**0.10**	**0.14**	**0.12**
Hazelnut	0.14	0.48	0.22	0.18	0.71	0.29	**0.35**	**0.88**	**0.50**
Metal Nut	0.19	0.30	0.23	0.29	0.28	0.29	**0.81**	**0.84**	**0.82**
Pill	0.06	0.24	0.09	0.19	0.11	0.14	**0.29**	**0.74**	**0.42**
Screw	0.03	**0.42**	0.06	0.01	0.07	0.01	**0.05**	0.29	**0.08**
Toothbrush	0.05	0.44	0.09	0.22	0.39	0.28	**0.46**	**0.59**	**0.52**
Transistor	0.08	0.11	0.09	**0.14**	0.08	0.10	0.13	**0.31**	**0.18**
Zipper	0.07	0.51	0.13	0.18	0.45	0.26	**0.66**	**0.70**	**0.68**
Carpet	0.04	0.42	0.08	0.33	0.62	0.43	**0.56**	**0.69**	**0.62**
Grid	0.01	**0.82**	0.02	0.07	0.51	0.12	**0.10**	0.62	**0.17**
Leather	0.01	0.61	0.02	0.11	0.78	0.20	**0.23**	**0.88**	**0.36**
Tile	0.18	0.24	0.21	0.31	0.46	0.37	**0.88**	**0.50**	**0.64**
Wood	0.11	0.28	0.16	0.28	0.49	0.36	**0.41**	**0.63**	**0.50**

Table 2. Performance of the evaluated methods on CrackForest and NanoTWICE. The best performing method in each dataset is **bolded** per metric.

	Unsupervised [3]			U-Net [17]			Proposed		
	Precision	Recall	F1	Precision	Recall	F1	Precision	Recall	F1
NanoTWICE	0.02	0.65	0.04	**0.37**	0.59	**0.45**	0.21	**0.80**	0.33
CrackForest	N/A	N/A	N/A	0.15	0.34	0.21	**0.26**	**0.62**	**0.36**

Qualitative inspection of the segmentation results produced by our proposed method shows why this is the case on NanoTWICE: our algorithm struggles with determining the exact size and shape of the anomalies. This doesn't come as a surprise, as the architecture of autoencoders compress spatial information during the encoding phase, which often leads to a loss in spatial resolution during decoding or reconstruction. Due to this, the reconstruction loss profiles of neighboring pixels are closely related and dependent, which makes the predicting of the exact anomalies' boundaries difficult. This behavior greatly impacts the precision of our method, as it produces many false positives that are not in the ground truth. An example of this is given for CrackForest and NanoTWICE, as depicted in Fig. 3. Looking at the visualizations in CrackForest, we can see that the predicted masks are almost always thicker or wider (often nearly twice as thick) than the ground truth, even though that the shapes are similar. Visualizations on the NanoTWICE dataset also shows that the predicted anomalies are

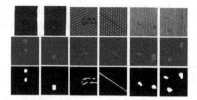

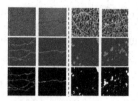

Fig. 2. Predicted labels on unseen modes of anomalies during training for MVTec AD. The three rows corresponds to the original images, the predictions, and the ground truth.

Fig. 3. Predicted labels on CrackForest (left) and NanoTWICE (right). The three rows corresponds to the original images, the predictions, and the ground truth.

almost always larger in size and shape. Since many anomalies in NanoTWICE are of extremely small with the size of just a handful of pixels, it makes the effect more pronounced, which is why the precision score of our proposed method falls behind U-Net on NanoTWICE. Despite this, we argue that this behavior is acceptable as we're usually more concerned about the location of the anomalies compared to the exact shape and size in practical applications.

Interestingly, our proposed method seems to be able to detect anomaly modes that are not present during training. An example of this behavior is given in Fig. 2. In this example, the presented modes of anomalies from different classes in MVTec were not sampled in the labeled set. While the segmentation masks are not as good when compared to other anomaly modes that are observed during training, we see that our proposed algorithm still has the capability to pick them out. This suggests that due to the statistically rare occurrence of anomalies, the loss profiles of different modes of anomalies have some common trait in them, which can be picked up and learned by our predictor, leading to some form of generalizability to unseen anomaly modes. We believe that this is highly beneficial as it can help combat the difficulty of identifying and collecting all modes of anomalous data during data collection in real-life scenarios.

5   Conclusions

We propose a novel semi-supervised learning algorithm for anomaly detection and segmentation tasks, which can be seen as a specific type of binary segmentation task with extreme data imbalance. The algorithm consists of a neural batch sampler and an anomaly classifier which operates on loss profiles, along with a periodically re-initialized and re-trained autoencoder that is used as a proxy to produce reconstruction loss profiles to transform the input space from RGB space to loss profile space for the classifier. From re-initializing and re-training the autoencoder with differently sampled batches, we're able to produce diversified inputs from limited supervision to successfully train a classifier.

Our algorithm is thoroughly evaluated and compared against other baselines on three datasets, which spans a large variety of different objects and textures. The experimental results show that by using the proposed semi-supervised algorithm, we can achieve better performance even with just a handful of collected anomalous samples, even with some generalization capabilities to unseen anomaly modes. Interestingly, this also suggests that there exists some meaningful information in loss profiles produced by neural networks during training which can possibly be utilized in different ways for other tasks.

Acknowledgements. This research is supported with funding from Shimizu Corporation.

References

1. Baur, C., Wiestler, B., Albarqouni, S., Navab, N.: Deep autoencoding models for unsupervised anomaly segmentation in brain MR images. In: Brainlesion: Glioma, Multiple Sclerosis, Stroke and Traumatic Brain Injuries-4th International Workshop (2018)
2. Bengio, S., Vinyals, O., Jaitly, N., Shazeer, N.: Scheduled sampling for sequence prediction with recurrent neural networks. In: Cortes, C., Lawrence, N.D., Lee, D.D., Sugiyama, M., Garnett, R. (eds.) Advances in Neural Information Processing Systems 28: Annual Conference on Neural Information Processing Systems (NIPS) (2015)
3. Bergmann, P., Fauser, M., Sattlegger, D., Steger, C.: Mvtec AD-A comprehensive real-world dataset for unsupervised anomaly detection. In: IEEE Conference on Computer Vision and Pattern Recognition, CVPR (2019)
4. Bergmann, P., Löwe, S., Fauser, M., Sattlegger, D., Steger, C.: Improving unsupervised defect segmentation by applying structural similarity to autoencoders. In: Proceedings of the 14th International Joint Conference on Computer Vision, Imaging and Computer Graphics Theory and Applications, VISIGRAPP 2019, vol. 5: VISAPP (2019)
5. Böttger, T., Ulrich, M.: Real-time texture error detection on textured surfaces with compressed sensing. Pattern Recogn. Image Anal. **26**(1), 88–94 (2016). https://doi.org/10.1134/S1054661816010053
6. Carrera, D., Manganini, F., Boracchi, G., Lanzarone, E.: Defect detection in SEM images of nanofibrous materials. IEEE Trans. Ind. Inf. **13**, 551 (2017)
7. Chen, L., Papandreou, G., Kokkinos, I., Murphy, K., Yuille, A.L.: Deeplab: Semantic image segmentation with deep convolutional nets, atrous convolution, and fully connected crfs. IEEE Trans. Pattern Anal. Mach. Intell. **40**(4), 834–848 (2018)
8. Cui, L., Qi, Z., Chen, Z., Meng, F., Shi, Y.: Pavement distress detection using random decision forests. In: Zhang, C., et al. (eds.) ICDS 2015. LNCS, vol. 9208, pp. 95–102. Springer, Cham (2015). https://doi.org/10.1007/978-3-319-24474-7_14
9. Deng, J., Dong, W., Socher, R., Li, L., Li, K., Li, F.: Imagenet: a large-scale hierarchical image database. In: 2009 IEEE Computer Society Conference on Computer Vision and Pattern Recognition (2009)
10. Eskin, E.: Anomaly detection over noisy data using learned probability distributions. In: Proceedings of the Seventeenth International Conference on Machine Learning (ICML) (2000)

11. He, K., Zhang, X., Ren, S., Sun, J.: Deep residual learning for image recognition. In: 2016 IEEE Conference on Computer Vision and Pattern Recognition, CVPR (2016)
12. Krähenbühl, P., Koltun, V.: Efficient inference in fully connected CRFS with gaussian edge potentials. In: Advances in Neural Information Processing Systems 24: 25th Annual Conference on Neural Information Processing Systems (NIPS) (2011)
13. Markou, M., Singh, S.: Novelty detection: a review—part 1: statistical approaches. Signal Process. **83**(12), 2481–2497 (2003)
14. Napoletano, P., Piccoli, F., Schettini, R.: Anomaly detection in nanofibrous materials by CNN-based self-similarity. Sensors **18**, 209 (2018)
15. Rahmani, M., Atia, G.K.: Coherence pursuit: fast, simple, and robust principal component analysis. IEEE Trans. Signal Process. **65**(23), 6260–6275 (2017)
16. Ravanbakhsh, M., Sangineto, E., Nabi, M., Sebe, N.: Training adversarial discriminators for cross-channel abnormal event detection in crowds. In: IEEE Winter Conference on Applications of Computer Vision, WACV (2019)
17. Ronneberger, O., Fischer, P., Brox, T.: U-Net: convolutional networks for biomedical image segmentation. In: Navab, N., Hornegger, J., Wells, W.M., Frangi, A.F. (eds.) MICCAI 2015. LNCS, vol. 9351, pp. 234–241. Springer, Cham (2015). https://doi.org/10.1007/978-3-319-24574-4_28
18. Ross, S., Gordon, G., Bagnell, D.: A reduction of imitation learning and structured prediction to no-regret online learning. In: Proceedings of the Fourteenth International Conference on Artificial Intelligence and Statistics, pp. 627–635 (2011)
19. Ruff, L., et al.: Deep semi-supervised anomaly detection (2020)
20. Sabokrou, M., Khalooei, M., Fathy, M., Adeli, E.: Adversarially learned one-class classifier for novelty detection. In: 2018 IEEE Conference on Computer Vision and Pattern Recognition, CVPR (2018)
21. Schlegl, T., Seeböck, P., Waldstein, S.M., Schmidt-Erfurth, U., Langs, G.: Unsupervised anomaly detection with generative adversarial networks to guide marker discovery. In: Information Processing in Medical Imaging-25th International Conference, IPMI (2017)
22. Shelhamer, E., Long, J., Darrell, T.: Fully convolutional networks for semantic segmentation. IEEE Trans. Pattern Anal. Mach. Intell. **39**(4), 640–651 (2017)
23. Shi, Y., Cui, L., Qi, Z., Meng, F., Chen, Z.: Automatic road crack detection using random structured forests. IEEE Trans. Intell. Transp. Syst. **17**(12), 3434–3445 (2016)
24. Steger, C., Ulrich, M., Wiedemann, C.: Machine Vision Algorithms and Applications. John Wiley & Sons, Hoboken (2018)
25. Sutton, R.S., Barto, A.G.: Reinforcement learning-an introduction. In: Adaptive Computation and Machine Learning MIT Press, New York (1998)
26. Williams, R.J.: Simple statistical gradient-following algorithms for connectionist reinforcement learning. Mach. Learn. **8**, 229–256 (1992)
27. Xu, H., Caramanis, C., Sanghavi, S.: Robust PCA via outlier pursuit. In: Advances in Neural Information Processing Systems 23: 24th Annual Conference on Neural Information Processing Systems (NIPS) (2010)
28. Yamanishi, K., Takeuchi, J.I., Williams, G., Milne, P.: On-line unsupervised outlier detection using finite mixtures with discounting learning algorithms. Data Min. Knowl. Disc. **8**(3), 275–300 (2004)

LEMMA: A Multi-view Dataset for LEarning Multi-agent Multi-task Activities

Baoxiong Jia$^{(\boxtimes)}$ (iD), Yixin Chen (iD), Siyuan Huang (iD), Yixin Zhu (iD), and Song-Chun Zhu (iD)

UCLA Center for Vision, Cognition, Learning, and Autonomy (VCLA), Los Angeles, USA
{baoxiongjia,ethanchen,huangsiyuan,yixin.zhu}@ucla.edu
sczhu@stat.ucla.edu

Abstract. Understanding and interpreting human actions is a longstanding challenge and a critical indicator of perception in artificial intelligence. However, a few imperative components of daily human activities are largely missed in prior literature, including the goal-directed actions, concurrent multi-tasks, and collaborations among multi-agents. We introduce the LEMMA dataset to provide a single home to address these missing dimensions with meticulously designed settings, wherein the number of tasks and agents varies to highlight different learning objectives. We densely annotate the atomic-actions with human-object interactions to provide ground-truths of the compositionality, scheduling, and assignment of daily activities. We further devise challenging compositional action recognition and action/task anticipation benchmarks with baseline models to measure the capability of compositional action understanding and temporal reasoning. We hope this effort would drive the machine vision community to examine goal-directed human activities and further study the task scheduling and assignment in the real world.

Keywords: Dataset · Multi-agent multi-task activities · Compositional action recognition · Action and task anticipations · Multiview

1 Introduction

Activity understanding is one of the most fundamental problems in artificial intelligence and computer vision. As the most readily available learning source, videos of daily human activities could be used to train intelligent agents and, in turn, to assist humans. However, compared to recent progress in learning from static images [2,23,24,44], current machine vision's ability to understand activities from videos still falls short. Admittedly, activity understanding is inherently more challenging, which requires reason about the complex structures in

Electronic supplementary material The online version of this chapter (https://doi.org/10.1007/978-3-030-58574-7_46) contains supplementary material, which is available to authorized users.

© Springer Nature Switzerland AG 2020
A. Vedaldi et al. (Eds.): ECCV 2020, LNCS 12371, pp. 767–786, 2020.
https://doi.org/10.1007/978-3-030-58574-7_46

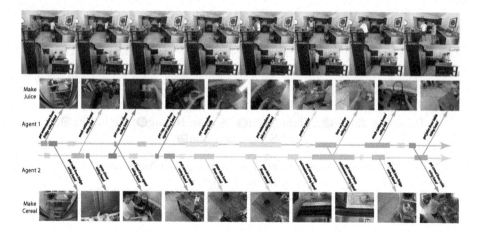

Fig. 1. Illustrations of the proposed multi-view dataset with annotations. From top to bottom: frames captured from the third-person primary view, frames captured from the third-person side view, annotated segments of each agent executing tasks, and corresponding frames captured from the first-person view.

activities along the additional temporal dimension; but we argue there are more profound reasons that we must look back to the origin of activity understanding.

The study and analysis of human motion perception are rooted in the field of neuroscience [58]. Using a dot-representation of human motions, Johansson [28] adopted a method to produce proximal patterns (*i.e.*, the moving light display experiment), which demonstrated that human perception of activities does not tightly couple with *pixel-based features*; human subjects can still perceive the semantics of activities from *sparse* representations of motions. Evidence from developmental psychology, the classic Heider-Simmel experiment, further suggests that we perceive human activities from as *goal-directed* behaviors [5,12,16,61]; it is the underlying intent, rather than the surface pixels or behavior, that matters when we observe motions [4]. Such a **goal-directed** [33] **perspective** of activity understanding has been largely left untouched in computer vision.

Daily human activities are intrinsically multi-tasked [38,47]; understanding activity naturally demands a learning system to interpret concurrent interactions. As agents' decision-making processes are deeply affected by their unique social values, task scheduling is significantly affected by interactions (*e.g.*, cooperation, competition, subordination) among multi-agents [30]. These observations implicate that the machine vision system must objectively understand how a given task should be decomposed into atomic-actions, how multi-tasks should be executed and coordinated in parallel among multi-agents, and take the perspective from human agents to understand why the observed human activities are optimal solutions. Such a **decompositional, multi-task, multi-agent, diagnostic-driven, social perspective** of activity understanding is critical for an intelligent agent to understand human behavior and team with humans collaboratively; yet it is broadly missing in activity understanding literature.

The semantics of human actions are intrinsically ambiguous when described in natural language. For instance, although both "opening the fridge" and "opening a book" use the action verb "open," their semantics of the actions are utterly different. In this paper, we take the stance of Grice's influential work on language act [21]—technical tools for reasoning about rational action should elucidate linguistic phenomena [18]. Specifically, the compositional relations between the verbs and nouns could reveal the functionality of the object and the patterns of human-object interactions, which subsequently facilitate the understanding of the observed human activities and the language that describes them. Though the previous work [20] attempted to address this issue, more general and flexible **compositional relations for describing human actions interacting with objects** are requisite for a goal-directed activity understanding.

Motivated by these deficiencies in prior work, we introduce the LEMMA dataset to explore the essence of complex human activities in a goal-directed, multi-agent, multi-task setting with ground-truth labels of compositional atomic-actions and their associated tasks. By quantifying the scenarios to up to two multi-step tasks with two agents, we strive to address human multi-task and multi-agent interactions in four scenarios: single-agent single-task (1×1), single-agent multi-task (1×2), multi-agent single-task (2×1), and multi-agent multi-task (2×2). Task instructions are only given to one agent in the 2×1 setting to resemble the robot-helping scenario, hoping that the learned perception models could be applied in robotic tasks (especially in HRI) in the near future.

Both the third-person views (TPVs) and the first-person views (FPVs) were recorded to account for different perspectives of the same activities; see Fig. 1. Such a setting potentially benefits future study on 3D holistic scene understanding [10,25], as well as action understanding and prediction [42,48]. We densely annotate atomic-actions (in the form of compositional verb-noun pairs) and tasks of each atomic-action, to facilitate the learning of multi-agent multi-task task scheduling and assignment; see more details in Sect. 2.

1.1 Related Work

In this section, we review and compare prior indoor activity datasets on the basis of tasks and captured video contents; see a detailed summary in Table 1.

Crowd-sourced from online videos and movie sharing platforms, typical large-scale video datasets [8,9,15,29,53] focus on **video-level summarization and classification**. Although activity classes exhibit a large inter-class variability, spanning from outdoor sports activities to indoor household activities, they generally lack sequential, goal-directed activities. Notably, they suffer from a major drawback [17]; activities are highly correlated to the general scene and object context, possessing a strong dataset bias for activity understanding.

Some datasets tackle the **human atomic-actions** using short clips or limited tasks, with a focus on the semantics of action verbs and objects [20], 3D action analysis [27,35,49], and action grounding with multi-modality inputs [37]. Although such datasets are suitable for atomic-actions, they are intrinsically impaired at studying the long-term reasoning of goal-directed human activities.

Recently, **concurrent actions** have been taken into consideration. For instance, Charades [52] is a large-scale benchmark for household activities, and

Table 1. Comparisons between LEMMA and relevant indoor activity datasets.

Dataset	Task annotation	Multi-agent	Multi-task	Multi-view	Samples	Frames	Action classes	Action segments	Actions per video	Modality	Year
MPII Cooking [45]	✓	✗	✗	✗	273	2.9M	88	14,105	51.7	RGB	2012
ADL [41]	✗	✗	✓	✗	20	1.0M	32	436	13.6	RGB	2012
50Salads [54]	✓	✗	✗	✗	50	0.5M	17	966	19.3	RGB-D	2013
CAD-120 [31]	✗	✗	✗	✗	120	0.1M	10	1,175	9.8	RGB-D	2013
Breakfast [32]	✓	✗	✗	✓	433	3.0M	50	3,078	7.1	RGB	2014
Watch-n-Patch [63]	✗	✗	✓	✗	458	0.1M	21	2978	6.5	RGB-D	2015
Charades [52]	✗	✗	✓	✗	9,848	7.4M	157	67,000	6.8	RGB	2016
Something-Something [20]	✗	✗	✗	✗	108,499	-	174	108,499	1.0	RGB	2017
EGTEA GAZE+ [36]	✓	✗	✗	✗	86	2.4M	106	10,325	120.1	RGB	2018
EPIC-KITCHENS [13]	✗	✗	✓	✗	432	11.5M	149	39,596	91.7	RGB	2018
LEMMA (proposed)	✓	✓	✓	✓	324	4.6M	641	11,781	36.4	RGB-D	2020

Charades-Ego [51] steps further with both FPVs and TPVs. However, the activities involved are mostly unrelated to specific goals due to the crowdsourced script generation process. Similarly, although Multi-THUMOS [64] and AVA [22] focus on highly paralleled activities, and some datasets look at the temporal order of activities [7,56], the unnaturally scripted activities result in the lack of meaningful goal-directed tasks exhibited in our daily life.

Conversely, **instructional video** datasets [1,31,32,46,54] tackle goal-directed multi-step tasks, mostly in cooking, repairing, and assembling activities. In spite of their relevance, they fail to account for multi-agent or multi-task problems. EPIC-KITCHENS [13] is perhaps the only exception; it records naturally paralleled task execution of agents in kitchen environments, but with no task specification or multi-agent interactions. Additionally, prior instructional video datasets have either drastic view perspective changes [1,55,57,65] or limited egocentric view with severe occlusions [36,41], hindering the activity understanding.

Another related stream of work is the learning of group-level activities in a **multi-agent** setting [26], such as detecting key actors [43], predicting future trajectories [34,40], and recognizing collective activities [11,39,50]. However, such coarse-grained multi-agent interactions leave the latent subtlety of collaboration and task assignment untouched. Although simulation-based multi-agent environments [3,6,59] can partially address such an issue, learning from noisy and real visual input in physical work is still essential for understanding collaborative planning behaviors of agents in the context of complex daily tasks.

The collected LEMMA dataset strives to address the shortcomings of the aforementioned works, capturing goal-directed, decompositional, multi-task activities with multi-agent collaborations. As shown in Table 1, the size, annotation, and actions per video of LEMMA are at a comparable scale to state-of-the-art benchmarks. We hope such a design will boost the study of human activity understanding and potentially motivate new cross-disciplinary research insights.

1.2 Contributions

This paper's contribution is three-fold. (i) We design and collect a multi-view video dataset, capturing multi-agent, multi-task activities with goal-directed daily tasks. (ii) We annotate the dataset, focusing on the compositionality of actions and the governing task for each atomic-action. (iii) We provide compositional action recognition and action/task anticipation benchmarks by considering the aforementioned features; we also compare and analyze multiple baseline models to promote future research on human activity understanding.

2   The LEMMA Dataset

This section describes the design, data collection, and data annotation process of the LEMMA dataset. The dataset is profiled by various statistics from diversified perspectives to highlight its potentials in activity understanding.[1]

---

[1] The dataset will be made publicly available at the following website with download links and util code: https://sites.google.com/view/lemma-activity.

2.1 Activities and Scenarios

We first build a task pool of 15 common tasks in the kitchen (*e.g.*, "make juice," "make cereal") and living room (*e.g.* "watch TV," "water plant"). On top of these tasks, we design four types of scenarios (with a different focus) to study goal-directed multi-step multi-task indoor activities in multi-agent settings.

1. **Single-agent Single-task** (1×1): Each participant was first asked to perform all tasks from the task pool independently; this ensures participants are clear with the goal of each task and could schedule and assign tasks efficiently in later multi-task or multi-agent scenarios. Participants were asked to read the instructions and walk around to get familiarized with the new environments.
2. **Single-agent Multi-task** (1×2): Each participant was then asked to simultaneously perform two tasks, randomly sampled from the task pool. The participants determined the order of task executions without any restrictions.
3. **Multi-agent Single-task** (2×1): Two participants were asked to perform a single task cooperatively; the task is randomly selected from the task pool. To emulate human-robot teaming accurately, only one participant (leader) was provided with task instructions; the other participant (helper), with no knowledge of the task, was asked to collaborate with the leader agent to finish the task efficiently. Only nonverbal communications (*e.g.*, gestures) were allowed between two participants; this design would open up new venues on nonverbal communications and the emergence of language in real-world environments.
4. **Multi-agent Multi-task** (2×2): Both participants were provided with task instructions. Since both participants were asked to accomplish two complex multi-step tasks collaboratively, this scenario has the most natural activity/task patterns and richest mechanisms for learning task scheduling and assignment.

In total, the LEMMA dataset includes 37 unique task combinations in the multi-task scenarios. Participants were explicitly instructed to perform tasks efficiently and provided with a brief task instruction with basic environment information. Except for the specification of the goal states for each task, we add no additional constraint to the order of task execution; participants perform tasks naturally and freely. Figure 2 shows a sample instruction for the 2×1 scenario.

In this task, you are asked to **make watermelon juice**. Here are things to know before your start: **Leader**
- All the items needed for this task can be found either in the **fridge**, on the **table**, or in one of the **drawers** or **closets**.
- Please **cut** the **watermelon** into pieces before blending it with the **juicer**.
- Please keep the kitchen clean; wash all the **tools/objects** you used.
- You will have an additional **helper** to collaborate with you.
  - Do **Not** speak with them. They do **NOT** know anything about the task you are working on.
  - Feel free to ask them for help, but only using **non-verbal** communication (e.g., gestures). For instance, you may point to something, or any other gestues you think may help instruct them.

In this task, you are asked to **collaborate** with your friend to finish a task in the kitchen.   **Helper**
Here are things to know before your start:
- All the items needed for this task can be found either in the **fridge**, on the **table**, or in one of the **drawers** or **closets**.
- Please keep the kitchen clean; wash all the **tools/objects** you used.
- As only your friend knows the task instruction, please try to infer what the task is and offer helps.
- **You may not speak with your friend.** You can only use **non-verbal** communication (e.g., gestures).

Fig. 2. An exemplar task instruction of making juice for two agents in a **Multi-agent Single-task** (2 × 1) scenario. Middle: Point clouds, TPVs, and FPVs.

2.2   Data Collection

We recorded the data in 7 different Airbnb houses, performed by 8 individuals in 14 unique kitchens/living rooms. To provide different views of performing the daily activities and avoid occlusion in narrow spaces, we set up two Kinect Azure cameras to capture the RGB-D videos of the global scene and human bodies. In addition, each participant was instructed to wear a head-mounted GoPro camera to capture detailed agent-specific actions in an egocentric view. In post-processing, we synchronize the camera recordings of all views at a frame rate of 24 FPS. Figure 2 shows an example of a scene with a point cloud merged from two Kinects and four RGB views from both Kinects and GoPros. Combining TPVs and FPVs captures most of the details of performing daily activities, provides sufficient data for understanding human activities, and benefits future research in embodied vision. The additional depth information and 3D human skeletons captured by Kinects can also be adopted for future 3D understanding tasks.

2.3   Ground-Truth Annotation

We used the Amazon Mechanical Turk (AMT) to annotate both human bounding boxes and action information in the synchronized recordings. Specifically, action information includes the temporal localization of segments, semantic labels, and the governing task of each atomic-action. The semantic labels of atomic-actions are composed of verbs and nouns, representing flexible compositional relations to describe human actions. Additional details are provided below.

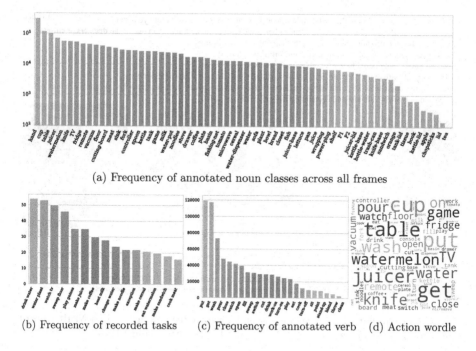

(a) Frequency of annotated noun classes across all frames

(b) Frequency of recorded tasks   (c) Frequency of annotated verb   (d) Action wordle

Fig. 3. Statistics of the LEMMA dataset.

Bounding Boxes and Segments: Bounding boxes of humans are annotated on the primary view of TPVs. Skeletons captured by Kinects are used to provide initial estimations of bounding boxes. Next, we use Vatic [60] to adjust bounding boxes and annotate the segments of atomic-actions. The segments of atomic-actions are defined by verbs without corresponding nouns, for example, "put __ to __ using __," "pour into __ from __." Each video was first annotated by two AMT workers; task-irrelevant actions (e.g., "walking," "holding") are ignored. We then compute the Intersection over Union (IoU) of both bounding boxes and temporal segments. A third AMT worker is asked to fine-tune the annotations if the IoU of bounding boxes or segments annotated is lower than 0.5.

Atomic-actions and Activities: Given the verbs of the atomic-action segments, two AMT workers were asked to fill in the blanks of the verb patterns and annotate the governing tasks in multi-task scenarios with a self-developed interactive annotation tool (see *supplementary material*). We allow concurrent actions for each agent with multiple nouns for the same verb; for example, "get spoon, cup from table using hand." As there might exist ambiguities in describing the atomic-actions with natural languages, such as the possible annotations of "wash cup using water" *vs.* "wash cup using sink," we manually go through all the annotations and resolve the ambiguous action annotations following a uniform criterion. Examples of annotation results are shown in *supplementary*.

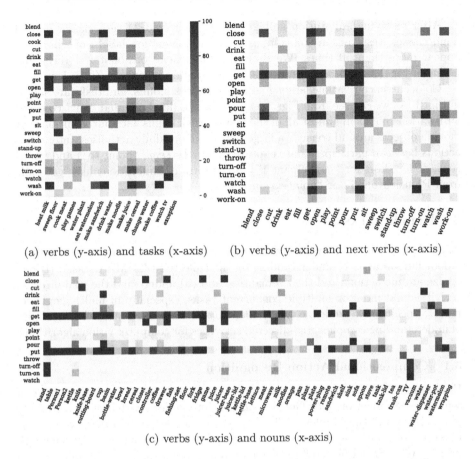

(a) verbs (y-axis) and tasks (x-axis)   (b) verbs (y-axis) and next verbs (x-axis)

(c) verbs (y-axis) and nouns (x-axis)

Fig. 4. The co-occurrence statistics for verbs, nouns, and tasks in LEMMA.

2.4 Dataset Statistics

In total, we recorded 324 activities, generating 324 × 2 TPV videos (from both Kinects) and 445 FPV videos. Among them, 136 activities were performed in kitchens and the remaining 188 in the living rooms. The collected LEMMA dataset consists of 127 1 × 1 activities, 76 1 × 2 activities, 66 2 × 1 activities, and 55 2 × 2 activities. The frequency of the recorded tasks is shown in Fig. 3b. The total duration of all the activities is 10.1 h, with an average duration of 2 min per video and the longest activity of 7 min.

We retrieved a total of 4.6 million images during post-processing, including 2.9 million RGB images captured by both GoPros and Kinects and 1.7 million depth images captured by Kinects. We annotated 0.9 million RGB frames captured by the primary view Kinect and gathered 0.8 million annotated frames with one or more actions performed by each of the agents (if multiple).

After resolving annotation ambiguities, we collected 24 verb classes and 64 noun classes, resulting in 862 compositional atomic-action labels, of which 641 appear more than 50 times. We show the frequencies of annotated verbs and nouns in Figs. 3a and 3c; both distributions roughly follow the Zipf's law.

Co-occurrence relations among annotated verbs, nouns, and tasks are shown in Fig. 4. As we can see from Figs. 4a and 4c, verbs like "get" and "put" co-occur with various nouns in almost all of the tasks, which aligns with our intuition that moving objects around consists a large portion of our daily activities. Interactive actions between participants are captured by verbs (e.g., "point-to") and nouns (e.g., "P1," short for "participant 1") in the form of annotations like "get knife from P1 using hand" or "point-to sink."

3   Benchmarks

Aligned with our motivations, two general goals are constructed to evaluate indoor human activity understanding on the collected LEMMA dataset: (i) recognize atomic-actions and their semantics; and (ii) understand the goal-directed activities and monitor multiple concurrent tasks, especially in multi-agent scenarios. Specifically, we define two challenging benchmarks to test the capability of understanding complex goal-directed activities for computer vision algorithms.

3.1   Compositional Action Recognition

Human indoor activities are composed of fine-grained action segments with rich semantics. As mentioned by Goyal et al. [20], interactions with objects are highly purposive. From the simplest verb of "put," we can generate a plethora of combinations of objects and target places, such as "put cup onto table," "put fork into drawer." Situations could become even more challenging when objects were used as tools; for example, "put meat into pan using fork."

Motivated by the above observation, we propose the compositional action recognition benchmark on the collected LEMMA dataset with each object attributed to a specific semantic position in the action label. Specifically, we build 24 compositional action templates; see Fig. 5a for some examples. In these action templates, each noun could denote an interacting object, a target or a source location, or a tool used by a human agent to perform certain actions.

The proposed compositional action recognition benchmark is challenging; it requires computational models to correctly detect the ongoing concurrent action verbs as well as the nouns at their correct semantic positions. We evaluate model performances by metrics on compositional action recognition in both FPVs and TPVs. Specifically, the model is asked to predict (i) multiple labels in verb recognition for concurrent actions (e.g., "watch tv" and "drink with cup" at the same time), and (ii) multiple labels in noun recognition for each semantic position given verbs, representing the interactions with multiple objects using the same action (e.g., "wash spoon, cup using sink"). Figure 5b shows the schematics of the evaluation process. For training and testing on TPVs, we provide ground-truth bounding boxes of humans as additional information on spatial localization.

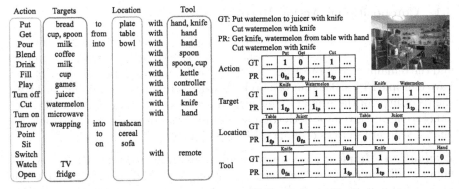

(a) Compositional action templates   (b) Prediction of verbs and nouns

Fig. 5. Compositional action recognition benchmark on LEMMA. (a) Examples of Compositional action templates. Yellow denotes verbs. Blue, green, and brown denote nouns for an interacting object, target/source location, and tool, respectively. (b) Examples of predictions of the verbs and nouns in compositional action recognition. Verbs and nouns are evaluated through multi-label classification. (Color figure online)

3.2 Action and Task Anticipation

As emphasized throughout the paper, the most significant factor of human activities is the goal-directed, teleological stand. An in-depth understanding of goal-directed tasks demands a predictive ability of latent goals, action preferences, and potential outcomes. To tackle these challenges, we propose the action and task anticipation benchmark on the collected LEMMA dataset. Specifically, we evaluate model performances for the anticipation (*i.e.*, predictions for the next action segment) of action and task with both FPV and TPV videos.

This benchmark provides both the training and testing data in all four scenarios of activities to study the goal-directed multi-task multi-agent problem. As there is an innate discrepancy of prediction difficulties among these four scenarios, we gradually increase the overall prediction difficulty, akin to a curriculum learning process, by setting the percentage of training videos to be 3/4, 1/4, 1/4, and 1/4 for 1×1, 1×2, 2×1 and 2×2 scenarios, respectively. Intuitively, with sufficient clean demonstrations of tasks in 1 × 1 scenario, interpreting tasks in more complex settings (*i.e.*, 1 × 2, 2 × 1, and 2 × 2) should be easier, thus requiring less learning samples; such a design encourages the model to generalize. The model performance is evaluated individually for each scenario.

4 Experiments

In this section, we conduct experiments on the two proposed benchmarks with details on evaluation metrics, experimental settings, and baseline results. We further discuss the results to highlight the underlying challenges of each task.

4.1   Compositional Action Recognition

Experimental Setup: We randomly split all the video samples into training and test sets with a ratio of 3:1, resulting in 243 recorded activities for training and the remaining 81 for testing. Due to the multi-agent setup, each activity may have multiple FPVs; 333 (out of 445) FPV videos are split into training. In TPVs, the recordings of the primary view with the ground-truth human bounding box annotations are given for both training and testing videos. Results are evaluated on two separate sources of inputs: FPVs and TPVs.

Evaluation Metrics: Model performances are evaluated separately for verbs, nouns, and compositional action recognition. Verb and compositional action recognition are treated as multi-label classifications with 25 verb classes and 863 compositional action classes (including a "null" action). After generating multi-hot labels for each semantic position in the presented verb, noun recognition is evaluated as multi-label classification (64 object classes). Average precision, recall, and F1-score for all predictions are reported on testing sets. During the evaluation, we sample image frames at 5 FPS and evaluate on these frames.

Methods: We adopt two recent 3D-CNN networks, I3D [9] and SlowFast Network [14], as the baseline models. The baseline models predict the compositional action directly. Considering compositionality of verbs and nouns, we propose two variants of the baseline models: (i) a multi-branch network (branching model) that builds on the bottleneck layer of the backbone models to leverage both verb and noun supervision, and (ii) a multi-step inference model (sequential model), wherein verbs are first inferred with a beam search and then fed into object inference with their verb embeddings for joint learning.

Implementation Details: The training procedure utilizes all annotated segments in the training set. Additionally, we re-scale all the images with the short side to 256 pixels. To feed data into 3D-CNN models, 4 frames are first sampled for each action segment as center frames, and an additional 8 frames are then uniformly sampled around center frames with a window length of 32. We train each model on 8 Titan RTX GPUs on a single computing node for 50 epochs (20k iterations) with a batch size of 96. We use warm-up strategy and perform large mini-batch batch normalization, as suggested in [19]. The learning rate is initially set to 0.0125 for each parallel branch and decays with a cosine annealing. Other settings of the backbone models are the same as in [14]. For the proposed sequential model, we use the beam search with a size of 5 for action inference. We extract bounding box features of humans with ROIAlign [23] for frames in TPVs. More implementation details are provided in *supplementary material.*

Results and Discussion: Table 2 shows quantitative results of predicting verbs, nouns, and compositional actions for the compositional action recognition task. For FPVs, rather than directly predicting the compositional actions (baseline models), predicting the verbs and nouns with their semantic positions boosts the performance on all metrics, indicating that understanding the compositional structures of human actions indeed supports the prediction. We also

Table 2. Comparisons of compositional action recognition on LEMMA.

View Type	Method	Verb			Noun			Compositional Action		
		Avg.Prec	Avg.Rec	Avg.F1	Avg.Prec	Avg.Rec	Avg.F1	Avg.Prec	Avg.Rec	Avg.F1
FPV	I3D	17.09	43.89	24.60	3.42	16.15	5.72	11.07	39.49	17.30
	Slowfast	22.27	56.42	31.94	4.31	20.60	7.13	18.68	**50.65**	27.3
	I3D sequential	25.04	**57.00**	34.80	**19.36**	**75.29**	**30.80**	18.00	50.04	26.47
	Slowfast sequential	24.30	49.71	32.64	17.95	59.11	27.54	26.80	38.41	31.57
	I3D branching	25.73	55.62	**35.8**	18.63	69.76	29.41	22.29	48.46	30.53
	Slowfast branching	**26.16**	56.33	35.73	18.18	73.46	29.15	**27.97**	48.87	**35.58**
TPV	I3D	14.18	36.34	20.40	2.29	11.05	3.79	6.85	**23.82**	10.64
	Slowfast	14.28	**37.38**	20.66	2.32	11.14	3.83	**7.76**	23.25	**16.31**
	I3D sequential	16.17	30.17	21.05	7.79	**25.41**	11.93	2.23	12.67	3.79
	Slowfast sequential	15.31	28.84	20.00	6.37	22.39	9.92	3.27	9.16	4.82
	I3D branching	12.92	32.09	18.43	12.75	17.70	14.82	4.67	20.76	7.6
	Slowfast branching	**16.64**	33.40	**22.21**	**17.29**	18.36	**17.81**	6.52	21.55	10.01

observe that the results of compositional action recognition in the sequential models are slightly lower than the branching model due to the aggregated error brought in by a relatively low precision (~25%) of the verb recognition.

In comparison, the results of compositional action recognition in TPVs are significantly lower than those in the FPVs due to severe occlusion. It also shows that predicting the composition of verbs and nouns makes no significant improvement compared with predicting compositional action directly. Such a result implies that current models could not capture the details of compositions between verbs and nouns from TPVs. Taken together, the results indicate that fusion among the representations of visual embodiment between TPVs and FPVs might be a crucial ingredient to tackle this problem in the future.

Figure 6 shows qualitative results for the composed action recognition task.

4.2 Action and Task Anticipations

Experimental Setup: We split the training and test sets with ratios 3 : 1, 1 : 3, 1 : 3, 1 : 3 for the four scenarios 1×1, 1×2, 2×1, 2×2, respectively. Such a spit results in training set with (96, 19, 16, 13) activities and a test set with (31, 57, 50, 42) activities in four scenarios. During training and testing, the computational models have access to both FPVs and TPVs, together with the ground-truth human bounding boxes annotations of the TPV primary view.

Evaluation Metrics: Model performances are evaluated individually (per agent) for the action and task anticipations task. Specifically, both action and task anticipations are evaluated as multi-label classifications with 863 compositional action classes (including a "null" action) and 15 task classes. Average precision, recall, and F1-score are reported individually for each of the four scenarios on the testing sets. Similar to the protocol used in the above compositional action recognition task, we re-sample image frames at 5 FPS and evaluate these sub-sampled frames during the testing phase.

Methods: We leverage the visual features extracted by the pre-trained SlowFast model in compositional action recognition for baseline models. Specifically, we

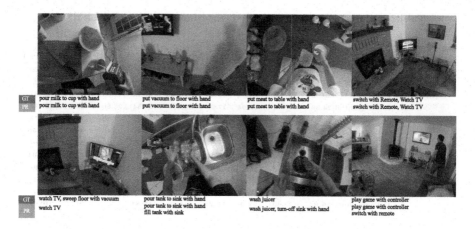

Fig. 6. Qualitative results of compositional action recognition on LEMMA. From top to bottom, we show correct predictions and failure examples. Red marks wrong verb or noun predictions, green indicates correct verb or noun predictions. (Color figure online)

compare two backbone models: (i) using segment-level recognition feature (SF) directly by adding an MLP on top of the features, and (ii) using long-term feature bank (LFB) with max pooling [62]. For activities with multi-agent interactions, we use the other agent's FPV features together with their own's to capture the joint task execution progress for learning and inference; these variants are denoted as M-SF (FPV) and M-LFB (FPV) For comparison, we also use the concatenation of the FPV feature and primary TPV feature as the input; the corresponding models are denoted as M-SF (TPV) and M-LFB (TPV).

Implementation Details: For the LFB model, we use a history window size of 10 and aggregate the features using max-pooling, as described in [62]. For the multi-agent variants, we use max-pooling to fuse features of two views and process them with a different branch as another temporal inference module. We train models on a single Titan Xp GPU for 50 epochs with a learning rate of 0.001. See *supplementary material* for more details on network architectures.

Results and Discussion: Table 3 shows quantitative results of action and task anticipation. The proposed multi-agent variants (M-) of baseline models perform the best among all models. For single-agent activities (1×1, 1×2), we have the following crucial observations. First, models that consider temporal relations between frames generally perform better than the models using segment features. Second, adding additional TPV features to single-agent activities slightly helps interpret the task being executed and therefore promotes anticipation. This result matches the intuition that computational models having access to both FPVs and TPVs would perceive more holistic scene information. We also find that the performances of task anticipation in the 1×1 single-task scenario

Table 3. Comparisons of the action and task anticipations on LEMMA.

Scenario	Method	1 × 1			1 × 2			2 × 1			2 × 2		
		Avg.Prec	Avg.Rec	Avg.F1	Avg.Prec	Avg.Rec	Avg.F1	Avg.Prec	Avg.Rec	Avg.F1	Avg.Prec	Avg.Rec	Avg.F1
Compositional action	SF	23.42	22.25	22.82	20.13	20.06	20.10	18.89	19.22	19.05	18.31	16.67	17.45
	LFB	23.03	28.67	25.54	20.48	25.4	22.67	18.31	22.30	20.11	18.53	20.97	19.68
	M-SF (TPV)	**24.22**	28.05	25.99	20.10	24.48	22.08	19.15	16.71	17.85	19.64	15.18	17.12
	M-LFB (TPV)	23.54	**37.81**	**29.01**	21.10	**31.86**	25.39	19.67	21.03	20.33	**20.11**	20.30	**20.15**
	M-SF (FPV)	23.30	25.41	24.31	**21.34**	23.18	22.22	**19.70**	17.46	18.51	19.82	15.8	17.58
	M-LFB (FPV)	23.26	31.07	26.60	20.78	27.40	23.63	19.42	**21.73**	**20.51**	19.49	20.12	19.8
Task	SF	50.53	79.08	61.66	48.07	67.78	56.25	39.05	57.43	46.49	44.88	62.09	52.1
	LFB	57.57	**84.31**	68.42	52.12	68.94	59.36	38.40	53.08	44.56	48.17	64.61	55.19
	M-SF (TPV)	58.61	79.96	67.05	55.45	67.24	60.78	**45.73**	58.98	**51.51**	**49.66**	64.47	56.10
	M-LFB (TPV)	**60.27**	82.19	**69.54**	**56.2**	**72.46**	**63.30**	43.94	61.41	51.23	48.85	**67.48**	**56.67**
	M-SF (FPV)	51.12	79.18	62.13	48.42	69.04	56.92	41.00	58.11	48.08	46.04	65.97	54.24
	M-LFB (FPV)	55.56	82.83	66.51	52.22	70.01	59.82	41.33	**64.49**	50.38	46.65	69.59	55.86

are better than the one in the 1×2 multi-task scenario, matching what we would expect from more complicated task execution patterns.

For multi-agent activities (2×1, 2×2), we observe that the aggregation of FPV and TPV features generally performs better. It supports our hypothesis that observing the other agents' actions helps the computational models to "understand" task scheduling and assignment. We also observe that, models' performances in 2×1 activities are slightly worse than in 2×2 activities. We hypothesize that task plans in the 2×2 scenarios change less frequently, with a clear task assignment coordinates the individual tasks. In comparison, in the 2×1 scenarios, the sequential ordering of the task requires more frequent communications between agents to coordinate. Such a performance gap calls for better modeling of multi-agent task assignments. Due to the page limit, we show qualitative results of action and task anticipation in the *supplementary material*.

5   Conclusions

In this paper, we introduce the LEMMA dataset with a focus on natural multi-agent multi-task daily activities. Dense annotations are provided on both compositional action and task for learning and inference on four different activity scenarios with increasing difficulty. Additionally, we propose two challenging tasks on LEMMA to measure existing models' competence in action understanding and temporal reasoning: (i) compositional action recognition, and (ii) action/task anticipations. We hope this effort would attract the computer vision community to look into natural and realistic goal-directed human activities and further study the task scheduling and assignment in real-world scenarios.

Acknowledgements. We thank (i) Tao Yuan at UCLA for designing the annotation tool, (ii) Lifeng Fan, Qing Li, Tengyu Liu at UCLA and Zhouqian Jiang for helpful discussions, and (iii) colleagues from UCLA VCLA for assisting the endeavor of post-processing this massive dataset. The work reported herein was supported by ONR MURI N00014-16-1-2007, ONR N00014-19-1-2153, and DARPA XAI N66001-17-2-4029.

References

1. Alayrac, J.B., Bojanowski, P., Agrawal, N., Sivic, J., Laptev, I., Lacoste-Julien, S.: Unsupervised learning from narrated instruction videos. In: Proceedings of the IEEE Conference on Computer Vision and Pattern Recognition (CVPR) (2016)
2. Antol, S., et al.: VQA: visual question answering. In: Proceedings of International Conference on Computer Vision (ICCV) (2015)
3. Baker, B., et al.: Emergent tool use from multi-agent autocurricula. In: International Conference on Learning Representations (ICLR) (2020)
4. Baldwin, D.A., Baird, J.A.: Discerning intentions in dynamic human action. Trends in Cognitive Sciences **5**(4), 171–178 (2001)
5. Baldwin, D.A., Baird, J.A., Saylor, M.M., Clark, M.A.: Infants parse dynamic action. Child Dev. **72**(3), 708–717 (2001)

6. Berner, C., et al.: Dota 2 with large scale deep reinforcement learning. arXiv preprint arXiv:1912.06680 (2019)
7. Bojanowski, P., et al.: Weakly supervised action labeling in videos under ordering constraints. In: Fleet, D., Pajdla, T., Schiele, B., Tuytelaars, T. (eds.) ECCV 2014. LNCS, vol. 8693, pp. 628–643. Springer, Cham (2014). https://doi.org/10.1007/978-3-319-10602-1_41
8. Caba Heilbron, F., Escorcia, V., Ghanem, B., Carlos Niebles, J.: Activitynet: a large-scale video benchmark for human activity understanding. In: Proceedings of the IEEE Conference on Computer Vision and Pattern Recognition (CVPR) (2015)
9. Carreira, J., Zisserman, A.: Quo vadis, action recognition? A new model and the kinetics dataset. In: Proceedings of the IEEE Conference on Computer Vision and Pattern Recognition (CVPR) (2017)
10. Chen, Y., Huang, S., Yuan, T., Qi, S., Zhu, Y., Zhu, S.C.: Holistic++ scene understanding: single-view 3d holistic scene parsing and human pose estimation with human-object interaction and physical commonsense. In: Proceedings of International Conference on Computer Vision (ICCV) (2019)
11. Choi, W., Shahid, K., Savarese, S.: What are they doing?: Collective activity classification using spatio-temporal relationship among people. In: International Conference on Computer Vision Workshops (ICCV Workshops) (2009)
12. Csibra, G., Gergely, G.: 'Obsessed with goals': functions and mechanisms of teleological interpretation of actions in humans. Acta Psychol. 124, 60–78 (2007)
13. Damen, D., et al.: Scaling egocentric vision: the epic-kitchens dataset. In: Proceedings of European Conference on Computer Vision (ECCV) (2018)
14. Feichtenhofer, C., Fan, H., Malik, J., He, K.: Slowfast networks for video recognition. In: Proceedings of the IEEE Conference on Computer Vision and Pattern Recognition (CVPR) (2019)
15. Fouhey, D.F., Kuo, W.C., Efros, A.A., Malik, J.: From lifestyle vlogs to everyday interactions. In: Proceedings of the IEEE Conference on Computer Vision and Pattern Recognition (CVPR) (2018)
16. Gergely, G., Bekkering, H., Király, I.: Rational imitation in preverbal infants. Nature 415(6873), 755–755 (2002)
17. Girdhar, R., Ramanan, D.: Cater: a diagnostic dataset for compositional actions and temporal reasoning (2020)
18. Goodman, N.D., Frank, M.C.: Pragmatic language interpretation as probabilistic inference. Trends Cogn. Sci. 20(11), 818–829 (2016)
19. Goyal, P., et al.: Accurate, large minibatch SGD: Training imagenet in 1 hour. arXiv preprint arXiv:1706.02677 (2017)
20. Goyal, R., et al.: The "something something" video database for learning and evaluating visual common sense. In: Proceedings of International Conference on Computer Vision (ICCV) (2017)
21. Grice, H.P.: Logic and conversation. In: Cole, P., Morgan, J.L. (eds.) Speech acts, pp. 41–58. Brill, Netherlands (1975)
22. Gu, C., et al.: Ava: a video dataset of spatio-temporally localized atomic visual actions. In: Proceedings of the IEEE Conference on Computer Vision and Pattern Recognition (CVPR) (2018)
23. He, K., Gkioxari, G., Dollár, P., Girshick, R.: Mask R-CNN. In: Proceedings of International Conference on Computer Vision (ICCV) (2017)
24. He, K., Zhang, X., Ren, S., Sun, J.: Deep residual learning for image recognition. In: Proceedings of the IEEE Conference on Computer Vision and Pattern Recognition (CVPR) (2016)

25. Huang, S., Qi, S., Zhu, Y., Xiao, Y., Xu, Y., Zhu, S.C.: Holistic 3D scene parsing and reconstruction from a single RGB image. In: Proceedings of European Conference on Computer Vision (ECCV) (2018)

26. Ibrahim, M.S., Muralidharan, S., Deng, Z., Vahdat, A., Mori, G.: A hierarchical deep temporal model for group activity recognition. In: Proceedings of the IEEE Conference on Computer Vision and Pattern Recognition (CVPR) (2016)

27. Ionescu, C., Papava, D., Olaru, V., Sminchisescu, C.: Human3. 6m: large scale datasets and predictive methods for 3D human sensing in natural environments. IEEE Trans. Pattern Anal. Mach. Intell. (TPAMI) 36(7), 1325–1339 (2013)

28. Johansson, G.: Visual perception of biological motion and a model for its analysis. Percept. Psychophysics 14(2), 201–211 (1973). https://doi.org/10.3758/BF03212378

29. Karpathy, A., Toderici, G., Shetty, S., Leung, T., Sukthankar, R., Fei-Fei, L.: Large-scale video classification with convolutional neural networks. In: Proceedings of the IEEE Conference on Computer Vision and Pattern Recognition (CVPR) (2014)

30. Kleiman-Weiner, M., Ho, M.K., Austerweil, J.L., Littman, M.L., Tenenbaum, J.B.: Coordinate to cooperate or compete: abstract goals and joint intentions in social interaction. In: Proceedings of the Annual Meeting of the Cognitive Science Society (CogSci) (2016)

31. Koppula, H.S., Gupta, R., Saxena, A.: Learning human activities and object affordances from RGB-D videos. Int. J. Robot. Res. (IJRR) 32(8), 951–970 (2013)

32. Kuehne, H., Arslan, A., Serre, T.: The language of actions: recovering the syntax and semantics of goal-directed human activities. In: Proceedings of the IEEE Conference on Computer Vision and Pattern Recognition (CVPR) (2014)

33. Land, M., Mennie, N., Rusted, J.: The roles of vision and eye movements in the control of activities of daily living. Perception 28(11), 1311–1328 (1999)

34. Lerner, A., Chrysanthou, Y., Lischinski, D.: Crowds by example. In: Proceedings of Computer Graphics Forum (2007)

35. Li, W., Zhang, Z., Liu, Z.: Action recognition based on a bag of 3d points. In: Proceedings of the IEEE Conference on Computer Vision and Pattern Recognition (CVPR) (2010)

36. Li, Y., Liu, M., Rehg, J.M.: In the eye of beholder: joint learning of gaze and actions in first person video. In: Proceedings of European Conference on Computer Vision (ECCV) (2018)

37. Monfort, M., et al.: Moments in time dataset: one million videos for event understanding. IEEE Trans. Pattern Anal. Mach. Intell. (TPAMI) 42, 502–508 (2019)

38. Monsell, S.: Task switching. Trends Cogn. Sci. 7(3), 134–140 (2003)

39. Oh, S., et al.: A large-scale benchmark dataset for event recognition in surveillance video. In: Proceedings of the IEEE Conference on Computer Vision and Pattern Recognition (CVPR) (2011)

40. Pellegrini, S., Ess, A., Schindler, K., Van Gool, L.: You'll never walk alone: modeling social behavior for multi-target tracking. In: Proceedings of International Conference on Computer Vision (ICCV) (2009)

41. Pirsiavash, H., Ramanan, D.: Detecting activities of daily living in first-person camera views. In: Proceedings of the IEEE Conference on Computer Vision and Pattern Recognition (CVPR) (2012)

42. Qi, S., Jia, B., Huang, S., Wei, P., Zhu, S.C.: A generalized earley parser for human activity parsing and prediction. IEEE Transactions on Pattern Analysis and Machine Intelligence (TPAMI), 1 (2020)

43. Ramanathan, V., Huang, J., Abu-El-Haija, S., Gorban, A., Murphy, K., Fei-Fei, L.: Detecting events and key actors in multi-person videos. In: Proceedings of the IEEE Conference on Computer Vision and Pattern Recognition (CVPR) (2016)

44. Ren, S., He, K., Girshick, R., Sun, J.: Faster R-CNN: towards real-time object detection with region proposal networks. In: Proceedings of Advances in Neural Information Processing Systems (NeurIPS) (2015)

45. Rohrbach, M., Amin, S., Andriluka, M., Schiele, B.: A database for fine grained activity detection of cooking activities. In: Proceedings of the IEEE Conference on Computer Vision and Pattern Recognition (CVPR) (2012)

46. Rohrbach, M., et al.: Recognizing fine-grained and composite activities using hand-centric features and script data. Int. J. Comput. Vis. (IJCV) **119**(3), 346–373 (2016). https://doi.org/10.1007/s11263-015-0851-8

47. Rubinstein, J.S., Meyer, D.E., Evans, J.E.: Executive control of cognitive processes in task switching. J. Exp. Psychol. Hum. Percept. Perform. **27**(4), 763 (2001)

48. Ryoo, M.S.: Human activity prediction: early recognition of ongoing activities from streaming videos. In: Proceedings of International Conference on Computer Vision (ICCV) (2011)

49. Savva, M., Chang, A.X., Hanrahan, P., Fisher, M., Nießner, M.: Pigraphs: learning interaction snapshots from observations. ACM Trans. Graph. (TOG) **35**(4), 1–12 (2016)

50. Shu, T., Xie, D., Rothrock, B., Todorovic, S., Chun Zhu, S.: Joint inference of groups, events and human roles in aerial videos. In: Proceedings of the IEEE Conference on Computer Vision and Pattern Recognition (CVPR) (2015)

51. Sigurdsson, G.A., Gupta, A., Schmid, C., Farhadi, A., Alahari, K.: Charades-ego: a large-scale dataset of paired third and first person videos. arXiv preprint arXiv:1804.09626 (2018)

52. Sigurdsson, G.A., Varol, G., Wang, X., Farhadi, A., Laptev, I., Gupta, A.: Hollywood in homes: crowdsourcing data collection for activity understanding. In: Proceedings of European Conference on Computer Vision (ECCV) (2016)

53. Soomro, K., Zamir, A.R., Shah, M.: Ucf101: a dataset of 101 human actions classes from videos in the wild. arXiv preprint arXiv:1212.0402 (2012)

54. Stein, S., McKenna, S.J.: Combining embedded accelerometers with computer vision for recognizing food preparation activities. In: ACM on Interactive, Mobile, Wearable and Ubiquitous Technologies (2013)

55. Tang, Y., et al.: Coin: a large-scale dataset for comprehensive instructional video analysis. In: Proceedings of the IEEE Conference on Computer Vision and Pattern Recognition (CVPR) (2019)

56. Tapaswi, M., Zhu, Y., Stiefelhagen, R., Torralba, A., Urtasun, R., Fidler, S.: Movieqa: understanding stories in movies through question-answering. In: Proceedings of the IEEE Conference on Computer Vision and Pattern Recognition (CVPR) (2016)

57. Toyer, S., Cherian, A., Han, T., Gould, S.: Human pose forecasting via deep markov models. In: International Conference on Digital Image Computing: Techniques and Applications (DICTA) (2017)

58. Turaga, P., Chellappa, R., Subrahmanian, V.S., Udrea, O.: Machine recognition of human activities: a survey. IEEE Trans. Pattern Anal. Mach. Intell. (TPAMI) **18**(11), 1473–1488 (2008)

59. Vinyals, O., et al.: Grandmaster level in starcraft ii using multi-agent reinforcement learning. Nature **575**(7782), 350–354 (2019)

60. Vondrick, C., Patterson, D., Ramanan, D.: Efficiently scaling up crowdsourced video annotation. Int. J. Comput. Vis. (IJCV) **101**(1), 184–204 (2013). https://doi.org/10.1007/978-3-642-15561-1_44

61. Woodward, A.L.: Infants selectively encode the goal object of an actor's reach. Cognition **69**(1), 1–34 (1998)

62. Wu, C.Y., Feichtenhofer, C., Fan, H., He, K., Krahenbuhl, P., Girshick, R.: Long-term feature banks for detailed video understanding. In: Proceedings of the IEEE Conference on Computer Vision and Pattern Recognition (CVPR) (2019)

63. Wu, C., Zhang, J., Savarese, S., Saxena, A.: Watch-n-patch: unsupervised understanding of actions and relations. In: Proceedings of the IEEE Conference on Computer Vision and Pattern Recognition (CVPR) (2015)

64. Yeung, S., Russakovsky, O., Jin, N., Andriluka, M., Mori, G., Fei-Fei, L.: Every moment counts: dense detailed labeling of actions in complex videos. Int. J. Comput. Vis. (IJCV) **126**(2–4), 375–389 (2018). https://doi.org/10.1007/s11263-017-1013-y

65. Zhou, L., Xu, C., Corso, J.J.: Towards automatic learning of procedures from web instructional videos. In: Proceedings of AAAI Conference on Artificial Intelligence (AAAI) (2018)

Author Index

Printed in the United States
By Bookmasters